2015
WRITER'S MARKET
DELUXE EDITION

includes a 1-year online subscription to

WritersMarket.com

Where & How to Sell What You Write

THE ULTIMATE MARKET RESEARCH TOOL FOR WRITERS

To register your *2015 Writer's Market Deluxe Edition* book and **start your 1-year online subscription**, scratch off the block below to reveal your activation code*, then go to www.WritersMarket.com. Find the box that says "Have an Activation Code?" then click on "Sign Up Now" and enter your contact information and activation code. It's that easy!

UPDATED MARKET LISTINGS FOR YOUR INTEREST AREA
EASY-TO-USE SEARCHABLE DATABASE • RECORD-KEEPING TOOLS
PROFESSIONAL TIPS & ADVICE • INDUSTRY NEWS

*valid through 12/31/15

WritersMarket.com
Where & How to Sell What You Write

Activate your WritersMarket.com subscription to get instant access to:

- **UPDATED LISTINGS IN YOUR WRITING GENRE:** Find additional listings that didn't make it into the book, updated contact information, and more. WritersMarket.com provides the most comprehensive database of verified markets available anywhere.

- **EASY-TO-USE SEARCHABLE DATABASE:** Looking for a specific magazine or book publisher? Just type in its name. Or widen your prospects with the Advanced Search. You can also search for listings that have been recently updated!

- **PERSONALIZED TOOLS:** Store your best-bet markets, and use our popular recording-keeping tools to track your submissions. Plus, get new and updated market listings, query reminders, and more—every time you log in!

- **PROFESSIONAL TIPS & ADVICE:** From pay-rate charts to sample query letters, and from how-to articles to Q&A's with literary agents, we have the resources writers need.

YOU'LL GET ALL OF THIS WITH YOUR INCLUDED SUBSCRIPTION TO

WMDE15

15TH ANNUAL EDITION

2015

WRITER'S MARKET

DELUXE EDITION

Robert Lee Brewer, *Editor*

WRITER'S DIGEST
BOOKS
WritersDigest.com
Cincinnati, Ohio

2015 Writer's Market. Copyright © 2014 F + W Media, Inc. Published by Writer's Digest Books, an imprint of F+W Media, Inc., 10151 Carver Road, Suite 200, Blue Ash, Ohio 45242. Printed and bound in the United States of America. All rights reserved. No part of this book may be reproduced in any form or by any electronic or mechanical means including information storage and retrieval systems without permission in writing from the publisher, except by a reviewer, who may quote brief passages in a review.

Publisher: Phil Sexton

Writer's Market website: www.writersmarket.com
Writer's Digest website: www.writersdigest.com

Distributed in Canada by Fraser Direct
100 Armstrong Avenue
Georgetown, Ontario, Canada L7G 5S4
Tel: (905) 877-4411

Distributed in the U.K. and Europe by F&W Media International
Brunel House, Newton Abbot, Devon, TQ12 4PU, England
Tel: (+44) 1626-323200, Fax: (+44) 1626-323319
E-mail: postmaster@davidandcharles.co.uk

Distributed in Australia by Capricorn Link
P.O. Box 704, Windsor, NSW 2756 Australia
Tel: (02) 4577-3555

Library of Congress Catalog Number 31-20772
ISSN: 0084-2729
ISBN-13: 978-1-59963-840-9
ISBN-13: 978-1-59963-845-4 (*Writer's Market Deluxe Edition*)
ISBN-10: 1-59963-840-1
ISBN-10: 1-59963-845-2 (*Writer's Market Deluxe Edition*)

Attention Booksellers: This is an annual directory of F + W Media, Inc.
Return deadline for this edition is December 31, 2015.

Edited by: Robert Lee Brewer
Cover designed by: Claudean Wheeler
Interior designed by: Geoff Raker
Production coordinated by: Greg Nock

CONTENTS

CONTESTS & AWARDS 783

RESOURCES

INDEX

FROM THE EDITOR

Are you ready to take those first steps as a freelancer? If you've already taken those first steps, are you ready to start running with your freelance business? I hope the answer is yes, because that's what *Writer's Market* is here to help you achieve.

In this edition of the book, we've completely updated the freelance pay rate chart in the "How Much Should I Charge?" piece by Aaron Belz. This chart collects the going freelance rates for tasks like creating press kits, paid blogging, nonprofit writing, and more.

New articles like "Pitch Like a PR Pro," by Dana W. Todd, and "How to Get Freelance Writing Gigs in Social Media," by Carol Tice, provide freelancers—new and experienced—fresh ways of finding and securing assignments. Plus, there are articles on writing perfect pitches, landing six-figure book deals, ghostwriting, and more.

If you're ready to take your freelance writing career to that next level, take my advice and read the articles first. They're inspirational and packed with advice that's been tested by successful freelancers. Then, dive into the market listings and do what so many freelance writers have done before you—use this book to find more success as a freelance writer. And don't forget to take advantage of your free webinar covering how to find more success freelancing at www.writersmarket.com/wm15-webinar.

Until next we meet, keep writing and marketing what you write.

Robert Lee Brewer
Senior Content Editor
Writer's Market and WritersMarket.com
http://writersdigest.com/editor-blogs/poetic-asides
http://blog.writersmarket.com
http://twitter.com/robertleebrewer

HOW TO USE
WRITER'S MARKET

Writer's Market is here to help you decide where and how to submit your writing to appropriate markets. Each listing contains information about the editorial focus of the market, how it prefers material to be submitted, payment information, and other helpful tips.

WHAT'S INSIDE?

Since 1921, *Writer's Market* has been giving you the information you need to knowledgeably approach a market. We've continued to develop improvements to help you access that information more efficiently.

NAVIGATIONAL TOOLS. We've designed the pages of *Writer's Market* with you, the writer, in mind. Within the pages you will find **readable market listings** and **accessible charts and graphs**. One such chart can be found in the ever-popular "How Much Should I Charge?" article.

Since 1921, *Writer's Market* has been giving you the information you need to knowledgeably approach a market. We've designed it with you, the writer, in mind.

We've taken all of the updated information in this feature and put it into an easy-to-read and navigate chart, making it convenient for you to find the rates that accompany the freelance jobs you're seeking.

ICONS. There are a variety of icons that appear before each listing. A complete Key to Icons & Abbreviations appears on the right. Icons let you know whether a listing is new to the book ([+]), a book publisher accepts only agented writers ([A]), comparative pay rates for a magazine ($-$$$$), and more.

ACQUISITION NAMES, ROYALTY RATES AND ADVANCES. In the Book Publishers section, we identify acquisition editors with the boldface word **Contact** to help you get your manuscript to the right person. Royalty rates and advances are also highlighted in boldface, as is other important information on the percentage of first-time writers and unagented writers the company publishes, the number of books published, and the number of manuscripts received each year.

EDITORS, PAY RATES, AND PERCENTAGE OF MATERIAL WRITTEN BY FREELANCE WRITERS. In the Consumer Magazines and Trade Journals sections, we identify to whom you should send your query or article with the boldface word **Contact**. The amount (percentage) of material accepted from freelance writers, and the pay rates for features, columns and departments, and fillers are also highlighted in boldface to help you quickly identify the information you need to know when considering whether to submit your work.

QUERY FORMATS. We asked editors how they prefer to receive queries and have indicated in the listings whether they prefer them by mail, e-mail, fax or phone. Be sure to check an editor's individual preference before sending your query.

ARTICLES. Many of the articles are new to this edition. Writers who want to improve their submission techniques should read the articles in the **Finding Work** section. The **Managing Work** section is geared more toward post-acceptance topics, such as contract negotiation and organization. With self-promotion a

KEY TO ICONS & ABBREVIATIONS

[+]	market new to this edition
[A]	market accepts agented submissions only
⊘	market does not accept unsolicited submissions
🏆	award-winning market
🍁	Canadian market
🌐	market located outside of the U.S. and Canada
🖱	online opportunity
$	market pays 0-9¢/word or $0-$150/article
$$	market pays 10-49¢/word or $151-$750/article
$$$	market pays 50-99¢/word or $751-$1,500/article
$$$$	market pays $1/word or over $1,500/article
💬	comment from the editor of *Writer's Market*
🔑	tips to break into a specific market
ms, mss	manuscript(s)
b&w	black & white (photo)
SASE	self-addressed, stamped envelope
SAE	self-addressed envelope
IRC	International Reply Coupon, for use when mailing to countries other than your own

big key in freelance success, there is a section of articles dedicated to this topic too: **Promoting Work**.

IMPORTANT LISTING INFORMATION

1) Listings are based on editorial questionnaires and interviews. They are not advertisements; publishers do not pay for their listings. The markets are not endorsed by *Writer's Market* editors. F + W Media, Inc., Writer's Digest Books, and its employees go to great effort to ascertain the validity of information in this book. However, transactions between users of the information and individuals and/or companies are strictly between those parties.

2) All listings have been verified before publication of this book. If a listing has not changed from last year, then the editor said the market's needs have not changed and the previous listing continues to accurately reflect its policies.

3) *Writer's Market* reserves the right to exclude any listing.

4) When looking for a specific market, check the index. A market may not be listed for one of these reasons:
   - It doesn't solicit freelance material.
   - It doesn't pay for material.
   - It has gone out of business.
   - It has failed to verify or update its listing for this edition.
   - It hasn't answered *Writer's Market* inquiries satisfactorily. (To the best of our ability, and with our readers' help, we try to screen fradulent listings.)

IF WRITER'S MARKET IS NEW TO YOU . . .

A quick look at the **Contents** pages will familiarize you with the arrangement of *Writer's Market*. The three largest sections of the book are the market listings of Book Publishers; Consumer Magazines; and Trade Journals. You will also find other sections of market listings for Literary Agents and Contests & Awards. More opportunities can be found on the WritersMarket.com website.

Narrowing your search

After you've identified the market categories that interest you, you can begin researching specific markets within each section.

Consumer Magazines and Trade Journals are categorized by subject within their respective sections to make it easier for you to identify markets for your work. If you want to publish an article dealing with parenting, you could look under the Child Care & Parental Guidance category of Consumer Magazines to find an appropriate market. You would want to keep in mind, however, that magazines in other categories might also be interested in your article. (For example, women's magazines publish such material.)

Contests & Awards are categorized by genre of writing. If you want to find journalism contests, you would search the Journalism category; if you have an unpublished novel, check the Fiction category.

Interpreting the markets

Once you've identified companies or publications that cover the subjects in which you're interested, you can begin evaluating specific listings to pinpoint the markets most receptive to your work and most beneficial to you.

In evaluating individual listings, check the location of the company, the types of material it is interested in seeing, submission requirements, and rights and payment policies. Depending on your personal concerns, any of these items could be a deciding factor as you determine which markets you plan to approach. Many listings also include a reporting time.

Check the Glossary for unfamiliar words. Specific symbols and abbreviations are explained in the Key to Icons & Abbreviations appearing on the back inside cover. The most important abbreviation is SASE—self-addressed, stamped envelope.

A careful reading of the listings will reveal that many editors are very specific about their needs. Your chances of success increase if you follow directions to the letter. Often companies do not accept unsolicited manuscripts and return them unread. If a company does not accept unsolicited manuscripts, it is indicated in the listing with a (⊘) icon. (Note: You may still be able to query a market that does not accept unsolicited manuscripts.)

Whenever possible, obtain submission guidelines before submitting material. You can usually obtain guidelines by sending a SASE to the address in the listing. Magazines often post their guidelines on their websites, and many book publishers do so as well. Most of the listings indicate how writer's guidelines are made available. You should also familiarize yourself with the company's publications. Many of the listings contain instructions on how to obtain sample copies, catalogs or market lists. The more research you do upfront, the better your chances of acceptance, publication and payment.

Guide to listing features

Following is an example of the market listings you'll find in each section of *Writer's Market*. Note the callouts that identify various format features of the listing.

EASY-TO-USE
REFERENCE ICONS

DIRECT E-MAIL
ADDRESSES

SPECIFIC
CONTACT NAMES

DETAILED
SUBMISSION
GUIDELINES

SPECIFIC
PAY RATES

💲 THE GEORGIA REVIEW

The University of Georgia, Athens GA 30602-9009. (706)542-3481. Fax: (706)542-0047. E-mail: garev@uga.edu. Website: www.uga.edu/garev. **Contact:** Stephen Corey, editor. **99% freelance written.** Quarterly journal. Our readers are educated, inquisitive people who read a lot of work in the areas we feature, so they expect only the best in our pages. All work submitted should show evidence that the writer is at least as well-educated and well-read as our readers. Essays should be authoritative but accessible to a range of readers. Estab. 1947. Circ. 3,500. Byline given. Pays on publication. No kill fee. Publishes ms an average of 6 months after acceptance. Accepts queries by mail. Responds in 2 weeks to queries. Responds in 2-3 months to mss. Sample copy for $10. Guidelines available online.

• No simultaneous or electronic submissions.

NONFICTION Needs essays. For the most part we are not interested in scholarly articles that are narrow in focus and/or overly burdened with footnotes. The ideal essay for *The Georgia Review* is a provocative, thesis-oriented work that can engage both the intelligent general reader and the specialist. **Buys 12-20 mss/year.** Send complete ms. **Pays $40/published page.**

PHOTOS Send photos. Reviews 5x7 prints or larger. Offers no additional payment for photos accepted with ms.

FICTION "We seek original, excellent writing not bound by type. Ordinarily we do not publish novel excerpts or works translated into English, and we strongly discourage authors from submitting these." **Buys 12-20 mss/year.** Send complete ms. **Pays $40/published page.**

POETRY "We seek original, excellent poetry. We do not accept submissions via fax or e-mail. If a submission is known to be included in a book already accepted by a publisher, please notify us of this fact (and of the anticipated date of book publication) in a cover letter." Reads year-round, but submissions postmarked May 15-August 15 will be returned unread. Guidelines available for SASE or on website. Responds in 2-3 months. Always sends prepublication galleys. Acquires first North American serial rights. Reviews books of poetry. "Our poetry reviews range from 500-word 'Book Briefs' on single volumes to 5,000-word essay reviews on multiple volumes." Buys 60-75 poems/year. Submit maximum 5 poems. **Pays $3/line.**

TIPS "Unsolicited manuscripts will not be considered from May 15-August 15 (annually); all such submissions received during that period will be returned unread. Check website for submission guidelines."

BEFORE YOUR FIRST SALE

Everything in life has to start somewhere and that somewhere is always at the beginning. Stephen King, Stephenie Meyer, John Grisham, Nora Roberts—they all had to start at the beginning. It would be great to say becoming a writer is as easy as waving a magic wand over your manuscript and "Poof!" you're published, but that's not how it happens. While there's no one true "key" to becoming successful, a long, well-paid writing career *can* happen when you combine four elements:

- Good writing
- Knowledge of writing markets
- Professionalism
- Persistence

Good writing is useless if you don't know which markets will buy your work or how to pitch and sell your writing. If you aren't professional and persistent in your contact with editors, your writing is just that—your writing. But if you are a writer who embraces the above four elements, you have a good chance at becoming a paid, published writer who will reap the benefits of a long and successful career.

As you become more involved with writing, you may read articles or talk to editors and authors with conflicting opinions about the right way to submit your work. The truth is, there are many different routes a writer can follow to get published, but no matter which route you choose, the end is always the same—becoming a published writer.

The following information on submissions has worked for many writers, but it is by no means the be-all-end-all of proper submission guidelines. It's very easy to get wrapped up in the specifics of submitting (Should I put my last name on every page of my manuscript?) and ignore the more important issues (Will this idea on ice fishing in Alaska be appropriate for a regional magazine in Seattle?). Don't allow yourself to become so blinded by submission procedures that you forget common sense. If you use your common sense and develop professional, courteous relations with editors, you will eventually find your own submission style.

DEVELOP YOUR IDEAS, THEN TARGET THE MARKETS

Writers often think of an interesting story, complete the manuscript, and then begin the search for a suitable publisher or magazine. While this approach is common for fiction, poetry and screenwriting, it reduces your chances of success in many nonfiction writing areas. Instead, try choosing categories that interest you and study those sections in *Writer's Market*. Select several listings you consider good prospects for your type of writing. Sometimes the individual listings will even help you generate ideas.

Next, make a list of the potential markets for each idea. Make the initial contact with markets using the method stated in the market listings. If you exhaust your list of possibilities, don't give up. Instead, reevaluate the idea or try another angle. Continue developing ideas and approaching markets. Identify and rank potential markets for an idea and continue the process.

As you submit to the various publications listed in *Writer's Market*, it's important to remember that every magazine is published with a particular audience and slant in mind. Probably the number one complaint we receive from editors is the submissions they receive are completely wrong for their magazines or book line. The first mark of professionalism is to know your market well. Gaining that knowledge starts with *Writer's Market*, but you should also do your own detective work. Search out back issues of the magazines you wish to write for, pick up recent issues at your local newsstand, or visit magazines' websites—anything that will help you figure out what subjects specific magazines publish. This research is also helpful in learning what topics have been covered ad nauseum—the topics you should stay away from or approach in a fresh way. Magazines' websites are invaluable as most post the current issue of the magazine, as well as back issues, and most offer writer's guidelines.

The same advice is true for submitting to book publishers. Research publisher websites for their submission guidelines, recently published titles and their backlist. You can use this information to target your book proposal in a way that fits with a publisher's other titles while not directly competing for sales.

Prepare for rejection and the sometimes lengthy wait. When a submission is returned, check your file folder of potential markets for that idea. Cross off the market that rejected the idea. If the editor has given you suggestions or reasons why the manuscript was not accepted, you might want to incorporate these suggestions when revising your manuscript.

After revising your manuscript mail it to the next market on your list.

Take rejection with a grain of salt

Rejection is a way of life in the publishing world. It's inevitable in a business that deals with such an overwhelming number of applicants for such a limited number of positions. Anyone who has published has lived through many rejections, and writers with thin skin are at a distinct disadvantage. A rejection letter is not a personal attack. It simply indicates your submission is not appropriate for that market. Writers who let rejection dissuade them from pursuing their dream or who react to an editor's "No" with indignation or fury do themselves a disservice. Writers who let rejection stop them do not get published. Resign yourself to facing rejection now. You will live through it, and you'll eventually overcome it.

QUERY AND COVER LETTERS

A query letter is a brief, one-page letter used as a tool to hook an editor and get him interested in your idea. When you send a query letter to a magazine, you are trying to get an editor to buy your idea or article. When you query a book publisher, you are attempting to get an editor interested enough in your idea to request your book proposal or your entire manuscript. (Note: Some book editors prefer to receive book proposals on first contact. Check individual listings for which method editors prefer.)

Here are some basic guidelines to help you create a query that's polished and well-organized. For more tips see "Query Letter Clinic" article.

- **LIMIT IT TO ONE PAGE, SINGLE-SPACED**, and address the editor by name (Mr. or Ms. and the surname). *Note*: Do not assume that a person is a Mr. or Ms. unless it is obvious from the name listed. For example, if you are contacting a D.J. Smith, do not assume that D.J. should be preceded by Mr. or Ms. Instead, address the letter to D.J. Smith.
- **GRAB THE EDITOR'S ATTENTION WITH A STRONG OPENING.** Some magazine queries, for example, begin with a paragraph meant to approximate the lead of the intended article.
- **INDICATE HOW YOU INTEND TO DEVELOP THE ARTICLE OR BOOK.** Give the editor some idea of the work's structure and content.
- **LET THE EDITOR KNOW IF YOU HAVE PHOTOS** or illustrations available to accompany your magazine article.
- **MENTION ANY EXPERTISE OR TRAINING THAT QUALIFIES YOU** to write the article or book. If you've been published before, mention it; if not, don't.
- **END WITH A DIRECT REQUEST TO WRITE THE ARTICLE.** Or, if you're pitching a book, ask for the go-ahead to send in a full proposal or the entire manuscript. Give the editor an idea of the expected length and delivery date of your manuscript.

A common question that arises is: If I don't hear from an editor in the reported response time, how do I know when I can safely send the query to another market? Many writers find it helpful to indicate in their queries that if they don't receive a response from the editor (slightly after the listed reporting time), they will assume the editor is not interested. It's best to take this approach, particularly if your topic is timely.

A brief, single-spaced cover letter is helpful when sending a manuscript as it helps personalize the submission. However, if you have previously queried the editor, use the cover letter to politely and briefly remind the editor of that query—when it was sent, what it contained, etc. "Here is the piece on low-fat cooking that I queried you about on December 12. I look forward to hearing from you at your earliest convenience." Do not use the cover letter as a sales pitch.

If you are submitting to a market that accepts unsolicited manuscripts, a cover letter is useful because it personalizes your submission. You can, and should, include information about the manuscript, yourself, your publishing history, and your qualifications.

In addition to tips on writing queries, the "Query Letter Clinic" article offers eight example query letters, some that work and some that don't, as well as comments on why the letters were either successful or failed to garner an assignment or contract.

Querying for fiction

Fiction is sometimes queried, but more often editors prefer receiving material. Many fiction editors won't decide on a submission until they have seen the complete manuscript. When submitting a fiction book idea, most editors prefer to see at least a synopsis and sample chapters (usually the first three). For fiction published in magazines, most editors want to see the complete short story manuscript. If an editor does request a query for fiction, it should include a description of the main theme and story line, including the conflict and resolution. Take a look at individual listings to see what editors prefer to receive.

QUERY LETTER RESOURCES

The following list of books provides you with more detailed information on writing query letters, cover letters, and book proposals. All titles are published by Writer's Digest Books.

- *Formatting & Submitting Your Manuscript*, 3rd Edition, by Chuck Sambuchino
- *How to Write Attention-Grabbing Query & Cover Letters*, by John Wood
- *How to Write a Book Proposal*, 4th Edition, by Michael Larsen
- *Writer's Market Companion*, 2nd Edition, by Joe Feiertag and Mary Cupito

---

THE SYNOPSIS

Most fiction books are sold by a complete manuscript, but most editors and agents don't have the time to read a complete manuscript of every wannabe writer. As a result, publishing decision-makers use the synopsis and sample chapters to help the screening process of fiction. The synopsis, on its most basic level, communicates what the book is about.

The length and depth of a synopsis can change from agent to agent or publisher to publisher. Some will want a synopsis that is 1-2 single-spaced pages; others will want a synopsis that can run up to 25 double-spaced pages. Checking your listings in *Writer's Market*, as well as double-checking with the listing's website, will help guide you in this respect.

The content should cover all the essential points of the novel from beginning to end and in the correct order. The essential points include main characters, main plot points, and, yes, the ending. Of course, your essential points will vary from the editor who wants a 1-page synopsis to the editor who wants a 25-page synopsis.

NONFICTION BOOK PROPOSALS

Most nonfiction books are sold by a book proposal—a package of materials that details what your book is about, who its intended audience is, and how you intend to write the book. It includes some combination of a cover or query letter, an overview, an outline, author's information sheet, and sample chapters. Editors also want to see information about the audience for your book and about titles that compete with your proposed book.

Submitting a nonfiction book proposal

A proposal package should include the following items:

- **A COVER OR QUERY LETTER.** This letter should be a short introduction to the material you include in the proposal.
- **AN OVERVIEW.** This is a brief summary of your book. It should detail your book's subject and give an idea of how that subject will be developed.
- **AN OUTLINE.** The outline covers your book chapter by chapter and should include all major points covered in each chapter. Some outlines are done in traditional outline form, but most are written in paragraph form.
- **AN AUTHOR'S INFORMATION SHEET.** This information should acquaint the editor with your writing background and convince him of your qualifications regarding the subject of your book.
- **SAMPLE CHAPTERS.** Many editors like to see sample chapters, especially for a first book. Sample chapters show the editor how you write and develop ideas from your outline.
- **MARKETING INFORMATION.** Facts about how and to whom your book can be successfully marketed are now expected to accompany every book proposal. If you can provide information about the audience for your book and suggest ways the book publisher can reach those people, you will increase your chances of acceptance.

- **COMPETITIVE TITLE ANALYSIS.** Check the *Subject Guide to Books in Print* for other titles on your topic. Write a one- or two-sentence synopsis of each. Point out how your book differs and improves upon existing topics.

For more information on nonfiction book proposals, read Michael Larsen's *How to Write a Book Proposal* (Writer's Digest Books).

A WORD ABOUT AGENTS

An agent represents a writer's work to publishers, negotiates contracts, follows up to see that contracts are fulfilled, and generally handles a writer's business affairs, leaving the writer free to write. Effective agents are valued for their contacts in the publishing industry, their knowledge about who to approach with certain ideas, their ability to guide an author's career, and their business sense.

While most book publishers listed in *Writer's Market* publish books by unagented writers, some of the larger houses are reluctant to consider submissions that have not reached them through a literary agent. Companies with such a policy are noted by an (Ⓐ) icon at the beginning of the listing, as well as in the submission information within the listing.

Writer's Market includes a list of literary agents who are all members of the Association of Authors' Representatives and who are also actively seeking new and established writers.

MANUSCRIPT FORMAT

You can increase your chances of publication by following a few standard guidelines regarding the physical format of your manuscript. It should be your goal to make your manuscript readable. Follow these suggestions as you would any other suggestions: Use what works for you and discard what doesn't.

In general, when submitting a manuscript, you should use white, 8½×11, 20 lb. paper, and you should also choose a legible, professional looking font (i.e., Times New Roman)—no all-italic or artsy fonts. Your entire manuscript should be double-spaced with a 1½-inch margin on all sides of the page. Once you are ready to print your manuscript, you should print either on a laser printer or an ink-jet printer.

MANUSCRIPT FORMATTING SAMPLE

(1) Your Name   50,000 Words (3)
Your Street Address
City State ZIP Code
Day and Evening Phone Numbers
E-mail Address

Website (if applicable)
(2)

TITLE

by

(4) Your Name

(1) Type your real name (even if you use a pseudonym) and contact information (2) Double-space twice (3) Estimated word count (4) Type your title in capital letters, double-space and type "by," double-space again, and type your name (or pseudonym if you're using one) (5) Double-space twice, then indent first paragraph and start text of your manuscript (6) On subsequent pages, type your name, a dash, and the page number in the upper left or right corner

(5) You can increase your chances of publication by following a few standard guidelines regarding the physical format of your article or manuscript. It should be your goal to make your manuscript readable. Use these suggestions as you would any other suggestions: Use what works for you and discard what doesn't.

In general, when submitting a manuscript, you should use white, 8½×11, 20-lb. bond paper, and you should also choose a legible, professional-looking font (i.e., Times New Roman)—no all-italic or artsy fonts. Your entire manuscript should be double-spaced with a 1½-inch margin on all sides of the page. Once you are ready to print your article or manuscript, you should print either on a laser printer or an inkjet printer.

Remember, articles should be written after you send a one-page query letter to an editor, and the editor then asks you to write the article. If, however, you are sending an article "on spec" to an editor, you should send both a query letter and the complete article.

Fiction and poetry is a little different from nonfiction articles, in that it is rarely queried. More often than not, poetry and fiction editors want to review the complete manuscript before making a final decision.

ESTIMATING WORD COUNT

All computers provide you with a word count of your manuscript. Your editor will count again after editing the manuscript. Although your computer is counting characters, an editor or production editor is more concerned about the amount of space the text will occupy on a page. Several small headlines or subheads, for instance, will be counted the same by your computer as any other word of text. However, headlines and subheads usually employ a different font size than the body text, so an editor may count them differently to be sure enough space has been estimated for larger type.

For short manuscripts, it's often quickest to count each word on a representative page and multiply by the number of pages. You can get a very rough count by multiplying the number of pages in your manuscript by 250 (the average number of words on a double-spaced typewritten page).

PHOTOGRAPHS AND SLIDES

In some cases, the availability of photographs and slides can be the deciding factor as to whether an editor will accept your submission. This is especially true when querying a publication that relies heavily on photographs, illustrations or artwork to enhance the article (e.g., craft magazines, hobby magazines, etc.). In some instances, the publication may offer additional payment for photographs or illustrations.

Check the individual listings to find out which magazines review photographs and what their submission guidelines are. Most publications prefer you do not send photographs with your submission. However, if photographs or illustrations are available, you should indicate that in your query. As with manuscripts, never send the originals of your photographs or illustrations. Instead, send digital images, which is what most magazine and book publishers prefer to use.

SEND PHOTOCOPIES

If there is one hard-and-fast rule in publishing, it's this: *Never* send the original (or only) copy of your manuscript. Most editors cringe when they find out a writer has sent the only copy of their manuscript. You should always send copies of your manuscript.

Some writers choose to send a self-addressed, stamped postcard with a photocopied submission. In their cover letter they suggest if the editor is not interested in their manuscript, it may be tossed out and a reply sent on the postcard. This method is particularly helpful when sending your submissions to international markets.

MAILING SUBMISSIONS

No matter what size manuscript you're mailing, always include a self-addressed, stamped envelope (SASE) with sufficient return postage. The website for the U.S. Postal Service (www.

usps.com) and the website for the Canadian Post (www.canadapost.ca) both have postage calculators if you are unsure how much postage to affix.

A book manuscript should be mailed in a sturdy, well-wrapped box. Enclose a self-addressed mailing label and paper clip your return postage to the label. However, be aware that some book publishers do not return unsolicited manuscripts, so make sure you know the practice of the publisher before sending any unsolicited material.

Types of mail service

There are many different mailing service options available to you whether you are sending a query letter or a complete manuscript. You can work with the U.S. Postal Service, United Parcel Service, Federal Express, or any number of private mailing companies. The following are the five most common types of mailing services offered by the U.S. Postal Service.

- **FIRST CLASS** is a fairly expensive way to mail a manuscript, but many writers prefer it. First-Class mail generally receives better handling and is delivered more quickly than Standard mail.
- **PRIORITY MAIL** reaches its destination within two or three days.
- **STANDARD MAIL** rates are available for packages, but be sure to pack your materials carefully because they will be handled roughly. To make sure your package will be returned to you if it is undeliverable, print "Return Postage Guaranteed" under your address.
- **CERTIFIED MAIL** must be signed for when it reaches its destination.
- **REGISTERED MAIL** is a high-security method of mailing where the contents are insured. The package is signed in and out of every office it passes through, and a receipt is returned to the sender when the package reaches its destination.

MAILING MANUSCRIPTS

- Fold manuscripts under five pages into thirds, and send in a #10 SASE.
- Mail manuscripts five pages or more unfolded in a 9×12 or 10×13 SASE.
- For return envelope, fold the envelope in half, address it to yourself, and add a stamp, or, if going to Canada or another international destination, International Reply Coupons (available at most post office branches).
- Don't send by Certified Mail—this is a sign of an amateur.

QUERY LETTER CLINIC

Many great writers ask year after year, "Why is it so hard to get published?" In many cases, these writers have spent years—and possibly thousands of dollars on books and courses—developing their craft. They submit to the appropriate markets, yet rejection is always the end result. The culprit? A weak query letter.

The query letter is often the most important piece of the publishing puzzle. In many cases, it determines whether an editor or agent will even read your manuscript. A good query letter makes a good first impression; a bad query letter earns a swift rejection.

THE ELEMENTS OF A QUERY LETTER

A query letter should sell editors or agents on your idea or convince them to request your finished manuscript. The most effective query letters get into the specifics from the very first line. It's important to remember that the query is a call to action, not a listing of features and benefits.

In addition to selling your idea or manuscript, a query letter can include information on the availability of photographs or artwork. You can include a working title and projected word count. Depending on the piece, you might also mention whether a sidebar might be appropriate and the type of research you plan to conduct. If appropriate, include a tentative deadline and indicate whether the query is being simultaneously submitted.

Biographical information should be included as well, but don't overdo it unless your background actually helps sell the article or proves that you're the only person who could write your proposed piece.

THINGS TO AVOID IN A QUERY LETTER

The query letter is not a place to discuss pay rates. This step comes after an editor has agreed to take on your article or book. Besides making an unprofessional impression on an editor, it can also work to your disadvantage in negotiating your fee. If you ask for too much, an editor may not even contact you to see if a lower rate might work. If you ask for too little, you may start an editorial relationship where you are making far less than the normal rate.

You should also avoid rookie mistakes, such as mentioning that your work is copyrighted or including the copyright symbol on your work. While you want to make it clear that you've researched the market, avoid using flattery as a technique for selling your work. It often has the opposite effect of what you intend. In addition, don't hint that you can rewrite the piece, as this only leads the editor to think there will be a lot of work involved in shaping up your writing.

Also, never admit several other editors or agents have rejected the query. Always treat your new audience as if they are the first place on your list of submission possibilities.

HOW TO FORMAT YOUR QUERY LETTER

It's OK to break writing rules in a short story or article, but you should follow the rules when it comes to crafting an effective query. Here are guidelines for query writing.

- Use a normal font and typeface, such as Times New Roman and 10- or 12-point type.
- Include your name, address, phone number, e-mail address and website, if possible.
- Use a one-inch margin on paper queries.
- Address a specific editor or agent. (Note: The listings in *Writer's Market* provide a contact name for most submissions. It's wise to double-check contact names online or by calling.)
- Limit query letter to one single-spaced page.
- Include self-addressed, stamped envelope or postcard for response with post submissions. Use block paragraph format (no indentations). Thank the editor for considering your query.

WHEN AND HOW TO FOLLOW UP

Accidents do happen. Queries may not reach your intended reader. Staff changes or interoffice mail snafus may end up with your query letter thrown away. Or the editor may have set your query off to the side for further consideration and forgotten it. Whatever the case may be, there are some basic guidelines you should use for your follow-up communication.

Most importantly, wait until the reported response time, as indicated in *Writer's Market* or their submission guidelines, has elapsed before contacting an editor or agent. Then, you should send a short and polite e-mail describing the original query sent, the date it was sent, and asking if they received it or made a decision regarding its fate.

The importance of remaining polite and businesslike when following up cannot be stressed enough. Making a bad impression on an editor can often have a ripple effect—as that editor may share his or her bad experience with other editors at the magazine or publishing company. Also, don't call.

HOW THE CLINIC WORKS

As mentioned earlier, the query letter is the most important weapon for getting an assignment or a request for your full manuscript. Published writers know how to craft a well-written, hard-hitting query. What follows are eight queries: four are strong; four are not. Detailed comments show what worked and what did not. As you'll see, there is no cut-and-dried "good" query format; every strong query works on its own merit.

GOOD NONFICTION MAGAZINE QUERY

Jimmy Boaz, editor
American Organic Farmer's Digest
8336 Old Dirt Road
Macon GA 00000

Dear Mr. Boaz,

There are 87 varieties of organic crops grown in the United States, but there's only one farm producing 12 of these—Morganic Corporation. ②

Located in the heart of Arkansas, this company spent the past decade providing great organic crops at a competitive price helping them grow into the ninth leading organic farming operation in the country. Along the way, they developed the most unique organic offering in North America.

As a seasoned writer with access to Richard Banks, the founder and president of Morganic, I propose writing a profile piece on Banks for your Organic Shakers department. After years of reading this riveting column, I believe the time has come to cover Morganic's rise in the organic farming industry. ③

This piece would run in the normal 800-1,200 word range with photographs available of Banks and Morganic's operation.

I've been published in *Arkansas Farmer's Deluxe, Organic Farming Today* and in several newspapers. ④

Thank you for your consideration of this article. I hope to hear from you soon.

Sincerely,

Jackie Service
34 Good St.
Little Rock AR 00000
jackie.service9867@email.com

① My name is only available on our magazine's website and on the masthead. This writer has done her research. ② Here's a story that hasn't been pitched before. I didn't know Morganic was so unique in the market. I want to know more. ③ The writer has access to her interview subject, and she displays knowledge of the magazine by pointing out the correct section in which her piece would run. ④ While I probably would've assigned this article based on the idea alone, her past credits do help solidify my decision.

BAD NONFICTION MAGAZINE QUERY

Dear Gentlemen, **1**

I'd like to write the next great article you'll ever publish. My writing credits include amazing pieces I've done for local and community newspapers and for my college English classes. I've been writing for years and years. **2**

Your magazine may not be a big one like *Rolling Stone* or *Sports Illustrated,* but I'm willing to write an interview for you anyway. I know you need material, and I need money. (Don't worry. I won't charge you too much.) **3**

Just give me some people to interview, and I'll do the best job you've ever read. It will be amazing, and I can re-write the piece for you if you don't agree. I'm willing to re-write 20 times if needed. **4**

You better hurry up and assign me an article though, because I've sent out letters to lots of other magazines, and I'm sure to be filled up to capacity very soon. **5**

Later gents,

Carl Bighead
76 Bad Query Lane
Big City NY 00000

1 This is sexist, and it doesn't address any contact specifically. **2** An over-the-top claim by a writer who does not impress me with his publishing background. **3** Insults the magazine and then reassures me he won't charge too much? **4** While I do assign material from time to time, I prefer writers pitch me their own ideas after studying the magazine. **5** I'm sure people aren't going to be knocking down his door anytime soon.

Marcus West
88 Piano Drive
Lexington KY 00000

August 8, 2011 **1**

Jeanette Curic, editor
Wonder Stories
45 Noodle Street
Portland OR 00000

Dear Ms. Curic,

Please consider the following 1,200-word story, "Turning to the Melon," a quirky coming-of-age story with a little magical realism thrown in the mix. **2**

After reading *Wonder Stories* for years, I think I've finally written something that would fit with your audience. My previous short story credits include *Stunned Fiction Quarterly* and *Faulty Mindbomb*. **3**

Thank you in advance for considering "Turning to Melon."

Sincerely,

Marcus West
(123) 456-7890
marcusw87452@email.com

Encl: Manuscript and SASE **4**

1 Follows the format we established in our guidelines. Being able to follow directions is more important than many writers realize. **2** Story is in our word count, and the description sounds like the type of story we would consider publishing. **3** It's flattering to know he reads our magazine. While it won't guarantee publication, it does make me a little more hopeful that the story I'm reading will be a good fit. Also, good to know he's been published before. **4** I can figure it out, but it's nice to know what other materials were included in the envelope. This letter is not flashy, but it gives me the basics and puts me in the right frame of mind to read the actual story.

BAD FICTION MAGAZINE QUERY

To: curic@wonderstories808.com (1)
Subject: A Towering Epic Fantasy

Hello there. (2)

I've written a great fantasy epic novel short story of about 25,000 words that may be included in your magazine if you so desire. (3)

More than 20 years, I've spent chained to my desk in a basement writing out the greatest story of our modern time. And it can be yours if you so desire to have it. (4)

Just say the word, and I'll ship it over to you. We can talk money and movie rights after your acceptance. I have big plans for this story, and you can be part of that success. (5)

Yours forever (if you so desire), (6)

Harold
(or Harry for friends)

(1) We do not consider e-mail queries or submissions. (2) This is a little too informal. (3) First off, what did he write? An epic novel or short story? Second, 25,000 words is way over our 1,500-word max. (4) I'm lost for words. (5) Money and movie rights? We pay moderate rates and definitely don't get involved in movies. (6) I'm sure the writer was just trying to be nice, but this is a little bizarre and kind of creepy. I do not so desire more contact with "Harry."

GOOD NONFICTION BOOK QUERY

To: corey@bigbookspublishing.com
Subject: Query: Become a Better Parent in 30 Days **1**

Dear Mr. Corey,

2 As a parent of six and a high school teacher for more than 20 years, I know first hand that being a parent is difficult work. Even harder is being a good parent. My proposed title, **3** *Taking Care of Yourself and Your Kids: A 30-day Program to Become a Better Parent While Still Living Your Life*, would show how to handle real-life situations and still be a good parent.

This book has been years in the making, as it follows the outline I've used successfully in my summer seminars I give on the topic to thousands of parents every year. It really works, because past participants contact me constantly to let me know what a difference my classes have made in their lives. **4**

In addition to marketing and selling *Taking Care of Yourself and Your Kids* at my summer seminars, I would also be able to sell it through my website and promote it through my weekly e-newsletter with over 25,000 subscribers. Of course, it would also make a very nice trade title that I think would sell well in bookstores and possibly retail outlets, such as Wal-Mart and Target. **5**

Please contact me for a copy of my full book proposal today. **6**

Thank you for your consideration.

Marilyn Parent
8647 Query St.
Norman OK 00000
mparent8647@email.com
www.marilynsbetterparents.com

1 Effective subject line. Lets me know exactly what to expect when I open the e-mail. **2** Good lead. Six kids and teaches high school. I already trust her as an expert. **3** Nice title that would fit well with others we currently offer. **4** Her platform as a speaker definitely gets my attention. **5** 25,000 e-mail subscribers? She must have a very good voice to gather that many readers. **6** I was interested after the first paragraph, but every paragraph after made it impossible to not request her proposal.

BAD NONFICTION BOOK QUERY

To: info@bigbookspublishing.com
Subject: a question for you **1**

I really liked this book by Mega Book Publishers called *Build Better Trains in Your Own Backyard*. It was a great book that covered all the basics of model train building. My father and I would read from it together and assemble all the pieces, and it was magical like Christmas all through the year. Why wouldn't you want to publish such a book? **2**

Well, here it is. I've already copyrighted the material for 2006 and can help you promote it if you want to send me on a worldwide book tour. As you can see from my attached digital photo, I'm not the prettiest person, but I am passionate. **3**

There are at least 1,000 model train builders in the United States alone, and there might be even more than that. I haven't done enough research yet, because I don't know if this is an idea that appeals to you. If you give me maybe $500, I could do that research in a day and get back to you on it. **4**

Anyway, this idea is a good one that brings back lots of memories for me.

Jacob **5**

1 The subject line is so vague I almost deleted this e-mail as spam without even opening it. **2** The reason we don't publish such a book is easy—we don't do hobby titles. **3** I'm not going to open an attachment from an unknown sender via e-mail. Also, copyrighting your work years before pitching is the sign of an amateur. **4** 1,000 possible buyers is a small market, and I'm not going to pay a writer to do research on a proposal. **5** Not even a last name? Or contact information? At least I won't feel guilty for not responding.

GOOD FICTION BOOK QUERY

Jeremy Mansfield, editor
Novels R Us Publishing
8787 Big Time Street
New York NY 00000

Dear Mr. Mansfield,

My 62,000-word novel, *The Cat Walk,* is a psychologically complex thriller in the same mold as James Patterson's Alex Cross novels, but with a touch of the supernatural a la Stephenie Meyer. **1**

Rebecca Frank is at the top of the modeling world, posing for magazines in exotic locales all over the world and living life to its fullest. Despite all her success, she feels something is missing in her life. Then she runs into Marcus Hunt, a wealthy bachelor with cold blue eyes and an ambiguous past.

Within 24 hours of meeting Marcus, Rebecca's understanding of the world turns upside down, and she finds herself fighting for her life and the love of a man who may not have the ability to return her the favor.

Filled with demons, serial killers, trolls, maniacal clowns and more, *The Cat Walk* follows Rebecca through a gauntlet of trouble and turmoil, leading up to a final climactic realization that may lead to her own unraveling. **2**

The Cat Walk should fit in well with your other titles, such as *Bone Dead* and *Carry Me Home*, though it is a unique story. Your website mentioned supernatural suspense as a current interest, so I hope this is a good match. **3**

My short fiction has appeared in many mystery magazines, including a prize-winning story in *The Mysterious Oregon Quarterly.* This novel is the first in a series that I'm working on (already half-way through the second). **4**

As stated in your guidelines, I've included the first 30 pages. Thank you for considering *The Cat Walk.*

Sincerely,

Merry Plentiful
54 Willow Road
East Lansing MI 00000
merry865423@email.com

1 Novel is correct length and has the suspense and supernatural elements we're seeking. **2** The quick summary sounds like something we would write on the back cover of our paperbacks. That's a good thing, because it identifies the triggers that draw a response out of our readers. **3** She mentions similar titles we've done and that she's done research on our website. She's not afraid to put in a little extra effort. **4** At the moment, I'm not terribly concerned that this book could become a series, but it is something good to file away in the back of my mind for future use.

BAD FICTION BOOK QUERY

Jeremy Mansfield
Novels R Us Publishing
8787 Big Time Street
New York NY 00000

Dear Editor,

My novel has an amazing twist ending that could make it a worldwide phenomenon overnight while you are sleeping. It has spectacular special effects that will probably lead to a multi-million dollar movie deal that will also spawn action figures, lunch boxes, and several other crazy subsidiary rights. I mean, we're talking big-time money here. **1**

I'm not going to share the twist until I have a signed contract that authorizes me to a big bank account, because I don't want to have my idea stolen and used to promote whatever new initiative "The Man" has in mind for media nowadays. Let it be known that you will be rewarded handsomely for taking a chance on me. **2**

Did you know that George Lucas once took a chance on an actor named Harrison Ford by casting him as Han Solo in Star Wars? Look at how that panned out. Ford went on to become a big actor in the Indiana Jones series, *The Fugitive, Blade Runner*, and more. It's obvious that you taking a risk on me could play out in the same dramatic way. **3**

I realize that you've got to make money, and guess what? I want to make money too. So we're on the same page, you and I. We both want to make money, and we'll stop at nothing to do so.

If you want me to start work on this amazing novel with an incredible twist ending, just send a one-page contract agreeing to pay me a lot of money if we hit it big. No other obligations will apply. If it's a bust, I won't sue you for millions. **4**

Sincerely,

Kenzel Pain
92 Bad Writer Road
Austin TX 00000

1 While I love to hear enthusiasm from a writer about his or her work, this kind of unchecked excitement is worrisome for an editor. **2** I need to know the twist to make a decision on whether to accept the manuscript. Plus, I'm troubled by the paranoia and emphasis on making a lot of money. **3** I'm confused. Does he think he's Harrison Ford? **4** So that's the twist: He hasn't even written the novel yet. There's no way I'm going to offer a contract for a novel that hasn't been written by someone with no experience or idea of how the publishing industry works.

PERFECT PITCH:

Pitches That Never Fail

....

by Marc Acito

"A first-time novelist sets the record at a writers conference for the most pitches, leading to a multiple-book deal, awards, translations, excellent reviews and a movie option. An inspiring true success story, a literary version of Seabiscuit, except the horse is a writer."

As pitches go, this one's devoid of conflict, but that's the point. This scenario actually happened to me. Hence my qualification for writing this article.

My writing students get nervous when I ask them to pitch their works-in-progress on the first day of class, particularly if they're just starting. "I wouldn't know how to describe it," they say. "I don't know what it's about."

A pitch is simply another story that you're telling. A very, very short one.

And therein lies the problem. To some degree, we can't know what our novel/memoir/screenplay/play/nonfiction book is entirely about until we've gotten it down. But I contend that thinking about the pitch ahead of time helps focus a writer's goals for a piece. It's not just a commercial concern, it's an artistic one.

Writers are storytellers and a pitch is simply another story that you're telling. A very, very short one. Rather than view pitching as if you were a salesman in a bad suit hawking used cars, imagine that you're a pitcher for the Yankees and that the agent or editor is the catcher: They're on your team, so they really want to catch the ball.

Or, put another way, you're a different kind of pitcher, this one full of cool, refreshing water that will fill their empty glass.

But first you've got to get their attention.

THE HOOK

"I need something to grab me right away that tells me exactly why I should want to read this submission (of all the submissions on my desk)," says Christina Pride, senior editor at Hyperion.

A hook is exactly what it sounds like—a way to grab a reader like a mackerel and reel them in. It's not a plot summary, but more like the ad campaign you'd see on a movie poster. Veteran Hollywood screenwriter Cynthia Whitcomb, who teaches the pitching workshop at the Willamette Writers Conference in Portland, Oregon, recommends that writers of all genres start with a hooky tagline like this one from *Raiders of the Lost Ark:*

> *"If adventure had a name, it'd be Indiana Jones."*

That's not just first-rate marketing, it's excellent storytelling.

Here are some of my other favorite taglines for movies based on books, so you can see how easily the concept works for novels:

- "Help is coming from above." (*Charlotte's Web*)
- "From the moment they met, it was murder." (*Double Indemnity*)
- "The last man on earth is not alone." (*I Am Legend*)
- "Love means never having to say you're sorry." (*Love Story*)

The last one actually isn't true; love means always saying you're sorry, even when you're not, but the thought is provocative and provocation is exactly what you want to do.

When I pitched my first novel, *How I Paid for College,* I always started the same way. First, I looked the catcher right in the eye (this is very important—how else are they going to catch the ball?). Then I said,

> *"Embezzlement. Blackmail. Fraud…High School."*

I began my query letters the same way.

"I always begin my proposals with a question," says Jennifer Basye Sander, co-author of *The Complete Idiot's Guide to Getting Published*. "I want to get editors nodding their heads in agreement right away."

No, you're not asking something like, "Are you ready to rock 'n roll?" but instead an open-ended conversation starter like, "Can you be forgiven for sending an innocent man to jail?" (Ian McEwan's *Atonement*) or "What does it take to climb Mount Everest?" (Jon Krakauer's *Into Thin Air).* Particularly useful are "what if?" questions like "What if an amnesiac didn't know he was the world's most wanted assassin?" (Robert Ludlum's *The Bourne Identity*) or "What if Franklin Delano Roosevelt had been defeated by Charles Lindbergh in 1940?" (*The Plot Against America*, Philip Roth).

Acito employs humor in his novels, but there's nothing funny about the effectiveness of his pitches.

The same also holds true for nonfiction. If you were to sit down in front of an agent and ask, "What if you could trim your belly fat and use it to fuel your car?" trust me, they'd listen. Questions like that make the catcher want to know more. Which is exactly what you do by creating...

THE LOG LINE

No, it's not a country-western dance done in a timber mill. And without realizing it, you're already a connoisseur of the genre, having read thousands of log lines in *TV Guide* or imdb.com or the *New York Times* Bestseller List. A log line is a one-sentence summary that states the central conflict of your story. For example:

> *"A teen runaway kills the first person she encounters, then is pursued by the dead woman's sister as she teams up with three strangers to kill again."*

Recognize it? That's *The Wizard of Oz*.
Here's another:

> *"The son of a carpenter leaves on an adventure of self-discovery, rejects sin, dies and rises again transformed."*

Obviously, that's *Pinocchio*.
Okay, seriously, here's the one I did for *How I Paid for College*:

> *"A talented but irresponsible teenager schemes to steal his college tuition money when his wealthy father refuses to pay for him to study acting at Juilliard."*

It's not genius, but it captured the story succinctly by identifying the protagonist, the antagonist, and the conflict between them. In other words, the essential element for any compelling story.

AND HERE'S THE PITCH...

Pitches are often referred to as "elevator pitches" because they should last the length of your average elevator ride—anywhere from 30 seconds to two minutes. Or, for a query letter, one single-spaced page . That's about 350 words, including "Dear Mr. William Morris" and "Your humble servant, Desperate Writer."

Essentially the pitch is identical to a book jacket blurb: it elaborates on the set-up, offers a few further complications on the central conflict, then gives an indication of how it wraps up. When it comes to the ending, "don't be coy," says Erin Harris, a literary agent at the Irene Skolnick Agency in Manhattan. "Spoil the secrets, and let me know what really happens." Agents and editors want a clear idea of what kind of ride they're getting on before investing hours in your manuscript. Make it easy for them to do their jobs selling it.

....

Agents and editors want a clear idea of what kind of ride they're getting on before investing hours in your manuscript.

....

Nowhere was this clearer to me than when I read the jacket copy of my first novel and saw that it was virtually identical to my query letter.

Indeed, your best practice for learning how to pitch is to read jacket descriptions (leaving out the part about the author being a "bold, original new voice"—that's for others to say).

Or think of it as a very short story, following the structure attributed to writer Alice Adams: Action, Backstory, Development, Climax, End.

It's as easy as ABDCE.

"The best queries convey the feeling that the author understands what the scope, structure, voice, and audience of the book really are," says Rakesh Satyal, senior editor at HarperCollins to authors such as Paul Coelho, Armistead Maupin and Clive Barker. "To misunderstand or miscommunicate any of these things can be truly detrimental."

That's the reason we often resort to the Hollywoody jargon of it's "This meets that," as in "It's *No Country for Old Men* meets *Little Women*." Or it's...

- ...*Die Hard* on a bus (*Speed*)
- ...*Die Hard* in a plane (*Con Air*)
- ...*Die Hard* in a phone booth (*Phone Booth*)
- ...*Die Hard* in a skyscraper (no, wait, that's *Die Hard*).

HOW I PAID FOR COLLEGE

A Tale of Sex, Theft, Friendship and Musical Theater

A novel by Marc Acito

Embezzlement...Blackmail...Fraud...High School.

How I Paid for College is a 97,000-word comic novel about a talented but irresponsible teenager who schemes to steal his college tuition money when his wealthy father refuses to pay for acting school. The story is just true enough to embarrass my family.

It's 1983 in Wallingford, New Jersey, a sleepy bedroom community outside of Manhattan. Seventeen-year-old Edward Zanni, a feckless Ferris Bueller type, is Peter Panning his way through a carefree summer of magic and mischief, sending underwear up flagpoles and re-arranging lawn animals in compromising positions. The fun comes to a screeching halt, however, when Edward's father remarries and refuses to pay for Edward to study acting at Juilliard.

In a word, Edward's screwed. He's ineligible for scholarships because his father earns too much. He's unable to contact his mother because she's off somewhere in Peru trying to commune with the Incan spirits. And, in a sure sign he's destined for a life in the arts, Edward's incapable of holding down a job. ("One little flesh wound is all it takes to get fired as a dog groomer, even if you artfully arrange its hair so the scar doesn't show.")

So Edward turns to his loyal (but immoral) misfit friends to help him steal the tuition money from his father. Disguising themselves as nuns and priests (because who's going to question the motives of a bunch of nuns and priests?) they merrily scheme their way through embezzlement, money laundering, identity theft, forgery and blackmail.

But along the way Edward also learns the value of friendship, hard work and how you're not really a man until you can beat up your father. (Metaphorically, that is.)

How I Paid for College is a farcical coming-of-age story that combines the first-person-smart-ass tone of David Sedaris with the byzantine plot twists of Armistead Maupin. I've written it with the HBO-watching, NPR-listening, Vanity Fair-reading audience in mind.

As a syndicated humor columnist, I'm familiar with this audience. For the past three years, my bi-weekly column, "The Gospel According to Marc," has appeared in 18 alternative newspapers in major markets, including Los Angeles, Chicago and Washington, DC. During that time I've amassed a personal mailing list of over 1,000 faithful readers.

How I Paid for College is a story for anyone who's ever had a dream...and a scheme.

www.MarcAcito.com
(503) 246-2208
Marc@MarcAcito.com
5423 SW Cameron Road, Portland, OR 97221

"I appreciate when agents and authors offer good comp titles," confirms Hyperion's Christina Pride. "It's good shorthand to help me begin to position the book in my mind right from the outset in terms of sensibility and potential audience."

Agent Erin Harris agrees. "For example," she says, "the premise of one book meets the milieu of another book." As in *Pride and Prejudice and Zombies*, an idea I will forever regret not thinking of myself.

When citing comp titles, be certain to invoke the most commercially successful and well-known works to which you can honestly liken yourself. No agent wants to earn 15 percent of *Obscure Literary Title* meets *Total Downer by Unknown Author*.

So I steered clear of my lesser-known influences and focused on the big names, saying, "*How I Paid for College* is a farcical coming-of-age story that combines the first-person-smart-ass tone of David Sedaris with the byzantine plot twists of Armistead Maupin."

That line also made it onto the jacket copy.

My book hasn't changed, but I continue to update the pitch as I develop the movie. What started as "*Ferris Bueller* meets *High School Musical*," turned into "A mash-up of *Ocean's 11* and *Glee*." By the time the movie actually gets made it'll be "*iTunes Implant Musical Experience* meets *Scheming Sentient Robots*."

"A word of caution," Harris adds. "Please do not liken your protagonist to Holden Caulfield or your prose style to that of Proust. Truly, it's best to steer clear of the inimitable."

Speaking of the inimitable, while the titles of *Catcher in the Rye* and *Remembrance of Things Past* are poetically evocative, they wouldn't distinguish themselves from the pack in the Too-Much-Information Age. Nowadays, your project is competing for attention with a video of a toddler trapped behind a couch. (I'm serious, Google it, it's got all the makings of great drama: a sympathetic protagonist, conflict, complications, laughter, tears and an uplifting ending. All in two minutes and 27 seconds.)

So while it's not a dictum of the publishing industry (though, given the nosedive the industry has taken, what do *they* know?), I think 21st century writers would do well to title their works in ways that accommodate the searchable keyword culture of the Internet.

In other words, *To Kill a Mockingbird* was fine for 1960, but if you tried promoting it today, you'd end up at the PETA website.

Like the logline, the catchiest titles actually describe what the book is about. Consider:

- *Eat, Pray, Love*
- *Diary of a Wimpy Kid*
- *Sh*t My Dad Says*
- *A Portrait of the Artist as a Young Man*

In those cases, the title is the synopsis. Similarly, some titles, while less clear, include an inherent mystery or question:

- *Sophie's Choice*

- *The Hunger Games*
- *And Then There Were None*
- *The Hitchhiker's Guide to the Galaxy*

Lastly, even if the reader can't know automatically what the title means, it helps if it's simple and memorable, like:

- *Twilight*
- *Valley of the Dolls*
- *The Thorn Birds*
- *Captain Underpants*

One way to tell if you've got an effective title is to submit it to the "Have you read…?" test. If it feels natural coming at the end of that sentence, you're on the right track.

Granted, straightforward titles are easier if you're writing nonfiction like *Trim Your Belly Fat and Use it to Fuel Your Car*. As is the final part of the pitch.

BUILDING A PLATFORM

Along with "branding," "platform" is one of the most overused buzzwords of the last decade. "If you are writing nonfiction," Erin Harris says, "it's important to describe your platform and to be a qualified expert on the subject about which you're writing"

In other words, if you're going to write *Teach Your Cat to Tap Dance* you better deliver a tap-dancing cat, along with research about the market for such a book.

For first-time novelists this can prove challenging. But Harris says that every credit truly helps: "If you have pieces published in literary magazines, if you have won awards, or if you have an MFA, my interest is piqued."

That last advice should also pique the interest of every fledgling writer out there. In my case, what actually got me an agent wasn't just the pitch, it was the fact that I met best-selling novelist Chuck Palahniuk at a workshop and he'd read a column of mine in a small alternative newspaper. Ultimately, it's not about who you know, it's about who knows you. So publish wherever you can. You never know who's reading.

Write on.

MARC ACITO is the award-winning author of the comic novels *How I Paid for College* and *Attack of the Theater People*. *How I Paid for College* won the Ken Kesey Award for Fiction, was a Top Teen Pick by the American Library Association and is translated into five languages the author cannot read. A regular contributor to NPR's *All Things Considered*, he teaches story structure online and at NYU. www.MarcAcito.com

LANDING THE SIX-FIGURE DEAL

What Makes Your Proposal Hot

by SJ Hodges

It's the question every first-time author wants to ask:

"If I sell my book, will the advance even cover my rent?"

Authors, I am happy to tell you that, yes, the six-figure book deal for a newbie still exists—even if you're not a celebrity with your own television show! As a ghostwriter, I work with numerous authors and personalities to develop both nonfiction and fiction proposals and I've seen unknown first-timers land life-changing deals even in a down economy. Is platform the ultimate key to their success? You better believe it's a huge consideration for publishers, but here's the good news: having a killer platform is only one element that transforms a "nice deal" into a "major deal."

You still have to ensure the eight additional elements of your proposal qualify as major attractions. Daniela Rapp, editor at St. Martin's Press explains, "In addition to platform, authors need to have a fantastic, original idea. They have to truly be an expert in their field and they must be able to write." So how do you craft a proposal that conveys your brilliance, your credentials, your talent and puts a couple extra zeroes on your check?

ONE: THE NARRATIVE OVERVIEW

Before you've even written word one of your manuscript, you are expected to, miraculously, summarize the entirety of your book in such a compelling and visceral way that a publisher or agent will feel as if they are reading the *New York Times* review. Sound impossible? That's because it is.

That's why I'm going to offer two unorthodox suggestions. First, consider writing the first draft of your overview after you've created your table of contents and your chapter outlines. You'll know much more about the content and scope of your material even if you're not 100% certain about the voice and tone. That's why you'll take another pass after you complete your sample chapters. Because then you'll be better acquainted with the voice of your book which brings me to unorthodox suggestion number two… treat your overview as literature.

I believe every proposal component needs to be written "in voice" especially because your overview is the first page the editor sees after the title page. By establishing your voice on the page immediately, your proposal becomes less of a sales document and more of a page-turner. Remember, not everyone deciding your fate works in marketing and sales. Editors still have some buying power and they are readers, first and foremost.

TWO: THE TABLE OF CONTENTS AND CHAPTER OUTLINES

Television writers call this "breaking" a script. This is where you break your book or it breaks you. This is where you discover if what you plan to share with the world actually merits 80,000 words and international distribution.

Regardless of whether you're writing fiction or nonfiction, this element of your proposal must take your buyer on a journey (especially if it's nonfiction) and once more, I'm a big fan of approaching this component with creativity particularly if you're exploring a specific historical time period, plan to write using a regional dialect, rely heavily on "slanguage" and especially if the material is highly-technical and dry.

This means you'll need to style your chapter summaries and your chapter titles as a form of dramatic writing. Think about the arc of the chapters, illuminating the escalating conflict, the progression towards a resolution, in a cinematic fashion. Each chapter summary should end with an "emotional bumper," a statement that simultaneously summarizes and entices in the same way a television show punches you in the gut before they cut to a commercial.

Is it risky to commit to a more creative approach? Absolutely. Will it be perfect the first time you write it? No. The fifth time you write it? No. The tenth time? Maybe. But the contents and chapter summary portion of your proposal is where you really get a chance to show off your skills as an architect of plot and structure and how you make an editor's job much, much easier. According to Lara Asher, Acquisitions Editor at Globe Pequot Press, it is the single most important component of your proposal. "If I can't easily understand what a book is trying to achieve then I can't present it to my colleagues. It won't make it through the acquisitions process."

THREE: YOUR AUTHOR BIO

Your author bio page must prove that you are more than just a pro, that you are recognized by the world at large as "the definitive expert" on your topic, that you have firsthand experience tackling the problems and implementing your solutions, and that you've seen positive results not only in your personal life but in the lives of others. You have to have walked the walk and talked the talk. You come equipped with a built-in audience, mass media attention, and a strong social network. Your bio assures your buyer that you are the right writer exploring the right topic at the right time.

FOUR: YOUR PLATFORM

Platform, platform, platform. Sit through any writing conference, query any agent, lunch with any editor and you'll hear the "P" word over and over again. What you won't hear is hard and fast numbers about just how large this platform has to be in order to secure a serious offer. Is there an audience to dollar amount ratio that seems to be in play? Are publishers paying per head?

"I haven't found this to be the case," says Julia Pastore, former editor for Random House. "It's easier to compel someone to 'Like' you on Facebook or follow you on Twitter than it is to compel them to plunk down money to buy your book. Audience engagement is more important than the sheer number of social media followers."

With that said, if you're shooting for six-figures, publishers expect you'll have big numbers and big plans. Your platform will need to include:

Cross-promotional partnerships

These are organizations or individuals that already support you, are already promoting your brand, your products or your persona. If you host a show on HGTV or Nike designed a tennis racket in your honor, they definitely qualify. If, however, you're not rolling like an A-lister just yet, you need to brainstorm any and every possible connection you have to organizations with reach in the 20,000 + range. Maybe your home church is only 200 people but the larger association serves 40,000 and you often write for their newsletter. Think big. Then think bigger.

Specific, verifiable numbers proving the loyalty of your audience

"Publishers want to see that you have direct contact with a loyal audience," says Maura Teitelbaum, agent Folio Literary Management. Meaning a calendar full of face-to-face speaking engagements, a personal mailing list, extensive database and verifiable traffic to your author website.

But how much traffic does there need to be? How many public appearances? How many e-mails in your Constant Contact newsletter? Publishers are loathe to quote concrete numbers for "Likes" and "Followers" so I'll stick my neck out and do it instead. At a minimum, to land a basic book deal, meaning a low five-figure sum, you'll need to prove that you've got 15 - 20,000 fans willing to follow you into hell and through high water.

For a big six-figure deal, you'll need a solid base of 100,000 rabid fans plus access to hundreds of thousands more. If not millions. Depressed yet? Don't be. Because we live in a time when things as trivial as angry oranges or as important as scientific TED talks can go viral and propel a writer out of obscurity in a matter of seconds. It is only your job to become part of the conversation. And once your foot is in the door, you'll be able to gather...

Considerable media exposure

Publishers are risk averse. They want to see that you're a media darling achieving pundit status. Organize and present all your clips, put together a DVD demo reel of your on-air appearances and be able to quote subscriber numbers and demographics about the publications running your articles or features about you.

Advance praise from people who matter

Will blurbs really make a difference in the size of your check? "I would include as many in a proposal as possible," says Teitelbaum. "Especially if those people are willing to write letters of commitment saying they will promote the book via their platform. That shows your efforts will grow exponentially."

FIVE: YOUR PROMOTIONAL PLANS

So what is the difference between your platform and your promotional plan? Your promotional plan must demonstrate specifically how you will activate your current platform and the expected sales results of that activation. These are projections starting three to six months before your book release date and continuing for one year after its hardcover publication. They want your guarantee to sell 15,000 books within that first year.

In addition, your promotional plan also issues promises about the commitments you are willing to make in order to promote the book to an even wider market. This is your expansion plan. How will you broaden your reach and who will help you do it? Publishers want to see that your goals are ambitious but doable.

Think about it this way. If you own a nail salon and you apply for a loan to shoot a movie, you're likely to be rejected. But ask for a loan to open your second salon and your odds get much better. In other words, keep your promotional plans in your wheelhouse while still managing to include:

- Television and Radio Appearances
- Access to Print Media
- A Massive Social Media Campaign
- Direct E-mail Solicitations

- E-Commerce and Back of Room Merchandising
- New Joint Partnerships
- Your Upcoming Touring & Speaking Schedule with Expected Audience

You'll notice that I did not include hiring a book publicist as a requirement. Gone are the days when an advance-sucking, three-month contract with a book publicist makes any difference. For a six-figure author, publishers expect there is a team in place: a powerful agent, a herd of assistants and a more generalized media publicist already managing the day-to-day affairs of building your brand, growing your audience. Hiring a book publicist at the last minute is useless.

SIX: YOUR MARKET ANALYSIS

It would seem the odds against a first-time author hitting the jackpot are slim but that's where market analysis provides a glimmer of hope. There are actually markets considered more desirable to publishers. "Broader is generally better for us," says Rapp. "Niche generally implies small. Not something we [St. Martin's Press] can afford to do these days. Current affairs books, if they are explosive and timely, can work. Neuroscience is hot. Animal books (not so much animal memoirs) still work. Military books sell."

"The health and diet category will always be huge," says Asher. "But in a category like parenting which is so crowded, we look for an author tackling a niche topic that hasn't yet been covered."

Niche or broad, your market analysis must position your book within a larger context, addressing the needs of the publishing industry, the relevant cultural conversations happening in the zeitgeist, your potential audience and their buying power and the potential for both domestic and international sales.

SEVEN: YOUR C.T.A.

Choose the books for your competitive title analysis not only for their topical similarities but also because the author has a comparable profile and platform to your own. Says Pastore, "It can be editorially helpful to compare your book to *Unbroken* by Hillenbrand, but unless your previous book was also a bestseller, this comparison won't be helpful to our sales force."

Limit your C.T.A. to five or six solid offerings then get on BookScan and make sure none of the books sold fewer than 10,000 copies. "Higher sales are preferable," says Rapp. "And you should leave it to the publisher to decide if the market can hold one more title or not. We always do our own research anyway, so just because the book is not mentioned in your line-up doesn't mean we won't know about it."

EIGHT: YOUR SAMPLE CHAPTERS

Finally, you have to/get to prove you can…write. Oh yeah, that!

This is the fun part, the pages of your proposal where you really get to shine. It is of upmost importance that these chapters, in harmony with your overview and chapter summaries, allow the beauty, wisdom and/or quirkiness of your voice to be heard. Loud and clear.

"Writing absolutely matters and strong sample chapters are crucial." Pastore explains, "An author must be able to turn their brilliant idea into engaging prose on the page."

Approach the presentation of these chapters creatively. Consider including excerpts from several different chapters and not just offering the standard Introduction, Chapter One and Two. Consider the inclusion of photographs to support the narrative, helping your editor put faces to names. Consider using sidebar or box quotes from the narrative throughout your proposal to build anticipation for the actual read.

NINE: YOUR ONE-PAGER

Lastly, you'll need a one-pager, which is a relatively new addition to the book proposal format. Publishers now expect an author to squeeze a 50- or 60-page proposal down to a one-page summary they can hand to their marketing and sales teams. In its brevity, the one-pager must provide your buyer with "a clear vision of what the book is, why it's unique, why you are the best person to write it, and how we can reach the audience," says Pastore. And it must do that in less than 1,000 words. There is no room to be anything but impressive.

And if you're shooting for that six-figure deal, impressive is what each component of your book proposal must be. Easy? No. But still possible? Yes.

SJ HODGES is an 11-time published playwright, ghostwriter and editor. Her most recent book, a memoir co-authored with Animal Planet's "Pit Boss" Shorty Rossi was purchased by Random House/Crown, hit #36 on the Amazon bestseller list and went into its 3rd printing less than six weeks after its release date. As a developmental editor, SJ has worked on books published by Vanguard Press, Perseus Book Group and St. Martin's Press. SJ is a tireless advocate for artists offering a free listing for jobs, grants and fellowships at her Facebook page: facebook.com/constantcreator. She can be reached through her website: sjhodges.com.

PITCH LIKE A PR PRO

Turn the Blinking Cursor Into Cash

....

by Dana W. Todd

Writing is not the most important part of making a living as a freelance writer. If you don't know how to catch the attention of a magazine editor, you can write as many pleasing words as you want. They'll go nowhere and fail to earn a dollar. To enjoy the monetary rewards of a successful freelance career, writers must think and act like a public relations (PR) practitioner.

What do PR practitioners know that writers can learn from them? They recognize:

- How to develop relationships with magazine editors;
- How to decide what feature ideas are relevant for particular publications;
- How to time pitches appropriately; and
- How to tailor queries to editors.

PITCH WHAT YOU KNOW AND WHO YOU KNOW

Compelling content is sovereign, but how you pitch that content to magazine editors makes the difference between silence and acceptance of a proposed article. PR pros represent clients in all types of industries. Even though it is impossible for a PR account manager to understand all the intricacies of every vertical market for which they pitch stories, they can lean on the expertise of their clients through "interviewing" conversations.

They are trained to recognize what is newsworthy about their clients' products, services, processes, and customers. Many times, clients don't know the gold mine of information they have to share with editors. PR pros know how to pull out the distinctive angles: Is there a customer in an industry using a product in a unique way? Has a company motivated employees using fresh techniques that led to increased profitability? Has a restaurant hired a new chef taking the cuisine in a new direction? Did the software entrepreneur's success begin by digging ditches for his cousin's company?

Finding these types of behind-the-scenes angles should be added to the freelancing toolbox. Activate your investigative nature (all writers have it). Begin by talking with your friends and business acquaintances to find out what is happening in their respective industries. One of my former college roommates, for example, works in my town. She introduced me to one of her clients in the funeral industry who explained a new consolidation trend. Despite the fact I had no personal knowledge or skill set in that area, I was able to interview my colleague and her client to understand more of the industry intricacies and successfully pitch the article idea to a business editor. The editor was willing to hear me out despite my inexperience in the funeral industry because of my proven experience writing business articles, which was the angle of the story.

> It's easier to branch out into writing for your dream magazine if you begin building a portfolio in your special area of expertise.

This example brings me to the next point: pitch what you know. To earn a full-time salary as a freelancer, you must either lean on others' expertise in particular market segments or pitch innovative angles on topics with which you are supremely familiar. It's easier to branch out into writing for your dream magazine if you begin building a portfolio in your special area of expertise. Were you a basketball player in college? You know the intricacies of the game's rules and opportunities that would make crafting pitches easier for a sports magazine. Do you work in a corporate department such as human resources? Use your knowledge of day-to-day HR responsibilities to craft a pitch to a business editor about how social media has changed today's face-to-face job interview process. Are you a master gardener? You are the most qualified to give advice about how to choose plants that deer detest.

When a publisher in one of the online writing groups to which I subscribe posted a notice about her search for a writer who lived on a Southern lake or river, I pitched my services immediately since I fit the profile. Because of my fishing, canoeing, and kayaking experience on a Southern waterway, she contracted with me to write an initial feature article for one of her magazines, which has turned into many other features over the last couple of years.

TARGET QUERIES TO SPECIFIC MEDIA OUTLETS

General pitches sent via a mass e-mail to 100 magazine editors do not work any better for PR account managers than generalized, mass queries sent by freelance writers. Effective PR professionals never distribute mass e-mails when pitching their clients or project ideas. They read six months' worth of back issues of the magazine, find the editor that covers the beat they wish to pitch, ensure the editor has not covered the topic in the last year, and pitch a precise angle that works with that magazine's particular readership.

"We choose the top three publications that might be interested in the story angle," says Lorri-Ann Carter, president of PR agency CarterTodd & Associates. "We pitch them one at a time, allowing about a week for the editor to consider the idea before we follow up. If the editor doesn't bite, we move on to the next top-tier publication."

One important way PR executives stay current is by consulting magazines' editorial calendars. You can find editorial calendars on most publications' websites under the advertising tab.

"Even though editorial calendars are more general than they were a decade ago, we still use them," says Carter. "Editors often don't list a particular angle, like they did in the past. Often that means they are open to hearing your pitches on that general topic."

What if an editorial calendar is not available? Editorial assistants usually are helpful. They have daily contact with all the magazine's editors and sit in editorial planning meetings. Editorial assistants are valuable to PR professionals because they will answer the phone and respond to e-mail questions, pointing PR managers to the correct method and place of sending queries and providing details about specific editors. PR professionals know not to be fooled by the "assistant" part of this title. Those in editorial assistant positions may still be learning the ropes, but they can provide insight into the magazine that is mostly unavailable to you as an outsider.

TIME IT RIGHT AND FOLLOW UP

Pitching a story at the appropriate time is the quickest way to show professionalism to an editor. For example, let's say you would like to pitch an Easter-themed story to *Family Circle* magazine. Using *Writer's Market*, you see the magazine's editorial lead time is four months, including seasonal material. Although that fact may lead you to decide to pitch your story idea in November, a PR practitioner would probably think the timing too late. Who wants to be the last one to the pitching party? Chances are, there are others with a similar idea, so why not bump up the timetable a bit? Plus, if you've done your homework by checking the editorial calendar or calling an editorial assistant, you will find out it takes about eight weeks for an editor to respond to queries. That changes your minimum pitch timetable to at least six months out from the publication date.

Writing for trade publications is a bit different from consumer magazines. Although it varies from publication to publication, many trade magazines operate three to four months ahead of print production. PR managers pitch to the same vertical trade editors repeatedly, since managers usually specialize and represent more than one client in that industry. It's a good idea for writers to do the same. If you have relationships with professionals in a particular industry, they may be happy to supply you on a regular basis with ideas for freelance articles. It is smart to become familiar with all the trade magazines for which these future queries may be well received.

You have your ideas, you have pitched them strategically, and now it's time to wait for the editor's call. Wait a minute; is that Fantasyland I hear calling?

Editors are busy. They receive lots of e-mails every day, just like you and me. Editors hear from lots of writers, too, on a daily basis. To be heard, you must be assertive.

Here's a shocking truth: If you don't plan to follow up, you might as well not e-mail a query at all. In all my years as a PR executive, I only recall a handful of times an editor enthusiastically embraced a story and proactively contacted me to follow through with article development. Editors are busy. They receive lots of e-mails every day, just like you and me. Editors hear from lots of writers, too, on a daily basis. To be heard, you must be assertive. In the PR world, one follow-up, whether by phone or e-mail, is not enough.

Yes, at some point you have to accept silence, but let it be after you have honestly reached out to the editor three or four times. Even a rejection is good news since most editors will tell you exactly why they are rejecting your proposal so you can write or time a pitch more appropriately next time.

Once my pitch to a well-known regional magazine was rejected, but only after I followed up three times. I received valuable feedback. I had pitched an interior design story. The editor commented positively on my experience with the subject matter but said the project I had pitched was too modern for her more traditionally minded-audience. Bingo! I had the answer I wanted, was freed to search for another home for the story, and had the feedback I needed to succeed with my next pitch to this editor.

The biggest lesson here: Think like a PR pro by refusing to let your pitch languish in La La Land.

DEVELOP TWO-WAY RELATIONSHIPS

PR practitioners also understand the intricacies of editorial relationships. They recognize the importance of timing pitches and working around editors' deadlines but also that editors arc people, too. They have dogs and cats and kids and housework and hobbies—things to which writers can relate. An editor I worked with in the past had a daughter who suffered from migraines, just like my son does, and we often began our query discussions with an update on our kids. If an editor is open to it, a little small talk will open the door to a stronger relationship, especially helpful if the physical distance is such that it cannot be bridged with face-to-face communication.

It's a fallacy that PR practitioners spend their days schmoozing clients and editors with lunches and happy hour cocktails. They are at their desks just like freelancers. What they do know is the power of goodwill. When they have a great news tip, they may call their favorite editor and give them the heads up first. They will match a journalist on assignment with a resource to provide last-minute information for a story, even if they or their clients do not immediately profit from the exchange.

Once I switched from full-time PR to full-time freelance writing, I used some of the PR techniques I learned in unique ways. I once filled in for a desperate editor who had a hole to fill when another writer did not deliver a feature story. I didn't charge a rush fee or make any extra money for writing the article in two days versus three weeks, but I banked a lot of goodwill and many future assignments.

A business editor for whom I regularly write introduced me to one of his colleagues at a mom's magazine. The mom's magazine editor was reworking the entire publication and was behind in her production schedule, with the holidays looming. In a goodwill gesture, I wrote a short 400-word article for no charge about a redesigned children's playroom I had previously promised to place somewhere for an interior designer friend. My friend was thrilled and the editor thankful and happy. The assignments rolled in from there.

While working for free is not ideal, a few articles free of charge will pay off handsomely in future assignments if the job is handled professionally and in a timely manner. Your takeaway is the beginning of a two-way relationship with the editor. Your future queries may not always receive the green light, but you will have the editor's ear, which is a big step in the right direction.

DANA W. TODD has 20 years of experience in public relations strategy and implementation, including serving as CEO of a high-tech PR agency. She has placed thousands of articles in publications for her clients over the years. More than a decade ago, she traded full-time PR for full-time freelance writing and now earns a living writing articles for business and consumer magazines nationwide.

HOW TO FIND SUCCESS IN THE MAGAZINE WORLD

by Kerrie Flanagan

Contrary to popular belief, magazines are still going strong. According to the latest study by the Magazine Publishers of America there are over 20,000 magazines in print. This is good news if you are looking to write for magazines. But before you jump in, there are a few things you should know that will increase your chances of getting an acceptance letter.

KNOW THE READER

Every magazine has a certain readership; teenage girl, mother of young children, budget traveler and so on. It is imperative you know as much about that reader as you can before submitting a query to the editor, because the more you know about who reads the magazine, the more you can tailor your query, article or essay to best reach that audience.

Geoff Van Dyke, Deputy Editor of the Denver magazine *5280* said, "I wish people would truly read the magazine, like cover to cover, and understand our readership and voice and mission before sending queries. Sometimes—more often than not—writers submit queries that make it clear that they don't really understand *5280*, don't understand our readers or our mission, and, thus, the query is a bad fit. If they just spend a little more time on the front end, it would make all the difference." So how can you find out who is the target audience for a specific magazine? The key is in the advertising. Companies spend thousands of dollars getting their messages out to their consumers. They are only going to invest their money in a magazine directed at their target market. By paying attention to the ads in a publication (and this goes for online too) you can learn a lot about the reader. What are the ages of the people in the ads? Are they families? Singles? What types of products are highlighted? Expensive clothes? Organic foods? Luxury cars and world travel or family cars and domestic travel?

Another way to find out the demographics of the reader is to locate the media kit on the magazine's website. This is a document intended to provide information to potential advertisers about their readership, but is a gold mine for freelance writers. The media kit provides information like the average age, income, gender, hobbies, home ownership, education and marital status.

This becomes invaluable when looking at ideas and topics to pitch to a magazine. For instance, in the media kit for *5280* magazine, 71% of the readers are married, 93% own their own home and 78% have lived in Colorado for more than 10 years or are natives of the state. With this little bit of information, pitching an article on where to find the best deals on apartments in Denver, is definitely not a good fit since most of their readers own their own home. An article on the best bars in Denver to meet other singles is also not a good idea for this publication, but one on the most romantic weekend getaways in Colorado to take your spouse is a possibility. It is also clear that, when writing the article, time does not have to be spent explaining to the reader things about Colorado that people who live in the state already know since 78% of the readers have been there for more than a decade.

KNOW THE MAGAZINE

Once you understand the reader, then you need to familiarize yourself with the actual magazine. Take the time to explore who are the writers, the length of the articles and the departments.

Tom Hess, editor with *Encompass Magazine* wishes more writers would take the time to know his magazine, in all its forms, before querying. "Too few writers make the effort, and those who do, get my immediate attention."

One way to do this with print magazines is to literally take apart the magazine. To see who writes for the magazine, find the masthead, the page in the front of the magazine that lists the editors and contributing writers. Tear it out so you have it as a reference. Now, go through the magazine, page by page and make a note by each article with a byline to find out who wrote the piece. Was it an editor? A contributing editor? If you can't find their names on the masthead, then they are typically freelance writers. A contributing editor is usually not on staff, but writes frequently for the magazine.

Now go through and pay attention to the length of articles and the various departments. How many feature stories are there? Is there a back page essay? Are there short department pieces in the front?

By knowing all of this information, you can better direct your query to the areas of the magazine that are more open to freelance writers and tailor your idea to better fit the type of articles they publish.

KNOW THE STYLE

Each magazine has its own style and tone. It's what makes the difference between *The New Yorker* and *Time Magazine*. Some magazines are very literary, others are more informational, so it is important to study the magazines to have a good understanding of their style.

Below are two travel writing examples portraying Ketchikan, Alaska, but with very different styles. As you read over each selection, pay attention to the style by looking at the use of quotes, the point of view (first person, third person…), the descriptions and the overall tone of the article.

Example 1

In Ketchikan, there are many great things to see and do. The roots of the three Native Alaskan tribes, the Tlingit, Haida, and Tsimshian run deep on this island where you can find the world's largest collection of totem poles. In a beautiful cove, eight miles north of downtown is Totem Bight State Park where 14 historic totems are found along with a native clanhouse. Totems can also be viewed at the Totem Heritage Center and the Southest Discovery Center. At the Saxman Tribal house and at the Metlakatla Long House, skilled groups bring Native dance to life with regular performances.

Example 2

The rest of the world disappeared when I entered this lush, green rainforest. Stillness and peace embraced me while I strolled on the wooden walkway, in awe of the surrounding beauty: moss hung from trees, foliage so dense it provided shelter from the rain and beautiful rivers flowed, in search of the ocean. Ketchikan, Alaska, is in the heart of the Tongass National Forest, and an unlikely place to find the Earth's largest remaining temperate rainforest.

The first article provides information and facts about traveling to Ketchikan to see the totem poles. This article would be a good fit for a magazine liek *Family Motor Coaching*. The second article definitely has a different style; one that is more poetic and descriptive and more likely to be found in *National Geographic Traveler*.

Both pieces are good but are unique in their style and tone. By understanding this aspect of a magazine, your query or article can better reflect the voice of the publication and increase your chances of an assignment and well-received article.

KNOW THE GUIDELINES

Most magazines put together submission guidelines, spelling out exactly what they are looking for with articles and how to submit your idea to them.

"I wish writers would understand exactly what kind of material we are looking for," said Russ Lumpkin, managing editor of *Gray's Sporting Journal*, "and that they would adhere strictly to our submission guidelines. We publish fly fishing and hunting stories and accept only digital submissions via e-mail. A poem about watching butterflies submitted through the mail creates work that falls out of my ordinary work flow. And that's aggravating."

The submission guidelines are usually found in the "About Us" or "Contact Us" section on a magazine's website as well as in great resources like *Writer's Market*. Read the guidelines carefully and follow them when submitting your query or article.

KNOW HOW TO WRITE AN EFFECTIVE QUERY LETTER

Once you have done all your upfront research and have found a magazine that is a good fit for your idea, it is time to write a good query letter. The letter should be professional and written in a style and tone similar to the article you are pitching.

Robbin Gould, editor of *Family Motor Coaching* believes a writer needs to submit as comprehensive a query as possible and be fully aware of the magazine's focus, particularly when dealing with a niche publication. "A writer who misuses terms or makes erroneous statements about the subject he or she proposes to cover indicates a lack of knowledge to the editor," says Gould. "Or a query that simply states, 'Would you be interested in an article about XXX?' with minimal explanation wastes everyone's time and suggests the writer is looking for any publication to take the article. If the writer doesn't show much attention to detail up front, the editor probably won't spend much time considering the idea."

There are basic components that should be included in every query letter.

- **Salutation (Dear Mr. Smith).** Find out who the correct editor is to direct your query. You should be able to find this information online. If not make a quick phone call to the publishing company and ask, "Who would I direct a travel query to?" Ask for spelling and the editor's e-mail. Unless you know the editor, use a formal salutation with Mr., Mrs., or Ms. If you are not sure if the editor is a man or woman, put their full name.
- **Good Hook.** You have about 10 seconds to catch the attention of an editor. The opening should be about one to three sentences in length and needs to lure the editor in right away.
- **Article Content.** This is the bulk of your query and should be about one paragraph. It will focus on the main points of the article and the topics you plan to cover.
- **Specifics.** Here you will include the specifics of the article: word count, department where you think it will fit, possible experts you are going to interview and other information pertinent to the piece.
- **Purpose.** In one sentence, share the purpose of your article. Will your article inform, educate, inspire, or entertain?

- **Qualifications.** This is not the place to be shy. You need to convince the editor that you are the perfect person to write this article. If you do not have any published clips, then really expand more on your experiences that relate to your article. If you are pitching a parenting article and you have six kids, mention that. It clearly positions you as an expert in the parenting field.
- **Sending.** Most magazines accept and want queries by e-mail. When sending a query via e-mail, include your information in the body of the message, not in an attachment. Make sure your contact information is at the bottom of the e-mail. Put something noticeable in the subject line. For example: "QUERY: The Benefits of Chocolate and the Creative Process."

By following all the steps in this article you will be ready set off on a magazine-writing journey equipped with the necessary tools and confidence to get your queries noticed, and, in the end, see your articles in print.

KERRIE FLANAGAN has 130+ published articles and essays to her credit. In addition she is the director of Northern Colorado Writers, a group she founded in 2007 that supports and encourages writers of all levels and genres through classes, networking events, retreats and an annual writer's conference. Kerrie is also available for writing coaching. Visit her website for more information about her and NCW. www.KerrieFlanagan.com

EARN A FULL-TIME INCOME FROM BLOGGING

....

by Carol Tice

It sounds like a dream: Instead of sending query letters and relying on editors to give you paying assignments, you start your own blog and turn it into a money-maker. No matter where in the world you want to live, you're able to earn a good living.

For a growing number of writers, it's not a dream. I know because I'm among the writers who now earn more from their own blogs than they do from freelance assignments.

But it's not easy, by any means. The vast majority of blogs never find an audience and their authors never earn a dime. It's hard to stand out—at the end of 2011, pollster Nielsen reported there were over 181 million blogs, up from 36 million in 2006.

In this vast sea of blogs, how can you write one that stands out and becomes the basis for a money-earning business? It begins with setting up the blog to attract a loyal readership. Once you build an audience, there are a limited number of ways you can earn income from your blog audience—I spotlight the five of the most popular methods below.

SETTING IT UP TO EARN

Many blogs don't attract readers because they lack basic elements of design and usability that make blogs appealing, says Seattle WordPress trainer Bob Dunn (www.bobwp.com). Dunn's own blog, BobWP, is the platform on which he's built his business.

How do you create an attractive blog?

Use a professional platform

Free blog platforms such as Blogger and Moveable Type have limitations that make it hard to look professional (and some free platforms prohibit commerce). If you're serious about blogging, pay for a host and use WordPress—it's now the dominant blogging platform, Technorati reports.

Offer contact information

Many bloggers cultivate an air of mystery, using a pen name and providing no contact info. But readers want to know who you are and be able to e-mail you questions, says Dunn.

Have an "About" page

With a million scams on the Internet, the About page has become a vital blog component—it's usually the most-visited page after the Home page, Dunn says. This is the place where readers get to know you and learn why you write your blog.

"I can't tell you how many times I go on a blog and there's no About page," says, Dunn. "It should be more than a resume, too—tell a story."

Clean up the design

No matter how wonderful your writing is, if your blog is a clutter of tiny type, dark backgrounds, multiple sidebars, and flashing ads, readers will leave, Dunn says. Begin with a simple, graphical header, title, and tagline that quickly communicate what your blog is about. You have just a few seconds in which to convey what you write about before readers leave, so be clear.

Make navigation simple

Many bloggers end up with multiple rows of tabs or long drop-down menus. Try to simplify—for every additional click you require, you will lose some readers, Dunn says.

Pick a niche topic

While most blogs ramble about whatever the author feels like discussing that day, business-focused blogs stick to a subject or a few related topics, notes Dunn. This allows you to attract and keep readers interested in your subject.

Create useful content

Write with your readers' needs in mind, rather than about your own interests, says Mexico-based Jon Morrow. His year-old blog Boost Blog Traffic (boostblogtraffic.com) earned $500,000 in 2012. If you don't know what readers want, Morrow says, take polls and ask questions to find out.

Write strong headlines

If you want readers to find your posts online, your headlines need key words and phrases that relate to your topic, to help them rank well in Google searches for your topic. You can do keyword research free using Google's tool (https://adwords.google.com/o/KeywordTool). Headlines also need to be lively and interesting to draw readers—Morrow offers a Headline Hacks report on his blog that dissects effective headline styles.

Use blog style

Blog posts are different from magazine articles because of how people read—make that skim—online, says Dunn. Good blog-post paragraphs are short, often just one or two sentences. Posts with bold subheads or bulleted or numbered lists are easy to scan and often enjoy higher readership.

Make sharing easy

To grow your audience, you'll need readers to spread the word, says Dunn. Make that easy with one-click sharing buttons for Twitter, Facebook and other popular social-media platforms. You should be active in these platforms, too, building relationships with influential people who might send you readers.

Start guest-posting

One of the fastest ways to build your blog audience is by guest-posting on popular blogs with lots of traffic. Your guest post will give you a link back to your own blog and allow new readers to find you. This is usually not paid work, but think of it as a marketing cost for your blog-based business. Many top blogs do accept guest posts—look for writer's guidelines on their sites.

"The big secret to making money from blogging is to get serious about marketing," Morrow says.

Build an e-mail list

The best way to stay in touch with readers is via an e-mail list visitors are encouraged to join, says Dunn. Subscribers who sign up through real simple syndication, or RSS, don't reveal their e-mail address, so it's hard to sell them anything.

START EARNING

Once your blog is set up to entice readers, you're ready to experiment with ways to generate income off your blog. Among the common approaches:

1. Freelance Gigs

Add a "Hire Me" tab to your site to begin attracting freelance blogging gigs from online businesses and publications. That's the approach U.K.-based writer Tom Ewer took when he quit his job and launched his blog Leaving Work Behind (www.leavingworkbehind.com) in 2011.

A brand-new writer at the time, Ewer quickly got a couple of freelance blogging clients by applying to online job ads. More clients approached him after seeing his guest posts on big blogs and finding his blog from there. Ewer was soon blogging for pay about topics including WordPress and government contracting. By late 2012, he was earning $4,000 a month as a paid blogger at $100 a post and up, working part-time hours.

A similar strategy worked for Nigerian blogger Bamidele Onibalusi, who began his online-earning themed blog YoungPrePro (www.youngprepro.com) in 2010, when he was just 16. By 2012, he was making $50,000 a year writing for blog owners who learned of him from his dozens of guest posts on top blogs including DailyBlogTips and ProBlogger.

He's blogged for paying clients in the U.S., U.K., Greece, and elsewhere about real estate, accounting, and weight loss, among other topics. Onibalusi says he impresses prospects with long, highly useful posts with strong key words that attract an ongoing stream of readers.

"Google has sent me most of my business," he says.

2. Books & eBooks

Build a major following on your blog, and you can earn well writing and selling your own books and e-books. That strategy has been successful for Jeff Goins of the writing and social-change blog GoinsWriter (goinswriter.com), who has two Kindle e-books and a traditionally published print book under his belt.

Launched in 2010 and now boasting 25,000 subscribers, GoinsWriter has loyal fans who help drive more than $3,500 a month in sales of his two low-priced e-books, including his co-authored *You Are a Writer (So Start Acting Like One)*, which goes for just $2.99.

Goins first creates excitement around his e-books by blogging about the upcoming release first. Then, as the publication date nears, he gives more than 100 diehard fans a free PDF of the e-book in exchange for Amazon reviews. When he officially publishes a few days later on Amazon and elsewhere, the glowing reviews help encourage thousands of purchases. The reviews and frequent downloads keep his e-books ranking highly for the writing category, which drives more sales. Links in the e-book also help bring more blog readers.

E-book sales also kicked off the blog-earning career of Pat Flynn, a southern Californian who first had modest blog-monetizing success with an e-book he wrote on how to pass an architectural exam. He started the Smart Passive Income (www.smartpassiveincome.com) blog in 2008 to dissect that success. This second blog went on to greatly surpass the original project, bringing in over $200,000 its first year alone.

3. Affiliate Sales

Flynn earns primarily through affiliate sales, a strategy in which a blogger receives a commission for selling someone else's product or service. It's an approach that works best with a large audience—Smart Passive Income has 57,000 subscribers and gets 100,000 visitors a month.

His audience includes many bloggers who need to set up their websites, so many of his affiliate products are tools or services that enable bloggers. Flynn's top-selling affiliate product in 2012 was website host Bluehost, from which he now typically earns $20,000 or more monthly. He receives a commission every time someone signs up for website hosting through his unique affiliate links.

"I find products that help them get from A to Z," he says. "They're recommended products I've actually used. You want to be sort of an expert in it."

Flynn builds loyalty by creating free blog posts that offer "high value content that would usually require payment." Rather than slapping up ads that might annoy readers, he simply states that site links earn him a commission. Fans are happy to click, and even send him thank-you notes about the products he sells.

Like many top-earning bloggers, Flynn uses videos and podcasts to help promote his blogs. Flynn's Smart Passive Income Podcast has brought many new readers—it's one of the top business-related podcasts on iTunes and has seen more than 2 million downloads.

4. Courses & Coaching

When you've built your reputation through delivering useful blog posts, you can sell your fans more advanced information on your topic. Courses and coaching are the main earners for Boost Blog Traffic's Morrow, who teaches a guest-blogging class and takes just 10 students at a time in his $10,000-a-head, five-month coaching course. The secret sauce in the guest-blogging class includes personal introductions by Morrow to top blog editors.

Build your authority enough, and customers pay just for the opportunity to learn from someone they respect, says Morrow.

"I'm not really selling products," he says. "I'm selling me."

Morrow attributes part of his earning success to hard work to improve the marketing campaigns for his paid programs. He says he's spent hundreds of hours testing and tinkering with marketing e-mails and promotional videos that help sell the courses. Now that he's refined his process, he says he needs to spend only five hours a week on his guest-blogging course. Affiliates do much of the selling of his blogging course for him.

An extension of this teaching niche is public speaking, for which top presenters can earn tens of thousands of dollars per appearance. Morrow recently presented at the New Media Expo (formerly known as BlogWorld), for instance.

5. Membership Community

Once they're publishing, teaching, speaking, and creating audio and video materials on a topic, bloggers can leverage all that content to earn even more through a paid membership community. Inside the community, members can access large amounts of training materials and their favorite expert's advice via chat forums for one low monthly rate, instead of paying for it piecemeal. The community model allows bloggers to earn more as additional members join without having to do much more work, as members mostly access existing content.

Large communities can be major money generators—for instance, A-List Blogger Club (www.alistbloggingbootcamps.com/alist-blogger-club-join), a blog-building training community started by top blogger Leo Babauta of Zen Habits that I used to learn how to build my own blog, had roughly 900 members in 2012 paying $20 apiece per month. The blog Write to Done (writetodone.com) serves as the main platform that introduces writers to the club.

Blogging is not for every writer. It's a lot of work coming up with post ideas and writing several posts a month or even a week. It can be many months until a blog starts to earn money, and there are no guarantees it will ever catch on. But for writers with the drive to stick with it and a willingness to learn about blog marketing, the rewards can be rich.

CAROL TICE writes the Make a Living Writing (www.makealivingwriting.com) blog and runs the writers learning community Freelance Writers Den (freelancewritersden.com). She has written two nonfiction business books and co-authored the Kindle e-book *13 Ways to Get the Writing Done Faster* (www.amazon.com/Ways-Writing-Done-Faster-ebook/dp/B009XM03SK).

GET WRITING GIGS IN SOCIAL MEDIA

Without Spending All Day Online

by Carol Tice

Tweets. Hangouts. Connections. Social media is a world with its own language, and each platform has its own vibe. If you're baffled by social media or feel it's too late to jump in, don't worry.

It's easy to learn how to get around, and definitely worth the effort. Social media can help you connect with editors or marketing managers you'd otherwise never have a chance to meet, especially if you live in a small town or outside the U.S.

Many writers view social media as a place to kill time with friends, but it can be a valuable marketing tool for freelancers who know how to use it and employ a focused approach.

Marketing on social media is a little tricky, because the main point of social media is not selling but socializing, notes Andrew Macarthy, U.K.-based author of 500 Social Media Marketing Tips. Overt sales pitches—"Hire me for freelance writing work!" are likely to get you the cold shoulder, which in social media takes the form of blocking your posts or "unfriending" you.

Successful social-media marketers focus on being helpful, Macarthy says. Make 80 percent of your posts simply useful information and links you think your connections or friends would like, and limit your sales pitches to 20 percent or less.

On any platform you join, be sure to completely fill out your profile and post status updates regularly, so that you appear active and visitors can learn about what you do, notes Macarthy.

With those basics, you're ready to get started in social media. Here's a look at how to get the most from four of the most popular platforms where freelance writers are reporting success finding clients:

LINKEDIN

If you're pressed for time but want to get involved in social media marketing, consider LinkedIn your first stop, says Boston-based freelance writer Susan Johnston, author of LinkedIn and Lovin' It (Rockable Press). This platform is all-business—no teenagers talking about where they partied last weekend—and you can do valuable marketing here in just a few minutes a week, once you get set up. Key features to know:

Profile—Be sure to include a picture and a headline with key words that are phrased the way prospects might search within LinkedIn for a writer of your type, says Johnston—i.e. "freelance science writer" rather than "freelance writing."

"LinkedIn is a big, giant search engine for freelancers," Johnston says.

Connections—Once your profile is set, start searching for colleagues, friends, and former editors. Send them invitations to connect. If they accept your invite, it will also connect you in a secondary way to all of their connections, broadening your network. When you spot 2nd-level connections to people you'd like to know, you can ask your connection to introduce you.

Atlanta freelance writer Lisa Baker struck gold on LinkedIn after refining her headline to read "freelance parenting writer." Soon after, she noticed a connection invite from an editor who turned out to work at one of Baker's target magazines, *Babytalk* (since discontinued).

"I couldn't believe she had asked to connect with me!" Baker says.

Baker accepted her invite and sent her an InMail—as LI's private e-mails are known—asking if the editor was looking for writers or ideas. She was, and Baker's followup story-idea query yielded invaluable tips on what the magazine was looking for. Baker got an assignment from the editor and broke into her first $1-a-word market, from following up on that LinkedIn connection.

Recommendations—You can request testimonials—or Recommendations, as LinkedIn calls them—from current and past clients. Flattering Recommendations can be approved and posted to your profile to be read by prospects.

One must-join is LinkedIn for Journalists. The group offers a free training on how to use LI. After taking the training, writers receive the Premium or paid level of LinkedIn free.

Groups—LinkedIn is loaded with interest groups that can be great places to learn, build connections, and potentially find clients, says Johnston. One must-join is LinkedIn for Journalists. The group offers a free training on how to use LI. After taking the training, writers receive the Premium or paid level of LinkedIn free. Premium access is valuable because it allows you to use InMail—LI's internal e-mail system—to contact unlimited prospects monthly, even people who are not connections.

Who's Viewed My Profile—This sidebar widget shows you which LI users have read your profile recently. With Premium access, you'll see enough information to InMail these prospects to see if they are looking for a writer.

FACEBOOK

The world's most popular social media site is one many writers already use. Facebook has a reputation as a place to chit-chat, game, and share videos, but writers are finding gigs on Facebook, when they tread carefully.

"The majority of content you post on Facebook should not be promotional in nature," warns author Macarthy. "Instead of selling yourself on Facebook, work towards getting your friends and fans to do it for you."

Groups—Let your Facebook friends know what you do, and you might find a referral to a gig. Keep an eye out for relevant groups to join. Groups paid off for freelance writer MeLinda Schnyder of Wichita, Kan., after she joined writer/entrepreneur Alexis Grant's private Facebook group Rockin' the Side Gig.

"I noticed the editor of a website that does app reviews posting to the group that she was looking to add a contributor," Schnyder relates. The resulting gig allowed Schnyder to break in to a new writing niche.

Pages—Facebook allows you to create a business page that can be a useful platform for promoting your writing. In late 2013, Facebook changed its policies to cut the number of people who views posts on pages unless their authors paid to "boost" or promote them, but writers are still getting results with their pages.

One feature that still works well despite Facebook's change is to simply raise awareness by inviting friends who use FB to "like" your page. Freelance writer Christy Mossburg of Frederick, Md., decided to do just that in late 2013, and sent an invite to all of her friends who had any business connection.

This paid off when a local dog trainer contacted her within an hour of his "like" invite to say, "Can we talk? I need your services." The resulting offer to write blog posts grew into a $750 web-content project.

"Now that is in my portfolio," she says, "and I'll be writing weekly blog posts for him."

GOOGLE PLUS

The social media platform created by search engine company Google is a relative newcomer to the scene, having just debuted in 2011. But Google+, as it's better known, is packed with unique potential to promote your writing career, says Google+/online search expert Johnny Base of Richmond, Va.

Because Google+ is owned by Google, posts here get more prominence in Google's search results than any other form of social media. That's a huge plus if you're trying to get your writer website to rank well on a niche search such as "Austin freelance writer," or trying to grow your blog audience.

Google+ is the only social media site where your posts are indexed by Google and findable on search almost immediately, Base notes. As Google+ users in your "circles" (as friends or connections are known here) share or vote for what you've posted by clicking the "+1" button, your content is ranked more highly, he notes. Other ways Google+ helps you become more prominent online:

Authorship—Google+ aims to be the central hub for everything you create online, says Base. The Authorship feature links your outside content to your Google+ profile to help give what you write elsewhere a search-results boost. Inserting a short "author" code on sites such as your blog makes your content there appear more prominently in Google search results and grabs attention because it includes your photo, notes Base.

....

Google+ is the only social media site where your posts are indexed by Google and findable on search almost immediately.

....

"All of a sudden, you come off as an authority," he says.

Google walks you through the steps for using Authorship at http://plus.google.com/authorship.

Communities—Base says some of the best connections are being made in Google+ Communities, which are similar to LI and FB groups. Base says prominent people have jumped on Google+ and are easily accessible on the platform, especially if you participate in their groups. Join communities, be helpful, share ideas, and you may find yourself with new writing opportunities.

Conversations on a private Google+ Communities group run by blogging and social media superstar Chris Brogan helped one freelance writer find clients. Web copywriter Tania Dakka of Toledo, Ohio, says offering tips to group members having website challenges led to several work offers, including a gig writing a single landing page for $1,000. She says business-to-business focused writers will do well on Google+.

"It's been a door-opener like I never thought," she says.

Hangouts—Google+ is thus far the only social media channel where you can jump on a live video chat with up to ten people. That feature gives Google+ users the chance to make intimate connections that aren't possible elsewhere, says Base.

"Having face to face engagement is like networking on steroids times 1,000," Base says. "After a Hangout, you feel like these people are your friends. I've never had that experience in any other social network."

TWITTER

If you think a place that limits your posts to 140 characters can't get you freelance gigs, think again. Twitter offers a strong search engine for finding prospects, and users reward those who help others.

"Use Twitter search to discover people asking questions you can easily answer," says social-media author Macarthy. "Selflessly provide assistance, and those good deeds will be seen by potential clients."

New freelance writer Edward Beaman of Canterbury, U.K., found his first client on Twitter, when he was still a newbie with only a half-dozen tweets to his name. By entering search terms such as "new website" and "website coming soon," he located and followed business owners who were in the process of launching a site.

One London electrical contractor responded when Beaman asked if he needed web content help. A $400 web content project was the result, which led to additional work on the client's LinkedIn profile.

"I got my first testimonial and gained a hell of a lot of confidence to push forward with my freelancing career," he says.

After you fill out your profile, take advantage of these features:

Follow and engage—You're free to "follow" or connect with anyone on Twitter, from Justin Bieber to the Dalai Lama. A difference between here and LI is that on Twitter, one of you can follow the other without reciprocation. If you both follow each other on Twitter, you can send private Direct Messages.

You can find other writers and editors to connect with using Muck Rack (muckrack. com), a site that tracks journalists on Twitter.

Once you're following someone, you'll be able to see their posts on your Twitter page. That will allow you to retweet or share their posts, comment, and ask questions.

Hashtags—It's easy to find people who might be good referrers or prospects for you by searching for topics and chat groups on Twitter. Subjects are organized using the "#" or hashtag mark. Popular writer hashtags include #amwriting and #WW or Writer Wednesday. Using these hashtags in Twitter's search engine gives you a custom tweetstream to browse of everyone who's been discussing that topic.

For instance, grant writer Micki Vandeloo has built her referral network by participating in #grantchat, which is for grant seekers, managers, and related consultants. She also landed a regular subcontracting gig writing grants for another writer who found her after seeing one of Vandeloo's blog post links on Twitter.

"I'm based in a town of 625 outside St. Louis, literally with cows in my back yard," says Vandeloo. "Twitter has been a great way for me to connect with people all over, even if it's a snowy day."

STAYING ORGANIZED

If you're jumping on multiple social networks, how do you keep social media marketing from eating your whole day? Planning campaigns and scheduling posts in batches is key, says author Macarthy.

Instead of popping on and off Twitter or Facebook all day, think carefully about your marketing goals for the coming weeks. Then use tools such as Buffer or HootSuite to create posts in a single session—and then schedule them to post a week or more ahead, across all your different social-media channels. Macarthy recommends creating a file for saving interesting links.

This allows you to do the bulk of your social media marketing in one session. Hop on briefly now and then to respond and help others, and you're done.

"Without thought and planning, social media can be a major time suck, complete with abject disappointment if no positive leads are forthcoming," says Macarthy. "But sites like Facebook and Twitter can improve your stature, audience, and paid work if approached in the right way."

CAROL TICE writes the Make a Living Writing (www.makealivingwriting.com) blog and runs the writers learning community Freelance Writers Den (freelancewritersden.com). She has written two nonfiction business books and co-authored the Kindle e-book *13 Ways to Get the Writing Done Faster* (www.amazon.com/Ways-Writing-Done-Faster-ebook/dp/B009XM03SK).

REPRINTS AND RESLANTS

More Money in the Bank

···

by Sue Bradford Edwards

Your goals this year include making more money with your writing, and it should be do-able. After all, you've been selling your work for some time now and have a solid resume. Deadlines pepper your calendar.

To increase your income, you can take on more assignments, but look at your calendar. You're working close to capacity now. If you take on much more, the quality of your work will suffer.

Fortunately, there is another solution. Maximize your efforts by selling both your research and your writing multiple times.

SELLING ONE PIECE REPEATEDLY

The easiest way to do this is by selling a piece of writing more than once. Selling a reprint is, in short, re-selling a piece of writing that has already been published. To make this work, you have to plan ahead in terms of what rights you sell.

"I sell a lot of reprints, so I always try to retain reprint rights, or nonexclusive reprint rights," says Kelly James-Enger, a long time freelancer and author of books including *Writer for Hire: 101 Secrets to Freelance Success*. "Sometimes markets will buy first N.A. serial rights and then I can reprint the story after the story first runs. In other cases, I'll sell all rights but see if I can negotiate retaining nonexclusive reprint rights. Markets don't always agree but it doesn't hurt to ask."

Jennifer Brown Banks, a freelancer who writes for blogs and magazines, agrees. "I typically extend 'one-time' rights or 'reprint' rights; thus I retain authorship to my pieces to place them as I wish in the future."

If you have kept the necessary rights, the next step is to find receptive markets. "Sometimes I Google 'reprint markets,'" Banks says. "Other times I simply check the writer's guidelines of popular publications to assess the possibilities. Checking by themes is another way."

While more smaller than larger publications accept reprints, some niche markets are also more receptive. "I look for smaller, regional, and/or specialty mags that need content about subjects I cover," James-Enger says. "I've had the most success selling to parenting, fitness/health, and bridal magazines."

Another possible market for reprints is anthologies. This is where Abigail Green, author of over 200 individual pieces, resells her essays.

If you are already making sales, an editor may contact you. "*Writer's Digest* once asked for a reprint of a piece I did for their magazine, for inclusion in a special edition annual publication, and I simply sold it for 25% of the original price," says C. Hope Clark, editor of Funds for Writers and author of the mystery *Lowcountry Bribe*. "We both recognized that as a fair price and didn't dicker on the payment. Very simple arrangement."

When an editor wants to reprint something that has appeared in another family of magazines, arrangements become more complicated. "Sometimes the editor has seen a particular story and wants to run it in her own magazine," says James-Enger. "If I own the rights, we negotiate from there. In others, an editor I've worked with before, or who knows I have hundreds of articles available, will contact me and ask for a story on a specific subject. If I have something that will work, I'll ask what they usually pay for reprints or ask for a specific amount to reprint it."

Banks has also been contacted by an editor. "I have been approached somewhat informally by a regular editor with whom I've worked for many years," says Banks. "Since she manages a print publication, she will sometimes request to use articles I have posted online for a similar niche."

Selling reprints takes very little work, but some writers wonder if the check you will receive is too small to bother. "I've actually made more money from my reprints in some cases than the original article," says Banks. "I've been paid $50 for a feature piece that I've later resold for $150."

The downside is that, because you are selling the same article, you will only be able to sell it so many times before you are looking at competing magazines. No editor wants to run content that a competitor has already published. Fortunately, you can also increase your income by reselling your research and basic knowledge on a topic.

COMING AT THE TOPIC IN A DIFFERENT WAY

Reslants offer more opportunities than reprints because, you are selling similar, not identical, pieces of writing. Explains Green, "Let's say you see a movie. You can write a movie review, or you can write a piece for writers on what they can learn from actors, or you can write an opinion piece on how shows like Glee and The Voice have influenced popular culture," she says. "You aren't taking the same article and selling it to *Parents* and *Parenting*. You're taking the same topic and reslanting it to different audiences. In most cases, the article will vary so much because you are writing for different audiences, different markets, and a different word count, that they are completely different articles."

Many writers worry that reslanting a topic will be just as much work as writing a whole new piece. "I usually end up with five times as much material as I can use in the finished piece," Green says. "Why let it go to waste? With practice, you go into an assignment thinking 'How else can I approach this topic for a different market?' It becomes second nature."

Banks agrees, "It is a means of 'working smarter, not harder,'" she says. "I typically do this with my relationship articles, as well as 'how-to' writing pieces. These are always popular reads."

THE DOWNSIDE TO RESLANTING

Do you dread writing two articles on the same topic, let alone four or five? You aren't alone.

"I'm not the normal voice of authority on this," says Clark. "I abhor having to take old material and reshape it. I'd much prefer to maybe take resources or research and write an entirely new piece. My voice is fresher, and I never have to worry about anyone saying they've seen it someplace before."

Says Clark, "My feelings about this go back to a fiasco that occurred years ago with two competing magazines. I took the same topic and wrote entirely different pieces for these two magazines. While the topic was similar, the pieces were original. However, these competing magazines just happened to decide to publish the pieces in the same month. I received my writer's copies in the mail the same day, and while I should've been ecstatic to see my name in print, I was devastated that they'd chosen the same month. Even though they were unique pieces, the editors were not happy. My name was the same. The topic was the same."

"I've never pitched competing magazines since. And if I ever decide to, it'll be with entirely different topics. One of the magazines wouldn't speak to me for five years. I totally get it. Magazine editors have their hands full trying to keep subscribers through novel and unique material, and situations like mine don't make their jobs easier. My advice to others is to avoid reslanting and refocusing pieces to competing publications. They watch each other like a hawk."

The moral of the story? Make sure no two stories appear the same. Change your approach. Change your audience. A humorous essay for a women's magazine doesn't duplicate a journalistic article for a men's fitness site. The editors won't feel cheated and you won't be bored writing two pieces that are too similar.

Change the market and the audience and you will have a piece that is only vaguely related to the others you have written on the same topic. "I wrote a piece for *Fit* on using heart rate monitors to lose weight," James-Enger says. "Then I did a story for *Experience Life* on using them to get more out of your workout. Several months later, I wrote a piece for a men's fitness magazine on using heart rate monitors to get more out of your cardio workout. Typically men prefer to lift weights and hate doing cardio. Then I wrote a piece for *Family Circle* on using your heart rate to get more out of your walks. What I do is come up with a specific angle for the story for a particular market, and see how many times I can reslant the topic—in this case, how heart rate monitors can help you get more from your workout." In this way, James-Enger wrote four unique articles using the same basic idea.

Green often reslants her work by changing her approach, penning both essays and articles. "I could write a first person essay about growing up in a TV-limited household," she says. "That's just a straight essay, but I have also reslanted that into a reported piece where I interviewed experts and included reports on the effects of screen time."

A new tone can also reslant a piece. "Even within just the essay genre, you can reslant," Green says. "You can take a more humorous slant and do a humor piece. I've written some essays in the style of a letter to my younger self. It's the same material but you alter how you approach it."

Using different sources for different markets is another way to reslant a piece. "If I'm writing for an online magazine and want to later submit a piece to a print publication, I may change the links that I provide as 'resources' to book recommendations," Banks says. "Additionally, I will sometimes lessen word counts for online readers and give shorter paragraphs and bullet points for easier skimming of material."

These authors aren't reslanting and then looking for a market. "Usually when I'm reslanting I'm doing it for a specific market such as one looking for letters to your younger self," says Green. Having a market in mind can help you find the new slant.

Once you know a topic, each subsequent piece comes together with less effort. "I think the best advice is to avoid what I call 'one-shots,' where you write about a subject only once," James-Enger says. "Come up with different angles and look for noncompeting markets that you can pitch the story to. You'll still have do additional research, typically interviewing more or different sources, but you already know a lot about the subject matter so the second, third, etc. stories take less time to write and make you more efficient. Even if you don't think of a second angle when you first come up with the initial idea, be open to finding more as you research and write the piece. That happens to me frequently. Or I will see something in the news or a recent study that makes me think of a new way to approach a story I have written in the past."

One final piece of advice. Periodically go through your files and take a look at what hasn't sold. "One example that I give in my class I had a work related anecdote that I reslanted 5 different ways over the course of several years before I finally sold it," Green says. "I tried a women's magazine, a business magazines, tweaking it slightly for the market. It finally sold to the career section of a newspaper when I slanted it to be about finding personal space at work. That wasn't the approach I took in the original but I eventually found a home for it." Reslanting your work opens up a variety of markets and increases sales.

You've heard the advice—work smarter, not harder. Apply this to your writing life by selling your research and your writing as many times as possible. If you do, you will find your by-lines and bank deposits adding up as you build a name for yourself as the go-to author on a variety of topics.

SUE BRADFORD EDWARDS works from her home in St. Louis, MIssouri. Her articles have appeared in *Writer's Digest, Children's Writer* newsletter, the *Writer's Guide,* and more publications. Find out more about her and her work at One Writer's Journey (suebe.wordpress.com).

FUNDS FOR WRITERS 101:

Find Money You Didn't Know Existed

....

by C. Hope Clark

When I completed writing my novel over a decade ago, I imagined the next step was simply to find a publisher and watch the book sell. Like most writers, my goal was to earn a living doing what I loved so I could walk away from the day job. No such luck. Between rejection and newfound knowledge that a novel can take years to sell enough for a single house payment, I opened my mind to other writing avenues. After researching in depth, I learned that there's no *one* way to find funds to support your writing; instead there are *many*. So many, in fact, that I felt the need to share the volume of knowledge I collected, and I called it FundsforWriters.com.

Funds are money. But obtaining those funds isn't necessarily a linear process, or a one-dimensional path. As a serious writer, you study all options at your fingertips, entertaining financial resources that initially don't make sense as well as the obvious. In the end, it's about publishing. In the interim, it's about identifying the fiscal resources to get you there.

GRANTS

Grants come from government agencies, nonprofits, businesses and even generous individuals. They do not have to be repaid, as long as you use the grant as intended. No two are alike. Therefore, you must do your homework to find the right match between your grant need and the grant provider's mission. Grantors like being successful at their mission just as you like excelling at yours. So they screen applicants, ensuring they fit the rules and show promise to follow through.

Don't fear grants. Sure, you're judged by a panel, and rejection is part of the game, but you already know that as a writer. Gigi Rosenberg, author of *The Artist's Guide to Grant Writing*, states, "If one funder doesn't want to invest in your project, find another who does.

And if nobody does, then begin it any way you can. Once you've started, that momentum will help your project find its audience and its financial support."

TYPES OF GRANTS

Grants can send you to retreats, handle emergencies, provide mentors, pay for conferences, or cover travel. They also can be called awards, fellowships, residencies, or scholarships. But like any aspect of your writing journey, define how any tool, even a grant, fits into your plans. Your mission must parallel a grantor's mission.

The cream-of-the-crop grants have no strings attached. Winning recipients are based upon portfolios and an application that defines a work-in-progress. You don't have to be a Pulitzer winner, but you must prove your establishment as a writer.

You find most of these opportunities in state arts commissions. Find them at www.nasaa-arts.org or as a partner listed at the National Endowment for the Arts website, www.nea.gov. Not only does your state's arts commission provide funding, but the players can direct you to other grant opportunities, as well as to artists who've gone before you. Speaking to grant winners gives you a wealth of information and a leg up in designing the best application.

Foundations and nonprofits fund the majority of grants. Most writers' organizations are nonprofits. Both the Mystery Writers of America (www.mysterywriters.org) and Society of Children's Book Writers and Illustrators (www.scbwi.org) offer scholarships and grants.

Many retreats are nonprofits. Journalist and freelancer Alexis Grant, (http://alexis-grant.com/) tries to attend a retreat a year. Some ask her to pay, usually on a sliding scale based upon income, and others provide scholarships. Each time, she applies with a clear definition of what she hopes to gain from the two to five-week trips. "It's a great way to get away from the noise of everyday responsibilities, focus on writing well and meet other people who prioritize writing. I always return home with a new perspective." A marvelous resource to find writing retreats is the Alliance of Artists Communities (http://www.artist-communities.org/).

Laura Lee Perkins won four artist-in-residence slots with the National Park Service (http://nps.gov). The federal agency has 43 locations throughout the United States where writers and artists live for two to four weeks. From Acadia National Park in Maine to Sleeping Bear Dunes National Lakeshore in Michigan, Laura spoke to tourists about her goals to write a book about Native American music. "Memories of the US National Parks' beauty and profound serenity will continue to enrich my work. Writers find unparalleled inspiration, quietude, housing, interesting staff, and a feeling of being in the root of your artistic desires."

Don't forget writers' conferences. While they may not advertise financial aid, many have funds available in times of need. Always ask as to the availability of a scholarship or work-share program that might enable your attendance.

Grants come in all sizes. FundsforWriters posts most emergency grants on its grants page (www.fundsforwriters.com/grants.htm) as well as periodic new grant opportunities such as the Sustainable Arts Foundation (www.sustainableartsfoundation.org) that offers grants twice a year to writers and artists with children under the age of 18, or the Awesome Foundation (www.awecomefoundation.org), which gives $1,000 grants to "awesome" creative projects.

Novelist Joan Dempsey won an Elizabeth George Foundation grant (http://www.elizabethgeorgeonline.com/foundation/index.htm) in early 2012. "I applied to the Foundation for a research grant that included three trips to places relevant to my novel-in-progress, trips I otherwise could not have afforded. Not only does the grant provide travel funds, but it also provides validation that I'm a serious writer worthy of investment, which is great for my psyche and my resume."

FISCAL SPONSORSHIP

Nonprofits have access to an incredibly large number of grants that individuals do not, and have the ability to offer their tax-exempt status to groups and individuals involved in activities related to their mission. By allowing a nonprofit to serve as your grant overseer, you may acquire funds for your project.

Deborah Marshall is President of the Missouri Writers Guild (www.missouriwritersguild.org) and founder of the Missouri Warrior Writers Project, with ample experience with grants in the arts. "Although grant dollars are available for individual writers, writing the grant proposal becomes difficult without significant publication credits. Partnering with a nonprofit organization, whether it is a writing group, service, community organization, or any 501(c)3, can fill in those gaps to make a grant application competitive. Partnering not only helps a writer's name become known, but it also assists in building that all-important platform."

Two excellent groups that offer fiscal sponsorship for writers are The Fractured Atlas (www.fracturedatlas.org) and Artspire (www.artspire.org) sponsored by the New York Foundation for the Arts and open to all US citizens. Visit The Foundation Center (www.foundationcenter.org) for an excellent tutorial guide to fiscal sponsorship.

CROWD SOURCING

Crowd sourcing is a co-op arrangement where people support artists directly, much like the agricultural co-op movement where individuals fund farming operations in exchange for fresh food. Kickstarter (www.kickstarter.com) has made huge strides in making this funding method successful in the arts.

Basically, the writer proposes his project, and for a financial endorsement as low as $1, donors receive some token in return, like an autographed book, artwork, or bookmark.

The higher the donation, the bigger the *wow* factor in the gift. Donors do not receive ownership in the project.

Meagan Adele Lopez (www.ladywholunches.net) presented her debut self-published book *Three Questions* to Kickstarter readers, requesting $4,400 to take her book on tour, create a book trailer, pre-order books, and redesign the cover. Eighty-eight backers pledged a total of $5,202. She was able to hire an editor and a company that designed film trailers. For every $750 she received over her plan, she added a new city to her book tour.

Other crowd sourcing companies are up and coming to include Culture 360 (www.culture360.org) that serves Asia and Europe, and Indiegogo (www.indiegogo.com), as well as Rocket Hub (www.rockethub.com). And nothing stops you from simply asking those you know to support your project. The concept is elementary.

CONTESTS

Contests offer financial opportunity, too. Of course you must win, place or show, but many writers overlook the importance that contests have on a career. These days, contests not only open doors to publishing, name recognition, and money, but listing such achievements in a query letter might make an agent or publisher take a second glance. Noting your wins on a magazine pitch might land a feature assignment. Mentioning your accolades to potential clients could clinch a freelance deal.

I used contests as a barometer when fleshing out my first mystery novel, *A Lowcountry Bribe*, Bell Bridge Books. After I placed in several contests, earned a total of $750, and reached the semi-finals of the Amazon Breakthrough Novel Award (www.createspace.com/abna), my confidence grew strong enough to pitch agents. My current agent admits that the contest wins drew her in.

Contests can assist in sales of existing books, not only aiding sales but also enticing more deals for future books . . . or the rest of your writing profession.

Whether writing short stories, poetry, novels or nonfiction, contests abound. As with any call for submission, study the rules. Double checking with entities that screen, like FundsforWriters.com and WinningWriters.com, will help alleviate concerns when selecting where to enter.

FREELANCING

A thick collection of freelancing clips can make an editor sit up and take notice. You've been vetted and accepted by others in the business, and possibly established a following. The more well known the publications, the brighter your aura.

Sooner or later in your career, you'll write an article. In the beginning, articles are a great way to gain your footing. As your career develops, you become more of an expert, and are expected to enlighten and educate about your journey and the knowledge you've acquired. Articles are, arguably, one of the best means to income and branding for writers.

Trade magazines, national periodicals, literary journals, newsletters, newspapers and blogs all offer you a chance to present yourself, earn money, and gain readers for a platform. Do not discount them as income earners.

Linda Formichelli, of Renegade Writer fame (www.therenegadewriter.com) leaped into freelance magazine writing because she simply loved to write, and that love turned her into an expert. "I never loved working to line someone else's pockets." A full-time freelancer since 1997, with credits like *Family Circle*, *Redbook*, and *Writer's Digest*, she also writes articles, books, e-courses, and e-books about her profession as a magazine writer.

JOBS

Part-time, full-time, temporary or permanent, writing jobs hone your skills, pad your resume, and present avenues to movers and shakers you wouldn't necessarily meet on your own. Government and corporate managers hire writers under all sorts of guises like Social Media Specialist and Communications Specialist, as well as the expected Reporter and Copywriter.

Alexis Grant considers her prior jobs as catapults. "Working at a newspaper (*Houston Chronicle*) and a news magazine (*US News & World Report*) for six years provided the foundation for what I'm doing now as a freelancer. Producing stories regularly on tight deadlines will always make you a better writer."

Joan Dempsey chose to return to full-time work and write her novel on the side, removing worries about her livelihood. "My creative writing was suffering trying to freelance. So, I have a day job that supports me now." She still maintains her Facebook presence to continue building her platform for her pending novel.

DIVERSIFICATION

Most importantly, however, is learning how to collect all your funding options and incorporate them into your plan. The successful writer doesn't perform in one arena. Instead, he thrives in more of a three-ring circus.

Grant states it well: "For a long while I thought of myself as only a journalist, but there are so many other ways to use my skills. Today my income comes from three streams: helping small companies with social media and blogging (the biggest source), writing and selling e-guides and courses (my favorite), and taking freelance writing or editing assignments."

Formichelli is proud of being flexible. "When I've had it with magazine writing, I put more energy into my e-courses, and vice versa. Heck, I'm even a certified personal trainer, so if I get really sick of writing I can work out. But a definite side benefit to diversifying is that I'm more protected from the feast-or-famine nature of writing."

Sometimes pursuing the more common sense or lucrative income opportunity can open doors for the dream. When my novel didn't sell, I began writing freelance articles. Then I established FundsforWriters, using all the grant, contest, publisher and market research I did for myself. A decade later, once the site thrived with over 45,000 readers, I used the very research I'd gleaned for my readers to find an agent and sign a publishing contract . . . for the original novel started so long ago.

You can fight to fund one project or study all resources and fund a career. Opportunity is there. Just don't get so wrapped up in one angle that you miss the chance to invest more fully in your future.

C. HOPE CLARK manages FundsforWriters.com, a site selected for *Writer's Digest's* 101 Best Websites for Writers for the past twelve years. She is also author of *A Lowcountry Bribe*, the first in The Palmetto State Mystery Series published by Bell Bridge Books . She lives on the banks of Lake Murray, South Carolina and presents to several writers conferences each year.

SELF-PUBLISHING CHECKLIST

Below is a checklist of essential hurdles to clear when self-publishing your book. This list makes the assumption that you've already completed and polished your manuscript. For more information on self-publishing, check out *The Complete Guide to Self-Publishing*, by Tom and Marilyn Ross (Writer's Digest).

☐ **CREATE PRODUCTION SCHEDULE.** Put a deadline for every step of the process of self-publishing your book. A good rule of thumb is to double your estimates on how long each step will take. It's better to have too much time and hit your dates than constantly have to extend deadlines.

☐ **FIND EDITOR.** Don't skimp on your project and do all the editing yourself. Even editors need editors. Try to find an editor you trust, whether through a recommendation or a search online. Ask for references if the editor is new to you.

☐ **FIND DESIGNER.** Same goes here. Find a good designer to at least handle the cover. If you can have a designer lay out the interior pages too, that's even better.

☐ **DEFINE THE TARGET AUDIENCE.** In nonfiction this is an important step, because knowing the needs of the audience can help with the editing process. Even if you're writing fiction or poetry, it's a good idea to figure out who your audience is, because this will help you with the next few steps.

☐ **FIGURE OUT A PRINT AND DISTRIBUTION PLAN.** This plan should first figure out what the end product will be: printed book, e-book, app, or a combination of options. Then, the plan will define how the products will be created and distributed to readers.

☐ **SET PUBLICATION DATE.** The publication date should be set on your production schedule above. Respect this deadline more than all the others, because the marketing and distribution plans will most likely hinge on this deadline being met.

☐ **PLOT OUT YOUR MARKETING PLAN.** The smartest plan is to have a soft launch date of a week or two (just in case). Then, hard launch into your marketing campaign, which could be as simple as a book release party and social networking mentions, or as involved as a guest blog tour and paid advertising. With self-publishing, it's usually more prudent to spend energy and ideas than money on marketing—at least in the beginning.

☐ **HAVE AN EXCELLENT TITLE.** For nonfiction, titles are easy. Describe what your book is covering in a way that is interesting to your target audience. For fiction and poetry, titles can be a little trickier, but attempt to make your title easy to remember and refer.

☐ **GET ENDORSEMENT.** Time for this should be factored into the production schedule. Contact some authors or experts in a field related to your title and send them a copy of your manuscript to review. Ask them to consider endorsing your book, and if they do, put that endorsement on the cover. Loop in your designer to make this look good.

☐ **REGISTER COPYRIGHT.** Protect your work. Go to http://copyright.gov for more information on how to register your book.

☐ **SECURE ISBN.** An ISBN code helps booksellers track and sell your book. To learn more about securing an ISBN, go to www.isbn.org.

☐ **CREATE TABLE OF CONTENTS AND INDEX (FOR NONFICTION).** The table of contents (TOC) helps organize a nonfiction title and give structure for both the author and the reader. An index serves a similar function for readers, making it easier for them to find the information they want to find. While an index is usually not necessary for fiction or poetry, most poetry collections do use a table of contents to make it easy to locate individual poems.

☐ **INCLUDE AUTHOR BIO.** Readers want to know about the authors of the books they read. Make this information easy to find in the back of the book.

☐ **INCLUDE CONTACT INFORMATION.** In the front of the book, preferably on the copyright and ISBN page, include all contact information, including mailing address and website. E-mail address is optional, but the more options you give the better chance you'll be contacted.

☐ **EXECUTE MARKETING PLAN.** Planning is important, but execution is critical to achieving success. If you're guest posting, finish posts on time and participate in comments section of your blog post. If you're making bookstore appearances, confirm dates and show up a little early—plus invite friends and family to attend.

☐ **KEEP DETAILED ACCOUNTING RECORDS.** For tax purposes, you'll need to keep records of how much money you invest in your project, as well as how much you receive back. Keep accurate and comprehensive records from day one, and you'll be a much happier self-published author.

PUBLISHERS & THEIR IMPRINTS

The publishing world is in constant transition. With all the buying, selling, reorganizing, consolidating, and dissolving, it's hard to keep publishers and their imprints straight. To help, here's a breakdown of major publishers (and their divisions), though this information changes frequently. For instance, HarperCollins and Harlequin are currently in the process of merging (and Penguin and Random House merged in 2013). The website of each publisher is provided to help you keep an eye on this ever-evolving business.

HACHETTE BOOK GROUP USA

www.hachettebookgroup.com

CENTER STREET

FAITHWORDS

GRAND CENTRAL PUBLISHING

Business Plus

5 Spot

Forever

Forever Yours

Grand Central Life & Style

Twelve

Vision

HACHETTE BOOK GROUP DIGITAL MEDIA

Hachette Audio

HYPERION

LITTLE, BROWN AND COMPANY

Back Bay Books

Mulholland Books

LITTLE, BROWN BOOKS FOR YOUNG READERS

LB Kids

Poppy

ORBIT

YEN PRESS

HARLEQUIN ENTERPRISES

www.harlequin.com

HARLEQUIN

    Harlequin American Romance

    Harlequin Bianca

    Harlequin Blaze

    Harlequin Desire

    Harlequin Historical

    Harlequin Intrigue

    Harlequin KISS

    Harlequin Medical Romance

    Harlequin Presents

    Harlequin Romance

    Harlequin Superromance

    Harlequin eBooks

    Harlequin Special Releases

    Harlequin Nonfiction

    Harlequin Teen

    Harlequin Romantic Suspense

    Heartsong Presents

    Love Inspired

HQN BOOKS

LUNA

MIRA

KIMANI PRESS

    Kimani Press Arabesque

    Kimani Press Kimani Romance

    Kimani Press Kimani TRU

    Kimani Press New Spirit

    Kimani Press Sepia

    Kimani Press Special Releases

    Kimani Press eBooks

SILHOUETTE

    Silhouette Desire

    Silhouette Nocturne

    Silhouette Nocturne Bites

    Silhouette Romantic Suspense

    Silhouette Special Edition

    Silhouette eBooks

SPICE

    SPICE Books

    SPICE Briefs

STEEPLE HILL

    Steeple Hill Café©

    Steeple Hill Love Inspired

    Steeple Hill Love Inspired Historical

    Steeple Hill Love Inspired Suspense

    Steeple Hill Women's Fiction

    Steeple Hill eBooks

WORLDWIDE LIBRARY

    Rogue Angel

    Worldwide Mystery

    Worldwilde Library eBooks

HARLEQUIN CANADA

HARLEQUIN U.K.

    Mills & Boon

HARPERCOLLINS

www.harpercollins.com

HARPERCOLLINS GENERAL BOOKS GROUP

    Amistad

    Avon

    Avon Impulse

    Avon Inspire

    Avon Red

    Bourbon Street Books

    Anthony Bourdain Books

    Broadside Books

    Dry Street Books

    Ecco

    Harper

Harper Business

Harper Design

Harper Luxe

Harper paperbacks

Harper Perennial

Harper Voyager

HarperAudio

HarperBibles

HarperCollins e-Books

HarperOne

Igniter

William Morrow

Witness

HARPERCOLLINS CHILDREN'S BOOKS

Amistad

Balzer + Bray

Greenwillow Books

HarperCollins Children's Audio

HarperFestival

HarperTeen

Katherine Tegen Books

Walden Pond Press

HARPERCOLLINS U.K.

Fourth Estate

HarperPress

HarperPerennial

The Friday Project

HarperThorsons/Element

HarperNonFiction

HarperTrue

HarperSport

HarperFiction

   Voyager

   Blue Door

   Angry Robot

   Avon U.K.

HarperCollins Childrens Books

Collins

Collins Geo

Collins Education

Collins Language

HARPERCOLLINS CANADA

HarperCollinsPublishers

Collins Canada

HarperPerennial Canada

HarperTrophyCanada

Phyllis Bruce Books

HARPERCOLLINS AUSTRALIA

HarperCollins

Angus & Robertson

HarperSports

Fourth Estate

Harper Perennial

Collins

Voyager

HARPERCOLLINS INDIA

HARPERCOLLINS NEW ZEALAND

HarperCollins

HarperSports

Flamingo

Voyager

Perennial

ZONDERVAN

Zonderkids

Editorial Vida

Youth Specialties

MACMILLAN US (HOLTZBRINCK)

http://us.macmillan.com

MACMILLAN

Farrar, Straus & Giroux

Faber and Faber, Inc

Farrar, Straus

Hill & Wang

HENRY HOLT & CO.
Henry Holt Books for Young Readers
Holt Paperbacks
Metropolitan
Times

MACMILLAN CHILDREN'S
Feiwel & Friends
Farrar, Straus and Giroux Books
   for Young Readers
Kingfisher
Holt Books for Young Readers
Priddy Books
Roaring Brook Press
First Second
Square Fish

PICADOR

PALGRAVE MACMILLAN

TOR/FORGE BOOKS
Tor
Forge
Orb
Tor/Seven Seas

ST. MARTIN'S PRESS
Minotaur Press
Thomas Dunne Books

BEDFORD, FREEMAN & WORTH
PUBLISHING GROUP

BEDFORD/ST. MARTIN'S

HAYDEN-MCNEIL

W.H. FREEMAN

WORTH PUBLISHERS

MACMILLAN KIDS

YOUNG LISTENERS

MACMILLAN AUDIO

PENGUIN GROUP (USA), INC.

www.penguingroup.com

PENGUIN ADULT DIVISION
Ace
Alpha
Amy Einhorn Books/Putnam
Avery
Berkley
Blue Rider Press
Current
Dutton
G.P. Putnam's Sons
Gotham
HP Books
Hudson Street Press
Jove
NAL
Pamela Dorman Books
Penguin
Penguin Press
Perigree
Plume
Portfolio
Prentice Hall Press

RIVERHEAD
Sentinel
Tarcher
Viking Press
Price Stern Sloan

YOUNG READERS DIVISION
Dial Books for Young Readers
Dutton Children's Books
Firebird

Frederick Warne

G.P. Putnam's Sons Books for Young Readers

Grosset & Dunlap

Philomel

PUFFIN BOOKS

Razorbill

Speak

Viking Books for Young Readers

RANDOM HOUSE, INC. (BERTELSMANN)

www.randomhouse.com

CROWN PUBLISHING GROUP

Amphoto Books

Backstage Books

Billboard Books

Broadway Business

Clarkson Potter

Crown

Crown Archetype

Crown Business

Crown Forum

Doubleday Religion

Harmony

Image Books

Potter Craft

Potter Style

Ten Speed Press

Three Rivers Press

Waterbrook Multnomah

Watson-Guptill

KNOPF DOUBLEDAY PUBLISHING GROUP

Alfred A. Knopf

Anchor Books

Doubleday

Everyman's Library

Nan A. Talese

Pantheon Books

Schocken Books

Vintage

RANDOM HOUSE PUBLISHING GROUP

Ballantine Books

Bantam

Del Rey

Del Rey/Lucas Books

Del Rey/Manga

Delacorte

Dell

The Dial Press

The Modern Library

One World

Presidio Press

Random House Trade Group

Random House Trade Paperbacks

Spectra

Spiegel and Grau

Triumph Books

Villard Books

RANDOM HOUSE AUDIO PUBLISHING GROUP

Listening Library

Random House Audio

RANDOM HOUSE CHILDREN'S BOOKS

Kids@Random

Golden Books

Princeton Review

Sylvan Learning

RANDOM HOUSE DIGITAL PUBLISHING GROUP

Books on Tape

Fodor's Travel

Living Language

Listening Library

Random House Audio

RH Large Print

RANDOM HOUSE INTERNATIONAL
  RH Australia
  RH of Canada Limited
  RH India
  RH Mondadori
  RH New Zealand
  RH South America
  RH Group (UK)
  Transworld Ireland
  Verlagsgruppe RH

SIMON & SCHUSTER

www.simonandschuster.com

SIMON & SCHUSTER ADULT PUBLISHING
  Atria Books
  Folger Shakespeare Library
  Free Press
  Gallery Books
  Howard Books
  Pocket Books

  Scribner
  Simon & Schuster
  Threshold Editions
  Touchstone
  Pimsleur
  Simon & Schuster Audioworks

SIMON & SCHUSTER CHILDREN'S PUBLISHING
  Aladdin Paperbacks
  Atheneum Books for Young Readers
  Bench Lane Books
  Little Simon®
  Margaret K. McElderry Books
  Paula Wiseman Books
  Simon & Schuster Books for Young Readers
  Simon Pulse
  Simon Spotlight®

SIMON & SCHUSTER INTERNATIONAL
  Simon & Schuster Australia
  Simon & Schuster Canada
  Simon & Schuster UK

THE WRITING ENTREPRENEUR

....

by J.M. Lacey

If you are writing full time, or even part time, and you claim the business on your taxes, you are an entrepreneur. Running a business comes with unique challenges and perks. If you are a sole proprietorship, or LLC, and you have no staff, you are marketing your own business, managing contracts and filing your own taxes. So how do you enjoy writing while simultaneously running a business? How can social networking ease your burden? Do your business cards scream amateur? How can you get a client to sign a contract—on your terms? And what really is considered tax deductible for a writer?

THE HAPPY WRITER

Before you even begin your writing business, there are some things to consider to help you build your career.

Kelly James-Enger, author of *Six Figure Freelancing–The Writer's Guide to Making More Money* and freelancer for the last 14 years, says that finding a niche, something you're good at, will help stem the tide of financial insecurity. "Specializing helps set you apart from everyone else and it's easier to get assignments."

To maintain a happy, balanced writing life, she also offers some tips for writers:

- **CHOOSE A MARKET YOU'D LIKE TO WRITE FOR MORE THAN ONCE,** then focus on building relationships.
- **HAVE A DAILY PRODUCTION GOAL,** such as how many queries you plan to send.
- **THINK LONG TERM.** Make sure what you do is leading you in the direction you want to reach.
- **CONSIDER WHAT THE MARKET WILL BEAR,** not just what you want to do. "Don't have all your money come from one source," she adds. "Diversify what you can do."

- **BE CAREFUL ABOUT WORKING NON-STOP.** Have a set time to turn off the e-mail and computer. Avoid working weekends and nights.

GETTING CLIENTS

Things that seem small to you—business cards, websites, stationery—can make a big impression. Prospects will never know how well you write if they can't get past a non-professional set-up.

Get simple, classy, clean and sophisticated cards professionally printed. Include your phone number, mailing, web and e-mail addresses, if you want paying clients to contact you. Your stationery should be the same.

Your website is going to be your most important marketing tool. Make sure your site is personalized, professional and provides the information your prospect will need, such as articles, client list, and portfolio.

Your website is going to be your most important marketing tool.

There are many books and articles that will tell you to save money and go ahead and design your own site. I disagree 100 percent. Unless you have had training in marketing, design, SEO and html construction, your site will look homemade. Plus, you are too intimate with your own business to have an objective outlook.

Websites aren't as expensive as they used to be, but you will have to dish out a few to several hundred dollars, depending on your needs. To run a business, you have to spend money, and if you pour your investment into anything, it should be your website. Write your own content and save money, but hand the rest over to the professionals. To keep more dollars in your wallet, offer to do a trade with your designer—materials for them and a website for you.

"But I'm a writer," you say, "what does design matter?" If your site looks thrown together, prospects will think your writing is treated the same. And frankly, if your site is difficult to navigate—too much scrolling, tiny fonts, unorganized, dark background—they'll give up looking. No one has that much time or patience.

You also need a professional e-mail address, so get rid of your Yahoo, Gmail and Hotmail, and use your real name. JMLacey@jmlacey.com sounds a lot better than trixie_partygirl@hotmail.com. Save that for your personal accounts.

Next, find work by writing letters, making cold calls, sending e-mails and getting out there. Target businesses (or magazines) for whom you'd like to write. My first major client came via a cold call to another prospect. After I met with the initial contact, she referred me to someone else. I contacted that business immediately, and within three days, I had snagged that client and am still with them over two years later working on multiple projects.

Can social networking help? Yes, if you use it wisely. Join groups like LinkedIn, Facebook and Twitter, but make sure anytime you type a comment or message, it's with the purpose of building your business. You can direct people to your site and blog, but don't ask for their business. Try to type messages and/or guide them to helpful articles and information. Remember the WIIFM—What's In It For Me? It's about *them,* not you. Eventually, your readers will gain confidence in your expert abilities. Be cautious that your networking habits do not become time suckers. Try to have a set time each day, and a set amount of time, to check in with all your networks and forums.

CONTRACTS

Once you have a client, how do you get paid on your terms?

As you establish your business and writing credentials, try to have a solid, though not inflexible idea, of how much you will be paid. Understand what to charge for your level of expertise and geographical area. Most clients, especially corporate clients, prefer project fees instead of hourly rates. So have a base in your head, if you can, of how long something will take you, and come up with a reasonable fee.

Figure out how much you're willing to go down if the client tries to negotiate. Be confident in your figure, but be agreeable with the client. Before I type the contract, I usually state the estimate then ask: "Will that work within your budget?" You want to avoid going too low just to get that project, but don't quote so high you quote yourself out of a job. It takes trial and error, but after a while, you'll learn and gain confidence.

Make sure your contract covers everything unexpected because once you quote a price you can't retract and ask for more. For example, my contracts outline the project and everything that goes with it—three edits, one additional meeting (even via phone), conception, content and design. If the project goes over what was agreed upon—additional edits, meetings, pages, etc.—I charge the additional fee stated in the contract. I also charge extra for commercial photos and anything that might crop up as I go along. But I have to have it covered or I lose money. And don't forget to include the deadline.

Most important, be certain the contract states what you will be paid and when. For my new clients, especially for large projects, I always ask for one-third to one-half down payment. If I'm hiring outside contractors, such as a web designer, I will ask for my contractor's fee in full, if I can, just in case the project flops. All my clients know they will receive an invoice when they've approved the final draft, and my invoice states "payment due upon receipt."

Some commercial clients have their own contracts written by lawyers who really should use writers. If you don't understand something, ask. Contracts are for negotiating. Include your requirements, like the additional charges for extra work. You want to be comfortable signing that contract.

Do not do the work or research until you have it in writing. People will try to get you to "look" at their stuff so you can get a handle on what they want. That's fine, but either wait until you have the contract, or tell them you charge for your research. The reason? You want people to respect you as a professional from the start. Otherwise, they will expect more for nothing.

....

Do not do the work or research until you have it in writing.

....

Target clients that will pay you what you are worth. Again, use your discretion, but be firm. If they start out by saying, "I don't have much money," run, because they don't and you have a business to operate. If they tell you, "We can market you," then unless they are a marketing agency, they can't do anything to help you that you can't do. To run your business effectively, establish yourself as a professional by not catering to the low-paying, time-sucking gigs that will get you nowhere except homeless.

TAX DEDUCTIONS

If you claim your writing on your taxes, then it isn't a hobby. This means that almost everything you do and buy for your business is tax deductible.

So what can you deduct? Pretty much anything office-related (computer, pens), books, magazine subscriptions and conferences are among your deductions. And anything you need that will help you in your research, such as travel expenses. In my case, CDs and concert tickets are included in my write-offs as a classical music writer.

Building your writing business takes time. It can take several months to a few years, but it will happen. The more effort you put into it, the sooner it will thrive. But above all, your professional habits will only increase your chances of being successful.

NEGOTIATING TIPS FOR WRITERS FROM AN EDITOR

While being an editor pays the bills around here, I always see a writer when I look in the mirror. And just to show you how much I care about my fellow writers, I'm going to make my life as an editor potentially more difficult by sharing my negotiating tips for writers.

Different editors surely approach negotiation in their own unique ways, but these are my tips for handling editors like myself.

- **ALWAYS TRY TO NEGOTIATE.** I loathe negotiating. Judging by the lack of negotiation from most of my freelancers, I've concluded that most of them loathe negotiating too. But I think it's important for writers to at least try to negotiate from the beginning, because I take those writers a little more seriously, especially if they...

- **DELIVER THE GOODS ON EACH ASSIGNMENT.** Write an amazing article with great sources and examples, and I'm more likely to offer you a better contract the next time around. If I don't, I may be trying to maintain the status quo, but you should try to nudge me again. And I emphasize nudging.

- **DON'T MAKE YOUR DEMANDS A "MY-WAY-OR-THE-HIGHWAY" SITUATION.** That is, don't make it that kind of situation unless you're willing to take the highway. There have been situations, especially when I'm working with a new freelancer, in which I'm not able or willing to go over my initial offer. There have been very good pitches that I let walk, because I couldn't (or wouldn't) go higher. Believe me, I always wish I could offer more, but I have to fill my pages with great content (not squander it all on a handful of articles). That said...

- **PITCH ME WITH AN IDEA THAT IS UNIQUE AND TRULY HELPFUL FOR MY AUDIENCE.** If you pitch me on an interview or list of query tips, I'm less likely to get excited than if you pitch me on an article that tells writers how to make a living off Twitter in 30 days (and actually have the track record to back up that claim). For instance, Lynn Wasnak, who puts together our "How Much Should I Charge?" piece, is far and away my top paid freelancer, because she has to survey professionals in several different fields of writing. It's a unique piece that is truly helpful for my audience. As such, she has greater negotiating power. Still...

- **CHOOSE YOUR BATTLES.** I advise negotiating each time you get a new assignment. Maybe I'll give a little, maybe I won't. But please pick your battles about what you want to negotiate. Don't fight over every single clause in your contract. That gets annoying on my end, and I'm just too busy to enjoy being annoyed. Related to that...

- **DON'T BE A PEST.** I'm more willing to negotiate with writers who complete their assignments on time and don't contact me every couple days with a revision of an already turned in piece or who try to re-negotiate the fee on an article after I've already assigned the piece. I like it when writers ask questions and want to make sure they understand an assignment, but I don't like to have to constantly haggle over things after we've come to an agreement. That's a good way to not receive any more assignments in the future.

- **THINK OF CREATIVE WAYS TO NEGOTIATE.** Offer to write a sidebar for an extra fee—or a series of blog posts. If the editor is unable to offer more money, ask for more complimentary copies. Or some other related comp that the editor may be able to send your way. Editors like to make writers happy (especially if they do a great job), so help them help you get more out of your relationship.

—ROBERT LEE BREWER

J.M. LACEY (http://jmlacey.com) is an independent writer, marketing and public relations professional. She has over 14 years worth of experience in journalism, marketing, public relations, and sales, working for both the corporate and non-profit sectors. She maintains a classical music blog (http://seasonkt.com) and works with small to large businesses creating websites, advertisements, biographies and other marketing and publicity needs. She is also a public speaker and teaches workshops on writing for businesses and on marketing at writing and corporate conferences.

CONTRACTS 101

....

by Cindy Ferraino

After you do a victory dance about getting the book deal you always dreamed about or your article hitting the top of the content list of a popular magazine, the celebration quickly comes to a halt when you realize you are not at the finish line yet. Your heart begins to beat faster because you know the next possible hurdle is just around the corner—the contract. For many, the idea of reviewing a contract is like being back in first grade. You know you have to listen to the teacher when you could be playing outside. You know you have to read this contract but why because there are terms in there that look like an excerpt from a foreign language syllabus.

Before I changed my status to self-employed writer, I was working as a grants and contracts administrator at a large medical university in Philadelphia. I helped shepherd the MD and PhD researchers through the channels of grants and contracts administration. While the researchers provided the technical and scientific pieces that could potentially be the next cure for diabetes, heart disease, or cancer, I was there to make sure they did their magic within the confines of a budget and imposed contractual regulations. The budget process was easy but when it came to contract regulations—oh well, that was a different story. I became familiar with the terms such as indemnifications, property and intellectual rights and conditions of payments. I was an integral part of reviewing and negotiating a grant or contract that had the best interests for every party involved.

After my son was born, I left the university and my contracts background went on a brief hiatus. Once my son went off to school, I began freelance writing. After a few writing gigs sprinkled with a few too many rejection slips, I landed an assignment for *Dog Fancy* magazine. I was thrilled and eagerly anticipated the arrival of a contract in my inbox. As I opened the document, the hiatus had lifted. I read through the contract and was able to send it back within a few hours.

For many new freelancers or writers who have been around the block, contract administration is not something that they can list as a perk on their resume. Instead of searching through the Yellow Pages for a contract lawyer or trying to call in a special favor to a writer friend, there are some easy ways for a newbie writer or even a seasoned writer to review a contract before putting a smiley face next to the dotted line.

TAKE A DEEP BREATH, THEN READ ON

Remember breaking those seals on test booklets and the voice in the background telling you, "Please read the directions slowly." As you tried to drown out the voice because your stomach was in knots, little did you know that those imparting words of wisdom would come in handy as you perspired profusely over the legal jargon that unfolded before your eyes. The same words go for contracts.

Many writers, including myself, are anxious to get an assignment underway, but the contract carrot continues to loom over our creative minds. "I'm surprised by writers who just skim a contract and then sign it without understanding what it means," says Kelly James-Enger. James-Enger is the author of books including *Six Figure Freelancing: The Writer's Guide to Making More* (Random House, 2005) and blog Dollarsanddeadlines.blogspot.com. "Most of the language in magazine contracts isn't that complicated, but it can be confusing when you're new to the business."

When I receive a contract from a new publisher or editor, I make a second copy. My children call it "my sloppy copy." I take out a highlighter and begin to mark up the key points of the contract: beginning and end date, conditions of payment, how my relationship is de fined by the publisher and what the outline of the article should look like.

The beginning and end date of a contract is crucial. After I recently negotiated a contract, the editor changed the due date of the article in an e-mail. I made sure the contract was changed to reflect the new due date. The conditions of the payments are important because it will describe when the writer will be paid and by what method. Most publishers

PAYMENT TYPES

There are any number of different arrangements for publishers to pay writers. However, here are three of the most common and what they mean.

- Pays on acceptance. This means that a publisher pays (or cuts a check) for the writer upon acceptance of the manuscript. This is usually the best deal a writer can hope to receive.
- Pays on publication. In these cases, a publisher pays (or cuts a check) for the writer by the publication date of the manuscript. For magazines, this could mean several months after the manuscript was accepted and approved. For books, this could mean more than a year.
- Pays after publication. Sometimes contracts will specify exactly how long after publication. Be wary of contracts that leave it open-ended.

have turned to incremental payment schedules or payments to be made online like Pay-Pal. How the publisher considers your contractor status is important. If you're a freelance contract writer, the contract should reflect that as well as identify you as an independent contractor for IRS tax purposes. Finally, the contract will highlight an outline of what your article or proposal should look like.

....

After I recently negotiated a contract, the editor changed the due date of the article in an e-mail. I made sure the contract was changed to reflect the new due date.

....

As you slowly digest the terms you are about to agree to for your assignment or book project, you gain a better understanding of what an editor or publisher expects from you and when.

CUTTING TO THE LEGAL CHASE

Once you have had a chance to review a contract, you may be scratching your head and saying, "Okay, now what does this all mean to me as a writer?" James-Enger describes three key areas where writers should keep sharp on when it comes to contracts—Indemnification, Pay and Exclusivity provisions.

INDEMNIFICATION is a publisher's way of saying if something goes wrong, we are not responsible. If a claim is brought against another writer's work, a publisher does not want to be responsible for the legal aftermath but you could be the one receiving a notice in the mail. James-Enger warns writers to be on the lookout for indemnification clauses. "In the U.S., anyone can sue anyone over just about anything," she says; "I'm okay with agreeing to indemnification clauses that specify breaches of contract because I know I'm not going to plagiarize, libel or misquote anyone. But I can't promise that the publication will never be sued by anyone whether or not I actually breached the contract."

CONTRACT TIPS

Even seasoned freelancers can find themselves intimidated by contracts. Here are a few things to consider with your contract:

- **KEEP COPY ON RECORD.** If the contract is sent via e-mail, keep a digital copy, but also print up a hard copy and keep it in an easy-to-find file folder.

- **CHECK FOR RIGHTS.** It's almost never a good idea to sell all rights. But you should also pay attention to whether you're selling any subsidiary or reprint rights. The more rights you release the more payment you should expect (and demand).
- **WHEN PAYMENT.** Make sure you understand when you are to be paid and have it specified in your contract. You may think that payment will come when the article is accepted or published, but different publishers have different policies. Get it in writing.
- **HOW MUCH PAYMENT.** The contract should specify exactly how much you are going to be paid. If there is no payment listed on the contract, the publisher could use your work for free.
- **TURN IN CONTRACT BEFORE ASSIGNMENT.** Don't start working until the contract is signed, and everything is official. As a freelancer, time is as important as money. Don't waste any of your time and effort on any project that is not yet contracted.

PAY is where you want the publisher "to show you the money." Writers need to be aware of how publishers will discuss the terms of payment in the contract. James-Enger advises to have "payment on acceptance." This means you will be paid when the editor agrees to accept your manuscript or article. If there is "no payment on acceptance," some publishers will pay when the article is published. "Push for payment whenever you can," she says.

EXCLUSIVITY PROVISIONS are where a particular publisher will not allow the writer to publish an article or manuscript that is "about the same or similar subject" during the time the publisher runs the piece. Because of the nature of the writing business, James-Enger feels writers need to negotiate this part of the contract. "I specialize in health, fitness and nutrition, and I'm always writing about a similar subject," she says.

WHEN TO HEAD TO THE BARGAINING TABLE

Recently, I became an independent contractor for the American Composites Manufacturing Association (ACMA). When I reviewed the terms of the contract, I was concerned how my independent contractor status was identified. Although I am not an ACMA employee, I wanted to know if I could include my ACMA publications on my resume. Before I signed the contract, I questioned this issue with my editor. My editor told me I may use this opportunity to put on my resume. I signed the contract and finished my assignment.

Writers should be able to talk to an editor or a publisher if there is a question about a term or clause in a contract. "Don't be afraid to talk to the editor about the changes you'd like to make to a contract," James-Enger says; "You don't know what you'll get or if an editor is willing to negotiate it, until you ask."

When writers have to approach an editor for changes to a contract, James-Enger advises writers to act professionally when it comes to the negotiations. "I start out with saying—I am really excited to be working with you on this story and I appreciate the assignment, but I have a couple of issues with the contract that I'd like to talk to you about," she says. "Sure I want a better contract but I also want to maintain a good working relationship with my editor. A scorched-earth policy doesn't benefit any freelancer in the long run."

> In today's economy, writers are a little more reluctant to ask for a higher rate for an article.

Negotiating payment terms is a tricky subject for some writers. Writers want to get the most bang for their buck but they don't want to lose a great writing assignment. Do your research first before you decide to ask an editor for more money to complete the assignment. Double check the publisher's website or look to see if the pay scale is equivalent to other publishers in the particular industry. Some publishers have a set publishing fee whereas others may have a little more wiggle room depending on the type of the assignment given. In today's economy, writers are a little more reluctant to ask for a higher rate for an article. If the publisher seems to be open to discussion about the pay scale, just make sure you approach the situation in a professional manner so as to not turn the publisher away from giving you another assignment.

WHO WILL OWN YOUR WRITING?

Besides payment terms, another area that writers may find themselves on the other end of the negotiation table is with ownership rights. We all want to take credit for the work that we have poured our heart and soul into. Unfortunately, the business of publishing has different ways of saying how a writer can classify their work. Ownership rights vary, but the biggest one that writers have a hard time trying to build up a good case against is "all rights." "All rights" is exactly what it means: *hope you are not in love with what you have just written because you will not be able to use it again.*

RIGHTS AND WHAT THEY MEAN

A creative work can be used in many different ways. As the author of the work, you hold all rights to the work in question. When you agree to have your work published, you are granting a publisher the right to use your work in any number of ways. Whether that right is to publish the manuscript for the first time in a publication, or to publish it as many times and in as many ways as a publisher wishes, is up to you—it all depends on the agreed-upon terms. As a general rule, the more rights you license away, the less control you have over your work and the money you're paid. You should strive to keep as many rights to your work as you can.

Writers and editors sometimes define rights in a number of different ways. Below you will find a classification of terms as they relate to rights.

- **FIRST SERIAL RIGHTS.** Rights that the writer offers a newspaper or magazine to publish the manuscript for the first time in any periodical. All other rights remain with the writer. Sometimes the qualifier "North American" is added to these rights to specify a geographical limitation to the license. When content is excerpted from a book scheduled to be published, and it appears in a magazine or newspaper prior to book publication, this is also called first serial rights.

- **ONE-TIME RIGHTS.** Nonexclusive rights (rights that can be licensed to more than one market) purchased by a periodical to publish the work once (also known as simultaneous rights). That is, there is nothing to stop the author from selling the work to other publications at the same time.

- **SECOND SERIAL (REPRINT) RIGHTS.** Nonexclusive rights given to a newspaper or magazine to publish a manuscript after it has already appeared in another newspaper or magazine.

- **ALL RIGHTS.** This is exactly what it sounds like. "All rights" means an author is selling every right he has to a work. If you license all rights to your work, you forfeit the right to ever use the work again. If you think you may want to use the article again, you should avoid submitting to such markets or refuse payment and withdraw your material.

- **ELECTRONIC RIGHTS.** Rights that cover a broad range of electronic media, including websites, CD/DVDs, video games, smart phone apps, and more. The contract should specify if—and which—electronic rights are included. The presumption is unspecified rights remain with the writer.

- **SUBSIDIARY RIGHTS.** Rights, other than book publication rights, that should be covered in a book contract. These may include various serial rights; movie, TV, audio, and other electronic rights; translation rights, etc. The book contract should specify who controls the rights (author or publisher) and what percentage of sales from the licensing of these rights goes to the author.

- **DRAMATIC, TV, AND MOTION PICTURE RIGHTS.** Rights for use of material on the stage, on TV, or in the movies. Often a one-year option to buy such rights is offered (generally for 10 percent of the total price). The party interested in the rights then tries to sell the idea to other people—actors, directors, studios, or TV networks. Some properties are optioned numerous times, but most fail to become full productions. In those cases, the writer can sell the rights again and again.

> Sometimes editors don't take the time to specify the rights they are buying. If you sense that an editor is interested in getting stories, but doesn't seem to know what his and the writer's responsibilities are, be wary. In such a case, you'll want to explain what rights you're offering (preferably one-time or first serial rights only) and that you expect additional payment for subsequent use of your work.
>
> The Copyright Law that went into effect January 1, 1978, states writers are primarily selling one-time rights to their work unless they—and the publisher—agree otherwise in writing. Book rights are covered fully by contract between the writer and the book publisher.

In recent months, I have written for two publications that I had given "all rights" to the company. My rationale is that I knew I would never need to use those articles again but I did make sure I was able to include those articles for my byline to show that I have publishing experience.

If you feel that you want to reuse or recycle an article that you had written a few years ago, you might want to consider negotiating an "all rights" clause or maybe going to another publisher. "We don't take all rights so there is no reason for authors to request we change the rights clause," says Angela Hoy, author and owner of WritersWeekly.com and Booklocker. com. "Our contracts were rated 'Outstanding' by Mark Levine (author of *The Fine Print of Self-Publishing*) and has also been called the clearest and fairest in the industry."

James-Enger is also an advocate of negotiating against contracts with an "all rights" clause. "I hate 'all rights' contracts, and try to avoid signing them as they preclude me from ever reselling the piece as a reprint to other markets," she says. "I explain that to editors, and I have been able to get editors to agree to let me retain nonexclusive reprint rights even when they buy all rights—which still lets me market the piece as a reprint." James-Enger also advises that "if the publisher demands all rights, then negotiate if the payment is sub-standard."

So if you are just receiving a contract in the mail for the first time or you are working with a new publisher, you should not be afraid of the legal lingo that blankets the message "we want to work with you." Contracts are meant to protect both the interests of the publishers and writers. Publishers want the commitment from writers that he or she will provide their best work and writers want to be recognized for their best work. But between those contracts lines, the legal lingo can cause writers to feel they need a law degree to review the contract. No, just sit back and relax and enjoy the prose that will take your writing to the next level.

CINDY FERRAINO has been blessed with a variety of assignments, including newspaper articles, magazine articles, ghost-written articles, stories for books, and most recently authoring a book on accounting and bookkeeping terminology, *The Complete Dictionary of Accounting & Bookkeeping Terms Explained Simply* (Atlantic Publishing Group).

7 HABITS OF FINANCIALLY SAVVY WRITERS

by Kate Meadows

We all know the stereotype of the starving artist. Fun work, little pay. But just how true is that stereotype?

For the writer, it depends on a few things. First, it depends on how you value yourself as a writer. Are you a hobbyist, writing on the side either strictly for pleasure or for a bit of extra income? Or are you a professional, going at the business of writing as a day job?

Make no mistake: There is nothing wrong with writing for pleasure. But if writing is your profession, or if you strive to make it your profession (goodbye, day job!), managing the financial side of your trade is crucial. How you handle money can make or break that notion of "starving artist."

Many writers don't take time to consider the importance of finances in their profession, acknowledges Hope Clark, an author who heads the popular website and newsletter, Funds for Writers (www.fundsforwriters.com). "If they do consider it," she says, "they treat it with trepidation."

Why? Perhaps it's because so often the creative overrules the practical aspect of making a living. Your burning desire to pen the next great American novel shouldn't be ignored. But writers who can balance the creative with the practical are the true professionals.

This is what "financially savvy" boils down to, says Mridu Khullar Relph, whose freelance articles appear in *The New York Times*, *Time Magazine*, *Christian Science Monitor* and elsewhere: "It's making sure you make the right decisions financially to be able to sustain your career and create time and space for yourself to work on projects you may believe in but that may not be lucrative."

Adds Clark: "We cannot just be artists. Writers have to be businesspeople, as well."

1. MARKET, MARKET, MARKET!

Marketing is crucial for two reasons. First, it pushes your ideas into the world. Second, it pushes you and your skill into the world. Not only must you market your work; you must also market yourself.

"Marketing is the number one thing you need to do to make it as a writer," says Linda Formichelli, a freelance writer whose articles have appeared in *Redbook, Family Circle,* and *Writer's Digest,* among others. "You can be the best writer ever, but if you don't market no one will ever know about it—or pay you."

Marketing is a never-ending process. Relph strives to make one marketing effort a day: an email, a follow-up phone call, a tweet.

"Finding an idea that gets you excited and then writing to an editor with the potential that idea holds, is the honeymoon phase of the project," she says, "when all possibilities exist and anything could happen."

Stay on top of your marketing efforts by having a system in place that tracks your ideas and potential markets for those ideas. I maintain two documents. My "Active Query Tracker" lists ideas I have pitched, the publication to which I sent the query and the appropriate editor's name and contact info, and the expected response date. My "Ideas List" includes all of my story ideas, each followed by a list of potential publications that fit the idea. When I receive a rejection, I delete that idea from my "Active Query Tracker" and strike out the publication on my "Ideas List." Then I pitch the idea to the next publication in line and update the "Active Query Tracker" as necessary.

2. THINK OF YOURSELF AS AN ENTREPRENEUR.

Anyone will concede that it's important for entrepreneurs to be financially savvy.

"The minute a writer decides to sell his work, he shifts from writer to entrepreneur," says Clark.

But too many writers fall short of this realization, focusing only on the creative output. The result? Lots of fantastic words and ideas that go nowhere.

Hate promoting yourself? Join the club. Feel clueless when it comes to the business end of writing? Take a class on accounting, marketing or running a home business. Such classes are often offered through community centers or colleges.

Relph draws these similarities between writers and entrepreneurs: "We come up with big ideas that others may or may not believe in and spend large chunks of time chasing them down and bringing them to fruition."

The difference, she says, is that entrepreneurs have a business model. Writers often don't.

Entrepreneurs invest in their trade. As a writer, it's important to put money into your venture, investing in supplies and experiences that will improve your craft.

Clark points out that many writers are so concerned with saving precious writing dollars that they don't pause to consider what might be reaped from spending. To save a few dollars, they won't pay for a cover design. They won't pay for a class they sorely need to improve a certain skill. They won't hire a professional to design their website, falling back on the mediocre skills of a friend who will do it for free.

Entrepreneurs know that quality up-front investments pay off in the long run. Becoming an entrepreneur means being proactive. It means recognizing opportunities when they arise and going after them wholeheartedly. Yes, there is risk involved. But what pursuit worth chasing doesn't involve some risk?

3. BE YOUR NO. 1 FAN.

You've heard it since grade school: A confident attitude goes a long way.

"A confident writer has no problem putting herself and her work out there," says Formichelli. "And that's where the money comes from."

Editors want to hire people who know what they're doing.

"I really believe that as independent professionals, how well we present ourselves plays a huge role in how much work we get and what we get paid for it," Relph says.

Relph once queried an editor at a UK-based Asian magazine and received a favorable response, under the condition that she would write the first article for free and then be paid a modest fee for each article thereafter. Relph declined the assignment. She couldn't afford to work for free, she explained, and her usual rate was twice what the editor offered for future pay, anyway. The editor responded, saying she would pay Relph that standard rate, for the first story and all stories thereafter.

Similarly, a lack of confidence can directly result in a lack of work. Procrastination and perfectionism are two big career killers, Formichelli says, both results of a lack of confidence.

If you don't believe in yourself, no one else will either.

4. KEEP RECEIPTS AND PAY STUBS, AND TRACK INCOME AND EXPENSES.

Writing is a numbers game.

"You need to know how much money you have coming in versus going out, how much you need to charge to earn what you want, and what your typical hourly rate is," says Formichelli.

Relying on hard numbers is crucial. How else will you know what sort of income you're earning, or where that hard-earned cash is going?

"Lots of writers assume or just want to believe that the only thing they have to do is write, and the rest of the stuff will take care of itself," says author John Scalzi. "It won't, and it doesn't."

Formichelli suggests using an accounting system like Freshbooks to make the in/out record keeping simple. I use an Excel spreadsheet, with one column that tracks income and another that tracks expenses. Allena Tapia, a freelance writer/editor and owner of Garden-Wall Publications, suggests using the week between Christmas and New Year's Day to prepare a chart for the coming year, so it's ready to go come January 1.

Crucial to your accounting system is sending invoices for every assignment. Many writers miss this important step and therefore chance losing payment for their work. Think about it: If you never received a bill from your utility provider, would you still write a check? A simple invoice takes just a few minutes to write and send.

Maintaining records requires diligence. And diligence is tough. But it is so worth it in the end.

5. DIVERSIFY YOUR PROJECTS.

Writers are wearers of many hats.

"Some things you do for the glamour, some you do for the money, some you do for personal satisfaction," says Relph. "Having that mix is what makes a freelancer successful."

Love to write fiction? Why not pitch to a writing magazine a service piece on how to sketch compelling characters? Have a penchant for realty? Consider offering your services as a copywriter or proofreader of newsletters and web content for realty companies in your area.

I recently started offering services as a freelance editor alongside my writing gigs. I contacted some nearby writing centers and offered to teach a series of workshops in my genre, nonfiction. The extra work keeps my business fund healthy when the writing assignments are slow in coming. What's more, the variety of projects is rewarding and keeps me on my toes.

Yes, you may have to venture into some work that's not as fun, to pad up your bank account. But treat those experiences as chances to expand your portfolio. Work such as technical writing or copywriting often pay better than the more creative end.

"You want to earn enough to create the time and space to work on projects that you truly enjoy," says Relph. "If you're earning great money in half of your working life, then you can dedicate the rest of it to writing whatever you want, without having to worry about the market."

6. ACKNOWLEDGE MISTAKES, AND THEN MOVE ON.

Face it. No one is going to write a winning query every time. Nor is everyone going to nail every assignment on the first draft. Stephen King pounded a nail into his wall, on which he hung every rejection letter he received. When that nail filled up, he got a bigger nail.

Good writers work hard. Good writers fail sometimes. But good writers also learn from their experiences.

I once pitched a strong query to a top children's magazine. Though I had never written for the children's market, the idea interested me, and the editor responded favorably, requesting the article on spec.

I rounded up sources and wrote the story. But, not being a children's writer, I struggled to fit the story to an audience of 6 to 12-year-olds. Consequently, the editor rejected the story, saying it was not suitable to the magazine's readership. Lesson learned? I am not a children's writer. Now I choose to focus on those markets I know I can handle.

7. READ CONTRACTS CAREFULLY, NEGOTIATE FAIR RATES, AND SIGN ONLY IF YOU UNDERSTAND AND AGREE WITH ALL OF THE TERMS.

Contracts are nothing to fear. They are simply documents that outline both the writer's and the client's terms regarding a specific assignment.

In other words, a contract is a communication tool.

Knowing what rights you give up as a writer for what financial return is part of being proactive—and professional. Know the difference between First North American Serial Rights (FNASR), which grants a publication the right to be the first to publish your work in a North American market (giving you the opportunity to sell reprints later on) and All Rights, which grants a publication exclusive rights to your work.

Don't want to give up exclusive rights to your work? Have the courage to say "no," or negotiate a different arrangement. Think five cents a word is not enough? Ask for more.

Negotiating fair rates is an act of confidence, Formichelli points out. It is the writer's way of advocating for himself and valuing his work.

Art must have two components to be professional: It must have a creative side, and it must have a business side. It's easy to fall back into the romanticized image of "starving artist" if you're a writer who just can't make ends meet. But before you toss in the towel and concede that writers are just undervalued professionals, ask yourself how well you practice these 7 habits.

The self-sustaining writers last the longest, says Clark. And being regarded as a self-sufficient wordsmith is a heck of a lot more rewarding than being regarded as a starving artist.

KATE MEADOWS is a freelance writer and editor who specializes in life stories and personal and small business histories. Her work has appeared in *Writer's Digest, Chicken Soup for the Soul, USAA Financial Magazine, Kansas City Parent,* and numerous trade and regional publications. Her book, *Tough Love: A Wyoming Childhood* (Pronghorn Press), was published in 2012.

MAKING THE MOST OF THE MONEY YOU EARN

by Sage Cohen

Writers who manage money well can establish a prosperous writing life that meets their short-term needs and long-term goals. This article will introduce the key financial systems, strategies, attitudes, and practices that will help you cultivate a writing life that makes the most of your resources and sustains you over time.

DIVIDING BUSINESS AND PERSONAL EXPENSES

If you are reporting your writing business to the IRS, it is important that you keep the money that flows from this source entirely separate from your personal finances. Here's what you'll need to accomplish this:

- **BUSINESS CHECKING ACCOUNT:** Only two types of money go into this account: money you have been paid for your writing and/or "capital investments" you make by depositing your own money to invest in the business. And only two types of payments are made from this account: business-related expenses (such as: subscriptions, marketing and advertisement, professional development, fax or phone service, postage, computer software and supplies), and "capital draws" which you make to pay yourself.

- **BUSINESS SAVINGS ACCOUNT OR MONEY MARKET ACCOUNT:** This account is the holding pen where your quarterly tax payments will accumulate and earn interest. Money put aside for your retirement account(s) can also be held here.

- **BUSINESS CREDIT CARD:** It's a good idea to have a credit card for your business as a means of emergency preparedness. Pay off the card responsibly every month and this will help you establish a good business credit record, which can be useful down the line should you need a loan for any reason.

When establishing your business banking and credit, shop around for the best deals, such as highest interest rates, lowest (or no) monthly service fees, and free checking. Mint.com is a good source for researching your options.

EXPENSE TRACKING AND RECONCILING

Once your bank accounts are set up, it's time to start tracking and categorizing what you earn and spend. This will ensure that you can accurately report your income and itemize your deductions when tax time rolls around every quarter. Whether you intend to prepare your taxes yourself or have an accountant help you, immaculate financial records will be the key to speed and success in filing your taxes.

For the most effective and consistent expense tracking, I highly recommend that you use a computer program such as QuickBooks. While it may seem simpler to do accounting by hand, I assure you that it isn't. Even a luddite such as I, who can't comprehend the most basic principles of accounting, can use QuickBooks with great aplomb to plug in the proper categories for income and expenses, easily reconcile bank statements, and with a few clicks prepare all of the requisite reports that make it easy to prepare taxes.

PAYING BILLS ONLINE

While it's certainly not imperative, you might want to check out your bank's online bill pay option if you're not using this already. Once you've set up the payee list, you can make payments in a few seconds every month or set up auto payments for expenses that are recurring. Having a digital history of bills paid can also come in handy with your accounting.

MANAGING TAXES

Self-employed people need to pay quarterly taxes. A quick, online search will reveal a variety of tax calculators and other online tools that can help you estimate what your payments should be. Programs such as TurboTax are popular and useful tools for automating and guiding you step-by-step through tax preparation. An accountant can also be helpful in understanding your unique tax picture, identifying and saving the right amount for taxes each quarter, and even determining SEP IRA contribution amounts (described later in this article). The more complex your finances (or antediluvian your accounting skills), the more likely that you'll benefit from this kind of personalized expertise.

Once you have forecasted your taxes either with the help of a specialized, tax-planning program or an accountant, you can establish a plan toward saving the right amount for quarterly payments. For example, once I figured out what my tax bracket was and the approximate percentage of income that needed to be set aside as taxes, I would immediately transfer a percentage of every deposit to my savings account, where it would sit and grow a little interest until quarterly tax time came around. When I could afford to do so, I would also set aside the appropriate percentage of SEP IRA contribution from each deposit so that I'd be ready at end-of-year to deposit as much as I possibly could for retirement.

THE PRINCIPLE TO COMMIT TO IS THIS: Get that tax-earmarked cash out of your hot little hands (i.e., checking account) as soon as you can, and create whatever deterrents you need to leave the money in savings so you'll have it when you need it.

INTELLIGENT INVESTING FOR YOUR CAREER

Your writing business will require not only the investment of your time but also the investment of money. When deciding what to spend and how, consider your values and your budget in these three, key areas:

EDUCATION	MARKETING AND PROMOTION	KEEPING THE WHEELS TURNING
Subscriptions to publications in your field	URL registration and hosting for blogs and websites	Technology and application purchase, servicing and back-up
Memberships to organizations in your field	Contact database subscription (such as Constant Contact) for communicating with your audiences	Office supplies and furniture
Books: on topics you want to learn, or in genres you are cultivating	Business cards and stationery	Insurance for you and/or your business
Conferences and seminars	Print promotions (such as direct mail), giveaways and schwag	Travel, gas, parking
Classes and workshops	Online or print ad placement costs	Phone, fax and e-mail

This is not an absolute formula for spending—just a snapshot of the types of expenses you may be considering and negotiating over time. My general rule would be: start small and modest with the one or two most urgent and/or inexpensive items in each list, and grow slowly over time as your income grows.

The good news is that these legitimate business expenses may all be deducted from your income—making your net income and tax burden less. Please keep in mind that the IRS allows losses as long as you make a profit for at least three of the first five years you are in business. Otherwise, the IRS will consider your writing a non-deductible hobby.

PREPARATION AND PROTECTION FOR THE FUTURE

As a self-employed writer, in many ways your future is in your hands. Following are some of the health and financial investments that I'd recommend you consider as you build and nurture The Enterprise of You. Please understand that these are a layperson's suggestions. I am by no means an accountant, tax advisor, or financial planning guru. I am simply a person who has educated herself on these topics for the sake of her own writing business, made the choices I am recommending, and benefited from them. I'd like you to benefit from them, too.

SEP IRAS

Individual Retirement Accounts (IRAs) are investment accounts designed to help individuals save for retirement. But I do recommend that you educate yourself about the Simplified Employee Pension Individual Retirement Account (SEP IRA) and consider opening one if you don't have one already.

A SEP IRA is a special type of IRA that is particularly beneficial to self-employed people. Whereas a Roth IRA has a contribution cap of $5,000 or $6,000, depending on your age, the contribution limit for self-employed people in 2011 is approximately 20% of adjusted earned income, with a maximum contribution of $49,000. Contributions for a SEP IRA are generally 100% tax deductible and investments grow tax deferred. Let's say your adjusted earned income this year is $50,000. This means you'd be able to contribute $10,000 to your retirement account. I encourage you to do some research online or ask your accountant if a SEP IRA makes sense for you.

CREATING A 9-MONTH SAVINGS BUFFER

When you're living month-to-month, you are extremely vulnerable to fluctuation in the economy, client budget changes, life emergencies and every other wrench that could turn a good working groove into a frightening financial rut. The best way to prepare for the unexpected is to start (or continue) developing a savings buffer. The experts these days are suggesting that we accumulate nine months of living expenses to help us navigate transition in a way that we feel empowered rather than scared and desperate to take the next thing that comes along.

....

When I paid off one of my credit cards in full, I added that monthly payment to the monthly savings transfer.

....

I started creating my savings buffer by opening the highest-interest money market account I could find and setting up a modest, monthly automatic transfer from my checking account. Then, when I paid off my car after five years of monthly payments, I added my car payment amount to the monthly transfer. (I'd been paying that amount for five years, so I was pretty sure I could continue to pay it to myself.) When I paid off one of my credit cards in full, I added that monthly payment to the monthly savings transfer. Within a year, I had a hefty sum going to savings every month before I had time to think about it, all based on expenses I was accustomed to paying, with money that had never been anticipated in the monthly cash flow.

What can you do today—and tomorrow—to put your money to work for your life, and start being as creative with your savings as you are with language?

DISABILITY INSURANCE

If writing is your livelihood, what happens if you become unable to write? I have writing friends who have become incapacitated and unable to work due to injuries to their brains, backs, hands and eyes. Disability insurance is one way to protect against such emergencies and ensure that you have an income in the unlikely event that you're not physically able to earn one yourself.

Depending on your health, age, and budget, monthly disability insurance payments may or may not be within your means or priorities. But you won't know until you learn more about your coverage options. I encourage you to investigate this possibility with several highly rated insurance companies to get the lay of the land for your unique, personal profile and then make an informed decision.

HEALTH INSURANCE

Self-employed writers face tough decisions about health insurance. If you are lucky, there is someone in your family with great health coverage that is also available to you. Without the benefit of group health insurance, chances are that self-insuring costs are high and coverage is low. Just as in disability insurance, age and health status are significant variables in costs and availability of coverage.

Ideally, of course, you'll have reasonably-priced health insurance that helps make preventive care and health maintenance more accessible and protects you in case of a major medical emergency. The following are a few possibilities to check out that could reduce costs and improve access to health coverage:

- Join a group that aggregates its members for group coverage, such as a Chamber of Commerce or AARP. Ask an insurance agent in your area if there are any other group coverage options available to you.
- Consider a high-deductible health plan paired with a Health Savings Account (HSA). Because the deductible is so high, these plans are generally thought to be

most useful for a major medical emergency. But an HSA paired with such a plan allows you to put aside a chunk of pre-tax change every year that can be spent on medical expenses or remain in the account where it can be invested and grow. 2011 HSA investment limits, for example, are: $3,050 for individual coverage and $6,150 for family coverage.

Establishing effective financial systems for your writing business will take some time and energy at the front end. I suggest that you pace yourself by taking an achievable step or two each week until you have a baseline of financial management that works for you. Then, you can start moving toward some of your bigger, longer-term goals. Once it's established, your solid financial foundation will pay you in dividends of greater efficiency, insight, and peace of mind for the rest of your writing career.

SAGE COHEN is the author of *The Productive Writer* and *Writing the Life Poetic*, both from Writer's Digest Books. She's been nominated for a Pushcart Prize, won first prize in the Ghost Road Press Poetry contest and published dozens of poems, essays and articles on the writing life. Sage holds an MFA in creative writing from New York University and a BA from Brown University. Since 1997, she has been a freelance writer serving clients including Intuit, Blue Shield, Adobe, and Kaiser Permanente..

PHOTO © Nyla Alisia

SUBMISSION TRACKER

Recordkeeping is an important tool for the successful freelance writer. It's important to keep accurate records for tax season, but it's equally important to keep accurate submission records. Failure to do so could lead to some embarrassing double submissions or result in missed opportunities to follow up. Plus, an organized writer always impresses editors and agents.

On the next page is a sample submission tracker spreadsheet. You can make copies of the one in this book to help you keep records, or you can create a similar spreadsheet on your computer using a spreadsheet program. WritersMarket.com also provides submission tracking tools as part of the My Markets feature of the site.

This submission tracker has nine columns:

- **MANUSCRIPT TITLE.** This is the title of your manuscript.
- **MARKET.** This is the name of the magazine, book publisher, contest, or other entity to which you've submitted your manuscript.
- **CONTACT NAME.** This is the name of the editor, agent, or other contact who's received your work.
- **DATE SENT.** The date you submitted your manuscript.
- **DATE RETURNED.** The date your manuscript was rejected.
- **DATE ACCEPTED.** The date your manuscript was accepted.
- **DATE PUBLISHED.** The date your manuscript was published.
- **PAYMENT RECEIVED.** Detail any payment received.
- **COMMENTS.** This column is for any other notes about your experience with the market.

SUBMISSION TRACKER

MANUSCRIPT TITLE	MARKET	CONTACT NAME	DATE SENT	DATE RETURNED	DATE ACCEPTED	DATE PUBLISHED	PAYMENT RECEIVED	COMMENTS

SHOULD YOUR WRITING BUSINESS BE AN LLC?

Business Structures Explained

by Carol Topp, CPA

A new member to my writers group told us her writing business was structured as a corporation. As a certified public accountant, I found that a little odd. I didn't know Connie well, but she had told us she had just written her first book, a self-published memoir. *Why would a brand new author want corporate status for her business?* I wondered. It seemed overly complex to me, so I asked her why she had formed a corporation. "I don't know," she said, "it's what my lawyer and CPA set up." Now I was really concerned. She'd had two professionals set her up in a complex business structure when she hadn't yet sold one copy of her book!

What was going on?

SOLE PROPRIETORSHIP

Most authors prefer the simplest business structure possible—what the IRS calls a sole proprietorship, meaning a business with one owner.

Sole proprietors may go by many names including:

- freelancer
- independent contractor
- self-employed writer
- independent publisher
- self-published or traditionally published author

During a consultation with a new author, I explained the advantages of sole proprietorship. She asked me, "Why would I want to be a sole proprietor? Why not just be a freelancer?" I explained that "sole proprietor" is a tax-related term to describe her profession as a freelance writer.

Sole proprietorships are easy and quick to start. You are in business as soon as you say that you are! Or at least when you are paid for your writing. I became a professional writer when I received $50 for writing a magazine article. A business had been born. Sole proprietorships have minimal government filings and licenses, if any. Usually a writer can use his or her own name as the business name, so business name filing is needed. Best of all, sole proprietorships have the simplest tax structure. Sole proprietors use a two-page form (Schedule C Business Income or Loss) and attach it to their Form 1040 tax return.

I would have thought that Connie's writing business would be structured as a sole proprietorship. Why then was she saying that her writing business was a corporation? I asked her a few more questions.

LIMITED LIABILITY STATUS

"Oh, they set up an LLC," she explained. Now I understood. Connie was talking about limited liability company (LLC) status. She had mistakenly thought that the "C" in LLC meant "corporation," but it means "company." They are quite different. LLC status is a legal standing granted by your state (not the IRS), and it offers limited liability to protect your personal assets from any business liabilities.

It's easy to get confused as Connie did; some advertising adds to the confusion. I've seen one ad that says "Get incorporated today" while showing a smiling woman holding a business card with "Your Business, LLC" circled in red. The ad confused incorporation with LLC status. Incorporating involves forming your business as a corporation for tax purposes; LLC status is a legal standing that limits liability.

LLCs are not one of the three business structures that the IRS recognizes for tax purposes. As a matter of fact, the IRS calls LLCs "disregarded entities." (We all wish the IRS would disregard us a little more!) Certainly, the IRS knows that LLCs exist, but for tax purposes, the LLC status is disregarded, and the business owner must choose one of three structures: sole proprietorship, partnership or corporation.

What LLC status will do for you

So why had Connie's lawyer and CPA set up her sole proprietorship with LLC status? Probably because they wanted to protect her personal assets from any business debts.

LLC status offers limited liability protection. When you read "liability," think "lawsuit" or, more specifically, the money you might owe if sued. LLC status cannot stop a lawsuit, but your liabilities may be limited to your business assets. As a writer, your business assets might include your laptop computer and the cash in your business checking account. The advantage of protecting your personal assets is the main reason why authors and other small business owners obtain LLC status for their businesses.

An example of how LLC status can help involved a ghostwriter who was sued for breach of contract. He was a sole proprietor with LLC status for his business. If he had lost, the lawsuit damages would have been limited to his business assets and could not have touched his personal assets, such as his house or savings. Fortunately, he won his case.

What LLC status won't do for you

Limited Liability Company status will not reduce your taxes. Your business files the same tax forms it did before having LLC status. "If an expense is business related, it's tax deductible, no matter what business structure you use," says tax attorney Julian Block, author of *Easy Tax Guide for Writers, Photographers and Other Freelancers.*

My tax client Russ showed me a handout from a seminar that claimed one of the benefits of LLC status was a health insurance tax deduction, leading Russ to believe he needed LLC status to receive this tax break. This health insurance deduction is available to all sole proprietorships, whether they have LLC status or not. The seminar handout had inadvertently confused him.

LLC STATUS IS NOT BULLETPROOF

For years the bulletproof vest of limited liability was only available to corporations. In the 1980s, LLC status became popular and sole proprietors signed up in droves. Finally, they could receive limited liability protection without the complexities of corporate status. It all seemed too good to be true, and perhaps it was.

Lately, limited liability status has been challenged in court, and several business owners found that their personal assets were at risk. The bulletproof vest has some cracks. "If an author were driving a car while on business and injured someone, he or she could still be sued," explains attorney Julian Block. "It's not a magic bullet."

To avoid piercing your limited liability, you must keep your business separate from your personal life. Mixing assets may lead a court to determine that your LLC status is weak and therefore hold you personally liable. "It isn't enough for business people merely to carry a liability shield; they must also take reasonable measures to this shield," cautions New Hampshire attorney John Cunningham.

There are several ways to protect your shield of limited liability:

- Don't commit fraud. Even LLC status can't protect you if you're a crook!
- Set up a separate checking account for your business.
- Avoid treating business assets as your own.
- Avoid personal guarantees on business loans.
- Purchase professional liability insurance.
- Sign contracts in the name of your LLC.
- Consider placing your home or investments into a trust to further protect your assets.

Disadvantages to LLC status

To obtain LLC status from your state, you file paperwork with an accompanying fee. Often, the paperwork is fairly straightforward, especially for single-member LLCs. Some individuals file for LLC status without assistance, but I recommend you seek professional advice to understand the pros and cons of LLC status for your business. If your LLC has multiple members or is a complex arrangement, you should hire a business attorney to assist you in establishing your LLC.

When should you consider LLC status for your writing business?

Consider LLC status when you wish to protect your personal assets. In Connie's case, her lawyer and CPA were possibly being overly cautious because she had no business income or assets yet.

I operated my accounting business as a sole proprietorship for its first six years. After that, I was attracting more clients and generating more income. I already had professional liability insurance, but I decided it was time to add limited liability status to my sole proprietorship. I applied to be a single member LLC in my state by filing the paperwork and paying a $125 fee. My business name is now Carol Topp, CPA, LLC (are you impressed?) but I still file the same tax forms I did before obtaining LLC status. I hope my limited liability status is never challenged in court, but I have it (and insurance) just in case I am ever sued.

PARTNERSHIPS ARE LIKE MARRIAGE

A second business structure is a partnership with two or more other people. Occasionally, a writer may coauthor a book, but these are usually collaborations, not formal business partnerships

I usually discourage coauthors from forming a business partnership, warning them that a partnership is like being married but not being in love. You may be responsible for debts the other person can take on. Partnerships have complex tax situations necessitating professional expertise, and they may require a lawyer to draft the partnership agreement.

"Forming a business partnership really isn't necessary, and that is especially true when it is a one-shot deal," explains Dr. Dennis Hensley, coauthor of more than six titles. Quite frequently a publisher will hire the coauthors and make all the business arrangements. "When I was teamed with Stanley Field to write *The Freelancer: A Writer's Guide to Success*, we signed an agreement defining our writing responsibilities, how we would share earnings, who would serve as lead writer for the project, and how we would communicate during the writing of the manuscript. The publisher was putting us together because we had separate areas of expertise that were needed for the book the publisher wanted to release."

Alternatively, you may come up with a book idea of your own. Dauna and Marcie, long-time friends, decided to write a book together, but they did not form a business partnership. Both women maintained separate sole proprietorships, agreeing on how to split expenses and share the royalties. This kept each of their businesses separate and made the book project easier to operate.

"Before jumping into a business partnership with your life partner, friend, family member or an entrepreneur you know, sit down and talk over expectations with each other,'" advises James Chartrand of Men With Pens. "Create an agreement for sharing work and profits. Decide who does what and when, and how to split up the money—or else you'll be splitting up, period."

WRITER, INC.

The third and most complex business structure is a corporation. There are two types of corporations, S corporations and C corporations. An S corporation has a limited number of shareholders and may have only one shareholder, the owner, while C corporations can have an unlimited number of shareholders and are typically run by a board of directors. If a writer forms a corporation, it is typically an S corporation.

S corporation status may be a desirable business structure for authors who form a publishing company. Felice Gerwitz self-published her books as a sole proprietor for many years. She started publishing other authors and found that forming an S corporation could save on taxes, particularly self-employment tax. "Self-employment taxes as a sole proprietor were killing me," says Gerwitz. "Fortunately, my CPA advised me to form an S corporation, and I saw my self-employment tax drop."

As an S corporation, Gerwitz takes some of her profit as wages and some as ordinary income, which is not subject to self-employment tax. An S corporation has more complex tax preparation than a sole proprietorship, so you should seek professional accounting advice for your record keeping and tax preparation.

CONCLUSION

A writer has three business structures from which to choose: sole proprietorship, partnership or corporate status (S or C). In addition, a writer may obtain limited liability company status to limit his or her liability. Each business structure has advantages and increasing complexity. For most writers, the sole proprietorship with LLC status will serve their needs well.

BUSINESS STRUCTURES

Word pictures can explain the different business structures an author might choose.

Picture a sole proprietorship as a single-family house. Single-family homes are very common, as is the sole proprietorship form of business (78 percent of all small businesses are sole proprietorships).

A partnership is like a duplex with two families living in one house. Living that close together can bring benefits but can also create friction, just like a business partnership.

A corporation is like an apartment building with many tenants in one building. In the same way, a corporation can have many owners called shareholders. Apartment buildings are expensive to start and can be difficult to maintain, just like a corporation.

A limited liability company (LLC) is not any of these. It is a legal status granted by your state, not a business structure in the eyes of the IRS. It is similar to a fence surrounding a building, providing protection. Picture the single family home with a fence protecting it. That would be a sole proprietorship with LLC status. A partnership or corporation can also have LLC protection, just as duplexes and apartment buildings may also have fences.

CAROL TOPP is a Certified Public Accountant and author of *Business Tips and Taxes for Writers* (Media Angels). She has authored 10 books, both as an indie publisher and author for a small press. Learn more at CarolToppCPA.com and TaxesForWriters.com.

HOW MUCH SHOULD I CHARGE?

....

by Aaron Belz

The first question most aspiring freelance writers ask themselves is, "Where do I find paying gigs?" But once a writer finds that first freelance gig, they often ask, "How much should I charge?"

They ask this question, because often their clients ask them. In the beginning, this can be one of the most stressful parts of the freelancing process: Trying to set rates that don't scare away clients, but that also help put dinner on the table.

Maybe that's why the "How Much Should I Charge?" pay rate chart is one of the most popular and useful pieces of the *Writer's Market*. Freelancers use the rates to justify their worth on the market to potential clients, and clients use the chart as an objective third party authority on what the current market is paying.

Use the following chart to help you get started in figuring out your freelance rates. If you're a beginner, it makes sense to price yourself closer to the lower end of the spectrum, but always use your gut in negotiating rates. The rate on that first assignment often helps set the expectations for future rates.

As you find success in securing work, your rates should naturally increase. If not, consider whether you're building relationships with clients that lead to multiple assignments. Also, take into account whether you're negotiating for higher rates on new assignments with familiar and newer clients.

Remember that smarter freelancers work toward the goal of higher rates, because better rates mean one of two things for writers: Either they're able to earn money, or they're able to earn the same money in less time. For some freelancers, having that extra time is worth more than anything money can buy.

Use the listings in *Writer's Market* to find freelance work for magazines, book publishers, and other traditional publishing markets. But don't restrict your search to the traditional markets if you want to make a serious living as a freelance writer.

As the pay rate chart shows, there are an incredible number of opportunities for writers to make a living doing what they love: writing. Maybe that writing critiques, editing anthologies, blogging, or something else entirely.

While this pay rate chart covers a wide variety of freelance writing gigs, there are some that are just too unique to get a going rate. If you can't find a specific job listed here, try to find something that is similar to use as a guide for figuring out a rate. There are times when you just have to create the going rate yourself.

Thank you, Aaron Belz, for assembling this pay rate chart and sharing your sources in the sidebar below. I know it will help more than one freelance writer negotiate the freelance rates they deserve.

—*Robert Lee Brewer*

PARTICIPATING ORGANIZATIONS

Here are the organizations surveyed to compile the "How Much Should I Charge?" pay rate chart. You can also find Professional Organizations in the Resources.

- American Medical Writers Association (AMWA), (301)294-5303. Website: www. amwa.org.
- American Society of Journalists & Authors (ASJA), (212)997-0947. Website: www. asja.org.
- American Society of Media Photographers (ASMP), (215)451-2767. Website: www. asmp.org.
- American Society of Picture Professionals (ASPP), (703)299-0219. Website: www. aspp.com.
- American Translators Association (ATA), (703)683-6100. Website: www.atanet.org.
- Association of Independents in Radio (AIR), (617)825-4400. Website: www.air media.org.
- Educational Freelancers Association (EFA), (212)929-5400. Website: www.the-efa.org.
- Freelance Success (FLX), (877) 731-5411. Website: www.freelancesucess.com.
- Investigative Reporters & Editors (IRE), (573)882-2042. Website: www.ire.org.
- Media Communicators Association International (MCA-I), (888)899-6224. Website: www.mca-i.org.
- National Cartoonists Society (NCS), (407)647-8839. Website: www.reuben.org/main.asp.

- National Writers Union (NWU), (212)254-0279. Website: www.nwu.org.
- National Association of Science Writers (NASW), (510)647-9500. Website: www.nasw.org.
- Society of Professional Journalists (SPJ), (317)927-8000. Website: www.spj.org.
- Women in Film (WIF). Website: www.wif.org.
- Writer's Guild of America East (WGAE), (212)767-7800. Website: www.wgaeast.org.
- Writer's Guild of America West (WGA), (323)951-4000. Website: www.wga.org.

AARON BELZ is the author of The Bird Hoverer (BlazeVOX), Lovely, Raspberry (Persea), and Glitter Bomb (Persea). A St. Louis native, he now lives and works in Hillsborough, North Carolina. Visit him online at belz.net or follow him on Twitter @aaronbelz..

	PER HOUR			PER PROJECT			OTHER		
	HIGH	LOW	AVG	HIGH	LOW	AVG	HIGH	LOW	AVG
ADVERTISING & PUBLIC RELATIONS									
Advertising copywriting	$156	$36	$84	$9,000	$160	$2,760	$3/word	30¢/word	$1.57/word
Advertising editing	$125	$20	$65	n/a	n/a	n/a	$1/word	30¢/word	66¢/word
Advertorials	$182	$51	$93	$1,890	$205	$285	$3/word	85¢/word	$1.58/word
Business public relations	$182	$30	$85	n/a	n/a	n/a	$500/day	$200/day	$356/day
Campaign development or product launch	$156	$36	$100	$8,755	$1,550	$4,545	n/a	n/a	n/a
Catalog copywriting	$156	$25	$71	n/a	n/a	n/a	$350/item	$30/item	$116/item
Corporate spokesperson role	$182	$72	$107	n/a	n/a	n/a	$1,200/day	$500/day	$740/day
Direct-mail copywriting	$156	$36	$85	$8,248	$500	$2,839	$4/word $400/page	$1/word $200/page	$2.17/word $315/page
Event promotions/publicity	$126	$30	$76	n/a	n/a	n/a	n/a	n/a	$500/day
Press kits	$182	$31	$81	n/a	n/a	n/a	$850/60sec	$120/60sec	$458/60sec
Press/news release	$182	$30	$80	$1,500	$125	$700	$2/word $750/page	50¢/word $150/page	$1.20/word $348/page
Radio commercials	$102	$30	$74	n/a	n/a	n/a	$850/60sec	$120/60sec	$456/60sec

	PER HOUR			PER PROJECT			OTHER		
	HIGH	LOW	AVG	HIGH	LOW	AVG	HIGH	LOW	AVG
Speech writing/editing for individuals or corporations	$168	$36	$92	$10,000	$2,700	$5,036	$355/minute	$105/minute	$208/minute
BOOK PUBLISHING									
Abstracting and abridging	$125	$30	$74	n/a	n/a	n/a	$2/word	$1/word	$1.48/word
Anthology editing	$80	$23	$51	$7,900	$1,200	$4,588	n/a	n/a	n/a
Book chapter	$100	$35	$60	$2,500	$1,200	$1,758	20¢/word	8¢/word	14¢/word
Book production for clients	$100	$40	$67	n/a	n/a	n/a	$17.50/page	$5/page	$10/page
Book proposal consultation	$125	$25	$66	$1,500	$250	$788	n/a	n/a	n/a
Book publicity for clients	n/a	n/a	n/a	$10,000	$500	$2,000	n/a	n/a	n/a
Book query critique	$100	$50	$72	$500	$75	$202	n/a	n/a	n/a
Children's book writing	$75	$35	$50	n/a	n/a	n/a	$5/word $5,000/adv	$1/word $450/adv	$2.75/word $2,286/adv
Content editing (scholarly/textbook)	$125	$20	$51	$15,000	$500	$4,477	$20/page	$3/page	$6.89/page
Content editing (trade)	$125	$19	$54	$20,000	$1,000	$6,538	$20/page	$3.75/page	$8/page
Copyediting (trade)	$100	$16	$46	$5,500	$2,000	$2,892	$6/page	$1/page	$4.22/page

	PER HOUR			PER PROJECT			OTHER		
	HIGH	LOW	AVG	HIGH	LOW	AVG	HIGH	LOW	AVG
Encyclopedia articles	n/a	n/a	n/a	n/a	n/a	n/a	50¢/word $3,000/item	15¢/word $50/item	35¢/word $933/item
Fiction book writing (own)	n/a	n/a	n/a	n/a	n/a	n/a	$40,000/adv	$525/adv	$14,193/adv
Ghostwriting, as told to	$125	$35	$67	$47,000	$5,500	$22,892	$100/page	$50/page	$87/page
Ghostwriting, no credit	$125	$30	$73	n/a	n/a	n/a	$3/word $500/page	50¢/word $50/page	$1.79/word $206/page
Guidebook writing/editing	n/a	n/a	n/a	n/a	n/a	n/a	$14,000/adv	$10,000/adv	$12,000/adv
Indexing	$60	$22	$35	n/a	n/a	n/a	$12/page	$2/page	$4.72/page
Manuscript evaluation and critique	$150	$23	$66	$2,000	$150	$663	n/a	n/a	n/a
Manuscript typing	n/a	n/a	$20	n/a	n/a	n/a	$3/page	95¢/page	$1.67/page
Movie novelizations	n/a	n/a	n/a	$15,000	$5,000	$9,159	n/a	n/a	n/a
Nonfiction book writing (collaborative)	$125	$40	$80	n/a	n/a	n/a	$110/page $75,000/adv	$50/page $1,300/adv	$80/page $22,684/adv
Nonfiction book writing (own)	$125	$40	$72	n/a	n/a	n/a	$110/page $50,000/adv	$50/page $1,300/adv	$80/page $14,057/adv
Novel synopsis (general)	$60	$30	$45	$450	$150	$292	$100/page	$10/page	$37/page

	PER HOUR			PER PROJECT			OTHER		
	HIGH	LOW	AVG	HIGH	LOW	AVG	HIGH	LOW	AVG
Personal history writing/editing (for clients)	$125	$30	$60	$40,000	$750	$15,038	n/a	n/a	n/a
Proofreading	$75	$15	$31	n/a	n/a	n/a	$5/page	$2/page	$3.26/page
Research for writers or book publishers	$150	$15	$52	n/a	n/a	n/a	$600/day	$400/day	$525/day
Rewriting/structural editing	$120	$25	$67	$50,000	$2,500	$13,929	14¢/word	5¢/word	10¢/word
Translation—literary	n/a	n/a	n/a	$95,000	$6,500	$8,000	17¢/target word	4¢/target word	8¢/target word
Translation—nonfiction/technical	n/a	n/a	n/a	n/a	n/a	n/a	30¢/target word	5¢/target word	12¢/target word
BUSINESS									
Annual reports	$185	$60	$102	$15,000	$500	$5,850	$600	$100	$349
Brochures, booklets, flyers	$150	$45	$91	$15,000	$300	$4,230	$2.50/word $800/page	35¢/word $50/page	$1.21/word $341/page
Business editing (general)	$155	$40	$80	n/a	n/a	n/a	n/a	n/a	n/a
Business letters	$155	$40	$79	n/a	n/a	n/a	$2/word	$1/word	$1.47/word
Business plan	$155	$40	$87	$15,000	$200	$4,115	n/a	n/a	n/a

	PER HOUR			PER PROJECT			OTHER		
	HIGH	LOW	AVG	HIGH	LOW	AVG	HIGH	LOW	AVG
Business writing seminars	$155	$70	$112	$8,600	$550	$2,919	n/a	n/a	n/a
Consultation on communications	$155	$50	$80	n/a	n/a	n/a	$1,300/day	$530/day	$830/day
Copyediting for business	$155	$35	$65	n/a	n/a	n/a	$4/page	$2/page	$3/page
Corporate histories	$155	$45	$91	160,000	$5,000	$54,525	$2/word	$1/word	$1.50/word
Corporate periodicals, editing	$155	$45	$74	n/a		n/a	$2.50/word	75¢/word	$1.42/word
Corporate periodicals, writing	$155	$45	$83	n/a	n/a	$1,880	$3/word	$1/word	$1.71/word
Corporate profiles	$155	$45	$93	n/a	n/a	$3,000	$2/word	$1/word	$1.50/word
Ghostwriting for business execs	$155	$45	$89	$3,000	$500	$1,400	$2.50/word	50¢/word	$2/word
Ghostwriting for businesses	$155	$45	$114	$3,000	$500	$1,790	n/a	n/a	n/a
Newsletters, desktop publishing/production	$155	$45	$75	$6,600	$1,000	$3,490	$750/page	$150/page	$429/page
Newsletters, editing	$155	$35	$72	n/a	n/a	$3,615	$230/page	$150/page	$185/page
Newsletters, writing	$155	$35	$82	$6,600	$800	$3,581	$5/word $1,250/page	$1/word $150/page	$2.31/word $514/page

	PER HOUR			PER PROJECT			OTHER		
	HIGH	LOW	AVG	HIGH	LOW	AVG	HIGH	LOW	AVG
Translation services for business use	$80	$45	$57	n/a	n/a	n/a	$35/ target word $1.41/ target line	7¢/ target word $1/ target line	$2.31/ target word $1.21/ target line
Resume writing	$105	$70	$77	$500	$150	$295	n/a	n/a	n/a
COMPUTER, INTERNET & TECHNICAL									
Blogging—paid	$150	$35	$100	$2,000	$500	$1,250	$500/post	$6/post	$49/post
E-mail copywriting	$135	$30	$85	n/a	n/a	$300	$2/word	30¢/word	91¢/word
Educational webinars	$500	$0	$195	n/a	n/a	n/a	n/a	n/a	n/a
Hardware/Software help screen writing	$95	$60	$81	$6,000	$1,000	$4,000	n/a	n/a	n/a
Hardware/Software manual writing	$165	$30	$80	$23,500	$5,000	$11,500	n/a	n/a	n/a
Internet research	$95	$25	$55	n/a	n/a	n/a	n/a	n/a	n/a
Keyword descriptions	n/a	n/a	n/a	n/a	n/a	n/a	$200/page	$130/page	$165/page
Online videos for clients	$95	$60	$76	n/a	n/a	n/a	n/a	n/a	n/a

	PER HOUR			PER PROJECT			OTHER		
	HIGH	LOW	AVG	HIGH	LOW	AVG	HIGH	LOW	AVG
Social media postings for clients	$95	$25	$62	n/a	n/a	$500	n/a	n/a	$10/word
Technical editing	$150	$30	$65	n/a	n/a	n/a	n/a	n/a	n/a
Technical writing	$160	$30	$80	n/a	n/a	n/a	n/a	n/a	n/a
Web editing	$100	$25	$57	n/a	n/a	n/a	$10/page	$4/page	$5.67/page
Webpage design	$150	$25	$80	$4,000	$200	$1,278	n/a	n/a	n/a
Website or blog promotion	n/a	$30	n/a	$650	$195	$335	n/a	n/a	n/a
Website reviews	n/a	$30	n/a	$900	$50	$300	n/a	n/a	n/a
Website search engine optimization	$89	$30	$76	$50,000	$8,000	$12,000	n/a	n/a	n/a
White papers	$135	$30	$82	$10,000	$2,500	$4,927	n/a	n/a	n/a
EDITORIAL/DESIGN PACKAGES									
Desktop publishing	$150	$18	$67	n/a	n/a	n/a	$750/page	$30/page	$202/page
Photo brochures	$125	$60	$87	$15,000	$400	$3,869	$65/picture	$30/picture	$48/picture
Photography	$100	$45	$71	$10,500	$50	$2,100	$2,500/day	$500/day	$1,340/day

	PER HOUR			PER PROJECT			OTHER		
	HIGH	LOW	AVG	HIGH	LOW	AVG	HIGH	LOW	AVG
Photo research	$75	$45	$49	n/a	n/a	n/a	n/a	n/a	n/a
Picture editing	$100	$45	$64	n/a	n/a	n/a	$65/picture	$30/picture	$53/picture
EDUCATIONAL & LITERARY SERVICES									
Author appearances at national events	n/a	n/a	n/a	n/a	n/a	n/a	$500/hour $30,000/ event	$100/hour $500/event	$285/hour $5,000/event
Author appearances at regional events	n/a	n/a	n/a	n/a	n/a	n/a	$1,500/event	$50/event	$615/event
Author appearances at local groups	$63	$40	$47	n/a	n/a	n/a	$400/event	$75/event	$219/event
Authors presenting in schools	$125	$25	$78	n/a	n/a	n/a	$350/class	$50/class	$183/class
Educational grant and proposal writing	$100	$35	$67	n/a	n/a	n/a	n/a	n/a	n/a
Manuscript evaluation for theses/dissertations	$100	$15	$53	$1,550	$200	$783	n/a	n/a	n/a
Poetry manuscript critique	$100	$25	$62	n/a	n/a	n/a	n/a	n/a	n/a
Private writing instruction	$60	$50	$57	n/a	n/a	n/a	n/a	n/a	n/a

	PER HOUR			PER PROJECT			OTHER		
	HIGH	LOW	AVG	HIGH	LOW	AVG	HIGH	LOW	AVG
Readings by poets, fiction writers	n/a	n/a	n/a	n/a	n/a	n/a	$3,000/event	$50/event	$225/event
Short story manuscript critique	$150	$30	$75	$175	$50	$112	n/a	n/a	n/a
Teaching adult writing classes	$125	$30	$82	n/a	n/a	n/a	$800/class $5,000/course	$115/class $500/course	$450/class $2,667/course
Writer's workshop panel or class	$220	$30	$92	n/a	n/a	n/a	$5,000/day	$60/day	$1,186/day
Writing for scholarly journals	$100	$40	$63	$450	$100	$285		n/a	n/a
FILM, VIDEO, TV, RADIO, STAGE									
Book/novel summaries for film producers	n/a	n/a	n/a	n/a	n/a	n/a	$34/page	$15/page	$23/page $120/book
Business film/video scriptwriting	$150	$50	$97	n/a	n/a	$600	$1,000/run min	$50/run min	$334/run min $500/day
Comedy writing for entertainers	n/a	n/a	n/a	n/a	n/a	n/a	$150/joke $500/group	$5/joke $100/group	$50/joke $283/group
Copyediting audiovisuals	$90	$22	$53	n/a	n/a	n/a	n/a	n/a	n/a
Educational or training film/video scriptwriting	$125	$35	$81	n/a	n/a	n/a	$500/run min	$100/run min	$245/run min

	PER HOUR			PER PROJECT			OTHER		
	HIGH	LOW	AVG	HIGH	LOW	AVG	HIGH	LOW	AVG
Feature film options	First 18 months, 10% WGA minimum; 10% minimum each 18-month period thereafter.								
TV options	First 180 days, 5% WGA minimum; 10% minimum each 180-day period thereafter.								
Industrial product film/video scriptwriting	$150	$30	$99	n/a	n/a	n/a	$500/run min	$100/run min	$300/run min
Playwriting for the stage	5-10% box office/Broadway, 6-7% box office/off-Broadway, 10% box office/regional theatre.								
Radio editorials	$70	$50	$60	n/a	n/a	n/a	$200/run min $400/day	$45/run min $250/day	$124/run min $325/day
Radio interviews	n/a	n/a	n/a	$1,500	$110	$645	n/a	n/a	n/a
Screenwriting (original screenplay-including treatment)	n/a	n/a	n/a	n/a	n/a	n/a	$118,745	$63,526	$92,153
Script synopsis for agent or film	$2,344/30 min, $4,441/60 min, $6,564/90 min								
Script synopsis for business	$75	$45	$62	n/a	n/a	n/a	n/a		n/a
TV commercials	$99	$60	$81	n/a	n/a	n/a	$2,500/30 sec	$150/30 sec	$1,204/30 sec
TV news story/feature	$1,550/5 min, $3,000/10 min, $4,200/15 min								
TV scripts (non-theatrical)	Prime Time: $33,700/60 min, $47,500/90 min Not Prime Time: $12,900/30 min, $23,500/60 min, $35,300/90 min								

	PER HOUR			PER PROJECT			OTHER		
	HIGH	LOW	AVG	HIGH	LOW	AVG	HIGH	LOW	AVG
TV scripts (teleplay/MOW)	$70,000/120 min								
MAGAZINES & TRADE JOURNALS									
Article manuscript critique	$130	$25	$69	n/a	n/a	n/a	n/a	n/a	n/a
Arts query critique	$105	$50	$80	n/a	n/a	n/a	n/a	n/a	n/a
Arts reviewing	$100	$65	$84	$335	$95	$194	$1.25/word	12¢/word	63¢/word
Book reviews	n/a	n/a	n/a	$900	$12	$348	$1.50/word	20¢/word	73¢/word
City magazine calendar	n/a	n/a	n/a	$250	$45	$135	$1/word	35¢/word	75¢/word
Comic book/strip writing	$225 original story, $525 existing story, $50 short script.								
Consultation on magazine editorial	$155	$35	$86	n/a	n/a	n/a	n/a	n/a	$100/page
Consumer magazine column	n/a	n/a	n/a	$2,500	$70	$898	$2.50/word	37¢/word	$1.13/word
Consumer front-of-book	n/a	n/a	n/a	$850	$320	$550	n/a	n/a	n/a
Content editing	$130	$30	$62	$6,500	$2,000	$3,700	15¢/word	6¢/word	11¢/word
Contributing editor	n/a	n/a	n/a	n/a	n/a	n/a	$160,000/contract	$22,000/contract	$53,000/contract

	PER HOUR			PER PROJECT			OTHER		
	HIGH	LOW	AVG	HIGH	LOW	AVG	HIGH	LOW	AVG
Copyediting magazines	$105	$18	$55	n/a	n/a	n/a	$10/page	$2.90/page	$5.78/page
Fact checking	$130	$15	$46	n/a	n/a	n/a	n/a	n/a	n/a
Gag writing for cartoonists	$35/gag; 25% sale on spec.								
Ghostwriting articles (general)	$225	$30	$107	$3,500	$1,100	$2,200	$10/word	65¢/word	$2.50/word
Magazine research	$125	$20	$53	n/a	n/a	n/a	$500/item	$100/item	$200/item
Proofreading	$80	$20	$40	n/a	n/a	n/a	n/a	n/a	n/a
Reprint fees	n/a	n/a	n/a	$1,500	$20	$439	$1.50/word	10¢/word	76¢/word
Rewriting	$130	$25	$74	n/a	n/a	n/a	$50/page	n/a	$50/page
Trade journal feature article	$128	$45	$80	$4,950	$150	$1,412	$3/word	20¢/word	$1.20/word
Transcribing interviews	$185	$95	$55	n/a	n/a	n/a	$3/min	$1/min	$2/min
MEDICAL/SCIENCE									
Medical/scientific conference coverage	$125	$50	$85	n/a	n/a	n/a	$800/day	$300/day	$600/day
Medical/scientific editing	$96	$15	$33	n/a	n/a	n/a	$12.50/page $600/day	$3/page $500/day	$4.40/page $550/day

	PER HOUR			PER PROJECT			OTHER		
	HIGH	LOW	AVG	HIGH	LOW	AVG	HIGH	LOW	AVG
Medical/scientific writing	$91	$20	$46	$4,000	$500	$2,500	$2/word	25¢/word	$1.12/word
Medical/scientific multimedia presentations	$100	$50	$75	n/a	n/a	n/a	$100/slide	$50/slide	$77/slide
Medical/scientific proofreading	$80	$18	$50	n/a	n/a	$500	$3/page	$2.50/page	$2.75/page
Pharmaceutical writing	$125	$100	$50	n/a	n/a	n/a	n/a	n/a	n/a
NEWSPAPERS									
Arts reviewing	$69	$30	$53	$200	$15	$101	60¢/word	6¢/word	36¢/word
Book reviews	$69	$45	$58	$350	$15	$140	60¢/word	25¢/word	44¢/word
Column, local	n/a	n/a	n/a	$600	$25	$206	$1/word	38¢/word	50¢/word
Column, self-syndicated	n/a	n/a	n/a	n/a	n/a	n/a	$35/insertion	$4/insertion	$16/insertion
Copyediting	$35	$15	$27	n/a	n/a	n/a	n/a	n/a	n/a
Editing/manuscript evaluation	$75	$25	$35	n/a	n/a	n/a	n/a	n/a	n/a
Feature writing	$79	$40	$63	$1,040	$85	$478	$1.60/word	10¢/word	59¢/word
Investigative reporting	n/a	n/a	n/a	n/a	n/a	n/a	$10,000/grant	$250/grant	$2.250/grant

	PER HOUR			PER PROJECT			OTHER		
	HIGH	LOW	AVG	HIGH	LOW	AVG	HIGH	LOW	AVG
Obituary copy	n/a	n/a	n/a	$225	$35	$124	n/a	n/a	n/a
Proofreading	$45	$15	$23	n/a	n/a	n/a	n/a	n/a	n/a
Stringing	n/a	n/a	n/a	$2,400	$40	$525	n/a	n/a	n/a
NONPROFIT									
Grant writing for nonprofits	$150	$12	$75	$3,000	$400	$1,852	n/a	n/a	n/a
Nonprofit annual reports	$100	$28	$60	n/a	n/a	n/a	n/a	n/a	n/a
Nonprofit writing	$150	$17	$65	$17,600	$100	$4,706	n/a	n/a	n/a
Nonprofit editing	$125	$16	$50	n/a	n/a	n/a	n/a	n/a	n/a
Nonprofit fundraising literature	$110	$35	$74	$3,500	$200	$1,597	$1,000/day	$300/day	$767/day
Nonprofit presentations	$100	$40	$73	n/a	n/a	n/a	n/a	n/a	n/a
Nonprofit public relations	$100	$30	$60	n/a	n/a	n/a	n/a	n/a	n/a
POLITICS/GOVERNMENT									
Government agency writing/editing	$110	$25	$64	n/a	n/a	n/a	$1.25/word	25¢/word	75¢/word

	PER HOUR			PER PROJECT			OTHER		
	HIGH	LOW	AVG	HIGH	LOW	AVG	HIGH	LOW	AVG
Government grant writing/editing	$150	$19	$72	n/a	n/a	n/a	n/a	n/a	n/a
Government-sponsored research	$110	$35	$66	n/a	n/a	n/a	n/a	n/a	$600/day
Public relations for political campaigns	$150	$40	$86	n/a	n/a	n/a	n/a	n/a	n/a
Speechwriting for government officials	$200	$40	$96	$4,550	$1,015	$2,755	$200/run min	$110/run min	$155/run min
Speechwriting for political campaigns	$155	$65	$101	n/a	n/a	n/a	$200/run min	$100/run min	$162/run min

BALANCE YOUR WRITING AND YOUR PLATFORM

in 8 Simple Steps

by Krissy Brady

Writers today have many hats to wear—writer, blogger, social media manager, publisher, marketer—so it's no wonder the balancing act becomes a challenge. This is especially the case when you're consumed by the *writing vs. platform* tug-of-war: either your writing is going well or your platform is going strong, but rarely do the two coexist peacefully.

If the quest for balance between your writing and platform hasn't been working out very well, strive for harmony instead. Both your writing and platform are important aspects of your career, but let's face it: nothing is *ever* more important than the writing itself. Your platform is supposed to complement your writing career, not distract you from it.

To prevent this from happening, follow these eight simple steps:

STEP 1: PLAN PLATFORM AROUND YOUR WRITING SCHEDULE

Your writing must *always* come first; otherwise, there's no point to building a platform. The further ahead you plan your writing schedule, the easier it will be to plan your blogging schedule. Doing so will give you a bird's eye view of how much time you'll have to devote to any blog- and social media-related tasks you want to take on.

The key to building a successful platform your followers will depend on is *consistency*. Always post blog posts when you say you're going to, and do the same with your social media profiles. To be (and stay) consistent, create your writing schedule, then take a look at the busiest portions of it: how much of your platform can you build during these times? Use this as your guide when creating your overall social media strategy.

You'll never have to feel like you're choosing between the two because you'll have planned a realistic amount of time for both. You'll also never have to worry about over-scheduling yourself. (Bonus: during assignment lulls, you can bank additional blog posts and social media content for upcoming busy periods.)

STEP 2: ALIGN YOUR WRITING TASKS WITH BLOGGING TASKS

The process of completing a blog post is identical to that of a freelance article, just on a smaller scale. Organize your workday based on each phase of the creative process, and batch similar tasks together:

- During brainstorming sessions, choose the next phase of article pitches you'd like to work on. While you're at it, create complementary blog post ideas. This will not only give you the opportunity to repurpose your research for multiple projects, it will spread your wings further within your chosen area of expertise.
- Speaking of research, after you've batched together the article and post ideas that are of similar scope, make a list of the holes that need to be filled for each angle you're focusing on. You'll be able to accomplish research for multiple pieces in one sitting instead of several.
- When outlining your query letters, create outlines for your guest post pitches.
- Create a production line of sorts for revising your pitches and researching markets, then go on a pitching frenzy!

By bunching tasks together that are similar in scope, you'll be able to seamlessly shift over to your blogging tasks without having to shift your entire mindset.

STEP 3: CREATE AN INDEX OF BLOG POST IDEAS

Some blog posts fly from our keyboards and onto the screen, while others just won't… come… out. This is a writer's worst nightmare. There's nothing more frustrating than taking four hours to write a blog post that should've only taken an hour, especially when we have paid writing deadlines waiting in the wings.

Alleviate the pressure by creating an index of blog post ideas. That way, when it's time to sit down and write a post, you can choose your next topic based on your current inspiration level. You'll look through your list of ideas and will be automatically drawn toward certain ideas over others, making the writing process more fluent and less forced.

You can keep track of your blog post ideas quickly and easily through your Wordpress dashboard, thanks to a plugin called *Ideas* (http://bit.ly/Mz1sVG). Before, you had to create blog post drafts to keep track of your ideas, making your dashboard look cluttered and messy. Now, with the *Ideas* plugin, you can keep track of your ideas in a separate area, create outlines for each in the summary section, and list the links you'd like to include in the resources section.

The more information you can prepare for each post in advance, the faster you'll write them, and the less conflicted you'll feel about your writing and blogging tasks.

STEP 4: WORK ON BLOG POSTS IN BATCHES

The word "balance" makes you feel like you have to split your days evenly between all aspects of your writing career, which leads to feelings of being torn and distracted. It's much easier to complete creative tasks when you're focusing on them individually rather than stringing yourself too thin.

Choose one day a week (or every two weeks depending on how often you plan to post) and *only* work on your blog posts. (A great plugin to help you with the planning process is the *Editorial Calendar* plugin from WordPress: http://bit.ly/4eP5W6.) By dividing your efforts instead of trying to maintain your writing and blogging simultaneously, your mind will always be clear to focus on the task at hand. No longer will you be writing while thinking about your blog, or blogging while thinking about your writing.

STEP 5: CREATE STRATEGY FOR SOCIAL MEDIA ACCOUNTS

An editorial calendar is just as important for your social media accounts as it is for your blog. In the social media world, sporadic, inconsistent social media posts are called "random acts of marketing." They confuse your audience and cause your platform to stagnate. Until you make vivid, concise goals for each of your social media profiles, there's no way to gauge the progress you're making because it's not clear what you're working toward.

Know your goals. Know your audience. Know their needs. If you recycle the same content over all of your profiles, you won't give them a reason to follow you across all platforms. Each social media platform has its own strengths you can use to create unique content:

- **Facebook** has become more and more visual with each upgrade. Focus on stunning visuals your target audience will immediately share with their friends and followers.
- **Twitter** is all about the headlines: focus on making your headlines irresistible and watch your content spread like wildfire.
- **LinkedIn** focuses on business networking and building your client base. Here you can concentrate on sharing intriguing articles and news that will help you establish credibility in your niche (and help you make quality connections).
- **YouTube** is perfect for the how-to guru. Create videos to help your audience improve their lives in big and small ways, and you'll stay top of mind when they need help in the future.
- **Pinterest** took the social media world by storm, combining stunning imagery with ultimate ideas in creativity (and causing other social media platforms to up the ante

with their own visual capabilities). Use Pinterest to help your followers make their dreams a reality.

Choose a specific focus for each of your social media accounts. For example, have each of your profiles represent a pressure point your target audience struggles with; this will encourage them to subscribe to all of your profiles. Clear profile definitions will ensure you won't become lost as you maintain them, and your followers won't as they visit them.

STEP 6: CURATE CONTENT FOR SOCIAL MEDIA ACCOUNTS

You know how important it is to share quality content through your social media profiles, but how do you go about doing so without it taking over your life? Browsing the Internet is a tricky business. Even if you subscribe to targeted blogs, you still have to sift through dozens of e-mails, dozens of shares and dozens of tweets. If you're not careful, hours could go by before you realize you're lost in the information sea.

Don't fret: there are now very handy, very convenient, and very free content curation tools at your disposal, including:

- **Google Alerts: google.com/alerts.** Choose search queries you want to be kept in the loop about, and have the results sent directly to your inbox as they happen, once a day, or once a week.
- **Social Mention: socialmention.com.** Similar to Google Alerts but for social media results—blogs, networks, comments, etc.—and you can have the results sent to your inbox on a daily basis.
- **News.me: news.me.** In an information overload society, we too easily miss out on fantastic content because it's buried underneath a pile of rubbish. When you sign up for News.me, it will keep track of your feeds and send you a daily newsletter of the five best links.
- **Prismatic: getprismatic.com.** Once you set up a Prismatic account, you'll wonder what you ever did without it. As you begin keeping track of the information that interests you and your followers, Prismatic keeps track of what you've read and what you're going to read, and uses this information to streamline a newsfeed that couldn't be more perfect for your needs.

Instead of spending hours scouring every blog for information to share, these tools will help you curate the best possible content for your readership (and in a fraction of the time).

STEP 7: CREATE A SEPARATE E-MAIL FOR SUBSCRIPTIONS

Admit it: there's nothing that clutters your mind more than a cluttered inbox. To alleviate said cluttered feeling, you spend hours reading and responding to all of your e-mails. Your inbox is eventually empty, and you feel a sense of accomplishment... for about five minutes, until the next flood of e-mails come in and you realize you haven't accomplished one word of writing.

If you want to boost your daily productivity level, the best decision you'll ever make is creating a separate e-mail account specifically for mailing list and blog subscriptions. Your primary inbox will then be dedicated to your writing assignments, which you'll be able to focus on distraction-free.

The same goes for when it's time to catch up on your reading: you'll be able to focus on the learning process without feeling guilty for not replying to work-related e-mails immediately.

STEP 8: SCHEDULE YOUR SOCIAL MEDIA POSTS IN ADVANCE

Once you have the editorial calendars for your blog and social media profiles in place, everything you post should be intentional toward your career goals. This is where scheduling your posts in advance comes in handy. Use a scheduling program like Buffer (bufferapp.com) or Hootsuite (hootsuite.com), and define a posting routine for each social media account.

Decide how many times you'll post to your Facebook page, Twitter account, and other social media profiles, and also decide on when. You can set up your scheduling program to automatically launch your posts at specific times so you can focus entirely on the quality of your content. To find out the best times to post—common times your following is online—sign up for a free Crowdbooster account (crowdbooster.com). Crowdbooster will continually analyze your Facebook and Twitter accounts and will regularly notify you of the best times to post content.

Scheduling your social media posts in advance means you'll have one less excuse to procrastinate during the week. Instead, unwind at the end of your productive day by engaging with your followers. (Just imagine!)

As you use the above steps to create harmony between your writing and platform, you'll naturally start refining each part of the process and making it your own. In no time, you'll be wearing all of your writing career hats in style.

KRISSY BRADY is a freelance writer from Gravenhurst, Ontario, Canada. Her articles have appeared in *Women's Health* and *The Writer*, and she's currently working on her first screenplay. You can learn more about Krissy at her website: www.writtenbykrissy.com.

HOW TO GET SOCIAL

20 Mistakes Writers Make When Using Social Media (& How to Avoid Them)

by Debbie Ridpath Ohi

Social media can be a great tool for writers but can also be damaging if misused. Here are the most common mistakes that authors tend to make, and how to avoid them:

1. Not deciding why they're using social media before using it.

Before you sign up for any social media network, think about why you're doing it. You need to be more specific than "I want to get published." Are you hoping to network with people in the industry who might be able to help you? For promotion purposes? To keep up with publishing industry trends and news? For mutual encouragement and fun chat with other writers? Knowing your goals will help you make the right choices.

2. Trying to be everywhere.

With so many social media networks to choose from, with new networks springing up every month, it's impossible and inadvisable for authors to join them all. Figuring out what you want (see Tip #1) will help you decide what networks to focus on and how to use them. At the time this article was written, Facebook and Twitter were the most popular social media venues, with Tumblr close behind and Google+ slowly gaining in popularity. My personal favorite is Twitter.

3. Not having a profile photo.

Some writers leave their profile photo blank, perhaps in a misguided effort to maintain privacy. My advice: If you're planning to use social media to network and promote yourself, you have to be willing to put yourself out there. I use a headshot photo, so people know what I look like. Some writers use the covers of their books while others use illustrations. Whatever you do, DON'T leave your profile photo blank—that tends to give the impression that you're a newbie who doesn't know what you're doing (even if that's true, you don't need to advertise the fact) or worse, that you're a spammer.

4. Having a blank or uninformative profile.

I'm amazed at how many writers don't bother filling in their profile bio info. This is one of the most important and useful opportunities for getting people interested in you and your work. As in a blank profile photo, a blank profile bio can give the impression that the user is a spammer, or may not be invested enough to put in the effort of writing a bio.

Some writers opt for one-sentence pithy profile bios which aim to be funny, mysterious or snarky. While this may intrigue some visitors enough to want to connect, writers need to think carefully about what kind of connections they're hoping to make. If you're hoping to be taken seriously by editors, publishers, agents and other writers, make sure your profile bio reflects your intention. This doesn't mean you can't inject some personality...just be wary of injecting too much. Always proofread your bio and keep it updated. Include a URL where people can find out more info about you and your work.

> I'm amazed at how many writers don't bother filling in their profile bio info. This is one of the most important and useful opportunities for getting people interested in you and your work.

5. Trying to be clever/funny when you're not.

Be wary of trying to be edgy, clever or funny in your social media unless you're very sure you ARE edgy, clever or funny. Because if you aren't, your post is more likely to fall flat and give readers the impression that you're trying too hard.

6. Missing opportunities to include links and tags, or over-tagging.

Social media platforms like Facebook and Twitter enable users to tag other users in posts, and can be a great way of connecting. Example: Suppose you're tweeting about a great blog post by author Gomer Glotz. Instead of "15 Tips for Dealing With Rejection by Gomer Glotz <link here>", it could be "15 Tips For Dealing With Rejection by @GomerGlotz <link here>". Gomer will get a notification in his Mentions feed of your tweet.

Tagging people in your posts can be an effective part of your networking efforts but it can also backfire if you overdo it. Tagging someone just because you want them to look at your post is like shouting their name across a crowded room. It may be fine once in a while if you're sure they would be interested and have the time to respond, but if you do it too often or inappropriately, people will start to ignore you. Or worse, get irritated.

7. Posting bare links or "check this out" on Twitter.

Never just post a bare link, expecting people to be curious enough to click through. Unless they're avid fans, most of them won't. Ditto for "check this out" posts with a link. What if a reader does click through and then feels let down or tricked when the page is something that doesn't interest him or her? Respect your readers' time and give them a reason to click the link.

Take the time to compose a succinct, informative and intriguing description when posting the link.

8. Spamming people's Facebook Walls.

Don't use other people's personal Facebook Walls as a billboard for your promo posts. That's like walking into someone's living room and slapping an advertising poster on their wall before leaving. And yes, this includes "I thought your readers would be interested in my FREE e-book giveaway and prize draw" type of posts.

9. Not taking the time to learn how a community works before they post.

Whether or not they're explicitly stated, every online community has its own rules of etiquette. Before you start participating, take the time to watch how other people behave and how they post. I've been in scheduled Twitter chats where someone kept posting "Buy my book!" promo throughout our discussion, oblivious. No one at the chat will buy his books.

My advice: Pick one or two social media channels in the beginning and focus on those. Learn how to use them properly. Find writers who write for a similar audience as you do, who are active and successful in social media. Watch what they do and how they do it.

....

Don't use other people's personal Facebook Walls as a billboard for your promo posts. That's like walking into someone's living room and slapping an advertising poster on their wall before leaving.

....

10. Only joining social media when they have a book to promote.

This is one of the most common errors I've seen writers make. "There's no point in me joining Twitter or Facebook yet," they'll say; "I don't have anything to promote yet." Big mistake. In my opinion, the best time to join social media is before you have anything to promote.

Why? Because then people won't think you're one of the many authors who join social media just because they have a book or books to sell.

For authors who have an upcoming book to promote, I strongly advise joining social media now (after you've finished reading this article, that is) instead of waiting until closer to launch date.

11. Over-promoting.

Posting "Buy my book" over and over again on your social media feed will not help sell your book. No matter what your posting schedule, anyone visiting your page is going to be turned off. I've also seen authors who also go through their entire follower list, tagging a different person with each repetitive post.

A a general rule, try to reign in your purely promotional posts to 20% or less. The rest of the time, you should be sharing useful or interesting content, interacting with other people.

There are exceptions, such as when your book actually launches. But even then, try to make your promo posts more personal and interesting. Instead of saying, "My book just launched! Buy it!", say, "I had so much fun at my book launch! Here are a few photos..."

12. Not proofreading before posting.

Proper spelling and grammar are especially important for writers. Even if you're posting from your mobile device, take the time to read over what you're about to post publicly before hitting Send. If you're posting a link, verify that the link works. When copying and pasting a link, it's easy to accidentally miss a character at the end of the URL. If you're tagging someone, make sure you're tagging the right person.

13. Forgetting that an online chat is still public.

When everyone in an online chat room or Twitter chat is exchanging casual chat or rapid-fire repartee, it can be easy to forget that what you post is still public. Unlike a private conversation in a friend's living room, parts of your conversation may be copied and pasted elsewhere, or saved on someone's hard drive. No matter how casual the atmosphere, always be aware of what you are saying in a public online venue.

14. Posting in anger.

Instead of blowing off steam in a public venue, call up a trusted friend instead. Sure, you get a momentary satisfaction for having vented, but chances are good that you'll regret making that post. Nearly everyone has heard the horror stories of well-known authors who have regretted a Twitter post and deleted it...only to find that it was too late since their tweet had already been shared with others.

If someone posts something upsetting about you, do not give in to the impulse to re-spond right away. Take a deep breath. Think hard about whether you need to reply at all. Is this something that would be better discussed in a private e-mail or a phone call? If a pub-lic reply is needed, always take the high road. Be brief and don't try to provoke, then switch to a more neutral topic.

15. Being overly negative.

Be aware that making a habit of whiny or complaining posts will give the impression that you are a whiny and complaining person. People who have not met you in person may as-sume that you're like this in real life as well, and may not want to work with you.

Never, ever bash a work or potential work colleague in public. It's unprofessional. I've heard agents and editors say they were about to sign on an author until they checked the author's blog or social media feed and were turned off by these kinds of posts.

Be aware of the image you are projecting. It's worth taking the time every so often and reviewing your posts to remind yourself how you are portraying yourself.

16. Obsessing about follower count.

Whatever the platform, don't let yourself get too hung up on follower count. I've seen Twit-ter profiles where the authors promise to follow back anyone who follows them...a sure sign that they're focus is on numbers instead of who their followers are. I would far rather have 100 people follow me who are actually interested in me and my work than 1,000 random strangers who are just after more followers.

Besides, be aware that what's popular in social media now may be old news next year when something shinier catches people's attention. A question to ask yourself: "If this so-cial media site shut down right now, would I still consider the time I've spent here worth it?"

I would far rather have 100 people follow me who are actually interested in me and my work than 1,000 random strangers who are just after more followers.

17. Forgetting the "social" in "social media."

Some authors use social media just to post links to their new blog posts. They may even have software set up so that these links are automatically posted to their social media feed in-stead of logging in manually. While there's nothing wrong with this in itself, people are less likely to want to follow this type of feed unless they're already fans. To attract new follow-ers and connections, you need to show you're interested and that you're genuinely engaged.

18. Believing that social media can replace engaging face-to-face.

As engaging and useful as social media can be, it can never replace face-to-face conversation. Engage in real-life: join your local writers' organization, attend writers' conferences and workshops.

19. Forcing themselves to use social media even if they hate it.

Given the potential benefits, I believe it's worth learning to use social media. However, if you've given it your best shot and still feel uncomfortable using it....then don't. Find other ways to achieve your goals that feel more natural.

If you force yourself to continue using social media just because everyone tells you that you should, your followers will be able to tell.

20. Spending too much time on social media.

It can be easy to convince yourself that the time you spend on social media is part of work. You're networking, after all, or doing promotion. Minutes can turn into hours before you know it, so keep track of your time. Be honest about what you're doing.

As fun and useful as social media can be, don't forget your first priority: writing.

DEBBIE RIDPATH OHI offers additional social media tips at inkygirl.com/a-writers-guide-to-twitter. Her illustrations appear in *I'M BORED,* a picture book written by Michael Ian Black (Simon & Schuster BFYR) chosen by The New York Times for its Notable Children's Books Of 2012 list. She is author of *Writer's Online Marketplace* (Writer's Digest Books). Twitter: @inkyelbows. Website: DebbieOhi.com.

HOW TO IMPROVE YOUR PRESENTATION SKILLS

....

by Brenda Collins

Given the emerging power and popularity of social media, do you still need to put your physical face on your author brand? Do you have to give presentations or workshops? According to many successful editors, agents, and writers, the answer is "yes". In this competitive publishing environment, authors have to be skilled marketers. The experts report that live events can be very beneficial to an author's career. The good news is you can learn how to present effectively even if the thought scares you.

"For certain audiences," notes Holly Root, of the Waxman Literary Agency, "it's absolutely expected that an author would be willing to appear—for instance, a very newsy nonfiction title, or a book with a huge publicity push, or a novel for kids, where school visits would be key. For the majority of novelists, it is optional, the kind of thing that if done well can be a terrific boost. The more people who know about you, the better your chances some of them will be your kind of readers." Root believes that appearances by one of her authors, Lisa Patton, absolutely contributed to her books becoming bestsellers.

If the thought of speaking in front of a crowd makes your stomach churn, you are not alone. Several studies have shown that public speaking is the number one fear for most people, followed by fear of death.

In my experience, though, even an introvert can become a great public speaker. When I was ten years old, I stood in front of my fifth grade class to give my first speech—and burst into tears. With practice and maturity, I now deliver talks to audiences of all sizes. You just need the right skills, techniques and experience.

PREPARATION

Preparation is the secret to successful presentations. Preparation will ease the jitters when first you look out at your audience. Preparation will help you hide the fact you've lost your place in your notes. Preparation will ensure your presentation doesn't run too long or too short. And, more than anything else, preparation will make sure you say something that is worth the time your audience spends listening to you.

DEFINE OBJECTIVE

Jot down, in plain language, one sentence stating what you want to achieve through the presentation. That is not the same as what you want to say. Ask yourself why you are giving this particular presentation to this particular audience. What should they take away from it? This becomes your *key message*, which will shape the rest of your presentation. For example, "My presentation objective is to give writers the tools they need to deliver effective presentations with confidence."

REFINE CONTENT & STRUCTURE

List the important points you want to make in the presentation. For some this may be a neat list of bullet points, but for less linear thinkers, also known as *pantsers*, it could be a mind map, bubble drawing, or just scribbles all over a page.

Guided by your key message, arrange your notes so that each point flows naturally into the next, like a story plot. Think—beginning, middle, and end. This is your opportunity to make sure your message is clear.

Presentation structure is standardized. Your opening is like a novel or magazine article. You need to hook your audience right from the beginning with a relevant quotation, personal anecdote, a rhetorical question or other device.

There's a saying, "Tell them what you're going to say—, tell them—, then tell them what you told them!" That forms the body of your presentation: your objective, main points and summary.

Finally, you wrap up your presentation by linking back to your opening. Think of your opening and closing as the bookends of your presentation holding it all together for your audience.

EDIT

Eliminate unnecessary information and conflicting messages. Presentations are rarely too short; often they are too long. As operatic soprano and self-help guru Dorothy Sarnoff once noted, "Make sure you have finished speaking before your audience has finished listening."

Some of your revisions can help you prepare for audience questions. Don't worry about anticipating all possible questions. If you do not have the answer, either throw the question out to the audience to generate discussion or ask for the questioner's card so you can get back with an answer later.

AVOID DEATH BY POWERPOINT

Decide if and where you are going to use slides, handouts or other aids. Slides are *not* mandatory. In fact, they can be a distraction, and there's always a risk that the technology won't work on the big day.

Only use a slide or handout if it illustrates something that is otherwise hard to visualize or if it will support audience participation.

If you do want to use slides, there are a few rules.

- Assume two minutes talk time per slide to calculate how many you should have. Remember to number them.
- A picture or graph is worth a thousand words. Use them where possible.
- No more than three or four short bullets per slide. Overwhelming detail or animation is confusing.
- Use a clear (sans serif), large (minimum 24 point) font size.
- Use a consistent color scheme, of three or four high contrast colors at most. Remember some people have difficulty distinguishing between certain color combinations (e.g., red-green, blue-yellow).

If you will be using slides, tell the organizers beforehand to ensure you'll have the equipment you need and that technical help will be available.

With or without technology, always have a contingency plan. Overhead lamps burn out. The projector provided might not work with your laptop, the thumb drive you had your presentation on could get lost. Bring a hard copy of your slides and notes so you can go ahead without a computer if need be.

The organizer may determine when handouts are distributed but, if you have a choice, consider these options.

BEFORE: Makes it easy for your audience to follow along with you and take notes. However, they also may be reading instead of listening to you and the paper rattling can be distracting.

DURING: This is my least favorite. It is difficult to distribute the handout quickly enough to be relevant to the point you're making without breaking the flow of your presentation.

AFTER: My preference is to let the audience know they will receive the slides at the end of the presentation so they can focus on what I'm saying but avoid taking unnecessary notes.

REHEARSE, REHEARSE, AND REHEARSE SOME MORE

One of the ways I learned to overcome the mind-numbing fear was to practice the presentation until I could give it in my sleep.

For notes, only write down key words, in large print so they are easy to read. Use these sparingly as memory joggers, not as a script. The fastest way to bore an audience is to read your presentation word for word.

Practice where you will pause throughout your presentation. You need time to take a breath and your audience needs time to digest your point before you move onto the next one.

Rehearse not only what you're going to say, but how. Use your voice and body language to make it interesting. Bob Mayer, best-selling author of over 40 books, publisher, and skilled professional speaker, notes, "as much as it is presenting information, it is also a form of entertainment. While content is important, presenting in an energetic and exciting manner is also important."

A run-through in front of the mirror is good. Even better is a trusted friend who will tell you if you unconsciously use any "ah, um, you know, like" empty fillers.

No friends available? Try recording your practice run, on video if possible. Early in my career, I was taped as part of a media training course. Watching that video was a shocker. As I spoke, my hands were flailing around as if I was swatting at wasps. You don't have to tie your hands behind your back but make sure you don't hold a pointer, pen or any other object you might play with if you're nervous. If you like putting your hands in your pockets, make sure there are no coins in there. You want your entire posture to project confidence and calm.

Your dress rehearsal should include the outfit you plan to wear for the presentation. What you wear should be appropriate and comfortable. You also want to be sure your shoes won't squeak and your jewelry won't rattle as you move.

THE BIG DAY

You are ready. Standing at the side of the stage, you hear your name called. Wait! If you want to deliver your presentation with energy and composure—I'm remembering my embarrassing episode of stage fright in Grade 5—the delivery of your presentation starts at least an hour before you get to the podium. You arrive before anyone else so that you can scope out the room in advance, place some water within easy reach, make sure your notes are in order, set up and test out any equipment you've requested.

With your environment arranged, you focus on making sure you are ready. My eldest brother had a long and successful career as an on-air morning show host on National Public Radio. He had to wake up his mouth and voice before flipping on the microphone. He might tighten and stretch his face muscles, rotate his lower jaw to loosen the jaw muscles, and recite a tongue twister, like "Rita wrote a ridiculous rhythm about racoons" or other sound combinations. Try it and your opening will slide out more smoothly.

Right before you begin is also the time to release any pent-up tension from your body by rolling your shoulders, stretching your neck, pulling your arms over your head and behind your back to open up your chest. Then take three deep abdominal breaths, straighten your shoulders and walk out to the podium with confidence.

While presenting, stay aware of your audience. If they are yawning or drooping, do not take it personally, especially if it's after lunch. Have you slipped into a monotone, or started reading your slides? Add an anecdote or stretch break to wake them up.

Presentations are both an art and a science. Consult your library or bookstore to learn more about giving presentations. I can add a few final lessons that the books often miss, and that I learned the hard way:

- Keep a bottle of water at hand for when your tongue threatens to stick to the roof of your mouth.
- Never drink coffee before you give a talk. Let's just say it makes men perspire and ladies glisten.
- When it comes to mistakes of any kind, laugh and the audience with laugh with you.
- If your talk is after lunch when everyone feels sluggish, turn down the thermostat a degree or two. You don't want to see their breath, but just enough to keep the audience feeling refreshed.
- Memorize your first three slides. I find that if nerves hit when I first look out at the audience, I can rely on rote to get started and usually by the fourth slide I've found my groove.

Writers are skilled wordsmiths. Presentations are one more way we can use our talent in crafting, polishing and delivering words to an audience. Any writer can learn to give presentations but Alicia Rasley, an award-winning author and nationally known teacher of writing workshops, advises, "Give presentations because it excites you, because it's fun, because you get to meet new people and see new places."

As Emily Ohanjanians, Associate Editor, HQN Books (Harlequin) says, "It is certainly not easy for everyone, but just be confident in who you are and what you have to say. After all, if people read your writing, you must have something good to say!"

....

BRENDA COLLINS has long believed that, for writers to succeed, writing talent must be supplemented with strong business skills. To support that view, she has published articles and delivered workshops to hundreds of writers on career planning, professional networking and presentation skills. Collins also serves annually as a judge for an international mystery / suspense fiction-writing contest. Her paranormal novella, *Witch in the Wind*, is available on Amazon. Prior to becoming a freelance writer, Collins spent 25 years in the corporate world where her work included award winning technical and corporate writing.

....

SAMIR HUSNI

Interview

....

by Angela Rogalski

When Elizabeth Barrett Browning wrote her famous poem, "How Do I Love Thee," most people believe she was referring to the love of her life, her husband Robert Browning. However, for others this poem reflects in a different way and on a variety of subjects. Samir Husni is one of those "others."

When you walk into Husni's office at the Magazine Innovation Center at the Meek School of Journalism and New Media, located on the campus of the University of Mississippi, you immediately discern why he's known as "Mr. Magazine™." Stacks, boxes and shelves are filled to capacity with magazines, most of them first editions. And he'll tell you, after God and his family, magazines are what he holds near and dear to his heart.

In fact, it has been said, by Husni himself first, that his heart began to pump ink at the tender age of nine, instead of blood. "At nine years old, I bought my first copy of Superman," Husni said. "From the moment I touched the cover of that magazine, a transformation began."

Due to this metamorphosis, Husni has become the leading expert on magazine launches and the world of magazine media in general. His expertise is called on by publishers and media executives all over the world, from Morris Corporation to the Finnish magazine group Sanoma and many, many others. So when it comes to tips for freelancers who are looking to break into the exciting world of magazine publishing; who better to go to than Mr. Magazine™ himself?

What do you think about current freelancer opportunities in the magazine media world?

As magazines and magazine media companies continue to downsize and continue to let staffers go, such as in the case of *Martha Stewart Living*, which right before the holidays fired 100 of their full-time staff and as bad as that is for the people who were let go, it opens up a lot of opportunities for freelance writers. However, when you have an abundance of writers and staffers from both newspapers and magazines laid off because everyone is discovering this downsizing and using it as a strategy for survival, the competition becomes tougher.

I recently was speaking at a travel writer's meeting in which they were telling me that there used to be at one stage around 300 travel writers at different newspapers in this country and now they're down to around a handful. So all these writers automatically became freelancers and the competition is stiff.

That's why I keep telling people, and this may sound like an old cliché, but you need to know the publication that you are trying to write for. You need to be on par with what's happening in the marketplace. It's not enough just to know that you are a good writer, it's not enough that you can collect the information and do some good reporting; you have to know the entire market. The good freelancer is the person who has his or her hand on the pulse of the nation, on the pulse of the audience and on the pulse of the pop culture. And understand those publications and magazines.

And you are going to have a much better chance freelancing for a new magazine than an established magazine. It's as simple as that. Because most people who come up with ideas for new magazines, and there is no shortage of ideas for those new magazines. We are averaging around 200 new magazines that are published with regular frequency and those folks don't have big staffs. They're probably Mom and Pop organizations with maybe four or five people working for them.

> It's not enough just to know that you are a good writer, it's not enough that you can collect the information and do some good reporting; you have to know the entire market.

And I can give you plenty of examples: look at *Covey Rise*, wonderful, beautiful magazine. But how many people do they have on staff; you can count them on one hand, the same thing with *First Coast Magazine* that was just launched in Jacksonville, Fla., they have very few people on staff.

So a lot of the new magazines that are coming out onto the marketplace are doing so as a labor of love, as a passion and they are looking for people who can fulfill their passions. If you have your hand on the pulse of the new magazines you already have a head start on those freelancers who don't.

As far as finding out what new magazines are out there; all you have to do is visit my Launch Monitor (launchmonitor.wordpress.com) every month, or search and Google and find those new magazines and approach them. There's plenty out there, but what's going to help you in our magazine world is for you to offer something different and better. But you can't do that if you don't know what's already out there first and if you don't spend time with a publication.

That may seem basic and just common sense, but that's one of the biggest problems we have in our industry. We have lost common sense. What I always like to say is that we've driven that car called common sense to the lowest garage, locked it and left the keys in it. And until we regain our common sense, until we regain our trust that it's not all doom and gloom and that print is not dead, we will continue to have problems.

Writers don't have to worry about the circulation of the magazine. Whether a magazine has a circulation of 10,000 or a million, the content has to be up to par with that audience and with that subject matter. So the least of the worries of a writer is how big the magazine is, leave that to the publishers. Because the bigger the magazine, the more competition you're going to have and the bigger the budget and they can afford their own staff.

One nice thing is we're moving away from the days where people used to say, "Ah, I read this in *Time*." Now we've become a society of bylines. Now it's, "Did you see what Nancy Gibbs wrote in *Time*," or whomever as opposed to just, "I read this in *Time* magazine."

So there's an opportunity for a freelancer to build up their name until their byline becomes bigger than the brand. And when you reach that stage you can write your own ticket.

How important is that initial approach to an editor of a magazine? Should freelancers talk much about their experience, what and whom they've written for, or should they approach a potential opportunity a bit more humbly?

Well, no one wants a newbie. By the same token, you can send me all your clips that are not relevant to my magazine or to my audience, and it may mean nothing to me. It will show me that you're published, but the important thing, and this is what I keep telling people time after time, understand the audience of the magazine. It's even more important than knowing the content of the magazine.

Freelancers must understand who the audience of that magazine is because we live and die today based on the knowledge of that audience, based on the knowledge of who are we trying to reach, because this myth about the audience of one no longer exists.

We live in a society where your publication cannot say I have an "average" reader anymore. Your publication today has an audience that's like a jury and that's what I like to tell people and my clients all the time, think about your audience like a jury and think about yourself as the prosecutor or the defense attorney. You have to deliver a presentation that will make each and every one of those twelve different people feel that you are talking to them, feel that if there's anybody in that room that this defense attorney or prosecutor is addressing, is you.

So how can you, as a freelancer, understand that audience and link it to the content of the magazine? If I get a query letter from somebody who shows me that they know my audience and what they are presenting, what they are telling me fits right smack in the heart of my magazine, like a laser-targeted query letter that reaches the crux of the content of the publication and my audience, that's when I give it the green light.

You have a mantra: "What is in it for me?" How important is that when it comes to the content a freelancer produces?

What we say is we're no longer in the business of the five W's and the H. We're now in the business of what is in it for me. The WIIIFM Factor is so important, and my challenge to all writers working with any magazine I consult with; I tell the editors to convey to all the writers that with every article you're going to give me make sure they outline or turn in what I refer to as four or five profit tips.

If I read this article as a reader, what are the profit tips that I'm going to gain from that article? Whether you want to put them in a sidebar or whether they are built within the article, but it's important that the writer provide those profit tips within the story, so the editor will know exactly what his or her readers are going to get.

> As a reader, I don't have time to go digging and try to find where that pot of gold is buried within the article. I want the gold sprinkled throughout the entire piece.

And that's very important. Consider it similar to the outline of your story, because if I don't have those profit tips, I don't really care about the article. The duty of the writer or the reporter, as they report the story, is to go after those profit tips knowing ahead of time who their audience is and what the content matter is going to be.

As a writer if I don't get A, B, C, and D first, for me as a freelancer, something that will give me an action plan or a roadmap so that I can move forward, go to the Launch Monitor, Google the magazines, research the audience, write the query letter, get my acceptance and then move forward and get to work, then I'm totally off balance in the structure of my attempts. You need those profit tips first.

Those profit tips have to be that obvious and that simple. As a reader, I don't have time to go digging and try to find where that pot of gold is buried within the article. I want the gold sprinkled throughout the entire piece.

You also refer to something known as the "WOW" Factor; tell me about that.

When someone is writing there is one this, I always tell them: there's no question that we've become an ADD society. We're bombarded with information, surrounded by it, everywhere you look somebody is trying to reach and grab your attention.

The only thing that neither technology nor innovation has not been able to do is add a single second or minute to the 24-hour, seven days in a week, we still have the same time. So if you think in reality who's your competitor; you'll discover our biggest competitor today is time and not the magazine either – time, as in seconds, minutes and hours.

The goal first is to value your time. If you give me $4.95 or $5.95 and buy my magazine, I better give you something worthy of that money. Plus, worthy of the 15 minutes you are going to give me. When was the last time you read an article and said, "Wow!" Or you looked at the cover or the photography inside and said, "Wow!" When was the last time you started reading something and you lost yourself and any sense of time and you said, "Wow, I've been reading this magazine for over an hour."

If you don't have this experience, and by the way, we are much more than just content providers, we are experience makers, because there is content everywhere as I said earlier. How can you form that content in such a way that you are actually creating an experience, an experience that your readers will lose themselves in?

One of the easiest ways to do that and the easiest way to see if you have that Wow moment, that lost sense of time, is to read your own article aloud. Then record the reaction your own mind tells you as you're reading it. Does it sound humdrum or is it something exciting, something where you can feel the tone of the conversation and suddenly you realize you have a smile on your lips and a feeling of completeness within your own skin.

That is the importance of the WOW Factor.

ANGELA ROGALSKI is a freelancer who writes regularly for *The Delta Business Journal*, *The Cleveland Current*, *Mud & Magnolias magazine*, *North Mississippi Parent* and also edits a website called Delta Posts through a grant funded through The Community Foundation of Northwest Mississippi and the University of Mississippi.

BOB MAYER

Author Interview

....

by Olivia Markham

In the fall of 2010, *New York Times* best-selling author Bob Mayer had already traditionally published over 40 books, but was frustrated with traditional publishing's slow schedule and unresponsiveness to change. So, he and now-business-partner Jen Talty formed what has become Cool Gus Publishing to publish his backlist as e-books. In January 2011, they sold 347 e-books. By July 2011, after a lot of hard work and long hours, they were selling 65,000 e-books a month, and by the end of 2011, they had sold over 400,000 e-books. In March of 2012, they were averaging 50,000 e-books a month, and had built a 7-figure indie publishing house in just two years.

This author has written a number of series—the Atlantis series, the Area-51 series, the Green Beret series, the Shadow Warrior series, the Presidential series, and, most recently, the Nightstalkers series. Some of his more recent titles have been *Chasing the Lost, The Jefferson Allegiance,* and *The Kennedy Endeavor.* From 2007 to 2011, he alsoco-wrote three books with New York Times best-selling author Jennifer Crusie: *Don't Look Down; Agnes and the Hitman;* and *Wild Ride.* He's also written a number of nonfiction titles, including *The Novel Writer's Toolkit; Write It Forward: From Writer to Successful Author;* and (as a former Green Beret) *Who Dares Wins: Special Operations Strategies for Success, and The Green Beret Survival Guide.*

Now, after four years of self-publishing and about a dozen more books written and released as e-books—more than half of those self-published—we're asking Bob about his success in self-publishing as a hybrid author (a term he coined), one who contracts with traditional publishers while also self-publishing.

What projects are you currently working on?

I'm writing my fourth Nightstalkers book. Which is interesting because although this interview is about self-publishing, my first three Nightstalker books were published by 47North, which is Amazon's science fiction imprint. This book is not part of that three-book contract, so the plus of self-publishing is, if Amazon doesn't pick it up, I can simply publish it myself. Even though I mainly "self" publish, I also believe in having multiple income streams. More importantly, publishing with Amazon increases my marketing footprint, as 47North has its own marketing arm.

What lead you to write Sci-Fi—the Atlantis series and the Area 51 series?

I just did a "True Lies" blog post (January 2014) about my four pillars of story: reading, my military background, history, and last, but not least, myths and legends. Atlantis is one of the most ancient myths, and Area 51 is a modern one. I'm interested in those stories. What's true? What's fiction? Is the line blurred? Actually, I put a lot more fact in my novels than most people suspect.

What would you liken your writing process to?

It's a creative flow. I trust my subconscious more and go with the flow. But I also focus more on pushing into the depth of my characters more. After almost 60 books written, I know a lot more about this than I did when I started. So if I'm starting to go in the wrong direction, I pick up on that immediately.

Any new projects on the horizon?

Series are the key to success. So I'm doing something momentous after 56 books. I'm wrapping several of my series into each other. I've already brought the main character from *The Green Berets: Chasing the Ghost* into my very successful Dave Riley Green Beret series, and they'll be together in future books. I've also brought my main two characters from my Cellar books into my Nightstalker books. In my current Nightstalkers, I'm also integrating some aspects of Psychic Warrior and eventually wrapping it back to my No.1 bestselling Atlantis series. My head hurts to think of it, because we're talking pulling together a lot of people and story-lines, but so far it's working.

How did you get started writing?

I was living in the Orient studying martial arts and had some time on my hands. So I simply began writing to keep sane. I didn't think about getting published. I was more focused on simply telling a story.

Why did you decide to self-publish?

In late 2009 I looked at the publishing landscape and saw a lot of change on the horizon. I'd always described publishing as slow and techno-phobic, and that didn't bode well. I also had the rights back to a lot of my backlist, and those books were sitting around doing nothing. Note that I didn't "self" publish. Jen Talty and I formed Cool Gus Publishing, because with the number of titles I have, it was impossible for me to do it myself. Also, I simply didn't want to do all that work because my primary work is being a writer. We now have published other authors. Jennifer Probst and Colin Falconer are doing quite well for us, and we have others whose sales are increasing.

In your opinion, what is the biggest benefit to self-publishing vs. traditional publishing?

Besides higher royalties [in self-publishing]? Creative and business control. We view ourselves as a publishing partnership where the author comes first. The author gets final say over content, cover, copy, marketing, price, etc. We advise the authors, but ultimately they are the ones who create story, which is the content that is sold to readers. We facilitate that.

It's also much, much faster. I still see announcements in Publishers Marketplace about deals for publication two years out. Who knows what the landscape will be two years out? We just launched a bunch of backlist for Janice Maynard, a rising star in romance, and got 7 titles out in two months from the time we agreed to do it. We're in the digital age, and the business has to reflect that.

How has self-publishing made a difference in your writing career?

It's totally transformed it. I earn more than I ever did in traditional publishing, even when I was a *New York Times* bestseller. I get paid every month. I know exactly how much is coming in and from where.

I also believe it's changed the actual writing. I was worried when *Nightstalkers: The Book of Truths* came out (2013), because it didn't fit the traditional novel style, but readers have really liked it. I've found that readers want more information, shorter books, and are more open to free-flowing narrative, rather than the traditional five-part structure.

What is the secret to your success?

Lots of books and hard work. Every successful indie author I know works very, very hard. The best promotion is a good book; better promotion is more good books.

In your opinion, what is the hardest part of self-publishing a book?

Writing a good book. I think because it's relatively easy to self-publish, people take short cuts. When you had to fight to get an agent, an editor, and a publisher, you had to work hard on craft. I don't see people doing that as much. They just slap stuff up there and are shocked when it doesn't sell. Readers are tougher than agents, editors, and publishers, so we have to work that much harder.

Where did you find your team of editors and cover artists?

We do our covers in-house. That was a steep learning curve, but one we've mastered. It involved a lot of back and forth with the author. We definitely want authors to be happy with their covers. And it has to pop in thumbnail.

We hire freelance editors as needed. It's the only thing we don't do inside of Cool Gus.

How do you market your books to reach readers and get real results?

That's the first question writers ask us when they consider Cool Gus. And we're honest—while there are things we can do, and we know how to work the system, it's extremely difficult to market fiction. While everything is happening faster, the truth is that marketing requires a long term plan. Consistency is key. Series are key. Finding your core group of readers and cultivating them is critical. My objective in 2014 is to focus much more on readers.

Any suggestions about how to find that core group of readers?

That's a big goal in 2014. To build up that core group, I'm doing my "True Lies" blog every Tuesday which is more personal than I have done in the past. We're building up our mailing list. I give out free Advance Reading Copies [ARCs] of upcoming books to fans, in the hope that they will write reviews.

....

Bottom line is that readers are the most important part of publishing, so we keep our focus on building our relationship with them.

....

Reviews are really important. What a lot of readers don't know is you can probably get a free e-book from an author if you promise to write a review. At least from authors who are "self" published.

Bottom line is that readers are the most important part of publishing, so we keep our focus on building our relationship with them.

How do you balance your writing time with everything else that goes with self-publishing?

The writing has to come first. I write in the mornings and spend the afternoon running my business. But I've learned you have to write whenever you can: on planes, in hotel rooms. Wherever. The easiest thing to slack off on is the writing. Everything about being an author is great; the writing is the hardest part.

What do you know now about the business that you wished you'd known when you started writing?

Take charge of your own career. No one else can do it for you. Network a lot. This is a people business. To think you can just sit back and write is naïve. I just got back from visiting my Amazon editor in New York City and Audible ACX in New Jersey (audiobooks). I learn from those meetings, and I also put a face on my books for them.

Practically speaking, I'd focus more on series. Very few authors can make a living doing stand alone books. Series, with intriguing characters, is key.

If you could pass on one piece of advice to other writers who are interested in self-publishing, what would it be?

Be willing to learn and change. Even in traditional publishing, I found few writers were willing to change what they were doing. I have my three rules of rule breaking for success:

1. Know the rule.
2. Have a good reason for breaking the rule.
3. Accept the consequences of breaking the rule.

We wrote a book on what we learned in digital publishing: How We Made Our First Million on Kindle: The Shelfless Book.

What advice would you give midlist authors who are looking to self-publish?

If you have more than a couple of titles, you really can't "self" publish. You can hire out a lot of it, but then you're dealing with multiple points of contacts. There are a lot of people trying to make money off writers. At Cool Gus we don't make money if our authors don't make money. They don't pay us anything. We have to believe in them, and we give them a single point of contact plus a lot of experience. We also provide the contacts we've cultivated over the years. We put our authors first, because they are the creators of content.

I'd recommend checking out many of the blogs about the business, and going to Kindleboards where there's a thread about pretty much every aspect of self-publishing with a lot of good information.

Understand you have to be an entrepreneur now, even if you're traditionally published. You're self-employed in the world of publishing. Focus on the business. Have a long-term goal and a business plan.

Distribution is no longer an issue; it's discoverability. I believe it's the best time ever to be a writer because the only person who can stop us is ourselves.

OLIVIA MARKHAM is a freelance writer with 10 years experience as a freelance editor, specializing in short stories and novels. She offers classes and workshops at conferences and elsewhere, to writers of all levels. She is a member of NW Independent Editors Guild, the National Writers Union, RWA, and the Oregon Writers Colony. Learn more at www.documentdriven.com.

HUGH HOWEY

Author Interview

....

by Maureen Dillman

Hugh Howey, best known for his popular sci-fi series *Wool*, made history when he refused to bow to traditional publishing pressures by the major houses, and instead issued his own terms. He's a shining example of what can happen when an indie creator sticks by their principles and doesn't lose sight of what writing is all about—telling a story.

But how did Howey get there, and why did he feel that a partnership between publishers and authors was so important? After hearing so much about him across the interwebs, I was eager for a chance to ask him about his journey through self-doubt and obscurity, to land a major publishing contract with Simon & Schuster on his own terms.

Did you ever have doubts that you would achieve success by publishing independently?

Every single day. I still do. But I would have these doubts however I published. I had these doubts as I queried my first book and signed with a small publisher. I never expected to make a living doing this. It's a passion. I feel the same way about photography, except that hobby costs me money. How's this: If writing was something that required monthly dues, I'd still pay to do it. I'm not in this to get rich, and I can't imagine anyone with that goal surviving the heartbreak of the years of obscurity. You have to write because you love it. That's my opinion, anyway.

How do you tackle self-doubt?

I don't. It tackles me. It's crippling. And the more success I have, the more I have to ignore the size of my audience and tell myself that I'm just writing for my wife and my mom. No one is ever going to see this. I'm safe here.

I'm like that kid who hides under the table and thinks if he can't see anyone, no one can see him back. That attitude gets me through the writing process. And then I tackle the publishing process as if millions of people will see this.

What would you say to someone else currently battling with self-doubt or the harsh critics and naysayers in their lives?

I've coined a new phrase to help myself deal with this: Huggers gonna hug. Fill yourself with love, even if you don't feel it at first, especially if you don't feel it at first. Understand that what people think of you has nothing to do with you. It has everything to do with them. It's not your business. Only you know who you are and what you're capable of. Concentrate on that. And feel love and pity for the people who bring negativity into the world. Be thankful that this isn't you.

Would you suggest that writers test their abilities in different styles, genres, or age categories?

Absolutely! Until you've tried it, you don't know if you like it or have an affinity for it. Don't keep punching the same ticket hoping for a different result. One of the biggest mistakes I see from new writers is sequelitis. Now that they have that first book and those characters they love, they keep writing in that world. Which leaves them selling their first book over and over, and that won't be their strongest book. Diversify. Explore. Try different POVs and tenses. Try different length works.

Do you agree that most writers generally can't make a living with their writing?

Yes, but only because most writers won't put the hours in. They won't dedicate themselves to this. This is like any other art. If you expect to pick up a paintbrush or a guitar and knock out a masterpiece, you aren't going to make it. You're going to get frustrated. How many people can write ten novels before they care about their first sale? Not many. And the reason people have this misconception about their chances is simple: We all spend a good amount of our lives writing. We think we have this nailed. But we haven't even started yet. Not until you get through that first draft.

The writers who approach this with passion and conviction can make a living at it. Those are precisely the ones I see doing well. How bad do you want this? Ask yourself that every day.

There's been a lot of speculation to this as of late, but do you feel the current abundance of self-published works is hurting the industry?

Not at all. Nor do I think my ability to surf the web and find interesting content is affected by the millions of new websites and blogs that go up every week. Stifling voices is a far greater concern. And as publishers move toward the Hollywood model of gambling on blockbusters instead of nurturing new writers, self-publishing becomes even more important. It's a fantastic way to start a career, build an audience, and improve one's craft. Musicians play small gigs and even street corners before they make it. Now authors have a similar path to success. It's no guarantee, but it has opened the door for thousands of writers to make a living doing what they love. And it has rewarded readers with affordable and exciting content."

Were you ever concerned that your independently published work would be judged as mediocre as compared to traditionally published work?

I don't know of anyone who assumes that every book in a bookstore is a great book. You have to read to know if it appeals to you. The opinions I care about are from those who pick up my book and give it a chance.

This is going to sound heretical and a bit nuts, and I totally get that, but one of the reasons I turned down offers from major publishers is that I worried about the stigma of being with a Random House or a HarperCollins. I explained this to editors at those houses during negotiations. My book was already a *New York Times* bestseller with a major film deal from Ridley Scott. These things mean more to me knowing that it was readers who made it happen, not a major publisher with a huge marketing budget. It happened organically. It was word of mouth. It may even have had something to do with the story I wrote. Signing all of that away would be to obscure the communal nature of the work's success. Even seven-figure offers weren't enough for me to turn my back on that.

As a small business owner and the employee of a large corporation, both of whom make the same amount and work the same hours, and see which of them takes more pride in their work.

Who do you feel truly determines success in the publishing industry? The publishers? The distributors? The public? Other writers?

The public, without a doubt. It isn't even close. I've watched publishers market the heck out of books only to see them flounder. The readers are in charge.

Now moving on to the thing a lot of our readers are probably curious about, your groundbreaking contract with Simon & Schuster. Can you tell us a little more about the contracts negotiations?

We told publishers what we wanted. They offered piles of money instead. We kept saying no.

Really? What were your reasons for holding out? What was missing from those first rounds of contracts?

All three rounds of offers wanted the digital rights to *Wool*. I don't think any author should sign those rights over until the 25% of net ceiling is broken. Publishers are making record profits right now because of the rise of e-books. They are raking in those profits by taking advantage of writers. Hollywood went through this a few years ago, and a strong union helped fight for fairer deals for streaming content. Unfortunately, writers are represented by a union that doesn't care about them. Our union spends all of its time fighting for bookstores and publishers. Because the people at the top are getting fat advances that effectively pay them higher royalties. New authors, meanwhile, are stuck. The rich get richer and the poor get poorer.

Even when my advance would've put me in the 'richer' category, I still believed this. We should stand together and demand change, demand that those record profits go toward helping nurture the careers of aspiring writers.

After you turned down the first round of offers from traditional publishers did you feel that you had made a terrible mistake?

I went back and forth. It wasn't easy. And we went through three rounds of offers over the course of a year, with five-figure deals turning into six-figure deals turning into seven-figure deals. It was never easy, but my agent and I held to our convictions. And our spouses were awesome and supportive (even if they gave us funny looks now and then).

What made you finally choose to sign with Simon & Schuster?

Simon & Schuster, which hadn't been a part of this exchange to that point, came to us with a brave and amazing deal. It was exactly what we had asked for. I think they deserve a lot of credit for treating us like partners rather than something to acquire. We got a print-only deal that left all other rights with me (digital, audio, foreign, everything). It also has a finite term, and so I get those print rights back six years from now. This is what authors deserve. It just requires walking away, which is scary. I can attest to that.

What excited you most about teaming up with a traditional publisher? What concerned you the most?

I was excited about trying something new. I love to diversify and experiment. I enjoy seeing so many sides of the publishing business. And even though my print on demand book was stocked in Barnes & Noble and indie bookstores like Powell's and elsewhere, I knew that this would help new readers discover my story. That was exciting.

What concerned me the most was all the extra work being with a traditional publisher entails! Book tours and promo videos and a surge of interviews. It was intense. I missed the self-publishing days when I could spend most of my time just writing.

And lastly before we let you go, what would you say to other writers who are embarking on their own self-pub journey?

> I'd really ask yourself why you are doing this. There are no guarantees. There is a lot of luck involved. Talent can go unnoticed. Hacks like me can have phenomenal success. Can you handle writing every day without promise of a single reader? If you can, and you stick with it, you can't lose.

MAUREEN DILLMAN is the author of *Crafting a Professional Independent Novel as an eBook* and a contributing author and layout and design editor of *The Writing Life*. Maureen currently lives in the San Francisco Bay area with her husband and rescue dog. When not writing, she enjoys exploring science and technology, cycling, and snapping pictures of the world around her.

BLOGGING BASICS:

Get the Most Out of Your Blog

....

by Robert Lee Brewer

In these days of publishing and media change, writers have to build platforms and learn how to connect to audiences if they want to improve their chances of publication and over-all success. There are many methods of audience connection available to writers, but one of the most important is through blogging.

Since I've spent several years successfully blogging—both personally and profession-ally—I figure I've got a few nuggets of wisdom to pass on to writers who are curious about blogging or who already are.

Here's my quick list of tips:

1. **START BLOGGING TODAY.** If you don't have a blog, use Blogger, WordPress, or some other blogging software to start your blog today. It's free, and you can start off with your very personal "Here I am, world" post.

2. **START SMALL.** Blogs are essentially simple, but they can get complicated (for peo-ple who like complications). However, I advise bloggers start small and evolve over time.

3. **USE YOUR NAME IN YOUR URL.** This will make it easier for search engines to find you when your audience eventually starts seeking you out by name. For instance, my url is http://robertleebrewer.blogspot.com. If you try Googling "Robert Lee Brewer," you'll notice that My Name Is Not Bob is one of the top 5 search results (behind my other blog: Poetic Asides).

4. **UNLESS YOU HAVE A REASON, USE YOUR NAME AS THE TITLE OF YOUR BLOG.** Again, this helps with search engine results. My Poetic Asides blog includes my name in the title, and it ranks higher than My Name Is Not Bob. However, I felt the play on my name was worth the trade off.

5. **FIGURE OUT YOUR BLOGGING GOALS.** You should return to this step every couple months, because it's natural for your blogging goals to evolve over time. Initially, your blogging goals may be to make a post a week about what you have written, submitted, etc. Over time, you may incorporate guests posts, contests, tips, etc.

6. **BE YOURSELF.** I'm a big supporter of the idea that your image should match your identity. It gets too confusing trying to maintain a million personas. Know who you are and be that on your blog, whether that means you're sincere, funny, sarcastic, etc.

7. **POST AT LEAST ONCE A WEEK.** This is for starters. Eventually, you may find it better to post once a day or multiple times per day. But remember: Start small and evolve over time.

8. **POST RELEVANT CONTENT.** This means that you post things that your readers might actually care to know.

9. **USEFUL AND HELPFUL POSTS WILL ATTRACT MORE VISITORS.** Talking about yourself is all fine and great. I do it myself. But if you share truly helpful advice, your readers will share it with others, and visitors will find you on search engines.

10. **TITLE YOUR POSTS IN A WAY THAT GETS YOU FOUND IN SEARCH ENGINES.** The more specific you can get the better. For instance, the title "Blogging Tips" will most likely get lost in search results. However, the title "Blogging Tips for Writers" specifies which audience I'm targeting and increases the chances of being found on the first page of search results.

11. **LINK TO POSTS IN OTHER MEDIA.** If you have an e-mail newsletter, link to your blog posts in your newsletter. If you have social media accounts, link to your blog posts there. If you have a helpful post, link to it in relevant forums and on message boards.

12. **WRITE WELL, BUT BE CONCISE.** At the end of the day, you're writing blog posts, not literary manifestos. Don't spend a week writing each post. Try to keep it to an hour or two tops and then post. Make sure your spelling and grammar are good, but don't stress yourself out too much.

13. **FIND LIKE-MINDED BLOGGERS.** Comment on their blogs regularly and link to them from yours. Eventually, they may do the same. Keep in mind that blogging is a form of social media, so the more you communicate with your peers the more you'll get out of the process.

14. **RESPOND TO COMMENTS ON YOUR BLOG.** Even if it's just a simple "Thanks," respond to your readers if they comment on your blog. After all, you want your readers to be engaged with your blog, and you want them to know that you care they took time to comment.

15. **EXPERIMENT.** Start small, but don't get complacent. Every so often, try something new. For instance, the biggest draw to my Poetic Asides blog are the poetry prompts

and challenges I issue to poets. Initially, that was an experiment—one that worked very well. I've tried other experiments that haven't panned out, and that's fine. It's all part of a process.

SEO TIPS FOR WRITERS

Most writers may already know what SEO is. If not, SEO stands for *search engine optimization*. Basically, a site or blog that practices good SEO habits should improve its rankings in search engines, such as Google and Bing. Most huge corporations have realized the importance of SEO and spend enormous sums of time, energy and money on perfecting their SEO practices. However, writers can improve their SEO without going to those same extremes.

In this section, I will use the terms of *site pages* and *blog posts* interchangeably. In both cases, you should be practicing the same SEO strategies (when it makes sense).

Here are my top tips on ways to improve your SEO starting today:

1. **USE APPROPRIATE KEYWORDS.** Make sure that your page displays your main keyword(s) in the page title, content, URL, title tags, page header, image names and tags (if you're including images). All of this is easy to do, but if you feel overwhelmed, just remember to use your keyword(s) in your page title and content (especially in the first and last 50 words of your page).

2. **USE KEYWORDS NATURALLY.** Don't kill your content and make yourself look like a spammer to search engines by overloading your page with your keyword(s). You don't get SEO points for quantity but for quality. Plus, one of the main ways to improve your page rankings is when you...

3. **DELIVER QUALITY CONTENT.** The best way to improve your SEO is by providing content that readers want to share with others by linking to your pages. Some of the top results in search engines can be years old, because the content is so good that people keep coming back. So, incorporate your keywords in a smart way, but make sure it works organically with your content.

4. **UPDATE CONTENT REGULARLY.** If your site looks dead to visitors, then it'll appear that way to search engines too. So update your content regularly. This should be very easy for writers who have blogs. For writers who have sites, incorporate your blog into your site. This will make it easier for visitors to your blog to discover more about you on your site (through your site navigation tools).

5. **LINK BACK TO YOUR OWN CONTENT.** If I have a post on Blogging Tips for Writers, for instance, I'll link back to it if I have a Platform Building post, because the two complement each other. This also helps clicks on my blog, which helps SEO. The one caveat is that you don't go crazy with your linking and that you make sure your links are relevant. Otherwise, you'll kill your traffic, which is not good for your page rankings.

6. **LINK TO OTHERS YOU CONSIDER HELPFUL.** Back in 2000, I remember being ordered by my boss at the time (who didn't last too much longer afterward) to ignore any competitive or complementary websites—no matter how helpful their content—because they were our competitors. You can try basing your online strategy on these principles, but I'm nearly 100 percent confident you'll fail. It's helpful for other sites and your own to link to other great resources. I shine a light on others to help them out (if I find their content truly helpful) in the hopes that they'll do the same if ever they find my content truly helpful for their audience.

7. **GET SPECIFIC WITH YOUR HEADLINES.** If you interview someone on your blog, don't title your post with an interesting quotation. While that strategy may help get readers in the print world, it doesn't help with SEO at all. Instead, title your post as "Interview With (insert name here)." If you have a way to identify the person further, include that in the title too. For instance, when I interview poets on my Poetic Asides blog, I'll title those posts like this: Interview With Poet Erika Meitner. Erika's name is a keyword, but so are the terms *poet* and *interview*.

8. **USE IMAGES.** Many expert sources state that the use of images can improve SEO, because it shows search engines that the person creating the page is spending a little extra time and effort on the page than a common spammer. However, I'd caution anyone using images to make sure those images are somehow complementary to the content. Don't just throw up a lot of images that have no relevance to anything. At the same time...

9. **OPTIMIZE IMAGES THROUGH STRATEGIC LABELING.** Writers can do this by making sure the image file is labeled using your keyword(s) for the post. Using the Erika Meitner example above (which does include images), I would label the file "Erika Meitner headshot.jpg"—or whatever the image file type happens to be. Writers can also improve image SEO through the use of captions and ALT tagging. Of course, at the same time, writers should always ask themselves if it's worth going through all that trouble for each image or not. Each writer has to answer that question for him (or her) self.

10. **USE YOUR SOCIAL MEDIA PLATFORM TO SPREAD THE WORD.** Whenever you do something new on your site or blog, you should share that information on your other social media sites, such as Twitter, Facebook, LinkedIn, online forums, etc. This lets your social media connections know that something new is on your site/blog. If it's relevant and/or valuable, they'll let others know. And that's a great way to build your SEO.

Programmers and marketers could get even more involved in the dynamics of SEO optimization, but I think these tips will help most writers out immediately and effectively while still allowing plenty of time and energy for the actual work of writing.

BLOG DESIGN TIPS FOR WRITERS

Design is an important element to any blog's success. But how can you improve your blog's design if you're not a designer? I'm just an editor with an English Lit degree and no formal training in design. However, I've worked in media for more than a decade now and can share some very fundamental and easy tricks to improve the design of your blog.

Here are my seven blog design tips for writers:

1. **USE LISTS.** Whether they're numbered or bullet points, use lists when possible. Lists break up the text and make it easy for readers to follow what you're blogging.
2. **BOLD MAIN POINTS IN LISTS.** Again, this helps break up the text while also highlighting the important points of your post.
3. **USE HEADINGS.** If your posts are longer than 300 words and you don't use lists, then please break up the text by using basic headings.
4. **USE A READABLE FONT.** Avoid using fonts that are too large or too small. Avoid using cursive or weird fonts. Times New Roman or Arial works, but if you want to get "creative," use something similar to those.
5. **LEFT ALIGN.** English-speaking readers are trained to read left to right. If you want to make your blog easier to read, avoid centering or right aligning your text (unless you're purposefully calling out the text).
6. **USE SMALL PARAGRAPHS.** A good rule of thumb is to try and avoid paragraphs that drone on longer than five sentences. I usually try to keep paragraphs to around three sentences myself.
7. **ADD RELEVANT IMAGES.** Personally, I shy away from using too many images. My reason is that I only like to use them if they're relevant. However, images are very powerful on blogs, so please use them—just make sure they're relevant to your blog post.

If you're already doing everything on my list, keep it up! If you're not, then you might want to re-think your design strategy on your blog. Simply adding a header here and a list there can easily improve the design of a blog post.

GUEST POSTING TIPS FOR WRITERS

Recently, I've broken into guest posting as both a guest poster and as a host of guest posts (over at my Poetic Asides blog). So far, I'm pretty pleased with both sides of the guest posting process. As a writer, it gives me access to an engaged audience I may not usually reach. As a blogger, it provides me with fresh and valuable content I don't have to create. Guest blogging is a rare win-win scenario.

That said, writers could benefit from a few tips on the process of guest posting:

1. **PITCH GUEST POSTS LIKE ONE WOULD PITCH ARTICLES TO A MAGAZINE.** Include what your hook is for the post, what you plan to cover, and a little about who you are.

Remember: Your post should somehow benefit the audience of the blog you'd like to guest post.

2. **OFFER PROMOTIONAL COPY OF BOOK (OR OTHER GIVEAWAYS) AS PART OF YOUR GUEST POST.** Having a random giveaway for people who comment on a blog post can help spur conversation and interest in your guest post, which is a great way to get the most mileage out of your guest appearance.

3. **CATER POSTS TO AUDIENCE.** As the editor of *Writer's Market* and *Poet's Market*, I have great range in the topics I can cover. However, if I'm writing a guest post for a fiction blog, I'll write about things of interest to a novelist—not a poet.

4. **MAKE PERSONAL, BUT PROVIDE NUGGET.** Guest posts are a great opportunity for you to really show your stuff to a new audience. You could write a very helpful and impersonal post, but that won't connect with readers the same way as if you write a very helpful and personal post that makes them want to learn more about you (and your blog, your book, your Twitter account, etc.). Speaking of which...

5. **SHARE LINKS TO YOUR WEBSITE, BLOG, SOCIAL NETWORKS, ETC.** After all, you need to make it easy for readers who enjoyed your guest post to learn more about you and your projects. Start the conversation in your guest post and keep it going on your own sites, profiles, etc. And related to that...

6. **PROMOTE YOUR GUEST POST THROUGH YOUR NORMAL CHANNELS ONCE THE POST GOES LIVE.** Your normal audience will want to know where you've been and what you've been doing. Plus, guest posts lend a little extra "street cred" to your projects. But don't stop there...

7. **CHECK FOR COMMENTS ON YOUR GUEST POST AND RESPOND IN A TIMELY MANNER.** Sometimes the comments are the most interesting part of a guest post (no offense). This is where readers can ask more in-depth or related questions, and it's also where you can show your expertise on the subject by being as helpful as possible. And guiding all seven of these tips is this one:

8. **PUT SOME EFFORT INTO YOUR GUEST POST.** Part of the benefit to guest posting is the opportunity to connect with a new audience. Make sure you bring your A-game, because you need to make a good impression if you want this exposure to actually help grow your audience. Don't stress yourself out, but put a little thought into what you submit.

ONE ADDITIONAL TIP: Have fun with it. Passion is what really drives the popularity of blogs. Share your passion and enthusiasm, and readers are sure to be impressed.

AUTHOR PLATFORM 2.0

....

by Jane Friedman

You've been through the drill already. You know about establishing your own website, being active on social media, plus networking up and down the food chain. You've heard all the advice about building your online and offline presence—and perhaps you've landed a book deal because of your strong platform.

But platform building is a career-long activity. It doesn't stop once your website goes live, or after you land a book deal. In fact, your continued career growth depends on extending your reach and uncovering new opportunities. So what's next?

I'll break it down into three categories:

- Optimize your online presence.
- Make your relationships matter.
- Diversify your content.

OPTIMIZE YOUR ONLINE PRESENCE

First things first. You need your own domain (e.g., JaneFriedman.com is the domain I own), and you should be self-hosted. If you're still working off Blogger or Wordpress.com, then you won't be able to implement all of my advice due to the limitations of having your site owned or hosted by someone else.

Once you truly own your site, hire a professional website designer to customize the look and feel to best convey your personality or brand. If you don't yet have a grasp on what your "personality" is, then hold off on a site revamp until you do. Or you might start simple, by getting a professionally designed header that's unique to your site.

Website and blog must-haves

Here's a checklist of things you should implement aside from a customized design.

- Readers should be able to subscribe to your blog posts via e-mail or RSS. You should be able to track the number of people who are signing up, and see when they are signing up.
- Customize the e-mails sent to anyone who subscribes to your blog posts. This can be done if you use Feedburner (free service) or MailChimp (free up to 2,000 names). Each e-mail that your readers receive should have the same look and feel as your website or whatever branding you typically use. You should also be able to see how many people open these e-mails and what they click on.
- If you do not actively blog, start an e-mail newsletter and post the sign-up form on your site. This way you can stay in touch with people who express interest in your news and updates. Again, MailChimp is a free e-mail newsletter delivery service for up to 2,000 names. You should also have e-newsletter sign-up forms with you at speaking engagements.
- Install Google Analytics, which offers valuable data on who visits your site, when they visit, what content they look at, how long they stay, etc.
- Add social sharing buttons to your site and each post, so people can easily share your content on Facebook, Google, etc. This functionality might have to be manually added if you have a self-hosted site.

Review your metrics

As I hope you noticed, many of the above items relate to metrics and measurement. Advance platform building requires that you study your numbers. Especially think about the following:

- How do people find your site? For example, if you're dumping a lot of energy into Twitter to drive traffic to your blog posts, but very few people visit your site from Twitter, that means your strategy is not working, and you might need to course correct.
- What content is the most popular on your site? This is like a neon sign, telling you what your readers want. Whatever it is, consider how you can build on it, repurpose it, or expand it.
- What causes a spike in traffic, followers, or subscribers? When you achieve spikes, you've done something right. How can you repeat the success?
- What's extending your reach? Most days, you're probably talking to the same crowd you were yesterday. But every so often, you'll be opened up to a new audience—and from that you can find new and loyal readers. Identify activities that have a broad ripple effect, and make you heard beyond your existing circles. (In Google Analytics, this would mean tracking how new visitors find you.)

Advanced social media monitoring and involvement

Just about everyone by now has a Facebook profile or page, a LinkedIn profile, a Twitter account, etc. But static profiles can only do so much for you. Social media becomes more valuable when you decide how to interact and how to facilitate valuable discussion among your followers. Here are a few areas to consider.

- Implement an advanced commenting system. Sometimes the most valuable part of a blog is having a comments section where people can contribute and interact with each other. But this usually means actively filtering the good comments from the bad. Using a robust system like Disqus or Livefyre (and paying for access to their filtering tools) can help you develop a quality discussion area that rewards the most thoughtful contributors.

- Add a forum or discussion board. Very popular bloggers, who may have hundreds of comments on a post, will often add a forum or discussion board so their community can interact in an extended way. If your site is Wordpress-based, plug-ins can help you add a forum to your site in one step. Or you can consider using a private Facebook group or Ning (ning.com) as the base for your community.

- Use HootSuite to be strategic with your social media updates. HootSuite is a free, Web-based software that helps you schedule updates primarily for Twitter, but also for other sites. It also helps you analyze the effectiveness of your tweets (e.g, how many people clicked on a link you tweeted?).

- Use Paper.li (free service) to automatically curate the best daily tweets, updates, and posts on whatever subject you're an expert on—based on the people or organizations you follow and trust. Sometimes curating is one of the best services you can provide for your community—not only do you provide valuable content, you help people understand *who else* provides valuable content!

A final word about social media: Everyone knows about the usual suspects (Facebook, Twitter, Google Plus). Make sure you're not missing a more niche, devoted community on your topic. For example, All About Romance (www.likesbooks.com) is a very popular site for readers and authors of romance.

MAKE YOUR RELATIONSHIPS MATTER

A key component to platform is the relationships you have and grow. Often when you see a successful author, it's only the *visible* aspects of their online presence or content that are apparent. What you can't see is all of the relationship-building and behind-the-scenes conversations that contribute to a more impactful and amplified reach.

Am I saying you have to know big-name people to have a successful platform? No! Do you need to build relationships with successful or authoritative people (or organizations/businesses) in your community? Yes. Here's how to amplify your efforts.

Make a list of who's interacting with you the most

Regardless of where it's happening (on your site or on social media), take note of who is reading, commenting on, or sharing your content. These are people who are already paying attention, like what you're doing, and are receptive to further interaction.

If you're ignoring these people, then you're missing an opportunity to develop a more valuable relationship (which will likely lead to new ones), as well as reward and empower those you're already engaged with.

What does "rewarding" and "empowering" look like? You might drop a personal note, offer an e-book or product for free, or involve them somehow in your online content. You might have a special newsletter for them. Do what makes sense—there are many ways to employ this principle. Christina Katz, who teaches classes to writers, creates "Dream Teams" of writers who are selected from previous students. It's a great idea that rewards both Christina and the students she coaches.

Make a list of your mentors and how you can help them

You should have a list (or wish list!) of mentors. If not, develop one. We all have people who are doing something we dream of, or operate a few steps beyond where we're currently at.

> Do not approach this as something you're going to "get something" out of, or it will backfire.

If you're not already closely following your mentors on their most active channels of communication (blog, Twitter, Facebook, etc.), then start. Begin commenting, sharing, and being a visible fan of what they do. Consider other ways you can develop the relationship, e.g., interview them on your blog or review their book. But most of all, brainstorm how you can serve them.

If you engage mentors in an intelligent way (not in a needy "look at me" sort of way), then you may develop a more meaningful relationship when they reach out to acknowledge your efforts. But be careful: Do not approach this as something you're going to "get something" out of, or it will backfire.

Do watch for opportunities that mentors will inevitably offer (e.g., "I'm looking for someone to help moderate my community. Who wants to help?") I once helped an author arrange a book event when he stopped in Cincinnati, and that helped solidify a relationship that had only been virtual up until that point.

Finally, don't forget a time-honored way to cozy up to mentors: offer a guest post for their blog. Just make sure that what you contribute is of the highest quality possible—more high quality than what you'd demand for your own site. If you bring a mentor considerable traffic, you'll earn their attention and esteem.

Look for partnerships with peers

Who is attempting to reach the same audience as you? Don't see them as competitors. Instead, align with them to do bigger and better things. You can see examples of partnership everywhere in the writing community, such as:

- Writer Unboxed website (where I participate)
- Jungle Red Writers blog
- The Kill Zone blog

We all have different strengths. Banding together is an excellent way to extend your platform in ways you can't manage on your own. When presented with opportunities to collaborate, say yes whenever you'll be exposed to a new audience or diversify your online presence.

Stay alert to your influencers and who you influence

There are many ways to identify important people in your community, but if you're not sure where to start, try the following.

- Blog rolls. Find just one blog that you know is influential. See who they're linking to and recommending. Identify sites that seem to be on everyone's "best of" list— or try searching for "best blogs" + your niche.
- Klout. This social media tool attempts to measure people's authority online by assigning a score. It will summarize who you influence, and who you are influenced by.
- If you use the Disqus commenting system, it will identify the most active commenters on your site.

DIVERSIFY YOUR CONTENT

Writers can easily fall into the trap of thinking only about new *written* content. It's a shame, because by repurposing existing content into new mediums, you can open yourself up to entirely new audiences.

For example, I have a friend who has a long solo commute by car, plus he walks his dogs while listening to his iPod. Nearly all of his media consumption is podcast driven. He rarely reads because his lifestyle doesn't support it. That means that if he can't get his content in audio form, he won't buy it.

Envision a day in the life of your readers. Are they likely to be using mobile devices? Tablets? (Guess what: Google Analytics tells you the percentage of mobile and tablet visits to your site!) Do your readers like to watch videos on YouTube? Do they buy e-books? Are they on Twitter?

If you adapt your content to different mediums, you will uncover a new audience who didn't know you existed. While not all content is fit for adaptation, brainstorm a list of all the content you currently own rights to, and think of ways it could be repurposed or redistributed.

> If you adapt your content to different mediums, you will uncover a new audience who didn't know you existed.

A popular repurposing project for longtime bloggers is to compile and edit a compilation of best blog posts, and make it available as an e-book (free or paid). Some bloggers will even do that with a handful of blog posts that can serve as a beginner or introductory guide to a specific topic. Fiction writers: How about a sampler of your work in e-book or PDF form? Poets: How about a podcast of you reading some of your favorite poems?

Some forms or mediums you might want to explore:

- Creating podcasts and distributing through your own site (or via iTunes)
- Creating videocasts and distributing through YouTube or Vimeo (did you know that YouTube is now the No. 2 search engine?)
- Creating tips or lessons in e-mail newsletter form
- Creating PDFs (free or paid), and using Scribd to help distribute
- Creating online tutorials or offering critiques through tools such as Google Hangouts, Google Docs, and/or Screencast.com
- Creating slide presentations and distributing through SlideShare

The only limit is your imagination!

HOUSEKEEPING

On a final note, I'd like to share a few housekeeping tips that can help boost your image and authority online. While they may seem trivial, they go a long way in making a good impression and spreading the word about what you do.

- Get professional headshots that accurately convey your brand or personality—what people know you and love you for.
- For your social media profiles, completely fill out *all* fields and maximize the functionality. This is important for search and discoverability. For instance, on LinkedIn, add keywords that cover all of your skill sets, pipe in your Twitter account and blog posts, and give complete descriptions of all positions you've held. On Google Plus, list all the sites that you're a contributor for. On Facebook, allow people to subscribe to your public updates even if they aren't your friends.

- Gather updated testimonials and blurbs, and use them on your site and/or your social media profiles if appropriate.

However you decide to tackle the next stage of your platform development, ensure consistency. Whether it's your website, e-newsletter, Facebook profile, business cards, or letterhead, be consistent in the look and feel of your materials and in the message you send. Unless you are appealing to different audiences with different needs, broadcast a unified message no matter where and how people find you. Believe me—it doesn't get boring. Instead, it helps people remember who you are and what you stand for.

JANE FRIEDMAN is a former publishing and media exec who now teaches full-time at the University of Cincinnati. She has spoken on writing, publishing, and the future of media at more than 200 events since 2001, including South by Southwest, BookExpo America, and the Association of Writers and Writing Programs. Find out more at http://janefriedman.com.

LITERARY AGENTS

The literary agencies listed in this section are open to new clients and are members of the Association of Authors' Representatives (AAR), which means they do not charge for reading, critiquing, or editing. Some agents in this section may charge clients for office expenses such as photocopying, foreign postage, long-distance phone calls, or express mail services. Make sure you have a clear understanding of what these expenses are before signing any agency agreement.

FOR MORE...

The *2015 Guide to Literary Agents* (Writer's Digest Books) offers more than 800 literary agents, as well as information on writers' conferences. It also offers a wealth of information on the author/agent relationship and other related topics. Also, WritersMarket.com offers hundreds of up-to-date listings for literary agents.

DOMINICK ABEL LITERARY AGENCY, INC.

146 W. 82nd St., #1A, New York NY 10024. (212)877-0710. **E-mail:** agency@dalainc.com. **Website:** dalainc.com/. Estab. 1975. Member AAR. Represents 100 clients. Currently handles: adult fiction and nonfiction.

REPRESENTS Considers these nonfiction areas: business, creative nonfiction. **Considers these fiction areas:** mystery, suspense.

HOW TO CONTACT Query via e-mail. Check website to learn when this agency reopens to new submissions.

TERMS Agent receives 15% commission on domestic sales. Agent receives 20% commission on foreign sales.

ADAMS LITERARY

7845 Colony Rd., C4 #215, Charlotte NC 28226. (704)542-1440. **Fax:** (704)542-1450. **E-mail:** info@adamsliterary.com. **E-mail:** submissions@adamsliterary.com. **Website:** www.adamsliterary.com. **Contact:** Tracey Adams, Josh Adams, Quinlan Lee. Member of AAR. Other memberships include SCBWI and WNBA. Currently handles: juvenile books.

REPRESENTS Considers these fiction areas: middle grade, picture books, young adult.

HOW TO CONTACT Contact through online form on website only. Send e-mail if that is not operating correctly. All submissions and queries should first be made through the online form on website. Will not review—and will promptly recycle—any unsolicited submissions or queries received by mail. Before submitting work for consideration, review complete guidelines. Responds in 6 weeks. "While we have an established client list, we do seek new talent—and we accept submissions from both published and aspiring authors and artists."

TERMS Agent receives 15% commission on domestic sales; 20% on foreign sales. Offers written contract.

ALIVE COMMUNICATIONS, INC.

7680 Goddard St., Suite 200, Colorado Springs CO 80920. (719)260-7080. **Fax:** (719)260-8223. **E-mail:** submissions@alivecom.com. **Website:** www.alivecom.com. **Contact:** Rick Christian. Member of AAR. Other memberships include Authors Guild. Represents 100+ clients. 5% of clients are new/unpublished writers. Currently handles: nonfiction books 50%, novels 40%, juvenile books 10%.

MEMBER AGENTS Rick Christian, president (blockbusters, bestsellers); Lee Hough (popular/commercial nonfiction and fiction, thoughtful spirituality, children's); Andrea Heinecke (thoughtful/inspirational nonfiction, women's fiction/nonfiction, popular/commercial nonfiction & fiction); Joel Kneedler (popular/commercial nonfiction and fiction, thoughtful spirituality, children's); Bryan Norman.

REPRESENTS Nonfiction books, novels, short story collections, novellas. **Considers these nonfiction areas:** autobiography, biography, business, child guidance, economics, how-to, inspirational, parenting, personal improvement, religious, self-help, women's issues, women's studies. **Considers these fiction areas:** adventure, contemporary issues, crime, family saga, historical, humor, inspirational, literary, mainstream, mystery, police, religious, satire, suspense, thriller.

HOW TO CONTACT "Because all our agents have full client loads, they are only considering queries from authors referred by clients and close contacts." New clients come through recommendations from others.

TERMS Agent receives 15% commission on domestic sales. Offers written contract; 2-month notice must be given to terminate contract.

BETSY AMSTER LITERARY ENTERPRISES

6312 SW Capitol Hwy #503, Portland OR 97239. **Website:** www.amsterlit.com. **Contact:** Betsy Amster (adult); Mary Cummings (children's and YA). Estab. 1992. Member of AAR. Represents more than 65 clients. 35% of clients are new/unpublished writers. Currently handles: nonfiction books 65%, novels 35%.

REPRESENTS Nonfiction books, novels. **Considers these nonfiction areas:** art & design, biography, business, child guidance, cooking/nutrition, current affairs, ethnic, gardening, health/medicine, history, memoirs, money, parenting, popular culture, psychology, science/technology, self-help, sociology, travelogues, social issues, women's issues. **Considers these fiction areas:** ethnic, literary, women's, high quality.

HOW TO CONTACT For adult titles: b.amster.assistant@gmail.com. "For fiction or memoirs, please embed the first three pages in the body of your e-mail. For nonfiction, please embed your proposal." For children's and YA: b.amster.kidsbooks@gmail.com. See submission requirements online at website. "For picture books, please embed the entire text in the body of your e-mail. For novels, please embed the first three pages." Accepts simultaneous submissions. Responds in 1 month to queries. Responds in 2 months to mss.

Obtains most new clients through recommendations from others, solicitations, conferences.

TERMS Agent receives 15% commission on domestic sales. Agent receives 20% commission on foreign sales. Offers written contract, binding for 1 year; 3-month notice must be given to terminate contract. Charges for photocopying, postage, messengers, galleys/books used in submissions to foreign and film agents and to magazines for first serial rights.

ARCADIA

31 Lake Place N., Danbury CT 06810. **E-mail:** arcadialit@sbcglobal.net. **Contact:** Victoria Gould Pryor. Member of AAR.

REPRESENTS Nonfiction books, literary and commercial fiction. **Considers these nonfiction areas:** biography, business, current affairs, health, history, psychology, science, true crime, women's, investigative journalism; culture; classical music; life transforming self-help.

HOW TO CONTACT No unsolicited submissions. Query with SASE. This agency accepts e-queries (no attachments).

THE AXELROD AGENCY

55 Main St., P.O. Box 357, Chatham NY 12037. (518)392-2100. **E-mail:** steve@axelrodagency.com. **Website:** www.axelrodagency.com. **Contact:** Steven Axelrod. Member of AAR. Represents 15-20 clients. Currently handles: novels 95%.

REPRESENTS Novels. **Considers these fiction areas:** crime, mystery, new adult, romance, women's.

HOW TO CONTACT Query. Accepts simultaneous submissions. Obtains most new clients through recommendations from others.

TERMS Agent receives 15% commission on domestic sales. Agent receives 20% commission on foreign sales. No written contract.

BARER LITERARY, LLC

20 W. 20th St., Suite 601, New York NY 10011. (212)691-3513. **E-mail:** submissions@barerliterary.com. **Website:** www.barerliterary.com. **Contact:** Julie Barer. Estab. 2004. Member of AAR.

MEMBER AGENTS Julie Barer, Anna Geller, William Boggess (literary fiction and narrative nonfiction).

REPRESENTS Nonfiction books, novels, short story collections., Julie Barer is especially interested in working with emerging writers and developing long-term relationships with new clients. **Considers these**

nonfiction areas: biography, ethnic, history, memoirs, popular culture, women's. **Considers these fiction areas:** contemporary issues, ethnic, historical, literary, mainstream.

HOW TO CONTACT Query; no attachments if query by e-mail. "We do not respond to queries via phone or fax."

TERMS Agent receives 15% commission on domestic sales. Agent receives 20% commission on foreign sales. Offers written contract. Charges for photocopying and books ordered.

LORETTA BARRETT BOOKS, INC.

220 E. 23rd St., 11th Floor, New York NY 10010. (212)242-3420. **E-mail:** query@lorettabarrettbooks.com. **Website:** www.lorettabarrettbooks.com. **Contact:** Loretta A. Barrett; Nick Mullendore; Gabriel Davis. Estab. 1990. Member of AAR. Currently handles: nonfiction books 50%, novels 50%.

REPRESENTS Nonfiction books, novels. **Considers these nonfiction areas:** biography, cooking, creative nonfiction, current affairs, gardening, health, history, humor, memoirs, politics, psychology, science, spirituality, sports, true crime, women's issues. **Considers these fiction areas:** commercial, literary, mainstream, metaphysical, mystery, romance, thriller, women's.

HOW TO CONTACT Query via snail mail or e-mail. No e-mail attachments. Paste all materials into the e-mail. "For hard-copy fiction queries, please send a 1-2 page query letter and a synopsis or chapter outline for your project. For hard-copy nonfiction queries, please send a 1-2 page query letter and a brief overview or chapter outline for your project." Accepts simultaneous submissions. Responds in 3-6 weeks to queries.

TERMS Agent receives 15% commission on domestic sales. Agent receives 20% commission on foreign sales. Offers written contract. Charges clients for shipping and photocopying.

BLEECKER STREET ASSOCIATES, INC.

217 Thompson St., #519, New York NY 10012. (212)677-4492. **Fax:** (212)388-0001. **E-mail:** bleeckerst@hotmail.com. **Contact:** Agnes Birnbaum. Member of AAR. Other memberships include RWA, MWA. Represents 60 clients. 20% of clients are new/unpublished writers. Currently handles: nonfiction books 75%, novels 25%.

HOW TO CONTACT Query by referral only. Accepts simultaneous submissions. Responds in 2 weeks to queries. Responds in 1 month to mss. "Obtains most new clients through recommendations from others, solicitations, conferences."

TERMS Agent receives 15% commission on domestic sales. Agent receives 25% commission on foreign sales. Offers written contract; 1-month notice must be given to terminate contract. Charges for postage, long distance, fax, messengers, photocopies (not to exceed $200).

BOOKENDS, LLC

136 Long Hill Rd., Gillette NJ 07933. **Website:** www. bookends-inc.com. **Contact:** Kim Lionetti, Jessica Alvarez, Beth Campbell. Member of AAR. RWA, MWA Represents 50+ clients. 10% of clients are new/unpublished writers. Currently handles: nonfiction books 50%, novels 50%.

REPRESENTS Nonfiction books, novels. **Considers these nonfiction areas:** business, ethnic, how-to, money, sex, true crime. **Considers these fiction areas:** detective, cozies, mainstream, mystery, romance, thrillers, women's.

HOW TO CONTACT Review website for guidelines, as they change. BookEnds is no longer accepting unsolicited proposal packages or snail mail queries. Send query in the body of e-mail to only 1 agent.

BOOKS & SUCH LITERARY AGENCY

52 Mission Circle, Suite 122, PMB 170, Santa Rosa CA 95409. **E-mail:** representation@booksandsuch.com. **Website:** www.booksandsuch.biz. **Contact:** Janet Kobobel Grant, Wendy Lawton, Rachel Kent, Mary Keeley, Rachelle Gardner. Member of AAR. Member of CBA (associate), American Christian Fiction Writers. Represents 150 clients. 5% of clients are new/unpublished writers. Currently handles: nonfiction books 50%, novels 50%.

REPRESENTS Nonfiction books, novels. **Considers these nonfiction areas:** humor, religion, self help, women's. **Considers these fiction areas:** historical, literary, mainstream, new adult, religious, romance, young adult.

HOW TO CONTACT Query via e-mail only; no attachments. Accepts simultaneous submissions. Responds in 1 month to queries. "If you don't hear from us asking to see more of your writing within 30 days after you have sent your e-mail, please know that we have read and considered your submission but determined that it would not be a good fit for us." Obtains most new clients through recommendations from others, conferences.

TERMS Agent receives 15% commission on domestic sales. Agent receives 20% commission on foreign sales. Offers written contract; 2-month notice must be given to terminate contract. No additional charges.

BRANDT & HOCHMAN LITERARY AGENTS, INC.

1501 Broadway, Suite 2310, New York NY 10036. (212)840-5760. **Fax:** (212)840-5776. **Website:** brandthochman.com. **Contact:** Gail Hochman. Member of AAR. Represents 200 clients.

MEMBER AGENTS Gail Hochman; Carl D. Brandt; Marianne Merola; Charles Schlessiger; Bill Contardi; Emily Forland (graphic novels); Emma Patterson (anything about the Yankees, stories set in Brooklyn); Jody Klein; Henry Thayer. The e-mail addresses and specific likes of each of these agents is listed on the agency website.

REPRESENTS **Considers these nonfiction areas:** biography, cooking, creative nonfiction, foods, history, memoirs, music, sports, young adult. **Considers these fiction areas:** commercial, crime, family saga, fantasy, historical, literary, middle grade, mystery, suspense, thriller, women's.

HOW TO CONTACT "We accept queries by e-mail and regular mail; however, we cannot guarantee a response to e-mailed queries. For queries via regular mail, be sure to include a self-addressed stamped envelope for our reply. Query letters should be no more than two pages and should include a convincing overview of the book project and information about the author and his or her writing credits. Address queries to the specific Brandt & Hochman agent whom you would like to consider your work. Agent e-mail addresses and query preferences may be found at the end of each agent profile on the AGENTS page of our website." Accepts simultaneous submissions. Responds in 1 month to queries. Obtains most new clients through recommendations from others.

TERMS Agent receives 15% commission on domestic sales. Agent receives 20% commission on foreign sales.

THE HELEN BRANN AGENCY, INC.

94 Curtis Rd., Bridgewater CT 06752. **Fax:** (860)355-2572. Member of AAR.

HOW TO CONTACT Query with SASE.

BARBARA BRAUN ASSOCIATES, INC.

7 E. 14th St., Suite 19F, New York NY 10003. **Fax:** (212)604-9023. **Website:** www.barbarabraunagency. com. **Contact:** Barbara Braun. Member of AAR.

MEMBER AGENTS Barbara Braun; John F. Baker.
REPRESENTS Nonfiction books, novels. **Considers these nonfiction areas:** architecture, art, biography, design, film, history, photography, psychology, women's issues. **Considers these fiction areas:** commercial, literary.
HOW TO CONTACT "We no longer accept submissions by regular mail. Please send all queries to bbasubmissions@gmail.com, marked 'Query' in the subject line. Your query should include: a brief summary of your book, word count, genre, any relevant publishing experience, and the first 5 pages of your ms pasted into the body of the e-mail. (NO attachments—we will not open these.)"
TERMS Agent receives 15% commission on domestic sales. Agent receives 20% commission on foreign sales.

CURTIS BROWN, LTD.

10 Astor Place, New York NY 10003-6935. (212)473-5400. **E-mail:** gknowlton@cbltd.com. **Website:** www.curtisbrown.com. **Contact:** Ginger Knowlton. Alternate address: Peter Ginsberg, president at CBSF, 1750 Montgomery St., San Francisco CA 94111; (415)954-8566. Member of AAR. Signatory of WGA.
REPRESENTS Nonfiction books, novels, short story collections, juvenile.
HOW TO CONTACT "Send us a query letter, a synopsis of the work, a sample chapter and a brief resume. Illustrators should send 1-2 samples of published work, along with 6-8 color copies (no original art). Please send all book queries to our address, Attn: Query Department. Please enclose a stamped, self-addressed envelope for our response and return postage if you wish to have your materials returned to you. We typically respond to queries within 6 to 8 weeks." Note that some agents list their e-mail on the agency website and are fine with e-mail submissions. Note if the submission/query is being considered elsewhere. Responds in 3 weeks to queries; 5 weeks to mss. Obtains most new clients through recommendations from others, solicitations, conferences.
TERMS Agent receives 15% commission on domestic sales; 20% on foreign sales. Offers written contract. 75-day notice must be given to terminate contract. Offers written contract. Charges for some postage (overseas, etc.).

KIMBERLEY CAMERON & ASSOCIATES

1550 Tiburon Blvd., #704, Tiburon CA 94920. **Fax:** (415)789-9191. **E-mail:** info@kimberleycameron. com. **Website:** www.kimberleycameron.com. **Contact:** Kimberley Cameron, Elizabeth Kracht, Pooja Menon, Amy Cloughley, Mary C. Moore, Ethan Vaughan. Member of AAR. 30% of clients are new/unpublished writers.
HOW TO CONTACT We accept e-mail queries only. Please address all queries to one agent only. Please send a query letter in the body of the e-mail, written in a professional manner and clearly addressed to the agent of your choice. Attach a one-page synopsis and the first fifty pages of your ms as separate Word or PDF documents. We have difficulties opening other file formats. Include "Author Submission" in the subject line. If submitting nonfiction, attach a nonfiction proposal. Obtains new clients through recommendations from others, solicitations.
TERMS Agent receives 15% on domestic sales; 10% on film sales. Offers written contract, binding for 1 year.

CASTIGLIA LITERARY AGENCY

1155 Camino Del Mar, Suite 510, Del Mar CA 92014. **E-mail:** castigliaagency-query@yahoo.com. **Website:** www.castigliaagency.com. Member of AAR. Other memberships include PEN. Represents 65 clients. Currently handles: nonfiction books 55%, novels 45%.
MEMBER AGENTS Julie Castiglia (not accepting queries at this time); Win Golden (fiction: thrillers, mystery, crime, science fiction, YA, commercial/literary fiction; nonfiction: narrative nonfiction, current events, science, journalism).
REPRESENTS Nonfiction books, novels. **Considers these nonfiction areas:** creative nonfiction, current affairs, investigative, science. **Considers these fiction areas:** commercial, crime, literary, mystery, science fiction, thriller, young adult.
HOW TO CONTACT Query via e-mail to CastigliaAgency-query@yahoo.com. Send no materials via first contact besides a one-page query. No snail mail submissions accepted. Obtains most new clients through recommendations from others, solicitations, conferences.
TERMS Agent receives 15% commission on domestic sales. Agent receives 25% commission on foreign sales. Offers written contract; 6-week notice must be given to terminate contract.

JANE CHELIUS LITERARY AGENCY

548 Second St., Brooklyn NY 11215. (718)499-0236. **Fax:** (718)832-7335. **E-mail:** queries@janechelius.com. **Website:** www.janechelius.com. Member of AAR.

MEMBER AGENTS Jane Chelius, Mark Chelius.

REPRESENTS Nonfiction books, novels. **Considers these nonfiction areas:** biography, humor, medicine, parenting, popular culture, satire, women's issues, women's studies, natural history; narrative. **Considers these fiction areas:** literary, mystery, suspense, women's.

HOW TO CONTACT E-query. Does not consider e-mail queries with attachments. No unsolicited sample chapters or mss. Responds if interested. Responds in 3-4-weeks usually.

CORNERSTONE LITERARY, INC.

4525 Wilshire Blvd., Suite 208, Los Angeles CA 90010. (323)930-6039. **Fax:** (323)930-0407. **E-mail:** info@cornerstoneliterary.com. **Website:** www.cornerstoneliterary.com. **Contact:** Helen Breitwieser. Member of AAR. Other memberships include Author's Guild, MWA, RWA, PEN, Poets & Writers. Represents 40 clients. 30% of clients are new/unpublished writers.

REPRESENTS Novels. **Considers these nonfiction areas:** creative nonfiction. **Considers these fiction areas:** commercial, literary.

HOW TO CONTACT "Submissions should consist of a one-page query letter detailing the book as well as the qualifications of the author. For fiction, submissions may also include the first ten pages of the novel pasted in the e-mail or one short story from a collection. We receive hundreds of queries each month, and make every effort to give each one careful consideration. We cannot guarantee a response to queries submitted electronically due to the volume of queries received." Obtains most new clients through recommendations from others.

TERMS Agent receives 15% commission on domestic sales. Agent receives 20% commission on foreign sales. Offers written contract, binding for 1 year; 2-month notice must be given to terminate contract.

THE CREATIVE CULTURE, INC.

47 E. 19th St., 3rd Floor, New York NY 10003. (212)680-3510. **Fax:** (212)680-3509. **E-mail:** submissions@thecreativeculture.com. **Website:** www.thecreativeculture.com. **Contact:** Debra Goldstein. Estab. 1998. Member of AAR.

REPRESENTS Nonfiction books, novels.

HOW TO CONTACT Query by e-mail or snail mail. "If you are submitting fiction, please send four to seven pages of the novel with the query. If you are sub-

mitting by mail, be sure to include a self-addressed, stamped envelope. All submissions will be read; however, because of the volume received, we will reply to e-mail submissions only if we are interested in seeing more material."

CYNTHIA CANNELL LITERARY AGENCY

833 Madison Ave., New York NY 10021. (212)396-9595. **Website:** www.cannellagency.com. **Contact:** Cynthia Cannell. Estab. 1997. Member of AAR. Other memberships include the Women's Media Group.

REPRESENTS Considers these nonfiction areas: biography, history, memoirs, science, self-help, spirituality. **Considers these fiction areas:** literary.

HOW TO CONTACT "Please query us with an e-mail or letter. If querying by e-mail, send a brief description of your project with relevant biographical information including publishing credits (if any) to info@cannellagency.com. Do not send attachments. If querying by conventional mail, enclose an SASE." Responds if interested.

DARHANSOFF & VERRILL LITERARY AGENTS

236 W. 26th St., Suite 802, New York NY 10001. (917)305-1300. **Fax:** (917)305-1400. **E-mail:** submissions@dvagency.com. **Website:** www.dvagency.com. Member of AAR. Represents 120 clients. 10% of clients are new/unpublished writers.

MEMBER AGENTS Liz Darhansoff; Chuck Verrill; Michele Mortimer; Catherine Luttinger.

REPRESENTS Considers these nonfiction areas: creative nonfiction, memoirs. **Considers these fiction areas:** fantasy, historical, literary, mystery, science fiction, suspense, thriller, young adult.

HOW TO CONTACT Send queries via e-mail (submissions@dvagency.com) or by snail mail with SASE. Obtains most new clients through recommendations from others.

◑ DEFIORE & CO.

47 E. 19th St., 3rd Floor, New York NY 10003. (212)925-7744. **Fax:** (212)925-9803. **E-mail:** info@defioreandco.com; submissions@defioreandco.com. **Website:** www.defioreandco.com. Member of AAR.

MEMBER AGENTS Brian DeFiore (popular nonfiction, business, pop culture, parenting, commercial fiction); Laurie Abkemeier (memoir, parenting, business, how-to/self-help, popular science); Kate Garrick (literary fiction, memoir, popular nonfiction); Matthew Elblonk (young adult, popular culture, narrative nonfiction); Caryn Karmatz-Rudy (popular fiction, self-help, narrative nonfiction); Adam Schear (commercial fiction, humor, YA, smart thrillers, historical fiction, and quirky debut literary novels. For nonfiction: popular science, politics, popular culture, and current events); Meredith Kaffel (smart upmarket women's fiction, literary fiction [especially debut] and literary thrillers, narrative nonfiction, nonfiction about science and tech, sophisticated pop culture/humor books); Rebecca Strauss (literary and commercial fiction, women's fiction, urban fantasy, romance, mystery, YA, memoir, pop culture, and select nonfiction); Debra Goldstein (nonfiction books on how to live better).

REPRESENTS Nonfiction books, novels. **Considers these nonfiction areas:** autobiography, biography, business, child guidance, cooking, economics, foods, how-to, inspirational, money, multicultural, parenting, popular culture, politics, psychology, religious, science, self-help, sports, young adult. **Considers these fiction areas:** ethnic, literary, mainstream, middle grade, mystery, paranormal, romance, short story collections, suspense, thriller, women's, young adult.

HOW TO CONTACT Query with SASE or e-mail to submissions@defioreandco.com. "Please include the word 'Query' in the subject line. All attachments will be deleted; please insert all text in the body of the e-mail. For more information about our agents, their individual interests, and their query guidelines, please visit our 'About Us' page on our website." There is more information (details, sales) for each agent on the agency website. Accepts simultaneous submissions. Obtains most new clients through recommendations from others.

TERMS Agent receives 15% commission on domestic sales. Agent receives 20% commission on foreign sales. Offers written contract; 10-day notice must be given to terminate contract. Charges clients for photocopying and overnight delivery (deducted only after a sale is made).

SANDRA DIJKSTRA LITERARY AGENCY

1155 Camino del Mar, PMB 515, Del Mar CA 92014. (858)755-3115. **Fax:** (858)794-2822. **E-mail:** elise@dijkstraagency.com. **Website:** www.dijkstraagency.com. Member of AAR. Other memberships include Authors Guild, PEN West, PEN USA, Organization of American Historians, Poets and Editors, MWA. Represents 100+ clients. 30% of clients are new/unpublished writers.

MEMBER AGENTS Sandra Dijkstra, president (adult only). Acquiring Sub-agents: Elise Capron (adult only), Jill Marr (adult only), Thao Le (adult and YA), Roz Foster (adult and YA), Jessica Watterson (adult and YA).

REPRESENTS Nonfiction books, novels. **Considers these nonfiction areas:** biography, business, creative nonfiction, design, history, memoirs, psychology, science, self-help, narrative. **Considers these fiction areas:** commercial, horror, literary, middle grade, science fiction, suspense, thriller, women's, young adult.

HOW TO CONTACT "Please see guidelines on our website, and note that we only accept e-mail submissions. Due to the large number of unsolicited submissions we receive, we are only able to respond those submissions in which we are interested." Accepts simultaneous submissions. Responds to queries of interest within 6 weeks.

TERMS Works in conjunction with foreign and film agents. Agent receives 15% commission on domestic sales and 20% commission on foreign sales. Offers written contract. No reading fee.

DONADIO & OLSON, INC.

121 W. 27th St., Suite 704, New York NY 10001. (212)691-8077. **Fax:** (212)633-2837. **E-mail:** mail@donadio.com. **Website:** donadio.com. **Contact:** Neil Olson. Member of AAR.

REPRESENTS Nonfiction books, novels. **Considers these fiction areas:** literary, young adult.

HOW TO CONTACT Please send a query letter, full synopsis, and the first three chapters/first 25 pages of the ms to mail@donadio.com. Please allow a few weeks for a reply. Obtains most new clients through recommendations from others.

JANIS A. DONNAUD & ASSOCIATES, INC.

525 Broadway, Second Floor, New York NY 10012. (212)431-2664. **Fax:** (212)431-2667. **E-mail:** jdonnaud@aol.com; donnaudassociate@aol.com. **Website:** www.publishersmarketplace.com/members/JanisDonnaud/. **Contact:** Janis A. Donnaud. Member of AAR. Signatory of WGA. Represents 40 clients. 5% of clients are new/unpublished writers. Currently handles: nonfiction books 100%.

REPRESENTS Nonfiction books. **Considers these nonfiction areas:** biography, business, cooking, creative nonfiction, ethnic, health, history, money, sports.

HOW TO CONTACT Query. For nonfiction, send a proposal; for fiction, paste a sample chapter into the e-mail. Prefers exclusive submissions. Responds in 1 month to queries and mss. Obtains most new clients through recommendations from others.

TERMS Agent receives 15% commission on domestic and film sales; 20% commission on foreign sales. Offers written contract; 1-month notice must be given to terminate contract.

DREISBACH LITERARY MANAGEMENT

PO Box 5379, El Dorado Hills CA 95762. (916)804-5016. **E-mail:** verna@dreisbachliterary.com. **Website:** www.dreisbachliterary.com. **Contact:** Verna Dreisbach. Estab. 2007.

REPRESENTS Considers these nonfiction areas: animals, biography, business, health, memoirs, multicultural, parenting, travel, true crime, women's issues. **Considers these fiction areas:** commercial, literary, mystery, thriller, young adult.

HOW TO CONTACT E-mail queries only. No attachments in the query; they will not be opened. No unsolicited mss. *Accepting new nonfiction clients only through a writers conference or a personal referral. Not accepting fiction.*

DUNHAM LITERARY, INC.

110 William St., Suite 2202, New York NY 10038. (212)929-0994. **E-mail:** dunhamlit@yahoo.com. **E-mail:** query@dunhamlit.com. **Website:** www.dunhamlit.com. **Contact:** Jennie Dunham. Member of AAR. SCBWI Represents 50 clients. 15% of clients are new/unpublished writers. Currently handles: nonfiction books 25%, novels 25%, juvenile books 50%.

REPRESENTS Nonfiction, fiction, novels, juvenile books. **Considers these nonfiction areas:** anthropology, archeology, biography, cultural interests, environment, ethnic, health, history, language, literature, medicine, popular culture, politics, psychology, science, technology, women's issues, women's studies. **Considers these fiction areas:** ethnic, juvenile, literary, mainstream, picture books, young adult.

HOW TO CONTACT Query with SASE. Responds in 3 weeks to queries; 2 months to mss. Obtains most new clients through recommendations from others, solicitations.

TERMS Agent receives 15% commission on domestic sales. Agent receives 20% commission on foreign sales.

DUNOW, CARLSON, & LERNER AGENCY

27 W. 20th St., Suite 1107, New York NY 10011. (212)645-7606. **E-mail:** mail@dclagency.com. **Website:** www.dclagency.com. Member of AAR.

REPRESENTS Nonfiction books, novels, juvenile. **Considers these nonfiction areas:** art, biography, creative nonfiction, cultural interests, current affairs, foods, health, history, memoirs, music, popular culture, psychology, science, sociology, sports. **Considers these fiction areas:** commercial, literary, mainstream, middle grade, mystery, picture books, thriller, young adult.

HOW TO CONTACT Query via snail mail with SASE, or by e-mail. No attachments. Responds if interested.

DYSTEL & GODERICH LITERARY MANAGEMENT

1 Union Square W., Suite 904, New York NY 10003. (212)627-9100. **Fax:** (212)627-9313. **Website:** www.dystel.com. Estab. 1994. Member of AAR. Represents 600+ clients.

REPRESENTS Nonfiction books, novels, cookbooks. **Considers these nonfiction areas:** animals, anthropology, archeology, autobiography, biography, business, child guidance, cultural interests, current affairs, economics, ethnic, gay/lesbian, health, history, humor, inspirational, investigative, medicine, metaphysics, military, New Age, parenting, popular culture, psychology, religious, science, technology, true crime, women's issues, women's studies. **Considers these fiction areas:** action, adventure, commercial, crime, detective, ethnic, family saga, gay, lesbian, literary, mainstream, middle grade, mystery, picture books, police, suspense, thriller, women's, young adult.

HOW TO CONTACT Query via e-mail. The varying e-mail addresses for each agent are on the agency website under "Who We Are and What We're Looking For." Accepts simultaneous submissions. Responds in 6 to 8 weeks to queries; within 8 weeks to mss. Obtains most new clients through recommendations from others, solicitations, conferences.

TERMS Agent receives 15% commission on domestic sales. Agent receives 19% commission on foreign sales. Offers written contract.

ANNE EDELSTEIN LITERARY AGENCY

404 Riverside Dr., #12D, New York NY 10025. (212)414-4923. **Fax:** (212)414-2930. **E-mail:** submissions@aeliterary.com. **Website:** www.aeliterary.com. Member of AAR. **Contact:** Anne Edelstein.

REPRESENTS Nonfiction, fiction. **Considers these nonfiction areas:** history, memoirs, psychology, religious, cultural history. **Considers these fiction areas:** commercial, literary.

HOW TO CONTACT E-mail queries only; consult website for submission guidelines.

THE LISA EKUS GROUP, LLC

57 North St., Hatfield MA 01038. (413)247-9325. **Fax:** (413)247-9873. **E-mail:** lisaekus@lisaekus.com. **Website:** www.lisaekus.com. **Contact:** Lisa Ekus-Saffer. Member of AAR.

REPRESENTS Nonfiction books. **Considers these nonfiction areas:** cooking, diet/nutrition, foods, occasionally health/well-being and women's issues.

HOW TO CONTACT Submit a one-page query via e-mail or submit complete hard copy proposal with title page, proposal contents, concept, bio, marketing, TOC, etc. Include SASE for the return of materials.

THE ELAINE P. ENGLISH LITERARY AGENCY

4710 41st St. NW, Suite D, Washington DC 20016. (202)362-5190. **Fax:** (202)362-5192. **E-mail:** queries@elaineenglish.com. **E-mail:** elaine@elaineenglish.com. **Website:** www.elaineenglish.com/literary.php. **Contact:** Elaine English, Lindsey Skouras. Member of AAR. Represents 20 clients. 25% of clients are new/unpublished writers. Currently handles: novels 100%.

REPRESENTS Novels. **Considers these fiction areas:** historical, multicultural, mystery, suspense, thriller, women's, romance (single title, historical, contemporary, romantic, suspense, chick lit, erotic), general women's fiction. The agency is slowly but steadily acquiring in all mentioned areas.

HOW TO CONTACT Not accepting queries as of 2014. Keep checking the website for further information and updates. Responds in 4-8 weeks to queries; 3 months to requested submissions. Obtains most new clients through recommendations from others, conferences, submissions.

TERMS Agent receives 15% commission on domestic sales. Agent receives 20% commission on foreign sales. Offers written contract; 30-day notice must be given to terminate contract. Charges only for shipping expenses; generally taken from proceeds.

FELICIA ETH LITERARY REPRESENTATION

555 Bryant St., Suite 350, Palo Alto CA 94301-1700. (650)375-1276. **E-mail:** feliciaeth.literary@gmail.com. **Website:** ethliterary.com. **Contact:** Felicia Eth. Member of AAR. Represents 25-35 clients. Currently handles: nonfiction books 75%, novels 25% adult.

REPRESENTS Nonfiction books, novels. **Considers these nonfiction areas:** animals, anthropology, autobiography, biography, business, child guidance, cultural interests, current affairs, economics, health, history, investigative, law, medicine, parenting, popular culture, politics, psychology, science, sociology, technology, women's issues, women's studies. **Considers these fiction areas:** literary, mainstream.

HOW TO CONTACT Query with SASE. Accepts simultaneous submissions. Responds in 3 weeks to queries. Responds in 4-6 weeks to mss.

TERMS Agent receives 15% commission on domestic sales. Agent receives 20% commission on foreign sales. Agent receives 20% commission on film sales. Charges clients for photocopying and express mail service.

FINEPRINT LITERARY MANAGEMENT

115 W. 29th, 3rd Floor, New York NY 10001. (212)279-1282. **E-mail:** stephany@fineprintlit.com. **Website:** www.fineprintlit.com. Member of AAR.

HOW TO CONTACT Query with SASE. Submit synopsis and first 3-5 pages of ms embedded in an e-mail proposal for nonfiction. Do not send attachments or mss without a request. See contact page onilne at website for e-mails. Obtains most new clients through recommendations from others, solicitations.

TERMS Agent receives 15% commission on domestic sales. Agent receives 20% commission on foreign sales.

FLETCHER & COMPANY

78 Fifth Ave., 3rd Floor, New York NY 10011. (212)614-0778. **Fax:** (212)614-0728. **E-mail:** info@fletcherandco.com. **Website:** www.fletcherandco.com. **Contact:** Christy Fletcher. Estab. 2003. Member of AAR.

MEMBER AGENTS Christy Fletcher; Melissa Chinchillo; Rebecca Gradinger (literary fiction, up-market commercial fiction, narrative nonfiction, self-help, memoir, women's studies, humor, and pop culture); Gráinne Fox (literary fiction and quality commercial authors, award-winning journalists and food writers); Lisa Grubka (fiction—literary, upmarket women's, and young adult; and nonfiction—narrative, food, science, and more); Donald Lamm (nonfiction—history, biography, investigative journalism, politics, current affairs, and business); Todd Sattersten (business books); Sylvie Greenberg (literary fiction, humor, history, sports writing and anything California-related); Rachel Crawford (international fiction, smart novels with a sci-fi/fantasy bent, big ideas, and great science writing).

REPRESENTS Nonfiction books, novels. **Considers these nonfiction areas:** biography, business, creative nonfiction, foods, history, humor, investigative, memoirs, popular culture, politics, science, self-help, sports, women's issues, women's studies. **Considers these fiction areas:** commercial, fantasy, literary, science fiction, women's, young adult.

HOW TO CONTACT To query, please send a letter, brief synopsis, and an SASE to our address, or you may also send queries to info@fletcherandco.com. Please do not include e-mail attachments with your initial query, as they will be deleted. Responds in 6 weeks to queries.

FOLIO LITERARY MANAGEMENT, LLC

The Film Center Building, 630 Ninth Ave., Suite 1101, New York NY 10036. (212)400-1494. **Fax:** (212)967-0977. **Website:** www.foliolit.com. Member of AAR. Represents 100+ clients.

REPRESENTS Nonfiction books, novels, short story collections. **Considers these nonfiction areas:** animals, art, biography, business, child guidance, cooking, creative nonfiction, economics, environment, foods, health, history, how-to, humor, inspirational, memoirs, military, parenting, popular culture, politics, psychology, religious, satire, science, self-help, technology, war, women's issues, women's studies. **Considers these fiction areas:** commercial, erotica, fantasy, horror, literary, middle grade, mystery, picture books, religious, romance, thriller, women's, young adult.

HOW TO CONTACT Query via e-mail only (no attachments). Read agent bios online for specific submission guidelines and e-mail addresses. Responds in 1 month to queries.

JEANNE FREDERICKS LITERARY AGENCY, INC.

221 Benedict Hill Rd., New Canaan CT 06840. (203)972-3011. **Fax:** (203)972-3011. **E-mail:** jeanne.fredericks@gmail.com. **Website:** www.jeannefredericks.com. **Contact:** Jeanne Fredericks. Estab. 1997. Member of AAR. Other memberships include Authors Guild. Represents 90 clients. 10% of clients are new/unpublished writers. Currently handles: nonfiction books 100%.

REPRESENTS Nonfiction books. **Considers these nonfiction areas:** animals, autobiography, biography, child guidance, cooking, decorating, foods, gardening, health, history, how-to, interior design, medicine, parenting, photography, psychology, self-help, women's issues.

HOW TO CONTACT Query first with SASE, then send outline/proposal, 1-2 sample chapters, SASE, or by e-mail, if requested. See submission guidelines online first. Accepts simultaneous submissions. Responds in 3-5 weeks to queries. Responds in 2-4 months to mss. Obtains most new clients through recommendations from others, solicitations, conferences.

TERMS Agent receives 15% commission on domestic sales. Agent receives 25% commission on foreign sales with co-agent. Offers written contract, binding for 9 months; 2-month notice must be given to terminate contract. Charges client for photocopying of whole proposals and mss, overseas postage, priority mail, express mail services.

THE FRIEDRICH AGENCY

19 W. 21st St., Suite 201, New York NY 10010. **E-mail:** mfriedrich@friedrichagency.com; lcarson@friedrichagency.com; nichole@friedrichagency.com; mmoretti@friedrichagency.com. **Website:** www.friedrichagency.com. **Contact:** Molly Friedrich; Lucy Carson. Member of AAR. Signatory of WGA. Represents 50+ clients.

MEMBER AGENTS Molly Friedrich, founder and agent (open to queries); Lucy Carson, foreign rights director and agent (open to queries); Nichole LeFebvre (foreign rights manager); Maureen Moretti (assistant).

REPRESENTS Full-length fiction and nonfiction. **Considers these nonfiction areas:** creative nonfiction, memoirs. **Considers these fiction areas:** commercial, literary.

HOW TO CONTACT Query by e-mail (strongly preferred), or by mail with SASE. See guidelines on website. Please query only one agent at this agency.

GELFMAN SCHNEIDER / ICM PARTNERS

850 7th Ave., Suite 903, New York NY 10019. (212)245-1993. **Fax:** (212)245-8678. **E-mail:** mail@gelfmanschneider.com. **Website:** www.gelfmanschneider.com. **Contact:** Jane Gelfman, Deborah Schneider. Member of AAR. Represents 300+ clients. 10% of clients are new/unpublished writers.

MEMBER AGENTS Jane Gelfman, Victoria Marini, Heather Mitchell.

REPRESENTS Fiction and nonfiction books. **Considers these nonfiction areas:** creative nonfiction, popular culture. **Considers these fiction areas:** historical, literary, mainstream, middle grade, mystery, suspense, women's, young adult.

HOW TO CONTACT Query. Send queries via snail mail only. No unsolicited mss. Please send a query letter, a synopsis, and a sample chapter only. Consult website for each agent's submission requirements. Responds in 1 month to queries. Responds in 2 months to mss.

TERMS Agent receives 15% commission on domestic sales. Agent receives 20% commission on foreign sales. Agent receives 15% commission on film sales. Offers written contract. Charges clients for photocopying and messengers/couriers.

FRANCES GOLDIN LITERARY AGENCY, INC.

57 E. 11th St., Suite 5B, New York NY 10003. (212)777-0047. **Fax:** (212)228-1660. **E-mail:** agency@goldinlit.com. **Website:** www.goldinlit.com. Estab. 1977. Member of AAR. Represents over 100 clients.

MEMBER AGENTS Frances Goldin, principal/agent; **Ellen Geiger**, agent (commercial and literary fiction and nonfiction, cutting-edge topics of all kinds); Matt McGowan, agent/rights director (innovative works of fiction and nonfiction); **Sam Stoloff**, agent, (literary fiction, memoir, history, accessible sociology and philosophy, cultural studies, serious journalism, narrative and topical nonfiction with a progressive orientation); **Sarah Bridgins**, agent/office manager, sb@goldinlit.com (voice-driven fiction and narrative nonfiction).

REPRESENTS Nonfiction books, novels. **Considers these nonfiction areas:** creative nonfiction, cultural interests, investigative, memoirs, philosophy, sociology. **Considers these fiction areas:** literary, mainstream.

HOW TO CONTACT Query by letter or e-mail. No unsolicited mss or work previously submitted to publishers. Prefers hard-copy queries. If querying by e-mail, put word "query" in subject line. For queries to Sam Stoloff or Ellen Geiger, please use online submission form. Responds in 4-6 weeks to queries.

IRENE GOODMAN LITERARY AGENCY

27 W. 24th St., Suite 700B, New York NY 10010. **E-mail:** irene.queries@irenegoodman.com. **Website:** www.irenegoodman.com. **Contact:** Irene Goodman, Miriam Kriss. Member of AAR.

MEMBER AGENTS Irene Goodman; Miriam Kriss; Barbara Poelle; Rachel Ekstrom.

REPRESENTS Nonfiction, novels. **Considers these nonfiction areas:** narrative nonfiction dealing with social, cultural and historical issues; an occasional memoir and current affairs book, parenting, social issues, francophilia, anglophilia, Judaica, lifestyles, cooking, memoir. **Considers these fiction areas:** historical, intelligent literary, modern urban fantasies, mystery, romance, thriller, women's.

HOW TO CONTACT Query. Submit synopsis, first 10 pages. E-mail queries only! See the website submission page. No e-mail attachments. Responds in 2 months to queries. Consult website for each agent's submission guidelines.

ASHLEY GRAYSON LITERARY AGENCY

1342 W. 18th St., San Pedro CA 90732. **E-mail:** graysonagent@earthlink.net. **Website:** www.publishersmarketplace.com/members/CGrayson/. Estab. 1976. Member of AAR. Represents 100 clients. 5% of clients are new/unpublished writers. Currently handles: nonfiction books 20%, novels 50%, juvenile books 30%.

MEMBER AGENTS Ashley Grayson (fantasy, mystery, thrillers, young adult); Carolyn Grayson (chick lit, mystery, children's, nonfiction, women's fiction, romance, thrillers); Lois Winston (women's fiction, chick lit, mystery).

REPRESENTS Nonfiction books, novels. **Considers these nonfiction areas:** business, computers, economics, history, investigative, popular culture, science, self-help, sports, technology, true crime. **Considers these fiction areas:** fantasy, juvenile, middle grade, multicultural, mystery, romance, science fiction, suspense, women's, young adult.

HOW TO CONTACT The agency is temporarily closed to queries from *fiction* writers who are not published at book length (self published or print-on-demand do not count). There are only three exceptions to this policy: (1) Unpublished authors who have received an offer from a reputable publisher, who need an agent before beginning contract negotiations; (2) Authors who are recommended by a published author, editor or agent who has read the work in question; (3) Authors whom we have met at conferences and from whom we have requested submissions. Nonfiction authors who are recognized within their field or area may still query with proposals.

TERMS Agent receives 15% commission on domestic sales. Agent receives 20% commission on foreign sales.

SANFORD J. GREENBURGER ASSOCIATES, INC.

55 Fifth Ave., New York NY 10003. (212)206-5600. **Fax:** (212)463-8718. **Website:** www.greenburger.com. Member of AAR. Represents 500 clients.

REPRESENTS Nonfiction books and novels.

HOW TO CONTACT E-query. "Please look at each agent's profile page for current information about what each agent is looking for and for the correct e-mail address to use for queries to that agent. Please be sure to use the correct query e-mail address for each agent." Accepts simultaneous submissions. Responds in 2 months to queries and mss. Obtains most new clients through recommendations from others.

TERMS Agent receives 15% commission on domestic sales. Agent receives 20% commission on foreign sales. Charges for photocopying and books for foreign and subsidiary rights submissions.

BLANCHE C. GREGORY, INC.

2 Tudor City Place, New York NY 10017. (212)697-0828. **E-mail:** info@bcgliteraryagency.com. **Website:** www.bcgliteraryagency.com. Member of AAR.

REPRESENTS Nonfiction books, novels, juvenile.

HOW TO CONTACT Submit via snail mail—query, brief synopsis, bio, SASE. No e-mail queries. Obtains most new clients through recommendations from others.

GREYHAUS LITERARY

3021 20th St., PL SW, Puyallup WA 98373. **E-mail:** scott@greyhausagency.com. **Website:** www.greyhausagency.com. **Contact:** Scott Eagan, member RWA. Estab. 2003.

REPRESENTS **Considers these fiction areas:** romance, women's.

HOW TO CONTACT Submissions to Greyhaus can be done in one of three ways: 1) Send a query, the first 3 pages and a synopsis of no more than 3 pages (and a SASE), using a snail mail submission. 2) A standard query letter via e-mail. If using this method, do not attach documents or send anything else other than a query letter. Or 3) use the Submission Form found on the website on the Contact page.

THE JOY HARRIS LITERARY AGENCY, INC.

381 Park Avenue S, Suite 428, New York NY 10016. (212)924-6269. **Fax:** (212)725-5275. **E-mail:** submissions@jhlitagent.com; contact@jhlitagent.com. **Website:** joyharrisliterary.com. **Contact:** Joy Harris. Estab. 1990. Member of AAR. Represents more than 100 cli-

ents. Currently handles: nonfiction books 50%, novels 50%.

REPRESENTS **Considers these nonfiction areas:** art, creative nonfiction, popular culture, science, technology. **Considers these fiction areas:** literary.

HOW TO CONTACT "Please send by regular mail a query letter, outline or sample chapter, and self-addressed stamped envelope to the address below. You may e-mail your submission to submissions@jhlitagent.com, however, we will only reply if interested." Do not send your full ms before it is requested. Accepts simultaneous submissions. Responds in 2 months to queries. Obtains most new clients through recommendations from clients and editors.

TERMS Agent receives 15% commission on domestic sales. Agent receives 20% commission on foreign sales. Charges clients for some office expenses.

JOHN HAWKINS & ASSOCIATES, INC.

71 W. 23rd St., Suite 1600, New York NY 10010. (212)807-7040. **Fax:** (212)807-9555. **E-mail:** jha@jhalit.com. **Website:** www.jhalit.com. **Contact:** Moses Cardona (rights and translations); Liz Free (permissions); Warren Frazier, literary agent; Anne Hawkins, literary agent. Member of AAR. Represents 100+ clients. 5-10% of clients are new/unpublished writers. Currently handles: nonfiction books 40%, novels 40%, juvenile books 20%.

REPRESENTS Nonfiction books, novels.

HOW TO CONTACT Query. Include the word "Query" in the subject line. For fiction, include 1-3 chapters of your book as a single Word attachment. For nonfiction, include your proposal as a single attachment. E-mail a particular agent directly if you are targeting one. Accepts simultaneous submissions. Responds in 1 month to queries. Obtains most new clients through recommendations from others.

TERMS Agent receives 15% commission on domestic sales. Agent receives 20% commission on foreign sales. Charges clients for photocopying.

HEACOCK HILL LITERARY AGENCY, INC.

West Coast Office, 1020 Hollywood Way, #439, Burbank CA 91505. (818)951-6788. **E-mail:** agent@heacockhill.com. **Website:** www.heacockhill.com. **Contact:** Catt LeBaigue or Tom Dark. Estab. 2009. Member of AAR. Other memberships include SCBWI.

MEMBER AGENTS Tom Dark (adult fiction, nonfiction); Catt LeBaigue (juvenile fiction, adult nonfiction including arts, crafts, anthropology, astronomy, nature studies, ecology, body/mind/spirit, humanities, self-help).

REPRESENTS Nonfiction, fiction. **Considers these nonfiction areas:** art, business, gardening, politics. **Considers these fiction areas:** juvenile, middle grade, picture books, young adult.

HOW TO CONTACT E-mail queries only. No unsolicited mss. No e-mail attachments. Responds in 1 week to queries. Obtains most new clients through recommendations from others, solicitations.

TERMS Offers written contract.

RICHARD HENSHAW GROUP

145 W. 28th St., 12th Floor, New York NY 10001. (212)414-1172. **E-mail:** submissions@henshaw.com. **Website:** www.richardhenshawgroup.com. **Contact:** Rich Henshaw. Member of AAR. Other memberships include SinC, MWA, HWA, SFWA, RWA. 20% of clients are new/unpublished writers. Currently handles: nonfiction books 35%, novels 65%.

REPRESENTS Nonfiction books, novels. **Considers these nonfiction areas:** animals, autobiography, biography, business, child guidance, cooking, current affairs, dance, economics, environment, foods, gay/lesbian, health, humor, investigative, money, music, New Age, parenting, popular culture, politics, psychology, science, self-help, sociology, sports, technology, true crime, women's issues, women's studies. **Considers these fiction areas:** crime, detective, fantasy, historical, horror, literary, mainstream, mystery, police, science fiction, supernatural, suspense, thriller, young adult.

HOW TO CONTACT "Please feel free to submit a query letter in the form of an e-mail of fewer than 250 words to submissions@henshaw.com address. As of December 1, 2013, we will no longer accept letters or partials at our physical address unless we have agreed in advance to make an exception." Responds in 3 weeks to queries. Responds in 6 weeks to mss. Obtains most new clients through recommendations from others, solicitations, conferences.

TERMS Agent receives 15% commission on domestic sales. Agent receives 20% commission on foreign sales. No written contract. Charges clients for photocopying and book orders.

HOPKINS LITERARY ASSOCIATES

2117 Buffalo Rd., Suite 327, Rochester NY 14624-1507. (585)352-6268. **Contact:** Pam Hopkins. Member of AAR. Other memberships include RWA. Represents 30 clients. 5% of clients are new/unpublished writers.

REPRESENTS Novels. **Considers these fiction areas:** romance, women's.

HOW TO CONTACT Regular mail with synopsis, 3 sample chapters (or first 50 pages), SASE. Accepts simultaneous submissions. Obtains most new clients through recommendations from others, solicitations, conferences.

TERMS Agent receives 15% commission on domestic sales. Agent receives 20% commission on foreign sales. No written contract.

ICM PARTNERS

730 Fifth Ave., New York NY 10019. (212)556-5600. **Website:** www.icmtalent.com. **Contact:** Literary Department. Member of AAR. Signatory of WGA.

REPRESENTS Nonfiction, fiction, novels, juvenile books.

HOW TO CONTACT This agency is generally not open to unsolicited submissions. However, some agents do attend conferences and meet writers then. The agents take referrals, as well. Obtains most new clients through recommendations from others.

TERMS Agent receives 15% commission on domestic sales. Agent receives 20% commission on foreign sales.

KIRCHOFF/WOHLBERG, INC.

897 Boston Post Rd., Madison CT 06443. (203)245-7308. **Fax:** (203)245-3218. **Website:** www.kirchoffwohlberg.com. **Contact:** Ronald Zollshan. Memberships include SCBWI, Society of Illustrators, SPAR, Bookbuilders of Boston, New York Bookbinders' Guild, AIGA.

REPRESENTS **Considers these fiction areas:** juvenile, middle grade, picture books, young adult.

HOW TO CONTACT "Submit by mail to address above. We welcome the submission of mss from firsttime or established children's book authors. Please enclose an SASE, but note that while we endeavor to read all submissions, we cannot guarantee a reply or their return." Accepts simultaneous submissions.

TERMS Offers written contract, binding for at least 1 year. Agent receives standard commission, depending upon whether it is an author only, illustrator only, or an author/illustrator.

HARVEY KLINGER, INC.

300 W. 55th St., Suite 11V, New York NY 10019. (212)581-7068. **Website:** www.harveyklinger.com. **Contact:** Harvey Klinger. Member of AAR. Repre-

sents 100 clients. 25% of clients are new/unpublished writers. Currently handles: nonfiction books 50%, novels 50%.

REPRESENTS Nonfiction books, novels. **Considers these nonfiction areas:** autobiography, biography, cooking, diet/nutrition, foods, health, investigative, medicine, psychology, science, self-help, spirituality, sports, technology, true crime, women's issues, women's studies. **Considers these fiction areas:** action, adventure, crime, detective, family saga, glitz, literary, mainstream, mystery, police, suspense, thriller.

HOW TO CONTACT Use online e-mail submission form on the website, or query with SASE via snail mail. No phone or fax queries. Don't send unsolicited mss or e-mail attachments. Responds in 2 months to queries and mss. Obtains most new clients through recommendations from others.

TERMS Agent receives 15% commission on domestic sales. Agent receives 25% commission on foreign sales. Offers written contract. Charges for photocopying mss and overseas postage for mss.

LINDA KONNER LITERARY AGENCY

10 W. 15th St., Suite 1918, New York NY 10011. (212)691-3419. **E-mail:** ldkonner@cs.com. **Website:** www.lindakonnerliteraryagency.com. **Contact:** Linda Konner. Member of AAR. Signatory of WGA. Other memberships include ASJA. Represents 85 clients. 30-35% of clients are new/unpublished writers. Currently handles: nonfiction books 100%.

REPRESENTS Nonfiction books. **Considers these nonfiction areas:** gay/lesbian, health, medicine, money, parenting, popular culture, psychology, science, self-help, women's issues, biography (celebrity), African American and Latino issues, relationships, popular science.

HOW TO CONTACT Query by e-mail or by mail with SASE, synopsis, author bio, sufficient return postage. Prefers to read materials exclusively for 2 weeks. Accepts simultaneous submissions. Obtains most new clients through recommendations from others, occasional solicitation among established authors/journalists.

TERMS Agent receives 15% commission on domestic sales. Agent receives 25% commission on foreign sales. Offers written contract. Charges one-time fee for domestic expenses; additional expenses may be incurred for foreign sales.

ELAINE KOSTER LITERARY AGENCY, LLC

55 Central Park W., Suite 6, New York NY 10023. (212)362-9488. **Fax:** (212)712-0164. **Website:** www. publishersmarketplace.com/members/ElaineKoster/. **Contact:** Elaine Koster, Stephanie Lehmann, Ellen Twaddell. Estab. 1998. Member of AAR. Other memberships include MWA, Author's Guild, Women's Media Group. Represents 40 clients. 10% of clients are new/unpublished writers. Currently handles: nonfiction books 10%, novels 90%.

REPRESENTS Nonfiction books, novels. **Considers these nonfiction areas:** autobiography, biography, business, child guidance, cooking, current affairs, diet/nutrition, economics, environment, ethnic, foods, health, history, how-to, medicine, money, parenting, popular culture, psychology, self-help, spirituality, women's issues, women's studies. **Considers these fiction areas:** contemporary issues, crime, detective, ethnic, family saga, feminist, historical, literary, mainstream, mystery, police, regional, suspense, thriller, young adult, chick lit.

HOW TO CONTACT This agency is currently closed to submissions. Responds in 3 weeks to queries. Responds in 1 month to mss. Obtains most new clients through recommendations from others.

TERMS Agent receives 15% commission on domestic sales. Bills back specific expenses incurred doing business for a client.

BARBARA S. KOUTS, LITERARY AGENT

P.O. Box 560, Bellport NY 11713. (631)286-1278. **Fax:** (631) 286-1538. **Contact:** Barbara S. Kouts. Member of AAR. Represents 50 clients. 10% of clients are new/unpublished writers.

REPRESENTS Juvenile.

HOW TO CONTACT Query with SASE. Accepts queries by mail only. Accepts simultaneous submissions. Responds in 1 week to queries; 2 months to mss. Obtains most new clients through recommendations from others, solicitations, conferences.

TERMS Agent receives 10% commission on domestic sales. Agent receives 20% commission on foreign sales. This agency charges clients for photocopying.

STUART KRICHEVSKY LITERARY AGENCY, INC.

381 Park Ave. S., Suite 428, New York NY 10016. (212)725-5288. **Fax:** (212)725-5275. **Website:** www. skagency.com. Member of AAR.

REPRESENTS Nonfiction books, novels.

HOW TO CONTACT Please send a query letter and the first few (up to 10) pages of your ms or proposal in the body of an e-mail (not an attachment) to one of the addresses below. For security reasons, we do not open attachments. Responds if interested. Obtains most new clients through recommendations from others, solicitations.

MICHAEL LARSEN/ELIZABETH POMADA, LITERARY AGENTS

1029 Jones St., San Francisco CA 94109. (415)673-0939. **E-mail:** larsenpoma@aol.com. **Website:** www.larsen-pomada.com. **Contact:** Mike Larsen, Elizabeth Pomada. Member of AAR. Other memberships include Authors Guild, ASJA, PEN, WNBA, California Writers Club, National Speakers Association. Represents 100 clients. 40-45% of clients are new/unpublished writers. Currently handles: nonfiction books 70%, novels 30%.
MEMBER AGENTS Michael Larsen (nonfiction); Elizabeth Pomada (fiction & narrative nonfiction); Lynn Brown (associate agent, new in 2014).
REPRESENTS Considers these nonfiction areas: anthropology, archeology, architecture, art, autobiography, biography, business, current affairs, diet/nutrition, design, economics, environment, ethnic, film, foods, gay/lesbian, health, history, how-to, humor, inspirational, investigative, law, medicine, memoirs, metaphysics, money, music, New Age, popular culture, politics, psychology, religious, satire, science, self-help, sociology, sports, travel, women's issues, women's studies, futurism. **Considers these fiction areas:** action, adventure, contemporary issues, crime, detective, ethnic, experimental, family saga, feminist, gay, glitz, historical, humor, inspirational, lesbian, literary, mainstream, mystery, police, religious, romance, satire, suspense, =.
HOW TO CONTACT Query with SASE. **Elizabeth Pomada** handles literary and commercial fiction, romance, thrillers, mysteries, narrative nonfiction and mainstream women's fiction. If you have completed a novel, **please e-mail the first 10 pages and 2-page synopsis to larsenpoma@aol.com.** Use 14-point typeface, double-spaced, as an e-mail letter with no attachments. For nonfiction, please read Michael's *How to Write a Book Proposal* book—available through your library or bookstore, and through our website—so you will know exactly what editors need. Then, before you start writing, send him the title, subtitle, and your promotion plan via conventional mail (with SASE) or e-mail. If sent as e-mail, please include the information in the body of your e-mail with no attachments. Please allow up to 2 weeks for a response. See each agent's page on the website for contact and submission information.
TERMS Agent receives 15% commission on domestic sales. Agent receives 20% (30% for Asia) commission on foreign sales. May charge for printing, postage for multiple submissions, foreign mail, foreign phone calls, galleys, books, legal fees.

THE NED LEAVITT AGENCY

70 Wooster St., Suite 4F, New York NY 10012. (212)334-0999. **Website:** www.nedleavittagency.com. **Contact:** Ned Leavitt; Jillian Sweeney. Member of AAR. Represents 40+ clients.
MEMBER AGENTS Ned Leavitt, founder and agent; Britta Alexander, agent; Jillian Sweeney, agent.
REPRESENTS Nonfiction books, novels.
HOW TO CONTACT This agency now only takes queries/submissions through referred clients. Do *not* cold query.

LEVINE GREENBERG LITERARY AGENCY, INC.

307 Seventh Ave., Suite 2407, New York NY 10001. (212)337-0934. **Fax:** (212)337-0948. **E-mail:** submit@levinegreenberg.com. **Website:** www.levinegreenberg.com. Member of AAR. Represents 250 clients.
MEMBER AGENTS Jim Levine; Stephanie Rostan (adult fiction, nonfiction, YA); Melissa Rowland; Daniel Greenberg (literary fiction; nonfiction: popular culture, narrative non-fiction, memoir, and humor); Victoria Skurnick; Danielle Svetcov; Elizabeth Fisher; Lindsay Edgecombe (narrative nonfiction, memoir, lifestyle and health, illustrated books, as well as literary fiction); Monika Verma (nonfiction: humor, pop culture, memoir, narrative nonfiction and style and fashion titles); Kerry Sparks (young adult and middle grade); Tim Wojcik; Jamie Maurer; Miek Coccia; Arielle Eckstut; Kirsten Wolf.
REPRESENTS Nonfiction books, novels. **Considers these nonfiction areas:** animals, art, biography, business, computers, cooking, creative nonfiction, gardening, health, humor, memoirs, money, New Age, science, sociology, spirituality, sports. **Considers these fiction areas:** literary, mainstream, middle grade, mystery, thriller, women's, young adult.
HOW TO CONTACT See website for full submission procedure at "How to Submit." Or use our e-mail address (submit@levinegreenberg.com) if you prefer, or

online submission form. Do not submit directly to agents. Prefers electronic submissions. Cannot respond to submissions by mail. Do not attach more than 50 pages. Obtains most new clients through recommendations from others.

TERMS Agent receives 15% commission on domestic sales. Agent receives 20% commission on foreign sales. Offers written contract. Charges clients for out-of-pocket expenses—telephone, fax, postage, photocopying—directly connected to the project.

LITERARY AND CREATIVE ARTISTS, INC.

3543 Albemarle St., N.W., Washington D.C. 20008-4213. (202)362-4688. **Fax:** (202)362-8875. **E-mail:** lca9643@lcadc.com. **Website:** www.lcadc.com. **Contact:** Muriel Nellis. Member of AAR. Other memberships include Authors Guild, American Bar Association, American Booksellers Association. Currently handles: nonfiction books 50%, novels 50%.

MEMBER AGENTS Prior to becoming an agent, Mr. Powell was in sales and contract negotiation.

REPRESENTS Nonfiction books, novels, art, biography, business, photography, popular culture, religion, self help, literary, regional, religious, satire. **Considers these nonfiction areas:** autobiography, biography, business, cooking, diet/nutrition, economics, foods, government, health, how-to, law, medicine, memoirs, philosophy, politics.

HOW TO CONTACT Query via e-mail first and include a synopsis. No attachments. **We do not accept unsolicited mss, faxed mss, mss sent by e-mail or mss on computer disk.** Accepts simultaneous submissions. Responds in 3 weeks to queries. Responds in 1 week to mss. Obtains new clients through recommendations from others.

TERMS Agent receives 15% commission on domestic sales. Agent receives 25% commission on foreign sales. Offers written contract. Charges clients for long-distance phone/fax, photocopying, shipping.

LIVING WORD LITERARY AGENCY

P.O. Box 40974, Eugene OR 97414. **E-mail:** livingwordliterary@gmail.com. **Website:** livingwordliterary.wordpress.com. **Contact:** Kimberly Shumate, agent. Estab. 2009. Member Evangelical Christian Publishers Association

REPRESENTS **Considers these nonfiction areas:** health, parenting, self-help, relationships. **Considers these fiction areas:** inspirational, adult fiction, Christian living.

HOW TO CONTACT Submit a query with short synopsis and first chapter via Word document. Agency only responds if interested.

LOWENSTEIN ASSOCIATES INC.

121 W. 27th St., Suite 501, New York NY 10001. (212)206-1630. **Fax:** (212)727-0280. **E-mail:** assistant@bookhaven.com. **Website:** www.lowensteinassociates.com. **Contact:** Barbara Lowenstein. Member of AAR. Represents 150 clients.

REPRESENTS Nonfiction books, novels.

HOW TO CONTACT "For fiction, please send us a one-page query letter, along with the first ten pages pasted in the body of the message by e-mail to assistant@bookhaven.com. If nonfiction, please send a one-page query letter, a table of contents, and, if available, a proposal pasted into the body of the e-mail to assistant@bookhaven.com. Please put the word QUERY and the title of your project in the subject field of your e-mail and address it to the agent of your choice. Please do not send an attachment as the message will be deleted without being read and no reply will be sent." Accepts simultaneous submissions. Responds in 6 weeks to queries. Obtains most new clients through recommendations from others, solicitations, conferences.

TERMS Agent receives 15% commission on domestic sales. Agent receives 20% commission on foreign sales. Offers written contract. Charges for large photocopy batches, messenger service, international postage.

DONALD MAASS LITERARY AGENCY

121 W. 27th St., Suite 801, New York NY 10001. (212)727-8383. **E-mail:** info@maassagency.com. **Website:** www.maassagency.com. Estab. 1980. Member of AAR. Other memberships include SFWA, MWA, RWA. Represents more than 100 clients. 5% of clients are new/unpublished writers. Currently handles: novels 100%.

MEMBER AGENTS Donald Maass (mainstream, literary, mystery/suspense, science fiction, romance); Jennifer Jackson (commercial fiction, romance, science fiction, fantasy, mystery/suspense); Cameron McClure (literary, mystery/suspense, urban, fantasy, narrative nonfiction and projects with multicultural, international, and environmental themes, gay/lesbian); Stacia Decker (fiction, memoir, narrative nonfiction, pop-culture [cooking, fashion, style, music, art], smart humor, upscale erotica/erotic memoir and multicultural fiction/nonfiction); Amy Boggs (fantasy and science fiction, especially urban fantasy, paranormal romance, steampunk, YA/children's, and alternate history. historical fiction, multicultural fiction, westerns); Katie Shea Boutillier (women's fiction/book club; edgy/dark, realistic/contemporary YA; commercial-scale literary fiction; and celebrity memoir); Jennifer Udden (speculative fiction (both science fiction and fantasy), urban fantasy, and mysteries, as well as historical, erotic, contemporary, and paranormal romance).

REPRESENTS Nonfiction, novels. **Considers these nonfiction areas:** creative nonfiction, memoirs, popular culture. **Considers these fiction areas:** crime, detective, fantasy, historical, horror, literary, mainstream, multicultural, mystery, paranormal, police, psychic, romance, science fiction, supernatural, suspense, thriller, westerns, women's, young adult.

HOW TO CONTACT E-query. All the agents have different submission addresses and instructions. See the website and each agent's online profile for exact submission instruction. Accepts simultaneous submissions.

TERMS Agent receives 15% commission on domestic sales. Agent receives 20% commission on foreign sales.

CAROL MANN AGENCY

55 Fifth Ave., New York NY 10003. (212)206-5635. **Fax:** (212)675-4809. **E-mail:** submissions@carolmannagency.com. **Website:** www.carolmannagency.com. **Contact:** Lydia Blyfield. Member of AAR. Represents roughly 200 clients. 15% of clients are new/unpublished writers.

MEMBER AGENTS Carol Mann (health/medical, religion, spirituality, self-help, parenting, narrative nonfiction, current affairs); Laura Yorke; Gareth Esersky; Myrsini Stephanides (nonfiction areas of interest: pop culture and music, humor, narrative nonfiction and memoir, cookbooks; fiction areas of interest: offbeat literary fiction, graphic works, and edgy YA fiction). Joanne Wyckoff (nonfiction areas of interest: memoir, narrative nonfiction, personal narrative, psychology, women's issues, education, health and wellness, parenting, serious self-help, natural history); fiction.

REPRESENTS Nonfiction books, novels. **Considers these nonfiction areas:** anthropology, archeology, architecture, art, autobiography, biography, business, child guidance, cultural interests, current affairs, design, ethnic, government, health, history, law, medicine, money, music, parenting, popular culture, politics, psychology, self-help, sociology, sports, women's issues, women's studies. **Considers these fiction areas:** commercial, literary, young adult.

HOW TO CONTACT Please see website for submission guidelines. Responds in 4 weeks to queries.

TERMS Agent receives 15% commission on domestic sales. Agent receives 20% commission on foreign sales. Offers written contract.

MANUS & ASSOCIATES LITERARY AGENCY, INC.

425 Sherman Ave., Suite 200, Palo Alto CA 94306. (650)470-5151. **Fax:** (650)470-5159. **E-mail:** manuslit@manuslit.com. **Website:** www.manuslit.com. **Contact:** Jillian Manus, Jandy Nelson, Penny Nelson. NYC address: 444 Madison Ave., 29th Floor, New York, NY 10022 Member of AAR. Represents 75 clients. 30% of clients are new/unpublished writers.

REPRESENTS Nonfiction books, novels.

HOW TO CONTACT Query via snail mail. Include proper SASE for a reply. Send print queries to the California address. Accepts simultaneous submissions. Responds in 3 months to queries. Responds in 3 months to mss. Obtains most new clients through recommendations from others, solicitations, conferences.

TERMS Agent receives 15% commission on domestic sales. Agent receives 20-25% commission on foreign sales. Offers written contract, binding for 2 years; 60-day notice must be given to terminate contract. Charges for photocopying and postage/UPS.

THE DENISE MARCIL LITERARY AGENCY, INC.

483 Westover Road, Stamford CT 06902. (203)327-9970. **E-mail:** dmla@DeniseMarcilAgency.com; AnneMarie@denisemarcilagency.com. **Website:** www.denisemarcilagency.com. **Contact:** Denise Marcil, Anne Marie O'Farrell. Address for Anne Marie O'Farrell: 86 Dennis Street, Manhasset, NY 11030. Member of AAR.

REPRESENTS **Considers these nonfiction areas:** business, health, parenting, self-help, women's issues.

HOW TO CONTACT E-query. At this time, the agency is no longer taking on new, unsolicited *fiction* clients that have not been referred or met at a conference. New nonfiction writers are welcome to query the appropriate agent.

TERMS Agent receives 15% commission on domestic sales. Agent receives 20% commission on foreign sales. Offers written contract, binding for 2 years. Charges

$100/year for postage, photocopying, long-distance calls, etc.

THE EVAN MARSHALL AGENCY

07068-1121, Roseland NJ 07068-1121. (973)287-6216. **Fax:** (973)488-7910. **E-mail:** evan@evanmarshallagency.com. **Contact:** Evan Marshall. Member of AAR. Other memberships include MWA, Sisters in Crime. Currently handles: novels 100%.

REPRESENTS Novels. **Considers these fiction areas:** action, adventure, erotica, ethnic, frontier, historical, horror, humor, inspirational, literary, mainstream, mystery, religious, satire, science fiction, suspense, western, romance (contemporary, gothic, historical, regency).

HOW TO CONTACT Do not query. Currently accepting clients only by referal from editors and our own clients. Responds in 1 week to queries. Responds in 1 month to mss. Obtains most new clients through recommendations from others.

TERMS Agent receives 15% commission on domestic sales. Agent receives 20% commission on foreign sales. Offers written contract.

MARTIN LITERARY MANAGEMENT

7683 SE 27th St., #307, Mercer Island WA 98040. (206)466-1773. **E-mail:** sharlene@martinliterarymanagement.com. **Website:** www.MartinLiterary-Management.com. **Contact:** Sharlene Martin.

MEMBER AGENTS Sharlene Martin (nonfiction); Clelia Martin (picture books, middle grade, young adult).

REPRESENTS Considers these nonfiction areas: autobiography, biography, business, child guidance, current affairs, economics, health, history, how-to, humor, inspirational, investigative, medicine, memoirs, parenting, popular culture, psychology, satire, self-help, true crime, women's issues, women's studies. **Considers these fiction areas:** middle grade, picture books, young adult.

HOW TO CONTACT Query via e-mail with MS Word only. No attachments on queries; place letter in body of e-mail. Accepts simultaneous submissions. Responds in 2 weeks to queries. Responds in 3-4 weeks to mss. Obtains most new clients through recommendations from others.

TERMS Agent receives 15% commission on domestic sales. Agent receives 25% commission on foreign sales. Offers written contract, binding for 1 year; 1-month notice must be given to terminate contract. Charges

author for postage and copying if material is not sent electronically. 99% of materials are sent electronically to minimize charges to author for postage and copying.

MARGRET MCBRIDE LITERARY AGENCY

P.O. Box 9128, La Jolla CA 92038. (858)454-1550. **Fax:** (858)454-2156. **E-mail:** staff@mcbridelit.com. **Website:** www.mcbrideliterary.com. **Contact:** Michael Daley, submissions manager. Member of AAR. Other memberships include Authors Guild.

REPRESENTS Nonfiction books, novels. **Considers these nonfiction areas:** autobiography, biography, business, cooking, cultural interests, current affairs, economics, ethnic, foods, government, health, history, how-to, law, medicine, money, popular culture, politics, psychology, science, self-help, sociology, technology, women's issues, style. **Considers these fiction areas:** action, adventure, crime, detective, historical, humor, literary, mainstream, mystery, police, satire, suspense, thriller.

HOW TO CONTACT Query via snail mail with SASE. Send a query and 1-2 page synopsis (for fiction). Accepts simultaneous submissions. Responds in 8 weeks to queries. Responds in 6-8 weeks to mss.

TERMS Agent receives 15% commission on domestic sales. Agent receives 25% commission on foreign sales. Charges for overnight delivery and photocopying.

THE MCCARTHY AGENCY, LLC

7 Allen St., Rumson NJ 07660. Phone/**Fax:** (732)741-3065. **E-mail:** McCarthylit@aol.com; ntfrost@hotmail.com. **Contact:** Shawna McCarthy. Member of AAR. Currently handles: nonfiction books 25%, novels 75%.

MEMBER AGENTS Shawna McCarthy, Nahvae Frost.

REPRESENTS Nonfiction books, novels. **Considers these nonfiction areas:** biography, history, philosophy, science. **Considers these fiction areas:** fantasy, juvenile, mystery, romance, women's.

HOW TO CONTACT Query via e-mail or regular mail to The McCarthy Agency, c/o Nahvae Frost, 101 Clinton Avenue, Apartment #2, Brooklyn, NY 11205 Accepts simultaneous submissions.

SALLY HILL MCMILLAN & ASSOCIATES, INC.

429 E. Kingston Ave., Charlotte NC 28203. (704)334-0897. **Website:** www.publishersmarketplace.com/

members/McMillanAgency/. **Contact:** Sally Hill Mc-Millan. Member of AAR.

REPRESENTS Considers these nonfiction areas: creative nonfiction, health, history, women's issues, women's studies. **Considers these fiction areas:** commercial, literary, mainstream, mystery.

HOW TO CONTACT "Please query first with SASE and await further instructions. E-mail queries will be read, but not necessarily answered."

MENDEL MEDIA GROUP, LLC

115 W. 30th St., Suite 800, New York NY 10001. (646)239-9896. **Fax:** (212)685-4717. **E-mail:** scott@mendelmedia.com. **Website:** www.mendelmedia.com. Member of AAR. Represents 40-60 clients.

REPRESENTS Nonfiction books, novels, scholarly, with potential for broad/popular appeal. **Considers these nonfiction areas:** Americana, animals, anthropology, architecture, art, biography, business, child guidance, cooking, current affairs, dance, diet/nutrition, education, environment, ethnic, foods, gardening, gay/lesbian, government, health, history, how-to, humor, investigative, language, medicine, memoirs, military, money, multicultural, music, parenting, philosophy, popular culture, psychology, recreation, regional, religious, science, self-help, sex, sociology, software, spirituality, sports, true crime, war, women's issues, women's studies, Jewish topics; creative nonfiction. **Considers these fiction areas:** action, adventure, contemporary issues, crime, detective, erotica, ethnic, feminist, gay, glitz, historical, humor, inspirational, juvenile, lesbian, literary, mainstream, mystery, picture books, police, religious, romance, satire, sports, thriller, young adult, Jewish fiction.

HOW TO CONTACT Query with SASE. Do not e-mail or fax queries. For nonfiction, include a complete, fully edited book proposal with sample chapters. For fiction, include a complete synopsis and no more than 20 pages of sample text. Responds in 2 weeks to queries. Responds in 4-6 weeks to mss. Obtains most new clients through recommendations from others.

TERMS Agent receives 15% commission on domestic sales. Agent receives 20% commission on foreign sales.

DORIS S. MICHAELS LITERARY AGENCY, INC.

1841 Broadway, Suite 903, New York NY 10023. (212)265-9474. **Fax:** (212)265-9480. **E-mail:** query@dsmagency.com. **Website:** www.dsmagency.com.

Contact: Doris S. Michaels, President. Member of AAR. Other memberships include WNBA.

REPRESENTS Novels. **Considers these fiction areas:** commercial, literary.

HOW TO CONTACT As of early 2014, they are not taking new clients. Check the website to see if this agency reopens to queries. Obtains most new clients through recommendations from others, conferences.

TERMS Agent receives 15% commission on domestic sales. Agent receives 20% commission on foreign sales. Offers written contract, binding for 1 year; 1-month notice must be given to terminate contract. Charges clients for office expenses, not to exceed $150 without written permission.

MARTHA MILLARD LITERARY AGENCY

50 W.67th St., #1G, New York NY 10023. **Contact:** Martha Millard. Estab. 1980. Member of AAR. Other memberships include SFWA. Represents 50 clients.

REPRESENTS Nonfiction books, novels. **Considers these nonfiction areas:** architecture, art, autobiography, biography, business, child guidance, cooking, cultural interests, current affairs, design, economics, education, ethnic, film, health, history, how-to, memoirs, metaphysics, money, music, New Age, parenting, photography, popular culture, psychology, self-help, theater, true crime, women's issues, women's studies. **Considers these fiction areas:** fantasy, mystery, romance, science fiction, suspense.

HOW TO CONTACT No unsolicited queries. **Referrals only.** Obtains most new clients through recommendations from others.

TERMS Agent receives 15% commission on domestic sales. Agent receives 20% commission on foreign sales. Offers written contract.

HOWARD MORHAIM LITERARY AGENCY

30 Pierrepont St., Brooklyn NY 11201. (718)222-8400. **Fax:** (718)222-5056. **Website:** www.morhaimliterary.com. Member of AAR.

MEMBER AGENTS Howard Morhaim, Kate McKean.

REPRESENTS Considers these nonfiction areas: cooking, crafts, creative nonfiction, design, humor, sports. **Considers these fiction areas:** fantasy, historical, literary, middle grade, new adult, romance, science fiction, women's, young adult, LGBTQ young adult, magical realism, fantasy should be high fantasy, historical fiction should be no earlier than the 20th century.

HOW TO CONTACT Query via e-mail with cover letter and three sample chapters. See each agent's listing for specifics.

WILLIAM MORRIS ENDEAVOR ENTERTAINMENT

1325 Avenue of the Americas, New York NY 10019. (212)586-5100. **Fax:** (212)246-3583. **Website:** www.wma.com. **Contact:** Literary Department Coordinator. Member of AAR.

REPRESENTS Nonfiction books, novels, tv, movie scripts, feature film.

HOW TO CONTACT This agency is generally closed to unsolicited literary submissions. Meet an agent at a conference, or query through a referral. Accepts simultaneous submissions.

TERMS Agent receives 15% commission on domestic sales. Agent receives 20% commission on foreign sales.

JEAN V. NAGGAR LITERARY AGENCY, INC.

216 E. 75th St., Suite 1E, New York NY 10021. (212)794-1082. **E-mail:** jweltz@jvnla.com; atasman@jvnla.com. **Website:** www.jvnla.com. **Contact:** Jean Naggar. Member of AAR. Other memberships include PEN, Women's Media Group, Women's Forum, SCBWI. Represents 450 clients. 20% of clients are new/unpublished writers.

REPRESENTS Nonfiction books, novels.

HOW TO CONTACT This agency now has an online submission form on its website. Accepts simultaneous submissions. Obtains most new clients through recommendations from others.

TERMS Agent receives 15% commission on domestic sales. Agent receives 20% commission on foreign sales. Offers written contract. Charges for overseas mailing, messenger services, book purchases, long-distance telephone, photocopying—all deductible from royalties received.

NELSON LITERARY AGENCY

1732 Wazee St., Suite 207, Denver CO 80202. (303)292-2805. **E-mail:** query@nelsonagency.com. **Website:** www.nelsonagency.com. **Contact:** Kristin Nelson, president and senior literary agent; Sara Megibow, associate literary agent. Estab. 2002. Member of AAR. RWA, SCBWI, SFWA.

MEMBER AGENTS Kristin Nelson; Sara Megibow.

REPRESENTS **Considers these fiction areas:** commercial, fantasy, literary, mainstream, middle grade, new adult, romance, science fiction, women's, young adult.

HOW TO CONTACT Query by e-mail. Put the word "Query" in the e-mail subject line. No attachments. Address your query to Sara or Kristin. Responds within 1 month.

HAROLD OBER ASSOCIATES

425 Madison Ave., New York NY 10017. (212)759-8600. **Fax:** (212)759-9428. **Website:** www.haroldober.com. **Contact:** Appropriate agent. Member of AAR. Represents 250 clients. 10% of clients are new/unpublished writers. Currently handles: nonfiction books 35%, novels 50%, juvenile books 15%.

MEMBER AGENTS Phyllis Westberg; Pamela Malpas; Craig Tenney (few new clients, mostly Ober backlist); Jake Elwell (previously with Elwell & Weiser).

HOW TO CONTACT Submit concise query letter addressed to a specific agent with the first 5 pages of the ms or proposal and SASE. No fax or e-mail. Does not handle filmscripts or plays. Responds as promptly as possible. Obtains most new clients through recommendations from others.

TERMS Agent receives 15% commission on domestic sales. Agent receives 20% commission on foreign sales. Charges clients for express mail/package services.

THE RICHARD PARKS AGENCY

P.O. Box 693, Salem NY 12865. (518)854-9466. **Fax:** (518)854-9466. **E-mail:** rp@richardparksagency.com. **Website:** www.richardparksagency.com. **Contact:** Richard Parks. Member of AAR.

REPRESENTS Nonfiction books, novels. **Considers these nonfiction areas:** animals, anthropology, archeology, art, autobiography, biography, business, child guidance, cooking, crafts, cultural interests, current affairs, dance, diet/nutrition, economics, environment, ethnic, film, foods, gardening, gay/lesbian, government, health, history, hobbies, how-to, humor, language, law, memoirs, military, money, music, parenting, popular culture, politics, psychology, science, self-help, sociology, technology, theater, travel, women's issues, women's studies.

HOW TO CONTACT Query with SASE. Does not accept queries by e-mail or fax. Other Responds in 2 weeks to queries. Obtains most new clients through recommendations/referrals.

TERMS Agent receives 15% commission on domestic sales. Agent receives 20% commission on foreign sales. Charges clients for photocopying or any unusual expense incurred at the writer's request.

L. PERKINS AGENCY

5800 Arlington Ave., Riverdale NY 10471. (718)543-5344. **Fax:** (718)543-5354. **E-mail:** submissions@lperkinsagency.com. **Website:** lperkinsagency.com. Member of AAR. Represents 90 clients. 10% of clients are new/unpublished writers.

MEMBER AGENTS Tish Beaty, ePub agent (erotic romance – including paranormal, historical, gay/lesbian/bisexual, and light-BDSM fiction; also, she seeks new adult and YA); **Sandy Lu**, sandy@lperkinsagency.com (fiction: she is looking for dark literary and commercial fiction, mystery, thriller, psychological horror, paranormal/urban fantasy, historical fiction, YA, historical thrillers or mysteries set in Victorian times; nonfiction: narrative nonfiction, history, biography, pop science, pop psychology, pop culture [music/theatre/film], humor, and food writing); **Lori Perkins** (not currently taking new clients).

REPRESENTS Nonfiction books, novels.

HOW TO CONTACT E-queries only. Include your query, a 1-page synopsis, and the first 5 pages from your novel pasted into the e-mail. No attachments. Submit to only one agent at the agency. No smail mail queries. Accepts simultaneous submissions. Responds in 12 weeks to queries. Responds in 3-6 months to mss. Obtains most new clients through recommendations from others, solicitations, conferences.

TERMS Agent receives 15% commission on domestic sales. Agent receives 20% commission on foreign sales. No written contract. Charges clients for photocopying.

AARON M. PRIEST LITERARY AGENCY

708 3rd Ave., 23rd Floor, New York NY 10017. (212)818-0344. **Fax:** (212)573-9417. **E-mail:** info@aaronpriest.com. **Website:** www.aaronpriest.com. Estab. 1974. Member of AAR. Currently handles: nonfiction books 25%, novels 75%.

HOW TO CONTACT Query one of the agents using the appropriate e-mail listed on the website. "Please do not submit to more than 1 agent at this agency. We urge you to check our website and consider each agent's emphasis before submitting. Your query letter should be about one page long and describe your work as well as your background. You may also paste the first chapter of your work in the body of the e-mail. Do not send attachments." Accepts simultaneous submissions. Responds in 4 weeks, only if interested.

TERMS Agent receives 15% commission on domestic sales.

HELEN REES LITERARY AGENCY

14 Beacon St., Suite 710, Boston MA 02108. (617)227-9014. **Fax:** (617)227-8762. **E-mail:** reesagency@reesagency.com. **Website:** reesagency.com. **Contact:** Joan Mazmanian, Ann Collette, Helen Rees, Lorin Rees. Estab. 1983. Member of AAR. Other memberships include PEN. Represents more than 100 clients. 50% of clients are new/unpublished writers. Currently handles: nonfiction books 60%, novels 40%.

REPRESENTS Nonfiction books, novels.

HOW TO CONTACT Consult website for each agent's submission guidelines, as they differ. Responds in 3-4 weeks to queries. Obtains most new clients through recommendations from others, conferences, submissions.

TERMS Agent receives 15% commission on domestic sales. Agent receives 20% commission on foreign sales.

REGAL LITERARY AGENCY

236 W. 26th St., #801, New York NY 10001. (212)684-7900. **Fax:** (212)684-7906. **E-mail:** info@regal-literary.com. **E-mail:** submissions@regal-literary.com. **Website:** www.regal-literary.com. London Office: 36 Gloucester Ave., Primrose Hill, London NW1 7BB, United Kingdom, uk@regal-literary.com Estab. 2002. Member of AAR. Represents 70 clients. 20% of clients are new/unpublished writers.

MEMBER AGENTS Michelle Andelman; Claire Anderson-Wheeler; Markus Hoffmann; Leigh Huffine; Lauren Pearson; Joseph Regal.

REPRESENTS Considers these nonfiction areas: creative nonfiction, memoirs, psychology, science. **Considers these fiction areas:** literary, middle grade, picture books, thriller, women's, young adult.

HOW TO CONTACT "Query with SASE or via e-mail. No phone calls. Submissions should consist of a 1-page query letter detailing the book in question, as well as the qualifications of the author. For fiction, submissions may also include the first 10 pages of the novel or one short story from a collection." Responds if interested. Accepts simultaneous submissions. Responds in 4-8 weeks.

TERMS Agent receives 15% commission on domestic sales. Agent receives 20% commission on foreign sales. "We charge no reading fees."

ANGELA RINALDI LITERARY AGENCY

P.O. Box 7877, Beverly Hills CA 90212-7877. (310)842-7665. **Fax:** (310)837-8143. **E-mail:** amr@rinaldiliterary.com. **Website:** www.rinaldiliterary.com. **Contact:** Angela Rinaldi. Member of AAR.

REPRESENTS Nonfiction books, novels, TV and motion picture rights (for clients only). **Considers these nonfiction areas:** biography, business, cooking, current affairs, health, psychology, self-help, true crime, women's issues, wine, lifestyle, career, personal finance, prescriptive and proactive self help books by journalists, academics, doctors and therapists, based on their research. **Considers these fiction areas:** commercial, literary, suspense, women's, upmarket women's fiction, book club women's fiction.

HOW TO CONTACT E-mail queries only. For fiction, please send a brief e-mail inquiry with the first 10 pages pasted into the e-mail—no attachments unless asked for. For nonfiction, query with detailed letter or outline/proposal, no attachments unless asked for. Accepts simultaneous submissions.

TERMS Agent receives 15% commission on domestic sales. Agent receives 25% commission on foreign sales. Offers written contract.

ANN RITTENBERG LITERARY AGENCY, INC.

15 Maiden Lane, Suite 206, New York NY 10038. **Website:** www.rittlit.com. **Contact:** Ann Rittenberg, president; Penn Whaling, associate. Member of AAR. Currently handles: fiction 75%, nonfiction 25%.

REPRESENTS Considers these nonfiction areas: memoirs, women's issues, women's studies. **Considers these fiction areas:** literary, mainstream, thriller, upmarket fiction.

HOW TO CONTACT Query with SASE. Submit outline, 3 sample chapters, SASE. Query via postal mail or e-mail to info@rittlit.com. Accepts simultaneous submissions. Responds in 6 weeks to queries. Responds in 2 months to mss. Obtains most new clients through referrals from established writers and editors.

TERMS Agent receives 15% commission on domestic sales. Agent receives 20% commission on foreign sales. Offers written contract. This agency charges clients for photocopying only.

RLR ASSOCIATES, LTD.

Literary Department, 7 W. 51st St., New York NY 10019. (212)541-8641. **Fax:** (212)262-7084. **E-mail:** sgould@rlrassociates.net. **Website:** www.rlrasso-ciates.net. **Contact:** Scott Gould. Member of AAR. Represents 50 clients. 25% of clients are new/unpublished writers. Currently handles: nonfiction books 70%, novels 25%, story collections 5%.

REPRESENTS Nonfiction books, novels, short-story collections, scholarly. **Considers these nonfiction areas:** creative nonfiction. **Considers these fiction areas:** commercial, literary, mainstream, middle grade, picture books, romance, women's, young adult.

HOW TO CONTACT Query by either e-mail or snail mail. For fiction, send a query and 1-3 chapters (pasted). For nonfiction, send query or proposal. Accepts simultaneous submissions. "If you do not hear from us within 3 months, please assume that your work is out of active consideration." Obtains most new clients through recommendations from others.

TERMS Agent receives 15% commission on domestic sales. Agent receives 20% commission on foreign sales. Offers written contract.

B.J. ROBBINS LITERARY AGENCY

5130 Bellaire Ave., North Hollywood CA 91607-2908. **E-mail:** Robbinsliterary@gmail.com. **E-mail:** angeline.bjrobbinsliterary@gmail.com. **Contact:** (Ms.) B.J. Robbins, or Amy Maldonado. Member of AAR. Represents 40 clients. 50% of clients are new/unpublished writers. Currently handles: nonfiction books 50%, novels 50%.

REPRESENTS Nonfiction books, novels. **Considers these nonfiction areas:** autobiography, biography, cultural interests, current affairs, dance, ethnic, film, health, humor, investigative, medicine, memoirs, music, popular culture, psychology, self-help, sociology, sports, theater, travel, true crime, women's issues, women's studies. **Considers these fiction areas:** crime, detective, ethnic, literary, mainstream, mystery, police, sports, suspense, thriller.

HOW TO CONTACT Query with SASE. Submit outline/proposal, 3 sample chapters, SASE. Accepts e-mail queries (no attachments). Accepts simultaneous submissions. Responds in 2-6 weeks to queries. Responds in 6-8 weeks to mss. Obtains most new clients through conferences, referrals.

TERMS Agent receives 15% commission on domestic sales. Agent receives 20% commission on foreign sales. Offers written contract; 3-month notice must be given to terminate contract. This agency charges clients for postage and photocopying (only after sale of ms).

THE ROSENBERG GROUP

23 Lincoln Ave., Marblehead MA 01945. (781)990-1341. **Fax:** (781)990-1344. **Website:** www.rosenberggroup. com. **Contact:** Barbara Collins Rosenberg. Estab. 1998. Member of AAR. Recognized agent of the RWA. Represents 25 clients. 15% of clients are new/unpublished writers. Currently handles: nonfiction books 30%, novels 30%, scholarly books 10%, 30% college textbooks.

REPRESENTS Nonfiction books, novels, textbooks, college textbooks only. **Considers these nonfiction areas:** current affairs, foods, popular culture, psychology, sports, women's issues, women's studies, women's health, wine/beverages. **Considers these fiction areas:** romance, women's, chick lit.

HOW TO CONTACT Query via snail mail. Your query letter should not exceed one page in length. It should include the title of your work, the genre and/or subgenre; the ms's word count; and a brief description of the work. If you are writing category romance, please be certain to let her know the line for which your work is intended. Responds in 2 weeks to queries. Responds in 4-6 weeks to mss. Obtains most new clients through recommendations from others, solicitations, conferences.

TERMS Agent receives 15% commission on domestic sales. Agent receives 15% commission on foreign sales. Offers written contract; 1-month notice must be given to terminate contract. Charges maximum of $350/year for postage and photocopying.

RITA ROSENKRANZ LITERARY AGENCY

440 West End Ave., #15D, New York NY 10024. (212)873-6333. **Website:** www.ritarosenkranzliteraryagency.com. **Contact:** Rita Rosenkranz. Member of AAR. Represents 35 clients. 30% of clients are new/ unpublished writers. Currently handles: nonfiction books 99%, novels 1%.

REPRESENTS Nonfiction books. **Considers these nonfiction areas:** animals, anthropology, art, autobiography, biography, business, child guidance, computers, cooking, crafts, cultural interests, current affairs, dance, decorating, economics, ethnic, film, gay, government, health, history, hobbies, how-to, humor, inspirational, interior design, language, law, lesbian, literature, medicine, military, money, music, nature, parenting, personal improvement, photography, popular culture, politics, psychology, religious, satire, science,

self-help, sports, technology, theater, war, women's issues, women's studies.

HOW TO CONTACT Send query letter only (no proposal) via regular mail or e-mail. Submit proposal package with SASE only on request. No fax queries. Accepts simultaneous submissions. Responds in 2 weeks to queries. Obtains most new clients through directory listings, solicitations, conferences, word of mouth.

TERMS Agent receives 15% commission on domestic sales. Agent receives 20% commission on foreign sales. Offers written contract, binding for 3 years; 3-month written notice must be given to terminate contract. Charges clients for photocopying. Makes referrals to editing services.

JANE ROTROSEN AGENCY LLC

318 E. 51st St., New York NY 10022. (212)593-4330. **Fax:** (212)935-6985. **Website:** www.janerotrosen.com. Estab. 1974. Member of AAR. Other memberships include Authors Guild. Represents more than 100 clients.

REPRESENTS Nonfiction books, novels.

HOW TO CONTACT Agent submissione-mail addresses are different. Send a query letter, a brief synopsis, and up to three chapters of your novel or the proposal for nonfiction. No attachments. Responds in 2 weeks to writers who have been referred by a client or colleague. Responds in 2 months to mss. Obtains most new clients through recommendations from others.

TERMS Agent receives 15% commission on domestic sales. Agent receives 20% commission on foreign sales. Offers written contract, binding for 3 years; 2-month notice must be given to terminate contract. Charges clients for photocopying, express mail, overseas postage, book purchase.

THE DAMARIS ROWLAND AGENCY

420 E. 23rd St., Suite 6F, New York NY 10010. **Contact:** Damaris Rowland. Member of AAR.

REPRESENTS Nonfiction books, novels.

HOW TO CONTACT Query with synopsis, SASE. Obtains most new clients through recommendations from others, solicitations, conferences.

TERMS Agent receives 15% commission on domestic sales. Agent receives 20% commission on foreign sales. Offers written contract.

THE SAGALYN AGENCY / ICM PARTNERS

1250 Connecticut Ave., 7th Floor, Washington DC 20036. **E-mail:** query@sagalyn.com. **Website:** www.

sagalyn.com. Estab. 1980. Member of AAR. Currently handles: nonfiction books 85%, novels 5%, scholarly books 10%.

MEMBER AGENTS Raphael Sagalyn; Shannon O'Neill.

REPRESENTS Considers these nonfiction areas: biography, business, creative nonfiction, economics, popular culture, science, technology. **Considers these fiction areas:** commercial, upmarket fiction.

HOW TO CONTACT Please send e-mail queries only (no attachments). Include 1 of these words in the subject line: query, submission, inquiry.

VICTORIA SANDERS & ASSOCIATES

241 Avenue of the Americas, Suite 11 H, New York NY 10014. (212)633-8811. **Fax:** (212)633-0525. **E-mail:** queriesvsa@gmail.com. **Website:** www.victoriasanders.com. **Contact:** Victoria Sanders. Estab. 1992. Member of AAR. Signatory of WGA. Represents 135 clients. 25% of clients are new/unpublished writers.

MEMBER AGENTS Tanya McKinnon, Victoria Sanders, Chris Kepner, Bernadette Baker-Baughman.

REPRESENTS Nonfiction books, novels. **Considers these nonfiction areas:** autobiography, biography, cultural interests, current affairs, ethnic, film, gay/lesbian, government, history, humor, law, literature, music, popular culture, politics, psychology, satire, theater, translation, women's issues, women's studies. **Considers these fiction areas:** action, adventure, contemporary issues, crime, ethnic, family saga, feminist, lesbian, literary, mainstream, mystery, new adult, picture books, thriller, young adult.

HOW TO CONTACT Query by e-mail only. "We will not respond to e-mails with attachments or attached files."

TERMS Agent receives 15% commission on domestic sales. Agent receives 20% commission on foreign/film sales. Offers written contract. Charges for photocopying, messenger, express mail. If in excess of $100, client approval is required.

HAROLD SCHMIDT LITERARY AGENCY

415 W. 23rd St., #6F, New York NY 10011. **Contact:** Harold Schmidt, acquisitions. Estab. 1984. Member of AAR. Represents 3 clients.

REPRESENTS Nonfiction, fiction. **Considers these fiction areas:** contemporary issues, gay, literary, original quality fiction with unique narrative voices, high quality psychological suspense and thrillers, likes offbeat/quirky.

HOW TO CONTACT Query with by mail with SASE or e-mail; do not send material without being asked. No telephone or e-mail queries. We will respond if interested. Do not send material unless asked as it cannot be read or returned.

SUSAN SCHULMAN LITERARY AGENCY

454 W. 44th St., New York NY 10036. (212)713-1633. **Fax:** (212)581-8830. **E-mail:** schulmanqueries@yahoo.com. **Website:** www.publishersmarketplace.com/members/Schulman/. **Contact:** Susan Schulman. Estab. 1980. Member of AAR. Signatory of WGA. Other memberships include Dramatists Guild. 10% of clients are new/unpublished writers. Currently handles: nonfiction books 50%, novels 25%, juvenile books 15%, stage plays 10%.

REPRESENTS Considers these nonfiction areas: biography, business, cooking, ethnic, health, history, money, religious, science, travel, women's issues, women's studies. **Considers these fiction areas:** juvenile, literary, mainstream, women's.

HOW TO CONTACT "For fiction: Query Letter with outline and three sample chapters, resume and SASE. For nonfiction: Query Letter with complete description of subject, at least one chapter, resume and SASE. Queries may be sent via regular mail or e-mail. Please do not submit queries via UPS or Federal Express .Please do not send attachments with e-mail queries." Accepts simultaneous submissions. Responds in 6 weeks to queries/mss. Obtains most new clients through recommendations from others, solicitations, conferences.

TERMS Agent receives 15% commission on domestic sales. Agent receives 20% commission on foreign sales. Offers written contract; 30-day notice must be given to terminate contract.

SCOVIL GALEN GHOSH LITERARY AGENCY, INC.

276 Fifth Ave., Suite 708, New York NY 10001. (212)679-8686. **Fax:** (212)679-6710. **E-mail:** info@sgglit.com. **Website:** www.sgglit.com. **Contact:** Russell Galen. Estab. 1992. Member of AAR. Represents 300 clients. Currently handles: nonfiction books 60%, novels 40%.

MEMBER AGENTS Jack Scovil, jackscovil@sgglit.com; **Russell Galen**, russellgalen@sgglit.com (novels that stretch the bounds of reality; strong, serious nonfiction books on almost any subject that teach something new; no books that are merely entertaining, such as diet or pop psych books; serious interests include science, history, journalism, biography, business, memoir, nature, politics, sports, contemporary culture, literary nonfiction, etc.); **Anna Ghosh**, annaghosh@sgglit.com (strong nonfiction proposals on all subjects, as well as adult commercial and literary fiction by both unpublished and published authors; serious interests include investigative journalism, literary nonfiction, history, biography, memoir, popular culture, science, adventure, art, food, religion, psychology, alternative health, social issues, women's fiction, historical novels and literary fiction); **Ann Behar**, annbehar@sgglit.com (juvenile books for all ages).

REPRESENTS Nonfiction books, novels.

HOW TO CONTACT E-mail queries strongly preferred. "If you prefer to mail a hard copy letter, please include your e-mail address so we can reply by e-mail. Do not send SASE or anything else." Note how each agent at this agency has their own submission e-mail. Accepts simultaneous submissions.

THE SEYMOUR AGENCY

475 Miner St., Canton NY 13617. (315)386-1831. **E-mail:** marysue@twcny.rr.com; nicole@theseymouragency.com. **Website:** www.theseymouragency.com. **Contact:** Mary Sue Seymour, Nicole Resciniti. Member of AAR. Signatory of WGA. Other memberships include RWA, Authors Guild. Represents 50 clients. 5% of clients are new/unpublished writers. Currently handles: nonfiction books 50%, other 50% fiction.

MEMBER AGENTS Mary Sue Seymour (accepts queries in Christian, inspirational, romance, and nonfiction); Nicole Resciniti (accepts all genres of romance, young adult, middle grade, new adult, suspense, thriller, mystery, sci-fi, fantasy).

REPRESENTS Nonfiction books, novels. **Considers these nonfiction areas:** business, health, how-to, self help, Christian books; cookbooks; any well-written nonfiction that includes a proposal in standard format and 1 sample chapter. **Considers these fiction areas:** action, fantasy, middle grade, mystery, new adult, religious, romance, science fiction, suspense, thriller, young adult.

HOW TO CONTACT For Mary Sue: E-query with synopsis, first 50 pages for romance. Accepts e-mail queries. For Nicole: E-mail the query plus first 5 pages of

the ms. Accepts simultaneous submissions. Responds in 1 month to queries. Responds in 3 months to mss.

TERMS Agent receives 12-15% commission on domestic sales.

DENISE SHANNON LITERARY AGENCY, INC.

20 W. 22nd St., Suite 1603, New York NY 10010. (212)414-2911. **Fax:** (212)414-2930. **E-mail:** info@deniseshannonagency.com. **E-mail:** submissions@deniseshannonagency.com. **Website:** www.deniseshannonagency.com. **Contact:** Denise Shannon. Estab. 2002. Member of AAR.

REPRESENTS Nonfiction books, novels. **Considers these nonfiction areas:** biography, business, health, narrative nonfiction; politics; journalism; memoir; social history. **Considers these fiction areas:** literary.

HOW TO CONTACT "Queries may be submitted by post, accompanied by a SASE, or by e-mail to submissions@deniseshannonagency.com. Please include a description of the available book project and a brief bio including details of any prior publications. We will reply and request more material if we are interested. We request that you inform us if you are submitting material simultaneously to other agencies."

WENDY SHERMAN ASSOCIATES, INC.

27 W. 24th St., Suite 700B, New York NY 10010. (212)279-9027. **E-mail:** wendy@wsherman.com. **E-mail:** submissions@wsherman.com. **Website:** www.wsherman.com. **Contact:** Wendy Sherman; Kim Perel. Member of AAR. Represents 50 clients.

MEMBER AGENTS Wendy Sherman (board member of AAR), Kim Perel.

REPRESENTS **Considers these nonfiction areas:** creative nonfiction, foods, humor, memoirs, parenting, popular culture, psychology, self-help, narrative nonfiction. **Considers these fiction areas:** mainstream, Mainstream fiction that hits the sweet spot between literary and commercial.

HOW TO CONTACT Query via e-mail only. "We ask that you include your last name, title, and the name of the agent you are submitting to in the subject line. For fiction, please include a query letter and your first 10 pages copied and pasted in the body of the e-mail. We will not open attachments unless they have been requested. For nonfiction, please include your query letter and author bio. Due to the large number of e-mail submissions that we receive, we can only reply to e-mail queries in the affirmative. We respectfully ask that you do not send queries to our individual e-mail addresses." Accepts simultaneous submissions. Responds in 1 month to queries. Obtains most new clients through recommendations from other writers.

TERMS Agent receives standard 15% commission. Offers written contract.

ROSALIE SIEGEL, INTERNATIONAL LITERARY AGENCY, INC.

1 Abey Dr., Pennington NJ 08534. (609)737-1007. **Fax:** (609)737-3708. **E-mail:** rosalie@rosaliesiegel.com. **Website:** rosaliesiegel.com. **Contact:** Rosalie Siegel. Member of AAR. Represents 35 clients. 10% of clients are new/unpublished writers.

HOW TO CONTACT "Please note that we are no longer accepting submissions of new material." Obtains most new clients through referrals from writers and friends.

TERMS Agent receives 15% commission on domestic sales. Agent receives 20% commission on foreign sales. Offers written contract; 2-month notice must be given to terminate contract. Charges clients for photocopying.

SPENCERHILL ASSOCIATES

P.O. Box 374, Chatham NY 12037. (518)392-9293. **Fax:** (518)392-9554. **E-mail:** submissions@spencerhillassociates.com. **Website:** www.spencerhillassociates.com. **Contact:** Karen Solem or Nalini Akolekar. Member of AAR. Represents 96 clients. 10% of clients are new/unpublished writers.

MEMBER AGENTS Karen Solem; Nalini Akolekar.

REPRESENTS Novels. **Considers these fiction areas:** commercial, erotica, literary, mainstream, mystery, paranormal, romance, thriller.

HOW TO CONTACT "We accept electronic submissions and are no longer accepting paper queries. Please send us a query letter in the body of an e-mail, pitch us your project and tell us about yourself: Do you have prior publishing credits? Attach the first three chapters and synopsis preferably in .doc, rtf or txt format to your e-mail. Send all queries to submission@spencerhillassociates.com. We do not have a preference for exclusive submissions, but do appreciate knowing if the submission is simultaneous. We receive thousands of submissions a year and each query receives our attention. Unfortunately, we are unable to respond to each query individually. If we are interested in your work, we will contact you within 8 weeks." Accepts simultaneous submissions.

TERMS Agent receives 15% commission on domestic sales. Agent receives 20% commission on foreign sales. Offers written contract; 3-month notice must be given to terminate contract.

PHILIP G. SPITZER LITERARY AGENCY, INC

50 Talmage Farm Lane, East Hampton NY 11937. (631)329-3650. **Fax:** (631)329-3651. **E-mail:** Luc.Hunt@spitzeragency.com. **Website:** www.spitzeragency.com. **Contact:** Luc Hunt. Member of AAR. Represents 60 clients. 10% of clients are new/unpublished writers. Currently handles: nonfiction books 35%, novels 65%.

REPRESENTS Nonfiction books, novels. **Considers these nonfiction areas:** biography, current affairs, history, politics, sports, travel. **Considers these fiction areas:** juvenile, literary, mainstream, suspense, thriller.

HOW TO CONTACT E-mail or mail query containing synopsis of work, brief biography, and two sample chapters. Responds in 2 weeks to queries. Responds in 6 weeks to mss. Obtains most new clients through recommendations from others.

TERMS Agent receives 15% commission on domestic sales. Agent receives 20% commission on foreign sales. Charges clients for photocopying.

STEELE-PERKINS LITERARY AGENCY

26 Island Ln., Canandaigua NY 14424. (585)396-9290. **Fax:** (585)396-3579. **E-mail:** pattiesp@aol.com. **Contact:** Pattie Steele-Perkins. Member of AAR. Other memberships include RWA. Currently handles: novels 100%.

REPRESENTS Novels. **Considers these fiction areas:** romance, women's, category romance, romantic suspense, historical, contemporary, multi-cultural, and inspirational.

HOW TO CONTACT Submit query along with synopsis and one chapter via e-mail (no attachments) or snail mail. Snail mail submissions require SASE. Accepts simultaneous submissions. Obtains most new clients through recommendations from others, queries/solicitations.

TERMS Agent receives 15% commission on domestic sales. Offers written contract, binding for 1 year; 1-month notice must be given to terminate contract.

STERLING LORD LITERISTIC, INC.

65 Bleecker St., 12th Floor, New York NY 10012. (212)780-6050. **Fax:** (212)780-6095. **E-mail:** info@sll.com. **Website:** www.sll.com. Estab. 1987. Member of AAR. Signatory of WGA. Represents 600 clients. Currently handles: nonfiction books 50%, novels 50%.

HOW TO CONTACT Query via snail mail. "Please submit a query letter, a synopsis of the work, a brief proposal or the first three chapters of the ms, a brief bio or resume, and a stamped self-addressed envelope for reply. Original artwork is not accepted. Enclose sufficient postage if you wish to have your materials returned to you. We do not respond to unsolicited e-mail inquiries." Responds in approximately 1 month.

TERMS Agent receives 15% commission on domestic sales; 20% commission on foreign sales. Offers written contract.

ROBIN STRAUS AGENCY, INC.

229 E. 79th St., Suite 5A, New York NY 10075. (212)472-3282. **Fax:** (212)472-3833. **E-mail:** info@robinstrausagency.com. **Website:** www.robinstrausagency.com. **Contact:** Ms. Robin Straus. Estab. 1983. Member of AAR.

REPRESENTS Considers these nonfiction areas: biography, cooking, creative nonfiction, current affairs, history, memoirs, parenting, popular culture, psychology, science. Considers these fiction areas: commercial, literary, mainstream, women's.

HOW TO CONTACT E-query or query via snail mail with SASE. "Send us a query letter with contact information, an autobiographical summary, a brief synopsis or description of your book project, submission history, and information on competition. If you wish, you may also include the opening chapter of your ms (pasted). Please let us know if you are showing the ms to other agents simultaneously."

TERMS Agent receives 15% commission on domestic sales. Agent receives 20% commission on foreign sales. Offers written contract. Charges for photocopying, express mail services, messenger and foreign postage, galleys and books for submissions, etc. as incurred.

PAM STRICKLER AUTHOR MANAGEMENT

P.O. Box 505, New Paltz NY 12561. (845)255-0061. **E-mail:** pamstrickleragency@gmail.com. **Website:** www.pamstrickler.com. **Contact:** Pamela Dean Strickler. Member of AAR. Also an associate member of the Historical Novel Society and member of RWA.

REPRESENTS Novels. Considers these fiction areas: historical, romance, women's.

HOW TO CONTACT This agency is currently closed to queries.

THE STRINGER LITERARY AGENCY, LLC

E-mail: stringerlit@comcast.net. **Website:** www.stringerlit.com. **Contact:** Marlene Stringer.

REPRESENTS Considers these fiction areas: fantasy, middle grade, mystery, romance, thriller, women's, young adult.

HOW TO CONTACT Electronic submissions through website submission form only. Accepts simultaneous submissions.

THE STROTHMAN AGENCY, LLC

P.O. Box 231132, Boston MA 02123. **E-mail:** info@strothmanagency.com. **Website:** www.strothmanagency.com. **Contact:** Wendy Strothman, Lauren MacLeod. Member of AAR. Other memberships include Authors' Guild. Represents 50 clients.

REPRESENTS Novels, juvenile books. **Considers these nonfiction areas:** business, current affairs, environment, government, history, language, law, literature, politics, travel. **Considers these fiction areas:** literary, middle grade, young adult.

HOW TO CONTACT Accepts queries only via e-mail at strothmanagency@gmail.com. See submission guidelines online. Accepts simultaneous submissions. Responds in 4 weeks to queries. Responds in 6 weeks to mss.

TERMS Agent receives 15% commission on domestic sales. Agent receives 20% commission on foreign sales. Offers written contract; 30-day notice must be given to terminate contract.

EMMA SWEENEY AGENCY, LLC

245 E 80th St., Suite 7E, New York NY 10075. **E-mail:** queries@emmasweeneyagency.com. **Website:** www.emmasweeneyagency.com. Member of AAR. Other memberships include Women's Media Group. Represents 80 clients. 5% of clients are new/unpublished writers. Currently handles: nonfiction books 50%, novels 50%.

REPRESENTS Nonfiction books, novels. **Considers these nonfiction areas:** biography, business, history, religious. **Considers these fiction areas:** literary, mainstream, mystery.

HOW TO CONTACT "We accept only electronic queries, and ask that all queries be sent to queries@emmasweeneyagency.com rather than to any agent directly. Please begin your query with a succinct (and hopefully catchy) description of your plot or proposal. Always include a brief cover letter telling us how you heard about ESA, your previous writing credits, and a few lines about yourself. We cannot open any attachments unless specifically requested, and ask that you paste the first 10 pages of your proposal or novel into the text of your e-mail."

TERMS Agent receives 15% commission on domestic sales. Agent receives 10% commission on foreign sales.

PATRICIA TEAL LITERARY AGENCY

2036 Vista Del Rosa, Fullerton CA 92831-1336. Phone/Fax: (714)738-8333. **Contact:** Patricia Teal. Member of AAR. Other memberships include RWA, Authors Guild. Represents 20 clients. Currently handles: non-fiction books 10%, 90% fiction .

REPRESENTS Nonfiction books, novels. **Considers these nonfiction areas:** animals, autobiography, biography, child guidance, health, how-to, investigative, medicine, parenting, psychology, self-help, true crime, women's issues, women's studies. **Considers these fiction areas:** glitz, mainstream, mystery, romance, suspense, women's.

HOW TO CONTACT Published authors only should submit. Query with SASE. Accepts simultaneous submissions. Obtains most new clients through conferences, recommendations from authors and editors.

TERMS Agent receives 10-15% commission on domestic sales. Agent receives 20% commission on foreign sales. Offers written contract, binding for 1 year. Charges clients for ms copies.

TESSLER LITERARY AGENCY, LLC

27 W. 20th St., Suite 1003, New York NY 10011. (212)242-0466. **Fax:** (212)242-2366. **Website:** www.tessleragency.com. **Contact:** Michelle Tessler. Estab. 2004. Member of AAR. Currently handles: 90% nonfiction books, 10% novels.

REPRESENTS **Considers these nonfiction areas:** biography, business, creative nonfiction, foods, memoirs, science, travel. **Considers these fiction areas:** commercial, literary, women's.

HOW TO CONTACT Submit query through online query form only. Accepts simultaneous submissions. New clients by queries/submissions through the website and recommendations from others.

TERMS Receives 15% commission on domestic sales; 20% on foreign sales. Offers written contract.

S©OTT TREIMEL NY

434 Lafayette St., New York NY 10003. (212)505-8353. **E-mail:** general@scotttreimelny.com. **Website:** ScottTreimelNY.blogspot.com; www.ScottTreimelNY.com. Estab. 1995. Member of AAR. Other memberships include Authors Guild, SCBWI. 10% of clients

are new/unpublished writers. Currently handles: other 100% juvenile/teen books.

REPRESENTS Nonfiction books, novels, juvenile, children's, picture books, young adult.

HOW TO CONTACT No longer accepts simultaneous submissions. Wants queries only from writers he has met at conferences.

TERMS Agent receives 15% commission on domestic sales. Agent receives 20% commission on foreign sales. Offers verbal or written contract. Charges clients for photocopying, express postage, messengers, and books needed to sell foreign, film and other rights.

TRIDENT MEDIA GROUP

41 Madison Ave., 36th Floor, New York NY 10010. (212)333-1511. **E-mail:** press@tridentmediagroup.com; info@tridentmediagroup.com. **E-mail:** ellen.assistant@tridentmediagroup.com. **Website:** www.tridentmediagroup.com. **Contact:** Ellen Levine. Member of AAR.

HOW TO CONTACT Preferred method of query is through the online submission form on the agency website. Query only one agent at a time.

VERITAS LITERARY AGENCY

601 Van Ness Ave., Opera Plaza, Suite E, San Francisco CA 94102. (415)647-6964. **Fax:** (415)647-6965. **E-mail:** submissions@veritasliterary.com. **Website:** www.veritasliterary.com. **Contact:** Katherine Boyle. Member of AAR. Other memberships include Author's Guild and SCBWI.

MEMBER AGENTS Katherine Boyle, Michael Carr.

REPRESENTS Nonfiction books, novels. **Considers these nonfiction areas:** current affairs, memoirs, popular culture, politics, true crime, women's issues, narrative nonfiction, art and music biography, natural history, health and wellness, psychology, serious religion (no New Age) and popular science. **Considers these fiction areas:** commercial, fantasy, literary, middle grade, mystery, science fiction, young adult.

HOW TO CONTACT This agency accepts short queries or proposals via e-mail only. "If you are sending a proposal or a ms after a positive response to a query, please write 'requested material' on the subject line and include the initial query letter."

RALPH M. VICINANZA LTD.

303 W. 18th St., New York NY 10011. (212)924-7090. **Fax:** (212)691-9644. Member of AAR.

MEMBER AGENTS Ralph M. Vicinanza; Chris Lotts; Christopher Schelling.

HOW TO CONTACT This agency takes on new clients by professional recommendation only.

TERMS Agent receives 15% commission on domestic sales. Agent receives 20% commission on foreign sales.

WALES LITERARY AGENCY, INC.

P.O. Box 9426, Seattle WA 98109. (206)284-7114. **E-mail:** waleslit@waleslit.com. **Website:** www.waleslit.com. **Contact:** Elizabeth Wales; Neal Swain. Member of AAR. Other memberships include Authors Guild, Pacific Northwest Writers Association. Represents 60 clients. 10% of clients are new/unpublished writers. Currently handles: nonfiction books 60%, novels 40%.

MEMBER AGENTS Elizabeth Wales; Neal Swain.

HOW TO CONTACT Accepts queries sent with cover letter and SASE, and e-mail queries with no attachments. No phone or fax queries. Guidelines and client list available on website. Accepts simultaneous submissions. Responds in 2 weeks to queries, 2 months to mss.

TERMS Agent receives 15% commission on domestic sales. Agent receives 20% commission on foreign sales.

WEED LITERARY

55 E. 65th St., Suite 4E, New York NY 10065. **E-mail:** info@weedliterary.com. **Website:** www.weedliterary.com. **Contact:** Elisabeth Weed. Estab. 2007.

REPRESENTS Fiction, novels. **Considers these fiction areas:** literary, women's.

HOW TO CONTACT Send a query letter. "Please do not send queries or submissions via snail, registered, certified mail, or by FedEx or UPS requiring signature."

WM CLARK ASSOCIATES

186 Fifth Ave., Second Floor, New York NY 10010. (212)675-2784. **Fax:** (347)-649-9262. **E-mail:** general@wmclark.com. **Website:** www.wmclark.com. Estab. 1997. Member of AAR. 50% of clients are new/unpublished writers. Currently handles: nonfiction books 50%, novels 50%.

REPRESENTS Nonfiction books, novels. **Considers these nonfiction areas:** architecture, art, autobiography, biography, cultural interests, current affairs, dance, design, ethnic, film, history, inspirational, memoirs, music, politics, popular culture, religious, science, sociology, technology, theater, translation, travel memoir, Eastern philosophy. **Considers these fiction areas:** contemporary issues, ethnic, historical, literary, mainstream, Southern fiction.

HOW TO CONTACT Accepts queries via online form only at www.wmclark.com/query-form.html. We respond to all queries submitted via this form. Responds in 1-2 months to queries.

TERMS Agent receives 15% commission on domestic sales. Agent receives 20% commission on foreign sales. Offers written contract.

WRITERS HOUSE

21 W. 26th St., New York NY 10010. (212)685-2400. **Fax:** (212)685-1781. **Website:** www.writershouse.com. **Contact:** Michael Mejias. Estab. 1973. Member of AAR. Represents 440 clients. 50% of clients are new/unpublished writers.

MEMBER AGENTS Amy Berkower; Stephen Barr, sbarr@writershouse.com; Susan Cohen; Dan Conaway; Lisa DiMona; Susan Ginsburg; Leigh Feldman; Merrilee Heifetz; Brianne Johnson; Daniel Lazar; Simon Lipskar; Steven Malk; Jodi Reamer, Esq.; Robin Rue; Rebecca Sherman; Geri Thoma; Albert Zuckerman.

REPRESENTS Nonfiction books, novels, juvenile. **Considers these nonfiction areas:** animals, art, autobiography, biography, business, child guidance, cooking, decorating, diet/nutrition, economics, film, foods, health, history, humor, interior design, juvenile nonfiction, medicine, military, money, music, parenting, psychology, satire, science, self-help, technology, theater, true crime, women's issues, women's studies. **Considers these fiction areas:** adventure, cartoon, contemporary issues, crime, detective, erotica, ethnic, family saga, fantasy, feminist, frontier, gay, hi-lo, historical, horror, humor, juvenile, literary, mainstream, middle grade, military, multicultural, mystery, New Age, occult, picture books, police, psychic, regional, romance, spiritual, sports, thriller, translation, war, women's, young adult.

HOW TO CONTACT Query with SASE. Do not contact two agents here at the same time. While snail mail is OK for all agents, some agents do accept e-queries. Check the website for individual agent bios. "Please send us a query letter of no more than 2 pages, which includes your credentials, an explanation of what makes your book unique and special, and a synopsis. (If submitting to Steven Malk: Writers House, 7660 Fay Ave., #338H, La Jolla, CA 92037. Note that Malk only accepts queries on an exclusive basis.)" Accepts simultaneous submissions. Obtains most new clients through recommendations from authors and editors.

TERMS Agent receives 15% commission on domestic sales. Agent receives 20% commission on foreign sales. Offers written contract, binding for 1 year. Agency charges fees for copying mss/proposals and overseas airmail of books.

BOOK PUBLISHERS

The markets in this year's Book Publishers section offer opportunities in nearly every area of publishing. Large, commercial houses are here as are their smaller counterparts.

When you have compiled a list of publishers interested in books in your subject area, read the detailed listings. Pare down your list by cross-referencing two or three subject areas and eliminating the listings only marginally suited to your book. When you have a good list, send for those publishers' catalogs and ms guidelines, or check publishers' websites, which often contain catalog listings, manuscript preparation guidelines, current contact names, and other information helpful to prospective authors. You want to use this information to make sure your book idea is in line with a publisher's list but is not a duplicate of something already published.

Publishers prefer different methods of submission on first contact. Most like to see a one-page query, especially for nonfiction. Others will accept a brief proposal package that might include an outline and/or a sample chapter. Some publishers will accept submissions from agents only. Each listing in the Book Publishers section includes specific submission methods, if provided by the publisher. Make sure you read each listing carefully to find out exactly what the publisher wants to receive.

When you write your one-page query, give an overview of your book, mention the intended audience, the competition for your book (check local bookstore shelves), and what sets your book apart from the competition. You should also include any previous publishing experience or special training relevant to the subject of your book. For more on queries, read "Query Letter Clinic."

Personalize your query by addressing the editor individually and mentioning what you know about the company from its catalog or books. Never send a form letter as a query.

Envelopes addressed to "Editor" or "Editorial Department" end up in the dreaded slush pile. When possible, we list the names of editors who acquire new books for each company, along with the editors' specific areas of expertise. Try your best to send your query to the appropriate editor. Editors move around all the time, so it's in your best interest to look online or call the publishing house to make sure the editor you are addressing your query to is still employed by that publisher.

Author-subsidy publishers' not included

Writer's Market is a reference tool to help you sell your writing, and we encourage you to work with publishers that pay a royalty. Subsidy publishing involves paying money to a publishing house to publish a book. The source of the money could be a government, foundation or university grant, or it could be the author of the book. If one of the publishers listed in this book offers you an author-subsidy arrangement (sometimes called "cooperative publishing," "co-publishing," or "joint venture"); or asks you to pay for part or all of the cost of any aspect of publishing (editing services, ms critiques, printing, advertising, etc.); or asks you to guarantee the purchase of any number of the books yourself, we would like you to inform us of that company's practices immediately.

What are my odds?

We've also highlighted important information in boldface, the "quick facts" you won't find in any other market guide but should know before you submit your work. These items include: how many mss a publisher buys per year; how many mss from first-time authors; how many mss from unagented writers; the royalty rate a publisher pays; and how large an advance is offered.

AARDVARK PRESS

P.O. Box 203, Onrus River Cape Town 7201, South Africa. **Fax:** (27)(86)514-0793. **E-mail:** publish@aardvarkpress.co.za. **Website:** www.aardvarkpress.co.za. Aardvark Press works with authors who are entrepreneurs and leaders and who are willing to take their belief in their message further than the pages of a book. **NONFICTION** Subjects include animals, health, sports, travel, leisure, recreation, young families. "We look at most nonfiction projects. If we can't offer to publish (for a myriad reasons including full lists, subject/genre outside our core focus, etc.), we try to provide advice on where an author might improve a proposal, or submit his or her work." Query via e-mail.

ABBEVILLE FAMILY

Abbeville Press, 137 Varick St., New York NY 10013. (212)366-5585. **Fax:** (212)366-6966. **E-mail:** abbeville@abbeville.com. **Website:** www.abbeville.com. Estab. 1977. "Our list is full for the next several seasons." **Publishes 8 titles/year. 10% of books from first-time authors.**

◯ *Not accepting unsolicited book proposals at this time.*

FICTION Picture books: animal, anthology, concept, contemporary, fantasy, folktales, health, hi-lo, history, humor, multicultural, nature/environment, poetry, science fiction, special needs, sports, suspense. Average word length 300-1,000 words. Please refer to website for submission policy.

ABC-CLIO

Acquisitions Department, P.O. Box 1911, Santa Barbara CA 93116. (805)968-1911. **Website:** www.abc-clio.com; www.greenwood.com. Estab. 1955. ABC-CLIO is an award-winning publisher of reference titles, academic and general interest books, electronic resources, and books for librarians and other professionals. **Publishes 600 titles/year. 20% of books from first-time authors. 90% from unagented writers. Pays variable royalty on net price.** Accepts simultaneous submissions. Catalog and Guidelines online. Online request form.

IMPRINTS ABC-CLIO; Greenwood Press; Praeger; Linworth and Libraries Unlimited.

NONFICTION Subjects include business, child guidance, education, government, history, humanities, language, music, psychology, religion, social sciences, sociology, sports, women's issues. No memoirs, drama. Query with proposal package, including scope, organization, length of project, whether a complete ms is available or when it will be, CV, and SASE. Check guidelines online for each imprint.

TIPS "Looking for reference materials and materials for educated general readers. Many of our authors are college professors who have distinguished credentials and who have published research widely in their fields."

ABDO PUBLISHING CO.

8000 W. 78th St., Suite 310, Edina MN 55439. (800)800-1312. **Fax:** (952)831-1632. **E-mail:** info@abdopub.com. **Website:** www.abdopub.com. **Contact:** Paul Abdo, editor-in-chief. Estab. 1985. Publishes hardcover originals. ABDO publishes nonfiction children's books (pre-kindergarten to 8th grade) for school and public libraries—mainly history, sports, biography, geography, science, and social studies. **Publishes 300 titles/year.**

IMPRINTS ABDO & Daughters; Buddy Books; Checkerboard Library; SandCastle.

◯ *No unsolicited mss.*

NONFICTION Subjects include animals, history, science, sports, geography, social studies. Submit résumé to pabdo@abdopub.com

ABINGDON PRESS

Imprint of The United Methodist Publishing House, 201 Eighth Ave. S., P.O. Box 801, Nashville TN 37202-0801. (615)749-6000. **Fax:** (615)749-6512. **Website:** www.abingdonpress.com. **Contact:** Robert Ratcliff, senior editor (professional clergy and academic); Judy Newman St. John (children's); Ron Kidd, senior editor (general interest). Neil M. Alexander, Pres. Estab. 1789. Publishes hardcover and paperback originals. "Abingdon Press, America's oldest theological publisher, provides an ecumenical publishing program dedicated to serving the Christian community—clergy, scholars, church leaders, musicians, and general readers—with quality resources in the areas of Bible study, the practice of ministry, theology, devotion, spirituality, inspiration, prayer, music and worship, reference, Christian education, and church supplies." **Publishes 120 titles/year. 3,000 queries received/year. 250 mss received/year. 85% from unagented writers. Pays 7 ½% royalty on retail price.** Publishes book 2 years after acceptance of ms. Responds in 2 months to queries. Book catalog available free. Guidelines online.

IMPRINTS Dimensions for Living; Kingswood Books; Abingdon Press.

NONFICTION Subjects include education, religion, theology. Query with outline and samples only. The author should retain a copy of any unsolicited material submitted.

HARRY N. ABRAMS, INC.

115 W. 18th St., 6th Floor, New York NY 10011. (212)206-7715. **Fax:** (212)519-1210. **E-mail:** abrams@abramsbooks.com. **Website:** www.abramsbooks.com. **Contact:** Managing Editor. Estab. 1951. Publishes hardcover and a few paperback originals. **Publishes 250 titles/year.**

IMPRINTS Stewart, Tabori & Chang: Abrams Appleseed; Abrams Books for Young Readers; Abrams Image; STC Craft/Melanie Falick Books; SelfMadeHero; Amulet Books.

Does not accept unsolicited materials.

ABRAMS BOOKS FOR YOUNG READERS

115 W. 18th St., New York NY 10011. **Website:** www.abramsyoungreaders.com.

Abrams no longer accepts unsolicted mss or queries.

ACADEMY CHICAGO PUBLISHERS

363 W. Erie St., Suite 4W, Chicago IL 60654. (312)751-7300. **Fax:** (312)751-7306. **E-mail:** zhanna@academy-chicago.com. **Website:** www.academychicago.com. **Contact:** Zhanna Vaynberg, managing editor. Estab. 1975. Publishes hardcover and some paperback originals and trade paperback reprints. "We publish quality fiction and nonfiction. Our audience is literate and discriminating. No novelized biography, history, or science fiction." No electronic submissions. **Publishes 10 titles/year. Pays 7-10% royalty on wholesale price.** Publishes book 18 months after acceptance of ms. Responds in 3 months. Catalog and guidelines online.

NONFICTION Subjects include history, travel. No religion, cookbooks, or self-help. Submit proposal package, outline, bio, 3 sample chapters.

FICTION Subjects include historical, mainstream, contemporary, military, war, mystery. "We look for quality work, but we do not publish experimental, avant garde, horror, science fiction, thrillers novels." Submit proposal package, synopsis, 3 sample chapters, and short bio.

TIPS "At the moment, we are looking for good nonfiction; we certainly want excellent original fiction, but we are swamped. No fax queries, no disks. No electronic submissions. We are always interested in reprinting good out-of-print books."

ACE SCIENCE FICTION AND FANTASY

Imprint of the Berkley Publishing Group, Penguin Group (USA), Inc., 375 Hudson St., New York NY 10014. (212)366-2000. **Website:** www.us.penguingroup.com. **Contact:** Ginjer Buchanan, editor-in-chief. Estab. 1953. Publishes hardcover, paperback, and trade paperback originals and reprints. Ace publishes science fiction and fantasy exclusively. **Publishes 75 titles/year. Pays royalty. Pays advance.**

As imprint of Penguin, Ace is not open to unsolicited submissions.

FICTION Subjects include fantasy, science fiction. No other genre accepted. No short stories. Due to the high volume of mss received, most Penguin Group (USA) Inc. imprints do not normally accept unsolicited mss.

ADAMS-BLAKE PUBLISHING

8041 Sierra St. #321, Fair Oaks CA 95628. (916)962-9296. **Website:** www.adams-blake.com. **Contact:** Monica Blane, acquisitions editor. Estab. 1992. Publishes only e-books. "We are getting away from doing trade titles and are doing more short-run/high-priced specialized publications targeted to corporations, law, medicine, engineering, computers, etc." **Publishes 5 titles/year. 50 queries received/year. 15 mss received/year. 80% of books from first-time authors. 99% from unagented writers. Pays 15% royalty on wholesale price.** Publishes book 2 months after acceptance. Accepts simultaneous submissions. Responds in 2 months.

NONFICTION Subjects include business, economics, computers, electronics, counseling, career guidance, labor, money, finance. "We like titles in sales and marketing, but which are targeted to a specific industry. We don't look for retail trade titles but more to special markets where we sell 10,000 copies to a company to give to their employees." Query. Does not review artwork/photos.

TIPS "If you have a book that a large company might buy and give away at sales meetings, send us a query. We like books on sales, especially in specific industries—Like 'How to Sell Annuities' or 'How to Sell High-Tech.' We look for the title that a company will buy several thousand copies of at a time. We often 'personalize' for the company. We especially like short books, 50,000 words (more or less)."

ADAMS MEDIA

Division of F+W Media, Inc., 57 Littlefield St., Avon MA 02322. (508)427-7100. **Fax:** (800)872-5628. **E-mail:** AdamsMediaSubmissions@fwmedia.com. **Website:** www.adamsmedia.com. **Contact:** Lisa Laing; Brendan O'Neill; Victoria Sandbrook; Ross Weisman; Halli Melnitsky. Estab. 1980. Publishes hardcover originals, trade paperback, eBook originals and reprints. Adams Media publishes commercial nonfiction, including self-help, women's issues, pop psychology, relationships, business, careers, pets, parenting, New Age, gift books, cookbooks, how-to, reference, and humor. Does not return unsolicited materials. **Publishes more than 250 books and eBooks/year titles/year. 5,000 queries received/year. 1,500 mss received/year. 40% of books from first-time authors. Pays standard royalty or makes outright purchase. Pays variable advance.** Publishes book 12-18 months after acceptance. Accepts simultaneous submissions. Responds in 3 months to queries. Guidelines online.

ADDICUS BOOKS, INC.

P.O. Box 45327, Omaha NE 68145. (402)330-7493. **Fax:** (402)330-1707. **E-mail:** info@addicusbooks.com. **Website:** www.addicusbooks.com. **Contact:** Acquisitions Editor. Estab. 1994. Addicus Books, Inc. seeks mss with strong national or regional appeal. "We are dedicated to producing high-quality nonfiction books. Our focus is on consumer health titles, but we will consider other topics. In addition to working with a master book distributor, IPG Books of Chicago, which delivers books to stores and libraries, we continually seek special sales channels, outside traditional bookstores." **Publishes 10 titles/year. 90% of books from first-time authors. 95% from unagented writers.** Publishes book 9 months after acceptance. Responds in 1 month to proposals. Catalog and guidelines online.

NONFICTION Subjects include business, economics, consumer health, investing. "We are expanding our line of consumer health titles." "Query with a brief e-mail. Tell us what your book is about, who the audience is, and how that audience would be reached. If we are interested, we may ask for a proposal, outlining the nature of your work. See proposal guidelines on our website. Do not send entire ms unless requested. When querying electronically, send only 1-page e-mail, giving an overview of your book and its market Please do not send hard copies by certified mail or return receipt requested. Additional submission guidelines online."

TIPS "We are looking for compact, concise books on consumer health topics."

AERONAUTICAL PUBLISHERS

1 Oakglade Circle, Hummelstown PA 17036-9525. **E-mail:** info@possibilitypress.com. **Website:** www.aeronauticalpublishers.com. **Contact:** Mike Markowski, publisher. Estab. 1981. Publishes trade paperback originals. "Our mission is to help people learn more about aviation and model aviation through the written word." **Pays variable royalty.** Responds in 2 months to queries. Guidelines online.

IMPRINTS American Aeronautical Archives, Aviation Publishers, Aeronautical Publishers.

NONFICTION Subjects include history, aviation, hobbies, recreation, radio control, free flight, indoor models, micro radio control, home-built aircraft, ultralights, and hang gliders. Prefers submission by mail. Include SASE. See guidelines online. Reviews artwork/photos. Do not send originals.

TIPS "Our focus is on books of short to medium length that will serve the emerging needs of the hobby. We also want to help youth get started, while enhancing everyone's enjoyment of the hobby. We are looking for authors who are passionate about the hobby, and will champion their book and the messages of their books, supported by efforts at promoting and selling their books."

AHSAHTA PRESS

MFA Program in Creative Writing, Boise State University, 1910 University Dr., MS 1525, Boise ID 83725. (208)426-4210. **E-mail:** ahsahta@boisestate.edu. **E-mail:** jholmes@boisestate.edu. **Website:** ahsahtapress.org. **Contact:** Janet Holmes, director. Estab. 1974. Publishes trade paperback originals. **Publishes 7 titles/year. 1,000 mss received/year. 15% of books from first-time authors. 100% from unagented writers. Pays 8% royalty on retail price for first 1,000 sold; 10% thereafter.** Publishes book 2 years after acceptance. Accepts simultaneous submissions. Responds in 3 months to mss. Book catalog online.

POETRY "We are booked years in advance and are not currently reading mss, with the exception of the Sawtooth Poetry Prize competition, from which we publish 2-3 mss per year." Submit complete ms. Considers multiple and simultaneous submissions. Reading period is temporarily suspended due to backlog, but the press publishes runners-up as well as winners of the Sawtooth Poetry Prize. Forthcoming, new, and backlist titles online. Most backlist titles: $9.95; most current titles: $18.

TIPS "Ahsahta's motto is that poetry is art, so our readers tend to come to us for the unexpected—poetry that makes them think, reflect, and even do something they haven't done before."

⊘ ALADDIN

Simon & Schuster, 1230 Avenue of the Americas, 4th Floor, New York NY 10020. (212)698-7000. **Website:** www.simonandschuster.com. **Contact:** Acquisitions Editor. Publishes hardcover/paperback imprints of Simon & Schuster Children's Publishing Children's Division. Aladdin publishes picture books, beginning readers, chapter books, middle grade and tween fiction and nonfiction, and graphic novels and nonfiction in hardcover and paperback, with an emphasis on commercial, kid-friendly titles.

FICTION Simon & Schuster does not review, retain or return unsolicited materials or artwork. "We suggest prospective authors and illustrators submit their mss through a professional literary agent."

ALGONQUIN BOOKS OF CHAPEL HILL

Workman Publishing, P.O. Box 2225, Chapel Hill NC 27515-2225. (919)967-0108. **Website:** www.algonquin. com. **Contact:** Editorial Department. Publishes hardcover originals. "Algonquin Books publishes quality literary fiction and literary nonfiction." **Publishes 24 titles/year.** Guidelines online.

NONFICTION Query by mail before submitting work. No phone, e-mail or fax queries or submissions. Visit our website for full submission policy to queries.

ALLWORTH PRESS

An imprint of Skyhorse Publishing, 307 West 36th St., 11th Floor, New York NY 10018. (212)643-6816. **Fax:** (212)643-6819. **Website:** www.allworth.com. **Contact:** Bob Porter, associate publisher; Tad Crawford, publisher. Estab. 1989. Publishes hardcover and trade paperback originals. "Allworth Press publishes business and self-help information for artists, designers, photographers, authors and film and performing artists, as well as books about business, money and the law for the general public. The press also publishes the best of classic and contemporary writing in art and graphic design. Currently emphasizing photography, graphic & industrial design, performing arts, fine arts and crafts, et al." **Publishes 12-18 titles/year. Pays advance.** Responds in 4-6 weeks. Book catalog and ms guidelines free.

NONFICTION Subjects include art, architecture, business, economics, film, cinema, stage, music, dance, photography, film, television, graphic design, performing arts, as well as business and legal guides for the public. "We are currently accepting query letters for practical, legal, and technique books targeted to professionals in the arts, including designers, graphic and fine artists, craftspeople, photographers, and those involved in film and the performing arts." Query with 1-2 page synopsis, chapter outline, market analysis, sample chapter, bio, SASE.

TIPS "We are helping creative people in the arts by giving them practical advice about business and success."

ALONDRA PRESS, LLC

4119 Wildacres Dr., Houston TX 77072. **E-mail:** lark@alondrapress.com. **Website:** www.alondrapress.com. **Contact:** Pennelope Leight, fiction editor; Solomon Tager, nonfiction editor. Estab. 2007. Publishes trade paperback originals and reprints. **Publishes 4 titles/year. 75% of books from first-time authors. 75% from unagented writers.** Publishes book 8 months after acceptance. Accepts simultaneous submissions. Responds in 1 month to queries/proposals; 3 months to mss. Guidelines online.

NONFICTION Subjects include anthropology, archaeology, history, philosophy, psychology, translation. Submit complete ms.

FICTION Subjects include literary, all fiction genres. "Just send us a few pages in an e-mail attachment, or the entire ms. We will look at it quickly and tell you if it interests us."

TIPS "Be sure to read our guidelines before sending a submission. We will not respond to authors who do not observe our simple guidelines. Send your submissions in an e-mail attachment only."

ALPINE PUBLICATIONS

38262 Linman Road, Crawford CO 81415. (970)921-5005. **Fax:** (970)921-5081. **E-mail:** editorialdept@alpinepub.com. **Website:** alpinepub.com. **Contact:** Ms. B.J. McKinney, publisher. Estab. 1975. Publishes hardcover and trade paperback originals and reprints. **Publishes 6-10 titles/year. 40% of books from first-time authors. 95% from unagented writers. Pays 8-15% royalty on wholesale price. Pays advance.** Publishes book 18 months after acceptance. Accepts simultaneous submissions. Responds in 1 month. Book catalog available free. Guidelines online.

IMPRINTS Blue Ribbon Books.

NONFICTION Subjects include animals. Alpine specializes in books that promote the enjoyment of and responsibility for companion animals with emphasis on dogs and horses. No biographies. Query with a brief synopsis, chapter outline, bio, 1-3 sample chapters, and market analysis.

TIPS "Our audience is pet owners, breeders, exhibitors, veterinarians, animal trainers, animal care specialists, and judges. Our books are in-depth and most are heavily illustrated. Look up some of our titles before you submit. See what is unique about our books. Write your proposal to suit our guidelines."

☼ THE ALTHOUSE PRESS

University of Western Ontario, Faculty of Education, 1137 Western Rd., London ON N6G 1G7, Canada. (519)661-2096. **Fax:** (519)661-3833. **E-mail:** press@ uwo.ca. **Website:** www.edu.uwo.ca/althousepress. **Contact:** Katherine Butson, editorial assistant. Publishes trade paperback originals and reprints. "The Althouse Press publishes both scholarly research monographs in education and professional books and materials for educators in elementary schools, secondary schools, and faculties of education. De-emphasizing curricular or instructional materials intended for use by elementary or secondary school students." **Publishes 1-5 titles/year. 50-100 queries received/year. 14 mss received/year. 50% of books from first-time authors. 100% from unagented writers. Pays $300 advance.** Publishes book 18 months after acceptance. Accepts simultaneous submissions. Responds in 1-2 months to queries; 4 months to mss. Book catalog available free. Guidelines online.

NONFICTION Subjects include education, scholarly. "Do not send incomplete mss that are only marginally appropriate to our market and limited mandate." Reviews artwork/photos. Send photocopies.

TIPS "Audience is practicing teachers and graduate education students."

AMACOM BOOKS

American Management Association, 1601 Broadway, New York NY 10019. (212)586-8100. **Fax:** (212)903-8168. **E-mail:** ekadin@amanet.org; rnirkind@amanet.org. **Website:** www.amacombooks.org. **Contact:** Ellen Kadin, executive editor (marketing, career, personal development); Robert Nirkind, senior editor (sales, customer service, project management, finance). Estab. 1923. Publishes hardcover and trade paperback originals, professional books. AMACOM is the publishing arm of the American Management Association, the world's largest training organization for managers and their organizations—advancing the skills of individuals to drive business success. AMACOM's books are intended to enhance readers' personal and professional growth, and to help readers meet the challenges of the future by conveying emerging trends and cutting-edge thinking.

NONFICTION Subjects include all business topics. Publishes books for consumer and professional markets, including general business, management, strategic planning, human resources, manufacturing, project management, training, finance, sales, marketing, customer service, career, technology applications, history, real estate, parenting, communications and biography. Submit proposals including brief book description and rationale, TOC, author bio and platform, intended audience, competing books and sample chapters. Proposals returned with SASE only.

TIPS "A proposal is usually between 10 and 20 pages in length."

AMERICAN BAR ASSOCIATION PUBLISHING

321 N. Clark St., Chicago IL 60654. (312)988-5000. **Fax:** (312)988-6030. **Website:** www.ababooks.org. **Contact:** Tim Brandhorst, director of new product development. Estab. 1878. Publishes hardcover and trade paperback originals. "We are interested in books that help lawyers practice law more effectively, whether it's how to handle clients, structure a real estate deal, or take an antitrust case to court." **Publishes 100 titles/year. 50 queries received/year. 20% of books from first-time authors. 95% from unagented writers.** Publishes book 6 months after acceptance. Accepts simultaneous submissions. Responds in 1 month to queries and proposals; 3 months to mss. Book catalog and ms guidelines online.

NONFICTION Subjects include business, economics, computers, electronics, money, finance, software, legal practice. "Our market is not, generally, the public. Books need to be targeted to lawyers who are seeking solutions to their practice problems. We rarely publish scholarly treatises." All areas of legal practice. Query with SASE.

TIPS "ABA books are written for practicing lawyers. The most successful books have a practical, reader-friendly voice. Features like checklists, exhibits, sample contracts, and flow charts are preferred. The Association also publishes over 80 major national periodicals in a variety of legal areas. Contact Tim Brandhorst, Director of New Product Development, at the above address with queries."

AMERICAN CARRIAGE HOUSE PUBLISHING

P.O. Box 1130, Nevada City CA 95959. (530)432-8860. **Fax:** (530)432-7379. **Website:** www.americancarriagehousepublishing.com. **Contact:** Lynn Taylor, editor (parenting, reference, child, women). Estab. 2004. Publishes trade paperback and electronic originals. **Publishes 10 titles/year. 10% of books from first-time authors. 100% from unagented writers. Pays outright purchase of $300-3,000.** Publishes book 1 year after acceptance. Accepts simultaneous submissions. Responds in 3 months. Catalog free on request.

NONFICTION Subjects include child guidance, education, parenting, womens issues, womens studies, young adult. Query with SASE. Reviews artwork/photos. Send photocopies.

FICTION Subjects include religious, spiritual, young adult. Query with SASE.

POETRY Wholesome poetry.

TIPS "We are looking for proposals, both fiction and nonfiction, preferably wholesome topics."

AMERICAN CATHOLIC PRESS

16565 S. State St., South Holland IL 60473. (312)331-5845. **Fax:** (708)331-5484. **E-mail:** acp@acpress.org. **Website:** www.acpress.org. **Contact:** Rev. Michael Gilligan, PhD, editorial director. Estab. 1967. Publishes hardcover originals and hardcover and paperback reprints. **Publishes 4 titles/year. Makes outright purchase of $25-100.** Guidelines online.

NONFICTION Subjects include education, music, dance, religion, spirituality. "We publish books on the Roman Catholic liturgy—for the most part, books on religious music and educational books and pamphlets. We also publish religious songs for church use, including Psalms, as well as choral and instrumental arrangements. We are interested in new music, meant for use in church services. Books, or even pamphlets, on the Roman Catholic Mass are especially welcome. We have no interest in secular topics and are not interested in religious poetry of any kind."

TIPS "Most of our sales are by direct mail, although we do work through retail outlets."

AMERICAN CHEMICAL SOCIETY

Publications/Books Division, 1155 16th St. NW, Washington DC 20036. (202)452-2120. **Fax:** (202)452-8913. **Website:** pubs.acs.org/books/. **Contact:** Bob Hauserman, acquisitions editor. Estab. 1876. Publishes hardcover originals. American Chemical Society publishes symposium-based books for chemistry. **Publishes 35 titles/year. Pays royalty.** Accepts simultaneous submissions. Responds in 2 months to proposals. Book catalog available free. Guidelines online.

NONFICTION Subjects include science. Emphasis is on meeting-based books. Log in to submission site online.

AMERICAN CORRECTIONAL ASSOCIATION

206 N. Washington St., Suite 200, Alexandria VA 22314. (703)224-0194. **Fax:** (703)224-0179. **E-mail:** aliceh@aca.org; susanc@aca.org; rgibson@aca.org. **Website:** www.aca.org. **Contact:** Alice Heiserman, manager of publications and research. Estab. 1870. Publishes trade paperback originals. "American Correctional Association provides practical information on jails, prisons, boot camps, probation, parole, community corrections, juvenile facilities and rehabilitation programs, substance abuse programs, and other areas of corrections." **Publishes 18 titles/year. 90% of books from first-time authors. 100% from unagented writers.** Publishes book 1 year after acceptance. Responds in 4 months to queries. Book catalog available free. Guidelines online.

NONFICTION "We are looking for practical, how-to texts or training materials written for the corrections profession. We are especially interested in books on management, development of first-line supervisors, and security-threat group/management in prisons." No autobiographies or true-life accounts by current or former inmates or correctional officers, theses, or dissertations. No fiction or poetry. Query with SASE. Reviews artwork/photos.

TIPS "Authors are professionals in the field of corrections. Our audience is made up of corrections professionals and criminal justice students. No books by inmates or former inmates. This publisher advises out-of-town freelance editors, indexers, and proofreaders to refrain from requesting work from them."

AMERICAN COUNSELING ASSOCIATION

5999 Stevenson Ave., Alexandria VA 22304. (703)823-9800. **Fax:** (703)823-4786. **E-mail:** cbaker@counseling.org. **Website:** www.counseling.org. **Contact:** Carolyn C. Baker, associate publisher. Estab. 1952. Publishes paperback originals. "The American Counseling Association is dedicated to promoting public confidence and trust in the counseling profession. We publish scholarly texts for graduate level students and mental health professionals. We do not publish books for the general public." **Publishes 8-10 titles/ year. 1% of books from first-time authors. 90% from unagented writers.** Accepts simultaneous submissions. Responds in 1 month to queries. Guidelines available free.

NONFICTION Subjects include education, gay, lesbian, health, multicultural, psychology, religion, sociology, spirituality, women's issues. ACA does not publish self-help books or autobiographies. Query with SASE. Submit proposal package, outline, 2 sample chapters, vitae.

TIPS "Target your market. Your books will not be appropriate for everyone across all disciplines."

AMERICAN FEDERATION OF ASTROLOGERS

6535 S. Rural Rd., Tempe AZ 85283. (480)838-1751. **Fax:** (480)838-8293. **E-mail:** info@astrologers.com. **Website:** www.astrologers.com. Estab. 1938. Publishes trade paperback originals and reprints. American Federation of Astrologers publishes astrology books, calendars, charts, and related aids. **Publishes 10-15 titles/year. 10 queries received/year. 20 mss received/ year. 50% of books from first-time authors. 100% from unagented writers. Pays 10% royalty.** Publishes book 10 months after acceptance of ms. after acceptance of ms. Accepts simultaneous submissions. Responds in 6 months to mss. Book catalog available free. Guidelines online.

NONFICTION "Our market for beginner books, Sun-sign guides, and similar material is limited and we thus publish very few of these. The ideal word count for a book-length ms published by AFA is about 40,000 words, although we will consider mss from 20,000 to 60,000 words." Submit complete ms.

TIPS "AFA welcomes articles for *Today's Astrologer*, our monthly journal for members, on any astrological subject. Most articles are 1,500-3,000 words, but we do accept shorter and longer articles. Follow the guidelines online for book mss. You also can e-mail your article to info@astrologers.com, but any charts or illustrations must be submitted as attachments and not embedded in the body of the e-mail or in an attached document."

AMERICAN QUILTER'S SOCIETY

5801 Kentucky Dam Road, Paducah KY 42003. (270)898-7903. **Fax:** (270)898-1173. **E-mail:** editor@ aqsquilt.com. **Website:** www.americanquilter.com. **Contact:** Andi Reynolds, executive book editor (primarily how-to and patterns, but other quilting books sometimes published, including quilt-related fiction). Estab. 1984. Publishes trade paperbacks. "American Quilter's Society publishes how-to and pattern books for quilters (beginners through intermediate skill level). We are not the publisher for non-quilters writing about quilts. We now publish quilt-related craft cozy romance and mystery titles, series only. Humor is good. Graphic depictions and curse words are bad." **Publishes 20-24 titles/year. 100 queries received/year. 60% of books from first-time authors. Pays 5% royalty on retail price fir both nonfiction and fiction.** Publishes book Publishes nonfiction ms 9-18 months after acceptance. Fiction published on a different schedule TBD. after acceptance of ms. Responds in 2 months to proposals. Nonfiction proposal guidelines online.

○ Accepts simultaneous nonfiction submissions. Does not accept simultaneous fiction submissions.

NONFICTION No queries; proposals only. Note: 1 or 2 completed quilt projects must accompany proposal.

FICTION Submit a synopsis and 2 sample chapters, plus an outline of the next 2 books in the series.

AMERICAN WATER WORKS ASSOCIATION

6666 W. Quincy Ave., Denver CO 80235. (303)347-6260. **Fax:** (303)794-7310. **E-mail:** submissions@ awwa.org. **Website:** www.awwa.org. **Contact:** David Plank, manager, business and product development. Estab. 1881. Publishes hardcover and trade paperback originals. "AWWA strives to advance and promote the safety and knowledge of drinking water and related issues to all audiences—from kindergarten through post-doctorate." **Publishes 25 titles/year.** Responds in 4 months to queries. Book catalog and ms guidelines free.

NONFICTION Subjects include nature, environment, science, software, drinking water- and wastewater-related topics, operations, treatment, sustainability. Query with SASE. Submit outline, bio, 3 sample chapters. Reviews artwork/photos. Send photocopies.

TIPS "See website to download submission instructions."

AMHERST MEDIA INC.

175 Rano St., Suite 200, Buffalo NY 14207. (716)874-4450. **Fax:** (716)874-4508. **E-mail:** submissions@amherstmedia.com. **Website:** www.amherstmedia.com. **Contact:** Craig Alesse, publisher. Estab. 1974. Publishes trade paperback originals and reprints. Amherst Media publishes how-to photography books. **Publishes 30 titles/year. 60% of books from first-time authors. 90% from unagented writers. Pays 6-8% royalty. Pays advance.** Publishes book 1 year after acceptance. Accepts simultaneous submissions. Responds in 2 months to queries. Book catalog free and online (catalog@amherstmedia.com). Guidelines free and online.

NONFICTION Subjects include photography. Looking for well-written and illustrated photo books. Query with outline, 2 sample chapters, and SASE. Reviews artwork/photos.

TIPS "Our audience is made up of beginning to advanced photographers. If I were a writer trying to market a book today, I would fill the need of a specific audience and self-edit in a tight manner."

AMIRA PRESS

2721 N. Rosedale St., Baltimore MD 21216. (704)858-7533. **E-mail:** submissions@amirapress.com. **Website:** www.amirapress.com. **Contact:** Yvette A. Lynn, CEO (any sub genre). Estab. 2007. Format publishes in paperback originals, e-books, POD printing. "We are a small press which publishes sensual and erotic romance. Our slogan is 'Erotic and Sensual Romance. Immerse Yourself.' Our authors and stories are diverse." **Published 30 new writers last year.** Averages 50 fiction titles/year. Member EPIC. Distributes/promotes titles through Amazon, Mobipocket, Fictionwise, BarnesandNoble.com, Target.com, Amirapress.com, AllRomance Ebooks, and Ingrams. **Pays royalties, 8.5% of cover price (print)—30-40% of cover price (e-books).** Publishes book 1-4 months after acceptance. Accepts simultaneous submissions. Responds in 3 months. Guildelines online.

FICTION Subjects include erotica. Submit complete ms with cover letter by e-mail. "No snail mail." Include estimated word count, heat level, brief bio, list of publishing credits. Accepts unsolicited mss. Sometimes critiques/comments on rejected mss.

TIPS "Please read our submission guidelines thoroughly and follow them when submitting. We do not consider a work until we have all the requested information and the work is presented in the format we outline."

AMULET BOOKS

115 W. 18th St., New York NY 10001. **Website:** www.amuletbooks.com. **Contact:** Susan Van Metre, vice president/publisher; Tamar Brazis, editorial director; Cecily Kaiser, publishing director. Estab. 2004. **10% of books from first-time authors.**

○ *Does not accept unsolicited mss or queries.*

FICTION Middle readers: adventure, contemporary, fantasy, history, science fiction, sports. Young adults/teens: adventure, contemporary, fantasy, history, science fiction, sports, suspense.

ANDREWS MCMEEL UNIVERSAL

1130 Walnut St., Kansas City MO 64106. (816)581-7500. **Website:** www.andrewsmcmeel.com. **Contact:** Christine Schillig, vice president/editorial director. Estab. 1973. Publishes hardcover and paperback originals. Andrews McMeel publishes general trade books, humor books, miniature gift books, calendars, and stationery products. **Publishes 300 titles/year. Pays royalty on retail price or net receipts. Pays advance.** Guidelines online.

NONFICTION Subjects include cooking, games, comics, puzzles. Submit proposal.

ANHINGA PRESS

P.O. Box 3665, Tallahassee FL 32315. Phone/**Fax:** (850)577-0745. **E-mail:** info@anhinga.org. **Website:** www.anhinga.org. **Contact:** Kristine Snodgrass, editor. Publishes hardcover and trade paperback originals. Publishes only full-length collections of poetry (60-80 pages). No individual poems or chapbooks. **Publishes 5 titles/year. Pays 10% royalty on retail price. Offers Anhinga Prize of $2,000.** Accepts simultaneous submissions. Responds in 3 months to queries, proposals, and mss. Book catalog and contest for #10 SASE or online. Guidelines online.

POETRY Query with SASE and 10-page sample (not full ms) by mail. No e-mail queries.

⊘☺ ANNICK PRESS, LTD.

15 Patricia Ave., Toronto ON M2M 1H9, Canada. (416)221-4802. **Fax:** (416)221-8400. **E-mail:** annickpress@annickpress.com. **Website:** www.annickpress.com. **Contact:** Rick Wilks, director; Colleen MacMil-

lan, associate publisher; Sheryl Shapiro, creative director. Publishes picture books, juvenile and YA fiction and nonfiction; specializes in trade books. "Annick Press maintains a commitment to high quality books that entertain and challenge. Our publications share fantasy and stimulate imagination, while encouraging children to trust their judgment and abilities." Publishes 5 picture books/year; 6 young readers/year; 8 middle readers/year; 9 young adult titles/year. **Publishes 25 titles/year. 5,000 queries received/year. 3,000 mss received/year. 20% of books from first-time authors. 80-85% from unagented writers. Pays authors royalty of 5-12% based on retail price. Offers advances (average amount: $3,000). Pays illustrators royalty of 5% minimum.** Publishes book Publishes a book 2 years after acceptance. Book catalog and Guidelines online.

○ *Does not accept unsolicited mss.*

NONFICTION Works with 20 illustrators/year. Illustrations only: Query with samples.

FICTION Publisher of children's books. Publishes hardcover and trade paperback originals. Average print order: 9,000. First novel print order: 7,000. Plans 18 first novels this year. Averages 25 total titles/year. Distributes titles through Firefly Books Ltd. Juvenile, young adult. Not accepting picture books at this time.

☺ ANVIL PRESS

P.O. Box 3008 MPO, Vancouver BC V6B 3X5, Canada. (604)876-8710. **Fax:** (604)879-2667. **E-mail:** info@anvilpress.com. **Website:** www.anvilpress.com. **Contact:** Brian Kaufman. Estab. 1988. Publishes trade paperback originals. "Anvil Press publishes contemporary adult fiction, poetry, and drama, giving voice to up-and-coming Canadian writers, exploring all literary genres, discovering, nurturing, and promoting new Canadian literary talent. Currently emphasizing urban/suburban themed fiction and poetry; de-emphasizing historical novels." **Publishes 8-10 titles/year. 300 queries received/year. 80% of books from first-time authors. 70% from unagented writers. Pays advance. Average advance is $500-2,000, depending on the genre.** Publishes book 8 months after acceptance of ms. after acceptance of ms. Accepts simultaneous submissions. Responds in 2 months to queries; 6 months to mss. Book catalog for 9×12 SAE with 2 first-class stamps. Guidelines online.

○ Canadian authors only. No e-mail submissions.

NONFICTION Query with 20-30 pages and SASE.

FICTION Subjects include experimental, literary, short story collections. Contemporary, modern literature; no formulaic or genre. Query with 20-30 pages and SASE.

POETRY "Get our catalog, look at our poetry. We do very little poetry-maybe 1-2 titles per year." Query with 8-12 poems and SASE.

TIPS "Audience is informed, educated, aware, with an opinion, culturally active (films, books, the performing arts). No U.S. authors. Research the appropriate publisher for your work."

APA BOOKS

American Psychological Association, 750 First St., NE, Washington DC 20002. (202)336-5792. **E-mail:** book-submissions@apa.org. **Website:** www.apa.org/books. Publishes hardcover and trade paperback originals. Catalog and guidelines online.

IMPRINTS Magination Press (children's books).

NONFICTION Subjects include education, gay, lesbian, multicultural, psychology, science, social sciences, sociology, women's issues, women's studies. Submit cv and prospectus with TOC, intended audience, selling points, and outside competition.

TIPS "Our press features scholarly books on empirically supported topics for professionals and students in all areas of psychology."

APPALACHIAN MOUNTAIN CLUB BOOKS

5 Joy St., Boston MA 02108. (617)523-0636. **Fax:** (617)523-0722. **E-mail:** amcbooks@outdoors.org. **Website:** www.outdoors.org. Estab. 1876. Publishes hardcover and trade paperback originals. "AMC Books are written and published by the experts in the Northeast outdoors. Our mission is to publish authoritative, accurate, and easy-to-use books and maps based on AMC's expertise in outdoor recreation, education, and conservation. We are committed to producing books and maps that appeal to novices and day visitors as well as outdoor enthusiasts in our core activity areas of hiking and paddling. By advancing the interest of the public in outdoor recreation and helping our readers to access backcountry trails and waterways, and by using our books to educate the public about safety, conservation, and stewardship, we support AMC's mission of promoting the protection, enjoyment, and wise use of the Northeast outdoors. We work with the best professional writers possible and draw upon the experience of our programs staff

and chapter leaders from Maine to Washington, D.C." Accepts simultaneous submissions. Guidelines online.

NONFICTION Subjects include nature, environment, recreation, regional, Northeast outdoor recreation, literary nonfiction, guidebooks, Maps that are based on our direct work with land managers and our on-the-ground collection of data on trails, natural features, and points of interest. AMC Books also publishes narrative titles related to outdoor recreation, mountaineering, and adventure, often with a historical perspective. "Appalachian Mountain Club publishes hiking guides, paddling guides, nature, conservation, and mountain-subject guides for America's Northeast. We connect recreation to conservation and education." Query with proposal and the first 3 chapters of your ms.

TIPS "Our audience is outdoor recreationists, conservation-minded hikers and canoeists, family outdoor lovers, armchair enthusiasts. Visit our website for proposal submission guidelines and more information."

ARCADE PUBLISHING

Skyhorse Publishing, 307 W. 36th St., 11th Floor, New York NY 10018. (212)643-6816. **Fax:** (212)643-6819. **E-mail:** arcadesubmissions@skyhorsepublishing.com. **Website:** www.arcadepub.com. **Contact:** Acquisitions Editor. Estab. 1988. Publishes hardcover originals, trade paperback reprints. "Arcade prides itself on publishing top-notch literary nonfiction and fiction, with a significant proportion of foreign writers." **Publishes 35 titles/year. 5% of books from first-time authors. Pays royalty on retail price and 10 author's copies. Pays advance.** Publishes book 18 months after acceptance. Responds in 2 months if interested. Book catalog and ms guidelines for #10 SASE.

NONFICTION Subjects include history, memoirs, nature, environment, travel, popular science, current events. Submit proposal with brief query, 1-2 page synopsis, chapter outline, market analysis, sample chapter, bio.

FICTION Subjects include literary, mainstream, contemporary, short story collections, translation. No romance, historical, science fiction. Submit proposal with brief query, 1-2 page synopsis, chapter outline, market analysis, sample chapter, bio.

ARCADIA PUBLISHING

420 Wando Park Blvd., Mt. Pleasant SC 29464. (843)853-2070. **Fax:** (843)853-0044. **E-mail:** publishingnortheast@arcadiapublishing.com; publishingsouth@arcadiapublishing.com; publishingwest@arcadiapublishing.com; publishingmidwest@arcadiapublishing.com; publishingmidatlantic@arcadiapublishing.com; publishingsouthwest@arcadiapublishing.com. **Website:** www.arcadiapublishing.com. Estab. 1993. Publishes trade paperback originals. "Arcadia publishes photographic vintage regional histories. We have more than 3,000 Images of America series in print. We have expanded our California program." **Publishes 600 titles/year. Pays 8% royalty on retail price.** Publishes book 9 months after acceptance. Accepts simultaneous submissions. Book catalog online. Guidelines available free.

NONFICTION Subjects include history, local, regional. "Arcadia accepts submissions year-round. Our editors seek proposals on local history topics and are able to provide authors with detailed information about our publishing program as well as book proposal submission guidelines. Due to the great demand for titles on local and regional history, we are currently searching for authors to work with us on new photographic history projects. Please contact one of our regional publishing teams if you are interested in submitting a proposal." Specific proposal form to be completed.

TIPS "Writers should know that we only publish history titles. The majority of our books are on a city or region, and contain vintage images with limited text."

ARCHAIA

Imprint of Boom! Studios, 5670 Wilshire Blvd., Suite 450, Los Angeles CA 90036. **Website:** www.archaia.com. **Contact:** Mark Smylie, chief creative officer. Use online submission form.

FICTION Subjects include adventure, fantasy, horror, mystery, science fiction. Looking for graphic novel submissions that include finished art. "Archaia is a multi-award-winning graphic novel publisher with more than 75 renowned publishing brands, including such domestic and international hits as *Artesia, Mouse Guard,* and a line of Jim Henson graphic novels including *Fraggle Rock* and *The Dark Crystal.*" Publishes creator-shared comic books and graphic novels in the adventure, fantasy, horror, pulp noir, and science fiction genres that contain idiosyncratic and atypical writing and art. *Archaia does not generally hire freelancers or arrange for freelance work, so submissions should only be for completed book and series proposals.*

A·R EDITIONS, INC.

8551 Research Way, Suite 180, Middleton WI 53562. (608)203-2565. **E-mail:** pamela.whitcomb@areditions. com. **Website:** www.areditions.com. **Contact:** Pamela Whitcomb, managing editor (Recent Researches Series). Estab. 1962. **Publishes 30 titles/year. 40 queries received/year. 30 mss received/year. 75% of books from first-time authors. 100% from unagented writers. Pays royalty or honoraria.** Responds in 1 month to queries; 3 months to proposals; 6 months to mss. Catalog and guidelines online.

NONFICTION Subjects include computers, electronics, music, dance, software, historical music editions. Computer Music and Digital Audio Series titles deal with issues tied to digital and electronic media, and include both textbooks and handbooks in this area. Query with SASE. Submit outline. "All material submitted in support of a proposal becomes the property of A-R Editions. Please send photocopies of all important documents (retain your originals). We suggest that you send your proposal either with delivery confirmation or by a service that offers package tracking to avoid misdirected packages."

⟳ ARSENAL PULP PRESS

#202-211 East Georgia St., Vancouver BC V6A 1Z6, Canada. (604)687-4233. **Fax:** (604)687-4283. **E-mail:** info@arsenalpulp.com. **Website:** www.arsenalpulp. com. **Contact:** Editorial Board. Estab. 1980. Publishes trade paperback originals, and trade paperback reprints. "We are interested in literature that traverses uncharted territories, publishing books that challenge and stimulate and ask probing questions about the world around us. With a staff of five, located in a second-floor office in the historic Vancouver district of Gastown, we publish between 14 and 20 new titles per year, as well as an average of 12 to 15 reprints." **Publishes 14-20 titles/year. 500 queries received/ year. 300 mss received/year. 30% of books from first-time authors. 100% from unagented writers.** Publishes book 1 year after acceptance of ms. Accepts simultaneous submissions. Responds in 2 months to queries. Responds in 4 months to proposals and mss. Book catalog for 9×12 SAE with IRCs or online. Guidelines online.

IMPRINTS Tillacum Library, Advance Editions.

NONFICTION Subjects include art, architecture, cooking, foods, nutrition, creative nonfiction, ethnic, Canadian, cultural studies, aboriginal issues, gay, health, lesbian, history, cultural, language, literature, multicultural, political/sociological studies, regional studies and guides, in particular for British Columbia, sex, sociology, travel, women's issues, women's studies, youth culture, film, visual art. Rarely publishes non-Canadian authors. No poetry at this time. "We do not publish children's books." Each submission must include: a synopsis of the work, a chapter by chapter outline for nonfiction, writing credentials, a 50-page excerpt from the ms (*do not send more, it will be a waste of postage; if we like what we see, we'll ask for the rest of the ms*), and a marketing analysis. If our editorial board is interested, you will be asked to send the entire ms. We do not accept discs or submissions by fax or e-mail, and we do not discuss concepts over the phone. Reviews artwork/photos.

FICTION Subjects include ethnic, general, feminist, gay, lesbian, literary, multicultural, short story collections. No children's books or genre fiction, i.e., westerns, romance, horror, mystery, etc. Submit proposal package, outline, clips, 2-3 sample chapters.

ARTE PUBLICO PRESS

University of Houston, 4902 Gulf Fwy, Bldg 19, Rm 100, Houston TX 77204-2004. **Fax:** (713)743-2847. **E-mail:** submapp@central.uh.edu. **Website:** artepublicopress.uh.edu/arte-publico-wp. **Contact:** Nicolas Kanellos, editor. Estab. 1979. Publishes hardcover originals, trade paperback originals and reprints. **Publishes 25-30 titles/year. 1,000 queries received/ year. 2,000 mss received/year. 50% of books from first-time authors. 80% from unagented writers. Pays 10% royalty on wholesale price. Provides 20 author's copies; 40% discount on subsequent copies. Pays $1,000-3,000 advance.** Publishes book 2 years after acceptance of ms. after acceptance of ms. Accepts simultaneous submissions. Responds in 1 month to queries and proposals. Responds in 4 months to mss. Book catalog available free. Guidelines online.

IMPRINTS Piñata Books.

NONFICTION Subjects include ethnic, language, literature, regional, translation, women's issues, women's studies. Hispanic civil rights issues for new series: The Hispanic Civil Rights Series. Submissions made through online submission form.

FICTION Subjects include contemporary, ethnic, literary, mainstream. "Written by U.S.-Hispanics." Submissions made through online submission form.

POETRY Submissions made through online submission form.

TIPS "Include cover letter in which you 'sell' your book—why should we publish the book, who will want to read it, why does it matter, etc. Use our ms submission online form. Format files accepted are: Word, plain/text, rich/text files. Other formats will not be accepted. Ms files cannot be larger than 5MB. Once editors review your ms, you will receive an e-mail with the decision. Revision process could take up to 4 months."

ASA, AVIATION SUPPLIES & ACADEMICS

7005 132 Place SE, Newcastle WA 98059. (425)235-1500. **E-mail:** feedback@asa2fly.com. **Website:** www.asa2fly.com. "ASA is an industry leader in the development and sales of aviation supplies, publications, and software for pilots, flight instructors, flight engineers and aviation technicians. All ASA products are developed by a team of researchers, authors and editors." Book catalog available free.

NONFICTION Subjects include education. "We are primarily an aviation publisher. Educational books in this area are our specialty; other aviation books will be considered." All subjects must be related to aviation education and training. Query with outline. Send photocopies.

TIPS "Two of our specialty series include ASA's *Focus Series*, and ASA *Aviator's Library*. Books in our *Focus Series* concentrate on single-subject areas of aviation knowledge, curriculum and practice. The *Aviator's Library* is comprised of titles of known and/or classic aviation authors or established instructor/authors in the industry, and other aviation specialty titles."

ASCE PRESS

American Society of Civil Engineers, 1801 Alexander Bell Dr., Reston VA 20191. (703)295-6275. **Fax:** (703)295-6278. **Website:** www.asce.org/pubs. Estab. 1989. "ASCE Press publishes technical volumes that are useful to practicing civil engineers and civil engineering students, as well as allied professionals. We publish books by individual authors and editors to advance the civil engineering profession. Currently emphasizing geotechnical, structural engineering, sustainable engineering and engineering history. De-emphasizing highly specialized areas with narrow scope." **Publishes 10-15 titles/year. 20% of books from first-time authors. 100% from unagented writers.** Guidelines online.

NONFICTION "We are looking for topics that are useful and instructive to the engineering practitioner." Query with proposal, sample chapters, CV, TOC, and target audience.

TIPS "As a traditional publisher of scientific and technical materials, ASCE Press applies rigorous standards to the expertise, scholarship, readability and attractiveness of its books."

ASHLAND POETRY PRESS

401 College Ave., Ashland OH 44805. (419)289-5957. **Fax:** (419)289-5255. **E-mail:** app@ashland.edu. **Website:** www.ashlandpoetrypress.com. **Contact:** Sarah M. Wells, managing editor. Estab. 1969. Publishes trade paperback originals. **Publishes 2-3 titles/year. 400 mss received/year in Snyder Prize. 50% of books from first-time authors. 100% from unagented writers. Makes outright purchase of $500-1,000.** Publishes book 10 months after acceptance. Accepts simultaneous submissions. Responds in 1 month to queries; 6 months to mss. Catalog and guidelines online.

POETRY "We accept unsolicited mss through the Snyder Prize competition each spring-the deadline is April 30. Judges are mindful of dedication to craftsmanship and thematic integrity."

TIPS "We rarely publish a title submitted off the transom outside of our Snyder Prize competition."

ASM PRESS

Book division for the American Society for Microbiology, 1752 N. St., NW, Washington DC 20036. (202)737-3600. **Fax:** (202)942-9342. **E-mail:** lwilliams@asmusa.org. **Website:** www.asmscience.org. **Contact:** Lindsay Williams, editorial and rights coordinator. Estab. 1899. Publishes hardcover, trade paperback and electronic originals. **Publishes 30 titles/year. 40% of books from first-time authors. 95% from unagented writers. Pays 5-15% royalty on wholesale price. Pays $1,000-10,000 advance.** Publishes book 6-9 months after acceptance. Accepts simultaneous submissions. Responds in 2 months. Catalog and guidelines online.

NONFICTION Subjects include agriculture, animals, education, health, medicine, history, horticulture, nature, environment, science, microbiology and related sciences. "Must have bona fide academic credentials in which they are writing." Query with SASE or by e-mail. Submit proposal package, outline, prospectus. Proposals for journal articles must be submitted to the journals department at: journals@asmusa.com. Reviews artwork/photos. Send photocopies.

TIPS "Credentials are most important."

⊘⊘ ATHENEUM BOOKS FOR YOUNG READERS

Simon & Schuster, 1230 Avenue of the Americas, New York NY 10020. **Website:** kids.simonandschuster.com. **Contact:** Caitlyn Dlouhy, editorial director; Justin Chanda, vice president/publisher; Namrata Tripathi, executive editor; Anne Zafian, vice president. Estab. 1961. Publishes hardcover originals. Accepts simultaneous submissions. Guidelines for #10 SASE.

NONFICTION Subjects include Americana, animals, art, architecture, business, economics, government, politics, health, medicine, history, music, dance, nature, environment, photography, psychology, recreation, religion, science, sociology, sports, travel. Publishes hardcover originals, picture books for young kids, nonfiction for ages 8-12 and novels for middle-grade and young adults. Types of books include biography, historical fiction, history, nonfiction. Publishes 60 titles/year. 100% require freelance illustration. Agented submissions only.

FICTION Subjects include adventure, ethnic, experimental, fantasy, gothic, historical, horror, humor, mainstream, contemporary, mystery, science fiction, sports, suspense, western, Animal. All in juvenile versions. "We have few specific needs except for books that are fresh, interesting and well written. Fad topics are dangerous, as are works you haven't polished to the best of your ability. We also don't need safety pamphlets, ABC books, coloring books and board books. In writing picture book texts, avoid the coy and 'cutesy,' such as stories about characters with alliterative names." Agented submissions only. No paperback romance-type fiction.

TIPS "Study our titles."

A.T. PUBLISHING

23 Lily Lake Rd., Highland NY 12528. (845)691-2021. **E-mail:** tjp2@optonline.net. **Contact:** Anthony Prizzia, publisher (education); John Prizzia, publisher. Estab. 2001. Publishes trade paperback originals. **Publishes 1-3 titles/year. 5-10 queries received/year. 100% of books from first-time authors. 100% from unagented writers. Pays 15-25% royalty on retail price. Makes outright purchase of $500-2,500. Pays $500-1,000 advance.** Accepts simultaneous submissions. Responds in 1 month to queries; 2 months to proposals; 4 months to mss.

NONFICTION Subjects include cooking, foods, nutrition, education, recreation, science, sports. Query with SASE. Submit complete ms. Reviews artwork/photos. Send photocopies.

TIPS "Audience is people interested in a variety of topics, general. Submit typed ms for consideration, including a SASE for return of ms."

AUTUMN HOUSE PRESS

87½ Westwood St., Pittsburgh PA 15211. (412)381-4261. **E-mail:** info@autumnhouse.org. **Website:** www.autumnhouse.org. **Contact:** Michael Simms, editor-in-chief (fiction). Sharon Dilworth, fiction editor. Estab. 1998. Publishes hardcover, trade paperback, and electronic originals. "We are a non-profit literary press specializing in high-quality poetry, fiction, and nonfiction. Our editions are beautifully designed and printed, and they are distributed nationally. Approximately one-third of our sales are to college literature and creative writing classes." Member CLMP, AWP, Academy of American Poets. "We distribute our own titles. We do extensive national promotion through ads, web-marketing, reading tours, bookfairs and conferences. We are open to all genres. The quality of writing concerns us, not the genre." You can also learn about our annual Fiction Prize, Poetry Prize, Nonfiction Prize, and Chapbook Award competitions, as well as our online journal, *Coal Hill Review.* (Please note that Autumn House accepts unsolicited mss *only* through these competitions.) **Publishes 8 titles/year. Receives 1,000 mss/year. 10% of books from first-time authors. 100% from unagented writers. Pays 7% royalty on wholesale price. Pays $0-2,500 advance.** Publishes book Publishes 9 months after acceptance. Accepts simultaneous submissions. Responds in 1-3 days on queries and proposals; 3 months on mss. Catalog free on request. Guidelines online at website; free on request; or for #10 SASE.

NONFICTION Subjects include memoirs. Enter the nonfiction contest.

FICTION Subjects include literary. Holds competition/award for short stories, novels, story collections, memoirs, nonfiction. *We ask that all submissions from authors new to Autumn House come through one of our annual contests.* "To identify and publish the best fiction, nonfiction, and poetry mss we can find." Annual. Prize: $2,500 and book publication. Entries should be unpublished. Open to all writers over the age of 18. Length: approx 200-300 pages. Results announced September. Winners notified by mail, by phone, by e-mail. Results made available to entrants with SASE, by fax, by e-mail, on website. Published *New World Order*, by Derek Green (collection of stories) and *Drift and Swerve*, by Samuel Ligon (collection of stories). All submissions come through our annual contests; deadline June 30 each year. See website for official guidelines. Responds to queries in 2 days. Accepts mss only through contest. Never critiques/comments on rejected mss. Responds to mss by August. "Submit only through our annual contest. See guidelines online. Submit completed ms. Cover letter should include name, address, phone, e-mail, novel/story title. The mss are judged blind, so please include two cover pages, one with contact information and one without. The competition is tough, so submit only your best work!"

POETRY Since 2003, the annual Autumn House Poetry Contest has awarded publication of a full-length ms and $2,500 to the winner. *We ask that all submissions from authors new to Autumn House come through one of our annual contests.* All finalists will be considered for publication. Submit only through our annual contest. See guidelines online.

TIPS "The competition to publish with Autumn House is very tough. Submit only your best work."

AVALON TRAVEL PUBLISHING

Avalon Publishing Group, 1700 4th St., Berkeley CA 94710. (510)595-3664. **Fax:** (510)595-4228. **E-mail:** avalon.acquisitions@perseusbooks.com. **Website:** www.travelmatters.com. Estab. 1973. Publishes trade paperback originals. "Avalon travel guides feature practicality and spirit, offering a traveler-to-traveler perspective perfect for planning an afternoon hike, around-the-world journey, or anything in between. ATP publishes 7 major series. Each one has a different emphasis and a different geographic coverage. We have expanded our coverage, with a focus on European and Asian destinations. Our main areas of interest are North America, Central America, South America, the Caribbean, and the Pacific. We are seeking only a few titles in each of our major series. Check online guidelines for our current needs. Follow guidelines closely." **Publishes 100 titles/year. 5,000 queries received/year. 25% of books from first-time authors. 95% from unagented writers. Pays up to $17,000**

advance. Publishes book an average of 9 months after acceptance of ms. Accepts simultaneous submissions. Responds in 4 months to queries. Responds in 4 months to proposals. Guidelines online.

NONFICTION Subjects include regional, travel. "We are not interested in fiction, children's books, and travelogues/travel diaries."

TIPS "ATP is only looking for books that fit into current series. Avalon travel guides range in size from 250-700 pages. The destination and focus of the guide determine its size, and the author typically has 6-12 months to research and write the book. Each book must conform to its respective series guidelines (we will provide guidelines only to those candidates who are selected to write a proposal). The author is also responsible for providing photos and map materials."

AVON ROMANCE

Harper Collins Publishers, 10 E. 53 St., New York NY 10022. **E-mail:** info@avonromance.com. **Website:** www.avonromance.com. **Contact:** Erika Tsang; Lucia Macro; May Chen; Tessa Woodward; Amanda Bergeron; Chelsey Emmelhainz; Nicole Fischer. Estab. 1941. Publishes paperback and digital originals and reprints. "Avon has been publishing award-winning books since 1941. It is recognized for having pioneered the historical romance category and continues to bring the best of commercial literature to the broadest possible audience." **Publishes 400 titles/year.**

FICTION Subjects include historical, literary, mystery, romance, science fiction, young adult. Submit a query and ms via the online submission form at www.avonromance.com/impulse.

TIPS Read the Meet the Editors feature online to learn interests and preferences.

⊘ AZRO PRESS

PMB 342, 1704 Llano St. B, Santa Fe NM 87505. (505)989-3272. **Fax:** (505)989-3832. **E-mail:** books@azropress.com; azropress@gmail.com. **Website:** www.azropress.com. **Contact:** Gae Eisenhardt. Estab. 1997. **Pays authors royalty of 5-10% based on wholesale price. Pays illustrators by the project ($2,000) or royalty of 5%.** Publishes book 1-2 years after acceptance. Accepts simultaneous submissions. Responds to queries/mss in 3-4 months. Catalog available for #10 SASE and 3 first-class stamps or online.

"We like to publish illustrated children's books by Southwestern authors and illustrators. We are always looking for books with a Southwestern look or theme."

NONFICTION Picture books: animal, geography, history. Young readers: geography, history.

FICTION Picture books: animal, history, humor, nature/environment. Young readers: adventure, animal, hi-lo, history, humor. Average word length: picture books—1,200; young readers—2,000-2,500.

TIPS "We are not currently accepting new mss. Please see our website for acceptance date."

Ⓐ B&H PUBLISHING GROUP

One Lifeway Plaza, Nashville TN 37234. (615)251-2000. **Website:** www.broadmanholman.com. "B&H Publishing Group is a non-profit publisher made up of people who are passionate about taking God's word to the world."

IMPRINTS CrossBooks; WORDsearch Bible.

◗ "At this time, B&H only accepts mss from literary agents."

BACKBEAT BOOKS

Hal Leonard Publishing Group, 33 Plymouth St., Suite 302, Montclair NJ 07042. (800)637-2852. **E-mail:** jcerullo@halleonard.com. **Website:** www.backbeatbooks.com. **Contact:** John Cerullo, group publisher. Publishes hardcover and trade paperback originals; trade paperback reprints. **Publishes 24 titles/year.**

NONFICTION Subjects include music (rock & roll), pop culture. Query with TOC, sample chapter, sample illustrations.

BACKCOUNTRY GUIDES

Imprint of The Countryman Press, P. O. Box 748, Woodstock VT 05091-0748. (802)457-4826. **Fax:** (802)457-1678. **E-mail:** khummel@wwnorton.com. **Website:** www.countrymanpress.com. **Contact:** Submissions. Estab. 1973. Publishes trade paperback originals. "We publish books of the highest quality that take the reader where they want to go. Our books are promoted and sold to bookstores and to specialty markets throughout the United States, Canada, and other parts of the world." **Publishes 70 titles/year.** Accepts simultaneous submissions. Responds in 3 months to proposals. Book catalog available free. Guidelines online.

NONFICTION Subjects include nature, environment, recreation, bicycling, hiking, canoeing, kayaking, fly fishing, walking, guidebooks, and series, sports, travel, food, gardening, country living, New England history. Query with SASE. Submit proposal package, outline, 2-3 sample chapters, market analysis. Reviews artwork/photos. Send transparencies.

TIPS Look at our existing series of guidebooks to see how your proposal fits in.

THE BACKWATERS PRESS

3502 N. 52nd St., Omaha NE 68104. **Website:** www.thebackwaterspress.org. **Contact:** Greg Kosmicki, editor.

POETRY Only considers submissions to Backwaters Prize. More details on website.

BAEN BOOKS

P.O. Box 1188, Wake Forest NC 27588. (919)570-1640. **E-mail:** info@baen.com. **Website:** www.baen.com. Estab. 1983. "We publish only science fiction and fantasy. Writers familiar with what we have published in the past will know what sort of material we are most likely to publish in the future: powerful plots with solid scientific and philosophical underpinnings are the sine qua non for consideration for science fiction submissions. As for fantasy, any magical system must be both rigorously coherent and integral to the plot, and overall the work must at least strive for originality." Responds to mss within 12-18 months.

FICTION "Style: Simple is generally better; in our opinion good style, like good breeding, never calls attention to itself. Length: 100,000-130,000 words Generally we are uncomfortable with mss under 100,000 words, but if your novel is really wonderful send it along regardless of length." "Query letters are not necessary. We prefer to see complete mss accompanied by a synopsis. We prefer not to see simultaneous submissions. Electronic submissions are strongly preferred. *We no longer accept submissions by e-mail.* Send ms by using the submission form at: ftp.baen.com/Slush/submit.aspx. No disks unless requested. Attach ms as a Rich Text Format (.rtf) file. Any other format will not be considered."

BAILIWICK PRESS

309 East Mulberry St., Fort Collins CO 80524. (970)672-4878. **Fax:** (970)672-4731. **E-mail:** info@bailiwickpress.com. **Website:** www.bailiwickpress.com. "We're a micro-press that produces books and other products that inspire and tell great stories. Our motto is 'books with something to say.' We are now considering submissions, agented and unagented, for children's and young adult fiction. We're looking for smart, funny, and layered writing that kids will clamor for. Authors who already have a following have a leg

up. We are only looking for humorous children's fiction. Please do not submit work for adults. Illustrated fiction is desired but not required. (Illustrators are also invited to send samples.) Make us laugh out loud, ooh and aah, and cry, 'Eureka!'" Accepts simultaneous submissions. Responds in 6 months.

FICTION "Please read the Aldo Zelnick series to determine if we might be on the same page, then fill out our submission form. Please do not send submissions via snail mail or phone calls. **You must complete the online submission form to be considered.** If, after completing and submitting the form, you also need to send us an e-mail attachment (such as sample illustrations or excerpts of graphics), you may e-mail them to aldozelnick@gmail.com."

⚠⊘ BAKER ACADEMIC

Division of Baker Publishing Group, 6030 E. Fulton Rd., Ada MI 49301. (616)676-9185. **Website:** baker-publishinggroup.com/bakeracademic. Estab. 1939. Publishes hardcover and trade paperback originals. **Publishes 50 titles/year. 10% of books from first-time authors. 85% from unagented writers. Pays advance.** Publishes book 1 year after acceptance.

⚲ "Baker Academic publishes religious academic and professional books for students and church leaders. Does not accept unsolicited queries. We will consider unsolicited work only through one of the following avenues. Materials sent to our editorial staff through a professional literary agent will be considered. In addition, our staff attends various writers' conferences at which prospective authors can develop relationships with those in the publishing industry."

NONFICTION Subjects include anthropology, archeology, education, psychology, religion, women's issues, women's studies, Biblical studies, Christian doctrine, books for pastors and church leaders, contemporary issues. Agented submissions only.

⚠⊘ BAKER BOOKS

Division of Baker Publishing Group, 6030 East Fulton Rd., Ada MI 49301. (616)676-9185. **Website:** baker-publishinggroup.com/bakerbooks. Estab. 1939. Publishes in hardcover and trade paperback originals, and trade paperback reprints. "We will consider unsolicited work only through one of the following avenues. Materials sent through a literary agent will be considered. In addition, our staff attends various writers'

conferences at which prospective authors can develop relationships with those in the publishing industry." Book catalog for 9½×12½ envelope and 3 first-class stamps. Guidelines online.

⚲ "Baker Books publishes popular religious nonfiction reference books and professional books for church leaders. Most of our authors and readers are evangelical Christians, and our books are purchased from Christian bookstores, mail-order retailers, and school bookstores. Does not accept unsolicited queries."

NONFICTION Subjects include childe guidance, psychology, religion, women's issues, women's studies, Christian doctrines.

TIPS "We are not interested in historical fiction, romances, science fiction, biblical narratives or spiritual warfare novels. Do not call to 'pass by' your idea."

⊘ BAKER PUBLISHING GROUP

6030 E. Fulton Rd., Ada MI 49301. (616)676-9185. **Fax:** (616)676-2315. **Website:** www.bakerpublishinggroup.com.

IMPRINTS Baker Academic; Baker Books; Bethany House; Brazos Press; Chosen; Fleming H. Revell.

⚲ *Does not accept unsolicited queries.*

BALCONY MEDIA, INC.

512 E. Wilson, Suite 213, Glendale CA 91206. (818)956-5313. **E-mail:** contact@balconypress.com. **Contact:** Ann Gray, publisher. Publishes hardcover and trade paperback originals. **Publishes 6-8 titles/year. 75% of books from first-time authors. 90% from unagented writers. Pays 10% royalty on wholesale price.** Accepts simultaneous submissions. Responds in 1 month to queries/proposals; 3 months to mss. Book catalog online.

⚲ "We also publish *Form: pioneering design magazine, bi-monthly to the architecture and design professions.* Editor: Alexi Drosu, www.form-mag.net."

NONFICTION Subjects include art, architecture, ethnic, gardening, history, relative to design, art, architecture, and regional. "We are interested in the human side of design as opposed to technical or how-to. We like to think our books will be interesting to the general public who might not otherwise select an architecture or design book." Query by e-mail or letter. Submit outline and 2 sample chapters with introduction, if applicable.

TIPS "Audience consists of architects, designers, and the general public who enjoy those fields. Our books typically cover California subjects, but that is not a restriction. It's always nice when an author has strong ideas about how the book can be effectively marketed. We are not afraid of small niches if a good sales plan can be devised."

Ⓐ BALLANTINE PUBLISHING GROUP

Imprint of Random House, Inc., 1745 Broadway, 18th Floor, New York NY 10019. (212)782-9000. **Website:** www.randomhouse.com. Estab. 1952. Publishes hardcover, trade paperback, mass market paperback originals. Ballantine Books publishes a wide variety of nonfiction and fiction. Guidelines online.

IMPRINTS Ballantine Books, Ballantine Reader's Circle, Del Rey, Del Rey/Lucas Books, Fawcett, Ivy, One World, Wellspring.

NONFICTION Subjects include animals, child guidance, community, cooking, foods, nutrition, creative nonfiction, education, gay, lesbian, health, medicine, history, language, literature, memoirs, military, war, recreation, religion, sex, spirituality, travel, true crime. Agented submissions only. Reviews artwork/photos. Send photocopies.

FICTION Subjects include confession, ethnic, fantasy, feminist, gay, lesbian, historical, humor, literary, mainstream, contemporary, womens, military, war, multicultural, mystery, romance, short story collections, spiritual, suspense, translation, general fiction. Agented submissions only.

Ⓐ BALZER & BRAY

HarperCollins Children's Books, 10 E. 53rd St., New York NY 10022. **Website:** www.harpercollinschildrens.com. Estab. 2008. "We publish bold, creative, groundbreaking picture books and novels that appeal directly to kids in a fresh way." **Publishes 10 titles/ year. Offers advances. Pays illustrators by the project.** Publishes book 18 months after acceptance.

NONFICTION Subjects include animals, cooking, dance, environment, history, multicultural, music, nature, science, social sciences, sports. "We will publish very few nonfiction titles, maybe 1-2 per year." Agented submissions only.

FICTION Picture Books, Young Readers: adventure, animal, anthology, concept, contemporary, fantasy, history, humor, multicultural, nature/environment, poetry, science fiction, special needs, sports, suspense. Middle readers, young adults/teens: adventure, animal, anthology, contemporary, fantasy, history, humor, multicultural, nature/environment, poetry, science fiction, special needs, sports, suspense. Agented submissions only.

Ⓐ BANCROFT PRESS

P.O. Box 65360, Baltimore MD 21209-9945. (410)358-0658. **Fax:** (410)764-1967. **E-mail:** bruceb@bancroft-press.com. **Website:** www.bancroftpress.com. **Contact:** Bruce Bortz, editor/publisher (health, investments, politics, history, humor, literary novels, mystery/thrillers, chick lit, young adult). Publishes hardcover and trade paperback originals. "Bancroft Press is a general trade publisher. We publish young adult fiction and adult fiction, as well as occasional nonfiction. Our only mandate is 'books that enlighten.'" **Publishes 4-6 titles/year. Pays 6-8% royalty. Pays various royalties on retail price. Pays $750 advance.** Publishes book up to 3 years after acceptance of ms. after acceptance of ms. Accepts simultaneous submissions. Responds in 6-12 months. Guidelines online.

NONFICTION Subjects include business, economics, government, politics, health, medicine, money, finance, regional, sports, women's issues, women's studies, popular culture. "We advise writers to visit the website." All quality books on any subject of interest to the publisher. Submit proposal package, outline, 5 sample chapters, competition/market survey.

FICTION Subjects include ethnic, general, feminist, gay, lesbian, historical, humor, literary, mainstream, contemporary, military, war, mystery, amateur sleuth, cozy, police procedural, private eye/hardboiled, regional, science fiction, hard science fiction/technological, soft/sociological, translation, frontier sage, traditional, young adult, historical, problem novels, series, thrillers. "Our current focuses are young adult fiction, women's fiction, and literary fiction." Submit complete ms.

TIPS "We advise writers to visit our website and to be familiar with our previous work. Patience is the number one attribute contributors must have. It takes us a very long time to get through submitted material, because we are such a small company. Also, we only publish 4-6 books per year, so it may take a long time for your optioned book to be published. We like to be able to market our books to be used in schools and in libraries. We prefer fiction that bucks trends and moves in a new direction. We are especially interested in mysteries and humor (especially humorous mysteries)."

Ⓐⓐ BANTAM BOOKS

Imprint of Random House, Inc., 1745 Broadway, New York NY 10019. (212)782-9000. **Website:** www.bantam dell.atrandom.com.

○ *Not seeking mss at this time.*

Ⓐⓐ BANTAM DELACORTE DELL BOOKS FOR YOUNG READERS

Random House Children's Publishing, Random House, Inc., 1745 Broadway, New York NY 10019. (212)782-9000. **Fax:** (212)782-8234. **Website:** www. randomhouse.com/kids. Publishes hardcover, trade paperback and mass market paperback series originals, trade paperback reprints. Bantam Delacorte Dell Books for Young Readers publishes award-winning books by distinguished authors and the most promising new writers. The best way to break into this market is through its 2 contests, the Delacrote/Yearling Contest and the Delacorte Press Contest for a First Young Adult Novel. **Publishes approximately 300 titles/year. Pays royalty.**

IMPRINTS Delacorte Press; Doubleday; Laurel Leaf (YA); Yearling (middle grade).

NONFICTION Bantam Delacorte Dell Books for Young Readers publishes a very limited number of nonfiction titles. *No unsolicited mss or queries.*

FICTION Subjects include adventure, fantasy, historical, humor, juvenile, mainstream, contemporary, mystery, picture books, suspense, chapter books, middle-grade. *No unsolicited mss or queri*

BARRICADE BOOKS, INC.

185 Bridge Plaza N., Suite 309, Fort Lee NJ 07024. (201)944-7600. **Fax:** (201)917-4951. **Website:** www. barricadebooks.com. **Contact:** Carole Stuart, publisher. Estab. 1991. Publishes hardcover and trade paperback originals, trade paperback reprints. "Barricade Books publishes nonfiction, mostly of the controversial type, and books we can promote with authors who can talk about their topics on radio and television and to the press." **Publishes 12 titles/year. 200 queries received/year. 100 mss received/year. 80% of books from first-time authors. 50% from unagented writers. Pays 10-12% royalty on retail price for hardcover. Pays advance.** Publishes book 18 months after acceptance. Responds in 1 month to queries.

NONFICTION Subjects include business, economics, ethnic, gay, lesbian, government, politics, health, medicine, history, nature, environment, psychology, sociology, true crime. We look for quality nonfiction mss—preferably with a controversial lean. Query with SASE. Submit outline, 1-2 sample chapters. Material will not be returned or responded to without SASE. We do not accept proposals on disk or via e-mail. Reviews artwork/photos. Send photocopies.

TIPS "Do your homework. Visit bookshops to find publishers who are doing the kinds of books you want to write. Always submit to a person—not just 'Editor.'"

BASIC BOOKS

Perseus Books, 387 Park Ave. S., 12th Floor, New York NY 10016. (212)340-8100. **Website:** www.basicbooks. com. **Contact:** Editor. Estab. 1952. Publishes hardcover and trade paperback originals and reprints. We want serious nonfiction by leading scholars, intellectuals, and journalists. No poetry, romance, children's books, conventional thrillers, or conventional horror. Accepts simultaneous submissions. Responds in at least 3 months to queries. Book catalog available free. Guidelines available free.

NONFICTION Subjects include history, psychology, sociology, politics, current affairs. Submit proposal package, outline, sample chapters, TOC, cv, SASE. No e-mail or disk submissions.

BAYLOR UNIVERSITY PRESS

One Bear Place 97363, Waco TX 76798. (254)710-3164. **Fax:** (254)710-3440. **E-mail:** carey_newman@baylor. edu. **Website:** www.baylorpress.com. **Contact:** Dr. Carey C. Newman, director. Estab. 1897. Publishes hardcover and trade paperback originals. "We publish contemporary and historical scholarly works about culture, religion, politics, science, and the arts." **Publishes 30 titles/year. Pays 10% royalty on wholesale price.** Publishes book 1 year after acceptance. Accepts simultaneous submissions. Responds in 2 months to proposals. Guidelines online.

NONFICTION Submit outline, 1-3 sample chapters via e-mail.

BAYWOOD PUBLISHING CO., INC.

26 Austin Ave., P.O. Box 337, Amityville NY 11701. (631)691-1270. **Fax:** (631)691-1770. **Website:** www. baywood.com. **Contact:** Stuart Cohen, managing editor. Estab. 1964. "Baywood Publishing publishes original and innovative books in the humanities and social sciences, including areas such as health scienc-

es, gerontology, death and bereavement, psychology, technical communications, and archaeology." **Pays 7-15% royalty on retail price.** Publishes book within 12 months of acceptance. after acceptance of ms. Book catalog and ms guidelines free or online.

NONFICTION Subjects include anthropology, archaeology, computers, electronics, education, health, environment, psychology, sociology, women's issues,, gerontology, technical writing, death and bereavement, environmental issues, recreational mathematics, health policy, labor relations, workplace rights. Submit proposal package.

BEACON PRESS

25 Beacon St., Boston MA 02108-2892. (617)742-2110. **Fax:** (617)723-3097. **Website:** www.beacon.org. **Contact:** Gayatri Patnaik, senior editor (African-American, Asian-American, Latino, Native American, Jewish, and gay and lesbian studies, anthropology); Joanne Wyckoff, executive editor (child and family issues, environmental concerns); Amy Caldwell, senior editor (poetry, gender studies, gay/lesbian studies, and Cuban studies); Christopher Vyce, assistant editor; Brian Halley, assistant editor. Estab. 1854. Publishes hardcover originals and paperback reprints. Beacon Press publishes general interest books that promote the following values: the inherent worth and dignity of every person; justice, equity, and compassion in human relations; acceptance of one another; a free and responsible search for truth and meaning; the goal of world community with peace, liberty, and justice for all; respect for the interdependent web of all existence. Currently emphasizing innovative nonfiction writing by people of all colors. De-emphasizing poetry, children's stories, art books, self-help. **Publishes 60 titles/year. 10% of books from first-time authors. Pays royalty. Pays advance.** Accepts simultaneous submissions. Responds in 3 months to queries.

IMPRINTS Bluestreak Series (innovative literary writing by women of color).

NONFICTION Subjects include anthropology, archeology, child guidance, education, ethnic, gay, lesbian, nature, environment, philosophy, religion, women's issues, women's studies, world affairs. General nonfiction including works of original scholarship, religion, women's studies, philosophy, current affairs, anthropology, environmental concerns, African-American, Asian-American, Native American, Latino, and Jew-

ish studies, gay and lesbian studies, education, legal studies, child and family issues, Irish studies. *Strongly prefers agented submissions.* Query with SASE. Submit outline, sample chapters, résumé, CV. *Strongly prefers referred submissions, on exclusive.*

TIPS "We probably accept only 1 or 2 mss from an unpublished pool of 4,000 submissions/year. No fiction, children's books, or poetry submissions invited. An academic affiliation is helpful."

BEARMANOR MEDIA

P.O. Box 1129, Duncan OK 73534. (580)252-3547. **Fax:** (814)690-1559. **E-mail:** books@benohmart.com. **Website:** www.bearmanormedia.com. **Contact:** Ben Ohmart, publisher. Estab. 2000. Publishes trade paperback originals and reprints. **Publishes 70 titles/year. 90% of books from first-time authors. 90% from unagented writers. Negotiable per project. Pays upon acceptance.** Accepts simultaneous submissions. Responds only if interested. Book catalog vailable online, or free with a 9 x 12 SASE submission.

NONFICTION Subjects include old-time radio, voice actors, old movies, classic television. Query with SASE. E-mail queries preferred. Submit proposal package, outline, list of credits on the subject.

TIPS "My readers love the past. Radio, old movies, old television. My own tastes include voice actors and scripts, especially of radio and television no longer available. I prefer books on subjects that haven't previously been covered as full books. It doesn't matter to me if you're a first-time author or have a track record. Just know your subject!"

BEAR STAR PRESS

185 Hollow Oak Dr., Cohasset CA 95973. (530)891-0360. **Website:** www.bearstarpress.com. **Contact:** Beth Spencer, publisher/editor. Estab. 1996. Publishes trade paperback originals. "Bear Star is committed to publishing the best poetry it can attract. Each year it sponsors the Dorothy Brunsman contest, open to poets from Western and Pacific states. From time to time we add to our list other poets from our target area whose work we admire." **Publishes 1-3 titles/year. Pays $1,000, and 25 copies to winner of annual Dorothy Brunsman contest.** Publishes book 9 months after acceptance. Accepts simultaneous submissions. Responds in 2 weeks to queries. Guidelines online.

FICTION Use our Online form. Mss should be between 50 and 65 pages in length. All work must be original and accompanied by a $20 reading fee. Previously published poems can be included in your ms if you retain the copyright (this is standard).

POETRY Wants well-crafted poems. No restrictions as to form, subject matter, style, or purpose. "Poets should enter our annual book competition. Other books are occasionally solicited by publisher, sometimes from among contestants who didn't win." Query and submit complete ms. Online form.

TIPS "Send your best work, consider its arrangement. A 'wow' poem early keeps me reading."

BEHRMAN HOUSE INC.

11 Edison Place, Springfield NJ 07081. (973)379-7200. **Fax:** (973)379-7280. **E-mail:** customersupport@behrmanhouse.com. **Website:** www.behrmanhouse.com. Estab. 1921. Publishes books on all aspects of Judaism: history, cultural, textbooks, holidays. "Behrman House publishes quality books of Jewish content—history, Bible, philosophy, holidays, ethics—for children and adults." **12% of books from first-time authors. Pays authors royalty of 3-10% based on retail price or buys ms outright for $1,000-5,000. Offers advance. Pays illustrators by the project (range: $500-5,000).** Publishes book 18 months after acceptance. Accepts simultaneous submissions. Responds in 1 month to queries; 2 months to mss. Book catalog free on request.

NONFICTION All levels: Judaism, Jewish educational textbooks. Average word length: young reader—1,200; middle reader—2,000; young adult—4,000. Submit outline/synopsis and sample chapters.

FICTION Submit outline/synopsis and sample chapters.

TIPS Looking for "religious school texts" with Judaic themes or general trade Judaica.

BELLEVUE LITERARY PRESS

New York University School of Medicine, Dept. of Medicine, NYU School of Medicine, 550 First Avenue, OBV 612, New York NY 10016. (212) 263-7802. **E-mail:** BLPsubmissions@gmail.com. **Website:** blpress.org. **Contact:** Erika Goldman, publisher/editorial director. Estab. 2005. "Publishes literary and authoritative fiction and nonfiction at the nexus of the arts and the sciences, with a special focus on medicine. As our authors explore cultural and historical representations of the human body, illness, and health, they address the impact of scientific and medical practice on the individual and society."

NONFICTION "If you have a completed ms, a sample of a ms or a proposal that fits our mission as a press feel free to submit it to us by postal mail. Please keep in mind that at this time we are unable to return mss. We will also accept short proposals by e-mail."

FICTION Subjects include literary. Submit complete ms.

TIPS "We are a project of New York University's School of Medicine and while our standards reflect NYU's excellence in scholarship, humanistic medicine, and science, our authors need not be affiliated with NYU. We are not a university press and do not receive any funding from NYU. Our publishing operations are financed exclusively by foundation grants, private donors, and book sales revenue."

BENBELLA BOOKS

10300 N. Central Expressway, Suite 530, Dallas TX 75231. **E-mail:** glenn@benbellabooks.com. **Website:** www.benbellabooks.com. **Contact:** Glenn Yeffeth, publisher. Estab. 2001. Publishes hardcover and trade paperback originals. **Publishes 30-40 titles/year. Pays 6-15% royalty on retail price.** Publishes book 10 months after acceptance. Accepts simultaneous submissions. Guidelines online.

NONFICTION Subjects include pop contemporary culture, cooking, foods, nutrition, health, medicine, literary criticism, money, finance, science. Submit proposal package, including: outline, 2 sample chapters (via e-mail).

BENTLEY PUBLISHERS

1734 Massachusetts Ave., Cambridge MA 02138. (617)547-4170. **Fax:** (617)876-9235. **E-mail:** michael.bentley@bentleypublishers.com. **Website:** www.bentleypublishers.com. **Contact:** Michael Bentley, president. Estab. 1950. Publishes hardcover and trade paperback originals and reprints. "Bentley Publishers publishes books for automotive enthusiasts. We are interested in books that showcase good research, strong illustrations, and valuable technical information." Automotive subjects only. Query with SASE. Submit sample chapters, bio, synopsis, target market. Reviews artwork/photos. Book catalog and ms guidelines online and with 9x12 SASE with 4 first-class stamps.

NONFICTION Subjects include Automotive subjects only. Query with SASE. Submit sample chapters, bio, synopsis, target market. Rreviews artwork/photos.

TIPS "Our audience is composed of serious, intelligent automobile, sports car, and racing enthusiasts, automotive technicians and high-performance tuners."

⊘⊘ BERKLEY BOOKS

Penguin Group (USA) Inc., 375 Hudson St., New York NY 10014. **Website:** us.penguingroup.com/. **Contact:** Leslie Gelbman, president and publisher. Estab. 1955. Publishes paperback and mass market originals and reprints. The Berkley Publishing Group publishes a variety of general nonfiction and fiction including the traditional categories of romance, mystery and science fiction. **Publishes 500 titles/year.**

IMPRINTS Ace; Berkley; Jove.

"Due to the high volume of mss received, most Penguin Group (USA) Inc. imprints do not normally accept unsolicited mss. The preferred and standard method for having mss considered for publication by a major publisher is to submit them through an established literary agent."

NONFICTION Subjects include business, economics, child guidance, creative nonfiction, gay, lesbian, health, medicine, history, New Age, psychology, true crime, job-seeking communication. No memoirs or personal stories. Prefers agented submissions.

FICTION Subjects include adventure, historical, literary, mystery, romance, spiritual, suspense, western, young adult. No occult fiction. Prefers agented submissions.

BERRETT-KOEHLER PUBLISHERS, INC.

235 Montgomery St., Suite 650, San Francisco CA 94104. (415)288-0260. **Fax:** (415)362-2512. **E-mail:** bkpub@bkpub.com. **Website:** www.bkconnection.com. **Contact:** Jeevan Sivasubramaniam, executive managing editor. Publishes hardcover & trade paperback originals, mass market paperback originals, hardcover & trade paperback reprints. "Berrett-Koehler Publishers' mission is to publish books that support the movement toward a world that works for all. Our titles promote positive change at personal, organizational and societal levels." Please see proposal guidelines online. **Publishes 40 titles/year. 1,300 queries received/year. 800 mss received/year. 20-30% of books from first-time authors. 70% from unagented writers. Pays 10-20% royalty.** Publishes book 10 months after acceptance. Accepts simulta-

neous submissions. Responds in 1 month to queries, proposals and mss. Catalog and guidelines online.

NONFICTION Subjects include business, economics, community, government, politics, New Age, spirituality. Submit proposal package, outline, bio, 1-2 sample chapters. Hard-copy proposals only. Do not e-mail, fax, or phone please. Reviews artwork/photos. Send photocopies or originals with SASE.

TIPS "Our audience is business leaders. Use common sense, do your research."

⊘ BETHANY HOUSE PUBLISHERS

Division of Baker Publishing Group, 6030 E. Fulton Rd., Ada MI 49301. (616)676-9185. **Fax:** (616)676-9573. **Website:** bakerpublishinggroup.com/bethanyhouse. Estab. 1956. Publishes hardcover and trade paperback originals, mass market paperback reprints. Bethany House Publishers specializes in books that communicate Biblical truth and assist people in both spiritual and practical areas of life. While we do not accept unsolicited queries or proposals via telephone or e-mail, we will consider 1-page queries sent by fax and directed to adult nonfiction, adult fiction, or young adult/children. **Publishes 90-100 titles/year. 2% of books from first-time authors. 50% from unagented writers. Pays royalty on net price. Pays advance.** Publishes book Publishes a book 1 year after acceptance. Accepts simultaneous submissions. Responds in 3 months to queries. Book catalog for 9 x 12 envelope and 5 first-class stamps. Guidelines online.

All unsolicited mss returned unopened.

NONFICTION Subjects include child guidance, Biblical disciplines, personal and corporate renewal, emerging generations, devotional, marriage and family, applied theology, inspirational.

FICTION Subjects include historical, young adult, contemporary.

TIPS "Bethany House Publishers' publishing program relates Biblical truth to all areas of life—whether in the framework of a well-told story, of a challenging book for spiritual growth, or of a Bible reference work. We are seeking high-quality fiction and nonfiction that will inspire and challenge our audience."

BETTERWAY HOME BOOKS

Imprint of F+W Media, Inc., 10151 Carver Rd., Suite 200, Cincinnati OH 45242. **E-mail:** jacqueline.musser@fwmedia.com. **Website:** www.betterwaybooks.com. **Contact:** Jacqueline Musser, senior content producer. Publishes trade paperback and hardcover originals. **Publishes 9 titles/year. 6 queries received/year. 60% of books from first-time authors. 95% from unagented writers. Pays 8-10% royalty on wholesale price. Pays $2,500-3,000 advance.** Publishes book 18 months after acceptance. Accepts simultaneous submissions. Responds in 3 month to queries and proposals.

NONFICTION Subjects include gardening, house and home, self-sufficiency, preparedness, home organization, homemaking, simple living, homesteading skills, personal finance. Query with SASE. Submit proposal package, outline, 1 sample chapter. Reviews artwork/photos. Send photocopies and PDFs (if submitting electronically).

TIPS "Looking for authors with a strong web following in their book topic."

BKMK PRESS

University of Missouri - Kansas City, 5101 Rockhill Rd., Kansas City MO 64110-2499. (816)235-2558. **Fax:** (816)235-2611. **E-mail:** bkmk@umkc.edu. **Website:** newletters.org. **Contact:** Ben Furnish, managing editor. Estab. 1971. Publishes trade paperback originals. "BkMk Press publishes fine literature. Reading period January-June." **Publishes 4/year titles/year.** Accepts simultaneous submissions. Responds in 4-6 months to queries. Guidelines online.

NONFICTION Creative nonfiction essays. Submit 25-50 sample pages and SASE.

FICTION Subjects include literary, short story collections. Query with SASE.

POETRY Submit 10 sample poems and SASE.

TIPS "We skew toward readers of literature, particularly contemporary writing. Because of our limited number of titles published per year, we discourage apprentice writers or `scattershot' submissions."

BLACK DOME PRESS CORP.

649 Delaware Ave., Delmar NY 12054. (518)439-6512. **Fax:** (518)439-1309. **E-mail:** blackdomep@aol.com. **Website:** www.blackdomepress.com. Estab. 1990. Publishes cloth and trade paperback originals and reprints. Accepts simultaneous submissions. Book catalog and Guidelines online.

Do not send the entire work. Mail a cover letter, table of contents, introduction, sample chapter (or 2), and your CV or brief biography to the Editor. Please do not send computer disks or submit your proposal via e-mail. If your book will include illustrations, please send us copies of sample illustrations. Do not send originals.

NONFICTION Subjects include history, nature, environment, photography, regional, New York state, Native Americans, grand hotels, genealogy, colonial life, French & Indian War (NYS), American Revolution (NYS), quilting, architecture, railroads, hiking and kayaking guidebooks. New York state regional material only. Submit proposal package, outline, bio.

TIPS "Our audience is comprised of New York state residents, tourists, and visitors."

BLACK HERON PRESS

P.O. Box 13396, Mill Creek WA 98082. **Website:** www.blackheronpress.com. **Contact:** Jerry Gold, publisher. Estab. 1984. Publishes hardcover and trade paperback originals, trade paperback reprints. "Black Heron Press publishes primarily literary fiction." **Publishes 4 titles/year. 1,500 queries received/year. 50% of books from first-time authors. 90% from unagented writers. Pays 8% royalty on retail price.** Publishes book 2 years after acceptance. Accepts simultaneous submissions. Responds in 6 months to queries and mss. Catalog available online and for 6x9 SAE with 3 first-class stamps. Guidelines available for #10 SASE.

NONFICTION Subjects include military, war. Submit proposal package, include cover letter and first 30-50 pages of your completed novel. "We do not review artwork."

FICTION Subjects include confession, erotica, literary (regardless of genre), military, war, sci-fi, young adult, Some science fiction—not fantasy, not Dungeons & Dragons—that makes or implies a social statement. "All of our fiction is character driven." "We don't want to see fiction written for the mass market. If it sells to the mass market, fine, but we don't see ourselves as a commercial press." Submit proposal package, including cover letter & first 40-50 pages pages of your completed novel.

TIPS "Our Readers love good fiction—they are scattered among all social classes, ethnic groups, and zip code areas. If you can't read our books, at least check out our titles on our website."

BLACK LAWRENCE PRESS

326 Bigham St., Pittsburgh PA 15211. **E-mail:** editors@blacklawrencepress.com. **Website:** www.blacklawrencepress.com. **Contact:** Diane Goettel, executive editor. Estab. 2003. Black Lawrence press seeks to publish intriguing books of literature—novels, short

story collections, poetry collections, chapbooks, anthologies, and creative nonfiction. Will also publish the occasional translation from German. Publishes 15-20 books/year, mostly poetry and fiction. Mss are selected through open submission and competition. Books are 20-400 pages, offset-printed or high-quality POD, perfect-bound, with 4-color cover. **Accepts submissions during the months of June and November. Pays royalties.** Responds in 6 months to mss.

FICTION Subjects include literary, short story collections, translation. Submit complete ms.

POETRY Submit complete ms.

BLACK MOUNTAIN PRESS

P.O. Box 9907, Asheville NC 28815. (828)273-3332. **E-mail:** jackmoe@theBlackMountainPress.com. **Website:** www.theBlackMountainPress.com. **Contact:** Jack Moe, editor (how-to, poetry); James Robiningski (short story collections, novels). Estab. 1994. Publishes hardcover, trade paperback, and electronic originals. **Publishes 4 titles/year. 150 mss received/year. 90% of books from first-time authors. 100% from unagented writers. Pays 5-10% royalty on retail price. Pays $100-500 advance.** Publishes book 5 months after acceptance. Accepts simultaneous submissions. Responds in 4-6 months to mss. Book catalog and ms guidelines online.

NONFICTION Subjects include architecture, art, language, literature, sports. "We are concentrating more on literary projects for the next 2 years." Submit complete ms. Reviews artwork. Send digital photos only on CD or DVD.

FICTION Subjects include comic books, experimental, literary, poetry, poetry in translation, short story collections, graphic novels. "Creative literary fiction and poetry or collection of short stories are wanted for the next few years." Submit complete ms.

POETRY Submit complete ms.

TIPS "Don't be afraid of sending your anti-government, anti-religion, anti-art, anti-literature, experimental, avant-garde efforts here. But don't send your work before it's fully cooked, we do, however, enjoy fresh, natural, and sometimes even raw material, just don't send in anything that is "glowing" unless it was savaged from a FoxNews book-burning event."

BLACK OCEAN

P.O. Box 52030, Boston MA 02205. **Fax:** (617)849-5678. **E-mail:** carrie@blackocean.org. **Website:** www.blackocean.org. **Contact:** Carrie Olivia Adams, poetry editor. Estab. 2006. **Publishes 3 titles/year.** Responds in 6 months to mss.

POETRY Wants poetry that is well-considered, risks itself, and by its beauty and/or bravery disturbs a tiny corner of the universe. Mss are selected through open submission. Books are 60+ pages. Book/chapbook mss may include previously published poems. "We have an open submission period in June of each year; specific guidelines are updated and posted on our website in the months preceding."

BLACK VELVET SEDUCTIONS PUBLISHING

1015 C Ave., Vinton IA 52349. (319)241-6556. **E-mail:** lauriesanders@blackvelvetseductions.com. **Website:** www.blackvelvetseductions.com. **Contact:** Laurie Sanders, acquisitions editor. Estab. 2005. Publishes trade paperback and electronic originals and reprints. "We publish two types of material: 1) romance novels and short stories and 2) romantic stories involving spanking between consenting adults. We look for well-crafted stories with a high degree of emotional impact. No first person point of view. All material must be in third person point of view." Publishes trade paperback and electronic originals. "We have a high interest in republishing backlist titles in electronic and trade paperback formats once rights have reverted to the author." Accepts only complete mss. Query with SASE. Submit complete ms. **Publishes about 20 titles/year. 500 queries received/year. 1,000 mss received/year. 90% of books from first-time authors. 100% from unagented writers. Pays 10% royalty for paperbacks; 50% royalty for electronic books.** Publishes book 6-12 months after acceptance. Accepts simultaneous submissions. Responds in 6 months to queries; 8 months to proposals; 8-12 months to mss. Catalog free or online. Guidelines online.

IMPRINTS Forbidden Experiences (erotic romance of all types); Tender Destinations (sweet romance of all types); Sensuous Journeys (sensuous romance of all types); Amorous Adventures (romantic suspense); Erotic relationship stories (erotic short stories, usually including spanking, with a romantic relationship at their core).

FICTION Subjects include romance, erotic romance, historical romance, multicultural romance, romance, short story collections romantic stories, romantic suspense, western romance. All stories must have a strong romance element. "There are very few sexual taboos in our erotic line. We tend to give our authors the widest latitude. If it is safe, sane, and consensual we will allow our authors latitude to show us the eroticism. However, we will not consider mss with any of the following: bestiality (sex with animals), necrophilia (sex with dead people), pedophillia (sex with children)." Only accepts electronic submissions.

TIPS "We publish romance and erotic romance. We look for books written in very deep point of view. Shallow point of view remains the number one reason we reject mss in which the storyline generally works."

JOHN F. BLAIR, PUBLISHER

1406 Plaza Dr., Winston-Salem NC 27103. (336)768-1374. **Fax:** (336)768-9194. **E-mail:** editorial@blairpub.com. **Website:** www.blairpub.com. **Contact:** Carolyn Sakowski, president. Estab. 1954. **Pays royalties. Pays negotiable advance.** Publishes book 18 months after acceptance. Responds in 3-6 months.

FICTION "We specialize in regional books, with an emphasis on nonfiction categories such as history, travel, folklore, and biography. We publish only one or two works of fiction each year. Fiction submitted to us should have some connection with the Southeast. We do not publish children's books, poetry, or category fiction such as romances, science fiction, or spy thrillers. We do not publish collections of short stories, essays, or newspaper columns." Accepts unsolicited mss. Any fiction submitted should have some connection with the Southeast, either through setting or author's background. Send a cover letter, giving a synopsis of the book. Include the first 2 chapters (at least 50 pages) of the ms. "You may send the entire ms if you wish. If you choose to send only samples, please include the projected word length of your book and estimated completion date in your cover letter. Send a biography of the author, including publishing credits and credentials."

TIPS "We are primarily interested in nonfiction titles. Most of our titles have a tie-in with North Carolina or the southeastern United States, we do not accept short-story collections. Please enclose a cover letter and outline with the ms. We prefer to review queries before we are sent complete mss. Queries should include an approximate word count."

BLAZEVOX [BOOKS]

131 Euclid Ave., Kenmore NY 14217. **E-mail:** editor@blazevox.org. **Website:** www.blazevox.org. **Contact:** Geoffrey Gatza, editor/publisher. Estab. 2005. "We are a major publishing presence specializing in innovative fictions and wide-ranging fields of innovative forms of poetry and prose. Our goal is to publish works that are challenging, creative, attractive, and yet affordable to individual readers. Articles of submission depend on many criteria, but overall items submitted must conform to one ethereal trait, your work must not suck. This put plainly, bad art should be punished; we will not promote it. However, all submissions will be reviewed and the author will receive feedback. We are human too." **Pays 10% royalties on fiction and poetry books, based on net receipts. This amount may be split across multiple contributors.** "We do not pay advances." Guidelines online.

FICTION Subjects include experimental, short story collections. Submit complete ms via e-mail.

POETRY Submit complete ms via e-mail.

TIPS "We actively contract and support authors who tour, read and perform their work, play an active part of the contemporary literary scene, and seek a readership."

BLOOMBERG PRESS

Imprint of John Wiley & Sons, Professional Development, 111 River St., Hoboken NJ 07030. **Website:** www.wiley.com. Estab. 1995. Publishes hardcover and trade paperback originals. Bloomberg Press publishes professional books for practitioners in the financial markets. We publish commercially successful, very high-quality books that stand out clearly from the competition by their brevity, ease of use, sophistication, and abundance of practical tips and strategies; books readers need, will use, and appreciate. **Publishes 18-22 titles/year. 200 queries received/year. 20 mss received/year. 45% from unagented writers. Pays negotiable, competitive royalty. Pays negotiable advance for trade books.** Publishes book 9 months after acceptance. Accepts simultaneous submissions.

NONFICTION Subjects include business, economics, money, finance, professional books on finance, investment and financial services, and books for financial advisors. We are looking for authorities and for experienced service journalists. Do not send us unfocused books containing general information already covered by books in the marketplace. We do not publish business, management, leadership, or career books. Submit outline, sample chapters, SAE with sufficient postage. Submit complete ms.

TIPS *Bloomberg Professional Library*: Audience is upscale, financial professionals—traders, dealers, brokers, planners and advisors, financial managers, money managers, company executives, sophisticated investors. Authors are experienced financial journalists and/or financial professionals nationally prominent in their specialty for some time who have proven an ability to write a successful book. Research Bloomberg and look at our books in a library or bookstore, and peruse our website.

Ⓐ BLOOMSBURY CHILDREN'S BOOKS

Imprint of Bloomsbury USA, 1385 Broadway, 5th Floor, New York NY 10008. **Website:** www.bloomsbury.com/us/childrens. **Contact:** Catherine Onder, editorial director; Caroline Abbey, senior director; Mary Kate Castellani, senior director; Donna Mark, art director. **Publishes 60 titles/year. 25% of books from first-time authors. Pays royalty. Pays advance.** Accepts simultaneous submissions. Responds in 6 months. Catalog and guidelines online.

◯ No phone calls or e-mails. *Agented submissions only.*

FICTION Subjects include adventure, fantasy, historical, humor, juvenile, multicultural, mystery, picture books, poetry, science fiction, sports, suspense, young adult, animal, anthology, concept, contemporary, folktales, problem novels. Agented submissions only.

BLUEBRIDGE

Imprint of United Tribes Media, Inc., P.O. Box 601, Katonah NY 10536. (914)301-5901. **E-mail:** janguerth@bluebridgebooks.com. **Website:** www.bluebridgebooks.com. **Contact:** Jan-Erik Guerth, publisher (general nonfiction). Estab. 2004. Publishes hardcover and trade paperback originals. BlueBridge is an independent publisher of international nonfiction based near New York City. The BlueBridge mission: Thoughtful Books for Mind and Spirit. **Publishes 6 titles/year. 1,000 queries received/year. Pays variable advance.** Accepts simultaneous submissions. Responds in 1 month to queries and proposals.

NONFICTION Subjects include Americana, anthropology, archaeology, art, architecture, business, economics, child guidance, contemporary culture, creative nonfiction, ethnic, gardening, gay, lesbian, government, politics, health, medicine, history, humanities, language, literature, literary criticism, multicultural, music, dance, nature, environment, philosophy, psychology, religion, science, social sciences, sociol-

ogy, spirituality, travel, women's issues, world affairs. Query with SASE or preferably by e-mail.

TIPS "We target a broad general nonfiction audience."

BLUE LIGHT PRESS

1563 45th Ave., San Francisco CA 94122. **E-mail:** bluelightpress@aol.com. **Website:** www.bluelightpress.com. **Contact:** Diane Frank, chief editor. Estab. 1988. "We like poems that are imagistic, emotionally honest, and push the edge—where the writer pushes through the imagery to a deeper level of insight and understanding. No rhymed poetry." Has published poetry by Alice Rogoff, Tom Centolella, Rustin Larson, Tony Krunk, Lisha Adela Garcia, Becky Sakellariou, and Christopher Buckley. "Books are elegantly designed and artistic." Chapbooks are 30 pages, digest-sized, professionally printed, with original cover art.

POETRY "We have an online poetry workshop with a wonderful group of American and international poets—open to new members 3 times/year. Send an e-mail for info. We work in person with local poets, and will edit/critique poems by mail; $40 for 4 poems." Does not accept e-mail submissions. Deadlines: January 30 full-sized ms. and June 15 for chapbooks. "Read our guidelines before sending your ms."

BLUE MOUNTAIN PRESS

Blue Mountain Arts, Inc., P.O. Box 4219, Boulder CO 80306. (800)525-0642. **E-mail:** BMPbooks@sps.com. **Website:** www.sps.com. **Contact:** Patti Wayant, editorial director. Estab. 1971. Publishes hardcover originals, trade paperback originals, electronic originals. **Pays royalty on wholesale price.** Publishes book 6-8 months after acceptance. Accepts simultaneous submissions. Responds in 2-4 months to queries, mss, and proposals. Guidelines available by e-mail.

◯ *"Please note: We are not accepting works of fiction, rhyming poetry, children's books, chapbooks, or memoirs."*

NONFICTION , Personal growth, teens/tweens, family, relationships, motivational, and inspirational but not religious. Query with SASE. Submit proposal package including outline and 3-5 sample chapters.

POETRY "We publish poetry appropriate for gift books, self-help books, and personal growth books. We do not publish chapbooks or literary poetry." Query. Submit 10+ sample poems.

BLUE POPPY PRESS

Imprint of Blue Poppy Enterprises, Inc., 1990 57th Court Unit A, Boulder CO 80301. (303)447-8372. **Fax:**

(303)245-8362. **E-mail:** info@bluepoppy.com. **Web-site:** www.bluepoppy.com. **Contact:** Bob Flaws, editor-in-chief. Estab. 1981. Publishes hardcover and trade paperback originals. **Publishes 3-4 titles/year. 50 queries received/year. 5-10 mss received/year. 30-40% of books from first-time authors. 100% from unagented writers. Pays 8-12% royalty.** Publishes book 1 year after acceptance. Responds in 1 month to queries. Book catalog available free. Guidelines online.

○ "Blue Poppy Press is dedicated to expanding and improving the English language literature on acupuncture and Asian medicine for both professional practitioners and lay readers."

NONFICTION Subjects include ethnic, health, medicine. We only publish books on acupuncture and Oriental medicine by authors who can read Chinese and have a minimum of 5 years clinical experience. We also require all our authors to use Wiseman's *Glossary of Chinese Medical Terminology* as their standard for technical terms. Query with SASE. Submit outline, 1 sample chapter.

TIPS "Audience is practicing acupuncturists interested in alternatives in healthcare, preventive medicine, Chinese philosophy, and medicine."

BLUE RIVER PRESS

Cardinal Publishers Group, 2402 N. Shadeland Ave., Suite A, Indianapolis IN 46219. (317)352-8200. **Fax:** (317)352-8202. **E-mail:** tdoherty@cardinalpub.com. **Website:** www.cardinalpub.com. **Contact:** Tom Doherty, president (adult nonfiction). Estab. 2000. Publishes hardcover, trade paperback and electronic originals and reprints. **Publishes 8-12 titles/year. 200 queries received/year. 25% of books from first-time authors. 80% from unagented writers. Pays 10-15% on wholesale price. Outright purchase of $500-5,000. Offers advance up to $5,000.** Publishes book 6 months after acceptance. Accepts simultaneous submissions. Responds to queries in 2 months. Book catalog for #10 SASE or online. Guidelines available by e-mail.

NONFICTION "Most non-religious adult nonfiction subjects are of interest. We like concepts that can develop into series products. Most of our books are paperback or hardcover in the categories of sport, business, health, fitness, lifestyle, yoga, and educational books for teachers and students."

BNA BOOKS

Imprint of The Bureau of National Affairs, Inc., 1801 S. Bell St., Arlington VA 22202. (703)341-5777. **Fax:** (703)341-1610. **E-mail:** books@bna.com. **Website:** www.bnabooks.com. **Contact:** Jim Fattibene, acquisitions manager. Estab. 1929. Publishes hardcover and softcover originals. Accepts simultaneous submissions. Catalog and guidelines online.

○ BNA Books publishes professional reference books written by lawyers, for lawyers.

NONFICTION No fiction, biographies, bibliographies, cookbooks, religion books, humor, or trade books. Submit detailed TOC or outline, cv, intended market, estimated word length.

TIPS "Our audience is made up of practicing lawyers and law librarians. We look for authoritative and comprehensive treatises that can be supplemented or revised every year or 2 on legal subjects of interest to those audiences."

BOA EDITIONS, LTD.

250 N. Goodman St., Suite 306, Rochester NY 14607. (585)546-3410. **Fax:** (585)546-3913. **E-mail:** conners@boaeditions.org; hall@boaeditions.org. **Website:** www.boaeditions.org. **Contact:** Peter Conners, editor. Melissa Hall, development director/office manager. Estab. 1976. Publishes hardcover and trade paperback originals. "BOA Editions publishes distinguished collections of poetry, fiction and poetry in translation. Our goal is to publish the finest American contemporary poetry, fiction and poetry in translation." **Publishes 11-13 titles/year. 1,000 queries received/year. 700 mss received/year. 15% of books from first-time authors. 90% from unagented writers. Negotiates royalties. Pays variable advance.** Publishes book 18 months after acceptance. Accepts simultaneous submissions. Responds in 1 week to queries; 5 months to mss. Catalog and guidelines online.

FICTION Subjects include literary, poetry, poetry in translation, short story collections. "We now publish literary fiction through our American Reader Series. While aesthetic quality is subjective, our fiction will be by authors more concerned with the artfulness of their writing than the twists and turns of plot. Our strongest current interest is in short story collections (and short-short story collections), although we will consider novels. We strongly advise you to read our first published fiction collections." *Temporarily closed to novel/collection submissions.*

POETRY "Readers who, like Whitman, expect of the poet to 'indicate more than the beauty and dignity which always attach to dumb real objects. They expect him to indicate the path between reality and their souls,' are the audience of BOA's books." BOA Editions, a Pulitzer Prize-winning, not-for-profit publishing house acclaimed for its work, reads poetry mss for the American Poets Continuum Series (new poetry by distinguished poets in mid- and late career), the Lannan Translations Selection Series (publication of 2 new collections of contemporary international poetry annually, supported by The Lannan Foundation of Santa Fe, NM), The A. Poulin, Jr. Poetry Prize (to honor a poet's first book; mss considered through competition), and The America Reader Series (short fiction and prose on poetics). Has published poetry by Naomi Shihab Nye, W.D. Snodgrass, Lucille Clifton, Brigit Pegeen Kelly, and Li-Young Lee. Check website for reading periods for the American Poets Continuum Series and The Lannan Translation Selection Series. "Please adhere to the general submission guidelines for each series." Guidelines available for SASE or on website.

BOLD STROKES BOOKS, INC.

P.O. Box 249, Valley Falls NY 12185. (518)677-5127. **Fax:** (518)677-5291. **E-mail:** publisher@boldstrokesbooks.com. **E-mail:** submissions@boldstrokesbooks.com. **Website:** www.boldstrokesbooks.com. **Contact:** Len Barot, president; Lee Ligon, operations manager; Cindy Cresap, senior consulting editor and production manager. Publishes trade paperback originals and reprints; electronic originals and reprints. **Publishes 85+ titles/year. 300 queries/year; 300 mss/year. 10-20% of books from first-time authors. Sliding scale based on sales volume and format.** Publishes book 6-16 months after acceptance. Responds in 1 month to queries; 2 months to proposals; 4 months to mss. Catalog free on request. Guidelines online.

IMPRINTS BSB Fiction; Matinee Books Romances; Victory Editions Lesbian Fiction; Liberty Editions Gay Fiction; Soliloquy Young Adult; Heat Stroke Erotica.

NONFICTION Subjects include gay, lesbian, memoirs, young adult. Submit completed ms with bio, cover letter, and synopsis electronically only. Does not review artwork.

FICTION Subjects include adventure, erotica, fantasy, gay, gothic, historical, horror, lesbian, literary, mainstream, mystery, romance, science fiction, suspense, western, young adult. "Submissions should have a gay, lesbian, transgendered, or bisexual focus and should be positive and life-affirming." Submit completed ms with bio, cover letter, and synopsis—electronically only.

TIPS "We are particularly interested in authors who are interested in craft enhancement, technical development, and exploring and expanding traditional genre definitions and boundaries and are looking for a long-term publishing relationship."

🎧 BOOKOUTURE

StoryFire Ltd., 23 Sussex Rd., Ickenham UB10 8P, United Kingdom. **E-mail:** questions@bookouture.com. **E-mail:** pitch@bookouture.com. **Website:** www.bookouture.com. **Contact:** Oliver Rhodes, founder and publisher. Estab. 2012. Publishes mass market paperback and electronic originals and reprints. **Publishes 20 titles/year. Receives 200 queries/year; 300 mss/year. Pays 45% royalty on wholesale price.** Publishes book 4 months after acceptance. Accepts simultaneous submissions. Responds in 1 month. Book catalog online.

IMPRINTS Imprint of StoryFire Ltd.

FICTION Subjects include contemporary, erotica, ethnic, fantasy, gay, historical, lesbian, mainstream, mystery, romance, science fiction, suspense, western. "We're looking for entertaining fiction targeted at modern women. That can be anything from Steampunk to Erotica, Historicals to thrillers. A distinctive author voice is more important than a particular genre or ms length." Submit complete ms.

TIPS "The most important question that we ask of submissions is why would a reader buy the next book? What's distinctive or different about your storytelling that will mean readers will want to come back for more. We look to acquire global English language rights for eBook and Print on Demand."

⊘♻ BOREALIS PRESS, LTD.

8 Mohawk Crescent, Napean ON K2H 7G6, Canada. (613)829-0150. **Fax:** (613)829-7783. **E-mail:** drt@borealispress.com. **Website:** www.borealispress.com. Estab. 1972. Publishes hardcover and paperback originals and reprints. "Our mission is to publish work that will be of lasting interest in the Canadian book market." Currently emphasizing Canadian fiction, nonfiction, drama, poetry. De-emphasizing children's books. **Publishes 20 titles/year. 80% of books**

from first-time authors. 95% from unagented writers. Pays 10% royalty on net receipts; plus 3 free author's copies. Publishes book 18 months after acceptance. Responds in 2 months to queries; 4 months to mss. Catalog and guidelines online.

IMPRINTS Tecumseh Press.

NONFICTION Subjects include government, politics, history, language, literature, regional. Only material Canadian in content. Looks for style in tone and language, reader interest, and maturity of outlook. Query with SASE. Submit outline, 2 sample chapters. *No unsolicited mss.* Reviews artwork/photos.

FICTION Subjects include adventure, ethnic, historical, juvenile, literary, mainstream, contemporary, romance, short story collections, young adult. Only material Canadian in content and dealing with significant aspects of the human situation. Query with SASE. Submit clips, 1-2 sample chapters. *No unsolicited mss.*

BOTTOM DOG PRESS, INC.

P.O. Box 425, Huron OH 44839. **E-mail:** LsmithDog@smithdocs.net. **Website:** smithdocs.net. **Contact:** Larry Smith, director; Allen Frost, Laura Smith, Susanna Sharp-Schwacke, associate editors. Bottom Dog Press, Inc., "is a nonprofit literary and educational organization dedicated to publishing the best writing and art from the Midwest and Appalachia."

○ "Query via e-mail first."

⊘ BRANDEN PUBLISHING CO., INC.

P.O. Box 812094, Wellesley MA 02482. (781)235-3634. **Fax:** (781)235-3634. **E-mail:** branden@brandenbooks.com. **Website:** www.brandenbooks.com. **Contact:** Adolph Caso, editor. Estab. 1909. Publishes hardcover and trade paperback originals, reprints, and software. "Branden publishes books by or about women, children, military, Italian-American, or African-American themes." **Publishes 15 titles/year. 80% of books from first-time authors. 90% from unagented writers.** Publishes book 10 months after acceptance. Responds in 1 month to queries.

IMPRINTS International Pocket Library and Popular Technology; Four Seas and Brashear; Branden Books.

NONFICTION Subjects include Americana, art, architecture, computers, electronics, contemporary culture, education, ethnic, government, politics, health, medicine, history, military, war, music, dance, photography, sociology, software, classics. "Especially looking for about 10 mss on national and international subjects, including biographies of well-known

individuals. Currently specializing in Americana, Italian-American, African-American." No religion or philosophy. *No unsolicited mss.* Paragraph query only with SASE. No telephone, e-mail, or fax inquiries. Reviews artwork/photos.

FICTION Subjects include ethnic, histories, integration, historical, literary, military, war, religious, historical-reconstructive, short story collections, translation. Looking for contemporary, fast pace, modern society. No science, mystery, experimental, horor, or pornography. *No unsolicited mss.* Query with SASE. Paragraph query only with author bio.

NICHOLAS BREALEY PUBLISHING

20 Park Plaza, Suite 610, Boston MA 02116. (617)523-3801. **Fax:** (617)523-3708. **E-mail:** info@nicholasbrealey.com. **E-mail:** submissions@nicholasbrealey.com. **Website:** www.nicholasbrealey.com. **Contact:** Attn: Aquisitions Editor. Estab. 1992. "Nicholas Brealey Publishing has a reputation for publishing high-quality and thought-provoking business books with international appeal. Over time our list has grown to focus also on careers, professional and personal development, travel narratives and crossing cultures. We welcome fresh ideas and new insights in all of these subject areas." Submit via e-mail and follow the guidelines on the website.

BREWERS PUBLICATIONS

Imprint of Brewers Association, P.O. Box 2072, Georgetown TX 78627. **E-mail:** kristi@brewersassociation.org. **Website:** www.brewerspublications.com. **Contact:** Kristi Switzer, publisher. Estab. 1986. Publishes hardcover and trade paperback originals. "BP is the largest publisher of contemporary and relevant brewing literature for today's craft brewers and homebrewers." **Publishes 2 titles/year. 50% of books from first-time authors. 100% from unagented writers. Pays small advance.** Publishes book 9 months after acceptance. Accepts simultaneous submissions. Responds in 3 months to relevant queries. "Only those submissions relevant to our needs will receive a response to queries.". Guidelines online.

NONFICTION "BP is the largest publisher of contemporary and relevant brewing literature for today's craft brewers and homebrewers. We seek to do this in a positive atmosphere, create lasting relationships and shared pride in our contributions to the brewing and beer community. The books we select to carry out this mission include titles relevant to homebrewing, professional brewing, starting a brewery, books on particular styles of beer, industry trends, ingredients, processes and the occasional broader interest title on cooking or the history/impact of beer in our society." Query first with proposal and sample chapter.

⊙ BRICK BOOKS

Box 20081, 431 Boler Rd., London ON N6K 4G6, Canada. (519)657-8579. **E-mail:** brick.books@sympatico.ca. **Website:** www.brickbooks.ca. **Contact:** Don McKay, Stan Dragland, Barry Dempster, editors. Estab. 1975. Publishes trade paperback originals. Brick Books has a reading period of January 1-April 30. Mss received outside that period will be returned. No multiple submissions. Pays 10% royalty in book copies only. **Publishes 7 titles/year. 30 queries received/ year. 100 mss received/year. 30% of books from first-time authors. 100% from unagented writers.** Publishes book 2 years after acceptance. Responds in 3-4 months to queries. Book catalog free or online. Guidelines online.

○ "We publish only poetry."

POETRY Submit only poetry.

TIPS "Writers without previous publications in literary journals or magazines are rarely considered by Brick Books for publication."

BRICK ROAD POETRY PRESS, INC.

P.O. Box 751, Columbus GA 31902. (706)649-3080. **Fax:** (706)649-3094. **E-mail:** editor@brickroadpoetrypress.com. **Website:** www.brickroadpoetrypress.com. **Contact:** Ron Self and Keith Badowski, co-editors/founders. Estab. 2009.

POETRY Publishes poetry only: books (single author collections), e-zine, and annual anthology. "We prefer poetry that offers a coherent human voice, a sense of humor, attentiveness to words and language, narratives with surprise twists, persona poems, and/or philosophical or spiritual themes explored through the concrete scenes and images." Does not want overemphasis on rhyme, intentional obscurity or riddling, highfalutin vocabulary, greeting card verse, overt religious statements of faith and/or praise, and/or abstractions. Publishes 10-12 poetry books/year and 1 anthology/year. Accepted poems meeting our theme requirements are published on our website. Mss accepted through open submission and competition. Books are 110 pages, print-on-demand, perfectbound, paperback with full color art or photograph covers. "We accept .doc, .rtf, or .pdf file formats. We prefer electronic submissions but will reluctantly consider hard copy submissions by mail if USPS Flat Rate Mailing Envelope is used and with the stipulation that, should the author's work be chosen for publication, an electronic version (.doc or .rtf) must be prepared in a timely manner and at the poet's expense." Please include cover letter with poetry publication/recognition highlights and something intriguing about your life story or ongoing pursuits. "We would like to develop a connection with the poet as well as the poetry." Please include the collection title in the cover letter. "We want to publish poets who are engaged in the literary community, including regular submission of work to various publications and participation in poetry readings, workshops, and writers' groups. That said, we would never rule out an emerging poet who demonstrates ability and motivation to move in that direction." Pays royalties and 15 author copies. Initial print run of 150, print-on-demand thereafter.

TIPS "The best way to discover all that poetry can be and to expand the limits of your own poetry is to read expansively. We recommend the following poets: Kim Addonizio, Ken Babstock, Coleman Barks, Billy Collins, Morri Creech, Alice Friman, Beth A. Gylys, Jane Hirshfield, Jane Kenyon, Ted Kooser, Stanley Kunitz, Thomas Lux, Barry Marks, Michael Meyerhofer, Linda Pastan, Mark Strand, and Natasha D. Trethewey."

⊘ BRIGHT RING PUBLISHING, INC.

P.O. Box 31338, Bellingham WA 98228. (360)592-9201. **Fax:** (360)592-4503. **E-mail:** maryann@brightring.com. **Website:** www.brightring.com. **Contact:** MaryAnn Kohl, editor. Estab. 1985.

○ *Bright Ring is no longer accepting ms submissions.*

⊙ BROADVIEW PRESS, INC.

P.O. Box 1243, Peterborough ON K9J 7H5, Canada. (705)743-8990. **Fax:** (705)743-8353. **E-mail:** customerservice@broadviewpress.com. **Website:** www.broadviewpress.com. **Contact:** See Editorial Guidelines online. Estab. 1985. "We publish in a broad variety of subject areas in the arts and social sciences. We are open to a broad range of political and philosophical viewpoints, from liberal and conservative to libertarian and Marxist, and including a wide range of feminist viewpoints." **Publishes over 40 titles/year. 500 queries received/year. 200 mss received/year. 10% of books from first-time authors. 99% from unagented writers. Pays royalty.** Publishes book 12 months after acceptance of ms. Accepts simultaneous submissions. Responds in 1 month to queries. Responds in 2 months to proposals. Responds in 4 months to mss. Book catalog available free. Guidelines online.

NONFICTION Subjects include language, literature, philosophy, religion, politics. Our focus is very much on English studies and Philosophy, but within those two core subject areas we are open to a broad range of academic approaches and political viewpoints. We welcome feminist perspectives, and we have a particular interest in addressing environmental issues. Our publishing program is internationally-oriented, and we publish for a broad range of geographical markets-but as a canadian company we also publish a broad range of titles with a canadian emphasis. Query with SASE. Submit proposal package. Reviews artwork/photos. Send photocopies.

TIPS "Our titles often appeal to a broad readership; we have many books that are as much of interest to the general reader as they are to academics and students."

❶ BROADWAY BOOKS

The Crown Publishing Group/Random House, 1745 Broadway, New York NY 10019. (212)782-9000. **Fax:** (212)782-9411. **Website:** crownpublishing.com/imprint/broadway-books. **Contact:** William Thomas, editor-in-chief. Estab. 1995. Publishes hardcover and trade paperback books. **Receives thousands of mss/year. Pays royalty on retail price. Pays advance.**

IMPRINTS Broadway Books; Broadway Business; Doubleday; Doubleday Image; Doubleday Religious Publishing; Main Street Books; Nan A. Talese.

◐ "Broadway publishes high quality general interest nonfiction and fiction for adults."

NONFICTION Subjects include business, economics, child guidance, contemporary culture, cooking, foods, nutrition, gay, lesbian, government, politics, health, medicine, history, memoirs, money, finance, multicultural, New Age, psychology, sex, spirituality, sports, travel, narrative, womens' issues, women's studies, current affairs, motivational/inspirational, popular culture, consumer reference. *Agented submissions only.*

◑ BROKEN JAW PRESS

Box 596, STN A, Fredericton NB E3B 5A6, Canada. (506)454-5127. **E-mail:** editors@brokenjaw.com. **Website:** www.brokenjaw.com. "Publishes almost exclusively Canadian-authored literary trade paperback

originals and reprints.". "We publish poetry, fiction, drama and literary nonfiction, including translations and multilingual books." **Publishes 3-6 titles/year. 20% of books from first-time authors. 100% from unagented writers. Pays 10% royalty on retail price. Pays $0-500 advance.** Publishes book 18 months after acceptance. Responds in 1 year to mss. Book catalog for 6×9 SAE with 2 first-class Canadian stamps in Canada or download PDF from website. Guidelines online.

IMPRINTS Book Rat; Broken Jaw Press; SpareTime Editions; Dead Sea Physh Products; Maritimes Arts Projects Productions.

◐ *Currently not accepting unsolicited mss and queries.*

NONFICTION Subjects include history, literature, literary criticism, regional, women's issues, women's studies, contemporary culture.

FICTION Subjects include Literary novel and short story collections, poetry.

TIPS "Unsolicited queries and mss are not welcome at this time."

BRONZE MANVV BOOKS

Millikin University, 1184 W. Main, Decatur IL 62522. (217)424-6264. **Website:** www.bronzemanbooks.com. **Contact:** Dr. Randy Brooks, editorial board; Edwin Walker, editorial board. Estab. 2006. Publishes hardcover, trade paperback, and mass market paperback originals. **Publishes 3-4 titles/year. 80% of books from first-time authors. 100% from unagented writers. Outright purchase based on wholesale value of 10% of a press run.** Publishes book 6 months after acceptance. Accepts simultaneous submissions. Responds in 1-3 months.

NONFICTION Subjects include architecture, art. Query with SASE.

FICTION Subjects include art, graphic design, exhibits, general. Submit completed ms.

POETRY Submit completed ms.

TIPS "The art books are intended for serious collectors and scholars of contemporary art, especially of artists from the Midwestern US. These books are published in conjunction with art exhibitions at Millikin University or the Decatur Area Arts Council. The children's books have our broadest audience, and the literary chapbooks are intended for readers of contemporary fiction, drama, and poetry."

BROOKS BOOKS

3720 N. Woodridge Dr., Decatur IL 62526. **E-mail:** brooksbooks@sbcglobal.net. **Website:** www.brooksbookshaiku.com. **Contact:** Randy Brooks, editor (haiku poetry, tanka poetry). Publishes hardcover, trade paperback, and electronic originals. "Brooks Books, formerly High/Coo Press, publishes English-language haiku books, chapbooks, magazines, and bibliographies." **Publishes 2-3 titles/year. 100 queries received/year. 25 mss received/year. 10% of books from first-time authors. 100% from unagented writers. Outright purchase based on wholesale value of 10% of a press run.** Publishes book 1 year after acceptance. Responds in 2 months to queries; 3 months to proposals and mss. Book catalog free on request or online. Guidelines free on request, for #10 SASE.

POETRY "We celebrate English language haiku by promoting & publishing in a variety of media. Our goal is to share our joy of the art of reading & writing haiku through our little chapbook-size magazine, *Mayfly*. Also, we celebrate the art of haiga, lifetime contributions of haiku writers, the integration of visual arts (photography or painting) and contemporary English language haiku by leading poets. Query.

TIPS "The best haiku capture human perception—moments of being alive conveyed through sensory images. They do not explain nor describe nor provide philosophical or political commentary. Haiku are gifts of the here and now, deliberately incomplete so that the reader can enter into the haiku moment to open the gift and experience the feelings and insights of that moment for his or her self. Our readership includes the haiku community, readers of contemporary poetry, teachers and students of Japanese literature and contemporary Japanese poetics."

☺ THE BRUCEDALE PRESS

P.O. Box 2259, Port Elgin ON N0H 2C0, Canada. (519)832-6025. **E-mail:** info@brucedalepress.ca. **Website:** brucedalepress.ca. Publishes hardcover and trade paperback originals. The Brucedale Press publishes books and other materials of regional interest and merit, as well as literary, historical, and/or pictorial works. **Publishes 3 titles/year. 50 queries received/year. 30 mss received/year. 75% of books from first-time authors. 100% from unagented writers. Pays royalty.** Publishes book 1 year after acceptance. Accepts simultaneous submissions. Book catalog for #10 SASE (Canadian postage or IRC) or online. Guidelines online.

⚫ *Accepts works by Canadian authors only. Submissions accepted in September and March ONLY.*

NONFICTION Subjects include history, language, literature, memoirs, military, war, nature, environment, photography. Reviews artwork/photos.

FICTION Subjects include fantasy, feminist, historical, humor, juvenile, literary, mainstream, contemporary, mystery, plays, poetry, romance, short story collections, young adult.

✚ BULLITT PUBLISHING

P.O. Box, Austin TX 78729. **E-mail:** bullittpublishing@yahoo.com. **E-mail:** submissions@bullittpublishing.com. **Website:** bullittpublishing.com. **Contact:** Pat Williams, editor. Estab. 2012. Publishes trade paperback and electronic originals. "Bullitt Publishing is a royalty-offering publishing house specializing in smart, contemporary romance. We are proud to provide print on demand distribution through the world's most comprehensive distribution channel including Amazon.com and BarnesandNoble.com. Digital distribution is available through the world's largest distibutor of e-books and can be downloaded to reading devices such as the iPhone, Ipod Touch, Amazon Kindle, Sony Reader or Barnes & Noble nook. E-books are distributed to the Apple iBookstore, Barnes & Noble, Sony, Kobo and the Diesel eBook Store. Whether this is your first novel or your 101st novel, Bullitt Publishing will treat you with the same amount of professionalism and respect. While we expect well-written entertaining mss from all of our authors, we promise to provide high quality, professional product in return." **Publishes 12 titles/year.**

IMPRINTS Includes imprint Tempo Romance.

☻ BUSTER BOOKS

9 Lion Yard, Tremadoc Rd., London WA SW4 7NQ, United Kingdom. 020 7720 8643. **Fax:** 022 7720 8953. **E-mail:** enquiries@michaclomarabooks.com. **Website:** www.busterbooks.co.uk. "We are dedicated to providing irresistible and fun books for children of all ages. We typically publish black-and-white nonfiction for children aged 8-12 novelty titles-including doodle books."

NONFICTION Prefers synopsis and sample text over complete ms.

FICTION Submit synopsis and sample text.

TIPS "We do not accept fiction submissions. Please do not send original artwork as we cannot guarantee its safety." Visit website before submitting.

BY LIGHT UNSEEN MEDIA

P.O. Box 1233, Pepperell MA 01463. (978) 433-8866. **Fax:** (978) 433-8866. **E-mail:** vyrdolak@bylightunseenmedia.com. **Website:** www.bylightunseenmedia.com. **Contact:** Inanna Arthen, owner/editor-in-chief. Estab. 2006. Publishes hardcover, paperback and electronic originals; trade paperback reprints. **Publishes 5 titles/year. 20 mss received/year; 5 queries received/year. 80% of books from first-time authors. 100% from unagented writers. Pays royalty of 20-50% on net as explicitly defined in contract. Payment quarterly. Pays $200 advance.** Publishes book 4 months after acceptance. Accepts simultaneous submissions. Responds in 3 months. Catalog online. Ms guidelines online.

NONFICTION Subjects include alternative lifestyles, contemporary culture, creative nonfiction, history, language, literary criticism, literature, New Age, science, social sciences, folklore, popular media. "We are a niche small press that will *only* consider nonfiction on the theme of vampires (vampire folklore, movies, television, literature, vampires in culture, etc.). We're especially interested in academic or other well-researched material, but will consider self-help/New Age types of books (e.g. the kind of material published by Llewellyn). We use digital printing so all interiors would need to be black and white, including illustrations." Submit proposal package including outline, 3 sample chapters, brief author bio. *All unsolicited mss will be returned unopened.* Reviews artwork. Send photocopies/scanned PDF/jpeg.

FICTION Subjects include fantasy, gay, gothic, horror, lesbian, mystery, occult, science fiction, short story collections, suspense, western, young adult, magical realism, thriller. "We are a niche small press that *only* publishes fiction relating in some way to vampires. Within that guideline, we're interested in almost any genre that includes a vampire trope, the more creative and innovative, the better. Restrictions are noted in the submission guidelines (no derivative fiction based on other works, such as Dracula, no gore-for-gore's-sake 'splatter' horror, etc.) We do not publish anthologies." Submit proposal package including synopsis, 3 sample chapters, brief author bio. *We encourage electronic submissions. All unsolicited mss will be returned unopened.*

TIPS "We strongly urge authors to familiarize themselves with the vampire genre and not imagine that they're doing something new and amazingly different just because they're not imitating the current fad."

C&R PRESS

812 Westwood Ave., Chattanooga TN 37405. (423)645-5375. **Website:** www.crpress.org. **Contact:** Chad Prevost, editorial director and publisher; Ryan G. Van Cleave, executive director and publisher. Estab. 2006. Publishes hardcover, trade paperback, mass market paperback, and electronic originals. **Publishes 8 titles/year. 20% of books from first-time authors. 75% from unagented writers.** Publishes book 1 year after acceptance. Accepts simultaneous submissions. Responds in up to 1 month on queries and proposals, 1-2 months on mss. Catalog and Guidelines online.

IMPRINTS Illumis Books.

NONFICTION Subjects include contemporary culture, creative nonfiction, memoirs. Submit complete ms and query via e-mail. "C&R is a green company and we prefer all submissions to be done electronically."

FICTION Subjects include experimental, literary, poetry, regional. "We want dynamic, exciting literary fiction and we want to work with authors (not merely books) who are engaged socially and driven to promote their work because of their belief in the product, and because it's energizing and exciting to do so and a vital part of the process." Submit complete ms via e-mail.

POETRY "We remain committed to our annual first book of poetry contest, the De Novo Award. However, we also feature 1-2 monthly paid reading periods when we consider any and all poetry projects. Please check the website for updated guidelines." Submit complete ms.

⊘ CALAMARI PRESS

Via Titta Scarpetta #28, Rome 00153, Italy. **E-mail:** derek@calamaripress.net. **Website:** www.calamaripress.com. Publishes paperback originals. Calamari Press publishes books of literary text and art. Publishes 1-2 books/year. Mss are selected by invitation. Occasionally has open submission period—check website. Helps to be published in *SleepingFish* first." Order books through the website, Powell's, or SPD. **Publishes 1-2/year titles/year. Pays in author's cop-**

ies. Publishes book Ms published 2-6 months after acceptance. Responds to mss in 2 weeks. Writer's guidelines on website.

FICTION Query with outline/synopsis and 3 sample chapters. Accepts queries by e-mail only. Include brief bio. Send SASE or IRC for return of ms.

CALKINS CREEK

Boyds Mills Press, 815 Church St., Honesdale PA 18431. **Website:** www.calkinscreekbooks.com. Estab. 2004. "We aim to publish books that are a well-written blend of creative writing and extensive research, which emphasize important events, people, and places in U.S. history." **Pays authors royalty or work purchased outright.** Guidelines online.

NONFICTION Subjects include history. Submit outline/synopsis and 3 sample chapters.

FICTION Subjects include historical. Submit outline/synopsis and 3 sample chapters.

TIPS "Read through our recently published titles and review our catalog. When selecting titles to publish, our emphasis will be on important events, people, and places in U.S. history. Writers are encouraged to submit a detailed bibliography, including secondary and primary sources, and expert reviews with their submissions."

CAMINO BOOKS, INC.

P.O. Box 59026, Philadelphia PA 19102. (215)413-1917. **Fax:** (215)413-3255. **Website:** www.caminobooks. com. **Contact:** E. Jutkowitz, publisher. Estab. 1987. Publishes hardcover and trade paperback originals. "Camino Books was founded in 1987 for the purpose of publishing quality nonfiction books of regional interest to people in the Middle Atlantic states. Our list is especially strong in titles about cooking, travel, gardening, and history, but we also publish biographies, local reference books, and books concerning parenting and important health issues. We occasionally publish books of national interest as well. We are always looking for new material and projects." **Publishes 6-10 titles/year. 20% of books from first-time authors. Pays $2,000 average advance.** Publishes book 1 year after acceptance. Responds in 2 weeks to queries. Guidelines online.

NONFICTION Subjects include agriculture, Americana, art, architecture, child guidance, cooking, foods, nutrition, ethnic, gardening, government, politics, history, regional, travel. Query with SASE. Submit outline, sample chapters.

TIPS "The books must be of interest to readers in the Middle Atlantic states, or they should have a clearly defined niche, such as cookbooks."

⊘ CANDLEWICK PRESS

99 Dover St., Somerville MA 02144. (617)661-3330. **Fax:** (617)661-0565. **E-mail:** bigbear@candlewick. com. **Website:** www.candlewick.com. Estab. 1991. Publishes hardcover and trade paperback originals, and reprints. "Candlewick Press publishes high-quality, illustrated children's books for ages infant through young adult. We are a truly child-centered publisher." **Publishes 200 titles/year. 5% of books from first-time authors. Pays authors royalty of 2½-10% based on retail price. Offers advance.**

○ *Candlewick Press is not accepting queries or unsolicited mss at this time.*

NONFICTION Picture books: concept, biography, geography, nature/environment. Young readers: biography, geography, nature/environment.

FICTION Subjects include juvenile, picture books, young adult. Picture books: animal, concept, contemporary, fantasy, history, humor, multicultural, nature/environment, poetry. Middle readers, young adults: contemporary, fantasy, history, humor, multicultural, poetry, science fiction, sports, suspense/mystery. "We do not accept editorial queries or submissions online. If you are an author or illustrator and would like us to consider your work, please read our submissions policy (online) to learn more."

TIPS *"We no longer accept unsolicited mss. See our* website for further information about us."

CANTERBURY HOUSE PUBLISHING, LTD.

7350 S. Tamiami Trail, Suite 215, Sarasota FL 34231. (941)312-6912. **Website:** www.canterburyhousepublishing.com. **Contact:** Wendy Dingwall, publisher; Sandra Horton, editor. Estab. 2009. Publishes hardcover, trade paperback, and electronic originals. "Our audience is made up of readers looking for wholesome fiction with good southern stories, with elements of mystery, romance, and inspiration and/or are looking for true stories of achievement and triumph over challenging circumstances." **Publishes 3-6 titles/year. 35% of books from first-time authors. 100% from unagented writers. Pays 10-15% royalty on wholesale price.** Publishes book 9-12 months after acceptance. Accepts simultaneous submissions. Responds in 1 month to queries; 3 months to mss. Book catalog online. Guidelines availably online, free on request by e-mail.

🔾 *"We are very strict on our submission guidelines due to our small staff, and our target market of Southern regional settings. The setting needs to be a strong component in the stories. Authors need to be willing to actively promote their books in the beginning 9 months of publication via signing events and social media."*

NONFICTION Subjects include memoirs, regional. Query with SASE and through website e-mail upon request. Reviews artwork. Send photocopies.

FICTION Subjects include contemporary, historical, literary, mainstream, mystery, regional, romance, suspense. Query with SASE and through website.

TIPS "Because of our limited staff, we prefer authors who have good writing credentials and submit edited mss. We also look at authors who are business and marketing savvy and willing to help promote their books."

CARDOZA PUBLISHING

5473 S. Eastern Ave., Las Vegas NV 89119. **E-mail:** submissions@cardozapub.com. **Website:** www.car-dozapub.com. **Contact:** Acquisitions Editor (gaming, gambling, card and casino games, and board games). Estab. 1981. Publishes trade paperback originals and reprints. **Publishes 35-40 titles/year. 20-30 queries received/year. 20-30 mss received/year. 50% of books from first-time authors. 90% from unagented writers. Pays 5-6% royalty on retail price. Pays $1,000-10,000 advance.** Publishes book 7 months after acceptance of ms. Accepts simultaneous submissions. Responds in 2-3 months to mss. Book catalog online. Guidelines available via e-mail.

NONFICTION Subjects include hobbies, gaming, gambling, backgammon chess, card games. "Cardoza Publishing publishes exclusively gaming and gambling titles. In the past, we have specialized in poker and chess titles. While we always need more of those, we are currently seeking more books on various non-casino card games, such as bridge, hearts, spades, gin rummy, or canasta." Submit complete ms. Reviews artwork/photos. Send photocopies.

TIPS "Audience is professional and recreational gamblers, chess players, card players. We prefer not to deal with agents whenever possible. We publish only titles in a very specific niche market; please do not send us material that will not be relevant to our business."

THE CAREER PRESS, INC.

220 West Parkway, Unit 12, Pompton Lakes NJ 07442. (201)848-0310 or (800)227-3371. **E-mail:** aschwartz@ careerpress.com. **Website:** www.careerpress.com; www.newpagebooks.com. **Contact:** Michael Pye, director of product development, Adam Schwartz, acquisitions editor. Estab. 1985. Publishes hardcover and paperback originals. Career Press publishes books for adult readers seeking practical information to improve themselves in careers, business, HR, sales, entrepreneurship, and other related topics, as well as titles on supervision, management and CEOs. New Page Books publishes in the areas of New Age, new science, paranormal, the unexplained, alternative history, spirituality. Accepts simultaneous submissions. Guidelines online.

IMPRINTS New Page Books.

NONFICTION Subjects include business, economics, money, finance, recreation, nutrition. Look through our catalog; become familiar with our publications. We like to select authors who are specialists on their topic. Submit outline, bio, table of contents, 2-3 sample chapters, marketing plan, SASE. Or, send complete ms (preferred).

CAROLINA WREN PRESS

120 Morris St., Durham NC 27701. (919)560-2738. **E-mail:** carolinawrenpress@earthlink.net. **Website:** www.carolinawrenpress.org. **Contact:** Andrea Selch, president. Estab. 1976. "We publish poetry, fiction, and memoirs by, and/or about people of color, women, gay/lesbian issues, and work by writers from, living in, or writing about the U.S. South." Publishes book 2 year after acceptance. Accepts simultaneous submissions. Responds in 3 months to queries; 6 months to mss. Guidelines online.

🔾 Accepts simultaneous submissions, but "let us know if work has been accepted elsewhere."

NONFICTION Subjects include ethnic, gay, lesbian, literature, multicultural, womens issues.

FICTION Subjects include ethnic, experimental, poetry, feminist, gay, lesbian, literary, short story collections. "We are no longer publishing children's literature of any topic." Books: 6×9 paper; typeset; various bindings; illustrations. **Published 1 debut author within the last year.** Distributes titles through Amazon.com, Barnes & Noble, Baker & Taylor, and on their website. "We very rarely accept any unsolicited mss, but we accept submissions for the Doris Bakwin Award for Writing by a Woman in Jan-March of even-numbered years." Starting in 2013, the Lee Smith Novel Prize contest will accept submissions in summer and fall of odd-numbered years for a novel by an author from, living in, or writing about the U.S. South. Query by mail. "We will accept e-mailed queries—a letter in the body of the e-mail describing your project—but please do not send large attachments."

POETRY Publishes 2 poetry books/year, "usually through the Carolina Wren Press Poetry Series Contest. Otherwise we primarily publish women, minorities, and authors from, living in, or writing about the U.S. South." Not accepting unsolicited submissions except through Poetry Series Contest. Accepts e-mail queries, but send only letter and description of work, no large files. Carolina Wren Press Poetry Contest for a First or Second Book takes submissions, electronically, from January to March of odd-numbered years.

TIPS "Best way to get read is to submit to a contest."

⊘ CAROLRHODA BOOKS, INC.

1251 Washington Ave. N., Minneapolis MN 55401. **Website:** www.lernerbooks.com. Estab. 1959. "We will continue to seek targeted solicitations at specific reading levels and in specific subject areas. The company will list these targeted solicitations on our website and in national newsletters, such as the SCBWI Bulletin."

> *Lerner Publishing Group no longer accepts submissions to any of their imprints except for Kar-Ben Publishing.*

CARSTENS PUBLICATIONS, INC.

Hobby Book Division, 108 Phil Hardin Rd., Newton NJ 07860. (973)383-3355. **Fax:** (973)383-4064. **Website:** www.carstens-publications.com. **Contact:** Henry R. Carstens, publisher. Estab. 1933. Publishes paperback originals. Carstens specializes in books about railroads, model railroads, and airplanes for hobbyists. **Publishes 8 titles/year. 100% from unagented writers. Pays 10% royalty on retail price. Pays advance.** Publishes book 1 year after acceptance. Responds in 2 months to queries. Book catalog for #10 SASE.

NONFICTION "Authors must know their field intimately because our readers are active modelers. Writers cannot write about somebody else's hobby with authority. If they do, we can't use them. Our railroad books presently are primarily photographic essays on specific railroads." Query with SASE. Reviews artwork/photos.

TIPS "We need lots of good photos. Material must be in model, hobby, railroad, and transportation field only."

Ⓐ⊘ CARTWHEEL BOOKS

Imprint of Scholastic Trade Division, 557 Broadway, New York NY 10012. (212)343-6100. **Website:** www.scholastic.com. Estab. 1991. Publishes novelty books, easy readers, board books, hardcover and trade paperback originals. Cartwheel Books publishes innovative books for children, up to age 8. "We are looking for 'novelties' that are books first, play objects second. Even without its gimmick, a Cartwheel Book should stand alone as a valid piece of children's literature." Accepts simultaneous submissions. Guidelines available free.

NONFICTION Subjects include animals, history, music, dance, nature, environment, recreation, science, sports. Cartwheel Books publishes for the very young, therefore nonfiction should be written in a manner that is accessible to preschoolers through 2nd grade. Often writers choose topics that are too narrow or "special" and do not appeal to the mass market. Also, the text and vocabulary are frequently too difficult for our young audience. *Accepts mss from agents only.* Reviews artwork/photos. Send Please do not send original artwork.

FICTION Subjects include humor, juvenile, mystery, picture books. Again, the subject should have mass market appeal for very young children. Humor can be helpful, but not necessary. Mistakes writers make are a reading level that is too difficult, a topic of no interest or too narrow, or mss that are too long. *Accepts mss from agents only.*

TIPS Audience is young children, ages 0-8. Know what types of books the publisher does. Some mss that don't work for one house may be perfect for another. Check out bookstores or catalogs to see where your writing would "fit" best.

CATHOLIC UNIVERSITY OF AMERICA PRESS

620 Michigan Ave. NE, 240 Leahy Hall, Washington DC 20064. (202)319-5052. **Fax:** (202)319-4985. **E-mail:** cua-press@cua.edu. **Website:** cuapress.cua.edu. **Contact:** James C. Kruggel, acquisitions editor (philosophy, theology); Trevor Lipscombe, director (all other fields). Estab. 1939. The Catholic University

of America Press publishes in the fields of history (ecclesiastical and secular), literature and languages, philosophy, political theory, social studies, and theology. "We have interdisciplinary emphasis on patristics, and medieval studies. We publish works of original scholarship intended for academic libraries, scholars and other professionals and works that offer a synthesis of knowledge of the subject of interest to a general audience or suitable for use in college and university classrooms." **Publishes 30-35 titles/ year. 50% of books from first-time authors. 100% from unagented writers. Pays variable royalty on net receipts.** Publishes book 18 months after acceptance. Responds in 5 days to queries. Book catalog on request. Guidelines online.

NONFICTION Subjects include government, politics, history, language, literature, philosophy, religion, Church-state relations. No unrevised doctoral dissertations. Length: 40,000-120,000 words. Query with outline, sample chapter, CV, and list of previous publications.

TIPS Scholarly monographs and works suitable for adoption as supplementary reading material in courses have the best chance.

CAVE HOLLOW PRESS

P.O. Drawer J, Warrensburg MO 64093. **E-mail:** gbcrump@cavehollowpress.com. **Website:** www. cavehollowpress.com. **Contact:** G.B. Crump, editor. Estab. 2001. Publishes trade paperback originals. **Publishes 1 titles/year. 70 queries received/ year. 6 mss received/year. 80% of books from first-time authors. 100% from unagented writers. Pays 7-12% royalty on wholesale price. Pays negotiable amount in advance.** Publishes book 1 year after acceptance of ms. Accepts simultaneous submissions. Responds in 1-2 months to queries and proposals; 3-6 months to mss. Book catalog for #10 SASE. Guidelines available free.

FICTION Subjects include contemporary, mainstream. "Our website is updated frequently to reflect the current type of fiction Cave Hollow Press is seeking." Query with SASE.

TIPS "Our audience varies based on the type of book we are publishing. We specialize in Missouri and Midwest regional fiction. We are interested in talented writers from Missouri and the surrounding Midwest. Check our submission guidelines on the website for what type of fiction we are interested in currently."

CEDAR FORT, INC.

2373 W. 700 S, Springville UT 84663. (801)489-4084. **Fax:** (801)489-1097. **Website:** www.cedarfort.com. **Contact:** Shersta Gatica, acquisitions editor. Estab. 1986. Publishes hardcover, trade paperback originals and reprints, mass market paperback and electronic reprints. "Each year we publish well over 100 books, and many of those are by first-time authors. At the same time, we love to see books from established authors. As one of the largest book publishers in Utah, we have the capability and enthusiasm to make your book a success, whether you are a new author or a returning one. We want to publish uplifting and edifying books that help people think about what is important in life, books people enjoy reading to relax and feel better about themselves, and books to help improve lives. Although we do put out several children's books each year, we are extremely selective. Our children's books must have strong religious or moral values, and must contain outstanding writing and an excellent storyline." **Publishes 120 titles/ year. Receives 200 queries/year; 600 mss/year. 60% of books from first-time authors. 95% from unagented writers. Pays 10-12% royalty on wholesale price. Pays $2,000-50,000 advance.** Publishes book 10-14 months after acceptance. Responds in 1 month on queries; 2 months on proposals; 4 months on mss. Catalog and guidelines online.

IMPRINTS Council Press, Sweetwater Books, Bonneville Books, Front Table Books, Hobble Creek Press, CFI.

NONFICTION Subjects include agriculture, Americana, animals, anthropology, archeology, business, child guidance, communications, cooking, crafts, creative nonfiction, economics, education, foods, gardening, health, history, hobbies, horticulture, house and home, military, nature, recreation, regional, religion, social sciences, spirituality, war, womens issues, young adult. Query with SASE; submit proposal package, including outline, 2 sample chapters; or submit completed ms. Reviews artwork as part of the ms package. Send photocopies.

FICTION Subjects include adventure, contemporary, fantasy, historical, humor, juvenile, literary, mainstream, military, multicultural, mystery, regional, religious, romance, science fiction, spiritual, sports, suspense, war, western, young adult. Submit completed ms.

TIPS "Our audience is rural, conservative, mainstream. The first page of your ms is very important because we start reading every submission, but good writing and plot keep us reading."

CENTER FOR THANATOLOGY RESEARCH & EDUCATION, INC.

391 Atlantic Ave., Brooklyn NY 11217. (718)858-3026. **E-mail:** thanatology@pipeline.com. **Website:** www. thanatology.org. Estab. 1980. **Publishes 7 titles/year. 10 queries received/year. 3 mss received/year. 15% of books from first-time authors. 100% from unagented writers. Pays 10% royalty on wholesale price.** Publishes book 9 months after acceptance. Responds in 1 month to queries and proposals. Book catalog and ms guidelines free.

NONFICTION Subjects include education, health, medicine, humanities, psychology, religion, social sciences, sociology, women's issues, women's studies, anthropology. All proposals we feel are applicable are sent to a board of professional readers for comment. Query with SASE. Reviews artwork/photos. Send photocopies.

POETRY "We are open to appropriate submissions." Query.

TIPS "We serve 2 different audiences: One is physicians/social workers/nurses dealing with dying patients and bereaved families. The second relates to all aspects of cemetery lore: recording, preservation, description, art of."

CENTERSTREAM PUBLISHING

P.O. Box 17878, Anaheim Hills CA 92817. (714)779-9390. **Fax:** (714)779-9390. **E-mail:** centerstrm@aol. com. **Website:** www.centerstream-usa.com. **Contact:** Ron Middlebrook, Cindy Middlebrook, owners. Estab. 1980. Publishes music hardcover and mass market paperback originals, trade paperback and mass market paperback reprints. Centerstream publishes music history and instructional books, all instruments plus DVDs. **Publishes 12 titles/year. 15 queries received/ year. 15 mss received/year. 80% of books from first-time authors. 100% from unagented writers. Pays 10-15% royalty on wholesale price. Pays $300-3,000 advance.** Publishes book 8 months after acceptance. Accepts simultaneous submissions. Responds in 3 months to queries. Book catalog and ms guidelines for #10 SASE.

NONFICTION Query with SASE.

CHALICE PRESS

483 E. Lockwood Ave., Suite 100, St. Louis MO 63119. (314)231-8500. **Fax:** (314)231-8524. **E-mail:** submissions@chalicepress.com. **Website:** www.chalicepress. com. **Contact:** Bradley Lyons, president and publisher. Publishes hardcover and trade paperback originals. **Publishes 60 titles/year. 300 queries received/year. 250 mss received/year. 10% of books from first-time authors. 100% from unagented writers.** Publishes book 1 year after acceptance. Accepts simultaneous submissions. Responds in 2 months to queries; 3 months to proposals and mss. Catalog and guidelines online.

NONFICTION Subjects include religion, Christian spirituality. Submit query.

TIPS "We publish for professors, church ministers, and lay Christian readers."

CHARLESBRIDGE PUBLISHING

85 Main St., Watertown MA 02472. (617)926-0329. **Fax:** (617)926-5720. **E-mail:** tradeart@charlesbridge. com. **Website:** www.charlesbridge.com. Estab. 1980. Publishes hardcover and trade paperback nonfiction and fiction, children's books for the trade and library markets. "Charlesbridge publishes high-quality books for children, with a goal of creating lifelong readers and lifelong learners. Our books encourage reading and discovery in the classroom, library, and home. We believe that books for children should offer accurate information, promote a positive worldview, and embrace a child's innate sense of wonder and fun. To this end, we continually strive to seek new voices, new visions, and new directions in children's literature." **Publishes 30 titles/year. 10-20% of books from first-time authors. 80% from unagented writers. Pays royalty. Pays advance.** Publishes book 2-4 years after acceptance. Responds in 3 months. Guidelines online.

IMPRINTS Charlesbridge, Imagine Publishing.

◯   "We're always interested in innovative approaches to a difficult genre, the nonfiction picture book."

NONFICTION Subjects include animals, creative nonfiction, history, multicultural, nature, environment, science, social science. Strong interest in nature, environment, social studies, and other topics for trade and library markets. *Exclusive submissions only.* "Charlesbridge accepts unsolicited mss submitted exclusively to us for a period of 3 months. 'Exclusive Submission' should be written on all envelopes and cover letters." Please submit only 1 or 2 chapters at a time. For nonfiction books longer than 30 ms pages, send a detailed proposal, a chapter outline, and 1 to 3 chapters of text. Mss should be typed and double-spaced. Please do not submit material by e-mail, by fax, or on a computer disk. Illustrations are not necessary. Please make a copy of your ms, as we cannot be responsible for submissions lost in the mail. Include your name and address on the first page of your ms and in cover letter. Be sure to list any previously published work or relevant writing experience.

FICTION Strong stories with enduring themes. Charlesbridge publishes both picture books and transitional bridge books (books ranging from early readers to middle-grade chapter books). Our fiction titles include lively, plot-driven stories with strong, engaging characters. No alphabet books, board books, coloring books, activity books, or books with audiotapes or CD-ROMs. *Exclusive submissions only.* "Charlesbridge accepts unsolicited mss submitted exclusively to us for a period of 3 months. 'Exclusive Submission' should be written on all envelopes and cover letters." Please submit only 1 or 2 mss at a time. For picture books and shorter bridge books, please send a complete ms. For fiction books longer than 30 ms pages, please send a detailed plot synopsis, a chapter outline, and 3 chapters of text. Mss should be typed and double-spaced. Please do not submit material by e-mail, by fax, or on a computer disk. Illustrations are not necessary. Please make a copy of your ms, as we cannot be responsible for submissions lost in the mail. Include your name and address on the first page of your ms and in your cover letter. Be sure to list any previously published work or relevant writing experience.

TIPS "To become acquainted with our publishing program, we encourage you to review our books and visit our website where you will find our catalog."

THE CHARLES PRESS, PUBLISHERS

230 North 21st St., #202, Philadelphia PA 19103. (215)561-2786. **Fax:** (215)561-0191. **E-mail:** submissions@charlespresspub.com. **Website:** www.charlespresspub.com. **Contact:** Lauren Meltzer, publisher. Estab. 1982. Publishes hardcover and trade paperback originals. Currently emphasizing mental and physical health (especially holistic, complementary and alternative healthcare), psychology, animals/pets/

veterinary medicine, how-to (especially relating to healthcare and wellness), comparative religion, aging/eldercare/geriatrics, medical reference books. Accepts simultaneous submissions. Responds in 1-2 months. Catalog and guidelines online.

NONFICTION Subjects include child guidance, health, mental health, physical health, medicine, psychology, religion, nursing, health care, how-to, aging/eldercare, criminology, true crime. No fiction, autobiographies, children's books, or poetry. Query first, then submit proposal package that includes a description of the book, a few representative sample chapters, intended audience, competing titles, author's qualifications/background and SASE. No e-mailed or faxed submissions. Reviews artwork/photos. Send photocopies or transparencies.

CHELSEA GREEN PUBLISHING CO.

85 N. Main St., Suite 120, White River Junction VT 05001. (802)295-6300. **Fax:** (802)295-6444. **E-mail:** editorial@chelseagreen.com. **E-mail:** submissions@chelseagreen.com. **Website:** www.chelseagreen.com. Estab. 1984. Publishes hardcover and trade paperback originals and reprints. "Since 1984, Chelsea Green has been the publishing leader for books on the politics and practice of sustainable living." **Publishes 18-25 titles/year. 600-800 queries received/year. 200-300 mss received/year. 30% of books from first-time authors. 80% from unagented writers. Pays royalty on publisher's net. Pays $2,500-10,000 advance.** Publishes book 18 months after acceptance. Responds in 2 weeks to queries; 1 month to proposals/mss. Book catalog free or online. Guidelines online.

NONFICTION Subjects include agriculture, alternative lifestyles, ethical & sustainable business, environment, foods, organic gardening, health, green building, progressive politics, science, social justice, simple living, renewable energy; and other sustainability topics. "We seldom publish cookbooks." Prefers electronic queries and proposals via e-mail (as a single attachment). If sending via snail mail, submissions will only be returned with SASE. Please review our guidelines carefully before submitting. Reviews artwork/photos.

TIPS "Our readers and our authors are passionate about finding sustainable and viable solutions to contemporary challenges in the fields of energy, food production, economics, and building. It would be helpful for prospective authors to have a look at several of our current books, as well as our website."

CHELSEA HOUSE PUBLISHERS

Infobase Publishing, 132 W. 31st St., 17th Floor, New York NY 10001. (800) 322-8755 or (212) 967-8800. **Fax:** (800)780-7300. **E-mail:** editorial@factsonfile. com. **Website:** www.chelseahouse.com. **Contact:** Editorial assistant. Publishes hardcover originals and reprints. We publish curriculum-based nonfiction books for middle school and high school students. Accepts simultaneous submissions. Book catalog online. Guidelines for #10 SASE.

NONFICTION Subjects include Americana, animals, anthropology, archeology, ethnic, gay, lesbian, government, politics, health, medicine, history, hobbies, language, literature, military, war, multicultural, music, dance, nature, environment, recreation, regional, religion, science, sociology, sports, travel, women's issues, women's studies. We are interested in expanding our topics to include more on the physical, life and environmental sciences. Query with SASE. Submit proposal package, outline, 2-3 sample chapters, résumé. Reviews artwork/photos. Send photocopies.

TIPS "Please review our products online or in our bi-annual catalog. Please be sure submissions fit our market of the middle and high school student. Be professional. Send clean, clear submissions that show you read the preferred submission format. Always include SASE."

CHEMICAL PUBLISHING CO., INC.

P.O. Box 676, Revere MA 02151. (888)439-3976. **Fax:** (888)439-3976. **E-mail:** info@chemical-publishing. com. **Website:** www.chemical-publishing.com. **Contact:** B. Carr, publisher. Estab. 1934. Publishes hardcover originals. Chemical Publishing Co., Inc., publishes professional chemistry-technical titles aimed at people employed in the chemical industry, libraries and graduate courses. **Publishes 10-15 titles/year. 20 queries received/year. 50% of books from first-time authors. 100% from unagented writers. Pays 10% royalty on retail price or makes negotiable outright purchase. Pays negotiable advance.** Publishes book 8 months after acceptance. Responds in 3 weeks to queries; 5 weeks to proposals; 1 months to mss. Book catalog available free. Guidelines online.

NONFICTION Subjects include agriculture, cooking, foods, nutrition, health, medicine, nature, environment, science, analytical methods, chemical technolo-

gy, cosmetics, dictionaries, engineering, environmental science, food technology, formularies, industrial technology, medical, metallurgy, textiles. Submit outline, a few pages of 3 sample chapters, SASE. Download CPC submission form online and include with submission. Reviews, artwork and photos should also be part of the ms package.

TIPS Audience is professionals in various fields of chemistry, corporate and public libraries, college libraries. We request a fax letter with an introduction of the author and the kind of book written. Afterwards, we will reply. If the title is of interest, then we will request samples of the ms.

CHICAGO REVIEW PRESS

814 N. Franklin St., Chicago IL 60610. (312)337-0747. **Fax:** (312)337-5110. **E-mail:** frontdesk@chicagoreviewpress.com. **Website:** www.chicagoreviewpress. com. **Contact:** Cynthia Sherry, publisher; Yuval Taylor, senior editor; Jerome Pohlen, senior editor; Lisa Reardon, senior editor. Estab. 1973. "Chicago Review Press publishes high-quality, nonfiction, educational activity books that extend the learning process through hands-on projects and accurate and interesting text. We look for activity books that are as much fun as they are constructive and informative." **Pays authors royalty of 7.5-12.5% based on retail price. Offers advances of $3,000-6,000. Pays illustrators by the project (range varies considerably). Pays photographers by the project (range varies considerably).** Publishes book Publishes a book 1-2 years after acceptance. Accepts simultaneous submissions. Responds in 2 months. Book catalog available for $3. Ms guidelines available for $3.

Chicago Review Press does not publish fiction.

NONFICTION Young readers, middle readers and young adults: activity books, arts/crafts, multicultural, history, nature/environment, science. "We're interested in hands-on, educational books; anything else probably will be rejected." Average length: young readers and young adults—144-160 pages. Enclose cover letter and no more than a table of contents and 1-2 sample chapters; prefers not to receive e-mail queries.

TIPS "We're looking for original activity books for small children and the adults caring for them—new themes and enticing projects to occupy kids' imaginations and promote their sense of personal creativity. We like activity books that are as much fun as they are constructive. Please write for guidelines so you'll know what we're looking for."

⊘ CHILDREN'S BRAINS ARE YUMMY (CBAY) BOOKS

P.O. Box 92411, Austin TX 78709. (512)789-1004. **Fax:** (512)473-7710. **E-mail:** submissions@cbaybooks.com. **Website:** www.cbaybooks.com. **Contact:** Madeline Smoot, publisher. Estab. 2008. "CBAY Books currently focuses on quality fantasy and science fiction books for the middle grade and teen markets." **Publishes 8 titles/year. 30% of books from first-time authors. Pays authors royalty 10%-15% based on wholesale price. Offers advances against royalties. Average amount $500.** Brochure and guidelines online.

○ "We are not currently accepting unsolicited submissions."

FICTION Subjects include adventure, mystery, science fiction, suspense, folktales.

⊘ CHILDREN'S PRESS/FRANKLIN WATTS

Imprint of Scholastic, Inc., 90 Old Sherman Turnpike, Danbury CT 06816. **Website:** www.scholastic.com/internationalschools/childrenspress.htm. Estab. 1946. Publishes nonfiction hardcover originals. Book catalog for #10 SASE.

NONFICTION Subjects include animals, anthropology, archeology, art, architecture, ethnic, health, medicine, history, hobbies, multicultural, music, dance, nature, environment, science, sports, general children's nonfiction. "We publish nonfiction books that supplement the school curriculum." No fiction, poetry, folktales, cookbooks or novelty books. Does not accept unsolicited mss.

TIPS Most of this publisher's books are developed in-house; less than 5% come from unsolicited submissions. However, they publish several series for which they always need new books. Study catalogs to discover possible needs.

◐⊘ CHILD'S PLAY (INTERNATIONAL) LTD.

Children's Play International, Ashworth Rd. Bridgemead, Swindon, Wiltshire SN5 7YD, United Kingdom. **E-mail:** allday@childs-play.com; neil@childs-play.com; office@childs-play.com. **Website:** www.childs-play.com. **Contact:** Sue Baker, Neil Burden, ms acquisitions. Art Director: Annie Kubler. Estab. 1972. Specializes in nonfiction, fiction, educational material, multicultural material. Produces 30 picture books/year; 10 young readers/year; 2 middle readers/year. "A child's early years are more important than any other. This is when children learn most about the world around them and the language they need to survive and grow. Child's Play aims to create exactly the right material for this all-important time." **Publishes 45 titles/year. 20% of books from first-time authors.** Publishes book 2 years after acceptance. Accepts simultaneous submissions.

○ "Due to a backlog of submissions, Child's Play is currently no longer able to accept anymore mss."

NONFICTION Picture books: activity books, animal, concept, multicultural, music/dance, nature/environment, science. Young readers: activity books, animal, concept, multicultural, music/dance, nature/environment, science. Average word length: picture books—2,000; young readers—3,000.

FICTION Picture books: adventure, animal, concept, contemporary, folktales, multicultural, nature/environment. Young readers: adventure, animal, anthology, concept, contemporary, folktales, humor, multicultural, nature/environment, poetry. Average word length: picture books—1,500; young readers—2,000.

TIPS "Look at our website to see the kind of work we do before sending. Do not send cartoons. We do not publish novels. We do publish lots of books with pictures of babies/toddlers."

CHILD WELFARE LEAGUE OF AMERICA

1726 M St. NW, Suite 500, Washington DC 20036. **E-mail:** books@cwla.org. **Website:** www.cwla.org/pubs. Publishes hardcover and trade paperback originals. CWLA is a privately supported, nonprofit, membership-based organization committed to preserving, protecting, and promoting the well-being of all children and their families. Accepts simultaneous submissions. Book catalog and ms guidelines online.

IMPRINTS CWLA Press (child welfare professional publications); Child & Family Press (children's books and parenting books for the general public).

NONFICTION Subjects include child guidance, sociology. Submit complete ms and proposal with outline, TOC, sample chapter, intended audience, and SASE.

TIPS "We are looking for positive, kid-friendly books for ages 3-9. We are looking for books that have a positive message—a feel-good book."

CHOSEN BOOKS

A division of Baker Publishing Group, 3985 Bradwater St., Fairfax VA 22031. (703)764-8250. **Fax:** (703)764-

3995. **E-mail:** jcampbell@chosenbooks.com. **Website:** www.chosenbooks.com. **Contact:** Jane Campbell, editorial director. Estab. 1971. Publishes hardcover and trade paperback originals. "We publish well-crafted books that recognize the gifts and ministry of the Holy Spirit, and help the reader live a more empowered and effective life for Jesus Christ." **Publishes 20 titles/year. 10% of books from first-time authors. 99% from unagented writers. Pays small advance.** Publishes book 12-18 months after acceptance. Accepts simultaneous submissions. Responds in 2-3 months to queries. Guidelines sent electronically on request.

NONFICTION "We publish books reflecting the current acts of the Holy Spirit in the world, books with a charismatic Christian orientation, or thematic first-person narrative. Query briefly by e-mail first." No New Age, poetry, fiction, autobiographies, biographies, compilations, Bible studies, booklets, academic, or children's books. Submit synopsis, chapter outline, 2 chapters, résumé and SASE or e-mail address. No computer disks. E-mail attachments OK.

TIPS "We look for solid, practical advice for the growing and maturing Christian. Platform essential. No chronicling of life events, please. Narratives have to be theme-driven. State the topic or theme of your book clearly in your query."

CHRISTIAN BOOKS TODAY LTD

136 Main St., Buckshaw Village Chorley, Lancashire PR7 7BZ, United Kingdom. **E-mail:** editme@christianbookstoday.com. **Website:** www.christianbookstoday.com. **Contact:** Jason Richardson, MD (nonfiction); Lynda McIntosh, editor (fiction). Estab. 2009. Publishes trade paperback originals/reprints and electronic originals/reprints. **Publishes 39 titles/year. 75% of books from first-time authors. 100% from unagented writers. Pays 10% royalty on Amazon retail price; 15% e-book; 5% wholesale trade.** Publishes book 6 months after acceptance. Accepts simultaneous submissions. Responds in 1 month to queries; 2 months to proposals and mss. Catalog and Guidelines online.

NONFICTION Subjects include spirituality, Christian/Catholic. "We are not looking for nonfiction at this time. Please send us your fiction."

FICTION Subjects include adventure, mainstream, poetry, religious, spiritual, Catholic/Christian. "Please send us your Christian or 'clean read' fiction. Nondenominational Christian romance, suspense, mystery, and contemporary fiction are always welcome." Submit query with synopsis and writing sample.

TIPS "We appeal to a general Christian readership. We are interested in 'clean read' mss only. No profanity, sexual content, gambling, substance abuse, or graphic violence. Please do not send us conspiracy-type stories."

CHRISTIAN FOCUS PUBLICATIONS

Geanies House, Fearn, Tain Ross-shire Scotland IV20 1TW, United Kingdom. 44 (0) 1862 871 011. **Fax:** 44 (0) 1862 871 699. **E-mail:** info@christianfocus.com. **Website:** www.christianfocus.com. **Contact:** Catherine Mackenzie, publisher. Estab. 1975. Specializes in Christian material, nonfiction, fiction, educational material. **Publishes 22-32 titles/year. 2% of books from first-time authors.** Publishes book 1 year after acceptance. Responds to queries in 2 weeks; mss in 3 months.

NONFICTION All levels: activity books, biography, history, religion, science. Average word length: picture books—5,000; young readers—5,000; middle readers—5,000-10,000; young adult/teens—10,000-20,000. Query or submit outline/synopsis and 3 sample chapters. Will consider electronic submissions and previously published work.

FICTION Picture books, young readers, adventure, history, religion. Middle readers: adventure, problem novels, religion. Young adult/teens: adventure, history, problem novels, religion. Average word length: young readers—5,000; middle readers—max 10,000; young adult/teen—max 20,000. Query or submit outline/synopsis and 3 sample chapters. Will consider electronic submissions and previously published work.

TIPS "Be aware of the international market as regards writing style/topics as well as illustration styles. Our company sells rights to European as well as Asian countries. Fiction sales are not as good as they were. Christian fiction for youngsters is not a product that is performing well in comparison to nonfiction such as Christian biography/Bible stories/church history, etc."

CHRONICLE BOOKS

680 Second St., San Francisco CA 94107. **E-mail:** submissions@chroniclebooks.com. **Website:** www.chroniclebooks.com. "We publish an exciting range of books, stationery, kits, calendars, and novelty for-

mats. Our list includes children's books and interactive formats; young adult books; cookbooks; fine art, design, and photography; pop culture; craft, fashion, beauty, and home decor; relationships, mind-body-spirit; innovative formats such as interactive journals, kits, decks, and stationery; and much, much more." **Publishes 90 titles/year. Generally pays authors in royalties based on retail price, "though we do occasionally work on a flat fee basis." Advance varies. Illustrators paid royalty based on retail price or flat fee.** Publishes book Publishes a book 1-3 years after acceptance. Responds to queries in 1 month. Book catalog for 9x12 SAE and 8 first-class stamps. Ms guidelines for #10 SASE.

NONFICTION Subjects include art, beauty, cooking, crafts, house and home, New Age, pop culture. "We're always looking for the new and unusual. We do accept unsolicited mss and we review all proposals. However, given the volume of proposals we receive, we are not able to personally respond to unsolicited proposals unless we are interested in pursuing the project." Submit via mail or e-mail (prefers e-mail for adult submissions; only by mail for children's submissions). Submit proposal (guidelines online) and allow 3 months for editors to review. If submitting by mail, do not include SASE since our staff will not return materials.

FICTION Only interested in fiction for children and young adults. No adult fiction. Submit complete ms (picture books); submit outline/synopsis and 3 sample chapters (for older readers). Will not respond to submissions unless interested. Will not consider submissions by fax, e-mail or disk. Do not include SASE; do not send original materials. No submissions will be returned.

CHRONICLE BOOKS FOR CHILDREN

680 Second St., San Francisco CA 94107. (415)537-4200. **Fax:** (415)537-4460. **E-mail:** submissions@chroniclebooks.com. **Website:** www.chroniclekids.com. Publishes hardcover and trade paperback originals. "Chronicle Books for Children publishes an eclectic mixture of traditional and innovative children's books. Our aim is to publish books that inspire young readers to learn and grow creatively while helping them discover the joy of reading. We're looking for quirky, bold artwork and subject matter. Currently emphasizing picture books. De-emphasizing young adult." **Publishes 50-60 titles/year. 30,000 queries received/year. 6% of books from first-time authors. 25% from unagented writers. Pays 8% royalty. Pays variable advance.** Publishes book Publishes a book 18-24 months after acceptance. Accepts simultaneous submissions. Responds in 2-4 weeks to queries; 6 months to mss. Book catalog for 9x12 envelope and 3 first-class stamps. Guidelines online.

NONFICTION Subjects include animals, art, architecture, multicultural, nature, environment, science. Query with synopsis. Reviews artwork/photos.

FICTION Subjects include mainstream, contemporary, multicultural, young adult, picture books. Does not accept proposals by fax, via e-mail, or on disk. When submitting artwork, either as a part of a project or as samples for review, do not send original art.

TIPS "We are interested in projects that have a unique bent to them—be it in subject matter, writing style, or illustrative technique. As a small list, we are looking for books that will lend our list a distinctive flavor. Primarily we are interested in fiction and nonfiction picture books for children ages up to 8 years, and nonfiction books for children ages up to 12 years. We publish board, pop-up, and other novelty formats as well as picture books. We are also interested in early chapter books, middle grade fiction, and young adult projects."

CHURCH PUBLISHING INC.

445 Fifth Ave., New York NY 10016. (800)223-6602. **Fax:** (212)779-3392. **E-mail:** nabryan@cpg.org. **Website:** www.churchpublishing.org. **Contact:** Nancy Bryan, editorial director. Estab. 1884. "With a religious publishing heritage dating back to 1918 and headquartered today in New York City, CPI is an official publisher of worship materials and resources for The Episcopal Church, plus a multi-faceted publisher and supplier to the broader ecumenical marketplace. In the nearly 100 years since its first publication, Church Publishing has emerged as a principal provider of liturgical and musical resources for The Episcopal Church, along with works on church leadership, pastoral care and Christian formation. With its growing portfolio of professional books and resources, Church Publishing was recognized in 1997 as the official publisher for the General Convention of the Episcopal Church in the United States. Simultaneously through the years, Church Publishing has consciously broadened its program, reach, and service to the church by publishing books for and about the worldwide Anglican Communion."

IMPRINTS Church Publishing, Morehouse Publishing, Seabury Books.

TIPS "Prefer using freelancers who are located in central Pennsylvania and are available for meetings when necessary."

CLARION BOOKS

Houghton Mifflin Co., 215 Park Ave. S., New York NY 10003. **Website:** www.houghtonmifflinbooks. com; www.hmco.com. **Contact:** Dinah Stevenson, vice president and publisher; Jennifer B. Greene, senior editor (contemporary fiction, picture books for all ages, nonfiction); Jennifer Wingertzahn, editor (fiction, picture books); Lynne Polvino, editor (fiction, nonfiction, picture books); Christine Kettner, art director. Estab. 1965. Publishes hardcover originals for children. "Clarion Books publishes picture books, nonfiction, and fiction for infants through grade 12. Avoid telling your stories in verse unless you are a professional poet." **Publishes 50 titles/year. Pays 5-10% royalty on retail price. Pays minimum of $4,000 advance.** Publishes book Publishes a book 2 years after acceptance. Responds in 2 months to queries. Guidelines for #10 SASE or online.

"We are no longer responding to your unsolicited submission unless we are interested in publishing it. Please do not include a SASE. Submissions will be recycled, and you will not hear from us regarding the status of your submission unless we are interested. We regret that we cannot respond personally to each submission, but we do consider each and every submission we receive."

NONFICTION Subjects include Americana, history, language, literature, nature, environment, photography, holiday. No unsolicited mss. Query with SASE. Submit proposal package, sample chapters, SASE. Reviews artwork/photos. Send photocopies.

FICTION Subjects include adventure, historical, humor, mystery, suspense, strong character studies, contemporary. "Clarion is highly selective in the areas of historical fiction, fantasy, and science fiction. A novel must be superlatively written in order to find a place on the list. Mss that arrive without an SASE of adequate size will *not* be responded to or returned. Accepts fiction translations." Submit complete ms. No queries, please. Send to only *one* Clarion editor.

TIPS "Looks for freshness, enthusiasm—in short, life."

CLARITY PRESS, INC.

3277 Roswell Rd. NE, Suite 469, Atlanta GA 30305. (404)647-6501. **Fax:** (877)613-7868. **E-mail:** claritypress@usa.net. **Website:** www.claritypress.com. **Contact:** Diana G. Collier, editorial director (contemporary social justice issues). Estab. 1984. Publishes hardcover and trade paperback originals. **Publishes 8 titles/year.** Accepts simultaneous submissions. Responds to queries only if interested.

NONFICTION Subjects include ethnic, world affairs, human rights/socioeconomic and minority issues, globalization, social justice. Publishes books on contemporary global issues in U.S., Middle East and Africa. No fiction. Query by e-mail only with synopsis, TOC, résumé, publishing history.

TIPS "Check our titles on the website at www.claritypress.com."

Ⓐ CLARKSON POTTER

The Crown Publishing Group, Random House, Inc., 1745 Broadway, 13th Floor, New York NY 10019. (212)782-9000. **Website:** www.clarksonpotter.com. Estab. 1959. Publishes hardcover and trade paperback originals. Accepts agented submissions only. Clarkson Potter specializes in publishing cooking books, decorating and other around-the-house how-to subjects.

NONFICTION Subjects include art, architecture, child guidance, cooking, foods, nutrition, language, literature, memoirs, nature, environment, photography, psychology, translation. Agented submissions only.

CLEIS PRESS

Cleis Press & Viva Editions, 2246 Sixth St., Berkeley CA 94710. (510)845-8000 or (800)780-2279. **Fax:** (510)845-8001. **E-mail:** cleis@cleispress.com. **E-mail:** bknight@cleispress.com. **Website:** www.cleispress. com and www.vivaeditions.com. **Contact:** Brenda Knight, publisher. Kara Wuest, managing editor; Frédérique Delacoste, president Estab. 1980. Publishes books that inform, enlighten, and entertain. Areas of interest include gift, inspiration, health, family and childcare, self-help, women's issues, reference, cooking. "We do our best to bring readers quality books that celebrate life, inspire the mind, revive the spirit, and enhance lives all around. Our authors are practical visionaries; people who offer deep wisdom in a hopeful and helpful manner.". Cleis Press publishes provocative, intelligent books in the areas of sexuality, gay and lesbian studies, erotica, fiction, gender studies, and human rights. **Publishes 45 titles/year. 10% of books from first-time authors. 90% from unagented writers. Pays royalty on retail price.** Publishes book 2 years after acceptance. Responds in 2 month to queries.

IMPRINTS Viva Editions.

NONFICTION Subjects include gay, lesbian, women's issues, women's studies, sexual politics. "Cleis Press is interested in books on topics of sexuality, human rights and women's and gay and lesbian literature. Please consult our website first to be certain that your book fits our list." Query or submit outline and sample chapters.

FICTION Subjects include feminist, gay, lesbian, literary. "We are looking for high quality fiction and nonfiction." Submit complete ms. Include brief bio, list of publishing credits. Send SASE for return of ms or send a disposable ms and SASE for reply only.

TIPS "Be familiar with publishers' catalogs; be absolutely aware of your audience; research potential markets; present fresh new ways of looking at your topic; avoid `PR' language and include publishing history in query letter."

CLEVELAND STATE UNIVERSITY POETRY CENTER

2121 Euclid Ave., RT 1841, Cleveland OH 44115. (216)687-3986. **Fax:** (216)687-6943. **E-mail:** poetrycenter@csuohio.edu. **Website:** www.csuohio.edu/poetrycenter. **Contact:** Frank Giampietro, manager. Estab. 1962.

POETRY The Cleveland State University Poetry Center publishes "full-length collections by established and emerging poets, through competition and solicitation, as well as occasional poetry anthologies, texts on poetics, and novellas. Eclectic in its taste and inclusive in its aesthetic, with particular interest in lyric poetry and innovative approaches to craft. Not interested in light verse, devotional verse, doggerel, or poems by poets who have not read much contemporary poetry. Most mss we publish are accepted through the competitions. All mss sent for competitions are considered for publication. Outside of competitions, mss are accepted by solicitation only."

○ COACH HOUSE BOOKS

80 bpNichol Lane, Toronto ON M5S 3J4, Canada. (416)979-2217. **Fax:** (416)977-1158. **E-mail:** editor@chbooks.com. **Website:** www.chbooks.com. **Contact:**

Alana Wilcox, editorial director. Publishes trade paperback originals by Canadian authors. **Publishes 16 titles/year. 80% of books from first-time authors. 100% from unagented writers. Pays 10% royalty on retail price.** Publishes book 1 year after acceptance. Responds in 6 months to queries. Guidelines online.

NONFICTION Query.

FICTION Subjects include experimental, literary, poetry. "Electronic submissions are welcome. Please send your complete ms, along with an introductory letter that describes your work and compares it to at least 2 current Coach House titles, explaining how your book would fit our list, and a literary CV listing your previous publications and relevant experience. If you would like your ms back, please enclose a large enough self-addressed envelope with adequate postage. If you don't want your ms back, a small stamped envelope or e-mail address is fine. We prefer electronic submissions. Please e-mail PDF files to editor@chbooks.com and include the cover letter and CV as a part of the ms. Please send your ms only once. Revised and updated versions will not be read, so make sure you're happy with your text before sending. You can also mail your ms. Please do not send it by Express-Post or Canada Post courier—regular Canada Post mail is much more likely to arrive here. Be patient. We try to respond promptly, but we do receive hundreds of submissions, so it may take us several months to get back to you. Please do not call or e-mail to check on the status of your submission. We will answer you as promptly as possible."

TIPS "We are not a general publisher, and publish only Canadian poetry, fiction, artist books and drama. We are interested primarily in innovative or experimental writing."

COFFEE HOUSE PRESS

79 13th NE, Suite 110, Minneapolis MN 55413. (612)338-0125. **Fax:** (612)338-4004. **E-mail:** info@coffeehousepress.org. **Website:** www.coffeehousepress.org. **Contact:** Anitra Budd, managing editor. Estab. 1984. Publishes hardcover and trade paperback originals. This successful nonprofit small press has received numerous grants from various organizations including the NEA, the McKnight Foundation and Target. Books published by Coffee House Press have won numerous honors and awards. Example: The Book of Medicines by Linda Hogan won the Colorado Book Award for Poetry and the Lannan Founda-

tion Literary Fellowship. **Publishes 16-18 titles/year.** Responds in 4-6 weeks to queries; up to 6 months to mss. Book catalog and ms guidelines online.

NONFICTION Subjects include creative nonfiction, memoirs, book-length essays, collections of essays. Query with outline and sample pages during annual reading periods (March 1-April 30 and September 1-October 31).

FICTION Seeks literary novels, short story collections and poetry. Query first with outline and samples (20-30 pages) during annual reading periods (March 1-April 30 and September 1-October 31).

POETRY Coffee House Press will not accept unsolicited poetry submissions. Please check our web page periodically for future updates to this policy.

TIPS "Look for our books at stores and libraries to get a feel for what we like to publish. No phone calls, e-mails, or faxes."

CONARI PRESS

Red Wheel/Weiser, LLC., 665 Third St., Suite 400, San Francisco CA 94107. **E-mail:** info@rwwbooks. com. **E-mail:** submissions@rwwbooks.com. **Website:** www.redwheelweiser.com. **Contact:** Pat Bryce, acquisitions editor. Estab. 1987. "Conari Press, an imprint of Red Wheel/Weiser, publishes books on topics ranging from spirituality, personal growth, and relationships to women's issues, parenting, and social issues. Our mission is to publish quality books that will make a difference in people's lives—how we feel about ourselves and how we relate to one another. We value integrity, compassion, and receptivity, both in the books we publish and in the way we do business."

NONFICTION Subjects include foods, health, parenting, spirituality, womens issues, womens studies. "Inspire, literally to breathe life into. That's what Conari Press books aim to do — inspire all walks of life, mind, body, and spirit; inspire creativity, laughter, gratitude, good food, good health, and all good things in life." Submit proposal, including: an overview of the book; a complete table of contents; a market/audience analysis, including similar titles; an up-to-date listing of your own marketing and publicity experience and/or plans; your vita and/or qualifications to write the book; and two or three sample chapters. Send cover letter including author information and brief description of proposed work.

TIPS "Review our website to make sure your work is appropriate."

CONCORDIA PUBLISHING HOUSE

3558 S. Jefferson Ave., St. Louis MO 63118. (314)268-1187. **Fax:** (314)268-1329. **E-mail:** publicity@cph.org; sarah.steiner@cph.org. **Website:** www.cph.org. **Contact:** Sarah Steiner, production editor for professional and academic books. Estab. 1869. Publishes hardcover and trade paperback originals. "Concordia Publishing House produces quality resources that communicate and nurture the Christian faith and ministry of people of all ages, lay and professional. These resources include curriculum, worship aids, books, and religious supplies. We publish approximately 30 quality children's books each year. We boldly provide Gospel resources that are Christ-centered, Bible-based and faithful to our Lutheran heritage." **Pays authors royalties based on retail price or work purchased outright ($750-2,000).** Responds in 1 month to queries; 3 months to mss. Ms guidelines for 1 first-class stamp and a #10 envelope.

NONFICTION Subjects include child guidance, religion, science, child guidance in Christian context, inspirational. Picture books, young readers, young adults: Bible stories, activity books, arts/crafts, concept, contemporary, religion. "All books must contain explicit Christian content." Submit complete ms (picture books); submit outline/synopsis and samples for longer mss. May also query.

TIPS "Do not send finished artwork with the ms. If sketches will help in the presentation of the ms, they may be sent. If stories are taken from the Bible, they should follow the Biblical account closely. Liberties should not be taken in fantasizing Biblical stories."

⊕⊕ CONSTABLE & ROBINSON, LTD.

55-56 Russell Square, London WC1B 4HP, United Kingdom. 0208-741-3663. **Fax:** 0208-748-7562. **E-mail:** reader@constablerobinson.com. **Website:** constablerobinson.co.uk. **Contact:** Krystyna Green, editorial director (crime fiction). Publishes hardcover and trade paperback originals. **Publishes 60 titles/year. 3,000 queries/year; 1,000 mss/year. Pays royalty. Pays advance.** Publishes book 1 year after acceptance. Accepts simultaneous submissions. Responds in 1 month to queries and proposals; 3 months to mss. Book catalog available free.

IMPRINTS Corsair; Constable Hardback; Robinson Paperback.

NONFICTION Subjects include health, history, medicine, military, photography, politics, psychology, science, travel, war. Query with SASE. Submit synopsis. Reviews artwork/photos. Send photocopies.

FICTION Subjects include historical, mystery. Publishes "crime fiction (mysteries) and historical crime fiction." Length 80,000 words minimum; 130,000 words maximum. *Agented submissions only.*

TIPS Constable & Robinson Ltd. is looking for "crime novels with good, strong identities. Think about what it is that makes your book(s) stand out from the others. We do not publish thrillers."

CORNELL UNIVERSITY PRESS

Sage House, 512 E. State St., Ithaca NY 14850. (607)277-2338. **Fax:** (607)277-2374. **Website:** www.cornellpress.cornell.edu. Estab. 1869. Publishes hardcover and paperback originals. "Cornell Press is an academic publisher of nonfiction with particular strengths in anthropology, Asian studies, biological sciences, classics, history, labor and business, literary criticism, politics and international relations, women's studies, Slavic studies, philosophy, urban studies, health care work, regional titles, and security studies. Currently emphasizing sound scholarship that appeals beyond the academic community." **Publishes 150 titles/year. Pays royalty. Pays $0-5,000 advance.** Publishes book 1 year after acceptance of ms. Accepts simultaneous submissions. Catalog and guidelines online.

IMPRINTS Comstock (contact Heidi Steinmetz Lovette); ILR Press (contact Frances Benson).

○ On occasion accepts simultaneous submissions.

NONFICTION Subjects include agriculture, anthropology, archeology, art, architecture, business, economics, ethnic, government, politics, history, language, literature, military, war, music, dance, philosophy, regional, sociology, translation, women's issues, women's studies, classics, life sciences. Submit résumé, cover letter, and prospectus.

CORWIN PRESS, INC.

2455 Teller Rd., Thousand Oaks CA 91320. (800)818-7243. **Fax:** (805)499-2692. **E-mail:** lisa.shaw@corwinpress.com. **Website:** www.corwinpress.com. **Contact:** Lisa Shaw, executive director, editorial. Hudson Perigo, executive editor (classroom management, new teacher induction, general teaching methods); Jessica Allan, senior acquisitions editor (science, special education, gifted education, early childhood education, and counseling). Estab. 1990. Publishes paperback originals. **Publishes 150 titles/year.** Publishes book

7 months after acceptance. Responds in 1-2 months to queries. Guidelines online.

○ "Corwin Press, Inc., publishes leading-edge, user-friendly publications for education professionals."

NONFICTION Subjects include education. Seeking fresh insights, conclusions, and recommendations for action. Prefers theory or research-based books that provide real-world examples and practical, hands-on strategies to help busy educators be successful. Professional-level publications for administrators, teachers, school specialists, policymakers, researchers and others involved with Pre K-12 education. No textbooks that simply summarize existing knowledge or mass-market books. Query with SASE.

☼ COTEAU BOOKS

Thunder Creek Publishing Co-operative Ltd., 2517 Victoria Ave., Regina SK S4P 0T2, Canada. (306)777-0170. **Fax:** (306)522-5152. **E-mail:** coteau@coteaubooks.com. **Website:** www.coteaubooks.com. **Contact:** Geoffrey Ursell, publisher. Estab. 1975. Publishes trade paperback originals and reprints. "Our mission is to publish the finest in Canadian fiction, nonfiction, poetry, drama, and children's literature, with an emphasis on Saskatchewan and prairie writers. De-emphasizing science fiction, picture books." **Publishes 12 titles/year. 200 queries received/year. 40 mss received/year. 25% of books from first-time authors. 90% from unagented writers. Pays 10% royalty on retail price.** Publishes book 1 year after acceptance. Responds in 3 months. Book catalog available free. Guidelines online.

NONFICTION Subjects include creative nonfiction, ethnic, history, language, literature, memoirs, regional, sports, travel. *Canadian authors only.* Submit hard copy query, bio, 3-4 sample chapters, SASE.

FICTION Subjects include ethnic, fantasy, feminist, gay, lesbian, historical, humor, juvenile, literary, mainstream, contemporary, multicultural, multimedia, mystery, plays, poetry, regional, short story collections, spiritual, sports, teen/young adult, novels/short fiction, adult/middle years. *Canadian authors only.* No science fiction. No children's picture books. Submit hard copy query, bio, complete ms, SASE.

POETRY Submit 20-25 sample poems.

TIPS "Look at past publications to get an idea of our editorial program. We do not publish romance, horror, or picture books but are interested in juvenile and teen fiction from Canadian authors. Submissions, even queries, must be made in hard copy only. We do not accept simultaneous/multiple submissions. Check our website for new submission timing guidelines."

COUNCIL ON SOCIAL WORK EDUCATION

1701 Duke St., Suite 200, Alexandria VA 22314. (703)683-8080. **Fax:** (703)683-8099. **E-mail:** info@ cswe.org. **Website:** www.cswe.org. **Contact:** Elizabeth Simon, publications manager. Estab. 1952. Publishes trade paperback originals. "Council on Social Work Education produces books and resources for social work educators, students and practitioners." **Publishes 4 titles/year. 12 queries received/year. 8 mss received/year. 25% of books from first-time authors. 100% from unagented writers. Pays sliding royalty scale, starting at 10%.** Publishes book 1 year after acceptance. Responds in 2 months to queries; 3 months to proposals and mss. Book catalog and ms guidelines free via website or with SASE.

NONFICTION Subjects include education, sociology, social work. Books for social work and other educators. Query via e-mail only with proposal package, including CV, outline, expected audience, and 2 sample chapters.

TIPS "Audience is Social work educators and students and others in the helping professions. Check areas of publication interest on website."

COVENANT COMMUNICATIONS, INC.

920 E. State Rd., American Fork UT 84003. (801)756-9966. **Fax:** (801)756-1049. **E-mail:** submissionsdesk@ covenant-lds.com. **Website:** www.covenant-lds.com. **Contact:** Kathryn Jenkins, managing editor. Estab. 1958. "Currently emphasizing inspirational, doctrinal, historical, biography. Our fiction is also expanding, and we are looking for new approaches to LDS literature and storytelling." **Publishes 80-100 titles/year. Receives 350 queries/year; 1,200 mss/year. 60% of books from first-time authors. 99% from unagented writers. Pays 6 1/2-15% royalty on retail price.** Publishes book 6-12 months after acceptance. Accepts simultaneous submissions. Responds in 1 month on queries and proposals; 4 months on mss. Guidelines online.

NONFICTION Subjects include history, religion, spirituality. "We target an exclusive audience of members of The Church of Jesus Christ of Latter-day Saints. All mss must be written for that audience." Submit complete ms. Reviews artwork. Send photocopies.

FICTION Subjects include adventure, historical, mystery, regional, religious, romance, spiritual, suspense. "We publish exclusively to the 'Mormon' (The Church of Jesus Christ of Latter-Day Saints) market. Fiction must feature characters who are members of that church, grappling with issues relevant to that religion." Submit complete ms.

TIPS "Our audience is exclusively LDS (Latter-Day Saints, 'Mormon'). We do not accept mss that do not have a strong LDS theme or feature strong LDS characters."

CQ PRESS

2300 N St., NW, Suite 800, Washington DC 20037. (202)729-1800. **E-mail:** ckiino@cqpress.com. **Website:** www.cqpress.com. **Contact:** Charisse Kiino, chief acquisitions editor. Estab. 1945. Publishes hardcover and online paperback titles. Accepts simultaneous submissions. Book catalog available free.

IMPRINTS College, Library/Reference, Staff Directories; CQ Electronic Library/CQ Researcher.

NONFICTION Subjects include government, politics, history. "We are interested in American government, public administration, comparative government, and international relations." Submit proposal package, including prospectus, TOC, 1-2 sample chapters.

TIPS "Our books present important information on American government and politics, and related issues, with careful attention to accuracy, thoroughness, and readability."

⊘ CRABTREE PUBLISHING COMPANY

PMB 59051, 350 Fifth Ave., 59th Floor, New York NY 10118. (212)496-5040; (800)387-7650. **Fax:** (800)355-7166. **Website:** www.crabtreebooks.com. Estab. 1978. Crabtree Publishing Company is dedicated to producing high-quality books and educational products for K-8+. Each resource blends accuracy, immediacy, and eye-catching illustration with the goal of inspiring nothing less than a life-long interest in reading and learning in children. The company began building its reputation in 1978 as a quality children's nonfiction book publisher with acclaimed author Bobbie Kalman's first series about the early pioneers. The Early Settler Life Series became a mainstay in schools as well as historic sites and museums across North America.

○ "Crabtree does not accept unsolicited mss. Crabtree Publishing has an editorial team in-house that creates curriculum-specific book series."

TIPS "Since our books are for younger readers, lively photos of children and animals are always excellent." Portfolio should be diverse and encompass several subjects rather than just 1 or 2; depth of coverage of subject should be intense so that any publishing company could, conceivably, use all or many of a photographer's photos in a book on a particular subject."

CRAFTSMAN BOOK CO.

6058 Corte Del Cedro, Carlsbad CA 92011. (760)438-7828 or (800)829-8123. **Fax:** (760)438-0398. **Website:** www.craftsman-book.com. **Contact:** Laurence D. Jacobs, editorial manager. Estab. 1957. Publishes paperback originals. Publishes how-to manuals for professional builders. Currently emphasizing construction software. **Publishes 12 titles/year. 85% of books from first-time authors. 98% from unagented writers. Pays 7 1/2-12 1/2% royalty on wholesale price or retail price.** Publishes book 2 years after acceptance. Accepts simultaneous submissions. Responds in 2 months to queries. Book catalog and ms guidelines free.

NONFICTION All titles are related to construction for professional builders. Reviews artwork/photos.

TIPS "The book submission should be loaded with step-by-step instructions, illustrations, charts, reference data, forms, samples, cost estimates, rules of thumb, and examples that solve actual problems in the builder's office and in the field. It must cover the subject completely, become the owner's primary reference on the subject, have a high utility-to-cost ratio, and help the owner make a better living in his chosen field."

CRAIGMORE CREATIONS

2900 SE Stark St., Suite 1A, Portland OR 97124. (503)477-9562. **E-mail:** info@craigmorecreations.com. **Website:** www.craigmorecreations.com. Estab. 2009. Accepts simultaneous submissions.

NONFICTION Subjects include animals, anthropology, archeology, creative nonfiction, environment, multicultural, nature, regional, science, young adult, Earth sciences, natural history. "We publish books that make time travel seem possible: nonfiction that explores pre-history and Earth sciences for children. Submit proposal package. See website for detailed submission guidelines. Send photocopies.

FICTION Subjects include juvenile, picture books, young adult. Submit proposal package. See website for detailed submission guidelines.

CREATIVE COMPANY

P.O. Box 227, Mankato MN 56002. (800)445-6209. **Fax:** (507)388-2746. **E-mail:** info@thecreativecompany.us. **Website:** www.thecreativecompany.us. **Contact:** Aaron Frisch. Estab. 1932. The Creative Company has two imprints: Creative Editions (picture books), and Creative Education (nonfiction series). **Publishes 140 titles/year.** Publishes book Publishes a book 2 years after acceptance. Responds in 3 months to queries/mss. Guidelines available for SAE.

"We are currently not accepting fiction submissions."

NONFICTION Picture books, young readers, young adults: animal, arts/crafts, biography, careers, geography, health, history, hobbies, multicultural, music/dance, nature/environment, religion, science, social issues, special needs, sports. Average word length: young readers—500; young adults—6,000. Submit outline/synopsis and 2 sample chapters, along with division of titles within the series.

TIPS "We are accepting nonfiction, series submissions only. Fiction submissions will not be reviewed or returned. Nonfiction submissions should be presented in series (4, 6, or 8) rather than single."

CRESCENT MOON PUBLISHING

P.O. Box 393, Maidstone Kent ME14 5XU, United Kingdom. (44)(162)272-9593. **E-mail:** cresmopub@yahoo.co.uk. **Website:** www.crescentmoon.org.uk. **Contact:** Jeremy Robinson, director (arts, media, cinema, literature); Cassidy Hushes (visual arts). Estab. 1988. Publishes hardcover and trade paperback originals. "Our mission is to publish the best in contemporary work, in poetry, fiction, and critical studies, and selections from the great writers. Currently emphasizing nonfiction (media, film, music, painting). De-emphasizing children's books." **Publishes 25 titles/year. 300 queries received/year. 400 mss received/year. 1% of books from first-time authors. 1% from unagented writers. Pays royalty. Pays negotiable advance.** Publishes book 18 months after acceptance. Accepts simultaneous submissions. Responds in 2 months to queries; 4 months to proposals and mss. Book catalog and ms guidelines free.

IMPRINTS *Joe's Press, Pagan America Magazine, Passion Magazine.*

NONFICTION Subjects include Americana, art, architecture, gardening, government, politics, language, literature, music, dance, philosophy, religion, travel, women's issues, women's studies, cinema, the media, cultural studies. Query with SASE. Submit outline, 2 sample chapters, bio. Reviews artwork/photos. Send photocopies.

FICTION Subjects include erotica, experimental, feminist, gay, lesbian, literary, short story collections, translation. "We do not publish much fiction at present but will consider high quality new work." Query with SASE. Submit outline, clips, 2 sample chapters, bio.

POETRY "We prefer a small selection of the poet's very best work at first. We prefer free verse or non-rhyming poetry. Do not send too much material." Query and submit 6 sample poems.

TIPS "Our audience is interested in new contemporary writing."

⊘ CRICKET BOOKS

Imprint of Carus Publishing, 70 E. Lake St., Suite 300, Chicago IL 60601. (603)924-7209. **Fax:** (603)924-7380. **Website:** www.cricketmag.com. **Contact:** Submissions Editor. Estab. 1999. Publishes hardcover originals. Cricket Books publishes picture books, chapter books, and middle-grade novels. **Publishes 5 titles/year. Pays up to 10% royalty on retail price. Average advance: $1,500 and up.** Publishes book 18 months after acceptance.

　◐　*Currently not accepting queries or mss. Check website for submissions details and updates.*

FICTION Subjects include juvenile, adventure, easy-to-read, fantasy/science fiction, historical, horror, mystery/suspense, problem novels, sports, westerns.

CRIMSON ROMANCE

Adams Media, a division of F+W Media, Inc., 57 Littlefield St., Avon MA 02322. (508)427-7100. **E-mail:** editorcrimson@gmail.com. **Website:** crimsonromance.com. **Contact:** Tara Gelsomino, editor. Publishes electronic originals. "Direct to e-book imprint of Adams Media."

FICTION Subjects include romance. "We're open to romance submissions in 5 popular subgenres: romantic suspense, contemporary, paranormal, historical, and erotic romance. Within those subgenres, we are flexible about what happens. It's romance, so there must be a happily-ever-after, but we're open to how your characters get there. You won't come up against preconceived ideas about what can or can't happen in romance or what kind of characters you can or can't have. Our only rule is everyone has to be a consenting adult. Other than that, we're looking for smart, savvy heroines, fresh voices, and new takes on old favorite themes. We're looking for full-length novels, and while we prefer to work on the shorter end of the spectrum (50,000 words, give or take), we're not going to rule you out because you go shorter or longer." Submit brief description of work–please, no attachments.

CROSS-CULTURAL COMMUNICATIONS

Cross-Cultural Literary Editions, Ltd.; Expressive Editions; Ostrich Editions, 239 Wynsum Ave., Merrick NY 11566. (516)869-5635. **Fax:** (516)379-1901. **E-mail:** cccbarkan@optonline.net. **Website:** www.cross-culturalcommunications.com. **Contact:** Stanley H. Barkan, publisher/editor-in-chief (bilingual poetry); Bebe Barkan, Mia Barkan Clarke, art editors (complementary art to poetry editions). Estab. 1971. Publishes hardcover and trade paperback originals. **Publishes 10 titles/year. 200 queries received/year. 50 mss received/year. 10-25% of books from first-time authors. 100% from unagented writers.** Publishes book 1 year after acceptance. Responds in 1 month to proposals; 2 months to mss. Book catalog (sample flyers) for #10 SASE.

IMPRINTS Expressive Editions (contact Mia Barkan Clarke).

NONFICTION Subjects include language, literature, memoirs, multicultural. "Query first; we basically do not want the focus on nonfiction." Query with SASE. Reviews artwork/photos. Send photocopies.

FICTION Subjects include historical, multicultural, poetry, poetry in translation, translation, bilingual poetry. Query with SASE.

POETRY For bilingual poetry submit 3-6 short poems in original language with English translation, a brief (3-5 lines) bio of the author and translator(s).

TIPS "Best chance: poetry from a translation."

❹ CROWN BUSINESS

Random House, Inc., 1745 Broadway, New York NY 10019. (212)572-2275. **Fax:** (212)572-6192. **E-mail:** crownbiz@randomhouse.com. **Website:** crownpublishing.com. Estab. 1995. Publishes hardcover and trade paperback originals. Accepts simultaneous submissions. Book catalog online.

　◐　*Agented submissions only.*

NONFICTION Subjects include business, economics, money, finance.

ⓐⓄ CROWN PUBLISHING GROUP

Random House, Inc., 1745 Broadway, New York NY 10019. (212)782-9000. **E-mail:** CrownBiz@randomhouse.com. **Website:** www.randomhouse.com/crown. Estab. 1933. Publishes popular fiction and nonfiction hardcover originals.

IMPRINTS Amphoto Books; Back Stage Books; Billboard Books; Broadway Books; Clarkson Potter; Crown; Crown Archetype; Crown Business; Crown Forum; Doubleday Religion; Harmony Books; Image Books; Potter Craft; Potter Style; Ten Speed Press; Three Rivers Press; Waterbrook Multnomah; Watson-Guptill.

○ *Agented submissions only.* See website for more details.

CRYSTAL SPIRIT PUBLISHING, INC.

P.O. Box 12506, Durham NC 27709. **E-mail:** crystalspiritinc@gmail.com. **Website:** www.crystalspiritinc.com. **Contact:** Vanessa S. O'Neal, senior editor; Elise L. Lattier, editor. Estab. 2004. Publishes hardcover, trade paperback, mass market paperback, and electronic originals. "Our readers are lovers of high-quality books that are sold in book and gift stores and placed in libraries and schools. They support independent authors and they expect works that will provide them with entertainment, inspiration, romance, and education. Our audience loves to read and will embrace niche authors that love to write." **Publishes 3-4 titles/year. Receives 30 mss/year. 80% of books from first-time authors. 100% from unagented writers. Pays 20-45% royalty on retail price.** Publishes book 3-6 months after acceptance. Accepts simultaneous submissions. Responds in 3-6 months to mss. Book catalog and ms guidelines online.

NONFICTION Subjects include business, creative nonfiction, economics, ethnic, memoirs, multicultural, New Age, religion, sex, spirituality, young adult, inspirational, Christian romance. Submit cover letter, synopsis, and 30 pages (or 30 chapters) by USPS mail ONLY.

FICTION Subjects include confession, contemporary, erotica, ethnic, feminist, gay, humor, juvenile, lesbian, literary, mainstream, multicultural, poetry, religious, romance, short story collections, spiritual, young adult, inspirational, Christian romance. Submit cover letter, synopsis, and 30 pages (or 30 chapters) **by USPS mail ONLY.**

POETRY "All poetry must have titles. Include a description of the collective works and type of poetry." Submit 10 sample poems.

TIPS "Submissions are accepted for publication throughout the year, but the decisions for publishing considerations are made in March, June, September, and December. Works should be positive and non-threatening. Typed pages only. Non-typed entries will not be reviewed or returned. Ensure that all contact information is correct, abide by the submission guidelines and do not send follow-up e-mails or calls."

CUP OF TEA BOOKS

PageSpring Publishing, P.O. Box 21133, Columbus OH 43221. **E-mail:** weditor@pagespringpublishing.com. **Website:** www.cupofteabooks.com. Estab. 2012. Publishes trade paperback and electronic originals. "Cup of Tea Books publishes novel-length women's fiction. We are interested in finely-drawn characters, a compelling story, and deft writing. We accept e-mail queries only; see our website for details." **Pays royalty.** Publishes book 6 months after acceptance. Accepts simultaneous submissions. Responds in 1 month to queries and mss. Guidelines online.

FICTION Subjects include adventure, contemporary, fantasy, feminist, historical, humor, literary, mainstream, mystery, regional, romance. Submit proposal package via e-mail. Include synopsis and the first 30 pages.

CYCLE PUBLICATIONS INC.

Van der Plas Publications, 1282 Seventh Ave., San Francisco CA 94112. (415)665-8214. **Fax:** (415)753-8572. **E-mail:** rvdp@cyclepublishing.com. **Website:** www.cyclepublishing.com. Estab. 1985. "Van der Plas Publications / Cycle Publishing was started in 1997 with four books. Since then, we have introduced about 4 new books each year, and in addition to our 'mainstay' of cycling books, we now also have books on manufactured housing, golf, baseball, and strength training. Our offices are located in San Francisco, where we do editorial work, as well as administration, publicity, and design. Our books are warehoused in Kimball, Michigan, which is close to the companies that print most of our books and is conveniently located to supply our book trade distributors and the major book wholesalers."

CYCLOTOUR GUIDE BOOKS

P.O. Box 10585, Rochester NY 14610. (585)244-6157. **E-mail:** cyclotour@cyclotour.com. **Website:** www.cyclotour.com. Estab. 1994. Publishes trade paperback originals. **Publishes 2 titles/year. Receives 25 queries/year and 2 mss/year. 50% of books from first-time authors. 100% from unagented writers.** Publishes book 2 years after acceptance. Accepts simultaneous submissions. Responds in 1 month to queries, proposals, and mss. Book catalog and ms guidelines online.

NONFICTION Subjects include sports (bicycle only), travel (bicycle tourism). No narrative accounts of their bicycle tour without distance indicators. Query with SASE. Reviews artwork/photos as part of ms package. Send photocopies.

TIPS Bicyclists. Folks with a dream of bicycle touring. "Check your grammar and spelling. Write logically."

⊘ DA CAPO PRESS

Perseus Books Group, 44 Farnsworth St., 3rd Floor, Boston MA 02210. (617)252-5200. **Website:** www.dacapopress.com. Estab. 1975. Publishes hardcover originals and trade paperback originals and reprints. **Publishes 115 titles/year. 500 queries received/year. 300 mss received/year. 25% of books from first-time authors. 1% from unagented writers. Pays 7-15% royalty. Pays $1,000-225,000 advance.** Publishes book 1 year after acceptance. Catalog and guidelines online.

NONFICTION Subjects include art, architecture, contemporary culture, creative nonfiction, government, politics, history, language, literature, memoirs, military, war, social sciences, sports, translation, travel, world affairs. No unsolicited mss or proposals.

➕😊 DARTON, LONGMAN & TODD

1 Spencer Ct., 140-142 Wandsworth High St., London SW18 4JJ, United Kingdom. (44)(208)875-0155. **Fax:** (44)(208)875-0133. **E-mail:** editorial@dartonlongman-todd.co.uk. **Website:** www.dltbooks.com. **Contact:** Editorial Department. Estab. 1959. Darton, Longman and Todd is an internationally-respected publisher of brave, ground-breaking, independent books and e-books on matters of heart, mind, and soul that meet the needs and interests of ordinary people. **Publishes 50 titles/year. Pays royalty.** Accepts simultaneous submissions. Guidelines available free.

NONFICTION Subjects include religion, spirituality. Simultaenous submissions accepted, but inform publisher if submitting elsewhere. Does not want poetry, scholarly monographs or children's books. Query with SASE.

TIPS "Our books are read by people inside and outside the Christian churches, by believers, seekers and sceptics, and by thoughtful non-specialists as well as students and academics. The books are widely sold throughout the religious and the general trade."

DAW BOOKS, INC.

Penguin Group (USA), 375 Hudson St., New York NY 10014-3658. (212)366-2096. **Fax:** (212)366-2090. **Website:** www.dawbooks.com. **Contact:** Peter Stampfel, submissions editor. Estab. 1971. Publishes hardcover and paperback originals and reprints. DAW Books publishes science fiction and fantasy. **Publishes 50-60 titles/year. Pays in royalties with an advance negotiable on a book-by-book basis.** Responds in 3 months. Guidelines online.

FICTION Subjects include fantasy, science fiction, "Currently seeking modern urban fantasy and paranormals. We like character-driven books with appealing protagonists, engaging plots, and well-constructed worlds. We accept both agented and unagented mss.". Submit entire ms, cover letter, SASE. Do not submit your only copy of anything. The average length of the novels we publish varies but is almost never less than 80,000 words.

DAWN PUBLICATIONS

12402 Bitney Springs Rd., Nevada City CA 95959. (530)274-7775. **Fax:** (530)274-7778. **Website:** www.dawnpub.com. **Contact:** Glenn Hovemann, editor. Estab. 1979. Publishes hardcover and trade paperback originals. "Dawn Publications is dedicated to inspiring in children a sense of appreciation for all life on earth. Dawn looks for nature awareness and appreciation titles that promote a relationship with the natural world and specific habitats, usually through inspiring treatment and nonfiction." **Publishes 6 titles/year. 2,500 queries or mss received/year. 15% of books from first-time authors. 90% from unagented writers. Pays advance.** Publishes book 1-2 years after acceptance. Accepts simultaneous submissions. Responds in 2 months to queries. Catalog and guidelines online.

🗨   Dawn accepts mss submissions by e-mail; follow instructions posted on website. Submissions by mail still OK.

NONFICTION Subjects include animals, nature, environment.

TIPS "Publishes mostly creative nonfiction with lightness and inspiration." Looking for "picture books expressing nature awareness with inspirational quality leading to enhanced self-awareness." Does not publish anthropomorphic works; no animal dialogue.

⚠️✅ DELACORTE PRESS

Imprint of Random House Publishing Group, 1745 Broadway, New York NY 10019. (212)782-9000. **Website:** www.randomhouse.com. Publishes middle grade and young adult fiction in hard cover, trade paperback, mass market and digest formats. Publishes middle grade and young adult fiction in hardcover, trade paperback, mass market and digest formats.

○ All other query letters or ms submissions must be submitted through an agent or at the request of an editor. No e-mail queries.

⚠️✅ DEL REY BOOKS

Imprint of Random House Publishing Group, 1745 Broadway, 18th Floor, New York NY 10019. (212)782-9000. **E-mail:** delrey@randomhouse.com. **Website:** www.randomhouse.com. Estab. 1977. Publishes hardcover, trade paperback, and mass market originals and mass market paperback reprints. Del Rey publishes top level fantasy, alternate history, and science fiction. **Pays royalty on retail price. Pays competitive advance.**

IMPRINTS Del Rey/Manga, Del Rey/Lucas Books.

FICTION Subjects include fantasy, should have the practice of magic as an essential element of the plot, science fiction, well-plotted novels with good characterizations, exotic locales and detailed alien creatures, alternate history. Agented submissions only.

TIPS "Del Rey is a reader's house. Pay particular attention to plotting, strong characters, and dramatic, satisfactory conclusions. It must be/feel believable. That's what the readers like. In terms of mass market, we basically created the field of fantasy bestsellers. Not that it didn't exist before, but we put the mass into mass market."

DEMONTREVILLE PRESS, INC.

P.O. Box 835, Lake Elmo MN 55042. **E-mail:** publisher@demontrevillepress.com. **Website:** www.demontrevillepress.com. **Contact:** Kevin Clemens, publisher (automotive fiction and nonfiction). Estab. 2006. Publishes trade paperback originals and reprints. **Publishes 4 titles/year. 150 queries received/year. 100 mss received/year. 90% of books from first-time authors. 90% from unagented writers. Pays 20% royalty on sale price.** Publishes book 18 months after acceptance. Accepts simultaneous submissions. Responds in 3 months to queries; 4 months to proposals; 6 months to mss. Catalog and guidelines online.

NONFICTION Subjects include current events, automotive, environment, motorcycle. "We want novel length automotive or motorcycle historicals and/or adventures. Environmental energy and infrastructure books wanted." Submit proposal package online, outline, 3 sample chapters, bio. Reviews artwork/photos. Do not send photos until requested.

FICTION Subjects include current events, environment, adventure, mystery, sports, young adult, automotive, motorcycle. "We want novel length automotive or motorcycle historicals and/or adventures." Submit proposal package, 3 sample chapters, clips, bio.

TIPS "Environmental, energy and transportation nonfiction works are now being accepted. Automotive and motorcycle enthusiasts, adventurers, environmentalists and history buffs make up our audience."

⚠️ DIAL BOOKS FOR YOUNG READERS

Imprint of Penguin Group USA, 375 Hudson St., New York NY 10014. (212)366-2000. **Website:** www.penguin.com/youngreaders. **Contact:** Lauri Hornik, president/publisher; Kathy Dawson, associate publisher; Kate Harrison, senior editor; Liz Waniewski, editor; Alisha Niehaus, editor; Jessica Garrison, editor; Lily Malcom, art director. Estab. 1961. Publishes hardcover originals. "Dial Books for Young Readers publishes quality picture books for ages 18 months-6 years; lively, believable novels for middle readers and young adults; and occasional nonfiction for middle readers and young adults." **Publishes 50 titles/year. 5,000 queries received/year. 20% of books from first-time authors. Pays royalty. Pays varies advance.** Responds in 4-6 months to queries. Book catalog for 9 X12 envelope and 4 first-class stamps.

NONFICTION "Due to the overwhelming number of unsolicited mss we receive, we at Dial Books for Young Readers have had to change our submissions policy: As of August 1, 2005, Dial will no longer respond to your unsolicited submission unless interested in publishing it. Please do not include SASE with your submission. You will not hear from Dial regarding the status of your submission unless we are interested, in which case you can expect a reply from us within four months. We accept entire picture book mss and a maximum of 10 pages for longer works (novels, easy-to-reads). When submitting a portion of a longer work, please provide an accompanying cover letter that briefly describes your ms's plot, genre (i.e. easy-to-read, middle grade or YA novel), the intended age group, and your publishing credits, if any."

FICTION Subjects include adventure, fantasy, juvenile, picture books, young adult. Especially looking for lively and well-written novels for middle grade and young adult children involving a convincing plot and believable characters. The subject matter or theme should not already be overworked in previously published books. The approach must not be demeaning to any minority group, nor should the roles of female characters (or others) be stereotyped, though we don't think books should be didactic, or in any way message-y. No topics inappropriate for the juvenile, young adult, and middle grade audiences. No plays. Accepts unsolicited queries and up to 10 pages for longer works and unsolicited mss for picture books.

TIPS "Our readers are anywhere from preschool age to teenage. Picture books must have strong plots, lots of action, unusual premises, or universal themes treated with freshness and originality. Humor works well in these books. A very well-thought-out and intelligently presented book has the best chance of being taken on. Genre isn't as much of a factor as presentation."

DIVERSION PRESS

P.O. Box 3930, Clarksville TN 37043. **E-mail:** diversionpress@yahoo.com. **Website:** www.diversionpress. com. Estab. 2008. Publishes hardcover, trade and mass market paperback originals. **Publishes 5-10 titles/year. 75% of books from first-time authors. 100% from unagented writers. Pays 10% royalty on wholesale price.** Publishes book 1-2 years after acceptance. Responds in 2 weeks to queries. Responds in 1 month to proposals. Guidelines online.

NONFICTION Subjects include Americana, animals, community, contemporary culture, education, ethnic, government, politics, health, medicine, history, hobbies, humanities, language, literature, literary criticism, memoirs, military, war, multicultural, philosophy, psychology, recreation, regional, science, social sciences, sociology, travel, women's issues, women's studies, world affairs. "The editors have doctoral degrees and are interested in a broad range of academic works. We are also interested in how-to, slice of life, and other nonfiction areas." Does not review works

that are sexually explicit, religious, or put children in a bad light. Send query/proposal first. Mss accepted by request only. Reviews artwork/photos. Send photocopies.

FICTION Subjects include adventure, fantasy, gothic, historical, horror, humor, literary, mainstream, contemporary, mystery, poetry, science fiction, short story collections, suspense, young adult. "We will happily consider any children's or young adult books if they are illustrated. If your story has potential to become a series, please address that in your proposal. Fiction short stories and poetry will be considered for our anthology series. See website for details on how to submit your ms."

POETRY "Poetry will be considered for anthology series and for our poetry award." Submit 5 sample poems.

TIPS "Read our website and blog prior to submitting. We like short, concise queries. Tell us why your book is different, not like other books. Give us a realistic idea of what you will do to market your book—that you will actually do. We will ask for more information if we are interested."

DIVERTIR

P.O. Box 232, North Salem NH 03073. **E-mail:** info@ divertirpublishing.com; query@divertirpublishing. com. **Website:** www.divertirpublishing.com. **Contact:** Kenneth Tupper, publisher. Estab. 2009. Publishes trade paperback and electronic originals. **Publishes 6-12 titles/year. 80% of books from first-time authors. 100% from unagented writers. Pays 10-15% royalty on wholesale price (for novels and nonfiction).** Publishes book 6-9 months after acceptance. Accepts simultaneous submissions. Responds in 1-2 months on queries; 3-4 months on proposals and mss. Catalog online. Guidelines online.

NONFICTION Subjects include contemporary culture, crafts, government, history, hobbies, New Age, politics, psychic, world affairs. "We are particularly interested in the following: political/social commentary, current events, history, humor and satire, and crafts and hobbies." Reviews artwork/photos as part of the ms package. Submit electronically.

FICTION Subjects include adventure, contemporary, fantasy, gothic, historical, horror, humor, literary, mainstream, mystery, occult, poetry, religious, romance, science fiction, young adult. "We are particularly interested in the following: science fiction, fan-

tasy, historical, alternate history, contemporary mythology, mystery and suspense, paranormal, and urban fantasy." Electronically submit proposal package,
including synopsis and query letter with author's bio.

TIPS "Please see our Author Info page (online) for
more information."

⚠️ DK PUBLISHING

Penguin Random House, 375 Hudson St., New York
NY 10014. **Website:** www.dk.com. "DK publishes
photographically illustrated nonfiction for children
of all ages."

○ *DK Publishing does not accept unagented mss
or proposals.*

DNA PRESS & NARTEA PUBLISHING

DNA Press, P.O. Box 9311, Glendale CA 91226. **E-
mail:** editors@dnapress.com. **Website:** www.dna-
press.com. Estab. 1998. Publishes hardcover and
trade paperback originals. Book publisher for young
adults, children, and adults. **Publishes 10 titles/year.
500 queries received/year. 400 mss received/year.
90% of books from first-time authors. 100% from
unagented writers. Pays 10-15% royalty.** Publishes
book 8 months after acceptance. Accepts simultaneous submissions. Responds in 6 weeks to mss. Book
catalog and ms guidelines free.

NONFICTION "We publish business, real estate and
investment books." Reviews artwork/photos.

FICTION Subjects include juvenile, science fiction,
young adult. All books should be oriented to explaining science even if they do not fall 100% under the category of science fiction. Submit complete ms.

TIPS Quick response, great relationships, high com-
mission/royalty.

⚠️ DOUBLEDAY RELIGION

The Crown Publishing Group, a Division of Random
House, Inc., 1745 Broadway, New York NY 10019.
(212)782-9000. **Website:** crownpublishing.com. Estab.
1897. Publishes hardcover and trade paperback originals and reprints. Accepts simultaneous submissions.

IMPRINTS Image Books; Galilee; New Jerusalem Bible; Three Leaves Press.

○ "Random House, Inc. does not accept unsolicited submissions, proposals, mss, or submission queries via e-mail at this time. If you
would like to have your work or ms considered
for publication by a major book publisher, we
recommend that you work with an established

literary agent. Each agency has ms submission
guidelines."

NONFICTION Agented submissions only.

DOVER PUBLICATIONS, INC.

31 E. Second St., Mineola NY 11501. (516)294-7000.
Fax: (516)873-1401. **E-mail:** hr@doverpublications.
com. **Website:** www.doverpublications.com. **Contact:** John Grafton (math/science reprints). Estab.
1941. Publishes trade paperback originals and reprints. **Publishes 660 titles/year. Makes outright
purchase.** Accepts simultaneous submissions. Book
catalog online.

○ Covers subjects from A - W, including Poetry -
Fine Art - Recipes - Games - Puzzles - Famous
Quotations - Clip Art - Great Literature - Craft
Projects - Photography - Coloring Pages.

NONFICTION Subjects include agriculture, Americana, animals, anthropology, archeology, art, architecture, cooking, foods, nutrition, health, medicine,
history, hobbies, language, literature, music, dance,
nature, environment, philosophy, photography, religion, science, sports, translation, travel. Publishes
mostly reprints. Accepts original paper doll collections, game books, coloring books (juvenile). Query
with SASE. Reviews artwork/photos.

DOWN EAST BOOKS

Imprint of Down East Enterprise, Inc., P.O. Box 679,
Camden ME 04843. (207)594-9544, 800-766-1670.
Fax: (207)594-7215. **E-mail:** editorial@downeast.com.
E-mail: submissions@downeast.com. **Website:** www.
downeast.com. **Contact:** Paul Doiron, editor-in-chief.
Estab. 1967. Publishes hardcover and trade paperback originals, trade paperback reprints. Down East
Books publishes books that capture and illuminate
the unique beauty and character of New England's
history, culture, and wild places. **Publishes 24-30 ti-
tles/year. 50% of books from first-time authors. 90%
from unagented writers. Pays $500 average advance.**
Publishes book 1 year after acceptance. Accepts simultaneous submissions. Responds in 3 months to
queries. Send SASE for ms guidelines. Send 9 x 12
SASE for guidelines, plus recent catalog.

NONFICTION Subjects include Americana, history, nature, environment, recreation, regional, sports.
Books about the New England region, Maine in particular. All of our regional books must have a Maine
or New England emphasis. Query with SASE. Do not
send CD, DVD, or disk. Reviews artwork/photos.

FICTION Subjects include juvenile, mainstream, contemporary, regional. We publish 2-4 juvenile titles/year (fiction and nonfiction), and 0-1 adult fiction titles/year. Query with SASE.

DOWN THE SHORE PUBLISHING

Box 100, West Creek NJ 08092. **Fax:** (609)597-0422. **E-mail:** info@down-the-shore.com; dtsbooks@comcast.net. **Website:** www.down-the-shore.com. Publishes hardcover and trade paperback originals and reprints. "Bear in mind that our market is regional-New Jersey, the Jersey Shore, the mid-Atlantic, and seashore and coastal subjects." **Publishes 4-10 titles/year. Pays royalty on wholesale or retail price, or makes outright purchase.** Accepts simultaneous submissions. Responds in 3 months to queries. Book catalog for 8×10 SAE with 2 first-class stamps or on website. Guidelines online.

NONFICTION Subjects include Americana, art, architecture, history, nature, environment, regional. Query with SASE. Submit proposal package, 1-2 sample chapters, synopsis. Reviews artwork/photos. Send photocopies.

FICTION Subjects include regional. Query with SASE. Submit proposal package, clips, 1-2 sample chapters.

POETRY "We do not publish poetry, unless it is to be included as part of an anthology."

TIPS "Carefully consider whether your proposal is a good fit for our established market."

⊕ DREAM OF THINGS

P.O. Box 872, Downers Grove IL 60515. **E-mail:** editor@dreamofthings.com. **Website:** dreamofthings.com. **Contact:** Mike O'Mary, owner. Estab. 2009. Publishes trade paperback originals and reprints, electronic originals and reprints. Publishes memoirs and creative nonfiction. **Publishes 3-4 titles/year. 90% of books from first-time authors. 90% from unagented writers. Pays 10% royalties on retail price. No advance.** Publishes book Accept to publish time is 6 months. after acceptance of ms. Accepts simultaneous submissions. Catalog available online at dreamofthings.com/dreamshop. Guidelines available online at dreamofthings.com/workshop-2.

NONFICTION Subjects include creative nonfiction, memoirs, anthologies of creative nonfiction/essays. Submit via online form. For memoirs, submit 1 sample chapter. For anthologies of creative nonfiction, submit essay. Does not review artwork.

DUFOUR EDITIONS

P.O. Box 7, 124 Byers Road, Chester Springs PA 19425. (610)458-5005 or (800)869-5677. **Fax:** (610)458-7103. **Website:** www.dufoureditions.com. Estab. 1948. Publishes hardcover originals, trade paperback originals and reprints. "We publish literary fiction by good writers which is well received and achieves modest sales. De-emphsazing poetry and nonfiction." **Publishes 3-4 titles/year. 200 queries received/year. 15 mss received/year. 20-30% of books from first-time authors. 80% from unagented writers. Pays $100-500 advance.** Publishes book 18 months after acceptance. Accepts simultaneous submissions. Responds in 3 months to queries and proposals; 6 months to mss. Book catalog available free.

NONFICTION Subjects include history, translation. Query with SASE. Reviews artwork/photos. Send photocopies.

FICTION Subjects include literary, short story collections, translation. "We like books that are slightly offbeat, different and well-written." Query with SASE.

POETRY Query.

TIPS Audience is sophisticated, literate readers especially interested in foreign literature and translations, and a strong Irish-Celtic focus, as well as work from U.S. writers. Check to see if the publisher is really a good match for your subject matter.

⊙ DUNDURN PRESS, LTD.

3 Church St., Suite 500, Toronto ON M5E 1M2, Canada. (416)214-5544. **E-mail:** info@dundurn.com. **Website:** www.dundurn.com. **Contact:** Acquisitions Editor. Estab. 1972. Publishes hardcover, trade paperback, and ebook originals and reprints. Dundurn publishes books by Canadian authors. **600 queries received/year. 25% of books from first-time authors. 50% from unagented writers.** Publishes book 1-2 year after acceptance. Accepts simultaneous submissions. Responds in 3 months to queries. Guidelines online.

⊙ "We *do not* publish poetry, short stories, children's books for readers under seven years of age, or picture books."

NONFICTION Subjects include art, architecture, history, Canadian and military, war, music, dance, drama, regional, art history, theater, serious and popular nonfiction. Submit cover letter, synopsis, CV, table of contents, writing sample, e-mail contact. Accepts submissions via postal mail only. Do not submit original materials. Submissions will not be returned.

FICTION Subjects include literary, mystery, young adult. No romance, science fiction, or experimental. "Until further notice, we will not be accepting any unsolicited fiction mss."

DUNEDIN ACADEMIC PRESS LTD

Hudson House, 8 Albany St., Edinburgh EH1 3QB, United Kingdom. (44)(131)473-2397. **E-mail:** mail@dunedinacademicpress.co.uk. **Website:** www.dunedinacademicpress.co.uk. **Contact:** Anthony Kinahan, director. Estab. 2001. **Publishes 15-20 titles/year. 10% of books from first-time authors. 90% from unagented writers. Pays royalty.** Book catalog and proposal Guidelines online.

○ "Read and respond to the proposal guidelines on our website before submitting. Do not send mss unless requested to do so. Do not send hard copy proposals. Approach first by e-mail, outlining proposal and identifying the market."

NONFICTION , earth science, education policy, health and social care, child protection. Reviews artwork/photos.

TIPS "Dunedin's list contains authors and subjects from across the international the academic world DAP's horizons are far broader than our immediate Scottish environment. One of the strengths of Dunedin is that we are able to offer our authors that individual support that comes from dealing with a small independent publisher committed to growth through careful treatment of its authors."

THOMAS DUNNE BOOKS

Imprint of St. Martin's Press, 175 Fifth Ave., New York NY 10010. (212)674-5151. **Website:** www.thomasdunnebooks.com. Estab. 1986. Publishes hardcover and trade paperback originals, and reprints. "Thomas Dunne Books publishes popular trade fiction and nonfiction. With an output of approximately 175 titles each year, his group covers a range of genres including commercial and literary fiction, thrillers, biography, politics, sports, popular science, and more. The list is intentionally eclectic and includes a wide range of fiction and nonfiction, from first books to international bestsellers." Accepts simultaneous submissions. Book catalog and ms guidelines free.

○ *Accepts agented submissions only.*

NONFICTION Subjects include government, politics, history, sports, political commentary. Agents submit query, or an outline and 1 sample pages.

FICTION Subjects include mainstream, contemporary, mystery, suspense, thrillers, women's. Agents submit query.

DUQUESNE UNIVERSITY PRESS

600 Forbes Ave., Pittsburgh PA 15282. (412)396-6610. **Fax:** (412)396-5984. **E-mail:** wadsworth@duq.edu. **Website:** www.dupress.duq.edu. **Contact:** Susan Wadsworth-Booth, director. Estab. 1927. Publishes hardcover and trade paperback originals. "Duquesne publishes scholarly monographs in the fields of literary studies (medieval & Renaissance), continental philosophy, ethics, religious studies and existential psychology. Interdisciplinary works are also of interest. Duquesne University Press does NOT publish fiction, poetry, children's books, technical or "hard" science works, or unrevised theses or dissertations." **Publishes 8-12 titles/year. 400 queries received/year. 65 mss received/year. 30% of books from first-time authors. 95% from unagented writers. Pays royalty on net price. Pays (some) advance.** Publishes book 1 year after acceptance. Responds in 1 month to proposals; 3 months to mss. Book catalog and ms guidelines for #10 SASE. Guidelines online.

NONFICTION Subjects include language, literature, philosophy, continental, psychology, existential, religion. "We look for quality of scholarship." For scholarly books, query or submit outline, 1 sample chapter, and SASE.

DUTTON ADULT TRADE

Imprint of Penguin Group (USA), Inc., 375 Hudson St., New York NY 10014. (212)366-2000. **Website:** us.penguingroup.com. Estab. 1852. Publishes hardcover originals. "Dutton currently publishes 45 hardcovers a year, roughly half fiction and half nonfiction." **Pays royalty. Pays negotiable advance.** Accepts simultaneous submissions. Book catalog for #10 SASE.

○ *Does not accept unsolicited ms. Agented submissions only.*

NONFICTION Agented submissions only. *No unsolicited mss.*

FICTION Subjects include adventure, historical, literary, mainstream, contemporary, mystery, short story collections, suspense. Agented submissions only. *No unsolicited mss.*

TIPS "Write the complete ms and submit it to an agent or agents. They will know exactly which editor will be interested in a project."

DUTTON CHILDREN'S BOOKS

Penguin Group (USA), Inc., 375 Hudson St., New York NY 10014. **E-mail:** duttonpublicity@ us.penguingroup.com. **Website:** www.penguin.com. **Contact:** Sara Reynolds, art director. Estab. 1852. Publishes hardcover originals as well as novelty formats. Dutton Children's Books publishes high-quality fiction and nonfiction for readers ranging from preschoolers to young adults on a variety of subjects. Currently emphasizing middle grade and young adult novels that offer a fresh perspective. De-emphasizing photographic nonfiction and picture books that teach a lesson. Approximately 80 new hardcover titles are published every year, fiction and nonfiction for babies through young adults. **Publishes 100 titles/year. 15% of books from first-time authors. Pays royalty on retail price. Pays advance.**

○ "Cultivating the creative talents of authors and illustrators and publishing books with purpose and heart continue to be the mission and joy at Dutton."

NONFICTION Subjects include animals, history, US, nature, environment, science. Query. Only responds if interested.

FICTION Subjects include juvenile, young adult. Dutton Children's Books has a diverse, general interest list that includes picture books; easy-to-read books; and fiction for all ages, from first chapter books to young adult readers. Query. Responds only if interested.

EAGLE'S VIEW PUBLISHING

168 W. 12th St., Ogden UT 84310. (801)393-3991. **Fax:** (801)393-4647. **E-mail:** sales@eaglefeathertrading. com. **Website:** www.eaglesviewpub.com. **Contact:** Denise Knight, editor-in-chief. Estab. 1982. Publishes trade paperback originals. "Eagle's View primarily publishes how-to craft books with a subject related to historical or contemporary Native American/Mountain Man/frontier crafts/bead crafts. Currently emphasizing bead-related craft books. De-emphasizing history except for historical Indian crafts." **Publishes 2-4 titles/year. 40 queries received/year. 20 mss received/year. 90% of books from first-time authors. 100% from unagented writers. Pays 8-10% royalty on net selling price.** Publishes book 1 year after acceptance. Accepts simultaneous submissions. Responds in 1 year to proposals. Book catalog and ms guidelines for $4.00.

NONFICTION Subjects include anthropology, archaeology, Native American crafts, ethnic, Native American, history, American frontier historical patterns and books, hobbies, crafts, especially beadwork. Submit outline, 1-2 sample chapters. Reviews artwork/photos. Send photocopies and sample illustrations.

TIPS "We will not be publishing any new beaded earrings books for the foreseeable future. We are interested in other craft projects using seed beads, especially books that feature a variety of items, not just different designs for 1 item."

EAKIN PRESS

P.O. Box 331779, Fort Worth TX 76163. Phone/**Fax:** (817)344-7036. **Website:** www.eakinpress.com. **Contact:** Kris Gholson, associate publisher. Estab. 1978. Publishes hardcover and paperback originals and reprints. "Our top priority is to cover the history and culture of the Southwest, especially Texas and Oklahoma. We also have successfully published titles related to ethnic studies. We publish very little fiction, other than for children." Accepts simultaneous submissions. Responds in up to 1 year to queries. Book catalog for $1.25. Guidelines online.

○ No electronic submissions.

NONFICTION Subjects include Americana, Western, business, economics, cooking, foods, nutrition, ethnic, history, military, war, regional, sports, African American studies. Juvenile nonfiction: includes biographies of historic personalities, prefer with Texas or regional interest, or nature studies; and easy-read illustrated books for grades 1-3. Submit sample chapters, bio, synopsis, publishing credits, SASE.

FICTION Subjects include historical, juvenile. Juvenile fiction for grades K-12, preferably relating to Texas and the Southwest or contemporary. No adult fiction. Query or submit outline/synopsis

EASTLAND PRESS

P.O. Box 99749, Seattle WA 98139. (206)217-0204. **Fax:** (206)217-0205. **E-mail:** info@eastlandpress.com. **Website:** www.eastlandpress.com. **Contact:** John O'Connor, Managing Editor. Estab. 1981. Publishes hardcover and trade paperback originals. "Eastland Press is interested in textbooks for practitioners of alternative medical therapies, primarily Chinese and physical therapies, and related bodywork." **Publishes 4-6 titles/year. 25 queries received/year. 30% of books from first-time authors. 90% from unagented writers. Pays 12-15% royalty on receipts.** Publishes book 12 to 24 months after acceptance. Accepts simultaneous submissions. Responds in 1 month to queries.

NONFICTION Subjects include health, medicine. "We prefer that a ms be completed or close to completion before we will consider publication. Proposals are rarely considered, unless submitted by a published author or teaching institution." Submit outline and 2-3 sample chapters. Reviews artwork/photos. Send photocopies.

THE ECCO PRESS

10 E. 53rd St., New York NY 10022. (212)207-7000. **Fax:** (212)702-2460. **Website:** www.harpercollins.com. **Contact:** Daniel Halpern, editor-in-chief. Estab. 1970. Publishes hardcover and trade paperback originals and reprints. **Publishes 60 titles/year. Pays royalty. Pays negotiable advance.** Publishes book 1 year after acceptance.

FICTION Literary, short story collections. "We can publish possibly one or two original novels a year." Published *Blonde*, by Joyce Carrol Oates; *Pitching Around Fidel*, by S.L. Price. *Does not accept unsolicited mss.*

TIPS "We are always interested in first novels and feel it's important that they be brought to the attention of the reading public."

ÉCRITS DES FORGES

992-A, rue Royale, Trois-Rivières QC G9A 4H9, Canada. (819)840-8492. **Website:** www.ecritsdesforges.com. **Contact:** Stéphane Despatie, director. Estab. 1971. **Pays royalties of 10-20%.** Responds to queries in 6 months.

POETRY Écrits des Forges publishes poetry only that is "authentic and original as a signature. We have published poetry from more than 1,000 poets coming from most of the francophone countries." Publishes 45-50 paperback books of poetry/year. Books are usually 80-88 pages, digest-sized, perfect-bound, with 2-color covers with art. Query first with a few sample poems and a cover letter with brief bio and publication credits. Order sample books by writing or faxing.

EDGE SCIENCE FICTION AND FANTASY PUBLISHING/TESSERACT BOOKS

Hades Publications, Box 1714, Calgary AB T2P 2L7, Canada. (403)254-0160. **Fax:** (403)254-0456. **E-mail:** publisher@hadespublications.com. **Website:** www.edgewebsite.com. **Contact:** Editorial Manager. Estab. 1996. "We are an independent publisher of science fiction and fantasy novels in hard cover or trade paperback format. We produce high-quality books with lots of attention to detail and lots of marketing effort. We want to encourage, produce and promote thought-provoking and fun-to-read science fiction and fantasy literature by 'bringing the magic alive: one world at a time' (as our motto says) with each new book released." Publishes hardcover and trade paperback originals. Books: natural offset paper; offset/web printing; HC/perfect binding; b&w illustration only. Average print order: 2,000-3,000. Plans 20 first novels this year. Averages 16-20 total titles/year. Member of Book Publishers Association of Alberta (BPAA), Independent Publishers Association of Canada (IPAC), Publisher's Marketing Association (PMA), Small Press Center. **Pays 10% royalty on wholesale price. Negotiable advance.** Publishes book 18-20 months after acceptance. Responds in 4-5 months to mss. Ms guidelines online.

FICTION Subjects include fantasy, science fiction. "We are looking for all types of fantasy and science fiction, horror except juvenile/young adlut, erotica, religious fiction, short stories, dark/gruesome fantasy, or poetry." Length: 75,000-100,000/words. Submit first 3 chapters and synopsis. Check website for guidelines. Include estimated word count.

TIPS "Send us your best, polished, completed ms. Use proper ms format. Take the time before you submit to get a critique from people who can offer you useful advice. When in doubt, visit our website for helpful resources, FAQs and other tips."

EDUPRESS, INC.

P.O. Box 8610, Madison WI 53708. (920)563-9571 ext. 332. **Fax:** (920)563-7395. **E-mail:** edupress@highsmith.com; LBowie@highsmith.com. **Website:** www.edupressinc.com. **Contact:** Liz Bowie. Estab. 1979. Edupress, Inc., publishes supplemental curriculum resources for PK-6th grade. Currently emphasizing reading and math materials, as well as science and social studies. **Work purchased outright from authors.** Publishes book 1-2 years after acceptance. Responds in 2-4 months. Catalog online.

"Our mission is to create products that make kids want to go to school!"

NONFICTION Submit complete ms via mail or e-mail with "Ms Submission" as the subject line.

TIPS "We are looking for unique, research-based, quality supplemental materials for Pre-K through eighth grade. We publish all subject areas in many different formats, including games. Our materials are intended for classroom and home schooling use."

EERDMANS BOOKS FOR YOUNG READERS

2140 Oak Industrial Dr. NE, Grand Rapids MI 49505. **E-mail:** youngreaders@eerdmans.com. **Website:** www.eerdmans.com/youngreaders. **Contact:** Acquisitions Editor. "We are seeking books that encourage independent thinking, problem-solving, creativity, acceptance, kindness. Books that encourage moral values without being didactic or preachy. Board books, picture books, middle reader fiction, young adult fiction, nonfiction, illustrated storybooks. A submission stands out when it's obvious that someone put time into it—the publisher's name and address are spelled correctly, the package is neat, and all of our submission requirements have been followed precisely. We look for short, concise cover letters that explain why the ms fits with our list, and/or how the ms fills an important need in the world of children's literature. Send exclusive ms submissions to acquisitions editor. We regret that due to the volume of material we receive, we cannot comment on ms we are unable to accept." **6,000 mss received/year. Pays 5-7% royalty on retail.** Publishes book Publishes middle reader and YA books 1 year after acceptance; publishes picture books in 2-3 years. after acceptance of ms. Responds to mss in 3-4 months.

○ "We seek to engage young minds with words and pictures that inform and delight, inspire and entertain. From board books for babies to picture books, nonfiction, and novels for children and young adults, our goal is to produce quality literature for a new generation of readers. We believe in books!"

NONFICTION Middle readers: biography, history, multicultural, nature/environment, religion, social issues. Young adults/teens: biography, history, multicultural, nature/environment, religion, social issues. Average word length: 35,000. Reviews artwork/photos. Send color photocopies rather than original art.

FICTION Picture books: animal, contemporary, folktales, history, humor, multicultural, nature/environment, poetry, religion, special needs, social issues, sports, suspense. Young readers: animal, contemporary, fantasy, folktales, history, humor, multicultural, poetry, religion, special needs, social issues, sports, suspense. Middle readers: adventure, contemporary, fantasy, history, humor, multicultural, nature/environment, problem novels, religion, social issues, sports, suspense. Young adults/teens: adventure, contemporary, fantasy, folktales, history, humor, multicultural, nature/environment, problem novels, religion, sports, suspense. Average word length: picture books—1,000; middle readers—15,000; young adult—45,000. "Right now we are not acquiring books that revolve around a holiday. (No Christmas, Thanksgiving, Easter, Halloween, Fourth of July, Hanukkah books.) We do not publish retold or original fairy tales, nor do we publish books about witches or ghosts or vampires." Send exclusive ms submissions (marked so on outside of envelope) to acquisitions editor.

TIPS "Find out who Eerdmans is before submitting a ms. Look at our website, request a catalog, and check out our books."

WILLIAM B. EERDMANS PUBLISHING CO.

2140 Oak Industrial Dr. NE, Grand Rapids MI 49505. (616)459-4591. **Fax:** (616)459-6540. **E-mail:** info@eerdmans.com. **Website:** www.eerdmans.com. **Contact:** Jon Pott, editor-in-chief. Estab. 1911. Publishes hardcover and paperback originals and reprints. "The majority of our adult publications are religious and most of these are academic or semi-academic in character (as opposed to inspirational or celebrity books), though we also publish general trade books on the Christian life. Our nonreligious titles, most of them in regional history or on social issues, aim, similarly, at an educated audience." Accepts simultaneous submissions. Responds in 4 weeks to queries, possibly longer for mss. Please include e-mail and/or SASE. Book catalog and ms guidelines free.

IMPRINTS Eerdmans Books for Young Readers.

○ Will not respond to or accept mss, proposals, or queries sent by e-mail or fax.

NONFICTION Subjects include history, religious, language, literature, philosophy, of religion, psychology, regional, history, religion, sociology, translation, Biblical studies. "We prefer that writers take the time to notice if we have published anything at all in the same category as their ms before sending it to us."

Query with TOC, 2-3 sample chapters, and SASE for return of ms. Reviews artwork/photos.

FICTION Subjects include religious, children's, general, fantasy. Query with SASE.

Ⓐⓞ EGMONT USA

443 Park Ave. S, New York NY 10016. (212)685-0102. **Website:** www.egmontusa.com. **Contact:** Elizabeth Law, vice president/publisher; Regina Griffin, executive editor; Greg Ferguson, senior editor; Alison Weiss, assistant editor. Estab 2008. Specializes in trade books. Publishes 1 picture book/year; 2 young readers/year; 20 middle readers/year; 20 young adult/year. "Egmont USA publishes quality commercial fiction. We are committed to editorial excellence and to providing first-rate care for our authors. Our motto is that we turn writers into authors and children into passionate readers." **25% of books from first-time authors. Pays authors royalties based on retail price.** Publishes book 18 months after acceptance. Accepts simultaneous submissions. Responds to queries in 4 weeks; mss in 6 weeks.

○ *"Unfortunately, Egmont USA is not currently able to accept unsolicited submissions; we only accept submissions from literary agents."*

FICTION Young readers: adventure, animal, contemporary, humor, multicultural. Middle readers: adventure, animal, contemporary, fantasy, humor, multicultural, problem novels, science fiction, special needs. Young adults/teens: adventure, animal, contemporary, fantasy, humor, multicultural, paranormal, problem novels, religion, science fiction, special needs. Query or submit completed ms.

EDWARD ELGAR PUBLISHING, INC.

The William Pratt House, 9 Dewey Court, Northampton MA 01060. (413)584-5551. **Fax:** (413)584-9933. **E-mail:** submissions@e-elgar.co.uk. **Website:** www.e-elgar.com. **Contact:** Alan Sturmer; Tara Gorvine. Estab. 1986. "Specializing in research monographs, reference books and upper-level textbooks in highly focused areas, we are able to offer a unique service in terms of editorial, production and worldwide marketing.We have three offices, Cheltenham and Camberley in the UK and Northampton, MA, US."

○ "We are actively commissioning new titles and are happy to consider and advise on ideas for monograph books, textbooks, professional law books and academic journals at any stage. Please complete a proposal form in as much detail as possible. We review all prososals with our academic advisors."

ELLORA'S CAVE PUBLISHING, INC.

1056 Home Ave., Akron OH 44310. **E-mail:** submissions@ellorascave.com. **Website:** www.ellorascave.com. Estab. 2000. Publishes electronic originals and reprints; print books. **Pays 45% royalty on amount received.** Accepts simultaneous submissions. Responds in 2-4 months to mss. No queries. Guidelines online. "Read and follow detailed submission instructions.".

FICTION Erotic romance and erotica fiction of every subgenre, including gay/lesbian, menage and more, and BDSM. All must have abundant, explicit, and graphic erotic content. Submit electronically only; cover e-mail as defined in our submission guidelines plus 1 attached .docx file containing full synopsis, first 3 chapters, and last chapter.

TIPS "Our audience is romance readers who want explicit sexual detail. They come to us because we offer sex with romance, plot, emotion. In addition to erotic romance with happy-ever-after endings, we also publish pure erotica, detailing sexual adventure, and experimentation."

EMIS, INC.

P.O. Box 270666, Fort Collins CO 80527. (214)349-0077; (800)225-0694. **Fax:** (970)672-8606. **Website:** www.emispub.com. **Contact:** Lynda Blake, president. Publishes trade paperback originals. **Publishes 2 titles/year. Pays 12% royalty on retail price.** Responds in 3 months to queries. Book catalog available free. Guidelines available free.

○ "Medical text designed for physicians; fit in the lab coat pocket as a quick reference. Currently emphasizing women's health."

NONFICTION Subjects include health, medicine, psychology, women's health/medicine. Submit 3 sample chapters with SASE.

TIPS Audience is medical professionals and medical product manufacturers and distributors.

Ⓐⓞ ENCOUNTER BOOKS

900 Broadway, Suite 601, New York NY 10003. (212)871-6310. **Fax:** (212)871-6311. **Website:** www.encounterbooks.com. **Contact:** Roger Kimball, editor and president. Publishes hardcover, trade paperback, and e-book originals and trade paperback reprints. Encounter Books publishes serious nonfiction—books that can alter our society, challenge our

morality, stimulate our imaginations—in the areas of history, politics, religion, biography, education, public policy, current affairs, and social sciences. Encounter Books is an activity of Encounter for Culture and Education, a tax-exempt, non profit corporation dedicated to strengthening the marketplace of ideas and engaging in educational activities to help preserve democratic culture. Accepts simultaneous submissions. Catalog and guidelines online.

○ *Accepts agented material only. No unsolicited mss/queries.*

NONFICTION Subjects include child guidance, education, ethnic, government, politics, health, medicine, history, language, literature, memoirs, military, war, multicultural, philosophy, psychology, religion, science, sociology, women's issues, women's studies, gender studies. Only considers agented submissions.

ENETE ENTERPRISES

3600 Mission #10, San Diego CA 92109. **E-mail:** EneteEnterprises@gmail.com. **Website:** www.EneteEnterprises.com. **Contact:** Shannon Enete, editor. Estab. 2011. Publishes trade paperback originals, mass market paperback originals, electronic originals. **Publishes 6 titles/year. 270 queries received/year. 95% of books from first-time authors. 100% from unagented writers. Pays royalties of 1-15%.** Publishes book 3-6 months after acceptance. Accepts simultaneous submissions. Responds to queries/proposals in 1 month; mss in 1-3 months. Guidelines online.

NONFICTION Subjects include alternative lifestyles, cooking, creative nonfiction, education, foods, gay, government, health, lesbian, medicine, memoirs, multicultural, nutrition, photography, politics, science, spirituality, travel, world affairs, travel guides, travel memoirs, life abroad, retired living abroad. "Actively seeking books about healthcare / medicine. More specifically: back care, emergency medicine, international medicine, healthcare, insurance, EMT or Paramedic, or alternative medicine." Submit query, proposal, or ms by e-mail. Reviews artwork.

FICTION Subjects include adventure, gay, lesbian, romance, science fiction. Submit query, proposal, or ms by e-mail according to guidelines (do not forget a marketing plan).

TIPS "Send me your best work. Do not rush a draft."

ENGLISH TEA ROSE PRESS

The Wild Rose Press, P.O. Box 708, Adams Basin NY 14410. (585)752-8770. **E-mail:** queryus@thewildrose-press.com. **Website:** www.thewildrosepress.com. **Contact:** Nicole D'Arienzo, editor. Estab. 2006. Publishes paperback originals, reprints, and e-books in a POD format. Member: EPIC, Romance Writers of America. Distributes/promotes titles through major distribution chains, including iTunes, Kobo, Sony, Amazon.com, Kindle, as well as smaller and online distributors. **Pays royalty of 7% minimum; 35% maximum.** Publishes book 1 year after acceptance. Responds in 4 weeks to queries; 3 months to mss. Guidelines online.

○ *Does not accept unsolicited mss.* Agented fiction less than 1%. Always comments on rejected mss. Sends prepublication galleys to author.

FICTION , Wants contemporary, futuristic/time travel, gothic, historical, regency, romantic suspense, erotic, and paranormal romances. "In the English Tea Rose line we have conquering heroes, high seas adventure, and scandalous gossip. The love stories that will take you back in time. From the windswept moors of Scotland, to the Emerald Isle, to the elegant ballrooms of Regency England, the men and women of this time are larger than life and willing to risk it all for the love of a lifetime. English Tea Rose stories encompass historical romances set before 1900 which are not set on American soil. Send us your medieval knights, Vikings, Scottish highlanders, marauding pirates, and ladies and gentlemen of the Ton. English Tea Rose romances should have strong conflict and be emotionally driven; and, whether the story is medieval, Regency, set during the renaissance, or any other pre-1900 time, they must stay true to their period in historical accuracy and flavor. English Tea Roses can range from sweet to spicy, but should not contain overly explicit language." Send query letter with outline and a list of publishing credits. Include estimated word count, brief bio, and list of publishing credits.

TIPS "Polish your ms, make it as error free as possible, and follow our submission guidelines."

ENSLOW PUBLISHERS, INC.

40 Industrial Rd., Box 398, Berkeley Heights NJ 07922. (973)771-9400. **E-mail:** customerservice@enslow.com. **Website:** www.enslow.com. **Contact:** Brian D. Enslow, editor. Estab. 1977. Publishes hardcover originals. 10% require freelance illustration. **Publishes 250 titles/year. Pays royalty on net price with advance or flat fee. Pays advance.** Publishes book 1 year after acceptance. Responds in 1 month to queries. Guidelines for #10 SASE.

IMPRINTS MyReportLinks.com Books, Enslow Elementary.

○ "Enslow publishes hardcover nonfiction series books for young adults and school-age children."

NONFICTION Subjects include health, medicine, history, recreation, sports, science, sociology. "Interested in new ideas for series of books for young people." No fiction, fictionalized history, or dialogue.

TIPS "We love to receive résumés from experienced writers with good research skills who can think like young people."

ENTREPRENEUR PRESS

2445 McCabe Way, Suite 400, Irvine CA 92614. (949)261-2325. **Fax:** (949)261-7729. **E-mail:** press@ entrepreneur.com. **Website:** www.entrepreneurpress. com. **Contact:** Jere L. Calmes, publisher. Publishes quality hardcover and trade paperbacks. "We are an independent publishing company that publishes titles focusing on starting and growing a business, personal finance, real estate and careers. **Publishes 60+ titles/year. 1,200 queries received/year. 600 mss received/year. 40% of books from first-time authors. 60% from unagented writers. Pays competitive net royalty.** Accepts simultaneous submissions. Guidelines online.

○ *Entrepreneur* continues to be the definitive guide to all the diverse challenges of business ownership. *Entrepreneur.com* is the most widely used website by entrepreneurs and emerging businesses worldwide."

NONFICTION Subjects include business, economics, start-up, small business management, marketing, finance, real estate, careers, personal finance, accounting, motivation, leadership, legal advise, business travel, and management. When submitting work to us, please send as much of the proposed book as possible. Proposal should include: cover letter, preface, marketing plan, analysis of competition and comparative titles, author bio, TOC, 2 sample chapters. Go to website for more details. Reviews artwork/photos. Send transparencies and all other applicable information.

TIPS We are currently seeking proposals covering sales, small business, startup, real estate, online businesses, marketing, etc.

⊙⊘ EOS

Imprint of HarperCollins General Books Group, 10 E. 53rd St., New York NY 10022. (212)207-7000. **Web-**

site: www.eosbooks.com. Estab. 1998. Publishes hardcover originals, trade and mass market paperback originals, and reprints. Eos publishes quality science fiction/fantasy with broad appeal. **Pays royalty on retail price. Pays variable advance.** Guidelines for #10 SASE.

FICTION Subjects include fantasy, science fiction. No horror or juvenile. Agented submissions only. *All unsolicited mss returned.*

EPICENTER PRESS, INC.

200 W. 34th Ave. #825, Anchorage AK 99503. **Fax:** (425)481-8253. **E-mail:** slay@epicenterpress.com. **Website:** www.epicenterpress.com. **Contact:** Lael Morgan, acquisitions editor. Estab. 1987. Publishes hardcover and trade paperback originals. "We are a regional press founded in Alaska whose interests include but are not limited to the arts, history, environment, and diverse cultures and lifestyles of the North Pacific and high latitudes." **Publishes 4-8 titles/year. 200 queries received/year. 100 mss received/year. 75% of books from first-time authors. 90% from unagented writers.** Publishes book 1-2 years after acceptance. Responds in 3 months to queries. Book catalog and ms guidelines on website.

○ "Our affiliated company, Aftershocks Media, provides a range of services to self-publisher industry distributors."

NONFICTION Subjects include animals, ethnic, history, nature, environment, recreation, regional, women's issues. "Our focus is Alaska and the Pacific Northwest. We do not encourage nonfiction titles from outside this region." Submit outline and 3 sample chapters. Reviews artwork/photos. Send photocopies.

TIPS *Bering Sea Blues*, by Joe Upton; *Surviving the Island of Grace*, by Leslie Leyland Fields.

F+W MEDIA, INC. (BOOK DIVISION)

10151 Carver Rd., Suite 200, Blue Ash OH 45242. (513)531-2690. **Website:** www.fwmedia.com. President: Sara Domville. President: David Blansfield. Estab. 1913. Publishes trade paperback originals and reprints. "In October 2008, F+W Media moved from a divisionally structured company to a community structure, wherein the publisher and editorial director for each community has full responsibility for the books, magazines, online, events, and educational products associated with their community. F+W Media produces more than 650 new books per year, maintains a backlist of more than 4,000 titles, publishes 46 magazines, owns and operates dozens of informational and subscription-based websites, and operates a growing number of successful consumer shows annually." **Publishes 400+ titles/year.** Guidelines online.

IMPRINTS Adams Media (general interest series); David & Charles (crafts, equestrian, railroads, soft crafts); HOW Books (graphic design, illustrated, humor, pop culture); IMPACT Books (fantasy art, manga, creative comics and popular culture); Interweave (knitting, beading, crochet, jewelry, sewing); Krause Books (antiques and collectibles, automotive, coins and paper money, comics, crafts, games, firearms, militaria, outdoors and hunting, records and CDs, sports, toys); Memory Makers (scrapbooking); North Light Books (crafts, decorative painting, fine art); Popular Woodworking Books (shop skills, woodworking); Tyrus Books (mystery and literary fiction); Warman's (antiques and collectibles, field guides); Writer's Digest Books (writing and reference).

○ Please see individual listings for specific submission information about the company's imprints.

FABER & FABER INC.

Farrar, Straus & Giroux, 18 W. 18th St., New York NY 10011. (212)741-6900. **E-mail:** fsg.editorial@fsgbooks.com. **Website:** us.macmillan.com/faberandfaber.aspx. Estab. 1976. Responds in 6-8 weeks.

NONFICTION "All submissions must be submitted through the mail—we do not accept electronic submissions, or submissions delivered in person. Please include a cover letter describing your submission, along with the first 50 pages of the ms."

POETRY "All submissions must be submitted through the mail—we do not accept electronic submissions, or submissions delivered in person. If you are submitting poems, please include 3-4 poems."

● FABER & FABER LTD

Bloomsbury House, 74-77 Great Russell St., London WC1B 3DA, United Kingdom. (020)7465-0045. **Fax:** (020)7465-0034. **Website:** www.faber.co.uk. **Contact:** Lee Brackstone, Hannah Griffiths, Angus Cargill, (fiction); Walter Donohue, (film); Dinah Wood, (plays); Julian Loose, Neil Belton, (nonfiction); Paul Keegan, (poetry); Belinda Matthews, (music); Suzy Jenvy, Julia Wells, (children's). Estab. 1925. Publishes hardcover and paperback originals and reprints. Faber & Faber have rejuvenated their nonfiction, music and children's

titles in recent years and the film and drama lists remain market leaders. **Publishes 200 titles/year. Pays royalty. Pays varying advances with each project.** Accepts simultaneous submissions. Responds in 3 months to mss. Book catalog online.

○ Faber & Faber will consider unsolicited proposals for poetry only.

NONFICTION Subjects include art, architecture, contemporary culture, cooking, foods, nutrition, creative nonfiction, government, politics, history, humanities, literary criticism, memoirs, military, war, multicultural, music, dance, psychology, recreation, science, sports, travel, world affairs, children's. *No unsolicited nonfiction submissions.*

FICTION Subjects include adventure, ethnic, experimental, fantasy, historical, humor, juvenile, literary, mystery, plays, poetry, short story collections, spiritual, sports, suspense, young adult, drama, screenplays. *No unsolicited fiction submissions.*

POETRY Address poetry to 'Poetry Submissions Department' and include an SAE for return. For more information, ring 020 7465 0045. Submit 6 sample poems.

TIPS "Explore the website and downloadable book catalogues thoroughly to get a feel for the lists in all categories and genres."

FACTS ON FILE, INC.

Infobase Learning, 132 W. 31st St., 17th Floor, New York NY 10001. (800)322-8755. **Fax:** (800)678-3633. **E-mail:** llikoff@factsonfile.com; custserv@factsonfile.com. **Website:** www.factsonfile.com. **Contact:** Laurie Likoff, editorial director (science, fashion, natural history); Justine Ciovacco (science, nature, juvenile); Owen Lancer, senior editor (American history, women's studies); James Chambers, trade editor (health, pop culture, true crime, sports); Jeff Soloway, acquisitions editor (language/literature). Estab. 1941. Publishes hardcover originals and reprints. Facts on File produces high-quality reference materials on a broad range of subjects for the school library market and the general nonfiction trade. **Publishes 135-150 titles/year. 25% from unagented writers. Pays 10% royalty on retail price. Pays $5,000-10,000 advance.** Accepts simultaneous submissions. Responds in 2 months to queries. Book catalog available free. Guidelines online.

IMPRINTS Checkmark Books.

NONFICTION Subjects include contemporary culture, education, health, medicine, history, language, literature, multicultural, recreation, religion, sports, careers, entertainment, natural history, popular culture. "We publish serious, informational books for a targeted audience. All our books must have strong library interest, but we also distribute books effectively to the trade. Our library books fit the junior and senior high school curriculum." No computer books, technical books, cookbooks, biographies (except YA), pop psychology, humor, fiction or poetry. Query or submit outline and sample chapter with SASE. No submissions returned without SASE.

TIPS "Our audience is school and public libraries for our more reference-oriented books and libraries, schools and bookstores for our less reference-oriented informational titles."

FAIRLEIGH DICKINSON UNIVERSITY PRESS

285 Madison Ave., M-GH2-01, Madison NJ 07940. (973)443-8564. **Fax:** (973)443-8364. **E-mail:** fdupress@fdu.edu. **Website:** www.fdupress.org. **Contact:** Harry Keyishian, director. Estab. 1967. Publishes hardcover originals and occasional paperbacks, and all existing electronic formats. Fairleigh Dickinson publishes scholarly books for the academic market, in the humanities and social sciences through a co-publishing partnership that was established in 2010 with The Rowman & Littlefield Publishing Group, Lanham, MD. **Publishes 35-45 titles/year. 33% of books from first-time authors. 95% from unagented writers.** Publishes book 6-7 months after acceptance. Responds in 2 weeks to queries.

○ "Contracts are arranged through The Rowman & Littlefield Publishing Group, which also handles editing and production. We are a selection committee."

NONFICTION Subjects include architecture, art, cinema, communications, contemporary culture, dance, economics, ethnic, film, gay, government, history, law, lesbian, literary criticism, multicultural, music, philosophy, psychology, regional, religion, sociology, womens issues, womens studies, world affairs, local, world literature, Italian Studies (series), Communication Studies (series), Willa Cather (series), American history and culture, Civil War, Jewish studies. "The Press discourages submissions of unrevised dissertations. We will consider scholarly editions of literary works in all fields, in English, or translation. We welcome inquiries about essay collections if the the material is previously unpublished, he essays have a unifying and consistent theme, and the edi-

tors provide a substantial scholarly introduction." No nonscholarly books. We do not publish textbooks, or original fiction, poetry or plays. Query with outline, detailed abstract, and sample chapters (if possible), and CV. Does not review artwork.

⊕ FAMILIUS

1254 Commerce Way, Sanger CA 93657. (559)876-2170. **Fax:** (559)876-2180. **E-mail:** bookideas@familius.com. **E-mail:** bookideas@familius.com. **Website:** familius.com. **Contact:** Michele Robbins, acquisitions editor. Estab. 2011. Publishes hardcover, trade paperback, and electronic originals and reprints. Familius is all about strengthening families. Collective, the authors and staff have experienced a wide slice of the family-life spectrum. Some come from broken homes. Some are married and in the throes of managing a bursting household. Some are preparing to start families of their own. Together, they publish books, articles, and videos that help families be happy. **Publishes 40 titles/year. 200 queries received/year. 100 mss received/year. 60% of books from first-time authors. 70% from unagented writers. Authors are paid 10-30% royalty on wholesale price.** Publishes book 12 months after acceptance. Accepts simultaneous submissions. Responds in 1 month to queries. Responds in 1 month to proposals. Responds in 2 months to mss. Catalog online. Guidelines online.

NONFICTION Subjects include Americana, child guidance, cooking, finance, foods, health, medicine, memoirs, money, nutrition, parenting, young adult. All mss must align with Familius mission statement to help families succeed. Submit a proposal package, including an outline, one sample chapter, competition evaluation, and your author platform. Reviews JPEGS if sent as part of the submission package.

FICTION Subjects include juvenile, picture books, young adult. All fiction must align with Familius values statement listed on the website footer. Submit a proposal package, including a synopsis, 3 sample chapters, and your author platform.

FANTAGRAPHICS BOOKS INC.

7563 Lake City Way, NE, Seattle WA 98115. (206)524-1967. **Fax:** (206)524-2104. **E-mail:** fbicomix@fantagraphics.com. **Website:** www.fantagraphics.com. **Contact:** Submissions Editor. Estab. 1976. Publishes original trade paperbacks. Publishes comics for thinking readers. Does not want mainstream genres of superhero, vigilante, horror, fantasy, or science fiction. Responds in 2-3 months to queries. Catalog and guidelines online.

FICTION Subjects include comic books. "Fantagraphics is an independent company with a modus operandi different from larger, factory-like corporate comics publishers. If your talents are limited to a specific area of expertise (i.e. inking, writing, etc.), then you will need to develop your own team before submitting a project to us. We want to see an idea that is fully fleshed-out in your mind, at least, if not on paper. Submit a minimum of 5 fully-inked pages of art, a synopsis, SASE, and a brief note stating approximately how many issues you have in mind."

TIPS "Take note of the originality and diversity of the themes and approaches to drawing in such Fantagraphics titles as *Love & Rockets* (stories of life in Latin America and Chicano L.A.), *Palestine* (journalistic autobiography in the Middle East), *Eightball* (surrealism mixed with kitsch culture in stories alternately humorous and painfully personal), and *Naughty Bits* (feminist humor and short stories which both attack and commiserate). Try to develop your own, equally individual voice; originality, aesthetic maturity, and graphic storytelling skill are the signs by which Fantagraphics judges whether or not your submission is ripe for publication."

FARCOUNTRY PRESS

P.O. Box 5630, Helena MT 59604. (800)821-3874. **Fax:** (406)443-5480. **E-mail:** will@farcountrypress.com. **Website:** www.farcountrypress.com. **Contact:** Will Harmon. Award-winning publisher Farcountry Press specializes in softcover and hardcover color photography books showcasing the nation's cities, states, national parks, and wildlife. Farcountry also publishes several children's series, as well as guidebooks, cookbooks, and regional history titles nationwide. **Publishes The staff produces about 30 books annually; the backlist has grown to more than 300 titles titles/year.** Submission guidelines online.

FARRAR, STRAUS & GIROUX

18 W. 18th St., New York NY 10011. (646)307-5151. **E-mail:** fsg.editorial@fsgbooks.com. **Website:** us.macmillan.com. **Contact:** Editorial Department. Estab. 1946. Publishes hardcover originals and trade paperback reprints. "We publish original and well-written material for all ages." **Publishes 75 titles/year. 6,000 queries and mss received/year. 5% of books from first-time authors. 50% from unagented writers. Pays 2-6% royalty on retail price for paperbacks, 3-10% for hardcovers. Pays $3,000-25,000 advance.** Publishes book 18 months after acceptance. Accepts simultaneous submissions. Responds in 2 months to queries; 3 months to mss. Catalog available by request. Guidelines online.

IMPRINTS Frances Foster Books.

NONFICTION All levels. Send cover letter describing submission with first 50 pages.

FICTION Subjects include juvenile, picture books, young adult. Do not query picture books; just send ms. Do not fax or e-mail queries or mss. Send cover letter describing submission with first 50 pages.

POETRY Send cover letter describing submission with 3-4 poems. By mail only.

FARRAR, STRAUS & GIROUX FOR YOUNG READERS

18 W. 18th St., New York NY 10011. (212)741-6900. **Fax:** (212)633-2427. **E-mail:** childrens-editorial@fsgbooks.com. **Website:** www.fsgkidsbooks.com. **Contact:** Margaret Ferguson, editorial director; Wesley Adams, executive editor; Janine O'Malley, senior editor; Frances Foster, Frances Foster Books; Robbin Gourley, art director. Estab. 1946. Book catalog available by request. Ms guidelines online.

NONFICTION All levels: all categories. "We publish only literary nonfiction." Submit cover letter, first 50 pages by mail only.

FICTION All levels: all categories. "Original and well-written material for all ages." Submit cover letter, first 50 pages by mail only.

POETRY Submit cover letter, 3-4 poems by mail only.

TIPS "Study our catalog before submitting. We will see illustrators' portfolios by appointment. Don't ask for criticism and/or advice—due to the volume of submissions we receive, it's just not possible. Never send originals. Always enclose SASE."

FATHER'S PRESS

2424 SE 6th St., Lee's Summit MO 64063. (816)600-6288. **E-mail:** mike@fatherspress.com. **Website:** www.fatherspress.com. **Contact:** Mike Smitley, owner (fiction, nonfiction). Estab. 2006. Publishes hardcover, trade paperback, and mass market paperback originals and reprints. **Publishes 6-10 titles/year. Pays 10-15% royalty on wholesale price.** Publishes book 6 months after acceptance of ms. Responds in 1 month to queries and proposals. Responds in 3 months to mss. Guidelines online.

NONFICTION Subjects include animals, cooking, foods, nutrition, creative nonfiction, history, military, war, nature, regional, religion, travel, women's issues, world affairs. Query with SASE. Unsolicited mss returned unopened. Call or e-mail first. Reviews artwork/photos. Send photocopies.

FICTION Subjects include adventure, historical, juvenile, literary, mainstream, contemporary, military, war, mystery, regional, religious, suspense, western, young adult. Query with SASE. Unsolicited mss returned unopened. Call or e-mail first.

◑⊘ FAWCETT

The Ballantine Publishing Group, A Division of Random House, Inc., 1745 Broadway, New York NY 10019. **E-mail:** bfi@randomhouse.com. **Website:** www.randomhouse.com. Estab. 1955. Publishes paperback originals and reprints. Major publisher of mystery mass market and trade paperbacks.

FICTION Subjects include mystery. Agented submissions only. *All unsolicited mss returned.*

FREDERICK FELL PUBLISHERS, INC.

2131 Hollywood Blvd., Suite 305, Hollywood FL 33020. (954)925-5242. **Fax:** (954)455-4243. **E-mail:** fellpub@aol.com. **Website:** www.fellpub.com. **Contact:** Barbara Newman, senior editor. Publishes hardcover and trade paperback originals. **Publishes 25 titles/year. 4,000 queries received/year. 1,000 mss received/year. 95% of books from first-time authors. 95% from unagented writers. Pays negotiable royalty on retail price. Pays up to $10,000 advance.** Publishes book 1 year after acceptance. Accepts simultaneous submissions. Responds in 1 month to queries; 3 months to proposals. Guidelines online.

○ "Fell is now publishing 50 e-books per year."

NONFICTION Subjects include business, economics, child guidance, education, ethnic, film, cinema, stage, health, medicine, hobbies, money, finance, spirituality. "We are reviewing in all categories. Advise us of the top 3 competitive titles for your work and the reasons why the public would benefit by having your book published." Submit proposal package, including outline, 3 sample chapters, author bio, publicity ideas, market analysis. Reviews artwork/photos. Send photocopies.

TIPS "We are most interested in well-written, timely nonfiction with strong sales potential. We will not consider topics that appeal to a small, select audience. Learn markets and be prepared to help with sales and promotion. Show us how your book is unique or better than the competition."

FENCE BOOKS

Science Library 320, Univ. of Albany, 1400 Washington Ave., Albany NY 12222. (518)591-8162. **E-mail:** fencesubmissions@gmail.com. **E-mail:** peter.n.fence@gmail.com. **Website:** www.fenceportal.org. **Contact:** Submissions Manager. Publishes hardcover originals. Closed to submissions until June 15. Check website for details. Guidelines online.

FICTION Subjects include literary, poetry. Submit via contests and occasional open reading periods.

POETRY Submit via contests and occasional open reading periods.

FERGUSON PUBLISHING CO.

Infobase Publishing, 132 W. 31st St., 17th Floor, New York NY 10001. (800)322-8755. **E-mail:** editorial@factsonfile.com. **Website:** www.infobasepublishing.com. Estab. 1940. Publishes hardcover and trade paperback originals. "We are primarily a career education publisher that publishes for schools and libraries. We need writers who have expertise in a particular career or career field (for possible full-length books on a specific career or field)." **Publishes 50 titles/year. Pays by project.** Responds in 6 months to queries. Guidelines online.

○ "Please provide an overview of the subject you wish to write on, the intended audience, a brief description of the contents, and a sample chapter or headword list. It is not advisable to send a complete ms at this point. Include a list of the relevant competition and an indication of how your book will improve upon the competition or fill a specific niche in the market. Include a brief curriculum vitae or your writing accomplishments and relevant experience. Send or e-mail your proposal to: Editorial Director."

NONFICTION "We publish work specifically for the elementary/junior high/high school/college library reference market. Works are generally encyclopedic in nature. Our current focus is career encyclopedias and young adult career sets and series. We consider mss that cross over into the trade market." No mass market, poetry, scholarly, or juvenile books, please. Query or submit an outline and 1 sample chapter.

TIPS "We like writers who know the market—former or current librarians or teachers or guidance counselors."

🌑 DAVID FICKLING BOOKS

31 Beamont St., Oxford En OX1 2NP, United Kingdom. (018)65-339000. **Fax:** (018)65-339009. **E-mail:** submissions@davidficklingbooks.com. **Website:** www.davidficklingbooks.co.uk. **Publishes 12-20 titles/year.** Responds to mss in 3 months. Guidelines online.

FICTION Considers all categories. Submit cover letter and 3 sample chapters as PDF attachment saved in format "Author Name_Full Title."

TIPS "We adore stories for all ages, in both text and pictures. Quality is our watch word."

☁ FIFTH HOUSE PUBLISHERS

Fitzhenry & Whiteside, 195 Allstate Parkway, Markham ON L3R 4T8, Canada. (403)571-5230; (800)387-9776. **E-mail:** tdettman@fitzhenry.ca. **Website:** www.fifthhousepublishers.ca. **Contact:** Tracey Dettman. Estab. 1982. "Fifth House Publishers, a Fitzhenry & Whiteside company, is committed to 'bringing the West to the rest' by publishing approximately 15 books a year about the land and people who make this region unique. Our books are selected for their quality and contribution to the understanding of western-Canadian (and Canadian) history, culture, and environment."

FILBERT PUBLISHING

140 3rd St. N., Kandiyohi MN 56251-0326. (320)444-5080. **E-mail:** filbertpublishing@filbertpublishing.com. **Website:** FilbertPublishing.com. **Contact:** Maurice Erickson, acquisitions. Estab. 2001. Publishes trade paperback and electronic originals and reprints. "We really like to publish books that creative people can use to help them make a living following their dream. This includes books on marketing, books that encourage living a full life, freelancing, we'll consider a fairly wide range of subjects under this umbrella. We will also give consideration to books on healthy living and plant-based cooking. Make sure your cookbook has a strong hook. We've got a few awesome books in this category on the horizon and are anxious to extend that line. The people who purchase our books (and visit our website) tend to be in their fifties, female, well-educated; many are freelancers who want to make a lviing writing. Any well-written title that would appeal to that audience is nearly a slam dunk to get added to our catalog. " **Publishes Publishes 6-12 titles/year. titles/year. 95% of books from first-time authors. 99% from unagented writers. Authors receive 10% royalty on retail price. E-books receive 50% net.** Publishes book 2-3 months

after acceptance. Accepts simultaneous submissions. Responds in 1 month on queries, 1 month on proposals, and 1 month on mss. Catalog available with SASE. Also available online at FilbertPublishing.com/our-titles/. Guidelines available with SASE. Also available online at FilbertPublishing.com/submissions/.

NONFICTION Subjects include communications, cooking, foods, health, medicine, nutrition, religion, spirituality, Reference books for freelancers and creative people, with an emphasis on marketing. "Our projects tend to be evergreen. If you've got a great project that's as relevant today as it will be ten years from now, something that you're passionate about, query." Submit a query via SASE with a proposal package, including an outline and 2 sample chapters. Will review artwork. Writers should send photocopies or query about sending electronically.

FICTION Subjects include contemporary, mainstream, mystery, romance, suspense. "We're slow to accept new fiction, however, we are thrilled when we find a story that sweeps us off our feet. Fiction queries have been very sparse the last couple of years, and we're keen on expanding that line in the coming months." Query via SASE with a proposal package, including a synopsis, 5 sample chapters, information regarding your web platform, and a brief mention of your current marketing plan.

TIPS "Get to know us. Subscribe to Writing Etc. to capture our preferred tone. Dig through our website, you'll get many ideas of what we're looking for. We love nurturing new writing careers and most of our authors have stuck with us since our humble beginning. We love words. We really love the publishing business. If you share those passions, feel free to query."

FILTER PRESS, LLC

P.O. Box 95, Palmer Lake CO 80133. (719)481-2420; (888)570-2663. **Fax:** (719)481-2420. **E-mail:** info@filterpressbooks.com. **Website:** www.filterpressbooks.com. **Contact:** Doris Baker, president. Estab. 1957. Publishes trade paperback originals and reprints. **Publishes 4-6 titles/year. Pays 10-12% royalty on wholesale price.** Publishes book 18 months after acceptance.

🗨 "Filter Press specializes in nonfiction of the West.",,"Please submit in hardcopy (not a computer disk) to our address."

NONFICTION Subjects include Americana, anthropology, archeology, ethnic, history, regional, crafts and crafts people of the Southwest. Query with outline and SASE. Reviews artwork/photos.

FINDHORN PRESS

Delft Cottage, Dyke, Forres Scotland IV36 2TF, United Kingdom. (44)(1309) 690-582. **Fax:** (44)(131) 777-2711. **E-mail:** submissions@findhornpress.com. **Website:** www.findhornpress.com. **Contact:** Thierry Bogliolo, publisher. Estab. 1971. Publishes trade paperback originals. **Publishes 20 titles/year. 1,000 queries received/year. 50% of books from first-time authors. 80% from unagented writers. Pays 10-15% royalty on wholesale price.** Publishes book 12-18 months after acceptance. Responds in 3-4 months to proposals. Book catalog and ms guidelines online.

NONFICTION Subjects include nature, spirituality, alternative health. No autobiographies.

FINNEY COMPANY, INC.

5995 149th St. W., Suite 105, Apple Valley MN 55124. **E-mail:** feedback@finneyco.com. **Website:** www.finneyco.com. **Contact:** Alan E. Krysan, president. Publishes trade paperback originals. **Publishes 2 titles/year. Pays 10% royalty on wholesale price. Pays advance.** Publishes book 1 year after acceptance. Responds in 2-3 months to queries.

NONFICTION Subjects include business, economics, education, career exploration/development. Finney publishes career development educational materials. Query with SASE. Reviews artwork/photos.

FIRE ENGINEERING BOOKS & VIDEOS

Imprint of PennWell Corp., 1421 S. Sheridan Rd., Tulsa OK 74112. (918)831-9410. **Fax:** (918)831-9555. **E-mail:** bookproposals@pennwell.com. **Website:** www.pennwellbooks.com. **Contact:** Maria Patterson. Publishes hardcover and softcover originals. "Fire Engineering publishes textbooks relevant to firefighting and training. Currently emphasizing strategy and tactics, reserve training, preparedness for terrorist threats, natural disasters, first response to fires and emergencies." Responds in 1 month to proposals. Book catalog available free.

NONFICTION Submit proposal via e-mail.

TIPS No human-interest stories; technical training only.

FIRST EDITION DESIGN PUBLISHING

P.O. Box 20217, Sarasota FL 34276. (941)921-2607. **Fax:** (617)866-7510. **E-mail:** support@firstedition-design.com. **E-mail:** submission@firsteditiondesign.com. **Website:** www.firsteditiondesignpublishing.com. **Contact:** Deborah E. Gordon, executive editor; Tom Gahan, marketing director. Estab. 1985. **Publishes 750+ titles/year. 45%% of books from first-time authors. 95%% from unagented writers. Pays royalty 30-70% on retail price.** Publishes book Accept to publish time is 1 week to 2 months. after acceptance of ms. Accepts simultaneous submissions. Guidelines available free on request or online.

NONFICTION Subjects include agriculture, alternative lifestyles, Americana, animals, architecture, art, business, career guidance, contemporary culture, counseling, creative nonfiction, education, ethnic, gay, government, health, history, humanities, language, law, memoirs, military, money, multicultural, nature, New Age, philosophy, psychology, recreation, regional, religion, science, sex, social sciences, sociology, spirituality, womens issues, womens studies, world affairs, young adult. Send complete ms electronically.

FICTION Subjects include adventure, confession, ethnic, experimental, fantasy, feminist, gay, gothic, historical, horror, humor, literary, mainstream, multicultural, mystery, occult, poetry, regional, religious, romance, science fiction, short story collections, spiritual, suspense, western, young adult. Submit complete ms electronically.

POETRY Submit complete ms electronically.

TIPS "Follow our FAQs listed on our website."

FITZHENRY & WHITESIDE LTD.

195 Allstate Pkwy., Markham ON L3R 4T8, Canada. (905)477-9700. **Fax:** (905)477-9179. **E-mail:** fitzkids@fitzhenry.ca; godwit@fitzhenry.ca; charkin@fitzhenry.ca. **Website:** www.fitzhenry.ca/. **Contact:** Sharon Fitzhenry, president; Cathy Sandusky, children's publisher; Christie Harkin, submissions editor. Emphasis on Canadian authors and illustrators, subject or perspective. **Publishes 15 titles/year. 10% of books from first-time authors. Pays authors 8-10% royalty with escalations. Offers "respectable" advances for picture books, split 50/50 between author and illustrator. Pays illustrators by project and royalty. Pays photographers per photo.** Publishes book 1-2 years after acceptance.

TIPS "We respond to quality."

FIVE STAR PUBLICATIONS, INC.

P.O. Box 6698, Chandler AZ 85246. (480)940-8182. **Fax:** (480)940-8787. **E-mail:** info@fivestarpublications.com. **Website:** www.fivestarpublications.com. **Contact:** Linda F. Radke, president. Estab. 1985. "Helps produce and market award-winning books."

O "Five Star Publications publishes and promotes award-winning fiction, nonfiction, cookbooks, children's literature and professional guides. More information about Five Star Publications, Inc., a 25-year leader in the book publishing/ book marketing industry, is available online at our website."

TIPS "Not only do we want to recognize and honor accomplished authors in the field of children's literature, but we also want to highlight and reward up-and-coming newly published authors, as well as younger published writers."

● FLARESTACK POETS

69 Beaks Hill Road, Birmingham B38 8BL, United Kingdom. **E-mail:** flarestackpoets@gmail.com. **Website:** www.flarestackpoets.co.uk. **Contact:** Meredith Andrea and Jacqui Rowe. Estab. 2008. **Pays 25% royalty and 6 contributor's copies.** Responds in 6 weeks.

POETRY Flarestack Poets wants "poems that dare outside current trends, even against the grain." Publishes 6 chapbooks/year. Chapbooks are 20-30 pages, professional photocopy, saddle-stitched, card cover. See website for current submission arrangements.

FLASHLIGHT PRESS

527 Empire Blvd., Brooklyn NY 11225. (718)288-8300. **Fax:** (718)972-6307. **E-mail:** editor@flashlightpress.com. **Website:** www.flashlightpress.com. **Contact:** Shari Dash Greenspan, editor. Estab. 2004. Publishes hardcover and trade paperback originals. **Publishes 2-3 titles/year. 1,200 queries received/year; 120 mss received/year. 50% of books from first-time authors. Pays 8-10% royalty on wholesale price.** Publishes book 3 years after acceptance. Accepts simultaneous submissions. "Due to the large number of queries we receive, we are no longer able to send individual replies for queries we do not wish to pursue. You will receive an automated reply that we received your query." Responds in 3 months to mss. Book catalog online.

FICTION Average word length: 1,000 words. Picture books: contemporary, humor, multicultural. "Query by e-mail only, after carefully reading our submission guidelines: www.flashlightpress.com/submissionguidelines.html. No e-mail attachments. Do not send anything by snail mail."

FLOATING BRIDGE PRESS

909 NE 43rd St., #205, Seattle WA 98105. **E-mail:** floatingbridgepress@yahoo.com. **Website:** www. floatingbridgepress.org. Estab. 1994.

POETRY Floating Bridge Press publishes chapbooks and anthologies by Washington State poets, selected through an annual competition.

ⒶⓄ FLUX

Llewellyn Worldwide, Ltd., Llewellyn Worldwide, Ltd., 2143 Wooddale Dr., Woodbury, MN 55125. (651)312-8613. **Fax:** (651)291-1908. **Website:** www. fluxnow.com; fluxnow.blogspot.com. **Contact:** Brian Farrey, acquisitions editor. Estab. 2005. "Flux seeks to publish authors who see YA as a point of view, not a reading level. We look for books that try to capture a slice of teenage experience, whether in real or imagined worlds." **Publishes 21 titles/year. 50% of books from first-time authors. Pays royalties of 10-15% based on wholesale price.** Book catalog and guidelines online.

O *Does not accept unsolicited mss.*

FICTION Young Adults: adventure, contemporary, fantasy, history, humor, problem novels, religion, science fiction, sports, suspense. Average word length: 50,000. Accepts agented submissions only.

TIPS "Read contemporary teen books. Be aware of what else is out there. If you don't read teen books, you probably shouldn't write them. Know your audience. Write incredibly well. Do not condescend."

FOCAL PRESS

Imprint of Elsevier (USA), Inc., 711 3rd Ave., 8th Floor, New York NY 10017. **Website:** www.focalpress.com. **Contact:** Amorette Petersen, publishing director; for further editorial contacts, visit the contacts page on the company's Website. Estab. US, 1981; UK, 1938. Publishes hardcover and paperback originals and reprints. "Focal Press provides excellent books for students, advanced amateurs, and working professionals involved in all areas of media technology. Topics of interest include photography (digital and traditional techniques), film/video, audio, broadcasting, and cinematography, through to journalism, radio, television, video, and writing. Currently emphasizing graphics, gaming, animation, and multimedia." **Publishes 80-120 UK-US titles/year; entire firm publishes over 1,000 titles/year. 25% of books from first-time authors. 90% from unagented writers.** Publishes book 6 months after acceptance. Accepts simultaneous submissions. Responds in 2 months to queries. Book catalog for #10 SASE. Guidelines online.

NONFICTION Subjects include film, cinema, stage, photography, film, cinematography, broadcasting, theater and performing arts, audio, sound and media technology. Does not publish collections of photographs or books composed primarily of photographs. To submit a proposal for consideration by Elsevier, complete the proposal form online. "Once we have had a chance to review your proposal in line with our publishing plan and budget, we will contact you to discuss the next steps." Reviews artwork/photos.

FODOR'S TRAVEL PUBLICATIONS, INC.

Imprint of Random House, Inc., 1745 Broadway, New York NY 10019. **E-mail:** editors@fodors.com. **Website:** www.fodors.com. Estab. 1936. Publishes trade paperback originals. Fodor's publishes travel books on many regions and countries. **Most titles are collective works, with contributions as works for hire. Most contributions are updates of previously published volumes.** Accepts simultaneous submissions. Responds in 2 months to queries. Book catalog available free.

○ "Remember that most Fodor's writers live in the areas they cover. Note that we do not accept unsolicited mss."

NONFICTION Subjects include travel. "We are interested in unique approaches to favorite destinations. Writers seldom review our catalog or our list and often query about books on topics that we're already covering. Beyond that, it's important to review competition and to say what the proposed book will add. Do not send originals without first querying as to our interest in the project. We're not interested in travel literature or in proposals for general travel guidebooks." Submit writing clips and résumé via mail or e-mail. In cover letter, explain qualifications and areas of expertise.

TIPS "In preparing your query or proposal, remember that it's the only argument Fodor's will hear about why your book will be a good one, and why you think it will sell; and it's also best evidence of your ability to create the book you propose. Craft your proposal well and carefully so that it puts your best foot forward."

FOLDED WORD

79 Tracy Way, Meredith NH 03253. **E-mail:** editors@foldedword.com. **Website:** www.foldedword.com. Editor-in-Chief: J.S. Graustein. Poetry Editor: Rose Auslander. Fiction Editor: Casey Tingle. Estab. 2008. "Folded Word is an independent literary press. Our focus? Connecting new voices to readers. Our goal? To make poetry and fiction accessible for the widest audience possible both on and off the page."

TIPS "We are seeking non-formulaic narratives that have a strong sense of place and/or time, especially the exploration of unfamiliar place/time."

FOREIGN POLICY ASSOCIATION

470 Park Ave. S., New York NY 10016. (212)481-8100. **Fax:** (212)481-9275. **E-mail:** krohan@fpa.org. **Website:** www.fpa.org. **Contact:** Karen Rohan, editorial department. Publishes 2 periodicals, an annual eight episode PBS Television series with DVD and an occasional hardcover and trade paperback original. The Foreign Policy Association, a nonpartisan, not-for-profit educational organization founded in 1918, is a catalyst for developing awareness, understanding of and informed opinion on US foreign policy and global issues. Through its balanced, nonpartisan publications, FPA seeks to encourage individuals in schools, communities and the workplace to participate in the foreign policy process. Accepts simultaneous submissions. Book catalog available free.

IMPRINTS Headline Series (quarterly); Great Decisions (annual).

NONFICTION Subjects include government, politics, history, foreign policy.

TIPS "Audience is students and people with an interest, but not necessarily any expertise, in foreign policy and international relations."

FORTRESS PRESS

P.O. Box 1209, Minneapolis MN 55440. (612)330-3300. **Website:** www.fortresspress.com. Publishes hardcover and trade paperback originals. "Fortress Press publishes academic books in Biblical studies, theology, Christian ethics, church history, and professional books in pastoral care and counseling." **Pays royalty on retail price.** Accepts simultaneous submissions. Book catalog free. Guidelines online.

NONFICTION Subjects include religion, women's issues, women's studies, church history, African-American studies. Use online form. Please study guidelines before submitting.

FORWARD MOVEMENT

412 Sycamore St., Cincinnati OH 45202. (513)721-6659; (800)543-1813. **Fax:** (513)721-0729. **E-mail:** rthompson@forwardmovement.org. **Website:** www.

forwardmovement.org. **Contact:** Richelle Thompson, managing editor. Estab. 1934. "Forward Movement was established to help reinvigorate the life of the church. Many titles focus on the life of prayer, where our relationship with God is centered, death, marriage, baptism, recovery, joy, the Episcopal Church and more. Currently emphasizing prayer/spirituality." **Publishes 30 titles/year.** Responds in 1 month. Book catalog and ms guidelines free. Guidelines online.

"Forward Movement is an official agency of the Episcopal Church. In addition to Forward Day by Day, our daily devotional guide, we publish other books and tracts related to the life and concerns of the Christian church, especially within the Anglican Communion. These typically include material introducing the Episcopal Church, meditations and spiritual readings, prayers, liturgical resources, biblical reflections, and material on stewardship, church history, issues before the church, and Christian healing."

NONFICTION Subjects include religion. "We are an agency of the Episcopal Church. There is a special need for tracts of under 8 pages. (A page usually runs about 200 words.) On rare occasions, we publish a full-length book." Query with SASE or by e-mail with complete ms attached.

FICTION Subjects include juvenile.

TIPS "Audience is primarily Episcopalians and other Christians."

WALTER FOSTER PUBLISHING, INC.

3 Wrigley, Suite A, Irvine CA 92618. (800)426-0099. **Fax:** (949)380-7575. **E-mail:** info@walterfoster.com. **Website:** www.walterfoster.com. Estab. 1922. Publishes trade paperback originals. "Walter Foster publishes instructional how-to/craft instruction as well as licensed products."

FOUR WAY BOOKS

Box 535, Village Station, New York NY 10014. **E-mail:** editors@fourwaybooks.com. **Website:** www.fourwaybooks.com. **Contact:** Martha Rhodes, director. Estab. 1993. "Four Way Books is a not-for-profit literary press dedicated to publishing poetry and short fiction by emerging and established writers. Each year, Four Way Books publishes the winners of its national poetry competitions, as well as collections accepted through general submission, panel selection, and solicitation by the editors."

FICTION Open reading period: June 1-30. Book-length story collections and novellas. Submission guidelines will be posted online at end of May. Does not want novels or translations.

POETRY Four Way Books publishes poetry and short fiction. Considers full-length poetry mss only. Books are about 70 pages, offset-printed digitally, perfect-bound, with paperback binding, art/graphics on covers. Does not want individual poems or poetry intended for children/young readers. See website for complete submission guidelines and open reading period in June. Book mss may include previously published poems. Responds to submissions in 4 months. Payment varies. Order sample books from Four Way Books online or through bookstores.

FOX CHAPEL PUBLISHING

1970 Broad St., East Petersburg PA 17520. (800)457-9112. **Fax:** (717)560-4702. **E-mail:** acquisitions@foxchapelpublishing.com. **Website:** www.foxchapelpublishing.com. **Contact:** Peg Couch, acquisitions editor. Publishes hardcover and trade paperback originals and trade paperback reprints. Fox Chapel publishes woodworking, woodcarving, and design titles for professionals and hobbyists. **Publishes 25-40 titles/year. 50% of books from first-time authors. 100% from unagented writers. Pays royalty or makes outright purchase. Pays variable advance.** Publishes book 18 months after acceptance. Accepts simultaneous submissions. Responds in 2 months to queries.

NONFICTION Submission guidelines on website. Reviews artwork/photos. Send photocopies.

TIPS "We're looking for knowledgeable artists, craftspeople and woodworkers, all experts in their fields, to write books of lasting value."

FRANCES LINCOLN CHILDREN'S BOOKS

Frances Lincoln, 74-77 White Lion St., Islington, London N1 9PF, United Kingdom. 00442072844009. **E-mail:** fl@franceslincoln.com. **Website:** www.franceslincoln.com. Estab. 1977. "Our company was founded by Frances Lincoln in 1977. We published our first books two years later, and we have been creating illustrated books of the highest quality ever since, with special emphasis on gardening, walking and the outdoors, art, architecture, design and landscape. In 1983, we started to publish illustrated books for children. Since then we have won many awards and prizes with both fiction and nonfiction children's books." **Pub-**

lishes 100 titles/year. 6% of books from first-time authors. Publishes book 18 months after acceptance. Accepts simultaneous submissions. Responds in 6 weeks to mss.

NONFICTION Subjects include animals, career guidance, cooking, environment, history, multicultural, nature, religion, young adult, social issues, special needs. Average word length: picture books—1,000; middle readers—29,768. Query by e-mail.

FICTION Subjects include adventure, fantasy, historical, humor, juvenile, multicultural, picture books, sports, young adult, antholoigy, folktales, nature. Average word length: picture books—1,000; young readers— 9,788; middle readers— 20,653; young adults— 35,407. Query by e-mail.

▲☯⊘ FRANKLIN WATTS

338 Euston Rd., London NW1 3BH, United Kingdom. +44 (0)20 7873 6000. **Fax:** +44 (0)20 7873 6024. **E-mail:** ad@hachettechildrens.co.uk. **Website:** www.franklinwatts.co.uk. Estab. 1942. Franklin Watts is well known for its high quality and attractive information books, which support the National Curriculum and stimulate children's enquiring minds. Reader Development is one of Franklin Watts' specialisations; the list offers titles on a wide array of subjects for beginner readers. It is also the proud publisher of many award-winning authors/illustrators, including Mick Manning and Brita Granstrom.

○   Generally does not accept unsolicited mss.

FREE SPIRIT PUBLISHING, INC.

217 Fifth Ave. N., Suite 200, Minneapolis MN 55401-1299. (612)338-2068. **Fax:** (612)337-5050. **E-mail:** acquisitions@freespirit.com. **Website:** www.freespirit.com. Estab. 1983. Publishes trade paperback originals and reprints. "We believe passionately in empowering kids to learn to think for themselves and make their own good choices." **Publishes 12-18 titles/year. 5% of books from first-time authors. 75% from unagented writers. Pays advance.** Responds to proposals in 4-6 months. Book catalog and ms guidelines online.

○   Free Spirit does not accept general fiction, poetry or storybook submissions.

NONFICTION Subjects include child guidance, education, pre-K-12, study and social sciences skills, special needs, differentiation but not textbooks or basic skills books like reading, counting, etc., health, medicine, mental/emotional health for/about children, psychology for/about children, sociology for/about children. "Many of our authors are educators, mental health professionals, and youth workers involved in helping kids and teens." No general fiction or picture storybooks, poetry, single biographies or autobiographies, books with mythical or animal characters, or books with religious or New Age content. "We are not looking for academic or religious materials, or books that analyze problems with the nation's school systems." Query with cover letter stating qualifications, intent, and intended audience and market analysis (how your book stands out from the field), along with your promotional plan, outline, 2 sample chapters, résumé, SASE. Do not send original copies of work.

FICTION "We will consider fiction that relates directly to select areas of focus. Please review catalog and author guidelines (both available online) for details before submitting proposal. If you'd like material returned, enclose a SASE with sufficient postage." Accepts queries only—not submissions—by e-mail.

TIPS "Our books are issue-oriented, jargon-free, and solution-focused. Our audience is children, teens, teachers, parents and youth counselors. We are especially concerned with kids' social and emotional well-being and look for books with ready-to-use strategies for coping with today's issues at home or in school—written in everyday language. We are not looking for academic or religious materials, or books that analyze problems with the nation's school systems. Instead, we want books that offer practical, positive advice so kids can help themselves, and parents and teachers can help kids succeed."

FREESTONE/PEACHTREE, JR.

1700 Chattahoochee Ave., Atlanta GA 30318. (404)876-8761. **Fax:** (404)875-2578. **E-mail:** hello@peachtree-online.com. **Website:** www.peachtree-online.com. **Contact:** Helen Harriss, acquisitions; Loraine Joyner, art director; Melanie McMahon Ives, production manager. Estab. 1977. **Publishes 4-8 titles/year.** Publishes book 1-2 years after acceptance. Accepts simultaneous submissions. Responds in 6 months-1 year.

○   Freestone and Peachtree, Jr. are imprints of Peachtree Publishers. See the listing for Peachtree for submission information. No e-mail or fax queries or submissions, please.

NONFICTION Picture books, young readers, middle readers, young adults: history, sports. Picture books:

animal, health, multicultural, nature/environment, science, social issues, special needs.

FICTION Middle Readers: adventure, animal, history, nature/environment, sports. Young Adults: fiction, history, biography, mystery, adventure. Does not want to see science fiction, religion, or romance. Submit 3 sample chapters by postal mail only. No query necessary.

FRONT ROW EXPERIENCE LLC

540 Discovery Bay Blvd., Discovery Bay CA 94505. (925)634-5710. **E-mail:** service@frontrowexperience. com. **Website:** www.frontrowexperience.com. **Contact:** Frank Alexander, editor. Estab. 1974. Publishes trade paperback originals and reprints. "Front Row publishes books on movement education and coordination activities for pre-K to 6th grade." **Publishes 1-2 titles/year.** Accepts simultaneous submissions. Responds in 1 month to queries.

IMPRINTS Kokono.

NONFICTION Subjects include movement education, perceptual-motor development, sensory motor development, hand-eye coordination activities. Query.

TIPS "Be on target—find out what we want, and only submit queries. If you want to send documents, send as a PDF file to our e-mail."

FULCRUM PUBLISHING

4690 Table Mountain Dr., Suite 100, Golden CO 80403. **E-mail:** info@fulcrum-books.com. **Website:** www.fulcrum-books.com. **Contact:** T. Baker, acquisitions editor. Estab. 1984. **Pays authors royalty based on wholesale price. Offers advances.** Catalog for SASE. Guidelines online.

NONFICTION Middle and early readers: Western history, nature/ environment, Native American. Submit complete ms or submit outline/synopsis and 2 sample chapters. "Publisher does not send response letters unless we are interested in publishing." Do not send SASE.

TIPS "Research our line first. We look for books that appeal to the school market and trade. "

FUTURECYCLE PRESS

Website: www.futurecycle.org. **Contact:** Diane Kistner, director/editor-in-chief. Estab. 2007. **Pays 10% royalty and 25 author's copies.** Responds to mss in 3 months. Guidelines online.

FICTION Flash fiction. Submit complete ms.

POETRY Wants "poetry from highly skilled poets, whether well known or emerging. With a few excep-

tions, we are eclectic in our editorial tastes." Does not want concrete or visual poetry. Has published David Chorlton, John Laue, Temple Cone, Neil Carpathios, Tania Runyan, Timothy Martin, Joanne Lowery. Publishes 4 poetry books/year and 2 chapbooks/year. Ms. selected through open submission and competition. "We read unsolicited mss. but also conduct a yearly poetry book competition." Books are 60-90 pages; offset print, perfect-bound, with glossy, full color cover stock, b&w inside. Chapbooks are 20-40 pages, offset print, saddle-stitched. Submit complete ms, no need to query.

GENEALOGICAL PUBLISHING CO., INC.

3600 Clipper Mill Rd., Suite 260, Baltimore MD 21211. (410)837-8271. **Fax:** (410)752-8492. **E-mail:** info@genealogical.com. **E-mail:** jgaronzi@genealogical.com. **Website:** www.genealogical.com. **Contact:** Joe Garonzik, mktg. dir. (history & genealogy). Estab. 1959. Publishes hardcover and trade paperback originals and reprints. **Publishes 100 titles/year. Receives 100 queries/year; 20 mss/year. 10% of books from first-time authors. 99% from unagented writers. Pays 10-15% royalty on wholesale price.** Publishes book 6 months after acceptance. Accepts simultaneous submissions. Responds in 1 month. Catalog free on request.

NONFICTION Subjects include Americana, ethnic, history, hobbies. Submit outline, 1 sample chapter. Reviews artwork/photos as part of the mss package.

TIPS "Our audience is genealogy hobbyists."

GIBBS SMITH

P.O. Box 667, Layton UT 84041. (801)544-9800. **Fax:** (801)544-8853. **E-mail:** duribe@gibbs-smith.com. **Website:** www.gibbs-smith.com. **Contact:** Suzanne Taylor, associate publisher and creative director (children's activity books); Jennifer Grillone, art acquisitions. Estab. 1969. **Publishes 3 titles/year. 50% of books from first-time authors. 50% from unagented writers. Pays authors royalty of 2% based on retail price or work purchased outright ($500 minimum). Offers advances (average amount: $2,000).** Publishes book 1-2 years after acceptance. Accepts simultaneous submissions. Responds to queries and mss in 2 months. Book catalog available for 9×12 SAE and $2.30 postage. Ms guidelines available by e-mail.

NONFICTION Middle readers: activity, arts/crafts, cooking, how-to, nature/environment, science. Average word length: picture books—under 1,000 words;

activity books—under 15,000 words. Submit an outline and writing samples for activity books; query for other types of books.

TIPS "We target ages 5-11. We do not publish young adult novels or chapter books."

⊘ GIFTED EDUCATION PRESS

10201 Yuma Ct., Manassas VA 20109. (703)369-5017. **E-mail:** mfisher345@comcast.net. **Website:** www. giftedpress.com. **Contact:** Maurice Fisher, publisher. Estab. 1981. Publishes trade paperback originals. "Searching for rigorous texts on teaching science, math and humanities to gifted students." **Publishes 5 titles/ year. 20 queries received/year. 10 mss received/year. 90% of books from first-time authors. 100% from unagented writers. Pays 10% royalty on retail price.** Publishes book 4 months after acceptance. Accepts simultaneous submissions. Responds in 1 month to queries, proposals and mss. Catalog and guidelines online.

NONFICTION Subjects include child guidance, computers, electronics, education, history, humanities, philosophy, science, teaching, math, biology, Shakespeare, chemistry, physics, creativity. Query with SASE. *All unsolicited mss returned unopened.* Reviews artwork/photos.

TIPS "Audience includes teachers, parents, gift program supervisors, professors. Be knowledgeable about your subject. Write clearly and don't use educational jargon."

◕⊘ GINNINDERRA PRESS

P.O. Box 3461, Port Adelaide 5015, Australia. **E-mail:** stephen@ginninderrapress.com.au. **Website:** www. ginninderrapress.com.au. **Contact:** Stephen Matthews, publisher. Estab. 1996. Ginninderra Press works "to give publishing opportunities to new writers." Has published poetry by Alan Gould and Geoff Page. Responds to queries within 1 week; mss in 2 months.

◑ *Publishes books by Australian authors only.*

POETRY Query first, with a few sample poems and a cover letter with brief bio and publication credits. Considers previously published poems.

GIVAL PRESS

Gival Press, LLC, P.O. Box 3812, Arlington VA 22203. (703)351-0079. **E-mail:** givalpress@yahoo.com. **Website:** www.givalpress.com. **Contact:** Robert L. Giron, editor-in-chief (area of interest: literary). Estab. 1998. Publishes trade paperback, electronic originals, and

reprints. **Publishes 5-6 titles/year. 200 queries received/year. 60 mss received/year. 50% of books from first-time authors. 70% from unagented writers. Pays royalty.** Publishes book 12 months after acceptance. Accepts simultaneous submissions. Responds in 1 month to queries, 3 months to proposals and mss. Catalog and guidelines online.

NONFICTION Subjects include gay, lesbian, memoirs, multicultural, translation, womens issues, womens studies, scholarly. Submit between October-December only. Always query first via e-mail; provide plan/ms content, bio, and supportive material. Reviews artwork/photos; query first.

FICTION Subjects include gay, lesbian, literary, multicultural, poetry, translation. Always query first via e-mail; provide description, author's bio, and supportive material.

POETRY Query via e-mail; provide description, bio, etc.; submit 5-6 sample poems via e-mail.

TIPS "Our audience is those who read literary works with depth to the work. Visit our website—there is much to be read/learned from the numerous pages."

GLENBRIDGE PUBLISHING, LTD.

19923 E. Long Ave., Centennial CO 80016. (800)986-4135; (720)870-8381. **Fax:** (720)230-1209. **Website:** www.glenbridgepublishing.com. Estab. 1986. Publishes hardcover originals and reprints, trade paperback originals. "Glenbridge has an eclectic approach to publishing. We look for titles that have long-term capabilities." **Publishes 6-8 titles/year. Pays 10% royalty.** Publishes book 1 year after acceptance. Accepts simultaneous submissions. Responds in 2 months to queries. Book catalog online. Guidelines for #10 SASE.

NONFICTION Subjects include Americana, animals, business, economics, education, environment, family, finance, parenting, writing, film, theatre, communication, cooking, foods, nutrition, health, medicine, history, philosophy, politics & government, psychology, sociology. Send e-mail on website. Query with outline/synopsis, sample chapters.

THE GLENCANNON PRESS

P.O. Box 1428, El Cerrito CA 94530. (510)528-4216. **Fax:** (510)528-3194. **E-mail:** merships@yahoo.com. **Website:** www.glencannon.com. **Contact:** Bill Harris (maritime, maritime children's). Estab. 1993. Publishes hardcover and paperback originals and hardcover reprints. "We publish quality books about ships and the sea." Average print order: 1,000. Member PMA,

BAIPA. Distributes titles through Baker & Taylor. Promotes titles through direct mail, magazine advertising and word of mouth. Accepts unsolicited mss. Often comments on rejected mss. **Publishes 4-5 titles/year. Pays 10-20% royalty.** Publishes book 6-24 months after acceptance. Accepts simultaneous submissions. Responds in 1 month to queries; 2 months to mss.

IMPRINTS Smyth: perfect binding; illustrations.

FICTION Submit complete ms. Include brief bio, list of publishing credits. Send SASE for return of ms or send a disposable ms and SASE for reply only.

TIPS "Write a good story in a compelling style."

🅐⊘ DAVID R. GODINE, PUBLISHER

15 Court Square, Suite 320, Boston MA 02108. (617)451-9600. **Fax:** (617)350-0250. **E-mail:** info@godine.com. **Website:** www.godine.com. Estab. 1970. "We publish books that matter for people who care."

> 🗨 This publisher is no longer considering unsolicited mss of any type. Only interested in agented material.

🅐⊘ GOLDEN BOOKS FOR YOUNG READERS GROUP

1745 Broadway, New York NY 10019. **Website:** www.randomhouse.com. Estab. 1935. "Random House Books aims to create books that nurture the hearts and minds of children, providing and promoting quality books and a rich variety of media that entertain and educate readers from 6 months to 12 years." **2% of books from first-time authors. Pays authors in royalties; sometimes buys mss outright.** Book catalog free on request.

> 🗨 Random House-Golden Books does not accept unsolicited mss, only agented material. They reserve the right not to return unsolicited material.

GOLDEN WEST BOOKS

P.O. Box 80250, San Marino CA 91118. (626)458-8148. **Fax:** (626)458-8148. **E-mail:** trainbook@earthlink.net. **Website:** www.goldenwestbooks.com. Publishes hardcover originals. "Golden West Books specializes in railroad history." **Publishes 3-4 titles/year. 8-10 queries received/year. 5 mss received/year. 75% of books from first-time authors. 100% from unagented writers. Pays 8-10% royalty on wholesale price.** Publishes book 3 months after acceptance. Responds in 3 months to queries. Book catalog and ms guidelines free.

> 🗨 "We are always interested in new material. Please use the form online to contact us; we will follow up with you as soon as possible."

NONFICTION Subjects include Americana, history. Use online form. Reviews artwork/photos.

GOODMAN BECK PUBLISHING

E-mail: info@goodmanbeck.com. **Website:** www.goodmanbeck.com. Estab. 2007. Publishes trade paperback originals. "Our primary interest at this time is mental health, personal growth, aging well, positive psychology, accessible spirituality, and self-help." **Publishes 5-6 titles/year. 65% of books from first-time authors. 90% from unagented writers. Pays 10% royalty on retail price.** Publishes book 6-9 months after acceptance. Accepts simultaneous submissions. "Due to high query volume, response not guaranteed.".

> 🗨 "Our audience is adults trying to cope with this 'upside down world.' With our self-help books, we are trying to improve the world one book at a time."

NONFICTION Subjects include creative nonfiction, health, medicine, philosophy, psychology, spirituality,. No religious or political works, textbooks, or how-to books at this time. Query by e-mail only. Reviews artwork/photos. Send photocopies.

POETRY "We are interested in zen-inspired haiku and non-embellished, non-rhyming, egoless poems. Read Mary Oliver." Query, submit 3 sample poems. E-mail submissions only.

TIPS "Your book should be enlightening and marketable. Be prepared to have a comprehensive marketing plan. You will be very involved."

⟳ GOOSE LANE EDITIONS

500 Beaverbrook Ct., Suite 330, Fredericton NB E3B 5X4, Canada. (506)450-4251. **Fax:** (506)459-4991. **E-mail:** submissions@gooselane.com. **Website:** www.gooselane.com. **Contact:** Angela Williams, publishing assistant. Estab. 1954. Publishes hardcover and paperback originals and occasional reprints. "Goose Lane publishes literary fiction and nonfiction from well-read and highly skilled Canadian authors." **Publishes 16-20 titles/year. 20% of books from first-time authors. 60% from unagented writers. Pays 8-10% royalty on retail price. Pays $500-3,000, negotiable advance.** Responds in 6 months to queries.

NONFICTION Subjects include art, architecture, history, language, literature, nature, environment, regional, women's issues, women's studies. Query with SASE.

FICTION Subjects include literary, novels, short story collections, contemporary. Our needs in fiction never change: Substantial, character-centered literary fiction. No children's, YA, mainstream, mass market, genre, mystery, thriller, confessional or science fiction. Query with SAE with Canadian stamps or IRCs. No U.S. stamps.

POETRY Considers mss by Canadian poets only. Submit cover letter, list of publications, synopsis, entire ms, SASE.

TIPS "Writers should send us outlines and samples of books that show a very well-read author with highly developed literary skills. Our books are almost all by Canadians living in Canada; we seldom consider submissions from outside Canada. We consider submissions from outside Canada only when the author is Canadian and the book is of extraordinary interest to Canadian readers. We do not publish books for children or for the young adult market."

THE GRADUATE GROUP

P.O. Box 370351, West Hartford CT 06137-0351. (860)233-2330. **Fax:** (860)233-2330. **E-mail:** graduategroup@hotmail.com. **Website:** www.graduategroup. com. **Contact:** Mara Whitman, partner; Robert Whitman, vice president. Estab. 1964. Publishes trade paperback originals. The Graduate Group helps college and graduate students better prepare themselves for rewarding careers and helps people advance in the workplace. Currently emphasizing test preparation, career advancement, and materials for prisoners, law enforcement, books on unique careers. **Publishes 50 titles/year. 100 queries received/year. 70 mss received/year. 60% of books from first-time authors. 85% from unagented writers. Pays 20% - royalty on retail price.** Publishes book 3 months after acceptance of ms. Accepts simultaneous submissions. Responds in 1 month to queries. Book catalog available free. Guidelines online.

NONFICTION Subjects include business, economics, education, government, politics, health, medicine, money, finance, law enforcement. Submit complete ms and SASE with sufficient postage.

TIPS "We are open to all submissions."

GRANITE PUBLISHING, LLC

P.O. Box 1429, Columbus NC 28722. (828)894-8444. **Fax:** (828)894-8454. **E-mail:** brian@granitepublish-

ing.us; eileen@souledout.org. **Website:** www.granitepublishing.us/index.html. **Contact:** Brian Crissey. Publishes trade paperback originals and reprints. "Granite Publishing strives to preserve the Earth by publishing books that develop new wisdom about our emerging planetary citizenship, bringing information from the outerworlds to our world. Currently emphasizing indigenous ideas, planetary healing." **Publishes 4 titles/year. 50 queries received/year. 150 mss received/year. 70% of books from first-time authors. 90% from unagented writers. Pays 7 1/2-10% royalty.** Publishes book 16 months after acceptance. Accepts simultaneous submissions. Responds in 6 months to mss.

IMPRINTS Wild Flower Press; Swan-Raven & Co.; Agents of Change.

"Granite Publishing accepts only a few very fine mss in our niches each year, and those that are accepted must follow our rigid guidelines online. Our Little Granite Books imprint publishes only our own writings for children."

NONFICTION Subjects include New Age, planetary paradigm shift. Submit proposal. Reviews artwork/photos. Send photocopies.

GRAYWOLF PRESS

250 Third Ave., N.,, Suite 600, Minneapolis MN 55401. **E-mail:** wolves@graywolfpress.org. **Website:** www. graywolfpress.org. **Contact:** Katie Dublinski, editorial manager (nonfiction, fiction). Estab. 1974. Publishes trade cloth and paperback originals. "Graywolf Press is an independent, nonprofit publisher dedicated to the creation and promotion of thoughtful and imaginative contemporary literature essential to a vital and diverse culture." **Publishes 23 titles/year. 3,000 queries received/year. 20% of books from first-time authors. 50% from unagented writers. Pays royalty on retail price. Pays $1,000-25,000 advance.** Publishes book Publishes 18 months after acceptance. Responds in 3 months to queries. Book catalog free. Guidelines online.

NONFICTION Subjects include contemporary culture, language, literature, culture. Agented submissions only.

FICTION Subjects include short story collections, literary novels. "Familiarize yourself with our list first." No genre books (romance, western, science fiction, suspense) Agented submissions only.

POETRY "We are interested in linguistically challenging work." Agented submissions only.

GREAT POTENTIAL PRESS

1325 N. Wilmot Ave., #300, Tucson AZ 85712. (520)777-6161. **Fax:** (520)777-6217. **Website:** www. giftedbooks.com. **Contact:** Janet Gore, editor; James T. Webb, Ph.D., president. Estab. 1986. Publishes trade paperback originals. Specializes in nonfiction books that address academic, social and emotional issues of gifted and talented children and adults. **Publishes 6-10 titles/year. 75 queries received/year. 20-30 mss received/year. 50% of books from first-time authors. 100% from unagented writers. Pays 10% royalty on retail price.** Publishes book 1 year after acceptance. Accepts simultaneous submissions. Responds in 2 months to queries; 3 months to proposals; 4 months to mss. Book catalog free or on website. Guidelines online.

NONFICTION Subjects include child guidance, education, multicultural, psychology, translation, travel, women's issues, gifted/talented children and adults, misdiagnosis of gifted, parenting gifted, teaching gifted, meeting the social and emotional needs of gifted and talented, and strategies for working with gifted children and adults. Use online submission form.

TIPS "Mss should be clear, cogent, and well-written and should pertain to gifted, talented, and creative persons and/or issues."

GREENHAVEN PRESS

27500 Drake Rd., Farmington Hills MI 48331. **E-mail:** betz.deschenes@cengage.com. **Website:** www.gale. com/greenhaven. **Contact:** Betz Des Chenes. Estab. 1970. Publishes 220 young adult academic reference titles/year. 50% of books by first-time authors. Greenhaven continues to print quality nonfiction anthologies for libraries and classrooms. "Our well-known Opposing Viewpoints series is highly respected by students and librarians in need of material on controversial social issues." Greenhaven accepts no unsolicited mss. Send query, résumé, and list of published works by e-mail. Work purchased outright from authors; write for-hire, flat fee.

NONFICTION Young adults (high school): controversial issues, social issues, history, literature, science, environment, health.

GREENWILLOW BOOKS

HarperCollins Publishers, 10 E. 53rd St., New York NY 10022. (212)207-7000. **Website:** www.greenwil-lowblog.com. **Contact:** Virginia Duncan, vice president/publisher; Paul Zakris, art director. Estab. 1974. Publishes hardcover originals, paperbacks, e-books, and reprints. **Publishes 40-50 titles/year. Pays 10% royalty on wholesale price for first-time authors. Offers variable advance.** Publishes book 2 years after acceptance.

○ Does not accept unsolicited mss. "Unsolicited mail will not be opened and will not be returned."

FICTION Subjects include fantasy, humor, literary, mystery, picture books.

GREENWOOD PRESS

ABC-CLIO, P.O. Box 1911, Santa Barbara CA 93116. (805)968-1911. **E-mail:** customerservice@abc-clio. com. **Website:** www.abc-clio.com. **Contact:** Vince Burns, vice president of editorial. Publishes hardcover originals. Greenwood Press publishes reference materials for high school, public and academic libraries in the humanities and the social and hard sciences. **Publishes 200 titles/year. 1,000 queries received/year. 25% of books from first-time authors. Pays variable royalty on net price. Pays rare advance.** Publishes book 1 year after acceptance. Accepts simultaneous submissions. Responds in 6 months to queries. Book catalog and ms guidelines online.

NONFICTION Subjects include humanities, literary criticism, social sciences, humanities and the social and hard sciences. Query with proposal package, including scope, organization, length of project, whether complete ms is available or when it will be, cv or résumé and SASE. *No unsolicited mss.*

GREY GECKO PRESS

565 S. Mason Rd., Suite 154, Katy TX 77450. (866)535-6078. **Fax:** (866)535-6078. **E-mail:** info@greygecko-press.com. **E-mail:** submissions@greygeckopress. com. **Website:** www.greygeckopress.com. **Contact:** Hilary Comfort, editor-in-chief; Jason Aydelotte, executive director. Estab. 2011. Publishes hardcover, trade paperback, and electronic originals. **Publishes 10-20 titles/year. 200+ queries received/year; 10-20 mss received/year. 100% of books from first-time authors. 100% from unagented writers. Pays 50-80% royalties on wholesale price.** Publishes book 3-6 months after acceptance. Accepts simultaneous submissions. Responds in 1-3 months. Book catalog and ms guidelines for #10 SASE, by e-mail or online.

NONFICTION Subjects include architecture, art, contemporary culture, cooking, creative nonfiction, environment, foods, history, marine subjects, military, nature, photography, travel, war. "All nonfiction submissions are evaluated on a case by case basis. We focus mainly on fiction, but we'll take a look at nonfiction works." "We prefer electronic submissions." Query with SASE. Submit proposal package including outline, detailed synopsis, and 3 sample chapters. Reviews artwork. Send photocopies or link to photo website.

FICTION Subjects include adventure, contemporary, ethnic, fantasy, feminist, gay, historical, horror, humor, juvenile, lesbian, literary, mainstream, military, multicultural, mystery, occult, regional, romance, science fiction, short story collections, sports, suspense, war, western, young adult. "We do not publish extreme horror, erotica, or religious fiction. New and interesting stories by unpublished authors will always get our attention. Innovation is a core value of our company. We prefer electronic submissions but will accept: Query with SASE. Submit proposal package including outline, detailed, synopsis, and 3 sample chapters."

TIPS "Be willing to be a part of the Grey Gecko family. Publishing with us is a partnership, not indentured servitude."

GROSSET & DUNLAP PUBLISHERS

Penguin Putnam Inc., 375 Hudson St., New York NY 10014. **Website:** www.penguingroup.com. **Contact:** Francesco Sedita, vice president/publisher. Estab. 1898. Publishes hardcover (few) and mass market paperback originals. Grosset & Dunlap publishes children's books that show children that reading is fun, with books that speak to their interests, and that are affordable so that children can build a home library of their own. Focus on licensed properties, series and readers. "Grosset & Dunlap publishes high-interest, affordable books for children ages 0-10 years. We focus on original series, licensed properties, readers and novelty books." **Publishes 140 titles/year. Pays royalty. Pays advance.**

NONFICTION Subjects include nature, environment, science. All book formats except for picture books. Submit a summary and the first chapter or 2 for longer works.

FICTION Subjects include juvenile. All book formats except for picture books. Submit a summary and the first chapter or 2 for longer works.

TIPS "Nonfiction that is particularly topical or of wide interest in the mass market; new concepts for novelty format for preschoolers; and very well-written easy readers on topics that appeal to primary graders have the best chance of selling to our firm."

○ GROUNDWOOD BOOKS

110 Spadina Ave. Suite 801, Toronto ON M5V 2K4, Canada. (416)363-4343. **Fax:** (416)363-1017. **E-mail:** ssutherland@groundwoodbooks.com. **Website:** www.houseofanansi.com. Publishes 13 picture books/year; 3 young readers/year; 5 middle readers/year; 5 young adult titles/year, approximately 2 nonfiction titles/year. **Offers advances.** Accepts simultaneous submissions. Responds to mss in 6-8 months. Visit website for guidelines: www.houseofanansi.com/Groundwoodsubmissions.aspx.

NONFICTION Recently published: *Looks Like Daylight- Voices of Indigenous Kids*, by Deborah Ellis. Picture books recently published: *Oy, Feh, So?*, by Cary Fagan, illustrated by Gary Clement; *once Upon a Northern Night*, by Jean E. Pendziwol, illustrated by Isabelle Arsenault; *Northwest Passage*, by Stan Rogers, illustrated by Matt James; *The Voyage*, by Veronica Salinas, illustrated by Camilla Engman; *Out the Window*, by Cybèle Young.

FICTION Submit synopsis and sample chapters.

GRYPHON HOUSE, INC.

P.O. Box 10, 6848 Leon's Way, Lewisville NC 27023. **Website:** www.gryphonhouse.com. **Contact:** Kathy Charner, editor-in-chief. Estab. 1981. Publishes trade paperback originals. "Gryphon House publishes books that teachers and parents of young children (birth-age 8) consider essential to their daily lives." Publishes parent and teacher resource books, textbooks. Recently published *Reading Games*, by Jackie Silberg; *Primary Art*, by MaryAnn F. Kohl; *Teaching Young Children with Autism Spectrum Disorder*, by Clarissa Willis; *The Complete Resource Book for Infants*, by Pam Schiller. "At Gryphon House, our goal is to publish books that help teachers and parents enrich the lives of children from birth through age 8. We strive to make our books useful for teachers at all levels of experience, as well as for parents, caregivers, and anyone interested in working with children." Query. Submit outline/synopsis and 2 sample chapters. Responds to queries/mss in 6 months. Publishes a book 18 months after acceptance. Will consider simultaneous submissions, e-mail submissions. Book catalog and ms guidelines available via website or with SASE. "We are looking for books of creative, participatory learning experiences that have a common conceptual theme to tie them together. The books should be on subjects that parents or teachers want to do on a daily basis." **Publishes 12-15 titles/year. Pays royalty on wholesale price.** Responds in 3-6 months to queries. Guidelines online.

NONFICTION Subjects include child guidance, education, early childhood. Currently emphasizing social-emotional intelligence and classroom management; de-emphasizing literacy after-school activities. "We prefer to receive a letter of inquiry and/or a proposal, rather than the entire ms. Please include: the proposed title, the purpose of the book, table of contents, introductory material, 20-40 sample pages of the actual book. In addition, please describe the book, including the intended audience, why teachers will want to buy it, how it is different from other similar books already published, and what qualifications you possess that make you the appropriate person to write the book. If you have a writing sample that demonstrates that you write clear, compelling prose, please include it with your letter."

⊘◌ GUERNICA EDITIONS

P.O. Box 76080, Abbey Market, Oakville ON L6M 3H5, Canada. (514)712-5304. **Fax:** (416)981-7606. **E-mail:** michaelmirolla@guernicaeditions.com. **Website:** www.guernicaeditions.com. **Contact:** Michael Mirolla, editor/publisher (poetry, nonfiction, short stories, novels). Estab. 1978. Publishes trade paperback originals and reprints. Guernica Editions is a literary press that produces works of poetry, fiction and nonfiction often by writers who are ignored by the mainstream. **Publishes 15 titles/year. Several hundred mss received/year. 20% of books from first-time authors. 99% from unagented writers. Pays 8-10% royalty on retail price, or makes outright purchase of $200-5,000. Pays $450-750 advance.** Publishes book Publishes 24-36 months after acceptance. Responds in 1 month to queries. Responds in 6 months to proposals. Responds in 1 year to mss. Book catalog online.

NONFICTION Subjects include art, architecture, creative nonfiction, ethnic, film, cinema, stage, gay, lesbian, government, politics, history, language, literature, lit-crit, memoirs, multicultural, music, dance, philosophy, psychology, regional, religion, sex, translation, women's issues. Query by e-mail only. Reviews artwork/photos. Send photocopies.

FICTION Subjects include feminist, gay, lesbian, literary, multicultural, plays, poetry, poetry in translation, translation. "We wish to open up into the fiction world and focus less on poetry. We specialize in European, especially Italian, translations." E-mail queries only.

POETRY Feminist, gay/lesbian, literary, multicultural, poetry in translation. We wish to have writers in translation. Any writer who has translated Italian poetry is welcomed. Full books only. No single poems by different authors, unless modern, and used as an anthology. First books will have no place in the next couple of years. Query.

GULF PUBLISHING COMPANY

2 Greenway Plaza, Suite 1020, Houston TX 77046. (713)529-4301. **Fax:** (713)520-4433. **E-mail:** svb@gulfpub.com. **Website:** www.gulfpub.com. **Contact:** Katie Hammon. Estab. 1916. Publishes hardcover originals and reprints; electronic originals and reprints. "Gulf Publishing Company is the leading publisher to the oil and gas industry. Our specialized publications reach over 100,000 people involved in energy industries worldwide. Our magazines and catalogs help readers keep current with information important to their field and allow advertisers to reach their customers in all segments of petroleum operations. More than half our editorial staff have engineering degrees. The others are thoroughly trained and experienced business journalists and editors." **Publishes 12-15 titles/year. 3-5 queries and mss received in a year. 30% of books from first-time authors. 80% from unagented writers. Royalties on retail price. Pays $1,000-1,500 advance.** Publishes book 8-9 months after acceptance. Accepts simultaneous submissions. Responds in 2 months to queries; 1 month to proposals and mss. Catalog free on request. Guidelines available by e-mail.

NONFICTION , Engineering. "We don't publish a lot in the year, therefore we are able to focus more on marketing and sales—we are hoping to grow in the future." Submit outline, 1-2 sample chapters, completed ms. Reviews artwork. Send high res file formats with high dpi in b&w.

TIPS "Our audience would be engineers, engineering students, academia, professors, well managers, construction engineers. We recommend getting contributors to help with the writing process—this provides a more comprehensive overview for technical and scientific books. Work harder on artwork. It's expensive and time-consuming for a publisher to redraw a lot of the figures."

HACHAI PUBLISHING

527 Empire Blvd., Brooklyn NY 11225. (718)633-0100. **Fax:** (718)633-0103. **Website:** www.hachai.com. **Contact:** Devorah Leah Rosenfeld, editor. Estab. 1988. Publishes hardcover originals. Hachai is dedicated to producing high quality Jewish children's literature, ages 2-10. Story should promote universal values such as sharing, kindness, etc. **Publishes 4 titles/year. 75% of books from first-time authors. Work purchased outright from authors for $800-1,000.** Accepts simultaneous submissions. Responds in 2 months to mss. Book catalog available free. Guidelines online.

○   "All books have spiritual/religious themes, specifically traditional Jewish content. We're seeking books about morals and values; the Jewish experience in current and Biblical times; and Jewish observance, Sabbath and holidays."

NONFICTION Subjects include ethnic, religion. Submit complete ms. Reviews artwork/photos. Send photocopies.

FICTION Picture books and young readers: contemporary, historical fiction, religion. Middle readers: adventure, contemporary, problem novels, religion. Does not want to see fantasy, animal stories, romance, problem novels depicting drug use or violence. Submit complete ms.

TIPS "We are looking for books that convey the traditional Jewish experience in modern times or long ago; traditional Jewish observance such as Sabbath and holidays and mitzvos such as mezuzah, blessings etc.; positive character traits (middos) such as honesty, charity, respect, sharing, etc. We are also interested in historical fiction for young readers (7-10) written with a traditional Jewish perspective and highlighting the relevance of Torah in making important choices. Please, no animal stories, romance, violence, preachy sermonizing. Write a story that incorporates a moral, not a preachy morality tale. Originality is the key. We feel Hachai publications will appeal to a wider readership as parents become more interested in positive values for their children."

HADLEY RILLE BOOKS

PO Box 25466, Overland Park KS 66225. **E-mail:** subs@hadleyrillebooks.com. **Website:** www.hrbpress. com. **Contact:** Eric T. Reynolds, editor/publisher. Estab. 2005.

○   Currently closed to submissions. Check website for future reading periods.

FICTION Subjects include fantasy, science fiction, short story collections.

TIPS "We aim to produce books that are aligned with current interest in the genres. Anthology markets are somewhat rare in SF these days, we feel there aren't enough good anthologies being published each year and part of our goal is to present the best that we can. We like stories that fit well within the guidelines of the particular anthology for which we are soliciting mss. Aside from that, we want stories with strong characters (not necessarily characters with strong personalities, flawed characters are welcome). We want a sense of wonder and awe. We want to feel the world around the character and so scene description is important (however, this doesn't always require a lot of text, just set the scene well so we don't wonder where the character is). We strongly recommend workshopping the story or having it critiqued in some way by readers familiar with the genre. We prefer clichés be kept to a bare minimum in the prose and avoid re-working old story lines."

HAMPTON ROADS PUBLISHING CO., INC.

665 Third St., Suite 400, San Francisco CA 94107. **E-mail:** submissions@rwwbooks.com. **Website:** www. redwheelweiser.com. **Contact:** Ms. Pat Bryce, Acquisitions Editor. Estab. 1989. Publishes and distributes hardcover and trade paperback originals on subjects including metaphysics, health, complementary medicine, visionary fiction, and other related topics. "Our reason for being is to impact, uplift, and contribute to positive change in the world. We publish books that will enrich and empower the evolving consciousness of mankind. Though we are not necessarily limited in scope, we are most interested in mss on the following subjects: Body/Mind/Spirit, Health and Healing, Self-Help. Please be advised that at the moment we are not accepting: Fiction or Novelized material that does not pertain to body/mind/spirit, Channeled writing." " **Publishes 35-40 titles/year. 1,000 queries received/year. 1,500 mss received/year. 50% of books from first-time authors. 70% from unagented writers. Pays royalty. Pays $1,000-50,000 advance.** Publishes book 1 year after acceptance. Accepts simultaneous submissions. Responds in 2-4 months to

queries; 1 month to proposals; 6-12 months to mss. Guidelines online.

○ "Please know that we only publish a handful of books every year, and that we pass on many well written, important works, simply because we cannot publish them all. We review each and every proposal very carefully. However, due to the volume of inquiries, we cannot respond to them all individually. Please give us 30 days to review your proposal. If you do not hear back from us within that time, this means we have decided to pursue other book ideas that we feel fit better within our plan."

NONFICTION Subjects include New Age, spirituality. Query with SASE. Submit synopsis, SASE. No longer accepting electronic submissions. Reviews artwork/photos. Send photocopies.

FICTION Subjects include literary, spiritual, visionary fiction, past-life fiction based on actual memories. Fiction should have 1 or more of the following themes: spiritual, inspirational, metaphysical, i.e., past-life recall, out-of-body experiences, near-death experience, paranormal. Query with SASE. Submit outline, 2 sample chapters, clips. Submit complete ms.

HANCOCK HOUSE PUBLISHERS

U.S. Office, 1431 Harrison Ave., Blaine WA 98230. (604)538-1114. **Fax:** (604)538-2262. **E-mail:** submissions@hancockhouse.com. **Website:** www.hancockhouse.com. Estab. 1971. Publishes hardcover, trade paperback, and eBook originals and reprints. "Hancock House Publishers is the largest North American publisher of wildlife and Native Indian titles. We also cover Pacific Northwest, fishing, history, Canadiana, biographies. We are seeking agriculture, natural history, animal husbandry, conservation, and popular science titles with a regional (Pacific Northwest), national, or international focus. Currently emphasizing nonfiction wildlife, cryptozoology, guide books, native history, biography, fishing." **Publishes 12-20 titles/year. 50% of books from first-time authors. 90% from unagented writers. Pays 10% royalty.** Publishes book 1 year after acceptance. Accepts simultaneous submissions. Responds to proposals in 3-6 months. Book catalog available free. Guidelines online.

NONFICTION Subjects include agriculture, animals, ethnic, history, horticulture, nature, environment, regional. Centered around Pacific Northwest, local history, nature guide books, international ornithology, and Native Americans. Query via e-mail, including outline with word count, a short author bio, table of contents, 3 sample chapters. Accepts double-spaced word .docs or PDFs. Reviews artwork/photos. Send photocopies.

HANSER PUBLICATIONS

6915 Valley Ave., Cincinnati OH 45244. (513)527-8800; (800)950-8977. **Fax:** (513)527-8801. **E-mail:** info@hanserpublications.com. **Website:** www.hanserpublications.com. **Contact:** Development Editor. Estab. 1993. Publishes hardcover and paperback originals, and digital educational and training programs. "Hanser Publications publishes books and electronic media for the manufacturing (both metalworking and plastics) industries. Publications range from basic training materials to advanced reference books." **Publishes 10-15 titles/year. 100 queries received/year. 10-20 mss received/year. 50% of books from first-time authors. 100% from unagented writers.** Publishes book 10 months after acceptance. Accepts simultaneous submissions. Responds in 2 weeks to queries; 1 month to proposals/mss. Book catalog available free. Guidelines online.

○ "Hanser Publications is currently seeking technical experts with strong writing skills to author training and reference books and related products focused on various aspects of the manufacturing industry. Our goal is to provide manufacturing professionals with insightful, easy-to-reference information, and to educate and prepare students for technical careers through accessible, concise training manuals. Do your publishing ideas match this goal? If so, we'd like to hear from you. Submit your detailed product proposals, résumé of credentials, and a brief writing sample to: Development Editor, Prospective Authors."

NONFICTION "We publish how-to texts, references, technical books, and computer-based learning materials for the manufacturing industries. Titles include award-winning management books, encyclopedic references, and leading references." Submit outline, sample chapters, résumé, preface, and comparison to competing or similar titles.

TIPS "E-mail submissions speed up response time."

⊛⊘ HARCOURT, INC., TRADE DIVISION

Imprint of Houghton Mifflin Harcourt Book Group, 215 Park Ave. S., New York NY 10003. **Website:** www.

harcourtbooks.com. Publishes hardcover and trade paperback originals and trade paperback reprints. **Publishes 120 titles/year. 5% of books from first-time authors. 5% from unagented writers. Pays 6-15% royalty on retail price. Pays $2,000 minimum advance.** Accepts simultaneous submissions. Book catalog for 9×12 envelope and first-class stamps. Guidelines online.

NONFICTION *No unsolicited mss.* Agented submissions only.

FICTION Agented submissions only.

◐⊘ HARPERBUSINESS

Imprint of HarperCollins General Books Group, 10 E. 53rd St., New York NY 10022. (212)207-7000. **Website:** www.harpercollins.com. Estab. 1991. Publishes hardcover, trade paperback originals and reprints. HarperBusiness publishes the inside story on ideas that will shape business practices with cutting-edge information and visionary concepts. **Pays royalty on retail price. Pays advance.** Accepts simultaneous submissions.

○ "The gold standard of business book publishing for 50 years, Harper Business brings you innovative, authoritative, and creative works from world-class thinkers. Building upon this rich legacy of paradigm-shifting books, Harper Business authors continue to help readers see the future and to lead and live successfully."

NONFICTION Subjects include business, economics, marketing subjects. "We don't publish how-to, textbooks or things for academic market; no reference (tax or mortgage guides), our reference department does that. Proposals need to be top notch. We tend not to publish people who have no business standing. Must have business credentials." Agented submissions only.

⊘◑ HARPERCOLLINS CANADA, LTD.

2 Bloor St. E., 20th Floor, Toronto ON M4W 1A8, Canada. (416)975-9334. **Fax:** (416)975-5223. **Website:** www.harpercollins.ca. Estab. 1989.

IMPRINTS HarperCollinsPublishers; HarperPerennialCanada (trade paperbacks); HarperTrophyCanada (children's); Phyllis Bruce Books.

○ HarperCollins Canada is not accepting unsolicited material at this time.

HARPERCOLLINS CHILDREN'S BOOKS/ HARPERCOLLINS PUBLISHERS

10 E. 53rd, New York NY 10022. (212)207-7000. **E-mail:** Dana.fritts@Harpercollins.com; Kate.engbring@Harpercollins.com. **Website:** www.harper-

collins.com. **Contact:** Kate Engbring, designer; Dana Fritts, picture book art supervisor. Publishes hardcover and paperback originals and paperback reprints. HarperCollins, one of the largest English language publishers in the world, is a broad-based publisher with strengths in academic, business and professional, children's, educational, general interest, and religious and spiritual books, as well as multimedia titles. **Publishes 500 titles/year. Negotiates payment upon acceptance.** Accepts simultaneous submissions. Responds in 1 month, will contact only if interested. Does not accept any unsolicited texts. Catalog online.

IMPRINTS HarperCollins Australia/New Zealand: Angus & Robertson, Fourth Estate, HarperBusiness, HarperCollins, HarperPerenniel, HarperReligious, HarperSports, Voyager; **HarperCollins Canada:** HarperFlamingoCanada, PerennialCanada; **HarperCollins Children's Books Group:** Amistad, Julie Andrews Collection, Avon, Joanna Cotler Books, Eos, Laura Geringer Books, Greenwillow Books, HarperAudio, HarperCollins Children's Books, HarperFestival, HarperTempest, HarperTrophy, Rayo, Katherine Tegen Books; **HarperCollins General Books Group:** Access, Amistad, Avon, Caedmon, Ecco, Eos, Fourth Estate, HarperAudio, HarperBusiness, HarperCollins, HarperEntertainment, HarperLargePrint, HarperResource, HarperSanFrancisco, HarperTorch, Harper Design International, Perennial, PerfectBound, Quill, Rayo, ReganBooks, William Morrow, William Morrow Cookbooks; **HarperCollins UK:** Collins Bartholomew, Collins, HarperCollins Crime & Thrillers, Collins Freedom to Teach, HarperCollins Children's Books, Thorsons/Element, Voyager Books; **Zondervan:** Inspirio, Vida, Zonderkidz, Zondervan.

NONFICTION *No unsolicited mss or queries.* Agented submissions only. Unsolicited mss returned unopened.

FICTION Subjects include picture books, young adult, chapter books, middle grade, early readers. "We look for a strong story line and exceptional literary talent." Agented submissions only. *All unsolicited mss returned.*

TIPS "We do not accept any unsolicited material."

◔ HARPERTEEN

10 E. 53rd St., New York NY 10022. (212)207-7000. **Fax:** (212)702-2583. **E-mail:** Jennifer.Deason@HARPERCOLLINS.com. **Website:** www.harpercollins.com. HarperTeen is a teen imprint that publishes

hardcovers, paperback reprints and paperback origi-nals. **Publishes 100 titles/year.**

⊙ *HarperCollins Children's Books is not accept-ing unsolicited and/or unagented mss or queries. Unfortunately the volume of these submissions is so large that they cannot receive the atten-tion they deserve. Such submissions will not be reviewed or returned.*

⊕ HARRINGTON & HARRINGTON PRESS

3400 Yosemite St., San Diego CA 92109. **E-mail:** press@harringtonandharrington.com. **E-mail:** sub-missions@harringtonandharrington.com. **Website:** www.harringtonandharrington.com. **Contact:** Lau-rie Champion, general manager and editor-in-chief; Stacy Bodus, acquisitions editor. Estab. 2013. Publish-es trade paperback originals. **Publishes 4-10 titles/ year. Receives 150 queries/year. Receives 50 mss/ year. 50% of books from first-time authors. 100% from unagented writers. Pays 10-15% royalties on retail price. Offers an advance between $100-1,000.** Publishes book 6 months after acceptance after accep-tance of ms. Accepts simultaneous submissions. Cata-log available for SASE. Guidelines available for SASE. **NONFICTION** Subjects include ethnic, memoirs, wo-mens issues, womens studies, young adult. Specializes in memoir and creative nonfiction. Query with SASE. **FICTION** Subjects include feminist, gay, lesbian, lit-erary, romance, short story collections, young adult. Specializes in literary fiction. Query with SASE.

THE HARVARD COMMON PRESS

535 Albany St., 5th Floor, Boston MA 02118. (617)423-5803. **Fax:** (617)695-9794. **E-mail:** info@harvardpress.com. **E-mail:** editorial@harvardcommonpress.com. **Website:** www.harvardcommonpress.com. **Contact:** Valerie Cimino, executive editor. Estab. 1976. Pub-lishes hardcover and trade paperback originals and reprints. "We want strong, practical books that help people gain control over a particular area of their lives. Currently emphasizing cooking, child care/parenting, health. De-emphasizing general instructional books, travel." **Publishes 16 titles/year. 20% of books from first-time authors. 40% from unagented writers. Pays royalty. Pays average $2,500-10,000 advance.** Publishes book 1 year after acceptance. Accepts si-multaneous submissions. Responds in 2 months to queries. Book catalog for 9x12 envelope and 3 first-class stamps. Guidelines for #10 SASE or online. **IMPRINTS** Gambit Books.

NONFICTION Subjects include child guidance, cooking, foods, nutrition, health, medicine. "A large percentage of our list is made up of books about cook-ing, child care, and parenting; in these areas we are looking for authors who are knowledgeable, if not ex-perts, and who can offer a different approach to the subject. We are open to good nonfiction proposals that show evidence of strong organization and writ-ing, and clearly demonstrate a need in the market-place. First-time authors are welcome." Submit out-line. Potential authors may also submit a query letter or e-mail of no more than 300 words, rather than a full proposal; if interested, will ask to see a proposal. Queries and questions may be sent via e-mail. "We will not consider e-mail attachments containing pro-posals. No phone calls, please."

TIPS "We are demanding about the quality of propos-als; in addition to strong writing skills and thorough knowledge of the subject matter, we require a detailed analysis of the competition."

⊘⊘ HARVEST HOUSE PUBLISHERS

990 Owen Loop N, Eugene OR 97402. (541)343-0123. **Fax:** (541)302-0731. **Website:** www.harvesthousepub-lishers.com. Estab. 1974. Publishes hardcover, trade paperback, and mass market paperback originals and reprints. **Publishes 160 titles/year. 1,500 queries re-ceived/year. 1,000 mss received/year. 1% of books from first-time authors. Pays royalty.**

NONFICTION Subjects include anthropology, arche-ology, business, economics, child guidance, health, medicine, money, finance, religion, women's issues, women's studies, Bible studies. *No unsolicited mss.*

FICTION *No unsolicited mss, proposals, or artwork.* Agented submissions only.

TIPS "For first time/nonpublished authors we sug-gest building their literary résumé by submitting to magazines, or perhaps accruing book contributions."

⊘ HAY HOUSE INC.

P.O. Box 5100, Carlsbad CA 92018. (760)431-7695. **Fax:** (760)431-6948. **E-mail:** editorial@hayhouse.com. **Website:** www.hayhouse.com. **Contact:** Patty Gift, East Coast acquisitions (pgift@hayhouse.com); Alex Freemon, West Coast acquisitions (afreemon@hay-house.com). Estab. 1985. Publishes hardcover, trade paperback and eBook/POD originals. "We publish books, audios, and videos that help heal the planet." **Publishes 50 titles/year. Pays standard royalty.** Ac-cepts simultaneous submissions. Guidelines online.

IMPRINTS Hay House Lifestyles; Hay House Insights; Hay House Visions; New Beginnings Press; SmileyBooks.

NONFICTION Subjects include cooking, foods, nutrition, education, health, medicine, money, finance, nature, environment, New Age, philosophy, psychology, sociology, women's issues, women's studies, mind/body/spirit. "Hay House is interested in a variety of subjects as long as they have a positive self-help slant to them. No poetry, children's books, or negative concepts that are not conducive to helping/healing ourselves or our planet." Accepts e-mail submissions from agents.

TIPS "Our audience is concerned with our planet, the healing properties of love, and general self-help principles. If I were a writer trying to market a book today, I would research the market thoroughly to make sure there weren't already too many books on the subject I was interested in writing about. Then I would make sure I had a unique slant on my idea. Simultaneous submissions from agents must include SASE's."

HEALTH PROFESSIONS PRESS

P.O. Box 10624, Baltimore MD 21285-0624. (410)337-9585. **Fax:** (410)337-8539. **E-mail:** mmagnus@health-propress.com. **Website:** www.healthpropress.com. **Contact:** Mary Magnus, director of publications (aging, long-term care, health administration). Publishes hardcover and trade paperback originals. "We are a specialty publisher. Our primary audiences are professionals, students, and educated consumers interested in topics related to aging and eldercare." **Publishes 6-8 titles/year. 70 queries received/year. 12 mss received/year. 50% of books from first-time authors. 100% from unagented writers. Pays 8-18% royalty on wholesale price.** Publishes book 10 months after acceptance. Accepts simultaneous submissions. Responds in 1 month to queries; 3 months to proposals; 4 months to mss. Book catalog free or online. Guidelines online.

NONFICTION Subjects include health, medicine, psychology. Query with SASE. Submit proposal package, outline, résumé, 1-2 sample chapters, cover letter.

WILLIAM S. HEIN & CO., INC.

2350 N. Forest Rd., Getzville NY 14068. (716)882-2600. **Fax:** (716)883-8100. **E-mail:** mail@wshein.com. **Website:** www.wshein.com. **Contact:** Sheila Jarrett, publications manager. Estab. 1961. "William S. Hein & Co. publishes reference books for law librarians, legal researchers, and those interested in legal writing. Currently emphasizing legal research, legal writing, and legal education." **Publishes 30 titles/year. 80 queries received/year. 40 mss received/year. 30% of books from first-time authors. 100% from unagented writers. Pays 10-20% royalty on net price.** Publishes book 9 months after acceptance. Accepts simultaneous submissions. Responds in 3 months to queries. Book catalog online. Guidelines by e-mail.

NONFICTION Subjects include education, government, politics, women's issues, world affairs, legislative histories.

HEINEMANN EDUCATIONAL PUBLISHERS

P.O. Box 781940, Sandton 2146, South Africa. (27)(11)322-8600. **Fax:** 086 687 7822. **E-mail:** customer-liaison@heinemann.co.za. **Website:** www.heinemann.co.za. Interested in textbooks for primary schools, literature and textbooks for secondary schools, and technical publishing for colleges/universities.

NONFICTION Subjects include animals, art, architecture, business, economics, education, ethnic, health, medicine, history, humanities, language, literature, music, dance, psychology, regional, religion, science, social sciences, sports, math, engineering, management, nursing, marketing.

HELLGATE PRESS

P.O. Box 3531, Ashland OR 97520. (541)973-5154. **E-mail:** harley@hellgatepress.com. **Website:** www.hellgatepress.com. **Contact:** Harley B. Patrick, editor. Estab. 1996. "Hellgate Press specializes in military history, other military topics, travel adventure, and historical/adventure fiction." **Publishes 15-20 titles/year. 85% of books from first-time authors. 95% from unagented writers. Pays royalty.** Publishes book 6-9 months after acceptance.

NONFICTION Subjects include history, memoirs, military, war, travel adventure. Query/proposal by e-mail only. *Do not send mss.*

HENDRICK-LONG PUBLISHING CO., INC.

10635 Tower Oaks, Suite D, Houston TX 77070. (832)912-READ. **Fax:** (832)912-7353. **E-mail:** hendrick-long@att.net. **Website:** hendricklongpublishing.com. **Contact:** Vilma Long. Estab. 1969. Publishes hardcover and trade paperback originals and hardcover reprints. "Hendrick-Long publishes historical fiction and nonfiction about Texas and the Southwest for children and young adults." **Publishes 4 titles/**

year. **90% from unagented writers. Pays royalty on selling price. Pays advance.** Publishes book 18 months after acceptance. Responds in 3 months to queries. Book catalog for 8½×11 or 9×12 SASE with 4 first-class stamps. Guidelines online.

NONFICTION Subjects include history, regional. Subject must be Texas related; other subjects cannot be considered. We are particularly interested in material from educators that can be used in the classroom as workbooks, math, science, history with a Texas theme or twist. Query, or submit outline and 2 sample chapters. Reviews artwork/photos. Send photocopies.

FICTION Subjects include juvenile, young adult. Query with SASE. Submit outline, clips, 2 sample chapters.

HENDRICKSON PUBLISHERS, INC.

P.O. Box 3473, Peabody MA 01961. **Fax:** (978)573-8276. **E-mail:** editorial@hendrickson.com; orders@hendrickson.com. **Website:** www.hendrickson.com. **Contact:** Shirley Decker-Lucke, editorial director. Estab. 1983. Publishes trade reprints, bibles, and scholarly material in the areas of New Testament; Hebrew Bible; religion and culture; patristics; Judaism; and practical, historical, and Biblical theology. "Hendrickson is an academic publisher of books that give insight into Bible understanding (academically) and encourage spiritual growth (popular trade). Currently emphasizing Biblical helps and reference, ministerial helps, and Biblical studies." **Publishes 35 titles/year. 800 queries received/year. 10% of books from first-time authors. 90% from unagented writers.** Publishes book 1 year after acceptance. Responds in 3-4 months to queries. Book catalog and ms guidelines for #10 SASE.

NONFICTION Subjects include religion. "No longer accepting unsolicited mss or book proposals. Cannot return material sent or respond to all queries." Submit outline, sample chapters, and CV.

HERITAGE BOOKS, INC.

518 Ruatan St., Berwyn Heights MD 20740. (301)345-2077. **E-mail:** info@heritagebooks.com. **E-mail:** submissions@heritagebooks.com. **Website:** www.heritagebooks.com. Estab. 1978. Publishes hardcover and paperback originals and reprints. "Our goal is to celebrate life by exploring all aspects of American life: settlement, development, wars, and other significant events, including family histories, memoirs, etc. Currently emphasizing early American life, early wars

and conflicts, ethnic studies." **Publishes 200 titles/year. 25% of books from first-time authors. 100% from unagented writers. Pays 10% royalty on list price.** Accepts simultaneous submissions. Responds in 3 months to queries. Book catalog and ms guidelines free.

NONFICTION Subjects include Americana, ethnic, origins and research guides, history, memoirs, military, war, regional, history. Query with SASE. Submit outline via e-mail. Reviews artwork/photos.

TIPS "The quality of the book is of prime importance; next is its relevance to our fields of interest."

HERITAGE HOUSE PUBLISHING CO., LTD.

103-1075 Pendergast St., Victoria BC V8V 0A1, Canada. (250)360-0829. **E-mail:** books@heritagehouse.ca. **Website:** www.heritagehouse.ca. **Contact:** Lara Kordic, senior editor. Publishes mostly trade paperback and some hardcovers. "Heritage House publishes books that celebrate the historical and cultural heritage of Canada, particularly Western Canada and the Pacific Northwest. We also publish some children's titles, titles of national interest and a series of books aimed at young and casual readers, called *Amazing Stories*. We accept simultaneous submissions, but indicate on your query that it is a simultaneous submission." **Publishes 25-30 titles/year. 200 queries received/year. 100 mss received/year. 50% of books from first-time authors. 90% from unagented writers. Pays 12-15% royalty on net proceeds. Advances are rarely paid.** Publishes book within 1-2 years of acceptance. after acceptance of ms. Accepts simultaneous submissions. Responds in 6 months to queries. Catalog and Guidelines online.

NONFICTION Subjects include history, regional, adventure, contemporary Canadian culture. Query by e-mail. Include synopsis, outline, 2-3 sample chapters with indication of illustrative material available, and marketing strategy.

TIPS "Our books appeal to residents of and visitors to the northwest quadrant of the continent. We're looking for good stories and good storytellers. We focus on work by Canadian authors."

HEYDAY BOOKS

c/o Acquisitions Editor, Box 9145, Berkeley CA 94709. **Fax:** (510)549-1889. **E-mail:** heyday@heydaybooks.com. **Website:** www.heydaybooks.com. **Contact:** Gayle Wattawa, acquisitions and editorial director.

Estab. 1974. Publishes hardcover originals, trade paperback originals and reprints. "Heyday Books publishes nonfiction books and literary anthologies with a strong California focus. We publish books about Native Americans, natural history, history, literature, and recreation, with a strong California focus." **Publishes 12-15 titles/year. 50% of books from first-time authors. 90% from unagented writers. Pays 8% royalty on net price.** Publishes book 18 months after acceptance. Responds in 3 months. Book catalog for 9 ×12 SAE with 4 first-class stamps.

NONFICTION Subjects include Americana, ethnic, history, nature, environment, recreation, regional, travel. Books about California only. Query with outline and synopsis. "Query or proposal by traditional post. Include a cover letter introducing yourself and your qualifications, a brief description of your project, a table of contents and list of illustrations, notes on the market you are trying to reach and why your book will appeal to them, a sample chapter, and a SASE if you would like us to return these materials to you." Reviews artwork/photos.

HIGHLAND PRESS PUBLISHING

P.O. Box 2292, High Springs FL 32655. (386) 454-3927. **Fax:** (386) 454-3927. **E-mail:** the.highland.press@gmail.com; submissions.hp@gmail.com. **Website:** www.highlandpress.org. **Contact:** Leanne Burroughs, CEO (fiction); she will forward all mss to appropriate editor. Estab. 2005. Publishes paperback originals. "With our focus on historical romances, Highland Press Publishing is known as your 'Passport to Romance.' We focus on historical romances and our award-winning anthologies. Our short stories/novellas are heart warming. As for our historicals, we publish historical novels like many of us grew up with and loved. History is a big part of the story and is tactfully woven throughout the romance." We have recently opened our submissions up to all genres, with the exception of erotica. Our newest lines are inspirational, regency, and young adult. **Publishes 30 titles/year. 90% from unagented writers. Pays royalties 7.5-8%.** Publishes book within 18 months of acceptance. after acceptance of ms. Accepts simultaneous submissions. Responds in 8 weeks to queries; 3-12 months to mss. Catalog and Guidelines online.

FICTION Query with outline/synopsis and sample chapters. Accepts queries by snail mail, e-mail. Include estimated word count, target market.

TIPS "I don't publish based on industry trends. We buy what we like and what we believe readers are looking for. However, often this proves to be the genres and time-periods larger publishers are not currently interested in. Be professional at all times. Present your ms in the best possible light. Be sure you have run spell check and that the ms has been vetted by at least one critique partner, preferably more. Many times we receive mss that have wonderful stories involved, but would take far too much time to edit to make it marketable."

HIGH PLAINS PRESS

P.O. Box 123, 403 Cassa Rd., Glendo WY 82213. (307)735-4370. **Fax:** (307)735-4590. **E-mail:** editor@highplainspress.com. **Website:** www.highplainspress.com. **Contact:** Nancy Curtis, publisher. Estab. 1984. Publishes hardcover and trade paperback originals. High Plains Press is a regional book publishing company specializing in books about the American West, with special interest in things relating to Wyoming. **Publishes 4 titles/year. 50 queries; 75 mss received/year. 75% of books from first-time authors. 100% from unagented writers. Pays 10% royalty on wholesale price. Pays $200-1,200 advance.** Publishes book 2 years after acceptance of ms. after acceptance of ms. Accepts simultaneous submissions. Responds in 3 months to queries and proposals; 12 months on mss. Catalog and guidelines online.

NONFICTION Subjects include agriculture, Americana, environment, history, horticulture, memoirs, nature, regional. "We consider only books with strong connection to the West." Query with SASE. Reviews artwork/photos. Send photocopies.

POETRY "We publish 1 poetry volume a year. Require connection to West. Consider poetry in August." Submit 5 sample poems.

TIPS "Our audience comprises general readers interested in history and culture of the Rockies."

HIGH TIDE PRESS

2081 Calistoga Dr., Suite 2N, New Lenox IL 60451. (815)717-3780. **Website:** www.hightidepress.com. **Contact:** Monica Regan, senior editor. Estab. 1995. Publishes hardcover and trade paperback originals. "High Tide Press is a leading provider of resources for disability and nonprofit professionals - publications and training materials on intellectual/developmental disabilities, behavioral health, and nonprofit management." **Publishes 2-3 titles/year. 20 queries received/**

year. 3 mss received/year. 50% of books from first-time authors. 100% from unagented writers. Pays royalty. Percentages vary. Publishes book up to 1 year after acceptance. Accepts simultaneous submissions. Responds in 6 months. Catalog and guidelines online.

NONFICTION Subjects include business, economics, education, health, medicine, how-to, human services, nonprofit management, psychology, reference, all of these topics as they relate to developmental, learning and intellectual disabilities, behavioral health, and human services management. "We do not publish personal stories. We produce materials for direct support staff, managers and professionals in the fields of disabilities and human services, as well as educators." Query via online form.

TIPS "Our readers are leaders and managers, mostly in the field of human services, and especially those who serve persons with intellectual disabilities or behavioral health needs."

HILL AND WANG

Farrar Straus & Giroux, Inc., 19 Union Square W., New York NY 10003. (212)741-6900. **Fax:** (212)633-9385. **E-mail:** fsg.editorial@fsgbooks.com. **Website:** www.fsgbooks.com. **Contact:** Thomas LeBien, publisher; Elisabeth Sifton, editor; June Kim, assistant editor. Estab. 1956. Publishes hardcover and trade paperbacks. "Hill and Wang publishes serious nonfiction books, primarily in history, science, mathematics and the social sciences. We are not considering new fiction, drama, or poetry." **Publishes 12 titles/year. 1,500 queries received/year. 50% of books from first-time authors. 50% from unagented writers. Pays 10% royalty on retail price to 5,000 copies sold, 12 ½% to 10,000 copies, 15% thereafter on hardcover; 7 ½% on retail price for paperback** Publishes book 1 year after acceptance of ms. Accepts simultaneous submissions. Book catalog available free.

NONFICTION Subjects include government, politics, history, American. Submit outline, sample chapters. SASE and a letter explaining rationale for book.

HIPPOCRENE BOOKS INC.

171 Madison Ave., New York NY 10016. (718)454-2366. **E-mail:** info@hippocrenebooks.com. **Website:** www.hippocrenebooks.com. Estab. 1971. "Over the last forty years, Hippocrene Books has become one of America's foremost publishers of foreign language reference books and ethnic cookbooks. As a small publishing house in a marketplace dominated by conglomerates, Hippocrene has succeeded by continually reinventing its list while maintaining a strong international and ethnic orientation."

⬤ HIPPOPOTAMUS PRESS

22 Whitewell Rd., Frome Somerset BA11 4EL, United Kingdom. (44)(173)466-6653. **E-mail:** rjhippopress@aol.com. **Contact:** R. John, editor; M. Pargitter (poetry); Anna Martin (translation). Estab. 1974. Publishes hardcover and trade paperback originals. "Hippopotamus Press publishes first, full collections of verse by those well represented in the mainstream poetry magazines of the English-speaking world." **Publishes 6-12 titles/year. 90% of books from first-time authors. 90% from unagented writers. Pays 7½-10% royalty on retail price. Pays advance.** Publishes book 10 months after acceptance. Accepts simultaneous submissions. Responds in 1 month to queries. Book catalog available free.

NONFICTION Subjects include language, literature, translation. Query with SASE. Submit complete ms.

POETRY "Read one of our authors—poets often make the mistake of submitting poetry without knowing the type of verse we publish." Query and submit complete ms.

TIPS "We publish books for a literate audience. We have a strong link to the Modernist tradition. Read what we publish."

⊕ HIPSO MEDIA

8151 E. 29th Ave., Denver CO 80238. **E-mail:** rob@hipsomedia.com. **Website:** www.hipsomedia.com. **Contact:** Rob Simon; Dan Cohen. Estab. 2012. Publishes trade and mass market paperback and electronic originals. **Publishes 6 titles/year. 10% of books from first-time authors. 100% from unagented writers. Authors receive between 15-30% on royalty.** Publishes book Averages 6 months between acceptance of a book-length ms and publication. after acceptance of ms. Accepts simultaneous submissions. Responds in 1 month. Catalog online. Guidelines online.

NONFICTION Subjects include alternative lifestyles, contemporary culture, cooking, foods, health, medicine, nutrition, travel. Looking for books that can be enhanced with media, video, audio, animation, and interactivity. Query with SASE. Reviews artwork as part of the ms package. Artwork or photos must be in JPG form.

FICTION Subjects include erotica, experimental, humor, multicultural, multimedia, mystery, short story collections, young adult. Query with SASE.

TIPS Describes ideal audience as "hip readers of e-books. We are going digital first, so tell us why someone would want to read your book."

HISTORY PUBLISHING COMPANY, INC.

P.O. Box 700, Palisades NY 10964. **Fax:** (845)231-6167. **Website:** www.historypublishingco.com. **Contact:** Don Bracken, editorial director. Estab. 2001. Publishes hardcover and trade paperback originals and electronic books. "History Publishing is looking for interesting stories that make up history. If you have a story about an aspect of history that would have an appeal to a large niche or broad readership, History Publishing is interested." **Publishes 20 titles/year. 50% of books from first-time authors. 50% from unagented writers. Pays 7-10% royalty on wholesale list price. Does not pay advances to unpublished authors.** Publishes book 1 year after acceptance. Responds in 2 months to full mss. Guidelines on website.

NONFICTION Subjects include Americana, business, contemporary culture, creative nonfiction, economics, government, history, military, politics, social sciences, sociology, war, world affairs. Query with SASE. Submit proposal package, outline, 3 sample chapters or submit complete ms. Reviews artwork/photos. Send photocopies.

TIPS "We focus on an audience interested in the events that shaped the world we live in and the events of today that continue to shape that world. Focus on interesting and serious events that will appeal to the contemporary reader who likes easy-to-read history that flows from one page to the next."

HOLIDAY HOUSE, INC.

425 Madison Ave., New York NY 10017. (212)688-0085. **Fax:** (212)421-6134. **E-mail:** info@holidayhouse.com. **Website:** holidayhouse.com. **Contact:** Mary Cash, editor-in-chief. Estab. 1935. Publishes hardcover originals and paperback reprints. "Holiday House publishes children's and young adult books for the school and library markets. We have a commitment to publishing first-time authors and illustrators. We specialize in quality hardcovers from picture books to young adult, both fiction and nonfiction, primarily for the school and library market." **Publishes 50 titles/year. 5% of books from first-time authors. 50% from unagented writers. Pays royalty on list price, range varies. Agent's royalty.** Publishes book Publishes 1-2 years after acceptance. Responds in 4 months. Guidelines for #10 SASE.

NONFICTION Subjects include Americana, history, science, Judaica. Please send the entire ms, whether submitting a picture book or novel. Send ms via U.S. Mail. "We do not accept certified or registered mail. There is no need to include a SASE. We do not consider submissions by e-mail or fax. Please note that you do not have to supply illustrations. However, if you have illustrations you would like to include with your submission, you may send detailed sketches or photocopies of the original art. Do not send original art." Reviews artwork/photos. Send photocopies-no originals.

FICTION Subjects include adventure, historical, humor, literary, mainstream, contemporary, Judaica and holiday, animal stories for young readers. Children's books only. Query with SASE. No phone calls, please.

TIPS "We need mss with strong stories and writing."

Ⓐ⊘ HENRY HOLT

175 Fifth Avenue, New York NY 10011. **Website:** www.henryholt.com.

 Agented submissions only.

HOLY CROSS ORTHODOX PRESS

Hellenic College, 50 Goddard Ave., Brookline MA 02445. (617)850-1321. **Fax:** (617)850-1457. **E-mail:** press@hchc.edu. **Contact:** Dr. Anton C. Vrame. Estab. 1974. Publishes trade paperback originals. "Holy Cross publishes titles that are rooted in the tradition of the Eastern Orthodox Church." **Publishes 8 titles/year. 10-15 queries received/year. 10-15 mss received/year. 85% of books from first-time authors. 100% from unagented writers. Pays 8-12% royalty on retail price.** Publishes book 2 years after acceptance. Accepts simultaneous submissions. Responds in 6 months to mss. Book catalog available online through Holy Cross Bookstore.

IMPRINTS Holy Cross Orthodox Press.

NONFICTION Subjects include ethnic, religion, Greek Orthodox. Holy Cross Orthodox Press publishes scholarly and popular literature in the areas of Orthodox Christian theology and Greek letters. Submissions are often far too technical usually with a very limited audiences. Submit outline. Submit complete ms. Reviews artwork/photos. Send photocopies.

Ⓐ HOPEWELL PUBLICATIONS

P.O. Box 11, Titusville NJ 08560. **Website:** www.hopepubs.com. **Contact:** E. Martin, publisher. Estab. 2002.

Format publishes in hardcover, trade paperback, and electronic originals; trade paperback and electronic reprints. "Hopewell Publications specializes in classic reprints—books with proven sales records that have gone out of print—and the occasional new title of interest. Our catalog spans from one to sixty years of publication history. We print fiction and nonfiction, and we accept agented and unagented materials. Submissions are accepted online only." **Publishes 20-30 titles/year. Receives 2,000 queries/year; 500 mss/year. 25% of books from first-time authors. 75% from unagented writers. Pays royalty on retail price.** Publishes book 6-12 months after acceptance. Accepts simultaneous submissions. Responds in 3 months to queries; 6 months to proposals; 9 months to mss. Catalog online. Guidelines online.

IMPRINTS Egress Books, Legacy Classics.

NONFICTION , All nonfiction subjects acceptable. Query online using our online guidelines.

FICTION Subjects include adventure, contemporary, experimental, fantasy, gay, historical, humor, juvenile, literary, mainstream, mystery, plays, short story collections, spiritual, suspense, young adult, All fiction subjects acceptable. Query online using our online guidelines.

HOUGHTON MIFFLIN HARCOURT BOOKS FOR CHILDREN

Imprint of Houghton Mifflin Trade & Reference Division, 222 Berkeley St., Boston MA 02116. (617)351-5000. **Fax:** (617)351-1111. **E-mail:** children's_books@hmco.com. **Website:** www.houghtonmifflinbooks.com. **Contact:** Erica Zappy, associate editor; Kate O'Sullivan, senior editor; Anne Rider, executive editor; Margaret Raymo, editorial director. Publishes hardcover originals and trade paperback originals and reprints. Houghton Mifflin Harcourt gives shape to ideas that educate, inform, and above all, delight. Query with SASE. Submit sample chapters, synopsis. Faxed or e-mailed mss and proposals are not considered. Complete submission guidelines online. **Publishes 100 titles/year. 5,000 queries received/year. 14,000 mss received/year. 10% of books from first-time authors. 60% from unagented writers. Pays 5-10% royalty on retail price. Pays variable advance.** Publishes book 2 years after acceptance. Accepts simultaneous submissions. Responds in 4-6 months to queries. Guidelines online.

IMPRINTS Sandpiper Paperback Books; Graphia.

Does not respond to or return mss unless interested.

NONFICTION Subjects include animals, anthropology, archeology, art, architecture, ethnic, history, language, literature, music, dance, nature, environment, science, sports. Interested in innovative books and subjects about which the author is passionate. Query with SASE. Submit sample chapters, synopsis. Reviews artwork/photos. Send photocopies.

FICTION Subjects include adventure, ethnic, historical, humor, juvenile, early readers, literary, mystery, picture books, suspense, young adult, board books. Submit complete ms.

TIPS Faxed or e-mailed mss and proposals are not considered.

HOUGHTON MIFFLIN HARCOURT CO.

222 Berkeley St., Boston MA 02116. (617)351-5000. **Website:** www.hmhco.com; www.hmhbooks.com. Estab. 1832. Publishes hardcover originals and trade paperback originals and reprints.

IMPRINTS American Heritage Dictionaries; Clarion Books; Great Source Education Group; Houghton Mifflin; Houghton Mifflin Books for Children; Houghton Mifflin Paperbacks; Mariner Books; McDougal Littell; Peterson Field Guides; Riverside Publishing; Sunburst Technology; Taylor's Gardening Guides; Edusoft; Promissor; Walter Lorraine Books; Kingfisher.

"Houghton Mifflin Harcourt gives shape to ideas that educate, inform and delight. In a new era of publishing, our legacy of quality thrives as we combine imagination with technology, bringing you new ways to know."

NONFICTION "We are not a mass market publisher. Our main focus is serious nonfiction. We do practical self-help but not pop psychology self-help." Agented submissions only. Unsolicited mss returned unopened.

HOUSE OF ANANSI PRESS

110 Spadina Ave., Suite 801, Toronto ON M5V 2K4, Canada. (416)363-4343. **Fax:** (416)363-1017. **Website:** www.anansi.ca. Estab. 1967. **Pays 8-10% royalties. Pays $750 advance and 10 author's copies.** Publishes book Responds to queries within 1 year, to mss (if invited) within 4 months. after acceptance of ms.

NONFICTION Avoids dry, jargon-filled academic prose and has a literary twist that will interest general readers and experts alike. Query with SASE.

FICTION Publishes literary fiction that has a unique flair, memorable characters, and a strong narrative voice. Query with SASE.

POETRY House of Anansi publishes literary fiction and poetry by Canadian and international writers. "We seek to balance the list between well-known and emerging writers, with an interest in writing by Canadians of all backgrounds. We publish Canadian poetry only, and poets must have a substantial publication record—if not in books, then definitely in journals and magazines of repute." Does not want "children's poetry or poetry by previously unpublished poets." Canadian poets should query first with 10 sample poems (typed double-spaced) and a cover letter with brief bio and publication credits. Considers simultaneous submissions. Poems are circulated to an editorial board. Often comments on rejected poems.

HOW BOOKS

F+W Media, Inc., 10151 Carver Rd., Suite 200, Blue Ash OH 45242. (513)531-2690. **E-mail:** scott.francis@fwmedia.com. **Website:** www.howdesign.com. **Contact:** Scott Francis, editor. Estab. 1985. Publishes hardcover and trade paperback originals. **Publishes 15 titles/year. 50 queries received/year. 5 mss received/year. 50% of books from first-time authors. 50% from unagented writers. Pays 10% royalty on wholesale price. Pays $2,000-6,000 advance.** Publishes book 18-24 months after acceptance. Accepts simultaneous submissions. Responds in 1 month to queries and proposals; 3 months to mss. Catalog and guidelines online.

NONFICTION , graphic design, creativity, pop culture. "We look for material that reflects the cutting edge of trends, graphic design, and culture. Nearly all HOW Books are intensely visual, and authors must be able to create or supply art/illustration for their books." Query with SASE. Submit proposal package, outline, 1 sample chapter, sample art or sample design. Reviews artwork/photos. Send photocopies and PDF's (if submitting electronically).

TIPS "Audience comprised of graphic designers. Your art, design, or concept."

HQN BOOKS

Imprint of Harlequin, 233 Broadway, Suite 1001, New York NY 10279. **Website:** harlequin.com. **Contact:** Tara Parsons, senior editor. Publishes hardcover, trade paperback, and mass market paperback originals. **Pays royalty. Pays advance.**

"HQN publishes romance in all subgenres—historical, contemporary, romantic suspense, paranormal—as long as the story's central focus is romance. Prospective authors can familiarize themselves with the wide range of books we publish by reading work by some of our current authors. The imprint is looking for a wide range of authors from known romance stars to first-time authors. At the moment, we are accepting only agented submissions—unagented authors may send a query letter to determine if their project suits our needs. Please send your projects to our New York Editorial Office."

FICTION Subjects include romance, contemporary and historical. Accepts unagented material. Length: 90,000 words.

HUNTER HOUSE PUBLISHERS

P.O. Box 2914, 1515 1/2 Park St., Alameda CA 94501. (510)865-5282. **E-mail:** ordering@hunterhouse.com. **E-mail:** acquisitions@hunterhouse.com. **Website:** www.hunterhouse.com. **Contact:** Jeanne Brondino, acquisitions editor; Kiran S. Rana, publisher. Estab. 1978. Publishes trade paperback originals and reprints. Hunter House publishes health books (especially women's health), self-help health, sexuality and couple relationships, violence prevention and intervention. De-emphasizing reference, self-help psychology. **Publishes 10-12 titles/year. 300 queries received/year. 100 mss received/year. 50% of books from first-time authors. 90% from unagented writers. Pays 10-20% royalty on net receipts. Pays $500-3,000 advance.** Publishes book 18 months after acceptance. Accepts simultaneous submissions. Responds in 2 months to queries; 3 months to proposals. Book catalog online. Guidelines online and by e-mail request.

NONFICTION Subjects include child guidance, community, health, medicine, nutrition, parenting, psychology, sex, women's issues, self-help, women's health, fitness, relationships, sexuality, personal growth, and violence prevention. Health books (especially women's health) should focus on self-help, health. Family books: Our current focus is sexuality and couple relationships, and alternative lifestyles to high stress. Community topics include violence prevention/violence intervention. We also publish specialized curriculam for counselors and educators in the areas of violence prevention and trauma in children. Query with proposal package, including synopsis, TOC, and chapter outline, two sample chapters, target audience information, competition, and what distinguishes the book. We look for computer printouts of good quality or e-mail. Please inform us if a ms is available on computer disk (IBM format is preferable). Reviews artwork/photos. Send photocopies. Proposals generally not returned, requested mss returned with SASE. Reviews artwork/photos as part of ms package.

TIPS "Audience is concerned people who are looking to educate themselves and their community about real-life issues that affect them. Please send as much information as possible about who your audience is, how your book addresses their needs, and how you reach that audience in your ongoing work. Include a marketing plan. Explain how you will help us market your book. Have a Facebook account, Twitter, or a blog. List any professional organization of which you are a member."

IBEX PUBLISHERS

P.O. Box 30087, Bethesda MD 20824. (301)718-8188. **Fax:** (301)907-8707. **E-mail:** info@ibexpub.com. **Website:** www.ibexpublishers.com. Estab. 1979. Publishes hardcover and trade paperback originals and reprints. "IBEX publishes books about Iran and the Middle East and about Persian culture and literature." **Publishes 10-12 titles/year. Payment varies.** Accepts simultaneous submissions. Book catalog available free.

IMPRINTS Iranbooks Press.

NONFICTION Subjects include cooking, foods, nutrition, language, literature. Query with SASE, or submit proposal package, including outline and 2 sample chapters.

POETRY "Translations of Persian poets will be considered."

ICONOGRAFIX, INC.

1830A Hanley Rd., P.O. Box 446, Hudson WI 54016. (715)381-9755. **Fax:** (715)381-9756. **E-mail:** dcfrautschi@iconografixinc.com. **Website:** www.cnthusiastbooks.com. **Contact:** Dylan Frautschi, editorial director. Estab. 1992. Publishes trade paperback originals. "Iconografix publishes special, historical-interest photographic books for transportation equipment enthusiasts. Currently emphasizing emergency vehicles, buses, trucks, railroads, automobiles, auto racing, construction equipment, snowmobiles." **Publishes 6-10 titles/year. 50 queries received/year. 20 mss received/year. 50% of books from first-time authors. 100% from unagented writers. Pays 8-12% royalty on wholesale price. Pays $1,000-3,000 advance.** Publishes book 1 year after acceptance. Accepts simultaneous submissions. Responds in 1 month to queries; 3 months to proposals and mss. Book catalog and ms guidelines free.

NONFICTION Subjects include Americana, photos from archives of historic places, objects, people, history, hobbies, military, war, transportation (older photos of specific vehicles). Interested in photo archives. Query with SASE, or submit proposal package, including outline. Reviews artwork/photos. Send photocopies.

IDEALS CHILDREN'S BOOKS AND CANDYCANE PRESS

2630 Elm Hill Pike, Suite 100, Nashville TN 37214. **Website:** www.idealsbooks.com. **Contact:** Submissions. Estab. 1944.

NONFICTION Ideals publishes for ages 4-8, no longer than 800 words; CandyCane publishes for ages 2-5, no longer than 500 words. Submit complete ms.

FICTION Picture books: animal, concept, history, religion. Board books: animal, history, nature/environment, religion. Ideals publishes for ages 4-8, no longer than 800 words; CandyCane publishes for ages 2-5, no longer than 500 words. Submit complete ms.

IDEALS PUBLICATIONS INC.

2630 Elm Hill Pike, Suite 100, Nashville TN 37214. (615)781-1451. **E-mail:** idealsinfo@guideposts.org. **Website:** www.idealsbooks.com. Estab. 1944. "Ideals Publications publishes 20-25 new children's titles a year, primarily for 2-8 year-olds. Our backlist includes more than 400 titles, and we publish picture books, activity books, board books, and novelty and sound books covering a wide array of topics, such as Bible stories, holidays, early learning, history, family relationships, and values. Our bestselling titles include *The Story of Christmas, The Story of Easter, Seaman's Journal, How Do I Love You?, God Made You Special* and *A View at the Zoo.* Through our dedication to publishing high-quality and engaging books, we never forget our obligation to our littlest readers to help create those special moments with books."

IMPRINTS Ideals, Ideals Children's Books, CandyCane Press, Williamson Books.

FICTION Ideals Children's Books publishes fiction and nonfiction picture books for children ages 4 to 8.

Subjects include holiday, inspirational, and patriotic themes; relationships and values; and general fiction. Mss should be no longer than 800 words. CandyCane Press publishes board books and novelty books for children ages 2 to 5. Subject matter is similar to Ideals Children's Books, with a focus on younger children. Mss should be no longer than 250 words.

IDW PUBLISHING

5080 Santa Fe, San Diego CA 92109. **E-mail:** letters@ idwpublishing.com. **Website:** www.idwpublishing. com. Estab. 1999. Publishes hardcover, mass market and trade paperback originals. IDW Publishing currently publishes a wide range of comic books and graphic novels including titles based on Angel, Doctor Who, GI Joe, Star Trek, Terminator: Salvation, and Transformers. Creator-driven titles include Fallen Angel by Peter David and JK Woodward, Locke & Key by Joe Hill and Gabriel Rodriguez, and a variety of titles by writer Steve Niles including Wake the Dead, Epilogue, and Dead, She Said.

IDYLL ARBOR, INC.

39129 264th Ave. SE, Enumclaw WA 98022. (360)825-7797. **Fax:** (360)825-5670. **E-mail:** editors@idyllarbor. com. **Website:** www.idyllarbor.com. **Contact:** Tom Blaschko. Estab. 1984. Publishes hardcover and trade paperback originals, and trade paperback reprints. "Idyll Arbor publishes practical information on the current state and art of healthcare practice. Currently emphasizing therapies (recreational, horticultural), and activity directors in long-term care facilities. Issues Press looks at problems in society from video games to returning veterans and their problems reintegrating into the civilian world. Pine Winds Press publishes books about strange phenomena such as Bigfoot and the life force." **Publishes 6 titles/year. 50% of books from first-time authors. 100% from unagented writers. Pays 8-15% royalty on wholesale price or retail price.** Publishes book 1 year after acceptance. Accepts simultaneous submissions. Responds in 1 month; 2 months to proposals; 6 months to mss. Book catalog and ms guidelines free.

IMPRINTS Issues Press; Pine Winds Press.

NONFICTION Subjects include health, medicine, for therapists, activity directors, psychology, recreational therapy, horticulture (used in long-term care activities or health care therapy). "Idyll Arbor is currently developing a line of books under the imprint Issues Press, which treats emotional issues in a clear-headed

manner. We look for mss from authors with recent clinical experience. Good grounding in theory is required, but practical experience is more important." Query preferred with outline and 1 sample chapter. Reviews artwork/photos. Send photocopies.

TIPS "The books must be useful for the health practitioner who meets face to face with patients or the books must be useful for teaching undergraduate and graduate level classes. Pine Winds Press books should be compatible with the model of the soul found on calculatingsoulconnections.com."

ILIUM PRESS

2407 S. Sonora Dr., Spokane WA 99037. (509)928-7950. **E-mail:** contact@iliumpress.com; submissions@iliumpress.com. **Website:** www.iliumpress. com. **Contact:** John Lemon, owner/editor (literature, epic poetry, how-to). Estab. 2010. Publishes trade paperback originals and reprints, electronic originals and reprints. **Publishes 1-3 titles/year. Pays 20%-50% royalties on receipts.** Publishes book up to 1 year after acceptance. Accepts simultaneous submissions. Responds in 6 months to queries/proposals/mss. Guidelines available on website www.iliumpress.com.

NONFICTION Subjects include contemporary culture, memoirs, music, alt-pop music bios, writing, and "practical small business how-to that appeals to the DIY ethic and promoting creative work". Query with SASE or submit proposal package, with outline, 3 sample chapters, and SASE.

FICTION Subjects include adventure, erotica, literary, science fiction, gritty/noir mystery, dystopian science fiction. "See website for guidelines and preferred styles." Query with SASE or submit proposal package with outline, first 20 pages, and SASE.

POETRY "Submit only book-length narrative epic poems in metered blank or sprung verse. All others will be rejected. See submission guidelines on website." Query with first 20 pages and SASE.

TIPS "Read submission guidelines and literary preferences on the website: www.iliumpress.com."

ILLUMINATION ARTS

P.O. Box 1865, Bellevue WA 98009. **Website:** www. illumin.com. **Contact:** Ruth Thompson, editorial director. Estab. 1987. **Pays authors and illustrators royalty based on wholesale price. Book fliers available for SASE.**

◐ "Note that our submission review process is on hold until notice on website so submissions are not currently being reviewed." Normal requirements include no electronic or CD submissions for text or art. Considers simultaneous submissions.

NONFICTION Uses color artwork only. Reviews both ms submissions from authors and illustration packages from artists. Artists may query with color samples, résumé and promotional material to be kept on file or returned with SASE only. Responds within 3 months with SASE only. Samples returned with SASE or filed.

FICTION Word length: Prefers under 1,000, but will consider up to 1,500 words.

TIPS "Read our books or visit website to see what our books are like. Follow submission guidelines found on website. Be patient. We are unable to track unsolicited submissions."

IMAGE COMICS

2001 Center St., 6th Floor, Berkeley CA 94704. E-mail: submissions@imagecomics.com. **Website:** www.imagecomics.com. **Contact:** Eric Stephenson, publisher. Estab. 1992. Publishes creator-owned comic books, graphic novels. See this company's website for detailed guidelines.

○ Does not accept writing samples without art.

FICTION Query with 1-page synopsis and 5 pages or more of samples. "We do not accept writing (that is plots, scripts, whatever) samples! If you're an established pro, we might be able to find somebody willing to work with you but it would be nearly impossible for us to read through every script that might find its way our direction. Do not send your script or your plot unaccompanied by art—it will be discarded, unread."

TIPS "We are not looking for any specific genre or type of comic book. We are looking for comics that are well written and well drawn, by people who are dedicated and can meet deadlines."

IMAGES SI, INC

109 Woods of Arden Rd., Staten Island NY 10312. (718)966-3964. **Fax:** (718)966-3695. **Website:** www.imagesco.com. Estab. 1990. **Publishes 4 titles/year. Pays 10-20% royalty on wholesale price.** Publishes book 6-24 months after acceptance.

NONFICTION Subjects include computers, electronics, science.

FICTION Subjects include science fiction.

IMMEDIUM

P.O. Box 31846, San Francisco CA 94131. (415)452-8546. **Fax:** (360)937-6272. **E-mail:** submissions@immedium.com. **Website:** www.immedium.com. **Contact:** Amy Ma, acquisitions editor. Estab. 2005. Publishes hardcover and trade paperback originals. "*Immedium* focuses on publishing eye-catching children's picture books, Asian American topics, and contemporary arts, popular culture, and multicultural issues." **Publishes 4 titles/year. 50 queries received/year. 25 mss received/year. 50% of books from first-time authors. 90% from unagented writers. Pays 5% royalty on wholesale price. Pays on publication.** Publishes book 2 years after acceptance. Accepts simultaneous submissions. Responds in 1 month to queries; 2 months to proposals; 3 months to mss. Catalog online. Guidelines online.

NONFICTION Subjects include art, architecture, multicultural. Submit complete ms. Reviews artwork/photos. Send photocopies.

FICTION Subjects include comic books, picture books. Submit complete ms.

TIPS "Our audience is children and parents. Please visit our site."

IMPACT BOOKS

F+W Media, Inc., 10151 Carver Rd., Suite 200, Blue Ash OH 45242. **Fax:** (513)531-2686. **E-mail:** mona.clough@fwmedia.com. **Website:** www.northlightshop.com; www.impact-books.com. **Contact:** Mona Clough, content director (art instruction for fantasy, comics, manga, anime, popular culture, graffiti, science fiction, cartooning and body art). Estab. 2004. Publishes trade paperback originals and reprints. **Publishes 8-9 titles/year. 50 queries received/year. 10-12 mss received/year. 80% of books from first-time authors. 100% from unagented writers.** Publishes book 11 months after acceptance of ms. Accepts simultaneous submissions. Responds in 4 months to queries. Responds in 4 months to proposals. Responds in 4 months to mss. Visit website for booklist. Guidelines available at www.artistsnetwork.com/contactus.

○ IMPACT Books publishes titles that emphasize illustrated how-to-draw-manga, graffiti, fantasy and comics art instruction. Currently emphasizing fantasy art, traditional American comics styles, including humor; and Japanese-style (manga and anime) and pop art. This market is for experienced artists who are willing to work with an IMPACT editor to produce a step-by-step how-to book about how to create the art and the artist's creative process. See also separate listing for F+W Media in this section.

NONFICTION Subjects include art, art instruction, contemporary culture, creative nonfiction, hobbies. Submit proposal package, outline, 1 sample chapter, at least 20 examples of sample art. Reviews artwork/photos. Send digital art.

TIPS "Audience comprised primarily of 12- to 18-year-old beginners along the lines of comic buyers, in general—mostly teenagers—but also appealing to a broader audience of young adults 19-30 who need basic techniques. Art must appeal to teenagers and be submitted in a form that will reproduce well. Authors need to know how to teach beginners step-by-step. A sample step-by-step demonstration is important."

IMPACT PUBLISHERS, INC.

P.O. Box 6016, Atascadero CA 93423. **E-mail:** submissions@impactpublishers.com. **Website:** www.impact-publishers.com. **Contact:** Freeman Porter, submissions editor. Estab. 1970. "Our purpose is to make the best human services expertise available to the widest possible audience. We publish only popular psychology and self-help materials written in everyday language by professionals with advanced degrees and significant experience in the human services." **Publishes 3-5 titles/year. 20% of books from first-time authors. Pays authors royalty of 10-12%. Offers advances.** Accepts simultaneous submissions. Responds in 3 months. Book catalog for #10 SASE with 2 first-class stamps. Guidelines for SASE.

IMPRINTS Little Imp Books, Rebuilding Books, The Practical Therapist Series.

NONFICTION Young readers, middle readers, young adults: self-help. Query or submit complete ms, cover letter, résumé.

TIPS "Please do not submit fiction, poetry or narratives."

INCENTIVE PUBLICATIONS, INC.

233 N. Michigan Ave., Suite 2000, Chicago IL 60601. **E-mail:** incentive@worldbook.com. **Website:** www.incentivepublications.com. **Contact:** Paul Kobasa, editor-in-chief. Estab. 1970. Publishes paperback originals. "Incentive publishes developmentally appropriate teacher/parent resource materials and educational workbooks for children in grades K-12. Actively seeking proposals for student workbooks, all grades/all

subjects, and professional development resources for pre K-12 classroom teachers and school administrators." **Publishes 25-30 titles/year. 25% of books from first-time authors. 100% from unagented writers. Pays royalty, or makes outright purchase.** Publishes book an average of 1 year after acceptance of ms. Responds in 1 month to queries.

NONFICTION Subjects include education. Instructional, teacher/administrator professional development books in pre-K through 12th grade. Query with synopsis and detailed outline.

INFORMATION TODAY, INC.

143 Old Marlton Pike, Medford NJ 08055. (609)654-6266. **Fax:** (609)654-4309. **E-mail:** jbryans@infotoday.com. **Website:** www.infotoday.com. **Contact:** John B. Bryans, editor-in-chief/publisher. Publishes hardcover and trade paperback originals. "We look for highly-focused coverage of cutting-edge technology topics. Written by established experts and targeted to a tech-savvy readership. Virtually all our titles focus on how information is accessed, used, shared, and transformed into knowledge that can benefit people, business, and society. Currently emphasizing Internet/online technologies, including their social significance: biography, how-to, technical, reference, scholarly. De-emphasizing fiction." **Publishes 15-20 titles/year. 200 queries received/year. 30 mss received/year. 30% of books from first-time authors. 90% from unagented writers. Pays 10-15% royalty on wholesale price. Pays $500-2,500 advance.** Publishes book 9 months after acceptance. Accepts simultaneous submissions. Responds in 1 month to queries; 2 months to proposals; 3 months to mss. Book catalog free or on website. Proposal guidelines free or via e-mail as attachment.

IMPRINTS ITI (academic, scholarly, library science); CyberAge Books (high-end consumer and business technology books-emphasis on Internet/WWW topics including online research).

NONFICTION Subjects include business, economics, computers, electronics, education, science, Internet and cyberculture. Query with SASE. Reviews artwork/photos. Send photocopies.

TIPS "Our readers include scholars, academics, indexers, librarians, information professionals (ITI imprint), as well as high-end consumer and business users of Internet/WWW/online technologies, and people interested in the marriage of technology with issues of social significance (i.e., cyberculture)."

INNOVATIVE PUBLISHERS INC.

44 Highland St., Boston MA 02119. (617)963-0886. **Fax:** (617)861-8533. **E-mail:** pub@innovative-publishers.com. **Website:** www.innovative-publishers.com. Estab. 2000. Publishes hardcover, trade paperback, mass market, and electronic originals; trade paperback and mass market reprints. **Publishes 350-600 titles/year. Receives 4,500 queries/year. Receives 800-1,000 mss/year. 45% of books from first-time authors. 50% from unagented writers. Pays 5-17% royalty on retail price. Offers $1,500-$125,000 advance.** Publishes book 2 years after acceptance. Accepts simultaneous submissions. Responds in 3 months to queries; 4-6 months to mss and proposals. Book catalog for 9x12 SASE with 7 first-class stamps. Guidelines for #10 SASE.

NONFICTION Subjects include Americana, anthropology, archeology, architecture, art, business, career guidance, child guidance, communications, community, contemporary culture, cooking, counseling, crafts, creative nonfiction, economics, education, entertainment, finance, foods, games, gardening, government, health, history, hobbies, house and home, humanities, language, law, literary criticism, literature, memoirs, money, multicultural, music, New Age, philosophy, photography, psychology, real estate, religion, science, social sciences, sociology, spirituality, translation, transportation, travel, womens issues, womens studies, world affairs, young adult. "We want books from dedicated writers and not those who are writing on the latest trend. Our audience is broad, educated, and insightful." Query with SASE. Reviews artwork.

FICTION Subjects include adventure, comic books, confession, contemporary, erotica, ethnic, experimental, fantasy, feminist, gothic, historical, horror, humor, juvenile, literary, mainstream, multicultural, mystery, picture books, plays, poetry, religious, romance, science fiction, short story collections, spiritual, suspense, translation, young adult. "Primarily seeking artists that are immersed in their topic. If you live, eat, and sleep your topic, it will show. Our focus is a wide demographic." Query with SASE.

POETRY "Some works may be slated for anthologies. Readers are from diverse demographic. Seeking innovative styles. Especially seeking emerging ethnic poets from Asia, Europe, and Spanish-speaking countries." Query. Submit 4 sample poems.

☺ INSOMNIAC PRESS

520 Princess Ave., London ON N6B 2B8, Canada. (416)504-6270. **E-mail:** mike@insomniacpress.com. **Website:** www.insomniacpress.com. **Contact:** Mike O'Connor, publisher. Estab. 1992. Publishes trade paperback originals and reprints, mass market paperback originals, and electronic originals and reprints. **Publishes 20 titles/year. 250 queries received/year. 1,000 mss received/year. 50% of books from first-time authors. 80% from unagented writers. Pays 10-15% royalty on retail price. Pays $500-1,000 advance.** Publishes book 6 months after acceptance. Accepts simultaneous submissions. Guidelines online.

NONFICTION Subjects include business, creative nonfiction, gay, lesbian, government, politics, health, medicine, language, literature, money, finance, multicultural, religion, true crime. Very interested in areas such as true crime and well-written and well-researched nonfiction on topics of wide interest. Query via e-mail, submit proposal package including outline, 2 sample chapters, or submit complete ms. Reviews artwork/photos. Send photocopies.

FICTION Subjects include comic books, ethnic, experimental, gay, lesbian, humor, literary, mainstream, multicultural, mystery, poetry, suspense. "We publish a mix of commercial (mysteries) and literary fiction." Query via e-mail, submit proposal.

POETRY "Our poetry publishing is limited to 2-4 books per year and we are often booked up a year or two in advance." Submit complete ms.

TIPS "We envision a mixed readership that appreciates up-and-coming literary fiction and poetry as well as solidly researched and provocative nonfiction. Peruse our website and familiarize yourself with what we've published in the past."

INTERLINK PUBLISHING GROUP, INC.

46 Crosby St., Northampton MA 01060. (413)582-7054. **Fax:** (413)582-7057. **E-mail:** info@interlinkbooks.com; editor@interlinkbooks.com. **Website:** www.interlinkbooks.com. **Contact:** Michel Moushabeck, publisher; Pam Thompson, editor. Estab. 1987. Publishes hardcover and trade paperback originals. Interlink is an independent publisher of general trade adult fiction and nonfiction with an emphasis on books that have a wide appeal while also meeting high intellectual and literary standards. **Publishes 90 titles/year. 30% of books from first-time authors. 50% from unagented writers. Pays 6-8% royalty on**

retail price. **Pays small advance.** Publishes book 18 months after acceptance. Accepts simultaneous submissions. Responds in 3-6 months to queries. Book catalog and guidelines online.

IMPRINTS Crocodile Books, USA; Codagan Guides, USA; Interlink Books; Olive Branch Press; Clockroot Books.

NONFICTION Subjects include world travel, world literature, world history and politics, art, world music & dance, international cooking, children's books from around the world. Submit outline and sample chapters.

FICTION Subjects include ethnic, international. "We are looking for translated works relating to the Middle East, Africa or Latin America." No science fiction, romance, plays, erotica, fantasy, horror. Query with SASE. Submit outline, sample chapters.

TIPS "Any submissions that fit well in our publishing program will receive careful attention. A visit to our website, your local bookstore, or library to look at some of our books before you send in your submission is recommended."

INTERNATIONAL FOUNDATION OF EMPLOYEE BENEFIT PLANS

18700 W. Bluemound Rd., Brookfield WI 53045. (262)786-6700. **Fax:** (262)786-8780. **E-mail:** bookstore@ifebp.org. **Website:** www.ifebp.org. **Contact:** Kelli Kolsrud, director, information services and publications. Estab. 1954. Publishes trade paperback originals. IFEBP publishes general and technical monographs on all aspects of employee benefits—pension plans, health insurance, etc. **Publishes 10 titles/year. 15% of books from first-time authors. 80% from unagented writers. Pays 5-15% royalty on wholesale and retail price.** Publishes book 1 year after acceptance. Responds in 3 months to queries. Book catalog available free. Guidelines online.

NONFICTION Subjects limited to health care, pensions, retirement planning and employee benefits and compensation. Query with outline.

TIPS "Be aware of interests of employers and the marketplace in benefits topics, for example, pension plan changes, healthcare cost containment."

INTERNATIONAL MARINE

The McGraw-Hill Companies, P.O. Box 220, Camden ME 04843-0220. (207)236-4838. **Fax:** (207)236-6314. **Website:** www.internationalmarine.com. **Contact:** Acquisitions Editor. Estab. 1969. Publishes hardcover and paperback originals. International Marine (publishes the best books about boats). **Publishes 50 titles/year. 500-700 mss received/year. 30% of books from first-time authors. 60% from unagented writers. Pays standard royalties based on net price. Pays advance.** Publishes book 1 year after acceptance of ms. Responds in 2 months to queries. Guidelines online.

IMPRINTS Ragged Mountain Press (sports and outdoor books that take you off the beaten path).

NONFICTION All books are illustrated. Material in all stages welcome. Publishes a wide range of subjects include: sea stories, seamanship, boat maintenance, etc. Query first with outline and 2-3 sample chapters. Reviews artwork/photos.

TIPS "Writers should be aware of the need for clarity, accuracy and interest. Many progress too far in the actual writing."

INTERNATIONAL PRESS

P.O. Box 502, Somerville MA 02143. (617)623-3855. **Fax:** (617)623-3101. **E-mail:** ipb-mgmt@intlpress.com. **Website:** www.intlpress.com. **Contact:** Brian Bianchini, general manager (research math and physics). Estab. 1992. Publishes hardcover originals and reprints. International Press of Boston, Inc. is an academic publishing company that welcomes book publication inquiries from prospective authors on all topics in Mathematics and Physics. International Press also publishes high-level mathematics and mathematical physics book titles and textbooks. **Publishes 12 titles/year. 200 queries received/year. 500 mss received/year. 10% of books from first-time authors. 100% from unagented writers. Pays 3-10% royalty.** Publishes book 6 months after acceptance. Responds in 5 months to queries and proposals; 1 year to mss. Book catalog available free. Guidelines online.

◯ With close ties to the Chinese math community and the community of Chinese American mathematicians, International Press is developing a strong partnership with publishers and distributors of academic books throughout China.

NONFICTION Subjects include science. All our books will be in research mathematics. Authors need to provide ready to print latex files. Submit complete ms. Reviews artwork/photos. Send EPS files.

TIPS "Audience is PhD mathematicians, researchers and students."

INTERNATIONAL WEALTH SUCCESS

P.O. Box 186, Merrick NY 11570. (516)766-5850. **Fax:** (516)766-5919. **Website:** www.iwsmoney.com. **Contact:** Tyler G. Hicks, editor. Estab. 1967. **Publishes 10 titles/year. 100% of books from first-time authors. 100% from unagented writers. Pays 10% royalty on wholesale or retail price. Offers usual advance of $1,000, but this varies depending on author's reputation and nature of book. Buys all rights.** Publishes book 4 months after acceptance. Responds in 1 month to queries. Book catalog and ms guidelines for 9x12 SAE with 3 first-class stamps.

◑ "Our mission is to publish books, newsletters, and self-study courses aimed at helping beginners and experienced business people start, and succeed in, their own small business in the fields of real estate, import-export, mail order, licensing, venture capital, financial brokerage, etc. The large number of layoffs and downsizings have made our publications of greater importance to people seeking financial independence in their own business, free of layoff threats and snarling bosses."

NONFICTION Subjects include business, economics, financing, business success, venture capital, etc. Techniques, methods, sources for building wealth. Highly personal, how-to-do-it with plenty of case histories. Books are aimed at wealth builders and are highly sympathetic to their problems. These publications present a wide range of business opportunities while providing practical, hands-on, step-by-step instructions aimed at helping readers achieve their personal goals in as short a time as possible while adhering to ethical and professional business standards. Length: 60,000-70,000 words. Query. Reviews artwork/photos.

TIPS "With the mass layoffs in large and medium-size companies there is an increasing interest in owning your own business. So we focus on more how-to, hands-on material on owning—and becoming successful in—one's own business of any kind. Our market is the BWB—Beginning Wealth Builder. This person has so little money that financial planning is something they never think of. Instead, they want to know what kind of a business they can get into to make some money without a large investment. Write for this market and you have millions of potential readers. Remember—there are a lot more people without money than with money."

INTERVARSITY PRESS

P.O. Box 1400, Downers Grove IL 60515. **E-mail:** e-mail@ivpress.com. **Website:** www.ivpress.com/submissions. **Contact:** David Zimmerman, associate editor (IVP Books); Cindy Bunch, senior editor (IVP Connect, Formatio, IVP Cresendo); Brannon Ellis, associate editor (academic, reference); David Congdon, senior editor (IVP Academic) or Dan Reid, senior editor (reference, academic); Al Hsu, associate editor (IVP Books, IVP Praxis). Estab. 1947. Publishes hardcover originals, trade paperback and mass market paperback originals. "InterVarsity Press publishes a full line of books from an evangelical Christian perspective targeted to an open-minded audience. We serve those in the university, the church, and the world, by publishing books from an evangelical Christian perspective." **Publishes 110-130 titles/year. 450 queries received/year. 900 mss received/year. 13% of books from first-time authors. 86% from unagented writers. Pays 14-16% royalty on retail price. Outright purchase is $75-1,500. Pays negotiable advance.** Publishes book 18 months after acceptance. Accepts simultaneous submissions. "We are unable to provide updates on the review process or personalized responses to unsolicited proposals. We regret that submissions will not be returned.". Book catalog for 9 ×12 SAE and 5 first-class stamps, or online. Guidelines online.

IMPRINTS IVP Academic; IVP Connect; IVP Books.

◑ "We think of ourselves as the leading publisher of thoughtful Christian books, and we envision our audience to be similarly thoughtful about their Christian lives—people who really want to think through what it means to be a Christ-follower and to live biblically, and then take some concrete steps toward living more in that direction."

NONFICTION Subjects include business, child guidance, contemporary culture, economics, ethnic, history, memoirs, multicultural, philosophy, psychology, religion, science, social sciences, sociology, spirituality. "InterVarsity Press publishes a full line of books from an evangelical Christian perspective targeted to an open-minded audience. We serve those in the university, the church, and the world, by publishing books from an evangelical Christian perspective." Very few business/economics, child guidance/parenting, memoirs. Submit proposal that includes chapter-by-chapter summary, 2 complete sample chapters, and bio. Does not review artwork.

TIPS "The best way to submit to us is to go to a conference where one of our editors are. Networking is key. We're seeking writers who have good ideas and a presence/platform where they've been testing their ideas out (a church, university, on a prominent blog). We need authors who will bring resources to the table for helping to publicize and sell their books (speaking at seminars and conferences, writing for national magazines or newspapers, etc.)."

INTERWEAVE PRESS

201 E. Fourth St., Loveland CO 80537. (970)669-7672. **Fax:** (970)667-8317. **Website:** www.interweave.com. Estab. 1975. Publishes hardcover and trade paperback originals. Interweave Press publishes instructive titles relating to the fiber arts and beadwork topics. **Publishes 40-45 titles/year. 60% of books from first-time authors. 90% from unagented writers.** Publishes book 6-18 months after acceptance. Accepts simultaneous submissions. Responds in 2 months to queries. Book catalog online. Guidelines available free.

NONFICTION Subjects limited to fiber arts (spinning, knitting, dyeing, weaving, sewing/stiching, art quilting, mixed media/collage) and jewelrymaking (beadwork, stringing, wireworking, metalsmithing). Submit outline, sample chapters. Accepts simultaneous submissions if informed of non-exclusivity. Reviews artwork/photos.

TIPS "We are looking for very clear, informally written, technically correct mss, generally of a how-to nature, in our specific fiber and beadwork fields only. Our audience includes a variety of creative self-starters who appreciate inspiration and clear instruction. They are often well educated and skillful in many areas."

⬤ IRISH ACADEMIC PRESS

8 Chapel Lane, Sallins Co. Kildare , Ireland. (353)(1)2989937. **Fax:** (353)(1)2982783. **E-mail:** info@iap.ie. **E-mail:** lisa.hyde@iap.ie. **Website:** www.iap.ie. **Contact:** Lisa Hyde, editor. Estab. 1974. **Publishes 15 titles/year. Pays royalty.** Accepts simultaneous submissions. Guidelines available free.

IMPRINTS Vallentine-Mitchell Publishers.

◓ Request submission guidelines before submitting.

NONFICTION Subjects include art, architecture, government, politics, history, literary criticism, military, war, womens issues, womens studies, genealogy, Irish history. Does not want fiction or poetry. Query with SASE. Submit proposal package, outline, résumé, publishing history, bio, target audience, competing books, 2-3 sample chapters, SASE.

IRON GATE PUBLISHING

P.O. Box 999, Niwot CO 80544. (303)530-2551. **Fax:** (303)530-5273. **E-mail:** editor@irongate.com. **Website:** www.irongate.com. **Contact:** Dina C. Carson, publisher (how-to, genealogy, local history). Publishes hardcover and trade paperback originals. "Our readers are people who are looking for solid, how-to advice on planning reunions or self-publishing a genealogy." **Publishes 6-10 titles/year. 100 queries received/year. 20 mss received/year. 30% of books from first-time authors. 10% from unagented writers. Pays royalty on a case-by-case basis.** Publishes book 1 year after acceptance. Accepts simultaneous submissions. Responds in 2 months to proposals. Book catalog and writer's guidelines free or online.

IMPRINTS Reunion Solutions Press; KinderMed Press.

NONFICTION , hobbies, genealogy, local history, reunions, party planning. Query with SASE, or submit proposal package, including outline, 2 sample chapters, and marketing summary. Reviews artwork/photos. Send photocopies.

TIPS "Please look at the other books we publish and tell us in your query letter why your book would fit into our line of books."

ITALICA PRESS

595 Main St., Suite 605, New York NY 10044-0047. (917)371-0563. **E-mail:** inquiries@italicapress.com. **Website:** www.italicapress.com. **Contact:** Ronald G. Musto and Eileen Gardiner, publishers. Estab. 1985. Publishes trade paperback originals. "Italica Press publishes English translations of modern Italian fiction and medieval and Renaissance nonfiction." **Publishes 6 titles/year. 600 queries received/year. 60 mss received/year. 5% of books from first-time authors. 100% from unagented writers. Pays 7-15% royalty on wholesale price; author's copies.** Publishes book 1 year after acceptance. Accepts simultaneous submissions. Responds in 1 month to queries; 4 months to mss. Book catalog and Guidelines online.

NONFICTION Subjects include translation. "We publish English translations of medieval and Renaissance source materials and English translations of modern Italian fiction." Query with SASE. Reviews artwork/photos. Send photocopies.

FICTION "First-time translators published. We would like to see translations of Italian writers who are well-known in Italy who are not yet translated for an American audience." Query with SASE.

POETRY Poetry titles are always translations and generally dual language. Query with 10 sample translations of medieval and Renaissance Italian poets. Include cover letter, bio, and list of publications.

TIPS "We are interested in considering a wide variety of medieval and Renaissance topics (not historical fiction), and for modern works we are only interested in translations from Italian fiction by well-known Italian authors." *Only* fiction that has been previously published in Italian. A *brief* call saves a lot of postage. 90% of proposals we receive are completely off base—but we are very interested in things that are right on target. Please send return postage if you want your ms returned.

JAIN PUBLISHING CO.

P.O. Box 3523, Fremont CA 94539. (510)659-8272. **Fax:** (510)659-0501. **E-mail:** mail@jainpub.com. **Website:** www.jainpub.com. **Contact:** M. Jain, editor-in-chief. Estab. 1989. Publishes hardcover and paperback originals and reprints. Jain Publishing Co. is a humanities and social sciences publisher that publishes college textbooks and supplements, as well as professional and scholarly references, e-books and e-courses. It also publishes in the areas of humanities and societies pertaining specifically to ask, commonly categorized as "Asian Studies." **Publishes 12-15 titles/year. 300 queries received/year. 100% from unagented writers. Pays 5-15% royalty on net sales.** Publishes book 1-2 years after acceptance. Responds in 3 months to mss. Book catalog and ms guidelines online.

NONFICTION Subjects include humanities, social sciences, Asian studies, medical, business, scientific/technical. Submit proposal package, publishing history. Reviews artwork/photos. Send photocopies.

ALICE JAMES BOOKS

114 Prescott St., Farmington ME 04938. (207)778-7071. **Fax:** (207)778-7766. **E-mail:** info@alicejamesbooks.org. **Website:** www.alicejamesbooks.org. **Contact:** Alyssa Neptune, managing editor; Carey Salerno, executive director; Nicole Wakefield, editorial assistant. Estab. 1973. Publishes trade paperback originals. "Alice James Books is a nonprofit cooperative poetry

press. The founders' objectives were to give women access to publishing and to involve authors in the publishing process. The cooperative selects mss for publication through both regional and national competitions." **Publishes 6 titles/year. Approximately 1,000 mss received/year. 50% of books from first-time authors. 100% from unagented writers. Pays through competition awards.** Publishes book 1 year after acceptance. Accepts simultaneous submissions. Responds promptly to queries; 4 months to mss. Book catalog for free or on website. Guidelines for #10 SASE or on website.

POETRY "Alice James Books is a nonprofit cooperative poetry press. The founders' objectives were to give women access to publishing and to involve authors in the publishing process. The cooperative selects mss for publication through both regional and national competitions." Seeks to publish the best contemporary poetry by both established and beginning poets, with particular emphasis on involving poets in the publishing process. Has published poetry by Jane Kenyon, Jean Valentine, B.H. Fairchild, and Matthea Harvey. Publishes flat-spined paperbacks of high quality, both in production and contents. Does not want children's poetry or light verse. Publishes 6 paperback books/year, 80 pages each, in editions of approximately 1,500. Query.

TIPS "Send SASE for contest guidelines or check website. Do not send work without consulting current guidelines."

JEWISH LIGHTS PUBLISHING

LongHill Partners, Inc., Sunset Farm Offices, Rt. 4, P.O. Box 237, Woodstock VT 05091. (802)457-4000. **Fax:** (802)457-4004. **E-mail:** editorial@jewishlights.com; sales@jewishlights.com. **Website:** www.jewishlights.com. **Contact:** Tim Holtz, art acquisitions. Estab. 1990. Publishes hardcover and trade paperback originals, trade paperback reprints. "Jewish Lights publishes books for people of all faiths and all backgrounds who yearn for books that attract, engage, educate and spiritually inspire. Our authors are at the forefront of spiritual thought and deal with the quest for the self and for meaning in life by drawing on the Jewish wisdom tradition. Our books cover topics including history, spirituality, life cycle, children, self-help, recovery, theology and philosophy. We do not publish autobiography, biography, fiction, haggadot, poetry or cookbooks. At this point we plan to do only two books for children annually, and one will be for younger children (ages 4-10)." **Publishes 30 titles/year. 50% of books from first-time authors. 75% from unagented writers. Pays authors royalty of 10% of revenue received; 15% royalty for subsequent printings.** Publishes book 1 year after acceptance. Accepts simultaneous submissions. Responds in 3 months to queries. Book catalog and ms guidelines online.

NONFICTION Subjects include business, economics, with spiritual slant, finding spiritual meaning in one's work, health, medicine, healing/recovery, wellness, aging, life cycle, history, nature, environment, philosophy, religion, theology, spirituality, and inspiration, women's issues, women's studies. Picture book, young readers, middle readers: activity books, spirituality. "We do *not* publish haggadot, biography, poetry, or cookbooks." Query. Reviews artwork/photos. Send photocopies.

FICTION Picture books, young readers, middle readers: spirituality. "We are not interested in anything other than spirituality." Query with outline/synopsis and 2 sample chapters; submit complete ms for picture books.

TIPS "We publish books for all faiths and backgrounds that also reflect the Jewish wisdom tradition. Explain in your cover letter why you're submitting your project to us in particular. Make sure you know what we publish."

JIST PUBLISHING

875 Montreal Way, St. Paul MN 55102. **E-mail:** educate@emcp.com. **Website:** www.jist.com. **Contact:** Susan Pines, associate publisher (career and education reference and library titles, assessments, videos, e-products); Lori Cates Hand, product line manager, trade and workbooks (career, job search, and education trade and workbook titles). Estab. 1981. Publishes hardcover and trade paperback originals. "Our purpose is to provide quality job search, career development, occupational, and life skills information, products, and services that help people manage and improve their lives and careers-and the lives of others. Publishes practical, self-directed tools and training materials that are used in employment and training, education, and business settings. Whether reference books, trade books, assessment tools, workbooks, or videos, JIST products foster self-directed job-search attitudes and behaviors." **Publishes 60 titles/year.**

Receives 40 submissions/year. 25% of books from first-time authors. 75% from unagented writers. Pays 8-10% royalty on net receipts. Pays advance: 12 months.** Accepts simultaneous submissions. Responds in 6 months to queries, proposals, and mss. Catalog and guidelines online.

NONFICTION Subjects include business, economics, education. Specializes in job search, career development, occupational information, character education, and domestic abuse topics. "We want text/workbook formats that would be useful in a school or other institutional setting. We also publish trade titles for all reading levels. Will consider books for professional staff and educators, appropriate software and videos." Submit proposal package, including outline, 1 sample chapter, and author résumé, competitive analysis, marketing ideas. Does not review artwork/photos.

TIPS "Our audiences are students, job seekers, and career changers of all ages and occupations who want to find good jobs quickly and improve their futures. We sell materials through the trade as well as to institutional markets like schools, colleges, and one-stop career centers."

THE JOHNS HOPKINS UNIVERSITY PRESS

2715 N. Charles St., Baltimore MD 21218. (410)516-6900. **Fax:** (410)516-6968. **E-mail:** jmm@press.jhu.edu. **Website:** www.press.jhu.edu. **Contact:** Jacqueline C. Wehmueller, executive editor (consumer health, psychology and psychiatry, and history of medicine; jcw@press.jhu.edu); Matthew McAdam, editor (mxm@jhu@press.edu); Robert J. Brugger, senior acquisitions editor (American history; rjb@press.jhu.edu); Vincent J. Burke, exec. editor (biology; vjb@press.jhu.edu); Juliana McCarthy, acquisitions editor (humanities, classics, and ancient studies; jmm@press.jhu.edu); Ashleigh McKown, assistant editor (higher education, history of technology, history of science; aem@press.jhu.edu); Suzanne Flinchbaugh, Associate Editor (Political Science, Health Policy, and Co-Publishing Liaison; skf@press.jhu.edu; Greg Nicholl, Assistant Editor (Regional Books, Poetry and Fiction, and Anabaptist and Pietist Studies; gan@press.jhu.edu). Estab. 1878. Publishes hardcover originals and reprints, and trade paperback reprints. **Publishes 140 titles/year. Pays royalty.** Publishes book 1 year after acceptance.

NONFICTION Subjects include government, politics, health, medicine, history, humanities, literary criticism, regional, religion, science. Submit proposal package, outline, 1 sample chapter, curriculum vita. Reviews artwork/photos. Send photocopies.

POETRY "One of the largest American university presses, Johns Hopkins publishes primarily scholarly books and journals. We do, however, publish short fiction and poetry in the series Johns Hopkins: Poetry and Fiction, edited by John Irwin."

JONATHAN DAVID PUBLISHERS, INC.

68-22 Eliot Ave., Middle Village NY 11379. (718)456-8611. **Fax:** (718)894-2818. **E-mail:** submission@jd-books.com. **Website:** www.jdbooks.com. **Contact:** David Kolatch, editorial director. Estab. 1948. Publishes hardcover and trade paperback originals and reprints. Jonathan David publishes popular Judaica. **Publishes 20-25 titles/year. 50% of books from first-time authors. 90% from unagented writers. Pays royalty, or makes outright purchase.** Publishes book 18 months after acceptance. Responds in 1 month to queries and proposals; 2 months to mss. Catalog and guidelines online.

NONFICTION Subjects include cooking, foods, nutrition, creative nonfiction, ethnic, multicultural, religion, sports. Query with SASE. Submit proposal package, outline, résumé, 3 sample chapters. Reviews artwork/photos. Send photocopies.

JOURNEYFORTH

Imprint of BJU Press, 1700 Wade Hampton Blvd., Greenville SC 29614. (864)242-5100, ext. 4350. **Fax:** (864)298-0268. **E-mail:** jb@bju.edu. **Website:** www.journeyforth.com. **Contact:** Nancy Lohr. Estab. 1974. Publishes paperback originals. "Small independent publisher of trustworthy novels and biographies for readers pre-school through high school from a conservative Christian perspective, Christian living books, and Bible studies for adults." **Publishes 25 titles/year. 10% of books from first-time authors. 8% from unagented writers. Pays royalty.** Publishes book 12-18 months after acceptance. Does accept simultaneous submissions. Responds in 1 month to queries. Responds in 3 months to mss. Book catalog available free. Guidelines online.

NONFICTION Subjects include animals, contemporary culture, creative nonfiction, environment, history, music, nature, religion, spirituality, sports, young adult. Christian living, Bible studies, church and ministry, church history. "We produce books for

the adult Christian market that are from a conservative Christian worldview."

FICTION Subjects include adventure, historical, animal, easy-to-read, series, mystery, sports, children's/juvenile, suspense, young adult, western. "Our fiction is all based on a moral and Christian worldview." Does not want short stories. Submit 5 sample chapters, synopsis, SASE.

TIPS "Study the publisher's guidelines. No picture books and no submissions by e-mail."

JUPITER GARDENS PRESS

Jupiter Gardens, LLC, PO Box 191, Grimes IA 50111. **E-mail:** submissions@jupitergardens.com. **Website:** www.jupitergardens.com. **Contact:** Mary Wilson, publisher (romance, sf/f, new age). Estab. 2007. Format publishes in trade paperback originals and reprints; electronic originals and reprints. **Publishes 30+ titles/year. Pays 40% royalty on retail price.** Publishes book 4 months after acceptance. Accepts simultaneous submissions. Responds in 1 months on proposals, 2 months on mss. Catalog online. Guidelines online.

NONFICTION Subjects include alternative lifestyles, animals, astrology, environment, gay, health, lesbian, medicine, nature, psychic, religion, sex, spirituality, womens issues, world affairs, young adult, romance, science fiction, fantasy, and metaphysical fiction & nonfiction. "We only publish metaphysical/New Age nonfiction, or nonfiction related to science fiction and fantasy." Submit proposal package, including: outline, 3 sample chapters, and promotional plan/market analysis. E-mail only for submissions. Does not review artwork.

FICTION Subjects include fantasy, gay, lesbian, occult, religious, romance, science fiction, spiritual, young adult, New Age/metaphysical. "We only publish romance (all sub-genres), science fiction & fantasy & metaphysical fiction. Our science fiction and fantasy covers a wide variety of topics, such as feminist fantasy, or more hard science fiction and fantasy which looks at the human condition. Our young adult imprint, Jupiter Storm, with thought provoking reads that explore the full range of speculative fiction, includes science fiction or fantasy and metaphysical fiction. These readers would enjoy edgy contemporary works. Our romance readers love seeing a couple, no matter the gender, overcome obstacles and grow in order to find true love. Like our readers, we believe that love can come in many forms." Submit via e-mail cover letter detailing writing experience (if any), and attach in DOC or RTF format, a 2-4 page synopsis, and the first 3 chapters.

TIPS "No matter which line you're submitting to, know your genre and your readership. We publish a diverse catalog, and we're passionate about our main focus. We want romance that takes your breath away and leaves you with that warm feeling that love does conquer all. Our science fiction takes place in wild and alien worlds, and our fantasy transports readers to mythical realms and finds strange worlds within our own. And our metaphysical nonfiction will help readers gain new skills and awareness for the coming age. We want authors who engage with their readers and who aren't afraid to use social media to connect. Read and follow our submission guidelines."

KAEDEN BOOKS

P.O. Box 16190, Rocky River OH 44116. **Website:** www.kaeden.com. **Contact:** Lisa Stenger, editor. Estab. 1986. Publishes paperback originals. "Children's book publisher for education K-3 market: reading stories, fiction/nonfiction, chapter books, science, and social studies materials." **Publishes 12-20 titles/year. 1,000 mss received/year. 30% of books from first-time authors. 95% from unagented writers. Work purchased outright from authors. Pays royalties to previous authors.** Publishes book 6-9 months after acceptance. Accepts simultaneous submissions. Responds only if interested. Book catalog and Guidelines online.

NONFICTION Subjects include animals, creative nonfiction, science, social sciences. Mss should have interesting topics and information presented in language comprehensible to young students. Content should be supported with details and accurate facts. Submit complete ms. "Can be as minimal as 25 words for the earliest reader or as much as 2,000 words for the fluent reader. Beginning chapter books are welcome. Our readers are in kindergarten to third grade, so vocabulary and sentence structure must be appropriate for young readers. Make sure that all language used in the story is of an appropriate level for the students to read independently. Sentences should be complete and grammatically correct." Reviews artwork/photos. Send photocopies.

FICTION Subjects include adventure, fantasy, historical, humor, mystery, short story collections, sports,

suspense. "We are looking for stories with humor, surprise endings, and interesting characters that will appeal to children in kindergarten through third grade." No sentence fragments. Please do not submit: queries, ms summaries, or résumés, mss that stereotype or demean individuals or groups, mss that present violence as acceptable behavior. Submit complete ms. "Can be as minimal as 25 words for the earliest reader or as much as 2,000 words for the fluent reader. Beginning chapter books are welcome. Our readers are in kindergarten to third grade, so vocabulary and sentence structure must be appropriate for young readers. Make sure that all language used in the story is of an appropriate level for the students to read independently. Sentences should be complete and grammatically correct."

TIPS "Our audience ranges from kindergarten-third grade school children. We are an educational publisher. We are particularly interested in humorous stories with surprise endings and beginning chapter books."

KALMBACH PUBLISHING CO.

21027 Crossroads Circle, P.O. Box 1612, Waukesha WI 53187. (262)796-8776. **Fax:** (262)798-6468. **E-mail:** books@kalmbach.com. **Website:** www.kalmbach. com. **Contact:** Ronald Kovach, senior editor. Estab. 1934. Publishes paperback originals and reprints. **Publishes 40-50 titles/year. 50% of books from first-time authors. 99% from unagented writers. Pays 7% royalty on net receipts. Pays $1,500 advance.** Publishes book 18 months after acceptance. Responds in 2 months to queries.

NONFICTION "Focus on beading, wirework, and one-of-a-kind artisan creations for jewelry-making and crafts and in the railfan, model railroading, plastic modeling and toy train collecting/operating hobbies. Kalmbach publishes reference materials and how-to publications for hobbyists, jewelry-makers, and crafters." Query with 2-3 page detailed outline, sample chapter with photos, drawings, and how-to text. Reviews artwork/photos.

TIPS "Our how-to books are highly visual in their presentation. Any author who wants to publish with us must be able to furnish good photographs and rough drawings before we'll consider his or her book."

KAMEHAMEHA PUBLISHING

567 S. King St., Honolulu HI 96813. **Website:** www. kamehamehapublishing.org. Estab. 1933. "Kamehameha Schools Press publishes in the areas of Hawai-

ian history, Hawaiian culture, Hawaiian language and Hawaiian studies." **Work purchased outright from authors or by royalty agreement.** Publishes book 2 years after acceptance. Responds in 3 months. Call or write for book catalog.

NONFICTION Young reader, middle readers, young adults: biography, history, multicultural, Hawaiian folklore.

FICTION Young reader, middle readers, young adults: biography, history, multicultural, Hawaiian folklore.

TIPS "Writers and illustrators must be knowledgeable in Hawaiian history/culture and be able to show credentials to validate their proficiency. Greatly prefer to work with writers/illustrators available in the Honolulu area."

ⒶKANE/MILLER BOOK PUBLISHERS

Kane/Miller: A Division of EDC Publishing, 4901 Morena Blvd., Suite 213, San Diego CA 92117. (858)456-0540. **Fax:** (858)456-9641. **E-mail:** submissions@kanemiller.com. **Website:** www.kanemiller.com. **Contact:** Editorial Department. Estab. 1985. "Kane/Miller Book Publishers is a division of EDC Publishing, specializing in award-winning children's books from around the world. Our books bring the children of the world closer to each other, sharing stories and ideas, while exploring cultural differences and similarities. Although we continue to look for books from other countries, we are now actively seeking works that convey cultures and communities within the US. We are looking for picture book fiction and nonfiction on those subjects that may be defined as particularly American: sports such as baseball, historical events, American biographies, American folk tales, etc. We are committed to expanding our early and middlegrade fiction list. We're interested in great stories with engaging characters in all genres (mystery, fantasy, adventure, historical, etc.) and, as with picture books, especially those with particularly American subjects. All submissions sent via USPS should be sent to: Editorial Department. Please do not send anything requiring a signature. Work submitted for consideration may also be sent via e-mail. Please send either the complete picture book ms, the published book (with a summary and outline in English, if that is not the language of origin) or a synopsis of the work and two sample chapters. Do not send originals. Illustrators may send color copies, tear sheets, or other non-returnable illustration samples. If you have

a website with additional samples of your work, please include the web address. Please do not send original artwork, or samples on CD. A SASE must be included if you send your submission via USPS; otherwise you will not receive a reply. If we wish to follow up, we will notify you." Responds in 90 days to queries.

NONFICTION Subjects include Americana, history, sports, young adult.

FICTION Subjects include adventure, fantasy, historical, juvenile, mystery, picture books. Picture Books: concept, contemporary, health, humor, multicultural. Young Readers: contemporary, multicultural, suspense. Middle Readers: contemporary, humor, multicultural, suspense.

KAR-BEN PUBLISHING

Lerner Publishing Group, 241 First Ave., N, Minneapolis MN 55401. (612)215-6229. **Fax:** 612-332-7615. **E-mail:** Editorial@Karben.com. **Website:** www.karben.com. Estab. 1974. Publishes hardcover, trade paperback and electronic originals. **Publishes 10-15 titles/year. 800 mss received/year. 20% of books from first-time authors. 70% from unagented writers. Pays 5% royalty on NET sale. Pays $500-2,500 advance.** Publishes book Most mss published within 2 years. after acceptance of ms. Accepts simultaneous submissions. Responds in 6 weeks. Book catalog available online; free upon request. Guidelines online.

NONFICTION Subjects include Jewish content children's books only. "In addition to traditional Jewish-themed stories about Jewish holidays, history, folktales and other subjects, we especially seek stories that reflect the rich diversity of the contemporary Jewish community." Picture books, young readers: activity books, arts/crafts, biography, careers, concept, cooking, history, how-to, multicultural, religion, social issues, special needs; must be of Jewish interest. No textbooks, games, or educational materials. Submit completed ms. Reviews artwork separately. Works with 10-12 illustrators/year. Prefers four-color art in any medium that is scannable. Reviews illustration packages from artists. Submit sample of art or online portfolio (no originals).

FICTION Subjects include juvenile; Jewish content only. "We seek picture book mss of about 1,000 words on Jewish-themed topics for children." Picture books: Adventure, concept, folktales, history, humor, multicultural, religion, special needs; must be on a Jewish theme. Average word length: picture books–1,000. Recently published titles: *The Count's Hanukkah Countdown, Sammy Spider's First Book of Jewish Holidays, The Cats of Ben Yehuda Street.* Submit full ms. Picture books only.

TIPS "Authors: Do a literature search to make sure similar title doesn't already exist. Illustrators: Look at our online catalog for a sense of what we like—bright colors and lively composition."

KELLY POINT PUBLISHING LLC

Martin Sisters Publishing LLC, P.O. Box 1154, Barbourville KY 40906. **E-mail:** publisher@kellypointpublishing.com. **E-mail:** submissions@kellypointpublishing.com. **Website:** www.kellypointpublishing.com. **Contact:** Melissa Newman, publisher. Estab. 2012. Publishes trade paperback, mass market, and electronic originals. Subsidiary of Martin Sisters Publishing LLC. **Publishes 12 titles/year. Receives 100 queries/year; 30 mss/year. 75% of books from first-time authors. 100% from unagented writers. Pays 7.5% royalty on retail price.** Publishes book 3-6 months after acceptance. Accepts simultaneous submissions. Responds in 1 month to queries; 2 months to proposals; 4 months to mss. Book catalog online. Guidelines available online or by e-mail.

IMPRINTS Kelly Point Books, KP Mystery, KP Romance.

◯ *All unsolicited mss returned unopened.*

NONFICTION Subjects include memoirs, young adult. "While Kelly Point Publishing focuses mainly on publishing fiction, we do look at a few memoirs and self-help mss if they are well written and researched." Query with SASE.

FICTION Subjects include adventure, contemporary, historical, humor, juvenile, literary, mainstream, mystery, romance, science fiction, short story collections, spiritual, sports, western, young adult, women's fiction, chick lit. "Please visit our website and read the submissions guidelines for aspiring authors before submitting your query." Query with SASE.

TIPS "Write a good query letter with a hook and follow the submissions guidelines on our website."

▲⊘ KENSINGTON PUBLISHING CORP.

850 Third Ave., 16th Floor, New York NY 10022. (212)407-1500. **Fax:** (212)935-0699. **Website:** www.kensingtonbooks.com. **Contact:** John Scognamiglio, editorial director, fiction (historical romance, Regency romance, women's contemporary fiction, gay and lesbian fiction and nonfiction, mysteries, suspense, mainstream fiction); Michaela Hamilton, editor-in-chief, Citadel Press (thrillers, mysteries, mainstream fiction, true crime, current events); Kate Duffy, editorial director, romance and women's fiction (historical romance, Regency romance, Brava erotic romance, women's contemporary fiction); Audrey LaFehr, editorial director (women's fiction, romance, romantic suspense, thrillers, erotica); Selena James, executive editor, Dafina Books (African American fiction and nonfiction, inspirational, young adult, romance); Gary Goldstein, senior editor (westerns, true crime, military, sports, how-to, narrative nonfiction); Richard Ember, editor, Citadel Press (biography, film, sports, New Age, spirituality); Danielle Chiotti, senior editor (Dating and relationships, pop culture, humor, women's issues, careers, memoirs, narrative nonfiction, biography, weddings, general self help, Contemporary women's fiction, romance, young adult); Mike Shohl, editor (pop culture, entertainment, music, male interest, fratire, sports, popular science/popular psychology, humor, martial arts, true crime); Peter Senftleben, assistant editor (mainstream fiction, women's contemporary fiction, gay and lesbian fiction, mysteries, suspense, thrillers, romantic suspense, paranormal romance). Estab. 1975. Publishes hardcover and trade paperback originals, mass market paperback originals and reprints. "Kensington focuses on profitable niches and uses aggressive marketing techniques to support its books." **Publishes over 500 titles/year. 5,000 queries received/year. 2,000 mss received/year. 10% of books from first-time authors. Pays 6-15% royalty on retail price. Makes outright purchase. Pays $2,000 and up advance.** Publishes book 9-12 months after acceptance of ms. Accepts simultaneous submissions. Responds in 1 month to queries and proposals. Responds in 4 months to mss. Book catalog online.

IMPRINTS Kensington Books; Brava Books; Citadel Press; Dafina Books; Pinnacle Books; Zebra Books.

◯ Kensington recently purchased the assets of Carol Publishing Group.

NONFICTION Subjects include alternative, Americana, animals, business, economics, child guidance, contemporary culture, cooking, foods, nutrition, gay, lesbian, health, medicine, history, hobbies, memoirs, military, war, money, finance, multicultural, nature, environment, philosophy, psychology, recreation, regional, sex, sports, travel, true crime, pop culture.

Agented submissions only. *No unsolicited mss.* Reviews artwork/photos. Send photocopies.

FICTION Subjects include ethnic, gay, lesbian, historical, horror, mainstream, multicultural, mystery, occult, romance, contemporary, historical, regency, suspense, western, epic, thrillers, women's. No science fiction/fantasy, experimental fiction, business texts or children's titles. Agented submissions only. *No unsolicited mss.*

TIPS "Agented submissions only, except for submissions to romance lines. For those lines, query with SASE or submit proposal package including 3 sample chapters, synopsis."

KENT STATE UNIVERSITY PRESS

P.O. Box 5190, 1118 University Library, 1125 Risman Dr., Kent OH 44242-0001. (330)672-8099. **Fax:** (330)672-3104. **E-mail:** ksupress@kent.edu. **Website:** www.kentstateuniversitypress.com. **Contact:** Joyce Harrison, acquiring editor. Estab. 1965. Publishes hardcover and paperback originals and some reprints. "Kent State publishes primarily scholarly works and titles of regional interest. Currently emphasizing US history, US literary criticism." **Publishes 30-35 titles/year. Non-author subsidy publishes 20% of books. Standard minimum book contract on net sales.** Responds in 4 months to queries. Book catalog available free.

NONFICTION Subjects include anthropology, archeology, art, architecture, history, language, literature, literary criticism, regional, true crime, literary criticism, material culture, textile/fashion studies, US foreign relations. "Especially interested in scholarly works in history (US and world) and US literary studies of high quality, any titles of regional interest for Ohio, scholarly biographies and general nonfiction. Send a letter of inquiry before submitting mss. Decisions based on in-house readings and 2 by outside scholars in the field of study." Please, no faxes, phone calls, or e-mail submissions. For your convenience, the Press provides the following downloadable guidelines in PDF format: Electronic Ms Guidelines for Authors, Illustration Submission Guidelines for Authors, Copyright Guidelines for Authors. Enclose return postage.

KIDS CAN PRESS

25 Dockside Dr., Toronto ON M5A 0B5, Canada. (416)479-7000. **Fax:** (416)960-5437. **E-mail:** info@kidscan.com; kkalmar@kidscan.com. **Website:** www.kidscanpress.com. **Contact:** Corus Quay, acquisitions. Estab. 1973. Publishes book 18-24 months after acceptance. Responds in 6 months only if interesed.

○ *Kids Can Press is currently accepting unsolicited mss from Canadian adult authors only.*

NONFICTION Picture books: activity books, animal, arts/crafts, biography, careers, concept, health, history, hobbies, how-to, multicultural, nature/environment, science, social issues, special needs, sports. Young readers: activity books, animal, arts/crafts, biography, careers, concept, history, hobbies, how-to, multicultural. Middle readers: cooking, music/dance. Average word length: picture books 500-1,250; young readers 750-2,000; middle readers 5,000-15,000. Submit outline/synopsis and 2-3 sample chapters. For picture books submit complete ms.

FICTION Picture books, young readers: concepts. "We do not accept young adult fiction or fantasy novels for any age." Adventure, animal, contemporary, folktales, history, humor, multicultural, nature/environment, special needs, sports, suspense/mystery. Average word length: picture books 1,000-2,000; young readers 750-1,500; middle readers 10,000-15,000; young adults over 15,000. Submit outline/synopsis and 2-3 sample chapters. For picture books submit complete ms.

○ KINDRED PRODUCTIONS

1310 Taylor Ave., Winnipeg MB R3M 3Z6, Canada. (204)669-6575. **Fax:** (204)654-1865. **E-mail:** kindred@mbconf.ca. **Website:** www.kindredproductions.com. **Contact:** Renita Kornelsen, acquisitions. Publishes trade paperback originals and reprints. "Kindred Productions publishes, promotes, and markets print and nonprint resources that will shape our Christian faith and discipleship from a Mennonite Brethren perspective. Currently emphasizing Mennonite Brethren Resources. De-emphasizing personal experience, biographical. No children's books or fiction." **Publishes 3 titles/year. 1% of books from first-time authors. 100% from unagented writers.** Publishes book 18 months after acceptance. Accepts simultaneous submissions. Responds in 3 months to queries; 5 months to mss. Guidelines available by e-mail request.

NONFICTION Subjects include religion, historical. "Our books cater primarily to our Mennonite Brethren denomination readers." Query with SASE. Submit outline, 2-3 sample chapters.

TIPS "Most of our books are sold to churches, religious bookstores, and schools. We are concentrating on books with a Mennonite Brethren perspective. We do not accept children's mss."

KIRKBRIDE BIBLE CO. INC.

1102 Deloss St., Indianapolis IN 46203. (800)428-4385. **Fax:** (317)633-1444. **E-mail:** info@kirkbride.com. **Website:** www.kirkbride.com. Estab. 1915. Publishes Thompson Chain-Reference Bible hardcover originals and quality leather bindings styles and translations of the Bible. Types of books include reference and religious. Specializes in reference and study material.

Ⓐ ALFRED A. KNOPF

Imprint of Random House, 1745 Broadway, New York NY 10019. **Website:** knopfdoubleday.com/imprint/knopf. **Contact:** The Editors. Estab. 1915. Publishes hardcover and paperback originals. **Publishes 200 titles/year. Royalties vary. Offers advance.** Publishes book 1 year after acceptance. Responds in 2-6 months to queries.

NONFICTION Usually only accepts mss submitted by agents. However, writers may submit sample 25-50 pages with SASE.

FICTION Publishes book-length fiction of literary merit by known or unknown writers. Length: 40,000-150,000 words. Usually only accepts mss submitted by agents. However, writers may submit sample 25-50 pages with SASE.

KNOPF PUBLISHING GROUP

Imprint of Random House, 1745 Broadway, New York NY 10019. (212)751-2600. **Website:** knopfdoubleday.com/imprint/knopf. **Contact:** The Editors. Estab. 1915. Publishes hardcover and paperback originals.

IMPRINTS Alfred A. Knopf; Everyman's Library; Pantheon Books; Schocken Books; Vintage Anchor Publishing (Vintage Books, Anchor Books); Doubleday; Black Lizard; Nan A. Talese.

◯   Knopf is a general publisher of quality nonfiction and fiction. "We usually only accept work through an agent, but you may still send a query to our slush pile."

NONFICTION Usually only accepts mss submitted by agents. However, writers may submit sample 25-50 pages with SASE.

FICTION Publishes book-length fiction of literary merit by known or unknown writers. Length: 40,000-150,000 words. Usually only accepts mss submitted by agents. However, writers may submit sample 25-50 pages with SASE.

KNOX ROBINSON PUBLISHING

244 Fifth Ave., Suite 1861, New York NY 10001. **E-mail:** subs@knoxrobinsonpublishing.com. **Website:** www.knoxrobinsonpublishing.com. **Contact:** Dana Celeste Robinson, managing director (historical fiction, historical romance, fantasy). Estab. 2010. Knox Robinson Publishing is an international, independent, specialist publisher of historical fiction, historical romance and fantasy. **Publishes 5 titles/year. Pays royalty.** Accepts simultaneous submissions. Responds in 2 months to submissions of first 3 chapters. "We do not accept proposals.". Guidelines free on request.

◯   "KRP publishes historical fiction and historical romance; any story set in an era prior to 1960 is acceptable. We also publish medieval fantasy. We do not publish science fiction. We do not publish fantasy with children and/or animal protagonists. We do not publish novels that involve any aspects of time travel. We welcome the submission of a well-written, detailed synopsis and the first 3 chapters of completed mss directly from authors."

NONFICTION Subjects include history, humanities, religion, general nonfiction, scholarly, history monographs. "Our goal is to publish history books, monographs and historical fiction that satisfies history buffs and encourages general readers to learn more." Submit first 3 chapters and author questionnaire found on website. Reviews artwork/photos. Send photocopies. Does not accept printed submissions; electronic only.

FICTION Subjects include historical, romance. "We are seeking historical fiction featuring obscure historical figures." Submit first 3 chapters and author questionnaire found on website.

KRAUSE PUBLICATIONS

A Division of F+W Media, Inc., 700 E. State St., Iola WI 54990. (715)445-2214. **Fax:** (715)445-4087. **Website:** www.krausebooks.com. **Contact:** Paul Kennedy (antiques and collectibles, music, sports, militaria, humor, numismatics); Corrina Peterson (firearms); Brian Lovett (outdoors); Brian Earnest (automotive). Publishes hardcover and trade paperback originals. "We are the world's largest hobby and collectibles publisher." **Publishes 80 titles/year. 200 queries received/year. 150 mss received/year. 50% of books from first-time authors. 95% from unagented writ-**

ers. **Pays advance. Photo budget.** Publishes book 18 months after acceptance. Responds in 3 months to proposals; 2 months to mss. Book catalog for free or on website. Guidelines available free upon request.

NONFICTION Submit proposal package, including outline, TOC, a sample chapter, and letter explaining your project's unique contributions. Reviews artwork/photos. Accepts only digital photography. Send sample photos.

TIPS Audience consists of serious hobbyists. "Your work should provide a unique contribution to the special interest."

⊘ KREGEL PUBLICATIONS

Kregel, Inc., P.O. Box 2607, Grand Rapids MI 49501. (616)451-4775. **Fax:** (616)451-9330. **E-mail:** kregelbooks@kregel.com. **Website:** www.kregelpublications.com. **Contact:** Dennis R. Hillman, publisher. Estab. 1949. Publishes hardcover and trade paperback originals and reprints. "Our mission as an evangelical Christian publisher is to provide—with integrity and excellence—trusted, Biblically based resources that challenge and encourage individuals in their Christian lives. Works in theology and Biblical studies should reflect the historic, orthodox Protestant tradition." **Publishes 90 titles/year. 20% of books from first-time authors. 35% from unagented writers. Pays royalty on wholesale price. Pays negotiable advance.** Publishes book 16 months after acceptance. Guidelines online.

IMPRINTS Editorial Portavoz (Spanish-language works); Kregel Academic & Professional; Kregel Kidzone.

○ Finds works through The Writer's Edge and Christian Ms Submissions ms screening services.

NONFICTION "We serve evangelical Christian readers and those in career Christian service."

FICTION Subjects include religious, children's, general, inspirational, mystery/suspense, relationships, young adult. Fiction should be geared toward the evangelical Christian market. Wants books with fast-paced, contemporary storylines presenting a strong Christian message in an engaging, entertaining style.

TIPS "Our audience consists of conservative, evangelical Christians, including pastors and ministry students."

KRIEGER PUBLISHING CO.

P.O. Box 9542, Melbourne FL 32902-9542. (321)724-9542. **Fax:** (321)951-3671. **E-mail:** info@krieger-pub-

lishing.com. **Website:** www.krieger-publishing.com. **Contact:** Sharan B. Merriam and Ronald M. Cervero, series editor (adult education); David E. Kyvig, series director (local history); James B. Gardner, series editor (public history). Also publishes in the fields of natural sciences, history and space sciences. Estab. 1969. Publishes hardcover and paperback originals and reprints. "We are a short-run niche publisher providing accurate and well-documented scientific and technical titles for text and reference use, college level and higher." **Publishes 30 titles/year. 30% of books from first-time authors. 100% from unagented writers. Pays royalty on net price.** Publishes book 9-18 months after acceptance of ms. Responds in 3 months to queries. Book catalog available free.

IMPRINTS Anvil Series; Orbit Series; Public History; Professional Practices in Adult Education and Lifelong Learning Series.

NONFICTION Subjects include agriculture, animals, education, adult, history, nature, environment, science, space, herpetology. Query with SASE. Reviews artwork/photos.

LAKE CLAREMONT PRESS

P.O. Box 711, Chicago IL 60690. (312)226-8400. **Fax:** (312)226-8420. **E-mail:** sharon@lakeclaremont.com. **Website:** www.lakeclaremont.com. **Contact:** Sharon Woodhouse, publisher. Estab. 1994. Publishes trade paperback originals. "We specialize in nonfiction books on the Chicago area and its history, particularly by authors with a passion or organizations with a mission." **Publishes 2-3 titles/year. 250 queries received/year. 100 mss received/year. 50% of books from first-time authors. 100% from unagented writers. Pays 10-15% royalty on net sales. Pays $500-1,000 advance.** Publishes book 12-18 months after acceptance. Accepts simultaneous submissions. Responds in 1 month to queries; 2 months to proposals; 2-6 months to mss. Book catalog online.

NONFICTION Subjects include Americana, ethnic, history, nature, environment, regional, travel, women's issues, film/cinema/stage (regional)—as long as it is primarily a Chicago book. Query with SASE, or submit proposal package, including outline and 2 sample chapters, or submit complete ms (e-mail queries and proposals preferred).

TIPS "Please include a market analysis in proposals (who would buy this book and where) and an analysis of similar books available for different regions. Please know what else is out there."

LAPWING PUBLICATIONS

1 Ballysillan Dr., Belfast BT14 8HQ, Northern Ireland. +44 2890 500 796. **Fax:** +44 2890 295 800. **E-mail:** lapwing.poetry@ntlworld.com. **Website:** www.lapwingpoetry.com. **Contact:** Dennis Greig, editor. Estab. 1989. **Pays 20 author's copies, no royalties.** Responds to queries in 1 month; mss in 2 months.

Lapwing will produce work only if and when resources to do so are available.

POETRY Lapwing publishes "emerging Irish poets and poets domiciled in Ireland, plus the new work of a suitable size by established Irish writers. Non-Irish poets are also published. Poets based in continental Europe have become a major feature. Emphasis on first collections preferrably not larger than 80 pages. Logistically, publishing beyond the British Isles is always difficult for 'hard copy' editions. PDF copies via e-mail are £3 or 3€ per copy. No fixed upperl limit to number of titles per year. Hard copy prices are £8 to £10 per copy. No e-reader required." Wants poetry of all kinds, but, "no crass political, racist, sexist propaganda, even of a positive or 'pc' tenor." Has published Alastair Thomson, Clifford Ireson, Colette Wittorski, Gilberte de Leger, Aubrey Malone, and Jane Shaw Holiday. Pamphlets up to 32 pages, chapbooks up to 44 pages, books 48-112 pages; New Belfast binding, simulated perfect binding for books, otherwise saddle stitching. "Submit 6 poems in the first instance; depending on these, an invitation to submit more may follow." Considers simultaneous submissions. Accepts e-mail submissions in body of message or in DOC format. Cover letter is required. "All submissions receive a first reading. If these poems have minor errors or faults, the writer is advised. If poor quality, the poems are returned. Those 'passing' first reading are retained, and a letter of conditional offer is sent." Often comments on rejected poems. "After initial publication, irrespective of the quantity, the work will be permanently available using 'print-on-demand' production; such publications will not always be printed exactly as the original, although the content will remain the same."

TIPS "At present we are unable to accept new work from beyond mainland Europe and the British Isles due to increased delivery costs."

LAUREL-LEAF

Imprint of Random House Children's Books/Random House, Inc., 1745 Broadway, New York NY 10019. (212)782-9000. **Website:** www.randomhouse.com/teens.

Quality reprint paperback imprint for young adult paperback books. *Does not accept unsolicited mss.*

LEDGE HILL PUBLISHING

P.O. Box 337, Alton NH 03809. **E-mail:** info@ledgehillpublishing.com. **Website:** www.ledgehillpublishing.com. **Contact:** Amanda Eason. Estab. 2011. Publishes hardcover, trade paperback, and mass market paperback originals. **Publishes 10-15 titles/year. 20-40 queries received/year. 15-30 mss received/year. 100% of books from first-time authors. 100% from unagented writers. Pays 2-15% royalty.** Publishes book 3 months after acceptance. Responds in 1 month to queries and proposals; 2 months to mss. Book catalog online. Guidelines free on request by e-mail or online.

NONFICTION Subjects include agriculture, animals, anthropology, archeology, astrology, automotive, career guidance, child guidance, contemporary culture, crafts, creative nonfiction, education, entertainment, environment, ethnic, games, gardening, health, history, hobbies, horticulture, humanities, marine subjects, medicine, memoirs, nature, New Age, sex, social sciences, womens issues, womens studies, young adult. Submit proposal package including an outline, 3 sample chapters or submit complete ms. Reviews artwork. Send photocopies or compressed .jpegs.

FICTION Subjects include adventure, confession, contemporary, experimental, hi-lo, humor, juvenile, literary, mainstream, mystery, occult, picture books, poetry, regional, religious, science fiction, short story collections, spiritual, suspense, young adult. Submit proposal package, including syopsis and 4 sample chapters or submit complete ms.

POETRY Submit complete ms.

LEE & LOW BOOKS

95 Madison Ave., #1205, New York NY 10016. (212)779-4400. **E-mail:** general@leeandlow.com. **Website:** www.leeandlow.com. **Contact:** Louise May, editor-in-chief (multicultural children's fiction/nonfiction). Jennifer Fox, senior editor; Emily Hazel, assistant editor Estab. 1991. Publishes hardcover originals and trade paperback reprints. "Our goals are to

meet a growing need for books that address children of color, and to present literature that all children can identify with. We only consider multicultural children's books. Currently emphasizing material for 5-12 year olds. Sponsors a yearly New Voices Award for first-time picture book authors of color. Contest rules online at website or for SASE." **Publishes 12-14 titles/year. Receives 100 queries/year; 1,200 mss/year. 20% of books from first-time authors. 50% from unagented writers. Pays net royalty. Pays authors advances against royalty. Pays illustrators advance against royalty. Photographers paid advance against royalty.** Publishes book 2 years after acceptance. Responds in 6 months to mss if interested. Book catalog online. Guidelines available online or by written request with SASE.

NONFICTION Picture books: concept. Picture books, middle readers: biography, history, multicultural, science and sports. Average word length: picture books-1,500-3,000. Submit complete ms. Reviews artwork/photos only if writer is also a professional illustrator or photographer. Send photocopies and nonreturnable art samples only.

FICTION Subjects include contemporary and historical fiction featuring people of color. Also accepts thematic or narrative poetry collections with a multicultural focus. Picture books, young readers: anthology, contemporary, history, multicultural, poetry. Picture book, middle reader: contemporary, history, multicultural, nature/environment, poetry, sports. Average word length: picture books—1,000-1,500 words. "We do not publish folklore or animal stories." Submit complete ms.

POETRY Submit complete ms.

TIPS "Check our website to see the kinds of books we publish. Do not send mss that don't fit our mission."

LEGACY PRESS

P.O. Box 261129, San Diego CA 92196. (858)277-1167. **E-mail:** john.gregory@rainbowpublishers.com. **Website:** www.rainbowpublishers.com Estab. 1979. Publishes 4 young readers/year; 4 middle readers/year; 4 young adult titles/year. 50% of books by first-time authors. "Our mission is to publish Bible-based, teacher resource materials that contribute to and inspire spiritual growth and development in kids ages 2-12." **For authors work purchased outright (range: $500 and up). Pays illustrators by the project (range: $300 and up). Sends galleys to authors.** Accepts simultaneous

submissions. Responds to queries in 6 weeks, mss in 3 months.

NONFICTION Young readers, middle readers, young adult/teens: activity books, arts/crafts, how-to, reference, religion. Works with 10 illustrators/year. Reviews ms/illustration packages from artists. Submit ms with 2-5 pieces of final art. Illustrations only: Query with samples. Responds in 6 weeks. Samples returned with SASE; samples filed.

TIPS "Our Rainbow imprint publishes reproducible books for teachers of children in Christian ministries, including crafts, activities, games and puzzles. Our Legacy imprint publishes titles for children such as devotionals, fiction and Christian living. Please see website and study the market before submitting material."

HAL LEONARD BOOKS

Hal Leonard Publishing Group, 33 Plymouth St.,, Suite 302, Montclair NJ 07042. (973)337-5034. **Fax:** (973)337-5227. **Website:** www.halleonardbooks.com. **Contact:** John Cerullo, publisher. **Publishes 30 titles/year.**

NONFICTION Subjects include music. Query with SASE.

LES FIGUES PRESS

P.O. Box 7736, Los Angeles CA 90007. **E-mail:** info@lesfigues.com. **Website:** www.lesfigues.com. **Contact:** Teresa Carmody and Vanessa Place, co-directors. Les Figues Press is an independent, nonprofit publisher of poetry, prose, visual art, conceptual writing, and translation. With amission is to create aesthetic conversations between readers, writers, and artists, Les Figues Press favors projects which push the boundaries of genre, form, and general acceptability. Submissions are only reviewed through its annual NOS Book Contest.

LETHE PRESS

118 Heritage Ave., Maple Shade NJ 08052. (609)410-7391. **E-mail:** editor@lethepressbooks.com. **Website:** www.lethepressbooks.com. **Contact:** Steve Berman, publisher. Estab. 2001. "Welcomes submissions from authors of any sexual or gender identity." Guidelines online.

NONFICTION Query via e-mail.

FICTION Subjects include gay, lesbian, occult, science fiction. "Named after the Greek river of memory and forgetfulness (and pronounced Lee-Thee), Lethe Press is a small press devoted to ideas that are often neglected or forgotten by mainstream, profit-oriented publishers." Distributes/promotes titles. Lethe Books are distributed by Ingram Publications and Bookazine, and are available at all major bookstores, as well as the major online retailers. Query via e-mail.

POETRY "Lethe Press is a small press seeking gay and lesbian themed poetry collections." Lethe Books are distributed by Ingram Publications and Bookazine, and are available at all major bookstores, as well as the major online retailers. Query with 7-10 poems, list of publications.

ARTHUR A. LEVINE BOOKS

Scholastic, Inc., 557 Broadway, New York NY 10012. (212)343-4436. **Fax:** (212)343-6143. **E-mail:** arthuralevinebooks@scholastic.com. **Website:** www.arthuralevinebooks.com. **Contact:** Arthur A. Levine, VP/publisher; Cheryl Klein, executive editor; Emily Clement, assistant editor. Estab. 1996. Publishes hardcover, paperback, and e-book editions. Imprint of Scholastic, Inc. Publishes book Publishes a book 18 months after acceptance. Responds in 1 month to queries; 5 months to mss. Guidelines online.

NONFICTION Please follow submission guidelines. Works with 8 illustrators/year. Will review ms/illustration packages from artists. Query first. Illustrations only: Send postcard sample with tearsheets. Samples not returned.

FICTION Subjects include juvenile, picture books, young adult. "Arthur A. Levine is looking for distinctive literature, for children and young adults, for whatever's extraordinary." Averages 18-20 total titles/year. Query.

LIFE CYCLE BOOKS

P.O. Box 799, Fort Collins CO 80522. **Website:** www.lifecyclebooks.com. **Contact:** Paul Broughton, general manager. Estab. 1973. Publishes trade paperback originals and reprints, and mass market reprints. **Publishes 6 titles/year. 100+ queries received/year. 50% of books from first-time authors. 100% from unagented writers. Pays 8-10% royalty on wholesale price. Pays $250-1,000 advance.** Publishes book 1 year after acceptance. Responds in 1 month. Book catalog online.

NONFICTION Subjects include health, medicine, religion, social sciences, womens issues, womens studies. "We specialize in human life issues." Query with SASE. Submit complete ms. Reviews artwork/photos.

LILLENAS PUBLISHING CO.

Imprint of Lillenas Drama Resources, P.O. Box 419527, Kansas City MO 64109. (816)931-1900. **Fax:** (816)412-8390. **E-mail:** drama@lillenas.com. **Website:** www.lillenasdrama.com. Publishes mass market paperback and electronic originals. "We purchase only original, previously unpublished materials. Also, we require that all scripts be performed at least once before it is submitted for consideration. We do not accept scripts that are sent via fax or e-mail. Direct all mss to the Drama Resources Editor." **Publishes 50+ titles/year. Pays royalty on net price. Makes outright purchase.** Responds in 4-6 months to material. Guidelines online.

NONFICTION Subjects include religion, life issues. No musicals. Query with SASE. Submit complete ms.

FICTION "Looking for sketch and monologue collections for all ages – adults, children and youth. For these collections, we request 12 - 15 scripts to be submitted at one time. Unique treatments of spiritual themes, relevant issues and biblical messages are of interest. Contemporary full-length and one-act plays that have conflict, characterization, and a spiritual context that is neither a sermon nor an apologetic for youth and adults. We also need wholesome so-called secular full-length scripts for dinner theatres and schools." No musicals.

TIPS "We never receive too many mss."

LINDEN PUBLISHING, INC.

2006 S. Mary, Fresno CA 93721. (559)233-6633. **Fax:** (559)233-6933. **E-mail:** richard@lindenpub.com. **Website:** www.lindenpub.com. **Contact:** Richard Sorsky, president; Kent Sorsky, vice president. Estab. 1976. Publishes trade paperback originals; hardcover and trade paperback reprints. **Publishes 10-12 titles/year. 30+ queries received/year. 5-15 mss received/year. 40% of books from first-time authors. 50% from unagented writers. Pays 7½ -12% royalty on wholesale price. Pays $500-6,000 advance.** Publishes book 18 months after acceptance. Responds in 1 month to queries and proposals. Book catalog online. Guidelines available via e-mail.

NONFICTION Subjects include history, regional, hobbies, woodworking, Regional California history. Submit proposal package, outline, 3 sample chapters, bio. Reviews artwork/photos. Send electronic files, if available.

R.C. LINNELL PUBLISHING

2100 Tyler Ln., Louisville KY 40205. **E-mail:** info@ LinnellPublishing.com. **Website:** www.linnellpublishing.com. **Contact:** Cheri Powell, owner. Estab. 2010. Publishes print on demand paperbacks. "We are currently very small and have published a limited number of books. We would review books on other subjects on a case-by-case basis. If a book is well-written and has an audience we would consider it." **Publishes 3 titles/year. 5 queries received/year. 5 mss received/year. 83% of books from first-time authors. 100% from unagented writers. Pays 10-40% royalty on retail price.** Publishes book 3 months after acceptance. Accepts simultaneous submissions. Responds in 1 month to mss. Book catalog and guidelines online.

NONFICTION Subjects include alternative lifestyles, Americana, astrology, career guidance, contemporary culture, cooking, counseling, creative nonfiction, ethnic, foods, language, literature, memoirs, multicultural, New Age, philosophy, psychic, psychology, regional, religion, sociology, spirituality, translation, travel, womens issues, womens studies, young adult. Submit complete ms.

FICTION Subjects include adventure, confession, contemporary, experimental, fantasy, feminist, gay, gothic, hi-lo, historical, humor, lesbian, literary, mainstream, multicultural, mystery, occult, regional, religious, romance, science fiction, short story collections, spiritual, suspense, translation, western, young adult. Submit complete ms.

TIPS "Visit our website to understand the business model and the relationship with authors. All sales are through the internet. Author should have a marketing plan in mind. We can help expand the plan but we do not market books. Author should be comfortable with using the internet and should know their intended readers. We offer translation services for English to Spanish and Spanish to English. We are especially interested in books that inspire, motivate, amuse and challenge readers."

LIQUID SILVER BOOKS

10509 Sedgegrass Dr., Indianapolis IN 46235. **E-mail:** acquisitions@liquidsilverbooks.com. **Website:** www. lsbooks.com. **Contact:** Tracey West, acquisitions editor; Terri Schaefer, editorial director. Estab. 1999. Liquid Silver Books is an imprint of Atlantic Bridge Publishing, a royalty paying, full-service ePublisher. Atlantic Bridge has been in business since June 1999. Liquid Silver Books is dedicated to bringing high quality erotic romance to our readers. Liquid Silver Books, Romance's Silver Lining. Publishes book 4-5 months after acceptance. Accepts simultaneous submissions. Responds to mss in 4-6 weeks.

"We are foremost an ePublisher. We believe the market will continue to grow for eBooks. It is our prime focus. At this time our print publishing is on hiatus. We will update the submission guidelines if we reinstate this aspect of our publishing."

FICTION Needs contemporary, gay and lesbian, paranormal, supernatural, sci-fi, fantasy, historical, suspense, and western romances. "We do not accept literary erotica submissions." E-mail entire ms as an attachment in .RTF format in Arial 12 pt. "Include in the body of the e-mail: author bio, your thoughts on ePublishing, a blurb of your book, including title and series title if applicable. Ms must include Pen name, real name, snail mail and e-mail contact information on the first page, top left corner."

LISTEN & LIVE AUDIO

1700 Manhattan Ave., Union City NJ 07087. **E-mail:** alfred@listenandlive.com. **Website:** www.listenandlive.com. **Contact:** Alfred C. Martino, president. Independent audiobook publisher. "We also license audiobooks for the download market. We specialize in the following genres: fiction, mystery, nonfiction, self-help, business, children's, and teen." **Publishes 10+ titles/year.** Catalog online.

LITTLE, BROWN AND CO. ADULT TRADE BOOKS

237 Park Ave., New York NY 10017. **E-mail:** publicity@littlebrown.com. **Website:** www.hachettebookgroup.com. **Contact:** Michael Pietsch, publisher. Estab. 1837. Publishes hardcover originals and paperback originals and reprints. "The general editorial philosophy for all divisions continues to be broad and flexible, with high quality and the promise of commercial success as always the first considerations." **Publishes 100 titles/year. Pays royalty. Offer advance.** Guidelines online.

NONFICTION *Agented submissions only.*

FICTION Subjects include contemporary, literary, mainstream. *Agented submissions only.*

⊘ LITTLE, BROWN AND CO. BOOKS FOR YOUNG READERS

Hachette Book Group USA, 237 Park Ave., New York NY 10017. (212)364-1100. **Fax:** (212)364-0925. **E-mail:** pamela.gruber@hbgusa.com. **Website:** www.lb-kids.com; www.lb-teens.com. Estab. 1837. "Little, Brown and Co. Children's Publishing publishes all formats including board books, picture books, middle grade fiction, and nonfiction YA titles. We are looking for strong writing and presentation, but no predetermined topics." *Only interested in solicited agented material.* **Publishes 100-150 titles/year. Pays authors royalties based on retail price. Pays illustrators and photographers by the project or royalty based on retail price. Sends galleys to authors; dummies to illustrators. Pays negotiable advance.** Publishes book 2 years after acceptance. Accepts simultaneous submissions. Responds in 1 month to queries; 2 months to proposals and mss.

NONFICTION Subjects include animals, art, architecture, ethnic, gay, lesbian, history, hobbies, nature, environment, recreation, science, sports. Writers should avoid looking for the 'issue' they think publishers want to see, choosing instead topics they know best and are most enthusiastic about/inspired by. Middle readers, young adults: arts/crafts, history, multicultural, nature, self help, social issues, sports, science. Average word length: middle readers—15,000-25,000; young adults—20,000-40,000. *Agented submissions only.*

FICTION Subjects include adventure, fantasy, feminist, gay, lesbian, historical, humor, mystery, science fiction, suspense, chick lit, multicultural. Picture books: humor, adventure, animal, contemporary, history, multicultural, folktales. Young adults: contemporary, humor, multicultural, suspense/mystery, chick lit. Multicultural needs include "any material by, for and about minorities." Average word length: picture books—1,000; young readers—6,000; middle readers—15,000- 50,000; young adults—50,000 and up. *Agented submissions only.*

TIPS "In order to break into the field, authors and illustrators should research their competition and try to come up with something outstandingly different."

⊘ LITTLE SIMON

Imprint of Simon & Schuster Children's Publishing Division, Simon & Schuster, 1230 Avenue of the Americas, New York NY 10020. (212)698-1295. **Fax:** (212)698-2794. **Website:** www.simonsayskids.com. Publishes novelty and branded books only. "Our goal is to provide fresh material in an innovative format for preschool to age 8. Our books are often, if not exclusively, format driven." **Offers advance and royalties.** Currently not accepting unsolicited mss.

NONFICTION "We publish very few nonfiction titles." No picture books. Query with SASE.

FICTION Novelty books include many things that do not fit in the traditional hardcover or paperback format, such as pop-up, board book, scratch and sniff, glow in the dark, lift the flap, etc. Children's/juvenile. No picture books. Large part of the list is holiday-themed.

🐾 LITTLE TIGER PRESS

1 The Coda Centre, 189 Munster Rd., London En SW6 6AW, United Kingdom. (44)20-7385 6333. **E-mail:** info@littletiger.co.uk; malperin@littletiger.co.uk. **Website:** www.littletigerpress.com.

FICTION Picture books: animal, concept, contemporary, humor. Average word length: picture books—750 words or less.

TIPS "Every reasonable care is taken of the mss and samples we receive, but we cannot accept responsibility for any loss or damage. Try to read or look at as many books on the Little Tiger Press list before sending in your material. Refer to our website for further details."

⊘ LIVINGSTON PRESS

University of West Alabama, Station 22, Livingston AL 35470. **E-mail:** jwt@uwa.edu. **Website:** www.livingstonpress.uwa.edu. **Contact:** Joe Taylor, director. Estab. 1974. Publishes hardcover and trade paperback originals. "Livingston Press, as do all literary presses, looks for authorial excellence in style. Currently emphasizing novels." No open reading period. Check back for details. **Publishes 10-12 titles/year. 50% of books from first-time authors. 100% from unagented writers. Pays 150 contributor's copies, after sales of 1,500, standard royalty.** Publishes book 18 months after acceptance. Accepts simultaneous submissions. Responds in 1 month to queries; 6-12 months to mss. Book catalog for SASE. Guidelines online.

IMPRINTS Swallow's Tale Press.

FICTION Subjects include experimental, literary, short story collections, off-beat or Southern. "We are interested in form and, of course, style."

TIPS "Our readers are interested in literature, often quirky literature that emphasizes form and style. Please visit our website for current needs."

LLEWELLYN PUBLICATIONS

Imprint of Llewellyn Worldwide, Ltd., 2143 Wooddale Dr., Woodbury MN 55125. (651)291-1970. **Fax:** (651)291-1908. **E-mail:** submissions@llewellyn.com. **Website:** www.llewellyn.com. Estab. 1901. Publishes trade and mass market paperback originals. "Llewellyn publishes New Age fiction and nonfiction exploring new worlds of mind and spirit. Currently emphasizing astrology, alternative health and healing, tarot. De-emphasizing fiction, channeling." **Publishes 100+ titles/year. 30% of books from first-time authors. 50% from unagented writers. Pays 10% royalty on wholesale or retail price.** Accepts simultaneous submissions. Responds in 3 months to queries. Book catalog for 9 x 12 SAE with 4 first-class stamps. **NONFICTION** Subjects include cooking, foods, nutrition, health, medicine, nature, environment, New Age, psychology, women's issues, women's studies. Submit outline, sample chapters. Reviews artwork/photos.

LONELY PLANET PUBLICATIONS

150 Linden St., Oakland CA 94607-2538. (510)893-8555. **Fax:** (510)893-8563. **E-mail:** info@lonelyplanet.com. **Website:** www.lonelyplanet.com. Estab. 1973. Publishes trade paperback originals. "Lonely Planet publishes travel guides, atlases, travel literature, phrasebooks, condensed pocket guides, diving and snorkeling guides." **Work-for-hire: on contract, 1/3 on submission, 1/3 on approval Pays advance.** Accepts simultaneous submissions. Responds in 3 months to queries. Catalog and guidelines online. **NONFICTION** Subjects include travel. Request our catalog first to make sure we don't already have a similar book or call and see if a similar book is on our production schedule. "We only work with contract writers on book ideas that we originate. We do not accept original proposals. Request our writer's guidelines. Send résumé and clips of travel writing." Query with SASE.

LOOSE ID

P.O. Box 425690, San Francisco CA 94142-5960. **E-mail:** submissions@loose-id.com. **Website:** www.loose-id.com. **Contact:** Treva Harte, editor-in-chief. Estab. 2004. "*Loose Id* is love unleashed. We're taking romance to the edge." Publishes e-books and some print books. Distributes/promotes titles. "The company promotes itself through web and print advertising wherever readers of erotic romance may be found, creating a recognizable brand identity as the place to let your id run free and the people who unleash your fantasies. It is currently pursuing licensing agreements for foreign translations, and has a print program of 2 to 5 titles per month." **Pays e-book royalties of 40%.** Publishes book within 1 year after acceptance. Responds to queries in 1 month. Guidelines online.

"Loose Id is actively acquiring stories from both aspiring and established authors."

FICTION Wants nontraditional erotic romance stories, including gay, lesbian, heroes and heroines, multi-culturalism, cross-genre, fantasy, and science fiction, straight contemporary or historical romances. Query with outline/synopsis and 3 sample chapters. Accepts queries by e-mail. Include estimated word count, list of publishing credits, and why your submission is love unleashed. "Before submitting a query or proposal, please read the guidelines on our website. Please don't hesitate to contact us by e-mail for any information you don't see there."

LOST HORSE PRESS

105 Lost Horse Lane, Sandpoint ID 83864. (208)255-4410. **E-mail:** losthorsepress@mindspring.com. **Website:** www.losthorsepress.org. **Contact:** Christine Holbert, publisher; Carolyne Wright, editor; Christi Kramer, editor. Estab. 1998. Publishes hardcover and paperback originals. Distributed by University of Washington Press. **Publishes 8-10 titles/year.** Publishes book 6-12 months after acceptance.

"*Does not accept unsolicited mss.* However, we welcome submissions for the *Idaho Prize for Poetry*, a national competition offering $1,000 prize money plus publication for a book-length ms. Please check the submission guidelines for the *Idaho Prize for Poetry* online."

FICTION Subjects include literary, poetry, regional, Pacific Northwest, short story collections.

LOUISIANA STATE UNIVERSITY PRESS

3990 W. Lakeshore Dr., Baton Rouge LA 70808. (225)578-6294. **Fax:** (225)578-6461. **E-mail:** mkc@lsu.edu. **Website:** www.lsupress.org. **Contact:** MK Callaway, director. John Easterly, executive editor (poetry, fiction, literary studies); Rand Dotson, senior editor (U.S. History & Southern Studies). Estab. 1935. Publishes hardcover and paperback originals, and reprints. Publishes 8 poetry titles per year and 2 works of original fiction as part of the Yellow Shoe Fiction series. Publishes in the fall and spring. **Publishes 80-90 titles/year. 33% of books from first-time authors. 95% from unagented writers. Pays royalty.** Publishes book 1 year after acceptance. Responds in 1 month to queries. Book catalog and ms guidelines free and online.

NONFICTION Subjects include Americana, animals, anthropology, archeology, art, architecture, ethnic, government, politics, history, language, literature, literary criticism, memoirs, military, war, Civil & WWII, music, dance, Southern, Jazz, nature, environment, philosophy, Political, photography, regional, sociology, women's issues, women's studies, world affairs, geography and environmental studies. "We publish general interest books about Louisiana and the South, Atlantic and European and World History. Prizes are regularly awarded to LSU Press authors for the excellence of their general body of work. All books must undergo a rigorous approval process." Query with SASE. Submit proposal package, outline, sample chapters, cover letter, résumé. *No unsolicited submissions by e-mail attachment.*

FICTION Query with SASE. Submit proposal package, sample chapters, résumé, clips, and cover letter.

POETRY A highly respected publisher of collections by poets such as Claudia Emerson, David Kirby, Brendan Galvin, Fred Chappell, Marilyn Nelson, and Henry Taylor. Publisher of the Southern Messenger Poets series edited by Dave Smith." "No unsolicited poetry mss. for the foreseeable future. We have filled our slots until 2014."

⊘ LOVING HEALING PRESS INC.

5145 Pontiac Trail, Ann Arbor MI 48105. (888)761-6268. **Fax:** (734)663-6861. **E-mail:** info@lovinghealing.com. **Website:** www.lovinghealing.com. **Contact:** Victor R. Volkman, senior editor (psychology, self-help, personal growth, trauma recovery). Estab. 2003. Publishes hardcover and trade paperback originals and reprints. **Publishes 20 titles/year. Receives 200 queries/year; 100 mss/year. 50% of books from first-time authors. 80% from unagented writers. Pays 6-12% royalty on retail price.** Publishes book 10 months after acceptance. Accepts simultaneous submissions. Responds in 1 month on queries and proposals, 2 months on mss. Catalog online. Guidelines online.

IMPRINTS Modern History Press, Marvelous Spirit Press.

◖ *Currently not accepting mss.*

NONFICTION Subjects include child guidance, health, memoirs, psychology, social work. "We are primarily interested in self-help books which are person-centered and non-judgmental." Submit proposal package, including: outline, 3 sample chapters; submit complete ms. Reviews artwork/photos as part of the ms package; send JPEG files.

FICTION Subjects include multicultural, social change. Submit complete ms.

LRP PUBLICATIONS, INC.

360 Hiatt Dr., Palm Beach Gardens FL 33418. **E-mail:** dshadovitz@lrp.com. **Website:** www.lrp.com. Estab. 1977. Publishes hardcover and trade paperback originals. **Pays royalty.** Book catalog free. Guidelines free.

◖ "LRP publishes two industry-leading magazines, *Human Resource Executive*® and *Risk & Insurance*®, as well as hundreds of newsletters, books, videos and case reporters in the fields of: human resources, federal employment, workers' compensation, public employment law, disability, bankruptcy, education administration and law."

NONFICTION Subjects include business, economics, education. Submit proposal package, outline.

LUCENT BOOKS

Attn: Publisher - Lucent Books, 27500 Drake Rd., Farmington Hills MI 48331. **E-mail:** betz.deschenes@cengage.com. **Website:** www.gale.com/lucent. **Contact:** Betz Des Chenes. Estab. 1988. Lucent Books is a nontrade publisher of nonfiction for the middle school audience providing students with resource material for academic studies and for independent learning.

NONFICTION Potential writers should familiarize themselves with the material. All are works for hire, by assignment only. *No unsolicited mss.* E-mail query with cover letter, résumé and list of publications.

LUCKY MARBLE BOOKS

PageSpring Publishing, P.O. Box 21133, Columbus OH 43221. **E-mail:** yaeditor@pagespringpublishing.com. **Website:** www.luckymarblebooks.com. Estab. 2012. Publishes trade paperback and electronic originals. "Lucky Marble Books publishes novel-length young adult and middle grade fiction. We are looking for engaging characters and well-crafted plots that keep our readers turning the page. We accept e-mail queries only; see our website for details." **Pays royalty.** Publishes book 6-9 months after acceptance. Accepts simultaneous submissions. Responds in 3 months to queries and mss. Guidelines online.

FICTION Subjects include adventure, contemporary, fantasy, feminist, historical, humor, juvenile, literary, mainstream, multicultural, mystery, regional, romance, science fiction, sports, suspense, young adult. Submit proposal package via e-mail. Include synopsis and 3 sample chapters.

TIPS "We love books that jump right into the story and sweep us along!"

⊘ LUNA BISONTE PRODS

137 Leland Ave., Columbus OH 43214-7505. **E-mail:** bennettjohnm@gmail.com. **Website:** www. johnmbennett.net. **Contact:** John M. Bennett, editor/publisher. Estab. 1967.

POETRY "Interested in avant-garde and highly experimental work only." Has published poetry by Jim Leftwich, Sheila E. Murphy, Al Ackerman, Richard Kostelanetz, Carla Bertola, Olchar Lindsann, and many others. Query first, with a few sample poems and cover letter with brief bio and publication credits. "Keep it brief. Chapbook publishing usually depends on grants or other subsidies, and is usually by solicitation. **Will also consider subsidy arrangements on negotiable terms.**" A sampling of various Luna Bisonte Prods products is available for $20.

⊘ THE LYONS PRESS

The Globe Pequot Press, Inc., Box 480, 246 Goose Ln., Guilford CT 06437. (203)458-4500. **Fax:** (203)458-4668. **E-mail:** info@globepequot.com. **Website:** www. lyonspress.com. Estab. 1984 (Lyons & Burford), 1997 (The Lyons Press). Publishes hardcover and trade paperback originals and reprints. The Lyons Press publishes practical and literary books, chiefly centered on outdoor subjects—natural history, all sports, gardening, horses, fishing, hunting, survival, self-reliant living, plus cooking, memoir, bio, nonfiction. "At this time, we are not accepting unsolicited mss or proposals." Check back for updates. **Pays $3,000-25,000 advance.** Catalog and guidelines online.

NONFICTION Subjects include agriculture, Americana, animals, art & reference, cooking, foods & wine, nutrition, history, military, war, nature, environment, recreation, sports, adventure, fitness, the sea, woodworking.

○ MAGENTA PUBLISHING FOR THE ARTS

151 Winchester St., Toronto ON M4X 1B5, Canada. **E-mail:** info@magentafoundation.org. **Website:** www. magentafoundation.org. **Contact:** Submissions. Estab. 2004. "The Magenta Foundation is Canada's pioneering non-profit arts publishing house. Magenta was created to organize promotional opportunities for Canadian artists in the international arts community through circulated exhibitions and publications. Projects mounted by Magenta are supported by credible international media coverage and critical reviews in all mainstream media formats (radio, television and print)."

MAGINATION PRESS

750 First St. NE, Washington DC 20002. (202)336-5618. **Fax:** (202)336-5624. **E-mail:** rteeter@apa.org. **Website:** www.apa.org. **Contact:** Kristine Enderle, managing editor. Estab. 1988. Magination Press is an imprint of the American Psychological Association. "We publish books dealing with the psycho/therapeutic resolution of children's problems and psychological issues with a strong self-help component." Submit complete ms. Materials returned only with SASE. **Publishes 12 titles/year. 75% of books from first-time authors.** Publishes book Publishes a book 18-24 months after acceptance. Accepts simultaneous submissions. Responds to queries in 1-2 months; mss in 2-6 months.

NONFICTION All levels: psychological and social issues, self-help, health, multicultural, special needs.

FICTION All levels: psychological and social issues, self-help, health, parenting concerns and, special needs. Picture books, middle school readers.

MAGNUS PRESS

1647 Shire Ave., Oceanside CA 92057. (760)806-3743. **Fax:** (760)806-3689. **E-mail:** magnuspres@aol.com. **Website:** www.magnuspress.com. **Contact:** Warren Angel, editorial director. Estab. 1997. Publishes trade paperback originals and reprints. **Publishes 1-3 titles/year. 120 queries received/year. 75 mss received/year. 44% of books from first-time authors. 89% from unagented writers. Pays 6-15% royalty on retail price.** Publishes book 1 year after acceptance. Accepts simultaneous submissions. Responds in 1 month. Book catalog and ms guidelines for #10 SASE. **IMPRINTS** Canticle Books.

NONFICTION Subjects include religion, from a Christian perspective. "Writers must be well-grounded in Biblical knowledge and must be able to communicate effectively with the lay person." Submit proposal package, outline, sample chapters, bio.

TIPS "Magnus Press's audience is mainly Christian lay persons, but also includes anyone interested in spirituality and/or Biblical studies and the church. Study our listings and catalog; learn to write effectively for an average reader; read any one of our published books."

MAIN STREET RAG PUBLISHING COMPANY

P.O. Box 690100, Charlotte NC 28227. (704)573-2516. **E-mail:** editor@mainstreetrag.com. **Website:** www.mainstreetrag.com. **Contact:** M. Scott Douglass, publisher, editor. Estab. 1996. "There are 4 ways to get a book of poetry published: 1) self-publish using our imprint; 2) Enter one of our contests; 3) Be invited; 4) Be recommended." Responds in 3-6 weeks to queries.

Main Street Rag (our poetry label); Mint Hill Books (fiction label); Pure Heart Press (self-publishing label).

NONFICTION Subjects include art (mostly photographs, prefer images of people in action), creative nonfiction, photography, interview, reviews, essays. "Pissing off politicians, corporations, zealots, and/or lawyers is acceptable and encouraged." Nothing derogatory on the basis of race, gender, sexual orientation, or religious persuasion. Query with SASE. Reviews artwork/photos.

FICTION Subjects include literary, poetry, cartoons, short fiction. "See Current themes online. Address to Short Fiction Anthology for consideration for our anthology. We are not open to unsolicited submissions of full-length mss of short fiction." Query with SASE. Submit 2 short stories.

POETRY "We are interested in any style, subject, with emphasis on edgier materials, and we enjoy humor. We prefer work alive with the poet's own experiences. We don't want much formal poetry, but will consider it if formal poems maintain the integrity of the form without becoming stiff, uninteresting, or losing their vitality. Poems of 40 lines or less are more acceptable. Submit 6 pages per submission, 1 typed page per 8.5 X 11 page. We are not interested in the graphic details of your love life. We are least likely to accept garden poetry, poetry about poems or Greek & Roman mythology." Query.

TIPS "You can request a free electronic newsletter which is a reference for writers, readers and publishers by providing limited information and directing them to links and e-mails. Current features include: Call for Submissions; Contests; and New Releases. (No e-mail submissions unless overseas, reviews, images, subscribers to *The Mainstreet Rag*.) In all cases, query prior to submitting for instructions."

MANDALA PUBLISHING

Mandala Publishing and Earth Aware Editions, 10 Paul Dr., San Rafael CA 94903. **E-mail:** info@mandalapublishing.com. **Website:** www.mandalapublishing.com. Estab. 1989. Publishes hardcover, trade paperback, and electronic originals. "In the traditions of the East, wisdom, truth, and beauty go hand in-hand. This is reflected in the great arts, music, yoga, and philosophy of India. Mandala Publishing strives to bring to its readers authentic and accessible renderings of thousands of years of wisdom and philosophy from this unique culture-timeless treasures that are our inspirations and guides. At Mandala, we believe that the arts, health, ecology, and spirituality of the great Vedic traditions are as relevant today as they were in sacred India thousands of years ago. As a distinguished publisher in the world of Vedic literature, lifestyle, and interests today, Mandala strives to provide accessible and meaningful works for the modern reader." **Publishes 12 titles/year. 200 queries received/year. 100 mss received/year. 40% of books from first-time authors. 100% from unagented writers. Pays 3-15% royalty on retail price.** Publishes book 8 months after acceptance. Accepts simultaneous submissions. Responds in 6 months. Book catalog online.

NONFICTION Subjects include alternative, cooking, foods, nutrition, education, health, medicine, philosophy, photography, religion, spirituality. Query with SASE. Reviews artwork/photos. Send photocopies and thumbnails.

FICTION Subjects include juvenile, religious, spiritual. Query with SASE.

MANOR HOUSE PUBLISHING, INC.

452 Cottingham Crescent, Ancaster ON L9G 3V6, Canada. **E-mail:** mbdavie@manor-house.biz. **Website:** www.manor-house.biz. **Contact:** Mike Davie, president (novels, poetry, and nonfiction). Estab. 1998. Publishes hardcover, trade paperback, and mass market paperback originals reprints. **Publishes 5-6 titles/year. 30 queries received/year; 20 mss**

received/year. **90% of books from first-time authors. 90% from unagented writers. Pays 10% royalty on retail price.** Publishes book 1 year after acceptance. Accepts simultaneous submissions. Queries and mss to be sent by e-mail only. "We will respond in 30 days if interested-if not, there is no response. Do not follow up unless asked to do so.". Book catalog online. Guidelines available via e-mail.

NONFICTION Subjects include alternative, anthropology, business, community, history, sex, social sciences, sociology, spirituality. "We are a Canadian publisher, so mss should be Canadian in content and aimed as much as possible at a wide, general audience. At this point in time, we are only publishing books by Canadian citizens residing in Canada." Query via e-mail. Submit proposal package, outline, bio, 3 sample chapters. Submit complete ms. Reviews artwork/photos. Send photocopies.

FICTION Subjects include adventure, experimental, gothic, historical, horror, humor, juvenile, literary, mystery, occult, poetry, regional, romance, short story collections, young adult. Stories should have Canadian settings and characters should be Canadian, but content should have universal appeal to wide audience. Query via e-mail. Submit proposal package, clips, bio, 3 sample chapters. Submit complete ms.

POETRY Poetry should engage, provoke, involve the reader.

TIPS "Our audience includes everyone-the general public/mass audience. Self-edit your work first, make sure it is well written with strong Canadian content."

MARINE TECHNIQUES PUBLISHING

126 Western Ave., Suite 266, Augusta ME 04330. (207)622-7984. **E-mail:** info@marinetechpublishing.com. **Website:** www.marinetechpublishing.com. **Contact:** James L. Pelletier, president/owner(commercial maritime); Maritime Associates Globally (commercial maritime). Estab. 1983. Trade paperback originals and reprints. "Publishes only books related to the commercial marine/maritime industry." **Publishes 2-5 titles/year. 20+ queries received/year. 40+ mss received/year. 50% of books from first-time authors. 75% from unagented writers. Pays 25-55% royalty on wholesale or retail price. Makes outright purchase.** Publishes book 1 year after acceptance. Accepts simultaneous submissions. Responds in 2 months. Book catalog available online, by

e-mail, and for #10 SASE for $5. Guidelines available by e-mail, and for #10 SASE for $5.

NONFICTION Subjects include maritime education, marine subjects, counseling, career guidance, maritime labor, marine engineering, global water transportation, marine subjects, water transportation. "We are concerned with 'maritime related works' and not recreational boating, but rather commercial maritime industries, such as deep-sea water transportation, offshore oil & gas, inland towing, coastal tug boat, 'water transportation industries.'" Submit proposal package, including all sample chapters; submit completed ms. Reviews artwork/photos as part of the ms package; send photocopies.

FICTION Subjects include adventure, military, war, maritime. Must be commercial maritime/marine related. Submit proposal package, including all sample chapters. Submit complete ms.

TIPS "Audience consists of commercial marine/maritime firms, persons employed in all aspects of the marine/maritime commercial water-transportation-related industries and recreational fresh and salt water fields, persons interested in seeking employment in the commercial marine industry; firms seeking to sell their products and services to vessel owners, operators, and managers; shipyards, vessel repair yards, recreational and yacht boat building and national and international ports and terminals involved with the commercial marine industry globally worldwide, etc."

MARTIN SISTERS PUBLISHING, LLC

P.O. Box 1749, Barbourville KY 40906-1499. **E-mail:** submissions@martinsisterspublishing.com. **Website:** www.martinsisterspublishing.com. **Contact:** Denise Melton, Publisher/Editor (Fiction/nonfiction); Melissa Newman, Publisher/Editor (Fiction/nonfiction). Estab. 2011. Firm/imprint publishes trade and mass market paperback originals; electronic originals. **Publishes 12 titles/year. 75% of books from first-time authors. 100% from unagented writers. Pays 7.5% royalty/max on retail price. No advance offered.** Publishes book Time between acceptance of ms and publication is 6 months. after acceptance of ms. Accepts simultaneous submissions. Responds in 1 month on queries, 2 months on proposals, 3-6 months on mss. Catalog and Guidelines online.

IMPRINTS Ivy House Books — literary/mainstream fiction; rainshower books — christian fiction and nonfiction; Skyvine Books — science fiction/fantasy/paranormal; romance; Martin Sisters Books — nonfiction/short story collections/coffee table books/ cookbooks; Barefoot Books — young adult. Query Ms. Newman or Ms. Melton for all Imprints listed.

NONFICTION Subjects include Americana, child guidance, contemporary culture, cooking, creative nonfiction, education, gardening, history, house and home, humanities, labor, language, law, literature, memoirs, money, nutrition, parenting, psychology, regional, sociology, spirituality, womens issues, womens studies, western. Send query letter only. Does not review artwork.

FICTION Subjects include adventure, confession, fantasy, historical, humor, juvenile, literary, mainstream, military, mystery, poetry in translation, regional, religious, romance, science fiction, short story collections, spiritual, sports, suspense, war, western, young adult. Send query letter only.

MARVEL COMICS

10 E. 40th St., New York NY 10016. **Website:** www. marvel.com. Publishes hardcover originals and re-prints, trade paperback reprints, mass market comic book originals, electronic reprints. **Pays on a per page work for hire basis or creator-owned which is then contracted. Pays negotiable advance.** Responds in 3-5 weeks to queries. Guidelines online.

FICTION Subjects include adventure, comic books, fantasy, horror, humor, science fiction, young adult. Our shared universe needs new heroes and villains; books for younger readers and teens needed. Submit inquiry letter, idea submission form (download from website), SASE.

TIPS Marvel currently appeals to 12 We're looking for strong voice

MASTER BOOKS

P.O. Box 726, Green Forest AR 72638. (870)438-5288. **Fax:** (870)438-5120. **E-mail:** submissions@newleafpress.net; craig@newleafpress.net. **Website:** www. masterbooks.net. **Contact:** Craig Froman, acquisitions editor. Estab. 1975. Publishes 3 middle readers/ year; 2 young adult nonfiction titles/year; 20 adult trade books/year. **10% of books from first-time authors. Pays authors royalty of 3-15% based on wholesale price.** Publishes book 1 year after acceptance. Responds in 4 months. Book catalog available upon request. Guidelines online.

NONFICTION Picture books: activity books, animal, nature/environment, creation. Young readers, middle

readers, young adults: activity books, animal, biography Christian, nature/environment, science, creation. Submission guidelines on website.

TIPS "All of our children's books are creation-based, including topics from the Book of Genesis. We look also for home school educational material that would be supplementary to a home school curriculum."

MAUPIN HOUSE PUBLISHING, INC.

1710 Roe Crest Dr., North Mankato MN 56003. **E-mail:** info@maupinhouse.com. **Website:** www.maupinhouse.com. **Contact:** Julie Graddy, publisher (areas of interest: education, professional development). Publishes trade paperback originals and reprints. "Maupin House publishes professional resource books for language arts teachers K-12." **Publishes 6-8 titles/ year. 60% of books from first-time authors. 100% from unagented writers. Pays 10% royalty on retail price.** Publishes book 18 months after acceptance. Accepts simultaneous submissions. Responds in less than 1 month. Catalog and guidelines online.

NONFICTION Subjects include education, language arts, literacy and the arts, reading comprehension, writing workshop. "Study the website to understand our pubilshing preferences. Successful authors are all teachers or former teachers." Query with SASE or via e-mail. Submit proposal package, including outline, 1-2 sample chapters, and TOC/marketing ideas. Reviews artwork/photos as part of the mss package. Writers should send photocopies, digital.

TIPS "Our audience is K-12 educators, teachers. Be familiar with our publishing areas and tell us why your book idea is better/different than what is out there. How do you plan to promote it? Successful authors help promote books via speaking engagements, conferences, etc."

MAVEN HOUSE PRESS

4 Snead Ct., Palmyra VA 22963. (610)883-7988. **Fax:** (888)894-3403. **E-mail:** jim@mavenhousepress.com. **Website:** www.mavenhousepress.com. **Contact:** Jim Pennypacker, publisher. Estab. 2012. Publishes hardcover, trade paperback, and electronic originals. Maven House Press publishes business books for executives and managers to help them lead their organizations to greatness. **Publishes 6 titles/year. Pays 10-50% royalty based on wholesale price.** Publishes book 9 months after acceptance. Accepts simultaneous submissions. Responds in 1 month.

NONFICTION Subjects include business, economics, Business/management. Submit proposal package including: outline, 1-2 sample chapters. See submission form online.

MAVERICK DUCK PRESS

E-mail: maverickduckpress@yahoo.com. **Website:** www.maverickduckpress.com. **Contact:** Kendall A. Bell, editor. Assistant Editors: Kayla Marie Middlebrook and Bronwyn E. Haynes. Estab. 2005. Maverick Duck Press is a "publisher of chapbooks from undiscovered talent. We arc looking for fresh and powerful work that shows a sense of innovation or a new take on passion or emotion. Previous publication in print or online journals could increase your chances of us accepting your ms." Does not want "unedited work." **Pays 20 author's copies (out of a press run of 50).**

POETRY Send ms in Microsoft Word format with a cover letter with brief bio and publication credits. Chapbook mss may include previously published poems. "Previous publication is always a plus, as we may be more familiar with your work. Chapbook mss should have 16-24 poems, but no more than 24 poems."

MAVERICK MUSICALS AND PLAYS

89 Bergann Rd., Maleny QLD 4552, Australia. Phone/**Fax:** (61)(7)5494-4007. **E-mail:** gail@mavmuse.com. **Website:** www.mavmuse.com. Estab. 1978. Guidelines online.

FICTION Subjects include plays and musicals. "Looking for two-act musicals and one- and two-act plays. See website for more details."

MCBOOKS PRESS

ID Booth Building, 520 N. Meadow St., Ithaca NY 14850. (607)272-2114. **Fax:** (607)273-6068. **E-mail:** mcbooks@mcbooks.com. **Website:** www.mcbooks.com. **Contact:** Alexander G. Skutt, publisher. Estab. 1979. Publishes trade paperback and hardcover originals and reprints. **Publishes 5 titles/year.** Accepts simultaneous submissions. Guidelines online.

"Currently not accepting submissions or queries for fiction or nonfiction."

FICTION Publishes Julian Stockwin, John Biggins, Colin Sargent, and Douglas W. Jacobson. Distributes titles through Independent Publishers Group.

TIPS "We are currently only publishing authors with whom we have a pre-existing relationship. If this policy changes, we will announce the change on our website."

THE MCDONALD & WOODWARD PUBLISHING CO.

431 E. College St., Granville OH 43023. (740)321-1140. **Fax:** (740)321-1141. **E-mail:** mwpubco@mwpubco.com. **Website:** www.mwpubco.com. **Contact:** Jerry N. McDonald, publisher. Estab. 1986. Publishes hardcover and trade paperback originals. McDonald & Woodward publishes books in natural history, cultural history, and natural resources. Currently emphasizing travel, natural and cultural history, and natural resource conservation. **Publishes 5 titles/year. 25 queries received/year. 20 mss received/year. Pays 10% royalty.** Accepts simultaneous submissions. Responds in less than 1 month. Book catalog online. Guidelines free on request; by e-mail.

NONFICTION Subjects include animals, architecture, environment, history, nature, science, travel, natural history. Query with SASE. Reviews artwork/photos. Photos are not required.

FICTION Subjects include historical. Query with SASE.

TIPS "Our books are meant for the curious and educated elements of the general population."

MARGARET K. MCELDERRY BOOKS

Imprint of Simon & Schuster Children's Publishing Division, 1230 Sixth Ave., New York NY 10020. (212)698-7200. **Website:** www.simonsayskids.com. **Contact:** Justin Chanda, vice president; Karen Wojtyla, editorial director; Gretchen Hirsch, associate editor; Emily Fabre, assistant editor; Ann Bobco, executive art director. Estab. 1971. "Margaret K. McElderry Books publishes hardcover and paperback trade books for children from pre-school age through young adult. This list includes picture books, middle grade and teen fiction, poetry, and fantasy. The style and subject matter of the books we publish is almost unlimited. We do not publish textbooks, coloring and activity books, greeting cards, magazines, pamphlets, or religious publications." **Publishes 30 titles/year. 15% of books from first-time authors. 50% from unagented writers. Pays authors royalty based on retail price. Pays illustrator royalty of by the project. Pays photographers by the project. Original artwork returned at job's completion. Offers $5,000-8,000 advance for new authors.** Guidelines for #10 SASE.

NONFICTION Subjects include history, adventure. Looks for originality of ideas, clarity and felicity of expression, well-organized plot and strong characterization (fiction) or clear exposition (nonfiction); quality. Accept query letters with SASE only for picture books; query letter with first 3 chapters, SASE for middle grades and young adult novels. *No unsolicited mss.*

FICTION Subjects include adventure, fantasy, historical, mainstream, contemporary, mystery, picture books, young adult, or middle grade, All categories (fiction and nonfiction) for juvenile and young adult. We will consider any category. Results depend on the quality of the imagination, the artwork, and the writing. Average word length: picture books—500; young readers—2,000; middle readers—10,000-20,000; young adults—45,000-50,000. *No unsolicited mss.* Send query letter with SASE.

POETRY *No unsolicited mss.* Query and submit 3 sample poems.

TIPS "Read! The children's book field is competitive. See what's been done and what's out there before submitting. We look for high quality: an originality of ideas, clarity and felicity of expression, a well organized plot, and strong character-driven stories. We're looking for strong, original fiction, especially mysteries and middle grade humor. We are always interested in picture books for the youngest age reader. Study our titles."

MCFARLAND & CO., INC., PUBLISHERS

Box 611, Jefferson NC 28640. (336)246-4460. **Fax:** (336)246-5018. **E-mail:** info@mcfarlandpub.com. **Website:** www.mcfarlandpub.com. **Contact:** Steve Wilson, editorial director (automotive, general); David Alff, editor (general); Gary Mitchem, acquisitions editor (general, baseball). Estab. 1979. Publishes hardcover and quality paperback originals; a nontrade publisher. "McFarland publishes serious nonfiction in a variety of fields, including general reference, performing arts, popular culture, sports (particularly baseball); women's studies, librarianship, literature, Civil War, history and international studies. Currently emphasizing medieval history, automotive history. De-emphasizing memoirs." **Publishes 350 titles/year. 50% of books from first-time authors. 95% from unagented writers.** Publishes book 10 months after acceptance. Responds in 1 month to queries. Guidelines online.

NONFICTION Subjects include art, architecture, automotive, health, medicine, history, military, war/war, popular contemporary culture, music, dance, recreation, sociology, world affairs, sports (very strong), African-American studies (very strong). Reference books are particularly wanted—fresh material (i.e., not in head-to-head competition with an established title). We prefer mss of 250 or more double-spaced pages or at least 75,000 words. No fiction, New Age, exposes, poetry, children's books, devotional/inspirational works, Bible studies, or personal essays. Query with SASE. Submit outline, sample chapters. Reviews artwork/photos.

TIPS "We want well-organized knowledge of an area in which there is not information coverage at present, plus reliability so we don't feel we have to check absolutely everything. Our market is worldwide and libraries are an important part."

MCGRAW-HILL/OSBORNE MEDIA

The McGraw-Hill Professional/Computing, 160 Spear St., Suite 700, San Francisco CA 94105. (800)227-0900. **E-mail:** megg_morin@mcgraw-hill.com. **Website:** www.osborne.com. **Contact:** Megg Morin, acq. ed., consumer computing. Estab. 1979. Publishes computer trade paperback originals. "Publishes self-paced computer training materials." Book catalog and ms guidelines online.

NONFICTION Subjects include computers, electronics, software, and hardware. Submit proposal package, outline, sample chapters, résumé, competition analysis, SASE. Reviews artwork/photos.

TIPS "A leader in self-paced training and skills development tools on information technology and computers."

MCGRAW-HILL PROFESSIONAL

Imprint of The McGraw-Hill Companies, 2 Penn Plaza, New York NY 10121-2298. **Website:** www.books.mcgraw-hill.com. McGraw Hill Professional is a publishing leader in business/investing, management, careers, self-help, consumer health, language reference, test preparation, sports/recreation, and general interest titles. Accepts simultaneous submissions. Guidelines online.

○ Publisher not responsible for returning mss or proposals.

NONFICTION Subjects include business, economics, child guidance, education, study guides, health, medicine, money, finance, sports, fitness, management, consumer reference, English and foreign language reference. Current, up-to-date, original ideas are needed. Good self-promotion is key. Submit proposal package, outline, concept of book, competition and market info, cv.

MC PRESS

3695 W. Quail Heights Ct., Boise ID 83703. **Fax:** (208)639-1231. **E-mail:** duptmor@mcpressonline. com. **Website:** www.mcpressonline.com. **Contact:** David Uptmor, publisher. Estab. 2001. Publishes trade paperback originals. **Publishes 40 titles/year. 100 queries received/year. 50 mss received/year. 5% of books from first-time authors. 5% from unagented writers. Pays 10-16% royalty on wholesale price.** Publishes book 5 months after acceptance. Accepts simultaneous submissions. Responds in 1 month. Book catalog and ms guidelines free.

IMPRINTS MC Press, IBM Press.

NONFICTION Subjects include computers, electronics. "We specialize in computer titles targeted at IBM technologies." Submit proposal package, outline, 2 sample chapters, abstract. Reviews artwork/photos. Send photocopies.

MEDALLION MEDIA GROUP

100 S. River St., Aurora IL 60506. (630)513-8316. **E-mail:** emily@medallionmediagroup.com. **E-mail:** submissions@medallionmediagroup.com. **Website:** medallionmediagroup.com. **Contact:** Emily Steele, editorial director. Estab. 2003. Publishes trade paperback, hardcover, e-book originals, book apps, and TREEbook™. "We are an independent, innovative publisher looking for compelling, memorable stories told in distinctive voices." **Offers advance.** Publishes book 1-2 years after acceptance. Responds in 2-3 months to mss. Guidelines online.

NONFICTION Subjects include art, health, design, fitness. *Agented only.* Please query.

FICTION Subjects include fantasy, historical, horror, literary, mainstream, mystery, romance, science fiction, suspense, young adult, thriller, Christian, YA-YA (YA written by young adults). Word count: 40,000-90,000 for YA; 60,000-120,000 for all others. No short stories, anthologies, erotica. Submit first 3 consecutive chapters and a synopsis through our online submission form.

TIPS "We are not affected by trends. We are simply looking for well-crafted, original, compelling works of fiction and nonfiction. Please visit our website for the most current guidelines prior to submitting anything to us."

MEDICAL GROUP MANAGEMENT ASSOCIATION

104 Inverness Terrace E., Englewood CO 80112. (303)799-1111. **E-mail:** support@mgma.com; connexion@mgma.com. **Website:** www.mgma.com. Estab. 1926. Publishes professional and scholarly hardcover, paperback, and electronic originals, and trade paperback reprints. **Publishes 6 titles/year. 18 queries received/year. 6 mss received/year. 30% of books from first-time authors. 100% from unagented writers. Pays 8-17% royalty on net sales (twice a year). Pays $2,000-5,000 advance.** Publishes book 6 months after acceptance. Accepts simultaneous submissions. Responds in less than 3 weeks to queries; months to proposals and mss. Book catalog online. Writer's guidelines online.

NONFICTION Subjects include audio, business, economics, education, health. Submit proposal package, outline, 3 sample chapters. Submit complete ms. Reviews artwork/photos. Send photocopies.

TIPS "Audience includes medical practice managers and executives. Our books are geared at the business side of medicine."

✪ MELANGE BOOKS, LLC

White Bear Lake MN 55110-5538. **E-mail:** melangebooks@melange-books.com. **E-mail:** submissions@melange-books.com. **Website:** www.melange-books. com. **Contact:** Nancy Schumacher, publisher and acquiring editor for Melange and Satin Romance; Caroline Andrus, acquiring editor for Fire and Ice for Young Adult. Estab. 2011. Publishes trade paperback originals and electronic originals. Melange is a royalty-paying company publishing e-books and print books. **Publishes 75 titles/year. Receives 1,000 queries/year. Receives 700 mss/year. 65% of books from first-time authors. 75% from unagented writers. Authors receive a minimum of 20% royalty on print sales, 40% on electronic book sales. Does not offer an advance.** Publishes book 12-15 months after acceptance. Accepts simultaneous submissions. Responds in 1 month on queries, 2 months on proposals, and 4-6 months on mss. Send SASE for book catalog. Send SASE for mss guidelines, or review them online.

IMPRINTS Imprints include Fire and Ice for Young and New Adults and Satin Romance.

FICTION Subjects include adventure, contemporary, erotica, fantasy, gay, gothic, historical, lesbian, mainstream, multicultural, mystery, romance, science fiction, suspense, western, young adult. Submit a clean mss by following guidelines on website. Query electronically by clicking on "submissions" on website. Include a synopsis and 4 chapters.

MERIWETHER PUBLISHING LTD.

885 Elkton Dr., Colorado Springs CO 80907. (719)594-9916. **Fax:** (719)594-4422. **E-mail:** editor@meriwether.com. **Website:** www.meriwether.com. **Contact:** Ted Zapel; Rhonda Wray. Estab. 1969. "Our niche is drama. Our books cover a wide variety of theatre subjects from play anthologies to theatrecraft. We publish books of monologs, duologs, short one-act plays, scenes for students, acting textbooks, how-to speech and theatre textbooks, improvisation and theatre games. We also publish anthologies of Christian sketches. We do not publish works of fiction or devotionals." **75% of books from first-time authors. Pays authors royalty of 10% based on retail or wholesale price.** Publishes book 6-12 months after acceptance. Accepts simultaneous submissions. Responds to queries in 3 weeks, mss in 2 months or less.

NONFICTION Middle readers: activity books, how-to, religion, textbooks. Young adults: activity books, drama/theater arts, how-to church activities, religion. Average length: 250 pages.

FICTION Middle readers, young adults: anthology, contemporary, humor, religion. "We publish plays, not prose-fiction. Our emphasis is comedy plays instead of educational themes."

TIPS "We are currently interested in finding unique treatments for theater arts subjects: scene books, how-to books, musical comedy scripts, monologs and short comedy plays for teens."

MERRIAM PRESS

133 Elm St., Suite 3R, Bennington VT 05201. (802)447-0313. **E-mail:** ray@merriam-press.com. **Website:** www.merriam-press.com. Estab. 1988. Publishes hardcover and softcover trade paperback originals and reprints. "Merriam Press specializes in military history, particularly World War II history. We are also branching out into other genres." **Publishes 20+ titles/year. 70-90% of books from first-time authors. 100% from unagented writers. Pays 10% royalty on actual selling price.** Publishes book 6 months or less after acceptance. Responds quickly (e-mail preferred) to queries. Book catalog available for $5 or visit website to view all available titles and access writer's guidelines and info.

NONFICTION Especially but not limited to: military, war, World War II. Query with SASE or by e-mail first. Send copies of sample chapters or entire ms by mail or on disk/flash drive or as an e-mail attachment (preferred in Word .doc/.docx file format). Reviews artwork/photos.

FICTION Especially but not limited to military, war, World War II. Query with SASE or by e-mail first.

POETRY Considers poetry related to military, war, World War II. Query.

TIPS "Our military history books are geared for military historians, collectors, model kit builders, wargamers, veterans, general enthusiasts. We now publish some historical fiction and poetry and will consider well-written books on a variety of non-military topics."

MESSIANIC JEWISH PUBLISHERS

6120 Day Long Lane, Clarksville MD 21029. (410)531-6644. **E-mail:** website@messianicjewish.net. **Website:** www.messianicjewish.net. **Contact:** Janet Chaier, managing editor. Publishes hardcover and trade paperback originals and reprints. **Publishes 6-12 titles/year. Pays 7-15% royalty on wholesale price.** Guidelines available via e-mail.

IMPRINTS Lederer Books.

NONFICTION Subjects include religion, Messianic Judaism, Jewish roots of the Christian faith. Text must demonstrate keen awareness of Jewish culture and thought, and Biblical literacy. Jewish themes only. Query with SASE. Unsolicited mss are not returned.

FICTION Subjects include religious. "We publish very little fiction. Jewish or Biblical themes are a must. Text must demonstrate keen awareness of Jewish culture and thought." Query with SASE. Unsolicited mss are not return

⊘ MIAMI UNIVERSITY PRESS

356 Bachelor Hall, Miami University, Oxford OH 45056. **E-mail:** tumakw@muohio.edu. **Website:** www.muohio.edu/mupress. **Contact:** Keith Tuma, editor; Amy Toland, managing editor. Estab. 1992. Publishes 1-2 books of poetry/year and 1 novella, in paperback editions.

POETRY Miami University Press is unable to respond to unsolicited mss and queries.

MICHIGAN STATE UNIVERSITY PRESS

1405 S. Harrison Rd., Suite 25, East Lansing MI 48823-5202. (517)355-9543. **Fax:** (517)432-2611. **E-mail:** msupress@msu.edu. **Website:** msupress.msu.

edu/. **Contact:** Alex Schwartz and Julie Loehr, acquisitions. Estab. 1947. Publishes hardcover and softcover originals. **Pays variable royalty.** Book catalog and ms guidelines for 9×12 SASE or online.

○ Michigan State University Press has notably represented both scholarly publishing and the mission of Michigan State University with the publication of numerous award-winning books and scholarly journals. In addition, they publish nonfiction that addresses, in a more contemporary way, social concerns, such as diversity and civil rights. They also publish literary fiction and poetry.

NONFICTION Subjects include Americana, American Studies, business, economics, creative nonfiction, ethnic, Afro-American studies, government, politics, history, contemporary civil rights, language, literature, literary criticism, regional, Great Lakes regional, Canadian studies, women's studies, environmental studies, and American Indian Studies. Distributes books for: University of Calgary Press, University of Alberta Press, and University of Manitoba Press. Submit proposal/outline and sample chapter. Hard copy is preferred but e-mail proposals are also accepted. Initial submissions to MSU Press should be in the form of a short letter of inquiry and a sample chapter(s), as well as our preliminary Marketing Questionnaire, which can be downloaded from their website. We do not accept: Festschrifts, conference papers, or unrevised dissertations. (Festschrift: A complimentary or memorial publication usually in the form of a collection of essays, addresses, or biographical, bibliographic, scientific, of other contributions). Reviews artwork/photos.

MICROSOFT PRESS

E-mail: 4bkideas@microsoft.com. **Website:** www.microsoft.com/learning/en/us/microsoft-press-books.aspx. **Publishes 80 titles/year. 25% of books from first-time authors. 90% from unagented writers.** Book proposal Guidelines online.

NONFICTION Subjects include software. A book proposal should consist of the following information: TOC, a résumé with author biography, a writing sample, and a questionnaire. "We place a great deal of emphasis on your proposal. A proposal provides us with a basis for evaluating the idea of the book and how fully your book fulfills its purpose."

MILKWEED EDITIONS

1011 Washington Ave. S., Suite 300, Minneapolis MN 55415. (612)332-3192. **Fax:** (612)215-2550. **E-mail:** submissions@milkweed.org. **Website:** www.milkweed.org. Estab. 1979. Publishes hardcover, trade paperback, and electronic originals; trade paperback and electronic reprints. "Milkweed Editions publishes with the intention of making a humane impact on society, in the belief that literature is a transformative art uniquely able to convey the essential experiences of the human heart and spirit. To that end, Milkweed Editions publishes distinctive voices of literary merit in handsomely designed, visually dynamic books, exploring the ethical, cultural, and esthetic issues that free societies need continually to address." **Publishes 15-20 titles/year. 25% of books from first-time authors. 75% from unagented writers. Pays authors variable royalty based on retail price. Offers advance against royalties. Pays varied advance from $500-10,000.** Publishes book in 18 months. after acceptance of ms. Accepts simultaneous submissions. Responds in 6 months. Catalog and guidelines online.

NONFICTION Subjects include agriculture, animals, archaeology, art, contemporary culture, creative nonfiction, environment, gardening, gay, government, history, humanities, language, literature, multicultural, nature, politics, literary, regional, translation, women's issues, world affairs. Does not review artwork.

FICTION Subjects include experimental, short story collections, translation, young adult. Novels for adults and for readers 8-13. High literary quality. For adult readers: literary fiction, nonfiction, poetry, essays. Middle readers: adventure, contemporary, fantasy, multicultural, nature/environment, suspense/mystery. Average length: middle readers—90-200 pages. No romance, mysteries, science fiction. Query with SASE, submit completed ms.

POETRY Milkweed Editions is "looking for poetry mss of high quality that embody humane values and contribute to cultural understanding." Not limited in subject matter. Open to writers with previously published books of poetry or a minimum of 6 poems published in nationally distributed commercial or literary journals. Considers translations and bilingual mss. Query with SASE; submit completed ms.

TIPS "We are looking for excellent writing with the intent of making a humane impact on society. Please read submission guidelines before submitting and acquaint yourself with our books in terms of style and quality before submitting. Many factors influence our selection process, so don't get discouraged. Nonfiction is focused on literary writing about the natural world, including living well in urban environments."

MILKWEED FOR YOUNG READERS

Milkweed Editions, Open Book Building, 1011 Washington Ave. S., Suite 300, Minneapolis MN 55415. (612)332-3192. **Fax:** (612)215-2550. **E-mail:** submissions@milkweed.org. **Website:** www.milkweed.org. Estab. 1984. Publishes hardcover and trade paperback originals. "We are looking first of all for high quality literary writing. We publish books with the intention of making a humane impact on society." **Publishes 3-4 titles/year. 25% of books from first-time authors. 50% from unagented writers. Pays 7% royalty on retail price. Pays variable advance.** Publishes book 1 year after acceptance. Accepts simultaneous submissions. Responds in 6 months to queries. Book catalog for $1.50. Guidelines for #10 SASE or on the website.
FICTION Subjects include adventure, fantasy, historical, humor, mainstream, contemporary, animal, environmental. Query with SASE. "Milkweed Editions now accepts mss online through our Submission Manager. If you're a first-time submitter, you'll need to fill in a simple form and then follow the instructions for selecting and uploading your ms. Please make sure that your ms follows the submission guidelines."

THE MILLBROOK PRESS

Lerner Publishing Group, 1251 Washington Ave N, Minneapolis MN 55401. **Website:** www.lernerbooks. com. **Contact:** Carol Hinz, editorial director. "Millbrook Press publishes informative picture books, illustrated nonfiction titles, and inspiring photo-driven titles for grades K–5. Our authors approach curricular topics with a fresh point of view. Our fact-filled books engage readers with fun yet accessible writing, high-quality photographs, and a wide variety of illustration styles. We cover subjects ranging from the parts of speech and other language arts skills; to history, science, and math; to art, sports, crafts, and other interests. Millbrook Press is the home of the best-selling Words Are CATegorical® series and Bob Raczka's Art Adventures."

○ "We do not accept unsolicited mss from authors. Occasionally, we may put out a call for submissions, which will be announced on our website."

MINNESOTA HISTORICAL SOCIETY PRESS

Minnesota Historical Society, 345 Kellogg Blvd. W., St. Paul MN 55102-1906. (651)259-3200. **Fax:** (651)297-1345. **Website:** shop.mnhs.org. **Contact:** Ann Regan, editor-in-chief. Estab. 1852. Publishes hardcover, trade paperback and electronic originals; trade paperback and electronic reprints. "Minnesota Historical Society Press publishes both scholarly and general interest books that contribute to the understanding of the Midwest." **Publishes 30 titles/year. 300 queries received/year. 150 mss received/year. 60% of books from first-time authors. 95% from unagented writers. Royalties are negotiated; 5-10% on wholesale price. Pays $1,000 and up.** Publishes book 16 months after acceptance. Accepts simultaneous submissions. Responds in 1 month to queries, 2 months on proposals, 2-4 months on mss. Book catalog online and available free. Guidelines available online and are free.
IMPRINTS Borealis Books, Minnesota Historical Society Press; Ann Regan, editor-in-chief.
NONFICTION Subjects include scholarly, Americana, anthropology, archaeology, art, architecture, community, cooking, foods, nutrition, creative nonfiction, ethnic, government, politics, history, memoirs, multicultural, nature, environment, photography, regional, women's issues, women's studies, Native American studies. Books must have a connection to the Midwest. Regional works only. Submit proposal package, outline, 1 sample chapter and other materials listed in our online website in author guidelines: CV, brief description, intended audience, readership, length of ms, schedule. Reviews artwork/photos. Send photocopies.

MITCHELL LANE PUBLISHERS, INC.

P.O. Box 196, Hockessin DE 19707. (302)234-9426. **Fax:** (866)834-4164. **E-mail:** barbaramitchell@mitchelllane.com. **Website:** www.mitchelllane.com. **Contact:** Barbara Mitchell, publisher. Estab. 1993. Publishes hardcover and library bound originals. **Publishes 80 titles/year. 100 queries received/year. 5 mss received/year. 0% of books from first-time authors. 90% from unagented writers. Work purchased outright from authors (range: $350-2,000). Pays illustrators by the project (range: $40-400).** Publishes book 1 year after acceptance. Responds only if interested to queries. Book catalog available free.

NONFICTION Subjects include ethnic, multicultural. Young readers, middle readers, young adults: biography, nonfiction, and curriculum-related subjects. Average word length: 4,000-50,000 words. Recently published: *My Guide to US Citizenship*, *Rivers of the World* and *Vote America*. Query with SASE. *All unsolicited mss discarded.*

TIPS "We hire writers on a 'work-for-hire' basis to complete book projects we assign. Send résumé and writing samples that do not need to be returned."

MOMENTUM BOOKS, LLC

117 W. Third St., Royal Oak MI 48067. (248)691-1800. **Fax:** (248)691-4531. **E-mail:** info@momentumbooks.com. **Website:** www.momentumbooks.com. **Contact:** Franklin Foxx, editor. Estab. 1987. Momentum Books publishes Midwest regional nonfiction. **Publishes 6 titles/year. 100 queries received/year; 30 mss received/year. 95% of books from first-time authors. 100% from unagented writers. Pays 10-15% royalty.** Guidelines online.

NONFICTION History, sports, travel, automotive, current events, biography, entertainment. Submit proposal package, outline, 3 sample chapters, marketing outline.

TIPS "Also, custom publishing services are available for authors who are considering self-publishing."

MONDIAL

203 W. 107th St., Suite 6C, New York NY 10025. (212)851-3252. **Fax:** (208)361-2863. **E-mail:** contact@mondialbooks.com. **Website:** www.mondialbooks.com; www.librejo.com. **Contact:** Andrew Moore, editor. Estab. 1996. Publishes hard cover, trade paperback originals and reprints. **Publishes 20 titles/year. 2,000 queries received/year. 500 mss received/year. 20%% of books from first-time authors. Pays 10% royalty on wholesale price.** Publishes book 4 months after acceptance. Accepts simultaneous submissions. Responds to queries in 3 months. Responds only if interested. Guidelines online.

NONFICTION Subjects include alternative, ethnic, gay, lesbian, history, language, literature, literary criticism, memoirs, multicultural, philosophy, psychology, sex, sociology, translation. Submit proposal package, outline, 1 sample chapters. Send only electronically by e-mail.

FICTION Subjects include adventure, erotica, ethnic, gay, lesbian, historical, literary, mainstream, contemporary, multicultural, mystery, poetry, romance, short story collections, translation. Query through online submission form.

Ⓐ⊘ MOODY PUBLISHERS

Moody Bible Institute, 820 N. LaSalle Blvd., Chicago IL 60610. (800)678-8812. **Fax:** (312)329-4157. **E-mail:** authors@moody.edu. **Website:** www.moodypublishers.org. Estab. 1894. Publishes hardcover, trade, and mass market paperback originals. "The mission of Moody Publishers is to educate and edify the Christian and to evangelize the non-Christian by ethically publishing conservative, evangelical Christian literature and other media for all ages around the world, and to help provide resources for Moody Bible Institute in its training of future Christian leaders." **Publishes 60 titles/year. 1,500 queries received/year. 2,000 mss received/year. 1% of books from first-time authors. 80% from unagented writers. Royalty varies.** Publishes book 1 year after acceptance. Responds in 2-3 months to queries. Book catalog for 9×12 envelope and 4 first-class stamps. Guidelines for SASE and on website.

IMPRINTS Northfield Publishing; Lift Every Voice (African American-interest).

NONFICTION Subjects include child guidance, money, finance, religion, spirituality, women's issues, women's studies. "We are no longer reviewing queries or unsolicited mss unless they come to us through an agent. Unsolicited proposals will be returned only if proper postage is included. We are not able to acknowledge the receipt of your unsolicited proposal." Does not accept unsolicited nonfiction submissions.

FICTION Subjects include fantasy, historical, mystery, religious, children's religious, inspirational, religious mystery/suspense, science fiction, young adult, adventure, fantasy/science fiction, historical, mystery/suspense, series. Agented submissions only.

TIPS "In our fiction list, we're looking for Christian storytellers rather than teachers trying to present a message. Your motivation should be to delight the reader. Using your skills to create beautiful works is glorifying to God."

MOON TIDE PRESS

P.O. Box 50184, Irvine CA 92619. **E-mail:** publisher@moontidepress.com. **Website:** www.moontidepress.com. **Contact:** Michael Miller, publisher. Estab. 2006. **POETRY** Query first.

TIPS "Keep in mind that when we open and read your ms, it will probably be in the middle of a large stack of other submissions, and many of those will be well-meaning but undistinguished collections about the same few themes. So don't be afraid to take risks. Surprise and entertain us. Give us something that the next ten poets in the stack won't."

MOREHOUSE PUBLISHING CO.

Church Publishing Incorporated, 4475 Linglestown Rd., Harrisburg PA 17112. **Fax:** (717)541-8136. **E-mail:** dperkins@cpg.org. **Website:** www.morehouse-publishing.org. **Contact:** Davis Perkins. Estab. 1884. Publishes hardcover and paperback originals. Morehouse Publishing publishes mainline Christian books, primarily Episcopal/Anglican works. Currently emphasizing Christian spiritual direction. **Publishes 35 titles/year. 50% of books from first-time authors. Pays small advance.** Publishes book 18 months after acceptance. Accepts simultaneous submissions. Responds in 2-3 months to queries. Guidelines online.

NONFICTION Subjects include religion, Christian, women's issues, women's studies, Christian spirituality, liturgies, congregational resources, issues around Christian life. Submit outline, résumé, 1-2 sample chapters, market analysis.

MOTORBOOKS

Quayside Publishing Group, Motorbooks, MBI Publishing Company, 400 First Ave. N., Suite 400, Minneapolis MN 55401. (612)344-8100. **Fax:** (612)344-8691. **E-mail:** zmiller@quaysidepub.com. **Website:** www.motorbooks.com. **Contact:** Zack Miller. Estab. 1973. Publishes hardcover and paperback originals. "Motorbooks is one of the world's leading transportation publishers, covering subjects from classic motorcycles to heavy equipment to today's latest automotive technology. We satisfy our customers' high expectations by hiring top writers and photographers and presenting their work in handsomely designed books that work hard in the shop and look good on the coffee table." **Publishes 200 titles/year. 300 queries received/year. 50 mss received/year. 95% from unagented writers. Pays $5,000 average advance.** Publishes book 1 year after acceptance. Accepts simultaneous submissions. Responds in 6-8 months to proposals. Book catalog available free. Guidelines for #10 SASE or online.

IMPRINTS Motorbooks International, Crestline.

NONFICTION Subjects include Americana, history, hobbies, military, war, photography, translation, nonfiction. State qualifications for doing book. Trans-

portation-related subjects. Query with SASE. Reviews artwork/photos. Send photocopies.

THE MOUNTAINEERS BOOKS

1001 SW Klickitat Way, Suite 201, Seattle WA 98134-1162. (206)223-6303. **Fax:** (206)223-6306. **E-mail:** mbooks@mountaineersbooks.org. **Website:** www.mountaineersbooks.org. **Contact:** Cassandra Conyers, acquisitions editor. Estab. 1961. Publishes 95% hardcover and trade paperback originals and 5% reprints. "Mountaineers Books specializes in expert, authoritative books dealing with mountaineering, hiking, backpacking, skiing, snowshoeing, etc. These can be either how-to-do-it or where-to-do-it (guidebooks). Currently emphasizing regional conservation and natural history." **Publishes 40 titles/year. 25% of books from first-time authors. 98% from unagented writers. Pays advance.** Publishes book 1 year after acceptance of ms. Responds in 3 months to queries. Book catalog for 9×12 envelope and $1.33 postage first-class stamps. Guidelines online.

○ See the Contests and Awards section for information on the Barbara Savage/'Miles From Nowhere' Memorial Award for outstanding adventure narratives offered by Mountaineers Books.

NONFICTION Subjects include nature, environment, recreation, regional, sports, non-competitive self-propelled, translation, travel, natural history, conservation. Accepts nonfiction translations. Looks for expert knowledge, good organization. Also interested in nonfiction adventure narratives. Does *not* want to see anything dealing with hunting, fishing or motorized travel. Submit outline, 2 sample chapters, bio.

TIPS "The type of book the writer has the best chance of selling to our firm is an authoritative guidebook (*in our field*) to a specific area not otherwise covered; or a how-to that is better than existing competition (again, *in our field*)."

MOUNTAIN PRESS PUBLISHING CO.

P.O. Box 2399, Missoula MT 59806. (406)728-1900 or (800)234-5308. **Fax:** (406)728-1635. **E-mail:** info@mtnpress.com. **Website:** www.mountain-press.com. **Contact:** Jennifer Carey, editor. Estab. 1948. Publishes hardcover and trade paperback originals. "We are expanding our Roadside Geology, Geology Underfoot, and Roadside History series (done on a state-by-state basis). We are interested in well-written regional field guides—plants and flowers—and readable history and natural history." **Publishes 15 titles/year. 50% of books from first-time authors. 90% from unagented writers. Pays 7-12% royalty on wholesale price.** Publishes book 2 years after acceptance. Responds in 3 months to queries. Book catalog online.

◯ Expanding children's/juvenile nonfiction titles.

NONFICTION Subjects include animals, history, Western, nature, environment, regional, science, Earth science. No personal histories or journals, poetry or fiction. Query with SASE. Submit outline, sample chapters. Reviews artwork/photos.

TIPS "Find out what kind of books a publisher is interested in and tailor your writing to them; research markets and target your audience. Research other books on the same subjects. Make yours different. Don't present your ms to a publisher—sell it. Give the information needed to make a decision on a title. Please learn what we publish before sending your proposal. We are a 'niche' publisher."

⊘ MOVING PARTS PRESS

10699 Empire Grade, Santa Cruz CA 95060. (831)427-2271. **E-mail:** frice@movingpartspress.com. **Website:** www.movingpartspress.com. **Contact:** Felicia Rice, poetry editor. Estab. 1977. Moving Part Press publishes handsome, innovative books, broadsides, and prints that "explore the relationship of word and image, typography and the visual arts, the fine arts and popular culture."

POETRY Does not accept unsolicited mss.

MSI PRESS

1760-F Airline Hwy, #203, Hollister CA 95023. **E-mail:** editor@msipress.com. **Website:** www.msipress.com. **Contact:** Betty Leaver, managing editor (foreign culture, self-help, spirituality, religion, memoir). Estab. 2003. Publishes trade paperback originals and corresponding e-books. **Publishes 8-12 titles/year. 10% of books from first-time authors. 100% from unagented writers. Pays 10% royalty on retail price.** Publishes book 6 months after acceptance. Accepts simultaneous submissions. Responds in 1 month to queries and proposals; 2 months to mss. Catalog online. Guidelines available by e-mail.

NONFICTION Subjects include education, health, humanities, language, medicine, psychology, spirituality. "We are hoping to expand our spirituality, psychology, and self-help line." Submit proposal package, including: outline, 1 sample chapter, and professional résumé. Prefers electronic submissions. Reviews artwork/photos; send computer disk, or, preferably, e-file.

TIPS "We are interested in helping to develop new writers who have good literacy skills and a strong story. We also have the capacity to work with authors with limited English skills whose first language is Arabic, Russian, Spanish, French, German, or Czech."

MVP BOOKS

MBI Publishing and Quayside Publishing Group, 400 First Ave. N, Suite 300, Minneapolis MN 55401. (612)344-8160. **E-mail:** jleventhal@mbipublishing.com. **Website:** www.mvpbooks.com. **Contact:** Josh Leventhal, publisher. Estab. 2009. Publishes hardcover and trade paperback originals. "We publish books for enthusiasts in a wide variety of sports, recreation, and fitness subjects, including heavily illustrated celebrations, narrative works, and how-to instructional guides." **Publishes 15-20 titles/year. Pays royalty or fees. Pays advance.** Publishes book 1 year after acceptance. Responds in 3 months to queries.

◯ "We seek authors who are strongly committed to helping us promote and sell their books. Please present as focused an idea as possible in a brief submission. Note your credentials for writing the book. Tell all you know about the market niche, existing competition, and marketing possibilities for proposed book."

NONFICTION Subjects include sports (baseball, football, basketball, hockey, surfing, golf, bicycling, martial arts, etc.); outdoor activities (hunting and fishing); health and fitness. No children's books. Query with SASE. "We consider queries from both first-time and experienced authors as well as agented or unagented projects. Submit outline." Reviews artwork/photos. Send sample digital images or transparencies (duplicates and tearsheets only).

◯ NAPOLEON & COMPANY

3 Church St., Suite 500, Toronto ON M5E 1M2, Canada. **E-mail:** submissions@dundurn.com. **Website:** www.napoleonandcompany.com. **Contact:** A. Thompson, editor. Estab. 1990. Publishes hardcover and trade paperback originals and reprints. Rendezvous publishes adult fiction. Napoleon publishes children's books. **Publishes 15 titles/year. 200 queries received/year. 100 mss received/year. 50% of books from first-time authors. 75% from unagented writers.** Publishes book 18 months after acceptance. Accepts simultaneous submissions. Responds in 1

month to queries; 3 months to proposals; 6 months to mss. Book catalog and guidelines online.

○ "Napoleon is not accepting children's picture books at this time. Rendezvous Crime is not accepting mysteries. Check website for updates. We are accepting general adult fiction only for RendezVous Press and Darkstar Fiction."

NONFICTION Query with SASE. Submit outline, 1 sample chapter.

TIPS Canadian resident authors only.

NATIONAL ASSOCIATION FOR MUSIC EDUCATION

1806 Robert Fulton Dr., Reston VA 20191-4348. **Fax:** (703)860-1531. **E-mail:** ellaw@nafme.org. **Website:** www.nafme.org. **Contact:** Ella Wilcox, editor; Linda Brown, editor. Sue Rarus, Dir. of Informaton Resources and Publications Estab. 1907. Publishes hardcover and trade paperback originals. "Our mission is to advance music education by encouraging the study and making of music by all." **Publishes 10 titles/year. 75 queries received/year. 50 mss received/year. 40% of books from first-time authors. 100% from unagented writers. Pays royalty on retail price.** Publishes book 1-2 years after acceptance. Responds in 2 months to queries; 4 months to proposals. Catalog and guidelines online.

NONFICTION Subjects include child guidance, education, multicultural, music, dance, music education. Mss evaluated by professional music educators. Submit proposal package, outline, 1-3 sample chapters, bio, CV, marketing strategy. For journal articles, submit electronically to mc.mscentral.com/mej. Authors will be required to set up an online account on the SAGETRACK system powered by ScholarOne (this can take about 30 minutes). From their account, a new submission can be initiated.

TIPS "Look online for book proposal guidelines. No telephone calls. We are committed to music education books that will serve as the very best resources for music educators, students and their parents."

NATUREGRAPH PUBLISHERS, INC.

P.O. Box 1047, Happy Camp CA 96039. **Fax:** (530)493-5240. **E-mail:** nature@sisqtel.net. **Website:** www.naturegraph.com. **Contact:** Barbara Brown, owner. Estab. 1946. Publishes trade paperback originals. **Publishes 2 titles/year. 300 queries received/year. 12 mss received/year. 80% of books from first-time authors.** Publishes book 2 years after acceptance. Accepts si-

multaneous submissions. Responds in 1 month to queries; 2 months to mss. Book catalog for #10 SASE.

NONFICTION Subjects include anthropology, archaeology, multicultural, nature, environment, science, natural history: biology, geology, ecology, astronomy, crafts.

THE NAUTICAL & AVIATION PUBLISHING CO.

845 A Low Country Blvd., Mt. Pleasant SC 29464. (843)856-0561. **Fax:** (843)856-3164. **Website:** www.nauticalaviation.bizland.com. **Contact:** Denise K. James. Estab. 1979. Publishes hardcover and trade paperback originals and reprints. **Publishes 6 titles/year. 200 queries received/year. Pays royalty.** Accepts simultaneous submissions.

NONFICTION Subjects include military, war, American, naval history. Query with SASE. Submit 3 sample chapters, synopsis.

FICTION Subjects include historical, military, war. Submit complete ms with cover letter and brief synopsis.

TIPS "We are primarily a nonfiction publisher, but we will review historical fiction of military interest with strong literary merit."

NAVAL INSTITUTE PRESS

US Naval Institute, 291 Wood Rd., Annapolis MD 21402. (410)268-6110. **Fax:** (410)295-1084. **E-mail:** books@usni.org. **Website:** www.usni.org. Estab. 1873. "The Naval Institute Press publishes trade and scholarly nonfiction. We are interested in national and international security, naval, military, military jointness, intelligence, and special warfare, both current and historical." **Publishes 80-90 titles/year. 50% of books from first-time authors. 90% from unagented writers.** Guidelines online.

NONFICTION Submit proposal package with outline, author bio, TOC, description/synopsis, sample chapter(s), page/word count, number of illustrations, ms completion date, intended market; or submit complete ms. Send SASE with sufficient postage for return of ms. Send by postal mail only. No e-mail submissions, please.

⊘ NAVPRESS

P.O. Box 35002, Colorado Springs CO 80935. **Fax:** (719)260-7223. **E-mail:** customerservice@navpress.com. **Website:** www.navpress.com. Estab. 1975. Publishes hardcover, trade paperback, direct and mass market paperback originals and reprints; electronic books and Bible studies. **Pays royalty. Pays low or no advances.** Book catalog available free.

NONFICTION Subjects include child guidance, parenting, sociology, spirituality and contemporary culture, Christian living, marriage.

NBM PUBLISHING

160 Broadway, Suite 700, East Bldg., New York NY 10038. **E-mail:** nbmgn@nbmpub.com. **Website:** nbmpub.com. **Contact:** Terry Nantier, editor/art director. Estab. 1976. Publishes graphic novels for an audience of YA/adults. Types of books include fiction, mystery and social parodies.

NEAL-SCHUMAN PUBLISHERS, INC.

50 E. Huron St., Chicago IL 60611. (312)280-5846. **Fax:** (312)280-5275. **E-mail:** info@neal-schuman.com. **Website:** www.neal-schuman.com. **Contact:** J. Michael Jeffers, vice president/ director of publishing. Estab. 1976. Publishes trade paperback originals. "Neal-Schuman publishes books about library management, archival science, records management, digital curation, information literary, the Internet and information technology. Especially submitting proposals for undergraduate information studies, archival science, records management, and knowledge management textbooks." **Publishes 36 titles/year. 150 queries received/year. 80% of books from first-time authors. 100% from unagented writers. Pays 10-15% royalty on wholesale price. Pays infrequent advance.** Publishes book 1 year after acceptance. Accepts simultaneous submissions. Responds in 1 month. Book catalog free.

NONFICTION Subjects include computers, electronics, education, software, Internet guides, library and information science, archival studies, records management. Submit proposal package, outline, 1 sample chapter. Reviews artwork. Send photocopies.

TIPS "Our audience are professional librarians, archivists, and records managers."

Ⓐ THOMAS NELSON, INC.

Box 141000, Nashville TN 37214-1000. (615)889-9000. **Website:** www.thomasnelson.com. **Contact:** Acquisitions Editor. Publishes hardcover and paperback orginals. Thomas Nelson publishes Christian lifestyle nonfiction and fiction, and general nonfiction. **Publishes 100-150 titles/year. Rates negotiated for each project Pays advance.** Publishes book 1-2 years after acceptance of ms. Accepts simultaneous submissions.

IMPRINTS Nelson Books; W Publishing; Rutledge Hill Press; J. Countryman; Cool Springs Press; Reference & Electronic Publishing; Editorial Caribe; Nelson Curriculum; Tommy Nelson; Nelson Current; WestBow Press.

Ⓞ *Does not accept unsolicited mss.* No phone queries.

NONFICTION Subjects include business, economics, business, economics development, cooking, foods, nutrition, gardening, health, medicine, and fitness, religion, spirituality, adult inspirational, motivational, devotional, Christian living, prayer and evangelism, Bible study, personal development, political, biography/autobiography.

FICTION Publishes authors of commercial fiction who write for adults from a Christian perspective.

➕⊘ TOMMY NELSON

Imprint of Thomas Nelson, Inc., P.O. Box 141000, Nashville TN 37214-1000. (615)889-9000. **Fax:** (615)902-2219. **Website:** www.tommynelson.com. Publishes hardcover and trade paperback originals. "Tommy Nelson publishes children's Christian nonfiction and fiction for boys and girls up to age 14. We honor God and serve people through books, videos, software and Bibles for children that improve the lives of our customers." **Publishes 50-75 titles/year.** Guidelines online.

Ⓞ *Does not accept unsolicited mss.*

NONFICTION Subjects include religion, Christian evangelical.

FICTION Subjects include adventure, juvenile, mystery, picture books, religious. No stereotypical characters.

TIPS "Know the Christian Booksellers Association market. Check out the Christian bookstores to see what sells and what is needed."

Ⓐ⊘ NEW AMERICAN LIBRARY

Penguin Putnam, Inc., 375 Hudson St., New York NY 10014. (212)366-2000. **Fax:** (212)366-2889. **Website:** www.penguinputnam.com. Estab. 1948. Publishes mass market and trade paperback originals and reprints. NAL publishes commercial fiction and nonfiction for the popular audience. **Pays negotiable royalty. Pays negotiable advance.** Book catalog for SASE.

IMPRINTS Onyx; ROC; Signet; Signet Classic; NAL trade paperback; Signet Eclipse.

NONFICTION Subjects include animals, child guidance, ethnic, health, medicine, military, war, psychology, sports, movie tie-in. Agented submissions only.

FICTION Subjects include erotica, ethnic, fantasy, historical, horror, mainstream, contemporary, mystery, romance, science fiction, suspense, western, chicklit. All kinds of commercial fiction. Query with SASE. Agented submissions only. State type of book and past publishing projects.

⊕ NEW DIRECTIONS

New Directions Publishing Corp., 80 Eighth Ave., New York NY 10011. **Fax:** (212)255-0231. **E-mail:** editorial@ndbooks.com. **Website:** www.ndpublishing.com. **Contact:** Editorial Assistant. Estab. 1936. Hardcover and trade paperback originals. "Currently, New Directions focuses primarily on fiction in translation, avant garde American fiction, and experimental poetry by American and foreign authors. If your work does not fall into one of those categories, you would probably do best to submit your work elsewhere." **Publishes 30 titles/year.** Responds in 3-4 months to queries. Book catalog and Guidelines online.

◯   Submit by post office mail.

FICTION Subjects include ethnic, experimental, historical, humor, literary, poetry, poetry in translation, regional, short story collections, suspense, translation. No juvenile or young adult, occult or paranormal, genre fiction (formula romances, sci-fi or westerns), arts & crafts, & inspirational poetry. Submit clips, cover letter, CV, writing credentials, professional experience or otherwise, 1-3 pages of work.

POETRY Query.

TIPS "Our books serve the academic community."

NEW FORUMS PRESS

New Forums, 1018 S. Lewis St., Stillwater OK 74074. (405)372-6158. **Fax:** (405)377-2237. **E-mail:** contact@newforums.com. **E-mail:** submissions@newforums.com. **Website:** www.newforums.com. **Contact:** Doug Dollar, president (interests: higher education, Oklahoma-Regional). Estab. 1981. Hardcover and trade paperback originals. "New Forums Press is an independent publisher offering works devoted to various aspects of professional development in higher education, home and office aides, and various titles of a regional interest. We welcome suggestions for thematic series of books and thematic issues of our academic journals—addressing a single issue, problem, or theory." **60% of books from first-time authors. 100% from unagented writers.** Use Author Guidelines online or call (800)606-3766 with any questions.

NONFICTION Subjects include business, finance, history, literature, money, music, politics, regional, sociology, young adult. "We are actively seeking new authors—send for review copies and author guidelines, and visit our website." Mss should be submitted as a Microsoft Word document, or a similar standard word processor document (saved in RTF rich text), as an attachment to an e-mail sent to submissions@newforums.com. Otherwise, submit your ms on 8 ½ x 11 inch white bond paper (one original). The name and complete address, telephone, fax number, and e-mail address of each author should appear on a separate cover page, so it can be removed for the blind review process.

NEW HARBINGER PUBLICATIONS

5674 Shattuck Ave., Oakland CA 94609. (510)652-0215. **Fax:** (510)652-5472. **E-mail:** proposals@newharbinger.com. **Website:** www.newharbinger.com. **Contact:** Catharine Meyers, VP of development. Estab. 1973. "We look for psychology and health self-help books that teach readers how to master essential life skills. Mental health professionals who want simple, clear explanations or important psychological techniques and health issues also read our books. Thus, our books must be simple ane easy to understand but also complete and authoritative. Most of our authors are therapists or other helping professionals." **Publishes 55 titles/year. 1,000 queries received/year. 300 mss received/year. 60% of books from first-time authors. 75% from unagented writers.** Publishes book 1 year after acceptance of ms. Accepts simultaneous submissions. Responds in 2 weeks to queries. Responds in 1 month to proposals. Responds in 2 months to mss. Book catalog available free. Guidelines online.

NONFICTION Subjects include health, medicine, psychology, women's issues, women's studies, psycho spirituality, anger management, anxiety, coping, mindfulness skills. Authors need to be qualified psychotherapists or health practitioners to publish with us. Submit proposal package, outline, 2 sample chapters, TOC, competing titles, and a compelling, supported reason why the book is unique.

TIPS "Audience includes psychotherapists and lay readers wanting step-by-step strategies to solve specific problems. Our definition of a self-help psychology or health book is one that teaches essential life skills. The primary goal is to train the reader so that, after reading the book, he or she can deal more effectively with health and/or psychological challenges."

NEW ISSUES POETRY & PROSE

Western Michigan University, 1903 W. Michigan Ave., Kalamazoo MI 49008-5463. (269)387-8185. **Fax:** (269)387-2562. **E-mail:** new-issues@wmich.edu. **Website:** wmich.edu/newissues. **Contact:** Managing Editor. Estab. 1996. **50% of books from first-time authors. 95% from unagented writers.** Publishes book Publishes 18 months after acceptance. Accepts simultaneous submissions. Guidelines online.

FICTION Subjects include literary, poetry. Only considers submissions to book contests.

POETRY New Issues Poetry & Prose offers two contests annually. The Green Rose Prize is awarded to an author who has previously published at least one full-length book of poems. The New Issues Poetry Prize, an award for a first book of poems, is chosen by a guest judge. Past judges have included Philip Levine, C.K. Williams, C.D. Wright, and Campbell McGrath. New Issues does not read mss outside our contests. Graduate students in the Ph.D. and M.F.A. programs of Western Michigan Univ. often volunteer their time reading mss. Finalists are chosen by the editors. New Issues often publishes up to 2 additional mss selected from the finalists.

🌐 NEW LIBRI PRESS

4230 95th Ave. SE, Mercer Island WA 98040. **E-mail:** query@newlibri.com. **Website:** www.newlibri.com. **Contact:** Michael Muller, editor; Stanislav Fritz, editor. Estab. 2011. Publishes trade paperback, electronic original, electronic reprints. **Publishes 10 titles/year. 80% of books from first-time authors. 100% from unagented writers. Pays 20-35% royalty on wholesale price. No advance.** Publishes book 9-12 months after acceptance. Responds in 1 month to mss. Catalog online. Guidelines online.

NONFICTION Subjects include agriculture, automotive, business, child guidance, computers, cooking, creative nonfiction, economics, electronics, environment, gardening, hobbies, house and home, nature, parenting, recreation, science, sex, software, translation, travel. "Writers should know we embrace ebooks. This means that some formats and types of books work well and others don't." Prefers e-mail. Submit proposal package, including outline, 2 sample chapters, and summary of market from author's perspective. Prefers complete ms.

FICTION Subjects include adventure, experimental, fantasy, historical, horror, literary, mainstream, military, mystery, science fiction, translation, war, western, young adult. "Open to most ideas right now; this will change as we mature as a press. As a new press, we are more open than most and time will probably shape the direction. That said, trite as it is, we want good writing that is fun to read. While we currently are not looking for some sub-genres, if it is well written and a bit off the beaten path, submit to us. We are e-book focused. We may not create a paper version if the e-book does not sell, which means some fiction may be less likely to currently sell (e.g. picture books would work only on an iPad or Color Nook as of this writing)." Submit proposal package, including synopsis. Prefers complete ms.

TIPS "Our audience is someone who is comfortable reading an e-book, or someone who is tired of the recycled authors of mainstream publishing, but still wants a good, relatively fast, reading experience. The industry is changing, while we accept for the traditional model, we are searching for writers who are interested in sharing the risk and controlling their own destiny. We embrace writers with no agent."

NEW RIVERS PRESS

MSU Moorhead, 1104 Seventh Ave. S., Moorhead MN 56563. **E-mail:** kelleysu@mnstate.edu. **Website:** www.newriverspress.com. **Contact:** Alan Davis. Suzzanne Kelley, managing editor. Estab. 1968. New Rivers Press publishes collections of poetry, novels, nonfiction, translations of contemporary literature, and collections of short fiction and nonfiction. "We continue to publish books regularly by new and emerging writers, but we also welcome the opportunity to read work of every character and to publish the best literature available nationwide. Each fall through the Many Voices Project competition, we choose 2 books: 1 poetry and 1 prose."

POETRY The Many Voices Project awards $1,000, a standard book contract, publication of a book-length ms by New Rivers Press, and national distribution. All previously published poems must be acknowledged. "We will consider simultaneous submissions if noted as such. If your ms is accepted elsewhere during the judging, you must notify New Rivers Press immediately. If you do not give such notification and your ms is selected, your entry gives New Rivers Press permission to go ahead with publication." Submit 50-80 pages of poetry. Entry form (required) and guidelines online. **Entry fee:** $25. **Deadline:** submit September 15-November 1 (postmark). Guidelines online.

NEWSAGE PRESS

P.O. Box 607, Troutdale OR 97060-0607. (503)695-2211. **E-mail:** info@newsagepress.com. **Website:** www.newsagepress.com. **Contact:** Maureen R. Michelson, publisher; Sherry Wachter, design. Estab. 1985. Publishes trade paperback originals. "We focus on nonfiction books. No 'how-to' books or cynical, despairing books. Photo-essay books in large format are no longer published by Newsage Press. No novels or other forms of fiction." Guidelines online.

NONFICTION Subjects include animals, multicultural, nature, environment, womens issues, womens studies, death/dying. Submit 2 sample chapters, proposal (no more than 1 page), SASE.

NEW VICTORIA PUBLISHERS

2455 W. Warner Ave., Chicago IL 60613. (773)793-2244. **E-mail:** newvictoriapub@att.net. **Website:** www.newvictoria.com. **Contact:** Patricia Feuerhaken, president. Estab. 1976. Publishes trade paperback originals. "Publishes mostly lesbian fiction—strong female protagonists. Most well known for Stoner McTavish mystery series." Distributes titles through Amazon Books, Bella books, Bulldog Books (Sydney, Australia), and Women and Children First Books (Chicago). Promotes titles "mostly through lesbian feminist media." **Publishes 3 titles/year. Pays 10% royalty.** Publishes book 1 year after acceptance. Accepts simultaneous submissions. Catalog free on request; for #10 SASE; or online. Guidelines free on request; for #10 SASE; or online.

NONFICTION Subjects include alternative, biography, lesbian, history, language, poetry, fiction, literature, memoirs, multicultural, music/dance, mystery, nature, environment, New Age, erotica, translation, women's issues/studies, world affairs, contemporary culture, autobiography, biography, general nonfiction, humor, reference, science fiction. "We will consider well-researched nonfiction of interest to women, as well as lesbian feminist herstory, or biography of interest to a general as well as academic audience." Query with SASE. Reviews artwork/photos; send photocopies.

FICTION Lesbian, feminist fiction including adventure, erotica, fantasy, historical, humor, mystery (amateur sleuth), or science fiction. Accepts unsolicited mss, but prefers query first. Submit outline, synopsis, and sample chapters (50 pages). No queries by e-mail or fax; please send SASE or IRC. No simultaneous submissions.

TIPS "We are especially interested in lesbian or feminist novels, ideally with a character or characters who can evolve through a series of books. Stories should involve a complex plot, accurate details, and protagonists with full emotional lives. Pay attention to plot and character development. Read guidelines carefully. We advise you to look through our catalog or visit our website to see our past editorial decisions as well as what we are currently marketing. Our books average 80-100,000 words, or 200-220 single-spaced pages."

NEW WORLD LIBRARY

14 Pamaron Way, Novato CA 94949. (415)884-2100. **Fax:** (415)884-2199. **E-mail:** submit@newworldlibrary.com. **Website:** www.newworldlibrary.com. **Contact:** Jonathan Wichmann, submissions editor. Estab. 1979. Publishes hardcover and trade paperback originals and reprints. "NWL is dedicated to publishing books that inspire and challenge us to improve the quality of our lives and our world." **Publishes 35-40 titles/year. 10% of books from first-time authors. 40% from unagented writers.** Accepts simultaneous submissions. Responds in 3 months to queries. Book catalog available free. Guidelines online.

IMPRINTS H.J. Kramer.

Prefers e-mail submissions. No longer accepting children's mss.

NONFICTION Submit outline, bio, 2-3 sample chapters, SASE.

NEW YORK UNIVERSITY PRESS

838 Broadway, New York NY 10003. (212)998-2575. **Fax:** (212)995-3833. **E-mail:** information@nyupress.org. **Website:** www.nyupress.org. **Contact:** Eric Zinner (cultural studies, literature, media, history); Jennifer Hammer (Jewish studies, psychology, religion, women's studies); Ilene Kalish (sociology, criminology, politics); Deborah Gershenowitz (law, American history). Estab. 1916. Hardcover and trade paperback originals. "New York University Press embraces ideological diversity. We often publish books on the same issue from different poles to generate dialogue, engender and resist pat categorizations." **Publishes**

100 titles/year. 800-1,000 queries received/year. 30% of books from first-time authors. 90% from unagented writers. Publishes book 9-11 months after acceptance of ms. Accepts simultaneous submissions. Responds in 1-4 months (peer reviewed) to proposals. Guidelines online.

NONFICTION Subjects include business, economics, ethnic, gay, lesbian, government, politics, language, literature, military, war, psychology, regional, religion, sociology, women's issues, women's studies, American history, anthropology. New York University Press is a publisher primarily of academic books and is a department of the New York University Division of Libraries. NYU Press publishes in the humanities and social sciences, with emphasis on sociology, law, cultural and American studies, religion, American history, anthropology, politics, criminology, media and film, and psychology. The Press also publishes books on New York regional history, politics, and culture. Query with SASE. Submit proposal package, outline, 1 sample chapter. Reviews artwork/photos. Send photocopies.

TIPS Make submissions to appropriate editor. E-mails go by first name.last name@nyupress.edu.

⊘ NINETY-SIX PRESS

Furman University, 3300 Poinsett Hwy., Greenville SC 29613. (864)294-3152. **Fax:** (864)294-2224. **E-mail:** gil.allen@furman.edu. **Website:** library.furman.edu/specialcollections/96Press/index.htm. **Contact:** Gilbert Allen, editor. Estab. 1991. For a sample, send $10.

TIPS "South Carolina poets only. Check our website for guidelines."

⊕ NOLO

950 Parker St., Berkeley CA 94710. (510)549-1976. **Fax:** (510)859-0025. **E-mail:** mantha@nolo.com. **Website:** www.nolo.com. **Contact:** Editorial Department. Estab. 1971. Publishes trade paperback originals. "We publish practical, do-it-yourself books, software and various electronic products on financial and legal issues that affect individuals, small business, and nonprofit organizations. We specialize in helping people handle their own legal tasks; i.e., write a will, file a small claims lawsuit, start a small business or nonprofit, or apply for a patent." **Publishes 75 new editions and 15 new titles/year. 20% of books from first-time authors. Pays advance.** Accepts simultaneous submissions. Responds in 3 weeks to queries. Responds in 5 weeks to proposals. Guidelines online.

NONFICTION Subjects include business, economics, money, finance, legal guides in various topics including employment, small business, intellectual property, parenting and education, finance and investment, landlord/tenant, real estate, and estate planning. Query with SASE. Submit outline, 1 sample chapter.

NOMAD PRESS

2456 Christain St., White River Junction VT 05001. (802)649-1995. **Fax:** (802)649-2667. **E-mail:** rachel@nomadpress.net; info@nomadpress.net. **Website:** www.nomadpress.net. **Contact:** Alex Kahan, publisher. Estab. 2001. "We produce nonfiction children's activity books that bring a particular science or cultural topic into sharp focus. Nomad Press does not accept unsolicited mss. If authors are interested in contributing to our children's series, please send a writing résumé that includes relevant experience/expertise and publishing credits." **Pays authors royalty based on retail price or work purchased outright. Offers advance against royalties.** Publishes book 1 year after acceptance. Responds to queries in 3-4 weeks. Catalog online.

◻ Nomad Press does not accept picture books or fiction.

NONFICTION Middle readers: activity books, history, science. Average word length: middle readers—30,000.

TIPS "We publish a very specific kind of nonfiction children's activity book. Please keep this in mind when querying or submitting."

NORTH ATLANTIC BOOKS

2526 MLK Jr. Way, Berkeley CA 94704. **Website:** www.northatlanticbooks.com. **Contact:** Douglas Reil, associate publisher; Erin Wiegand, senior acquisitions editor. Estab. 1974. Publishes hardcover, trade paperback, and electronic originals; trade paperback and electronic reprints. **Publishes 60 titles/year. Receives 200 mss/year. 50% of books from first-time authors. 75% from unagented writers. Pays royalty percentage on wholesale price.** Publishes book 14 months after acceptance. Accepts simultaneous submissions. Responds in 3-6 months. Book catalog free on request (if available). Guidelines online.

IMPRINTS Evolver Editions, Blue Snake Books.

NONFICTION Subjects include agriculture, anthropology, archeology, architecture, art, astrology, business, child guidance, community, contemporary culture, cooking, economics, electronics, environment, finance, foods, gardening, gay, health, horticulture, lesbian, medicine, memoirs, money, multicultural, nature, New Age, nutrition, philosophy, politics, psychic, psychology, public affairs, religion, science, social sciences, sociology, spirituality, sports, travel, womens issues, womens studies, world affairs. "See our submission guidelines on our website." Submit proposal package including an outline, 3-4 sample chapters, and "a 75-word statement about the book, your qualifications as an author, marketing plan/audience, for the book, and comparable titles." Reviews artwork with ms package.

FICTION Subjects include adventure, literary, multicultural, mystery, regional, science fiction, spiritual. "We only publish fiction on rare occasions." Submit proposal package including an outline, 3-4 sample chapters, and "a 75-word statement about the book, your qualifications as an author, marketing plan/audience, for the book, and comparable titles."

POETRY Submit 15-20 sample poems.

NORTH CAROLINA OFFICE OF ARCHIVES AND HISTORY

Historical Publications Section, 4622 Mail Service Center, Raleigh NC 27699. (919)733-7442. **Fax:** (919)733-1439. **E-mail:** historical.publications@ncdcr.gov. **Website:** www.ncpublications.com. **Contact:** Donna E. Kelly, administrator (North Carolina and southern history). Publishes hardcover and trade paperback originals. "We publish *only* titles that relate to North Carolina. The North Carolina Office of Archives and History also publishes the *North Carolina Historical Review*, a quarterly scholarly journal of history." **Publishes 4 titles/year. 20 queries received/year. 25 mss received/year. 5% of books from first-time authors. 100% from unagented writers. Makes one-time payment upon delivery of completed ms.** Publishes book 2 years after acceptance. Accepts simultaneous submissions. Responds in 1 week to queries and to proposals; 2 months to mss. Guidelines for $3.

NONFICTION Subjects include history, related to North Carolina, military, war, related to North Carolina, regional, North Carolina and Southern history. Query with SASE. Reviews artwork/photos. Send photocopies.

NORTH LIGHT BOOKS

F+W Media, Inc., 10151 Carver Rd., Suite 200, Blue Ash OH 45242. **Fax:** (513)891-7153. **E-mail:** mona.

clough@fwmedia.com. **Website:** www.fwmedia.com, www.artistsnetwork.om. **Contact:** Mona Clough, content director art and mixed media. Publishes hardcover and trade paperback how-to books. "North Light Books publishes art books, including watercolor, drawing, mixed media, acrylic that emphasize illustrated how-to art instruction. Currently emphasizing drawing including traditional as well as creativity and inspiration." **Publishes 70-75 titles/year. Pays 8% royalty on net receipts and $3,000 advance.** Accepts simultaneous submissions. Responds in 2 months to queries. visit www.northlightshop.com.

○ This market is for experienced fine artists who are willing to work with an North Light editor to produce a step-by-step how-to book that teaches readers how to accomplish art techniques. See also separate listing for F+W Media, Inc., in this section.

NONFICTION Subjects include hobbies,, watercolor, realistic drawing, creativity, decorative painting, paper arts, collage and other craft instruction books. Interested in books on acrylic painting, basic drawing and sketching, journaling, pen and ink, colored pencil, decorative painting, art and how-to. Do not submit coffee table art books without how-to art instruction. Query via e-mail only. Submit outline with JPEG low-resolution images. Submissions via snail mail will not be returned.

NORTH POINT PRESS

Imprint of Farrar Straus & Giroux, Inc., 19 Union Square W., New York NY 10003. (212)741-6900. **E-mail:** fsg.editorial@fsgbooks.com. **Website:** www.fsgbooks.com. Estab. 1980. Publishes hardcover and paperback originals. "We are a broad-based literary trade publisher-high quality writing only." **Pays standard royalty. Pays varied advance.** Accepts simultaneous submissions. Guidelines for #10 SASE.

NONFICTION Subjects include history, nature, environment, religion;no New Age, travel, cultural criticism, music, cooking/food. Be familiar with our list. No genres. Query with SASE. Submit outline, 1-2 sample chapters.

NORTIA PRESS

Santa Ana CA **E-mail:** acquisitions@nortiapress.com. **Website:** www.nortiapress.com. Estab. 2009. Publishes trade paperback and electronic originals. **Publishes 6 titles/year. 0% of books from first-time authors. 80% from unagented writers. Pays negotiable roy-**

alties on wholesale price. Publishes book 7 months after acceptance. Accepts simultaneous submissions. Responds in 1 month to queries and proposals.

NONFICTION Subjects include ethnic, government, humanities, military, public affairs, religion, social sciences, sociology, war, womens issues.

FICTION Subjects include ethnic, historical, literary, military, war. "We focus mainly on nonfiction as well as literary and historical fiction, but are open to other genres. No vampire stories, science fiction, or erotica, please." Submit a brief e-mail query. Please include a short bio, approximate word count of book, and expected date of completion (fiction titles should be completed before sending a query, and should contain a sample chapter in the body of the e-mail). All unsolicited snail mail or attachments will be discarded without review.

TIPS "We specialize in working with experienced authors who seek a more collaborative and fulfilling relationship with their publisher. As such, we are less likely to accept pitches form first-time authors, no matter how good the idea. As with any pitch, please make your e-mail very brief and to the point, so the reader is not forced to skim it. Always include some biographic information. Your life is interesting."

Ⓐ⊘ W.W. NORTON & COMPANY, INC.

500 Fifth Ave., New York NY 10110. (212)354-5500. **Fax:** (212)869-0856. **Website:** www.wwnorton.com. **Contact:** Trish Marks. Estab. 1923. "W. W. Norton & Company, the oldest and largest publishing house owned wholly by its employees, strives to carry out the imperative of its founder to 'publish books not for a single season, but for the years' in fiction, nonfiction, poetry, college textbooks, cookbooks, art books and professional books."

○ "Due to the workload of our editorial staff and the large volume of materials we receive, *Norton is no longer able to accept unsolicited submissions*. If you are seeking publication, we suggest working with a literary agent who will represent you to the house."

NO STARCH PRESS, INC.

38 Ringold St., Suite 250, San Francisco CA 94103. (415)863-9900. **Fax:** (415)863-9950. **E-mail:** info@nostarch.com. **Website:** www.nostarch.com. **Contact:** William Pollock, publisher. Estab. 1994. Publishes trade paperback originals. "No Starch Press publishes the finest in geek entertainment—unique books on technology, with a focus on open source, security, hacking, programming, alternative operating systems, LEGO, science, and math. Our titles have personality, our authors are passionate, and our books tackle topics that people care about. No Starch Press titles have received numerous awards, including gold medals from the Independent Publisher Book Awards (the 'IPPYs') and ForeWord's Book of the Year Awards, and have been showcased in the prestigious STEP Inside Design 100 and Communication Arts Design Annual. Visit www.nostarch.com for a complete catalog." **Publishes 20-25 titles/year. 100 queries received/year. 5 mss received/year. 80% of books from first-time authors. 90% from unagented writers. Pays 10-15% royalty on wholesale price. Pays advance.** Publishes book 4 months after acceptance. Accepts simultaneous submissions. Book catalog online.

NONFICTION Subjects include science, technology, computing, lego. Submit outline, bio, 1 sample chapter, market rationale. Reviews artwork/photos. Send photocopies.

TIPS "Books must be relevant to tech-savvy, geeky readers."

NOVA PRESS

9058 Lloyd Place, West Hollywood CA 90069. (310)275-3513. **Fax:** (310)281-5629. **E-mail:** novapress@aol.com. **Website:** www.novapress.net. **Contact:** Jeff Kolby, president. Estab. 1993. Publishes trade paperback originals. "Nova Press publishes only test prep books for college entrance exams (SAT, GRE, GMAT, LSAT, etc.), and closely related reference books, such as college guides and vocabulary books." **Publishes 4 titles/year.** Publishes book 6 months after acceptance. Book catalog available free.

NONFICTION Subjects include education, software.

NURSESBOOKS.ORG

American Nurses Association, 8515 Georgia Ave., Suite 400, Silver Spring MD 20901. (800)274-4ANA. **Fax:** (301)628-5003. **E-mail:** anp@ana.org. **Website:** www.nursesbooks.org. **Contact:** Rosanne Roe, publisher; Eric Wurzbacher, editor/project manager; Camille Walker, business operations coordinator/project manager. Publishes professional paperback originals and reprints. "Nursebooks.org publishes books designed to help professional nurses in their work and careers. Through the publishing program, Nursebooks.org provides nurses in all practice settings with publications that address cutting edge issues and form a basis for debate and exploration of this century's most critical health care trends." **Publishes 10 titles/ year. 50 queries received/year. 8-10 mss received/ year. 75% of books from first-time authors. 100% from unagented writers.** Publishes book 4 months after acceptance. Responds in 3 months. Book catalog online. Guidelines available free.

NONFICTION Subjects include advanced practice, computers, continuing education, ethics, health care policy, nursing administration, psychiatric and mental health, quality, nursing history, workplace issues, key clinical topics, such as geriatrics, pain management, public health, spirituality and home health. Submit outline, 1 sample chapter, CV, list of 3 reviewers and paragraph on audience and how to reach them. Reviews artwork/photos. Send photocopies.

OAK KNOLL PRESS

310 Delaware St., New Castle DE 19720. (302)328-7232. **Fax:** (302)328-7274. **E-mail:** Laura@oakknoll. com. **Website:** www.oakknoll.com. **Contact:** Laura R. Williams, publishing director. Estab. 1976. Publishes hardcover and trade paperback originals and reprints. "Oak Knoll specializes in books about books and manuals on the book arts: preserving the art and lore of the printed word." **Publishes 40 titles/year. 250 queries received/year. 100 mss received/year. 50% of books from first-time authors. 100% from unagented writers.** Publishes book 1 year after acceptance. Accepts simultaneous submissions. Guidelines online.

NONFICTION Reviews artwork/photos. Send photocopies.

OAK TREE PRESS

1820 W. Lacy Blvd., #220, Hanford CA 93230. **E-mail:** query@oaktreebooks.com. **Website:** www.oaktreebooks.com. **Contact:** Billie Johnson, publisher (mysteries, romance, nonfiction); Sarah Wasson, acquisitions editor (all); Barbara Hoffman, senior editor (children's, young adult, educational). Estab. 1998. Publishes trade paperback and hardcover books. "Oak Tree Press is an independent publisher that celebrates writers, and is dedicated to the many great unknowns who are just waiting for the opportunity to break into print. We're looking for mainstream, genre fiction, narrative nonfiction, how-to. Sponsors 3 contests annually: Dark Oak Mystery, Timeless Love Romance and CopTales for true crime and other stories of law enforcement professionals." **Royalties based on sales. No advance.** Publishes book 9-18 months after acceptance. Responds in 4-6 weeks. Catalog and guidelines online.

⍉ "I am always on the lookout for good mysteries, ones that engage quickly. I definitely want to add to our Timeless Love list. I am also looking at a lot of nonfiction, especially in the 'how-to' category. We are one of a few publishers who will consider memoirs, especially memoirs of folks who are not famous, and this is because I enjoy reading them myself. In addition, plans are in progress to launch a political/current affairs imprint, and I am actively looking for titles to build this list. Then, of course, there is always that 'special something' book that you can't quite describe, but you know it when you see it. "

FICTION Subjects include adventure, confession, contemporary, ethnic, fantasy, feminist, humor, mainstream, mystery, picture books, suspense, young adult. Emphasis on mystery and romance novels. "No science fiction or fantasy novels, or stories set far into the future. Next, novels substantially longer than our stated word count are not considered, regardless of genre. We look for mss of 70-90,000 words. If the story really charms us, we will bend some on either end of the range. No right-wing political or racist agenda, gratuitous sex or violence, especially against women, or depict harm of animals." Does not accept or return unsolicited mss. Query with SASE. Accepts queries by e-mail. Include estimated word count, brief bio, list of publishing credits, brief description of ms.

TIPS "Perhaps my most extreme pet peeve is receiving queries on projects which we've clearly advertised we don't want: science fiction, fantasy, epic tomes, bigoted diatribes and so on. Second to that is a practice I call 'over-taping,' or the use of yards and yards of tape, or worse yet, the filament tape so that it takes forever to open the package. Finding story pitches on my voice mail is also annoying."

OBERLIN COLLEGE PRESS

50 N. Professor St., Oberlin College, Oberlin OH 44074. (440)775-8408. **Fax:** (440)775-8124. **E-mail:** oc.press@oberlin.edu. **Website:** www.oberlin.edu/ ocpress. **Contact:** Marco Wilkinson, managing editor. Estab. 1969. Publishes hardcover and trade paperback originals. **Publishes 2-3 titles/year. Pays**

7½-10% royalty. Accepts simultaneous submissions. Responds promptly to queries; 2 months to mss.

IMPRINTS *FIELD: Contemporary Poetry & Poetics*, a magazine published twice annually, FIELD Translation Series, FIELD Poetry Series, FIELD Editions Anthologies.

POETRY *FIELD Magazine*—submit 2-6 poems through website "submissions" tab; FIELD Translation Series—query with SASE and sample poems; FIELD Poetry Series—*no unsolicited mss.* Enter mss in FIELD Poetry Prize ($1,000 and a standard royalty contract) held annually in May. Submit complete ms.

TIPS "Queries for the FIELD Translation Series: send sample poems and letter describing project. Winner of the annual FIELD poetry prize determines publication. Do not send unsolicited mss."

OCEANVIEW PUBLISHING

595 Bay Isles Rd., Suite 120-G, Longboat Key FL 34228. **E-mail:** submissions@oceanviewpub.com. **Website:** www.oceanviewpub.com. **Contact:** Robert Gussin, CEO. Estab. 2006. Publishes hardcover and electronic originals. "Independent publisher of nonfiction and fiction, with primary interest in original mystery, thriller and suspense titles. Accepts new and established writers." Responds in 3 months on mss. Catalog and Guidelines online.

NONFICTION Accepts nonfiction but specializes in original mystery, thriller and suspense titles. Query first.

FICTION Subjects include mystery, suspense, thriller. Accepting adult mss with a primary interest in the mystery, thriller and suspense genres—from new & established writers. No children's or YA literature, poetry, cookbooks, technical manuals or short stories. Within body of e-mail only, include author's name and brief bio (Indicate if this is an agent submission), ms title and word count, author's mailing address, phone number and e-mail address. Attached to the e-mail should be the following: A synopsis of 750 words or fewer. The first 30 pages of the ms. Please note that we accept only Word documents as attachments to the submission e-mail. Do not send query letters or proposals.

OHIO STATE UNIVERSITY PRESS

1070 Carmack Rd., 180 Pressey Hall, Columbus OH 43210-1002. (614)292-6930. **Fax:** (614)292-2065. **E-mail:** ohiostatepress@osu.edu. **Website:** www.ohiostatepress.org. **Contact:** Malcolm Litchfield, director;

Sandy Crooms, acquisitions editor. Estab. 1957. The Ohio State University Press publishes scholarly nonfiction, and offers short fiction and short poetry prizes. Currently emphasizing history, literary studies, political science, women's health, classics, Victoria studies. **Publishes 30 titles/year. Pays royalty. Pays advance.** Responds in 3 months to queries. Guidelines online.

NONFICTION Subjects include business, economics, education, government, politics, history, American, language, literature, literary criticism, multicultural, regional, sociology, women's issues, women's studies, criminology, literary criticism, women's health. Query with SASE.

OHIO UNIVERSITY PRESS

19 Circle Dr., The Ridges, Athens OH 45701. (740)593-1155. **Fax:** (740)593-4536. **Website:** www.ohioswallow.com. **Contact:** Gillian Berchowitz, senior editor (American history and popular culture, ecology and history, law and society, International studies, Latin American studies, Southern Asian studies, Polish and Polish-American studies, African studies, Appalachian studies); David Sanders, director (literature, literary criticism, midwest studies, Ohioana). Estab. 1964. Publishes hardcover and trade paperback originals and reprints. "Ohio University Press publishes and disseminates the fruits of research and creative endeavor, specifically in the areas of literary studies, regional works, philosophy, contemporary history, and African studies. Its charge to produce books of value in service to the academic community and for the enrichment of the broader culture is in keeping with the university's mission of teaching, research and service to its constituents." **Publishes 45-50 titles/year. 500 queries received/year. 50 mss received/year. 20% of books from first-time authors. 95% from unagented writers.** Publishes book 1 year after acceptance of ms. Responds in 1 month to queries and proposals. Responds in 3 months to mss. Book catalog available free. Guidelines online.

IMPRINTS Ohio University Research in International Studies (Gillian Berchowitz); Swallow Press (David Sanders).

NONFICTION Subjects include Americana, anthropology, archaeology, government, history, language, literature, military, nature, politics, regional, sociology, women's issues, women's studies, African studies. We prefer queries or detailed proposals, rather than mss, pertaining to scholarly projects that might have a general interest. Proposals should explain the thesis and details of the subject matter, not just sell a title. Query with SASE. Reviews artwork/photos. Send photocopies.

TIPS Rather than trying to hook the editor on your work, let the material be compelling enough and well-presented enough to do it for you.

➕ OLD HARBOUR PRESS

1723 Forest Hill Dr., Greenville NC 27858. **E-mail:** editor@oldharbourpress.com. **E-mail:** editor@old-harbourpress.com. **Website:** www.oldharbourpress.com. **Contact:** Paul Morin, editor. Estab. 2013. Publishes hardcover originals, trade paperback originals and reprints, and electronic originals and reprints. Old Harbour Press is a small, independent publisher located in Greenville, North Carolina that aims to deliver quality, contemporary travel and cross-cultural literature, both fiction and nonfiction. **Publishes 2-5 titles/year. Authors are paid between 5-50% on wholesale price.** Accepts simultaneous submissions. Responds in 1 month on queries and 2 months on proposals. Send self-addressed envelope for catalog. Send self-addressed envelope for ms guidelines.

NONFICTION Subjects include creative nonfiction, travel. Especially interested in travel, but if a book is for a general audience, and tells a story, please submit. Query with SASE. Writers should send photocopies of artwork/photos with proposals, if available.

FICTION Subjects include adventure, contemporary, experimental, historical, humor, literary, mainstream, military, multicultural, multimedia, mystery, regional, religious, spiritual, sports, suspense, translation, war, young adult. "We're generally not interested in genre fiction; otherwise, we'll look at anything with a good story. We're especially interested in travel fiction and fiction featuring other cultures." Query with SASE.

TIPS "Writers are welcome to query by e-mail with a brief description of the book. (No attachments, please.) We're a newer company, and so we're more open than most to fiction and nonfiction that doesn't fit into any neat category."

🌐 ONEWORLD PUBLICATIONS

10 Bloomsbury St., London WC1B 3SR, United Kingdom. (44)(20)7307-8900. **E-mail:** submissions@oneworld-publications.com. **Website:** www.oneworld-publications.com. Estab. 1986. Publishes hardcover and trade paperback originals and mass market pa-

perback reprints. "We publish general trade nonfiction, which must be accessible but authoritative, mainly by academics or experts for a general readership and where appropriate a cross-over student market. Currently emphasizing current affairs, popular science, history, psychology and business; de-emphasizing self-help. We also publish literary fiction by international authors, both debut and established, throughout the English language world as well as selling translation rights. Our focus is on well-written literary and high-end commercial fiction from a variety of cultures and periods, many exploring interesting issues and global problems. In addition we publish fiction in translation." **Publishes 50 titles/year. 300 queries received/year; 200 mss received/year. 20% of books from first-time authors. 50% from unagented writers. Pays 10% royalty on wholesale price for academic books; standard royalties for trade titles. Pays $1,000-50,000 advance.** Publishes book 12-15 months after acceptance.

NONFICTION Subjects include business, economics. Submit through online proposal form.

FICTION Subjects include politics, history, multicultural, philosophy, psychology, religion, science, sociology, women's issues, women's studies. Submit through online proposal forms.

TIPS "We don't require agents—just good proposals with enough hard information."

ONSTAGE PUBLISHING

190 Lime Quarry Rd., Suite 106-J, Madison AL 35758-8962. (256)461-0661. **E-mail:** onstage123@knology.net. **Website:** www.onstagepublishing.com. **Contact:** Dianne Hamilton, senior editor. Estab. 1999. At this time, we only produce fiction books for ages 8-18. We are adding an eBook only side of the house for mysteries for grades 6-12. See our website for more information. We will not do anthologies of any kind. Query first for nonfiction projects as nonfiction projects must spark our interest. Now accepting e-mail queries and submissions. For submissions: Put the first 3 chapters in the body of the e-mail. Do not use attachments! We will no longer return any mss. Only an SASE envelope is needed. Send complete ms if under 20,000 words, otherwise send synopsis and first 3 chapters. **80% of books from first-time authors. Pays authors/illustrators/photographers advance plus royalties.**

FICTION Middle readers: adventure, contemporary, fantasy, history, nature/environment, science fiction, suspense/mystery. Young adults: adventure, contemporary, fantasy, history, humor, science fiction, suspense/mystery. Average word length: chapter books—4,000-6,000 words; middle readers—5,000 words and up; young adults—25,000 and up. Recently published *China Clipper* by Jamie Dodson (an adventure for boys ages 12+); *Huntsville, 1892: Clara* (a chapter book for grades 3-5). "We do not produce picture books."

TIPS "Study our titles and get a sense of the kind of books we publish, so that you know whether your project is likely to be right for us."

○ ON THE MARK PRESS

15 Dairy Ave., Napanee ON K7R 1M4, Canada. (800)463-6367. **Fax:** (800)290-3631. **E-mail:** product-development@onthemarkpress.com. **Website:** www.onthemarkpress.com. Estab. 1986. Publishes books for the Canadian curriculum. **15% of books from first-time authors.**

OOLIGAN PRESS

369 Neuberger Hall, 724 SW Harrison St., Portland OR 97201. (503)725-9410. **E-mail:** acquisitions@ooliganpress.pdx.edu. **Website:** www.ooliganpress.pdx.edu. Estab. 2001. Publishes trade paperback, and electronic originals and reprints. **Publishes 4-6 titles/year. 250-500 queries received/year. 100 mss received/year. 90% of books from first-time authors. 90% from unagented writers. Pays negotiable royalty on retail price.** Catalog and guidelines online.

NONFICTION Subjects include agriculture, alternative, anthropology, archeology, art, architecture, community, contemporary culture, cooking, foods, nutrition, creative nonfiction, education, ethnic, film, cinema, stage, gay, lesbian, government, politics, history, humanities, language, literature, literary criticism, memoirs, multicultural, music, dance, nature, environment, philosophy, regional, religion, social sciences, sociology, spirituality, translation, travel, women's issues, women's studies, world affairs, young adult. Young adult: open to all categories. Query with SASE. Submit proposal package, outline, 4 sample chapters, projected page count, audience, marketing ideas and a list of similar titles. Reviews artwork/photos.

FICTION Subjects include adventure, ethnic, experimental, fantasy, feminist, gay, lesbian, historical, horror, humor, literary, mainstream, contemporary, multicultural, mystery, plays, poetry, poetry in translation, regional, science fiction, short story collections, spiritual, suspense, translation, young adult, and middle grade. "Ooligan Press is a general trade press at Portland State University. As a teaching press, Ooligan makes as little distinction as possible between the press and the classroom. Under the direction of professional faculty and staff, the work of the press is done by students enrolled in the Book Publishing graduate program at PSU. We are especially interested in works with social, literary, or educational value. Though we place special value on local authors, we are open to all submissions, including translated works and writings by children and young adults. We do not currently publish picture books, board books, easy readers, or pop-up books or middle grade readers." Query with SASE. *"At this time we cannot accept science fiction or fantasy submissions."*

POETRY Ooligan is a general trade press that "specializes in publishing authors from the Pacific Northwest and/or works that have specific value to that community. We are limited in the number of poetry titles that we publish as poetry represents only a small percentage of our overall acquisitions. We are open to all forms of style and verse; however, we give special preference to translated poetry, prose poetry, and traditional verse. Although spoken word, slam, and rap poetry are of interest to the press, we will not consider such work if it does not translate well to the written page. Ooligan does not publish chapbooks." Query, submit 20 sample poems, submit complete ms.

TIPS "For children's books, our audience will be middle grades and young adult, with marketing to general trade, libraries, and schools. Good marketing ideas increase the chances of a ms succeeding."

OPEN COURT PUBLISHING CO.

70 E. Lake St., Suite 800, Chicago IL 60601. **Website:** www.opencourtbooks.com. Estab. 1887. Publishes hardcover and trade paperback originals. **Publishes 20 titles/year. Pays 5-15% royalty on wholesale price.** Publishes book 2 years after acceptance. Catalog and guidelines online.

○   Only accepting submissions to Popular Culture and Philosophy series.

NONFICTION Subjects include philosophy, Asian thought, religious studies and popular culture. Query with SASE. Submit proposal package, outline, 1 sample chapter, TOC, author's cover letter, intended audience.

TIPS "Audience consists of philosophers and intelligent general readers."

OPEN ROAD TRAVEL GUIDES

P.O. Box 284, Cold Spring Harbor NY 11724. (631)692-7172. **E-mail:** jonathan@openroadguides.com. **Website:** www.openroadguides.com. Estab. 1993. Publishes trade paperback originals. "Open Road publishes travel guides and, in its Cold Spring Press imprint, now publishes genealogy books (8 in print to date) and welcomes submissions in this area." **Publishes 20-22 titles/year. 200 queries received/year. 75 mss received/year. 30% of books from first-time authors. 98% from unagented writers. Pays 5-6% royalty on retail price. Pays $1,000-3,500 advance.** Publishes book 3 months after acceptance. Accepts simultaneous submissions. Responds in 1 month to queries; 2 months to proposals. Book catalog online. Ms guidelines sent if proposal is accepted.

NONFICTION Subjects include travel guides and travelogues. Query with SASE.

ORANGE FRAZER PRESS, INC.

P.O. Box 214, 37½ W. Main St., Wilmington OH 45177. (937)382-3196. **Fax:** (937)383-3159. **E-mail:** publisher@orangefrazer.com. **Website:** www.orangefrazer.com; www.orangefrazercustombooks.com. **Contact:** Marcy Hawley (custom book publishing); John Baskin (trade publishing). Publishes hardcover and trade paperback originals. "Orange Frazer Press accepts nonfiction only: corporate histories, town celebrations, and anniversary books. We now focus mostly on custom books/self-publishing, but do still take on some trade books." **Publishes 25 titles/year. 50 queries received/year. 35 mss received/year. 80% of books from first-time authors. 100% from unagented writers. Pays 10% royalty on wholesale price. "50% of our books are author-subsidy published/year if the author can afford it." Pays advance.** Publishes book an average of 10 months after acceptance. Accepts simultaneous submissions. Responds in 6 months to proposals. Book catalog and guidelines free.

NONFICTION Subjects include audio, anthropology, archaeology, art, architecture, business, economics, cooking, foods, nutrition, education, history, nature, environment, photography, regional, sports, travel. "Sports and personalities are our main focus. Accepts Ohio nonfiction only." Submit proposal package, out-

line, 3 sample chapters, and marketing plan. Reviews artwork/photos. Send photocopies.

TIPS "For our commercial titles, we focus mainly on sports and biographies. Our readers are interested in sports or curious about famous persons/personalities. Also, we mainly publish custom books now—90% custom titles, 10% trade titles."

☺ ORCA BOOK PUBLISHERS

P.O. Box 5626, Stn. B, Victoria BC V8R 6S4, Canada. **Fax:** (877)408-1551. **E-mail:** orca@orcabook.com. **Website:** www.orcabook.com. **Contact:** Amy Collins, editor (picture books); Sarah Harvey, editor (young readers); Andrew Wooldridge, editor (juvenile and teen fiction); Bob Tyrrell, publisher (YA, teen). Estab. 1984. Publishes hardcover and trade paperback originals, and mass market paperback originals and reprints. **Publishes 30 titles/year. 2,500 queries received/year. 1,000 mss received/year. 20% of books from first-time authors. 75% from unagented writers. Pays 10% royalty.** Publishes book 12-18 months after acceptance. Responds in 1 month to queries; 2 months to proposals and mss. Book catalog for 8½x11 SASE. Guidelines online.

○ Only publishes Canadian authors.

NONFICTION Subjects include multicultural, picture books. Only publishes Canadian authors. Query with SASE.

FICTION Subjects include hi-lo, juvenile (5-9), literary, mainstream, contemporary, young adult (10-18). Picture books: animals, contemporary, history, nature/environment. Middle readers: contemporary, history, fantasy, nature/environment, problem novels, graphic novels. Young adults: adventure, contemporary, hi-lo (Orca Soundings), history, multicultural, nature/environment, problem novels, suspense/mystery, graphic novels. Average word length: picture books—500-1,500; middle readers—20,000-35,000; young adult—25,000-45,000; Orca Soundings—13,000-15,000; Orca Currents—13,000-15,000. No romance, science fiction. Query with SASE. Submit proposal package, outline, clips, 2-5 sample chapters, SASE.

TIPS "Our audience is students in grades K-12. Know our books, and know the market."

▲⊘ ORCHARD BOOKS

557 Broadway, New York NY 10012. **E-mail:** mcroland@scholastic.com. **Website:** www.scholastic.com. **Contact:** Ken Geist, vice president/editorial director;

David Saylor, vice president/creative director. **Publishes 20 titles/year. 10% of books from first-time authors. Most commonly offers an advance against list royalties.**

◯ *Orchard is not accepting unsolicited mss.*

FICTION Picture books, early readers, and novelty: animal, contemporary, history, humor, multicultural, poetry.

TIPS "Read some of our books to determine first whether your ms is suited to our list."

⊘ ORCHISES PRESS

P.O. Box 320533, Alexandria VA 22320. (703)683-1243. **E-mail:** lathbury@gmu.edu. **Website:** mason.gmu.edu/~lathbury. **Contact:** Roger Lathbury, editor-in-chief. Estab. 1983. Publishes hardcover and trade paperback originals and reprints. Orchises Press is a general literary publisher specializing in poetry with selected reprints and textbooks. No new fiction or children's books. **Publishes 2-3 titles/year. 1% of books from first-time authors. 95% from unagented writers. Pays 36% of receipts after Orchises has recouped its costs.** Publishes book 1 year after acceptance. Accepts simultaneous submissions. Responds in 3 months to queries. Guidelines online.

NONFICTION No real restrictions on subject matter. Query with SASE. Reviews artwork/photos. Send photocopies.

POETRY Poetry must have been published in respected literary journals. *Orchises Press no longer reads unsolicited mss.* Publishes free verse, but has strong formalist preferences. Query and submit 5 sample poems.

OREGON STATE UNIVERSITY PRESS

121 The Valley Library, Corvallis OR 97331. (541)737-3873. **Fax:** (541)737-3170. **E-mail:** mary.braun@oregonstate.edu. **Website:** oregonstate.edu/dept/press. **Contact:** Mary Elizabeth Braun, acquiring editor. Estab. 1962. Publishes hardcover, paperback, and e-book originals. **Publishes 20-25 titles/year. 75% of books from first-time authors.** Publishes book 1 year after acceptance. Responds in 3 months to queries. Book catalog for 6x9 SAE with 2 first-class stamps. Guidelines online.

NONFICTION Subjects include regional, science. Publishes scholarly books in history, biography, geography, literature, natural resource management, with strong emphasis on Pacific or Northwestern topics and Native American and indigenous studies. Submit outline, sample chapters.

⊕ O'REILLY MEDIA

1005 Gravenstein Highway N., Sebastopol CA 95472. (707)827-7000. **Fax:** (707)829-0104. **E-mail:** proposals@oreilly.com. **Website:** www.oreilly.com. **Contact:** Acquisitions Editor. "We're always looking for new authors and new book ideas. Our ideal author has real technical competence and a passion for explaining things clearly." Guidelines online.

NONFICTION Subjects include computers, electronics. At the same time as you might say that our books are written 'by and for smart people,' they also have a down to earth quality. We like straight talk that goes right to the heart of what people need to know. Submit proposal package, outline, publishing history, bio.

TIPS "It helps if you know that we tend to publish 'high end' books rather than books for dummies, and generally don't want yet another book on a topic that's already well covered."

OUR SUNDAY VISITOR, INC.

200 Noll Plaza, Huntington IN 46750. **E-mail:** jlindsey@osv.com. **Website:** www.osv.com. **Contact:** Jacquelyn Lindsey; David Dziena; Bert Ghezzi; Cindy Cavnar; Tyler Ottinger, art director. Publishes paperback and hardbound originals. "We are a Catholic publishing company seeking to educate and deepen our readers in their faith. Currently emphasizing devotional, inspirational, Catholic identity, apologetics, and catechetics." **Publishes 40-50 titles/year. Pays authors royalty of 10-12% net. Pays illustrators by the project (range: $25-1,500).** Publishes book 1-2 years after acceptance. Accepts simultaneous submissions. Responds in 2 months. Book catalog for 9×12 envelope and first-class stamps; ms Guidelines online.

◯ Our Sunday Visitor, Inc. is publishing only those children's books that are specifically Catholic. See website for submission guidelines.

NONFICTION Prefers to see well-developed proposals as first submission with annotated outline and definition of intended market; Catholic viewpoints on family, prayer, and devotional books, and Catholic heritage books. Picture books, middle readers, young readers, young adults. Query, submit complete ms, or submit outline/synopsis and 2-3 sample chapters. Reviews artwork/photos.

TIPS "Stay in accordance with our guidelines."

Ⓐⵔ THE OVERLOOK PRESS

141 Wooster St., New York NY 10012. (212)673-2210.
Fax: (212)673-2296. **E-mail:** sales@overlookny.com.
Website: www.overlookpress.com. Estab. 1971. Publishes hardcover and trade paperback originals and hardcover reprints. "Overlook Press publishes fiction, children's books, and nonfiction." **Publishes 100 titles/year.** Book catalog available free.

NONFICTION Subjects include art, architecture, film, cinema, stage, history, regional, New York State, current events, design, health/fitness, how-to, lifestyle, martial arts. The Overlook Press is an independent general-interest publisher. The publishing program consists of nearly 100 new books per year, evenly divided between hardcovers and trade paperbacks. The list is eclectic, but areas of strength include interesting fiction, history, biography, drama, and design. No pornography. Agented submissions only.

FICTION Subjects include literary, some commercial, foreign literature in translation. Agented submissions only.

RICHARD C. OWEN PUBLISHERS, INC.

P.O. Box 585, Katonah NY 10536. (914)232-3903;
(800)262-0787. **E-mail:** richardowen@rcowen.com.
Website: www.rcowen.com. **Contact:** Richard Owen, publisher. Estab. 1982. "We publish child-focused books, with inherent instructional value, about characters and situations with which five-, six-, and seven-year-old children can identify—books that can be read for meaning, entertainment, enjoyment and information. We include multicultural stories that present minorities in a positive and natural way. Our stories show the diversity in America." Not interested in lesson plans, or books of activities for literature studies or other content areas. Submit complete ms and cover letter. **Pays authors royalty of 5% based on net price or outright purchase (range: $25-500). Offers no advances. Pays illustrators by the project (range: $100-2,000) or per photo (range: $100-150).** Publishes book 2-3 years after acceptance. Accepts simultaneous submissions. Responds to mss in 1 year. Book catalog available with SASE. Ms guidelines with SASE or online.

🖵 "Due to high volume and long production time, we are currently limiting to nonfiction submissions only."

NONFICTION Subjects include art, architecture, history, nature, environment, recreation, science, sports, women's issues, women's studies, music, diverse culture, nature. "Our books are for kindergarten, first- and second-grade children to read on their own. The stories are very brief—under 1,000 words—yet well structured and crafted with memorable characters, language, and plots. Picture books, young readers: animals, careers, history, how-to, music/dance, geography, multicultural, nature/environment, science, sports. Multicultural needs include: Good stories respectful of all heritages, races, cultural—African-American, Hispanic, American Indian." Wants lively stories. No "encyclopedic" type of information stories. Average word length: under 500 words.

TIPS "We don't respond to queries or e-mails. Please do not fax or e-mail us. Because our books are so brief, it is better to send an entire ms. We publish story books with inherent educational value for young readers—books they can read with enjoyment and success. We believe students become enthusiastic, independent, life-long learners when supported and guided by skillful teachers using good books. The professional development work we do and the books we publish support these beliefs."

ⵔ PETER OWEN PUBLISHERS

20 Holland Park Ave., London W11 3 QU, United Kingdom. (44)(208)350-1775. **Fax:** (44)(208)340-9488.
E-mail: admin@peterowen.com. **Website:** www.peterowen.com. **Contact:** Antonia Owen, editorial director. Publishes hardcover originals and trade paperback originals and reprints. "We are far more interested in proposals for nonfiction than fiction at the moment. No poetry or short stories." **Publishes 20-30 titles/year. 3,000 queries received/year. 800 mss received/year. 70% from unagented writers. Pays 7½-10% royalty. Pays negotiable advance.** Publishes book 1 year after acceptance. Responds in 2 months to queries; 3 months to proposals and mss. Book catalog for SASE, SAE with IRC or on website.

NONFICTION Subjects include history, literature, memoirs, translation, travel, art, drama, literary, biography. Query with synopsis, sample chapters.

FICTION Subjects include literary and translation. "No first novels. Authors should be aware that we publish very little new fiction these days." Query with synopsis, sample chapters.

OXFORD UNIVERSITY PRESS

198 Madison Ave., New York NY 10016. (212)726-6000. **E-mail:** custserv.us@oup.com. **Website:** www.

oup.com/us. World's largest university press with the widest global audience. Guidelines online.

NONFICTION Query with outline, proposal, sample chapters.

OZARK MOUNTAIN PUBLISHING, INC.

P.O. Box 754, Huntsville AR 72740. (479)738-2348. **Fax:** (479)738-2448. **E-mail:** info@ozarkmt.com. **Website:** www.ozarkmt.com. **Contact:** Julia Degan, director (New Age/metaphysics/spiritual). Estab. 1992. Publishes trade paperback originals. **Publishes 8-10 titles/year. 50-75 queries; 150-200 mss. 50% of books from first-time authors. 95% from unagented writers. Pays 10-15% royalty on retail or wholesale price. Pays $250-500 advance.** Publishes book 6-9 months after acceptance. Accepts simultaneous submissions. Responds in 6 months to queries; 7 months to mss. Book catalog free on request. Guidelines online.

NONFICTION Subjects include new age/metaphysical/body-mind-spirit, philosophy, spirituality. No phone calls please. Query with SASE. Submit 4-5 sample chapters.

TIPS "We envision our audience to be open minded, spiritually expanding. Please do not call to check on submissions. Do not submit electronically. Send hard copy only."

P & R PUBLISHING CO.

P.O. Box 817, Phillipsburg NJ 08865. **Fax:** (908)859-2390. **E-mail:** editorial@prpbooks.com. **Website:** www.prpbooks.com. Estab. 1930. Publishes hardcover originals and trade paperback originals and reprints. **Publishes 40 titles/year. Up to 300 queries received/year. 100 mss received/year. 5% of books from first-time authors. 95% from unagented writers. Pays 10-16% royalty on wholesale price.** Accepts simultaneous submissions. Responds in 3 months to proposals. Guidelines online.

NONFICTION Subjects include history, religion, spirituality, translation. Only accepts electronic submission with completion of online Author Guidelines. Hard copy mss will not be returned.

TIPS "Our audience is evangelical Christians and seekers. All of our publications are consistent with Biblical teaching, as summarized in the Westminster Standards."

PACIFIC PRESS PUBLISHING ASSOCIATION

Trade Book Division, 1350 N. Kings Rd., Nampa ID 83687. (208)465-2500. **Fax:** (208)465-2531. **E-mail:** booksubmissions@pacificpress.com. **Website:** www.pacificpress.com. **Contact:** Scott Cady, acquisitions editor (children's stories, biography, Christian living, spiritual growth); David Jarnes, book editor (theology, doctrine, inspiration). Estab. 1874. Publishes hardcover and trade paperback originals and reprints. "We publish books that fit Seventh-day Adventist beliefs only. All titles are Christian and religious. For guidance, see www.adventist.org/beliefs/index.html. Our books fit into the categories of this retail site: www.adventistbookcenter.com." **Publishes 35 titles/year. 35% of books from first-time authors. 100% from unagented writers. Pays 8-16% royalty on wholesale price.** Publishes book 2 years after acceptance. Responds in 3 months to queries. Guidelines online.

NONFICTION Subjects include child guidance, cooking, foods, nutrition, vegetarian only, health, history, nature, environment, philosophy, religion, spirituality, women's issues, family living, Christian lifestyle, Bible study, Christian doctrine, prophecy. Query with SASE or e-mail, or submit 3 sample chapters, cover letter with overview of book. Electronic submissions accepted. Reviews artwork/photos.

FICTION Subjects include religious. "Pacific Press rarely publishes fiction, but we're interested in developing a line of Seventh-day Adventist fiction in the future. Only proposals accepted; no full mss."

TIPS "Our primary audience is members of the Seventh-day Adventist denomination. Almost all are written by Seventh-day Adventists. Books that do well for us relate the Biblical message to practical human concerns and focus more on the experiential rather than theoretical aspects of Christianity. We are assigning more titles, using less unsolicited material—although we still publish mss from freelance submissions and proposals."

PAGESPRING PUBLISHING

P.O. Box 2113, Columbus OH 43221. **E-mail:** ps@pagespringpublishing.com. **E-mail:** yaeditor@pagespringpublishing.com; weditor@pagespringpublishing.com. **Website:** www.pagespringpublishing.com. Estab. 2012. Publishes trade paperback and electronic originals. "PageSpring Publishing publishes young adult and middle grade titles under the Lucky Marble Books imprint and women's fiction under the Cup of Tea imprint. See imprint websites for submission details." **Publishes 10-20 titles/year. Pays royalty on wholesale price.** Publishes book 6 months after acceptance. Accepts simultaneous submissions. Responds to queries in 1 month. Guidelines online.

IMPRINTS Lucky Marble Books, Cup of Tea Books.

FICTION Subjects include adventure, contemporary, fantasy, feminist, historical, humor, literary, mainstream, mystery, regional, romance, young adult. Submit proposal package including synopsis and 3 sample chapters.

PALADIN PRESS

7077 Winchester Circle, Boulder CO 80301. (303)443-7250. **Fax:** (303)442-8741. **E-mail:** editorial@paladin-press.com. **Website:** www.paladin-press.com. Estab. 1970. Publishes hardcover originals and paperback originals and reprints, videos. "Paladin Press publishes the action library of nonfiction in military science, police science, weapons, combat, personal freedom, self-defense, survival." **Publishes 50 titles/year. 50% of books from first-time authors. 95% from unagented writers. "We pay royalties in full and on time." Pays advance.** Publishes book 1 year after acceptance of ms. Accepts simultaneous submissions. Responds in 2 months to proposals. Book catalog available free.

IMPRINTS Sycamore Island Books; Flying Machines Press; Outer Limits Press; Romance Book Classics.

NONFICTION Subjects include government, politics, military, war. If applicable, send sample photographs and line drawings with complete outline and sample chapters. Paladin Press primarily publishes original mss on military science, weaponry, self-defense, personal privacy, financial freedom, espionage, police science, action careers, guerrilla warfare, and fieldcraft. To submit a book proposal to Paladin Press, send an outline or chapter description along with 1-2 sample chapters (or the entire ms) to the address below. If applicable, samples of illustrations or photographs are also useful. Do not send a computer disk at this point, and be sure keep a copy of everything you send us. We are not accepting mss as electronic submissions at this time. Please allow 2-6 weeks for a reply. If you would like your sample material returned, a SASE with proper postage is required. Editorial Department, Paladin Press Gunbarrel Tech Center, 7077 Winchester Circle, Boulder, CO 80301, or e-mail us at: editorial@paladin-press.com. Query with SASE. Submitting a proposal for a video project is not much different than a book proposal. See guidelines online and send to: All materials related to video proposals should be addressed directly to: David Dubrow, Video Production Manager.

TIPS "We need lucid, instructive material aimed at our market and accompanied by sharp, relevant illustrations and photos. As we are primarily a publisher of 'how-to' books, a ms that has step-by-step instructions, written in a clear and concise manner (but not strictly outline form) is desirable. No fiction, first-person accounts, children's, religious, or joke books. We are also interested in serious, professional videos and video ideas (contact Michael Rigg)."

PALARI PUBLISHING

107 S. West St., PMB 778, Alexandria VA 22314. (866)570-6724. **Fax:** (866)570-6724. **E-mail:** dave@palaribooks.com. **Website:** www.palaribooks.com. **Contact:** David Smitherman, publisher/editor. Estab. 1998. Publishes hardcover and trade paperback originals. "Palari provides authoritative, well-written nonfiction that addresses topical consumer needs and fiction with an emphasis on intelligence and quality. We accept solicited and unsolicited mss, however we prefer a query letter and SASE, describing the project briefly and concisely. This letter should include a complete address and telephone number. Palari Publishing accepts queries or any other submissions by e-mail, but prefers queries submitted by US mail. All queries must be submitted by mail according to our guidelines. Promotes titles through book signings, direct mail and the Internet." **Pays royalty.** Publishes book 1 year after acceptance. Responds in 1 month to queries; 2-3 months to mss. Guidelines online.

◒ Member of Publishers Marketing Association.

NONFICTION Subjects include business, economics, memoirs.

FICTION Subjects include adventure, ethnic, gay, lesbian, historical, literary, mainstream, contemporary, multicultural. "Tell why your idea is unique or interesting. Make sure we are interested in your genre before submitting." Query with SASE. Submit bio, estimated word count, list of publishing credits. Accepts queries via e-mail (prefer US Mail), fax.

TIPS "Send a good bio. I'm interested in a writer's experience and unique outlook on life."

PALETTES & QUILLS

1935 Penfield Road, Penfield NY 14526. (585)456-0217. **E-mail:** palettesnquills@gmail.com. **Website:** www.palettesnquills.com. **Contact:** Donna M. Marbach, publisher/owner. Estab. 2002.

NONFICTION Does not want political and religious diatribes.

POETRY Palettes & Quills "is at this point, a poetry press only, and produces only a handful of publications each year, specializing in anthologies, individual chapbooks, and broadsides." Wants "work that should appeal to a wide audience." Does not want "poems that are sold blocks of text, long-lined and without stanza breaks. Wildly elaborate free-verse would be difficult and in all likelihood fight with art background, amateurish rhyming poem, overly sentimental poems, poems that use excessive profanity, or which denigrate other people, or political and religious diatribes." Query first with 3-5 poems and a cover letter with brief bio and publication credits for individual unsolicited chapbooks. May include previously published poems. Chapbook poets would get 20 copies of a run; broadside poets and artists get 5-10 copies and occasionally paid $10 for reproduction rights. Anthology poets get 1 copy of the anthology. All poets and artists get a discount on purchases that include their work.

PALGRAVE MACMILLAN

St. Martin's Press, 175 Fifth Ave., New York NY 10010. (212)982-3900. **Fax:** (212)777-6359. **Website:** www.palgrave-usa.com. **Contact:** Airié Stuart (history, business, economics, current events, psychology, biography); Anthony Wahl (political science, current events, Asian studies, international relations); Farideh Koohi-Kamali (literature, anthropology, cultural studies, performing arts, Islamic World & Middle East); Amanda Johnson (education, religion, women's studies/history); Ella Pearce (African studies, Latin American studies); Alessandra Bastagli (American history, American studies, world history); Heather Van Dusen (political science, political economy, political theory). Publishes hardcover and trade paperback originals. "Palgrave wishes to expand on our already successful academic, trade, and reference programs so that we will remain at the forefront of publishing in the global information economy of the 21st century. We publish high-quality academic works and a distinguished range of reference titles, and we expect to see many of our works available in electronic form. We do not accept fiction or poetry." Accepts simultaneous submissions. Book catalog and ms guidelines online.

○ Palgrave Macmillan is a cross-market publisher specializing in cutting edge academic and trade nonfiction titles. Our list consists of top authors ranging from academics making original contributions in their disciplines to trade authors, including journalists and experts, writing news-making books for a broad, educated readership.

NONFICTION Subjects include business, economics, creative nonfiction, education, ethnic, gay, lesbian, government, politics, history, language, literature, military, war, money, finance, multicultural, music, dance, philosophy, regional, religion, sociology, spirituality, translation, women's issues, women's studies, humanities. We are looking for good solid scholarship. Query with proposal package including outline, 3-4 sample chapters, prospectus, cv and SASE. Reviews artwork/photos.

⊘ PANTHEON BOOKS

Random House, Inc., 1745 Broadway, 3rd Floor, New York NY 10019. **E-mail:** pantheonpublicity@randomhouse.com. **Website:** www.pantheonbooks.com. Estab. 1942. Publishes hardcover and trade paperback originals and trade paperback reprints.

○ Pantheon Books publishes both Western and non-Western authors of literary fiction and important nonfiction. "We only accept mss submitted by an agent."

NONFICTION *Does not accept unsolicited mss.* Agented submissions only.

FICTION *Does not accept unsolicited mss.* Agented submissions only.

PARADISE CAY PUBLICATIONS

P.O. Box 29, Arcata CA 95518-0029. (800)736-4509. **Fax:** (707)822-9163. **E-mail:** info@paracay.com; james@paracay.com. **Website:** www.paracay.com. **Contact:** Matt Morehouse, publisher. Publishes hardcover and trade paperback originals and reprints. "Paradise Cay Publications, Inc. is a small independent publisher specializing in nautical books, videos, and art prints. Our primary interest is in mss that deal with the instructional and technical aspects of ocean sailing. We also publish and will consider fiction if it has a strong nautical theme." **Publishes 5 titles/year. 360-480 queries received/year. 240-360 mss received/year. 10% of books from first-time authors. 100% from unagented writers. Pays 10-15% royalty on wholesale price. Makes outright purchase of $1,000-10,000. Does not normally pay advances to first-time or little-known authors.** Publishes book

4 months after acceptance. Responds in 1 month to queries/proposals; 2 months to mss. Book catalog and ms guidelines free on request or online.

IMPRINTS Pardey Books.

NONFICTION Subjects include cooking, foods, nutrition, recreation, sports, travel. Must have strong nautical theme. Include a cover letter containing a story synopsis and a short bio, including any plans to promote their work. The cover letter should describe the book's subject matter, approach, distinguishing characteristics, intended audience, author's qualifications, and why the author thinks this book is appropriate for Paradise Cay. Call first. Reviews artwork/photos. Send photocopies.

FICTION Subjects include adventure, nautical, sailing. All fiction must have a nautical theme. Query with SASE. Submit proposal package, clips, 2-3 sample chapters.

TIPS "Audience is recreational sailors. Call Matt Morehouse (publisher)."

PARADISE RESEARCH PUBLICATIONS, INC.

P.O. Box 837, Kihei HI 96753. (808)874-4876. **Fax:** (808)874-4876. **E-mail:** dickb@dickb.com. **Website:** www.dickb.com/index.shtml. Publishes trade paperback originals. Paradise Research Publications wants only books on Alcoholics Anonymous and its spiritual roots. **Publishes 3 titles/year. 5 queries received/year. 1 mss received/year. 20% of books from first-time authors. 100% from unagented writers. Pays 10% royalty.** Publishes book 3 months after acceptance. Accepts simultaneous submissions. Responds in 1 month to queries. Book catalog online.

NONFICTION Subjects include health, medicine, psychology, religion, spirituality, recovery, alcoholism, addictions, Christian recovery, history of Alcoholics Annonymous. Query with SASE.

PARAGON HOUSE PUBLISHERS

1925 Oakcrest Ave., Suite 7, St. Paul MN 55113. (651)644-3087. **Fax:** (651)644-0997. **E-mail:** paragon@paragonhouse.com. **Website:** www.paragonhouse.com. **Contact:** Gordon Anderson, acquisitions editor. Estab. 1962. Publishes hardcover and trade paperback originals and trade paperback reprints and eBooks. "We publish general-interest titles and textbooks that provide the readers greater understanding of society and the world. Currently emphasizing religion, philosophy, economics, and society." **Publishes 5-10 ti-** tles/year. 1,500 queries received/year. 150 mss received/year. 7% of books from first-time authors. 90% from unagented writers. Pays $500-1,000 advance. Publishes book 1 year after acceptance. Accepts simultaneous submissions. Guidelines online.

IMPRINTS *Series:* Paragon Issues in Philosophy, Genocide and Holocaust Studies; Omega Books.

NONFICTION Subjects include government, politics, multicultural, nature, environment, philosophy, psychology, religion, sociology, women's issues, world affairs. Submit proposal package, outline, 2 sample chapters, market breakdown, SASE.

PASSKEY PUBLICATIONS

27762 Antonio Parkway, Suite L1, #238, Ladera Ranch CA 92694. (916)712-7446. **Fax:** (916)427-5765. **Website:** www.passkeypublications.com. **Contact:** Christine P. Silva, president. Estab. 2007. Publishes trade paperback originals. **Publishes 15 titles/year. Receives 375 queries/year; 120 mss/year. 15% of books from first-time authors. 90% from unagented writers. Pay varies on retail price.** Publishes book 1 year after acceptance. Accepts simultaneous submissions. Responds in 1 month. Catalog and guidelines online.

IMPRINTS Passkey Publications, PassKey EA Review.

NONFICTION Subjects include business, economics, finance, money, real estate, accounting, taxation, study guides for professional examinations. "Books on taxation and accounting are generally updated every year to reflect tax law changes, and the turnaround on a ms must be less than 3 months for accounting and tax subject matter. Books generally remain in publication only 11 months and are generally published every year for updates." Submit complete ms. Nonfiction mss only. Reviews artwork/photos as part of ms package. Send electronic files on disk, via e-mail, or jump drive.

TIPS "Accepting business, accounting, tax, finance and other related subjects only."

PAUL DRY BOOKS

1700 Sansom St., Suite 700, Philadelphia PA 19103. (215)231-9939. **Fax:** (215)231-9942. **E-mail:** pdry@pauldrybooks.com; editor@pauldrybooks.com. **Website:** pauldrybooks.com. Hardcover and trade paperback originals, trade paperback reprints. "We publish fiction, both novels and short stories, and nonfiction, biography, memoirs, history, and essays, covering subjects from Homer to Chekhov, bird watching to jazz music, New York City to shogunate Japan." Catalog and guidelines online.

○ "Take a few minutes to familiarize yourself with the books we publish. Then if you think your book would be a good fit in our line, we invite you to submit the following: A one- or two-page summary of the work. Be sure to tell us how many pages or words the full book will be; a sample of 20-30 pages; your bio. A brief description of how you think the book (and you, the author) could be marketed."

NONFICTION Subjects include agriculture, contemporary culture, history, literary criticism, memoirs, multicultural, philosophy, religion, translation, popular mathematics. Submit proposal package.

FICTION Subjects include literary, short story collections, translation, young adult, novels. Submit sample chapters, clips, bio.

TIPS "Our aim is to publish lively books 'to awaken, delight, and educate'—to spark conversation. We publish fiction and nonfiction, and essays covering subjects from Homer to Chekhov, bird watching to jazz music, New York City to shogunate Japan."

PAULINE BOOKS & MEDIA

50 St. Paul's Ave., Boston MA 02130. (617)522-8911. **Fax:** (617)541-9805. **E-mail:** design@paulinemedia. com; editorial@paulinemedia.com. **Website:** www. pauline.org. Estab. 1932. Publishes trade paperback originals and reprints. "Submissions are evaluated on adherence to Gospel values, harmony with the Catholic tradition, relevance of topic, and quality of writing." For board books and picture books, the entire ms should be submitted. For easy-to-read, young readers, and middle reader books and teen books, please send a cover letter accompanied by a synopsis and two sample chapters. "Electronic submissions are encouraged. We make every effort to respond to unsolicited submissions within 2 months." **Publishes 40 titles/ year. 15% of books from first-time authors. 5% from unagented writers. Varies by project, but generally are royalties with advance. Flat fees sometimes considered for smaller works.** Publishes book Publishes a book approximately 11-18 months after acceptance. Accepts simultaneous submissions. Responds in 2 months to queries, proposals, & mss. Book catalog online. Guidelines available online & by e-mail.

NONFICTION Subjects include child guidance, religion, spirituality. Picture books, young readers, middle readers, teen: religion and fiction. Average word length: picture books—500-1,000; young readers—8,000-10,000; middle readers—15,000-25,000; teen—30,000-50,000. No memoir/autobiography, poetry, or strictly nonreligious works considered. Submit proposal package, including outline, 1-2 sample chapters, cover letter, synopsis, intended audience and proposed length. Reviews artwork; send photocopies.

FICTION Subjects include juvenile. Children's and teen fiction only. We are now accepting submissions for easy-to-read and middle reader chapter, and teen fiction. Please see our Writer's Guidelines. "Submit proposal package, including synopsis, 2 sample chapters, and cover letter; complete ms."

TIPS "Mss may or may not be explicitly catechetical, but we seek those that reflect a positive worldview, good moral values, awareness and appreciation of diversity, and respect for all people. All material must be relevant to the lives of readers and must conform to Catholic teaching and practice."

PAULIST PRESS

997 MacArthur Blvd., Mahwah NJ 07430. (201)825-7300. **Fax:** (201)825-8345. **Website:** www.paulistpress. com. **Contact:** Mark-David Janus, CSP, publisher. Estab. 1865. "Paulist Press publishes ecumenical theology, Roman Catholic studies, and books on scripture, liturgy, spirituality, church history, and philosophy, as well as works on faith and culture. Our publishing is oriented toward adult-level nonfiction. We do not publish poetry or works of fiction, and we have scaled back our involvement in children's publishing." **Receives 250 submissions/year. Royalties and advances are negotible. Illustrators sometimes receive a flat fee when all we need are spot illustrations.** Publishes book Publishes a book 18-24 months after acceptance. Responds in 3 months to queries and proposals; 3-4 months on mss. Book catalog online. Guidelines available online and by e-mail.

PAYCOCK PRESS

3819 N. 13th St., Arlington VA 22201. (703)525-9296. **E-mail:** gargoyle@gargoylemagazine.com. **Website:** www.gargoylemagazine.com. **Contact:** Richard Peabody. Estab. 1976. "Too academic for the underground, too outlaw for the academic world. We tend to be edgy and look for ultra-literary work." Publishes paperback originals. Books: POD printing. Average print order: 500. Averages 1 total title/year. Member

CLMP. Distributes through Amazon and website. Publishes book 1 year after acceptance. Accepts simultaneous submissions. Responds to queries in 1 month; mss in 4 months.

FICTION Wants: experimental, literary, short story or poetry collections. Accepts unsolicited mss. Accepts queries by e-mail. Include brief bio. Send SASE for return of ms or send a disposable ms and SASE for reply only.

POETRY Considers experimental, cdgy poetry collections. Accepts unsolicited mss. Accepts queries by e-mail. Include brief bio. Send SASE for return of ms or send a disposable ms and SASE for reply only.

TIPS "Check out our website. Two of our favorite writers are Paul Bowles and Jeanette Winterson."

PEACE HILL PRESS

Affiliate of W.W. Norton, 18021 The Glebe Ln., Charles City VA 23030. (804)829-5043. **Fax:** (804)829-5704. **E-mail:** info@peacehillpress.com. **Website:** www. peacehillpress.com. **Contact:** Peter Buffington, acquisitions editor. Estab. 2001. Publishes hardcover and trade paperback originals. **Publishes 4-8 titles/ year. Pays 6-10% royalty on retail price. Pays $500-1,000 advance.** Publishes book Publishes a book 18 months after acceptance.

NONFICTION Subjects include education, history, language, literature. Does not take submissions. Reviews artwork/photos. Send photocopies.

FICTION Subjects include historical, juvenile, picture books, young adult. Does not take submissions.

PEACHTREE CHILDREN'S BOOKS

Peachtree Publishers, Ltd., 1700 Chattahoochee Ave., Atlanta GA 30318-2112. (404)876-8761. **Fax:** (404)875-2578. **E-mail:** hello@peachtree-online.com. **Website:** www.peachtree-online.com. **Contact:** Helen Harriss, submissions editor. Publishes hardcover and trade paperback originals. "We publish a broad range of subjects and perspectives, with emphasis on innovative plots and strong writing." **Publishes 30 titles/year. 25% of books from first-time authors. 25% from unagented writers. Pays royalty on retail price.** Publishes book 1 year after acceptance. Accepts simultaneous submissions. Responds in 6 months and mss. Book catalog for 6 first-class stamps. Guidelines online.

IMPRINTS Freestone; Peachtree Jr.

NONFICTION Subjects include animals, child guidance, creative nonfiction, education, ethnic, gardening, health, medicine, history, language, literature, literary criticism, multicultural, music, dance, nature, environment, recreation, regional, science, social sciences, sports, travel. No e-mail or fax queries of mss. Submit complete ms with SASE, or summary and 3 sample chapters with SASE.

FICTION Subjects include juvenile, picture books, young adult. Looking for very well-written middle grade and young adult novels. No adult fiction. No collections of poetry or short stories; no romance or science fiction. Submit complete ms with SASE.

PEACHTREE PUBLISHERS, LTD.

1700 Chattahoochee Ave., Atlanta GA 30318. (404)876-8761. **Fax:** (404)875-2578. **E-mail:** hello@ peachtree-online.com; jackson@peachtree-online. com. **Website:** www.peachtree-online.com. **Contact:** Helen Harriss, acquisitions editor; Loraine Joyner, art director; Melanie McMahon Ives, production manager. Estab. 1977. **Publishes 30-35 titles/year.** Publishes book 1-2 years after acceptance. Accepts simultaneous submissions. Responds in 6-7 months.

NONFICTION Picture books: animal, history, nature/environment. Young readers, middle readers, young adults: animal, biography, nature/environment. Does not want to see religion. Submit complete ms or 3 sample chapters by postal mail only.

FICTION Picture books, young readers: adventure, animal, concept, history, nature/environment. Middle readers: adventure, animal, history, nature/environment, sports. Young adults: fiction, mystery, adventure. Does not want to see science fiction, romance. Submit complete ms or 3 sample chapters by postal mail only.

PEDLAR PRESS

113 Bond St., St. John's NL A16 1T6, Canada. (709)738-6702. **E-mail:** feralgrl@interlog.com. **Website:** www. pedlarpress.com. **Contact:** Beth Follett, owner/editor. Distributes in Canada through LitDistCo. **Publishes 7 titles/year. Pays 10% royalty on retail price. Average advance: $200-400.** Publishes book 1 year after acceptance.

FICTION Experimental, feminist, gay/lesbian, literary, short story collections. Canadian writers only. Query with SASE, sample chapter(s), synopsis.

TIPS "I select mss according to my taste, which fluctuates. Be familiar with some if not most of Pedlar's recent titles."

PELICAN PUBLISHING COMPANY

1000 Burmaster St., Gretna LA 70053. (504)368-1175. **Fax:** (504)368-1195. **E-mail:** editorial@pelicanpub. com. **Website:** www.pelicanpub.com. **Contact:** Nina Kooij, editor-in-chief. Estab. 1926. Publishes hardcover, trade paperback and mass market paperback originals and reprints. "We believe ideas have consequences. One of the consequences is that they lead to a best-selling book. We publish books to improve and uplift the reader. Currently emphasizing business and history titles." Publishes 20 young readers/year; 1 middle reader/year. "Our children's books (illustrated and otherwise) include history, biography, holiday, and regional. Pelican's mission is to publish books of quality and permanence that enrich the lives of those who read them." **Pays authors in royalties; buys ms outright "rarely." Illustrators paid by "various arrangements." Advance considered.** Publishes book Publishes a book 9-18 months after acceptance. Responds in 1 month to queries; 3 months to mss. Book catalog and ms guidelines online.

NONFICTION Subjects include Americana, especially Southern regional, Ozarks, Texas, Florida, and Southwest, art, architecture, ethnic, government, politics, special interest in conservative viewpoint, history, popular, multicultural, American artforms, but will consider others: jazz, blues, Cajun, R&B, regional, religion, for popular audience mostly, but will consider others, sports, motivational (with business slant). "We look for authors who can promote successfully. We require that a query be made first. This greatly expedites the review process and can save the writer additional postage expenses." Young readers: biography, history, holiday, multicultural. Middle readers: Louisiana history, holiday, regional. No multiple queries or submissions. Query with SASE. Reviews artwork/photos.

FICTION Subjects include historical, juvenile, regional or historical focus. We publish no adult fiction. Young readers: history, holiday, science, multicultural and regional. Middle readers: Louisiana History. Multicultural needs include stories about African-Americans, Irish-Americans, Jews, Asian-Americans, and Hispanics. Does not want animal stories, general Christmas stories, "day at school" or "accept yourself" stories. Maximum word length: young readers—1,100; middle readers—40,000. No young adult, romance, science fiction, fantasy, gothic, mystery, erotica, confession, horror, sex, or violence. Also no psychological novels. Query with SASE. Submit outline, clips, 2 sample chapters, SASE.

POETRY Pelican Publishing Company is a medium-sized publisher of popular histories, cookbooks, regional books, children's books, and inspirational/motivational books. Considers poetry for "hardcover children's books only (1,100 words maximum), preferably with a regional focus. However, our needs for this are very limited; we publish 20 juvenile titles per year, and most of these are prose, not poetry." Two of Pelican's popular series are prose books about Gaston the Green-Nosed Alligator by James Rice, and Clovis Crawfish by Mary Alice Fontenot. Books are 32 pages, magazine-sized, include illustrations.

TIPS "We do extremely well with cookbooks, popular histories, and business. We will continue to build in these areas. The writer must have a clear sense of the market and knowledge of the competition. A query letter should describe the project briefly, give the author's writing and professional credentials, and promotional ideas."

🅐⊘ PENGUIN GROUP USA

375 Hudson St., New York NY 10014. (212)366-2000. **Website:** www.penguin.com. **Contact:** Peter Stampfel, submission editor (DAW Books). General interest publisher of both fiction and nonfiction. Guidelines online.

IMPRINTS Penguin Adult Division: Ace Books, Alpha Books, Avery, Berkley Books, Dutton, Gotham Books, HPBooks, Hudson Street Press, Jove, New American Library, Penguin, The Penguin Press, Perigee, Plume, Portfolio, G.P. Putnam's Sons, Riverhead, Sentinel, Jeremy P. Tarcher, Viking; **Penguin Children's Division:** Dial Books for Young Readers, Dutton Children's Books, Firebird, Grosset & Dunlap, Philomel, Price Stern Sloan, Puffin Books, G.P. Putnam's Sons, Speak, Viking Children's Books, Frederick Warne.

🅞 *No unsolicited mss.* Submit work through a literary agent. Exceptions are DAW Books and Penguin Young Readers Group.

PENNY-FARTHING PRESS INC.

One Sugar Creek Center Blvd., Suite 820, Sugar Land TX 77478. (713)780-0300 or (800)926-2669. **Fax:** (713)780-4004. **E-mail:** submissions@pfpress.com; corp@pfpress.com. **Website:** www.pfpress.com. **Contact:** Ken White, publisher; Marlaine Maddox, editor-in-chief. Estab. 1998. "Penny-Farthing Press officially opened its doors in 1998 with a small staff and a plan to create comic books and children's books that exemplified quality storytelling, artwork, and printing. Starting with only one book, The Victorian, Penny-Farthing Press has expanded its line to six titles, but keeps its yearly output small enough to maintain the highest quality. This 'boutique approach' to publishing has won the recognition of the comics and fine arts industries, and PFP has won numerous awards including the Gutenberg D'Argent Medal and several Spectrum Awards." Guidelines online.

FICTION "Please make sure all submissions include a synopsis that is brief and to the point. Remember, the synopsis is the 'first impression' of your submission and you know what they say about first impressions. If you are submitting just one single-issue story (standard 32 pp.), you may send the full script with your submission. If you are submitting a story for any kind of series or graphic novel, please send only the first chapter of the series. If we like what we see, we will contact you to see more. If you are submitting a completed work (script, art work and lettering) copies of this may be sent instead."

⊗⊘ PERENNIAL

HarperCollins Publishers, 10 E. 53rd St., New York NY 10022. (212)207-7000. **Website:** www.harpercollins.com. **Contact:** Acquisitions Editor. Estab. 1963. Publishes trade paperback originals and reprints. Perennial publishes a broad range of adult literary fiction and nonfiction paperbacks that create a record of our culture. Book catalog available free.

○ "With the exception of Avon romance, HarperCollins does not accept unsolicited submissions or query letters. Please refer to your local bookstore, the library, or a book entitled *Literary Marketplace* on how to find the appropriate agent for you."

NONFICTION Subjects include Americana, animals, business, economics, child guidance, cooking, foods, nutrition, education, ethnic, gay, lesbian, history, language, literature, military, war, money, finance, music, dance, nature, environment, and environment, philosophy, psychology, self-help psychotherapy, recreation, regional, religion, spirituality, science, sociology, sports, translation, travel, womens issues, womens studies, mental health, health, classic literature. Our focus is ever-changing, adjusting to the marketplace. Mistakes writers often make are not giving their

background and credentials-why they are qualified to write the book. A proposal should explain why the author wants to write this book; why it will sell; and why it is better or different from others of its kind. Agented submissions only.

FICTION Subjects include ethnic, feminist, literary. Agented submissions only.

POETRY Don't send poetry unless you have been published in several established literary magazines already. *Agented submissions only.*

TIPS "See our website for a list of titles or write to us for a free catalog."

THE PERMANENT PRESS

Attn: Judith Shepard, 4170 Noyac Rd., Sag Harbor NY 11963. (631)725-1101. **Fax:** (631)725-8215. **E-mail:** judith@thepermanentpress.com; shepard@thepermanentpress.com. **Website:** www.thepermanentpress.com. **Contact:** Judith and Martin Shepard, acquisitions/co-publishers. Blog: www.thecockeyedpessimist.com. Estab. 1978. Publishes hardcover originals. Midsize, independent publisher of literary fiction. "We keep titles in print and are active in selling subsidiary rights." Average print order: 1,000-2,500. Averages 16 total titles. Accepts unsolicited mss. Pays 10-15% royalty on wholesale price. Offers $1,000 advance. **Pays 10-15% royalty on wholesale price. Offers $1,000 advance.** Publishes book within 18 months after acceptance. Responds in weeks or months to queries and submissions.

○ *Will NOT accept simultaneous submissions.*

FICTION Promotes titles through reviews. Literary, mainstream/contemporary, mystery. Especially looking for high-line literary fiction, "artful, original and arresting." Accepts any fiction category as long as it is a "well-written, original full-length novel."

TIPS "We are looking for good books—be they 10th novels or first ones, it makes little difference. The fiction is more important than the track record. Send us the first 25 pages; it's impossible to judge something that begins on page 302. Also, no outlines—let the writing present itself."

PERSEA BOOKS

277 Broadway, Suite 708, New York NY 10007. (212)260-9256. **Fax:** (212)267-3165. **E-mail:** info@perseabooks.com. **Website:** www.perseabooks.com. Estab. 1975. The aim of Persea is to publish works that endure by meeting high standards of literary merit and relevance. "We have often taken on important

books other publishers have overlooked, or have made significant discoveries and rediscoveries, whether of a single work or writer's entire oeuvre. Our books cover a wide range of themes, styles, and genres. We have published poetry, fiction, essays, memoir, biography, titles of Jewish and Middle Eastern interest, women's studies, American Indian folklore, and revived classics, as well as a notable selection of works in translation." Responds in 8 weeks to proposals; 10 weeks to mss. Guidelines online.

NONFICTION Subjects include contemporary culture, literary criticism, literature, memoirs, translation, travel, young adult. Queries should include a cover letter, author background and publication history, a detailed synopsis of the proposed work, and a sample chapter. Please indicate if the work is simultaneously submitted.

FICTION Subjects include contemporary, literary, short story collections, translation, young adult. Queries should include a cover letter, author background and publication history, a detailed synopsis of the proposed work, and a sample chapter. Please indicate if the work is simultaneously submitted.

POETRY "We have a longstanding commitment to publishing extraordinary contemporary poetry and maintain an active poetry program. At this time, due to our commitment to the poets we already publish, we are limited in our ability to add new collections." Send an e-mail to poetry@perseabooks.com describing current project and publication history, attaching a pdf or Word document with up to 12 sample pages of poetry. "If the timing is right and we are interested in seeing more work, we will contact you."

⊘ PERUGIA PRESS

P.O. Box 60364, Florence MA 01062. **Website:** www.perugiapress.com. **Contact:** Susan Kan, director. Estab. 1997. Celebrating poetry by women since 1997. "Contact us through our website."

PETER PAUPER PRESS, INC.

202 Mamaroneck Ave., White Plains NY 10601. **E-mail:** customerservice@peterpauper.com. **Website:** www.peterpauper.com. **Contact:** Barbara Paulding, editorial director. Estab. 1928. Publishes hardcover originals. "PPP publishes small and medium format, illustrated gift books for occasions and in celebration of specific relationships such as mom, sister, friend, teacher, grandmother, granddaughter. PPP has expanded into the following areas: books for teens and tweens, activity books for children, organizers, books on popular topics of nonfiction for adults and licensed books by best-selling authors." **Publishes 40-50 titles/year. 100 queries received/year. 150 mss received/year. 5% from unagented writers. Makes outright purchase only. Pays advance.** Publishes book 1 year after acceptance. Responds in 2 months to queries. Ms guidelines for #10 SASE or may request via e-mail.

NONFICTION "We do not publish fiction or poetry. We publish brief, original quotes, aphorisms, and wise sayings. Please do not send us other people's quotes." Submit cover letter and hard copy ms.

TIPS "Our readers are primarily female, age 10 and over, who are likely to buy a 'gift' book or gift book set in a stationery, gift, book, or boutique store or national book chain. Writers should become familiar with our previously published work. We publish only small- and medium-format, illustrated, hardcover gift books and sets of between 1,000-4,000 words. We have much less interest in work aimed at men."

⊕ PETERSON'S

2000 Lenox Dr., Princeton Pike Corporate Center, 3rd Floor, Lawrenceville NJ 08648. (609)896-1800. **Website:** www.petersons.com. Estab. 1966. Publishes trade and reference books. Peterson's publishes guides to graduate and professional programs, colleges and universities, financial aid, distance learning, private schools, summer programs, international study, executive education, job hunting and career opportunities, educational and career test prep, as well as online products and services offering educational and career guidance and information for adult learners and workplace solutions for education professionals. **Pays royalty. Pays advance.** Book catalog available free.

IMPRINTS Arco, Peterson's

NONFICTION Subjects include business, economics, education, careers. Looks for appropriateness of contents to our markets, author's credentials, and writing style suitable for audience.

TIPS Many of Peterson's reference works are updated annually. Peterson's markets strongly to libraries and institutions, as well as to the corporate sector.

PFLAUM PUBLISHING GROUP

2621 Dryden Rd., Suite 300, Dayton OH, 45439. **Contact:** Cullen W. Schippe, president and publisher Pflaum Publishing Division. "Pflaum Publishing Group, a division of Peter Li, Inc., serves the specialized market of religious education, primarily Roman Catholic. We provide high quality, theologically sound, practical, and affordable resources that assist religious educators of and ministers to children from preschool through senior high school." **Publishes 20 titles/year. Payment by outright purchase.** Book catalog and ms guidelines free.

NONFICTION Query with SASE.

PHILOMEL BOOKS

Imprint of Penguin Group (USA), Inc., 375 Hudson St., New York NY 10014. (212)414-3610. **Website:** www.us.penguingroup.com. **Contact:** Michael Green, president/publisher; Annie Ericsson, junior designer. Estab. 1980. Publishes hardcover originals. "We look for beautifully written, engaging mss for children and young adults." **Publishes 8-10 titles/year. 5% of books from first-time authors. 20% from unagented writers. Pays authors in royalties. Average advance payment "varies." Illustrators paid by advance and in royalties. Pays negotiable advance.** Accepts simultaneous submissions. Book catalog for 9×12 envelope and 4 first-class stamps. Guidelines for #10 SASE.

NONFICTION Picture books.

FICTION Subjects include adventure, ethnic, fantasy, historical, juvenile, literary, picture books, regional, short story collections, translation, western, young adult. All levels: adventure, animal, boys, contemporary, fantasy, folktales, historical fiction, humor, sports, multicultural. Middle readers, young adults: problem novels, science fiction, suspense/mystery. No concept picture books, mass-market "character" books, or series. Average word length: picture books—1,000; young readers—1,500; middle readers—14,000; young adult—20,000. No series or activity books. No generic, mass-market oriented fiction. *No unsolicited mss.*

TIPS Wants "unique fiction or nonfiction with a strong voice and lasting quality. Discover your own voice and own story and persevere." Looks for "something unusual, original, well written. Fine art or illustrative art that feels unique. The genre (fantasy, contemporary, or historical fiction) is not so important as the story itself and the spirited life the story allows its main character."

PIANO PRESS

P.O. Box 85, Del Mar CA 92014. (619)884-1401. **Fax:** (858)755-1104. **E-mail:** pianopress@pianopress.com. **Website:** www.pianopress.com. **Contact:** Elizabeth C.

Axford, editor. Estab. 1998. "We publish music-related books, either fiction or nonfiction, coloring books, songbooks, and poetry." **Pays authors, illustrators, and photographers royalty of 5-10% based on retail price.** Publishes book 1 year after acceptance. Accepts simultaneous submissions. Responds to queries in 3 months; mss in 6 months. Book catalog available for #10 SASE and 2 first-class stamps.

NONFICTION Picture books, young readers, middle readers, young adults: multicultural, music/dance. Average word length: picture books—1,500-2,000.

FICTION Picture books, young readers, middle readers, young adults: folktales, multicultural, poetry, music. Average word length: picture books—1,500-2,000.

TIPS "We are looking for music-related material only for any juvenile market. Please do not send non-music-related materials. Query first before submitting anything."

PIATKUS BOOKS

Little, Brown Book Group, 100 Victoria Embankment, London WA EC4Y 0DY, United Kingdom. 0207 911 8000. **Fax:** 0207 911 8100. **E-mail:** info@littlebrown.co.uk. **Website:** piatkus.co.uk. **Contact:** Emma Beswetherick, senior editor. Donna Condon, editor; Kim Mackay, editorial assistant Estab. 1979. Publishes hardcover originals, paperback originals, and paperback reprints. "Until 2007, Piatkus operated as an independent publishing house. Now it exists as a commercial imprint of Hachette-owned Little, Brown Book Group." **10% from unagented writers.** Publishes book 1 year after acceptance. Responds in 3 months to mss. Guidelines online.

Piatkus no longer accepts fiction proposals.

NONFICTION Agented submissions only.

FICTION Quality family saga, historical, literary. Agented submissions only.

PICADOR USA

MacMillan, 175 Fifth Ave., New York NY 10010. (212)674-5151. **E-mail:** david.saint@picadorusa.com; pressinquiries@macmillanusa.com. **Website:** www.picadorusa.com. **Contact:** Frances Coady, publisher (literary fiction). Joshua Kendall, associate editor (literary fiction); Sam Douglas, associate editor; David Rogers, assistant editor Estab. 1994. Picador publishes high-quality literary fiction and nonfiction. "We are open to a broad range of subjects, well written by authoritative authors." Publishes hardcover and trade paperback originals and reprints. Titles distributed through Von Holtzbrinck Publishers. Titles promoted through national print advertising and bookstore co-op. **Publishes 70-80 titles/year. Pays 7-15% on royalty. Advance varies.** Publishes book 18 months after acceptance. Accepts simultaneous submissions. Responds to queries in 2 months. Book catalog for 9×12 SASE and $2.60 postage. Ms guidelines for #10 SASE or online.

Does not accept unsolicited mss. *Agented submissions only.*

PICCADILLY BOOKS, LTD.

P.O. Box 25203, Colorado Springs CO 80936. (719)550-9887. **Fax:** (719) 550-8810. **E-mail:** info@piccadillybooks.com. **Website:** www.piccadillybooks.com. Estab. 1985. Publishes hardcover originals and trade paperback originals and reprints. "Piccadilly publishes nonfiction, diet, nutrition, and health-related books with a focus on alternative and natural medicine." **Publishes 5-8 titles/year. 70% of books from first-time authors. 95% from unagented writers. Pays 6-10% royalty on retail price.** Publishes book 1 year after acceptance. Accepts simultaneous submissions. Responds only if interested, unless accompanied by a SASE to queries.

NONFICTION Subjects include cooking, foods, nutrition, health, medicine, performing arts. "Do your research. Let us know why there is a need for your book, how it differs from other books on the market, and how you will promote the book. No phone calls." "We prefer to see the entire ms, but will accept a minimum of 3 sample chapters on your first inquiry. A cover letter is also required; please provide a brief overview of the book, information about similar books already in print and explain why yours is different or better. Tell us the prime market for your book and what you can do to help market it. Also, provide us with background information on yourself and explain what qualifies you to write this book."

TIPS "We publish nonfiction, general interest, self-help books currently emphasizing alternative health."

PICCADILLY PRESS

5 Castle Rd., London NW1 8PR, United Kingdom. (44)(207)267-4492. **Fax:** (44)(207)267-4493. **E-mail:** books@piccadillypress.co.uk. **Website:** www.piccadillypress.co.uk. "Piccadilly Press is the perfect choice for variety of reading for everyone aged 2-16! We're an independent publisher, celebrating 26 years of specialising in teen fiction and nonfiction, children's fiction, picture books and parenting books by highly acclaimed authors and illustrators and fresh new talents too. We hope you enjoy reading the books as much as we enjoy publishing them." Responds to mss in 6 weeks.

NONFICTION Young adults: self help (humorous). Average word length: young adults—25,000-35,000. Submit outline/synopsis and 2 sample chapters.

FICTION Picture books: animal, contemporary, fantasy, nature/environment. Young adults: contemporary, humor, problem novels. Average word length: picture books—500-1,000; young adults—25,000-35,000. Submit complete ms for picture books or submit outline/synopsis and 2 sample chapters for YA. Enclose a brief cover letter and SASE for reply.

TIPS "Take a look in bookshops to see if there are many other books of a similar nature to yours—this is what your book will be competing against, so make sure there is something truly unique about your story. Looking at what else is available will give you ideas as to what topics are popular, but reading a little of them will also give you a sense of the right styles, language and length appropriate for the age-group."

PICTON PRESS

Picton Corp., 814 E. Elkcam Circle, Marco Island FL 34145. **E-mail:** sales@pictonpress.com. **Website:** www.pictonpress.com. Publishes hardcover and mass market paperback originals and reprints, DVDs, and CDs. "Picton Press is one of America's oldest, largest, and most respected publishers of genealogical and historical books specializing in research tools for the 17th, 18th, and 19th centuries." **Publishes 15 titles/year. 30 queries received/year. 15 mss received/year. 20% of books from first-time authors. 100% from unagented writers. Pays 0-10% royalty on wholesale price. Makes outright purchase.** Publishes book 6 months after acceptance. Responds in 1 month. Book catalog available free.

IMPRINTS Cricketfield Press; New England History Press; Penobscot Press; Picton Press.

NONFICTION Subjects include Americana, history, genealogy. Query with SASE. Submit outline.

PIÑATA BOOKS

Imprint of Arte Publico Press, University of Houston, 4902 Gulf Fwy, Bldg 19, Rm 100, Houston TX 77204-2004. (713)743-2845. **Fax:** (713)743-3080. **E-mail:** submapp@mail.uh.edu. **Website:** www.latinoteca.

com/arte-publico-press. **Contact:** Nicolas Kanellos, director. Estab. 1994. Publishes hardcover and trade paperback originals. "Piñata Books is dedicated to the publication of children's and young adult literature focusing on U.S. Hispanic culture by U.S. Hispanic authors. Arte Publico's mission is the publication, promotion and dissemination of Latino literature for a variety of national and regional audiences, from early childhood to adult, through the complete gamut of delivery systems, including personal performance as well as print and electronic media." **Publishes 10-15 titles/year. 80% of books from first-time authors. Pays 10% royalty on wholesale price. Pays $1,000-3,000 advance.** Publishes book 2 years after acceptance. Accepts simultaneous submissions. Responds in 2-3 months to queries; 4-6 months to mss. Book catalog and ms guidelines available via website or with #10 SASE.

○ Accepts material from U.S./Hispanic authors only (living abroad OK). Mss, queries, synopses, etc., are accepted in either English or Spanish.

NONFICTION Subjects include ethnic. Piñata Books specializes in publication of children's and young adult literature that authentically portrays themes, characters and customs unique to U.S. Hispanic culture. Submissions made through online submission form.

FICTION Subjects include adventure, juvenile, picture books, young adult. Submissions made through online submission form.

POETRY Appropriate to Hispanic theme. Submissions made through online submission form.

TIPS "Include cover letter with submission explaining why your ms is unique and important, why we should publish it, who will buy it, etc."

PINEAPPLE PRESS, INC.

P.O. Box 3889, Sarasota FL 34230. (941)739-2219. **Fax:** (941)739-2296. **E-mail:** info@pineapplepress.com. **Website:** www.pineapplepress.com. **Contact:** June Cussen, executive editor. Estab. 1982. Publishes hardcover and trade paperback originals. "We are seeking quality nonfiction on diverse topics for the library and book trade markets. Our mission is to publish good books about Florida." **Publishes 25 titles/year. 1,000 queries received/year. 500 mss received/year. 50% of books from first-time authors. 95% from unagented writers. Pays authors royalty of 10-15%.** Publishes

book Publishes a book 1 year after acceptance. Accepts simultaneous submissions. Responds to queries/samples/mss in 2 months. Book catalog for 9×12 SAE with $1.25 postage. Guidelines online.

NONFICTION Subjects include regional, Florida. Picture books: animal, history, nature/environmental, science. Young readers, middle readers, young adults: animal, biography, geography, history, nature/environment, science. Recently published *Those Magical Manatees,* by Jan Lee Wicker and *Those Beautiful Butterflies,* by Sarah Cussen. We will consider most nonfiction topics when related to Florida. Query or submit outline/synopsis and intro and 3 sample chapters. Reviews artwork/photos. Send photocopies.

FICTION Subjects include regional, Florida. Picture books, young readers, middle readers, young adults: animal, folktales, history, nature/environment. Query or submit outline/synopsis and 3 sample chapters.

TIPS "Quality first novels will be published, though we usually only do one or two novels per year and they must be set in Florida. We regard the author/editor relationship as a trusting relationship with communication open both ways. Learn all you can about the publishing process and about how to promote your book once it is published. A query on a novel without a brief sample seems useless."

⊘ PLAN B PRESS

P.O. Box 4067, Alexandria VA 22303. (215)732-2663. **E-mail:** planbpress@gmail.com. **Website:** www.planbpress.com. **Contact:** Steven Allen May, president. Estab. 1999. Plan B Press is a "small publishing company with an international feel. Our intention is to have Plan B Press be part of the conversation about the direction and depth of literary movements and genres. Plan B Press's new direction is to seek out authors rarely-to-never published, sharing new voices that might not otherwise be heard. Plan B Press is determined to merge text with image, writing with art." Publishes poetry and short fiction. Wants "experimental poetry, concrete/visual work." Has published poetry by Lamont B. Steptoe, Michele Belluomini, Jim Mancinelli, Lyn Lifshin, Robert Miltner, and Steven Allen May. Publishes 1 poetry book/year and 5-10 chapbooks/year. Mss are selected through open submission and through competition (see below). Books/chapbooks are 24-48 pages, with covers with art/graphics. **Pays author's copies.** Responds to queries in 1 month; mss in 3 months.

POETRY Wants to see: experimental, concrete, visual poetry. Does not want "sonnets, political or religious poems, work in the style of Ogden Nash."

PLANNERS PRESS

Imprint of the American Planning Association, 205 N. Michigan Ave., Suite 1200, Chicago IL 60601. (312)431-9100. **Fax:** (312)786-6700. **E-mail:** planners-press@planning.org. **Website:** www.planning.org/plannerspress/index.htm. **Contact:** Timothy Mennel, Ph.D. (planning practice, urban issues, land use, transportation). Estab. 1970. Publishes hardcover, electronic, and trade paperback originals; and trade paperback and electronic reprints. "Our books often have a narrow audience of city planners and frequently focus on the tools of city planning." **Publishes 12 titles/year. 50 queries received/year. 35 mss received/year. 25% of books from first-time authors. 100% from unagented writers. Pays 10-15% royalty on net receipts. Pays advance.** Publishes book 15 months after acceptance. Accepts simultaneous submissions. Responds in 1 month to queries; 2 months to proposals and mss. Book catalog online. Guidelines available by e-mail.

NONFICTION Subjects include agriculture, business, economics, community, contemporary culture, economics, environment, finance, government, politics, history, horticulture, law, money, finance, nature, environment, politics, real estate, science, social sciences, sociology, transportation, world affairs. Submit proposal package, including: outline, 1 sample chapter and c.v. Submit completed ms. Reviews artwork/photos. Send photocopies.

TIPS "Our audience is professional planners but also anyone interested in community development, urban affairs, sustainability, and related fields."

PLEXUS PUBLISHING, INC.

143 Old Marlton Pike, Medford NJ 08055. (609)654-6500. **Fax:** (609)654-4309. **E-mail:** jbryans@plexuspublishing.com. **Website:** www.plexuspublishing.com. **Contact:** John B. Bryans, editor-in-chief/publisher. Estab. 1977. Publishes hardcover and paperback originals. Plexus publishes regional-interest (southern New Jersey and the greater Philadelphia area) fiction and nonfiction including mysteries, field guides, nature, travel and history. Also a limited number of titles in health/medicine, biology, ecology, botany, astronomy. **Pays $500-1,000 advance.** Accepts simultaneous submissions. Responds in 3 months to proposals. Book catalog and book proposal guidelines for 10x13 SASE.

NONFICTION Query with SASE.

FICTION Mysteries and literary novels with a strong regional (southern New Jersey) angle. Query with SASE.

⊘⊘ POCKET BOOKS

Simon & Schuster, 1230 Avenue of the Americas, New York NY 10020. (212)698-7000. **Website:** www.simonandschuster.com. **Contact:** Jennifer Bergstrom, editor-in-chief. Estab. 1939. Publishes paperback originals and reprints, mass market and trade paperbacks. Pocket Books publishes commercial fiction and genre fiction (WWE, Downtown Press, Star Trek). Book catalog available free. Guidelines online.

NONFICTION Subjects include cooking, foods, nutrition. *Agented submissions only.*

FICTION Subjects include mystery, romance, suspense, psychological suspense, thriller, western. *Agented submissions only.*

POCOL PRESS

Box 411, Clifton VA 20124. (703)830-5862. **Website:** www.pocolpress.com. **Contact:** J. Thomas Hetrick, editor. Estab. 1999. Publishes trade paperback originals. "Pocol Press is dedicated to producing high-quality print books and e-books from first-time, non-agented authors. However, all submissions are welcome. We're dedicated to good storytellers and to the written word, specializing in short fiction and baseball. Several of our books have been used as literary texts at universities and in book group discussions around the nation. Pocol Press does not publish children's books, romance novels, or graphic novels." **Publishes 6 titles/year. 90 queries received/year. 20 mss received/year. 90% of books from first-time authors. 100% from unagented writers. Pays 10-12% royalty on wholesale price.** Publishes book less than 1 year after acceptance. Responds in 1 month to queries; 2 months to mss. Book catalog and Guidelines online.
"Our authors are comprised of veteran writers and emerging talents."

FICTION Subjects include historical, horror, literary, mainstream, contemporary, military, war, mystery, short story collections, thematic, spiritual, sports, western, baseball fiction. "We specialize in thematic short fiction collections by a single author and baseball fiction. Expert storytellers welcome." Horror (psychological, supernatural), literary, mainstream/

contemporary, short story collections, baseball. Does not accept or return unsolicited mss. Query with SASE or submit 1 sample chapter(s).

TIPS "Our audience is aged 18 and over. Pocol Press is unique; we publish good writing and great storytelling. Write the best stories you can. Read them to you friends/peers. Note their reaction. Publishes some of the finest fiction by a small press."

THE POISONED PENCIL

Poisoned Pen Press, 6962 E. 1st Ave., Suite 103, Scottsdale AZ 85251. (480)945-3375. **Fax:** (480)949-1707. **E-mail:** info@thepoisonedpencil.com. **E-mail:** www.thepoisonedpencil.submittable.com/submit. **Website:** www.thepoisonedpencil.com. **Contact:** Ellen Larson, editor. Estab. 2012. Publishes trade paperback and electronic originals. **250 submissions received/year. Pays 9-15% for trade paperback; 25-35% for eBooks. Pays advance of $1,000.** Publishes book 15 months after acceptance. Responds in 6 weeks to mss. Guidelines online.

Accepts young adult mysteries only.

FICTION Subjects include mystery, young adult. "We publish only young adult mystery novels, 45,000 to 90,000 words in length. For our purposes, a young adult book is a book with a protagonist between the ages of 13 and 18. We are looking for both traditional and cross-genre young adult mysteries. We encourage off-beat approaches and narrative choices that reflect the complexity and ambiguity of today's world. Submissions from teens are very welcome. Avoid serial killers, excessive gore, and vampires (and other heavy supernatural themes). We only consider authors who live in the US or Canada, due to practicalities of marketing promotion. Avoid coincidence in plotting. Avoid having your sleuth leap to conclusions rather than discover and deduce. Pay attention to the resonance between character and plot; between plot and theme; between theme and character. We are looking for clean style, fluid storytelling, and solid structure. Unrealistic dialogue is a real turn-off." Submit proposal package including synopsis, complete ms, and cover letter.

TIPS "Our audience is young adults and adults who love YA mysteries."

POISONED PEN PRESS

6962 E. 1st Ave., Suite 103, Scottsdale AZ 85251. (480)945-3375. **Fax:** (480)949-1707. **E-mail:** submissions@poisonedpenpress.com. **Website:** www.poisonedpenpress.com. **Contact:** Jessica Tribble, publisher; Barbara Peters, editor-in-chief. Estab. 1996. Publishes hardcover originals, and hardcover and trade paperback reprints. "Our publishing goal is to offer well-written mystery novels of crime and/or detection where the puzzle and its resolution are the main forces that move the story forward." **Publishes 36 titles/year. 1,000 queries received/year. 300 mss received/year. 35% of books from first-time authors. 65% from unagented writers. Pays 9-15% royalty on retail price.** Publishes book 10-12 months after acceptance. Responds in 2-3 months to queries and proposals; 6 months to mss. Book catalog and guidelines online.

IMPRINTS The Poisoned Pencil.

Not currently accepting submissions. Check website.

FICTION Subjects include mystery. Mss should generally be longer than 65,000 words and shorter than 100,000 words. Member Publishers Marketing Associations, Arizona Book Publishers Associations, Publishers Association of West. Distributes through Ingram, Baker & Taylor, Brodart. Does not want novels centered on serial killers, spousal or child abuse, drugs, or extremist groups, although we do not entirely rule such works out. Accepts unsolicited mss. Electronic queries only. "Query with SASE. Submit clips, first 3 pages. We must receive both the synopsis and ms pages electronically as separate attachments to an e-mail message or as a disk or CD which we will not return."

TIPS "Audience is adult readers of mystery fiction."

POPULAR WOODWORKING BOOKS

Imprint of F+W Media, Inc., 10151 Carver Rd., Suite 200, Blue Ash OH 45242. (513)531-2690. **Website:** www.popularwoodworking.com. **Contact:** David Thiel, executive editor. Publishes trade paperback and hardcover originals and reprints. "Popular Woodworking Books is one of the largest publishers of woodworking books in the world. From perfecting a furniture design to putting on the final coat of finish, our books provide step-by-step instructions and trusted advice from the pros that make them valuable tools for both beginning and advanced woodworkers. Currently emphasizing woodworking jigs and fixtures, furniture and cabinet projects, smaller finely crafted boxes, all styles of furniture. De-emphasizing woodturning, woodcarving, scroll saw projects." **Publishes 6-8 titles/year. 20 queries received/year. 10**

mss received/year. **20% of books from first-time authors. 95% from unagented writers.** Accepts simultaneous submissions. Responds in 1 month to queries.
NONFICTION Subjects include hobbies, woodworking/wood crafts. "We publish heavily illustrated how-to woodworking books that show, rather than tell, our readers how to accomplish their woodworking goals." Query with SASE, or electronic query. Proposal package should include an outline and digital photos.
TIPS "Our books are for beginning to advanced woodworking enthusiasts."

POSSIBILITY PRESS

1 Oakglade Circle, Hummelstown PA 17036. **E-mail:** info@possibilitypress.com. **Website:** www.possibilitypress.com. **Contact:** Mike Markowski, publisher. Estab. 1981. Publishes trade paperback originals. "Our mission is to help the people of the world grow and become the best they can be, through the written and spoken word." **Publishes 2-3 titles/year. 90% of books from first-time authors. 100% from unagented writers. Royalties vary.** Responds in 1 month to queries. Catalog online. Guidelines online.
IMPRINTS Aeronautical Publishers; Possibility Press; Markowski International Publishers.
NONFICTION Subjects include psychology, pop psychology, self-help, leadership, relationships, attitude, business, success/motivation, inspiration, entrepreneurship, sales marketing, MLM and home-based business topics, and human interest success stories. Prefers submissions to be mailed. Include SASE. Submit ms in Microsoft Word. Your submission needs to be made both in hard copy and on a CD. Label it clearly with the book title and your name. Be sure to keep a backup CD for yourself. See guidelines online. Reviews artwork/photos. Do not send originals.
FICTION Needs: parables that teach lessons about life and success.
TIPS "Our focus is on co-authoring and publishing short (15,000-40,000 words) bestsellers. We're looking for kind and compassionate authors who are passionate about making a difference in the world, and will champion their mission to do so, especially by public speaking. Our dream author writes well, knows how to promote, will champion their mission, speaks for a living, has a following and a platform, is cooperative and understanding, humbly handles critique and direction, is grateful, intelligent, and has a good sense of humor."

POTOMAC BOOKS, INC.

Attn: KO, 22841 Quicksilver Dr., Dulles VA 20166. (703)661-1548. **Fax:** (703)661-1547. **Website:** www.potomacbooksinc.com. **Contact:** Editorial Department. Estab. 1984. Publishes hardcover and trade paperback originals and reprints. "Potomac Books specializes in national and international affairs, history (especially military and diplomatic), intelligence, biography, reference, and sports. We are particularly interested in authors who can communicate a sophisticated understanding of their topic to general readers, as well as specialists." **Publishes 60 titles/year. 900 queries received/year. 20% of books from first-time authors. 70% from unagented writers. Pays royalty on wholesale price. Pays five figure maximum advance.** Publishes book 1 year after acceptance of ms. Accepts simultaneous submissions. Responds in 2 months to queries. Book catalog available free. Guidelines online.
IMPRINTS Potomac Sports.
NONFICTION Subjects include government, politics, history, military, war, sports, world affairs, national and international affairs. When submitting nonfiction, be sure to include sufficient biographical information (e.g., track records of previous publications), and make clear in the query letter how your work might differ from other such works already published and with which yours might compete. "Query letter should provide a summary of the project, a description of the author's credentials and an analysis of the work's competition. "We are encouraging prospective authors to submit book proposals via e-mail."
TIPS "Our audience consists of general nonfiction readers, as well as students, scholars, policymakers and the military."

PPI (PROFESSIONAL PUBLICATIONS, INC.)

1250 Fifth Ave., Belmont CA 94002. (650)593-9119. **Fax:** (650)592-4519. **E-mail:** info@ppi2pass.com. **Website:** www.ppi2pass.com. Estab. 1975. Publishes hardcover, paperback, and electronic products, CD-ROMs and DVDs. "PPI publishes professional, reference, and licensing preparation materials. PPI wants submissions from both professionals practicing in the field and from experienced instructors. Currently emphasizing engineering, interior design, architecture, landscape architecture and LEED exam review." **Publishes 10 titles/year. 5% of books from first-time**

authors. 100% from unagented writers. Publishes book 4-18 months after acceptance. Accepts simultaneous submissions. Responds in 1 month to queries. Book catalog and ms guidelines free.

NONFICTION Subjects include architecture, science, landscape architecture, engineering mathematics, engineering, surveying, interior design, greenbuilding, sustainable development, and other professional licensure subjects. Especially needs review and reference books for all professional licensing examinations. Please submit ms and proposal outlining market potential, etc. Proposal template available upon request. Reviews artwork/photos.

TIPS "We specialize in books for those people who want to become licensed and/or accredited professionals: engineers, architects, surveyors, interior designers, LEED APs, etc. Exam Prep Lines generally include online and print products such as review manuals, practice problems, sample exams, E-Learning Modules, IPhone Apps, and more. Demonstrating your understanding of the market, competition, appropriate delivery methods, and marketing ideas will help sell us on your proposal."

PRAKKEN PUBLICATIONS, INC.

P.O. Box 8623, Ann Arbor MI 48107. (734)975-2800. **Fax:** (734)975-2787. **E-mail:** pam@eddigest.com. **E-mail:** susanne@eddigest.com. **Contact:** Susanne Peckham, book editor; Sharon K. Miller, art/design/production manager. Estab. 1934. Publishes educational hardcover and paperback originals, as well as educational magazines. "We publish books for educators in career/vocational and technology education, as well as books for the machine trades and machinists' education. Currently emphasizing machine trades." **Publishes 3 titles/year.** Accepts simultaneous submissions. Responds in 2 months to queries. Book catalog for #10 SASE.

NONFICTION Subjects include education. "We are currently interested in mss with broad appeal in any of the specific subject areas of machine trades, technology education, career-technical education, and reference for the general education field." Submit outline, sample chapters.

TIPS "We have a continuing interest in magazine and book mss which reflect emerging issues and trends in education, especially career-technical, industrial, and technology education."

PRESA :S: PRESS

P.O. Box 792, 8590 Belding Rd. NE, Rockford MI 49341. **E-mail:** presapress@aol.com. **Website:** www.presapress.com. **Contact:** Roseanne Ritzema, editor. Estab. 2003. Presa :S: Press publishes "perfect-bound paperbacks and saddle-stitched chapbooks of poetry. Wants "imagistic poetry where form is an extension of content, surreal, experimental, and personal poetry." Does not want "overtly political or didactic material." **Pays 10-25 author\quotes copies.** Publishes book Time between acceptance and publication is 8-12 weeks. after acceptance of ms. Responds to queries in 2-4 weeks; to mss in 8-12 weeks. Guidelines available in magazine, for SASE, and by e-mail.

POETRY Needs poems, reviews, essays, photos, criticism, and prose. Dedicates 6-8 pages of each issue to a featured poet. Considers previously published poems. (Considers poetry posted on a public website/blog/forum and poetry posted on a private, password-protected forum as published.) Acquires first North American serial rights and the right to reprint in anthologies. Rights revert to poets upon publication. Accepts postal submissions only. Cover letter is preferred. Reads submissions year round. Poems are circulated to an editorial board. Never comments on rejected poems. Never publishes theme issues. Reviews books and chapbooks of poetry. Send materials for review consideration to Roseanne Ritzema. Query first, with a few sample poems and a cover letter with brief bio and publication credits. Book/chapbook mss may include previously published poems.

PRESS 53

P.O. Box 30314, Winston-Salem NC 27101. **E-mail:** kevin@press53.com. **Website:** www.press53.com. **Contact:** Kevin Morgan Watson, publisher. "Press 53 was founded in October 2005 and quickly began earning a reputation as a quality publishing house of short story and poetry collections." Open submission period in November each year. **Publishes 16-18 titles/year.** Responds in 6 months to mss. Guidelines online.

FICTION Subjects include literary, short story collections. "We publish roughly 8 short story collections each year by writers who are active and earning recognition through publication and awards." Collections should include 10-15 short stories with 70% or more of those stories previously published. Does not want novels. November submission period. Submit via Submittable on site a letter of introduction (information about yourself and your collection), where the stories have been published, a few ideas for marketing your book, and the complete ms.

POETRY "We love working with poets who have been widely published and are active in the poetry community. We publish only full-length poetry collections of roughly 70 pages or more." Prefers that at least 30-40% of the poems in the collection be previously published. In November, submit via Submittable on site: letter of introduction with info about yourself and poetry collection, the number of poems in collection, where the poems have been published, and a few ideas for marketing book, along with complete ms.

TIPS "We are looking for writers who are actively involved in the writing community, writers who are submitting their work to journals, magazines and contests, and who are getting published and earning a reputation for their work."

⊙ PRESSES DE L'UNIVERSITÉ DE MONTREAL

3744, rue Jean Brillant, local 6310, Montreal QC H3T 1P1, Canada. (514)343-6933. **Fax:** (514)343-2232. **E-mail:** pum@umontreal.ca. **E-mail:** hh@editionspum.ca. **Website:** www.pum.umontreal.ca. **Contact:** Sylvie Brousseau, rights and sales. Publishes hardcover and trade paperback originals. **Publishes 40 titles/year.** Publishes book 6 months after acceptance. Responds in 1 month to queries and proposals; months to mss. Book catalog and ms guidelines free.

NONFICTION Subjects include education, health, medicine, history, language, literature, philosophy, psychology, sociology, translation. Submit outline, 2 sample chapters.

⊙⊘ PRICE STERN SLOAN, INC.

Penguin Group, 375 Hudson St., New York NY 10014. (212)366-2000. **Website:** us.penguingroup.com/static/pages/publishers/index.html. **Contact:** Francesco Sedita, vice-president/publisher. Estab. 1963. "Price Stern Sloan publishes quirky mass market novelty series for childrens as well as licensed movie tie-in books." Price Stern Sloan only responds to submissions it's interested in publishing. Book catalog online.

○ Price Stern Sloan does not accept e-mail submissions.

FICTION Publishes picture books and novelty/board books including Mad Libs Movie and Television Tie-ins, and unauthorized biographies. All book formats except for picture books. "We publish unique novel-ty formats and fun, colorful paperbacks and activity books. We also publish the Book with Audio Series *Wee Sing* and *Baby Loves Jazz*." Agented submissions only.

TIPS "Price Stern Sloan publishes unique, fun titles."

PRINCETON ARCHITECTURAL PRESS

37 E. 7th St., New York NY 10003. (212)995-9620. **Fax:** (212)995-9454. **E-mail:** submissions@papress.com. **Website:** www.papress.com. Publishes hardcover and trade paperback originals. **Publishes 50 titles/year. 300 queries received/year. 150 mss received/year. 65% of books from first-time authors. 95% from unagented writers. Pays royalty on wholesale price.** Publishes book 1 year after acceptance. Accepts simultaneous submissions. Responds in 2 months. Catalog and guidelines online.

NONFICTION Subjects include art, architecture. Submit proposal package, outline, 1 sample chapter, TOC, sample of art, and survey of competitive titles. Reviews artwork/photos. Do not send originals.

TIPS "Princeton Architecture Press publishes fine books on architecture, design, photography, landscape, and visual culture. Our books are acclaimed for their strong and unique editorial vision, unrivaled design sensibility, and high production values at affordable prices."

PRINCETON UNIVERSITY PRESS

41 William St., Princeton NJ 08540. (609)258-4900. **Fax:** (609)258-6305. **Website:** www.pupress.princeton.edu. **Contact:** Hanne Winarsky, editor. "The Lockert Library of Poetry in Translation embraces a wide geographic and temporal range, from Scandinavia to Latin America to the subcontinent of India, from the Tang Dynasty to Europe of the modern day. It especially emphasizes poets who are established in their native lands and who are being introduced to an English-speaking audience. The series, many of whose titles are bilingual editions, calls attention to some of the most widely-praised poetry available today. In the Lockert Library series, each book is given individual design treatment rather than stamped into a series mold. We have published a wide range of poets from other cultures, including well-known writers such as Hoölderlin and Cavafy, and those who have not yet had their due in English translation, such as Goöran Sonnevi. Mss are judged with several criteria in mind: the ability of the translation to stand on its own as poetry in English; fidelity to the tone and spirit

of the original, rather than literal accuracy; and the importance of the translated poet to the literature of his or her time and country." Responds in 3-4 months. Guidelines online.

NONFICTION Query with SASE.

POETRY Submit hard copy of proposal with sample poems or full ms. Cover letter is required. Reads submissions year round. Mss will not be returned. Comments on finalists only.

PRINTING INDUSTRIES OF AMERICA

200 Deer Run Rd., Sewickley PA 15143. (412)741-6860. **Fax:** (412)741-2311. **E-mail:** awoodall@printing.org. **Website:** www.printing.org. **Contact:** Amy Woodall, director (printing, graphic arts, communication). Estab. 1921. Publishes trade paperback originals and reference texts. "Printing Industries of America, along with its affiliates, delivers products and services that enhance the growth and profitability of its members and the industry through advocacy, education, research, and technical information." Printing Industries of America's mission is to serve the graphic communications community as the major resource for technical information and services through research and education. **Publishes 8-10 titles/year. 20 mss received/year; 30 queries received/year. 50% of books from first-time authors. 100% from unagented writers. Pays 15% royalty on wholesale price.** Publishes book 18 months after acceptance. Accepts simultaneous submissions. Responds in 1 month to queries.

NONFICTION Subjects include business, communications, economics, education, printing and graphic arts reference, technical, textbook. Currently emphasizing technical textbooks as well as career guides for graphic communications and turnkey training curricula. Query with SASE, or submit outline, sample chapters, and SASE. Reviews artwork. Send photocopies.

PROMETHEUS BOOKS

59 John Glenn Dr., Amherst NY 14228-2119. (800)421-0351. **Fax:** (716)564-2711. **E-mail:** editorial@prometheusbooks.com. **Website:** www.prometheusbooks.com. **Contact:** Steven L. Mitchell, editor-in-chief. Estab. 1969. Publishes hardcover originals, trade paperback originals and reprints. "Prometheus Books is a leading independent publisher in philosophy, social science, popular science, and critical thinking. We publish authoritative and thoughtful books by distinguished authors in many categories.

Currently emphasizing popular science, health, psychology, social science, current events, business and economics, atheism and critiques of religion." **Publishes 90-100 titles/year. 30% of books from first-time authors. 40% from unagented writers.** Accepts simultaneous submissions. Responds in 2 months to queries. Responds in 3 months to proposals. Responds in 4 months to mss. Book catalog free or online. Guidelines for #10 SASE or online.

IMPRINTS Humanity Books (scholarly and professional monographs in philosophy, social science, sociology, archaeology, black studies, women's studies); PYR (science fiction/fantasy—accepts agented works only by previously published authors—send to the attention of Lou Anders).

NONFICTION Subjects include education, government, politics, health, medicine, history, language, literature, New Age, critiquing of, philosophy, psychology, religion, contemporary issues. Ask for a catalog, go to the library or our website, look at our books and others like them to get an idea of what our focus is. Submit proposal package including outline, synopsis, potential market, tentative ms length, résumé, and a well-developed query letter with SASE, two or three of author's best chapters. Reviews artwork/photos. Send photocopies.

TIPS "Audience is highly literate with multiple degrees; an audience that is intellectually mature and knows what it wants. They are aware, and we try to provide them with new information on topics of interest to them in mainstream and related areas."

PROSTAR PUBLICATIONS INC.

East Coast, 3 Church Circle, Suite 109, Annapolis MD 21401. (800)481-6277. **Fax:** (800)487-6277. **E-mail:** editor@prostarpublications.com. **Website:** www.prostarpublications.com. Estab. 1991. "ProStar Publications, Inc. is the largest publisher and distributor of U.S. Nautical publications world wide. Our titles include all U.S. Sailing Directions, U.S.C.G. Light Lists, Navigation Rules (International & Inland), NOAA Tide & Tidal Current Tables, Code of Federal Regulations (CFR™s), Boating Almanacs and the U.S. Notice to Mariners on a weekly basis."

PRUFROCK PRESS, INC.

P.O. Box 8813, Waco TX 76714. (800)988-2208. **Fax:** (800)240-0333. **E-mail:** info@prufrock.com. **Website:** www.prufrock.com. **Contact:** Joel McIntosh, publisher and marketing director. "Prufrock Press offers award-winning products focused on gifted education, gifted children, advanced learning, and special needs learners. For more than 20 years, Prufrock has supported gifted children and their education and development. The company publishes more than 300 products that enhance the lives of gifted children and the teachers and parents who support them." **50 queries received/year. 40 mss received/year. 20% of books from first-time authors. 100% from unagented writers.** Publishes book 1-2 year after acceptance. Accepts simultaneous submissions. Book catalog for 10×12 envelope and 2 first-class stamps. Guidelines online.

○ Accepts simultaneous submissions, but must be notified about it.

NONFICTION Subjects include education, language, literature. "We are always looking for truly original, creative materials for teachers." Query with SASE. Submit outline, 1-3 sample chapters.

FICTION Prufrock Press "offers award-winning products focused on gifted education, gifted children, advanced learning, and special needs learners. For more than 20 years, Prufrock has supported gifted children and their education and development. The company publishes more than 300 products that enhance the lives of gifted children and the teachers and parents who support them." No picture books. "Prufrock Press does not consider unsolicited mss."

PUFFIN BOOKS

Imprint of Penguin Group (USA), Inc., 375 Hudson St., New York NY 10014. (212)366-2000. **Website:** www.penguinputnam.com. **Contact:** Kristin Gilson, editorial director. Sharyn November, senior editor Publishes trade paperback originals and reprints. "Puffin Books publishes high-end trade paperbacks and paperback reprints for preschool children, beginning and middle readers, and young adults." **Publishes 175-200 titles/year. Receives 600 queries and mss/year. 1% of books from first-time authors. 5% from unagented writers. Royalty varies. Pays varies advance.** Publishes book 1 year after acceptance. Responds in 5 months. Book catalog for 9×12 SAE with 7 first-class stamps.

IMPRINTS Speak, Firebird, Sleuth.

NONFICTION Subjects include education, for teaching concepts and colors, not academic, history, women's issues, women's studies. "Women in history books interest us." *No unsolicited mss.* Agented submissions only.

FICTION Subjects include fantasy, picture books, science fiction, young adult, middle grade, easy-to-read grades 1-3, graphic novels, classics. *No unsolicited mss.* Agented submissions only.

TIPS "Our audience ranges from little children 'first books' to young adult (ages 14-16). An original idea has the best luck."

PURDUE UNIVERSITY PRESS

504 West State St., West Lafayette IN 47907-2058. (765)494-2038. **E-mail:** rlcorbin@purdue.edu. **Website:** www.thepress.purdue.edu. **Contact:** Rebecca Corbin, administrative assistant. Estab. 1960. Publishes hardcover and trade paperback originals and trade paperback reprints. "We look for books that look at the world as a whole and offer new thoughts and insights into the standard debate. Currently emphasizing technology, human-animal issues, business. De-emphasizing literary studies." **Publishes 20-25 titles/year.** Book catalog and ms guidelines for 9×12 SASE.

IMPRINTS PuP Books.

NONFICTION Subjects include agriculture, Americana, business, government, politics, health, history, language, literary criticism, philosophy, regional, science, social sciences, sociology. Dedicated to the dissemination of scholarly and professional information, Purdue University Press provides quality resources in several key subject areas including business, technology, health, veterinary medicine, and other selected disciplines in the humanities and sciences. As the scholarly publishing arm of Purdue University and a unit of Purdue Libraries, the Press is also a partner for university faculty and staff, centers and departments, wishing to disseminate the results of their research. Query before submitting.

✪ PURICH PUBLISHING

Box 23032, Market Mall Post Office, Saskatoon SK S7J 5H3, Canada. (306)373-5311. **Fax:** (306)373-5315. **E-mail:** purich@sasktel.net. **Website:** www.purichpublishing.com. **Contact:** Donald Purich, publisher; Karen Bolstad, publisher. Estab. 1992. Publishes trade paperback originals. "Purich publishes books on law, Aboriginal/Native American issues, and Western Canadian history for the academic and professional trade reference market." **Publishes 3-5 titles/year. 20% of books from first-time authors. 100% from unagented writers. Pays 8-12% royalty on retail price.** Publishes book 4 months after acceptance.

Responds in 1 month to queries. Book catalog available free.

NONFICTION , Aboriginal and social justice issues, Western Canadian history. "We are a specialized publisher and only consider work in our subject areas." Query with SASE.

Ⓐ PUSH

Scholastic, 557 Broadway, New York NY 10012. **E-mail:** dlevithan@scholastic.com. **Website:** www.thisispush.com. Estab. 2002. PUSH publishes new voices in teen literature. **Publishes 6-9 titles/year. 50% of books from first-time authors.**

Ⓞ   PUSH does not accept unsolicited mss or queries, only agented or referred fiction/memoir.

NONFICTION Subjects include memoirs, young adult.

FICTION Subjects include contemporary, multicultural, poetry, young adult. *Does not accept unsolicited mss.*

TIPS "We only publish first-time writers (and then their subsequent books), so authors who have published previously should not consider PUSH. Also, for young writers in grades 7-12, we run the PUSH Novel Contest with the Scholastic Art & Writing Awards. Every year it begins in October and ends in March. Rules can be found on our website."

Ⓐ Ⓞ G.P. PUTNAM'S SONS HARDCOVER

Imprint of Penguin Group (USA), Inc., 375 Hudson, New York NY 10014. (212)366-2000. **Fax:** (212)366-2664. **Website:** www.penguinputnam.com. Publishes hardcover originals. **Pays variable royalties on retail price. Pays varies advance.** Accepts simultaneous submissions. Request book catalog through mail order department.

NONFICTION Subjects include animals, business, economics, child guidance, contemporary culture, cooking, foods, nutrition, health, medicine, military, war, nature, environment, religion, science, sports, travel, women's issues, women's studies, celebrity-related topics. Agented submissions only. *No unsolicited mss.*

FICTION Subjects include adventure, literary, mainstream, mystery, suspense, women's. Agented submissions only.

QUE

Pearson Education, 800 E. 96th St., Indianapolis IN 46240. (317)581-3500. **E-mail:** proposals@quepublishing.com. **Website:** www.quepublishing.com. Es-

tab. 1981. Publishes hardcover, trade paperback and mass market paperback originals and reprints. **Publishes 100 titles/year. 80% from unagented writers. Pays variable royalty on wholesale price or makes work-for-hire arrangements. Pays varying advance.** Accepts simultaneous submissions. Book catalog and ms guidelines online.

NONFICTION Subjects include computers, electronics, technology, certification. Submit proposal package, résumé, TOC, writing sample, competing titles.

QUEST BOOKS

Imprint of Theosophical Publishing House, 306 W. Geneva Rd., P.O. Box 270, Wheaton IL 60187. **E-mail:** submissions@questbooks.net. **Website:** www.questbooks.net. **Contact:** Richard Smoley, editor. Estab. 1965. Publishes hardcover and trade paperback originals and reprints. "Quest Books is the imprint of the Theosophical Publishing House, the publishing arm of the Theosophical Society in America. Since 1965, Quest books has sold millions of books by leading cultural thinkers on such increasingly popular subjects as transpersonal psychology, comparative religion, deep ecology, spiritual growth, the development of creativity, and alternative health practices." **Publishes 10 titles/year. 150 mss received/year; 350 queries received/year. 20% of books from first-time authors. 80% from unagented writers. Pays royalty on retail price. Pays varying advance.** Publishes book 1 year after acceptance. Accepts simultaneous submissions. Responds in 2 months to queries, proposals, and mss. Book catalog available free. Guidelines online.

NONFICTION Subjects include philosophy, psychology, religion, spirituality, New Age, astrology/psychic. "Our speciality is high-quality spiritual nonfiction with a self-help aspect. Great writing is a must. We seldom publish 'personal spiritual awakening' stories. No submissions accepted that do not fit the needs outlined above. No fiction, poetry, children's books, or any literature based on channeling or personal psychic impressions." Submit proposal package, including outline, 1 sample chapter. Prefer online submissions; attachments must be sent as a single file in Microsoft Word, Rich Text, or PDF formats. Reviews artwork/photos. Hard copies of mss. and artwork will not be returned. Reviews artwork/photos. Writers should send photocopies or transparencies, but note that none will be returned.

TIPS "Our audience includes readers interested in spirituality, particularly the world's mystical traditions. Read a few recent Quest titles and submission guidelines before submitting. Know our books and our company goals. Explain how your book or proposal relates to other Quest titles. Quest gives preference to writers with established reputations/successful publications. Please be advised that proposals or mss will not be accepted if they fall into any of the following categories: Works intended for or about children, teenagers, or adolescents; Fiction or literary works (novels, short stories, essays, or poetry); Autobiographical material (memoirs, personal experiences, or family stories; Works received through mediumship, trance, or channeling; Works related to UFOs or extraterrestrials; Works related to self-aggrandizement (e.g., 'how to make a fortune') or 'how-to' books. Nor do we publish books from fundamentalist Christian perspectives."

⊘ QUITE SPECIFIC MEDIA GROUP, LTD.

7373 Pyramid Place, Hollywood CA 90046. (323)851-5797. **Fax:** (323)851-5798. **E-mail:** info@quitespecificmedia.com. **Website:** www.quitespecificmedia.com. **Contact:** Ralph Pine, editor-in-chief. Estab. 1967. Publishes hardcover originals, trade paperback originals and reprints. "Quite Specific Media Group is an umbrella company of 5 imprints specializing in costume and fashion, theater and design." **Publishes 12 titles/year. 75 queries received/year. 30 mss received/year. 75% of books from first-time authors. 85% from unagented writers. Pays royalty on wholesale price. Pays varies advance.** Publishes book 18 months after acceptance. Accepts simultaneous submissions. Responds to queries. Book catalog online. Guidelines available free.

IMPRINTS Imprints: Costume & Fashion Press; Drama Publishers; By Design Press; Entertainment Pro; Jade Rabbit.

NONFICTION Subjects include fashion, film, cinema, stage, history, literary criticism, translation. Accepts nonfiction and technical works in translations also. For and about performing arts theory and practice: acting, directing; voice, speech, movement; makeup, masks, wits; costumes, sets, lighting, sound; design and execution; technical theater, stagecraft, equipment; stage management; producing; arts management, all varieties; business and legal aspects; film, radio, television, cable, video; theory, criticism, reference; theater and performance history; costume and fashion. Query by e-mail please. Reviews artwork/photos.

QUIXOTE PRESS

3544 Blakslee St., Wever IA 52658. (800)571-2665. **Fax:** (319)372-7485. **Website:** www.heartsntummies.com. **Contact:** Bruce Carlson. Publishes trade paperback originals and reprints. **Pays 10% royalty on wholesale price.** Publishes book 1 year after acceptance. Accepts simultaneous submissions.

NONFICTION Query with SASE.

FICTION Subjects include humor, short story collections. Query with SASE.

TIPS "Carefully consider marketing considerations. Audience is women in gift shops, on farm sites, direct retail outlets, wineries, outdoor sport shops, etc. Contact us at *you idea* stage, not complete ms stage. Be receptive to design input by us."

☻ RADCLIFFE PUBLISHING LTD

Unit C5, Sunningdale House, 43 Caldecotte Lake Dr., Caldecotte Lake Business Park, Milton Keynes MK7 8LF, United Kingdom. (44)(0)1908-326-941. **Fax:** (44)(0)-1908-326-960. **E-mail:** louise.crowe@radcliffe-publishing.com. **Website:** www.radcliffe-oxford.com. **Contact:** Louise Crowe, publishing director. Estab. 1987. **Publishes 90 or fewer titles/year. Pays royalty.** Guidelines available via e-mail.

NONFICTION Subjects include health, medicine, sociology, nursing, midwifery, health services management and policy. Submit proposal package, outline, résumé, publishing history, bio.

TIPS "Receive book proposal guidelines by e-mail and study them."

RAGGED SKY PRESS

P.O. Box 312, Annandale NJ 08801. **E-mail:** info@raggedsky.com. **Website:** www.raggedsky.com. **Contact:** Ellen Foos, publisher; Vasiliki Katsarou, managing editor; Arlene Weiner, editor. Produces poetry anthologies and single-author poetry collections along with inspired prose. Ragged Sky is a small, highly selective cooperative press. "We work with our authors closely." Single-author submissions currently by invitation only. Learn more online.

RAINBOW PUBLISHERS

P.O. Box 261129, San Diego CA 92196. (858)277-1167. **E-mail:** editor@rainbowpublishers.com. **Website:** www.rainbowpublishers.com; www.legacypresskids.

com. Estab. 1979. "Our mission is to publish Bible-based, teacher resource materials that contribute to and inspire spiritual growth and development in kids ages 2-12." **For authors work purchased outright (range: $500 and up).** Accepts simultaneous submissions. Responds to queries in 6 weeks; mss in 3 months.

NONFICTION Young readers, middle readers, young adult/teens: activity books, arts/crafts, how-to, reference, religion.

TIPS "Our Rainbow imprint publishes reproducible books for teachers of children in Christian ministries, including crafts, activities, games and puzzles. Our Legacy imprint publishes titles for children such as devotionals, fiction and Christian living. Please write for guidelines and study the market before submitting material."

RAINCOAST BOOK DISTRIBUTION, LTD.

2440 Viking Way, Richmond BC V6V 1N2, Canada. (604)448-7100. **Fax:** (604)270-7161. **E-mail:** info@raincoast.com. **Website:** www.raincoast.com. Publishes hardcover and trade paperback originals and reprints. **Publishes 60 titles/year. 3,000 queries received/year. 10% of books from first-time authors. 40% from unagented writers. Pays 8-12% royalty on retail price. Pays $1,000-6,000 advance.** Publishes book within 2 years of acceptance. after acceptance of ms. Book catalog for #10 SASE.

IMPRINTS Raincoast Books; Polestar Books (fiction, poetry, literary nonfiction).

NONFICTION Subjects include animals, art, architecture, ethnic, history, nature, environment, photography, recreation, regional, sports, travel. *No unsolicited mss.* Query with SASE.

FICTION Subjects include literary, short story collections, young adult. *No unsolicited mss.*

RAIN TOWN PRESS

1111 E. Burnside St. #309, Portland OR 97214. (503)962-9612. **E-mail:** submissions@raintownpress.com. **Website:** www.raintownpress.com. **Contact:** Misty V'Marie, acquisitions editor; Ellery Harvey, art director. Estab. 2009. **Publishes 1-4 middle readers; 1-4 young adult titles/year. 100% of books from first-time authors. Pays 8-15% royalty on net sales. Does not pay advance.** Publishes book 1 year after acceptance. Accepts simultaneous submissions.

Responds in 1-6 months. Catalog online. Guidelines online.

IMPRINTS Raintown Kids, Mary Darcy, Misty V'Marie, William Softich, Leah Brown.

"We are Portland, Oregon's first independent press dedicated to publishing literature for middle grade and young adult readers. We hope to give rise to their voice, speaking directly to the spirit they embody through our books and other endeavors. The gray days we endure in the Pacific Northwest are custom-made for reading a good book—or in our case, making one. The rain inspires, challenges, and motivates us. To that end, we say: Let it drizzle. We will soon publish picture books."

NONFICTION Subjects include animals, contemporary culture, environment, health, history, multicultural, nature, sports. Middle Readers/YA/Teens: biography, concept, graphic novels, hi-lo, how-to. Query. Submit outline/synopsis and 2 sample chapters.

FICTION Subjects include fantasy, folktales, graphic novels, hi-lo, problem novels, science fiction, special needs, concept. Middle Readers/YA/Teens: Wants adventure, animal, contemporary, fantasy, folktales, graphic novels, health, hi-lo, history, humor, multicultural, nature/environment, problem novels, sci-fi, special needs, sports. Catalog online. Query. Submit complete ms.

TIPS "The middle grade and YA markets have sometimes very stringent conventions for subject matter, theme, etc. It's most helpful if an author knows his/her genre inside and out. Read, read, read books that have successfully been published for your genre. This will ultimately make your writing more marketable. Also, follow a publisher's submission guidelines to a tee. We try to set writers up for success. Send us what we're looking for."

RANDOM HOUSE, INC.

Division of Bertelsmann Book Group, 1745 Broadway, New York NY 10019. (212)782-9000. **Website:** www.randomhouse.com. Estab. 1925. Random House has long been committed to publishing the best literature by writers both in the United States and abroad. **Pays royalty. Pays advance.**

IMPRINTS **Ballantine Publishing Group:** Ballantine Books, Ballantine Reader's Circle, Del Rey, Del Rey/Lucas Books, Fawcett, Ivy, One World, Wellspring; **Bantam Dell Publishing Group:** Bantam

Hardcover, Bantam Mass Market, Bantam Trade Paperback, Crimeline, Delacorte Press, Dell, Delta, The Dial Press, Domain, DTP, Fanfare, Island, Spectra; **Crown Publishing Group:** Bell Tower, Clarkson Potter, Crown Business, Crown Forum, Crown Publishers, Inc., Harmony Books, Shaye Arehart Books, Three Rivers Press; **Doubleday Broadway Publishing Group:** Broadway Books, Currency, Doubleday, Doubleday Image, Doubleday Religious Publishing, Main Street Books, Nan A. Talese; **Knopf Publishing Group:** Alfred A. Knopf, Everyman's Library, Pantheon Books, Schocken Books, Vintage Anchor Publishing (Vintage Books, Anchor Books); **Random House Audio Publishing Group:** Listening Library, Random House Audible, Random House Audio, Random House Audio Assets, Random House Audio Dimensions, Random House Audio Roads, Random House Audio Voices, Random House Price-less; **Random House Children's Books:** BooksReportsNow.com, GoldenBooks.com, Junie B. Jones, Kids@Random, Seusville, Teachers@Random, Teens@Random, Knopf/Delacorte/Dell Young Readers Group (Alfred A. Knopf, Bantam, Crown, David Fickling Books, Delacorte Press, Dell Dragonfly, Dell Laurel-Leaf, Dell Yearling Books, Doubleday, Wendy Lamb Books), Random House Young Readers Group (Akiko, Arthur, Barbie, Beginner Books, The Berenstain Bears, Bob the Builder, Disney, Dragon Tales, First Time Books, Golden Books, Landmark Books, Little Golden Books, Lucas Books, Mercer Mayer, Nickelodeon, Nick, Jr., pat the bunny, Picturebacks, Precious Moments, Richard Scarry, Sesame Street Books, Step Into Reading, Stepping Stones, Star Wars, Thomas the Tank Engine and Friends), **Random House Direct, Inc.:** Bon Appetit, Gourmet Books, Pillsbury; **Random House Information Group:** Fodor's Travel Publications, House of Collectibles, Living Language, Prima Games, The Princeton Review, Random House Espanol, Random House Puzzles & Games, Random House Reference; **Random House International:** Arete, McClelland & Stewart Ltd., Plaza & Janes, Random House Australia, Random House of Canada Ltd., Random House Mondadori, Random House South Africa, Random House South America, Random House United Kingdom, Transworld UK, Verlagsgruppe Random House; **Random House Value Publishing:** Children's Classics, Crescent, Derrydale, Gramercy, Testament, Wings; **Waterbrook Press:** Fisherman Bible Study Guides, Shaw Books, Waterbrook Press.

○ *Agented submissions only. No unsolicited mss.*

Ⓐⵁ RANDOM HOUSE AUDIO PUBLISHING GROUP

Subsidiary of Random House, Inc., 1745 Broadway, New York NY 10019. (212)782-9720. **Fax:** (212)782-9600. **Website:** www.randomhouse.com. "Audio publishing for adults and children, offering titles in both abridged and unabridged formats on cassettes, compact discs, and by digital delivery."

IMPRINTS Listening Library; Random House Audible; Random House Audio; Random House Audio Assets; Random House Audio Dimensions; Random House Audio Roads; Random House Audio Voices; Random House Price-less.

Ⓐⵁ RANDOM HOUSE CHILDREN'S BOOKS

1745 Broadway, New York NY 10019. (212)782-9000. **Website:** www.randomhouse.com. Estab. 1925. "Producing books for preschool children through young adult readers, in all formats from board to activity books to picture books and novels, Random House Children's Books brings together world-famous franchise characters, multimillion-copy series and top-flight, award-winning authors, and illustrators."

IMPRINTS BooksReportsNow.com, GoldenBooks.com, Junie B. Jones, Kids@Random, Seusville, Teachers@Random, Teens@Random; **Knopf/Delacorte/Dell Young Readers Group:** Bantam, Crown, David Fickling Books, Delacorte Press, Dell Dragonfly, Dell Laurel-Leaf, Dell Yearling, Doubleday, Alfred A. Knopf, Wendy Lamb Books; **Random House Young Readers Group:** Akiko, Arthur, Barbie, Beginner Books, The Berenstain Bears, Bob the Builder, Disney, Dragon Tales, First Time Books, Golden Books, Landmark Books, Little Golden Books, Lucas Books, Mercer Mayer, Nickelodeon, Nick, Jr., pat the bunny, Picturebacks, Precious Moments, Richard Scarry, Sesame Street Books, Step Into Reading, Stepping Stones, Star Wars, Thomas the Tank Engine and Friends.

○ Submit mss through a literary agent.

FICTION "Random House publishes a select list of first chapter books and novels, with an emphasis on fantasy and historical fiction." Chapter books, middle-grade readers, young adult. *Does not accept unsolicited mss.*

TIPS "We look for original, unique stories. Do something that hasn't been done before."

A ✎ ∅ RANDOM HOUSE CHILDREN'S BOOKS

61-63 Uxbridge Rd., London En W5 5SA, United Kingdom. (44)(208)231-6000. **Fax:** (44)(208)231-6737. **E-mail:** enquiries@randomhouse.co.uk; lduffy@randomhouse.co.uk. **Website:** www.kidsatrandomhouse.co.uk. **Contact:** Philippa Dickinson, managing director. **Publishes 250 titles/year. Pays authors royalty. Offers advances.**

IMPRINTS Doubleday, Corgi, Johnathan Cape, Hutchinson, Bodley Head, Red Fox, David Fickling Books, Tamarind Books.

○ *Only interested in agented material.*

FICTION Picture books: adventure, animal, anthology, contemporary, fantasy, folktales, humor, multicultural, nature/environment, poetry, suspense/mystery. Young readers: adventure, animal, anthology, contemporary, fantasy, folktales, humor, multicultural, nature/environment, poetry, sports, suspense/mystery. Middle readers: adventure, animal, anthology, contemporary, fantasy, folktales, humor, multicultural, nature/environment, problem novels, romance, sports, suspense/mystery. Young adults: adventure, contemporary, fantasy, humor, multicultural, nature/environment, problem novels, romance, science fiction, suspense/mystery. Average word length: picture books—800; young readers—1,500-6,000; middle readers—10,000-15,000; young adults—20,000-45,000.

TIPS "Although Random House is a big publisher, each imprint only publishes a small number of books each year. Our lists for the next few years are already full. Any book we take on from a previously unpublished author has to be truly exceptional. Mss should be sent to us via literary agents."

A ∅ RANDOM HOUSE LARGE PRINT

Division of Random House, Inc., 1745 Broadway, New York NY 10019. (212)782-9720. **Fax:** (212)782-9600. **Website:** www.randomhouse.com. Estab. 1990. "Acquires and publishes general interest fiction and nonfiction in large print editions." **Publishes 60 titles/year.**

A ∅ RANDOM HOUSE PUBLISHING GROUP

Division of Random House, Inc., 1745 Broadway, New York NY 10019. (212)782-9000. **E-mail:** kmarino@randomhouse.com. **Website:** www.randomhouse.com. Estab. 1925. Publishes hardcover and paperback trade books. Random House is the world's largest English-language general trade book publisher. It includes an array of prestigious imprints that publish some of the foremost writers of our time—in hardcover, trade paperback, mass market paperback, electronic, multimedia and other formats. **Publishes 120 titles/year.**

IMPRINTS Ballantine Books; Del Rey; Modern Library; One World; Presidio Press; Random House; Random House Trade Paperbacks; Villard.

○ See website for details.

NONFICTION Agented submissions only.

FICTION Agented submissions only.

✎ RANSOM PUBLISHING

Radley House, 8 St. Cross Road, Winchester Hampshire SO23 9HX, United Kingdom. +44 (0) 01962 862307. **Fax:** +44 (0) 05601 148881. **E-mail:** ransom@ransom.co.uk. **Website:** www.ransom.co.uk. **Contact:** Jenny Ertle, editor. Estab. 1995. Publishes paperback originals. Independent UK publisher with distribution in English speaking markets throughout the world. Specializes in books for reluctant and struggling readers. "Our high quality, visually stimulating, age appropriate material has achieved wide acclaim for its ability to engage and motivate those who either can't or won't read." One of the few English language publishers to publish books with very high interest age and very low reading age. Has a developing list of children's books for home and school use. Specializes in phonics and general reading programs. **Pays 10% royalty on net receipts.** Responds to mss in 3-4 weeks. Ms guidelines by e-mail.

FICTION Easy reading for young adults. Books for reluctant and struggling readers. Accepts unsolicited mss. Query with SASE or submit outline/proposal. Prefers queries by e-mail. Include estimated word count, brief bio, list of publishing credits.

RAZORBILL

Penguin Group, 375 Hudson St., New York NY 10014. (212)414-3448. **Fax:** (212)414-3343. **E-mail:** laura.schechter@us.penguingroup.com; ben.schrank@us.penguingroup.com. **Website:** www.razorbillbooks.com. **Contact:** Gillian Levinson, assistant edtor; Jessica Rothenberg, editor; Brianne Mulligan, editor. Estab. 2003. "This division of Penguin Young Readers is looking for the best and the most original of commercial contemporary fiction titles for middle grade and YA readers. A select quantity of nonfiction titles will also be considered." **Publishes 30 titles/year. Offers advance against royalties.** Publishes book 1-2 after acceptance. Responds in 1-3 months.

NONFICTION Middle readers and young adults/teens: concept. Submit cover letter with up to 30 sample pages.

FICTION Middle Readers: adventure, contemporary, graphic novels, fantasy, humor, problem novels. Young adults/teens: adventure, contemporary, fantasy, graphic novels, humor, multicultural, suspense, paranormal, science fiction, dystopian, literary, romance. Average word length: middle readers—40,000; young adult—60,000. Submit cover letter with up to 30 sample pages.

TIPS "New writers will have the best chance of acceptance and publication with original, contemporary material that boasts a distinctive voice and well-articulated world. Check out www.razorbillbooks.com to get a better idea of what we're looking for."

◐⊘ REALITY STREET

63 All Saints St., Hastings, E. Sussex TN34 3BN, United Kingdom. +44(0)1424 431271. **E-mail:** info@realitystreet.co.uk. **Website:** www.realitystreet.co.uk. **Contact:** Ken Edwards, editor and publisher. Estab. 1993. Publishes trade paperback originals. Reality Street is based in Hastings, UK, publishing new and innovative writing in English and in translation from other languages. Some established writers whose books they have published are Nicole Brossard, Allen Fisher, Barbara Guest, Fanny Howe, Denise Riley, Peter Riley, and Maurice Scully. **Publishes 3-4 titles/year.** Book catalog online.

○ *Does not accept unsolicited submissions.*

FICTION Subjects include poetry, poetry in translation, translation, experimental fiction, anthologies.

TIPS No unsolicited submissions.

◯ RED DEER PRESS

195 Allstate Pkwy., Markham ON L3R 4TB, Canada. (905)477-9700. **Fax:** (905)477-9179. **E-mail:** rdp@reddeerpress.com; dionne@reddeerpress.com; val@reddeerpress.com. **Website:** www.reddeerpress.com. **Contact:** Richard Dionne, publisher. Estab. 1975. **Pays 8-10% royalty.** Publishes book 18 months after acceptance. Accepts simultaneous submissions. Responds to queries in 6 months. Book catalog for 9 x 12 SASE.

○ Red Deer Press has received numerous honors and awards from the Book Publishers Association of Alberta, Canadian Children's Book Centre, the Governor General of Canada and the Writers Guild of Alberta.

NONFICTION Submit query with outline and sample chapter.

FICTION Publishes young adult, adult science fiction, fantasy, and paperback originals "focusing on books by, about, or of interest to Canadians." Books: offset paper; offset printing; hardcover/perfect-bound. Average print order: 5,000. First novel print order: 2,500. Distributes titles in Canada and the US, the UK, Australia and New Zealand. Young adult (juvenile and early reader), contemporary. No romance or horror. Accepts unsolicited mss. Query with SASE. No submissions on disk.

TIPS "We're very interested in young adult and children's fiction from Canadian writers with a proven track record (either published books or widely published in established magazines or journals) and for mss with regional themes and/or a distinctive voice. We publish Canadian authors exclusively."

RED HEN PRESS

P.O. Box 3537, Granada Hills CA 91394. (818)831-0649. **Fax:** (818)831-6659. **E-mail:** redhenpressbooks.com. **Website:** www.redhen.org. **Contact:** Mark E. Cull, publisher/editor (fiction). Estab. 1993. Publishes trade paperback originals. "At this time, the best opportunity to be published by Red Hen is by entering one of our contests. Please find more information in our award submission guidelines." **Publishes 22 titles/year. 2,000 queries received/year. 500 mss received/year. 10% of books from first-time authors. 90% from unagented writers.** Publishes book 1 year after acceptance. Accepts simultaneous submissions. Responds in 1 month to queries; 2 months to proposals and mss. Book catalog available free. Guidelines online.

NONFICTION Subjects include ethnic, gay, lesbian, language, literature, memoirs, women's issues, women's studies, political/social interest. Query with synopsis and either 20-30 sample pages or complete ms using online submission manager.

FICTION Subjects include ethnic, experimental, feminist, gay, lesbian, historical, literary, mainstream, contemporary, poetry, poetry in translation, short story collections. Query with synopsis and either 20-

30 sample pages or complete ms using online submission manager.

POETRY Submit to Benjamin Saltman Poetry Award.

TIPS "Audience reads poetry, literary fiction, intelligent nonfiction. If you have an agent, we may be too small since we don't pay advances. Write well. Send queries first. Be willing to help promote your own book."

RED MOON PRESS

P.O. Box 2461, Winchester VA 22604. (540)722-2156. **E-mail:** jim.kacian@redmoonpress.com. **Website:** www.redmoonpress.com. **Contact:** Jim Kacian, editor/publisher. Estab. 1993. Red Moon Press "is the largest and most prestigious publisher of English-language haiku and related work in the world." Publishes 6-8 volumes/year, usually 3-5 anthologies and individual collections of English-language haiku, as well as 1-3 books of essays, translations, or criticism of haiku. Under other imprints, the press also publishes chapbooks of various sizes and formats.

POETRY Query with book theme and information, and 30-40 poems or draft of first chapter. Responds to queries in 2 weeks, to mss (if invited) in 3 months. "Each contract separately negotiated."

RED ROCK PRESS

331 W. 57th St., Suite 175, New York NY 10019. **Fax:** (212)362-6216. **E-mail:** info@redrockpress.com. **Website:** www.redrockpress.com. **Contact:** Ilene Barth. Estab. 1998. Publishes hardcover and trade paperback originals. **Publishes 6-8 titles/year. Pays royalty on wholesale price. The amount of the advance offered depends on the project.** Responds in 3-4 months to queries. Book catalog for #10 SASE.

NONFICTION Subjects include creative nonfiction. All of our books are pegged to gift-giving holidays.

RED SAGE PUBLISHING, INC.

P.O. Box 4844, Seminole FL 33775. (727)391-3847. **E-mail:** submissions@eredsage.com. **Website:** www. eredsage.com. **Contact:** Alexandria Kendall, publisher; Theresa Stevens, managing editor. Estab. 1995. Publishes books of romance fiction, written for the adventurous woman. **Publishes 4 titles/year. 50% of books from first-time authors. Pays advance.** Guidelines online.

FICTION Read guidelines.

RED TUQUE BOOKS, INC.

477 Martin St., Unit #6, Penticton BC V2A 5L2, Canada. (778)476-5750. **Fax:** (778)476-5651. **E-mail:** dave@ redtuquebooks.ca. **Website:** www.redtuquebooks.ca. **Contact:** David Korinetz, executive editor. **Pays 5-7% royalties on net sales. Pays $250 advance.** Publishes book 1 year after acceptance. Responds in 3 weeks.

FICTION Subjects include adventure, fantasy, science fiction, short story collections, young adult. Submit a query letter and first five pages. Include total word count. A one-page synopsis is optional. Accepts queries by e-mail and mail. SASE for reply only.

TIPS "Well-plotted, character-driven stories, preferably with happy endings, will have the best chance of being accepted. Keep in mind that authors who like to begin sentences with 'and, or, and but' are less likely to be considered. Don't send anything gruesome or overly explicit; tell us a good story, but think PG."

RED WHEEL/WEISER, CONARI PRESS, HAMPTON ROADS

665 Third St., Suite 400, San Francisco CA 94107. (415)978-2665. **Fax:** (415)359-0142. **Website:** www. redwheelweiser.com. **Contact:** Pat Bryce, acquisitions editor. Estab. 1956. Publishes hardcover and trade paperback originals and reprints. **Publishes 60-75 titles/year. 2,000 queries received/year; 2,000 mss received/year. 20% of books from first-time authors. 50% from unagented writers. Pays royalty.** Publishes book 1 year after acceptance of ms. Accepts simultaneous submissions. Responds in 3 months to queries; 3-6 months to proposals and mss. Book catalog available free. Guidelines online.

IMPRINTS Conari Press; Weiser.

NONFICTION Subjects include New Age, spirituality, womens issues, womens studies, parenting. Query with SASE. Submit proposal package, outline, 2 sample chapters, table of contents. Reviews artwork/ photos. Send photocopies.

ROBERT D. REED PUBLISHERS

P.O. Box 1992, Bandon OR 97411. (541)347-9882. **Fax:** (541)347-9883. **Website:** www.rdrpublishers.com. **Contact:** Cleone L. Reed. Editor: Kate Rakini. Estab. 1991. Publishes hardcover and trade paperback originals. **Publishes 25-35 titles/year. 75% of books from first-time authors. 90% from unagented writers. Pays 12-17% royalty on wholesale price.** Publishes book 5 months after acceptance. Accepts simultaneous submissions. Responds in 1 month. Catalog and guidelines online.

NONFICTION Subjects include alternative lifestyles, business, career guidance, child guidance, communications, contemporary culture, counseling, education, ethnic, gay, health, history, language, lesbian, literature, memoirs, military, money, multicultural, New Age, philosophy, psychology, sex, sociology, spirituality, travel, womens issues, womens studies, world affairs. "We want titles that have a large audience with at least 10-year sales potential, and author's workshop, speaking and seminar participation. We like titles that are part of author's career." Submit proposal package with outline. Reviews artwork.

FICTION Subjects include adventure, fantasy, feminist, historical, humor, literary, military, multicultural, mystery, romance, science fiction, spiritual, war, western. "We look for high quality work from authors who will work hard to display their work and travel, selling books." Query with SASE or via e-mail.

TIPS "Target trade sales and sales to corporations, organizations, and groups. Read over our website and see what we have done."

REFERENCE SERVICE PRESS

5000 Windplay Dr., Suite 4, El Dorado Hills CA 95762. (916)939-9620. **Fax:** (916)939-9626. **E-mail:** info@rspfunding.com. **Website:** www.rspfunding.com. **Contact:** Stuart Hauser, acquisitions editor. Estab. 1977. Publishes hardcover originals. "Reference Service Press focuses on the development and publication of financial aid resources in any format (print, electronic, e-book, etc.). We are interested in financial aid publications aimed at specific groups (e.g., minorities, women, veterans, the disabled, undergraduates majoring in specific subject areas, specific types of financial aid, etc.)." **Publishes 10-20 titles/year. 100% from unagented writers. Pays 10% royalty. Pays advance.** Publishes book 6 months after acceptance. Accepts simultaneous submissions. Responds in 2 months to queries. Book catalog for #10 SASE.

NONFICTION Subjects include agriculture, art, architecture, business, economics, education, ethnic, health, medicine, history, religion, science, sociology, women's issues, women's studies, disabled. Submit outline, sample chapters.

TIPS "Our audience consists of librarians, counselors, researchers, students, re-entry women, scholars, and other fundseekers."

RENAISSANCE HOUSE

465 Westview Ave., Englewood NJ 07631. (201)408-4048. **E-mail:** info@renaissancehouse.net. **Website:** www.renaissancehouse.net. Publishes biographies, folktales, coffee table books, instructional, textbooks, adventure, picture books, juvenile and young adult. Specializes in multicultural and bilingual titles, Spanish-English. Submit ms; e-mail submissions. Children's, educational, multicultural, and textbooks. Represents 80 illustrators. 95% of artwork handled is children's book illustration. Currently open to illustrators seeking representation. Open to both new and established illustrators. Publishes book 1 year after acceptance. Accepts simultaneous submissions. Responds to queries/mss in 2 weeks.

FICTION Subjects include fantasy, juvenile, picture books, legends, fables. Picture books: animal, folktales, multicultural. Young readers: animal, anthology, folktales, multicultural. Middle readers, young adult/teens: anthology, folktales, multicultural, nature/environment.

RING OF FIRE PUBLISHING LLC

6523 California Ave. SW #409, Seattle WA 98136. **E-mail:** contact@ringoffirebooks.com. **E-mail:** submissions@ringoffirebooks.com. **Website:** www.ringoffirebooks.com. Estab. 2011. "Our audience is comprised of well read fiction enthusiasts. Let us tell your story." **Publishes 6-12 titles/year. 75% of books from first-time authors. 100% from unagented writers. Pays royalties.** Publishes book 6 months after acceptance. Accepts simultaneous submissions. Responds in 1 month to queries; 2 months to mss. Book catalog and ms Guidelines online.

IMPRINTS Publishes trade paperback and electronic originals.

FICTION Subjects include adventure, contemporary, experimental, fantasy, gothic, horror, juvenile, literary, mainstream, mystery, occult, romance, science fiction, short story collections, suspense, western, young adult. Query online. Submit synopsis and 3 sample chapters.

RIO NUEVO PUBLISHERS

Imprint of Treasure Chest Books, P.O. Box 5250, Tucson AZ 85703. **Fax:** (520)624-5888. **E-mail:** info@rionuevo.com. **Website:** www.rionuevo.com. Estab. 1975. Publishes hardcover and trade paperback originals and reprints. **Publishes 12-20 titles/year. 20 queries received/year. 10 mss received/year. 30% of** books from first-time authors. **100% from unagented writers. Pays $1,000-4,000 advance.** Publishes book 1 year after acceptance. Accepts simultaneous submissions. Responds in 6 months. Book catalog online. Guidelines available via e-mail.

NONFICTION Subjects include animals, cooking, foods, nutrition, gardening, history, nature, environment, regional, religion, spirituality, travel. "We cover the Southwest but prefer titles that are not too narrow in their focus. We want our books to be of broad enough interest that people from other places will also want to read them." Query with SASE. Submit proposal package, outline, 2 sample chapters. Reviews artwork/photos. Send photocopies.

TIPS "We have a general audience of intelligent people interested in the Southwest-nature, history, culture. Many of our books are sold in gift shops throughout the region; we are also distributed nationally by W.W. Norton."

➕ RIPPLE GROVE PRESS

P.O. Box 491, Hubbardston MA 01452. **E-mail:** submit@ripplegrovepress.com. **Website:** www.ripplegrovepress.com. Estab. 2013. Publishes hardcover originals. Ripple Grove Press is a family-owned children's picture book publishing company started in 2013. "Our mission is to create picture books that come from life experiences, elegant imagination, and the deep passion in our hearts. We want each book to enlighten a child's mind with fun and wonder. Ripple Grove Press searches for a powerful 'timeless' feel in each book we publish. Our stories will make you laugh, think, or keep you guessing and dreaming." **Publishes 3-10 titles/year. Authors receive between 10-12% royalty on net receipt.** Publishes book Average length of time between acceptance of a book-length ms and publication is 12-18 months. after acceptance of ms. Accepts simultaneous submissions. Responds to queries within 3 months. Guidelines online.

NONFICTION Submit completed mss only. Accepts submissions by mail and e-mail. Please submit a cover letter including a summary of your story, the age range of the story, a brief biography of yourself, and contact information. Does review artwork. Writers should send photo copies or links to their website and online portfolio.

FICTION Subjects include contemporary, humor, juvenile, literary, mainstream, multicultural, picture books. "Our focus is picture books for children aged 2-6. We want something unique, sweet, funny, touching, offbeat, colorful, surprising, charming, different, and creative." Submit completed ms. Accepts submissions by mail and e-mail. Please submit a cover letter including a summary of your story, the age range of the story, a brief biography of yourself, and contact information.

TIPS Also targeting the adults reading to the children. "We create books that children and adults want to read over and over again. Our books showcase art as well as stories and tie them together to create a unique and creative product."

RIVER CITY PUBLISHING

1719 Mulberry St., Montgomery AL 36106. **E-mail:** fnorris@rivercitypublishing.com. **Website:** www.rivercitypublishing.com. **Contact:** Fran Norris, editor. Estab. 1989. Publishes hardcover and trade paperback originals. Midsize independent publisher (8-10 books per year). River City primarily publishes narrative nonfiction that reflects the South. "We are looking for mainly for narrative histories, sociological accounts, and travel. Only biographies and memoirs from noted persons will be considered; we are closed to all personal memoir submissions." **Publishes 6 titles/year. Pays 10-15% royalty on retail price. Pays $500-5,000 advance.** Publishes book 1 year after acceptance. Accepts simultaneous submissions. Responds to mss in 9 months.

NONFICTION "We do not publish self-help, how-to, business, medicine, religion, education, or psychology." Accepts unsolicited submissions and submissions from unagented authors, as well as those from established and agented writers. Submit 5 consecutive sample chapters or entire ms for review. "Please include a short biography that highlights any previous writing and publishing experience, sales opportunities the author could provide, ideas for marketing the book, and why you think the work would be appropriate for River City." Send appropriate-sized SASE or IRC, "otherwise, the material will be recycled." Also accepts queries by e-mail at: jgilbert@rivercitypublishing.com. "Please include your electronic query letter as inline text and not an as attachment; we do not open unsolicited attachments of any kind. Please do not include sample chapters or your entire ms as inline text. We do not field or accept queries by telephone. Please wait at least 3 months before contacting us about your submission." No multiple submissions. Rarely comments on rejected mss.

FICTION Subjects include literary, regional, short story collections. No poetry, memoir, or children's books. Send appropriate-sized SASE or IRC, "otherwise, the material will be recycled." Also accepts queries by e-mail at: jgilbert@rivercitypublishing.com. "Please include your electronic query letter as inline text and not an as attachment; we do not open unsolicited attachments of any kind. Please do not include sample chapters or your entire ms as inline text. We do not field or accept queries by telephone. Please wait at least 3 months before contacting us about your submission." No multiple submissions. Rarely comments on rejected mss.

TIPS "Only send your best work after you have received outside opinions. From approximately 1,000 submissions each year, we publish no more than 8 books and few of those come from unsolicited material. Competition is fierce, so follow the guidelines exactly. All first-time novelists should submit their work to the Fred Bonnie Award contest."

RIVERHEAD BOOKS

Penguin Putnam, 375 Hudson St., Office #4079, New York NY 10014. **E-mail:** ecommerce@ us.penguingroup.com. **E-mail:** riverhead.web@ us.penguingroup.com. **Website:** www.riverhead-books.com. **Contact:** Megan Lynch, senior editor.

FICTION Subjects include contemporary, literary, mainstream. *Submit through agent only. No unsolicited mss.*

ROARING BROOK PRESS

175 Fifth Ave., New York NY 10010. (646)307-5151. **E-mail:** david.langva@roaringbrookpress.com. **E-mail:** press.inquiries@macmillanusa.com. **Website:** us.macmillan.com/RoaringBrook.aspx. **Contact:** David Langva. Estab. 2000. Roaring Brook Press is an imprint of MacMillan, a group of companies that includes Henry Holt and Farrar, Straus & Giroux. Roaring Brook is not accepting unsolicited mss. **Pays authors royalty based on retail price.**

NONFICTION Picture books, young readers, middle readers, young adults: adventure, animal, contemporary, fantasy, history, humor, multicultural, nature/environment, poetry, religion, science fiction, sports, suspense/mystery. *Not accepting unsolicited mss or queries.*

FICTION Picture books, young readers, middle readers, young adults: adventure, animal, contemporary, fantasy, history, humor, multicultural, nature/environment, poetry, religion, science fiction, sports, suspense/mystery. *Not accepting unsolicited mss or queries.*

TIPS "You should find a reputable agent and have him/her submit your work."

ROCKY MOUNTAIN BOOKS

414 13th Ave. NE, Calgary AB T2E 1C2, Canada. (403)249-9490. **Fax:** (403)249-2968. **E-mail:** don@ rmbooks.com. **Website:** www.rmbooks.com. **Contact:** Don Gorman, publisher. Publishes trade paperback and hardcover books. "RMB is a dynamic book publisher located in western Canada. We specialize in quality nonfiction on the outdoors, travel, environment, social and cultural issues." **Rarely offers advance.** Accepts simultaneous submissions. Responds in 2-6 months to queries. Book catalog and ms guidelines online.

NONFICTION Subjects include nonfiction outdoors, environment, travel & tourism and international mountain culture/history. "Our main area of publishing is outdoor recreation guides to Western and Northern Canada."

RECENT TITLE(S) *Caves of the Canadian Rockies and Columbia Mountains*, by Jon Rollins; *Exploring Prince George*, by Mike Nash.

RODALE BOOKS

33 E. Minor St., Emmaus PA 18098. (610)967-5171. **Fax:** (610)967-8961. **Website:** www.rodale.com. Estab. 1932. "Rodale Books publishes adult trade titles in categories such health & fitness, cooking, spirituality and pet care."

RONSDALE PRESS

3350 W. 21st Ave., Vancouver BC V6S 1G7, Canada. (604)738-4688. **Fax:** (604)731-4548. **E-mail:** ronsdale@shaw.ca. **Website:** ronsdalepress.com. **Contact:** Ronald B. Hatch (fiction, poetry, nonfiction, social commentary); Veronica Hatch (YA novels and short stories). Estab. 1988. Publishes trade paperback originals. "Ronsdale Press is a Canadian literary publishing house that publishes 12 books each year, four of which are young adult titles. Of particular interest are books involving children exploring and discovering new aspects of Canadian history." **Publishes 12 titles/year. 40 queries received/year. 800 mss re-**

ceived/year. **40% of books from first-time authors. 95% from unagented writers. Pays 10% royalty on retail price.** Publishes book 1 year after acceptance. Accepts simultaneous submissions. Responds to queries in 2 weeks; mss in 2 months. Book catalog for #10 SASE. Guidelines online.

NONFICTION Subjects include history, Canadian, language, literature, nature, environment, regional. Middle readers, young adults: animal, biography, history, multicultural, social issues. Average word length: young readers—90; middle readers—90. "We publish a number of books for children and young adults in the age 10 to 15 range. We are especially interested in YA historical novels. We regret that we can no longer publish picture books." Submit complete ms.

FICTION Subjects include literary, short story collections, novels. Young adults: Canadian novels. Average word length: middle readers and young adults—50,000. Recently published *Torn from Troy*, by Patrick Bowman (ages 10-14); *Hannah & The Salish Sea*, by Carol Anne Shaw (ages 10-14); *Dark Times*, edited by Ann Walsh (anthology of short stories, ages 10 and up); *Outlaw in India*, by Philip Roy; *Freedom Bound*, by Jean Rae Baxter (ages 10-14). Submit complete ms.

POETRY Poets should have published some poems in magazines/journals and should be well-read in contemporary masters. Submit complete ms.

RECENT TITLE(S) *I'll Be Home Soon*, by Luanne Armstrong (YA historical fiction); *When Eagles Call*, by Susan Dobbie (novel).

TIPS "Ronsdale Press is a literary publishing house, based in Vancouver, and dedicated to publishing books from across Canada, books that give Canadians new insights into themselves and their country. We aim to publish the best Canadian writers."

ROSE ALLEY PRESS

4203 Brooklyn Ave. NE, #103A, Seattle WA 98105. (206)633-2725. **E-mail:** rosealleypress@juno.com. **Website:** www.rosealleypress.com. **Contact:** David D. Horowitz. Estab. 1995. "Rose Alley Press primarily publishes books featuring rhymed metrical poetry and an annually updated booklet about writing and publication. We do not read or consider unsolicited mss."

● ROTOVISION

Sheridan House, 114 Western Rd., Hove East Sussex BN3 IDD, England. (44)(127)371-6010. **Fax:** (44)

(127)372-7269. **E-mail:** isheetam@rotovision.com. **Website:** www.rotovision.com. **Contact:** Isheeta Mustafi. Publishes hardcover and trade paperback originals, and trade paperback reprints. Accepts simultaneous submissions. Book catalog available free. Guidelines available free.

"RotoVision books showcase the works of top writers and designers reflecting excellence and innovation in the visual arts. If you wish to submit a book proposal, in the first instance please familiarise yourself with our publishing portfolio to ensure your proposal fits into our focus area."

NONFICTION Subjects include art, creative nonfiction, design, fashion, graphic design, photography. "Our books are aimed at keen amateurs and professionals who want to improve their skills." Submit an e-mail with "Book Proposal" in the subject line. Reviews artwork/photos. Send transparencies and PDFs.

RECENT TITLE(S) *Art Directors Annual 83*; *Motion Design*, by Matt Woolman; *Underwater Photography*, by Larry and Denise Tackett.

TIPS "Our audience includes professionals, keen amateurs, and students of visual arts including graphic design, general design, advertising, and photography. Make your approach international in scope. Content not to be less than 35% US."

ROWMAN & LITTLEFIELD PUBLISHING GROUP

4501 Forbes Blvd., Suite 200, Lanham MD 20706. (301)459-3366. **Fax:** (301)429-5748. **E-mail:** jsisk@rowmanlittlefield.com. **Website:** www.rowmanlittlefield.com. **Contact:** Jonathan Sisk, vice president/executive editor (American government, public policy, political theory); Susan McEachern, vice president/editorial director (international studies); Sarah Stanton and Patti Davis, acquisitions editors. Estab. 1949. Publishes hardcover and trade paperback originals and reprints. "We are an independent press devoted to publishing scholarly books in the best tradition of university presses; innovative, thought-provoking texts for college courses; and crossover trade books intended to convey scholarly trends to an educated readership. Our approach emphasizes substance and quality of thought over ephemeral trends. We offer a forum for responsible voices representing the diversity of opinion on college campuses, and take special pride in several series designed to provide students with the pros and cons of hotly contested issues." **Pays advance.** Catalog and guidelines online.

IMPRINTS Lexington Books; Rowman & Littlefield Publishers; Madison Books; Scarecrow Press; Cooper Square.

NONFICTION "Rowman & Littlefield is seeking proposals in the serious nonfiction areas of history, politics, current events, religion, sociology, philosophy, communication and education. All proposal inquiries can be e-mailed or mailed to the respective acquisitions editor listed on the contacts page on our website."

RECENT TITLE(S) *Crime, Punishment, and Policing in China*, by Børge Bakken; *The Making of Arab News*, by Noha Mellor; *African Americans in the U.S. Economy*, edited by Cecilia A. Conrad, John Whitehead, Patrick Mason, and James Stewart.

RUKA PRESS

P.O. Box 1409, Washington DC 20013. **E-mail:** contact@rukapress.com. **E-mail:** submissions@rukapress.com. **Website:** www.rukapress.com. **Contact:** Daniel Kohan, owner. Estab. 2010. Publishes in trade paperback originals, electronic. "We publish nonfiction books with a strong environmental component for a general audience. We are looking for books that explain things, that make an argument, that demystify. We are interested in economics, science, nature, climate change, and sustainability. We like building charts and graphs, tables and timelines. Our politics are progressive, but our books need not be political." **Publishes 2-4 titles/year. Pays advance. Royalties are 10-25% on wholesale price.** Publishes book an average of 9-12 months after acceptance of ms. after acceptance of ms. Accepts simultaneous submissions. Responds in 1 month to queries and proposals. Catalog and guidelines online.

NONFICTION Subjects include environment, nature, science. Submit proposal package, including outline, résumé, bio, or CV, and 1 sample chapter.

TIPS "We appeal to an audience of intelligent, educated readers with broad interests. Be sure to tell us why your proposal is unique, and why you are especially qualified to write this book. We are looking for originality and expertise."

RUTGERS UNIVERSITY PRESS

100 Joyce Kilmer Ave., Piscataway NJ 08854-8099. (732)445-7762. **Fax:** (732)445-7039. **Website:** rutgerspress.rutgers.edu. **Contact:** Leslie Mitchner, editor-in-chief/associate director (humanities); Adi Hovav,

editor (social sciences); Doreen Valentine, editor (science, health & medicine); Beth Kressel, associate editor (Jewish studies). Estab. 1936. Publishes hardcover and trade paperback originals, and reprints. Our Press aims to reach audiences beyond the academic community with accessible scholarly and regional books. **Publishes 100 titles/year. 1,500 queries received/year. 300 mss received/year. 30% of books from first-time authors. 70% from unagented writers. Pays 7 1/2-15% royalty. Pays $1,000-10,000 advance.** Publishes book 1 year after acceptance of ms. Responds in 1 month to proposals. Book catalog online or with SASE. Guidelines online.

NONFICTION Subjects include art, architecture, art, architecture history, ethnic, film, cinema, stage, gay, lesbian, government, politics, health, medicine, history, multicultural, nature, environment, regional, religion, sociology, womens issues, womens studies, African-American studies. Books for use in undergraduate courses. Submit outline, 2-3 sample chapters. Reviews artwork/photos. Send photocopies.

RECENT TITLE(S) *Wrestling with Starbucks: Conscience, Capital, Cappuccino*, by Kim Fellner; *Mama, PhD.: Women Write About Motherhood and Academic Life*, by Elrena Evans and Caroline Grant; *A Shore History of Film*, by Wheeler Winston Dixon and Gwendolyn Audrey Foster.

TIPS Both academic and general audiences. Many of our books have potential for undergraduate course use. We are more trade-oriented than most university presses. We are looking for intelligent, well-written, and accessible books. Avoid overly narrow topics.

SAE INTERNATIONAL

400 Commonwealth Dr., Warrendale PA 15096-0001. (724)776-4841. **E-mail:** writeabook@sae.org. **Website:** www.sae.org/writeabook. **Contact:** Martha Swiss, intellectual property manager; Kevin Jost, editorial director. Estab. 1905. Publishes hardcover and trade paperback originals, e-books. Automotive means anything self-propelled. "We are a professional society serving engineers, scientists, and researchers in the automobile, aerospace, and off-highway industries." **Publishes approximately 10 titles/year. 50 queries received/year. 20 mss received/year. 70% of books from first-time authors. 100% from unagented writers. Pays royalty. Pays possible advance.** Publishes book 9-10 months after acceptance. Accepts

simultaneous submissions. Responds in 4 months to queries. Book catalog free. Guidelines online.

NONFICTION Query with proposal.

RECENT TITLE(S) *Advanced Hybrid Powertrains for Commercial Vehicles; Laser Diagnostics and Optical Measurement Techniques in Internal Combustion Engines; Engine Failure Analysis.*

TIPS "Audience is automotive and aerospace engineers and managers, automotive safety and biomechanics professionals, students, educators, enthusiasts, and historians."

SAFARI PRESS, INC.

15621 Chemical Lane, Building B, Huntington Beach CA 92649. (714)894-9080. **Fax:** (714)894-4949. **E-mail:** info@safaripress.com. **Website:** www.safaripress.com. **Contact:** Jacqueline Neufeld, editor. Estab. 1985. Publishes hardcover originals and reprints, and trade paperback reprints. Safari Press publishes books only on big-game hunting, sporting, firearms, and wingshooting; this includes African, North American, European, Asian, and South American hunting and wingshooting. Does not want books on 'outdoors' topics (hiking, camping, canoeing, etc.). **Publishes 25-30 titles/year. 70% of books from first-time authors. 80% from unagented writers. Pays 8-15% royalty on wholesale price.** Book catalog for $1. Guidelines online.

The editor notes that she receives many mss outside the areas of big-game hunting, wingshooting, and sporting firearms, and these are always rejected.

NONFICTION "We discourage autobiographies, unless the life of the hunter or firearms maker has been exceptional. We routinely reject mss along the lines of 'Me and my buddies went hunting for. and a good time was had by all!" No outdoors topics (hiking, camping, canoeing, fishing, etc.). Query with SASE. Submit outline.

RECENT TITLE(S) *Royal Quest: The Hunting Saga of H.I.H. Prince Abdorreza of Iran; The Best of Holland & Holland: England's Premier Gunmaker.*

ST. AUGUSTINE'S PRESS

P.O. Box 2285, South Bend IN 46680. (574)-291-3500. **Fax:** (574)291-3700. **E-mail:** bruce@staugustine.net. **Website:** www.staugustine.net. **Contact:** Bruce Fingerhut, president (philosophy). Publishes hardcover originals and trade paperback originals and reprints. "Our market is scholarly in the humanities. We publish

in philosophy, religion, cultural history, and history of ideas only." **Publishes 20 titles/year. 350 queries received/year. 300 mss received/year. 2% of books from first-time authors. 95% from unagented writers. Pays 6-15% royalty. Pays $500-5,000 advance.** Publishes book 8 months after acceptance. Accepts simultaneous submissions. Responds in 2-6 months to queries; 3-8 months to proposals; 4-8 months to mss. Book catalog available free.

IMPRINTS Carthage Reprints.

NONFICTION Query with SASE. Reviews artwork/photos. Send photocopies.

RECENT TITLE(S) *The Last Superstition: A Refutation of the New Atheism* by Edward Feser; *Socrates in the Underworld: On Plato's Gorgias,* by Nalin Ranasinghe; *What Catholics Believe,* by Josef Pieper.

TIPS "Scholarly and college student audience."

ST. JOHANN PRESS

P.O. Box 241, Haworth NJ 07641. (201)387-1529. **E-mail:** d.biesel@verizon.net. **Website:** www.stjohannpress.com. Estab. 1991. Publishes hardcover originals, trade paperback originals and reprints. **Publishes 6-8 titles/year. Receives 15 submissions/year. 50% of books from first-time authors. 95% from unagented writers. Pays 10-15% royalty on wholesale price.** Publishes book 15 months after acceptance. Accepts simultaneous submissions. Responds in 1 month on queries. Catalog online. Guidelines free on request.

NONFICTION Subjects include cooking, crafts, foods, history, hobbies, memoirs, military, nutrition, religion, sports (history), war (USMC), Black history in sports. "We are a niche publisher with interests in titles that will sell over a long period of time. For example, the World Football League Encyclopedia, Chicago Showcase of Basketball, will not need to be redone. We do baseball but prefer soccer, hockey, etc." Query with SASE. Reviews artwork/photos as part of the ms package. Send photocopies.

TIPS "Our readership is libraries, individuals with special interests, (e.g. sports historians); we also do specialized reference."

ST. MARTIN'S PRESS, LLC

Holtzbrinck Publishers, 175 Fifth Ave., New York NY 10010. (212)674-5151. **Fax:** (212)420-9314. **Website:** www.stmartins.com. Estab. 1952. Publishes hardcover, trade paperback and mass market originals. General interest publisher of both fiction and nonfiction. **Publishes 1,500 titles/year. Pays royalty. Pays advance.**

IMPRINTS Minotaur; Thomas Dunne Books; Griffin; Palgrave MacMillan (division); Priddy Books; St. Martin's Press Paperback & Reference Group; St. Martin's Press Trade Division; Truman Talley Books.

NONFICTION Subjects include business, economics, cooking, foods, nutrition, sports, general nonfiction. Agented submissions only. *No unsolicited mss.*

FICTION Subjects include fantasy, historical, horror, literary, mainstream, contemporary, mystery, science fiction, suspense, western, contemporary, general fiction. Agented submissions only. *No unsolicited mss.*

SAINT MARY'S PRESS

702 Terrace Heights, Winona MN 55987. (800)533-8095. **Fax:** (800)344-9225. **E-mail:** submissions@smp.org. **Website:** www.smp.org. Ms guidelines online or by e-mail.

NONFICTION Subjects include religion, prayers, spirituality. Titles for Catholic youth and their parents, teachers, and youth ministers. High school Catholic religious education textbooks and primary source readings. Query with SASE. Submit proposal package, outline, 1 sample chapter, SASE. Brief author biography.

RECENT TITLE(S) *The Catholic Faith Handbook for Youth*; *The Catholic Youth Bible*; *The Catholic Family Connections Bible.*

TIPS "Request product catalog and/or do research online of Saint Mary Press book lists before submitting proposal."

ST PAULS

Society of St. Paul, 2187 Victory Blvd., Staten Island NY 10314. (718)761-0047. **Fax:** (718)761-0057. **E-mail:** edmund_lane@juno.com. **Website:** www.stpauls.us. **Contact:** Edmund C. Lane, SSP, acquisitions editor. Estab. 1957. Publishes trade paperback and mass market paperback originals and reprints. **Publishes 22 titles/year. 250 queries received/year. 150 mss received/year. 10% of books from first-time authors. 100% from unagented writers. Pays 5-10% royalty.** Publishes book 10 months after acceptance. Responds in 1 month to queries and proposals; 2 months to mss. Book catalog and ms guidelines free.

NONFICTION Subjects include philosophy, religion, spirituality. Alba House is the North American publishing division of the Society of St. Paul, an International Roman Catholic Missionary Religious Congregation dedicated to spreading the Gospel message via the media of communications. Does not want fiction, children's books, poetry, personal testimonies, or autobiographies. Submit complete ms. Reviews artwork/photos. Send photocopies.

RECENT TITLE(S) *I Believe in One God*, by Pope Benedict XVI; *The Story of Friendship*, by Robert Nugent; *Everything Has Been Loaned to You*, by J. Robert Ouimet.

TIPS "Our audience is educated Roman Catholic readers interested in matters related to the Church, spirituality, Biblical and theological topics, moral concerns, lives of the saints, etc."

SAKURA PUBLISHING & TECHNOLOGIES

P.O. Box 1681, Hermitage PA 16148. (330)360-5131. **E-mail:** skpublishing124@gmail.com. **Website:** www.sakura-publishing.com. **Contact:** Derek Vasconi, talent finder and CEO. Estab. 2007. Publishes hardcover, trade paperback, mass market paperback and electronic originals and reprints. Mss that don't follow guidelines will not be considered. **Publishes 10-12 titles/year. 90% of books from first-time authors. 99% from unagented writers. Pays royalty of 20-60% on wholesale price or retail price.** Publishes book 6 months after acceptance. Accepts simultaneous submissions. Responds in 1 month to queries, mss, proposals. Book catalog available for #10 SASE. Guidelines online.

NONFICTION Subjects include alternative lifestyles, Americana, animals, architecture, art, contemporary culture, creative nonfiction, entertainment, games, gay, history, hobbies, humanities, memoirs, military. Follow guidelines online.

FICTION Subjects include horror, poetry. Follow guidelines online.

POETRY Follow guidelines online.

TIPS "Sakura Publishing is looking to publish primarily authors who have a marketing plan in place for their books and a strong support network behind them. Also, Sakura Publishing has a preference for fiction/nonfiction books specializing in Asian culture."

SALMON POETRY

Knockeven, Cliffs of Moher, County Clare , Ireland. 353(0)85-231-809. **E-mail:** info@salmonpoetry.com. **E-mail:** jessie@salmonpoetry.com. **Website:** www.salmonpoetry.com. **Contact:** Jessie Lendennie, editor. Estab. 1981. Publishes mass market paperback originals and e-books.

POETRY "Salmon Press has become one of the most important publications in the Irish literary world, specialising in the promotion of new poets, particularly women poets. Established as an alternative voice. Walks tightrope between innovation and convention. Was a flagship for writers in the west of Ireland. Salmon has developed a cross-cultural, internatonal literary dialog, broadening Irish Literature and urging new perspectives on established traditions."

RECENT TITLE(S) *Boogeyman Dawn*, by Raina Leon; *The Hidden World of Poetry: Unravelling Celtic Mythology in Contemporary Irish Poetry*, by Adam Wyeth; *A Shed for Wood*, by Daniel Thomas.

TIPS "If we are broad minded and willing to nurture the individual voice inherent in the work, the artist will emerge."

⊘ SALVO PRESS

E-mail: info@salvopress.com. **E-mail:** submissions@start-media.com. **Website:** www.salvopress.com. **Contact:** Scott Schmidt, publisher. Estab. 1998. **Publishes 6-12 titles/year. 75% from unagented writers. Pays 10% royalty.** Publishes book 9-12 months after acceptance. Responds in 5 minutes to 1 month to queries; 2 months to mss. Book catalog and ms guidelines online.

FICTION Subjects include adventure, literary, mystery, science fiction, suspense, thriller/espionage. "We are a small press specializing in mystery, suspense, espionage and thriller fiction. Our press publishes in trade paperback and most e-book formats." Publishes hardcover, trade paperback originals and e-books in most formats. **Published 6 debut authors within the last year.** "Our needs change, check our website." Query by e-mail.

RECENT TITLE(S) *Crown of Thorns*, by Hank Luce (religious thriller); *Terralus 4*, by Lee Gimenez (sci-fi); *Gift of the Bouda*, by Richard Farnsworth (horror).

SAMHAIN PUBLISHING, LTD

11821 Mason Montgomery Rd., Cincinnati OH 45249. (478)314-5144. **Fax:** (478)314-5148. **E-mail:** editor@samhainpublishing.com. **Website:** www.samhainpublishing.com. **Contact:** Heather Osborn, editorial director. Estab. 2005. Publishes e-books and paperback originals. POD/offset printing; line illustrations. "A small, independent publisher, Samhain's motto is 'It's all about the story.' We look for fresh, unique voices who have a story to share with the world. We encourage our authors to let their muse have its way and to create tales that don't always adhere to current trends. One never knows what the next hot genre will be or when it will start, so write what's in your soul. These are the books that, whether the story is based on formula or is an original, when written from the heart will earn you a life-time readership." **Pays royalties 30-40% for e-books, average of 8% for trade paper, and author's copies (quantity varies).** Publishes book 18 months after acceptance. Responds in 4 months. Guidelines online.

FICTION Needs erotica and all genres and all heat levels of romance (contemporary, futuristic/time travel, gothic, historical, paranormal, regency period, romantic suspense, fantasy, action/adventure, etc.), as well as fantasy, urban fantasy or science fiction with strong romantic elements, with word counts between 12,000 and 120,000 words. "Samhain is now accepting submissions for our line of horror novels. We are actively seeking talented writers who can tell an exciting, dramatic and frightening story, and who are eager to promote their work and build their community of readers. We are looking for novels 'either supernatural or non-supernatural, contemporary or historical' that are original and compelling. Authors can be previously unpublished or established, agented or un-agented. Content can range from subtle and unsettling to gory and shocking. The writing is what counts." Accepts unsolicited mss. Query with outline/synopsis and either 3 sample chapters or the full ms. Accepts queries by e-mail only. Include estimated word count, brief bio, list of publishing credits, and "how the author is working to improve craft: association, critique groups, etc."

TIPS "Because we are an e-publisher first, we do not have to be as concerned with industry trends and can publish less popular genres of fiction if we believe the story and voice are good and will appeal to our customers. Please follow submission guidelines located on our website, include all requested information and proof your query/ms for errors prior to submission."

SANTA MONICA PRESS LLC

P.O. Box 850, Solana Beach CA 92075. (858)793-1890; (800)784-9553. **E-mail:** books@santamonicapress.com. **Website:** www.santamonicapress.com. Estab. 1994. Publishes hardcover and trade paperback originals. "At Santa Monica Press, we're not afraid to cast a wide editorial net. Our eclectic list of lively and modern nonfiction titles includes books in such categories as popular culture, film history, photography, humor, biography, travel, and reference." **Publishes 15 titles/year. 25% of books from first-time authors. 75% from unagented writers. Pays 6-10% royalty on net price. Pays $500-10,000+ advance.** Publishes book 1 year after acceptance. Accepts simultaneous submissions. Responds in 1-2 months to proposals. Guidelines online.

NONFICTION Subjects include Americana, architecture, art, contemporary culture, creative nonfiction, education, entertainment, film, games, humanities, language, literature, memoirs, regional, social sciences, sports, travel, Biography, coffee table book, general nonfiction, gift book, humor, illustrated book, reference. Submit proposal package, including outline, 2-3 sample chapters, biography, marketing and publicity plans, analysis of competitive titles, SASE with appropriate postage. Reviews artwork/photos. Send photocopies.

RECENT TITLE(S) *Turn Up the Radio! Rock, Pop, and Roll in Los Angeles 1956-1972,* by Harvey Kubernik with a foreword by Tom Petty; *Tower Stories: An Oral History of 9/11,* by Damon Dimarco; *Route 66 Adventure Handbook: Turbocharged* 4th Edition, by Drew Knowles.

TIPS "Visit our website before submitting to view our author guidelines and to get a clear idea of the types of books we publish. Carefully analyze your book's competition and tell us what makes your book different—and what makes it better. Also let us know what promotional and marketing opportunities you, as the author, bring to the project."

SARABANDE BOOKS, INC.

2234 Dundee Rd., Suite 200, Louisville KY 40205. (502)458-4028. **Fax:** (502)458-4065. **E-mail:** info@sarabandebooks.org. **Website:** www.sarabandebooks.org. **Contact:** Sarah Gorham, editor-in-chief. Estab. 1994. Publishes trade paperback originals. "Sarabande Books was founded to publish poetry, short fiction, and creative nonfiction. We look for works of lasting literary value. Please see our titles to get an idea of our taste. Accepts submissions through contests and open submissions." **Publishes 10 titles/year. 1,500 queries received/year. 3,000 mss received/year. 35% of books from first-time authors. 75% from unagented writers. Pays royalty. 10% on actual income received. Also pays in author's copies. Pays $500-1,000 advance.** Publishes book 18 months after acceptance. Accepts simultaneous submissions. Book catalog available free. Contest guidelines for #10 SASE or on website.

○ Charges $10 handling fee with alternative option of purchase of book from website (e-mail confirmation of sale must be included with submission).

FICTION Subjects include literary, short story collections, novellas, short novels (300 pages maximum, 150 pages minimum). "We consider novels and nonfiction in a wide variety of genres and subject matters with a special emphasis on mysteries and crime fiction. We do not consider science fiction, fantasy, or horror. Our target length is 70,000-90,000 words." Queries can be sent via e-mail, fax, or regular post.

POETRY Poetry of superior artistic quality; otherwise no restraints or specifications. Sarabande Books publishes books of poetry of 48 pages minimum. Wants "poetry that offers originality of voice and subject matter, uniqueness of vision, and a language that startles because of the careful attention paid to it—language that goes beyond the merely competent or functional." Mss selected through literary contests, invitation, and recommendation by a well-established writer.

RECENT TITLE(S) *Portrait of My Mother Who Posed Nude in Wartime,* by Marjorie Sandor; *October,* by Louise Glück.

TIPS "Sarabande publishes for a general literary audience. Know your market. Read-and buy-books of literature. Sponsors contests for poetry and fiction. Make sure you're not writing in a vacuum, that you've read and are conscious of contemporary literature. Have someone read your ms, checking it for ordering, coherence. Better a lean, consistently strong ms than one that is long and uneven. We like a story to have good narrative, and we like to be engaged by language."

SASQUATCH BOOKS

1904 Third Ave., Suite 710, Seattle WA 98101. (206)467-4300. **Fax:** (206)467-4301. **E-mail:** ttabor@sasquatchbooks.com. **Website:** www.sasquatchbooks.com. **Contact:** Gary Luke, editorial director; Terence Maikels, acquisitions editor; Heidi Lenze, acquisitions editor. Estab. 1986. Publishes regional hardcover and trade paperback originals. "Sasquatch Books publishes books for and from the Pacific Northwest, Alaska, and California is the nation's premier regional press. Sasquatch Books' publishing program is a veritable celebration of regionally written words. Undeterred by political or geographical borders, Sasquatch defines its region as the magnificent area that stretches from the Brooks Range to the Gulf of California and from the Rocky Mountains to the Pacific Ocean. Our top-selling Best Places® travel guides serve the most popular destinations and locations of the West. We also publish widely in the areas of food and wine, gardening, nature, photography, children's books, and regional history, all facets of the literature of place. With more than 200 books brimming with insider information on the West, we offer an energetic eye on the lifestyle, landscape, and worldview of our region. Considers queries and proposals from authors and agents for new projects that fit into our West Coast regional publishing program. We can evaluate query letters, proposals, and complete mss." **Publishes 30 titles/year. 20% of books from first-time authors. 75% from unagented writers. Pays royalty on cover price. Pays wide range advance.** Publishes book 6-9 months after acceptance. Accepts simultaneous submissions. Responds to queries in 3 months. Book catalog for 9×12 envelope and 2 first-class stamps. Guidelines online.

◯   "When you submit to Sasquatch Books, please remember that the editors want to know about you *and* your project, along with a sense of who will want to read your book."

NONFICTION Subjects include animals, art, architecture, business, economics, cooking, foods, nutrition, gardening, history, nature, environment, recreation, regional, sports, travel, women's issues, women's studies, outdoors. "We are seeking quality nonfiction works about the Pacific Northwest and West Coast regions (including Alaska to California). The literature of place includes how-to and where-to as well as history and narrative nonfiction." Picture books: activity books, animal, concept, nature/environment. Query first, then submit outline and sample chapters with SASE. Send submissions to The Editors. E-mailed submissions and queries are not recommended. Please include return postage if you want your materials back.

FICTION Young readers: adventure, animal, concept, contemporary, humor, nature/environment.

RECENT TITLE(S) *Amazing Alaska*, by Deb Vanasse, Illustrated by Karen Lewis; *Sourdough Man*, by Barbara Lavallee; *Larry Gets Lost in New York*, by John Skewes (picture book).

TIPS "We sell books through a range of channels in addition to the book trade. Our primary audience consists of active, literate residents of the West Coast."

SATURNALIA BOOKS

105 Woodside Rd., Ardmore PA 19003. (267) 278-9541. **E-mail:** info@saturnaliabooks.com. **Website:** www.saturnaliabooks.org. **Contact:** Henry Israeli, publisher. Estab. 2002. Publishes trade paperback originals and digital versions for e readers. "We do not accept unsolicited submissions. We hold a contest, the Saturnalia Books Poetry Prize, annually in which 1 anonymously submitted title is chosen by a poet with a national reputation for publication. Submissions are accepted during the month of March. The submission fee is $30, and the prize is $2,000 and 20 copies of the book. See website for details." **Publishes 4 titles/year. Receives 500 mss a year. 33% of books from first-time authors. 100% from unagented writers. Pays authors 4-6% royalty on retail price. Pays $400-2,000 advance.** Accepts simultaneous submissions. Responds in 4 months on mss. Catalog on website. Guidelines on website.

POETRY "Saturnalia Books has no bias against any school of poetry, but we do tend to publish writers who take chances and push against convention in some way, whether it's in form, language, content, or musicality." Submit complete ms to contest only.

RECENT TITLE(S) *My Scarlet Ways*, by Tanya Larkin; *The Girls of Peculiar*, by Catherine Pierce; *Ladies & Gentlemen*, by Michael Robins; *Xing*, by Debora Kuan.

TIPS "Our audience tend to be young avid readers of contemporary poetry. Read a few sample books first."

⊕ SCARECROW PRESS, INC.

Imprint of Rowman & Littlefield Publishing Group, 4501 Forbes Blvd., Suite 200, Lanham MD 20706. (301)459-3366. **Fax:** (301)429-5748. **Website:** www.scarecrowpress.com. **Contact:** April Snyder, acquisitions editor (information studies, interdisciplinary studies, general reference); Renee Camus, acquisitions editor (music); Stephen Ryan (film and theater); Corinne O. Burton (young adult literature). Estab. 1955. Publishes hardcover originals. Scarecrow Press publishes several series: Historical Dictionaries (includes countries, religions, international organizations, and area studies); Studies and Documentaries on the History of Popular Entertainment (forthcoming); Society, Culture and Libraries. Emphasis is on any title likely to appeal to libraries. Currently emphasizing jazz, Africana, and educational issues of contemporary interest. **Publishes 165 titles/year. 70% of books from first-time authors. 99% from unagented writers. Pays 8% royalty on net of first 1,000 copies; 10% of net price thereafter.** Publishes book 18 months after acceptance of ms. Responds in 2 months to queries. Catalog and ms guidelines online.

NONFICTION Subjects include film, cinema, stage, language, literature, religion, sports, annotated bibliographies, handbooks and biographical dictionaries in the areas of women's studies and ethnic studies, parapsychology, fine arts and handicrafts, genealogy, sports history, music, movies, stage, library and information science. Query with SASE.

⊕ SCARLETTA PRESS

10 S. 5th St., Suite 1105, Minneapolis MN 55402. (612)455-0252. **Website:** www.scarlettapress.com. Estab. 2005. **Publishes 8-12 titles/year. 50% of books from first-time authors. 85% from unagented writers. Pays 10-20% royalty.** Accepts simultaneous submissions. Guidelines online.

○ "We accept submissions only during our reading period September 1-June 1."

NONFICTION Subjects include creative nonfiction, education, memoirs. Submit cover letter with synopsis, 1-2 sample chapters.

FICTION Subjects include juvenile, picture books, educational, autobiographical, psychological, middle grade. Does not publish plays, screenplays, short story collections, or poetry. Submit cover letter with synopsis, 1-2 sample chapters.

RECENT TITLE(S) *My Brother's Name* (psychological fiction); *Monster Needs a Costume* (picture book); *Cool World Cooking* (middle grade nonfiction).

TIPS "Read our submission guidelines carefully before submitting."

SCHIFFER PUBLISHING, LTD.

4880 Lower Valley Rd., Atglen PA 19310. (610)593-1777. **Fax:** (610)593-2002. **E-mail:** info@schifferbooks.com; schifferbk@aol.com. **Website:** www.schifferbooks.com. **Contact:** Tina Skinner. Estab. 1975. **Publishes 10-20 titles/year. Pays royalty on wholesale price.** Responds in 2 weeks to queries. Book catalog available free. Guidelines online.

NONFICTION Art-quality illustrated regional histories. Looking for informed, entertaining writing and

lots of subject areas to provide points of entry into the text for non-history buffs who buy a beautiful book because they are from, or love, an area. Full color possible in the case of historic postcards. Fax or e-mail outline, photos, and book proposal.

RECENT TITLE(S) *Antique Enameled Jewelry*, by Dale Nicholls with Robin Allison; *Mannequins*, by Steven M. Richman; *The Long Campaign*, by John W. Lambert.

TIPS "We want to publish books for towns or cities with relevant population or active tourism to support book sales. A list of potential town vendors is a helpful start toward selling us on your book idea."

Ⓐⵔ SCHOCKEN BOOKS

Imprint of Knopf Publishing Group, Division of Random House, Inc., 1745 Broadway, New York NY 10019. (212)572-9000. **Fax:** (212)572-6030. **Website:** www.schocken.com. Estab. 1945. Publishes hardcover and trade paperback originals and reprints. "Schocken publishes quality Judaica in all areas-fiction, history, biography, current affairs, spirituality and religious practices, popular culture, and cultural studies." **Publishes 9-12 titles/year. Pays varied advance.** Accepts simultaneous submissions.

○ Does not accept unsolicited mss. Agented submissions only.

RECENT TITLE(S) *The Wicked Son*, by David Mamet; *Marc Chagall*, by Jonathan Wilson; *The Promise of Politics*, by Hannah Arendt.

SCHOLASTIC INC.

557 Broadway, New York NY 10012. (212)343-6100. **Website:** www.scholastic.com.

IMPRINTS Arthur A. Levine Books, Cartwheel Books®, Chicken House®, Graphix™, Little Scholastic™, Little Shepherd™, Michael di Capua Books, Orchard Books®, Point™, PUSH, Scholastic en Español, Scholastic Licensed Publishing, Scholastic Nonfiction, Scholastic Paperbacks, Scholastic Press, Scholastic Reference™, and The Blue Sky Press® are Imprints of the Scholastic Trade Books Division. In addition, Scholastic Trade Books included Klutz®, a highly innovative publisher and creator of "books plus" for children.

○ Scholastic Trade Books is an award-winning publisher of original children's books. Scholastic publishes more than 600 new hardcover, paperback and novelty books each year. The list includes the phenomenally successful publishing properties Harry Potter®, Goosebumps®,

The 39 Clues™, I Spy™, and *The Hunger Games*; best-selling and award-winning authors and illustrators, including Blue Balliett, Jim Benton, Meg Cabot, Suzanne Collins, Christopher Paul Curtis, Ann M. Martin, Dav Pilkey, J.K. Rowling, Pam Muñoz Ryan, Brian Selznick, David Shannon, Mark Teague, and Walter Wick, among others; as well as licensed properties such as Star Wars® and Rainbow Magic®.

Ⓐ SCHOLASTIC LIBRARY PUBLISHING

90 Old Sherman Turnpike, Danbury CT 06816. (203)797-3500. **Fax:** (203)797-3197. **E-mail:** slpservice@scholastic.com. **Website:** www.scholastic.com/librarypublishing. **Contact:** Phil Friedman, vice president/publisher; Kate Nunn, editor-in-chief; Marie O'Neil, art director. Estab. 1895. Publishes hardcover and trade paperback originals. "Scholastic Library is a leading publisher of reference, educational, and children's books. We provide parents, teachers, and librarians with the tools they need to enlighten children to the pleasure of learning and prepare them for the road ahead. Publishes informational (nonfiction) for K-12; picture books for young readers, grades 1-3." **Pays authors royalty based on net or work purchased outright. Pays illustrators at competitive rates.**

IMPRINTS Grolier; Children's Press; Franklin Watts; Grolier Online.

🖸 *Accepts agented submissions only.*

NONFICTION Photo-illustrated books for all levels: animal, arts/crafts, biography, careers, concept, geography, health, history, hobbies, how-to, multicultural, nature/environment, science, social issues, special needs, sports. Average word length: young readers—2,000; middle readers—8,000; young adult—15,000. Query; submit outline/synopsis, résumé, and/or list of publications, and writing sample. SASE required for response.

FICTION Publishes 1 picture book series, Rookie Readers, for grades 1-2. Does not accept unsolicited mss. *Does not accept fiction proposals.*

Ⓐ SCHOLASTIC PRESS

Imprint of Scholastic, Inc., 557 Broadway, New York NY 10012. (212)343-6100. **Fax:** (212)343-4713. **Website:** www.scholastic.com. **Contact:** David Saylor, editorial director, Scholastic Press, creative director and associate publisher for all Scholastic hardcover imprints. David Levithan, executive editorial director; Lisa Sandell, acquiring editor; Dianne Hess, executive editor; Tracy Mack, executive editor; Rachel Griffiths, editor; Jennifer Rees, associate editor. Publishes hardcover originals. Scholastic Press publishes fresh, literary picture book fiction and nonfiction; fresh, literary nonseries or nongenre-oriented middle grade and young adult fiction. Currently emphasizing subtly handled treatments of key relationships in children's lives; unusual approaches to commonly dry subjects, such as biography, math, history, or science. De-emphasizing fairy tales (or retellings), board books, genre, or series fiction (mystery, fantasy, etc.). **Publishes 60 titles/year. 2,500 queries received/year. 1% of books from first-time authors. Pays royalty on retail price. Pays variable advance.** Publishes book 2 years after acceptance. Responds in 3 months to queries; 6-8 months to mss.

NONFICTION Agented submissions and previously published authors only.

FICTION Subjects include juvenile, picture books, novels. Looking for strong picture books, young chapter books, appealing middle grade novels (ages 8-11) and interesting and well-written young adult novels. Wants fresh, exciting picture books and novels—inspiring, new talent.

TIPS "Read *currently* published children's books. Revise, rewrite, rework and find your own voice, style and subject. We are looking for authors with a strong and unique voice who can tell a great story and have the ability to evoke genuine emotion. Children's publishers are becoming more selective, looking for irresistible talent and fairly broad appeal, yet still very willing to take risks, just to keep the game interesting."

◗ SCRIBE PUBLICATIONS

18-20 Edward St., Brunswick VIC 3056, Australia. (61)(3)9388-8780. **Fax:** (61)(3)9388-8787. **E-mail:** info@scribepub.com.au. **Website:** www.scribepublications.com.au. Estab. 1976. **Publishes 70 titles/year. 10-25% of books from first-time authors. 10-20% from unagented writers.** Submission guidelines available on website under About Us.

NONFICTION Subjects include environment, government, politics, history, memoirs, nature, environment, psychology, current affairs, social history. "Please refer first to our website before contacting us or submitting anything, because we explain there who we will accept proposals from."

FICTION Submit synopsis, sample chapters, CV.

RECENT TITLE(S) *Behind the Beautiful Forevers,* by Katherine Boo; *Brain Rules,* by John Medina; *In the Garden of Beasts,* by Erik Larson; *Daniel Stein, Interpreter,* by Ludmila Ulitskaya.

Ⓐ SCRIBNER

Imprint of Simon & Schuster Adult Publishing Group, 1230 Avenue of the Americas, 12th Floor, New York NY 10020. (212)698-7000. **E-mail:** paul.whitlatch@simonandschuster.com. **Website:** www.simonsays.com. **Contact:** Nan Graham (literary fiction, nonfiction); Beth Wareham (fiction); Alexis Gargagliano (literary fiction, nonfiction); Brant Rumble (nonfiction); Colin Harrison (fiction, nonfiction); Samantha Martin (fiction, nonfiction); Whitney Frick (fiction, nonfiction); Kara Watson (fiction, nonfiction); Paul Whitlatch (fiction, nonfiction). Publishes hardcover originals. **Publishes 70-75 titles/year. Thousands queries received/year. 20% of books from first-time authors. 0% from unagented writers. Pays 7 1/2-15% royalty. Pays variable advance.** Publishes book 9 months after acceptance of ms. Accepts simultaneous submissions. Responds in 3 months to queries.

IMPRINTS Lisa Drew Books; Scribner Classics (reprints only); Scribner Poetry (by invitation only).

NONFICTION Subjects include education, ethnic, gay, lesbian, health, medicine, history, language, literature, nature, environment, philosophy, psychology, religion, science, criticism. Agented submissions only.

FICTION Subjects include literary, mystery, suspense. Agented submissions only.

RECENT TITLE(S) *Under the Dome,* by Stephen King; *The Ultramind Solution,* by Mark Hyman; *Raymond Carver,* by Carol Sklenicka; `` ``, by Alex Lemon.

SEAL PRESS

1700 4th St., Berkeley CA 94710. (510)595-3664. **E-mail:** seal.press@perseusbooks.com. **E-mail:** sealacquisitions@avalonpub.com. **Website:** www.sealpress.com. Estab. 1976. Publishes trade paperback originals. "Seal Press is an imprint of Avalon Publishing Group, feminist book publisher interested in original, lively, radical, empowering and culturally diverse nonfiction by women addressing contemporary issues from a feminist perspective or speaking positively to the experience of being female. Currently emphasizing women outdoor adventurists, young feminists, political issues for women, health issues, and surviving abuse. *Not accepting fiction at this time.*" **Publishes 30 titles/year. 1,000 queries received/year. 750 mss received/year. 25% of books from first-time authors. 50% from unagented writers. Pays 7-10% royalty on retail price. Pays variable royalty on retail price. Pays $3,000-10,000 advance. Pays variable advance.** Publishes book 1 year after acceptance. Accepts simultaneous submissions. Responds in 2 months to queries. Book catalog and ms guidelines for SASE or online.

NONFICTION Subjects include Americana, child guidance, contemporary culture, creative nonfiction, ethnic, gay, lesbian, memoirs, multicultural, nature, environment, sex, travel, women's issues, women's studies, popular culture, politics, domestic violence, sexual abuse. Query with SASE. Reviews artwork/photos. Send photocopies. No original art or photos accepted.

FICTION Ethnic, feminist, gay/lesbian, literary, multicultural. "We are interested in alternative voices." *Does not accept fiction at present.* Query with SASE or submit outline, 2 sample chapters, synopsis.

RECENT TITLE(S) *Confessions of a Naughty Mommy,* by Heidi Raykeil; *Invisible Girls,* by Dr. Patti Ferguson; *The Risks of Sunbathing Topless,* by Kate Chynoweth.

TIPS "Our audience is generally composed of women interested in reading about women's issues addressed from a feminist perspective."

SEARCH INSTITUTE PRESS

Search Institute, 615 First Ave. NE, Suite 125, Minneapolis MN 55413. (612)399-0200. **Fax:** (612)692-5553. **E-mail:** acquisitions@search-institute.org. **Website:** www.search-institute.org. Estab. 1958. Publishes trade paperback originals. **Publishes 12-15 titles/year. Pays royalty.** Publishes book 1 year after acceptance. Accepts simultaneous submissions. Responds in 6 months to queries, proposals, mss. Catalog free on request, online. Guidelines online.

NONFICTION Subjects include career guidance, child guidance, community, counseling, education, entertainment, games, parenting, public affairs, social sciences, youth leadership, prevention, activities. Does not want children's picture books, poetry, New Age and religious-themes, memoirs, biographies, and autobiographies. Query with SASE. Does not review artwork/photos.

RECENT TITLE(S) *Helping Teens Handle Tough Experiences, Great Preschools, Engage Every Parent!, Parenting Preteens With a Purpose.*

TIPS "Our audience is educators, youth program leaders, mentors, parents."

SEAWORTHY PUBLICATIONS, INC.

2023 N. Atlantic Ave., #226, Cocoa Beach FL 32931. (321)610-3634. **Fax:** (321)400-1006. **E-mail:** queries@ seaworthy.com. **Website:** www.seaworthy.com. **Contact:** Joseph F. Janson, publisher. Publishes trade paperback originals, hardcover originals, and reprints. "Seaworthy Publications is a nautical book publisher that primarily publishes books of interest to recreational boaters and bluewater cruisers, including cruising guides, how-to books about boating. Currently emphasizing cruising guides." **Publishes 8 titles/year. 150 queries received/year. 40 mss received/ year. 60% of books from first-time authors. 100% from unagented writers. Pays 15% royalty on wholesale price. Pays $1,000 advance.** Publishes book 6 months after acceptance. Responds in 1 month to queries. Book catalog and Guidelines online.

NONFICTION Subjects include regional, sailing, boating, regional, boating guide books. Regional guide books, first-person adventure, reference, technical—all dealing with boating. Query with SASE. Submit 3 sample chapters, TOC. Prefers electronic query via e-mail. Reviews artwork/photos. Send photocopies or color prints.

TIPS "Our audience consists of sailors, boaters, and those interested in the sea, sailing, or long-distance cruising."

SECOND STORY PRESS

20 Maud St., Suite 401, Toronto ON M5V 2M5, Canada. (416)537-7850. **Fax:** (416)537-0588. **E-mail:** info@ secondstorypress.ca; marketing@secondstorypress. com. **Website:** www.secondstorypress.ca.

NONFICTION Picture books: biography. Accepts appropriate material from residents of Canada only. Submit complete ms or submit outline and sample chapters by postal mail only. No electronic submissions or queries.

FICTION Considers non-sexist, non-racist, and non-violent stories, as well as historical fiction, chapter books, picture books.

SEEDLING CONTINENTAL PRESS

520 E. Bainbridge St., Elizabethtown PA 17022. **E-mail:** bspencer@continentalpress.com. **Website:** www.continentalpress.com. **Contact:** Megan Bergonzi. Publishes books for classroom use only for the beginning reader in English. "Natural language and predictable text are requisite. Patterned text is acceptable, but must have a unique story line. Poetry, books in rhyme and full-length picture books are not being accepted. Illustrations are not necessary." **Work purchased outright from authors.** Publishes book 1-2 years after acceptance. Accepts simultaneous submissions. Responds to mss in 6 months.

NONFICTION Young readers: animal, arts/crafts, biography, careers, concept, multicultural, nature/environment, science. Does not accept texts longer than 12 pages or over 300 words. Average word length: young readers—100. Submit complete ms.

FICTION Young readers: adventure, animal, folktales, humor, multicultural, nature/environment. Does not accept texts longer than 12 pages or over 300 words. Average word length: young readers—100. Submit complete ms.

TIPS "See our website. Follow writers' guidelines carefully and test your story with children and educators."

⊕ SELF-COUNSEL PRESS

1704 N. State St., Bellingham WA 92225. (360)676-4530. **Website:** www.self-counsel.com. **Contact:** Richard Day, managing editor. Estab. 1971. Publishes trade paperback originals. Self-Counsel Press publishes a range of quality self-help books written in practical, nontechnical style by recognized experts in the fields of business, financial, or legal guidance for people who want to help themselves. **Publishes 30 titles/year. 1,500 queries received/year. 30% of books from first-time authors. 90% from unagented writers. Pays rare advance.** Publishes book 8 months after acceptance of ms. Accepts simultaneous submissions. Responds in 2 months to queries. Book catalog via website or upon request. Guidelines online.

NONFICTION Subjects include business, economics, computers, electronics, money, finance, legal issues for lay people. Submit proposal package, outline, résumé, 2 sample chapters.

SENTIENT PUBLICATIONS

1113 Spruce St., Boulder CO 80302. **E-mail:** contact@ sentientpublications.com. **Website:** www.sentient-publications.com. **Contact:** Connie Shaw, acquisitions editor. Estab. 2001. Publishes hardcover and trade paperback originals; trade paperback reprints. **Publishes 4 titles/year. 200 queries received/year. 100 mss received/year. 70% of books from first-time authors. 50% from unagented writers. Pays royalty** on wholesale price. **Sometimes pays advance.** Publishes book 6 months after acceptance. Accepts simultaneous submissions. Responds in 1 month to queries; 2 months to proposals and mss. Book catalog online.

NONFICTION Subjects include child guidance, contemporary culture, creative nonfiction, education, gardening, history, memoirs, philosophy, photography, psychology, science, social sciences, sociology, spirituality, travel. "We're especially looking for holistic health books that have something new to say." Submit proposal package, See our website. Submit complete ms. Does not review artwork/photos.

RECENT TITLE(S) *Me, My Cells, and I,* by Dave Ames (holistic health); *The Alchemy of Teaching*, by Jeremiah Conway (alternative education); *The Open Path,* by Elias Amidon (spirituality).

SERIOUSLY GOOD BOOKS

999 Vanderbilt Beach Rd., Naples FL 34119. **E-mail:** seriouslygoodbks@aol.com. **Website:** www.seriouslygoodbks.net. Estab. 2010. Publishes trade paperback and electronic originals. Publishes historial fiction only. **Publishes 2-5 titles/year. Pays 15% minimum royalties.** Responds in 1 month to queries. Book catalog and guidelines online.

FICTION Subjects include historical. Query by e-mail.

TIPS "Looking for historial fiction with substance. We seek well-researched historical fiction in the vein of Rutherfurd, Mary Renault, Maggie Anton, Robert Harris, etc. Please don't query with historical fiction mixed with other genres (romance, time travel, vampires, etc.)."

SEVEN STORIES PRESS

140 Watts St., New York NY 10013. (212)226-8760. **Fax:** (212)226-1411. **E-mail:** info@sevenstories.com. **Website:** www.sevenstories.com. **Contact:** Daniel Simon; Anna Lui. Estab. 1995. Publishes hardcover and trade paperback originals. Founded in 1995 in New York City, and named for the seven authors who committed to a home with a fiercely independent spirit, Seven Stories Press publishes works of the imagination and political titles by voices of conscience. While most widely known for its books on politics, human rights, and social and economic justice, Seven Stories continues to champion literature, with a list encompassing both innovative debut novels and National Book Award–winning poetry collections, as well as prose and poetry translations from the French, Spanish, German, Swedish, Italian, Greek, Polish, Korean, Vietnamese, Russian, and Arabic. **Publishes 40-50 titles/year. 15% of books from first-time authors. 50% from unagented writers. Pays 7-15% royalty on retail price. Pays advance.** Publishes book 1-3 years after acceptance. Accepts simultaneous submissions. Responds in 1 month to queries and mss. Book catalog and ms guidelines free.

NONFICTION Responds only if interested. Submit cover letter with 2 sample chapters.

FICTION Subjects include literary. Submit cover letter with 2 sample chapters.

TIPS "Each year we also publish an annual compilation of censored news stories by Project Censored. Features of this series include the Top 25 Censored News Stories of the year—which has a history of identifying important neglected news stories and which is widely disseminated in the alternative press—as well as the 'Junk Food News' chapter and chapters on hot-button topics for the year. Seven Stories also maintains a publishing partnership with Human Rights Watch through the yearly publication of the World Report, a preeminent account of human rights abuse around the world—a report card on the progress of the world's nations towards the protection of human rights for people everywhere."

SEVERN HOUSE PUBLISHERS

Salatin House, 19 Cedar St., Sutton, Surrey SM2 5DA, United Kingdom. (44)(208)770-3930. **Fax:** (44)(208)770-3850. **Website:** www.severnhouse.com. **Contact:** Amanda Stewart, editorial director. Publishes hardcover and trade paperback originals and reprints. Severn House is currently emphasizing suspense, romance, mystery. Large print imprint from existing authors. **Publishes 150 titles/year. 400-500 queries received/year. 50 mss received/year. Pays 7 1/2-15% royalty on retail price. Pays $750-5,000 advance.** Accepts simultaneous submissions. Responds in 3 months to proposals. Book catalog available free.

IMPRINTS Creme de la Crime.

FICTION Subjects include adventure, fantasy, historical, horror, mainstream, contemporary, mystery, romance, short story collections, suspense. *Agented submissions only.*

SHAMBHALA PUBLICATIONS, INC.

300 Massachusetts Ave., Boston MA 02115. (617)424-0030. **Fax:** (617)236-1563. **E-mail:** editors@shambhala.com. **Website:** www.shambhala.com. Estab. 1969. Publishes hardcover and trade paperback originals

and reprints. **Publishes 90-100 titles/year. 500 queries received/year. 1,200 mss/proposals received/year. 30% of books from first-time authors. 70% from unagented writers. Pays 8% royalty on retail price.** Publishes book 1 year after acceptance. Accepts simultaneous submissions. Responds in 4 months to queries, proposals, and mss. Book catalog and ms guidelines free.

IMPRINTS Roost Books.

NONFICTION Subjects include cooking, crafts, parenting, Buddhism, martial arts, yoga, natural health, Eastern philosophy, creativity, green living, nature writing. To send a book proposal, include a synopsis of the book, TOC or outline, a copy of the author's résumé or some other brief biographical statement, along with two or three sample chapters (they do not need to be in consecutive order). The chapters should be double-spaced. Include SASE. Publishes very little fiction or poetry.

FICTION Submit proposal package, outline, résumé, 2 sample chapters, TOC.

● SHEARSMAN BOOKS, LTD

50 Westons Hills Dr., Emersons Green Bristol BS16 7DF, United Kingdom. **E-mail:** editor@shearsman.com. **Website:** www.shearsman.com. **Contact:** Tony Frazer, editor. Estab. 1981. Publishes trade paperback originals. **Publishes 45-60 titles/year. Pays 10% royalty on retail price after 150 copies have sold; authors also receive 10 free copies of their books.** Responds in 2-3 months to mss. Catalog and guidelines online.

NONFICTION Subjects include memoirs, translation, essays.

POETRY "Shearsman only publishes poetry, poetry collections, and poetry in translation (from any language but with an emphasis on work in Spanish & in German). Some critical work on poetry and also memoirs and essays by poets. Mainly poetry by British, Irish, North American, and Australian poets." No children's books.

TIPS "Book ms submission: most of the ms must have already appeared in the UK or USA magazines of some repute, and it has to fill 70-72 pages of half letter or A5 pages. You must have sufficient return postage. Submissions can also be made by e-mail. It is unlikely that a poet with no track record will be accepted for publication as there is no obvious audience for the work. Try to develop some exposure to UK and US magazines and try to assemble a ms only later."

➕ ⊘ SHIPWRECKT BOOKS PUBLISHING COMPANY LLC

115(B) Parkway Ave., P.O. Box 20, Lanesboro MN 55949. (507)458-8190. **E-mail:** publisher@shipwrecktbooks.com. **E-mail:** contact@shipwrecktbooks.com. **Website:** www.shipwrecktbooks.com. **Contact:** Tom Driscoll, managing editor. Publishes trade paperback originals, mass market paperback originals, and electronic originals. **Publishes 6 titles/year. 50%% of books from first-time authors. 100%% from unagented writers. Authors receive a maximum of 50% royalties.** Publishes book Average length of time between acceptance of a book-length ms and publication is 6 months. after acceptance of ms. Accepts simultaneous submissions. Responds to queries within a month. Send SASE for book catalog. Send SASE for ms guidelines.

IMPRINTS Rocket Science Press (literary); Up On Big Rock Poetry Series; Lost Lake Folk Art (fee-based publishing).

NONFICTION Subjects include agriculture, alternative lifestyles, Americana, animals, creative nonfiction, environment, ethnic, foods, gardening, gay, government, health, history, hobbies, horticulture, house and home, lesbian, medicine, memoirs, military, multicultural, nature, nutrition, politics, recreation, regional, spirituality, sports, war, womens issues, world affairs, young adult. E-mail query at contact@shipwrecktbooks.com. All unsolicited mss returned unopened. Does not review artwork.

FICTION Subjects include adventure, comic books, ethnic, experimental, fantasy, historical, humor, literary, multicultural, mystery, poetry, regional, science fiction, suspense, young adult. E-mail query. All unsolicited mss returned unopened.

POETRY Submit 3 sample poems by e-mail.

TIPS Quality writing to be considered for royalty contract. Offers full-time editorial services for new and unpublished writers.

⊘ SIERRA CLUB BOOKS

85 Second St., San Francisco CA 94105. (415)977-5500. **Fax:** (415)977-5792. **E-mail:** books.publishing@sierraclub.org. **Website:** www.sierraclub.org/books. **Contact:** Danny Moses, editor-in-chief. Estab. 1962. Publishes hardcover and paperback originals and reprints. "The Sierra Club was founded to help people to explore, enjoy, and preserve the nation's forests, waters, wildlife, and wilderness. The books program

publishes quality trade books about the outdoors and the protection of the natural world." **Publishes approximately 15 titles/year. 50% from unagented writers. Pays royalty. Pays $5,000-15,000 average advance.** Publishes book 1 year after acceptance of ms. Accepts simultaneous submissions. Responds in 1 month to queries. Responds in 2 months to proposals. Responds in 3 months to mss. Catalog and guidelines online.

IMPRINTS Sierra Club Books for Children.

Currently not accepting unsolicited mss or proposals for children's books.

NONFICTION Subjects include nature, environment. A broad range of environmental subjects: outdoor adventure, women in the outdoors; literature, including travel and works on the spiritual aspects of the natural world; natural history and current environmental issues. Does not want proposals for large, color-photographic books without substantial text; how-to books on building things outdoors; books on motorized travel; or any but the most professional studies of animals. No fiction or poetry. Query with SASE. Reviews artwork/photos. Send photocopies.

SILVERFISH REVIEW PRESS

P.O. Box 3541, Eugene OR 97403. (541)344-5060. **E-mail:** sfrpress@earthlink.net. **Website:** www.silverfishreviewpress.com. **Contact:** Rodger Moody, series editor. Estab. 1978. Publishes trade paperback originals. "Sponsors the Gerald Cable Book Award. This prize is awarded annually to a book length ms of original poetry by an author who has not yet published a full-length collection. There are no restrictions on the kind of poetry or subject matter; translations are not acceptable. Winners will receive $1,000, publication, and 25 copies of the book. Entries must be postmarked by October 15. Entries may be submitted by e-mail. See website for instructions." **Publishes 2-3 titles/year. 50% of books from first-time authors. 100% from unagented writers.** Guidelines online.

RECENT TITLE(S) *Going to Seed: Dispatches From the Garden,* by Charles Goodrich; *Best Western and Other Poems,* by Eric Gudas; *Close By,* by Gigi Marks.

TIPS "Read recent Silverfish titles."

SILVER LEAF BOOKS, LLC

P.O. Box 6460, Holliston MA 01746. **E-mail:** editor@silverleafbooks.com. **Website:** www.silverleafbooks.com. **Contact:** Brett Fried, editor. "Silver Leaf Books is a small press featuring primarily new and upcoming talent in the fantasy, science fiction, mystery, thrillers, suspense, and horror genres. Our editors work closely with our authors to establish a lasting and mutually beneficial relationship, helping both the authors and company continue to grow and thrive." Average print order: 3,000. Debut novel print order: 3,000. Distributes/promotes titles through Baker & Taylor Books and Ingram. **Publishes 6 titles/year. 75% from unagented writers. Pays royalties, and provides author's copies.** Publishes book 1-2 years after acceptance. Responds to queries in 6 months; mss in 4 months. Guidelines online.

Publishes hardcover originals, trade paperback originals, paperback originals, electronic/digital books.

FICTION Subjects include fantasy, horror, mystery, science fiction, suspense, young adult. Query with outline/synopsis and 3 sample chapters. Accepts queries by snail mail. Include estimated word count, brief bio and marketing plan. Send SASE or IRC for return of ms or disposable copy of ms and SASE/IRC for reply only.

TIPS "Follow the online guidelines, be thorough and professional."

⊘⊘ SIMON & SCHUSTER

1230 Avenue of the Americas, New York NY 10020. (212)698-7000. **Website:** www.simonandschuster.com.

Accepts agented submissions only.

⊘⊘ SIMON & SCHUSTER ADULT PUBLISHING GROUP

1230 Avenue of the Americas, New York NY 10020. **E-mail:** ssonline@simonsays.com; Lydia.Frost@simonandschuster.com. **Website:** www.simonandschuster.com. Estab. 1924. The Simon & Schuster Adult Publishing Group includes a number of publishing units that offer books in several formats. Each unit has its own publisher, editorial group and publicity department. Common sales and business departments support all the units. The managing editorial, art, production, marketing, and subsidiary rights departments have staff members dedicated to the individual imprints.

FICTION *Agented submissions only.*

⊘⊘ SIMON & SCHUSTER BOOKS FOR YOUNG READERS

Imprint of Simon & Schuster Children's Publishing, 1230 Avenue of the Americas, New York NY 10020.

(212)698-7000. **Fax:** (212)698-2796. **Website:** www. simonsayskids.com. Publishes hardcover originals. "Simon and Schuster Books For Young Readers is the Flagship imprint of the S&S Children's Division. We are committed to publishing a wide range of contemporary, commercial, award-winning fiction and nonfiction that spans every age of children's publishing. BFYR is constantly looking to the future, supporting our foundation authors and franchises, but always with an eye for breaking new ground with every publication. We publish high-quality fiction and nonfiction for a variety of age groups and a variety of markets. Above all, we strive to publish books that we are passionate about." **Publishes 75 titles/year. Pays variable royalty on retail price.** Publishes book 2-4 years after acceptance. Accepts simultaneous submissions. Guidelines online.

IMPRINTS Paula Wiseman Books.

⚪ *No unsolicited mss.* All unsolicited mss returned unopened.

NONFICTION Subjects include history, nature, environment, biography. Picture books: concept. All levels: narrative, current events, biography, history. "We're looking for picture books or middle grade nonfiction that have a retail potential. No photo essays." Agented submissions only.

FICTION Subjects include fantasy, historical, humor, juvenile, mystery, picture books, science fiction, young adult, adventure, historical, mystery, contemporary fiction. Agented submissions only.

TIPS "We're looking for picture books centered on a strong, fully-developed protagonist who grows or changes during the course of the story; YA novels that are challenging and psychologically complex; also imaginative and humorous middle-grade fiction. And we want nonfiction that is as engaging as fiction. Our imprint's slogan is 'Reading You'll Remember.' We aim to publish books that are fresh, accessible and family-oriented; we want them to have an impact on the reader."

Ⓐ⊘🌎 SIMON & SCHUSTER UK LTD.

Division of Simon & Schuster, Inc., 222 Gray's Inn Rd., 1st Floor, London WC1X 8HB, United Kingdom. (44) (207)316-1900. **Fax:** (44)(207)316-0332. **E-mail:** editorial.enquiries@simonandschuster.co.uk. **Website:** www.simonandschuster.co.uk. Estab. 1987. "Publisher committed to ongoing literary and commercial suc-

cess across a wide range of imprints. Does not accept unsolicited material."

IMPRINTS Simon & Schuster (fiction, memoir, travel, sport, biography, pop culture); Simon & Schuster Illustrated; Simon & Schuster Children's.

SKINNER HOUSE BOOKS

The Unitarian Universalist Association, 25 Beacon St., Boston MA 02108. (617)742-2100 ext. 603. **Fax:** (617)742-7025. **E-mail:** bookproposals@uua.org. **Website:** www.uua.org/publications/skinnerhouse. **Contact:** Betsy Martin. Estab. 1975. Publishes trade paperback originals and reprints. "We publish titles in Unitarian Universalist faith, liberal religion, history, biography, worship, and issues of social justice. Most of our children's titles are intended for religious education or worship use. They reflect Unitarian Universalist values. We also publish inspirational titles of poetic prose and meditations. Writers should know that Unitarian Universalism is a liberal religious denomination committed to progressive ideals. Currently emphasizing social justice concerns." **Publishes 10-20 titles/year. 50% of books from first-time authors. 100% from unagented writers.** Publishes book 1 year after acceptance. Accepts simultaneous submissions. Responds to queries in 3 weeks. Book catalog for 6×9 SAE with 3 first-class stamps. Guidelines online.

NONFICTION Subjects include gay, lesbian, memoirs, religion, women's issues, women's studies, inspirational, church leadership. All levels: activity books, multicultural, music/dance, nature/environment, religion. Query or submit proposal with cover letter, TOC, 2 sample chapters. Reviews artwork/photos. Send photocopies.

FICTION All levels: anthology, multicultural, nature/environment, religion. Query or submit proposal with cover letter, TOC, 2 sample chapters.

TIPS "From outside our denomination, we are interested in mss that will be of help or interest to liberal churches, Sunday School classes, parents, ministers, and volunteers. Inspirational/spiritual and children's titles must reflect liberal Unitarian Universalist values."

SLACK, INC.

6900 Grove Rd., Thorofare NJ 08086. (856)848-1000. **Fax:** (856)853-5991. **E-mail:** editor@healio.com. **Website:** www.healio.com. **Contact:** John Bond, publisher. Estab. 1960. Publishes hardcover and paperback originals. SLACK INC. publishes academic textbooks and professional reference books on various medical topics in an expedient manner. **Publishes 35 titles/year. 80 queries received/year. 23 mss received/year. 75% of books from first-time authors. 100% from unagented writers. Pays 10% royalty. Pays advance.** Publishes book 8 months after acceptance. Accepts simultaneous submissions. Responds in 1 month to queries/proposals; 3 months to mss. Book catalog and ms guidelines free.

NONFICTION Subjects include health, medicine, ophthalmology. Submit proposal package, outline, 2 sample chapters, market profile and CV. Reviews artwork/photos. Send photocopies.

⊘ SLEEPING BEAR PRESS

315 East Eisenhower Pkwy, Suite 200, Ann Arbor MI 48108. (800)487-2323. **Fax:** (734)794-0004. **E-mail:** customerservice@sleepingbearpress.com. **Website:** www.sleepingbearpress.com. **Contact:** Heather Hughes. Estab. 1998. Book catalog available via e-mail.

○ *Currently not accepting ms submissions or queries at this time.* "Please check back for further updates."

FICTION Picture books: adventure, animal, concept, folktales, history, multicultural, nature/environment, religion, sports. Young readers: adventure, animal, concept, folktales, history, humor, multicultural, nature/environment, religion, sports. Average word length: picture books—1,800.

SMALL BEER PRESS

150 Pleasant St., #306, Easthampton MA 01027. (413)203-1636. **Fax:** (413)203-1636. **E-mail:** info@smallbeerpress.com. **Website:** www.smallbeerpress.com. **Contact:** Gavin J. Grant, acquisitions. Estab. 2000.

○ Small Beer Press also publishes the zine *Lady Churchill's Rosebud Wristlet.* "SBP's books have recently received the Tiptree and Crawford Awards."

FICTION Subjects include experimental, literary, short story collections, speculative. Does not accept unsolicited novel or short story collection mss. Send queries with an SASE by mail.

TIPS "Please be familiar with our books first to avoid wasting your time and ours, thank you."

SME

One SME Dr., Dearborn MI 48128. (313)425-3278. **E-mail:** publications@sme.org. **Website:** www.sme.org.

Publishes hardcover and trade paperback originals. **Publishes 6 titles/year. 20 queries received/year. 10 mss received/year. 90% of books from first-time authors. 90% from unagented writers. Pays 10% or more royalty on wholesale or retail price.** Publishes book 6 months after acceptance. Responds in 1 month to queries and mss; 2 months to proposals. Book catalog and ms guidelines online.

NONFICTION Seeking mss that would assist manufacturing practitioners in increasing their productivity, quality, and/or efficiency. Reviews artwork/photos. Send photocopies.

TIPS "Audience is manufacturing practitioners, managers, and individuals wishing to advance their careers in the industry or to enhance productivity, quality, and efficiency within a manufacturing operation."

GIBBS SMITH, PUBLISHER

P.O. Box 667, Layton UT 84041. (801)544-9800. **Fax:** (801)546-8853. **E-mail:** info@gibbs-smith.com. **Website:** www.gibbs-smith.com. **Contact:** Suzanne Taylor, editorial director. Estab. 1969. Publishes hardcover and trade paperback originals. "We publish books that enrich and inspire humankind. Currently emphasizing interior decorating and design, home reference. De-emphasizing novels and short stories." **Publishes 80 titles/year. 3,000-4,000 queries received/year. 50% of books from first-time authors. 75% from unagented writers. Pays 8-14% royalty on gross receipts. Offers advance based on first year saleability projections.** Publishes book 1-2 years after acceptance of ms. Accepts simultaneous submissions. Responds in 1 month to queries. Responds in 10 weeks to proposals and mss. Book catalog for 9×12 SAE and $2.13 in postage. Guidelines online.

NONFICTION Subjects include art, architecture, nature, environment, regional, interior design, cooking, business, western, outdoor/sports/recreation. Query with SASE. Submit outline, several completed chapters, author's cv. Reviews artwork/photos. Send sample illustrations, if applicable.

FICTION Only short works oriented to gift market. No novels or short stories. Submit synopsis with sample illustration.

RECENT TITLE(S) *Secrets of French Design*, by Betty Lou Phillips (nonfiction); *101 More Things to Do with a Slow Cooker*, by Stephanie Ashcraft and Janet Eyring (cookbook).

SOFT SKULL PRESS INC.

Counterpoint, 1919 Fifth St., Berkeley CA 94710. (510)704-0230. **Fax:** (510)704-0268. **E-mail:** info@ softskull.com. **Website:** www.softskull.com. Publishes hardcover and trade paperback originals. "Here at Soft Skull we love books that are new, fun, smart, revelatory, quirky, groundbreaking, cage-rattling and/ or/otherwise unusual." **Publishes 40 titles/year. Pays 7-10% royalty. Average advance: $100-15,000.** Publishes book 6 months after acceptance. Responds in 2 months to proposals; 3 months to mss. Book catalog and guidelines on website.

NONFICTION Subjects include contemporary culture, creative nonfiction, entertainment, literature, pop culture. Send a cover letter describing your project and a full proposal along with 2 sample chapters.

FICTION Subjects include comic books, confession, contemporary, erotica, experimental, gay, lesbian, literary, mainstream, multicultural, short story collections. Does not consider poetry. Soft Skull Press no longer accepts digital submissions. Send a cover letter describing your project in detail and a completed ms. For graphic novels, send a minimum of five fully inked pages of art, along with a synopsis of your storyline. "Please do not send original material, as it will not be returned."

TIPS "See our website for updated submission guidelines."

SOHO PRESS, INC.

853 Broadway, New York NY 10003. **E-mail:** soho@ sohopress.com. **Website:** www.sohopress.com. **Contact:** Bronwen Hruska, publisher; Katie Herman, editor. Mark Doten, editor Estab. 1986. Publishes hardcover and trade paperback originals; trade paperback reprints. Soho Press publishes primarily fiction, as well as some narrative literary nonfiction and mysteries set abroad. No electronic submissions, only queries by e-mail. **Publishes 60-70 titles/year. 15-25% of books from first-time authors. 10% from unagented writers. Pays 10-15% royalty on retail price (varies under certain circumstances).** Publishes book 18 months after acceptance. Accepts simultaneous submissions. Responds in 3 months. Guidelines online.

IMPRINTS Soho Press; Soho Crime; Soho Teen.

NONFICTION Subjects include creative nonfiction, ethnic, memoirs. "Independent publisher known for sophisticated fiction, mysteries set abroad, women's interest (no genre) novels and multicultural novels."

Publishes hardcover and trade paperback originals and reprint editions. Books: perfect binding; halftone illustrations. First novel print order varies. We do not buy books on proposal. We always need to see a complete ms before we buy a book, though we prefer an initial submission of 3 sample chapters. We do not publish books with color art or photographs or a lot of graphical material." No self-help, how-to, or cookbooks. Submit 3 sample chapters and a cover letter with a synopsis and author bio; SASE. Send photocopies.

FICTION Subjects include ethnic, historical, humor, literary, mystery, In mysteries, we only publish series with foreign or exotic settings, usually procedurals. Adventure, ethnic, feminist, historical, literary, mainstream/contemporary, mystery (police procedural), suspense, multicultural. Submit 3 sample chapters and cover letter with synopsis, author bio, SASE. *No e-mailed submissions.*

RECENT TITLE(S) *Murder in the Latin Quarter*, by Cara Black (mystery); *Chose By a Horse*, by Susan Richards (memoir); *Light Fell*, by Evan Fallenberg (literary fiction).

TIPS "Soho Press publishes discerning authors for discriminating readers, finding the strongest possible writers and publishing them. Before submitting, look at our website for an idea of the types of books we publish, and read our submission guidelines."

SOLAS HOUSE/TRAVELERS' TALES

2320 Bowdoin St., Palo Alto CA 94306. (650)462-2110. **Fax:** (650)462-2114. **E-mail:** submit@travelerstales.com. **Website:** www.travelerstales.com; www.besttravelwriting.com. **Contact:** James O'Reilly; Larry Habegger; Sean O'Reilly, series editors. Publishes inspirational travel books, mostly anthologies and travel advice books. **Publishes 8-10 titles/year. Pays $100 honorarium for anthology pieces.** Accepts simultaneous submissions. Guidelines online. Sponsors and operates annual Solas Awards for Best Travel Writing.

IMPRINTS Travelers' Tales; Solas House.

○ "Due to the volume of submissions, we do not respond unless the material submitted meets our immediate editorial needs. All stories are read and filed for future use contingent upon meeting editorial guidelines."

NONFICTION Subjects include all aspects of travel.

RECENT TITLE(S) *Leave the Lipstick, Take the Iguana*; *Kin to the Wind*; *Akhmed and the Atomic Matzo Balls.*

TIPS "We publish personal nonfiction stories and anecdotes—funny, illuminating, adventurous, frightening, or grim. Stories should reflect that unique alchemy that occurs when you enter unfamiliar territory and begin to see the world differently as a result. Stories that have already been published, including book excerpts, are welcome as long as the authors retain the copyright or can obtain permission from the copyright holder to reprint the material. We publish nonfiction for the most part, but in 2012 we published our first novel."

⊘ SOURCEBOOKS, INC.

P.O. Box 4410, Naperville IL 60567. (630)961-3900. **Fax:** (630)961-2168. **Website:** www.sourcebooks.com. **Contact:** Todd Stocke, VP/editorial director (nonfiction trade); Deborah Werksman (Sourcebooks Casablanca); Peter Lynch (nonfiction); Daniel Ehrenhaft (Sourcebooks Jabberwocky). Estab. 1987. Publishes hardcover and trade paperback originals. "Sourcebooks publishes many forms of fiction and nonfiction titles, including books on parenting, self-help/psychology, business, and health. Focus is on practical, useful information and skills. It also continues to publish in the reference, New Age, history, current affairs, and humor categories. Currently emphasizing gift, women's interest, history, reference, historical fiction, romance genre, and children's." **Publishes 300 titles/year. 30% of books from first-time authors. 25% from unagented writers. Pays royalty on wholesale or list price. Pays advance.** Publishes book 1 year after acceptance of ms. Accepts simultaneous submissions. Responds in 3 months to queries. Catalog and guidelines online.

IMPRINTS Sourcebooks Casablanca (romance fiction and love/relationships); Sourcebooks Hysteria (women's humor/gift book); Sourcebooks Landmark (fiction); Sourcebooks MediaFusion (multimedia); Sphinx Publishing (self-help legal); Sourcebooks Jabberwocky (children's).

NONFICTION Subjects include biography, gift book, how-to, illustrated book, multimedia, reference, self-help, business, economics, child guidance, history, military, war, money, finance, psychology, science, sports, women's issues, women's studies, contemporary culture. Books for small business owners, entrepreneurs, and students. A key to submitting books to us is to explain how your book helps the reader, why it is different from the books already out there (please do your homework), and the author's credentials for writing this book. Books likely to succeed with us are self-help, parenting and childcare, psychology, women's issues, how-to, history, reference, biography, humor, gift books, or books with strong artwork. "We seek unique books on traditional subjects and authors who are smart and aggressive." Query with SASE, 2-3 sample chapters (not the first). *No complete mss.* Reviews artwork/photos.

RECENT TITLE(S) *Child's Journey Out of Autism*, by LeAnn Whiffen; *In the Land of Invisible Women*, by Qanta Ahmed.

TIPS "Our market is a decidedly trade-oriented bookstore audience. We also have very strong penetration into the gift-store market. Books which cross over between these 2 very different markets do extremely well with us. Our list is a solid mix of unique and general audience titles and series-oriented projects. We are looking for products that break new ground either in their own areas or within the framework of our series of imprints."

⊕ SOURCEBOOKS CASABLANCA

Sourcebooks, Inc., 1935 Brookdale Rd., Naperville IL 60564. **E-mail:** romance@sourcebooks.com. **Website:** www.sourcebooks.com. **Contact:** Deb Werksman, Mary Altman, Cat Clyne. "Our romance imprint, Sourcebooks Casablanca, publishes single title romance in all subgenres." Responds in 2-3 months. Guidelines online and by e-mail (deb.werksman@sourcebooks.com). "Please allow 21 days for a response.".

● "We are actively acquiring single-title and single-title series romance fiction (90,000-100,000 words) for our Casablanca imprint. We are looking for strong writers who are excited about marketing their books and building their community of readers, and whose books have something fresh to offer in the genre of romance."

FICTION "Our editorial criteria call for: a heroine the reader can relate to, a hero she can fall in love with, a world gets created that the reader can escape into, there's a hook that we can sell within 2-3 sentences, and the author is out to build a career with us."

SOURCEBOOKS LANDMARK

Sourcebooks, Inc., 232 Madison Ave., Suite 1100, New York NY 10016. **E-mail:** editorialsubmissions@ sourcebooks.com. **Website:** www.sourcebooks.com. **Contact:** Shana Drehs, Stephanie Bowen, Deb Werksman, Anna Klenke. "Our fiction imprint, Sourcebooks Landmark, publishes a variety of commercial fiction, including specialties in historical fiction and Austenalia. We are interested first and foremost in books that have a story to tell." Responds in 2-3 months.

FICTION "We are actively acquiring contemporary, book club, and historical fiction for our Landmark imprint. We are looking for strong writers who are excited about marketing their books and building their community of readers." Submit synopsis and full ms preferred. Receipt of e-mail submissions acknowledged within 3 weeks of e-mail.

SOUTH END PRESS

P.O. Box 382132, Cambridge MA 02238. (718)874-0089. **Fax:** (800)960-0778. **E-mail:** southend@southendpress.org. **Website:** www.southendpress.org. Estab. 1977. Publishes library and trade paperback and eBook originals and reprints, in English and some Spanish. "South End Press publishes nonfiction political books with a left/feminist/antiracist perspective." **Publishes 10 titles/year. 400 queries received/year. 100 mss received/year. 30% of books from first-time authors. 95% from unagented writers. Pays 11% royalty on wholesale price. Pays occasionally $500-2,500 advance.** Publishes book 9 months after acceptance. Accepts simultaneous submissions. Responds in up to 3 months. Book catalog available free. Guidelines online.

NONFICTION Subjects include economics, environment, government, health, history, medicine, nature, philosophy, science, sociology, womens issues, womens studies, world affairs, critical ethnic studies, queer studies, disability studies, culture & media studies. Query with SASE. Submit 2 sample chapters, intro or conclusion, and annotated TOC. Reviews artwork/photos. Send photocopies.

RECENT TITLE(S) *The Revolution Will Not Be Funded: Beyond the Nonprofit Industrial Complex*, by IN-CITE! Women of Color Against Violence; *Heat: How to Stop the Planet from Burning*, by George Monbiot; *In Kashmir: Gender, Militarization and the Nation-State*, by Seema Kazi.

SOUTHERN ILLINOIS UNIVERSITY PRESS

1915 University Press Dr., SIUC Mail Code 6806, Carbondale IL 62901. (618)453-6626. **Fax:** (618)453-1221. **Website:** www.siu.edu/~siupress. **Contact:** Karl Kageff, editor-in-chief (film, regional history, rhetoric); Kristine Priddy, editor (theater, composition); Sylvia Rodrigue, executive editor (Civil War, Reconstruction); Bridget Brown, assistant editor (communication, poetry, popular culture). Estab. 1956. Publishes hardcover and trade paperback originals and reprints. Scholarly press specializes in film and theater studies, rhetoric and composition studies, American history, Civil War, regional and nonfiction trade, poetry. No fiction. Currently emphasizing film, theater and American history, especially Civil War. **Publishes 50-60 titles/year. 700 queries received/year. 300 mss received/year. 40% of books from first-time authors. 99% from unagented writers. Pays 5-10% royalty on wholesale price. Rarely offers advance.** Publishes book 1-1 1/2 years after acceptance of ms. Responds in 2 months to queries. Book catalog and ms guidelines free.

IMPRINTS Shawnee Books; Shawnee Classics (regional reprint); Crab Orchard Series in Poetry; Theater in the Americas; Studies in Rhetorics and Feminisms; Studies in Writing and Rhetoric; Civil War Campaign in the Heartland.

RECENT TITLE(S) *The Man Who Emptied Death row: Governor George Ryan and the Politics of Crime*, by James L. Merriner; *Marketing to Moviegoers: A Handbook of Strategies and Tactics*, 2nd edition, by Robert Marich; *Lincoln Lessons: Reflections on America's Greatest Leader*, ed. by Frank J. Williams and William D. Pederson; *A Rhetoric of Style*, by Barry Brummett.

SPINNER BOOKS

University Games, 2030 Harrison St., San Francisco CA 94107. (415)503-1600. **Fax:** (415)503-0085. **E-mail:** info@ugames.com. **Website:** www.ugames.com. Estab. 1985. "Spinners Books publishes books of puzzles, games and trivia." Publishes book 6 months after acceptance. Responds to queries in 3 months; mss in 2 months only if interested.

NONFICTION Picture books: games & puzzles. Query.

STACKPOLE BOOKS

5067 Ritter Rd., Mechanicsburg PA 17055. **Fax:** (717)796-0412. **E-mail:** jschnell@stackpolebooks.com. **E-mail:** kweaver@stackpolebooks.com; mallison@stackpolebooks.com; jnichols@stackpolebooks.com. **Website:** www.stackpolebooks.com. **Contact:** Judith Schnell, editorial director (outdoor sports); Mark Allison, editor (nature); Kyle Weaver, editor (regional/Pennsylvania); Jay Nichols, editor (fly fishing); Pam Hoenig, editor (crafts). Estab. 1935. Publishes hardcover and trade paperback originals, reprints, and e-books. "Stackpole maintains a growing and vital publishing program by featuring authors who are experts in their fields." **Publishes 100 titles/year. Pays industry standard advance.** Publishes book 1 year after acceptance. Responds in 1 month to queries. Catalog and guidelines online.

NONFICTION Subjects include history, military, outdoor sports. "First of all, send your query to an individual editor. The more information you can supply, the better." Reviews artwork/photos.

RECENT TITLE(S) *Band of Sisters*; *Fishing Knots*; *True Crime New Jersey*.

TIPS "Stackpole seeks well-written, authoritative mss for specialized and general trade markets. Proposals should include chapter outline, sample chapter, illustrations, and author's credentials."

STANDARD PUBLISHING

Standex International Corp., 8805 Governor's Hill Dr., Suite 400, Cincinnati OH 45249. (800)543-1353. **E-mail:** customerservice@standardpub.com. **E-mail:** adultministry@standardpub.com; ministrytochildren@standardpub.com; ministrytoyouth@standardpub.com. **Website:** www.standardpub.com. Mark Taylor, adult ministry resources; Ruth Frederick, children and youth ministry resources; Diane Stortz, family resources. Estab. 1866. Publishes resources that meet church and family needs in the area of children's ministry. Guidelines and current publishing objectives online.

RECENT TITLE(S) *Second Guessing God*, by Brian Jones; *Devotions by Dead People*, by Lynn Lusby Pratt; *My Little Good Night Storybook*, by Susan Lingo.

STANFORD UNIVERSITY PRESS

425 Broadway St., Redwood City CA 94063. (650)723-9434. **Fax:** (650)725-3457. **E-mail:** info@www.sup.org. **Website:** www.sup.org. **Contact:** Eric Brandt (Asian studies, US foreign policy, Asian-American studies); Kate Wahl (law, political science, public policy); Margo Beth Fleming (economics, finance, business). Estab. 1925. "Stanford University Press publishes scholarly books in the humanities and social sciences, along with professional books in business, economics and management science; also high-level textbooks and some books for a more general audience." **Pays variable royalty (sometimes none). Pays occasional advance.** Guidelines online.

○ Submit to specific editor.

NONFICTION Subjects include anthropology, archeology, business, economics, ethnic, studies, gay, lesbian, government, politics, history, humanities, language, literature, literary criticism, and literary theory, nature, environment, philosophy, psychology, religion, science, social sciences, sociology, political science, law, education, history and culture of China, Japan and Latin America, European history, linguistics, geology, medieval and classical studies. Query with prospectus and an outline. Reviews artwork/photos.

RECENT TITLE(S) *Culture and Public Action*; *The Sovereignty Revolution*; *Maps, Myths, and Men*.

TIPS "The writer's best chance is a work of original scholarship with an argument of some importance."

STARCHERONE BOOKS

Dzanc Books, P.O. Box 303, Buffalo NY 14201. (716)885-2726. **E-mail:** starcherone@gmail.com; publisher@starcherone.com. **Website:** www.starcherone.com. **Contact:** Ted Pelton, publisher; Carra Stratton, acquisitions editor. Estab. 2000. Non-profit publisher of literary and experimental fiction. Publishes paperback originals and reprints. Books: acid-free paper; perfect bound; occasional illustrations. Average print order: 1,000. Average first novel print order: 1,000. **Published 2 debut authors within the last year.** Member CLMP. Titles distributed through website, Small Press Distribution, Amazon, independent bookstores. **Pays 10-12.5% royalty.** Publishes book 18 months after acceptance. Responds in 2 months to queries; 6-10 months to mss. Catalog and guidelines online.

FICTION Accepts queries by mail or e-mail during August and September of each year. Submissions of unsolicited mss will risk being returned or discarded, unread. Include brief bio, list of publishing credits. Always query before sending ms.

RECENT TITLE(S) Published *Quinnehtukqut,* by Joshua Harmon (debut author, novel); *Hangings*, by Nina Shope (debut author, short stories); *My Body in Nine Parts*, by Raymond Federman (experimental).

TIPS "During the late summer/early fall each year, after our contest has concluded, we have an open consideration period of approximately 6 weeks. During this time, we read queries from authors who already have established their credentials in some way, generally through prior publication, awards, and the like. We ask for queries from writers describing their projects and their writing credentials. From these, we invite submissions. Our next period for receiving queries will be in the late summer/early fall."

STEEL TOE BOOKS

Department of English, Western Kentucky University, 1906 College Heights Blvd. #11086, Bowling Green KY 42101. (270)745-5769. **E-mail:** tom.hunley@wku.edu. **Website:** www.steeltoebooks.com. **Contact:** Dr. Tom C. Hunley, director. Estab. 2003. Steel Toe Books publishes "full-length, single-author poetry collections. Our books are professionally designed and printed. We look for workmanship (economical use of language, high-energy verbs, precise literal descriptions, original figurative language, poems carefully arranged as a book); a unique style and/or a distinctive voice; clarity; emotional impact; humor (word plays, hyperbole, comic timing); performability (a Steel Toe poet is at home on the stage as well as on the page)." Does not want "dry verse, purposely obscure language, poetry by people who are so wary of being called 'sentimental' they steer away from any recognizable human emotions, poetry that takes itself so seriously that it's unintentionally funny." Has published poetry by Allison Joseph, Susan Browne, James Doyle, Martha Silano, Mary Biddinger, John Guzlowski, Jeannine Hall Gailey, and others. Publishes 1-3 poetry books/year. Mss are normally selected through open submission.

POETRY "Check the website for news about our next open reading period." Book mss may include previously published poems. Responds to mss in 3 months. Pays $500 advance on 10% royalties and 10 author's copies. Order sample books by sending $12 to Steel Toe Books. *Must purchase a ms in order to submit.* See website for submission guidelines.

STEMMER HOUSE PUBLISHERS

4 White Brook Rd., P.O. Box 89, Gilsum NH 03448. (800)345-6665. **Fax:** (603)357-2073. **E-mail:** pbs@stemmer.com; editor@stemmer.com. **Website:** www.stemmer.com. Estab. 1975. **Pays advance.** Publishes book 1-2 years after acceptance. Accepts simultaneous submissions. Book catalog for 5 1/2x8 1/2 envelope and 2 first-class stamps. Guidelines for #10 SASE.

IMPRINTS The International Design Library®; The NatureEncyclopedia Series.

NONFICTION Subjects include animals, arts, multicultural, nature, environment. Query with SASE.

STENHOUSE PUBLISHERS

480 Congress St., Portland ME 04101. **E-mail:** editors@stenhouse.com. **Website:** www.stenhouse.com. **Contact:** Jill Cooley, editorial assistant. Estab. 1993. Publishes paperback originals. Stenhouse publishes exclusively professional books for teachers, K-12. **Publishes 15 titles/year. 300 queries received/year. 30% of books from first-time authors. 99% from unagented writers. Pays royalty on wholesale price.** Accepts simultaneous submissions. Responds in 2 weeks to queries; 1 month to mss. Book catalog free or online. Guidelines online.

NONFICTION Subjects include education, specializing in literary with offerings in elementary and middle level math and science. All of our books are a combination of theory and practice. No children's books or student texts. Query by e-mail (preferred) or SASE. Reviews artwork/photos. Send photocopies.

RECENT TITLE(S) *Write Like This*, by Kelly Gallagher; *So What Do They Really Know?*, by Cris Tovani; *Opening Minds*, by Peter Johnston.

STERLING PUBLISHING CO., INC.

387 Park Ave. S., 11th Floor, New York NY 10016. (212)532-7160. **Fax:** (212)981-0508. **E-mail:** ragis@sterlingpublishing.com. **E-mail:** info@sterlingpublishing.com. **Website:** www.sterlingpublishing.com. Brett Duquette Publishes hardcover and paperback originals and reprints. "Sterling publishes highly illustrated, accessible, hands-on, practical books for adults and children." **15% of books from first-time authors. Pays royalty or work purchased outright. Offers advances (average amount: $2,000).** Accepts simultaneous submissions. Catalog online. Guidelines online.

IMPRINTS Sterling/Books; Sterling/Ethos; Lark; Sterling/Children's; Sterling/Epicure; Ecosystem; Puzzlewright Press; Union Square Press; Ecosystem; Sandy Creek; Sterling/Innovation; Fall River Press; Metro Books; Flashkids; Quamut; Silver Lining Calendars; Hearst Books.

○ "Our mission is to publish high-quality books that educate, entertain, and enrich the lives of our readers."

NONFICTION Subjects include alternative, animals, art, architecture, ethnic, gardening, health, medicine, hobbies, New Age, recreation, science, sports, fiber arts, games and puzzles, children's humor, children's science, nature and activities, pets, wine, home decorating, dolls and puppets, ghosts, UFOs, woodworking, crafts, medieval, Celtic subjects, alternative health and healing, new consciousness. Proposals on subjects such as crafting, decorating, outdoor living, and photography should be sent directly to Lark Books at their Asheville, North Carolina offices. Complete guidelines can be found on the Lark site: www.larkbooks.com/submissions. Publishes nonfiction only. Submit outline, publishing history, 1 sample chapter (typed and double-spaced), SASE. "Explain your idea. Send sample illustrations where applicable. For children's books, please submit full mss. We do not accept electronic (e-mail) submissions. Be sure to include information about yourself with particular regard to your skills and qualifications in the subject area of your submission. It is helpful for us to know your publishing history—whether or not you've written other books and, if so, the name of the publisher and whether those books are currently in print." Reviews artwork/photocopies.

FICTION "At present we do not accept fiction."

RECENT TITLE(S) *AARP Crash Course in Estate Planning*, by Michael Palermo and Ric Edelman.

TIPS "We are primarily a nonfiction activities-based publisher. We have a picture book list, but we do not publish chapter books or novels. Our list is not trend-driven. We focus on titles that will backlist well. "

STIPES PUBLISHING LLC

P.O. Box 526, Champaign IL 61824. (217)356-8391. **Fax:** (217)356-5753. **E-mail:** stipes01@sbcglobal.net. **Website:** www.stipes.com. **Contact:** Benjamin H. Watts, (engineering, science, business); Robert Watts (agriculture, music, and physical education). Estab. 1925. Publishes hardcover and paperback originals. "Stipes Publishing is oriented towards the education market and educational books with some emphasis in the trade market." **Publishes 15-30 titles/year. 50% of books from first-time authors. 95% from unagented writers. Pays 15% maximum royalty on re-**tail price. Publishes book 4 months after acceptance. Responds in 2 months to queries. Guidelines online.

NONFICTION Subjects include agriculture, business, economics, music, dance, nature, environment, recreation, science. "All of our books in the trade area are books that also have a college text market. No books unrelated to educational fields taught at the college level." Submit outline, 1 sample chapter.

RECENT TITLE(S) *Keyboard Musicianship: Piano For Adults, Book One, 9th edition* by James Lyke, *et. al; Manual Of Woody Landscape Plants, 6th edition*, by Michael Dirr; *Health Ethics*, by John M. Charles.

STONE BRIDGE PRESS

P.O. Box 8208, Berkeley CA 94707. **E-mail:** sbp@stonebridge.com. **Website:** www.stonebridge.com. **Contact:** Peter Goodman, publisher. Estab. 1989. "Independent press focusing on books about Japan and Asia in English (business, language, culture, literature, animation)." Publishes hardcover and trade paperback originals. Books: 60-70 lb. offset paper; web and sheet paper; perfect bound; some illustrations. Distributes titles through Consortium. Promotes titles through Internet announcements, special-interest magazines and niche tie-ins to associations. **Publishes 12 titles/year. 75% from unagented writers. Pays royalty on wholesale price.** Publishes book 2 years after acceptance. Responds to queries in 4 months; mss in 8 months. Book catalog for 2 first-class stamps and SASE. Ms guidelines online.

FICTION Experimental, gay/lesbian, literary, Japan-themed. "Primarily looking at material relating to Japan. Translations only." Does not accept unsolicited mss. Query with SASE. Accepts queries by e -mail, fax.

TIPS "Fiction translations only for the time being. No poetry."

STONESLIDE BOOKS

Stoneslide Media LLC, P.O. Box 8331, New Haven CT 06530. **E-mail:** editors@stoneslidecorrective.com. **E-mail:** submissions@stoneslidecorrective.com. **Website:** www.stoneslidecorrective.com. **Contact:** Jonathan Weisberg, editor; Christopher Wachlin, editor. Estab. 2012. Publishes trade paperback and electronic originals. **Publishes 3-5 titles/year. Receives 300 queries/year; 150 mss/year. Pays 20-80% royalty.** Publishes book 8 months after acceptance. Responds in 1-2 months. Book catalog and guidelines online.

FICTION Subjects include adventure, contemporary, experimental, fantasy, gothic, historical, humor, literary, mainstream, mystery, science fiction, short story collections, suspense. "We will look at any genre. The importatn factor for us is that the story use plot, characters, emotions, and other elements of storytelling to think and move the mind forward." Submit proposal package via e-mail including: synopsis and 3 sample chapters.

RECENT TITLE(S) *Shock to Equilibrium*, by Jonathan T.F. Weisberg (thriller); *Red Mask Stories*, by B. Clim (fantasy).

TIPS "Read the Stoneslide Corrective to see if your work fits with our approach."

STOREY PUBLISHING

210 MASS MoCA Way, North Adams MA 01247. (800)793-9396. **Fax:** (413)346-2196. **E-mail:** webmaster@storey.com. **Website:** www.storey.com. **Contact:** Deborah Balmuth, editorial director (building, sewing, gift). Estab. 1983. Publishes hardcover and trade paperback originals and reprints. "The mission of Storey Publishing is to serve our customers by publishing practical information that encourages personal independence in harmony with the environment. We seek to do this in a positive atmosphere that promotes editorial quality, team spirit, and profitability. The books we select to carry out this mission include titles on gardening, small-scale farming, building, cooking, homebrewing, crafts, part-time business, home improvement, woodworking, animals, nature, natural living, personal care, and country living. We are always pleased to review new proposals, which we try to process expeditiously. We offer both work-for-hire and standard royalty contracts." **Publishes 40 titles/year. 600 queries received/year. 150 mss received/year. 25% of books from first-time authors. 60% from unagented writers. We offer both work-for-hire and standard royalty contracts. Pays advance.** Publishes book 2 years after acceptance. Accepts simultaneous submissions. Responds in 1 month to queries; 3 months to proposals/mss. Book catalog available free. Guidelines online.

NONFICTION Subjects include animals, gardening, nature, environment, home, mind/body/spirit, birds, beer and wine, crafts, building, cooking. Reviews artwork/photos.

RECENT TITLE(S) *The Veggie Gardener's Answer Book*, by Barbara W. Ellis; *The Home Creamery*, by Kathy Farrell-Kingsley; *Happy Dog, Happy You*, by Arden Moore.

STRATEGIC MEDIA BOOKS

782 Wofford St., Rock Hill SC 29730. (803)366-5440. **E-mail:** contactstrategicmediabooks.com. **Website:** strategicmediabooks.com. **Contact:** Ron Chepesiuk, president. Estab. 2010. Publishes hardcover, trade paperback, and electronic originals. "Strategic Media Books, LLC is an independent U.S. publisher that aims to bring extraordinary true-life stories to the widest possible audience. Founded in 2010, Strategic Media Books intends to be one of the most energetic and hard-hitting nonfiction publishers in the business. While we currently specialize in true crime, we plan to expand and publish great books in any nonfiction genre." **Publishes 16-20 titles/year. 100 queries received/year. 30-35 mss received/year. 20% of books from first-time authors. 85% from unagented writers. Authors receive 15-20% royalty on retail price.** Publishes book 8-9 months after acceptance. Accepts simultaneous submissions. Responds in 1 month to queries, 1 month to proposals, and 2 months on mss. Catalog is free on request, send #10 SASE. Also online. Guidelines available for free by e-mail.

NONFICTION Subjects include Americana, contemporary culture, environment, ethnic, government, history, memoirs, military, multicultural, nature, politics, regional, war, world affairs, True Crime. Planning to increase the number of books for the 2014 and 2015 seasons. Query with SASE. Will review artwork. Writers should send photocopies.

FICTION Subjects include mystery, suspense. "We are very selective in our publication of fiction. If writers want to submit, make sure mss fits the mystery or suspense genres." Query with SASE.

RECENT TITLE(S) *Diary of a Motor City Hit Man: The Chester Wheeler Campbell Story*, by Christian Cipolliani (True Crime); *Wild Times in Skidaway Island*, by Karen Dove Barr (Nature); *Liberating Iraq: The Untold Story of the Assyrian Christains*, by Amire George (Government/Politics); *The Gospel According to Prissy*, by Barbara Casey (Mystery)

SUBITO PRESS

University of Colorado at Boulder, Dept. of English, 226 UCB, Boulder CO 80309-0226. **E-mail:** subitopressucb@gmail.com. **Website:** www.subitopress.org. Publishes trade paperback originals. Subito Press is a non-profit publisher of literary works. Each year Subito publishes one work of fiction and one work of poetry through its contest. Accepts simultaneous submissions. Guidelines online.

FICTION Subjects include experimental, literary, translation. Submit complete ms to contest.

POETRY Submit complete ms to contest.

TIPS "We publish 2 books of innovative writing a year through our poetry and fiction contests. All entries are also considered for publication with the press."

SUN BOOKS / SUN PUBLISHING

P.O. Box 5588, Santa Fe NM 87502. (505)471-5177. **E-mail:** info@sunbooks.com. **Website:** www.sunbooks.com. **Contact:** Skip Whitson, director. Estab. 1973. Publishes trade paperback originals and reprints. **Publishes 10-15 titles/year. 5% of books from first-time authors. 90% from unagented writers. Pays 5% royalty on retail price. Occasionally makes outright purchase.** Publishes book 16-18 months after acceptance. "Will respond within 2 months, via e-mail, to queries if interested.". Book catalog online. Queries via e-mail only, please.

NONFICTION , self-help, leadership, motivational, recovery, inspirational.

RECENT TITLE(S) *Eight Pillars of Prosperity*, by James Allen; *Ambition and Success*, by Orson Swett Marden; *Cheerfulness as a Life Power*, by Orson Swett Marden.

SUNBURY PRESS, INC.

P.O. Box 548, Boiling Springs PA 17007. **E-mail:** info@sunburypress.com. **E-mail:** proposals@sunburypress.com. **Website:** www.sunburypress.com. Estab. 2004. Publishes trade paperback originals and reprints; electronic originals and reprints. **Publishes 75 titles/year. 750 queries/year; 500 mss/year. 40% of books from first-time authors. 90% from unagented writers. Pays 10% royalty on wholesale price.** Publishes book 3 months after acceptance. Accepts simultaneous submissions. Responds in 2 months. Catalog and guidelines online.

○ "Please use our online submission form."

NONFICTION Subjects include Americana, animals, anthropology, archeology, architecture, art, astrology, business, career guidance, child guidance, communications, computers, contemporary culture, counseling, crafts, creative nonfiction, dance, economics, education, electronics, entertainment, ethnic, government, health, history, hobbies, house and home, humanities, language, literature, memoirs, military, money, multicultural, music, nature, New Age, photography, regional, religion, science, sex, spirituality, sports, transportation, travel, war, world affairs, young adult. "We are currently seeking Civil War era memoirs and unpublished or new material regarding the Civil War. We are also seeking biographies / histories of local/regional figures who were noteworthy but unpublished or sparsely published." Reviews artwork.

FICTION Subjects include adventure, confession, contemporary, ethnic, experimental, fantasy, gothic, historical, horror, humor, juvenile, mainstream, military, multicultural, mystery, occult, picture books, poetry, regional, religious, romance, science fiction, short story collections, spiritual, sports, suspense, western, young adult. "We are especially seeking historical fiction regarding the Civil War and books of regional interest."

POETRY Submit complete ms.

RECENT TITLE(S) *Amelia Earhart: The Truth at Last*, by Mike Campbell (biography); *Teen Mom Prom*, by Tammy Berberick (self-help); *The Lurking Man*, by Keith Rommel (horror).

TIPS "Our books appeal to very diverse audiences. We are building our list in many categories, focusing on many demographics. We are not like traditional publishers—we are digitally adept and very creative. Don't be surprised if we move quicker than you are accustomed to!"

SUNRISE RIVER PRESS

39966 Grand Ave., North Branch MN 55056. (800)895-4585. **Fax:** (651)277-1203. **E-mail:** editorial@sunriverpress.com. **Website:** www.sunriverpress.com. Estab. 1992. "E-mail is preferred method of contact." **Publishes 30 titles/year. Pays advance.** Accepts simultaneous submissions. Guidelines online.

○ Sunrise River Press is part of a 3-company publishing house that also includes CarTech Books and Specialty Press. "Sunrise River Press is currently seeking book proposals from health/medical writers or experts who are interested in authoring consumer-geared trade paperbacks on healthcare, fitness, and nutrition topics."

NONFICTION Subjects include cooking, foods, nutrition, health, medicine, genetics, immune system maintenance, fitness; also some professional healthcare titles. Check website for submission guidelines. No phone calls, please; no originals.

FICTION "Although we don't solicit article-length mss, short humour contributions or jokes are welcome." Submit online at: www2.readersdigest.ca/laugh_submit.html.

SUPERCOLLEGE

2713 Newlands Ave., Belmont CA 94002. Phone/**Fax:** (650)618-2221. **E-mail:** supercollege@supercollege. com. **Website:** www.supercollege.com. Estab. 1998. Publishes trade paperback originals. "We only publish books on admission, financial aid, scholarships, test preparation, student life, and career preparation for college and graduate students." **Publishes 8-10 titles/year. 50% of books from first-time authors. 70% from unagented writers. Pays royalty on wholesale price or makes outright purchase.** Publishes book 7-9 months after acceptance. Book catalog and writers guidelines online.

NONFICTION Subjects include education, admissions, financial aid, scholarships, test prep, student life, career prep. Submit complete ms. Reviews artwork/photos. Send photocopies.

RECENT TITLE(S) *The Ultimate Scholarship Book*; *How to Write a Winning Scholarship Essay*.

TIPS "We want titles that are student and parent friendly, and that are different from other titles in this category. We also seek authors who want to work with a small but dynamic and ambitious publishing company."

SWAN ISLE PRESS

P.O. Box 408790, Chicago IL 60640. (773)728-3780. **E-mail:** info@swanislepress.com. **Website:** www. swanislepress.com. Estab. 1999. Publishes hardcover and trade paperback originals. **Publishes 3 titles/year. 1,500 queries received/year. Pays 7 1/2-10% royalty on wholesale price.** Publishes book 18 months after acceptance. Responds in 6 months to queries; 12 months to mss. Catalog and guidelines online.

🖉 *"We do not accept unsolicited mss."*

NONFICTION Subjects include art, architecture, creative nonfiction, ethnic, history, humanities, language, literature, literary criticism, memoirs, multicultural, translation. Query with SASE. Submit complete mss only if author receives affirmative response to query. Reviews artwork/photos. Send photocopies.

FICTION Subjects include ethnic, historical, literary, multicultural, poetry, poetry in translation, short story collections, translation. Query with SASE. Submit complete mss.

POETRY Query and submit complete ms.

RECENT TITLE(S) *Sebastian's Arrows: Letters and Mementos of Salvador Dalí and Federico Garcia Lora*, Edited, translated with Prologue by Christopher Maurer; *Malambo*, by Lucía Charan Illescas.

SWAN SCYTHE PRESS

1468 Mallard Way, Sunnyvale CA 94087. **E-mail:** robert.pesich@gmail.com. **Website:** www.swanscythe. com. **Contact:** Robert Pesich, editor. Estab. 1999.

POETRY "After publishing 25 chapbooks, a few full-sized poetry collections, and 1 anthology, then taking a short break from publishing, Swan Scythe Press is now re-launching its efforts with some new books, under a new editorship. We have also begun a new series of books, called Poetas/Puentes, from emerging poets writing in Spanish, translated into English. We will also consider mss in indigenous languages from North, Central and South America, translated into English." Query first before submitting a ms via e-mail or through website.

SWEDENBORG FOUNDATION

320 N. Church St., West Chester PA 19380. (610)430-3222. **Fax:** (610)430-7982. **E-mail:** editor@swedenborg.com. **Website:** www.swedenborg.com. **Contact:** Lisa Lapp, editor. Estab. 1849. Publishes trade paperback originals and reprints. The Swedenborg Foundation publishes books by and about Emanuel Swedenborg (1688-1772), his ideas, how his ideas have influenced others, and related topics. Appropriate topics include Swedenborgian concepts, such as: near-death experience, angels, Biblical interpretation, mysteries of good and evil, etc. A work must actively engage the thought of Emanuel Swedenborg and show an understanding of his philosophy in order to be accepted for publication. **Publishes 5 titles/year.** Responds in 1 month to queries. Responds in 3 months to proposals and mss. Book catalog available free. Guidelines online.

NONFICTION Subjects include philosophy, psychology, religion, science. Query with SASE. Submit proposal package, outline, sample chapters, synopsis. "I personally prefer e-mail." Reviews artwork/photos. Send photocopies.

RECENT TITLE(S) *Our Life After Death*, by Emanuel Swedenborg; *The Lives of Angels*, by Emanuel Swedenborg; *12 Miracles of Spiritual Growth*, by E. Kent Rogers.

SYLVAN DELL PUBLISHING

612 Johnnie Dodds, Suite A2, Mt. Pleasant SC 29464. (843)971-6722. **Fax:** (843)216-3804. **E-mail:** katie-hall@sylvanpublishing.com. **E-mail:** donnagerman@sylvandellpublishing.com. **Website:** www.sylvandell-publishing.com. **Contact:** Donna German and Katie Hall, editors. Estab. 2004. Publishes hardcover, trade paperback, and electronic originals. "The picture books we publish are usually, but not always, fictional stories that relate to animals, nature, the environment, math, and science. All books should subtly convey an educational theme through a warm story that is fun to read and that will grab a child's attention. Each book has a 3-5 page '*For Creative Minds*' section to reinforce the educational component. This section will have a craft and/or game as well as 'fun facts' to be shared by the parent, teacher, or other adult. Authors do not need to supply this information. Mss. should be less than 1,500 words and meet all of the following 4 criteria: Fun to read—mostly fiction with nonfiction facts woven into the story; National or regional in scope; Must tie into early elementary school curriculum; must be marketable through a niche market such as a zoo, aquarium, or museum gift shop." **Publishes 20 titles/year. 2,000 mss received/year. 50% of books from first-time authors. 100% from unagented writers. Pays 6-8% royalty on wholesale price. Pays small advance.** Publishes book 18 months after acceptance. May hold onto mss of interest for 1 year until acceptance. after acceptance of ms. Accepts simultaneous submissions. Acknowledges receipt of ms submission within 1 week. Book catalog and Guidelines online.

NONFICTION Subjects include science, math. "We are not looking for mss. about: pets (dogs or cats in particular); new babies; local or state-specific; magic; biographies; history-related; ABC books; poetry; series; young adult books or novels; holiday-related books. We do not consider mss. that have been previously published in any way, including e-books or self-published." Accepts electronic submissions only. Snail mail submissions are discarded without being opened. Reviews artwork/photos. Send 1-2 JPEGS.

FICTION Subjects include picture books. Picture books: animal, folktales, nature/environment, math-related. Word length—picture books: no more than 1,500. Accepts electronic submissions only. Snail mail submissions are discarded without being opened.

RECENT TITLE(S) *The Shape Family Babies*, by Kristin Haas, illustrated by Shennen Bersani; *Balloon Trees*, by Dana Smith, illustrated by Laurie Allen Klein; *The Great Divide*, by Suzanne Slade, illustrated by Erin Hunter.

TIPS "Please make sure that you have looked at our website to read our complete submission guidelines and to see if we are looking for a particular subject. Mss must meet all four of our stated criteria. We look for fairly realistic, bright and colorful art-no cartoons. We want the children excited about the books. We envision the books being used at home and in the classroom."

SYNERGEBOOKS

948 New Highway 7, Columbia TN 38401. (863)956-3015. **Fax:** (863)588-2198. **E-mail:** synergebooks@aol.com. **Website:** www.synergebooks.com. **Contact:** Debra Staples, publisher/acquisitions editor. Estab. 1999. Publishes trade paperback and electronic originals. "SynergEbooks is first and foremost a digital publisher, so most of our marketing budget goes to those formats. Authors are required to direct-sell a minimum of 100 digital copies of a title before it's accepted for print." **Publishes 40-60 titles/year. 250 queries received/year. 250 mss received/year. 95% of books from first-time authors. 99.9% from unagented writers. Pays 15-40% royalty; makes outright purchase.** Accepts simultaneous submissions. Book catalog and guidelines online.

NONFICTION Subjects include New Age, philosophy, spirituality, travel, young adult. Submit proposal package, 1-3 sample chapters. Reviews artwork/photos. Send JPEG via attached mail.

FICTION Subjects include fantasy, historical, horror, humor, mainstream, contemporary, military, magic, mystery, philosophy, poetry, religious, romance, science fiction, short story collections, spiritual, suspense, western, young adult, and audio books. SynergEbooks publishes at least 40 new titles a year, and only 1-5 of those are put into print in any given year. "SynergEbooks is first and foremost a digital publisher, so most of our marketing budget goes to those formats. Authors are required to direct-sell a minimum of 100 digital copies of a title before it's accepted for print." Submit proposal package, including synopsis, 1-3 sample chapters, and marketing plans.

POETRY Anthologies must be a unique topic or theme. Query and submit 1-5 sample poems.

RECENT TITLE(S) *A Talent to Deceive*, by William Norris (True Crime); *LOBO: The Strange Life of William Jameson*, by John H. Manhold (Historical Fiction); *Lucky Dog: The True Story of a Little Mexico Street Dog Who Goes International* (Travel/Humor).
TIPS "At SynergEbooks, we work with the author to promote their work."

SYRACUSE UNIVERSITY PRESS

621 Skytop Rd., Suite 110, Syracuse NY 13244. (315)443-5534. **Fax:** (315)443-5545. **E-mail:** seguiod@syr.edu; dhmccay@syr.edu; jsbaines@syr.edu. **Website:** syracuseuniversitypress.syr.edu. **Contact:** Suzanne Guiod, editor-in-chief; Deanna McCay, acquisitions editor; Jennika Baines, acquisitions editor. Estab. 1943. "Currently emphasizing Middle East studies, Jewish studies, Irish studies, peace studies, disability studies, television and popular culture, sports and entertainment, Native American studies, gender and ethnic studies, New York State." **Publishes 50 titles/year. 25% of books from first-time authors. 95% from unagented writers.** Publishes book 15 months after acceptance. Catalog and guidelines online.
NONFICTION "Special opportunity in our nonfiction program for books on New York state, sports history, Jewish studies, Irish studies, the Middle East, religion and politics, television, and popular culture, disability studies, peace studies, Native American studies. Provide precise descriptions of subjects, along with background description of project. The author must make a case for the importance of his or her subject." Submit query via e-mail with the book proposal form found on our website and a copy of your CV. Reviews artwork/photos.
RECENT TITLE(S) *Walking Seasonal Roads*, by M. Hood; *Memory Ireland, Volume 2: Diaspora and Memory Practices*, edited by O. Frawley; *Collaborative Dubliners: Joyce in Dialogue*, edited by V. Mahaffey.
TIPS "We're seeking well-written and thoroughly researched books that will make a significant contribution to the subject areas listed above and will be favorably received in the marketplace."

🌑 TAFELBERG PUBLISHERS

Imprint of NB Publishers, P.O. Box 879, Cape Town 8000, South Africa. (27)(21)406-3033. **Fax:** (27)(21)406-3812. **E-mail:** kristin@nb.co.za. **Website:** www.tafelberg.com. **Contact:** Danita van Romburgh, editorial secretary; Louise Steyn, publisher. General publisher best known for Afrikaans fiction, authoritative political works, children's/youth literature, and a variety of illustrated and nonillustrated nonfiction. **Publishes 10 titles/year. Pays authors royalty of 15-18% based on wholesale price.** Publishes book 1 year after acceptance. Responds to queries in 2 weeks; mss in 6 months.
NONFICTION Subjects include health, medicine, memoirs, politics. Submit outline, information on intended market, bio, and 1-2 sample chapters.
FICTION Subjects include juvenile, romance. Picture books, young readers: animal, anthology, contemporary, fantasy, folktales, hi-lo, humor, multicultural, nature/environment, scient fiction, special needs. Middle readers, young adults: animal (middle reader only), contemporary, fantasy, hi-lo, humor, multicultural, nature/environment, problem novels, science fiction, special needs, sports, suspense/mystery. Average word length: picture books—1,500-7,500; young readers—25,000; middle readers—15,000; young adults—40,000. Submit complete ms.
RECENT TITLE(S) *Switch on Your Brain*, by Caroline Leaf (nonfiction); *How Many?*, by Ann Walton (children's); *Boomplaats*, by Gilbert Gibson (fiction).
TIPS "Writers: Story needs to have a South African or African style. Illustrators: I'd like to look, but the chances of getting commissioned are slim. The market is small and difficult. Do not expect huge advances. Editorial staff attended or plans to attend the following conferences: IBBY, Frankfurt, SCBWI Bologna."

🅐⊘ NAN A. TALESE

Imprint of Doubleday, Random House, Inco,, 1745 Broadway, New York NY 10019. (212)782-8918. **Fax:** (212)782-8448. **Website:** www.nanatalese.com. **Contact:** Nan A. Talese, publisher and editorial director; Ronit Feldman, assistant editor. Publishes hardcover originals. Nan A. Talese publishes nonfiction with a powerful guiding narrative and relevance to larger cultural interests, and literary fiction of the highest quality. **Publishes 15 titles/year. 400 queries received/year. 400 mss received/year. Pays variable royalty on retail price. Pays varying advance.**
NONFICTION Subjects include contemporary culture, history, philosophy, sociology. Agented submissions only.
FICTION Subjects include literary. Well-written narratives with a compelling story line, good characterization and use of language. We like stories with an edge. Agented submissions only.

RECENT TITLE(S) *Saturday*, by Ian McEwan; *Albion: The Origins of the English Imagination*, by Peter Ackroyd; *Oryx and Crake*, by Margaret Atwood.

TIPS "Audience is highly literate people interested in story, information and insight. We want well-written material submitted by agents only. See our website."

⊘ TANGLEWOOD BOOKS

P.O. Box 3009, Terre Haute IN 47803. **E-mail:** ptierney@tanglewoodbooks.com. **Website:** www.tanglewoodbooks.com. **Contact:** Kairi Hamlin, acquisitions editor; Peggy Tierney, publisher. Estab. 2003. "Tanglewood Press strives to publish entertaining, kid-centric books." **Publishes 10 titles/year. 20% of books from first-time authors.** Publishes book 2 years after acceptance. Accepts simultaneous submissions. Responds to mss in up to 18 months. Guidelines online.

FICTION Picture books: adventure, animal, concept, contemporary, fantasy, humor. Average word length: picture books—800. Not currently accepting submissions.

RECENT TITLE(S) *68 Knots*, by Micheal Robert Evans (young adult); *The Mice of Bistrot des Sept Freres*, written and illustrated by Marie Letourneau; *Chester Raccoon and the Acorn Full of Memories*, by Audrey Penn and Barbara Gibson.

TIPS "Please see lengthy 'Submissions' page on our website."

⊕ TANTOR MEDIA

2 Business Park Road, Old Saybrook CT 06475. (860)395-1155. **Fax:** (860)395-1154. **E-mail:** rightsemail@tantor.com. **Website:** www.tantor.com. **Contact:** Ron Formica, director of acquisitions. Estab. 2001. Publishes hardcover, trade paperback, mass market paperback, and electronic originals and reprints. Also publishes audiobooks. Tantor is a leading indepedent audiobook publisher, producing more than 50 new titles every month. **Publishes 600 titles/year. 50% of books from first-time authors. 50% from unagented writers. Pays 5-15% royalty on wholesale price.** Publishes book 3 months after acceptance. Accepts simultaneous submissions. Responds in 2 months to queries, proposals, and mss. Catalog online.

NONFICTION Subjects include agriculture, alternative lifestyles, Americana, animals, anthropology, astrology, business, child guidance, communications, contemporary culture, cooking, creative nonfiction, economics, education, entertainment, foods, games, gay, government, health, history, horticulture, law, lesbian, literary criticism, marine subjects, memoirs, military, money, multicultural, music, New Age, philosophy, psychology, religion, science, sex, social sciences, sociology, spirituality, sports, womens issues, womens studies, world affairs, young adult. Query with SASE, or submit proposal package, including outline and 3 sample chapters.

FICTION Subjects include adventure, contemporary, erotica, experimental, fantasy, feminist, gay, gothic, historical, horror, humor, juvenile, lesbian, literary, mainstream, military, multicultural, multimedia, mystery, occult, religious, romance, science fiction, short story collections, spiritual, sports, suspense, western, young adult. Query with SASE, or submit proposal package including synopsis and 3 sample chapters.

JEREMY P. TARCHER, INC.

Imprint of Penguin Group (USA), Inc., 375 Hudson St., New York NY 10014. (212)366-2000. **Website:** www.penguin.com. **Contact:** Mitch Horowitz, editor-in-chief; Sara Carder, senior editor. Estab. 1972. Publishes hardcover and trade paperback originals and reprints. "Tarcher's vision is to publish ideas and works about human consciousness that are large enough to include all aspects of human experience." **Publishes 40-50 titles/year. 1,000 queries received/year. 1,000 mss received/year. 20% of books from first-time authors. 20% from unagented writers. Pays royalty. Pays advance.** Accepts simultaneous submissions.

NONFICTION Subjects include health, medicine, nature, environment, philosophy, psychology, religion, Eastern and Western religions, metaphysics. Query with SASE.

RECENT TITLE(S) *Catching the Big Fish*, by David Lynch; *The Writing Diet*, by Julia Cameron; *Zolz*, by Daniel Pinchbeck.

TIPS "Our audience seeks personal growth through books. Understand the imprint's focus and categories."

TARPAULIN SKY PRESS

P.O. Box 189, Grafton VT 05146. **E-mail:** editors@tarpaulinsky.com. **Website:** www.tarpaulinsky.com. **Contact:** Colie Collen, editor-in-chief. Estab. 2006. Tarpaulin Sky Press publishes cross- and trans-genre works as well as innovative poetry and prose. Produces full-length books and chapbooks, hand-bound books and trade paperbacks, and offers both hand-bound and perfect-bound paperback editions of full-length books. "We're a small, author-centered press endeavoring to create books that, as objects, please our authors as much their texts please us."

POETRY Writers whose work has appeared in or been accepted for publication in *Tarpaulin Sky* may submit chapbook or full-length mss at any time, with no reading fee. Tarpaulin Sky Press also considers chapbook and full-length mss from writers whose work has not appeared in the journal, but **asks for a $20 reading fee**. Make checks/money orders to Tarpaulin Sky Press. Cover letter is preferred. Reads periods may be found on the website.

TAYLOR TRADE PUBLISHING

The Rowman & Littlefield Publishing Group, 5360 Manhattan Circle, #101, Boulder CO 80303. (303)543-7835. **Fax:** (303)543-0043. **E-mail:** tradeeditorial@rowman.com. **Website:** www.rowman.com/taylortrade. **Contact:** Acquisitions Editor. Publishes hardcover originals, trade paperback originals and reprints. Taylor Trade Publishing does not publish fiction or poetry. "Proposals from institutions such as museums or galleries pertaining to their collections are strongly encouraged." **Publishes 70 titles/year. 15% of books from first-time authors. 65% from unagented writers.** Publishes book 1 year after acceptance of ms. after acceptance of ms. Responds in 2 months to queries. See catalog online. Submission guidelines online.

NONFICTION Subjects include art, child guidance, cooking, entertainment, gardening, history, nature, regional, sports. "Proposals should be limited to a query letter; an e-mail will generate the quickest response. If querying by e-mail, please note in the memo box 'book proposal.' Send no attachments unless requested. If using postal mail, query with SASE. What we look for at this stage is suitability of the proposed book to our publishing program (see categories) as well as the author's unique qualifications for writing his or her book."

⊘ TEBOT BACH

P.O. Box 7887, Huntington Beach CA 92615. (714)968-0905. **E-mail:** info@tebotbach.org. **Website:** www.tebotbach.org. **Contact:** Mifanwy Kaiser, editor/publisher. Publishes book Publishes mss 2 years after acceptance. Responds in 3 months.

POETRY Offers 2 contests per year. The Patricia Bibby First Book Contest and The Clockwise Chapbook contest. Go to www.tebotbach.org and www.spillway.org for further information on programs and guidelines for submission. Query first via e-mail, with a few sample poems and cover letter with brief bio.

RECENT TITLE(S) *One Breath*, by Catharine Clark-Sayles, *Monkey Journal,* by Holly Prado; *Swagger and Remorse* by Richard Fox.

TEMPLE UNIVERSITY PRESS

1852 N. 10th St., Philadelphia PA 19122. (215)926-2140. **Fax:** (215)926-2141. **E-mail:** tempress@temple.edu. **Website:** www.temple.edu/tempress/. **Contact:** Alex Holzman, director; Janet Francendese, editor-in-chief; Micah Kleit, executive editor. Estab. 1969. "Temple University Press has been publishing path-breaking books on Asian-Americans, law, gender issues, film, women's studies and other interesting areas for nearly 40 years." **Publishes 60 titles/year. Pays advance.** Publishes book 10 months after acceptance. Responds in 2 months to queries. Book catalog available free. Guidelines online.

NONFICTION Subjects include ethnic, government, politics, health, medicine, history, photography, regional, Philadelphia, sociology, labor studies, urban studies, Latin American/Latino, Asian American, African American studies, public policy, women's studies. No memoirs, fiction or poetry. Query with SASE. Reviews artwork/photos.

RECENT TITLE(S) *From Black Power to Hip Hop*, by Patricia Hill Collins; *Pictures From A Drawer: Prison and the Art of Portraiture*, by Bruce Jackson.

♦ TEN SPEED PRESS

The Crown Publishing Group, Attn: Acquisitions, 2625 Alcatraz Ave. #505, Berkeley CA 94705. (510)559-1600. **Fax:** (510)524-1052. **E-mail:** crown-biz@randomhouse.com. **Website:** crownpublishing.com/imprint/ten-speed-press. Estab. 1971. Publishes trade paperback originals and reprints. "Ten Speed Press publishes authoritative books for an audience interested in innovative ideas. Currently emphasizing cookbooks, career, business, alternative education, and offbeat general nonfiction gift books." **Publishes 120 titles/year. 40% of books from first-time authors. 40% from unagented writers. Pays $2,500 average advance.** Publishes book 1 year after acceptance. Accepts simultaneous submissions. Responds in 3 months to queries; 6-8 weeks to proposals. Book catalog for 9×12 envelope and 6 first-class stamps. Guidelines online.

NONFICTION Subjects include business, career guidance, cooking, crafts, relationships, how-to, humor, and pop culture. No fiction. "Please read our submission guidelines online. Before submitting your ms, you should first familiarize yourself with our publishing areas and imprints. Note that we do not consider certain genres, including fiction, poetry, memoir, and most photography." Agented submissions only.

RECENT TITLE(S) *How to Be Happy, Dammit*, by Karen Salmansohn; *The Bread Baker's Apprentice*, by Peter Reinhart.

TIPS "We like books from people who really know their subject, rather than people who think they've spotted a trend to capitalize on. We like books that will sell for a long time, rather than 9-day wonders. Our audience consists of a well-educated, slightly weird group of people who like food, the outdoors, and take a light, but serious, approach to business and careers. Study the backlist of each publisher you're submitting to and tailor your proposal to what you perceive as their needs. Nothing gets a publisher's attention like someone who knows what he or she is talking about, and nothing falls flat like someone who obviously has no idea who he or she is submitting to."

TEXAS TECH UNIVERSITY PRESS

P.O. Box 41037, 3003 15th St., Suite 901, Lubbock TX 79409. (806)834-5821. **Fax:** (806)742-2979. **E-mail:** joanna.conrad@ttu.edu. **Website:** www.ttupress.org. **Contact:** Joanna Conrad, editor-in-chief. Estab. 1971. Texas Tech University Press, the book publishing office of the university since 1971 and an AAUP member since 1986, publishes nonfiction titles in the areas of natural history and the natural sciences; 18th century and Joseph Conrad studies; studies of modern Southeast Asia, particularly the Vietnam War; costume and textile history; Latin American literature and culture; and all aspects of the Great Plains and the American West, especially history, biography, memoir, sports history, and travel. In addition, the Press publishes several scholarly journals, acclaimed series for young readers, an annual invited poetry collection, and literary fiction of Texas and the West. Guidelines online.

NONFICTION Subjects include environment, ethnic, history, law, literary criticism, literature, regional, sports. Submit proposal that includes introduction, 2 sample chapters, cover letter, working title, anticipated ms length, description of audience, comparison of book to others published on the subject, brief bio or CV.

FICTION Subjects include ethnic, multicultural, religious, western. Fiction rooted in the American West and Southwest, Jewish literature, Latin American and Latino fiction (in translation or English).

POETRY "TTUP publishes an annual invited first-book poetry ms (please note that we cannot entertain unsolicited poetry submissions)."

⊘ TEXAS WESTERN PRESS

The University of Texas at El Paso, 500 W. University Ave., El Paso TX 79968. (915)747-5688. **Fax:** (915)747-5345. **E-mail:** twpress@utep.edu; ctavarez@utep.edu. **Website:** twp.utep.edu. **Contact:** Carmen P. Tavarez. Estab. 1952. Publishes hardcover and paperback originals. "Texas Western Press publishes books on the history and cultures of the American Southwest, particularly historical and biographical works about West Texas, New Mexico, northern Mexico, and the U.S. borderlands. The Press also publishes selected books in the areas of regional art, photography, Native American studies, geography, demographics, border issues, politics, and natural history." **Publishes 1 titles/year. Pays standard 10% royalty. Pays advance.** Responds in 2 months to queries. Book catalog available free. Guidelines online.

IMPRINTS Southwestern Studies.

NONFICTION Subjects include education, health, medicine, history, language, literature, nature, environment, regional, science, social sciences. "Historic and cultural accounts of the Southwest (West Texas, New Mexico, northern Mexico). Also art, photographic books, Native American and limited regional fiction reprints. Occasional technical titles. Our *Southwestern Studies* use mss of up to 30,000 words. Our hardback books range from 30,000 words and up. The writer should use good exposition in his work. Most of our work requires documentation. We favor a scholarly, but not overly pedantic, style. We specialize in superior book design." Not currently seeking mss.

RECENT TITLE(S) *Jose Cisneros Immigrant Artist*, by John O. West; *Showtime! From Opera Houses to Picture Palaces in El Paso*, by Cynthia Farah Haines.

TIPS "Texas Western Press is interested in books relating to the history of Hispanics in the US. Will experiment with photo-documentary books, and is interested in seeing more contemporary books on border issues. We try to treat our authors professionally, produce handsome, long-lived books and aim for quality, rather than quantity of titles carrying our imprint."

⊕ THISTLEDOWN PRESS LTD.

401 2nd Ave., Saskatoon SK S7K 2C3, Canada. (306)244-1722. **Fax:** (306)244-1762. **E-mail:** editorial@thistledownpress.com. **Website:** www.thistledownpress.com. **Contact:** Allan Forrie, publisher. **Pays authors royalty of 10-12% based on net dollar sales. Pays illustrators and photographers by the project (range: $250-750).** Publishes book 1 year after acceptance. Responds to queries in 4 months. Book catalog free on request. Guidelines available for #10 envelope and IRC.

○ "Thistledown originates books by Canadian authors only, although we have co-published titles by authors outside Canada. We do not publish children's picture books."

FICTION Middle readers, young adults: adventure, anthology, contemporary, fantasy, humor, poetry, romance, science fiction, suspense/mystery, short stories. Average word length: young adults—40,000. Submit outline/synopsis and sample chapters. *Does not accept mss.* Do not query by e-mail.

POETRY "We do not publish cowboy poetry, inspirational poetry, or poetry for children."

TIPS "Send cover letter including publishing history and SASE."

⊕ THOMSON CARSWELL

One Corporate Plaza 2075 Kennedy Rd., Toronto ON M1T 3V4, Canada. (416)298-5024. **Fax:** (416)298-5094. **Website:** www.carswell.com. **Contact:** Robert Freeman, vice president, legal, accounting and finance, and corporate groups. Publishes hardcover originals. "Thomson Carswell is Canada's national resource of information and legal interpretations for law, accounting, tax and business professionals." **Publishes 150-200 titles/year. 30-50% of books from first-time authors. Pays 5-15% royalty on wholesale price.** Publishes book 6 months after acceptance of ms. Accepts simultaneous submissions. Responds in 3 months to queries. Book catalog and ms guidelines free.

NONFICTION Canadian information of a regulatory nature is our mandate. Submit proposal package, outline, résumé.

TIPS "Audience is Canada and persons interested in Canadian information; professionals in law, tax, accounting fields; business people interested in regulatory material."

TIA CHUCHA PRESS

P.O. Box 328, San Fernando CA 91341. **E-mail:** info@tiachucha.com. **Website:** www.tiachucha.com. **Contact:** Luis Rodriguez, director. Estab. 1989. Publishes hardcover and trade paperback originals. Tia Chucha's Centro Cultural is a nonprofit learning and cultural arts center. "We support and promote the continued growth, development and holistic learning of our community through the many powerful means of the arts. Tia Centra provides a positive space for people to activate what we all share as humans: the capacity to create, to imagine and to express ourselves in an effort to improve the quality of life for our community." **Publishes 2-4 titles/year. 25-30 queries received/year. 150 mss received/year. Pays 10% royalty on wholesale price.** Publishes book 1 year after acceptance. Responds in 9 months to mss. Guidelines online.

POETRY No restrictions as to style or content. "We only publish poetry at this time. We do cross-cultural and performance-oriented poetry. It has to work on the page, however." Query and submit complete ms.

TIPS "We will cultivate the practice. Audience is those interested."

⊕⊘ TIGHTROPE BOOKS

602 Markham St., Toronto ON M6G 2L8, Canada. (647)348-4460. **E-mail:** tightropeasst@gmail.com. **E-mail:** info@tightropebooks.com. **Website:** www.tightropebooks.com. **Contact:** Shirarose Wilensky, editor. Estab. 2005. Publishes hardcover and trade paperback originals. **Publishes 12 titles/year. 70% of books from first-time authors. 100% from unagented writers. Pays 5-15% royalty on retail price. Pays advance of $200-300.** Publishes book 1 year after acceptance. Accepts simultaneous submissions. Responds if interested. Catalog and guidelines online.

○ Accepting submissions for new mystery imprint, Mysterio.

NONFICTION Subjects include alternative lifestyles, architecture, art, contemporary culture, creative nonfiction, ethnic, gay, language, lesbian, literary criticism, literature, multicultural, womens issues.

FICTION Subjects include contemporary, ethnic, experimental, fantasy, feminist, gay, horror, juvenile, lesbian, literary, mainstream, multicultural, poetry,

poetry in translation, short story collections, translation, young adult.

RECENT TITLE(S) *She's Shameless: Women write about growing up, rocking out and fighting back*, editing by Stacey May Fowles and Megan Griffith-Greene (anthology); *Wrong Bar*, by Nathaniel G. Moore (experimental, post-modern novel); *Contents of a Mermaid's Purse*, by Phoebe Tsang (lyric poetry; debut collection).

TIPS "Audience is young, urban, literary, educated, unconventional."

TILBURY HOUSE

Wordsplice Studio, Inc., Tilbury House Publishers, 12 Starr Street, Thomaston ME 04861. (800)582-1899. **Fax:** (207)582-8227. **E-mail:** tilbury@tilburyhouse. com. **Website:** www.tilburyhouse.com. **Contact:** Karen Fisk, associate children's book editor; Jonathan Eaton, publisher. Estab. 1990. **Publishes 10 titles/year. Pays royalty based on wholesale price.** Publishes book 1 year after acceptance. Responds to mss in 2 months. Book catalog available free. Guidelines online.

NONFICTION Regional adult biography/history/maritime/nature, and children's picture books that deal with issues, such as bullying, multiculturalism, etc. Submit complete ms or outline/synopsis. Reviews artwork/photos. Send photocopies.

FICTION Picture books: multicultural, nature/environment. Special needs include books that teach children about tolerance and honoring diversity. Recently published *The Eye of the Whale*, by Jennifer O'Connell, illustrated by Jennifer O'Connell; *The Secret Pool*, by Kimberly Ridley, illustrated by Rebekah Raye Submit complete ms or outline/synopsis.

RECENT TITLE(S) *Unplugged*, by Laura Pedersen; *Say Something* 10th Anniversary Edition, by Peggy Moss; *The Eye of the Whale*, by Jennifer O'Connell; *The Secret Pool*, by Kimberly Ridley

TIPS "We are always interested in stories that will encourage children to understand the natural world and the environment, as well as stories with social justice themes. We really like stories that engage children to become problem solvers as well as those that promote respect, tolerance and compassion." We do not publish books with personified animal characters; historical fiction; chapter books; fantasy."

TIMBERLINE PRESS

5710 S. Kimbark #3, Chicago IL 60637. **E-mail:** timberline@vacpoetry.org. **Website:** vacpoetry.org/timberline. Estab. 1975. "Since January 2011, Timberline Press (founded by Clarence Wolfshohl in 1975) has been the fine press imprint of Virtual Artists Collective. We print chapbooks—usually poetry—usually 20-30 pages, hand bound, limited editions of 50-100. We generally print no more than 2 or 3 books a year."

"Please note that we are not currently accepting new submissions."

TIN HOUSE BOOKS

2617 NW Thurman St., Portland OR 97210. (503)473-8663. **Fax:** (503)473-8957. **E-mail:** meg@tinhouse. com. **Website:** www.tinhouse.com. **Contact:** Meg Storey, editor; Tony Perez, editor; Masie Cochran, associate editor. Publishes hardcover originals, paperback originals, paperback reprints. "We are a small independent publisher dedicated to nurturing new, promising talent as well as showcasing the work of established writers. Our Tin House New Voice series features work by authors who have not previously published a book." Distributes/promotes titles through Publishers Group West. **Publishes 10-12 titles/year. 20% from unagented writers.** Publishes book 1 year after acceptance. Accepts simultaneous submissions. Responds to queries in 2-3 weeks; mss in 2-3 months. Guidelines online.

NONFICTION *Agented mss only.* We no longer read unsolicited submissions by authors with no representation. We will continue to accept submissions from agents.

FICTION *Agented mss only.* We no longer read unsolicited submissions by authors with no representation. We will continue to accept submissions from agents.

RECENT TITLE(S) *Glaciers*, by Alexis Smith; *American Dream Machine*, by Matthew Specktor; *The Celestials*, by Karen Shepard.

TITAN PRESS

PMB 17897, Encino CA 91416. **E-mail:** titan91416@ yahoo.com. **Website:** www.calwriterssfv.com. **Contact:** Stefanya Wilson, editor. Estab. 1981. Publishes hardcover and paperback originals. **Publishes 12 titles/year. 50% from unagented writers. Pays 20-40% royalty.** Publishes book 1 year after acceptance. Responds to queries in 3 months. Ms guidelines for #10 SASE.

FICTION Literary, mainstream/contemporary, short story collections. Published *Orange Messiahs*, by Scott Sonders (fiction). Does not accept unsolicited mss. Query with SASE. Include brief bio, social security number, list of publishing credits.

TIPS "Look, act, sound, and *be* professional."

⊘ TOP COW PRODUCTIONS, INC.

3812 Dunn Dr., Culver City CA 90232. **Website:** www. topcow.com.

FICTION *No unsolicited submissions.* Prefers submissions from artists. See website for details and advice on how to break into the market.

TOP PUBLICATIONS, LTD.

12221 Merit Dr., Suite 950, Dallas TX 75251. (972)628-6414. **Fax:** (972)233-0713. **E-mail:** info@toppub.com. **E-mail:** submissions@toppub.com. **Website:** www. toppub.com. Estab. 1999. Publishes hardcover and paperback originals. Primarily a mainstream fiction publisher. **Publishes 2-3 titles/year. 200 queries received/year. 20 mss received/year. 90% of books from first-time authors. 95% from unagented writers. Pays 15% royalty on wholesale price. Pays $250-$1,000 advance.** Publishes book 6 months after acceptance. Accepts simultaneous submissions. Acknowledges receipt of queries but only responds if interested in seeing ms. Responds in 6 months to mss. Guidelines online.

○ "It is imperative that our authors realize they will be required to promote their book extensively for it to be a success. Unless they are willing to make this commitment, they shouldn't submit to TOP."

FICTION Subjects include adventure, contemporary, historical, horror, juvenile, military, mystery, regional, romance, science fiction, short story collections, suspense, young adult.

RECENT TITLE(S) *Unconscionable: A Rich Coleman Novel,* by William Manchee; *Ghosts of Malhado,* by H.J. Ralles; *Crime Montage,* by Patricia L. Morin.

TIPS "We recommend that our authors write books that appeal to a large mainstream audience to make marketing easier and increase the chances of success. We only publish a few titles a year so the odds at getting published at TOP are slim. If we don't offer you a contract it doesn't mean we didn't like your submission. We have to pass on a lot of good material each year simply by the limitations of our time and budget."

⊘ TOR BOOKS

175 Fifth Ave., New York NY 10010. **Website:** www. tor-forge.com. **Contact:** Juliet Pederson, publishing coordinator. Susan Change, senior editor **Publishes Publishes 5-10 middle readers/year; 5-10 young adult titles/year. titles/year. Pays author royalty. Pays illustrators by the project.** Book catalog available for 9x12 SAE and 3 first-class stamps. See website for latest submission guidelines.

IMPRINTS Forge, Orb, Starscape, Tor Teen.

○ Tor Books is the "world's largest publisher of science fiction and fantasy, with strong category publishing in historical fiction, mystery, western/Americana, thriller, YA."

NONFICTION Middle readers and young adult: geography, history, how-to, multicultural, nature/environment, science, social issues. Does not want to see religion, cooking. Average word length: middle readers—25,000-35,000; young adults—70,000.

FICTION Subjects include Middle readers, young adult titles: adventure, animal, anthology, concept, contemporary, fantasy, history, humor, multicultural, nature/environment, problem novel, science fiction, suspense/mystery. Average word length: middle readers—30,000; young adults—60,000-100,000. "We do not accept queries."

RECENT TITLE(S) *Hidden Talents, Flip*, by David Lubar (ages 10 and up, fantasy); *Briar Rose*, by Jane Yolen (ages 12 and up).

TIPS "Know the house you are submitting to, familiarize yourself with the types of books they are publishing. Get an agent. Allow him/her to direct you to publishers who are most appropriate. It saves time and effort."

TORQUERE PRESS

1380 Rio Rancho Blvd., #1319, Rio Rancho NM 87124. **E-mail:** editor@torquerepress.com. **E-mail:** submissions@torquerepress.com. **Website:** www.torquere-press.com. **Contact:** Shawn Clements, submissions editor (homoerotica, suspense, gay/lesbian); Lorna Hinson, senior editor (gay/lesbian romance, historicals). Estab. 2003. Publishes trade paperback originals and electronic originals and reprints. "We are a gay and lesbian press focusing on romance and genres of romance. We particularly like paranormal and western romance." **Publishes 140 titles/year. 500 queries received/year. 200 mss received/year. 25% of books from first-time authors. 100% from unagented writ-**

ers. **Pays 8-40% royalty. Pays $35-75 for anthology stories.** Publishes book 6 months after acceptance. Responds in 1 month to queries and proposals; 2-4 months to mss. Catalog and guidelines online.

IMPRINTS Top Shelf (Shawn Clements, editor); Single Shots (Kil Kenny, editor); Screwdrivers (M. Rode, editor); High Balls (Vincent Diamond, editor).

FICTION Subjects include adventure, erotica, gay, lesbian, historical, horror, mainstream, contemporary, multicultural, mystery, occult, romance, science fiction, short story collections, suspense, western. All categories gay and lesbian themed. Submit proposal package, 3 sample chapters, clips.

RECENT TITLE(S) *Filet Gumbo* by B.A. Tortuga (contemporary romance); *X-Factor*, by Sean Michael (contemporary romance).

TIPS "Our audience is primarily people looking for a familiar romance setting featuring gay or lesbian protagonists. Please read guidelines carefully and familiarize yourself with our lines."

TORREY HOUSE PRESS, LLC

2806 Melony Dr., Salt Lake City UT 84124. (801)810-9THP. **E-mail:** mark@torreyhouse.com. **Website:** torreyhouse.com. **Contact:** Mark Bailey, publisher. Estab. 2010. Publishes hardcover, trade paperback, and electronic originals. "Torrey House Press (THP) publishes literary fiction and creative nonfiction about the world environment with a tilt toward the American West. Want submissions from experienced and agented authors only." **Publishes 10 titles/year. 500 queries/year; 200 mss/year. 80% of books from first-time authors. 80% from unagented writers. Pays 5-15% royalty on retail price.** Publishes book 6-12 months after acceptance. Accepts simultaneous submissions. Responds in 3 months. Catalog online. Guidelines online.

NONFICTION Subjects include anthropology, creative nonfiction, environment, nature. Query; submit proposal package, including: outline, ms, bio. Does not review artwork.

FICTION Subjects include historical, literary. "Torrey House Press publishes literary fiction and creative nonfiction about the world environment and the American West." Submit proposal package including: synopsis, complete ms, bio.

POETRY Query; submit complete ms.

TIPS "Include writing experience (none okay)."

☼ TOUCHWOOD EDITIONS

The Heritage Group, 103-1075 Pendergast St., Victoria BC V8V 0A1, Canada. (250)360-0829. **Fax:** (250)386-0829. **E-mail:** edit@touchwoodeditions.com. **Website:** www.touchwoodeditions.com. Ruth Linka Publishes trade paperback originals and reprints. **Publishes 20-25 titles/year. 40% of books from first-time authors. 70% from unagented writers. Pays 15% royalty on net price.** Publishes book 12-24 months after acceptance. Accepts simultaneous submissions. Responds in 3 months to queries. Book catalog and submission guidelines online.

NONFICTION Subjects include anthropology, archeology, art, architecture, creative nonfiction, government, politics, history, nature, environment, recreation, regional, nautical. Submit TOC, outline, word count, 2-3 sample chapters, synopsis. Reviews artwork/photos. Send photocopies.

FICTION Subjects include historical, mystery. Submit TOC, outline, word count.

RECENT TITLE(S) *Somebody's Child: Stories About Adoption*, edited by Lynne Van Luven and Bruce Gillespie; *Cravings: Comfort Eats and Favourite Treats*, by Debbie Harding; *The End of the Line*, by Stephen Legault.

TIPS "Our area of interest is Western Canada. We would like more creative nonfiction and books about people of note in Canada's history."

TOWER PUBLISHING

588 Saco Rd., Standish ME 04084. (207)642-5400. **Fax:** (207)642-5463. **E-mail:** info@towerpub.com. **Website:** www.towerpub.com. **Contact:** Michael Lyons, president. Estab. 1772. Publishes hardcover originals and reprints, trade paperback originals. Tower Publishing specializes in business and professional directories and legal books. **Publishes 22 titles/year. 60 queries received/year. 30 mss received/year. 10% of books from first-time authors. 90% from unagented writers.** Publishes book 6 months after acceptance. Accepts simultaneous submissions. Responds in 1 month to queries; 2 months to proposals and mss. Book catalog and ms guidelines online.

NONFICTION Subjects include business, economics. Looking for legal books of a national stature. Query with SASE. Submit outline.

⊘ TOY BOX PRODUCTIONS

7532 Hickory Hills Ct., Whites Creek TN 37189. (615)299-0822. **Fax:** (615)876-3931. **E-mail:** toybox@

crttoybox.com. **Website:** www.crttoybox.com. Estab. 1995. Publishes mass market paperback originals. **Publishes 4 titles/year. 100% of books from first-time authors. 100% from unagented writers. Pays 10-15% royalty on wholesale price.** Book catalog online.

◯   We are not accepting new submissions at this time.

NONFICTION Subjects include audio, Americana, education, religion. *All unsolicited mail returned unopened.*

RECENT TITLE(S) *Rosa Parks: Not Giving In*, by James Collins; *The Legend Of Pocahontas & Captain John Smith*, by Joe Loesch.

☼ TRADEWIND BOOKS

202-1807 Maritime Mews, Granville Island, Vancouver BC V6H 3W7, Canada. (604)662-4405. **E-mail:** tradewindbooks@mail.lycos.com. **Website:** www.tradewindbooks.com. **Contact:** Michael Katz, publisher; Carol Frank, art director; R. David Stephens, senior editor. Publishes hardcover and trade paperback originals. "Tradewind Books publishes juvenile picture books and young adult novels. Requires that submissions include evidence that author has read at least 3 titles published by Tradewind Books." **Publishes 5 titles/year. 15% of books from first-time authors. 50% from unagented writers. Pays 7% royalty on retail price. Pays variable advance.** Publishes book 3 years after acceptance. Accepts simultaneous submissions. Responds to mss in 2 months. Book catalog and ms guidelines online.

FICTION Subjects include juvenile, picture books. Picture books: adventure, multicultural, folktales. Average word length: 900 words. Send complete ms for picture books. *YA novels by Canadian authors only. Chapter books by US authors considered.*

POETRY Please send a book-length collection only.

RECENT TITLE(S) *Zig Zag*, by Robert San Souci, illustrated by Stefan Czernecki; *Pacific Seashores*, by Marja Dion Westman, illustrated by George Juharz; *Bamboo*, by Paul Yee, illustrated by Shaoli Wang.

TRAFALGAR SQUARE BOOKS

P.O. Box 257, 388 Howe Hill Road, North Pomfret VT 05053. (802)457-1911. **Website:** www.horseandrider-books.com. **Contact:** Martha Cook, managing director; Rebecca Didier, senior editor. Estab. 1985. Publishes hardcover and trade paperback originals. "We publish high quality instructional books for horsemen and horsewomen, always with the horse's welfare in mind." **Publishes 12 titles/year. 50% of books from first-time authors. 80% from unagented writers. Pays royalty. Pays advance.** Publishes book 18 months after acceptance. Responds in 1 month to queries, 2 months to proposals, 2-3 months to mss. Catalog free on request and by e-mail.

NONFICTION Subjects include animals, horses/dogs. "We rarely consider books for complete novices." Query with SASE. Submit proposal package including outline, 1-3 sample chapters, letter of introduction including qualifications for writing on the subject and why the proposed book is an essential addition to existing publications. Reviews artwork/photos as part of the ms package. We prefer color laser thumbnail sheets or duplicate prints (do not send original photos or art!).

RECENT TITLE(S) *The Rider's Pain-Free Back*, by James Warson; *The Ultimate Horse Behavior and Training Book*, by Linda Tellington-Jones.

TIPS "Our audience is horse lovers and riders interested in doing what is best in the interest of horses."

TRISTAN PUBLISHING

2355 Louisiana Ave. N, Golden Valley MO 55427. (763)545-1383. **Fax:** (763)545-1387. **E-mail:** info@tristanpublishing.com or mss@tristanpublishing.com. **Website:** www.tristanpublishing.com. **Contact:** Brett Waldman, publisher. Estab. 2002. Publishes hardcover originals. **Publishes 6-10 titles/year. 1,000 queries and mss/year. 15% of books from first-time authors. 100% from unagented writers. Pays royalty on wholesale or retail price; outright purchase.** Publishes book 2 years after acceptance. Accepts simultaneous submissions. Responds in 3 months. Catalog and guidelines online.

IMPRINTS Tristan Publishing; Waldman House Press; Tristan Outdoors.

NONFICTION , inspirational. "Our mission is to create books with a message that inspire and uplift in typically 1,000 words or less." Query with SASE; submit completed mss. Reviews artwork/photos; send photocopies.

FICTION , inspirational, gift books. Query with SASE; submit completed mss.

RECENT TITLE(S) *Paw Prints in the Stars*, by Warren Hanson (gift book); *An Imperfect Life*, and *I'm Not Too Busy* by Jodi Hills (gift books).

TIPS "Our audience is adults and children."

TRIUMPH BOOKS

814 N. Franklin St., Chicago IL 60610. (312)939-3330; (800)335-5323. **Fax:** (312)663-3557. **Website:** www.triumphbooks.com. **Contact:** Tom Bast, editorial director. Estab. 1990. Publishes hardcover originals and trade paperback originals and reprints. Accepts simultaneous submissions. Book catalog available free.

IMPRINTS Triumph Entertainment (pop culture, current events).

NONFICTION Subjects include recreation, sports, health, sports business/motivation. Query with SASE. Reviews artwork/photos. Send photocopies.

RECENT TITLE(S) *Laker Girl* by Jeannie Buss, *The Golden Jet* by Bobby Hull, *The Fire Within* by Jim Taylor.

TRUMAN STATE UNIVERSITY PRESS

100 E. Normal Ave., Kirksville MO 63501. (660)785-7336. **Fax:** (660)785-4480. **E-mail:** tsup@truman.edu. **Website:** tsup.truman.edu. **Contact:** Barbara Smith-Mandell, copy editor/acquisitions editor; Judith Sharp, production editor; Janet Blohm Pultz, director/editor-in-chief. Estab. 1986. Truman State University Press (TSUP) publishes peer-reviewed research in the humanities for the scholarly community and the broader public, and publishes creative literary works. Guidelines online.

NONFICTION , contemporary nonfiction, early modern, American studies, poetry. Submit book ms proposals in American Studies to Barbara Smith-Mandell, at bsm@truman.edu; nonfiction to Monica Barron at tsupnonfiction@truman.edu; early modern studies to wolfem1@stjohns.edu.

TUPELO PRESS

P.O. Box 1767, North Adams MA 01247. (413)664-9611. **E-mail:** publisher@tupelopress.org. **E-mail:** www.tupelopress.org/submissions. **Website:** www.tupelopress.org. **Contact:** Jeffrey Levine, publish/editor-in-chief; Elyse Newhouse, associate publisher; Jim Schley, managing editor. Estab. 2001. "We're an independent nonprofit literary press. We accept book-length poetry, poetry collections (48+ pages), short story collections, novellas, literary nonfiction/memoirs and up to 80 pages of a novel." Guidelines online.

NONFICTION Subjects include memoirs. No cookbooks, children's books, inspirational books, graphic novels, or religious books. **Charges $45 reading fee.**

FICTION Subjects include poetry, short story collections, Novels. "For Novels—submit no more than 100 pages along with a summary of the entire book. If we're interested we'll ask you to send the rest. We accept very few works of prose (1 or 2 per year)." Submit complete ms. **Charges a $45 reading fee.**

POETRY "Our mission is to publish thrilling, visually and emotionally and intellectually stimulating books of the highest quality, inside and out. We want contemporary poetry, etc. by the most diverse list of emerging and established writers in the U.S." Submit complete ms. **Charges $28 reading fee.**

RECENT TITLE(S) *After the Gold Rush*, by Lewis Buzbee (fiction); *The Animal gospels*, by Brian Barker (poetry); *Invitation to a Secret Feast*, by Joumana Haddad.

○ TURNSTONE PRESS

206-100 Arthur St., Winnipeg MB R3B 1H3, Canada. (204)947-1555. **Fax:** (204)942-1555. **E-mail:** info@turnstonepress.com. **E-mail:** editor@turnstonepress.com. **Website:** www.turnstonepress.com. Estab. 1976. "Turnstone Press is a literary publisher, not a general publisher, and therefore we are only interested in literary fiction, literary nonfiction—including literary criticism—and poetry. We do publish literary mysteries, thrillers, and noir under our Ravenstone imprint. We publish only Canadian authors or landed immigrants, we strive to publish a significant number of new writers, to publish in a variety of genres, and to have 50% of each year's list be Manitoba writers and/or books with Manitoba content." Publishes book 2 years after acceptance. Responds in 4-7 months. Guidelines online.

NONFICTION "Samples must be 40 to 60 pages, typed/printed in a minimum 12 point serif typeface such as Times, Book Antiqua, or Garamond."

FICTION "Samples must be 40 to 60 pages, typed/printed in a minimum 12 point serif typeface such as Times, Book Antiqua, or Garamond."

POETRY Poetry mss should be a minimum 70 pages. Submit complete ms. Include cover letter.

TIPS "As a Canadian literary press, we have a mandate to publish Canadian writers only. Do some homework before submitting works to make sure your subject matter/genre/writing style falls within the publishers area of interest."

TURN THE PAGE PUBLISHING LLC

P.O. Box 3179, Upper Montclair NJ 07043. **E-mail:** rlentin@turnthepagepublishing.com. **E-mail:** inquiry@turnthepagepublishing.com. **Website:** www.turnthepagepublishing.com. **Contact:** Roseann Lentin, editor-in-chief; Ann Kolakowski, editor. Estab. 2009. Publishes hardcover, trade paperback, electronic originals and trade paperback, electronic reprints. **Publishes 12-15 titles/year. Receives 100 queries/year; 50 mss/year. 95% of books from first-time authors. 100% from unagented writers. Pays 8-15% royalty on retail price.** Publishes book 8 months after acceptance. Accepts simultaneous submissions. Responds in 2-3 months. Book catalog online. Guidelines by e-mail.

NONFICTION Subjects include alternative lifestyles, Americana, animals, astrology, child guidance, cooking, creative nonfiction, finance, foods, memoirs, military, money, New Age, parenting, spirituality, war, womens studies, young adult. Submit proposal package including outline, 3 sample chapters, author bio. Reviews artwork. Send photocopies.

FICTION Subjects include contemporary, humor, juvenile, literary, mainstream, military, picture books, spiritual, suspense, war, young adult. "We like new, fresh voices who are not afraid to 'step outside the box,' with unique ideas and storylines. We prefer 'edgy' rather than 'typical.'" Submit proposal package including synopsis and 3 sample chapters.

RECENT TITLE(S) *The Only Buddha in Town,* by Alanna Maure; *Cinderella's Housework: Families in Crisis, Households at the Edge of Chaos!,* by Paul Meinhardt; *Fate, Love, Tears,* by Lauren Bishop.

TIPS "Our audience is made up of intelligent, sophisticated, forward-thinking, progressive readers, who are not afraid to consider reading something different to Turn the Page of their lives. We're an independent publisher, we're avant-garde, so if you're looking for run of the mill, don't submit here."

TUTTLE PUBLISHING

364 Innovation Dr., North Clarendon VT 05759. (802)773-8930. **Fax:** (802)773-6993. **E-mail:** submissions@tuttlepublishing.com. **Website:** www.tuttlepublishing.com. Estab. 1832. Publishes hardcover and trade paperback originals and reprints. Tuttle is America's leading publisher of books on Japan and Asia. **Publishes 125 titles/year. 1,000 queries received/year. 20% of books from first-time authors. 40% from unagented writers. Pays 5-10% royalty on net or retail price, depending on format and kind of book. Pays advance.** Publishes book 18 months after acceptance. Accepts simultaneous submissions. Responds in 2-3 months to proposals.

"Familiarize yourself with our catalog and/or similar books we publish. Send complete book proposal with cover letter, table of contents, 1-2 sample chapters, target audience description, SASE. No e-mail submissions."

NONFICTION Query with SASE.

RECENT TITLE(S) *The Complete Book of Sushi*, by Hideo Dekura, Brigid Treloar, and Ryuichi Yoshii; *Aikido Basics*, by Phong Thong Dany and Lynn Seiser; *Contemporary Asian Kitchens and Dining Rooms*, by Chami Jotisalikorn and Karina Zabihi.

TWILIGHT TIMES BOOKS

P.O. Box 3340, Kingsport TN 37664. **E-mail:** publisher@twilighttimesbooks.com. **Website:** www.twilighttimesbooks.com. **Contact:** Andy M. Scott, managing editor. Estab. 1999. "We publish compelling literary fiction by authors with a distinctive voice." Published 5 debut authors within the last year. Averages 120 total titles; 15 fiction titles/year. Member: AAP, PAS, SPAN, SLF. **90% from unagented writers. Pays 8-15% royalty.** Responds in 4 weeks to queries; 2 months to mss. Guidelines online.

FICTION Accepts unsolicited mss. Do not send complete mss. Queries via e-mail only. Include estimated word count, brief bio, list of publishing credits, marketing plan.

RECENT TITLE(S) *Equity of Evil*, by Rudy Mazzocchi; *The Coal Elf*, by Maria DeVivo; *The Nameless Prince*, by Dominick Domingo; *The Patriot Spy*, by S. W. O'Connell.

TIPS "The only requirement for consideration at Twilight Times Books is that your novel must be entertaining and professionally written."

TYNDALE HOUSE PUBLISHERS, INC.

351 Executive Dr., Carol Stream IL 60188. (800)323-9400. **Fax:** (800)684-0247. **Website:** www.tyndale.com. **Contact:** Katara Washington Patton, acquisitions; Talinda Iverson, art acquisitions. Estab. 1962. Publishes hardcover and trade paperback originals and mass paperback reprints. "Tyndale House publishes practical, user-friendly Christian books for the home and family." **Publishes 15 titles/year. Pays negotiable royalty. Pays negotiable advance.** Accepts simultaneous submissions. Guidelines online.

NONFICTION Subjects include child guidance, religion, devotional/inspirational.

FICTION Subjects include juvenile, romance, Christian (children's, general, inspirational, mystery/suspense, thriller, romance). "Christian truths must be woven into the story organically. No short story collections. Youth books: character building stories with Christian perspective. Especially interested in ages 10-14. We primarily publish Christian historical romances, with occasional contemporary, suspense, or standalones." Agented submissions only. No unsolicited mss.

RECENT TITLE(S) *Danzig Passage*, by Bodie & Brock Thoene; *Croutons for Breakfast*, by Lissa Halls Johnson and Kathy Wierenga; *Stolen Secrets*, by Jerry B. Jenkins and Chris Fabry.

TIPS "All accepted mss will appeal to Evangelical Christian children and parents."

⊕ TYRUS BOOKS

F+W Media, 1213 N. Sherman Ave., #306, Madison WI 53704. (508)427-7100. **Fax:** (508)427-6790. **E-mail:** submissions@tyrusbooks.com. **Website:** tyrusbooks.com. **Contact:** Ashley Myers, editor. Publisher: Benjamin LeRoy. "We publish crime and literary fiction. We believe in the life changing power of the written word." Accepts simultaneous submissions.

FICTION Subjects include literary, mystery. Submit query, synopsis, and up to 20 sample pages.

UNBRIDLED BOOKS

200 N. Ninth St., Suite A, Columbia MO 65201. **E-mail:** michalsong@unbridledbooks.com. **Website:** unbridledbooks.com. **Contact:** Greg Michalson. Estab. 2004. "Unbridled Books is a premier publisher of works of rich literary quality that appeal to a broad audience."

FICTION Please query first by e-mail. Due to the heavy volume of submissions, we regret that at this time we are not able to consider uninvited mss.

TIPS "We try to read each ms that arrives, so please be patient."

UNION SQUARE PUBLISHING

Sterling, 387 Park Ave. S., 11th Floor, New York NY 10016-8810. **E-mail:** submissions@cardozapub.com. **Website:** www.sterlingpublishing.com. **Contact:** Acquisition Editor (biographies, word books, cultural studies, sports, general nonfiction and fiction). Estab. 2002. Publishes hardcover originals, trade paperback originals and reprints, mass market paperback originals. **Publishes 5-10 titles/year. 10 queries received/year. 5 mss received/year. 80% of books from first-time authors. 95% from unagented writers. Pays 5-6% royalty on retail price. Pays $1,000-10,000 advance.** Publishes book 7 months after acceptance. Accepts simultaneous submissions. Responds in 1-3 months. Guidelines via e-mail.

NONFICTION Subjects include anthropology, archeology, community, contemporary culture, cooking, foods, nutrition, education, ethnic, government, politics, history, hobbies, humanities, language, literature, memoirs, multicultural, music, dance, nature, environment, philosophy, recreation, religion, social sciences, sociology, spirituality, sports, translation. "Union Square Publishing is a new imprint of a long-established company, and we have yet to determine the exact role it will fill in the publishing world. We began by publishing books on writing, words, and language." Query with SASE. Submit complete ms. Reviews artwork/photos. Send photocopies.

RECENT TITLE(S) *The Complete Guide to Successful Publishing*, by Avery Cardoza; *Drinking Companion*, by Kelly Boler; *Write in Style*, by Bobbie Christmas.

TIPS "We will never reject a book based solely on genre. Our audience is the general market interested in original concepts."

UNITY HOUSE

Unity, 1901 N.W. Blue Pkwy., Unity Village MO 64065-0001. (816)524-3550. **Fax:** (816)347-5518. **E-mail:** unity@unityonline.org. **E-mail:** sartinson@unityonline.org. **Website:** www.unityonline.org. **Contact:** Sharon Sartin, executive assistant. Estab. 1889. Publishes hardcover, trade paperback, and electronic originals. Unity House publishes metaphysical Christian books based on Unity principles, as well as inspirational books on metaphysics and practical spirituality. All mss must reflect a spiritual foundation and express the Unity philosophy, practical Christianity, universal principles, and/or metaphysics. **Publishes 5-7 titles/year. 50 queries received/year. 5% of books from first-time authors. 95% from unagented writers. Pays 10-15% royalty on retail price. Pays advance.** Publishes book 13 months after acceptance. Responds in 6-8 months. Catalog and guidelines online.

NONFICTION Subjects include religion, spirituality, metaphysics, new thought. "Writers should be familiar with principles of metaphysical Christianity but not feel bound by them. We are interested in works in the related fields of holistic health, spiritual psychology, and the philosophy of other world religions." Submit proposal package, including: outline, 50 sample chapters. Reviews artwork/photos. Writers should send photocopies.

FICTION Subjects include spiritual, inspirational, metaphysical, visionary fiction. "We are a bridge between traditional Christianity and New Age spirituality. Unity is based on metaphysical Christian principles, spiritual values and the healing power of prayer as a resource for daily living." Submit complete mss (3 copies).

RECENT TITLE(S) *Sacred Secrets*, edited by Paula Godwin Goppel; *I of the Storm*, by Gary Simmons; *That's Just How My Spirit Travels*, by Rosemary Fillmore Rhea.

TIPS "We target an audience of spiritual seekers."

THE UNIVERSITY OF AKRON PRESS

120 E. Mill St., Suite 415, Akron OH 44325. (330)972-6953. **Fax:** (330)972-8364. **E-mail:** uapress@uakron.edu. **Website:** www.uakron.edu/uapress. **Contact:** Thomas Bacher, director and acquisitions. Estab. 1988. Publishes hardcover and paperback originals and reissues. "The University of Akron Press is the publishing arm of The University of Akron and is dedicated to the dissemination of scholarly, professional, and regional books and other content." **Publishes 10-12 titles/year. 100 queries received/year. 50-75 mss received/year. 40% of books from first-time authors. 80% from unagented writers. Pays 7-15% royalty.** Publishes book 9-12 months after acceptance. Accepts simultaneous submissions. Responds in 2 weeks to queries/proposals; 3-4 months to solicited mss. Query prior to submitting. Guidelines online.

NONFICTION Subjects include Applied politics, early American literature, emerging technologies, history of psychology, history of technology, interdisciplinary studies, Northeast Ohio history and culture, Ohio politics, poetics. Query by e-mail. Mss cannot be returned unless SASE is included.

POETRY Follow the guidelines and submit mss only for the contest: www.uakron.edu/uapress/poetry.html. "We publish two books of poetry annually, one of which is the winner of The Akron Poetry prize. We also are interested in literary collections based around one theme, especially collections of translated works." If you are interested in publishing with The University of Akron Press, please fill out form online.

RECENT TITLE(S) *Signaletics*, by Emilia Phillips; *Orbit of Discovery, The All-Ohio Space Shuttle Mission*, by Don Thomas.

THE UNIVERSITY OF ALABAMA PRESS

200 Hackberry Lane, 2nd Floor, Tuscaloosa AL 35487. (205)348-5180 or (205)348-1571. **Fax:** (205)348-9201. **E-mail:** waterman@uapress.ua.edu. **Website:** www.uapress.ua.edu. **Contact:** Daniel Waterman, editor-in-chief; Michele Myatt Quinn, designer; Kaci Lane Hindman, production editor. Publishes nonfiction hardcover and paperbound originals, and fiction paperback reprints. **Publishes 70-75 titles/year. 70% of books from first-time authors. 95% from unagented writers. Pays advance.** Responds in 2 weeks to queries. Book catalog available free.

NONFICTION Subjects include anthropology, archeology, community, government, politics, history, language, literature, literary criticism, religion, translation. Considers upon merit almost any subject of scholarly interest, but specializes in communications, military history, public administration, literary criticism and biography, history, Jewish studies, and American archaeology. Accepts nonfiction translations. Query with SASE. Reviews artwork/photos.

FICTION Reprints of works by contemporary, Southern writers. Distributor of Fiction Collective 2 (FC@), avant garde fiction. Query with SASE.

TIPS "Please direct inquiry to appropriate acquisitions editor. University of Alabama Press responds to an author within 2 weeks upon receiving the ms. If they think it is unsuitable for Alabama's program, they tell the author at once. If the ms warrants it, they begin the peer-review process, which may take 2-4 months to complete. During that process, they keep the author fully informed."

UNIVERSITY OF ARIZONA PRESS

355 S. Euclid Ave., Suite 103, Tucson AZ 85719. (520)621-1441. **Fax:** (520)621-8899. **E-mail:** uap@uapress.arizona.edu. **Website:** www.uapress.arizona.edu. **Contact:** Patti Hartmann, acquiring editor (humanities); Allyson Carter, acquiring editor (social sciences and science). Estab. 1959. Publishes hardcover and paperback originals and reprints. "University of Arizona is a publisher of scholarly books and books of the Southwest." **Royalty terms vary; usual starting point for scholarly monography is after sale of first 1,000 copies. Pays advance.** Responds in 3 months

to queries. Book catalog available via website or upon request. Guidelines online.

NONFICTION Subjects include Americana, anthropology, archeology, ethnic, nature, environment, regional, environmental studies, western, and environmental history. Scholarly books about anthropology, Arizona, American West, archeology, Native American studies, Latino studies, environmental science, global change, Latin America, Native Americans, natural history, space sciences, and women's studies. Submit sample chapters, résumé, TOC, ms length, audience, comparable books. Reviews artwork/photos.

RECENT TITLE(S) *Elegy for Desire*, by Luis Omar Salinas; *In-Between Places*, by Diane Glancy; *Beyond Desert Walls: Essays from Prison*, by Ken Lamberton.

TIPS "Perhaps the most common mistake a writer might make is to offer a book ms or proposal to a house whose list he or she has not studied carefully. Editors rejoice in receiving material that is clearly targeted to the house's list ('I have approached your firm because my books complement your past publications in') and presented in a straightforward, businesslike manner."

THE UNIVERSITY OF ARKANSAS PRESS

McIlroy House, 105 N. McIlroy Ave., Fayetteville AR 72701. (479)575-3246. **Fax:** (479)575-6044. **E-mail:** mbieker@uark.edu. **Website:** uapress.com. **Contact:** Mike Bieker, director. Estab. 1980. Publishes hardcover and trade paperback originals and reprints. "The University of Arkansas Press publishes series on Ozark studies, the Civil War in the West, poetry and poetics, and sport and society." **Publishes 30 titles/year. 30% of books from first-time authors. 95% from unagented writers.** Publishes book 1 year after acceptance. Responds in 3 months to proposals. Book catalog and ms guidelines online.

NONFICTION Subjects include government, politics, history, Southern, humanities, literary criticism, nature, environment, regional, Arkansas. Accepted mss must be submitted on disk. Query with SASE. Submit outline, sample chapters, résumé.

POETRY University of Arkansas Press publishes 4 poetry books per year through the Miller Williams Poetry Prize.

RECENT TITLE(S) *Reading With Oprah*, by Kathleen Rooney; *Looking Back to See*, by Maxine Brown; *Chattahoochee*, by Patrick Phillips.

☉ UNIVERSITY OF CALGARY PRESS

2500 University Dr. NW, Calgary AB T2N 1N4, Canada. (403)220-7578. **Fax:** (403)282-0085. **Website:** www.uofcpress.com. **Contact:** John Wright, interim director. Publishes scholarly and trade paperback originals and reprints. **Publishes 10 titles/year.** Publishes book 20 months after acceptance. Book catalog available for free. Guidelines online.

NONFICTION Subjects include art, architecture, philosophy women's studies, world affairs,, Canadian studies, post-modern studies, native studies, history, international relations, arctic studies, Africa, Latin American and Caribbean studies, and heritage of the Canadian and American heartland.

UNIVERSITY OF CALIFORNIA PRESS

2120 Berkeley Way, Berkeley CA 94720-1012. (510)642-4247. **Fax:** (510)643-7127. **E-mail:** askucp@ucpress.edu. **Website:** www.ucpress.edu. **Contact:** Lynne Withey (public health); Reed Malcolm (religion, politics, Asian studies); Niels Hooper (history); Deborah Kirshman (museum copublications); Sheila Levine (food, regional); Jenny Wapner (natural history, organismal biology); Naomi Schneider (sociology, politics, anthropology, Latin American studies); Blake Edgar (biology, archaeology, viticulture & enology); Stephanie Fay (art); Stan Holwitz (anthropology, public health, Jewish studies); Laura Cerruti (literature, poetry, classics); Mary Francis (music, film); Chuck Crumly (evolution, environment, ecology, biology). Estab. 1893. Publishes hardcover and paperback originals and reprints. "University of California Press publishes mostly nonfiction written by scholars." **Pays advance.** Response time varies, depending on the subject. Enclose return postage to queries. Guidelines online.

NONFICTION Subjects include history, nature, environment, translation, art, literature, natural sciences, some high-level popularizations. No length preference. Submit sample chapters, letter of introduction, cv, TOC.

FICTION Publishes fiction only in translation.

RECENT TITLE(S) *William Dean Howells: A Writer's Life*, by Susan Goodman and Carl Dawson; *A History of Wine in America: From Prohibition to the Present*, by Thomas Pinney; *Biology of Gila Monsters and Beaded Lizards*, by Daniel Beck.

⊘ THE UNIVERSITY OF CHICAGO PRESS

1427 E. 60th St., Chicago IL 60637. Voice-mail: (773)702-7700. **Fax:** (773)702-9756. **Website:** www.

press.uchicago.edu. **Contact:** Randolph Petilos, poetry and medieval studies editor. Estab. 1891. "The University of Chicago Press has been publishing scholarly books and journals since 1891. Annually, we publish an average of four books in our Phoenix Poets series and two books of poetry in translation. Occasionally, we may publish a book of poetry outside Phoenix Poets, or as a paperback reprint from another publisher." Has recently published work by Charles Bernstein, Peter Campion, Milo De Angelis, Mark Halliday, Benjamin Landry, Pier Paolo Pasolini, Katie Peterson, Alan Shapiro, and Joshua Weiner.

UNIVERSITY OF GEORGIA PRESS

Main Library, Third Floor, 320 S. Jackson St., Athens GA 30602. (706)369-6130. **Fax:** (706)369-6131. **E-mail:** books@ugapress.uga.edu. **Website:** www.ugapress.org. Estab. 1938. Publishes hardcover originals, trade paperback originals, and reprints. University of Georgia Press is a midsized press that publishes fiction only through the Flannery O'Connor Award for Short Fiction competition. **Publishes 85 titles/year. Pays 7-10% royalty on net receipts. Pays rare, varying advance.** Publishes book 1 year after acceptance. Responds in 2 months to queries. Book catalog and ms guidelines for #10 SASE or online.

NONFICTION Subjects include government, politics, history, American, nature, environment, regional, environmental studies, literary nonfiction. Query with SASE. Submit bio, 1 sample chapter. Reviews artwork/photos. Send if essential to book.

FICTION Short story collections published in Flannery O'Connor Award Competition. Mss for Flannery O'Connor Award for Short Fiction accepted in April and May.

RECENT TITLE(S) *Equiano, the African: Biography of a Self-Made Man*, by Vincent Carretta; *The Civil Rights Movement in American Memory*, edited by Renee Romano and Leigh Raiford; *Sabbath Creole*, by Juddun Mitcham.

TIPS "Please visit our website to view our book catalogs and for all ms submission guidelines."

UNIVERSITY OF ILLINOIS PRESS

1325 S. Oak St., Champaign IL 61820-6903. (217)333-0950. **Fax:** (217)244-8082. **E-mail:** uipress@uillinois.edu. **Website:** www.press.uillinois.edu. **Contact:** Willis Regier, director (literature, classics, ancient religion, sports history); Larin McLaughlin, senior acquisitions editor (women's studies, American studies, religion); Laurie Matheson, senior acquisitions editor (history, appalachian studies, labor studies, music, folklore); Daniel Nasset, acquisitions editor (film studies, anthropology, communication studies. Estab. 1918. Publishes hardcover and trade paperback originals and reprints. University of Illinois Press publishes scholarly books and serious nonfiction with a wide range of study interests. Currently emphasizing American history, especially immigration, labor, African-American, and military; American religion, music, women's studies, and film. **Publishes 150 titles/year. 35% of books from first-time authors. 95% from unagented writers. Pays $1,000-1,500 (rarely) advance.** Publishes book 1 year after acceptance. Responds in 1 month to queries. Book catalog for 9x12 envelope and 2 first-class stamps. Guidelines online.

NONFICTION Subjects include Americana, animals, cooking, foods, nutrition, government, politics, history, especially American history, language, literature, military, war, music, especially American music, dance, philosophy, regional, sociology, sports, translation, film/cinema/stage. "Always looking for solid, scholarly books in American history, especially social history; books on American popular music, and books in the broad area of American studies." Query with SASE. Submit outline.

RECENT TITLE(S) *Philosophical Writings*, by Simone de Beauvoir (philosophy); *Women for President: Media Bias in Eight Campaigns*, by Erica Falk; *Herndon's Lincoln*, edited by Douglas L. Wilson and Rodney D. Davis.

TIPS "As a university press, we are required to submit all mss to rigorous scholarly review. Mss need to be clearly original, well written, and based on solid and thorough research. We cannot encourage memoirs or autobiographies."

UNIVERSITY OF IOWA PRESS

100 Kuhl House, 119 W. Park Rd., Iowa City IA 52242. (319)335-2000. **Fax:** (319)335-2055. **E-mail:** uipress@uiowa.edu. **Website:** www.uiowapress.org. **Contact:** Holly Carver, director; Joseph Parsons, acquisitions editor. Estab. 1969. Publishes hardcover and paperback originals. "We publish authoritative, original nonfiction that we market mostly by direct mail to groups with special interests in our titles, and by advertising in trade and scholarly publications." **Publishes 35 titles/year. 30% of books from first-time authors. 95% from unagented writers. Pays 7-10% royalty on net receipts.**

Publishes book 1 year after acceptance. Book catalog available free. Guidelines online.

NONFICTION Subjects include anthropology, archeology, creative nonfiction, history, regional, language, literature, nature, environment, American literary studies, medicine and literature. "Looks for evidence of original research, reliable sources, clarity of organization, complete development of theme with documentation, supportive footnotes and/or bibliography, and a substantive contribution to knowledge in the field treated. Use *Chicago Manual of Style*." Query with SASE. Submit outline. Reviews artwork/photos.

FICTION Currently publishes the Iowa Short Fiction Award selections.

POETRY Currently publishes winners of the Iowa Poetry Prize Competition, Kuhl House Poets, poetry anthologies. Competition guidelines online.

RECENT TITLE(S) *First We Read, Then We Write: Emerson on the Creative Process*, by Robert D. Richardson.

UNIVERSITY OF MICHIGAN PRESS

839 Greene St., Ann Arbor MI 48106. **Website:** www. press.umich.edu.

TIPS "Aside from work published through the Michigan Literary Fiction Awards, we seek only fiction set in the Great Lakes region."

UNIVERSITY OF NEBRASKA PRESS

1111 Lincoln Mall, Lincoln NE 68588. (800)755-1105. **Fax:** (402)472-6214. **E-mail:** pressmail@unl.edu. **E-mail:** arold1@unl.edu. **Website:** nebraskapress.unl. edu. **Contact:** Heather Lundine, editor-in-chief; Alison Rold, production manager. Publishes hardcover and trade paperback originals and trade paperback reprints. "We primarily publish nonfiction books and scholarly journals, along with a few titles per season in contemporary and regional prose and poetry. On occasion, we reprint previously published fiction of established reputation, and we have several programs to publish literary works in translation." Book catalog available free. Guidelines online.

IMPRINTS Bison Books (paperback reprints of classic books).

NONFICTION Subjects include agriculture, animals, anthropology, archeology, creative nonfiction, history, memoirs, military, war, multicultural, nature, environment, religion, sports, translation, women's issues, women's studies, Native American studies, American Lives series, experimental fiction by American-Indian writers. Submit book proposal with overview, audience, format, detailed chapter outline, sample chapters, sample bibliography, timetable, CV.

FICTION Series and translation only. Occasionally reprints fiction of established reputation.

POETRY Publishes contemporary, regional.

RECENT TITLE(S) *Mondo and Other Stories*, by J. M. G. CleZIO; *Sleep in My*, by Jon Pineda; *Scoreboard, Baby*, by Ken Armstrong and Nick Perry.

UNIVERSITY OF NEVADA PRESS

Morrill Hall, Mail Stop 0166, Reno NV 89557. (775)784-6573. **Fax:** (775)784-6200. **Website:** www. unpress.nevada.edu. **Contact:** Joanne O'Hare, director. Estab. 1961. Publishes hardcover and paperback originals and reprints. "Small university press. Publishes fiction that primarily focuses on the American West." Member: AAUP **Publishes 25 titles/year.** Publishes book 18 months after acceptance. Responds in 2 months. Guidelines online.

NONFICTION Subjects include anthropology, archeology, ethnic, studies, history, regional and natural, nature, environment, regional, history and geography, western literature, current affairs, gambling and gaming, Basque studies. No juvenile books. Submit proposal. No online submissions. Reviews artwork/photos. Send photocopies.

FICTION "We publish in Basque Studies, Gambling Studies, Western literature, Western history, Natural science, Environmental Studies, Travel and Outdoor books, Archeology, Anthropology, and Political Studies, all focusing on the West". The Press also publishes creative nonfiction and books on regional topics for a general audience. Submit proposal package, outline, clips, 2-4 sample chapters. Include estimated word count, brief bio, list of publishing credits. Send SASE or IRC. No e-mail submissions.

UNIVERSITY OF NEW MEXICO PRESS

1717 Roma Ave., Albuquerque NM 87106. (505)277-3324 or (800)249-7737. **Fax:** (505)277-3343. **E-mail:** clarkw@unm.edu. **E-mail:** wcwhiteh@unm.edu. **Website:** www.unmpress.com. **Contact:** W. Clark Whitehorn, editor-in-chief. Estab. 1929. Publishes hardcover originals and trade paperback originals and reprints. "The Press is well known as a publisher in the fields of anthropology, archeology, Latin American studies, art and photography, architecture and the history and culture of the American West, fiction, some poetry, Chicano/a studies and works by and about American Indians. We focus on American West, Southwest and

Latin American regions." **Pays variable royalty. Pays advance.** Book catalog available for free. Please read and follow the submission query guidelines on the Author Information page online. Do not send your entire ms or additional materials until requested. If your book is accepted for publication, you will be notified.

NONFICTION Subjects include Americana, anthropology, archeology, art, architecture, biography, creative nonfiction, ethnic, gardening, gay, lesbian, government, politics, history, language, literature, memoirs, military, war, multicultural, music, dance, nature, environment, photography, regional, religion, science, translation, travel, women's issues, women's studies, contemporary culture, cinema/stage, true crime, general nonfiction. No how-to, humor, juvenile, self-help, software, technical or textbooks. Query with SASE. Reviews artwork/photos. Send photocopies.

RECENT TITLE(S) *Constructing Lives at Mission San Francisco: Native Californians and Hispanic Colonists, 1776-1821,* by Quincy Newell; *The American Military Frontiers: The United States Army in the West, 1783-1900,* by Robert Wooster; *Country of Bullets, Chronicles of War,* by Juanita León, Translated by Guillermo Bleichmar.

THE UNIVERSITY OF NORTH CAROLINA PRESS

116 S. Boundary St., Chapel Hill NC 27514. (919)966-3561. **Fax:** (919)966-3829. **E-mail:** uncpress@unc.edu. **Website:** www.uncpress.unc.edu. **Contact:** David Perry, editor-in-chief (regional trade, Civil War); Charles Grench, senior editor (American history, European history, law and legal studies, business and economic history, classics, political or social science); Elaine Maisner, senior editor (Latin American studies, religious studies, anthropology, regional trade, folklore); Sian Hunter, senior editor (literary studies, gender studies, American studies, African American studies, social medicine, Appalachian studies, media studies); Mark Simpson-Vos, associate editor (electronic publishing and special projects, American-Indian studies). Publishes hardcover originals, trade paperback originals and reprints. "UNC Press publishes nonfiction books for academic and general audiences. We have a special interest in trade and scholarly titles about our region. We do not, however, publish original fiction, drama, or poetry, memoirs of living persons, or festshriften." **Publishes 90 titles/year. 500 queries received/year. 200 mss received/year. 50% of books from first-time authors. 90% from unagented writers.**

Pays variable royalty on wholesale price. Offers variable advance. Publishes book 1 year after acceptance of ms. Responds in 3-4 weeks to queries and proposals. Responds in 2 weeks to mss. Book catalog free or on website. Guidelines online.

NONFICTION Subjects include Americana, anthropology, archeology, art, architecture, cooking, foods, nutrition, gardening, government, politics, health, medicine, history, language, literature, military, war, multicultural, music, dance, nature, environment, philosophy, photography, regional, religion, translation, womens issues, women's studies, African-American studies, American studies, cultural studies, Latin-American studies, American-Indian studies, media studies, gender studies, social medicine, Appalachian studies. Submit proposal package, outline, CV, cover letter, abstract, and TOC. Reviews artwork/photos. Send photocopies.

UNIVERSITY OF NORTH TEXAS PRESS

1155 Union Circle, #311336, Denton TX 76203. (940)565-2142. **Fax:** (940)565-4590. **E-mail:** ronald.chrisman@unt.edu; karen.devinney@unt.edu. **Website:** untpress.unt.edu. **Contact:** Ronald Chrisman, director; Paula Oates, assistant editor; Lori Belew, administrative assistant. Estab. 1987. Publishes hardcover and trade paperback originals and reprints. "We are dedicated to producing the highest quality scholarly, academic, and general interest books. We are committed to serving all peoples by publishing stories of their cultures and experiences that have been overlooked. Currently emphasizing military history, Texas history and literature, music, Mexican-American studies." **Publishes 14-16 titles/year. 500 queries received/year. 50% of books from first-time authors. 95% from unagented writers.** Publishes book 1-2 years after acceptance. Responds in 1 month to queries. Book catalog for 8 ½×11 SASE. Guidelines online.

NONFICTION Subjects include Americana, ethnic, government, politics, history, music, dance, biography, military, war, nature, regional, women's issues/studies. Query with SASE. Reviews artwork/photos. Send photocopies.

FICTION "The only fiction we publish is the winner of the Katherine Anne Porter Prize in Short Fiction, an annual, national competition with a $1,000 prize, and publication of the winning ms each Fall."

POETRY "The only poetry we publish is the winner of the Vassar Miller Prize in Poetry, an annual, national competition with a $1,000 prize and publication of the winning ms each Spring." Query.

TIPS "We publish series called War and the Southwest; Texas Folklore Society Publications; the Western Life Series; Practical Guide Series; Al-Filo: Mexican-American studies; North Texas Crime and Criminal Justice; Katherine Anne Porter Prize in Short Fiction; and the North Texas Lives of Musicians Series."

UNIVERSITY OF OKLAHOMA PRESS

2800 Venture Dr., Norman OK 73069. **E-mail:** cerankin@ou.edu. **Website:** www.oupress.com. **Contact:** Charles E. Rankin, editor-in-chief. Estab. 1928. Publishes hardcover and paperback originals and reprints. University of Oklahoma Press publishes books for both scholarly and nonspecialist readers. **Publishes 90 titles/year. Pays standard royalty.** Responds promptly to queries. Book catalog for 9×12 SAE with 6 first-class stamps.

IMPRINTS Plains Reprints.

NONFICTION Subjects include political science (Congressional, area and security studies), history (regional, military, natural), language/literature (American Indian, US West), American Indian studies, classical studies. Query with SASE or by e-mail. Submit outline, résumé, 1-2 sample chapters. Use *Chicago Manual of Style* for ms guidelines. Reviews artwork/photos.

RECENT TITLE(S) *So Rugged and Mountainous: Blazing Trails to Oregon and California, 1812-1848,* by Will Bagley; *Plains Indian Art: The Pioneering Work of John C. Ewers,* edited by Jane Ewers Robinson; *Iroquois Art, Power, and History,* by Neal B. Keating.

◑ UNIVERSITY OF OTTAWA PRESS

542 King Edward, Ottawa ON K1N 6N5, Canada. (613)562-5246. **Fax:** (613)562-5247. **E-mail:** puo-uop@uottawa.ca. **Website:** www.press.uottawa.ca. Estab. 1936. "UOP publishes books and journals, in French and English, and in any and all editions and formats, that touch upon the human condition: anthropology, sociology, political science, psychology, criminology, media studies, economics, education, language and culture, law, history, literature, translation studies, philosophy, public administration, health sciences, and religious studies." Accepts simultaneous submissions. Book catalog and ms guidelines online.

NONFICTION Submit outline, proposal form (please see website), CV, 1-2 sample chapters (for monographs only), ms (for collected works only), TOC, 2-5 page proposal/summary, contributor names, short bios, and citizenships (for collected works only)."

RECENT TITLE(S) *Sexual Assault in Canada*, edited by Elizabeth Sheehy; *Worlding Sei Shonagon*, by Valerie Henitiuk; *Braaaiiinnnsss!*, edited by Robert Smith.

TIPS "Please note that the University of Ottawa Press does not accept: bilingual works (texts must be either entirely in English or entirely in French), undergraduate or masters theses, or doctoral theses that have not been substantially revised."

◉ UNIVERSITY OF PENNSYLVANIA PRESS

3905 Spruce St., Philadelphia PA 19104. (215)898-6261. **Fax:** (215)898-0404. **Website:** www.pennpress.org. **Contact:** Jerome Singerman, humanities editor; Peter Agree, editor-in-chief and social sciences editor; Jo Joslyn, art and architecture editor; Robert Lockhart, history editor; Bill Finan, politics, international relations; John Hubbard, art director. Estab. 1890. Publishes hardcover and paperback originals, and reprints. "Ms submissions are welcome in fields appropriate for Penn Press's editorial program. The Press's acquiring editors, and their fields of responsibility, are listed in the Contact Us section of our Web site. Although we have no formal policies regarding ms proposals and submissions, what we need minimally, in order to gauge our degree of interest, is a brief statement describing the ms, a copy of the contents page, and a reasonably current vita. Initial inquiries are best sent by letter, in paper form, to the appropriate acquiring editor." **Publishes 100+ titles/year. 20-30% of books from first-time authors. 95% from unagented writers. Royalty determined on book-by-book basis. Pays advance.** Publishes book 10 months after acceptance. Responds in 3 months to queries. Catalog and guidelines online.

NONFICTION Subjects include Americana, art, architecture, history, American, art, architecture, literary criticism, sociology, anthropology, literary criticism, cultural studies, ancient studies, medieval studies, urban studies, human rights. Follow the *Chicago Manual of Style*. "Serious books that serve the scholar and the professional, student and general reader." *No unsolicited mss.* Query with SASE. Submit outline, résumé. Reviews artwork/photos. Send photocopies.

UNIVERSITY OF SOUTH CAROLINA PRESS

1600 Hampton St., 5th Floor, Columbia SC 29208. (803)777-5243. **Fax:** (803)777-0160. **Website:** www.sc.edu/uscpress. **Contact:** Linda Fogle, assistant director for operations (trade books); Jim Denton, acquisitions editor (literature, religious studies, rhetoric, communication, social work); Alexander Moore, acquisitions editor (history, regional studies). Estab. 1944. Publishes hardcover originals, trade paperback originals and reprints. "We focus on scholarly monographs and regional trade books of lasting merit." **Publishes 50 titles/year. 500 queries received/year. 150 mss received/year. 30% of books from first-time authors. 95% from unagented writers.** Publishes book 1 year after acceptance of ms. Accepts simultaneous submissions. Responds in 3 months to mss. Book catalog available free. Guidelines online.

NONFICTION Subjects include art, architecture, history, American, Civil War, culinary, maritime, women's studies, language, literature, regional, religion, rhetoric, communication. Do not submit entire unsolicited mss or projects with limited scholarly value. Query with SASE, or submit proposal package and outline, and 1 sample chapter and résumé with SASE Reviews artwork/photos. Send photocopies.

RECENT TITLE(S) *Mary Black's Family Quilts*, by Laurel Horton; *Sons of Privilege*, by W. Eric Emerson; *Jesus in the Mist: Stories*, by Paul Ruffin.

UNIVERSITY OF TAMPA PRESS

University of Tampa, 401 W. Kennedy Blvd., Box 19F, Tampa FL 33606-1490. (813)253-6266. **Fax:** (813)258-7593. **E-mail:** utpress@ut.edu. **Website:** www.utpress. ut.edu. **Contact:** Richard Mathews, editor. Publishes hardcover originals and reprints; trade paperback originals and reprints. Responds in 3-4 months to queries. Book catalog online.

NONFICTION , Florida history. Reviews artwork/photos.

FICTION Subjects include literary, poetry.

POETRY Submit 3-6 sample poems.

RECENT TITLE(S) *Yesteryear I Lived in Paradise: The Story of Caladesi Island*, by Myrtle Scharrer Betz; *The Shape of Poetry*, by Peter Meinke; *White Shirt*, by Christopher Buckley.

TIPS "We only consider book-length poetry submitted through the annual Tampa Review Prize for Poetry, and rarely publish excerpts. No e-mail or handwritten submissions. Submit between Sept. 1 and Dec. 31."

⊕ THE UNIVERSITY OF TENNESSEE PRESS

110 Conference Center, Knoxville TN 37996. (865)974-3321. **Fax:** (865)974-3724. **Website:** www.utpress.org. **Contact:** Scot Danforth, acquisitions editor (scholarly

books); Jennifer Siler, director (regional trades, fiction). Estab. 1940. "Our mission is to stimulate scientific and scholarly research in all fields; to channel such studies, either in scholarly or popular form, to a larger number of people; and to extend the regional leadership of the University of Tennessee by stimulating research projects within the South and by nonuniversity authors." **Publishes 35 titles/year. 35% of books from first-time authors. 99% from unagented writers. Pays negotiable royalty on net receipts.** Book catalog for 12×16 envelope and 2 first-class stamps. Guidelines online.

NONFICTION Subjects include Americana, anthropology, archeology, historical, art, architecture, vernacular, history, language, literature, literary criticism, regional, religion, history sociology, anthropology, archeology, biography only, women's issues, women's studies, African-American studies, Appalachian studies, folklore/folklife, material culture. Prefers scholarly treatment and a readable style. Authors usually have PhDs. Submissions in other fields, and submissions of poetry, textbooks, plays and translations are not invited Submit outline, bio, 2 sample chapters. Reviews artwork/photos.

FICTION Query with SASE. Submit clips, bio.

RECENT TITLE(S) *Dictionary of Smoky Mountain English*, by Michael B. Montgomery and Joseph S. Hall.

TIPS "Our market is in several groups: scholars; educated readers with special interests in given scholarly subjects; and the general educated public interested in Tennessee, Appalachia, and the South. Not all our books appeal to all these groups, of course, but any given book must appeal to at least one of them."

UNIVERSITY OF TEXAS PRESS

P.O. Box 7819, Austin TX 78713-7819. (512)471-4278, ext. 3. **Fax:** (512)232-7178. **E-mail:** utpress@uts. cc.utexas.edu. **Website:** www.utexaspress.com. **Contact:** Theresa May, assistant director/editor-in-chief (social sciences, Latin American studies); James Burr, sponsoring editor (humanities, classics); William Bishel, sponsoring editor (natural sciences, Texas history); Allison Faust, sponsoring editor (Texana, geography, art, music). Estab. 1952. "In addition to publishing the results of advanced research for scholars worldwide, UT Press has a special obligation to the people of its state to publish authoritative books on Texas. We do not publish fiction or poetry, except as invited by a series editor, and some Latin American and Middle Eastern literature in translation." **Publishes 90 titles/year.**

50% of books from first-time authors. 99% from un-agented writers. **Pays occasional advance.** Publishes book 18-24 months after acceptance of ms. Responds in 3 months to queries. Book catalog available free. Guidelines online.

NONFICTION Subjects include anthropology, archeology, art, architecture, ethnic, film, cinema, stage, history, language, literature, literary criticism, nature, environment, regional, science, translation, women's issues, women's studies, natural history, American, Latin American, Native American, Latino, and Middle Eastern studies; classics and the ancient world, film, contemporary regional architecture, geography, ornithology, biology. Also uses specialty titles related to Texas and the Southwest, national trade titles and regional trade titles. Reviews artwork/photos.

RECENT TITLE(S) *The Memory of Bones*, by Houston; *Who Guards the Guardians and How*, by Bruneau; *Women Embracing Islam*, edited by van Nieuwkerk.

TIPS "It's difficult to make a ms over 400 double-spaced pages into a feasible book. Authors should take special care to edit out extraneous material. We look for sharply focused, in-depth treatments of important topics."

⊕ UNIVERSITY OF WASHINGTON PRESS

P.O. Box 50096, Seattle WA 98145-5096. (206)543-4050. **Fax:** (206)543-3932. **E-mail:** uwpress@u.washington.edu. **E-mail:** mkedlang@u.washington.edu. **Website:** www.washington.edu/uwpress/. **Contact:** Marianne Keddington-Lang (Western History, Environmental and Native American Studies). Hardcover originals. **Publishes 70 titles/year.** Book catalog Guidelines online.

NONFICTION Subjects include anthropology, archeology, art, architecture, ethnic, Groups in China, history, Western, multicultural, nature, environment, photography, regional, social sciences. Go to our Book Search page for complete subject listing. We publish academic and general books, especially in anthropology, Asian studies, art, environmental studies, Middle Eastern Studies & regional interests. International Studies with focus on Asia; Jewish Studies; Art & Culture of the Northwest coast; Indians & Alaskan Eskimos; The Asian-American Experience; Southeast Asian Studies; Korean and Slavic Studies; Studies in Modernity & National Identity; Scandinavian Studies. Query with SASE. Submit proposal package, outline, sample chapters,.

RECENT TITLE(S) *Do Glaciers Listen? Local Knowledge, Colonial Encounters, and Social Imagination*, by Julie Cruikshank; *Making Mountains: New York City and the Catskills*, by David Stradling; *Road to Freedom*, by Julian Cox (Photographs of the Civil Rights Movement 1956-1968).

UNIVERSITY OF WISCONSIN PRESS

1930 Monroe St., 3rd Floor, Madison WI 53711. (608)263-1110. **Fax:** (608)263-1132. **E-mail:** gcwalker@uwpress.wisc.edu. **E-mail:** kadushin@wisc.edu. **Website:** uwpress.wisc.edu. **Contact:** Raphael Kadushin, senior acquisitions editor; Gwen Walker, acquisitions editor. Estab. 1937. Publishes hardcover originals, paperback originals, and paperback reprints. **Publishes 98 titles/year. Pays royalty.** Publishes book 9-18 months after acceptance. Responds in 2 weeks to queries; 8 weeks to mss. Rarely comments on rejected mss. Guidelines online.

◗ Check online guidelines for latest submission guidelines.

NONFICTION Subjects include anthropology, dance, environment, film, foods, gay, history, lesbian, memoirs, travel, African Studies, classical studies, human rights, Irish studies, Jewish studies, Latin American studies, Latino/a memoirs, modern Western European history, performance studies, Slavic studies, Southeast Asian studies. Does not accept unsolicited mss. Query with SASE or submit outline, 1-2 sample chapter(s), synopsis. Accepts queries by e-mail, mail, fax. Include estimated word count, brief bio. Send copy of ms and SASE. Direct your inquiries to the appropriate editor. See website for more info.

FICTION Subjects include gay, hi-lo, lesbian, mystery, regional, short story collections. Query with SASE or submit outline, 1-2 sample chapter(s), synopsis.

POETRY The University of Wisconsin Press Awards the Brittingham Prize in Poetry and Felix Pollack Prize in Poetry. Each winning poet receives $2,500 ($1,000 cash prize and $1,500 honorarium to cover expenses of reading in Madison). Prizes awarded annually for the two best book-length mss of original poetry submitted in the open competition. Submission period September 1-30. More details online.

TIPS "Make sure the query letter and sample text are well-written, and read guidelines carefully to make sure we accept the genre you are submitting."

UNIVERSITY PRESS OF KANSAS

2502 Westbrooke Circle, Lawrence KS 66045. (785)864-4154. **Fax:** (785)864-4586. **E-mail:** upress@ku.edu. **Website:** www.kansaspress.ku.edu; www.facebook.com/kansaspress. **Contact:** Michael J. Briggs, editor-in-chief; Fred Woodward, senior editor; Charles T. Myers, director. Estab. 1946. Publishes hardcover originals, trade paperback originals and reprints. "The University Press of Kansas publishes scholarly books that advance knowledge and regional books that contribute to the understanding of Kansas, the Great Plains, and the Midwest." **Publishes 55 titles/year. 600 queries received/year. 20% of books from first-time authors. 98% from unagented writers. Pays selective advance.** Publishes book 10 months after acceptance. Responds in 1 month to proposals. Book catalog and ms guidelines free.

NONFICTION Subjects include Americana, archeology, environment, government, military, nature, politics, regional, war, American History, Native Studies, American Cultural Studies. "We are looking for books on topics of wide interest based on solid scholarship and written for both specialists and informed general readers. Do not send unsolicited, complete mss." Submit outline, sample chapters, cover letter, CV, prospectus. Reviews artwork/photos. Send photocopies.

RECENT TITLE(S) *Writing the Gettysburg Address*, by Martin P. Johnson; *Obesity Rules*, by Whitney Strub; *West Side Story as Cinema*, by Ernesto R. Acevedo-Munoz.

UNIVERSITY PRESS OF KENTUCKY

663 S. Limestone St., Lexington KY 40508-4008. (859)257-8434. **Fax:** (859)323-1873. **Website:** www.kentuckypress.com. **Contact:** Joyce Harrison, editor-in-chief. Estab. 1943. Publishes hardcover and paperback originals and reprints. "We are a scholarly publisher, publishing chiefly for an academic and professional audience, as well as books about Kentucky, the upper South, Appalachia, and the Ohio Valley." **Publishes 60 titles/year. Royalty varies.** Publishes book 1 year after acceptance of ms. Responds in 2 months to queries. Book catalog available free. Guidelines online.

NONFICTION Subjects include history, military, war, history, regional, political science. No textbooks, genealogical material, lightweight popular treatments, how-to books, or books unrelated to our major areas of interest. The Press does not consider original works of fiction or poetry. Query with SASE.

UNIVERSITY PRESS OF MISSISSIPPI

3825 Ridgewood Rd., Jackson MS 39211. (601)432-6205. **Fax:** (601)432-6217. **E-mail:** press@mississippi.edu. **Website:** www.upress.state.ms.us. **Contact:** Craig Gill, editor-in-chief (regional studies, history, folklore, music). Estab. 1970. Publishes hardcover and paperback originals and reprints and e-books. "University Press of Mississippi publishes scholarly and trade titles, as well as special series, including: American Made Music; Conversations with Comic Artists; Conversations with Filmmakers; Faulkner and Yoknapatawpha; Literary Conversations; Hollywood Legends; Caribbean Studies." **Publishes 70 titles/year. 80% of books from first-time authors. 90% from unagented writers. Competitive royalties and terms. Pays advance.** Publishes book 1 year after acceptance. Responds in 3 months to queries.

NONFICTION Subjects include Americana, art, architecture, ethnic, minority studies, politics, history, literature, literary criticism, music, photography, regional, Southern, folklife, literary criticism, popular culture with scholarly emphasis, literary studies. "We prefer a proposal that describes the significance of the work and a chapter outline." Submit outline, sample chapters, CV.

RECENT TITLE(S) *The Painted Screens of Baltimore*, by Elaine Eff; *Gloria Swanson*, by Tricia Welsch.

UPPER ACCESS, INC.

87 Upper Access Rd., Hinesburg VT 05461. (802)482-2988. **Fax:** (802)304-1005. **E-mail:** info@upperaccess.com. **Website:** www.upperaccess.com. **Contact:** Steve Carlson, publisher. Estab. 1986. Publishes hardcover and trade paperback originals; hardcover and trade paperback reprints. Publishes nonfiction to improve the quality of life. **Publishes 2-3 titles/year. 200 queries received/year. 40 mss received/year. 50% of books from first-time authors. 80% from unagented writers. Pays 10-20% royalty on wholesale price. Pays $200-500 advance. "Advances are tokens of our good faith; author earnings are from royalties a book sells."** Publishes book 8 months after acceptance. Accepts simultaneous submissions. Responds in 1 month to queries/mss. Catalog online. Guidelines online.

NONFICTION Subjects include alternative lifestyles, child guidance, community/public affairs, contemporary culture, cooking, foods, nutrition, creative nonfiction, education, ethnic, gardening, government, politics/politics, health, medicine, history, humor, humanities, language, literature, multicultural, nature, environment, philosophy, psychology, science, sex, social sciences, sociology, womens issues, womens studies, world affairs affairs, (gay, lesbian possible). "We are open to considering almost any nonfiction topic that has some potential for national general trade sales." Query with SASE. "We strongly prefer an initial e-mail describing your proposed title. No attachments please. We will look at paper mail if there is no other way, but e-mail will be reviewed much more quickly and thoroughly." Will request artwork, etc. if and when appropriate. "Discuss this with us in your initial e-mail query."

FICTION "Note: Please do not submit fiction, even if it relates to nonfiction subjects. We cannot take novels or poetry of any kind at this time."

RECENT TITLE(S) *Editing Made Easy: Simple Rules for Effective Writing*, by Bruce Kaplan; *Final Rights: Reclaiming the American Way of Death*, by Joshua Slocum and Lisa Carlson; *True North: Journeys Into the Great Northern Ocean*, by Myron Arms.

TIPS "We target intelligent adults willing to challenge the status quo, who are interested in more self-sufficiency with respect for the environment. Most of our books are either unique subjects or unique or different ways of looking at major issues or basic education on subjects that are not well understood by most of the general public. We make a long-term commitment to each book that we publish, trying to find its market as long as possible. Please note that as a tiny company, we go through periods when we cannot even look at new mss while we catch up with the projects we are committed to. During such periods, we will respond to e-mail queries, but with standardized responses."

URJ PRESS

633 Third Ave., 7th Floor, New York NY 10017. (212)650-4120. **Fax:** (212)650-4119. **E-mail:** press@urj.org. **Website:** www.urjbooksandmusic.com. **Contact:** Michael H. Goldberg, editor-in-chief. Publishes hardcover and trade paperback originals. "URJ publishes textbooks for the religious classroom, children's tradebooks and scholarly work of Jewish education import—no adult fiction and no YA fiction." **Publishes 22 titles/year. 500 queries received/year. 400 mss received/year. 70% of books from first-time authors. 90% from unagented writers. Pays 3-5% royalty on retail price. Makes outright purchase of $500-2,000. Pays $500-2,000 advance.** Publishes book 18-24 months after acceptance. Responds in 4 months. Book catalog and ms guidelines online.

○ *URJ Press publishes books related to Judaism.*

NONFICTION Subjects include art, architecture, synagogue, child guidance, cooking, foods, nutrition, Jewish, education, ethnic, Judaism, government, politics, Israeli/Jewish, history, language, literature, Hebrew, military, war, as relates to Judaism, music, dance, nature, environment, philosophy, Jewish, religion, Judaism only, sex, as it relates to Judaism, spirituality, Jewish. Picture books, young readers, middle readers: religion. Average word length: picture books—1,500. Submit proposal package, outline, bio, 1-2 sample chapters.

RECENT TITLE(S) *Talmud for Everyday Living: Employer-Employee Relations*, by Hillel Gamoran (nonfiction); *The Gift of Wisdom*, by Steven E. Steinbock (textbook for grades 5-7); *Solomon and the Trees*, by Matt Biers-Ariel (picture book).

TIPS "Look at some of our books. Have an understanding of the Reform Judaism community. In addition to bookstores, we sell to Jewish congregations and Hebrew day schools."

USBORNE PUBLISHING

83-85 Saffron Hill, London En EC1N 8RT, United Kingdom. (44)207430-2800. **Fax:** (44)207430-1562. **E-mail:** mail@usborne.co.uk. **Website:** www.usborne.com. "Usborne Publishing is a multiple-award winning, world-wide children's publishing company publishing almost every type of children's book for every age from baby to young adult." **Pays authors royalty.**

FICTION Young readers, middle readers: adventure, contemporary, fantasy, history, humor, multicultural, nature/environment, science fiction, suspense/mystery, strong concept-based or character-led series. Average word length: young readers—5,000-10,000; middle readers—25,000-50,000; young adult—50,000-100,000.

TIPS "Do not send any original work and, sorry, but we cannot guarantee a reply."

VANDERBILT UNIVERSITY PRESS

PMB 351813, 2301 Vanderbilt Place, Nashville TN 37235. (615)322-3585. **Fax:** (615)343-8823. **E-mail:** vupress@vanderbilt.edu. **Website:** www.vanderbiltuniversitypress.com. **Contact:** Michael Ames, director. Publishes hardcover originals and trade paperback originals and reprints. "Vanderbilt University Press publishes books on healthcare, social sciences, education, and regional studies, for both academic and general audiences that are intellectually significant, socially relevant, and of practical importance." **Publishes 20-25 titles/year. 500 queries received/year. 25% of books from first-time authors. 90% from unagented writers. Pays rare advance.** Publishes book 10 months after acceptance. Accepts simultaneous submissions. Responds in 2 weeks to proposals. Catalog and guidelines online.

○ Also distributes for and co-publishes with Country Music Foundation.

NONFICTION Subjects include Americana, anthropology, archeology, education, ethnic, government, politics, health, medicine, history, language, literature, multicultural, music, dance, nature, environment, philosophy, women's issues, women's studies. Submit prospectus, sample chapter, CV. Does not accept electronic submissions. Reviews artwork/photos. Send photocopies.

RECENT TITLE(S) *A Life of Control: Stories of Living With Diabetes*, by Alan L. Graber, Anne W. Brown, and Kathleen Wolff; *Lost Delta Found*, edited by Robert Gordon and Bruce Nemerov.

TIPS "Our audience consists of scholars and educated, general readers."

◑ VÉHICULE PRESS

P.O.B. 42094 BP Roy, Montreal QC H2W 2T3, Canada. (514)844-6073. **Fax:** (514)844-7543. **E-mail:** vp@vehiculepress.com. **E-mail:** esplanade@vehiculepress.com. **Website:** www.vehiculepress.com. **Contact:** Simon Dardick, president/publisher. Estab. 1973. Publishes trade paperback originals by Canadian authors mostly. "Montreal's Véhicule Press has published the best of Canadian and Quebec literature-fiction, poetry, essays, translations, and social history." **Publishes 15 titles/year. 20% of books from first-time authors. 95% from unagented writers. Pays 10-15% royalty on retail price. Pays $200-500 advance.** Publishes book 1 year after acceptance. Responds in 4 months to queries. Book catalog for 9 x 12 SAE with IRCs.

IMPRINTS Signal Editions (poetry); Dossier Quebec (history, memoirs); Esplanade Editions (fiction).

NONFICTION Subjects include government, politics, history, language, literature, memoirs, regional, sociology. Especially looking for Canadian social history. Query with SASE. Reviews artwork/photos.

FICTION Subjects include feminist, literary, regional, translation, literary novels. No romance or formula writing. Query with SASE.

POETRY Vehicle Press is a "literary press with a poetry series, Signal Editions, publishing the work of Canadian poets only." Publishes flat-spined paperbacks. Publishes Canadian poetry that is "first-rate, original, content-conscious."

RECENT TITLE(S) *Mirabel*, by Pierre Nepreu, translated by Judith Cowan; *Seventeen Tomatoes*, by Jasprect Singh; *The Man Who Killed Houdini*, by Don Bell.

TIPS "Quality in almost any style is acceptable. We believe in the editing process."

⊘ VERTIGO

DC Universe, Vertigo-DC Comics, 1700 Broadway, New York NY 10019. **Website:** www.dccomics.com.

FICTION "The DC TALENT SEARCH program is designed to offer aspiring artists the chance to present artwork samples directly to the DC Editors and Art Directors. The process is simple: during your convention visit, drop off photocopied samples of your work and enjoy the show! No lines, no waiting. If the DC folks like what they see, a time is scheduled for you the following day to meet a DC representative personally and discuss your artistic interests and portfolio. At this time, DC Comics does not accept unsolicited writing submissions by mail. See submission guidelines online. "We're seeking artists for all our imprints, including the DC Universe, Vertigo, WildStorm, Mad magazine, Minx, kids comics and more!"

ⒶⓄ VIKING

Imprint of Penguin Group (USA), Inc., 375 Hudson St., New York NY 10014. (212)366-2000. **Website:** us.penguingroup.com/static/pages/publishers/adult/viking.html. Estab. 1925. Publishes hardcover and originals. Viking publishes a mix of academic and popular fiction and nonfiction. **Publishes 100 titles/year. Pays 10-15% royalty on retail price.** Publishes book 18 months after acceptance. Accepts simultaneous submissions.

NONFICTION Subjects include business, economics, child guidance, cooking, foods, nutrition, health, medicine, history, language, literature, music, dance, philosophy, womens issues, womens studies. Agented submissions only.

FICTION Subjects include literary, mainstream, contemporary, mystery, suspense. Agented submissions only.

RECENT TITLE(S) *The Mermaid Chair*, by Sue Monk Kidd; *Mountain Peril*, by Tom Eslick; *House*, by Michael Ruhlman.

Ⓐⵁ VIKING CHILDREN'S BOOKS

375 Hudson St., New York NY 10014. **E-mail:** averystudiopublicity@us.penguingroup.com. **Website:** www.penguingroup.com. **Contact:** Catherine Frank, executive editor. Joy Peskin, Anne Gunton, Tracy Gates, associate editorial editors; Joy Peskin, executive editor; Janet Pascal, editor; Kendra Levin, associate editor; Leila Sales, editorial assistant. Publishes hardcover originals. "Viking Children's Books is known for humorous, quirky picture books, in addition to more traditional fiction. We publish the highest quality fiction, nonfiction, and picture books for pre-schoolers through young adults." **Publishes 70 titles/year. Pays 2-10% royalty on retail price or flat fee. Pays negotiable advance.** Publishes book 1-2 years after acceptance. Responds in 6 months.

Ⓞ *Does not accept unsolicited submissions.*

NONFICTION All levels: biography, concept, history, multicultural, music/dance, nature/environment, science, and sports. Agented submissions only.

FICTION All levels: adventure, animal, contemporary, fantasy, history, humor, multicultural, nature/environment, poetry, problem novels, romance, science fiction, sports, suspense/mystery. *Accepts agented mss only.*

TIPS "No 'cartoony' or mass-market submissions for picture books."

Ⓐⵁ VILLARD BOOKS

Imprint of Random House Publishing Group, 1745 Broadway, New York NY 10019. (212)572-2600. **Website:** www.atrandom.com. Estab. 1983. "Villard Books is the publisher of savvy and sometimes quirky, best-selling hardcovers and trade paperbacks." **Pays negotiable royalty. Pays negotiable advance.**

NONFICTION Agented submissions only.

FICTION Commercial fiction. Agented submissions only.

RECENT TITLE(S) *Dog Days*, by Jon Katz; *Walking in Circles Before Lying Down*, by Merrill Markoe; *Have You Found Her*, by Janice Erlbaum.

Ⓐⵁ VINTAGE ANCHOR PUBLISHING

Imprint of Random House, 1745 Broadway, New York NY 10019. **Website:** www.randomhouse.com. **Contact:** Furaha Norton, editor. **Pays 4-8% royalty on retail price. Average advance: $2,500 and up.** Publishes book 1 year after acceptance.

FICTION Literary, mainstream/contemporary, short story collections. *Agented submissions only.*

VIVISPHERE PUBLISHING

675 Dutchess Turnpike, Poughkeepsie NY 12603. (845)463-1100, ext. 314. **Fax:** (845)463-0018. **E-mail:** cs@vivisphere.com. **Website:** www.vivisphere.com. **Contact:** Submissions. Estab. 1995. Publishes trade paperback originals and reprints and e-books. Vivisphere Publishing is now considering new submissions from any genre as follows: game of bridge (cards), nonfiction, history, military, new age, fiction, feminist/gay/lesbian, horror, contemporary, self-help, science fiction and cookbooks. **Pays royalty.** Publishes book 6 months-2 years after acceptance. Accepts simultaneous submissions. Responds in 6-12 months. Book catalog and ms guidelines online.

Ⓞ "Cookbooks should have a particular slant or appeal to a certain niche. Also publish out-of-print books."

NONFICTION Subjects include history, military, New Age, game of bridge. "Query with SASE. Please submit a proposal package (printed paper copy) including: outline and 1st chapter along with your contact information."

FICTION Subjects include feminist, gay, lesbian, historical, horror, literary, contemporary, military, self help, science fiction. Query with SASE.

VIZ MEDIA LLC

P.O. Box 77010, San Francisco CA 94107. (415)546-7073. **Website:** www.viz.com. "VIZ Media, LLC is one of the most comprehensive and innovative companies in the field of manga (graphic novel) publishing, animation and entertainment licensing of Japanese content. Owned by three of Japan's largest creators and licensors of manga and animation, Shueisha Inc., Shogakukan Inc., and Shogakukan-Shueisha Productions, Co., Ltd., VIZ Media is a leader in the publishing and distribution of Japanese manga for English speaking audiences in North America, the United Kingdom, Ireland, and South Africa and is a global ex-Asia licensor of Japanese manga and animation. The company offers an integrated product line including magazines such as *Shonen Jump* and *Shojo Beat*, graphic novels, and DVDs, and develops, markets, licenses, and distributes animated entertainment for audiences and consumers of all ages."

FICTION VIZ Media is currently accepting submissions and pitches for original comics. Keep in mind that all submissions must be accompanied by a signed release form.

VOYAGEUR PRESS

Quayside Publishing Group, 400 First Ave., N., Suite 300, Minneapolis MN 55401. (800)458-0454. **Fax:** (612)344-8691. **E-mail:** mdregni@voyageurpress.com. **Website:** voyageurpress.com. **Contact:** Michael Dregni, publisher. Estab. 1972. Publishes hardcover and trade paperback originals. "Voyageur Press (and its sports imprint MVP Books) is internationally known as a leading publisher of quality music, sports, country living, crafts, natural history, and regional books. No children's or poetry books." **Publishes 80 titles/year. 1,200 queries received/year. 500 mss received/year. 10% of books from first-time authors. 90% from unagented writers. Pays royalty. Pays advance.** Publishes book 1 year after acceptance. Accepts simultaneous submissions. Responds in 3 months to queries.

IMPRINTS MVP Books.

NONFICTION Subjects include Americana, cooking, environment, history, hobbies, music, nature, regional, sports, collectibles, country living, knitting and quilting, outdoor recreation. Query with SASE. Submit outline. Send sample digital images or transparencies (duplicates and tearsheets only).

RECENT TITLE(S) *The Snowflake* (popular science and microphotography look at snow crystals); *The Replacements* (oral history of post-punk rock'n'roll band); *The Surfboard* (history of surfboards); *How to Raise Chickens.*

TIPS "We publish books for an audience interested in regional, natural, and cultural history on a wide variety of subjects. We seek authors strongly committed to helping us promote and sell their books. Please present as focused an idea as possible in a brief submission (1-page cover letter; 2-page outline or proposal). Note your credentials for writing the book. Tell all you know about the market niche and marketing possibilities for proposed book. We use more book designers than artists or illustrators, since most of our books are illustrated with photographs."

⊘ WAKE FOREST UNIVERSITY PRESS

P.O. Box 7333, Winston-Salem NC 27109. (336)758-5448. **Fax:** (336)758-5636. **E-mail:** wfupress@wfu.edu. **Website:** www.wfu.edu/wfupress. **Contact:** Jefferson Holdridge, director/poetry editor; Dillon Johnston, advisory editor. Estab. 1976. "We publish only poetry from Ireland. I am able to consider only poetry written by native Irish poets. I must return, unread, poetry from American poets." Query with 4-5 samples and cover letter. Sometimes sends prepublication galleys. Buys North American or U.S. rights. **Publishes 4-6 titles/year. Pays on 10% royalty contract, plus 6-8 author's copies. Negotiable advance.** Responds to queries in 1-2 weeks; to submissions (*if invited*) in 2-3 months.

RECENT TITLE(S) *Collected Poems* by John Montague; *Ghost Orchid* by Michael Longley; *Selected Poems* by Medbh McGuckian; and *The Wake Forest Book of Irish Women's Poetry.*

WALCH PUBLISHING

P.O. Box 658, Portland ME 04104-0658. (207)772-3105. **Fax:** (207)774-7167. **Website:** www.walch.com. **Contact:** Susan Blair, editor-in-chief. Estab. 1927. "We focus on English/language arts, math, social studies and science teaching resources for middle school through adult assessment titles." **Publishes 100 titles/year. 10% of books from first-time authors. 95% from unagented writers. Pays 5-8% royalty on flat rate.** Publishes book 6 months after acceptance of ms. Accepts simultaneous submissions. Responds in 2 months to queries. Book catalog for 9×12 envelope and 5 first-class stamps. Guidelines for #10 SASE.

NONFICTION Subjects include education, mathematics, middle school, social sciences studies, remedial and special education, government, politics, history, language, literature, science, technology. Most titles are assigned by us, though we occasionally accept an author's unsolicited submission. We have a great need for author/artist teams and for authors who can write at third- to seventh-grade levels. Looks for sense of organization, writing ability, knowledge of subject, skill of communicating with intended audience. Formats include teacher resources, reproducibles. We do *not* want textbooks or anthologies. All authors should have educational writing experience. *Query first.* Query with SASE. Reviews artwork/photos.

WALKER AND CO.

Walker Publishing Co., 175 Fifth Ave., 7th Floor, New York NY 10010. (212)727-8300. **Fax:** (212)727-0984. **E-mail:** rebecca.mancini@bloomsburyusa.com. **Website:** bloomsbury.com/us/childrens. **Contact:** Emily Easton, publisher (picture books, middle grade & young adult novels); Stacy Cantor, associate editor (picture books, middle grade, and young adult novels); Mary Kate Castellani, assistant editor (picture books, middle grade, and young adult novels). Estab. 1959. Publishes hardcover trade originals. "Walker publishes general nonfiction on a variety of subjects, as well as children's books." **Pays 5-10% royalty.** Publishes book 1 year after acceptance. Book catalog for 9×12 envelope and 3 first-class stamps.

NONFICTION Subjects include business, economics, health, medicine, history, (science and technology), nature, environment, science, sports, mathematics, self-help. *Adult: agented submissions only*; Juvenile: send synopsis.

FICTION Subjects include juvenile, mystery, adult, picture books. Accepts unsolicited mss. Query with SASE. Include "a concise description of the story line, including its outcome, word length of story, writing experience, publishing credits, particular expertise on this subject and in this genre. Common mistake: not researching our publishing program and forgetting SASE." Query with SASE. Send complete ms for picture books.

RECENT TITLE(S) Published *Stolen Car,* by Patrick Jones; *Skinny*by Ibi Kaslik, *Violent Raines Almost Got Struck by Lightning*, by Danette Haworth, *Gimme Cracked Corn and I Will Share*, by Kevin O'Malley.

WALTSAN PUBLISHING

Fort Worth TX (817)845-1251. **E-mail:** sandra@waltsan.com. **Website:** www.waltsanpublishing.com. **Contact:** William Kercher, acquisitions editor. Estab. 2010. Trade paperback, mass market paperback, and electronic originals. Waltsan publishing publishes biographies, general nonfiction, how-tos, and illustrated, reference, scholary, self-help, technical books, and textbooks. **Publishes 12 titles/year. Accepts electronic submissions ONLY. "See website for details." Pays royalty minimum of 20%, maximum of 50% Does not pay advance.** Accepts simultaneous submissions. Responds in 1 month. Cataog available for SAE with 1 first class stamp. Guidelines online.

○ "Waltsan looks at author credentials, ms length, suitability of topic, believability, marketability, and writing skills. Looking for appropriate number and quality of graphics when appropriate."

NONFICTION Interested in all topics. Reviews artwork as part of the ms package.

FICTION Interested in all topics. "Make sure your writing is polished, believable, and the ms is not too short. Pay attention to details and don't try to fool the readers. Check for continuity of details by making sure what is written in one chapter coincides with what is written in other chapters. Don't guess. Check your facts." Accepts electronic submissions only.

POETRY Accepts electronic submissions only.

RECENT TITLE(S) Fiction: *Pup Fiction,* by Sherry Gottlieb; *Wildcat,* by William Kercher; *Fragments From a Writer's Notebook,* by Dr. Howeton Morris. Poetry: *Corn Woman/Mujer Maiz,* by Sue Littleton.

TIPS "Waltsan Publishing's audience is the 'on-the-go' person, electronic reader or android in hand, that wants to read whenever and wherever they get a chance. Generally younger, technologically savvy, and intelligent. Truly a 21st century individual."

WASHINGTON STATE UNIVERSITY PRESS

P.O. Box 645910, Pullman WA 99164-5910. (800)354-7360. **Fax:** (509)335-8568. **E-mail:** robert.clark@wsu.edu. **Website:** wsupress.wsu.edu. **Contact:** Robert A. Clark, acquisitions editor. Estab. 1928. Publishes hardcover originals, trade paperback originals, and reprints. WSU Press publishes scholarly nonfiction books on the history, pre-history, culture, and politics of the West, particularly the Pacific Northwest. **Publishes 4-6 titles/year. 40% of books from first-time authors. 95% from unagented writers. Pays 5% royalty graduated according to sales.** Publishes book 18 months after acceptance. Responds in 2 months to queries. Submission guidelines online.

NONFICTION Subjects include archaeology, cultural studies, cooking and food history, environment, government, history, politics, nature, railroads, science, essays. "We welcome engaging and thought-provoking mss that focus on the greater Pacific Northwest (primarily Washington, Oregon, Idaho, British Columbia, western Montana, and southeastern Alaska). Currently we are not accepting how-to books, literary criticism, memoirs, novels, or poetry." Submit outline, sample chapters. Reviews artwork/photos.

RECENT TITLE(S) *Made in Hanford: The Bomb that Changed the World; Governing Washington: Politics and Government in the Evergreen State; Planet Rock Doc: Nuggets from Explorations of the Natural World; Greenscapes: Olmsted's Pacific Northwest.*

TIPS "We have developed our marketing in the direction of regional and local history, and use this as the base upon which to expand our publishing program. For history, the secret is to write strong narratives on significant topics or events. Stories should be told in imaginative, clever ways and be substantiated factually. Have visuals (photos, maps, etc.) available to help the reader envision what has happened. Explain stories in ways that tie them to wider-ranging regional, national—or even international—events. Weave them into the large pattern of history."

WASHINGTON WRITERS' PUBLISHING HOUSE

P.O. Box 15271, Washington DC 20003. **E-mail:** wwphpress@gmail.com. **Website:** www.washingtonwriters.org. **Contact:** Patrick Pepper, president. Estab. 1975. Guidelines for SASE or on website.

FICTION Washington Writers' Publishing House considers book-length mss for publication by fiction writers living within 75 driving miles of the U.S. Capitol, Baltimore area included, through competition only. Has published fiction books by Andrew Wingfield, David Taylor, Elizabeth Bruce, Phil Kurata, Gretchen Roberts, Denis Collins, Elisavietta Ritchie, Laura Brylawski-Miller, Hilary Tham, Catherine Kimrey. Offers $1,000 and 50 copies of published book plus additional copies for publicity use. Mss may include previously published stories and excerpts. "Author should indicate where they heard about WWPH." **Entry fee:** $25. **Deadline:** July 1-November 1 (postmark). Order sample fiction books on website or by sending $16, plus $3 shipping. Submit an electronic copy by e-mail (use PDF, .doc, or rich text format) or 2 hard copies by snail mail of a short story collection or novel (no more than 350 pages, double or 1-1/2 spaced; author's name should not appear on any ms pages). Include separate page of publication acknowledgments plus 2 cover sheets: one with ms title, poet's name, address, telephone number, and e-mail address, the other with ms title only. Include SASE for results only; mss will not be returned (will be recycled).

POETRY Washington Writers' Publishing House considers book-length mss for publication by poets living within 75 driving miles of the U.S. Capitol (Baltimore area included) through competition only. Publishes 1-2 poetry books/year. "No specific criteria, except literary excellence."

RECENT TITLE(S) Has published books by David Ebenbach, Melanie S. Hatter, Andrew Wingfield, David Taylor, and Gray Jacobik.

ⒶⓄ WATERBROOK MULTNOMAH PUBLISHING GROUP

Random House, 12265 Oracle Blvd.,, Suite 200, Colorado Springs CO 80921. (719)590-4999. **Fax:** (719)590-8977. **Website:** www.waterbrookmultnomah.com. Es-

tab. 1996. Publishes hardcover and trade paperback originals. **Publishes 70 titles/year. 2,000 queries received/year. 15% of books from first-time authors. Pays royalty.** Publishes book 1 year after acceptance. Accepts simultaneous submissions. Responds in 2-3 months. Book catalog online.

NONFICTION Subjects include child guidance, money, finance, religion, spirituality, marriage, Christian living. "We publish books on unique topics with a Christian perspective." Agented submissions only.

FICTION Subjects include adventure, historical, literary, mainstream, contemporary, mystery, religious, inspirational, religious mystery/suspense, religious thriller, religious romance, romance, contemporary, historical, science fiction, spiritual, suspense. Agented submissions only.

RECENT TITLE(S) *The Greatest Words Ever Spoken* by Steven K. Scott; *When the Soul Mends,* by Cindy Woodsmall; *One Month to Live*, by Kerry & Chris Schook.

Ⓐ WATSON-GUPTILL PUBLICATIONS

Crown Publishing Group/Random House, The Crown Publishing Group, 1745 Broadway, New York NY 10019. (646)654-5000. **Fax:** (646)654-5486. **Website:** www.watsonguptill.com. **Contact:** The Editors. Publishes hardcover and trade paperback originals and reprints. "Watson-Guptill is an arts book publisher." **150 queries received/year. 50 mss received/year. 50% of books from first-time authors. 75% from unagented writers. Pays royalty on wholesale price.** Publishes book 9 months after acceptance of ms. Responds in 2 months to queries. Responds in 3 months to proposals. Book catalog available free. Guidelines online.

IMPRINTS Watson-Guptill; Amphoto; Whitney Library of Design; Billboard Books; Back Stage Books.

NONFICTION Subjects include art, architecture, music, dance, photography, lifestyle. "Writers should be aware of the kinds of books (arts, crafts, graphic designs, instructional) Watson-Guptill publishes before submitting. Although we are growing and will consider new ideas and approaches, we will not consider a book if it is clearly outside of our publishing program." "Query with SASE. Submit proposal package, outline, 1-2 sample chapters. Not accepting unsolicited submissions mss, proposals, or submissions queries via e-mail right now. Send inquiries in writing on your letterhead by mail or fax to (212)940-7868." Reviews artwork/photos. Send photocopies and transparencies.

RECENT TITLE(S) *Manga Mania Shoujo*, by Christopher Hart; *Scared! How to Draw Horror Comic Characters*, by Steve Miller and Bryan Baugh; *Days of Hope and Dreams: An Intimate Portrait of Bruce Springsteen*, by Frank Stefanko.

TIPS "We are an art book publisher."

WAVE BOOKS

1938 Fairview Ave. E., Suite 201, Seattle WA 98102. (206)676-5337. **E-mail:** info@wavepoetry.com. **Website:** www.wavepoetry.com. **Contact:** Charlie Wright, publisher; Joshua Beckman and Matthew Zapruder, editors; Heidi Broadhead, managing editor. Estab. 2005. Publishes hardcover and trade paperback originals. "Wave Books is an independent poetry press based in Seattle, Washington, dedicated to publishing the best in contemporary American poetry, poetry in translation, and writing by poets. The Press was founded in 2005, merging with established publisher Verse Press. By publishing strong innovative work in finely crafted trade editions and handmade ephemera, we hope to continue to challenge the values and practices of readers and add to the collective sense of what's possible in contemporary poetry." Catalog online.

⬭   "Please no unsolicited mss or queries. We will post calls for submissions on our website."

RECENT TITLE(S) *Traces of the Blast*, by Mary Ruefle; *People on Sunday*, by Geoffrey G. O'Brien; *Poems (1962-1997)*, by Robert Lax, translated by John Beer.

WAVELAND PRESS, INC.

4180 Illinois Route 83, Suite 101, Long Grove IL 60047-9580. (847)634-0081. **Fax:** (847)634-9501. **E-mail:** info@waveland.com. **Website:** www.waveland.com. Estab. 1975. Waveland Press, Inc. is a publisher of college textbooks and supplements. We are committed to providing reasonably priced teaching materials for the classroom and actively seek to add new titles to our growing lists in a variety of academic disciplines. If you are currently working on a project you feel serves a need and would have promise as an adopted text in the college market, we would like to hear from you.

⊙ WEIGL EDUCATIONAL PUBLISHERS, LTD.

350 5th Ave., 59th Floor, New York NY 10118. (403)233-7747. **Fax:** (403)233-7769. **E-mail:** linda@weigl.com; av2books@weigl.com. **Website:** www.weigl.ca. Estab. 1979. Publishes hardcover originals and reprints, school library softcover. "Textbook publisher catering to juvenile and young adult audience (K-12)." Makes outright purchase. Responds ASAP to queries. Query with SASE. **Publishes 40 titles/year. 100% from unagented writers.** Book catalog available for free.

NONFICTION Animals, education, government, politics, history, nature, environment, science.

WEIGL PUBLISHERS INC.

350 Fifth Ave. 59th Floor, New York NY 10118. (866)649-3445. **Fax:** (866)449-3445. **E-mail:** linda@weigl.com. **Website:** www.weigl.com. **Contact:** Heather Kissock, acquisitions. Estab. 2000. Publishes 25 young readers/year; 40 middle readers/year; 20 young adult titles/year. "Our mission is to provide innovative high-quality learning resources for schools and libraries worldwide at a competitive price." **Publishes 85 titles/year. 15% of books from first-time authors.** Publishes book 6-9 months after acceptance. Accepts simultaneous submissions. Catalog online.

NONFICTION Young readers: animal, biography, geography, history, multicultural, nature/environment, science. Middle readers: animal, biography, geography, history, multicultural, nature/environment, science, social issues, sports. Young adults: biography, careers, geography, history, multicultural, nature/environment, social issues. Average word length: young readers—100 words/page; middle readers—200 words/page; young adults—300 words/page. Query by e-mail only.

WESLEYAN PUBLISHING HOUSE

P.O. Box 50434, Indianapolis IN 46250. **E-mail:** submissions@wesleyan.org. **Website:** www.wesleyan.org/wg. **Contact:** Rachael Stevenson, associate production editor. Estab. 1843. Publishes hardcover and trade paperback originals. **150-175 submissions received/year. Pays royalty on wholesale price.** Publishes book 11 months after acceptance. Accepts simultaneous submissions. Responds within 2 months to proposals. Catalog online. Guidelines online.

NONFICTION Subjects include Christianity/religion. No hard-copy submissions. Submit proposal package, including outline, 5 sample chapters, bio. See writer's guidelines. Does not review artwork.

RECENT TITLE(S) *Jaded Faith*, by Jarod Osborne (spiritual growth); *SoulShift*, by Steve DeNeff and David Drury (Christian living); *Faith Legacy for Couples*, by Jim and Jerolyn Bogear (Christian living/marriage).

TIPS "Our books help evangelical Christians learn about the faith or grow in their relationship with God."

⊘ WESLEYAN UNIVERSITY PRESS

215 Long Lane, Middletown CT 06459. (860)685-7711. **Fax:** (860)685-7712. **E-mail:** stamminen@wesleyan.edu. **E-mail:** psmathers@wesleyan.edu. **Website:** www.wesleyan.edu/wespress. **Contact:** Suzanna Tamminen, director and editor-in-chief; Parker Smathers, editor. Estab. 1959. Publishes hardcover originals and paperbacks. "Wesleyan University Press is a scholarly press with a focus on poetry, music, dance and cultural studies." Wesleyan University Press is one of the major publishers of poetry in the nation. Poetry publications from Wesleyan tend to get widely (and respectfully) reviewed. **"We are accepting mss by invitation only until further notice."** Pays royalties, plus 10 author's copies. Accepts simultaneous submissions. Responds to queries in 2 months; to mss in 4 months. Book catalog available free. Guidelines online.

NONFICTION Subjects include music, dance, film/TV & media studies, science fiction studies, dance and poetry. Submit proposal package, outline, sample chapters, cover letter, CV, TOC, anticipated length of ms and date of completion. Reviews artwork/photos. Send photocopies.

POETRY Does not accept unsolicited mss.

RECENT TITLE(S) *Sex and the Slayer*, by Lorna Jarrett; *Door in the Mountain*, by Jean Valentine; *The Begum's Millions*, by Jules Verne.

WESTERN PSYCHOLOGICAL SERVICES

625 Alaska Ave., Torrance CA 90503. (424)201-8800 or (800)648-8857. **Fax:** (424)201-6950. **E-mail:** review@wpspublish.com. **Website:** www.wpspublish.com; www.creativetherapystore.com. Estab. 1948. Publishes psychological and educational assessments and some trade paperback originals. "Western Psychological Services publishes psychological and educational assessments that practitioners trust. Our products allow helping professionals to accurately screen, diagnose, and treat people in need. WPS publishes practical books and games used by therapists, counselors, social workers, and others in the helping professionals who work with children and adults." **Publishes 2 titles/year. 60 queries received/year. 30 mss received/year. 90% of books from first-time authors. 95% from unagented writers. Pays 5-10% royalty on wholesale price.** Publishes book 1 year after acceptance. Accepts simultaneous submissions. Responds in 2 months to queries. Book catalog available free. Guidelines online.

NONFICTION Subjects include child guidance, psychology, autism, sensory processing disorders. "We publish children's books dealing with feelings, anger, social skills, autism, family problems." Submit complete ms. Reviews artwork/photos. Send photocopies.

FICTION Children's books dealing with feelings, anger, social skills, autism, family problems, etc. Submit complete ms.

RECENT TITLE(S) *Sensory Integration and the Child*, by A. Jean Ayres, PhD; *To Be Me*, by Rebecca Etlinger.

WESTMINSTER JOHN KNOX PRESS

Division of Presbyterian Publishing Corp., 100 Witherspoon St., Louisville KY 40202. **Fax:** (502)569-5113. **E-mail:** submissions@wjkbooks.com. **Website:** www.wjkbooks.com. **Contact:** Editorial Department. Publishes hardcover and paperback originals and reprints. "All WJK books have a religious/spiritual angle, but are written for various markets-scholarly, professional, and the general reader. Westminster John Knox is affiliated with the Presbyterian Church USA. No phone queries. We do not publish fiction, poetry, memoir, children's books, or dissertations. We will not return or respond to submissions without an accompanying SASE with sufficient postage." **Publishes 70 titles/year. 2,500 queries received/year. 750 mss received/year. 10% of books from first-time authors. Pays royalty on net price.** Responds in 3 months. Proposal guidelines online.

NONFICTION Subjects include religion, spirituality. Submit proposal package according to the WJK book proposal guidelines found online.

WHITAKER HOUSE

1030 Hunt Valley Circle, New Kensington PA 15068. **E-mail:** publisher@whitakerhouse.com. **Website:** www.whitakerhouse.com. **Contact:** Editorial Department. Estab. 1970. Publishes hardcover, trade paperback, and mass market originals. **Publishes 50 titles/year. 600 queries received/year. 200 mss received/year. 15% of books from first-time authors. 60% from unagented writers. Pays 5-15% royalty on wholesale price.** Publishes book 7 months after acceptance. Accepts simultaneous submissions. Responds in 3 months. Catalog and guidelines online.

NONFICTION Subjects include religion, Christian. Accepts submissions on topics with a Christian perspective. Query with SASE. Does not review artwork/photos.

FICTION Subjects include religious, Christian, historial romance, African American romance and Amish fiction. All fiction must have a Christian perspective. Query with SASE.

RECENT TITLE(S) *Glory of God*, by Guillermo Maldonado (charasmatic); *Prayers That Get Results*, by Tom Brown (Christian living); *Faith, Family & Finances*, by Henry Ferdnandez (Christian living).

TIPS "Audience includes those seeking uplifting and inspirational fiction and nonfiction."

☺ WHITECAP BOOKS, LTD.

210 - 314 W. Cordova St., Vancouver BC V6B 1 E8, Canada. (604)681-6181. **Fax:** (905)477-9179. **E-mail:** jeffreyb@whitecap.ca. **Website:** www.whitecap.ca. Publishes hardcover and trade paperback originals. "Whitecap Books is a general trade publisher with a focus on food and wine titles. Although we are interested in reviewing unsolicited ms submissions, please note that we only accept submissions that meet the needs of our current publishing program. Please see some of most recent releases to get an idea of the kinds of titles we are interested in." **Publishes 40 titles/year. 500 queries received/year; 1,000 mss received/year. 20% of books from first-time authors. 90% from unagented writers. Pays royalty. Pays negotiated advance.** Publishes book 1 year after acceptance. Accepts simultaneous submissions. Responds in 2-3 months to proposals. Catalog and guidelines online.

NONFICTION Subjects include animals, cooking, foods, nutrition, gardening, history, nature, environment, recreation, regional, travel. Young children's and middle reader's nonfiction focusing mainly on nature, wildlife and animals. "Writers should take the time to research our list and read the submission guidelines on our website. This is especially important for children's writers and cookbook authors. We will only consider submissions that fall into these categories: cookbooks, wine and spirits, regional travel, home and garden, Canadian history, North American natural history, juvenile series-based fiction." "At this time, we are not accepting the following categories: self-help or inspirational books, political, social commentary, or issue books, general how-to books, biographies or memoirs, business and finance, art and architecture, religion and spirituality." Submit cover letter, synopsis, SASE via ground mail. See guidelines online. Reviews artwork/photos. Send photocopies.

FICTION No children's picture books or adult fiction. See guidelines.

TIPS "We want well-written, well-researched material that presents a fresh approach to a particular topic."

WHITE MANE KIDS

73 W. Burd St., P.O. Box 708, Shippensburg PA 17257. (717)532-2237. **Fax:** (717)532-6110. **E-mail:** marketing@whitemane.com. **Website:** www.whitemane.com. **Contact:** Harold Collier, acquisitions editor. Estab. 1987. **Pays authors royalty of 7-10%. Pays illustrators and photographers by the project.** Publishes book 18 months after acceptance. Accepts simultaneous submissions. Responds to queries in 1 month, mss in 3 months. Book catalog and writer's guidelines available for SASE.

IMPRINTS White Mane Books, Burd Street Press, White Mane Kids, Ragged Edge Press.

NONFICTION Middle readers, young adults: history. Average word length: middle readers—30,000. Does not publish picture books. Submit outline/synopsis and 2-3 sample chapters.

FICTION Middle readers, young adults: history (primarily American Civil War). Average word length: middle readers—30,000. Does not publish picture books. Query.

TIPS "Make your work historically accurate. We are interested in historically accurate fiction for middle and young adult readers. We do *not* publish picture books. Our primary focus is the American Civil War and some America Revolution topics."

WHITE PINE PRESS

P.O. Box 236, Buffalo NY 14201. (716)627-4665. **Fax:** (716)627-4665. **E-mail:** wpine@whitepine.org. **Website:** www.whitepine.org. **Contact:** Dennis Maloney, editor. Estab. 1973. Publishes trade paperback originals. **Publishes 10-12 titles/year. 500 queries/yearly 1% of books from first-time authors. 100% from unagented writers. Pays contributor's copies.** Publishes book 18 months after acceptance. Accepts simultaneous submissions. Responds in 1 month to queries and proposals; 4 months to mss. Catalog available online at website; for #10 SASE. Guidelines online.

NONFICTION Subjects include language, literature, multicultural, translation, poetry. *"We are currently not considering nonfiction mss."* "We do not review artwork/photos."

FICTION Subjects include poetry, poetry in translation, translation. For fiction and poetry in translation

ONLY-query with SASE; submit proposal package, including synopsis and 2 sample chapters.

POETRY "We are currently not reading U.S. fiction. We are currently reading unsolicited poetry only as part of our Annual Poetry Contest. The reading period is July 1 - November 30 for fiction and poetry in translation only." Query with SASE.

ALBERT WHITMAN & COMPANY

250 S. Northwest Hwy., Suite 320, Park Ridge IL 60068. (800)255-7675. **Fax:** (847)581-0039. **E-mail:** submissions@awhitmanco.com. **Website:** www.albertwhitman.com. Estab. 1919. Publishes in original hardcover, paperback, boardbooks. Albert Whitman & Company publishes books for the trade, library, and school library market. Interested in reviewing the following types of projects: Picture book mss for ages 2-8; novels and chapter books for ages 8-12; young adult novels; nonfiction for ages 3-12 and YA; art samples showing pictures of children. Best known for the classic series The Boxcar Children® Mysteries. **Publishes 60 titles/year. 10% of books from first-time authors. 50% from unagented writers.** Accepts simultaneous submissions. Guidelines online.

○ "We are no longer reading unsolicited queries and mss sent through the US mail. We now require these submissions to be sent by e-mail. You must visit our website for our guidelines, which include instructions for formatting your e-mail. E-mails that do not follow this format may not be read. We read every submission within 4 months of receipt, but we can no longer respond to every one. If you do not receive a response from us after four months, we have declined to publish your submission."

WILD CHILD PUBLISHING

PO Box 4897, Culver City CA 90231. (310) 721-4461. **E-mail:** admin@wildchildpublishing.com. **Website:** www.wildchildpublishing.com. **Contact:** Marci Baun, editor-in-chief (genres not covered by other editors); Faith Bicknell-Brown, managing editor (horror and romance); S.R. Howen, editor (science fiction and nonfiction). Estab. 1999. Wild Child Publishing is a small, independent press that started out as a magazine in September 1999. We are known for working with newer/unpublished authors and editing to the standards of NYC publishers. Publishes paperback originals, e-books. Format: POD printing; perfect bound. Average print order: 50-200. Member EPIC. Distributes/promotes titles through Ingrams and own website, Mobipocket Kindle, Amazon, and soon with Fictionwise. Freya's Bower already distributes through Fictionwise. **Publishes 12 titles/year. Pays royalties 10-40%.** Publishes book 2-4 months after acceptance. Responds in 1 month to queries and mss. Book catalogs on website.

FICTION Adventure, children's/juvenile, erotica for Freya's Bower only, ethnic/multicultural, experimental, fantasy, feminist, gay, historical, horror, humor/satire, lesbian, literary, mainstream, military/war, mystery/suspense, New Age/mystic, psychic/supernatural, romance, science fiction, short story collections, thriller/espionage, western, young adult/teen (fantasy/science fiction). Multiple anthologies planned. Query with outline/synopsis and 1 sample chapter. Accepts queries by e-mail only. Include estimated word count, brief bio. Often critiques/comments on rejected mss.

TIPS "Read our submission guidelines thoroughly. Send in entertaining, well-written stories. Be easy to work with and upbeat."

THE WILD ROSE PRESS

P.O. Box 708, Adams Basin NY 14410. (585) 752-8770. **E-mail:** queryus@thewildrosepress.com; rpenders@thewildrosepress.com. **Website:** www.thewildrosepress.com. **Contact:** Nicole D'Arienzo, editor. Estab. 2006. Publishes paperback originals, reprints, and e-books in a POD format. **Publishes 10 titles/year. Pays royalty of 7% minimum; 35% maximum.** Publishes book 1 year after acceptance. Responds in 1 month to queries; 3 months to mss. Guidelines online.

○ "The American Rose line publishes stories about the French and Indian wars; Colonial America; the Revolutionary War; the war of 1812; the War Between the States; the Reconstruction era; the dawn of the new century. These are the struggles at the heart of the American Rose story. The central romantic relationship is the key driving force, set against historically accurate backdrop. These stories are for those who long for the courageous heroes and heroines who fought for their freedom and settled the new world; for gentle southern belles with spines of steel and the gallant gentlemen who sweep them away. This line is wide open for writers with a love of American history."

FICTION Subjects include contemporary, erotica, gothic, historical, regional, romance, suspense, war, futuristic/time travel, regency, romantic suspense, and paranormal. Plans several anthologies "in several lines of the company in the next year, including Cactus Rose, Yellow Rose, American Rose, Black Rose, and Scarlet Rose.". Please do not submit women's fiction, poetry, science fiction, fanfiction, or any type of nonfiction. *Does not accept unsolicited mss.* Send query letter with outline and synopsis of up to 5 pages. Accepts all queries by e-mail. Include estimated word count, brief bio, and list of publishing credits. Agented fiction less than 1%. Always comments on rejected mss. Sends prepublication galleys to author. Only our full length (over 65K words) will go to print.

TIPS "Polish your ms, make it as error free as possible, and follow our submission guidelines."

⊘ WILDSTORM

DC Universe, 1700 Broadway, New York NY 10019. **Website:** www.dccomics.com/wildstorm.

○ *Does not accept unsolicited mss.*

JOHN WILEY & SONS, INC.

Wiley-Blackwell, 111 River St., Hoboken NJ 07030. (201)748-6000. **Fax:** (201)748-6088. **Website:** www.wiley.com. **Contact:** Editorial Department. Estab. 1807. Publishes hardcover originals, trade paperback originals and reprints. "The General Interest group publishes nonfiction books for the consumer market. There is also a Higher Education Division. See proposal guidelines online." **Pays competitive rates. Pays advance.** Accepts simultaneous submissions. Catalog and guidelines online.

IMPRINTS Jossey-Bass, Pfeiffer, Capstone.

NONFICTION Subjects include history, memoirs, psychology, science, popular, African-American interest, health/self-improvement, technical, medical. "If you have an idea for a new book, journal, or electronic product that falls into the chemistry, the life sciences, medicine, mathematical and physical sciences, humanities, and social sciences arena, please send your proposal or ms to Wiley-Blackwell." See website for more details.

TIPS "Include a brief description of the publication and overall objective. Describe exactly what the publication will be about. What will there be about your selection, organization, or treatment of the subject that will make the readers buy the publication? Address why there is a need for the proposed publication."

▲⊘ WILLIAM MORROW

HarperCollins, 10 E. 53rd St., New York NY 10022. (212)207-7000. **Fax:** (212)207-7145. **Website:** www.harpercollins.com. Estab. 1926. "William Morrow publishes a wide range of titles that receive much recognition and prestige—a most selective house." **Pays standard royalty on retail price. Pays varying advance.** Book catalog available free.

NONFICTION Subjects include art, architecture, cooking, foods, nutrition, history. Length 50,000-100,000 words. *No unsolicited mss or proposals.* Agented submissions only.

FICTION Publishes adult fiction. Morrow accepts only the highest quality submissions in adult fiction. *No unsolicited mss or proposals.* Agented submissions only.

WILLIAMSON BOOKS

2630 Elm Hill Pike, Suite 100, Nashville TN 37214. **E-mail:** pjay@guideposts.org. **Website:** www.idealsbooks.com. Estab. 1983. Publishes "very successful nonfiction series (Kids Can! Series) on subjects such as history, science, arts/crafts, geography, diversity, multiculturalism. Little Hands series for ages 2-6, Kaleidoscope Kids series (age 7 and up) and Quick Starts for Kids! series (ages 8 and up). Our goal is to help every child fulfill his/her potential and experience personal growth." **Pays authors advance against future royalties based on wholesale price or purchases outright. Pays illustrators by the project. Pays photographers per photo.** Publishes book 1 year after acceptance. Responds in 4 months. Guidelines available for SASE.

NONFICTION Hands-on active learning books, animals, African-American, arts/crafts, Asian, biography, diversity, careers, geography, health, history, hobbies, how-to, math, multicultural, music/dance, nature/environment, Native American, science, writing and journaling. Does not want to see textbooks, picture books, fiction. "Looking for all things African American, Asian American, Hispanic, Latino, and Native American including crafts and traditions, as well as their history, biographies, and personal retrospectives of growing up in U.S. for grades pre K-8th. We are looking for books in which learning and doing are inseparable." Query with annotated TOC/synopsis and 1 sample chapter.

TIPS "Please do not send any fiction or picture books of any kind—those should go to Ideals Children's Books. Look at our books to see what we do. We're interested in interactive learning books with a creative approach packed with interesting information, written for young readers ages 3-7 and 8-14. In nonfiction children's publishing, we are looking for authors with a depth of knowledge shared with children through a warm, embracing style. Our publishing philosophy is based on the idea that all children can succeed and have positive learning experiences. Children's lasting learning experiences involve their participation."

WILLOW CREEK PRESS

P.O. Box 147, Minocqua WI 54548. (715)358-7010. **Fax:** (715)358-2807. **E-mail:** jpetrie@willowcreekpress.com. **Website:** www.willowcreekpress.com. **Contact:** Managing Editor. Estab. 1986. Publishes hardcover and trade paperback originals and reprints. "We specialize in nature, outdoor, and sporting topics, including gardening, wildlife, and animal books. Pets, cookbooks, and a few humor books and essays round out our titles. Currently emphasizing pets (mainly dogs and cats), wildlife, outdoor sports (hunting, fishing). De-emphasizing essays, fiction." **Publishes 25 titles/year. 400 queries received/year. 150 mss received/year. 15% of books from first-time authors. 50% from unagented writers. Pays 6-15% royalty on wholesale price. Pays $2,000-5,000 advance.** Publishes book 18 months after acceptance. Accepts simultaneous submissions. Responds in 2 months to queries. Guidelines online.
NONFICTION Subjects include animals, cooking, foods, nutrition, gardening, nature, environment, recreation, sports, travel, wildlife, pets. Submit cover letter, chapter outline, 1-2 sample chapters, brief bio, SASE. Reviews artwork/photos.

WILSHIRE BOOK CO

9731 Variel Ave., Chatsworth CA 91311. (818)700-1522. **Fax:** (818)700-1527. **E-mail:** mpowers@mpowers.com. **Website:** www.mpowers.com. **Contact:** Rights Department. Estab. 1947. Publishes trade paperback originals and reprints. **Publishes 25 titles/year. 1,200 queries received/year. 70% of books from first-time authors. 90% from unagented writers. Pays standard royalty. Pays advance.** Publishes book 6-9 months after acceptance. Accepts simultaneous submissions. Responds in 2 months. Ms guidelines online.
NONFICTION Subjects include psychology, personal success. Minimum 30,000 words. Submit 3 sample chapters. Submit complete ms. Include outline, author bio, analysis of book's competition and SASE. No e-mail or fax submissions. Reviews artwork/photos. Send photocopies.
FICTION "You are not only what you are today, but also what you choose to become tomorrow." Looking for adult fables that teach principles of psychological

growth. Distributes titles through wholesalers, bookstores and mail order. Promotes titles through author interviews on radio and television.Wants adult allegories that teach principles of psychological growth or offer guidance in living. Minimum 30,000 words. No standard fiction. Submit 3 sample chapters. Submit complete ms. Include outline, author bio, analysis of book's, competition and SASE.
TIPS "We are vitally interested in all new material we receive. Just as you are hopeful when submitting your ms for publication, we are hopeful as we read each one submitted, searching for those we believe could be successful in the marketplace. Writing and publishing must be a team effort. We need you to write what we can sell. We suggest you read the successful books similar to the one you want to write. Analyze them to discover what elements make them winners. Duplicate those elements in your own style, using a creative new approach and fresh material, and you will have written a book we can catapult onto the bestseller list. You are welcome to telephone or e-mail us for immediate feedback on any book concept you may have. To learn more about us and what we publish, and for complete ms guidelines, visit our website."

⊘ WINDRIVER PUBLISHING, INC.

3280 Madison Ave., Ogden UT 84403. (801)689-7440. **E-mail:** info@windriverpublishing.com. **Website:** www.windriverpublishing.com. **Contact:** E. Keith Howick, Jr., president; Gail Howick, vice president/editor-in-chief. Estab. 2003. Publishes hardcover originals and reprints, trade paperback originals, and mass market originals. "Authors who wish to submit book proposals for review must do so according to our Submissions Guidelines, which can be found on our website, along with an on-line submission form, which is our preferred submission method. *We do not accept submissions of any kind by e-mail.*" **Publishes 8 titles/year. 1,000 queries received/year. 300 mss received/year. 95% of books from first-time authors. 90% from unagented writers.** Publishes book 1 year after acceptance. Accepts simultaneous submissions. Responds in 1-2 months to queries; 4-6 months to proposals/mss. Catalog and guidelines online.
NONFICTION Subjects include business, computers, education, environment, gardening, government, health, history, hobbies, language, literature, medicine, nature, philosophy, religion, science, spirituality,

sports, true crime, antiques/collectibles. Does not accept unsolicited mss. Reviews artwork/photos.

FICTION Subjects include adventure, fantasy, historical, horror, humor, juvenile, literary, military, war, mystery, occult, religious, romance, science fiction, short story collections, spiritual, sports, suspense, western, young adult, drama; espionage; political; psychological; fairy tales/folklore; graphic novels. Not accepting submissions at this time.

TIPS "We do not accept mss containing graphic or gratuitous profanity, sex, or violence. See online instructions for details."

WINDWARD PUBLISHING

Finney Company, 5995 149th St. W., Suite 105, Apple Valley MN 55124. **E-mail:** feedback@finneyco.com. **Website:** www.finneyco.com. **Contact:** Alan E. Krysan, president. Estab. 1973. Publishes trade paperback originals. Windward publishes illustrated natural history, recreation books, and children's books. "Covers topics of natural history and science, outdoor recreation, and children's literature. Its principal markets are book, retail, and specialty stores. While primarily a nonfiction publisher, we will occasionally accept fiction books with educational value." **Publishes 6-10 titles/year. 120 queries received/year. 50 mss received/year. 50% of books from first-time authors. 100% from unagented writers. Pays 10% royalty on wholesale price. Pays advance.** Publishes book 1 year after acceptance. Accepts simultaneous submissions. Responds in 8-10 weeks to queries.

NONFICTION Subjects include agriculture, animals, gardening, nature, environment, recreation, science, sports, natural history. Young readers, middle readers, young adults: activity books, animal, careers, nature/environment, science. Young adults: textbooks. Query with SASE. Does not accept e-mail or fax submissions. Reviews artwork/photos.

WISCONSIN HISTORICAL SOCIETY PRESS

816 State St., Madison WI 53706. (608)264-6465. **Fax:** (608)264-6486. **E-mail:** whspress@wisconsinhistory.org. **Website:** www.wisconsinhistory.org/whspress/. **Contact:** Kate Thompson, editor. Estab. 1855. Publishes hardcover and trade paperback originals; trade paperback reprints. **Publishes 12-14 titles/year. 60-75 queries received/year. 20% of books from first-time authors. 90% from unagented writers. Pays royalty on wholesale price.** Publishes book 2 years after acceptance. Book catalog available free. Guidelines online.

IMPRINTS Wisconsin Magazine of History.

NONFICTION Subjects include Wisconsin history and culture: archaeology, architecture, cooking, foods, ethnic, history (Wisconsin), memoirs, regional, sports. Submit proposal package, form from website. Reviews artwork/photos. Send photocopies.

TIPS "Our audience reads about Wisconsin. Carefully review the book."

WISDOM PUBLICATIONS

199 Elm St., Somerville MA 02144. (617)776-7416, ext. 28. **Fax:** (617)776-7841. **E-mail:** editors@wisdompubs.org. **Website:** www.wisdompubs.org. **Contact:** David Kittlestrom, senior editor. Estab. 1976. Publishes hardcover originals and trade paperback originals and reprints. "Wisdom Publications is dedicated to making available authentic Buddhist works for the benefit of all. We publish translations, commentaries, and teachings of past and contemporary Buddhist masters and original works by leading Buddhist scholars. Currently emphasizing popular applied Buddhism, scholarly titles." **Publishes 20-25 titles/year. 300 queries received/year. 50% of books from first-time authors. 95% from unagented writers. Pays 4-8% royalty on wholesale price. Pays advance.** Publishes book within 2 years of acceptance. after acceptance of ms. Book catalog and ms guidelines online.

NONFICTION Subjects include philosophy, Buddhist or comparative Buddhist/Western, psychology, religion, Buddhism, Tibet. Submissions should be made electronically.

TIPS "We are basically a publisher of Buddhist books-all schools and traditions of Buddhism. Please see our catalog or our website before you send anything to us to get a sense of what we publish."

✿⊘ PAULA WISEMAN BOOKS

1230 Sixth Ave., New York NY 10020. (212)698-7272. **Fax:** (212)698-2796. **E-mail:** paula.wiseman@simonandschuster.com; sylvie.frank@simonandschuster.com. **Website:** kids.simonandschuster.com. **Publishes 20 titles/year. 10% of books from first-time authors.**

NONFICTION Picture books: animal, biography, concept, history, nature/environment. Young readers: animal, biography, history, multicultural, nature/environment, sports. Average word length: picture books— 500; others standard length. Does not accept unsolicited or unagented mss.

FICTION Considers all categories. Average word length: picture books—500; others standard length.

WOODBINE HOUSE

6510 Bells Mill Rd., Bethesda MD 20817. (301)897-3570. **Fax:** (301)897-5838. **E-mail:** info@woodbinehouse. com. **Website:** www.woodbinehouse.com. **Contact:** Nancy Gray Paul, acquisitions editor. Estab. 1985. Publishes trade paperback originals. Woodbine House publishes books for or about individuals with disabilities to help those individuals and their families live fulfilling and satisfying lives in their homes, schools, and communities. **Publishes 10 titles/year. 15% of books from first-time authors. 90% from unagented writers. Pays 10-12% royalty.** Publishes book 18 months after acceptance. Accepts simultaneous submissions. Responds in 3 months to queries. Book catalog for 6x9 SAE with 3 first-class stamps. No metered mail or international reply coupons (IRCs) please. Guidelines online.

NONFICTION Subjects include specific issues related to a given disability (e.g., communication skills, social sciences skills, feeding issues) and practical guides to issues of concern to parents of children with disabilities (e.g., special education, sibling issues). Publishes books for and about children with disabilities. No personal accounts or general parenting guides. Submit outline, and at least 3 sample chapters. Reviews artwork/photos.

FICTION Subjects include picture books, children's. Receptive to stories re: developmental and intellectual disabilities, e.g., autism and cerebral palsy. Submit complete ms with SASE.

TIPS "Do not send us a proposal on the basis of this description. Examine our catalog or website and a couple of our books to make sure you are on the right track. Put some thought into how your book could be marketed (aside from in bookstores). Keep cover letters concise and to the point; if it's a subject that interests us, we'll ask to see more."

WORDSONG

815 Church St., Honesdale PA 18431. **Fax:** (570)253-0179. **E-mail:** submissions@boydsmillspress.com; eagarrow@boydsmillspress.com. **Website:** www. wordsongpoetry.com. Estab. 1990. "We publish fresh voices in contemporary poetry." **Pays authors royalty or work purchased outright.** Responds to mss in 3 months.

NONFICTION Submit complete ms or submit through agent. Label package "Ms Submission" and include SASE. "Please send a book-length collection of your own poems. Do not send an initial query."

FICTION Submit complete ms or submit through agent. Label package "Ms Submission" and include SASE. "Please send a book-length collection of your own poems. Do not send an initial query."

POETRY Submit complete ms or submit through agent. Label package "Ms Submission" and include SASE. "Please send a book-length collection of your own poems. Do not send an initial query."

TIPS "Collections of original poetry, not anthologies, are our biggest need at this time. Keep in mind that the strongest collections demonstrate a facility with multiple poetic forms and offer fresh images and insights. Check to see what's already on the market and on our website before submitting."

WORKMAN PUBLISHING CO.

225 Varick St., New York NY 10014. **Website:** www. workman.com. **Contact:** Suzanne Rafer, executive editor (cookbook, child care, parenting, teen interest); Ruth Sullivan, Margot Herrera, Kylie Foxx-McDonald, Jay Schaefer, senior editors. Raquel Jaramillo, senior editor (juvenile); Megan Nicolay, Savannah Ashour (associate editors). Estab. 1967. Publishes hardcover and trade paperback originals, as well as calendars. "We are a trade paperback house specializing in a wide range of popular nonfiction. We publish no adult fiction and very little children's fiction. We also publish a full range of full-color wall and Page-A-Day calendars." **Publishes 40 titles/year. thousands of queries received/year. Open to first-time authors. Pays variable royalty on retail price. Pays variable advance.** Publishes book approximately 1 year after acceptance of ms. Accepts simultaneous submissions. Responds in 5 months to queries. Guidelines online.

IMPRINTS Algonquin, Artisan, Greenwich Workshop Press, Storey, Timber.

NONFICTION Subjects include business, economics, child guidance, cooking, foods, nutrition, gardening, health, medicine, sports, travel. Query with SASE first for guidelines.

TIPS "No phone calls, please. We do not accept submissions via fax."

WORLD BOOK, INC.

233 N. Michigan Ave., Suite 2000, Chicago IL 60601. (312)729-5800. **Fax:** (312)729-5600. **Website:** www. worldbook.com. **Contact:** Paul A. Kobasa, editor-in-chief. World Book, Inc. (publisher of The World Book Encyclopedia), publishes reference sources and nonfiction series for children and young adults in the areas

of science, mathematics, English-language skills, basic academic and social skills, social studies, history, and health and fitness. "We publish print and non-print material appropriate for children ages 3-14. WB does not publish fiction, poetry, or wordless picture books." **Payment negotiated on project-by-project basis.** Publishes book 18 months after acceptance. Responds to queries in 2 months.

NONFICTION Young readers: animal, arts/crafts, careers, concept, geography, health, reference. Middle readers: animal, arts/crafts, careers, geography, health, history, hobbies, how-to, nature/environment, reference, science. Young adult: arts/crafts, careers, geography, health, history, hobbies, how-to, nature/environment, reference, science. Submit outline/synopsis only; no mss.

⊕ WRITELIFE PUBLISHING, LLC

2323 S. 171st St., Suite 202, Omaha NE 68130. (402)934-1412. **Fax:** (402)519-2173. **E-mail:** info@writelife.com. **E-mail:** queries@writelife.com. **Website:** www.writelife.com. **Contact:** Cindy Grady, publisher; Erin Reel, senior editor/in-house agent. Estab. 2008. Publishes hardcover originals, trade paperback originals, mass market paperback originals, and electronic originals. WriteLife, LLC, is an independent publisher offering a uniquely collaborative approach to publishing, marketing, and supporting writers serious about their work. **Publishes 12 titles/year. Authors are paid 50% of net royalties on wholesale and retail price.** Publishes book 6-12 months after acceptance. Accepts simultaneous submissions. Book catalog available for SASE or online. Ms guidelines available for SASE or online.

NONFICTION Subjects include astrology, business, career guidance, counseling, creative nonfiction, economics, education, history, memoirs, psychic, spirituality, womens issues, womens studies, lifestyle, wellness. Only interested in publishing nonfiction in the selected genres by authors with substantial platforms. Querying writers should provide a complete and thorough book proposal, should a submission be requested. Submit a proposal package with an outline and 3 sample chapters. Reviews artwork. Send photocopies.

FICTION Subjects include adventure, contemporary, historical, humor, juvenile, literary, mainstream, multicultural, mystery, picture books, regional, science fiction, spiritual, suspense, young adult. Open to receiving queries from writers who have yet to publish their first book, but would like to see evidence of previously published work in literary journals, newspapers, websites, anthologies, etc., included in the book proposal. Submit proposal package with synopsis and 3 sample chapters.

TIPS "Please describe the audience you envision for your books. We know from talking with our readers that they have just as eclectic tastes in books as we have. When it comes to fiction, our readers love vivid, authentic, and memorable characters and engaging plots. In nonfiction, our readers want books that will help them gain perspective, learn something new, make them feel good, help them to heal and improve their lives, and show them real life characters who have made or are making a difference in the world."

WRITER'S DIGEST BOOKS

Imprint of F+W Media, Inc., 10151 Carver Rd., Suite #200, Cincinnati OH 45242. **E-mail:** writersdigest@fwmedia.com. **Website:** www.writersdigest.com. **Contact:** Rachel Randall; James Duncan. Estab. 1920. Publishes hardcover originals and trade paperbacks. "Writer's Digest Books is the premiere source for instructional books on writing and publishing for an audience of aspirational writers. Typical mss are 80,000 words. E-mail queries strongly preferred; no phone calls please." **Publishes 18-20 titles/year. 300 queries received/year. 50 mss received/year. 30% from unagented writers. Pays average $3,000 advance.** Publishes book 1 year after acceptance. Accepts simultaneous submissions. Responds in 3 months to queries. "Our catalog of titles is available to view online at www.WritersDigestShop.com.".

◗ Writer's Digest Books accepts query letters and complete proposals via e-mail at writersdigest@fwmedia.com.

NONFICTION "Our instruction books stress results and how specifically to achieve them. Should be well-researched, yet lively and readable. We do not want to see books telling readers how to crack specific nonfiction markets: *Writing for the Computer Market* or *Writing for Trade Publications,* for instance. We are most in need of fiction-technique books written by published authors. Be prepared to explain how the proposed book differs from existing books on the subject." No fiction or poetry. Query with SASE. Submit outline, sample chapters, SASE.

TIPS "Most queries we receive are either too broad (how to write fiction) or too niche (how to write erotic horror), and don't reflect a knowledge of our large backlist of 150 titles. We rarely publish new books on journalism, freelancing, magazine article writing or marketing/promotion. We are actively seeking fiction and nonfiction writing technique books with fresh perspectives, interactive and visual writing instruction books, similar to *Pocket Muse* by Monica Wood, and general reference works that appeal to an audience beyond writers."

YALE UNIVERSITY PRESS

P.O. Box 209040, New Haven CT 06520. (203)432-0960. **Fax:** (203)432-0948. **E-mail:** christopher.rogers@yale. edu. **Website:** www.yale.edu/yup. **Contact:** Christopher Rogers, editorial director. Estab. 1908. Publishes hardcover and trade paperback originals. "Yale University Press publishes scholarly and general interest books." Accepts simultaneous submissions. Book catalog and ms guidelines online.

NONFICTION Subjects include Americana, anthropology, archeology, art, architecture, business, economics, education, health, medicine, history, language, literature, military, war, music, dance, philosophy, psychology, religion, science, sociology, women's issues, women's studies. Our nonfiction has to be at a very high level. Most of our books are written by professors or journalists, with a high level of expertise. *Submit proposals only.* We'll ask if we want to see more. *No unsolicited mss.* We won't return them. Submit sample chapters, cover letter, prospectus, cv, table of contents, SASE. Reviews artwork/photos. Send photocopies.

POETRY Publishes 1 book each year. Submit to Yale Series of Younger Poets Competition. Open to poets under 40 who have not had a book previously published. Submit ms of 48-64 pages by November 15. Rules and guidelines available online or with SASE. Submit complete ms.

TIPS "Audience is scholars, students and general readers."

○○ YEARLING BOOKS

Imprint of Random House Children's Books/Random House, Inc., 1745 Broadway, New York NY 10019. (212)782-9000. **Website:** www.randomhouse.com/kids.

IMPRINTS *Does not accept unsolicited mss.*

○ "Quality reprint paperback imprint for middle grade paperback books."

YELLOW SHOE FICTION SERIES

P.O. Box 25053, Baton Rouge LA 70894. **Website:** www. lsu.edu/lsupress. **Contact:** Michael Griffith, editor. Es-

tab. 2004. **Publishes 2 titles/year. Pays royalty. Offers advance.**

○ "Looking first and foremost for literary excellence, especially good mss that have fallen through the cracks at the big commercial presses. I'll cast a wide net."

FICTION Does not accept unsolicited mss. Accepts queries by mail, Attn: Rand Dotson. No electronic submissions.

YMAA PUBLICATION CENTER

P.O. Box 480, Wolfeboro NH 03894. (603)569-7988. **Fax:** (603)569-1889. **E-mail:** info@ymaa.com. **Contact:** David Ripianzi, director. Estab. 1982. Publishes trade paperback originals and reprints. YMAA publishes books on Chinese Chi Kung (Qigong), Taijiquan, (Tai Chi) and Asian martial arts. We are expanding our focus to include books on healing, wellness, meditation and subjects related to Asian culture and Asian medicine. De-emphasizing fitness books. **Publishes 6 titles/ year. 50 queries received/year. 20 mss received/year. 25% of books from first-time authors. 100% from unagented writers.** Publishes book 18 months after acceptance. Accepts simultaneous submissions. Responds in 3 months to proposals. Book catalog online. Guidelines available free.

NONFICTION Subjects include ethnic, health, medicine, Chinese, history, philosophy, spirituality, sports, Asian martial arts, Chinese Qigong. "We no longer publish or solicit books for children. We also produce instructional DVDs and videos to accompany our books on traditional Chinese martial arts, meditation, massage, and Chi Kung. We are most interested in Asian martial arts, Chinese medicine, and Chinese Qigong. We publish Eastern thought, health, meditation, massage, and East/West synthesis." Submit proposal package, outline, bio, 1 sample chapter, SASE. Reviews artwork/photos. Send Send photocopies and 1-2 originals to determine quality of photo/line art.

FICTION "We are excited to announce a new category: **martial arts fiction**. We are seeking mss that bring the venerated tradition of true Asian martial arts to readers. Your novel length ms should be a thrilling story that conveys insights into true martial techniques and philosophies."

TIPS "If you are submitting health-related material, please refer to an Asian tradition. Learn about author publicity options as your participation is mandatory."

YOGI IMPRESSIONS BOOKS PVT. LTD.

1711, Centre 1, World Trade Centre, Cuffe Parade Mumbai 400 005, India. **E-mail:** yogi@yogiimpressions.com. **Website:** www.yogiimpressions.com. Estab. 2000. "Yogi Impressions are Self-help, Personal Growth and Spiritual book publishers based in Mumbai, India. Established at the turn of the millennium, at Mumbai, Yogi Impressions publishes books which seek to revive interest in spirituality, enhance the quality of life and, thereby, create the legacy of a better world for future generations." Guidelines online.

NONFICTION Subjects include audio, child guidance, multicultural, religion, spirituality, alternative health, enlightened business, self-improvement/personal growth. Submit outline/proposal, bio, 2-3 sample chapters, market assessment, SASE.

ZEBRA BOOKS

Kensington, 119 W. 40th St., New York NY 10018. (212)407-1500. **E-mail:** mrecords@kensingtonbooks.com. **Website:** www.kensingtonbooks.com. **Contact:** Megan Records, associate editor. Publishes hardcover originals, trade paperback and mass market paperback originals and reprints. Zebra Books is dedicated to women's fiction, which includes, but is not limited to romance. Publishes book 12-18 months after acceptance. Accepts simultaneous submissions. Book catalog online.

NONFICTION Send cover letter/query, including the author's qualifications and connections relevant to the book's content and marketing, and summary or outline of book's content. All submissions should be double-spaced, paginated, cleanly printed and readable. Do not bind pages together.

FICTION Mostly historical romance. Some contemporary romance, westerns, horror, and humor. Send cover letter, first 3 chapters, and synopsis (no more than five pages). Note that we do not publish science fiction or fantasy.

ZENITH PRESS

Quayside Publishing Group, 400 First Avenue N., Suite 300, Minneapolis MN 55401. (612)344-8100; (800)328-0590. **Fax:** (612)344-8691. **E-mail:** egilg@quaysidepub.com. **E-mail:** spearson@quaysidepub.com. **Website:** www.qbookshop.com; zenithpress.com. **Contact:** Eric Gilg, editorial director; Scott Pearson, acquisitions editor; Richard Kane, senior acquisitions editor. Estab. 2004. Publishes hardcover and trade paperback originals, electronic originals and reprints, hardcover and trade paperback reprints. "Zenith Press publishes an eclectic collection of historical nonfiction and current affairs in both narrative and illustrated formats. Building on a core of military history, particularly from World War II forward, Zenith reaches out to other historical, aviation, and science topics with compelling narrative hooks or eye-catching photography. From a history of WWII aviation wrecks to an illustrated celebration of the space shuttle program, Zenith books are engaging true stories with historical, military, or science foundations—sometimes all 3 at once." **Publishes 210 titles/year. Receives 250 queries/year; 100 mss/year. 25% of books from first-time authors. 50% from unagented writers. Pays authors 8-15% royalty on wholesale price.** Publishes book 1 year after acceptance. Accepts simultaneous submissions. Responds in 1 month. Catalog and guidelines online.

NONFICTION Subjects include history, military, politics, science, world affairs, aviation. Submit proposal package, including outline, 1-3 sample chapters, and author biography. Reviews artwork. Send digital files.

ZONDERVAN

Division of HarperCollins Publishers, 3900 Sparks Dr., Grand Rapids MI 49546. (616)698-6900. **Fax:** (616)698-3454. **E-mail:** submissions@zondervan.com. **Website:** www.zondervan.com. Estab. 1931. Publishes hardcover and trade paperback originals and reprints. "Our mission is to be the leading Christian communications company meeting the needs of people with resources that glorify Jesus Christ and promote biblical principles." **Publishes 200 titles/year. 10% of books from first-time authors. 60% from unagented writers. Pays 14% royalty on net amount received on sales of cloth and softcover trade editions; 12% royalty on net amount received on sales of mass market paperbacks. Pays variable advance.** Responds in 2 months to queries; 3 months to proposals; 4 months to mss. Guidelines online.

IMPRINTS Zondervan, Zonderkidz, Youth Specialties, Editorial Vida.

NONFICTION Subjects include history, humanities, memoirs, religion, Christian living, devotional, bible study resources, preaching, counseling, college and seminary textbooks, discipleship, worship, church renewal for pastors, professionals and lay leaders in ministry, theological, and biblical reference books. *No longer accepts unsolicited mailed submissions. Instead,* submissions may be submitted electronically to (ChristianMsSubmissions.com).

FICTION Will not consider collections of short stories or poetry. Submit TOC, curriculum vitae, chapter outline, intended audience.

ZUMAYA PUBLICATIONS, LLC

3209 S. Interstate 35, Austin TX 78741. **E-mail:** business@zumayapublications.com. **E-mail:** acquisitions@zumayapublications.com. **Website:** www.zumayapublications.com. **Contact:** Adrienne Rose, acquisitions editor. Estab. 1999. Publishes trade paperback and electronic originals and reprints. **Publishes 20-25 titles/year. 1,000 queries received/year. 100 mss received/year. 5% of books from first-time authors. 98% from unagented writers.** Publishes book 2 years after acceptance. Responds in 6 months to queries and proposals; 9 months to mss. Guidelines online.

IMPRINTS Zumaya Arcane (New Age, inspirational fiction & nonfiction), Zumaya Boundless (GLBT); Zumaya Embraces (romance/women's fiction); Zumaya Enigma (mystery/suspense/thriller); Zumaya Thresholds (YA/middle grade); Zumaya Otherworlds (SF/F/H), Zumaya Yesterdays (memoirs, historical fiction, fiction, western fiction); Zumaya Fabled Ink (graphic and illustrated novels).

○ "We accept only electronic queries; all others will be discarded unread. A working knowledge of computers and relevant software is a necessity, as our production process is completely digital."

NONFICTION Subjects include creative nonfiction, memoirs, New Age, spirituality, true ghost stories. "The easiest way to figure out what we're looking for is to look at what we've already done. Our main nonfiction interests are in collections of true ghost stories, ones that have been investigated or thoroughly documented, memoirs that address specific regions and eras from a 'normal person' viewpoint and books on the craft of writing. That doesn't mean we won't consider something else." Electronic query only. Reviews artwork/photos. Send digital format.

FICTION Subjects include adventure, fantasy, bisexual, gay, lesbian, historical, horror, humor, juvenile, literary, mainstream, contemporary, multicultural, mystery, occult, romance, science fiction, short story collections, spiritual, suspense, transgender, western, young adult. "We are currently oversupplied with speculative fiction and are reviewing submissions in SF, fantasy and paranormal suspense by invitation only. We are much in need of GLBT and YA/middle grade, historical and western, New Age/inspirational (no overtly Christian materials, please), non-category romance, thrillers. As with nonfiction, we encourage people to review what we've already published so as to avoid sending us more of the same, at least, insofar as the plot is concerned. While we're always looking for good specific mysteries, we want original concepts rather than slightly altered versions of what we've already published."

TIPS "We're catering to readers who may have loved last year's best seller but not enough to want to read 10 more just like it. Have something different. If it does not fit standard pigeonholes, that's a plus. On the other hand, it has to have an audience. And if you're not prepared to work with us on promotion and marketing, particularly via social media, it would be better to look elsewhere."

CONSUMER MAGAZINES

Selling your writing to consumer magazines is as much an exercise of your marketing skills as it is of your writing abilities. Editors of consumer magazines are looking for good writing which communicates pertinent information to a specific audience—their readers.

APPROACHING THE CONSUMER MAGAZINE MARKET

Marketing skills will help you successfully discern a magazine's editorial slant, and write queries and articles that prove your knowledge of the magazine's readership. You can gather clues about a magazine's readership—and establish your credibility with the magazine's editor—in a number of ways:

- **Read** the magazine's listing in *Writer's Market*.
- **Study** a magazine's writer's guidelines.
- **Check** a magazine's website.
- **Read** several current issues of the target magazine.
- **Talk** to an editor by phone.

Writers who can correctly and consistently discern a publication's audience and deliver stories that speak to that target readership will win out every time over writers who submit haphazardly.

What editors want

In nonfiction, editors continue to look for short feature articles covering specialized topics. Editors want crisp writing and expertise. If you are not an expert in the area about which you are writing, make yourself one through research. Always query before sending your ms unless the listing mentions doing otherwise.

Fiction editors prefer to receive complete mss. Writers must keep in mind that marketing fiction is competitive, and editors receive far more material than they can publish. For this reason, they often do not respond to submissions unless they are interested in using the story. More comprehensive information on fiction markets can be found in *Novel & Short Story Writer's Market* (Writer's Digest Books).

Payment

Most magazines listed here have indicated pay rates; some give very specific payment-per-word rates, while others state a range. (Note: All of the magazines listed in the Consumer Magazines section are paying markets. However, some of the magazines are not identified by payment icons (**$**) because the magazines preferred not to disclose specific payment information.) Any agreement you come to with a magazine, whether verbal or written, should specify the payment you are to receive and when you are to receive it. Some magazines pay writers only after the piece in question has been published (on publication). Others pay as soon as they have accepted a piece and are sure they are going to use it (on acceptance).

So what is a good pay rate? There are no standards; the principle of supply and demand operates at full throttle in the business of writing and publishing. As long as there are more writers than opportunities for publication, wages for freelancers will never skyrocket. Rates vary widely from one market to the next. Smaller circulation magazines and some departments of the larger magazines will pay a lower rate.

Editors know these listings are read and used by writers with a wide range of experience, from those unpublished writers just starting out, to those with a successful, profitable freelance career. As a result, many magazines publicly report pay rates in the lower end of their actual pay ranges. Experienced writers will be able to successfully negotiate higher pay rates for their material. Newer writers should be encouraged that as their reputation grows (along with their clip file), they will be able to command higher rates.

ANIMAL

$$ APPALOOSA JOURNAL

2720 West Pullman Rd., Moscow ID 83843. (208)882-5578. **Fax:** (208)882-8150. **E-mail:** editor@appaloosajournal.com; designer2@appaloosajournal.com. **Website:** www.appaloosajournal.com. **Contact:** Dana Russell, editor; John Langston, art director. **40% freelance written.** Monthly magazine covering Appaloosa horses. "*Appaloosa Journal* is the authoritative, association-based source for information about the Appaloosa Horse Club, the Appaloosa breed and the Appaloosa industry. Our mission is to cultivate a broader membership base and instill enthusiasm for the breed by recognizing the needs and achievements of the Appaloosa, ApHC members, enthusiasts and our readers. The Appaloosa Horse Club is a not-for-profit organization. Serious inquiries within specified budget only." Estab. 1946. Circ. 25,000. Byline given. Pays on publication. Publishes ms an average of 3 months after acceptance. Responds in 1 month to queries. Responds in 2 months to mss. Sample copy free. Guidelines online.

Appaloosa Journal no longer accepts material for columns.

NONFICTION Needs historical, interview, photo feature, breeders, trainers, specific training methods, influential horses, youth and non-pro competitors, breed history, trail riding, and artists using Appaloosa subjects. **Buys 15-20 mss/year.** Send complete ms. *Appaloosa Journal* is not responsible for unsolicited materials. All freelance correspondence should be directed to editor Dana Russell via e-mail, with the subject line "'Freelance.' Article-length reports of timely and newsworthy events, such as shows, races, and overseas competition, are welcome but must be pre-approved by the editor. Mss exceeding the preferred word length will be evaluated according to relevance and content matter. Lengthy stories, opinion pieces, or poorly written pieces will be rejected. Mss may be sent on a CD or via e-mail in Microsoft Word or text-only format. If sent via CD, an accompanying hard copy should be printed, double spaced, following the guidelines." Length: 1,500-1,800 words (features); 600-800 words (article-length). **Pays $200-400.**

PHOTOS In photographer's samples, wants to see "high-quality color photos of world-class, characteristic (coat patterned) Appaloosa horses in appealing, picturesque outdoor environments.". Send photos. Captions, identification of subjects required. Payment varies. Pays $200 for color cover; $25 minimum for color inside. Pays on publication. Credit line given.

TIPS "Articles by writers with horse knowledge, news sense, and photography skills are in great demand. If it's a strong article about an Appaloosa, the writer has a pretty good chance of publication. A good understanding of the breed and the industry, breeders, and owners is helpful. Make sure there's some substance and a unique twist."

$$ CAT FANCY

I-5 Publishing, P.O. Box 6050, Mission Viejo CA 92690. (949)855-8822. **Fax:** (949)855-3045. **E-mail:** slogan@bowtieinc.com. **E-mail:** query@catfancy.com. **Website:** www.catchannel.com. **Contact:** Susan Logan, editor. **90% freelance written.** Monthly magazine covering all aspects of responsible cat ownership. "*Cat Fancy* is the undisputed premier feline magazine that is dedicated to better lives for pet cats. Always a presence within the cat world, *Cat Fancy* and its sister website, CatChannel.com, are where cat owners, lovers, and rescue organizations go for education and entertainment. With a readership that is highly receptive to its credible advice, news, lifestyle information, *Cat Fancy* and CatChannel.com are the ultimate places to read about cat news, breeds, care and products and services." Estab. 1965. Circ. 290,000. Pays on publication. Editorial lead time 6 months. Accepts queries by mail, e-mail. Responds in 3 months to queries. Guidelines online.

Cat Fancy does not accept unsolicited mss and only accepts queries from January-May. Queries sent after May will be returned or discarded. "Show us how you can contribute something new and unique. No phone queries."

NONFICTION Needs how-to, humor, photo feature, travel, behavior, health, lifestyle, cat culture, entertainment. "We no longer publish any fiction or poetry." **Buys 70 mss/year.** Feature Articles: "We are open to working with new contributors and fresh voices in addition to drawing from a talented crop of established contributors. Each month, we provide our readers with a mix of informative articles on various topics, including breed profiles, feline health, nutrition, grooming, behavior, training, as well as lifestyle and special interest articles on cat culture, the human-animal bond and personalities. Query first." Length: 100-1,000 words. **Pays $50-450.**

CONSUMER MAGAZINES

PHOTOS "Seeking photos of happy, healthy, well-groomed cats and kittens in indoor settings.". Captions, identification of subjects, model releases required. Pays $200 maximum for color cover; $25-200 for inside. Negotiates payment individually. Credit line given. Buys first North American serial rights.

TIPS "Please read recent issues to become acquainted with our style and content."

⊗⊗ THE CHRONICLE OF THE HORSE

P.O. Box 46, Middleburg VA 20118. (540)687 6341. **Fax:** (540)687-3937. **E-mail:** slieser@chronofhorse.com. **E-mail:** bethr@chronofhorse.com (feature stories); results@chronofhorse.com (news stories). **Website:** www.chronofhorse.com. **Contact:** Sara Lieser, managing editor; Beth Rasin, executive editor. **80% freelance written.** Weekly magazine covering horses. "We cover English riding sports, including horse showing, grand prix jumping competitions, steeplechase racing, foxhunting, dressage, endurance riding, handicapped riding, and combined training. We are the official publication for the national governing bodies of many of the above sports. We feature news, how-to articles on equitation and horse care and interviews with leaders in the various fields." Estab. 1937. Circ. 18,000. Byline given. Pays for features on acceptance; news and other items on publication. Publishes ms an average of 4 months after acceptance. Submit seasonal material 3 months in advance. Accepts queries by mail, e-mail. Responds in 5-6 weeks to queries. Sample copy for $2 and 9x12 SASE. Guidelines online.

NONFICTION Needs general interest, historical, history of breeds, use of horses in other countries and times, art, etc., how-to, trailer, train, design a course, save money, etc., humor, centered on living with horses or horse people, interview, of nationally known horsemen or the very unusual, technical, horse care, articles on feeding, injuries, care of foals, shoeing, etc. Special issues: Steeplechase Racing (January); American Horse in Sport and Grand Prix Jumping (February); Horse Show (March); Intercollegiate (April); Kentucky 4-Star Preview (April); Junior and Pony (April); Dressage (June); Horse Care (July); Combined Training (August); Hunt Roster (September); Amateur (November); Stallion (December). No poetry, Q&A interviews, clinic reports, Western riding articles, personal experience or wild horses. **Buys 300 mss/year.** Send complete ms. Length: 1,500-2,500 words. **Pays $150-250.**

PHOTOS State availability. Identification of subjects required. Photo captions required with every subject identified. Reviews e-mailed image, prints or color slides; accepts color for color reproduction. Pays $30 base rate. Pays on publication. Buys one-time rights. Credit line given. Prefers first North American rights.

COLUMNS/DEPARTMENTS Dressage, Combined Training, Horse Show, Horse Care, Racing over Fences, Young Entry (about young riders, geared for youth), Horses and Humanities, Hunting, Vaulting, Handicapped Riding, Trail Riding, 1,000-1,225 words; News of major competitions (clear assignment with us first), 1,500 words. Query with or without published clips or send complete ms. **Pays $25-200.**

TIPS "Get our guidelines. Our readers are sophisticated, competitive horsemen. Articles need to go beyond common knowledge. Freelancers often attempt too broad or too basic a subject. We welcome well-written news stories on major events, but clear the assignment with us. We do not want to see portfolio or samples. Contact us first, preferably by letter; include SASE for reply. Know horse sports."

⊗ COONHOUND BLOODLINES

United Kennel Club, Inc., 100 E. Kilgore Rd., Kalamazoo MI 49002-5584. (269)343-9020. **Fax:** (269)343-7037. **E-mail:** vrand@ukcdogs.com. **Website:** www.ukcdogs.com. **Contact:** Vicki Rand, editor. **40% freelance written.** Monthly magazine covering all aspects of the 7 Coonhound dog breeds. Estab. 1925. Circ. 10,000. Byline given. Pays on publication. Publishes ms an average of 6 months after acceptance. Please include e-mail address with submissions. Editorial lead time 6 months. Submit seasonal material 6 months in advance. Accepts queries by mail, e-mail, fax, phone. Accepts simultaneous submissions. Responds in 6 weeks to queries. Sample copy for $7.

NONFICTION Needs general interest, historical, humor, interview, new product, personal experience, photo feature; breed-specific. Special issues: Seven of the magazine's 12 issues are each devoted to a specific breed of Coonhound. American Leopard Hound (January); Treeing Walker (February); English (July); Black & Tan (April); Bluetick (May); Redbone (June); Plott Hound (August), 1,000-3,000 words and photos. **Buys 12-36 mss/year.** Query. Length: 1,000-5,000 words. **Pays variable amount.** Sometimes pays expenses of writers on assignment.

PHOTOS State availability. Captions, identification of subjects required. Reviews contact sheets. Negotiates payment individually.

FICTION Must be about the Coonhound breeds or hunting with hounds. Needs adventure, historical, humorous, mystery. **Buys 3-6 mss/year.** Query. Length: 1,000-3,000 words. **Pay varies.**

⊗⊗ DOG FANCY

BowTie Inc., P.O. Box 6050, Mission Viejo CA 92690. (949)855-8822. **Fax:** (949)855-3045. **E-mail:** barkback@dogfancy.com. **Website:** www.dogfancy.com; www.dogchannel.com. **95% freelance written.** Monthly magazine for men and women of all ages interested in all phases of dog ownership. Estab. 1970. Circ. 268,000. Byline given. Pays on publication. Offers kill fee. Publishes ms an average of 6 months after acceptance. Accepts queries by e-mail. Responds in 2 months to queries. Guidelines online.

○ Reading period from January through April.

NONFICTION Needs general interest, how-to, humor, inspirational, interview, photo feature, travel. "No stories written from a dog's point of view." **Buys 10 or fewer from new writers; 80 mss/year.** Query. Length: 850-1,200 words. **Pays 40¢/word.**

PHOTOS State availability of photos. Digital images, only. Offers no additional payment for photos accepted with ms.

COLUMNS/DEPARTMENTS News hound, fun dog. **Buys 6 mss/year.** Query by e-mail. **Pays 40¢/word.**

TIPS "We're looking for the unique experience that enhances the dog/owner relationship. Medical articles are assigned to veterinarians. Note that we write for a lay audience (nontechnical), but we do assume a certain level of intelligence. Read the magazine before making a pitch. Make sure your query is clear, concise, and relevant."

⊗ DOG SPORTS MAGAZINE

Cher Car Kennels, 4215 S. Lowell Rd., St. Johns MI 48879. (989)224-7225. **Fax:** (989)224-6033. **E-mail:** suggestions@dogsports.com; info@chercarkennels.com. **Website:** www.dogsports.com. **Contact:** Cheryl Carlson, editor. **5% freelance written.** Monthly tabloid covering working dogs. *Dog Sports* online magazine is for all dog trainers. Focuses on the "how" of dog training. You will find articles on Police K-9 training, Narcotics detection, Herding, Weight Pull, Tracking, Search and Rescue, and how to increase your dog training Business. Brings the latest in techniques from the field, actual dog trainers that are out there, working, titling and training. French Ring, Mondio, Schutzhund, N.A.P.D. PPDA, K-9 Pro Sports all are featured, as well as spotlight articles on breeds, trainers, judges, or events. Estab. 1979. Circ. 2,000. Byline given. Pays on publication. Publishes ms an average of 1 month after acceptance. Editorial lead time 1 month. Submit seasonal material 1 month in advance. Accepts queries by mail, e-mail. Accepts simultaneous submissions. Sample copy free or online.

NONFICTION Needs essays, general interest, how-to, working dogs, humor, interview, technical. **Buys 5 mss/year.** Send complete ms. **Pays $50.**

PHOTOS State availability of photos. Captions, identification of subjects required. Reviews prints. Offers no additional payment for photos accepted with ms.

TIPS "If you have ideas about topics, articles, or areas of interest, please drop us an e-mail and let us know how we can make this online magazine the best training tool you've ever had!"

⊗ THE GREYHOUND REVIEW

P.O. Box 543, Abilene KS 67410. (785)263-4660. **E-mail:** nga@ngagreyhounds.com. **Website:** www.ngagreyhounds.com. **20% freelance written.** Monthly magazine covering greyhound breeding, training, and racing. Estab. 1911. Circ. 3,500. Byline given. Pays on acceptance. Submit seasonal material 2 months in advance. Responds in 2 weeks to queries. Responds in 1 month to mss. Sample copy for $3. Guidelines free.

NONFICTION Needs how-to, interview, personal experience. Do not submit gambling systems. **Buys 24 mss/year.** Query. Length: 1,000-10,000 words. **Pays $85-150.**

REPRINTS Send photocopy. Pays 100% of amount paid for original article.

PHOTOS State availability. Identification of subjects required. Reviews digital images. Pays $10-50 photo.

⊗⊗⊗ THE HORSE

P.O. Box 919003, Lexington KY 40591. (800)866-2361. **Fax:** (859)276-4450. **E-mail:** editorial@thehorse.com. **Website:** www.thehorse.com. **85% freelance written.** Monthly magazine covering equine health, care, management and welfare. *The Horse* is an educational/news magazine geared toward the hands-on horse owner. Estab. 1983. Circ. 55,000. Byline given. Pays on acceptance. Publishes ms an average of 6 months after acceptance. Accepts queries by mail, e-mail. Responds in 3 months to queries. Sample copy for $3.95 or online. Guidelines online.

NONFICTION Needs how-to, technical, topical interviews. No first-person experiences not from professionals; this is a technical magazine to inform horse owners. **Buys 90 mss/year.** Query with published clips. Length: 250-4,000 words. **Pays $60-850.**

PHOTOS Send photos. Captions, identification of subjects required. Reviews transparencies. Offers $35-350.

COLUMNS/DEPARTMENTS News Front (news on horse health), 100-500 words; Equinomics (economics of horse ownership); Step by Step (feet and leg care); Nutrition; Reproduction; Back to Basics, all 1,500-2,200 words. **Buys Accepts 50 column articles/year. mss/year.** Query with published clips. **Pays $50-450.**

TIPS "We publish reliable horse health care and management information from top industry professionals and researchers around the world. Ms must be submitted electronically."

HORSE ILLUSTRATED

I-5 Publishing, P.O. Box 12106, Lexington KY 40580. (800)546-7730. **E-mail:** horseillustrated@i5publishing.com. **Website:** www.horseillustrated.com. **Contact:** Elizabeth Moyer, editor. **90% freelance written. Prefers to work with published/established writers, but will work with new/unpublished writers.** Monthly magazine covering all aspects of horse ownership. "Our readers are adults, mostly women, between the ages of 18 and 40; stories should be geared to that age group and reflect responsible horse care." Estab. 1976. Circ. 160,660. Byline given. Pays on publication. Publishes ms an average of 8 months after acceptance. Submit seasonal material 6 months in advance. Accepts queries by mail. Responds in 3 months to queries. Guidelines available at www.horsechannel.com/horse-magazines/horse-illustrated/submission-guidelines.aspx.

NONFICTION Needs general interest, how-to, horse care, training, veterinary care, inspirational, photo feature. "No little girl horse stories, cowboy and Indian stories, or anything not *directly* relating to horses." **Buys 20 mss/year.** Query or send complete ms. Length: 1,000-2,000 words. **Pays $200-475.**

TIPS "Freelancers can break in at this publication with feature articles on Western and English training methods; veterinary and general care how-to articles;

and horse sports articles. We rarely use personal experience articles. Submit photos with training and how-to articles whenever possible. We have a very good record of developing new freelancers into regular contributors/columnists. We are always looking for fresh talent, but certainly enjoy working with established writers who know the ropes as well. We are accepting less unsolicited freelance work—much is now assigned and contracted."

MUSHING.COM MAGAZINE

P.O. Box 1195, Willow AK 99688. (907)495-2468. **E-mail:** editor@mushing.com. **Website:** www.mushing.com. **Contact:** Greg Sellentin, managing editor. Bimonthly magazine covering "all aspects of the growing sports of dogsledding, skijoring, carting, dog packing, and weight pulling. *Mushing* promotes responsible dog care through feature articles and updates on working animal health care, safety, nutrition, and training." Estab. 1987. Circ. 10,000. Byline given. Pays within 3 months of publication. Publishes ms an average of 4 months after acceptance. Submit seasonal material 4 months in advance. Accepts queries by mail, e-mail, fax, phone. Responds in 8 months to queries. Sample copy for $5 ($6 US to Canada). Guidelines online.

NONFICTION Needs historical, how-to. Special issues: Iditarod and Long-Distance Racing (January/February); Ski or Sprint Racing (March/April); Health and Nutrition (May/June); Musher and Dog Profiles, Summer Activities (July/August); Equipment, Fall Training (September/October); Races and Places (November/December). Query with or without published clips. "We prefer detailed queries but also consider unsolicited mss. Please make proposals informative yet to the point. Spell out your qualifications for handling the topic. We like to see clips of previously published material but are eager to work with new and unpublished authors, too." Considers complete ms with SASE. Length: 1,000-2,500 words. **Pays $50-250.** Sometimes pays expenses of writers on assignment.

PHOTOS "We look for good quality color for covers and specials." Send photos. Captions, identification of subjects. Reviews digital images only. Pays $20-165/photo.

COLUMNS/DEPARTMENTS Query with or without published clips or send complete ms.

FILLERS Needs anecdotes, facts, newsbreaks, short humor, cartoons, puzzles. Length: 100-250 words. **Pays $20-35.**

TIPS "Read our magazine. Know something about dog-driven, dog-powered sports."

⊖⊖ USDF CONNECTION

United States Dressage Federation, 4051 Iron Works Pkwy., Lexington KY 40511. **E-mail:** connection@usdf.org. **E-mail:** editorial@usdf.org. **Website:** www.usdf.org. **40% freelance written.** Magazine published 10 times/year covering dressage (an equestrian sport). All material must relate to the sport of dressage in the U.S. Estab. 2000. Circ. 35,000. Byline given. Pays on acceptance. Offers 50% kill fee. Publishes ms an average of 3 months after acceptance. Editorial lead time 3 months. Submit seasonal material 6 months in advance. Accepts queries by mail, e-mail. Responds in 1 month to queries. Responds in 1-2 months to mss. Sample copy for $5. Guidelines online.

NONFICTION Needs book excerpts, essays, how-to, interview, opinion, personal experience. Does not want general-interest equine material or stories that lack a U.S. dressage angle. **Buys 20 mss/year.** Query. Length: 500-2,000 words. **Pays $100-400 for assigned articles. Pays $100-300 for unsolicited articles.** Sometimes pays expenses of writers on assignment.

PHOTOS State availability. Captions, identification of subjects required. Reviews JPEG files. Negotiates payment individually.

COLUMNS/DEPARTMENTS Amateur Hour (profiles of adult amateur USDF members), 1,200-1,500 words; Under 21 (profiles of young USDF members), 1,200-1,500 words; Horse-Health Connection (dressage-related horse health), 1,500-2,500 words; Mind-Body-Spirit Connection (rider health/fitness, sport psychology), 1,500-2,500 words. **Buys 12 mss/year.** Query with published clips. **Pays $150-400.**

TIPS "Know the organization and the sport. Most successful contributors are active in the horse industry and bring valuable perspectives and insights to their stories and images."

ART AND ARCHITECTURE

ARCHITECTURAL DIGEST

Condé Nast Publications, Inc., 4 Times Square, 18th Floor, New York NY 10036. (323)965-3700. **Fax:** (323)965-4975. **Website:** www.architecturaldigest.

com. Monthly magazine covering architecture. A global magazine that offers a look at the homes of the rich and famous. Other topics include travel, shopping, automobiles, and technology. Estab. 1920. Circ. 800,000. Accepts queries by mail, e-mail. Sample copy for $5 on newsstands.

○ Query before submitting. Difficult market to break into.

NONFICTION Query with published clips.

⊖⊖ THE ARTIST'S MAGAZINE

F+W Media, Inc., 10151 Carver Rd., Blue Ash OH 45242. (513)531-2690, ext. 11731. **Fax:** (513)891-7153. **Website:** www.artistsmagazine.com. **Contact:** Maureen Bloomfield, editor-in-chief; Brian Roeth, senior art director. **80% freelance written.** Magazine published 10 times/year covering primarily two-dimensional art for working artists. Maureen Bloomfield says, "Ours is a highly visual approach to teaching serious amateur and professional artists techniques that will help them improve their skills and market their work. The style should be crisp and immediately engaging, written in a voice that speaks directly to artists. We do not accept unsolicited mss. Artists should send digital images of their work; writers should send clips of previously published work, along with a query letter." Circ. 100,000. Bionote given for feature material. Pays on publication. Offers 8% kill fee. Publishes ms an average of 6 months-1 year after acceptance. Responds in 6 months to queries. Sample copy for $5.99. Guidelines online.

○ Sponsors 3 annual contests. Look online for information on contests.

NONFICTION No unillustrated articles. **Buys 60 mss/year.** Length: 500-1,200 words. **Pays $300-500 and up.**

PHOTOS Images of artwork must be in the form of 35mm slides, larger transparencies, or high-quality, high-resolution digital files. Full captions must accompany these.

TIPS "Look at several current issues and read the author's guidelines carefully. Remember that our readers are professional artists. Pitch an article; send clips. Do not send a finished article."

⊖⊖ THE MAGAZINE ANTIQUES

Brant Publications, 110 Greene St, New York NY 10012. (212)941-2800. **Fax:** (212)941-2819. **E-mail:** tmaedit@brantpub.com (JavaScript required to view). **Website:** www.themagazineantiques.com. **Contact:**

Editorial. **75% freelance written.** Bimonthly. "Articles should present new information in a scholarly format (with footnotes) on the fine and decorative arts, architecture, historic preservation, and landscape architecture." Estab. 1922. Circ. 40,000. Byline given. Pays on publication. Publishes ms an average of 6 months after acceptance. Editorial lead time 6 months. Submit seasonal material 6 months in advance. Responds in 3 weeks to queries. Responds in 6 months to mss. Sample copy $12 plus shipping costs. Contact tmae-mail@brantpub.com.

NONFICTION Needs historical, scholarly. **Buys 50 mss/year.** "For submission guidelines and questions about our articles, please contact the editorial department at tmaedit@brantpub.com; you need JavaScript enabled to view it." Length: 2,850-3,500 words. **Pays $250-500.** Sometimes pays expenses of writers on assignment.

PHOTOS State availability. Captions, identification of subjects required. Reviews contact sheets, negatives, transparencies, prints.

SOUTHWEST ART

10901 W. 120th Ave., Suite 350, Broomfield CO 80021. (303)442-0427. **Fax:** (303)449-0279. **E-mail:** southwestart@fwmedia.com. **Website:** www.southwestart.com. **Contact:** Kristin Hoerth, editor-in-chief. **60% freelance written.** Monthly magazine directed to art collectors interested in artists, market trends, and art history of the American West. Estab. 1971. Circ. 60,000. Byline given. Pays on acceptance. Publishes ms an average of 1 year after acceptance. Submit seasonal material 8 months in advance. Accepts queries by mail, fax. Responds in 6 months to mss.

NONFICTION Needs book excerpts, interview. No fiction or poetry. **Buys 70 mss/year.** Query with published clips. Length: 1,400-1,600 words.

PHOTOS Photographs, color print-outs, and videotapes will not be considered. Captions, identification of subjects required. Reviews 35mm, 2¼x2¼, 4x5 transparencies.

TIPS "Research the Southwest art market, send slides or transparencies with queries, and send writing samples demonstrating knowledge of the art world."

ASSOCIATIONS

🟢🟢🟢🟢 AAA LIVING

Pace Communications, 1301 Carolina St., Greensboro NC 27401. **Fax:** (336)383-8272. **E-mail:** martha.leonard@paceco.com. **Website:** www.aaa.com/aaaliving. **Contact:** Martha Leonard. **20% freelance written.** Published 4 times a year/print; 6 times a year/digital. AAA Living magazine, published for the Auto Club Group of Dearborn, Michigan, is for members of AAA clubs in 8 Midwest states (IL, N. IN, IA, MI, MN, NE, ND, & WI). Magazine features lifestyle & travel articles about each state, written by knowledgeable resident writers. This is the best opportunity for freelancers. Estab. 1917. Circ. 2.5 million. Pays on acceptance. Offers 10% kill fee. Editorial lead time 6 months. Accepts queries by mail, e-mail. Responds in 6 months to mss. Samples online. Guidelines are not online.

NONFICTION Needs travel. Query with published clips. Length: 150-1,600 words. **Pays $1/word for assigned articles.** Sometimes pays expenses of writers on assignment.

PHOTOS Send photos. Captions, identification of subjects required. Reviews GIF/JPEG files. Negotiates payment individually.

TIPS "We are most interested in sharing with our readers in each state the new experiences, sites, destinations, entertainment, etc., that they can enjoy on weekend getaways within their state. If you are on the ground in 1 of these states and can loop us into a hot new ziplining site, hiking trail, scenic drive, railway-turned-bike path, museum exhibition, etc., let us know. We're based in North Carolina, so we value your local knowledge. Keep in mind our readers tend to be slightly older—median age is around 50."

🟢🟢 DAC NEWS

Detroit Athletic Club, 241 Madison Ave., Detroit MI 48226. (313)442-1034. **Fax:** (313)442-1047. **E-mail:** kenv@thedac.com. **Website:** www.thedac.com. **20% freelance written.** *DAC News* is the magazine for Detroit Athletic Club members. It covers club news and events, plus general interest features. Published 10 times/year. Estab. 1916. Circ. 5,000. Byline given. Pays on publication. Publishes ms an average of 3 months after acceptance. Editorial lead time 3 months. Submit seasonal material 3 months in advance. Accepts queries by mail, phone. Responds in 1 month to queries. Sample copy free.

NONFICTION Needs general interest, historical, photo feature. "No politics or social issues—this is an entertainment magazine. We do not acccept unsolicited mss or queries for travel articles." **Buys 2-3**

mss/year. Length: 1,000-2,000 words. **Pays $100-500.** Sometimes pays expenses of writers on assignment.

PHOTOS Illustrations only. State availability. Captions, identification of subjects, model releases required. Reviews transparencies, 4x6 prints. Negotiates payment individually.

TIPS "Review our editorial calendar. It tends to repeat from year to year, so a freelancer with a fresh approach to one of these topics will get our attention quickly. It helps if articles have some connection with the DAC, but this is not absolutely necessary. We also welcome articles on Detroit history, Michigan history, or automotive history."

$ $ THE ELKS MAGAZINE

The Elks Magazine, 425 W. Diversey Parkway, Chicago IL 60614. (773)755-4740. **E-mail:** magnews@elks.org. **Website:** www.elks.org/elksmag. **Contact:** Cheryl T. Stachura, editor/publisher. **25% freelance written.** Magazine covers nonfiction only; published 10 times/year with basic mission of being the voice of the elks. All material is written in-house. Estab. 1922. Circ. 1,037,000. Pays on acceptance. Accepts queries by mail, e-mail. Responds in 1 month with a /no on ms purchase. Guidelines online.

Each year, the editors buy 20 to 30 articles. Thesearticles consist of previously unpublished, informative, upbeat, entertaining writing on a variety of subjects, including science, technology, nature, Americana, sports, history, health, retirement, personal finance, leisure-time activities, and seasonal topics. Articles should be authoritative (please include sources) and appeal to the lay person.

NONFICTION No fiction, religion, controversial issues, first-person, fillers, or verse. **Buys 20-30 mss/year.** Send complete ms. Length: 1,200-2,000 words. **Pays 25¢/word.**

PHOTOS "If possible, please advise where photographs may be found. Photographs taken and submitted by the writer are paid for separately at $25 each. Send transparencies, slides. Pays $475 for one-time cover rights.". Pays $25/photo.

COLUMNS/DEPARTMENTS "The invited columnists are already selected."

TIPS "Please try us first. We'll get back to you soon."

$ $ $ KIWANIS

Kiwanis International, 3636 Woodview Trace, Indianapolis IN 46268-3196. (317)217-6223; (317)875-8755; (800)549-2647 [dial 411] (US and Canada only). **Fax:** (317)879-0204. **E-mail:** magazine@kiwanis.org; shareyourstory@kiwanis.org. **Website:** www.kiwanis.org. **Contact:** Stan D. Soderstorm, editor; Kasey Jackson, managing editor. **10% freelance written.** Magazine published 6 times/year for business and professional persons and their families. Estab. 1917. Circ. 240,000. Byline given. Pays on acceptance. Offers 40% kill fee. Publishes ms an average of 6 months after acceptance. Accepts queries by mail, e-mail, fax. Responds in 1 month to queries. Sample copy and writer's guidelines for 9x12 SAE with 5 first class stamps. Guidelines online.

No unsolicited mss.

NONFICTION Needs "Most *Kiwanis* content is related to the activities of our Kiwanis clubs.". No fiction, personal essays, profiles, travel pieces, fillers, or verse of any kind. A light or humorous approach is welcomed where the subject is appropriate and all other requirements are observed. **Buys 20 mss/year.** "See guidelines under Share Your Story in the Media Center section on the website. You must be 13 or older to submit your story and/or photographs. If you are age 18 or younger, you must have the permission of your parent or guardian to complete your submission." Length: 500-1,200 words. **Pays $300-600.** Sometimes pays expenses of writers on assignment.

PHOTOS We accept photos submitted with mss. Our rate for a ms with good photos is higher than for one without. Identification of subjects, model releases required.

TIPS We will work with any writer who presents a strong feature article idea applicable to our magazine's audience and who will prove he or she knows the craft of writing. First, obtain writer's guidelines and a sample copy. Study for general style and content. When querying, present detailed outline of proposed ms's focus and editorial intent. Indicate expert sources to be used, as well as possible Kiwanis sources for quotations and anecdotes. Present a well-researched, smoothly written ms that contains a 'human quality' with the use of anecdotes, practical examples, quotations, etc.

$ $ LION

Lions Clubs International, 300 W. 22nd St., Oak Brook IL 60523-8842. (630)468-6909; (630)468-6805. **Fax:** (630)571-1685. **E-mail:** magazine@lionsclubs.org. **Website:** www.lionsclubs.org. **Contact:** Jay

Copp, senior editor. **35% freelance written. Works with a small number of new/unpublished writers each year.** Monthly magazine covering service club organization for Lions Club members and their families. Estab. 1918. Circ. 490,000. Byline given. Pays on acceptance. Publishes ms an average of 5 months after acceptance. Accepts queries by mail, e-mail, fax, phone. Responds in 1 month to queries. Sample copy and writer's guidelines free.

○ "*LION* magazine welcomes freelance article submissions with accompanying photos that depict the service goals and projects of Lions clubs on the local, national, and international level. Contributors may also submit general interest articles that reflect the humanitarian, community betterment, and service activism ideals of the worldwide association. Lions Clubs International is the world's largest service club organization. Lions are recognized globally for their commitment to projects that benefit the blind, visually impaired, and people in need."

NONFICTION Needs photo feature, must be of a Lions Club service project, informational (issues of interest to civic-minded individuals). No travel, biography, or personal experiences. **Buys 40 mss/year.** "Article length should not exceed 2,000 words, and is subject to editing. No gags, fillers, quizzes or poems are accepted. Photos must be color prints or sent digitally. *LION* magazine pays upon acceptance of material. Advance queries save your time and ours. Address all submissions to Jay Copp, senior editor, by mail or e-mail text and .tif or .jpg (300 dpi) photos." Length: 500-2,000 words. **Pays $100-750.** Sometimes pays expenses of writers on assignment.

PHOTOS Purchased with accompanying ms. Photos should be at least 5x7 glossies; color prints or slides are preferred. "We also accept digital photos by e-mail. Be sure photos are clear and as candid as possible.". Captions required. Total purchase price for ms includes payment for photos accepted with ms.

TIPS "Send detailed description of proposed article. Query first and request writer's guidelines and sample copy. Incomplete details on how the Lions involved actually carried out a project and poor quality photos are the most frequent mistakes made by writers in completing an article assignment for us. No gags, fillers, quizzes, or poems are accepted. We are geared increasingly to an international audience. Writers who travel internationally could query for possible assignments, although only locally related expenses could be paid."

⊖⊖ PENN LINES

Pennsylvania Rural Electric Association, 212 Locust St., P.O. Box 1266, Harrisburg PA 17108. **E-mail:** editor@prea.com. **Website:** www.prea.com/content/penn_lines_2012.asp. Monthly magazine covering rural life in Pennsylvania. News magazine of Pennsylvania electric cooperatives. Features should be balanced, and they should have a rural focus. Electric cooperative sources (such as consumers) should be used. Estab. 1966. Circ. 165,000. Byline given. Pays on publication. Publishes ms an average of 3 months after acceptance. Editorial lead time 4 months. Submit seasonal material 4 months in advance. Accepts queries by mail, e-mail. Sample copy online.

NONFICTION Needs general interest, historical, how-to, interview, travel; rural PA only. Query or send complete ms. Length: 500-2,000 words. **Negotiates payment individually.**

PHOTOS Captions required. Reviews prints and GIF/JPEG files. Negotiates payment individually.

TIPS "Find topics of statewide interest to rural residents. Detailed information on *Penn Lines'* readers, gleaned from a reader survey, is online."

THE ROTARIAN

Rotary International, One Rotary Center, 1560 Sherman Ave., Evanston IL 60201. (847)866-3000. **Fax:** (847)328-8554. **E-mail:** rotarian@rotary.org. **Website:** www.rotary.org. **40% freelance written.** Monthly magazine for Rotarian business and professional men and women and their families, schools, libraries, hospitals, etc. "Articles should appeal to an international audience and in some way help Rotarians help other people. The organization's rationale is one of hope, encouragement, and belief in the power of individuals talking and working together." Estab. 1911. Circ. 510,000. Byline sometimes given. Pays on acceptance. Offers kill fee. Kill fee negotiable. Editorial lead time 4-8 months. Accepts queries by mail, e-mail. Sample copy for $1 (edbrookc@rotaryintl.org). Guidelines online.

NONFICTION Needs general interest, humor, inspirational, photo feature, technical, science, travel, lifestyle, sports, business/finance, environmental, health/medicine, social issues. No fiction, religious, or political articles. Query with published clips. Length: 1,500-2,500 words. **Pays negotiable rate.**

REPRINTS "Send tearsheet, photocopy or typed ms with rights for sale noted and information about when and where the material previously appeared." Negotiates payment.

PHOTOS State availability. Reviews contact sheets, transparencies.

COLUMNS/DEPARTMENTS Health; Management; Finance; Travel, all 550-900 words. Query.

TIPS "The chief aim of *The Rotarian* is to report Rotary international news. Most of this information comes through Rotary channels and is staff written or edited. The best field for freelance articles is in the general interest category. We prefer queries with a Rotary angle. These stories run the gamut from humor pieces and how-to stories to articles about such significant concerns as business management, technology, world health, and the environment."

$ $ $ SCOUTING

Boy Scouts of America, 1325 W. Walnut Hill Lane, P.O. Box 152079, Irving TX 75015-2079. **Website:** www.scoutingmagazine.org. **Contact:** Mike Goldman, managing editor; Bryan Wendell, senior editor; Gretchen Sparling, associate editor. **80% freelance written.** Magazine published 6 times/year covering Scouting activities for adult leaders of the Boy Scouts, Cub Scouts, and Venturing. Estab. 1913. Circ. 1 million. Byline given. Pays on acceptance for major features and some shorter features. Publishes ms an average of 18 months after acceptance. Editorial lead time 1 year. Submit seasonal material 1 year in advance. Accepts queries by mail. Accepts simultaneous submissions. Responds in 3 weeks to queries. Responds in 2 months to mss. Sample copy for $2.50 and 9x12 SAE with 4 first-class stamps, or online. Guidelines online.

NONFICTION Needs inspirational, interview. **Buys 20-30 mss/year.** Query with published clips and SASE. A query with a synopsis or outline of a proposed story is essential. Include a SASE. Purchases first rights unless otherwise specified (purchase does not necessarily guarantee publication). Photos, if of acceptable quality, are usually included in payment for certain assignments. (Normally assign professional photographers to take photographs for major story assignments.) Writers or photographers should be familiar with the Scouting program and *Scouting* magazine. Length: short features, 500-700 words; some longer features, up to 1,200 words, usually the result of a definite assignment to a professional writer. **Pays $650-800 for major articles, $300-500 for shorter features. Rates depend on professional quality an article.** Pays expenses of writers on assignment.

REPRINTS Send photocopy of article and information about when and where the article previously appeared. First-person accounts of meaningful Scouting experiences (previously published in local newspapers, etc.) are a popular subject.

PHOTOS State availability. Identification of subjects required. Reviews transparencies, prints.

COLUMNS/DEPARTMENTS Way It Was (Scouting history), 600-750 words; Family Talk (family, raising kids, etc.), 600-750 words. **Buys 8-12 mss/year.** Query. **Pays $300-500.**

FILLERS Limited to personal accounts of humorous or inspirational Scouting experiences. Needs anecdotes, short humor. **Buys 15-25 mss/year.** Length: 50-150 words. **Pays $25 on publication.**

TIPS "*Scouting* magazine articles are mainly about successful program activities conducted by or for Cub Scout packs, Boy Scout troops, and Venturing crews. We also include features on winning leadership techniques and styles, profiles of outstanding individual leaders, and inspirational accounts (usually first person) of *Scouting*'s impact on an individual, either as a youth or while serving as a volunteer adult leader. Because most volunteer Scout leaders are also parents of children of Scout age, *Scouting* is also considered a family magazine. We publish material we feel will help parents in strengthening their families (because they often deal with communicating and interacting with young people, many of these features are useful to a reader in both roles as parent and Scout leader)."

$ $ $ VFW MAGAZINE

Veterans of Foreign Wars of the United States, 406 W. 34th St., Kansas City MO 64111. (816)756-3390. **Fax:** (816)968-1169. **E-mail:** kgibson@vfw.org; magazine@vfw.org. **Website:** www.vfwmagazine.org. **Contact:** Kelly Gibson, senior writer. **40% freelance written.** Monthly magazine on veterans' affairs, military history, patriotism, defense, and current events. *VFW Magazine* goes to its members worldwide, all having served honorably in the armed forces overseas from World War II through the Iraq and Afghanistan Wars. Estab. 1904. Circ. 1.5 million. Byline given. Pays on acceptance. Offers 50% kill fee. Publishes ms

3-6 months after acceptance. Editorial lead time is 6 months. Submit seasonal material 6 months in advance. Accepts queries by mail, e-mail, fax. Responds in 2 months to queries. Sample copy for 9x12 SAE with 5 first-class stamps. Guidelines online.

💬 Unsolicited mss and photographs must be accompanied by return postage and no responsibility is assumed for safe handling. Poetry submissions not accepted.

NONFICTION Needs general interest, historical, inspirational. **Buys 25-30 mss/year.** Query with 1-page outline, résumé, and published clips. Do not send unsolicited mss. Length: 1,000 words. **Pays up to $500-$1,000 maximum for assigned articles; $500-$750 maximum for unsolicited articles.**

PHOTOS Send photos. Reviews contact sheets, negatives, hi-res, GIF/JPEG files, 5x7 or 8x10 prints.

TIPS "Absolute accuracy and quotes from relevant individuals are a must. Bibliographies useful if subject required extensive research and/or is open to dispute. Consult *The Associated Press Stylebook* for correct grammar and punctuation. Please enclose a brief and your military experience (if applicable) in the field in which you are writing. No phone queries."

ASTROLOGY & NEW AGE

$ WHOLE LIFE TIMES

Whole Life Media, LLC, 23705 Vanowen St., #306, West Hills CA 91307. (877)807-2599. **Fax:** (310)933-1693. **E-mail:** editor@wholelifemagazine.com. **Website:** www.wholelifemagazine.com. Bimonthly regional glossy on holistic living. *Whole Life Times* relies almost entirely on freelance material. Open to stories on natural health, alternative healing, green living, sustainable and local food, social responsibility, conscious business, the environment, spirituality and personal growth—anything that deals with a progressive, healthy lifestyle. Estab. 1978. Circ. 42,000 (print); 5,000 (digital). Byline given. Pays within 30-45 days of publication. 50% kill fee on assigned stories. No kill fee to first-time *WLT* writers, or for unsolicited submissions. Publishes ms 2-4 months after acceptance. Accepts queries by e-mail only. Sample copy for $3. Guidelines online and via e-mail.

NONFICTION Special issues: Special issues include: Healing Arts, Food and Nutrition, Spirituality, New Beginnings, Relationships, Longevity, Arts/Cultures Travel, Vitamins and Supplements, Women's Issues, Sexuality, Science and Metaphysics, eco lifestyle. **Buys 60 mss/year.** Send complete ms. Submissions are accepted via e-mail. Artwork should also be sent via e-mail as hard copies will not be returned. "Queries should be professionally written and show an awareness of current topics of interest in our subject area. We welcome investigative reporting and are happy to see queries that address topics in a political context. We are especially looking for articles on health and nutrition. No regular columns sought. Submissions should be double-spaced in AP style as an attached unformatted MS Word file (.doc). If you do not have Microsoft Word and must e-mail in another program, please also copy and paste your story in the message section of your e-mail." **Payment varies.**

REPRINTS Rarely publishes reprints.

COLUMNS/DEPARTMENTS Local News, Taste of Health, Yoga & Spirit, Healthy Living, Art & Soul. Length: 750-900 words. Send complete ms. Submissions are accepted via e-mail. Artwork should also be sent via e-mail as hard copies will not be returned. "Queries should be professionally written and show an awareness of current topics of interest in our subject area. We welcome investigative reporting and are happy to see queries that address topics in a political context. We are especially looking for articles on health and nutrition. No regular columns sought. Submissions should be double-spaced in AP style as an attached unformatted MS Word file (.doc). If you do not have Microsoft Word and must e-mail in another program, please also copy and paste your story in the message section of your e-mail."

TIPS "We accept articles at any time by e-mail. If you would like your article to be considered for a specific issue, we should have it in hand 2-4 months before the issue of publication."

$ WITCHES AND PAGANS

BBI Media, Inc., P.O. Box 687, Forest Grove OR 97116. (888)724-3966. **E-mail:** editor2@bbimedia.com. **Website:** www.witchesandpagans.com. Quarterly magazine covering paganism, wicca, and earth religions. "*Witches and Pagans* is dedicated to witches, wiccans, neo-pagans, and various other earth-based, pre-Christian, shamanic, and magical practitioners. We hope to reach not only those already involved in what we cover, but the curious and completely new as well." Estab. 2002. Circ. 10,000. Byline given. No cash payment, but 4 contributor copies and 1-year subscription given for published submissions. Editorial lead time 3-4 months. Submit seasonal material 6 months in advance. Accepts queries by mail, e-mail, fax, phone. Responds in 1-2 weeks to queries. Responds in 1 month to mss. Sample copy for $6. Guidelines online.

NONFICTION Needs book excerpts, essays, historical, how-to, humor, inspirational, interview, new product, opinion, personal experience, photo feature, religious, travel. Special issues: Features (articles, essays, fiction, interviews, and rituals) should range between 1,000-5,000 words. "We most often publish items between 1500-3000 words; we prefer in-depth coverage to tidbits in most cases, and the upper ranges are usually reserved for lead pieces assigned to specific writers.". Send complete ms. "Submit all written material in electronic format. Our first choice is Open Office writer file attachments e-mailed directly to editor2@bbimedia.com. This e-mail address is being protected from spambots. You need JavaScript enabled to view it; other acceptable file attachment formats include text files and commonly used word processing programs; you may also paste the text of your ms directly into an e-mail message. Use a plain, legible font or typeface large enough to read easily. Sidebars can be 500-1,300 words or so. Reviews have specific lengths and formats; e-mail editor2@bbimedia.com." Length: 1,000-4,000 words.

FICTION Needs adventure, erotica, ethnic, fantasy, historical, horror, humorous, mainstream, mystery, novel concepts, religious, romance, suspense. Does not want faction (fictionalized retellings of real events). Avoid gratuitous sex, violence, sentimentality, and pagan moralizing. Don't beat our readers with the Rede or the Threefold Law. **Buys 3-4 mss/year.** Send complete ms. Length: 1,000-5,000 words.

POETRY Needs avant-garde, free verse, haiku, light verse, traditional. Submit maximum 3-5 poems.

TIPS "Read the magazine, do your research, write the piece, send it in. That's really the only way to get started as a writer; everything else is window dressing."

AUTOMOTIVE AND MOTORCYCLE

AMERICAN MOTORCYCLIST

American Motorcyclist Association, 13515 Yarmouth Dr., Pickerington OH 43147. (614)856-1900. **E-mail:** submissions@ama-cycle.org. **Website:** www.americanmotorcyclist.com. **Contact:** Grant Parsons, director of communications; James Holter, managing editor. **25% freelance written.** Monthly magazine for enthusiastic motorcyclists investing considerable time and money in the sport, emphasizing the motorcyclist, not the vehicle. Monthly magazine of the American Motorcyclist Association. Emphasizes people involved in, and events dealing with, all aspects of motorcycling. Readers are "enthusiastic motorcyclists, investing considerable time in road riding or all aspects of the sport." Estab. 1947. Circ. 200,000. Byline given. Pays on publication. Editorial lead time 3 months. Submit seasonal material 4 months in advance. Accepts queries by mail, e-mail. Responds in 5 weeks to queries. Responds in 6 weeks to mss. Sample copy for $1.50. Guidelines free.

NONFICTION Needs interview, with interesting personalities in the world of motorcycling, personal experience, travel. **Buys 8 mss/year.** Send complete ms. Length: 1,000-2,500 words. **Pays minimum $8/ published column inch.**

PHOTOS Buys 10-20 photos/issue. Subjects include: travel, technical, sports, humorous, photo essay/feature and celebrity/personality. Photo captions preferred. Send photos. Captions, identification of subjects required. Reviews transparencies, prints. Pays $50/photo minimum. Pays $50-150/photo; $250 minimum for cover. Also buys photos in photo/text packages according to same rate; pays $8/column inch minimum for story. Pays on publication.

TIPS "Our major category of freelance stories concerns motorcycling trips to interesting North American destinations. Prefers stories of a timeless nature."

AUTO RESTORER

BowTie, Inc., 3 Burroughs, Irvine CA 92618. (213)385-2222. **Fax:** (213)385-8565. **E-mail:** tkade@ bowtieinc.com. **Website:** www.autorestorermagazine.com. **Contact:** Ted Kade, editor. **85% freelance written.** Monthly magazine covering auto restoration. "Our readers own old cars and they work on them. We help our readers by providing as much practical, how-to information as we can about restoration and old cars." Estab. 1989. Circ. 60,000. Pays on publication. Publishes mss 3 months after acceptance. Submit seasonal material 4 months in advance. Accepts queries by mail, e-mail, fax. Responds in 2 months to queries. Sample copy for $7. Guidelines free.

🔑 Areas most open to freelance work are technical illustrations for feature articles and renderings of classic cars for various sections.

NONFICTION Needs how-to, auto restoration, new product, photo feature, technical product evaluation. **Buys 60 mss/year.** Query first. Length: 250-2,000/ words. **Pays $150/published page, including photos and illustrations.**

PHOTOS Emphasizes restoration of collector cars and trucks. Readers are 98% male, professional/ technical/managerial, ages 35-65. Buys 47 photos from freelancers/issue; 564 photos/year. Send photos. Model/property release preferred. Photo captions required; include year, make and model of car; identification of people in photo. Reviews photos with accompanying ms only. Reviews contact sheets, transparencies, 5x7 prints. Looks for "technically proficient or dramatic photos of various automotive subjects, auto portraits, detail shots, action photos, good angles, composition and lighting. We're also looking for photos to illustrate how-to articles such as how to repair a damaged fender or how to repair a carburetor.". Pays $50 for b&w cover; $35 for b&w inside. Pays on publication. Credit line given.

TIPS "Interview the owner of a restored car. Present advice to others on how to do a similar restoration. Seek advice from experts. Go light on history and nonspecific details. Make it something that the magazine regularly uses. Do automotive how-tos."

⊘ $ $ $ $ CAR AND DRIVER

Hearst Communications, Inc., 1585 Eisenhower Place, Ann Arbor MI 48108. (734)971-3600. **Fax:** (734)971-9188. **E-mail:** editors@caranddriver.com. **Website:** www.caranddriver.com. **Contact:** Eddie Alterman, editor-in-chief; Mike Fazioli, managing editor. Monthly magazine for auto enthusiasts; college-educated, professional, median 24-35 years of age. Estab. 1956. Circ. 1,212,555. Byline given. Pays on acceptance. Offers 25% kill fee. Accepts queries by mail, e-mail. Responds in 2 months to queries.

NONFICTION Query with published clips before submitting. Pays expenses of writers on assignment.

PHOTOS Color slides and b&w photos sometimes purchased with accompanying ms.

TIPS "It is best to start off with an interesting query and to stay away from nuts-and-bolts ideas, because that will be handled in-house or by an acknowledged expert. Our goal is to be absolutely without flaw in our presentation of automotive facts, but we strive to be every bit as entertaining as we are informative. We do not print this sort of story: 'My Dad's Wacky, Lovable Beetle.'"

MOTOR TREND

Source Interlink Media, Inc., 831 S. Douglas St., El Segundo CA 90245. **Website:** www.motortrend.com. **5-10% freelance written. Only works with published/established writers.** Monthly magazine for automotive enthusiasts and general interest consumers. Estab. 1949. Circ. 1,250,000. Publishes ms an average of 3 months after acceptance. Accepts queries by mail. Responds in 1 month to queries.

NONFICTION Query before submitting. Send typed mss and photos with accompanying captions with SASE.

PHOTOS Buys photos of prototype cars and assorted automotive matter.

$ $ RIDER MAGAZINE

1227 Flynn Rd., Ste. 304, Camarillo CA 93010. (805)978-5500. **Website:** www.ridermagazine.com. **60% freelance written.** Monthly magazine covering motorcycling. *Rider* serves the all-brand motorcycle lifestyle/enthusiast with a slant toward travel and touring. Estab. 1974. Circ. 135,000. Byline given. Pays on publication. Publishes ms an average of 6-18 months after acceptance. Editorial lead time 3 months. Submit seasonal material 6 months in advance. Accepts queries by mail only. Responds in 2 months to queries. Sample copy for $2.95. Guidelines online.

NONFICTION Needs general interest, historical, how-to, humor, interview, personal experience, travel. Does not want to see fiction or "How I Began Motorcycling" articles. **Buys 40-50 mss/year.** Query. Length: 750-1,800 words. **Pays $150-750.**

PHOTOS Send photos. Captions required. Reviews high-resolution (4MP+) digital images. Offers no additional payment for photos accepted with ms.

COLUMNS/DEPARTMENTS Favorite Rides (short trip), 850-1,000 words. **Buys 12 mss/year.** Query. **Pays $150-750.**

TIPS "We rarely accept mss without photos. Query first. Follow guidelines available on request. We are most open to favorite rides, feature stories (must include excellent photography) and material for Rides, Rallies and Clubs. Include a map, information on routes, local attractions, restaurants, and scenery in favorite ride submissions."

AVIATION

$ AFRICAN PILOT

Wavelengths 10 (Pty) Ltd., 6 Barbeque Heights, 9 Dytchley Rd., Barbeque Downs, Midrand 1684 South Africa. +27 11 466-8524. **Fax:** +27 11 466 8496. **E-mail:** editor@africanpilot.co.za. **Website:** www.africanpilot.co.za. **Contact:** Athol Franz, editor. **50% freelance written.** "*African Pilot* is southern Africa's premier monthly aviation magazine. It publishes a high-quality magazine that is well-known and respected within the aviation community of southern Africa. The magazine offers a number of benefits to readers and advertisers, including a weekly e-mail, Aviation News, annual service guide, aviation training supplement, executive wall calendar and an extensive website. The monthly aviation magazine is also online as an exact replica of the paper edition, but where all major advertising pages are hyperlinked to the advertisers website. The magazine offers clean layouts with outstanding photography and reflects editorial professionalism as well as a responsible approach to journalism. The magazine offers a complete and tailored promotional solution for all aviation businesses operating in the African region." Estab. 2001. Circ. 7,000+ online; 6,600+ print. Byline given. Editorial lead time 2-3 months. Accepts queries by e-mail. Accepts simultaneous submissions. Responds only if interested, send nonreturnable samples. Sample copies available upon request. Writer's guidelines online or via e-mail.

NONFICTION Needs general interest, historical, interview, new product, personal experience, photo feature, technical. No articles on aircraft accidents. **Buys up to 60 mss/year.** Send complete ms. Length: 1,200-2,800 words. Sometimes pays expenses of writers on assignment.

PHOTOS Send photos. Captions required. Negotiates payment individually.

TIPS "The website is updated monthly and all articles are fully published online."

$$ AVIATION HISTORY

Weider History Group, 19300 Promenade Dr., Leesburg VA 20176. **E-mail:** aviationhistory@weiderhistorygroup.com. **Website:** www.historynet.com/aviation-history. **95% freelance written.** Bimonthly magazine covering military and civilian aviation from first flight to the space age. "It aims to make aeronautical history not only factually accurate and complete, but also enjoyable to a varied subscriber and newsstand audience." Estab. 1990. Circ. 40,000. Byline given. Pays on publication. Publishes ms an average of 2 years after acceptance. Editorial lead time 6 months. Submit seasonal material 1 year in advance. Accepts queries by mail, e-mail, fax. Accepts simultaneous submissions. Responds in 2 months to queries. Responds in 3 months to mss. Sample copy for $5. Guidelines with #10 SASE or online.

NONFICTION Needs historical, interview, personal experience. **Buys 24 mss/year.** Query. Feature articles should be 3,000-3,500 words, each with a 500-word sidebar where appropriate, author's biography, and book suggestions for further reading **Pays $300 and up.**

PHOTOS State availability of art and photos with submissions, cite sources. We'll order. Identification of subjects required. Reviews contact sheets, negatives, transparencies.

COLUMNS/DEPARTMENTS Aviators, Restored, Extremes all 1,500 words or less. Pays $150 and up. Book reviews, 250-500 words, pays minimum $50.

TIPS "Choose stories with strong narrative and art possibilities. Include a hard copy as well as an IBM- or Macintosh-compatible CD. Write an entertaining, informative, and unusual story that grabs the reader's attention and holds it. All stories must be true. We do not publish fiction or poetry."

$$ FLYING ADVENTURES

Aviation Publishing Corporation, El Monte Airport (EMT), P.O. Box 93613, Pasadena CA 91109-3613. (626)618-4000. **E-mail:** editor@flyingadventures.com; info@flyingadventures.com. **Website:** www.flyingadventures.com. **20% freelance written.** Bimonthly magazine covering lifestyle travel for owners and passengers of private aircraft. Articles cover upscale travelers. Estab. 1994. Circ. 135,858. Byline given for features. Pays on acceptance. Editorial lead time 2 weeks to 2 months. Accepts queries by e-mail. Accepts simultaneous submissions. Responds immediately. Sample copy and guidelines free.

NONFICTION Needs travel, lifestyle. "Nothing non-relevant or not our style. See magazine." Query with published clips. Length: 500-1,500 words. **Pays $150-300 for assigned and unsolicited articles.** Sometimes pays expenses of writers on assignment.

PHOTOS Contact: Photography director. State availability. Captions, identification of subjects, model releases required. Reviews GIF/JPEG files. Negotiates payment individually.

COLUMNS/DEPARTMENTS Contact: Editor. Numerous departments; see magazine. **Buys 100+ mss/yr. mss/year.** Query with published clips. **Pays $150.**

TIPS "Send clip that fits our content and style. Must fit our style!"

BUSINESS AND FINANCE

BUSINESS NATIONAL

FAST COMPANY

7 World Trade Center, New York NY 10007-2195. **E-mail:** pr@fastcompany.com. **Website:** www.fastcompany.com. **Contact:** Lori Hoffman, managing editor. Magazine published 10 times/year that inspires readers and users to think beyond traditional boundaries, lead conversations, and create the future of business. *Fast Company* is the world's leading progressive business media brand, with a unique editorial focus on innovation in technology, ethonomics (ethical economics), leadership, and design. Estab. 1996. Circ. 750,000. Accepts queries by e-mail. No formal guidelines. Familiarize yourself with the magazine.

🗨 Difficult market to break into.

NONFICTION Rarely accepts unsolicited freelancer contributions. If you have a person, company, product, or any other story idea you'd like to see in *Fast Company*, query with a pitch. If interested, *Fast Company* will contact you.

FORBES

Forbes, Inc., 60 5th Ave., New York NY 10011. **Website:** www.forbes.com. Biweekly magazine. Edited for top business management professionals and for those aspiring to positions of corporate leadership. Circ. 1,000,000. Editorial lead time 2 months.

🗨 Query before submitting.

FORTUNE

Time, Inc., 1271 Avenue of the Americas, New York NY 10020. (212)522-1212. **Fax:** (212)522-0810. **E-mail:** letters@fortune.com. **Website:** www.fortune.com. Biweekly magazine covering business and finance. Edited primarily for high-demographic business people. Specializes in big stories about companies, business personalities, technology, managing, Wall Street, media, marketing, personal finance, politics, and policy. Circ. 1,066,000. Editorial lead time 6 weeks.

🗨 Query before submitting.

MONEY

Time, Inc., 1271 Avenue of the Americas, 17th Floor, New York NY 10020. (212)522-1212. **Fax:** (212)522-0189. **E-mail:** managing_editor@moneymail.com; editor@money.timeinc.com. **Website:** money.cnn.com. Monthly magazine covering finance. *Money* magazine offers sophisticated coverage in all aspects of personal finance for individuals, business executives, and personal investors. Estab. 1972. Circ. 1,967,420.

🗨 Query before submitting.

💲💲 TECHNICAL ANALYSIS OF STOCKS & COMMODITIES

4757 California Ave., SW, Seattle WA 98116. (206)938-0570. **E-mail:** editor@traders.com. **Website:** www.traders.com. **Contact:** Jayanthi Gopalakrishnan, editor; Christine Morrison, art director. **90% freelance written.** "Magazine covers methods of investing and trading stocks, bonds and commodities (futures), options, mutual funds, and precious metals using technical analysis." Estab. 1982. Circ. 60,000. Byline given. Pays on publication. Publishes ms an average of 4 months after acceptance. Responds in 2 months to queries. Sample copy for $5. Guidelines online.

🗨 "Eager to work with new/unpublished writers."

NONFICTION Needs how-to, trade, technical, cartoons, trading and software aids to trading, Product reviews, utilities, real-world trading (actual case studies of trades and their results). No newsletter-type, buy-sell recommendations. The article subject must relate to technical analysis, charting or a numerical technique used to trade securities or futures. Almost universally requires graphics with every article. **Buys 150 mss/year.** Send complete ms. Length: 1,000-4,000 words. **Pays $100-500.**

REPRINTS Send tearsheet with rights for sale noted and information about when and where the material previously appeared.

PHOTOS State availability. Captions, identification of subjects, model releases required. Pays $60-350 for b&w or color negatives with prints or positive slides.

COLUMNS/DEPARTMENTS Length: 800-1,600 words. **Buys 100 mss/year.** Query. **Pays $50-300**

FILLERS Contact: Karen Wasserman, fillers editor. "Must relate to trading stocks, bonds, options, mutual funds, commodities, or precious metals." **Buys 20 mss/year.** Length: 500 words. **Pays $20-50.**

TIPS "Describe how to use technical analysis, charting, or computer work in day-to-day trading of stocks, bonds, commodities, options, mutual funds, or precious metals. A blow-by-blow account of how a trade was made, including the trader's thought processes, is the very best-received story by our subscribers. One of our primary considerations is to instruct in a manner that the layperson can comprehend. We are not hypercritical of writing style."

BUSINESS REGIONAL

BLOOMBERG BUSINESSWEEK

Bloomberg LP, 731 Lexington Ave., New York NY 10022. **E-mail:** letters@bloomberg.net. **Website:** www.businessweek.com. Weekly business magazine that provides information and interpretation about what is happening in the business world. Estab. 1929.

Query before submitting. Difficult market to break into.

BUSINESS NH MAGAZINE

55 S. Commercial St., Manchester NH 03101. (603)626-6354. **Fax:** (603)626-6359. **E-mail:** hcopeland@BusinessNHmagazine.com. **Website:** www.millyardcommunications.com. **Contact:** Heidi Copeland, publisher. **25% freelance written.** Monthly magazine covering business, politics, and people of New Hampshire. "Our audience consists of the owners and top managers of New Hampshire businesses." Estab. 1983. Circ. 15,000. Byline given. Pays on publication. Publishes ms an average of 2 months after acceptance. Accepts queries by e-mail, fax.

NONFICTION Needs how-to, interview. No unsolicited mss; interested in New Hampshire writers only. **Buys 24 mss/year.** Query with published clips and résumé. Length: 750-2,500 words. **Payment varies.**

PHOTOS Both b&w and color photos are used. Model/property release preferred. Photo captions required; include names, locations, contact phone number. Payment varies. Pays $450 for color cover; $100 for color or b&w inside. Credit line given. Buys one-time rights. Pays on publication.

TIPS "We always want clips and résumés with queries. Freelance stories are almost always assigned. Stories must be local to New Hampshire."

THE ECONOMIST

The Economist Group, 25 St. James's St., London SW1A 1HG England. +44(0) 20 7830 7000. **Fax:** +44(0) 20 7839 2968. **Website:** www.economist.com. **Contact:** Adrian Woolridge, management editor. Weekly newspaper that is not just a chronicle of economics. Takes "part in a severe contest between intelligence, which presses forward, and an unworthy, timid ignorance obstructing our progress." Targets highly educated readers. Offers authoritative insight and opinion on international news, politics, business, finance, science, and technology. Estab. 1843.

Query before submitting.

PACIFIC COAST BUSINESS TIMES

14 E. Carrillo St., Suite A, Santa Barbara CA 93101. (805)560-6950. **E-mail:** hdubroff@pacbiztimes.com. **Website:** www.pacbiztimes.com. **Contact:** Henry Dubroff, founder and editor. **10% freelance written.** Weekly tabloid covering financial news specific to Santa Barbara, Ventura, San Luis Obispo counties in California. Estab. 2000. Circ. 5,000. Byline given. Editorial lead time 1 month. Accepts queries by e-mail, phone. Sample copy free. Guidelines free.

NONFICTION Needs interview, opinion, personal finance. Does not want first person, promo or fluff pieces. **Buys 20 mss/year.** Query. Length: 500-800 words. **Pays $75-175.** Pays expenses of writers on assignment.

SMARTCEO MEDIA

SmartCEO, 2700 Lighthouse Point E., Suite 220A, Baltimore MD 21224. (410)342-9510. **Fax:** (410)675-5280. **E-mail:** editorial@smartceo.com. **Website:** www.smartceo.com. **25% freelance written.** Publishes four bi-monthly print magazines covering regional business in the Baltimore, MD, Philadelphia, PA, New York, NY, and Washington, DC areas. Nearly 50,000 offensive-minded, growth-oriented CEOs turn to *SmartCEO* magazine to find ideas and inspiration to help them grow their businesses. Each issue includes behind-the-scenes looks at local success stories, columns written by key opinion leaders and other resources to help the region's middle-market CEOs conquer the daily challenges of running a business. *SmartCEO* magazine is published on a bi-monthly basis with editions in four major markets: *Baltimore SmartCEO*, *New York SmartCEO*, *Philadelphia SmartCEO* and *Washington SmartCEO*. Estab. 2001. Circ. 45,000. Byline given. Pays on publication. Publishes ms an average of 2 months after acceptance. Editorial lead time 5 months. Submit seasonal material 5 months in advance. Accepts queries by e-mail, phone. Responds in 4 weeks to queries. Responds in 2 months to mss. Sample copy online. Guidelines by e-mail.

NONFICTION Needs interview, Business features or tips. "We do not want pitches on CEOs or companies outside the Baltimore, MD, Philadelphia, PA, New York, NY or Washington, DC areas; no product reviews, lifestyle content or book reviews, please." **Buys 20 mss/year.** Query. Length: varies. **Pays varies.** Sometimes pays expenses of writers on assignment.

PHOTOS Contact: Erica Fromherz, art director. State availability. Identification of subjects required. Reviews GIF/JPEG files.

COLUMNS/DEPARTMENTS Project to Watch (overview of a local development project in progress and why it is of interest to the business community), 600 words; Q&A and tip-focused coverage of business issues and challenges (each article includes the opinions of 10-20 CEOs), 500-1,000 words. **Buys 0-5 mss/year.** Query.

TIPS "When pitching a local CEO, tell us why his/her accomplishments tell an inspiring story with applicable lessons for other CEOs. *SmartCEO* is not news; we are a resource full of smart ideas to help educate and inspire decision-makers in the Baltimore and DC areas. Send your pitch via e-mail and follow up with a phone call."

CAREER, COLLEGE AND ALUMNI

💲💲 EQUAL OPPORTUNITY

Equal Opportunity Publications, Inc., 445 Broad Hollow Rd., Suite 425, Melville NY 11747. (631)421-9421. **Fax:** (631)421-0359. **E-mail:** jschneider@eop.com. **Website:** www.eop.com. **Contact:** James Schneider, director, editorial and production. **70% freelance written. Prefers to work with published/established writers.** Triannual magazine dedicated to advancing the professional interests of African Americans, Hispanics, Asian Americans, and Native Americans. Audience is 90% college juniors and seniors; 10% working graduates. An understanding of educational and career problems of minorities is essential. Estab. 1967. Circ. 11,000. Byline given. Pays on publication. Publishes ms an average of 6 months after acceptance. Editorial lead time 6 months. Submit seasonal material 6 months in advance. Accepts queries by mail, e-mail,

fax, phone. Responds in 2 weeks to queries. Responds in 1 month to mss. Sample copy and writer's guidelines for 9x12 SAE with 5 first-class stamps.

◑ Distributed through college guidance and placement offices.

NONFICTION Needs general interest, specific minority concerns, how-to, job hunting skills, personal finance, better living, coping with discrimination, interview, minority role models, opinion, problems of minorities, personal experience, professional and student study experiences, technical, on career fields offering opportunities for minorites, coverage of minority interests. **Buys 10 mss/year.** Send complete ms. Length: 1,000-2,000 words. **Pays 10¢/word.** Sometimes pays expenses of writers on assignment.

REPRINTS Send information about when and where the material previously appeared. Pays 10¢/word.

PHOTOS Captions, identification of subjects required. Reviews 35mm color slides and b&w.

TIPS "Articles must be geared toward questions and answers faced by minority and women students. We would like to see role-model profiles of professions."

💲💲💲💲 NOTRE DAME MAGAZINE

University of Notre Dame, 500 Grace Hall, Notre Dame IN 46556-5612. (574)631-5335. **E-mail:** ndmag@nd.edu. **Website:** magazine.nd.edu. **Contact:** Kerry Temple, editor; Kerry Prugh, art director. **50% freelance written.** "We are a university magazine with a scope as broad as that found at a university, but we place our discussion in a moral, ethical, and spiritual context reflecting our Catholic heritage." Estab. 1972. Circ. 150,000. Byline given. Pays on acceptance. Publishes ms an average of 1 year after acceptance. Accepts queries by mail, e-mail, fax. Responds in 2 months to queries. Sample copy online and by request. Guidelines online.

NONFICTION Needs opinion, personal experience, religious. **Buys 35 mss/year.** Query with published clips. Length: 600-3,000 words. **Pays $250-3,000.** Sometimes pays expenses of writers on assignment.

PHOTOS State availability. Identification of subjects, model releases required.

COLUMNS/DEPARTMENTS CrossCurrents (essays, deal with a wide array of issues—some topical, some personal, some serious, some light). Query with or without published clips or send complete ms.

TIPS "The editors are always looking for new writers and fresh ideas. However, the caliber of the magazine and frequency of its publication dictate that the writing meet very high standards. The editors value articles strong in storytelling quality, journalistic technique, and substance. They do not encourage promotional or nostalgia pieces, stories on sports, or essays that are sentimentally religious."

💲💲 OREGON QUARTERLY

5228 University of Oregon, Eugene OR 97403. (541)346-5048. **E-mail:** quarterly@uoregon.edu. **Website:** www.oregonquarterly.com. **85% freelance written.** Quarterly magazine covering people and ideas at the University of Oregon and the Northwest. Estab. 1919. Circ. 100,000. Byline given. Pays on acceptance. Offers 20% kill fee. Publishes ms an average of 3 months after acceptance. Accepts queries by e-mail (preferred), mail ("grumpily"). Limited to works by UO faculty and alumni authors. Responds in 2 months to queries. Guidelines online.

NONFICTION Buys 30 mss/year. Query with published clips. Length: 300-3,000 words. **Payment varies—75¢-$1/per word**

PHOTOS State availability of story-related images. Identification of subjects required. Prefers hi-res digital.

FICTION Rarely publishes novel excerpts by UO professors or grads.

TIPS "Query with pitches appropriate to the magazin's mission, character, and focus, with strong, colorful writing on clear display; clips. And please, demonstrate you have a familiarity with our publication."

THE PENN STATER

Penn State Alumni Association, Hintz Family Alumni Center, University Park PA 16802. (814)865-2709. **Fax:** (814)863-5690. **E-mail:** pennstater@psu.edu. **Website:** www.alumni.psu.edu. **60% freelance written.** Bimonthly magazine covering Penn State and Penn Staters. Estab. 1910. Circ. 130,000. Byline given. Pays on acceptance. Offers 50% kill fee. Publishes ms an average of 4 months after acceptance. Editorial lead time 3 months. Submit seasonal material 8 months in advance. Accepts queries by mail, e-mail, fax. Accepts simultaneous submissions. Responds in 3 months to queries. Sample copy and writer's guidelines free.

NONFICTION Needs book excerpts, by or about Penn Staters, general interest, historical, interview, personal experience, photo feature, book reviews, science/research. No unsolicited mss. **Buys 20 mss/year.**

Query with published clips. Length: 200-3,000 words. **Pays competitive rates.** Pays expenses of writers on assignment.

REPRINTS Send photocopy and information about when and where the material previously appeared. Payment varies

PHOTOS Send photos. Captions required.

TIPS "We are especially interested in attracting writers who are savvy in creative nonfiction/literary journalism. Most stories must have a Penn State tie-in. No phone calls, please."

CHILD CARE & PARENTAL GUIDANCE

💲💲💲 AMERICAN BABY

Meredith Corp., 375 Lexington Ave., 9th Floor, New York NY 10017. **E-mail:** abletters@americanbaby.com. **Website:** www.americanbaby.com. **Contact:** Dana Points, editor-in-chief. **70% freelance written.** Monthly magazine covering health, medical, and child care concerns for expectant and new parents, particularly those having their first child or those whose child is between the ages of birth and 2 years old. Mothers are the primary readers, but fathers' issues are equally important. Estab. 1938. Circ. 2,000,000. Byline given. Pays on acceptance. Offers 25% kill fee. Publishes ms an average of 6 months after acceptance. Editorial lead time 5 months. Submit seasonal material 6 months in advance. Accepts queries by mail. Responds in 3 months to queries. Responds in 3 months to mss. Sample copy for 9x12 SAE with 6 first-class stamps. Guidelines for #10 SASE.

Prefers to work with published/established writers; works with a small number of new/unpublished writers each year.

NONFICTION Needs book excerpts, essays, general interest, how-to, some aspect of pregnancy or child care, humor, new product, personal experience, fitness, beauty, health. No "hearts and flowers" or fantasy pieces. **Buys 60 mss/year.** Send complete ms. Length: 1,000-2,000 words. **Pays $750-1,200 for assigned articles. Pays $600-800 for unsolicited articles.** Pays expenses of writers on assignment.

REPRINTS Send photocopy and information about when and where the material previously appeared. Pays 50% of original price.

PHOTOS State availability. Identification of subjects, model releases required. Reviews transparencies, prints.

COLUMNS/DEPARTMENTS Personal essays (700-1,000 words) and shorter items for Crib Notes (news and features) and Health Briefs (50-150 words) are also accepted. **Pays $200-1,000.**

TIPS "Get to know our style by thoroughly reading a recent issue of the magazine. Don't send something we recently published. Our readers want to feel connected to other parents, both to share experiences and to learn from one another. They want reassurance that the problems they are facing are solvable and not uncommon. They want to keep up with the latest issues affecting their new family, particularly health and medical news, but they don't have a lot of spare time to read. We forgo the theoretical approach to offer quick-to-read, hands-on information that can be put to use immediately. A simple, straightforward, clear approach is mandatory."

🌎🌎 CHICAGO PARENT

141 S. Oak Park Ave., Oak Park IL 60302. (708)386-5555. **Website:** www.chicagoparent.com. **Contact:** Tamara O'Shaughnessy, editor. **60% freelance written.** Monthly tabloid. *Chicago Parent* has a distinctly local approach. Offers information, inspiration, perspective, and empathy to Chicago-area parents. Lively editorial mix has a "we're all in this together" spirit, and articles are thoroughly researched and well written. Estab. 1988. Circ. 125,000 in 3 zones, covering the 6-county Chicago metropolitan area. Byline given. Pays on publication. Offers 10-50% kill fee. Publishes ms an average of 2 months after acceptance. Editorial lead time 4 months. Submit seasonal material 4 months in advance. Accepts queries by e-mail. Responds in 6 weeks to queries. Sample copy for $4.95 and 11×17 SAE with $1.65 postage direct to circulation. Guidelines online.

NONFICTION Needs essays, expose, how-to, parent-related, humor, interview, travel. No pot-boiler parenting pieces, simultaneous submissions, previously published pieces or non-local writers (from outside the 6-county Chicago metropolitan area). **Buys 40-50 mss/year.** Query with links published clips. Length: 200-2,500 words. **Pays $25-300 for assigned articles.**

FAMILYFUN

Meredith, 47 Pleasant St., Northampton MA 01060. (413)585-0444. **Website:** www.parents.com/family-fun-magazine. Family magazine published 10 times/year. Written for parents with children ages 3-12, focusing on family cooking, vacations, parties, holidays, crafts, and learning. Estab. 1991. Circ. 2.1 million. Accepts queries by mail, e-mail. Guidelines available upon request.

NONFICTION Interested in stories that will appeal to a wide variety of parents. Query before submitting. Queries should describe the content, structure, and tone of a proposed article. Include published clips with query. Works only with experienced writers.

🌎 GRAND RAPIDS FAMILY MAGAZINE

Gemini Publications, 549 Ottawa Ave. NW, Suite 201, Grand Rapids MI 49503-1444. (616)459-4545. **Fax:** (616)459-4800. **E-mail:** cvalade@geminipub.com. **Website:** www.grfamily.com. **Contact:** Carole Valade, editor. Monthly magazine covering local parenting issues. *Grand Rapids Family* seeks to inform, instruct, amuse, and entertain its readers and their families. Circ. 30,000. Byline given. Pays on publication. Offers $25 kill fee. Editorial lead time 3 months. Submit seasonal material 4 months in advance. Accepts simultaneous submissions. Responds in 2 months to queries. Responds in 6 months to mss. Guidelines with #10 SASE.

NONFICTION Query. **Pays $25-50.**

PHOTOS State availability. Captions, identification of subjects, model releases required. Reviews contact sheets. Offers $25/photo.

COLUMNS/DEPARTMENTS All local: law, finance, humor, opinion, mental health. **Pays $25.**

🌎 HOME EDUCATION MAGAZINE

P.O. Box 1083, Tonasket WA 98855. (800)236-3278; (509)486-1351. **Fax:** (509)486-2753. **E-mail:** articles@homeedmag.com. **Website:** www.homeedmag.com. **Contact:** Jeanne Faulconer, articles editor. **80% freelance written.** Bimonthly magazine covering home-based education. "We feature articles which address the concerns of parents who want to take a direct involvement in the education of their children—concerns such as socialization, how to find curriculums and materials, testing and evaluation, how to tell when your child is ready to begin reading, what to do when homeschooling is difficult, teaching advanced subjects, etc." Estab. 1983. Circ. 120,000. Byline given. Pays on publication. Publishes ms an average of 6 months after acceptance. Submit seasonal material 6 months in advance. Accepts queries by mail. Responds in 2 months to queries. Sample copy for $6.50. Writer's guidelines with #10 SASE, via e-mail, or online.

NONFICTION Needs essays, how-to, related to homeschooling, humor, interview, personal experience, photo feature, technical. **Buys 40-50 mss/year.** Send complete ms. Length: 750-2,500 words. **Pays $50-150.**

PHOTOS Send photos. Identification of subjects required. Reviews enlargements, 35mm prints, CDs. Pays $100/cover; $12/inside photos.

TIPS "We would like to see how-to articles (that don't preach, just present options); articles on testing, accountability, working with the public schools, socialization, learning disabilities, resources, support groups, legislation, and humor. We need answers to the questions that homeschoolers ask. Please, no teachers telling parents how to teach. Personal experience with homeschooling is the preferred approach."

🌐 MEDIA FOR LIVING, VALLEY LIVING MAGAZINE

Shalom Foundation, 1251 Virginia Ave., Harrisonburg VA 22802. (540)433-5351. **E-mail:** mediaforliving@gmail.com. **Website:** www.mediaforliving.org. **90% freelance written.** Quarterly tabloid covering family living. Articles focus on giving general encouragement for families of all ages and stages. Estab. 1985. Circ. 11,000. Byline given. Pays on publication. Publishes ms an average of 6-12 months after acceptance. Editorial lead time 4-6 months. Submit seasonal material 6 months in advance. Accepts queries by mail, e-mail. Accepts simultaneous submissions. Responds in 2 months to queries. Responds in 2-4 months to mss. Sample copy for SAE with 9x12 envelope and 4 first-class stamps. Guidelines free.

🔑 "We want our stories and articles to be very practical and upbeat. We do not assume a Christian audience. Writers need to take this into account. Personal experience stories are welcome but are not the only approach. Our audience? Children, teenagers, singles, married couples, right on through to retired persons. We cover the wide variety of subjects that people face in the home and workplace. (See theme list in our guidelines online.)"

NONFICTION Needs general interest, how-to, humor, inspirational, personal experience. "We do not use devotional materials intended for Christian audiences. We seldom use pet stories and receive way too many grief/death/dealing with serious illness stories to use. We publish in March, June, September, and December so holidays that occur in other months are not usually the subject of articles." **Buys 48-52 mss/year.** Query. Length: 500-1,200 words. **Pays $35-60.**

PHOTOS Contact: Lindsey Shantz. State availability. Captions, identification of subjects, model releases required. Reviews 4x6 prints, GIF/JPEG files. Offers $15-25/photo.

TIPS "We prefer 'good news' stories that are uplifting and noncontroversial in nature. We want articles that tell stories of people solving problems and dealing with personal issues rather than essays or 'preaching.' If you submit electronically, it is very helpful if you put the specific title of the submission in the subject line and please include your e-mail address in the body of the e-mail or on your ms. Also, always please include your address and phone number."

🌐 METROKIDS

Kidstuff Publications, Inc., 1412-1414 Pine St., Philadelphia PA 19102. (215)291-5560, ext. 102. **Fax:** (215)291-5563. **E-mail:** editor@metrokids.com. **Website:** www.metrokids.com. **Contact:** Cheryl Krementz, managing editor. **25% freelance written.** Monthly magazine providing information for parents and kids in Philadelphia and surrounding counties, South Jersey, and Delaware. "*MetroKids*, a free monthly magazine, is a resource for parents living in the greater Delaware Valley. The Pennsylvania, South Jersey, and Delaware editions of *MetroKids* are available in supermarkets, libraries, daycares, and hundreds of other locations. The magazine and website feature the area's most extensive calendar of day-by-day family events; child-focused camp, day care, and party directories; local family fun suggestions; and articles that offer parenting advice and insights. Other *MetroKids* publications include *The Ultimate Family Guide*, a guide to area attractions, service providers and community resources; SpecialKids, a resource guide for families of children with special needs; and Educator's Edition, a directory of field trips, assemblies, and school enrichment programs." Estab. 1990. Circ. 115,000. Byline given. Pays on publication. Submit seasonal material 4 months in advance. Accepts queries by e-mail. Guidelines available by e-mail.

💬 Responds only if interested.

NONFICTION Needs general interest, how-to, new product, travel, parenting, health. Special issues: Educator's Edition—field trips, school enrichment, teacher, professional development (March and September); SpecialKids—children with special needs (August). **Buys 40 mss/year.** Query with published clips. Length: 575-1,500 words. **Pays $50.**

REPRINTS E-mail summary or complete article and information about when and where the material previously appeared. Pays $35, or $50 if localized after discussion.

COLUMNS/DEPARTMENTS Tech Talk, Mom Matters, Health, Money, Your Home, Parenting, Toddlers, Tweens/Teens, Education, Food & Nutrition, Play, Toddlers, Camp, Classes, Features, all 650-850 words. **Buys 25 mss/year.** Query. **Pays $25-50.**

TIPS "We prefer e-mail queries or submissions. Because they're so numerous, we don't reply unless interested. We are interested in feature articles (on specified topics) or material for our regular departments (with a regional/seasonal base). Articles should cite expert sources, preferably from the Philadelphia/South Jersey/Delaware area, and the most up-to-date theories and facts. We are looking for a journalistic style of writing. We are also interested in finding local writers for assignments."

PARENTS

Meredith Corp., 375 Lexington Ave., 10th Floor, New York NY 10017. (212)499-2000. **Fax:** (212)499-2077. **Website:** www.parents.com. **Contact:** Dana Points, editor-in-chief. Monthly magazine that focuses on the daily needs and concerns of mothers with young children. Provides high quality content that informs, entertains and joins parents in celebrating the joys of parenthood. Features information about child health, safety, behavior, discipline, and education. There are also stories on women's health, nutrition, pregnancy, marriage, and beauty. Estab. 1926. Circ. 2,215,645. Pays on acceptance. Offers 25% kill fee. Submit seasonal material 6-8 months in advance. Accepts queries by mail, e-mail. Responds in 4-6 weeks to queries.

NONFICTION Query before submitting.

COLUMNS/DEPARTMENTS As They Grow (issues on different stages of development), 1,000 words.

TIPS "We're a national publication, so we're mainly interested in stories that will appeal to a wide variety of parents. We're always looking for compelling human-interest stories, so you may want to check your local newspaper for ideas. Keep in mind that we can't pursue stories that have appeared in competing national publications."

PEDIATRICS FOR PARENTS

Pediatrics for Parents, Inc., 120 Western Ave., Gloucester MA 01930. (215)253-4543. **Fax:** (973)302-4543. **E-mail:** editor@pedsforparents.com. **E-mail:** submissions@pedsforparents.com. **Website:** www.pedsforparents.com. **Contact:** Richard J. Sagall, M.D., editor. **50% freelance written.** Monthly newsletter covering children's health. "*Pediatrics For Parents* emphasizes an informed, common-sense approach to childhood health care. We stress preventative action, accident prevention, when to call the doctor, and when and how to handle a situation at home. We are also looking for articles that describe general, medical, and pediatric problems, advances, new treatments, etc. All articles must be medically accurate and useful to parents with children—prenatal to adolescence." Estab. 1981. Circ. 120,000. Byline given. Pays on publication. Publishes ms an average of 4 months after acceptance. Accepts queries by mail, e-mail, fax. Accepts simultaneous submissions. Responds in 1 month to queries. Sample copy online. Guidelines online.

NONFICTION No first person or experience. **Buys 25 mss/year.** Send complete ms with cover letter containing contact info. Prefers electronic submissions: Send to submissions@pedsforparents.com. Length: 1,000-1,500 words. **Pays $10-25.**

SCREAMINMAMAS

Harmoni Productions, LLC, 1911 Cleveland St., Hollywood FL 33020. **E-mail:** screaminmamas@gmail.com. **Website:** www.screaminmamas.com. Editor: Darlene Pistocchi. Managing Editor: Denise Marie. Monthly magazine designed and created by and for moms. "We are the voice of everyday moms. We share their stories, revelations, humorous rants, photos, talent, children, ventures, etc." Estab. 2012. Circ. 500. Byline given. Publishes ms 1-3 months after acceptance. Editorial lead time: 3 months. Submit seasonal material 3 months in advance. Accepts queries by mail, e-mail. Accepts simultaneous submissions. Responds in 3-6 weeks on queries; 1-3 months on mss. Sample copy online. Guidelines online.

NONFICTION Needs humor, inspirational, personal experience, religious, anything to do with being a mom. Special issues: Each issue has a theme, which we list on the website. Does not want vulgar, derogatory, negative pieces. Send complete ms. Length: 500-2,000 words.

PHOTOS State availability or send photos with submission. Requires model releases, identification of subjects. Reviews contact sheets, GIF/JPEG files. Offers no additional payment for photos accepted with ms.

FICTION Needs adventure, fantasy, historical, humorous, mainstream, novel excerpts, religious, romance, science fiction, serialized novels, slice-of-life vignettes, suspense. Does not want vulgar, obscene, derogatory, or negative fiction. Send complete ms. Length: 800-3,000 words.

POETRY Needs avant-garde, free verse, haiku, light verse, traditional. Submit maximum 3 poems. Length: 2-20 lines.

FILLERS Needs anecdotes, facts, short humor. Length: 10-100 words.

TIPS "Visit our submissions page and themes page on our website."

🍁➡$$$$ TODAY'S PARENT

Rogers Media, Inc., One Mt. Pleasant Rd., 8th Floor, Toronto ON M4Y 2Y5 Canada. (416)764-2883. **Fax:** (416)764-2894. **E-mail:** editors@todaysparent.com. **Website:** www.todaysparent.com. **Contact:** Alicia Kowalewski, art director. Monthly magazine for parents with children up to the age of 12. Circ. 2,000,000. Editorial lead time 5 months.

NONFICTION Length: 1,800-2,500 words. **Pays $1,500-2,200.**

COLUMNS/DEPARTMENTS What's New (games/apps/movies/toys); Health (parents and children); Behaviour; Relationships; Steps and Stages; How Does He/She Do It; Bright Idea; Food/In the Kitchen.

TIPS "Because we promote ourselves as a Canadian magazine, we try to use only Canadian writers and focus on Canadian content."

WORKING MOTHER

Bonnier Corporation, 2 Park Ave., 10th Floor, New York NY 10016. (212)779-5000. **Website:** www.workingmother.com. **90% freelance written. Prefers to work with published/established writers; works with a small number of new/unpublished writers each year.** Magazine published 8 times/year for women who balance a career, home, and family. Estab. 1981. Circ. 760,000. Byline given. Offers kill fee. Publishes ms an average of 4 months after acceptance. Submit seasonal material 6 months in advance. Accepts queries by e-mail. Sample copy available. Guidelines online.

NONFICTION Needs humor, service, child development, material pertinent to the working mother's predicament. **Buys 9-10 mss/year.** Query with published clips. Feature queries should specifically relate to the working mom, whether geared to her work, family, personal well-being, or a mixture of these. Length: 1,000-2,000 words.

COLUMNS/DEPARTMENTS Most of columns are staff written, but some are assigned out occasionally. E-mail queries, including links or files of clips of previously published work. Include all contact info. If pitching about a specific working mom, include recent photographs/JPGs (at least 300 dpi) if possible. Unsolicited mss will not be returned. Does not respond to every proposal, only if interested. If interested, will respond in 90 days. Columns topics (sorted by editor): All Best Companies initiatives (krista.carothers@workingmother.com); non-initiatives features, working-mom balance, parenting, travel, food, money and finance, LOL, Moms @ Work (barbara.turvett@workingmother.com); celebrities, workplace issues, entrepeneur moms, child health, pregnancy, romance, family sleep, child care (lela.nargi@workingmother.com); beauty, mom and kid fashion, kid fitness and activities, mom and kid books, toys and games, apps (irene.chang@workingmother.com); news, fashion and beauty, for online (maricar.santos@bonniercorp.com).

COMIC BOOKS

NTH DEGREE

3502 Fernmoss Ct., Charlotte NC 28269. **E-mail:** submissions@nthzine.com. **Website:** www.nthzine.com. **Contact:** Michael Pederson. Free online fanzine to promote up-and-coming new science fiction and fantasy authors and artists. Also supports the world of fandom and conventions. Estab. 2002. Pays on publication. Accepts queries by mail. Accepts simultaneous submissions. Responds in 2 weeks to queries; 2 months to mss. Guidelines online.

💬 No longer accepts hard copy submissions.

FICTION Needs adventure, fantasy, horror, humorous, mystery, science fiction, short stories. Submit complete ms via e-mail. Length: no more than 7,500 words. **Pays in contributor's copies.**

POETRY Submit through e-mail. Looking for poetry about science fiction, fantasy, horror, alternate history, well-crafted mystery, and humor. **Pays in contributor's copies.**

TIPS "Don't submit anything that you may be ashamed of 10 years later."

CONTEMPORARY CULTURE

😊😊 A&U

Art & Understanding, Inc., 25 Monroe St., Suite 205, Albany NY 12210-2729. (518)426-9010. **Fax:** (518)436-5354. **E-mail:** mailbox@aumag.org; chaelneedle@mac.com. **Website:** www.aumag.org. **Contact:** Chael Needle, managing editor. **50% freelance written.** Monthly national nonprofit print magazine covering cultural, political, and medical responses to HIV/AIDS. Estab. 1991. Circ. 180,000. Byline given. Pays 1-3 months after publication. Publishes ms an average of 1-3 months after acceptance. Editorial lead time 6 months. Accepts queries by mail, e-mail. Accepts simultaneous submissions. Responds in 1 month to queries. Responds in 2 months to mss. Sample copy for $5. Guidelines online.

NONFICTION Needs AIDS-related articles, essays, general interest, how-to, humor, interview, opinion, personal experience, photo feature, travel, reviews (film, theater, art exhibits, video, music, other media), medical news, artist profiles. **Buys 6 mss/year.** Query with published clips. Length: 800-1,200 words. **Pays $150-300 for assigned articles.**

COLUMNS/DEPARTMENTS The Culture of AIDS (reviews of books, music, film), 300 words; Viewpoint (personal opinion), 750 words. **Buys 8 mss/year.** Send complete ms. **Pays $50-150.**

FICTION Literary electronic submissions, as Word attachments, may be mailed to Brent Calderwood, literary editor, at aumaglit@gmail.com. Pay rate schedule available upon request. Send complete ms. Length: less than 1,500 words. **Pays $50.**

POETRY Any length/style (shorter works preferred). **Pays $25.**

TIPS "We're looking for more articles on youth and HIV/AIDS; more international coverage; celebrity interviews; more coverage of how the pandemic is affecting historically underrepresented communities."

😊 BOSTON REVIEW

PO Box 425786, Cambridge MA 02142. (617)324-1360. **Fax:** (617)452-3356. **E-mail:** review@bostonreview. net. **Website:** www.bostonreview.net. **90% freelance written.** Bimonthly magazine of cultural and political analysis, reviews, fiction, and poetry. "The editors are committed to a society and culture that foster human diversity and a democracy in which we seek common grounds of principle amidst our many differences. In the hope of advancing these ideals, the *Review* acts as a forum that seeks to enrich the language of public debate." Estab. 1975. Circ. 20,000. Byline given. Publishes ms an average of 4 months after acceptance. Accepts queries by online submission form. Accepts simultaneous submissions. Responds in 4 months to queries. Sample copy for $6.95 plus shipping or online. Guidelines online.

🔑 Reads submissions September 15-May 15.

NONFICTION Needs essays (book reviews). "*We do not accept unsolicited book reviews.* If you would like to be considered for review assignments, please send your résumé along with several published clips." **Buys 50 mss/year.** Query with published clips. "You may submit query letters and unsolicited nonfiction up to 5,000 words via the online submissions system."

FICTION Looking for "stories that are emotionally and intellectually substantive and also interesting on the level of language. Things that are shocking, dark, lewd, comic, or even insane are fine so long as the fiction is *controlled* and purposeful in a masterly way. Subtlety, delicacy, and lyricism are attractive, too. Simultaneous submissions are fine as long as we are notified of the fact." Needs ethnic, experimental, contemporary, prose poem. No romance, erotica, genre fiction. **Buys 5 mss/year.** Send complete ms. Length: 1,200-5,000 words. Average length: 2,000 words. **Pays $25-300 and contributor's copies.**

POETRY "We are open to both traditional and experimental forms. What we value most is originality and a strong sense of voice." Send materials for review consideration. Reads poetry between September 15 and May 15 each year. Submit maximum 6 poems. **Payment varies.**

TIPS "The best way to get a sense of the kind of material *Boston Review* is looking for is to read the magazine."

😊😊😊 FLAUNT

1422 N. Highland Ave., Los Angeles CA 90028. (323)836-1000. **E-mail:** info@flauntmagazine.com. **Website:** www.flaunt.com. **Contact:** Luis Barajas, editor-in-chief. **40% freelance written.** Monthly magazine covering culture, arts, entertainment, music, fashion, and film. *"Flaunt* features the bold work of emerging photographers, writers, artists and musicians. The quality of the content is mirrored in the sophisticated, interactive format of the magazine, using advanced printing techniques, fold-out articles, beautiful papers and inserts to create a visually stimulating, surprisingly readable, and intelligent book that pushes the magazine into the realm of art-object. *Flaunt* has, since 1998, made it a point to break new ground, earning itself a reputation as an engine of the avant-garde and an outlet for the culture of the cutting edge. *Flaunt* takes pride in reinventing itself each month, while consistently representing a hybrid of all that is interesting in entertainment, fashion, music, design, film, art, and literature." Estab. 1998. Circ. 100,000. Byline given. Publishes ms an average of 3 months after acceptance. Editorial lead time 3 months. Submit seasonal material 3 months in advance. Accepts queries by mail, e-mail. Accepts simultaneous submissions. Responds in 2 weeks to queries. Responds in 1 month to mss. Guidelines by e-mail.

NONFICTION Needs book excerpts, essays, expose, general interest, historical, humor, interview, new product, opinion, personal experience, photo feature, travel. Special issues: September and March (fashion issues); February (men's issue); May (music issue). **Buys 20 mss/year.** Query with published clips. Length: 500-5,000 words. **Pays up to $500.** Sometimes pays expenses of writers on assignment.

PHOTOS State availability. Identification of subjects, model releases required. Reviews contact sheets, transparencies, prints, GIF/JPEG files.

FICTION Contact: Contact Andrew Pogany, senior editor. **Buys 4 mss/year.**

⊖⊖⊖⊖ MOTHER JONES

Foundation for National Progress, 222 Sutter St., Suite 600, San Francisco CA 94108. (415)321-1700. **E-mail:** mmurrmann@motherjones.com; query@motherjones.com. **Website:** www.motherjones.com. **Contact:** Mark Murrmann, associate photo editor; Monika Bauerlein and Clara Jeffery, editors. **80% freelance written.** Bimonthly magazine covering politics, investigative reporting, social issues, and pop culture. *"Mother Jones* is a 'progressive' magazine—but the core of its editorial well is reporting (i.e., fact-based). No slant required. MotherJones.com is an online sister publication." Estab. 1976. Circ. 240,000. Byline giv-

en. Pays on publication. Offers 33% kill fee. Publishes ms an average of 4 months after acceptance. Editorial lead time 4 months. Submit seasonal material 6 months in advance. Responds in 2 months to queries. Sample copy for $6 and 9x12 SASE. Guidelines online.

NONFICTION Needs exposé, interview, photo feature, current issues, policy, investigative reporting. **Buys 70-100 mss/year.** Query with published clips. "Please also include your résumé and two or three of your most relevant clips. If the clips are online, please provide the complete URLs. Web pieces are generally less than 1,500 words. Because we have staff reporters it is extremely rare that we will pay for a piece whose timeliness or other qualities work for the Web only. Magazine pieces can range up to 5,000 words. There is at least a two-month lead time. No phone calls please." Length: 2,000-5,000 words. **Pays $1/word.** Sometimes pays expenses of writers on assignment.

COLUMNS/DEPARTMENTS Outfront (short, newsy and/or outrageous and/or humorous items), 200-800 words; Profiles of Hellraisers, 500 words. **Pays $1/word.**

TIPS "We're looking for hard-hitting, investigative reports exposing government cover-ups, corporate malfeasance, scientific myopia, institutional fraud or hypocrisy; thoughtful, provocative articles which challenge the conventional wisdom (on the right or the left) concerning issues of national importance; and timely, people-oriented stories on issues such as the environment, labor, the media, healthcare, consumer protection, and cultural trends. Send a great, short query and establish your credibility as a reporter. Explain what you plan to cover and how you will proceed with the reporting. The query should convey your approach, tone and style, and should answer the following: What are your specific qualifications to write on this topic? What 'ins' do you have with your sources? Can you provide full documentation so that your story can be fact-checked?"

PEOPLE STYLEWATCH

Time Inc., 1271 Avenue of the Americas, 27th Floor, New York NY 10020. (212)522-1388. **Fax:** (212)467-3127. **E-mail:** editors@people.com. **Website:** www.peoplestylewatch.com. **Contact:** Susan Kaufman, editor. Monthly magazine focusing on celebrity style, fashion, and beauty. *People StyleWatch* is an extension of *People Magazine's* StyleWatch column. Estab. 2002. ◐ Query before submitting.

$$$ THE SUN

107 N. Roberson St., Chapel Hill NC 27516. (919)942-5282. **Fax:** (919)932-3101. **Website:** www.thesunmagazine.org. **Contact:** Sy Safransky, editor. **90% freelance written.** Monthly magazine publishing essays, interviews, fiction, poetry, and b&w photography. "We are open to all kinds of writing, though we favor work of a personal nature." Estab. 1974. Circ. 72,000. Byline given. Pays on publication. Publishes ms an average of 6-12 months after acceptance. Accepts queries by mail. Responds in 3-6 months to queries. Responds in 3-6 months to mss. Sample copy for $5. Guidelines online.

NONFICTION Contact: Sy Safransky, editor. Needs essays, memoir, personal experience, spiritual fields, in-depth philosophical. Also needs thoughtful essays on political, cultural, and philosophical themes. **Buys 50. mss/year.** Send complete ms. 7,000 words maximum **Pays $300-2,000.** .

REPRINTS Send photocopy and information about when and where the material previously appeared.

PHOTOS Model releases required. Offers $100-500/photo.

FICTION Contact: Sy Safransky, editor. Open to all fiction. Receives 800 unsolicited mss/month. Accepts 20 short stories/year. Recently published work by Sigrid Nunez, Susan Straight, Lydia Peelle, Stephen Elliott, David James Duncan, Linda McCullough Moore, Brenda Miller. No science fiction, horror, fantasy, or other genre fiction. "Read an issue before submitting." **Buys 20/year mss/year.** Send complete ms. Accepts reprint submissions. Length: 7,000 words maximum. **Pays $300-1,500.**

POETRY Contact: Sy Safransky, editor. Needs free verse. Submit up to 6 poems at a time. Considers previously published poems but strongly prefers unpublished work. "Poems should be typed and accompanied by a cover letter and SASE." Recently published poems by Tony Hoagland, Ellen Bass, Steve Kowit, Brian Doyle and Alison Luterman. Guidelines available with SASE or online. Responds within 3-6 months. Acquires first serial or one-time rights. Rarely publishes poems that rhyme. **Pays $100-500 on publication plus contributor's copies and subscription.**

TIPS "Do not send queries except for interviews. We're open to unusual work. Read the magazine to get a sense of what we're about. Our submission rate is extremely high. Please be patient after sending us your work and include return postage."

⊘ VANITY FAIR

Conde Nast Publications, Inc., 1472 Broadway, New York NY 10036. **E-mail:** letters@vf.com. **Website:** www.vanityfair.com. Monthly magazine. *Vanity Fair* is edited for readers with an interest in contemporary society.

💬 Does not buy freelance material, use freelance writers, or respond to queries.

DISABILITIES

$$ DIABETES SELF-MANAGEMENT

R.A. Rapaport Publishing, Inc., 150 W. 22nd St., Suite 800, New York NY 10011. (212)989-0200. **Fax:** (212)989-4786. **E-mail:** editor@rapaportpublishing.com. **Website:** www.diabetesselfmanagement.com. **20% freelance written.** Bimonthly magazine. "We publish how-to health care articles for motivated, intelligent readers who have diabetes and who are actively involved in their own health care management. All articles must have immediate application to their daily living." Estab. 1983. Circ. 410,000. Byline given. Pays on publication. Offers 20% kill fee. Submit seasonal material 6 months in advance. Accepts queries by mail, e-mail, fax. Responds in 6 weeks to queries. Sample copy for $4 and 9x12 SAE with 6 first-class stamps, or online. Guidelines for #10 SASE.

NONFICTION Needs how-to, exercise, nutrition, diabetes self-care, product surveys, technical, reviews of products available, foods sold by brand name, pharmacology, travel, considerations and prep for people with diabetes. No personal experiences, personality profiles, exposés, or research breakthroughs. **Buys 10-12 mss/year.** Query with published clips. Length: 2,000-2,500 words. **Pays $400-700 for assigned articles. Pays $200-700 for unsolicited articles.**

TIPS "The rule of thumb for any article we publish is that it must be clear, concise, useful, and instructive, and it must have immediate application to the lives of our readers. If your query is accepted, expect heavy editorial supervision."

$ KALEIDOSCOPE

Kaleidoscope, 701 S. Main St., Akron OH 44311-1019. (330)762-9755. **Fax:** (330)762-0912. **E-mail:** kaleidoscope@udsakron.org. **Website:** www.kaleidoscope-online.org. **Contact:** Gail Willmott, editor-in-chief. **75% freelance written. Eager to work with new/unpublished writers.** Semiannual free online magazine. "*Kaleidoscope* magazine creatively focuses on the experiences of disability through literature and the fine arts. Unique to the field of disability studies, this award-winning publication expresses the diversity of the disablty experience from a variety of perspectives including: individuals, families, friends, caregivers and healthcare professionals, among others." Estab. 1979. Byline given. Pays on publication. Accepts queries by submissions and queries electronically via website and e-mail. Accepts simultaneous submissions. Responds within 6-9 months. Guidelines online.

NONFICTION Needs essays, interview, personal experience, reviews, articles relating to both literary and visual arts. For book reviews: "Reviews that are substantive, timely, powerful works about publications in the field of disability and/or the arts. The writer's opinion of the work being reviewed should be clear. The review should be a literary work in its own right.". **Buys 40-50 mss/year.** Length: no more than 5,000 words. **Pays $10-100.**

REPRINTS Send double-spaced typed ms with complete author's/artist's contact information, rights for sale noted and information about when and where the material previously appeared. Reprints permitted with credit given to original publication. All rights revert to author upon publication

PHOTOS Send digital images.

FICTION Short stories with a well-crafted plot and engaging characters. Needs short stories. No fiction that is stereotypical, patronizing, sentimental, erotic, or maudlin. No romance, religious or dogmatic fiction; no children's literature. Submit complete ms by website or e-mail. Include cover letter. Length: no more than 5,000 words. All rights revert to author upon publication. **Pays $10-100.**

POETRY Wants poems that have strong imagery, evocative language. Submit up to 5 poems. "Do not get caught up in rhyme scheme. High quality with strong imagery and evocative language. Reviews any style."

TIPS "The material chosen for Kaleidoscope challenges and overcomes stereotypical, patronizing, and sentimental attitudes about disability. We accept the work of writers with and without disabilities, however the work of a writer without a disability must focus on some aspect of disability.The criteria for good writing apply: effective technique, thought-provoking subject matter, and in general, a mature grasp of the art of sto-

ry-telling. Writers should avoid using offensive language and always put the person before the disability."

😊😊 SPECIALIVING

P.O. Box 1000, Bloomington IL 61702. (309)962-2003. **E-mail:** gareeb@aol.com. **Website:** www.specialiving.com. **90% freelance written.** Quarterly online magazine covering the physically disabled/mobility impaired. "We are now an online-only magazine. There is no subscription fee. Subject matter is the same. Payment is still the same, (max 800 words). Need photos with ms." Estab. 2001. Circ. 12,000. Byline given. Pays on publication. Editorial lead time 3 months. Submit seasonal material 6 months in advance. Accepts queries by mail, e-mail, fax, phone. Accepts simultaneous submissions. Responds in 3 weeks to queries.

NONFICTION Needs how-to, humor, inspirational, interview, new product, personal experience, technical, travel. **Buys 40 mss/year.** Query. Length: 800 words. **Pays 10¢/word.**

PHOTOS State availability. Captions, identification of subjects required. Reviews GIF/JPEG files. Offers $10/photo; $50/cover photo.

COLUMNS/DEPARTMENTS Shopping Guide; Items. **Buys 30 mss/year.** Query.

ENTERTAINMENT

😊 CINEASTE

Cineaste Publishers, Inc., 708 Third Avenue, 5th Floor, New York NY 10017-4201. (212)209-3856. **E-mail:** cineaste@cineaste.com. **Website:** www.cineaste.com. **30% freelance written.** Quarterly magazine covering motion pictures with an emphasis on social and political perspective on cinema. Estab. 1967. Circ. 11,000. Byline given. Pays on publication. Offers 50% kill fee. Publishes ms an average of 4 months after acceptance. Editorial lead time 3 months. Submit seasonal material 4 months in advance. Accepts queries by mail, e-mail, fax. Responds in 1 month to queries. Sample copy for $7. Writer's guidelines online.

NONFICTION Needs book excerpts, essays, expose, historical, humor, interview, opinion. **Buys 20-30 mss/year.** Query with published clips. Length: 2,000-5,000 words. **Pays $30-100.**

PHOTOS State availability. Identification of subjects required. Reviews transparencies, 8x10 prints. Offers no additional payment for photos accepted with ms.

COLUMNS/DEPARTMENTS Homevideo (topics of general interest or a related group of films); A Second

Look (new interpretation of a film classic or a reevaluation of an unjustly neglected release of more recent vintage); Lost and Found (film that may or may not be released or otherwise seen in the US but which is important enough to be brought to the attention of our readers); all 1,000-1,500 words. Query with published clips. **Pays $50 minimum.**

TIPS "We dislike academic jargon, obtuse Marxist terminology, film buff trivia, trendy 'buzz' phrases, and show biz references. We do not want our writers to speak of how they have 'read' or 'decoded' a film, but to view, analyze, and interpret. Warning the reader of problems with specific films is more important to us than artificially 'puffing' a film because its producers or politics are agreeable. One article format we encourage is an omnibus review of several current films, preferably those not reviewed in a previous issue. Such an article would focus on films that perhaps share a certain political perspective, subject matter, or generic concerns (i.e., films on suburban life, or urban violence, or revisionist Westerns). Like individual film reviews, these articles should incorporate a very brief synopsis of plots for those who haven't seen the films. The main focus, however, should be on the social issues manifested in each film, and how it may reflect something about the current political/social/esthetic climate."

🍁 $ DANCE INTERNATIONAL

Scotiabant Dance Centre, Level 6 677 Davie St., Vancouver BC V6B 2G6 Canada. (604)681-1525. **Fax:** (604)681-7732. **E-mail:** Editor@DanceInternational.org. **Website:** www.danceinternational.org. **100% freelance written.** Quarterly magazine covering dance arts. Articles and reviews on current activities in world dance, with occasional historical essays; reviews of dance films, DVDs, and books. Estab. 1973. Circ. 3,000. Byline given. Pays on publication. Offers 50% kill fee. Publishes ms an average of 3 months after acceptance. Editorial lead time 3 months. Submit seasonal material 6 weeks in advance. Accepts queries by mail, e-mail. Responds in 2 weeks to queries. Responds in 1 month to mss. Sample copy for $7.50 plus p&p.

NONFICTION Needs book excerpts, essays, historical, interview, personal experience, photo feature. **Buys 100 mss/year.** Query. Length: 1,200-2,200 words. **Pays $40-150.**

PHOTOS Send photos. Identification of subjects required. Reviews prints. Offers no additional payment for photos accepted with ms.

COLUMNS/DEPARTMENTS Mediawatch (recent books, DVDs, media reviewed), 700-800 words; Regional Reports (events in each region), 800 words. **Buys 100 mss/year.** Query. **Pays $80.**

TIPS Send résumé and samples of recent writings.

ENTERTAINMENT WEEKLY

Time, Inc., 1675 Broadway, 30th Floor, New York NY 10019. (212)522-5600. **Fax:** (212)522-0074. **Website:** www.ew.com. **Contact:** Matt Bean, editor. Weekly magazine. *Entertainment Weekly* is an all-access pass to Hollywood's most creative minds and fascinating stars. Written for readers who want the latest reviews, previews and updates of the entertainment world. Circ. 1,600,000. Editorial lead time 4 weeks.

💬 Query before submitting.

🌐 METRO MAGAZINE (AUSTRALIA)

P.O. Box 2040, St. Kilda West VIC 3182 Australia. (61)(3)9525-5302. **Fax:** (61)(3)9537-2325. **E-mail:** metro@atom.org.au. **Website:** www.metromagazine.com.au. Quarterly magazine specializing in critical essays on film, TV and media from Australia, New Zealand, and the Asia-Pacific region. Estab. 1968. Guidelines online.

NONFICTION Needs essays, general interest, interview, reviews. Send complete ms via e-mail. Length: 1,000-3,000 words.

PHOTOS Send photos. Reviews TIFF/JPEG files.

STAR

American Media, Inc., 1000 American Media Way, Boca Raton FL 33464-1000. **E-mail:** letters@starmagazine.com. **Website:** www.starmagazine.com. *Star* is a weekly celebrity tabloid/gossip magazine. Estab. 1974.

💬 Query before submitting.

TV GUIDE

11 W. 42nd St., 16th Floor, New York NY 10036. (212)852-7500. **Fax:** (212)852-7470. **Website:** www.tvguide.com. **Contact:** Debra Birnbaum, editor-in-chief. Weekly magazine. Focuses on all aspects of network, cable, and pay television programming and how it affects and reflects audiences. Estab. 1953. Circ. 9 million.

💬 Query before submitting.

US WEEKLY

Wenner Media LLC, 1290 Avenue of the Americas, New York NY 10104. (212)484-1616. **Fax:** (212)484-4242. **E-mail:** letters@usmagazine.com. **Website:** www.usmagazine.com. Weekly celebrity and entertainment magazine. Estab. 1977. Circ. 2 million.

💬 Query to gauge interest before submitting unsolicited mss.

ETHNIC AND MINORITY

AFRICAN VOICES

African Voices Communications, Inc., 270 W. 96th St., New York NY 10025. (212)865-2982. **Fax:** (212)316-3335. **E-mail:** africanvoicesmag@gmail.com. **Website:** www.africanvoices.com. **85% freelance written.** Quarterly magazine covering art, film, culture. *African Voices*, published quarterly, is an "art and literary magazine that highlights the work of people of color. We publish ethnic literature and poetry on any subject. We also consider all themes and styles: avant-garde, free verse, haiku, light verse, and traditional. We do not wish to limit the reader or author." Estab. 1992. Circ. 20,000. Byline given. Pays on publication. Publishes ms an average of 3-6 months after acceptance. Editorial lead time 3 months. Submit seasonal material 3 months in advance. Accepts queries by mail. Accepts simultaneous submissions. Responds in 3 months to queries. Sample copy for $5.

NONFICTION Needs book excerpts, essays, historical, humor, inspirational, interview, photo feature, travel. Query with published clips. Length: 500-2,500 words. **Pays in contributor's copies.**

PHOTOS State availability. Pays in contributor copies.

FICTION Contact: Contact Kim Horne, fiction editor. Needs adventure, cond novels, erotica, ethnic, experimental, fantasy, historical, general, horror, humorous, mainstream, mystery, novel concepts, religious, romance, science fiction, serialized, slice-of-life vignettes, suspense, African-American. **Buys 4 mss/year.** Send complete ms. Include short bio. Send SASE for return of ms. Responds in 3 months to queries. Length: 500-2,500 words. **Pays $25-50. Pays on publication for first North American serial rights.**

POETRY Contact: Contact: Ekere Tallie, poetry editor. Needs avant-garde, free verse, haiku, traditional. Submit no more than 2 poems at any 1 time. Accepts submissions by e-mail (in text box), by fax, and by postal mail. Cover letter and SASE required. Seldom comments on rejected poems. Reviews books of poetry in 500-1,000 words. Send materials for review consideration to Ekere Tallie. Buys 10 poems/year. Submit maximum 5 poems. Length: 5-100 lines. **Pays 2 contributor copies.**

TIPS "A ms stands out if it is neatly typed with a well-written and interesting storyline or plot. Originality is encouraged. We are interested in more horror, erotic, and drama pieces. *AV* wants to highlight the diversity in our culture. Stories must touch the humanity in us all. We strongly encourage new writers/poets to send in their work. Accepted contributors are encouraged to subscribe."

$ $ AMBASSADOR MAGAZINE

National Italian American Foundation, 1860 19th St. NW, Washington DC 20009. (202)939-3108. **Fax:** (202)387-0800. **E-mail:** don@niaf.org. **Website:** www.niaf.org. **Contact:** Don Oldenburg, editor. **50% freelance written.** Quarterly magazine for Italian-Americans covering Italian-American history and culture. We publish nonfiction articles on little known events in Italian-American history and articles on Italian-American culture, traditions, and personalities living and dead. Estab. 1989. Circ. 25,000. Byline given. Pays on approval of final draft. Offers $50 kill fee. Editorial lead time 3 months. Accepts queries by mail, e-mail, fax. Accepts simultaneous submissions. Responds in 2 months to queries. Sample copy and writer's guidelines free.

NONFICTION Needs historical, interview, photo feature. **Buys 12 mss/year.** Send complete ms. Length: 800-1,500 words. **Pays $250 for photos and article.**

PHOTOS Send photos. Captions, identification of subjects required. Reviews contact sheets, prints. Offers no additional payment for photos accepted with ms.

TIPS Good photos, clear prose, and a good storytelling ability are all prerequisites.

🍁 $ CELTIC LIFE INTERNATIONAL

Clansman Publishing, Ltd., P.O. Box 8805, Station A, Halifax NS B3K 5M4 Canada. (902)835-2358. **Fax:** (902)835-0080. **E-mail:** editor@celticlife.ca. **Website:** www.celticlifeintl.com. **Contact:** Carels Mandel, editor. **95% freelance written.** Quarterly magazine covering culture of those with an interest in Celtic culture around the world. Celtic Life International is a global community for a living, breathing Celtic culture. Home to an extensive collection of feature stories, interviews, history, heritage, news, views, reviews, recipes, events, trivia, humour and tidbits from across all Seven Celtic Nations and beyond. The flagship publication, *Celtic Life International Magazine*, is published four times a year in both print and digital formats, and is distributed around the world. Our online abode, CelticLife.ca, is an informative and interactive community that engages Celts from all walks of life. Estab. 1987. Circ. distribution: 201,340; readership: 1,026,834. Byline given. Pays after publication. Editorial lead time 2 months. Submit seasonal material 3 months in advance. Accepts queries by e-mail only. Responds in 1 week to queries. Responds in 1 month to mss.

NONFICTION Needs essays, general interest, historical, interview, opinion, personal experience, travel, Gaelic language, Celtic music reviews, profiles of Celtic musicians, Celtic history, traditions, and folklore. Also buys short fiction. No fiction, poetry, historical stories already well publicized. **Buys 100 mss/year.** Query or send complete ms. Length: 800-2,500 words. **All writers receive a complimentary subscription.**

PHOTOS State availability. Captions, identification of subjects, model releases required. Reviews 35mm transparencies, 5x7 prints, JPEG files (300 dpi). "We pay for photographs.".

COLUMNS/DEPARTMENTS Query.

$ $ GERMAN LIFE

Zeitgeist Publishing, Inc., 1068 National Hwy., LaVale MD 21502. (301)729-6190. **Fax:** (301)729-1720. **E-mail:** mslider@germanlife.com. **Website:** www.germanlife.com. **Contact:** Mark Slider. **50% freelance written.** Bimonthly magazine covering German-speaking Europe. "*German Life* is for all interested in the diversity of German-speaking culture—past and present—and in the various ways that the US (and North America in general) has been shaped by its German immigrants. The magazine is dedicated to solid reporting on cultural, historical, social, and political events." Estab. 1994. Circ. 40,000. Byline given. Pays on publication. Editorial lead time 4 months. Submit seasonal material 6 months in advance. Accepts queries by mail, e-mail. Responds in 2 months to queries. Responds in 3 months to mss. Sample copy for $4.95 and SASE with 4 first-class stamps. Guidelines online.

NONFICTION Needs general interest, historical, interview, photo feature, travel. Special issues: Okto-berfest-related (October); Seasonal Relative to Germany, Switzerland, or Austria (December); Travel to German-speaking Europe (April). **Buys 50 mss/year.** Query with published clips. Length: 800-1,500 words. **Pays $200-500 for assigned articles. Pays $200-350 for unsolicited articles.**

PHOTOS State availability. Identification of subjects required. Reviews color transparencies, 5×7 color or b&w prints. Offers no additional payment for photos accepted with ms.

COLUMNS/DEPARTMENTS German-Americana (regards specific German-American communities, organizations, and/or events past or present), 1,200 words; Profile (portrays prominent Germans, Americans, or German-Americans), 1,000 words; At Home (cuisine, etc. relating to German-speaking Europe), 800 words; Library (reviews of books, videos, CDs, etc.), 300 words. **Buys 30 mss/year.** Query with published clips. **Pays $50-150.**

FILLERS Needs facts, newsbreaks. Length: 100-300 words. **Pays $50-150.**

TIPS "The best queries include several informative proposals. Writers should avoid overemphasizing autobiographical experiences/stories."

$ $ HADASSAH MAGAZINE

50 W. 58th St., New York NY 10019. (212)688-0227. **Fax:** (212)446-9521. **E-mail:** magazine@hadassah.org. **Website:** www.hadassah.org/magazine. **Contact:** Elizabeth Goldberg. **90% freelance written.** Monthly magazine. "*Hadassah* is a general interest Jewish feature and literary magazine. We speak to our readers on a vast array of subjects ranging from politics to parenting, to midlife crisis to Mideast crisis. Our readers want coverage on social and economic issues, Jewish women's (feminist) issues, the arts, travel and health." Circ. 243,000. Pays on acceptance. Responds in 4 months to mss. Sample copy and writer's guidelines with 9x12 SASE.

NONFICTION Buys 10 unsolicited mss/year. Query. Length: 1,500-2,000 words. Sometimes pays expenses of writers on assignment.

PHOTOS "We buy photos only to illustrate articles. Always interested in striking cover photos.". Offers $50 for first photo, $35 for each additional photo.

COLUMNS/DEPARTMENTS "We have a family column and a travel column, but a query for topic or destination should be submitted first to make sure the area is of interest and the story follows our format."

FICTION Contact: Zelda Shluker, managing editor. Short stories with strong plots and positive Jewish values. Needs ethnic, Jewish. No personal memoirs, schmaltzy or shelter magazine fiction. Length: 1,500-2,000 words. **Pays $500 minimum.**

TIPS "Stories on a Jewish theme should be neither self-hating nor schmaltzy."

😊😊 ITALIAN AMERICA

219 E St. NE, Washington DC 20002. (202)547-2900. **Fax:** (202)546-8168. **E-mail:** ddesanctis@osia.org. **Website:** www.osia.org. **Contact:** Dona De Sanctis, editor. **20% freelance written.** Quarterly magazine. *Italian America* provides timely information about OSIA, while reporting on individuals, institutions, issues, and events of current or historical significance in the Italian-American community. Estab. 1996. Circ. 65,000. Byline given. Pays on publication. Offers 50% kill fee. Publishes ms an average of 3 months after acceptance. Editorial lead time 3 months. Accepts queries by mail, e-mail, fax. Accepts simultaneous submissions. Sample copy free. Guidelines online.

NONFICTION Needs historical, little known historical facts that must relate to Italian Americans, interview, opinion, current events. **Buys 8 mss/year.** Query with published clips. Length: 750-1,000 words. **Pays $50-250.**

TIPS "We pay particular attention to the quality of graphics that accompany the stories. We are interested in little known facts about historical/cultural Italian America."

😊😊 JEWISH ACTION

Orthodox Union, 11 Broadway, New York NY 10004. (212)613-8146. **Fax:** (212)613-0646. **E-mail:** ja@ou.org. **Website:** www.ou.org/jewish_action. **Contact:** Nechama Carmel, editor; Rashel Zywica, assistant editor. **80% freelance written.** Quarterly magazine covering a vibrant approach to Jewish issues, Orthodox lifestyle, and values. Estab. 1986. Circ. 40,000. Byline given. Pays 2 months after publication. Submit seasonal material 4 months in advance. Accepts queries by mail, e-mail, fax. Responds in 3 months to queries. Sample copy online. Guidelines with #10 SASE or by e-mail.

○   Prefers queries by e-mail. Mail and fax OK.

NONFICTION "We are not looking for Holocaust accounts. We welcome essays about responses to personal or societal challenges." **Buys 30-40 mss/year.** Query with published clips. Length: 1,000-3,000 words.

Pays $100-400 for assigned articles. Pays $75-150 for unsolicited articles.

PHOTOS Send photos. Identification of subjects required.

COLUMNS/DEPARTMENTS Just Between Us (personal opinion on current Jewish life and issues), 1,000 words. **Buys 4 mss/year.**

FICTION Must have relevance to Orthodox reader. Length: 1,000-2,000 words.

POETRY Buys limited number of poems/year. **Pays $25-75.**

TIPS "Remember that your reader is well educated and has a strong commitment to Orthodox Judaism. Articles on the holidays, Israel, and other common topics should offer a fresh insight. Because the magazine is a quarterly, we do not generally publish articles which concern specific timely events."

😊😊 NATIVE PEOPLES MAGAZINE

5333 N. Seventh St., Suite C-224, Phoenix AZ 85014. (602)265-4855. **Fax:** (602)265-3113. **E-mail:** dgibson@nativepeoples.com; kcoochwytewa@nativepeoples.com. **Website:** www.nativepeoples.com. **Contact:** Daniel Gibson, editor; Kevin Coochwytewa, art director. Bimonthly magazine covering Native Americans. High-quality reproduction with full color throughout. The primary purpose of this magazine is to offer a sensitive portrayal of the arts and lifeways of native peoples of the Americas. Estab. 1987. Circ. 40,000. Byline given. Pays on publication. Accepts queries by mail, e-mail, fax. Responds in 2 months to queries. Guidelines by request.

NONFICTION Needs interviews of interesting and leading Natives from all walks of life, with an emphasis on arts, personal experience. **Buys 35 mss/year.** Length: 1,000-2,500 words. **Pays 25¢/word.**

PHOTOS State availability. Identification of subjects required. Reviews transparencies, prefers high-res digital images and 35mm slides. Inquire for details. Offers $45-150/page rates, $250/cover photos.

TIPS "We are focused upon authenticity and a positive portrayal of present-day Native American life and cultural practices. Our stories portray role models of Native people, young and old, with a sense of pride in their heritage and culture. Therefore, it is important that the Native American point of view be incorporated in each story."

$$$$ PAKN TREGER

National Yiddish Book Center, 1021 West St., Amherst MA 01002. (413)256-4900. **E-mail:** aatherley@bikher.org; pt@bikher.org;. **Website:** www.yiddishbookcenter.org. **Contact:** Anne Atherley, editor's assistant. **50% freelance written.** Literary magazine published 3 times/year; focuses on modern and contemporary Jewish and Yiddish culture. Estab. 1980. Circ. 20,000. Byline given. Pays on publication. Publishes ms an average of 3 months after acceptance. Editorial lead time 4 months. Submit seasonal material 3 months in advance. Accepts queries by mail, e-mail, fax. Accepts simultaneous submissions. Responds in 4 weeks to queries. Responds in 3 months to mss. Sample copy online. Guidelines by e-mail.

NONFICTION Needs pre-publication book excerpts, essays, humor, interview, travel, graphic novels. Does not want personal memoirs, fiction, or poetry. **Buys 6-10 mss/year.** Query. Length: 1,200-4,000 words. **Pays $800-2,000 for assigned articles. Pays $350-1,000 for unsolicited articles.** Sometimes pays expenses of writers on assignment.

PHOTOS State availability. Identification of subjects required. Reviews GIF/JPEG files. Negotiates payment individually.

COLUMNS/DEPARTMENTS Let's Learn Yiddish (Yiddish lesson), 1 page Yid/English; Translations (Yiddish-English), 1,200-2,500 words. **Pays $350-1,000.**

TIPS "Read the magazine and visit our website."

$$ RUSSIAN LIFE

RIS Publications, P.O. Box 567, Montpelier VT 05601. **Website:** www.russianlife.com. **75% freelance written.** Bimonthly magazine covering Russian culture, history, travel, and business. "Our readers are informed Russophiles with an avid interest in all things Russian. But we do not publish personal travel journals or the like." Estab. 1956. Circ. 15,000. Byline given. Pays on publication. Publishes ms an average of 3-6 months after acceptance. Editorial lead time 2 months. Submit seasonal material 3 months in advance. Accepts queries by mail. TrueResponds in 1 month to queries. Sample copy with 9x12 SASE and 6 first-class stamps. Guidelines online.

NONFICTION Needs general interest, photo feature, travel. No personal stories, i.e., How I came to love Russia. **Buys 15-20 mss/year.** Query. Length: 1,000-6,000 words. **Pays $100-300.**

REPRINTS Accepts previously published submissions rarely.

PHOTOS Send photos. Captions required. Model/property release preferred. Words with local freelancers only. Reviews contact sheets. Negotiates payment individually. Pays $20-50 (color photo with accompanying story), depending on placement in magazine. Pays on publication. Credit line given.

FOOD AND DRINK

AMERICAN WINE SOCIETY JOURNAL

American Wine Society, 2800 S. Lake Leelanau Dr., Lake Leelanau MI 49653. (586)946-0049. **E-mail:** rink@americanwinesociety.org. **Website:** www.americanwinesociety.org. **Contact:** Jim Rink, editor. **100% freelance written.** The non-profit American Wine Society is the largest consumer based wine education organization in the U.S. The *Journal* reflects the varied interests of AWS members, which may include wine novices, experts, grape growers, amateur and professional winemakers, chefs, wine appreciators, wine educators, restauranteurs, and anyone wanting to learn more about wine and gastronomy. Estab. 1967. Circ. 5,000. Byline given. Pays on publication. Publishes 3 months after acceptance. Editorial lead time is 3 months. Accepts queries by mail, e-mail. Accepts simultaneous submissions. Responds in 2 weeks on queries, 3 months on mss. Sample copy online. Writer's guidelines available by e-mail at rink@americanwinesociety.org.

NONFICTION Needs general interest, historical, how-to, nostalgic, technical, travel. Submit query with published clips.

PHOTOS Freelancers should send photos with submission. Requires captions and identification of subjects. Reviews GIF/JPEG files. Offers no additional payment for photos accepted with ms.

COLUMNS/DEPARTMENTS Columns include wine reviews, book reviews, food and wine articles. Writer should send query with published clips.

TIPS Suggests "requesting a sample copy, which we can provide in PDF format. The readership is diverse, and you see may see a travel piece next to a technical piece on malolactic fermentation. Use proper grammar and spelling. Please proofread copy before sending. Always looking for engaging pieces related to winemaking, grape growing, food and wine, wine and travel, book reviews, recipes, and new developments in the field."

BON APPETIT

Conde Nast Publications, Inc., 4 Times Square, 5th Floor, New York NY 10036. (212)286-3535. **E-mail:** askba@bonappetit.com. **Website:** www.bonappetit. com. **50% freelance written.** Monthly magazine covering fine food, restaurants, and home entertaining. *Bon Appetit* celebrates the world of great food and the pleasure of sharing it with others. Every issue invites readers into a hands-on experience, engaging them in all aspects of the epicurean lifestyle-cooking, dining, travel, entertaining, shopping and design. Estab. 1956. Circ. 1,529,385. Byline given. Pays on acceptance. Submit seasonal material 1 year in advance. Accepts queries by mail. Guidelines for #10 SASE.

NONFICTION Needs travel, food-related, food feature, personal essays. No cartoons, quizzes, poetry, historic food features, or obscure food subjects. **Buys 50 mss/year.** Query with résumé and published clips. No phone calls or e-mails. Length: 150-2,000 words. Pays expenses of writers on assignment.

TIPS "Writers must have a good knowledge of *Bon Appetit* and the related topics of food, travel, and entertaining (as shown in accompanying clips). A light, lively style is a plus."

COOKING LIGHT

Southern Progress Corporation (Time Inc.), P.O. Box 1748, Birmingham AL 35201. (205)445-6000. **Fax:** (205)445-6600. **Website:** www.cookinglight.com. Monthly American food and lifestyle magazine. Each magazine issue includes approximately 100 original recipes, plus editorial content covering food trends, fitness tips, and other culinary and health-related news. Estab. 1987. Circ. 1.8 million.

Query before submitting. Difficult market to break into.

EVERY DAY WITH RACHAEL RAY

Meredith Corporation, **E-mail:** comments@rachaelraymag.com. **Website:** www.rachaelraymag.com. **Contact:** Lauren Purcell, editor-in-chief. Magazine published 10 times/year, providing recipes, shopping tricks to save time and money, and new ideas for fun things to do with friends and family. Estab. 2005. Circ. 1.2 million.

Currently closed to submissions.

FOOD & FAMILY

Kraft, Three Lakes Dr., Northfield IL 60093. (877)535-5666. **Website:** www.kraftrecipes.com/foodfamilyarchive. Magazine published 4 times/year that includes recipes, quick family favorites and how-to's, desserts and treats, and more. Circ. 1 million.

Currently closed to freelance submissions.

FOOD & WINE

American Express Publishing Corp., 1120 Avenue of the Americas, 9th Floor, New York NY 10036. (212)382-5600. **Fax:** (212)764-2177. **Website:** www. foodandwine.com. **Contact:** Mary Ellen Ward, managing editor. Monthly magazine for the reader who enjoys the finer things in life. Editorial focuses on upscale dining, covering resturants, entertaining at home, and travel destinations. Circ. 964,000. Editorial lead time 6 months.

Query before submitting to ensure magazine is currently accepting mss.

FOOD NETWORK MAGAZINE

Hearst Corporation, 75 Ninth Ave., New York NY 10011. **Website:** www.foodnetwork.com. Food Network Magazine is a food entertainment magazine published 10 times/year based on the popular television network. The only magazine in the epicurean category to offer unprecedented access to many of America's favorite TV chefs and personalities. Circ. 1.4 million.

Query before submitting. Difficult market to break into.

GOURMET TRAVELLER WINE

Bauer Media Pty Limited, 54-58 Park St., GPO Box 4088, Sydney NSW 2000 Australia. (61)(2)9282-8000. **Fax:** (61)(2)9267-4361. **Website:** www.gourmettravellerwine.com.au. **Contact:** Judy Sarris, editor. Bimonthly magazine for the world of wine, celebrating both local and overseas industries. *"Gourmet Traveller WINE* is for wine lovers: It's for those who love to travel, to eat out, and to entertain at home, and for those who want to know more about the wine in their glass."* Circ. 22,088.

Target men 25-54, professionals and managers.

NONFICTION Needs general interest, how-to, interview, new product, travel. Query.

KASHRUS MAGAZINE

The Kashrus Institute, P.O. Box 204, Brooklyn NY 11204. (718)336-8544. **E-mail:** editorial@kashrusmagazine.com. **Website:** www.kashrusmagazine.com. **Contact:** Rabbi Wikler, editor. Estab. 1981. Circ. 10,000. Byline given. Pays on publication. Offers 50% kill fee. Publishes ms an average of 2 months after acceptance. Submit seasonal material 2 months in advance. Accepts queries by mail, phone. Accepts simultaneous submissions. Responds in 2 weeks. Sample copy - e-mail kashrus@aol.com and ask for "writer's sample copy.".

NONFICTION Needs health, travel, new product, personal experience, photo feature, religious, technical. Special issues: International Kosher Travel (October); Passover Shopping Guide (March); Domestic Kosher Travel Guide (June). **Buys 8-12 mss/ year.** Query with published clips. Length: 1,000-1,500 words. **Pays $100-250 for assigned articles. Pays up to $100 for unsolicited articles.** Sometimes pays expenses of writers on assignment.

REPRINTS Send tearsheet or photocopy and information about when and where the material previously appeared. Pays 25-50% of amount paid for an original article.

PHOTOS No guidelines; send samples or call. State availability. Offers no additional payment for photos accepted with ms.

COLUMNS/DEPARTMENTS Health/Diet/Nutrition, 1,000-1,500 words; Book Review (cookbooks, food technology, kosher food), 250-500 words; People In the News (interviews with kosher personalities), 1,000-1,500 words; Regional Kosher Supervision (report on kosher supervision in a city or community), 1,000-1,500 words; Food Technology (new technology or current technology with accompanying pictures), 1,000-1,500 words; Kosher Travel (international, national—must include Kosher information and Jewish communities), 1,000-1,500 words; Regional Kosher Cooking, 1,000-1,500 words. **Buys 8-12 mss/year.** Query with published clips. **Pays $50-250.**

TIPS "*Kashrus Magazine* will do more writing on general food technology, production, and merchandising as well as human interest travelogs and regional writing in 2013 than we have done in the past. Areas most open to freelancers are interviews, food technology, cooking and food preparation, dining, regional reporting, and travel, but we also feature healthy eating and lifestyles, redecorating, catering, and hospitals and health care. We welcome stories on the availability and quality of kosher foods and services in communities across the US and throughout the world. Some of our best stories have been by non-Jewish writers about kosher observance in their region. We also enjoy humorous articles. Just send a query with clips and we'll try to find a storyline that's right for you, or better yet, call us to discuss a storyline."

TASTE OF HOME

Reader's Digest Association, Inc., 5400 S. 60th St., Greendale WI 53129. (414)423-0100. **Fax:** (414)423-8463. **E-mail:** editors@tasteofhome.com. **Website:** www.tasteofhome.com. Bimonthly magazine. *Taste of Home* is dedicated to home cooks, from beginners to the very experienced. Editorial includes recipes and serving suggestions, interviews and ideas from the publication's readers and field editors based around the country, and reviews of new cooking tools and gadgets. Circ. 3.5 million.

Query before submitting.

VEGETARIAN JOURNAL

P.O. Box 1463, Baltimore MD 21203-1463. (410)366-8343. **E-mail:** vrg@vrg.org. **Website:** www.vrg.org. **Contact:** Debra Wasserman, editor. Quarterly non-profit vegetarian magazine that examines the health, ecological and ethical aspects of vegetarianism. "Highly-educated audience including health professionals." Estab. 1982. Circ. 20,000. Sample: $4.

Vegetarian Journal is 36 pages, magazine-sized, professionally printed, saddle-stapled, with glossy card cover. Press run is 20,000.

POETRY "Please, no submissions of poetry from adults; 18 and under only."

TIPS Areas most open to freelancers are recipe section and feature articles. "Review magazine first to learn our style. Send query letter with photocopy sample of line drawings of food."

GAMES AND PUZZLES

THE BRIDGE BULLETIN

American Contract Bridge League, 6575 Windchase Dr., Horn Lake MS 38637-1523. (662)253-3156. **Fax:** (662)253-3187. **E-mail:** editor@acbl.org. **E-mail:** brent.manley@acbl.org. **Website:** www.acbl.org. Paul Linxwiler, managing editor. **Contact:** Brent Manley, editor. **20% freelance written.** Monthly magazine covering duplicate (tournament) bridge. Estab. 1938. Circ. 155,000. Byline given. Pays on publication. Publishes ms an average of 3 months after acceptance. Editorial lead time 2 months. Accepts queries by mail, e-mail. Accepts simultaneous submissions.

NONFICTION Needs book excerpts, essays, how-to, play better bridge, humor, interview, new product, personal experience, photo feature, technical, travel. **Buys 6 mss/year.** Query. Length: 500-2,000 words. **Pays $100/page.**

PHOTOS State availability. Identification of subjects required. Reviews photos with or without a ms. Pays $200 or more for suitable work. Pays on publication. Negotiates payment individually.

TIPS "Articles must relate to contract bridge in some way. Cartoons on bridge welcome."

💲💲 CHESS LIFE

P.O. Box 3967, Crossville TN 38557. (931)787-1234. **Fax:** (931)787-1200. **E-mail:** dlucas@uschess.org; fbutler@uschess.org. **Website:** www.uschess.org. **Contact:** Daniel Lucas, editor; Francesca "Frankie" Butler, art director. **15% freelance written. Works with a small number of new/unpublished writers/year.** Monthly magazine. "*Chess Life* is the official publication of the United States Chess Federation, covering news of most major chess events, both here and abroad, with special emphasis on the triumphs and exploits of American players." Estab. 1939. Circ. 85,000. Byline given. Publishes ms an average of 6 months after acceptance. Submit seasonal material 6 months in advance. Accepts queries by e-mail only to dlucas@uschess.org. Accepts simultaneous submissions. Responds in 3 months to mss. Sample copy via PDF is available.

NONFICTION Needs general interest, historical, humor, interview, of a famous chess player or organizer, photo feature, chess centered, technical. No stories about personal experiences with chess. **Buys 30-40 mss/year.** Query with samples if new to publication. 3,000 words maximum. **Pays $100/page (800-1,000 words).** Sometimes pays expenses of writers on assignment.

PHOTOS Uses about 15 photos/issue; 7-8 supplied by freelancers. Captions, identification of subjects, model releases required. Reviews b&w contact sheets and prints, and color prints and slides. Pays $25-100 inside; covers negotiable. Pays on publication. Buys one-time rights; "we occasionally purchase all rights for stock mug shots." Credit line given.

FILLERS Submit with samples and clips. Buys first or negotiable rights to cartoons and puzzles. **Pays $25 upon acceptance.**

TIPS "Articles must be written from an informed point of view. Freelancers in major population areas (except NY and LA) who are interested in short personality profiles and perhaps news reporting have the best opportunities. We're looking for more personality pieces on chess players around the country; not just the stars, but local masters, talented youths, and dedicated volunteers. Freelancers interested in such pieces might let us know of their interest and their range. Could be we know of an interesting story in their territory that needs covering. Examples of published articles include a locally produced chess television program, a meeting of chess set collectors from around the world, chess in our prisons, and chess in the works of several famous writers."

⊘ GAME INFORMER

GameStop, 724 N. First St., 4th Floor, Minneapolis MN 55401. (612)486-6154. **Fax:** (612)486-6101. **Website:** www.gameinformer.com. **Contact:** Andy McNamara, editor-in-chief; Matt Bertz, managing editor. Monthly video game magazine featuring articles, news, strategy, and reviews of video games and associated consoles. Estab. 1991. Circ. 7.6 million.

○ *Game Informer* is closed to freelance submissions.

GAY & LESBIAN INTEREST

💲💲 INSTINCT MAGAZINE

11856 Balboa Blvd., #312, Granada Hills CA 91344. (818)284-4525. **E-mail:** editor@instinctmag.com. **Website:** instinctmagazine.com. **Contact:** Mike Wood, editor-in-chief. **40% freelance written.** Gay men's monthly lifestyle and entertainment magazine. "*Instinct* is a blend of *Cosmo* and *Maxim* for gay men. We're smart, sexy, irreverent, and we always have a sense of humor—a unique style that has made us the #1 gay men's magazine in the US." Estab. 1997. Circ. 115,000. Byline given. Pays on publication. Offers 20% kill fee. Editorial lead time 2-3 months. Accepts queries by mail, e-mail. NoAccepts simultaneous submissions. Sample copy online. Guidelines online. Register online first.

NONFICTION Needs expose, general interest, humor, interview, celebrity and non-celebrity, travel, basically anything of interest to gay men will be considered. Does not want first-person accounts or articles. Send complete ms via online submissions manager. Length: 850-2,000 words. **Pays $50-300.** Sometimes pays expenses of writers on assignment.

PHOTOS Captions, identification of subjects, model releases required. Negotiates payment individually.

COLUMNS/DEPARTMENTS Health (gay, off-kilter), 800 words; Fitness (irreverent), 500 words; Movies, Books (edgy, sardonic), 800 words; Music, Video Games (indie, underground), 800 words. **Pays $150-250.**

TIPS "While *Instinct* publishes a wide variety of features and columns having to do with gay men's issues, we maintain our signature irreverent, edgy tone throughout. When pitching stories (e-mail is preferred), be as specific as possible, and try to think beyond the normal scope of 'gay relationship' features. An article on 'Dating Tips,' for example, will not be considered, while an article on 'Tips on Dating Two Guys At Once' is more our slant. We rarely accept finished articles. We keep a special eye out for pitches on investigational/expose-type stories geared toward our audience."

⊖⊖ MENSBOOK JOURNAL

CQS Media, Inc., P.O. Box 418, Sturbridge MA 01566. **Fax:** (508)347-8150. **E-mail:** features@mensbook. com. **Website:** www.mensbook.com. **Contact:** P.C. Carr, editor/publisher. **100% freelance written.** Online anthology updated with offerings as they come in and are accepted by our editors. "We target bright, inquisitive, discerning gay men who want more non-commercial substance from gay media. We seek primarily first-person autobiographical pieces—then: biographies, political and social analysis, cartoons, short fiction, commentary, travel, and humor." Estab. 2008. Circ. variable. Byline given. Editorial lead time 4 months. Accepts queries by e-mail. Responds in 8 weeks to queries. Sample copy sent free by PDF. Publisher splits download fee with authors 50/50. Submit finished material anytime by e-mail. Do not call. Guidelines online at www.mensbook.com/writers-guidelines.htm.

NONFICTION Needs first-person pieces; essays; think-pieces; exposé; humor; inspirational profiles of courage and triumph over adversity; interview/profile; religion/philosophy vis-à-vis the gay experience; opinion; travel. "We do not want celebrity profiles/commentary, chatty, campy gossip; sexual conjecture

about famous people; or film reviews." Buys variably throughout the year. Query by e-mail. Length: 750-3,500 words.

FICTION Needs adventure, erotica, fantasy, mystery/suspense, slice-of-life vignettes. Buys variable amounts of fiction mss/year. Send complete ms. Length: 750-3,500 words.

POETRY Needs avant-garde, free verse, haiku, light verse, traditional. Buys 8 poems/year.

TIPS "Be a tight writer with a cogent, potent message. Structure your work with well-organized progressive sequencing. Edit everything down before you send it over so we know it is the best you can do, and we'll work together from there."

⊖⊖ METROSOURCE MAGAZINE

137 W. 19th St., 2nd Floor, New York NY 10011. (212)691-5127. **E-mail:** letters@metrosource.com. **Website:** www.metrosource.com. **75% freelance written.** Magazine published 6 times/year. "*MetroSource* is an upscale, glossy, 4-color lifestyle magazine targeted to an urban, professional gay and lesbian readership." Estab. 1990. Circ. 145,000. Byline given. Pays on publication. Publishes ms an average of 2 months after acceptance. Editorial lead time 4 months. Submit seasonal material 4 months in advance. Accepts queries by mail, e-mail, fax, phone. Accepts simultaneous submissions. Sample copy for $5.

NONFICTION Needs exposé, interview, opinion, photo feature, travel. **Buys 20 mss/year.** Query with published clips. Length: 1,000-1,800 words. **Pays $100-400.**

PHOTOS State availability. Captions, model releases required. Negotiates payment individually.

COLUMNS/DEPARTMENTS Book, film, television, and stage reviews; health columns; and personal diary and opinion pieces. Word lengths vary. Query with published clips. **Pays $200.**

⊖ RAINBOW RUMPUS

P.O. Box 6881, Minneapolis MN 55406. (612)721-6442. **E-mail:** fictionandpoetry@rainbowrumpus. org; admin@rainbowrumpus.org. **Website:** www. rainbowrumpus.org. **Contact:** Beth Wallace, fiction editor. "*Rainbow Rumpus* is the world's only online literary magazine for children and youth with lesbian, gay, bisexual, and transgender (LGBT) parents. We are creating a new genre of children's and young adult fiction. Please carefully read and observe the guidelines on our website. All fiction and poetry submissions should be sent via our contact page. Be sure to select the 'Submissions' category. A staff member will be in touch with you shortly to obtain a copy of your ms." Estab. 2005. Circ. 300 visits/day. Byline given. Pays on publication. Writer's guidelines online.

NONFICTION Needs interview, profile, social issues. Query. Length: 800-5,000 words. **Pays $75/story.**

FICTION Needs All levels: adventure, animal, contemporary, fantasy, folktales, history, humorous, multicultural, nature/environment, problem solving, science fiction, sports, suspense/mystery. **Buys 24 mss/year.** "Stories should be written from the point of view of children or teens with lesbian, gay, bisexual, or transgender parents or other family members, or who are connected to the LGBT community. Stories featuring families of color, bisexual parents, transgender parents, family members with disabilities, and mixed-race families are particularly welcome." Length: "Stories for 4- to 12-year-old children should be approximately 800 to 2,500 words in length. Stories for 13- to 18-year-olds may be as long as 5,000 words." **Pays $300/story.**

TIPS "Emerging writers encouraged to submit. You do not need to be a member of the LGBT community to participate."

⊖ THE WASHINGTON BLADE

P.O. Box 53352, Washington DC 20009. (202)747-2077. **Fax:** (202)747-2070. **E-mail:** knaff@washblade.com. **Website:** www.washblade.com. **Contact:** Kevin Naff, editor. **20% freelance written.** Nation's oldest and largest weekly newspaper covering the lesbian, gay, bisexual and transgender issues. Articles (subjects) should be written from or directed to a gay perspective. Estab. 1969. Circ. 30,000. Byline given. Submit seasonal material one month in advance. Accepts queries by mail, e-mail, fax. Responds in within one month to queries.

REPRINTS Send typed ms with rights for sale noted and information about when and where the material previously appeared.

PHOTOS A photo or graphic with feature articles is particularly important. Photos with news stories are appreciated. Send photos by mail or e-mail to mkey@washblade.com. Captions required. Pay varies. Photographers on assignment are paid mutually agreed upon fee.

COLUMNS/DEPARTMENTS Send feature submissions to Joey DiGuglielmo, arts editor (joeyd@wash-

blade.com). Sent opinion submissions to Kevin Naff, editor (knaff@washblade.com). Pay varies. No sexually explicit material.

TIPS "We maintain a highly competent and professional staff of news reporters, and it is difficult to break in here as a freelancer covering news. Include a résumé, good examples of your writing, and know the paper before you send a ms for publication. We look for writers who are credible and professional, and for copy that is accurate, fair, timely, and objective in tone. We do not work with writers who play fast and loose with the facts, or who are unprofessional in presentation. Before you send anything, become familiar with our publication. Do not send sexually explicit material."

GENERAL INTEREST

⊖⊖ THE AMERICAN LEGION MAGAZINE

P.O. Box 1055, Indianapolis IN 46206-1055. (317)630-1200. **Fax:** (317)630-1280. **E-mail:** magazine@legion. org. **E-mail:** mgrills@legion.org; hsoria@legion.org. **Website:** www.legion.org. **Contact:** Matt Grills, cartoon editor; Holly Soria, art director. **70% freelance written. Prefers to work with published/established writers, but works with a small number of new/unpublished writers each year.** Monthly magazine. Working through 15,000 community-level posts, the honorably discharged wartime veterans of The American Legion dedicate themselves to God, country, and traditional American values. They believe in a strong defense; adequate and compassionate care for veterans and their families; community service; and the wholesome development of our nation's youth. Publishes articles that reflect these values. Informs readers and their families of significant trends and issues affecting the nation, the world and their way of life. Major features focus on the American flag, national security, foreign affairs, business trends, social issues, health, education, ethics, and the arts. Also publishes selected general feature articles, articles of special interest to veterans, and question-and-answer interviews with prominent national and world figures. Estab. 1919. Circ. 2,550,000. Byline given. Pays on acceptance. Publishes ms an average of 6 months after acceptance. Accepts queries by mail, e-mail, fax. Responds in 2 months to queries. Sample copy for $3.50

and 9x12 SAE with 6 first-class stamps. Guidelines for #10 SASE.

NONFICTION Needs general interest, interview. No regional topics or promotion of partisan political agendas. No personal experiences or war stories. **Buys 50-60 mss/year.** Query with SASE should explain the subject or issue, article's angle and organization, writer's qualifications, and experts to be interviewed. Length: 300-2,000 words. **Pays 40¢/word and up.**

TIPS "Queries by new writers should include clips/background/expertise; no longer than 1 1/2 pages. Submit suitable material showing you have read several issues. *The American Legion Magazine* considers itself 'the magazine for a strong America.' Reflect this theme (which includes economy, educational system, moral fiber, social issues, infrastructure, technology and national defense/security). We are a general interest, national magazine, not a strictly military magazine. We are widely read by members of the Washington establishment and other policy makers."

THE ATLANTIC MONTHLY

The Watergate, 600 New Hampshire Ave., NW, Washington DC 20037. (202)266-6000. **Website:** www.theatlantic.com. **Contact:** James Bennet, editor; C. Michael Curtis, fiction editor; David Barber, poetry editor. Covers poetry, fiction, and articles of the highest quality. General magazine for an educated readership with broad cultural and public-affairs interests. "*The Atlantic* considers unsolicited mss, either fiction or nonfiction. A general familiarity with what we have published in the past is the best guide to our needs and preferences." Estab. 1857. Circ. 500,000. Byline given. Pays on acceptance. Accepts queries by mail, e-mail. Responds in 4-6 weeks to mss. Guidelines online.

NONFICTION Needs book excerpts, essays, general interest, humor, travel. Query with or without published clips or send complete ms to "Editorial Department" at address above or send pitches to pitches@theatlantic.com. All unsolicited mss must be accompanied by SASE. A general familiarity with what we have published in the past is the best guide to our needs and preferences. Simply send your ms—typewritten, double-spaced—to the Editorial Director, The Atlantic. Receipt of mss will be acknowledged if accompanied by a self-addressed stamped envelope. Mss will not be returned. Length: 1,000-6,000 words **Payment varies.** Sometimes pays expenses.

FICTION Contact: C. Michael Curtis, fiction editor. "Seeks fiction that is clear, tightly written with strong sense of 'story' and well-defined characters." No longer publishes fiction in the regular magazine. Instead, it will appear in a special newsstand-only fiction issue. Submit via e-mail with Word document attachment to submissions@theatlantic.com. Mss submitted via postal mail must be typewritten and double-spaced. Receipt of mss will be acknowledged if accompanied by a self-addressed stamped envelope. Mss will not be returned. TheAtlantic.com no longer accepts unsolicited submissions." Receives 1,000 unsolicited mss/month. Accepts 7-8 mss/year. **Publishes 3-4 new writers/year.** Needs literary, contemporary. Send complete ms. Preferred length: 2,000-6,000 words **True.**

POETRY Contact: David Barber, poetry editor. *The Atlantic Monthly* publishes some of the most distinguished poetry in American literature. "We read with interest and attention every poem submitted to the magazine and, quite simply, we publish those that seem to us to be the best." Has published poetry by Maxine Kumin, Stanley Plumly, Linda Gregerson, Philip Levine, Ellen Bryant Voigt, and W.S. Merwin. Receives about 60,000 poems/year. Buys 30-35 poems/year. Submit maximum 2-6 poems.

TIPS "Writers should be aware that this is not a market for beginner's work (nonfiction and fiction), nor is it truly for intermediate work. Study this magazine before sending only your best, most professional work. When making first contact, cover letters are sometimes helpful, particularly if they cite prior publications or involvement in writing programs. Common mistakes: melodrama, inconclusiveness, lack of development, unpersuasive characters and/or dialogue."

💲 CAPPER'S/GRIT

Ogden Publications, Inc., 1503 SW 42nd St., Topeka KS 66609-1265. Capper's: (800)678-4883; Grit: (800)803-7096. **E-mail:** editor@cappers.com; editor@grit.com. **Website:** www.cappers.com; www.grit.com. **Contact:** Caleb Regan, managing editor. **80% freelance written.** "*CAPPER's* and *Grit* are bi-monthly rural lifestyle magazines that focus on small town life, country and rural lifestyles and 'hobby' farms. Buys shared rights, which grants the publisher the right to publish or republish the work in any form in any country at any time. Does not publish poetry or fiction. Send queries via e-mail (cregan@grit.com). Include complete contact information. Articles (except Heart of the Home) are assigned in most cases; no editorial calendar is published. A great way to have a first article published is to become a blogger. For blogger information, send e-mail to tsmith@grit.com." Estab. 1879. Circ. 250,000. Byline given. Pays for articles on publication. Publishes mss an average of 2-15 months after acceptance. Submit seasonal queries 6-8 months in advance. Accepts queries by e-mail only, with "Query" and the subject of the query in the subject line. Responds in 2-3 weeks to queries. Sample copies and guidelines online or by e-mailing ireid@grit.com.

NONFICTION Needs feature-length articles (1,000-1,750 words with photos) on topics of interest to those living in rural areas, on farms or ranches, or those simply interested in the rural lifestyle; department articles (500-1,500 words with photos) on nostalgia, farm equipment and animals, DIY projects, gardening and cooking. Paid upon publication.

PHOTOS Photos paid upon publication. Pay is negotiable. Photo captions required. E-mail managing editor Caleb Regan (cregan@grit.com) to be added to the photo call-out list. Image requests sent for each issue. Send low-res digital images or lightboxes in response to call-out to jteller@grit.com. If images are purchased, send digital images via e-mail, one at a time as JPEG files at 300 dpi resolution to jteller@grit.com Send digital images via e-mail, one at a time, as JPEG files at 300 dpi resolution. Buys shared rights.

COLUMNS/DEPARTMENTS Departments include Gazette (news and quirky briefs of interest to lifestyle farmers); Heart of the Home (nostalgic remembrances on specific topics asked for in each issue); Country Tech (looking at equipment necessary for the farm life); Looking Back (nostalgic look at life on the farm); and In the Shop (how-to for those specialty farm items). Other departments are Comfort Foods, Recipe Box, In the Wild and Sow Hoe (gardening topics). A query should be sent via e-mail to cregan@grit.com for all departments except Heart of the Home. Send complete article via e-mail to tsmith@cappers.com or mail them to CAPPER's and Grit, Heart of the Home Dept., 1503 SW 42nd St., Topeka KS 66609. **Payment varies depending on experience and expertise. Payment will also include two contributor's copies. We pay a standard $25 rate for Heart of the Home stories and a standard $5 payment for Heart**

of the Home articles that appear on our website but not in the magazines.

TIPS "Study a few issues of the magazine. Most rejections are for material that is unsuitable or out of character for our magazine. Do not try to write for CAPPER's and Grit if you know nothing about rural life, gardening or urban farming. We intend to be an authoritative and sometimes playful voice for rural lifestyle farmers and country or small-town dwellers, and we require our freelance writers to be informed about that way of life. On occasion, we must cut material to fit column space. Electronic submissions preferred."

CONTINENTAL NEWSTIME

Continental Features/Continental News Service, Inc., 501 W. Broadway, Plaza A, PMB #265, San Diego CA 92101-3802. (858) 492-8696. **E-mail:** continental-newsservice@yahoo.com. **Website:** www.continental-newsservice.com. **Contact:** Gary P. Salamone, editor-in-chief. Twice-monthly general interest magazine of news and commentary on U.S. national and world news, with travel columns, entertainment features, humor pieces, comic strips, general humor panels, and editorial cartoons. "Writers who offer the kind and quality of writing we seek stand an equal chance regardless of experience. *CF/CNS* specializes in covering the unreported/under-reported news/information and requires 3 letters of recommendation, 1 of which must be from a current subscriber to our general-interest newsmagazine, *Continental Newstime*, to ensure consistency with this mission and with our quality and format standards." Estab. 1987. Responds in 1 month. Sample copy available for $4.50 in US and $6.50 CAN/foreign. Guidelines for #10 SASE.

NONFICTION Needs "Feature material should fit the equivalent of 1/4-1/2 standard newspaper page, and *Continental News* considers an ultra-liberal or ultra-conservative slant inappropriate.".

TIPS "*CNS* is working to develop a feature package of greater interest and value to an English-speaking international audience. That is, those writers who can accompany their economic-social-political analyses (of foreign countries) with photo(s) of the key public figure(s) involved are particularly in demand. Official photos (8x10 down to 3x5) of key government leaders available from the information ministry/press office/embassy will be acceptable. *CNS* emphasizes analytical/explanatory articles, but muckraking articles minus official photos are also encouraged."

EBONY

Johnson Publishing Co., Inc., 820 S. Michigan Ave., Chicago IL 60605. **E-mail:** editors@ebony.com. **Website:** www.ebonyjet.com. **Contact:** Kierna Mayo, editorial director. Monthly magazine covering topics ranging from education and history to entertainment, art, government, health, travel, sports and social events. *Ebony* is the top source for an authoritative perspective on the Black-American community. *Ebony* features the best thinkers, trendsetters, hottest celebrities and next-generation leaders of Black-America. It ignites conversation, promotes empowerment and celebrates aspiration. Circ. 1,280,000. Editorial lead time 3 months.

Query before submitting.

🌑🌑🌑🌑 HARPER'S MAGAZINE

666 Broadway, 11th Floor, New York NY 10012. (212)420-5720. **Fax:** (212)228-5889. **E-mail:** readings@harpers.org; scg@harpers.org. **Website:** www.harpers.org. **90% freelance written.** Monthly magazine for well-educated, socially concerned, widely read men and women who value ideas and good writing. *Harper's Magazine* encourages national discussion on current and significant issues in a format that offers arresting facts and intelligent opinions. By means of its several shorter journalistic forms—Harper's Index, Readings, Forum, and Annotation—as well as with its acclaimed essays, fiction, and reporting, *Harper's* continues the tradition begun with its first issue in 1850: to inform readers across the whole spectrum of political, literary, cultural, and scientific affairs. Estab. 1850. Circ. 230,000. Pays on acceptance. Offers negotiable kill fee. Publishes ms an average of 3 months after acceptance. Responds in 6 weeks to queries. Sample copy for $5.95.

Harper's Magazine will neither consider nor return unsolicited nonfiction mss that have not been preceded by a written query. *Harper's* will consider unsolicited fiction. Unsolicited poetry will not be considered or returned. No queries or mss will be considered unless they are accompanied by a SASE. All submissions and written queries (with the exception of Readings submissions) must be sent by mail to above address.

NONFICTION Needs humor. No interviews; no profiles. **Buys 2 mss/year.** Query. Length: 4,000-6,000 words.

REPRINTS Accepted for Readings section. Send typed ms with rights for sale ted and information about when and where the article previously appeared.

PHOTOS Occasionally purchased with ms; others by assignment. State availability. Pays $50-500.

FICTION Will consider unsolicited fiction. Needs humorous. **Buys 12 mss/year.** Query. Length: 3,000-5,000 words. **Generally pays 50¢-$1/word.**

TIPS Some readers expect their magazines to clothe them with opinions in the way that Bloomingdale's dresses them for the opera. The readers of *Harper's Magazine* belong to a different crowd. They strike me as the kind of people who would rather think in their own voices and come to their own conclusions.

🌑🌑🌑🌑 NATIONAL GEOGRAPHIC

1145 17th St. NW, Washington DC 20036. (202)857-7000. **Fax:** (202)492-5767. **Website:** www.nationalgeographic.com. **60% freelance written. Prefers to work with published/established writers.** Monthly magazine for members of the National Geographic Society. Looking for timely articles written in a compelling, "eyewitness" style. Arresting photographs that speak to the beauty, mystery, and harsh realities of life on earth. Maps of unprecedented detail and accuracy. These are the hallmarks of *National Geographic* magazine. Estab. 1888. Circ. 6,800,000. Accepts queries by mail. Guidelines online.

NONFICTION Query (500 words with clips of published articles) by mail to editor. Do not send mss. Length: 2,000-8,000 words. Pays expenses of writers on assignment.

PHOTOS Query in care of the Photographic Division.

TIPS "State the theme(s) clearly, let the narrative flow, and build the story around strong characters and a vivid sense of place. Give us rounded episodes, logically arranged."

🌑🌑🌑 NEWSWEEK

The Daily Beast, 251 W. 57th St., New York NY 10019. (212)445-4000. **Website:** www.newsweek.com. **Contact:** Kira Bindrim, managing editor. *Newsweek* is edited to report the week's developments on the newsfront of the world and the nation through news, commentary, and analysis. Estab. 1933. Circ. 3.2 million.

Query before submitting.

COLUMNS/DEPARTMENTS Contact: myturn@newsweek.com. No longer accepting submissions for the print edition. To submit an essay to website, please e-mail. The My Turn essay should be: A) an original piece, B) 850-900 words, C) generally personal in tone, and D) about any topic, but not framed as a response to a Newsweek story or another My Turn essay. Submissions must not have been published elsewhere. Please include full name, phone number, and address with your entry. The competition is very stiff. Receives 600 entries per month and only prints 1 a week. **Pays $1,000 on publication.**

THE NEW YORKER

4 Times Square, New York NY 10036. (212)286-5900. **Website:** www.newyorker.com. **Contact:** David Remnick, editor-in-chief. A quality weekly magazine of distinct news stories, articles, essays, and poems for a literate audience. Estab. 1925. Circ. 938,600. Pays on acceptance. Accepts queries by mail, e-mail. Responds in 3 months to mss.

○ *The New Yorker* receives approximately 4,000 submissions per month. Subscription: $59.99/year (47 issues), $29.99 for 6 months (23 issues).

NONFICTION Submissions should be sent as pdf attachments. Do not paste them into the message field. Due to volume, cannot consider unsolicited "Talk of the Town" stories or other nonfiction.

FICTION Publishes 1 ms/issue. Send complete ms. Fiction, poetry, Shouts & Murmurs, and newsbreaks should be sent as pdf attachments. **Payment varies.**

POETRY Contact: poetry@newyorker.com. Send poetry to Poetry Department. Submit no more than 6 poems at a time. No previously published poems or simultaneous submissions. Use online e-mail source and upload as pdf attachment. Include poet's name in the subject line and as the title of attached document. **Pays top rates.**

TIPS "Be lively, original, not overly literary. Write what you want to write, not what you think the editor would like."

⊖⊖⊖ THE NEW YORK TIMES MAGAZINE

620 8th Ave., New York NY 10018. (212)556-1234. **Fax:** (212)556 3830. **E-mail:** magazine@nytimes.com; nytnews@nytimes.com; executive-editor@nytimes.com. **Website:** www.nytimes.com/pages/magazine. **Contact:** Margaret Editor, public editor. *The New York Times Magazine* appears in *The New York Times* on Sunday. The *Arts and Leisure* section appears during the week. The *Op Ed* page appears daily. Circ. 1.8 million.

○ "Because of the volume of submissions for the Lives column, the magazine cannot return or respond to unsolicited mss. If you have a query about about the "Lives" page, please write to lives@nytimes.com. For Randy Cohen/The Ethicist, please write to ethicist@nytimes.com."

PEOPLE

Time, Inc., 1271 Avenue of the Americas, 28th Floor, New York NY 10020. (212)522-1212. **Fax:** (212)522-1359. **E-mail:** editor@people.com. **Website:** www.people.com. Weekly magazine. Designed as a forum for personality journalism through the use of short articles on contemporary news events and people. Circ. 3.7 million. Editorial lead time 3 months.

○ Query before submitting.

PORTLAND MONTHLY

165 State St., Portland ME 04101. (207)775-4339. **E-mail:** staff@portlandmonthly.com. **Website:** www.portlandmagazine.com. **Contact:** Colin Sargent, editor. Monthly city lifestyle magazine—fiction, style, business, real estate, controversy, fashion, cuisine, interviews, and art relating to the Maine area. Estab. 1985. Circ. 100,000. Pays on publication. Accepts queries by mail, e-mail.

NONFICTION Needs Wants interviews and features. Submit via online submission manager. Length: up to 1,500 words.

FICTION Submit via online submission manager. Length: up to 1,000 words.

TIPS "Our target audience is our 100,000 readers, ages 18-90. We write for our readers alone, and while in many cases we're delighted when our interview subjects enjoy our stories once they're in print, we are not writing for them but only for our readers. Interview subjects may not ever read or hear any portion of our stories before the stories are printed, and in the interest of objective distance, interview subjects are never to be promised complimentary copies of the magazine. It is the writer's responsibility to return all materials such as photos or illustrations to the interview subjects providing them."

⊖⊖ READER'S DIGEST

The Reader's Digest Association, Inc., Box 100, Pleasantville NY 10572. **E-mail:** letters@rd.com. **E-mail:** articleproposals@rd.com. **Website:** www.rd.com. *Reader's Digest* is an American general interest family magazine, published monthly. Estab. 1922. Circ. 4.6 million. Accepts queries by e-mail. Guidelines online.

💬 Query before submitting.

NONFICTION Accepts 1-page queries that clearly detail the article idea, with special emphasis on the arc of the story, interview access to the main characters, access to documents, etc. Looks for dramatic narratives, articles about everyday heroes, crime dramas, adventure stories. Include a separate page for writing credentials.

COLUMNS/DEPARTMENTS Life; @Work; Off Base, **pays $300**. Laugh; Quotes, **pays $100**. Address your submission to the appropriate humor category.

TIPS "Full-length, original articles are usually assigned to regular contributors to the magazine. We do not accept or return unpublished mss. We do, however, accept 1-page queries that clearly detail the article idea—with special emphasis on the arc of the story, your interview access to the main characters, your access to special documents, etc. We look for dramatic narratives, articles about everyday heroes, crime dramas, adventure stories. Do include a separate page of your writing credits. We are not interested in poetry, fiction, or opinion pieces. Please submit article proposals on the website."

$ REUNIONS MAGAZINE

P.O. Box 11727, Milwaukee WI 53211-0727. (414)263-4567. **Fax:** (414)263-6331. **E-mail:** editor@reunionsmag.com. **Website:** www.reunionsmag.com. **Contact:** Edith Wagner, editor. **85% freelance written.** Quarterly magazine covering reunions—all aspects and types. "*Reunions Magazine* is primarily for people actively planning family, class, military, and other reunions. We want easy, practical ideas about organizing, planning, researching/searching, attending, or promoting reunions." Estab. 1990. Circ. 20,000. Byline given. publication. Publishes ms an average of 1 year after acceptance. Editorial lead time 6 months. Submit seasonal material 1 year in advance. Accepts queries by mail, e-mail, fax; prefers Word attachments to e-mail. Responds in about 1 year. Sample copy and writer's guidelines for #10 SASE or online.

NONFICTION Needs reunions, how-to, humor, history/genealogy, interview, new product, personal experience, photo feature, travel, reunion recipes with reunion anecdote. **Buys 40 mss/year.** Query with published clips. Length: 500-2,500 (prefers work on the short side) **"Rarely able to pay anymore, but when we can pays $25-50."**

REPRINTS Send tearsheet, photocopy or typed ms with rights for sale noted and information about when and where the material previously appeared. Usually pays $10.

PHOTOS Always looking for vertical cover photos screaming *Reunion!* Prefers print or e-mail pictures. State availability. Captions, identification of subjects, model releases required. Reviews contact sheets, negatives, 35mm transparencies, prints, TIFF/JPEG files (300 dpi or higher) as e-mail attachments. Send to reunionsmag@gmail.com. Offers no additional payment for photos accepted with ms.

FILLERS Must be reunion-related. Needs anecdotes, facts, short humor. **Buys 20-40 fillers/year mss/year.** Length: 50-250 words. **Pays $5.**

TIPS "All copy must be reunion-related with strong, real reunion examples and experiences. Write a lively account of an interesting or unusual reunion, either upcoming or soon after while it's hot. Tell readers why the reunion is special, what went into planning it, and how attendees reacted. Our 'Masterplan' section, about family reunion planning, is a great place for a freelancer to start by telling her/his own reunion story. Send us how-tos or tips about any of the many aspects of reunion organizing or activities. Open your minds to different types of reunions—they're all around!"

$$$$ SMITHSONIAN MAGAZINE

Capital Gallery, Suite 6001, MRC 513, P.O. Box 37012, Washington DC 20013. (202)275-2000. **E-mail:** smithsonianmagazine@si.edu. **Website:** www.smithsonianmag.com. **Contact:** Molly Roberts, photo editor; Jeff Campagna, art services coordinator. **90% freelance written.** Monthly magazine for associate members of the Smithsonian Institution; 85% with college education. *Smithsonian Magazine's* mission is to inspire fascination with all the world has to offer by featuring unexpected and entertaining editorial that explores different lifestyles, cultures and peoples, the arts, the wonders of nature and technology, and much more. The highly educated, innovative readers of *Smithsonian* share a unique desire to celebrate life, seeking out the timely as well as timeless, the artistic as well as the academic, and the thought-provoking as well as the humorous. Circ. 2.3 million. Pays on acceptance. Offers 33% kill fee. Publishes ms an average of 6 months after acceptance. Editorial lead time 2 months. Submit seasonal material 3 months in advance. Accepts queries by online submission form only. Responds in 3 weeks to queries from the web form. Sample copy for $5. Guidelines online.

NONFICTION Buys 120-130 feature (up to 5,000 words) and 12 short (500-650 words) mss/year. Use online submission form. *Smithsonian* magazine accepts unsolicited proposals from established freelance writers for features and some departments. Submit a proposal of 250 to 300 words as a preliminary query. Background information and writing credentials are helpful. The proposal text box on the Web submission form holds 10,000 characters (approximately 2,000 words), ample room for a cover letter and proposal. All unsolicited proposals are sent on speculation. Responds in 3 weeks. Supporting material or clips of previously published work can be provided with links. Article length ranges from a 700-word humor column to a 4,000-word full-length feature. Considers focused subjects that fall within the general range of Smithsonian Institution interests, such as: cultural history, physical science, art and natural history. **Pays various rates per feature, $1,500 per short piece.** Pays expenses of writers on assignment.

PHOTOS Purchased with or without ms and on assignment. Illustrations are not the responsibility of authors, but if you do have photographs or illustration materials, please include a selection of them with your submission. In general, 35mm color transparencies or black-and-white prints are perfectly acceptable. Photographs published in the magazine are usually obtained through assignment, stock agencies, or specialized sources. No photo library is maintained and photographs should be submitted only to accompany a specific article proposal. Send photos. Captions required. Pays $400/full color page.

COLUMNS/DEPARTMENTS Length: 1,000-2,000 words. Last Page humor, 550-700 words. **Buys 12-15 mss/year.** Use online submission form. **Pays $1,000-1,500.**

TIPS "Send proposals through online submission form only. No e-mail or mail queries, please."

TIME

1271 Avenue of the Americas, New York NY 10020. **E-mail:** letters@time.com. **Website:** www.time.com. **Contact:** Nancy Gibbs, managing editor. Weekly magazine. *TIME* covers the full range of information that is important to people today—breaking news, na-

tional and world affairs, business news, societal and lifestyle issues, culture and entertainment news and reviews. Estab. 1923. Circ. 4 million.

Query before submitting.

HEALTH AND FITNESS

AMERICAN FITNESS

15250 Ventura Blvd., Suite 200, Sherman Oaks CA 91403. (800)446-2322, ext. 200. **E-mail:** americanfitness@afaa.com. **Website:** www.afaa.com. **Contact:** Meg Jordan, editor. **75% freelance written.** Bimonthly magazine covering exercise and fitness, health, and nutrition. "We need timely, in-depth, informative articles on health, fitness, aerobic exercise, sports nutrition, age-specific fitness, and outdoor activity. Absolutely no first-person accounts. Need well-researched articles for professional readers." Estab. 1983. Circ. 42,900. Byline given. Pays 30 days after publication. Publishes ms an average of 6 months after acceptance. Submit seasonal material 4 months in advance. Accepts queries by mail, fax. Accepts simultaneous submissions. Responds in 2 months to queries. Sample copy for $4.50 and SASE with 6 first-class stamps.

NONFICTION Needs historical, history of various athletic events, inspirational, sport's leaders motivational pieces, interview, fitness figures, new product, plus equipment review, personal experience, successful fitness story, photo feature, on exercise, fitness, new sport, travel, activity adventures. No articles on unsound nutritional practices, popular trends, or unsafe exercise gimmicks. **Buys 18-25 mss/year.** Send complete ms. Length: 800-1,200 words. **Pays $200 for features, $80 for news.** Sometimes pays expenses of writers on assignment.

PHOTOS Sports, action, fitness, aquatic aerobics competitions, and exercise class. We are especially interested in photos of high-adrenalin sports like rock climbing and mountain biking. Captions, identification of subjects, model releases required. Reviews transparencies, prints. Pays $35 for transparencies.

COLUMNS/DEPARTMENTS Research (latest exercise and fitness findings); Alternative paths (nonmainstream approaches to health, wellness, and fitness); Strength (latest breakthroughs in weight training); Clubscene (profiles and highlights of fitness club industry); Adventure (treks, trails, and global challenges); Food (low-fat/nonfat, high-flavor dishes); Homescene (home-workout alternatives); Clip 'n' Post (concise exercise research to post in health clubs, offices or on refrigerators). Length: 800-1,000 words. Query with published clips or send complete ms. **Pays $100-200.**

TIPS "Make sure to quote scientific literature or good research studies and several experts with good credentials to validate exercise trend, technique, or issue. Cover a unique aerobics or fitness angle, provide accurate and interesting findings, and write in a lively, intelligent manner. Please, no first-person accounts of 'how I lost weight or discovered running.' *AF* is a good place for first-time authors or regularly published authors who want to sell spin-offs or reprints."

💲💲💲💲 FITNESS MAGAZINE

Meredith Corp., 805 Third Ave., 25th Floor, New York NY 10022. **E-mail:** fitquestions@fitnessmagazine. com. **Website:** www.fitnessmagazine.com. **Contact:** Kathy Green, managing editor. Monthly magazine for women in their 20s and 30s who are interested in fitness and living a healthy life. Fitness magazine motivates women to move—for fun, for health, for life. With workouts and diet plans that get results, plus inspiring beauty and health tips, *Fitness* empowers women to be fierce about reaching for and achieving body success, however they define it. Circ. 1.5 million. Byline given. Pays on acceptance. Offers 20% kill fee. Responds in 2 months to queries.

NONFICTION Buys 60-80 mss/year. Query. Length: 1,500-2,500 words. Pays expenses of writers on assignment.

REPRINTS Send photocopy. Negotiates fee.

COLUMNS/DEPARTMENTS Length: 600-1,200 words. **Buys 30 mss/year.** Query.

TIPS "Our pieces must get inside the mind of the reader and address her needs, hopes, fears, and desires. *Fitness* acknowledges that getting and staying fit is difficult in an era when we are all time-pressured."

💲💲💲💲 HEALTH

Time, Inc., Southern Progress Corp., 1271 Avenue of Americas, New York NY 10020. **Website:** www.health. com. **Contact:** Christine Mattheis, senior editor; Theresa Tamkins, editor-in-chief. Magazine published 10 times/year covering health, fitness, and nutrition. Readers are predominantly college-educated women in their 30s, 40s, and 50s. Edited to focus not on illness, but on wellness news, events, ideas, and people. Estab. 1987. Circ. 1,360,000. Byline given. Pays on acceptance. Offers 33% kill fee. Accepts queries by mail,

fax. Accepts simultaneous submissions. Responds in 2 months to queries. Sample copy for $5 to Back Issues. Guidelines for #10 SASE or via e-mail.

💭 Query before submitting.

NONFICTION No unsolicited mss. **Buys 25 mss/ year.** Query with published clips and SASE. 1,200 words Pays expenses of writers on assignment.

COLUMNS/DEPARTMENTS Body, Mind, Fitness, Beauty, Food.

TIPS "We look for well-articulated ideas with a narrow focus and broad appeal. A query that starts with an unusual local event and hooks it legitimately to some national trend or concern is bound to get our attention. Use quotes, examples and statistics to show why the topic is important and why the approach is workable. We need to see clear evidence of credible research findings pointing to meaningful options for our readers. Stories should offer practical advice and give clear explanations."

💲💲💲 IMPACT MAGAZINE

IMPACT Productions, 2007 2nd St. SW, Calgary AB T2S 1S4 Canada. (403)228-0605. **E-mail:** editor@impactmagazine.ca; info@impactmagazine.ca. **Website:** www.impactmagazine.ca. **Contact:** Chris Welner, editor. **10% freelance written.** Bimonthly magazine covering fitness and sport performance. A leader in the industry, *IMPACT Magazine* is committed to publishing content provided by the best experts in their fields for those who aspire to higher levels of health, fitness, and sport performance. Estab. 1992. Circ. 90,000. Byline given. Pays 30 days after publication. Offers 25% kill fee. Publishes ms an average of 4-6 months after acceptance. Editorial lead time 6 months. Submit seasonal material 6 months in advance. Accepts queries by e-mail. Accepts simultaneous submissions. Responds in 4 weeks to queries. Sample copy and guidelines online.

💭 "Query first, outlining the parameters of the article, the length, sources, etc., before submitting a completed ms. We do not accept as editorial articles that profile and promote a specific business or service. *IMPACT Magazine* is a bi-monthly publication; submission deadlines are16 weeks prior to the publishing date. E-mail the article in a MS Word or text format (Mac or PC format). *IMPACT Magazine* compensates writers whose qualifications and work meet our specific guidelines (available from the editor). We are happy to accept photos or illustrations and will give photos credit where due. Digital images must be a minimum of 300 dpi."

NONFICTION Needs general interest, how-to, interview, new product, opinion, technical. **Buys 4 mss/ year.** Query before submitting. Length: 600-1,800 words. **Pays $0.25/max. for assigned articles. Pays $0.25/max. for unsolicited articles.**

PHOTOS State availability. Identification of subjects, model releases required. Reviews contact sheets, GIF/ JPEG files (300 dpi or greater). Negotiates payment individually.

☢❸❸❸ OXYGEN

Robert Kennedy Publishing, 400 Matheson Blvd. W., Mississauga ON L5R 3M1 Canada. (905)507-3545; (888)254-0767. **Fax:** (905)507-2372. **Website:** www. oxygenmag.com. **70% freelance written.** Monthly magazine covering women's health and fitness. *Oxygen* encourages various exercise, good nutrition to shape, and condition the body. Estab. 1997. Circ. 340,000. Byline given. Pays on acceptance. Offers 25% kill fee. Publishes ms an average of 4 months after acceptance. Editorial lead time 3 months. Submit seasonal material 6 months in advance. Accepts queries by mail, fax. Responds in 5 weeks to queries. Responds in 2 months to mss. Sample copy for $5.

NONFICTION Needs expose, how-to, training and nutrition, humor, inspirational, interview, new product, personal experience, photo feature. No poorly researched articles that do not genuinely help the readers toward physical fitness, health, and physique. **Buys 100 mss/year.** Send complete ms with SASE and $5 for return postage. Length: 1,400-1,800 words. **Pays $250-1,000.** Sometimes pays expenses of writers on assignment.

PHOTOS State availability of or send photos. Identification of subjects required. Reviews contact sheets, 35mm transparencies, prints. Offers $35-500.

COLUMNS/DEPARTMENTS Nutrition (low-fat recipes), 1,700 words; Weight Training (routines and techniques), 1,800 words; Aerobics (how-tos), 1,700 words. **Buys 50 mss/year.** Send complete ms. **Pays $150-500.**

TIPS "Every editor of every magazine is looking, waiting, hoping and praying for the magic article. The beauty of the writing has to spring from the page; the edge imparted has to excite the reader because of its unbelievable information."

❸❸❸❸ POZ

CDM Publishing, LLC, 462 Seventh Ave., 19th Floor, New York NY 10018. (212)242-2163. **Fax:** (212)675-8505. **E-mail:** website@poz.com; editor-in-chief@ poz.com. **Website:** www.poz.com. **Contact:** Doriot Kim, art director. **25% freelance written.** Monthly national magazine for people impacted by HIV and AIDS. "*POZ* is a trusted source of conventional and alternative treatment information, investigative features, survivor profiles, essays and cutting-edge news for people living with AIDS and their caregivers. *POZ* is a lifestyle magazine with both health and cultural content." Estab. 1994. Circ. 125,000. Byline given. Pays 30 days after publication. Offers 25% kill fee. Publishes ms an average of 3 months after acceptance. Editorial lead time 4 months. Submit seasonal material 4 months in advance. Accepts simultaneous submissions. Sample copy and writer's guidelines free.

NONFICTION Needs book excerpts, essays, exposé, historical, how-to, humor, inspirational, interview, opinion, personal experience, photo feature. Query with published clips. "We take unsolicited mss on speculation only." Length: 200-3,000 words. **Pays $1/word.** Sometimes pays expenses of writers on assignment.

PHOTOS Send photos. Identification of subjects required. Reviews contact sheets, negatives. Negotiates payment individually.

PREVENTION

Rodale, Inc., 33 E. Minor St., Emmaus PA 18098-0099. **E-mail:** editor@prevention.com. **Website:** www.prevention.com. Monthly magazine covering health and fitness. Written to motivate, inspire and enable male and female readers ages 35 and over to take charge of their health, to become healthier and happier, and to improve the lives of family and friends. Estab. 1950. Circ. 3,150,000.

❸ Query before submitting.

❸❸❸❸ SHAPE

American Media, 4 New York Plaza, 4th Floor, New York NY 10004. (212)545-4800. **Website:** www.shape. com. **70% freelance written. Prefers to work with published/established writers.** Monthly magazine covering health, fitness, nutrition, and beauty for women ages 18-34. *Shape* reaches women who are committed to healthful, active lifestyles. Readers are participating in a variety of fitness-related activities, in the gym, at home and outdoors, and they are also proactive about their health and are nutrition conscious. Estab. 1981. Circ. 1.6 million. Pays on acceptance. Offers 33% kill fee. Submit seasonal material 8 months in advance. Accepts queries by mail. Responds in 2 months to queries. Sample copy for SAE with 9x12 envelope and 4 First-Class stamps.

💬 Query before submitting.

NONFICTION Needs book excerpts, expose, health, fitness, nutrition related, how-to, get fit, health/fitness, recipe. Rarely publishes celebrity question and answer stories, celebrity profiles, or menopausal/hormone replacement therapy stories. Query with published clips. Length: 2,500 words/features; 1,000 words/shorter pieces. **Pays $1.50/word (on average).**

TIPS "Review a recent issue of the magazine. Not responsible for unsolicited material. We reserve the right to edit any article."

$$$ SPIRITUALITY & HEALTH MAGAZINE

Spirituality & Health Media, LLC, 444 Hana Hwy., Suite D, Kahului HI 96732. (231)933-5660. **E-mail:** editors@spiritualityhealth.com. **Website:** www.spiritualityhealth.com. **Contact:** Karen Bouris, editor-in-chief; Ilima Loomis, managing editor. Bimonthly magazine covering research-based spirituality and health. "We look for formally credentialed writers in their fields. We are nondenominational and non-proselytizing. We are not New Age. We appreciate well-written work that offers spiritual seekers from all different traditions help in their unique journeys." Estab. 1998. Circ. 95,000. Byline given. Pays on acceptance. Offers 25% kill fee. Editorial lead time 4 months. Submit seasonal material 6 months in advance. Accepts queries by e-mail. Accepts simultaneous submissions. Responds in 3-4 months to queries. Responds in 2-4 months to mss. Sample copy and writer's guidelines online.

💬 The most open department is Inner & Outer Worlds. Read it to see what is used. (All back issues are on the website.) News must be current with a 4-month lead time.

NONFICTION Does not want proselytizing, New Age cures with no scientific basis, "how I recovered from a disease personal essays," psychics, advice columns, profiles of individual healers or practitioners, pieces promoting one way or guru, reviews, poetry or columns.

TIPS "Start by pitching really interesting, well-researched news shorts for Inner & Outer Worlds. Before you pitch, do a search of our website to see if we've already covered it. Provide links to 2 or 3 clips that represent your published work."

WEBMD THE MAGAZINE

WebMD, 111 8th Ave, 7th Floor, New York NY 10011. (212)624-3700. **Website:** www.webmd.com/magazine. **80% freelance written.** Bimonthly magazine covering health, lifestyle health and well-being, some medical. Published by WebMD Health, *WebMD the Magazine* is the print sibling of the website WebMD.com. It aims to broaden thecompany-wide mandate: "Better information, better health." It is a health magazine, with a difference. It is specifically designed and written for people who are about to have what may be the most important conversation of the year with their physician or other medical professional. The magazine's content is therefore developed to be most useful at this critical point of care, to improve and enhance the dialogue between patient and doctor. Readers are adults (65% women, 35% men) in their 30s, 40s, and 50s (median age is 41) who care about their health, take an active role in their own and their family's wellness, and want the best information possible to make informed healthcare decisions. Estab. 2005. Circ. 1 million. Byline given. Pays on acceptance. Offers 30% kill fee. Publishes ms an average of 3 months after acceptance. Editorial lead time 3-4 months. Submit seasonal material 3-4 months in advance. Accepts queries by e-mail. Sample copy online.

💬 Query before submitting.

TIPS "We only want experienced magazine writers, in the topic areas of consumer health. Writers with experience writing for national women's health magazines preferred. Relevant clips required. Fresh, witty, smart, well-written style, with solid background in health. This is not a publication for writers breaking into the field."

WEIGHT WATCHERS

14 W. 23rd St. #2, New York NY 10010. (212)929-7054. **Website:** www.weightwatchers.com/magazine. The official magazine of Weight Watchers International, an international company that offers various products and services to assist weight loss and service. Estab. 1963.

Query before submitting.

WOMEN'S HEALTH

Rodale Inc., 400 South 10th St., Emmaus PA 18098. **E-mail:** womenshealth@rodale.com; whonline@womenshealthmag.com. **Website:** www.womenshealthmag.com. Magazine published 10 times/year for the woman who wants to reach a healthy, attractive weight. *Women's Health* reaches a new generation of women who don't like the way most women's magazines make them feel. Estab. 2005. Circ. 1.5 million. Accepts queries by e-mail.

Query before submitting.

HISTORY

AMERICA'S CIVIL WAR

Weider History Group, 19300 Promenade Dr., Leesburg VA 20176-6500. (703)771-9400. **Fax:** (703)779-8345. **E-mail:** acw@weiderhistorygroup.com. **Website:** www.historynet.com; AmericasCivilWarMag.com. **60% freelance written.** Bimonthly magazine covering popular history and straight historical narrative for both the general reader and the American Civil War buff featuring firsthand accounts, remarkable photos, expert commentary, and maps in making the whole story of the most pivotal era in American history accessible and showing why it still matters in the 21st century. Estab. 1988. Circ. 78,000. Byline given. Pays on publication. Accepts queries by e-mail. Sample copy for $5.99. Guidelines available by e-mail. **NONFICTION** Needs historical, book notices, preservation news. **Buys 18 mss/year.** "Query. Submit a page outlining the subject and your approach to it, and why you believe this would be an important article for the magazine. Briefly summarize your prior writing experience in a cover note." Length: 3,500 words; 250-word sidebar. **Pays $300 and up.**
PHOTOS Send photos with submission or cite sources. Captions, identification of subjects required.
TIPS "All stories must be true. We do not publish fiction or poetry. Write an entertaining, well-researched, informative and unusual story that grabs the reader's attention and holds it. Submit queries or mss by e-mail. All submissions are on speculation."

THE ARTILLERYMAN

Historical Publications, Inc., 234 Monarch Hill Rd., Tunbridge VT 05077. (802)889-3500. **Fax:** (802)889-5627. **E-mail:** mail@artillerymanmagazine.com.

Website: www.artillerymanmagazine.com. **Contact:** Kathryn Jorgensen, editor. **60% freelance written.** Quarterly magazine covering antique artillery, fortifications, and crew-served weapons 1750-1900 for competition shooters, collectors, and living history reenactors using artillery. Estab. 1979. Circ. 1,200. Byline given. Pays on publication. Publishes ms an average of 6 months after acceptance. Accepts queries by mail, e-mail, fax. Accepts simultaneous submissions. Responds in 3 weeks to queries. Sample copy and writer's guidelines for 9x12 SAE with 4 first-class stamps.
NONFICTION Needs historical, how-to, interview, photo feature, technical, travel. **Buys 12 mss/year.** Send complete ms. Length: 300 words minimum. **Pays $40-60.**
PHOTOS Send photos. Captions, identification of subjects required. Pays $15 for color or b&w digital prints.
TIPS "We regularly use freelance contributions for Places-to-Visit and Unit Profiles departments and welcome pieces on unusual cannon or cannon with a known and unique history. Writers should ask themselves if they could knowledgeably talk artillery with an expert."

GATEWAY

Missouri History Museum, P.O. Box 11940, St. Louis MO 63112. (314)746-4558. **Fax:** (314)746-4548. **E-mail:** vwmonks@mohistory.org. **Website:** www.mohistory.org. **Contact:** Victoria Monks, editor. **75% freelance written.** Annual magazine covering Missouri history and culture. *Gateway* is a popular cultural history magazine that is primarily a member benefit of the Missouri History Museum. Thus, we have a general audience with an interest in the history and culture of Missouri and St. Louis in particular. Estab. 1980. Circ. 9,000. Byline given. Publishes ms an average of 6 months to 1 year after acceptance. Editorial lead time 6 months. Accepts queries by mail, e-mail, fax. Responds in 1 month to queries. Responds in 2 months to mss. Sample copy for $10, online or send #10 SASE.
NONFICTION Needs book excerpts, essays, interview, photo feature, historical, scholarly essays, Missouri biographies, photo essays, viewpoints on events, first-hand historical accounts, regional architectural history, literary history. No genealogies. **Buys 4-6 mss/year.** Query with writing samples. Length: 2,000-5,000 words.

PHOTOS State availability with submission.

TIPS "You'll get our attention with queries reflecting new perspectives on historical and cultural topics."

$ GOOD OLD DAYS

Annie's, 306 E. Parr Rd., Berne IN 46711. **Fax:** (260)589-8093. **E-mail:** editor@goodolddaysmagazine.com. **Website:** www.goodolddaysmagazine.com. **Contact:** Mary Beth Weisenburger, editor. **75% freelance written.** Bimonthly magazine of first-person nostalgia, 1935-1965. "We look for strong narratives showing life as it was in the middle decades of the 20th century. Our readership is composed of nostalgia buffs, history enthusiasts, and the people who actually lived and grew up in this era." Byline given. Pays on contract. Publishes ms an average of 8 months after acceptance. Submit seasonal material 10 months in advance. Accepts queries by e-mail, fax. Responds in 2 months to queries. Sample copy for $2. Guidelines online.

💬 Queries accepted, but are not necessary.

NONFICTION Needs historical, humor, personal experience, photo feature, favorite food/recipes, year-round seasonal material, biography, memorable events, fads, fashion, sports, music, literature, entertainment. No fiction accepted. **Buys 350 mss/year.** Query or send complete ms. Length: 500-1,500 words. **Pays $15-50, depending on quality and photos.**

PHOTOS Do not send original photos until we ask for them. You may send photocopies or duplicates. Do not submit laser-copied prints. Send photos. Identification of subjects required.

TIPS "Most of our writers are not professionals. We prefer the author's individual voice, warmth, humor, and honesty over technical ability."

$ LEBEN

City Seminary Press, 2150 River Plaza Dr., Suite 150, Sacramento CA 95833. **E-mail:** editor@leben.us. **Website:** www.leben.us. **40% freelance written.** Quarterly magazine presenting the people and events of Christian history from a Reformation perspective. Not a theological journal, per se, but rather a popular history magazine. Estab. 2004. Circ. 5,000. Byline given. Pays on acceptance. Offers 25% kill fee. Publishes ms an average of 6 months after acceptance. Editorial lead time 6 months. Submit seasonal material 6 months in advance. Accepts queries by online submission form. Accepts simultaneous submissions. Responds in 3 weeks to queries. Responds in 2 months to mss. Sample copy for $1.50 (order online or request via e-mail). Guidelines by e-mail.

NONFICTION Needs historical and biographical material related to Protestand and Reformation subjects. Does not want articles that argue theological issues. "There is a place for that, but not in a popular history/biography magazine aimed at general readership." Query. Length: 500-2,500 words. **Pays 5¢/word for original material.**

TIPS "Visit our website and read our publication. We are a niche magazine, but a person knowledgeable about the Reformation should be able to write for."

$$ PERSIMMON HILL

1700 NE 63rd St., Oklahoma City OK 73111. (405)478-2250, ext. 213. **Fax:** (405)478-4714. **E-mail:** editor@nationalcowboymuseum.org. **Website:** www.nationalcowboymuseum.org. **Contact:** Judy Hilovsky. **70% freelance written. Prefers to work with published/established writers; works with a small number of new/unpublished writers each year.** Biannual magazine for an audience interested in Western art, Western history, ranching, and rodeo, including historians, artists, ranchers, art galleries, schools, and libraries. Publication of the National Cowboy and Western Heritage Museum. Estab. 1970. Circ. 7,500. Byline given. Pays on publication. Publishes ms an average of 18 months after acceptance. Responds in 3 months to queries. Sample copy for $11. Writer's guidelines online.

NONFICTION **Buys 50-75 mss/year.** Query with clips. Length: 1,500 words. **Pays $150-300.**

PHOTOS Purchased with ms or on assignment. Captions required. Reviews digital images and b&w prints. Pays according to quality and importance for b&w and color photos.

TIPS "Send us a story that captures the spirit of adventure and indvidualism that typifies the Old West or reveals a facet of the Western lifestyle in comtemporary society. Excellent illustrations for articles are essential! We lean towards scholarly, historical, well-researched articles. We're less focused on Western celebrities than some of the other contemporary Western magazines."

REMINISCE

Reiman Media Group, Inc., 5400 S. 60th St., Greendale WI 53129-1404. **E-mail:** editors@reminisce.com; editors@reminisceextra.com. **Website:** www.reminisce.com. **Reader-written magazine.** Magazine published 7 times/year that covers the 20th century. Reminisce helps readers "bring abck the good times" through true stories and vintage photographs. Estab. 1991. Does not provide payment. Accepts queries by mail, e-mail. Guidelines online.

NONFICTION Any appropriate memory or photo is welcome, as long as it originated from 1900 through the 1970s. Editorial style is relaxed and conversational; write the way you'd relate to a friend. Length: 700 words.

HOBBY AND CRAFT

⊕ BEADWORK

Interweave Press, 201 E. Fourth St., Loveland CO 80537. **E-mail:** beadworksubmissions@interweave.com. **Website:** www.beadingdaily.com. "*Beadwork* is a bimonthly magazine devoted to everything about beads and beadwork. Our pages are filled with projects for all levels of beaders, with a focus on the learning needs of those who seek to master beadweaving stitches. We pride ourselves on our easy-to-follow instructions and technical illustrations as well as our informative and entertaining features." Pays on publication. Accepts simultaneous submissions. Guidelines online.

NONFICTION Needs step-by-step beading projects, features on beading and bead artists. Query by e-mail or mail. If submitting a project idea, include high-resolution photo of project and contact info. If querying for a feature, submit proposal and contact info.

💲💲 BLADE MAGAZINE

F+W Media, Inc., 700 E. State St., Iola WI 54990-0001. (715)445-2214. **Fax:** (715)445-4087. **E-mail:** joe.kertzman@fwmedia.com. **Website:** www.blademag.com. **Contact:** Joe Kertzman, managing editor. **5% freelance written.** Monthly magazine covering working and using collectible, popular knives. *Blade* prefers in-depth articles focusing on groups of knives, whether military, collectible, high-tech, pocket knives or hunting knives, and how they perform. Estab. 1973. Circ. 39,000. Byline given. Pays on publication. Publishes ms an average of 9 months after acceptance. Editorial lead time 9 months. Submit seasonal material 9 months in advance. Accepts queries by mail, e-mail, fax. Responds in 3 months to queries. Responds in 6 months to mss. Sample copy for $4.99. Guidelines for SAE with 8x11 envelope and 3 first-class stamps.

NONFICTION Needs general interest, historical, how-to, interview, new product, photo feature, technical. "We assign profiles, show stories, hammer-in stories, etc. We don't need those. If you've seen the story on the Internet or in another knife or knife/gun magazine, we don't need it. We don't do stories on knives used for self-defense." Send complete ms. Length: 700-1,400 words. **Pays $150-300.**

PHOTOS Send photos. Captions, identification of subjects required. Reviews transparencies, prints, digital images (300 dpi at 1200x1200 pixels). Offers no additional payment for photos accepted with ms.

FILLERS Needs anecdotes, facts, newsbreaks. **Buys 1-2 mss/year.** Length: 50-200 words. **Pays $25-50.**

TIPS "We are always willing to read submissions from anyone who has read a few copies and studied the market. The ideal article for us is a piece bringing out the romance, legend, and love of man's oldest tool—the knife. We like articles that place knives in peoples' hands—in life saving situations, adventure modes, etc. (Nothing gory or with the knife as the villain.) People and knives are good copy. We are getting more well-written articles from writers who are reading the publication beforehand. That makes for a harder sell for the quickie writer not willing to do his homework. Go to knife shows and talk to the makers and collectors. Visit knifemakers' shops and knife factories. Read anything and everything you can find on knives and knifemaking."

⊕ CLOTH PAPER SCISSORS

Interweave Press, ATTN: CPS Submissions, 490 Boston Post Road, Suite 15, Sudbury MA 01776. **E-mail:** mjibson@interweave.com. **E-mail:** submissions@clothpaperscissors.com. **Website:** www.clothpaperscissors.com. **Contact:** Michelle Jibson. "*Cloth Paper Scissors* is most interested in publishing articles that cover unique collage and mixed-media techniques geared to beginner, intermediate, or advanced artists. Feature articles may explore motifs and methods that will inspire and inform collage, fiber, and mixed media artists. We are interested in articles focusing on fabric and paper collage techniques; paint and dye applications; handmade books; creative sketchbook keeping; art journaling; altered books techniques; ways of working with polymer clay; stitching on paper, fabric, and other media; crafting as a business and way of life; embossing techniques; digital imagery for collage; working with found objects; crafting 'green';

and stories about creating inspired studios for mixed-media artists." Guidelines online.

NONFICTION "If you have a technique, project, or body of work to share, *Cloth Paper Scissors* would like to know about it. We want to show other artists—from beginners to the advanced—the latest, edgiest, most unusual collage and mixed-media techniques and applications." Query by e-mail (submissions@ clothpaperscissors.com) or mail.

⊛⊛ DOLLHOUSE MINIATURES

68132 250th Ave., Kasson MN 55944. (507)634-3143. **E-mail:** usoffice@ashdown.co.uk. **Website:** www. dhminiatures.com. **70% freelance written.** Monthly magazine covering dollhouse scale miniatures. *Dollhouse Miniatures* is America's best-selling miniatures magazine and the definitive resource for artisans, collectors, and hobbyists. It promotes and supports the large national and international community of miniaturists through club columns, short reports, and by featuring reader projects and ideas. Estab. 1971. Circ. 25,000. Byline given. Pays on acceptance. Editorial lead time 6 months. Submit seasonal material 6 months in advance. Accepts queries by mail. Responds in 1 month to queries. Responds in 2 months to mss. Sample copy for $6.95, plus shipping. Guidelines available by e-mailing submissions editor at traci@ashdown.co.uk.

NONFICTION Needs how-to, miniature projects of various scales in variety of media, interview, artisans, collectors, photo feature, dollhouses, collections, museums. No articles on miniature shops or essays. **Buys 50-60 mss/year.** Send complete ms. Length: 500-1,500 words. **Pays $30-250 for assigned articles. Pays $0-150 for unsolicited articles.**

PHOTOS Send digital photos. Captions, identification of subjects required. Reviews 3x5 prints. Photos are paid for with ms. Seldom buys individual photos.

TIPS "Familiarity with the miniatures hobby is very helpful. Accuracy to scale is extremely important to our readers. A complete digital package (ms/photos) has a better chance of publication."

F+W MEDIA, INC. (MAGAZINE DIVISION)

(formerly F+W Publications, Inc.), 10151 Carver Rd., Suite 200, Cincinnati OH 45242. (513)531-2690. **E-mail:** dave.pulvermacher@fwmedia.com. **Website:** www.fwmedia.com. **Contact:** Dave Pulvermacher, marketing research supervisor. "Each month, millions of enthusiasts turn to the magazines from F+W

for inspiration, instruction, and encouragement. Readers are as varied as our categories, but all are assured of getting the best possible coverage of their favorite hobby." Publishes magazines in the following categories: **antiques and collectibles** (*Antique Trader*); **automotive** (*Military Vehicles, Old Cars Report Price Guide, Old Cars Weekly*); **beading** (*Beadwork*); coins and paper money (*Bank Note Reporter, Coins Magazine, Numismatic News, World Coin News*); **construction** (*Frame Building News, Metal Roofing, Rural Builder*); **crocheting** (*Interweave Crochet*); **fine art** (*Collector's Guide, Drawing, Pastel Journal, Southwest Art, The Artist's Magazine, Watercolor Artist*); **firearms and knives** (*Blade, Gun Digest*); **genealogy** (*Family Tree Magazine*); **graphic design** (*HOW Magazine, PRINT*); **horticulture** (*Horticulture*); **jewelry** (*Jewelry Stringing, Lapidary Journal Jewelry Artist, Step by Step Wire Jewelry*); **knitting** (*Interweave Knits*) **militaria** (*Military Trader*); **outdoors and hunting** (*Deer & Deer Hunting, Trapper & Predator Caller*); **quilting** (*Quilting Arts Magazine*); **records and CDs** (*Goldmine*); **sewing** (*Sew Beautiful*); **spinning** (*Spinoff*) **sports** (*Sports Collectors Digest*); **woodworking** (*Popular Woodworking Magazine*); **writing** (*Writer's Digest*).

Please see individual listings in the Consumer Magazines and Trade Journals sections for specific submission information about each magazine.

⊛⊛⊛ FAMILY TREE MAGAZINE

F+W Media, Inc., 10151 Carver Rd., Suite 200, Cincinnati OH 45242. (513)531-2690. **Fax:** (513)891-7153. **E-mail:** ftmedit@fwpubs.com. **Website:** www.familytreemagazine.com. **75% freelance written.** Magazine covering family history, heritage, and genealogy research. "*Family Tree Magazine* is a special-interest consumer magazine that helps readers discover, preserve, and celebrate their family's history. We cover genealogy, ethnic heritage, genealogy websites and software, photography and photo preservation, and other ways that families connect with their past." Estab. 1999. Circ. 75,000. Byline given. Pays on acceptance. Offers 25% kill fee. Publishes ms an average of 6 months after acceptance. Editorial lead time 8 months. Submit seasonal material 8 months in advance. Accepts queries by mail, e-mail. Responds in 6-8 weeks to queries. Sample copy for $8 from website. Guidelines online.

NONFICTION Needs book excerpts, historical, how-to, genealogy, new product, photography, computer, technical, genealogy software, photography equipment. Does not publish personal experience stories (except brief stories in Everything's Relative column) or histories of specific families. **Buys 60 mss/year.** Query with a specific story idea and published clips. Length: 250-4,500 words. **Pays $25-800.** Does not pay expenses.

PHOTOS State availability. Captions required. Reviews color transparencies. Negotiates payment individually.

TIPS "Always query with a specific story idea. Look at sample issues before querying to get a feel for appropriate topics and angles. We see too many broad, general stories on genealogy or records and personal accounts of 'How I found great-aunt Sally' without how-to value."

FINE BOOKS & COLLECTIONS

OP Media, LLC, 101 Europa Dr., Suite 150, Chapel Hill NC 27517. (800)662-4834. **Fax:** (919)945-0700. **E-mail:** rebecca@finebooksmagazine.com. **Website:** www.finebooksmagazine.com. **90% freelance written.** Bimonthly magazine covering used and antiquarian bookselling and book collecting. Covers all aspects of selling and collecting out-of-print books. Emphasizes good writing, interesting people, and unexpected viewpoints. Estab. 2002. Circ. 5,000. Byline given. Pays on publication. Offers negotiable kill fee. Publishes ms an average of 4 months after acceptance. Editorial lead time 6+ months. Submit seasonal material 4 months in advance. Accepts queries by mail, e-mail. Accepts simultaneous submissions. Responds in 2 months to queries and mss. Sample copy for $6.50 plus shipping. Guidelines online.

NONFICTION Needs book excerpts, essays, expose, general interest, historical, how-to, travel. Does not want tales of the "gold in my attic" vein. **Buys 25 mss/ year.** Query with published clips. Length: 500-2,000 words. **Pays $125-400.** Sometimes pays expenses of writers on assignment.

PHOTOS State availability. Captions, identification of subjects required. Reviews GIF/JPEG files. Negotiates payment individually.

COLUMNS/DEPARTMENTS Digest (news about collectors, booksellers, and bookselling), 500 words.

TIPS "We like good journalism on most any topic related to collectible books or fine art. Written for an educated general reader."

FINESCALE MODELER

Kalmbach Publishing Co., 21027 Crossroads Circle, P.O. Box 1612, Waukesha WI 53187-1612. (414)796-8776. **Website:** www.finescale.com. **80% freelance written. Eager to work with new/unpublished writers.** Magazine published 10 times/year devoted to how-to-do-it modeling information for scale model builders who build non-operating aircraft, tanks, boats, automobiles, figures, dioramas, and science fiction and fantasy models. Circ. 60,000. Byline given. Pays on acceptance. Publishes ms an average of 14 months after acceptance. Responds in 6 weeks to queries. Responds in 3 months to mss. Sample copy with 9x12 SASE and 3 first-class stamps. Guidelines online.

Finescale Modeler is especially looking for how-to articles for armor and aircraft modelers.

NONFICTION Needs how-to, build scale models, technical, research information for building models. Query or send complete ms via www.contribute.kalmbach.com. Length: 750-3,000 words. **Pays $60/ published page minimum.**

PHOTOS "Send original high-res digital images, slides, or prints with submission. You can submit digital images at www.contribute.kalmbach.com.". Captions, identification of subjects required. Reviews transparencies, color prints. Pays $7.50 minimum for transparencies and $5 minimum for color prints.

COLUMNS/DEPARTMENTS *FSM* Showcase (photos plus description of model); *FSM* Tips and Techniques (model building hints and tips). **Buys 25-50 mss/year.** Send complete ms. **Pays $25-50.**

TIPS "A freelancer can best break in first through hints and tips, then through feature articles. Most people who write for *FSM* are modelers first, writers second. This is a specialty magazine for a special, quite expert audience. Essentially, 99% of our writers will come from that audience."

THE FINE TOOL JOURNAL LLC

P.O. Box 737, 9325 Dwight Boyer Rd., Watervliet MI 49098. (269)463-8255. **Fax:** (269)463-3767. **E-mail:** finetoolj@gmail.com; jim@finetooljournal.net. **Website:** www.finetooljournal.net. **Contact:** Jim Gehring. **90% freelance written.** "Quarterly magazine specializing in older or antique hand tools from all traditional trades. Readers are primarily interested in woodworking tools, but some subscribers have interests in such areas as leatherworking, wrenches, kitchen, and machinist tools. Readers range from beginners just getting into the hobby to advanced collectors and organizations.". Estab. 1970. Circ. 2,500. Byline given. Pays on publication. Offers $50 kill fee. Publishes ms an average of 6 months after acceptance. Editorial lead time 9 months. Submit seasonal material 6 months in advance. Accepts queries by mail, online submission form. Responds in 2 months to queries; 3 months to mss. Sample copy for $6. Guidelines for #10 SASE.

NONFICTION Needs general interest, historical, how-to, make, use, fix and tune tools, interview, personal experience, photo feature, technical. **Buys 24 mss/year.** Send complete ms. Length: 1,000-3,000 words. **Pays $50-200.** Pays expenses of writers on assignment.

PHOTOS Send photos. "Photographs and illustrations should be submitted in JPEG or PDF files—we can scan them if necessary, but this sometimes leads to loss of resolution. If you are writing about a patented tool and wish to illustrate it with the patent drawing, these can be downloaded as PDF files from Google Patents.". Identification of subjects, model releases required. Reviews 4x5 prints. Negotiates payment individually.

COLUMNS/DEPARTMENTS Stanley Tools (new finds and odd types), 300-400 words; Tips of the Trade (how to use tools), 100-200 words. **Buys 12 mss/year.** Send complete ms. **Pays $30-60.**

TIPS "The easiest way to get published in the *Journal* is to have personal experience or know someone who can supply the detailed information. We are seeking articles that go deeper than general interest, and that knowledge requires experience and/or research. Short of personal experience, find a subject that fits our needs and that interests you. Spend some time learning the ins and outs of the subject, and with hard work and a little luck you will earn the right to write about it."

⊕ HANDWOVEN

Interweave Press, 24520 Melott Rd., Hillsboro OR 97123. **E-mail:** aosterhaug@interweave.com. **Website:** www.weavingdaily.com. **Contact:** Anita Osterhaug. "The main goal of *Handwoven* articles is to inspire our readers to weave. Articles and projects should be accessible to weavers of all skill levels, even when the material is technical. The best way to prepare an article for *Handwoven* is to study the format and style of articles in recent issues." Pays on publica-

tion. Editorial lead time is 6-12 months. Responds in 6 weeks to queries. Guidelines online.

NONFICTION Special issues: Query or submit full ms by e-mail or mail. Include written intro, relevant photos or other visuals (include photo credits), 25-word author bio and photo.

⊕ INTERWEAVE CROCHET

Interweave Press, 201 E. Fourth St., Loveland CO 80537. **E-mail:** lindsay.jarvis@fwmedia.com (queries only). **Website:** www.crochetme.com. "*Interweave Crochet* is a quarterly publication of Interweave for all those who love to crochet. In each issue we present beautifully finished projects, accompanied by clear step-by-step instructions, as well as stories and articles of interest to crocheters. The projects range from quick but intriguing projects that can be accomplished in a weekend to complex patterns that may take months to complete. Engaging and informative feature articles come from around the country and around the world. Fashion sensibility and striking examples of craft technique are important to us." Pays on publication. Guidelines online.

NONFICTION Special issues: "We are interested in articles on a broad range of topics, including: technical pieces, profiles of inspiring crochet designers, and features about regions of the world where crochet has played or continues to play an important role.". Query by mail. Include submission form (online). "Please send a detailed proposal—complete outline, written description—to give us a clear idea of what to expect in the finished piece."

⊕ INTERWEAVE KNITS

Interweave Press, 201 E. Fourth St., Loveland CO 80537. **Website:** www.knittingdaily.com. *Interweave Knits* is a quarterly publication of Interweave Press for all those who love to knit. In each issue we present beautifully finished projects, accompanied by clear step-by-step instruction, and stories and articles of interest to knitters. The projects range from quick but intriguing items that can be accomplished in a weekend, to complex patterns that may take months to complete. Feature articles (personally arresting but information-rich) come from around the country and around the world. Fashion sensibility and striking examples of craft technique are important to us. *Interweave Knits* is published quarterly. Pays on publication. Editorial lead time is 6-12 months. Responds in 6 weeks to queries. Guidelines online.

NONFICTION Special issues: "We are interested in articles of all lengths on a broad range of topics, including technical pieces; profiles of inspiring knit-wear designers and others in textile industries; and features about regions of the world where knitting has played or continues to play an important role. We take knitting seriously and want articles that do the same. The best way to understand what we're looking for is to read a recent issue of the magazine carefully. For all article queries, send a detailed proposal: For shorter submissions, a brief description will do; for feature articles, send an outline and a sample paragraph or two. If the proposal is accepted, and once we've made any adjustments to the concept and agreed on the details, you will begin work on the article.". Query by mail. Include submission form (online). Do not address queries to Eunny Jang. "Beyond the Basics" (useful, accurate, high-quality technical information; 2,000-2,200 words); "Ravelings" (the personal side of knitting; 700-750 words, send whole articles)

COLUMNS/DEPARTMENTS "Knitted Artifact" (examines a knitted artifact, exploring the societal and cultural importance of the craft; 250-300 words); "Where it Comes From (educates readers about fiber and yarn; 250-300 words); "Yarn Review" (1,200-1,400 words); Profiles (showcasing a designer; 1,500-1,800 words).

TIPS "Remember that your submission is a representation of who you are and how you work—if you send us a thoughtful, neat, and well-organized submission, we are likely to be intrigued."

🌑🌑 KITPLANES

P.O. Box 1295, Dayton NV 89403. (832)851-6665. **E-mail:** editorial@kitplanes.com. **Website:** www. kitplanes.com. **Contact:** Paul Dye, editor-in-chief. **50% freelance written. Eager to work with new/un-published writers.** Monthly magazine covering self-construction of private aircraft for pilots and builders. Estab. 1984. Circ. 72,000. Byline given. Pays on publication. Publishes ms an average of 3 months after acceptance. Submit seasonal material 6 months in advance. Accepts queries by mail, e-mail. Responds in 4 weeks to queries. Responds in 6 weeks to mss. Sample copy for $6. Guidelines online.

NONFICTION Needs general interest, how-to, interview, new product, personal experience, photo feature, technical. No general-interest aviation articles, or "My First Solo" type of articles. **Buys 80 mss/year.**

Query. Length: 500-3,000 words. **Pays $250-1,000, including story photos.**

PHOTOS State availability of or send photos. Captions, identification of subjects required. Pays $300 for cover photos.

TIPS "*Kitplanes* contains very specific information—a writer must be extremely knowledgeable in the field. Major features are entrusted only to known writers. We cannot emphasize enough that articles must be directed at the individual aircraft builder. We need more 'how-to' photo features in all areas of home-built aircraft."

LAPIDARY JOURNAL JEWELRY ARTIST

300 Chesterfield Parkway, Suite 100, Malvern PA 19355. (610)232-5700. **Fax:** (610)232-5756. **E-mail:** ljeditorial@interweave.com. **Website:** www.lapidaryjournal.com. **70% freelance written.** Monthly magazine covering gem, bead, and jewelry arts. Our audience is hobbyists who usually have some knowledge of and proficiency in the subject before they start reading. Our style is conversational and informative. There are how-to projects and profiles of artists and materials. Estab. 1947. Circ. 53,000. Byline given. Pays on acceptance. Publishes ms an average of 4 months after acceptance. Editorial lead time 3 months. Accepts queries by mail, e-mail. Sample copy online.

NONFICTION Needs how-to, jewelry/craft, interview, new product, personal experience, technical, travel. **Buys 100 mss/year.** Query. 1,500-2,500 words preferred; 1,000-3,500 words acceptable; longer works occasionally published serially.

REPRINTS Send photocopy.

TIPS "Some knowledge of jewelry, gemstones, and/or minerals is a definite asset. Step-by-Step is a section within *Lapidary Journal* that offers illustrated, step-by-step instruction in gem-cutting, jewelry-making, and beading. Please request a copy of the Step-by-Step guidelines for greater detail."

🌑 LINN'S STAMP NEWS

Amos Press, P.O. Box 29, Sidney OH 45365. (937)498-0801. **Fax:** (937)498-0886. **E-mail:** linns@linns.com. **Website:** www.linns.com. **Contact:** Charles Snee, editor. **50% freelance written.** Weekly tabloid on the stamp collecting hobby. "All articles must be about philatelic collectibles. Our goal at *Linn's* is to create the number one website for stamp collectors and a weekly print publication that is indispensable to stamp collectors." Estab. 1928. Circ. 20,000. Byline given. Pays within 1 month of publication. Publishes ms an average of 4 months after acceptance. Submit seasonal material 2 months in advance. Responds in 6 weeks to queries. Sample copy online. Guidelines online.

NONFICTION Needs general interest, historical, how-to, interview, technical, club and show news, current issues, auction realization, and recent discoveries. No articles merely giving information on background of stamp subject. Must have philatelic information included. **Buys 25 mss/year.** Send complete ms. Length: 1,200 words maximum. **Pays $40-100.** Sometimes pays expenses of writers on assignment.

PHOTOS "Good illustrations are a must. Send scans with submission.". Captions required. Reviews digital color at twice actual size (300 dpi). Offers no additional payment for photos accepted with ms.

TIPS "Check and double check all facts. Footnotes and bibliographies are not appropriate to newspaper style. Work citation into the text. Even though your subject might be specialized, write understandably. Explain terms. *Linn's* features are aimed at a broad audience of novice and intermediate collectors. Keep this audience in mind. Provide information in such a way to make stamp collecting more interesting to more people."

$ MODEL CARS MAGAZINE

Golden Bell Press, 2403 Champa St., Denver CO 80205. (808)754-1378. **E-mail:** gregg@modelcarsmag.com. **Website:** www.modelcarsmag.com. **25% freelance written.** Magazine published 9 times year covering model cars, trucks, and other automotive models. *Model Cars Magazine* is the hobby's how-to authority for the automotive modeling hobbiest. This magazine is on the forefront of the hobby, the editorial staff are model car builders, and every single one of the writers has a passion for the hobby that is evident in the articles and stories that we publish. This is the model car magazine written by and for model car builders. Estab. 1999. Circ. 7,000. Byline given. Pays on publication. Publishes ms an average of 2-3 months after acceptance. Editorial lead time 2-3 months. Accepts queries by mail, e-mail. Sample copy online.

NONFICTION Needs how-to. Length: 600-3,000 words. **Pays $50/page. Pays $25/page for unsolicited articles.**

⊘ OLD CARS REPORT PRICE GUIDE

F+W Media, Inc., 700 E. State St., Iola WI 54990-0001. (715)445-2214. **Fax:** (715)445-4087. **E-mail:** report@fwmedia.com. **Website:** www.oldcarspriceguide.net. **Contact:** Brian Earnest, editor. Bimonthly magazine covering collector vehicle values from 1930-2004. Estab. 1978. Circ. 60,000. Sample copy free.

🗨 This publication is not accepting freelance submissions at this time.

$ PIECEWORK MAGAZINE

Interweave Press, Inc., 201 E. Fourth St., Loveland CO 80537. (800) 272-2193. **Fax:** (970)669-6117. **E-mail:** piecework@interweave.com. **Website:** www.interweave.com. **90% freelance written.** Bimonthly magazine covering needlework history. *PieceWork* celebrates the rich tradition of needlework and the history of the people behind it. Stories and projects on embroidery, cross-stitch, knitting, crocheting, and quilting, along with other textile arts, are featured in each issue. Estab. 1993. Circ. 30,000. Byline given. Pays on publication. Offers 25% kill fee. Editorial lead time 6 months. Submit seasonal material 6 months in advance. Accepts queries by mail, e-mail, fax, phone. Responds in 6 months to queries. Sample copy and writer's guidelines free.

NONFICTION Needs book excerpts, historical, how-to, interview, new product. No contemporary needlework articles. **Buys 25-30 mss/year.** Send complete ms. Length: 1,500-4,000 words.

PHOTOS State availability of or send photos. Captions, identification of subjects, model releases required. Reviews transparencies, prints.

TIPS Submit a well-researched article on a historical aspect of needlework complete with information on visuals and suggestion for accompanying project.

$$$$ POPULAR MECHANICS

Hearst Corp., 300 W. 57th St., New York NY 10019-5899. (212)649-2000. **E-mail:** popularmechanics@hearst.com; pmwebmaster@hearst.com. **Website:** www.popularmechanics.com. **Contact:** Jim Meigs, editor-in-chief. **Up to 50% freelance written.** Monthly magazine on technology, science, automotive, home, outdoors. A men's service magazine that addresses the diverse interests of today's male, providing him with information to improve the way he lives. Covers stories from do-it-yourself projects to technological advances in aerospace, military, automotive, and so on. Estab. 1902. Circ. 1,200,000. Byline given. Pays on acceptance. Offers 25% kill fee. Publishes ms an average of 6 months after acceptance. Submit seasonal material 6 months in advance. Guidelines online.

NONFICTION Query before submitting a ms. Send ms to the appropriate departmental editor. In any article query, be specific as to what makes the development new, better, different, interesting, or less expensive. All articles must be submitted in a word processing app. Editorial interests include automotive, home journal, science/technology/aerospace, boating/outdoors, electronics/photography/telecommunications, and general interest articles. **Pays $300-1,000 for features.**

$ $ POPULAR WOODWORKING MAGAZINE

F+W Media, Inc., 8469 Blue Ash Rd., Suite 100, Cincinnati OH 45236. (513)531-2690, ext. 11348. **E-mail:** glen.huey@fwmedia.com. **Website:** www.popularwoodworking.com. **Contact:** Glen Huey. **45% freelance written.** Magazine published 7 times/year. "*Popular Woodworking Magazine* invites woodworkers of all skill levels into a community of professionals who share their hard-won shop experience through in-depth projects and technique articles, which help the readers hone their existing skills and develop new ones for both hand and power tools. Related stories increase the readers' understanding and enjoyment of their craft. Any project submitted must be aesthetically pleasing, of sound construction, and offer a challenge to readers. On the average, we use 2 freelance features per issue. Our primary needs are 'how-to' articles on woodworking. Our secondary need is for articles that will inspire discussion concerning woodworking. Tone of articles should be conversational and informal but knowledgeable, as if the writer is speaking directly to the reader. Our readers are the woodworking hobbyist and small woodshop owner. Writers should have an extensive knowledge of woodworking and excellent woodworking techniques and skills." Estab. 1981. Circ. 150,000. Byline given. Pays on acceptance. Publishes ms an average of 10 months after acceptance. Submit seasonal material 6 months in advance. Accepts queries by mail, e-mail, phone. Responds in 2 months to queries. Sample copy for $5.99 and 9x12 SAE with 6 first-class stamps or online. Guidelines online.

NONFICTION Needs how-to (on woodworking projects, with plans), humor (woodworking anecdotes), technical (woodworking techniques). No tool reviews. **Buys 12 mss/year.** Query first; see guidelines and sample query online. Length: 1,200-2,500 words. **Pay starts at $250/published page.**

REPRINTS Send photocopy with rights for sale noted and information about when and where the material previously appeared. Pays 25% of amount paid for an original article.

PHOTOS Photographic quality affects acceptance. Need professional quality, high-resolution digital images of step-by-step construction process. Send photos. Captions, identification of subjects required. Pays $75/image.

COLUMNS/DEPARTMENTS Tricks of the Trade (helpful techniques), End Grain (thoughts on woodworking as a profession or hobby, can be humorous or serious), 500-550 words. **Buys 20 columns/yr mss/year.** Query. **Pays $275 for End Grain and $50-100 for Tricks of the Trade.**

TIPS "Write an 'End Grain' column for us and then follow up with photos of your projects. Submissions should include materials list, complete diagrams (blueprints not necessary), and discussion of the step-by-step process. We select attractive, practical projects with quality construction for which the authors can supply quality digital photography."

⊕ QUILTING ARTS MAGAZINE

Interweave Press, 201 E. Fourth St., Loveland CO 80537. **E-mail:** submissions@quiltingarts.com. **Website:** www.quiltingdaily.com. "At *Quilting Arts*, we celebrate contemporary art quilting, surface design, mixed media, fiber art trends, and more. We are always looking for new techniques, innovative processes, and unique approaches to the art of quilting." Pays on publication. Editorial lead time is 12 months. Responds in 3 months to queries. Guidelines online.

NONFICTION Special issues: Wants "beautiful and inspiring contemporary quilts and exhibits; sketchbook-inspired quilts for our Off The Page series; artists with inspiring portfolios of work to be featured in our In The Spotlight, Artist Profile, and Q&A articles; unique techniques, new ways to use existing tools and supplies, and ideas we've never featured before.". Query by e-mail. Include brief description of idea and contact info.

$ SHUTTLE SPINDLE & DYEPOT

Handweavers Guild of America, Inc., 1255 Buford Hwy., Suite 211, Suwanee GA 30024. (678)730-0010.

Fax: (678)730-0836. **E-mail:** hga@weavespindye.org. **Website:** www.weavespindye.org. **60% freelance written.** Quarterly magazine. Quarterly membership publication of the Handweavers Guild of America, Inc., *Shuttle Spindle & Dyepot* magazine seeks to encourage excellence in contemporary fiber arts and to support the preservation of techniques and traditions in fiber arts. It also provides inspiration for fiber artists of all levels and develops public awareness and appreciation of the fiber arts. *Shuttle Spindle & Dyepot* appeals to a highly educated, creative, and very knowledgeable audience of fiber artists and craftsmen, weavers, spinners, dyers, and basket makers. Estab. 1969. Circ. 30,000. Byline given. Pays on publication. Publishes ms an average of 6 months after acceptance. Editorial lead time 8 months. Submit seasonal material 8 months in advance. Accepts queries by mail, e-mail, fax, phone. Sample copy for $8 plus shipping. Guidelines online.

NONFICTION Needs inspirational, interview, new product, personal experience, photo feature, technical, travel. No self-promotional and no articles from those without knowledge of area/art/artists. **Buys 40 mss/year.** Query with published clips. Length: 1,000-2,000 words. **Pays $75-150.**

PHOTOS State availability. Captions, identification of subjects, model releases required. Offers no additional payment for photos accepted with ms.

COLUMNS/DEPARTMENTS Books and Videos, News and Information, Calendar and Conference, Travel and Workshop (all fiber/art related).

TIPS "Become knowledgeable about the fiber arts and artists. The writer should provide an article of importance to the weaving, spinning, dyeing and basket making community. Query by telephone (once familiar with publication) by appointment helps editor and writer."

SPIN-OFF

Interweave Press, 201 E. Fourth St., Loveland CO 80537. **E-mail:** spinoff@interweave.com. **Website:** www.spinningdaily.com. "*Spin-Off* is a quarterly magazine devoted to the interests of handspinners at all skill levels. Informative articles in each issue aim to encourage the novice, challenge the expert, and increase every spinner's working knowledge of this ancient and complex craft." Pays on publication. Editorial lead time is 6-12 months. Responds in 6 weeks to queries. Guidelines online.

"If you are not a spinner, it will be difficult for you to write effectively for this magazine. If you are a spinner whose idea interests us, but you're an inexperienced writer, we will work with you on presenting your thoughts."

NONFICTION Special issues: Wants articles on the following subjects: spinning tips (400 words or less); spinning basics (1,200 words); Armchair Traveler (800 words); Behind the Scenes (800 words); back page essay (650 words); methods for dyeing with natural and chemical d; tools for spinning and preparing fibers; fiber basics (2,000 words); ideas for using handspun yarn in a variety of techniques; profiles of people who spin; a gallery of your work; tips on blending fibers; the history and/or cultural role of spinning. Query or submit full ms by e-mail or mail. Length: 200-2,700 words. **Pays $50/published page. If images are provided, pays $10/published photo.**

TIPS "*Spin-Off* is many things. As a contributor, think of it as a forum where you can share your experiences and knowledge with your community. Consider how your contribution will serve the reader."

STEP BY STEP WIRE JEWELRY

630 Freedom Business Center Dr., 3rd Floor, King of Prussia PA 19406. **E-mail:** dpeck@interweave.com. **Website:** www.jewelrymakingdaily.com. **Contact:** Denise Peck. *Step by Step Wire Jewelry* is published 6 times/year by Interweave Press. The magazine is project-oriented, with step-by-step instructions for creating wire jewelry, as well as tips, tools, and techniques. Articles range from beginner to expert level. Writers must be able to substantiate that material submitted is accurate and must make sure that all steps involved in the creation of the piece are feasible using the tools listed. Pays on publication. Editorial lead time is 6-12 months. Responds in 6 weeks to queries. Guidelines online.

NONFICTION Needs step-by-step jewelry projects. Submit ms by e-mail. Include name, contact info, project title, level of experience required, brief bio, complete list of tools, and project text. Length: 700-2,500 words. **Pays nominal fee for article based on length and complexity and determined by editor.**

STITCH

Interweave Press, 201 E. Fourth St., Loveland CO 80537. **E-mail:** stitchsubmissions@interweave.com. **Website:** www.sewdaily.com. "*Stitch* is a special issue sewing magazine all about creating with fabric and thread., it's sewing but oh so much more. It's loaded with clever projects and modern designs for your wardrobe and home, inspiring designer profiles, plus hot trends, news, and inspiration from the global community of sewing. Whether you're just learning to sew or have been sewing forever, *Stitch* will inspire you to make beautiful things that showcase your unique point of view." Pays on publication. Editorial lead time is 12 months. Responds in 3 months to queries. Guidelines online.

NONFICTION Needs original sewing projects, feature articles on sewing, design, and textiles. "We accept queries for feature articles on timely topics related to sewing, design, and textiles." Query by e-mail. Include brief description of idea and contact info. Length: 1,000-1,500 words.

HOME AND GARDEN

$$ THE AMERICAN GARDENER

7931 E. Boulevard Dr., Alexandria VA 22308-1300. (703)768-5700. **Fax:** (703)768-7533. **E-mail:** editor@ahs.org; myee@ahs.org. **Website:** www.ahs.org. **Contact:** Mary Yee, art director. **60% freelance written.** Bimonthly, 64-page, four-color magazine covering gardening and horticulture. "This is the official publication of the American Horticultural Society (AHS), a national, nonprofit, membership organization for gardeners, founded in 1922. The AHS mission is 'to open the e of all Americans to the vital connection between people and plants, and to inspire all Americans to become responsible caretakers of the earth, to celebrate America's diversity through the art and science of horticulture, and to lead this effort by sharing the society's unique national resources with all Americans.' All articles are also published on members-only website." Estab. 1922. Circ. 20,000. Byline given. Pays on publication. Offers 25% kill fee. Publishes ms an average of 6 months after acceptance. Editorial lead time 6 months. Submit seasonal material at least 1 year in advance. Accepts queries by mail with SASE. Responds in 3 months to queries. Sample copy for $5. Writer's guidelines by e-mail and online.

NONFICTION Buys 20 mss/year. Query with published clips. No fax, phone, or e-mail submissions. Length: 1,500-2,500 words. **Pays $300-500, depending on complexity and author's experience.**

REPRINTS Rarely purchases second rights. Send photocopy of article with information about when and where the material previously appeared. Payment varies.

PHOTOS E-mail or check website for guidelines before submitting. It is very important to include some kind of plant list for your stock so we can determine if you specialize in the types of plants we cover. The list does not have to be comprehensive, but it should give some idea of the breadth of your photo archive. If, for instance, your list contains mostly tulips, pansies, roses, and other popular plants like these, your stock will not be a good match for our articles. Also, if your list does not include the botanical names for all plants, we will not be able to use the photos. Identification of subjects required. Photo captions required; include complete botanical names of plants including genus, species and botanical variety or cultivar. Pays $350 maximum for color cover; $80-130 for color inside. Pays on publication. Credit line given. Buys one-time North American and nonexclusive rights.

COLUMNS/DEPARTMENTS Natural Connections (explains a natural phenomenon—plant and pollinator relationships, plant and fungus relationships, parasites—that may be observed in nature or in the garden), 750-1,200 words. Homegrown Harvest (articles on edible plants delivered in a personal, reassuring voice. Each issue focuses on a single crop, such as carrots, blueberries, or parsley), 800-900 words; Plant in the Spotlight (profiles of a single plant species or cultivar, including a personal perspective on why it's a favored plant), 600 words. **Buys 5 mss/year.** Query with published clips. **Pays $100-250.**

TIPS "The majority of our readers are advanced, passionate amateur gardeners; about 20 percent are horticultural professionals. Most prefer not to use synthetic chemical pesticides. Our articles are intended to bring this knowledgeable group new information, ranging from the latest scientific findings that affect plants, to in-depth profiles of specific plant groups and leading horticulturalists, and the history of gardening and gardens in America."

$$ ATLANTA HOMES AND LIFESTYLES

Network Communications, Inc., 1100 Johnson Ferry Rd., Suite 685, Atlanta GA 30342. (404)252-6670. **Fax:** (404)252-6673. **E-mail:** gchristman@nci.com. **Website:** www.atlantahomesmag.com. **Contact:** Elizabeth Ralls, editor; Elizabeth Anderson, art director. **65%**

freelance written. Magazine published 12 times/year. *Atlanta Homes and Lifestyles* is designed for the action-oriented, well-educated reader who enjoys his/her shelter, its design and construction, its environment, and living and entertaining in it. Estab. 1983. Circ. 30,000. Byline given. Pays on publication. Publishes ms an average of 6 months after acceptance. Accepts queries by mail, fax. Responds in 3 months to queries. Sample copy for $3.95.

NONFICTION Needs interview, new product, photo feature, well-designed homes, gardens, local art, remodeling, food, preservation, entertaining. "We do not want articles outside respective market area, not written for magazine format, or that are excessively controversial, investigative, or that cannot be appropriately illustrated with attractive photography." **Buys 35 mss/year.** Query with published clips. Length: 500-1,200 words. **Pays $100-500.** Sometimes pays expenses of writer on assignment.

PHOTOS Most photography is assigned. State availability. Captions, identification of subjects, model releases required. Reviews transparencies. Pays $40-50/photo.

COLUMNS/DEPARTMENTS Pays $50-200.

TIPS "Query with specific new story ideas rather than previously published material."

$ BACKHOME

Wordsworth Communications, Inc., P.O. Box 70, Hendersonville NC 28793. (828)696-3838. **Fax:** (828)696-0700. **E-mail:** backhome2622@att.net. **Website:** www.backhomemagazine.com. **80% freelance written.** Bimonthly magazine. "*BackHome* encourages readers to take more control over their lives by doing more for themselves: productive organic gardening; building and repairing their homes; utilizing renewable energy systems; raising crops and livestock; building furniture; toys and games and other projects; creative cooking. *BackHome* promotes respect for family activities, community programs, and the environment." Estab. 1990. Circ. 42,000. Byline given. Pays on publication. Offers $25 kill fee at publisher's discretion. Publishes ms an average of 1 year after acceptance. Editorial lead time 3 months. Submit seasonal material 6 months in advance. Accepts queries by mail, e-mail, fax, phone. Responds in 6 weeks to queries. Responds in 2 months to mss. Sample copy $5 or online. Guidelines online.

💬 The editor reports an interest in seeing more renewable energy experiences, *good* small houses, workshop projects (for handy persons, not experts), and community action others can copy.

NONFICTION Needs how-to, gardening, construction, energy, homebusiness, interview, personal experience, technical, self-sufficiency. No essays or old-timey reminiscences. **Buys 80 mss/year.** Query. Length: 750-5,000 words. **Pays $35 (approximately)/printed page.**

REPRINTS Send photocopy and information about when and where the material previously appeared. Pays $35/printed page.

PHOTOS Send photos. Identification of subjects required. Reviews color prints, 35mm slides, JPEG photo attachments of 300 dpi. Offers additional payment for photos published.

TIPS "Very specific in relating personal experiences in the areas of gardening, energy and homebuilding how-to. Third-person approaches to others' experiences are also acceptable but somewhat less desirable. Clear color photo prints, especially those in which people are prominent, help immensely when deciding upon what is accepted."

$ $ $ $ BETTER HOMES AND GARDENS

1716 Locust St., Des Moines IA 50309-3023. (515)284-3044. **Fax:** (515)284-3763. **Website:** www.bhg.com. Brenda Lesch, creative director. **Contact:** Gayle Goodson Butler, editor-in-chief. **10-15% freelance written.** Magazine providing home service information for people who have a serious interest in their homes. Reads all freelance articles, but prefers to see a query letter rather than a finished ms. Estab. 1922. Circ. 7,605,000. Pays on acceptance.

NONFICTION Needs travel, education, gardening, health, cars, home, entertainment. Does not deal with political subjects or with areas not connected with the home, community, and family. No poetry or fiction. **Pay rates vary.**

TIPS "Most stories published by this magazine go through a lengthy process of development involving both editor and writer. Some editors will consider only query letters, not unsolicited mss. Direct queries to the department that best suits your storyline."

$ $ BIRDS & BLOOMS

Reiman Media Group, 5400 S. 60th St., Greendale WI 53129-1404. (414)423-0100. **E-mail:** editors@birdsandblooms.com. **Website:** www.birdsandblooms. com. **15% freelance written.** Bimonthly magazine focusing on "the beauty in your own backyard.". *Birds & Blooms* is a sharing magazine that lets backyard enthusiasts chat with each other by exchanging personal experiences. This makes *Birds & Blooms* more like a conversation than a magazine, as readers share tips and tricks on producing beautiful blooms and attracting feathered friends to their backyards. Estab. 1995. Circ. 1,900,000. Byline given. Pays on publication. Publishes ms an average of 7 months after acceptance. Editorial lead time 2 months. Submit seasonal material 4 months in advance. Accepts queries by mail, online submission form. Accepts simultaneous submissions. Responds in 2 months to queries and mss. Sample copy for $2, 9x12 SAE and $1.95 postage. Guidelines online.

NONFICTION Needs essays, how-to, humor, inspirational, personal experience, photo feature, natural crafting and plan items for building backyard accents. No bird rescue or captive bird pieces. **Buys 12-20 mss/ year.** Send complete ms, along with full name, daytime phone number, e-mail address and mailing address. If submitting for a particular column, note that as well. Each reader contributor whose story, photo, or short item is published receives a *Birds & Blooms* tote bag. See guidelines online. Length: 250-1,000 words. **Pays $100-400.**

PHOTOS Send photos. Identification of subjects required. Reviews transparencies, prints.

COLUMNS/DEPARTMENTS Bird Tales (birding experiences); Front Porch (gardening and birding tips and tricks, reader-created gardening, birding DIYs, etc.); From Your Backyard (more casual writing). **Buys 12-20 mss/year.** Send complete ms. **Pays $50-75.**

FILLERS Needs anecdotes, facts, gags. **Buys 25 mss/ year.** Length: 10-250 words. **Pays $10-75.**

TIPS "Focus on conversational writing, like you're chatting with a neighbor over your fence. Mss full of tips and ideas that people can use in backyards across the country have the best chance of being used. Photos that illustrate these points also increase chances of being used."

CANADIAN HOMES & COTTAGES

The In-Home Show, Ltd., 2650 Meadowvale Blvd., Unit 4, Mississauga ON L5N 6M5 Canada. (905)567-1440. **Fax:** (905)567-1442. **E-mail:** jnaisby@homesandcottages.com; editorial@homesandcottages.

com. **Website:** www.homesandcottages.com. **Contact:** Janice E. Naisby, editor-in-chief. **75% freelance written.** Magazine published 6 times/year covering home building and renovating in Canada. "*Homes & Cottages* is Canada's largest home improvement magazine. Publishes articles that have a technical slant, as well as those with a more general lifestyle feel." Estab. 1987. Circ. 92,340. Byline given. Pays on acceptance. Offers 10% kill fee. Publishes ms an average of 6 months after acceptance. Editorial lead time 3 months. Submit seasonal material 6 months in advance. Accepts queries by mail. Sample copy for SAE. Guidelines for #10 SASE.

NONFICTION Needs humor, building and renovation related, new product, technical. **Buys 32 mss/ year.** Query. Length: 800-1,500 words. **Pays $3500-650.** Sometimes pays expenses of writers on assignment.

PHOTOS Bimonthly. Canada's largest building, renovation and home improvement magazine. Send photos. Captions, identification of subjects required. Reviews transparencies, prints. Negotiates payment individually. Pays on acceptance. Credit line given.

TIPS "Read our magazine before sending in a query. Remember that you are writing to a Canadian audience."

COUNTRY LIVING

The Hearst Corp., 300 W. 57th St., New York NY 10019. (212)649-3501. **E-mail:** countryliving@hearst. com. **Website:** www.countryliving.com. **Contact:** Sarah Gray Miller, editor-in-chief; Shelly Ridenour, managing editor. Monthly magazine covering home design and interior decorating with an emphasis on country style. A lifestyle magazine for readers who appreciate the warmth and traditions associated with American home and family life. Each monthly issue embraces American country decorating and includes features on furniture, antiques, gardening, home building, real estate, cooking, entertaining and travel. Estab. 1978. Circ. 1,600,000.

NONFICTION Buys 20-30 mss/year. Query to see if market is currently accepting submissions. Then, send complete ms and SASE. **Payment varies.**

COLUMNS/DEPARTMENTS Query first.

TIPS "Know the magazine, know the market, and know how to write a good story that will interest *our* readers."

THE FAMILY HANDYMAN

Reader's Digest Association, 2915 Commers Dr., #700, Eagan MN 55121. **E-mail:** editors@thefamilyhandyman.com. **Website:** www.familyhandyman.com. *The Family Handyman* is an American home-improvement magazine. Estab. 1951. Circ. 1.1 million. Byline given. Pays on acceptance. Accepts queries by online submission form.

NONFICTION Submit to *Family Handyman* via online submission form. Accepts mss for home projects that writers want to share. **Pays $100/ms.**

COLUMNS/DEPARTMENTS Accepts mss for Handy Hint, Great Goof, and Shop Tips. Accepts submissions online. **Pays $100/ms.**

HGTV MAGAZINE

Hearst Corporation, 300 W. 57th St., New York NY 10019-5915. **Website:** hgtvmagonline.com. **Contact:** Sarah Peterson, editor-in-chief. *HGTV Magazine* is a fresh, new home lifestyle magazine that gives readers inspiring, real-life solutions for all the things that homeowners deal with every day in an upbeat and engaging way. The magazine offers value of insider advice from trusted experts, as well as the enjoyment of taking a look inside real people's homes.

○ Query before submitting. Difficult market to break into.

⊙ HOME DESIGN

Universal Magazines, Ltd., Unit 5, 6-8 Byfield St., North Ryde NSW 2113 Australia. (61)(2)9887-0399. **Fax:** (61)(2)9805-0714. **E-mail:** kstjames@universalmagazines.com.au. **Website:** www.luxuryhome.com.au. Bi-monthly magazine dedicated to providing readers with a comprehensive overview of design directions in the upper end of the residential market.

NONFICTION Needs general interest, how-to, new product, photo feature. Query.

⊙⊙⊙⊙ HORTICULTURE

F+W Media, Inc., 10151 Carver Rd., Suite #200, Blue Ash OH 45242. (513)531-2690. **Fax:** (513)891-7153. **E-mail:** edit@hortmag.com. **Website:** www.hortmag.com. Bimonthly magazine. *Horticulture*, the country's oldest gardening magazine, is designed for active home gardeners. Our goal is to offer a blend of text, photographs and illustrations that will both instruct and inspire readers. Circ. 160,000. Byline given. Offers kill fee. Submit seasonal material 10 months in advance. Accepts queries by mail, e-mail, fax. Responds in 3 months to queries. Guidelines for SASE or by e-mail.

NONFICTION **Buys 70 mss/year.** Query with published clips, subject background material and SASE. Length: 800-1,000 words. **Pays $500.**

COLUMNS/DEPARTMENTS Length: 200-600 words. Query with published clips, subject background material and SASE. Include disk where possible. **Pays $250.**

TIPS "We believe every article must offer ideas or illustrate principles that our readers might apply on their own gardens. Our readers want to become better, more creative gardeners."

⊙⊙⊙⊙ HOUSE BEAUTIFUL

The Hearst Corp., 300 W. 57th St., 27th Floor, New York NY 10019. (212)903-5000. **E-mail:** readerservices@housebeautiful.com. **Website:** www.housebeautiful.com. **Contact:** Jeffrey Bauman, executive managing editor. Monthly magazine covering home decoration and design. Targeted toward affluent, educated readers ages 30-40. Covers home design and decoration, gardening and entertaining, interior design, architecture, and travel. Circ. 865,352. Editorial lead time 3 months.

○ Query before submitting.

LOG HOME LIVING

Home Buyer Publications, Inc., 4125 Lafayette Center Dr., Suite 100, Chantilly VA 20151. (703)222-9411; (800)826-3893. **Fax:** (703)222-3209. **E-mail:** editor@timberhomeliving.com. **Website:** www.loghomeliving.com. **90% freelance written.** Monthly magazine for enthusiasts who are dreaming of, planning for, or actively building a log home. Estab. 1989. Circ. 132,000. Byline given. Pays on acceptance. Offers $100 kill fee. Publishes ms an average of 6 months after acceptance. Editorial lead time 6 months. Submit seasonal material 6 months in advance. Accepts queries by mail, e-mail. Responds in 6 weeks to queries. Sample copy for $4. Guidelines online.

○ Also publishes *Timber Home Living, Log Home Design Ideas* and *Building Systems*.

NONFICTION Needs how-to (build or maintain log home), interview of log home owners, personal experience, photo feature (log homes), technical, design/decor topics, travel. **Buys 60 mss/year.** Query with SASE. Length: 1,000-2,000 words. **Payment depends on length, nature of the work, and writer's expertise.** Pays expenses of writers on assignment.

REPRINTS Send tearsheet, photocopy or typed ms and information about when and where the material previously appeared.

PHOTOS State availability. Reviews contact sheets, 4x5 transparencies, 4x6 prints. Negotiates payment individually.

TIPS "*Log Home Living* is devoted almost exclusively to modern manufactured and handcrafted kit log homes. Our interest in historical or nostalgic stories of very old log cabins, reconstructed log homes, or one-of-a-kind owner-built homes is secondary and should be queried first."

$$ MOUNTAIN LIVING

Network Communications, Inc., 1780 S. Bellaire St., Suite 505, Denver CO 80222. (303)248-2060. **Fax:** (303)248-2066. **E-mail:** hscott@mountainliving.com; cdeorio@mountainliving.com. **Website:** www.mountainliving.com. **Contact:** Holly Scott, publisher; Christine DeOrio, editor-in-chief. **50% freelance written.** Magazine published 10 times/year covering architecture, interior design, and lifestyle issues for people who live in, visit, or hope to live in the mountains. Estab. 1994. Circ. 48,000. Byline given. Pays on acceptance. Offers 15% kill fee. Publishes ms an average of 4 months after acceptance. Editorial lead time 6 months. Submit seasonal material 8-12 months in advance. Accepts queries by mail, e-mail. Responds in 6 weeks to queries. Responds in 2 months to mss. Sample copy for $7. Guidelines by e-mail.

NONFICTION Needs photo feature, travel, home features. **Buys 30 mss/year.** Query with published clips. Length: 500-1,000 words. **Pays $250-600.** Sometimes pays expenses of writers on assignment.

PHOTOS Provide photos (slides, transparencies, or on disk, saved as TIFF and at least 300 dpi). State availability. All features photography is assigned to photographers who specialize in interior photography. Negotiates payment individually.

COLUMNS/DEPARTMENTS ML Recommends; Short Travel Tips; New Product Information; Art; Insider's Guide; Entertaining. Length: 300-800 words. **Buys 35 mss/year.** Query with published clips. **Pays $50-500.**

TIPS "A deep understanding of and respect for the mountain environment is essential. Think out of the box. We love to be surprised. Write a brilliant, short query, and always send clips. Before you query, please read the magazine to get a sense of who we are and what we like."

$$ ROMANTIC HOMES

Y-Visionary Publishing, 22840 Savi Ranch Parkway, Suite 200, Yorba Linda CA 92887. **E-mail:** jdemontravel@beckett.com. **Website:** www.romantichomes.com. **Contact:** Jacqueline DeMontravel, editor. **70% freelance written.** Monthly magazine covering home decor. *Romantic Homes* is the magazine for women who want to create a warm, intimate, and casually elegant home—a haven that is both a gathering place for family and friends and a private refuge from the pressures of the outside world. The *Romantic Homes* reader is personally involved in the decor of her home. Features offer unique ideas and how-to advice on decorating, home furnishings, and gardening. Departments focus on floor and wall coverings, paint, textiles, refinishing, architectural elements, artwork, travel, and entertaining. Every article responds to the reader's need to create a beautiful, attainable environment, providing her with the style ideas and resources to achieve her own romantic home. Estab. 1994. Circ. 200,000. Byline given. Pays 30-60 days upon receipt of invoice. Publishes ms an average of 4 months after acceptance. Editorial lead time 5 months. Submit seasonal material 6 months in advance. Accepts queries by mail, fax. Accepts simultaneous submissions. Responds in 2 weeks to queries. Responds in 2 months to mss. Guidelines for #10 SASE.

NONFICTION Needs essays, how-to, new product, personal experience, travel. **Buys 150 mss/year.** Query with published clips. Length: 1,000-1,200 words. **Pays $500.**

PHOTOS State availability of or send photos. Captions, identification of subjects, model releases required. Reviews transparencies.

COLUMNS/DEPARTMENTS Departments cover antiques, collectibles, artwork, shopping, travel, refinishing, architectural elements, flower arranging, entertaining, and decorating. Length: 400-600 words. **Pays $250.**

TIPS Submit great ideas with photos.

MARTHA STEWART LIVING

Omnimedia, 601 W. 26th St., New York NY 10001. (212)827-8000. **Fax:** (212)827-8204. **Website:** livingblog.marthastewart.com; www.marthastewart.com. Monthly magazine for gardening, entertaining, renovating, cooking, collecting, and creating. Magazine, featuring Martha Stewart, that focuses on the domestic arts. Estab. 1990. Circ. 2 million.

◒ Query before submitting. Difficult market to break into.

🟢🟢 TEXAS GARDENER

Suntex Communications, Inc., P.O. Box 9005, 10566 North River Crossing, Waco TX 76714. (254)848-9393. **Fax:** (254)848-9779. **E-mail:** info@texasgardener.com. **Website:** www.texasgardener.com. **80% freelance written. Works with a small number of new/unpublished writers each year.** Bimonthly magazine covering vegetable and fruit production, ornamentals, and home landscape information for home gardeners in Texas. Estab. 1981. Circ. 20,000. Byline given. Pays on publication. Publishes ms an average of 4 months after acceptance. Submit seasonal material 6 months in advance. Accepts queries by mail, e-mail, fax. Responds in 2 months to queries. Sample copy for $4.25 and SAE with 5 first-class stamps. Writers' guidelines online at website.

NONFICTION Needs how-to, humor, interview, photo feature. **Buys 50-60 mss/year.** Query with published clips. Length: 800-2,400 words. **Pays $50-200.**

PHOTOS "We prefer superb color and b&w photos; 90% of photos used are color. Send low resolution jpgs files for review to info@texasgardener.com. High resolution jpg files are required for publication if photos are accepted.". Send photos. Identification of subjects, model releases required. Reviews contact sheets, 2 1/4x2 1/4 or 35mm color transparencies, 8x10 b&w prints. Pays negotiable rates.

COLUMNS/DEPARTMENTS Between Neighbors. **Pays $25.**

TIPS First, be a Texan. Then come up with a good idea of interest to home gardeners in this state. Be specific. Stick to feature topics like 'How Alley Gardening Became a Texas Tradition.' Leave topics like 'How to Control Fire Blight' to the experts. High quality photos could make the difference. We would like to add several writers to our group of regular contributors and would make assignments on a regular basis. Fillers are easy to come up with in-house. We want good writers who can produce accurate and interesting copy. Frequent mistakes made by writers in completing an article assignment for us are that articles are not slanted toward Texas gardening, show inaccurate or too little gardening information, or lack good writing style.

🟢🟢🟢🟢 THIS OLD HOUSE

Time Inc., 135 W. 50th St., 10th Floor, New York NY 10020. (212)522-9465. **Fax:** (212)522-9435. **E-mail:** toh_letters@thisoldhouse.com. **Website:** www.thisoldhouse.com. **40% freelance written.** Magazine published 10 times/year covering home design, renovation, and maintenance. *This Old House* is the ultimate resource for readers whose homes are their passions. The magazine's mission is threefold: to inform with lively service journalism and reporting on innovative new products and materials, to inspire with beautiful examples of fine craftsmanship and elegant architectural design, and to instruct with clear step-by-step projects that will enhance a home or help a homeowner maintain one. The voice of the magazine is not that of a rarefied design maven or a linear Mr. Fix It, but rather that of an e-wide-open, in-the-trenches homeowner who's eager for advice, tools, and techniques that'll help him realize his dream of a home. Estab. 1995. Circ. 960,000. Byline given. Pays on acceptance. Publishes ms an average of 3-6 months after acceptance. Editorial lead time 3-12 months. Submit seasonal material 1 year in advance. Accepts queries by mail, e-mail.

NONFICTION Needs essays, how-to, new product, technical; must be house-related. **Buys 70 mss/year.** Query with published clips. Length: 250-2,500 words. **Pays $1/word.** Sometimes pays expenses of writers on assignment.

COLUMNS/DEPARTMENTS Around the House (news, new products), 250 words. **Pays $1/word.**

TRADITIONAL HOME

Meredith Corp., 1716 Locust St., Des Moines 50309-3023. (515)284-3762. **Fax:** (515)284-2083. **E-mail:** traditionalhome@meredith.com. **Website:** www.traditionalhome.com. Magazine published 8 times/year. Features articles on building, renovating, and decorating homes in the traditional style. From home, garden, and green living to fashion, beauty, entertaining, and travel, *Traditional Home* is a celebration of quality, craftsmanship, authenticity, and family. Estab. 1989. Circ. 950,000. Editorial lead time 6 months.

◒ Query before submitting.

HUMOR

🟢 FUNNY TIMES

Funny Times, Inc., P.O. Box 18530, Cleveland Heights OH 44118. (216)371-8600. **Fax:** (216)371-8696. **E-**

mail: info@funnytimes.com. **Website:** www.funnytimes.com. **Contact:** Ray Lesser and Susan Wolpert, editors. **50% freelance written.** Monthly tabloid for humor. "*Funny Times* is a monthly review of America's funniest cartoonists and writers. We are the *Reader's Digest* of modern American humor with a progressive/peace-oriented/environmental/politically activist slant." Estab. 1985. Circ. 70,000. Byline given. Pays on publication. Publishes ms an average of 3 months after acceptance. Editorial lead time 2 months. Accepts simultaneous submissions. Responds in 3 months to mss. Sample copy for $3 or 9x12 SAE with 3 first-class stamps ($1.14 postage). Guidelines online.

NONFICTION Needs essays, funny, humor, interview, opinion, humorous, personal experience, absolutely funny. **Buys 60 mss/year.** Send complete ms. Length: 500-700 words. **Pays $60 minimum.**

COLUMNS/DEPARTMENTS Query with published clips.

FICTION Wants anything funny. Needs humorous. **Buys 6 mss/year.** Query with published clips. Length: 500-700 words. **Pays $50-150.**

TIPS "Send us a small packet (1-3 items) of only your very funniest stuff. If this makes us laugh, we'll be glad to ask for more. We particularly welcome previously published material that has been well received elsewhere."

INFLIGHT

$$$ GO

INK Publishing, 68 Jay St., Suite 315, Brooklyn NY 11201. (347)294-1220. **Fax:** (917)591-6247. **E-mail:** editorial@airtranmagazine.com. **Website:** www.airtranmagazine.com. **Contact:** Orion Ray-Jones, editor-in-chief; Jaime Lowe, executive editor; Sophie-Claire Hoeller, assistant editor. **80% freelance written.** Monthly magazine covering travel. "*Go* is an inflight magazine covering travel, general interest and light business." Estab. 2003. Circ. 100,000. Byline given. net 45 days upon receipt of invoice. Offers 50% kill fee. Publishes ms an average of 3 months after acceptance. Editorial lead time 4 months. Submit seasonal material 5 months in advance. Accepts queries by e-mail.

[O] Does not accept unsolicited mss.

NONFICTION Needs general interest, interview, photo feature, travel, light business. Does not want first-person travelogues. **Buys 200 mss/year.** Query with published clips. Length: 400-2,000 words. **Pay is negotiable.**

PHOTOS State availability. Reviews GIF/JPEG files. Offers no additional payment for photos accepted with ms.

TIPS "Review past issues online and study the guidelines to get a true sense of the types of features we are looking for."

$$$ HEMISPHERES

Ink Publishing, 68 Jay St., Brooklyn NY 11201. (347)294-1220. **Fax:** (917)591-6247. **E-mail:** editorial@hemispheresmagazine.com. **Website:** www.hemispheresmagazine.com. **Contact:** Joe Keohane, editor-in-chief. **95% freelance written.** Monthly magazine for the educated, business, and recreational frequent traveler on an airline that spans the globe. "*Hemispheres* is an inflight magazine that interprets 'inflight' to be a mode of delivery rather than an editorial genre. *Hemispheres'* task is to engage, intrigue and entertain its primary readers—an international, culturally diverse group of affluent, educated professionals and executives who frequently travel for business and pleasure on United Airlines. The magazine offers a global perspective and a focus on topics that cross borders as often as the people reading the magazine. Emphasizes ideas, concepts, and culture rather than products, presented in a fresh, artful, and sophisticated graphic environment." Estab. 1992. Circ. 12.3 million. Byline given. Pays on acceptance. Offers 20% kill fee. Publishes ms an average of 4-6 months after acceptance. Editorial lead time 8 months. Submit seasonal material 8 months in advance. Accepts queries by mail. Responds in 2 months to queries. Responds in 4 months to mss. Sample copy for $7.50. Guidelines online.

NONFICTION Needs general interest, humor, personal experience. No "in this country" phraseology. "Too American" is a frequent complaint for queries. Query with published clips. Length: 500-3,000 words. **Pays 50¢/word and up.**

PHOTOS Reviews photos only when we request them. State availability. Captions, identification of subjects, model releases required. Negotiates payment individually.

FICTION Needs adventure, ethnic, historical, humorous, mainstream, mystery, explorations of those issues common to all people but within the context of a particular culture. **Buys 14 mss/year.** Send complete ms. Length: 1,000-4,000 words. **Pays 50¢/word and up.**

JUVENILE

$ BABYBUG

70 East Lake St., Suite 800, Chicago IL 60601. **E-mail:** babybug@babybugmagkids.com. **Website:** www.cricketmag.com/babybug; www.babybugmagkids.com. **Contact:** Submissions editor. **50% freelance written.** *Babybug* is a look-and-listen magazine for babies and toddlers ages 6 months-3 years. Publishes 9 issues per year. Estab. 1994. Circ. 45,000. Byline given. Accepts simultaneous submissions. Responds in 6 months to mss. Guidelines online.

NONFICTION Needs very short clear fiction. **Buys 10-20 mss/year.** submittable.cricketmag.com; www.cricketmag.com/submissions Six sentence maximum **Pays up to 25¢ per word. Payment after publication. Rights vary.**

PHOTOS Pays $500/spread; $250/page.

FICTION Very short, clear fiction. Needs rhythmic, rhyming. **Buys 10-20 mss/year.** Length: 6 sentences maximum. **Up to 25¢/word. Payment after publication. Rights vary.**

POETRY "We are especially interested in rhythmic and rhyming poetry. Poems may explore a baby's day or they may be more whimsical." **Pays up to $3/line; $25 minimum. Payment after publication. Rights vary.**

TIPS "Imagine having to read your story or poem—out loud—50 times or more! That's what parents will have to do. Babies and toddlers demand, 'Read it again!' Your material must hold up under repetition. And humor is much appreciated by all."

$$$$ BOYS' LIFE

Boy Scouts of America, P.O. Box 152079, 1325 West Walnut Hill Lane, Irving TX 75015. (972)580-2366. **Fax:** (972)580-2079. **Website:** www.boyslife.org. **Contact:** J.D. Owen, editor-in-chief; Michael Goldman, managing editor; Paula Murphey, senior editor. **75% freelance written. Prefers to work with published/established writers; works with small number of new/unpublished writers each year.** *Boys' Life* is a monthly 4-color general interest magazine for boys 7-18, most of whom are Cub Scouts, Boy Scouts or Venturers. Estab. 1911. Circ. 1.1 million. Byline given. Pays on acceptance. Publishes approximately one year after acceptance. Accepts queries by mail. Responds to queries/mss in 2 months. Sample copies for $3.95 plus 9x12 SASE. Guidelines online.

NONFICTION Contact: Send article queries to the attention of the senior editor; column queries to the attention of the associate editor. Needs Scouting activities and general interests (nature, Earth, health, cars, sports, science, computers, space and aviation, entertainment, history, music, animals, how-to's, etc.). **Buys 60 mss/year.** Query with SASE. No phone queries. Averge word length for articles: 500-1,500 words, including sidebars and boxes. Average word length for columns: 300-750. **Pay ranges from $400-1,500.** Pays expenses of writers on assignment.

PHOTOS Photo guidelines free with SASE. Boy Scouts of America Magazine Division also publishes *Scouting* magazine. "Most photographs are from specific assignments that freelance photojournalists shoot for *Boys' Life*. Interested in all photographers, but do not send unsolicited images.". Pays $500 base editorial day rate against placement fees, plus expenses. **Pays on acceptance.** Buys one-time rights.

FICTION Needs All fiction is assigned.

TIPS "We strongly recommend reading at least 12 issues of the magazine before submitting queries. We are a good market for any writer willing to do the necessary homework. Write for a boy you know who is 12. Our readers demand punchy writing in relatively short, straightforward sentences. The editors demand well-reported articles that demonstrate high standards of journalism. We follow the *Associated Press* manual of style and usage. Learn and read our publications before submitting anything."

BOYS' QUEST

P.O. Box 227, Bluffton OH 45817-0227. (419)358-4610, ext. 101. **Fax:** (419)358-8020. **Website:** www.funforkidzmagazines.com. **Contact:** Marilyn Edwards, editor. Bimonthly magazine. "*Boys' Quest* is a magazine created for boys from 5 to 14 years, with youngsters 8, 9 and 10 the specific target age. Our point of view is that every young boy deserves the right to be a young boy for a number of years before he becomes a young adult." Estab. 1995. Circ. 10,000. Byline given. Pays on publication. Accepts queries by mail. Responds to queries in 2 weeks; mss in 2 weeks (if rejected); 6 weeks (if scheduled). Guidelines and open themes available for SASE, or visit www.funforkidz.com and click on 'Writers' at the bottom of the homepage.

NONFICTION Needs Needs nonfiction pieces that are accompanied by clear photos. Articles accompanied by photos with high resolution are far more likely to be accepted than those that need illustrations. Query or send complete ms (preferred). Send SASE with correct postage. No faxed or e-mailed material. Length: 500 words.

PHOTOS "We use a number of photos, printed in b&w, inside the magazine. These photos support the articles.". $5/photo.

FICTION Picture-oriented material, young readers, middle readers: adventure, animal, history, humorous, multicultural, nature/environment, problem-solving, sports. Does not want to see violence, teenage themes. Buys 30 mss/year. Query or send complete ms (preferred). Send SASE with correct postage. No faxed or e-mailed material. Length: 200-500 words.

POETRY Reviews poetry. Limit submissions to 6 poems. Length: 21 lines maximum.

TIPS "First be familiar with our magazines. We are looking for lively writing, most of it from a young boy's point of view—with the boy or boys directly involved in an activity that is both wholesome and unusual. We need nonfiction with photos and fiction stories—around 500 words—puzzles, poems, cooking, carpentry projects, jokes and riddles. Nonfiction pieces that are accompanied by b&w photos are far more likely to be accepted than those that need illustrations. We will entertain simultaneous submissions as long as that fact is noted on the ms."

CADET QUEST MAGAZINE

1333 Alger St. SE, Grand Rapids MI 49507. (616)241-5616. **Fax:** (616)241-5558. **E-mail:** submissions@calvinistcadets.org. **Website:** www.calvinistcadets.org. **Contact:** G. Richard Broene, editor. **40% freelance written. Works with a small number of new/unpublished writers each year.** Magazine published 7 times/year. *Cadet Quest Magazine* shows boys 9-14 how God is at work in their lives and in the world around them. Estab. 1958. Circ. 6,000. Byline given. Pays on acceptance. Publishes ms an average of 4-11 months after acceptance. Accepts simultaneous submissions. Responds in 2 months to mss. Sample copy for 9x12 SASE. Guidelines for #10 SASE.

Accepts submissions by mail or by e-mail (must include ms in text of e-mail). Will not open attachments.

NONFICTION Needs how-to, humor, inspirational, interview, personal experience, informational. Special issues: Write for new-themes list in January. **Buys 6-12 mss/year.** Send complete ms. Length: 500-1,500 words. **Pays 4-6¢/word.**

REPRINTS Send typed ms with rights for sale noted. Payment varies.

PHOTOS Pays $20-30 for photos purchased with ms.

COLUMNS/DEPARTMENTS Freelance column: Project Page (uses simple projects boys 9-14 can do on their own, made with easily accessible materials; must provide clear, accurate instructions).

FICTION Middle readers, boys/early teens: adventure, arts/craft, games/puzzles, hobbies, humorous, multicultural, religious, science, sports. Fast-moving stories that appeal to a boy's sense of adventure or sense of humor are welcome. Needs adventure, religious, spiritual, sports. Avoid preachiness. Avoid simplistic answers to complicated problems. Avoid long dialogue and little action. No fantasy, science fiction, fashion, horror, or erotica. **Buys 14 mss/year.** Send complete ms. Length: 900-1,500 words. **Pays 4-6¢/word, and 1 contributor's copy.**

TIPS "Best time to submit stories/articles is early in the year (January-April). Also remember readers are boys ages 9-14. Stories must reflect or add to the theme of the issue and be from a Christian perspective."

CALLIOPE

30 Grove St., Suite C, Peterborough NH 03458-1454. (603)924-7209. **Fax:** (603)924-7380. **E-mail:** customerservice@caruspub.com. **Website:** www.cobblestonepub.com. **Contact:** Rosalie Baker and Charles Baker, co-editors; Lou Waryncia, editorial director; Ann Dillon, art director. **50% freelance written.** Magazine published 9 times/year covering world history (East and West) through 1800 AD for 8 to 14-year-old kids. Articles must relate to the issue's theme. Lively, original approaches to the subject are the primary concerns of the editors in choosing material. Estab. 1990. Circ. 13,000. Byline given. Pays on publication. Kill fee. Accepts queries by mail. If interested, responds 5 months before publication date. Sample copy for $5.95, $2 shipping and handling, and 10x13 SASE. Guidelines online.

NONFICTION Needs essays, general interest, historical, how-to, crafts/woodworking, humor, interview, personal experience, photo feature, technical, travel, recipes. No religious, pornographic, biased, or sophisticated submissions. **Buys 30-40 mss/year.** Query with writing sample, 1-page outline, bibliography, SASE. Length: 400-1000 words/feature articles; 300-600 words/supplemental nonfiction. **Pays 20-25¢/word.**

PHOTOS If you have photographs pertaining to any upcoming theme, please contact the editor by mail or fax, or send them with your query. You may also send images on speculation. Model/property release preferred. Reviews b&w prints, color slides. Reviews photos with or without accompanying ms. We buy one-time use. Our suggested fee range for professional quality photographs follows: ¼ page to full page b/w $15-100; color $25-100. Please note that fees for non-professional quality photographs are negotiated. Cover fees are set on an individual basis for one-time use, plus promotional use. All cover images are color. Prices set by museums, societies, stock photography houses, etc., are paid or negotiated. Photographs that are promotional in nature (e.g., from tourist agencies, organizations, special events, etc.) are usually submitted at no charge. Pays on publication. Credit line given. Buys one-time rights; negotiable.

FICTION Middle readers and young adults: adventure, folktales, plays, history, biographical fiction. Material must relate to forthcoming themes. Needs adventure, historical, biographical, retold legends. **Buys 10 mss/year.** Length: no more than 1,000 words. **Pays 20-25¢/word.**

FILLERS Crossword and other word puzzles (no word finds), mazes, and picture puzzles that use the vocabulary of the issue's theme or otherwise relate to the theme. **Pays on an individual basis.**

TIPS "A query must consist of the following to be considered: a brief cover letter stating subject and word length of the proposed article; a detailed one-page outline explaining the information to be presented in the article; a bibliography of materials the author intends to use in preparing the article; a SASE. Writers new to *Calliope* should send a writing sample with query. In all correspondence, please include your complete address as well as a telephone number where you can be reached. A writer may send as many queries for one issue as he or she wishes, but each query must have a separate cover letter, outline and bibliography as well as a SASE. Telephone and e-mail queries are not accepted. Handwritten queries will not be considered. Queries may be submitted at

any time, but queries sent well in advance of deadline may not be answered for several months."

⑨⑨ COBBLESTONE

Carus Publishing, 30 Grove St., Suite C, Peterborough NH 03458. (800)821-0115. **Fax:** (603)924-7380. **E-mail:** customerservice@caruspub.com. **Website:** www.cobblestonepub.com. **50% freelance written.** Covers American history for ages 9-14. "We are interested in articles of historical accuracy and lively, original approaches to the subject at hand. Writers are encouraged to study recent *Cobblestone* back issues for content and style. All material must relate to the theme of a specific upcoming issue in order to be considered. To be considered, a query must accompany each individual idea (however, you can mail them all together) and must include the following: a brief cover letter stating the subject and word length of the proposed article, a detailed one-page outline explaining the information to be presented in the article, an extensive bibliography of materials the author intends to use in preparing the article, a SASE. Authors are urged to use primary resources and up-to-date scholarly resources in their bibliography. Writers new to COBBLESTONE® should send a writing sample with the query. If you would like to know if your query has been received, please also include a stamped postcard that requests acknowledgment of receipt. In all correspondence, please include your complete address as well as a telephone number where you can be reached. A writer may send as many queries for one issue as he or she wishes, but each query must have a separate cover letter, outline, bibliography, and SASE. All queries must be typed. Please do not send unsolicited mss—queries only! Prefers to work with published/ established writers. Each issue presents a particular theme, making it exciting as well as informative. Half of all subscriptions are for schools. All material must relate to monthly theme." Circ. 15,000. Byline given. Pays on publication. Offers 50% kill fee. Accepts queries by mail, fax. Accepts simultaneous submissions. Guidelines online or with SASE; sample copy for $6.95, $2 shipping/handling, 10x13 SASE.

NONFICTION Needs historical, humor, interview, personal experience, photo feature, travel, crafts, recipes, activities. No material that editorializes rather than reports. **Buys 45-50 mss/year.** Query with writing sample, 1-page outline, bibliography, SASE. Length: 800 words/feature articles; 300-600 words/

supplemental nonfiction; 700 words maximum/activities. **Pays 20-25¢/word.**

PHOTOS Captions, identification of subjects required, model release. Reviews contact sheets, transparencies, prints. $15-100/b&w. Pays on publication. Credit line given. Buys one-time rights. Our suggested fee range for professional quality photographs follows: ¼ page to full page b/w $15 to $100; color $25 to $100. Please note that fees for non-professional quality photographs are negotiated.

FICTION Needs adventure, historical, biographical, retold legends, folktales, multicultural. **Buys 5 mss/year.** Query. Length: 800 words maximum. **Pays 20-25¢/word.**

POETRY Contact: Meg Chorlian. Needs free verse, light verse, traditional. Serious and light verse considered. Must have clear, objective imagery. Buys 3 poems/year. Length: 100 lines maximum. **Pays on an individual basis. Acquires all rights.**

FILLERS "Crossword and other word puzzles (no word finds), mazes, and picture puzzles that use the vocabulary of the issue's theme or otherwise relate to the theme." **Pays on an individual basis.**

TIPS "Review theme lists and past issues to see what we're looking for."

💲💲 CRICKET

70 E. Lake St., Suite 800, Chicago IL 60601. **E-mail:** cricket@cricketmagkids.com. **Website:** www.cricketmag.com/ckt-cricket-magazine-for-kids-ages-9-14; www.cricketmagkids.com. **Contact:** Submissions editor. Monthly magazine for children ages 9-14. "*Cricket* is a monthly literary magazine for ages 9-14." Publishes 9 issues per year. Estab. 1973. Circ. 73,000. Byline given. Pays on publication. Accepts queries by mail. Responds in 3-6 months to mss. Guidelines online at submittable.cricketmag.com or www.cricketmag.com/submissions.

NONFICTION Needs Biography, history, science, technology, natural history, social science, geography, foreign culture, travel, adventure, sports. Submittable. cricketmag.com; www.cricketmag.com/submissions Length: 1,200-1,800 words. **Pays up to 25¢/word.**

FICTION Needs realistic, contemporary, historic, humor, mysteries, fantasy, science fiction, folk/fairy tales, legend, myth. No didactic, sex, religious, or horror stories. **Buys 75-100 mss/year.** Submit complete ms. Length: 1,200-1,800 words. **Pays up to 25¢/word.**

POETRY Reviews poems. Serious, humorous, nonsense rhymes. Buys 20-30 poems/year. Length: 35 lines maximum. **Pays up to $3/line.**

FILLERS Crossword puzzles, logic puzzles, math puzzles, crafts, recipes, science experiments, games and activities from other countries, plays, music, art.

TIPS Writers: "Read copies of back issues and current issues. Adhere to specified word limits. *Please* do not query." Would currently like to see more fantasy and science fiction. Illustrators: "Send only your best work and be able to reproduce that quality in assignments. Put name and address on *all* samples. Know a publication before you submit."

💲💲 FACES

Cobblestone Publishing, 30 Grove St., Suite C, Peterborough NH 03458. (603)924-7209; (800)821-0115. **Fax:** (603)924-7380. **E-mail:** customerservice@caruspub.com. **Website:** www.cobblestonepub.com. **90-100% freelance written.** "Published 9 times/year, *Faces* covers world culture for ages 9-14. It stands apart from other children's magazines by offering a solid look at one subject and stressing strong editorial content, color photographs throughout, and original illustrations. *Faces* offers an equal balance of feature articles and activities, as well as folktales and legends." Estab. 1984. Circ. 15,000. Byline given. Pays on publication. Offers 50% kill fee. Accepts queries by mail, e-mail. Accepts simultaneous submissions. Sample copy for $6.95, $2 shipping and handling, 10 x 13 SASE. Guidelines with SASE or online.

NONFICTION Needs historical, humor, interview, personal experience, photo feature, travel, recipes, activities, crafts. **Buys 45-50 mss/year.** Query with writing sample, 1-page outline, bibliography, SASE. Length: 800 words/feature articles; 300-600/supplemental nonfiction; 700 words maximum/activities. **Pays 20-25¢/word.**

PHOTOS "Contact the editor by mail or fax, or send photos with your query. You may also send images on speculation.". Captions, identification of subjects, model releases required. Reviews contact sheets, transparencies, prints. Pays $15-100/b&w; $25-100/color; cover fees are negotiated.

FICTION Needs ethnic, historical, retold legends/folktales, original plays. Length: 800 words maximum. **Pays 20-25¢/word.**

POETRY Serious and light verse considered. Must have clear, objective imagery. Length: 100 lines maximum. **Pays on an individual basis.**

FILLERS "Crossword and other word puzzles (no word finds), mazes, and picture puzzles that use the vocabulary of the issue's theme or otherwise relate to the theme." **Pays on an individual basis.**

TIPS "Writers are encouraged to study past issues of the magazine to become familiar with our style and content. Writers with anthropological and/or travel experience are particularly encouraged; *Faces* is about world cultures. All feature articles, recipes and activities are freelance contributions."

🟢🟢 GIRLS' LIFE

Monarch Publishing, 4529 Harford Rd., Baltimore MD 21214. (410)426-9600. **Fax:** (866)793-1531. **E-mail:** writeforGL@girlslife.com. **Website:** www.girlslife.com. **Contact:** Jessica D'Argenio Waller, fashion editor; Chun Kim, art director. Bimonthly magazine covering girls ages 9-15. Estab. 1994. Circ. 363,000. Byline given. Pays on publication. Publishes ms an average of 3 months after acceptance. Editorial lead time 4 months. Submit seasonal material 5 months in advance. Accepts queries by mail, e-mail. Responds in 1 month to queries. Sample copy for $5 or online. Guidelines online.

NONFICTION Needs book excerpts, essays, general interest, how-to, humor, inspirational, interview, new product, travel. Special issues: Special issues: Back to School (August/September); Fall, Halloween (October/November); Holidays, Winter (December/January); Valentine's Day, Crushes (February/March); Spring, Mother's Day (April/May); and Summer, Father's Day (June/July). **Buys 40 mss/year.** Query by mail with published clips. Submit complete mss on spec only. "Features and articles should speak to young women ages 10-15 looking for new ideas about relationships, family, friends, school, etc. with fresh, savvy advice. Front-of-the-book columns and quizzes are a good place to start." Length: 700-2,000 words. **Pays $350/regular column; $500/feature.**

PHOTOS State availability. Captions, identification of subjects, model releases required. Reviews contact sheets, negatives, transparencies. Negotiates payment individually.

COLUMNS/DEPARTMENTS Buys 20 mss/year. Query with published clips. **Pays $150-450.**

FICTION "We accept short fiction. They should be stand-alone stories and are generally 2,500-3,500 words."

TIPS "Send thought-out queries with published writing samples and detailed résumé. Have fresh ideas and a voice that speaks to our audience-not down to them. And check out a copy of the magazine or visit girlslife.com before submitting."

🟢 HIGHLIGHTS FOR CHILDREN

803 Church St., Honesdale PA 18431. (570)253-1080. **Fax:** (570)251-7847. **Website:** www.highlights.com. **Contact:** Christine French Cully, editor-in-chief. **80% freelance written.** Monthly magazine for children up to ages 3-12. "This book of wholesome fun is dedicated to helping children grow in basic skills and knowledge, in creativeness, in ability to think and reason, in sensitivity to others, in high ideals, and worthy ways of living—for children are the world's most important people. We publish stories for beginning and advanced readers. Up to 500 words for beginning readers, up to 800 words for advanced readers." Estab. 1946. Circ. approximately 1.5 million. Pays on acceptance. Accepts queries by mail. Responds in 2 months to queries. Sample copy free. Guidelines online in "Company" area.

NONFICTION "Generally we prefer to see a ms rather than a query. However, we will review queries regarding nonfiction." Length: 800 words maximum. **Pays $25 for craft ideas and puzzles; $25 for fingerplays; $150 and up for articles.**

PHOTOS Reviews electronic files, color 35mm slides, photos.

FICTION Meaningful stories appealing to both girls and boys, up to age 12. Vivid, full of action. Engaging plot, strong characterization, lively language. Prefers stories in which a child protagonist solves a dilemma through his or her own resources. Seeks stories that the child ages 8-12 will eagerly read, and the younger child will like to hear when read aloud (500-800 words). Stories require interesting plots and a number of illustration possiblities. Also need rebuses (picture stories 100 words), stories with urban settings, stories for beginning readers (100-500 words), sports and humorous stories, adventures, holiday stories, and mysteries. We also would like to see more material of 1-page length (300 words), both fiction and factual. Needs adventure, fantasy, historical, humorous, animal, contemporary, folktales, multi-cultural, problem-solving, sports. No sotries glorifying war, crime or violence. Send complete ms. **Pays $100 minimum plus 2 contributor's copies.**

POETRY Lines/poem: 16 maximum ("most poems are shorter"). Considers simultaneous submissions ("please indicate"); no previously published poetry. No e-mail submissions. "Submit typed ms with very brief cover letter." Occasionally comments on submissions "if ms has merit or author seems to have potential for our market." Guidelines available for SASE. Responds "generally within one month." Always sends prepublication galleys. Pays 2 contributor's copies; "money varies." Acquires all rights.

TIPS "Know the magazine's style before submitting. Send for guidelines and sample issue if necessary." Writers: "At *Highlights* we're paying closer attention to acquiring more nonfiction for young readers than we have in the past." Illustrators: "Fresh, imaginative work encouraged. Flexibility in working relationships a plus. Illustrators presenting their work need not confine themselves to just children's illustrations as long as work can translate to our needs. We also use animal illustrations, real and imaginary. We need crafts, puzzles and any activity that will stimulate children mentally and creatively. Know our publication's standards and content by reading sample issues, not just the guidelines. Avoid tired themes, or put a fresh twist on an old theme so that its style is fun and lively. Write what inspires you, not what you think the market needs. We are pleased that many authors of children's literature report that their first published work was in the pages of *Highlights*. It is not our policy to consider fiction on the strength of the reputation of the author. We judge each submission on its own merits. Query with simple letter to establish whether the nonfiction subject is likely to be of interest. Expert reviews and complete bibliography required for nonfiction. A beginning writer should first become familiar with the type of material that *Highlights* publishes. Include special qualifications, if any, of author. Write for the child, not the editor. Write in a voice that children understand and relate to. Speak to today's kids, avoiding didactic, overt messages. Even though our general principles haven't changed over the years, we are contemporary in our approach to issues. Avoid worn themes."

HOPSCOTCH

P.O. Box 164, Bluffton OH 45817. (419)358-4610. **Fax:** (419)358-8020. **E-mail:** customerservice@funforkidz.com ("we do not accept submissions via e-mail"). **Website:** www.hopscotchmagazine.com. **Contact:** Marilyn Edwards, editor. "For girls from ages 5-14, featuring traditional subjects—pets, games, hobbies, nature, science, sports, etc.—with an emphasis on articles that show girls actively involved in unusual and/or worthwhile activities." Estab. 1989. Circ. 14,000. Byline given. Pays on publication. Responds in 2 weeks to queries; 5 weeks to mss.

NONFICTION Needs Picture-oriented material, young readers, middle readers: animal, arts/crafts, biography, cooking, games/puzzles, geography, hobbies, how-to, humorous, math, nature/environment, science. "Need more nonfiction with quality photos about a *Hopscotch*-age girl involved in a worthwhile activity.". Does not want to see pieces dealing with dating, sex, fashion, hard rock music. **Buys 60-70 mss/year.** Query or submit complete ms. Length: 400-700 words.

FICTION Needs picture-oriented material, young readers, middle readers: adventure, animal, history, humorous, nature/environment, sports, suspense/mystery. Does not want to see stories dealing with dating, sex, fashion, hard rock music. **Buys 30 mss/year.** Submit complete ms. Length: 300-700 words.

TIPS "Remember we publish only 6 issues a year, which means our editorial needs are extremely limited. Please look at our guidelines and our magazine. Remember, we use far more nonfiction than fiction. Guidelines and current theme list can be downloaded from our website. If decent photos accompany the piece, it stands an even better chance of being accepted. We believe it is the responsibility of the contributor to come up with photos. Please remember, our readers are 6-12 years—most are 8-10—and your text should reflect that. Many magazines try to entertain first and educate second. We try to do the reverse. Our magazine is more simplistic, like a book to be read from cover to cover. We are looking for wholesome, nondated material."

🏵🏵 JACK AND JILL

U.S. Kids, 1100 Waterway Blvd., Indianapolis IN 46206-0567. (317)634-1100. **E-mail:** editor@saturdayeveningpost.com. **Website:** www.jackandjillmag.org. **50% freelance written.** Bimonthly magazine published for children ages 8-12. Estab. 1938. Circ. 200,000. Byline given. Pays on publication. Publishes ms an average of 8 months after acceptance. Submit seasonal material 8 months in advance. Responds to mss in 3 months. Guidelines online.

○ "Please do not send artwork. We prefer to work with professional illustrators of our own choosing."

NONFICTION Needs Young readers, middle readers: animal, arts, crafts, cooking, games, puzzles, history, hobbies, how-to, humorous, interviews, profile, nature, science, sports. **Buys 8-10 mss/year.** Submit complete ms via postal mail; no e-mail submissions. Queries not accepted. "We are especially interested in features or Q&As with regular kids (or groups of kids) in the *Jack and Jill* age group who are engaged in unusual, challenging, or interesting activities. No celebrity pieces please." Length: 700 words. **Pays 30¢/word.**

FICTION Submit complete ms via postal mail; no e-mail submissions. "The tone of the stories should be fun and engaging. Stories should hook readers right from the get-go and pull them through the story. Humor is very important! Dialogue should be witty instead of just furthering the plot. The story should convey some kind of positive message. Possible themes could include self-reliance, being kind to others, appreciating other cultures, and so on. There are a million positive messages, so get creative! Kids can see preachy coming from a mile away, though, so please focus on telling a good story over teaching a lesson. The message—if there is one—should come organically from the story and not feel tacked on." Needs Young readers and middle readers: adventure, contemporary, folktales, health, history, humorous, nature, sports. **Buys 30-35 mss/year.** Length: 600-800 words. **Pays 30¢/word.**

POETRY Submit via postal mail; no e-mail submissions. Wants light-hearted poetry appropriate for the age group. Mss must be typewritten with poet's contact information in upper right-hand corner of each poem's page. SASE required. **Pays $25-50.**

TIPS "We are constantly looking for new writers who can tell good stories with interesting slants—stories that are not full of outdated and time-worn expressions. We like to see stories about kids who are smart and capable, but not sarcastic or smug. Problem-solving skills, personal responsibility, and integrity are good topics for us. Obtain current issues of the magazine and study them to determine our present needs and editorial style."

⊖⊖ LADYBUG

700 E. Lake St., Suite 800, Chicago IL 60601. **E-mail:** ladybug@ladybugmagkids.com. **Website:** www.cricketmag.com/ladybug; ladybugmagkids.com. **Contact:** Submissions editor. Monthly magazine for children ages 3-6. *LADYBUG Magazine* is an imaginative magazine with art and literature for young children (ages 3-6). Publishes 9 issues per year. Estab. 1990. Circ. 125,000. Byline given. Pays on publication. Responds in 6 months to mss. Guidelines online at submittable.cricketmag.com or www.cricketmag.com/submissions.

NONFICTION Needs gentle nonfiction, action rhymes, finger plays, crafts and activities. **Buys 35 mss/year.** Send complete ms, SASE. Length: 400-700 words. **Pays 25¢/word minimum.**

FICTION Needs imaginative contemporary stories, original retellings of fairy and folk tales, multicultural stories. **Buys 30 mss/year.** Submit complete ms, include SASE. Length: 800 words maximum. **Pays up to 25¢/word.**

POETRY Needs light verse, traditional. Wants poetry that is "rhythmic, rhyming; serious, humorous." Length: 20 lines maximum. **Pays up to $3/line ($25 minimum).**

FILLERS Learning activities, games, crafts, songs, finger games. See back issues for types, formats, and length.

⊖⊖⊖⊘ MUSE

Cricket Magazine Group, 70 E. Lake St., Suite 800, Chicago IL 60601. **E-mail:** muse@musemagkids.com. **Website:** www.cricketmag.com. "The goal of *Muse* is to give as many children as possible access to the most important ideas and concepts underlying the principal areas of human knowledge. Articles should meet the highest possible standards of clarity and transparency aided, wherever possible, by a tone of skepticism, humor, and irreverence." All articles are commissioned. To be considered for assignments, experienced science writers may send a résumé and 3 published clips. Estab. 1996. Circ. 40,000.

○ *Muse is not accepting unsolicited mss or queries.*

NONFICTION Needs Middle readers, young adult: animal, arts, history, math, nature/environment, problem-solving, science, social issues.

⊖ NATURE FRIEND MAGAZINE

4253 Woodcock Lane, Dayton VA 22821. (540)867-0764. **E-mail:** info@naturefriendmagazine.com; editor@naturefriendmagazine.com; photos@naturefriendmagazine.com. **Website:** www.naturefriendmagazine.com. **Contact:** Kevin Shank, editor. **80% freelance written.** Monthly children's magazine covering creation-based nature. "*Nature Friend* includes stories, puzzles, science experiments, nature experiments—all submissions need to honor God as creator." Estab. 1982. Circ. 13,000. Byline given. Pays on publication. Editorial lead time 4 months. Submit seasonal material 6 months in advance. Accepts simultaneous submissions. Responds in 6 months to mss. Sample copy for $5 postage paid. Guidelines online.

💬 Picture-oriented material and conversational material needed.

NONFICTION Needs how-to, nature, photo feature, science experiments (for ages 8-12), articles about interesting/unusual animals. No poetry, evolution, animals depicted in captivity, talking animal stories, or evolutionary material. **Buys 50 mss/year.** Send complete ms. Length: 250-900 words. **Pays 5¢/word.**

PHOTOS Send photos. Captions, identification of subjects required. Reviews prints. Offers $20-75/photo.

COLUMNS/DEPARTMENTS Learning By Doing, 500-900 words. **Buys 12 mss/year.** Send complete ms.

FILLERS Needs facts, puzzles, short essays on something current in nature. **Buys 35 mss/year.** Length: 150-250 words. **5¢/word.**

TIPS "We want to bring joy and knowledge to children by opening the world of God's creation to them. We endeavor to create a sense of awe about nature's Creator and a respect for His creation. We'd like to see more submissions on hands-on things to do with a nature theme (not collecting rocks or leaves—real stuff). Also looking for good stories that are accompanied by good photography."

$$ POCKETS

The Upper Room, P.O. Box 340004, Nashville TN 37203. (615)340-7333. **Fax:** (615)340-7267. **E-mail:** pockets@upperroom.org. **Website:** pockets.upperroom.org. **Contact:** Lynn W. Gilliam, editor. **60% freelance written.** Magazine published 11 times/year. "*Pockets* is a Christian devotional magazine for children ages 8-12. All submissions should address the broad theme of the magazine. Each issue is built around one theme with material which can be used by children in a variety of ways. Scripture stories, fiction, poetry, prayers, art, graphics, puzzles and activities are included. Submissions do not need to be overtly religious. They should help children experience a Christian lifestyle that is not always a neatly-wrapped moral package, but is open to the continuing revelation of God's will. Seasonal material, both secular and liturgical, is desired." Estab. 1981. Byline given. Pays on acceptance. Publishes ms an average of 1 year after acceptance. Submit seasonal material 1 year in advance. Responds in 8 weeks to mss. Each issue reflects a specific theme. Guidelines online.

💬 Does not accept e-mail or fax submissions.

NONFICTION Needs Picture-oriented, young readers, middle readers: cooking, games/puzzles. "*Pockets* seeks biographical sketches of persons, famous or unknown, whose lives reflect their Christian commitment, written in a way that appeals to children." Does not accept how-to articles. "Nonfiction reads like a story." Multicultural needs include: stories that feature children of various racial/ethnic groups and do so in a way that is true to those depicted. **Buys 10 mss/year.** Length: 400-1,000 words. **Pays 14¢/word.**

REPRINTS Accepts one-time previously published submissions. Send ms with rights for sale noted and information about when and where the material previously appeared.

PHOTOS Send 4-6 close-up photos of children actively involved in peacemakers at work activities. Send photos, contact sheets, prints, or digital images. Must be 300 dpi. Pays $25/photo.

COLUMNS/DEPARTMENTS Poetry and Prayer (related to themes), maximum 20 lines; Family Time, 200-300 words; Peacemakers at Work (profiles of children working for peace, justice, and ecological concerns), 400-600 words. **Pays 14¢/word.** Activities/Games (related to themes). **Pays $25 and up.** Kids Cook (simple recipes children can make alone or with minimal help from an adult). **Pays $25.**

POETRY Considers poetry by children. Buys 14 poems/year. Length: 4-20 lines. **Pays $25 minimum.**

TIPS "Theme stories, role models, and retold scripture stories are most open to freelancers. Poetry is also open. It is very helpful if writers read our writers' guidelines and themes on our website."

$ SHINE BRIGHTLY

GEMS Girls' Clubs, 1333 Alger St., SE, Grand Rapids MI 49507. (616)241-5616. **Fax:** (616)241-5558. **E-mail:** shinebrightly@gemsgc.org. **Website:** www.gemsgc.org. **Contact:** Kathryn Miller, executive director;

Kelli Gilmore, managing editor. **80% freelance written. Works with new and published/established writers.** Monthly magazine (with combined June/July, August summer issue). "Our purpose is to lead girls into a living relationship with Jesus Christ and to help them see how God is at work in their lives and the world around them. Puzzles, crafts, stories, and articles for girls ages 9-14." Estab. 1970. Circ. 17,000. Byline given. Pays on publication. Publishes ms an average of 1 year after acceptance. Submit seasonal material 1 year in advance. Accepts simultaneous submissions. Responds in 2 months to mss. Sample copy with 9x12 SASE with 3 first class stamps and $1. Guidelines online.

NONFICTION Needs humor, inspirational, seasonal and holiday, interview, personal experience, photo feature, religious, travel, adventure, mystery. Avoid the testimony approach. **Buys 35 unsolicited mss/year.** Submit complete ms in body of e-mail. No attachments. Length: 100-800 words. **Pays up to $35, plus 2 copies.**

REPRINTS Send typed ms with rights for sale noted and information about when and where the material previously appeared.

PHOTOS Purchased with or without ms. Appreciate multicultural subjects. Reviews 5x7 or 8x10 clear color glossy prints. Pays $25-50 on publication.

COLUMNS/DEPARTMENTS How-to (crafts); puzzles and jokes; quizzes. Length: 200-400 words. Send complete ms. **Pay varies.**

FICTION Does not want "unrealistic stories and those with trite, easy endings. We are interested in mss that show how girls can change the world." Needs adventure experiences girls could have in their hometowns or places they might realistically visit, ethnic, historical, humorous, mystery, religious, omance, slice-of-life vignettes, suspense,. Believable only. Nothing too preachy. **Buys 30 mss/year.** Submit complete ms in body of e-mail. No attachments. Length: 700-900 words. **Pays up to $35, plus 2 copies.**

POETRY Needs free verse, haiku, light verse, traditional. **Limited need for poetry. Pays $5-15.**

TIPS Writers: "Please check our website before submitting. We have a specific style and theme that deals with how girls can impact the world. The stories should be current, deal with pre-adolescent problems and joys, and help girls see God at work in their lives through humor as well as problem-solving." Prefers not to see anything on the adult level, secular material, or violence. Writers frequently oversimplify the articles and often write with a Pollyanna attitude. An author should be able to see his/her writing style as exciting and appealing to girls ages 9-14. The style can be fun, but also teach a truth. Subjects should be current and important to *SHINE brightly* readers. Use our theme update as a guide. We would like to receive material with a multicultural slant."

SPARKLE

GEMS Girls' Clubs, 1333 Alger St. SE, Grand Rapids MI 49507. (616)241-5616. **Fax:** (616)241-5558. **E-mail:** kelli@gemsgc.org. **Website:** www.gemsgc.org. **Contact:** Kelli Gilmore, managing editor; Lisa Hunter, art director/photo editor. **80% freelance written.** Bimonthly magazine for girls ages 6-9. Mission is to prepare young girls to live out their faith and become world-changers. Strives to help girls make a difference in the world. Looks at the application of scripture to everyday life. Also strives to delight the reader and cause the reader to evalute her own life in light of the truth presented. Finally, attempts to teach practical life skills. Estab. 2002. Circ. 9,000. Byline given. Pays on publication. Offers $20 kill fee. Editorial lead time 3 months. Submit seasonal material 1 year in advance. Accepts queries by mail, e-mail. Accepts simultaneous submissions. Responds in 3 weeks to queries; 3 months to mss. Sample copy for 9x13 SAE, 3 first-class stamps, and $1 for coverage/publication cost. Writer's guidelines for #10 SASE or online.

NONFICTION Needs Young readers: animal, arts/crafts, biography, careers, cooking, concept, games/puzzles, geography, health, history, hobbies, how-to, humor, inspirational, interview/profile, math, multicultural, music/drama/art, nature/environment, personal experience, photo feature, problem-solving, quizzes, recipes, religious, science, social issues, sports, travel. Looking for inspirational biographies, stories from Zambia, and ideas on how to live a green lifestyle. Constant mention of God is not necessary if the moral tone of the story is positive. **Buys 15 mss/year.** Send complete ms. Length: 100-400 words. **Pays $35 maximum.**

PHOTOS Send photos. Identification of subjects required. Reviews at least 5X7 clear color glossy prints, GIF/JPEG files on CD. Offers $25-50/photo.

COLUMNS/DEPARTMENTS Crafts; puzzles and jokes; quizzes, all 200-400 words. Send complete ms. **Payment varies.**

FICTION Young readers: adventure, animal, contemporary, ethnic/multcultural, fantasy, folktale, health, history, humorous, music and musicians, mystery, nature/environment, problem-solving, religious, recipes, service projects, slice-of-life, sports, suspense/mystery, vignettes, interacting with family and friends. **Buys 10 mss/year.** Send complete ms. Length: 100-400 words. **Pays $35 maximum.**

POETRY Prefers rhyming. "We do not wish to see anything that is too difficult for a first grader to read. We wish it to remain light. The style can be fun, but also teach a truth." No violence or secular material. Buys 4 poems/year. Submit maximum 4 poems.

FILLERS Needs facts, short humor. **Buys 6 mss/year.** Length: 50-150 words. **Pays $10-15.**

TIPS "Keep it simple. We are writing to 1st-3rd graders. It must be simple yet interesting. Mss should build girls up in Christian character but not be preachy. They are just learning about God and how He wants them to live. Mss should be delightful as well as educational and inspirational.Writers should keep stories simple but not write with a 'Pollyanna' attitude. Authors should see their writing style as exciting and appealing to girls ages 6-9. Subjects should be current and important to *Sparkle* readers. Use our theme as a guide. We would like to receive material with a multicultural slant."

ⓢ STONE SOUP

Children's Art Foundation, P.O. Box 83, Santa Cruz CA 95063-0083. (831)426-5557. **E-mail:** editor@stonesoup.com. **Website:** stonesoup.com. **Contact:** Ms. Gerry Mandel, editor. **100% freelance written.** Bimonthly magazine of writing and art by children age 13 under, including fiction, poetry, book reviews, and art. *Stone Soup* is 48 pages, 7x10, professionally printed in color on heavy stock, saddle-stapled, with coated cover with full-color illustration. Receives 5,000 poetry submissions/year, accepts about 12. Press run is 15,000. Subscription: $37/year (U.S.). "We have a preference for writing and art based on real-life experiences; no formula stories or poems. We only publish writing by children ages 8 to 13. We do not publish writing by adults." Estab. 1973. Pays on publication. Publishes ms an average of 4 months after acceptance. Submit seasonal material 6 months in advance. Sample copy by phone only. Guidelines online.

○   "Stories and poems from past issues are online."

NONFICTION Needs historical, personal experience, book reviews. **Buys 12 mss/year.** Submit complete ms; no SASE. **Pays $40, a certificate and 2 contributor's copies, plus discounts.**

FICTION Needs adventure, ethnic, experimental, fantasy, historical, humorous, mystery, science fiction, slice-of-life vignettes, suspense. "We do not like assignments or formula stories of any kind." **Buys 60 mss/year.** Send complete ms; no SASE. Length: 150-2,500 words. **Pays $40 for stories, a certificate and 2 contributor's copies, plus discounts.**

POETRY Needs avant-garde, free verse. Wants free verse poetry. Does not want rhyming poetry, haiku, or cinquain. Buys 12 poems/year. **Pays $40/poem, a certificate, and 2 contributor's copies, plus discounts.**

TIPS "All writing we publish is by young people ages 13 and under. We do not publish any writing by adults. We can't emphasize enough how important it is to read a couple of issues of the magazine. You can read stories and poems from past issues online. We have a strong preference for writing on subjects that mean a lot to the author. If you feel strongly about something that happened to you or something you observed, use that feeling as the basis for your story or poem. Stories should have good descriptions, realistic dialogue, and a point to make. In a poem, each word must be chosen carefully. Your poem should present a view of your subject, and a way of using words that are special and all your own."

LITERARY & LITTLE

ACM (ANOTHER CHICAGO MAGAZINE)

P.O. Box 408439, Chicago IL 60640. **E-mail:** editors@anotherchicagomagazine.net. **Website:** www.anotherchicagomagazine.net. **Contact:** Jacob S. Knabb, editor-in-chief; Caroline Eick Kasner, managing editor. "*Another Chicago Magazine* is a biannual literary magazine that publishes work by both new and established writers. We look for work that goes beyond the artistic and academic to include and address the larger world. The editors read submissions in fiction, poetry, creative nonfiction, etc. year round. We often publish special theme issues and sections. We will post upcoming themes on our website. Fiction: Short stories and novel excerpts of 15-20 pages or less. Poetry: Usually no more than 4 pages. Creative Nonfiction: Usually no more than 20 pages. Et Al.: Work that doesn't quite fit into the other genres such as Word &

Image Texts, Satire, and Interviews." Estab. 1977. Circ. 2,000. Byline given. Accepts queries by mail. Accepts simultaneous submissions. Responds in 3 months to queries; 6 months to mss. Sample copy available for $8.

NONFICTION Contact: Ling Ma, nonfiction editor. "Please include the following contact information in your cover letter and on your ms: Byline (name as you want it to appear if published), mailing address, phone number, and e-mail. Include a self-addressed stamped envelope (SASE). If a SASE is not enclosed, you will only hear from us if we are interested in your work. Include the genre (e.g., nonfiction, et al.) of your work in the address." Accepts simultaneous, multiple submissions.

FICTION Contact: Paul Genesius Durica, fiction editor. Needs ethnic, experimental, contemporary, feminist, gay, lesbian, literary. "Please include the following contact information in your cover letter and on your ms: Byline (name as you want it to appear if published), mailing address, phone number, and e-mail. Include a self-addressed stamped envelope (SASE). If a SASE is not enclosed, you will only hear from us if we are interested in your work. Include the genre (e.g., fiction) of your work in the address." Short stories and novel excerpts of 15-20 pages or less. **Pays small honorarium when possible, contributor's copies and 1 year subscription.**

POETRY Contact: David Welch, poetry editor. Submit 3-4 typed poems at a time, usually no more than 4 pages. Considers simultaneous submissions with notification; no previously published poems. Reads submissions year-round. Guidelines online; however, "The best way to know what we publish is to read what we publish. If you haven't read *ACM* before, order a sample copy to know if your work is appropriate." Responds in 3 months. Sends prepublication galleys. Pays monetary amount "if funds permit," and/or one contributor's copy and one-year subscription. Acquires first serial rights. Reviews books of poetry in 250-800 words. Send materials for review consideration. No more than 4 pages.

TIPS "Support literary publishing by subscribing to at least one literary journal—if not ours, another. Get used to rejection slips, and don't get discouraged. Keep introductory letters short. Make sure ms has name and address on every page, and that it is clean, neat, and proofread. We are looking for stories with freshness and originality in subject angle and style and work that encounters the world."

ACUMEN MAGAZINE

Ember Press, 6 The Mount, Higher Furzeham, Brixham, South Devon TQ5 8QY United Kingdom. **E-mail:** patriciaoxley6@gmail.com. **Website:** www.acumen-poetry.co.uk. **Contact:** Patricia Oxley, general editor. *Acumen*, published 3 times/year in January, May, and September, is "a general literary magazine with emphasis on good poetry." Wants "well-crafted, high-quality, imaginative poems showing a sense of form." Does not want "experimental verse of an obscene type." Has published poetry by Ruth Padel, William Oxley, Hugo Williams, Peter Porter, Danielle Hope, and Leah Fritz. Estab. 1971. Accepts queries by mail. Accepts simultaneous submissions. Responds in 3 months. Submission guidelines online at website.

Acumen is 120 pages, A5, perfect-bound.

NONFICTION Needs "*Acumen* is always on the look out for new and unusual articles, etc. However, the magazine likes quality writing in its prose. It will consider articles on poetry and poetry-related subjects (eg. criticism, use of language, poetry from past-masters re-evaluated, etc.) , the main criteria being they are relevant, well-written, interesting and readable (ie. with a minimum of jargon throughout the text).". Length: 1,500-3,000 words.

POETRY Submit 5-6 poems at a time. All submissions should be accompanied by SASE. Include name and address on each separate sheet. Accepts e-mail submissions, but see guidelines on the website. Will send rejections, acceptances, proofs, and other communications via e-mail overseas to dispense with IRCs and other international postage. Any poem that may have chance of publication is shortlisted, and from list final poems are chosen. All other poems returned within 2 months. "If a reply is required, please send IRCs. One IRC for a decision, 3 IRCs if work is to be returned." Willing to reply by e-mail to save IRCs. **Pays "by negotiation" and 1 contributor's copy.**

TIPS "Read *Acumen* carefully to see what kind of poetry we publish. Also, read widely in many poetry magazines, and don't forget the poets of the past— they can still teach us a great deal."

AGNI

Creative Writing Program, Boston University, 236 Bay State Rd., Boston MA 02215. (617)353-7135. **Fax:** (617)353-7134. **E-mail:** agni@bu.edu. **Website:** www.agnimagazine.org. **Contact:** Sven Birkerts, editor. Bi-annual literary magazine. "Eclectic literary magazine publishing first-rate poems, essays, translations, and stories." Estab. 1972. Circ. 3,000 in print, plus more than 60,000 distinct readers online per year. Byline given. Pays on publication. Publishes ms an average of 6 months after acceptance. Editorial lead time 1 year. Accepts queries by mail. Accepts simultaneous submissions. Responds in 2 weeks to queries. Responds in 4 months to mss. Sample copy for $10 or online. Guidelines online.

◑ Reading period is September 1-May 31 only. Online magazine carries original content not found in print edition. All submissions are considered for both. Founding editor Askold Melnyczuk won the 2001 Nora Magid Award for Magazine Editing. Work from *AGNI* has been included and cited regularly in the *Pushcart Prize* and *Best American* anthologies.

FICTION Buys stories, prose poems. "No science fiction or romance." **Buys 20+ mss/year.** Query by mail. **Pays $10/page up to $150, a 1-year subscription, and for print publication: 2 contributor's copies and 4 gift copies.**

POETRY Submit no more than 5 poems at a time. No e-mail submissions. Cover letter is required ("brief, sincere"). "No fancy fonts, gimmicks. Include SASE or e-mail address; no preformatted reply cards." Buys 120+ poems/year. **Pays $20/page up to $150.**

TIPS "We're also looking for extraordinary translations from little-translated languages. It is important to read work published in *AGNI* before submitting, to see if your own might be compatible."

⊛⊛ ALASKA QUARTERLY REVIEW

University of Alaska-Anchorage, 3211 Providence Dr. (ESH 208), Anchorage AK 99508. (907)786-6916. **E-mail:** aqr@uaa.alaska.edu. **Website:** www.uaa.alaska.edu/aqr. **Contact:** Ronald Spatz, editor-in-chief. **95% freelance written.** Semiannual magazine publishing fiction, poetry, literary nonfiction, and short plays in traditional and experimental styles. *"Alaska Quarterly Review* is a literary journal devoted to contemporary literary art, publishing fiction, short plays, poetry, photo essays, and literary nonfiction in traditional and experimental styles. The editors encourage new and emerging writers, while continuing to publish award-winning and established writers." Estab. 1982. Circ. 2,700. Byline given. Honorariums on publication when funding permits. Publishes ms an average of 6 months after acceptance. Accepts queries by

mail. Accepts simultaneous submissions. Responds in 4 months to queries; responds in 4 months to mss. Sample copy for $6. Guidelines online.

◑ Magazine: 6×9; 232-300 pages; 60 lb. Glatfelter paper; 12 pt. C15 black ink or 4-color; varnish cover stock; photos on cover and photo essays

NONFICTION Buys 0-5 mss/year. Query. Length: 1,000-20,000 words. **Pays $50-200 subject to funding.**

FICTION "Works in *AQR* have certain characteristics: freshness, honesty, and a compelling subject. The voice of the piece must be strong—idiosyncratic enough to create a unique persona. We look for craft, putting it in a form where it becomes emotionally and intellectually complex. Many pieces in *AQR* concern everyday life. We're not asking our writers to go outside themselves and their experiences to the absolute exotic to catch our interest. We look for the experiential and revelatory qualities of the work. We will champion a piece that may be less polished or stylistically sophisticated, if it engages me, surprises me, and resonates for me. The joy in reading such a work is in discovering something true. Moreover, in keeping with our mission to publish new writers, we are looking for voices our readers do not know, voices that may not always be reflected in the dominant culture and that, in all instances, have something important to convey." Needs experimental and traditional literary forms., contemporary, prose poem, novel excerpts, drama: experimental and traditional one-acts. No romance, children's, or inspirational/religious. **Buys 20-26 mss/year; 0-2 mss/year drama. mss/year.** Length: 100 pages maximum. **Pays $50-200 subject to funding; pays in contributor's copies and subscriptions when funding is limited.**

POETRY Needs avant-garde, free verse, traditional. No light verse. Buys 10-30 poems/year. Submit maximum 10 poems. **Pays $10-50 subject to availability of funds; pays in contributor's copies and subscriptions when funding is limited.**

TIPS "Although we respond to e-mail queries, we cannot review electronic submissions."

◑ AMBIT

Staithe House, Main Road, Brancaster Staithe, Norfolk PE31 8PB United Kingdom. **E-mail:** info@ambitmagazine.co.uk. **Website:** www.ambitmagazine.co.uk. **Contact:** Briony Bax, editor; Liz Berry and Declan Ryan, poetry editors. *Ambit* magazine is a literary and artwork quarterly created in London, published in the UK, and read internationally. *Ambit* is put together entirely from unsolicited, previously unpublished poetry and short fiction submissions. Responds in 3-4 months. Sample copy £9. Submit using Submittable portal online on www.ambitmagazine.co.uk. There are 2 windows for submissions: February 1-April 1 and September 1-November 1. Please only submit during these windows. No e-mail submissions. Guidelines available in magazine or online.

POETRY No previously published poems (including onlines or blogs) or simultaneous submissions. Poems should be typed, double-spaced. Never comments on rejected poems. Does not want "indiscriminately centre-justified poems; jazzy fonts; poems all in italics for the sake of it." **Payment details online.**

TIPS "Read a copy of the magazine before submitting!"

THE AMERICAN POETRY REVIEW

1700 Sansom St., Suite 800, Philadelphia PA 19103. E-mail: sberg@aprweb.org. **Website:** www.aprweb.org. **Contact:** Stephen Berg, editor. "*The American Poetry Review* is dedicated to reaching a worldwide audience with a diverse array of the best contemporary poetry and literary prose. *APR* also aims to expand the audience interested in poetry and literature, and to provide authors, especially poets, with a far-reaching forum in which to present their work." Estab. 1972. Circ. 5,000-8,000. Accepts queries by mail. Responds in 3 months. Sample: $4.50. Guidelines online. Submit via postal mail (include SASE) or online submissions manager ($3 fee).

> *APR* has included the work of over 1,500 writers, among whom there are 9 Nobel Prize laureates and 33 Pulitzer Prize winners.

NONFICTION Needs essays, interview, literary criticism. Mss should be typewritten or computer-printed on white, 8.5x11 paper.

FICTION Mss should be typewritten or computer-printed on white, 8.5x11 paper.

POETRY Mss should be typewritten or computer-printed on white, 8.5x11 paper. Has published poetry by D.A. Powell, James Franco, Dean Faulwell, and Caroline Pittman. Submit maximum 5 poems.

THE ANTIGONISH REVIEW

St. Francis Xavier University, P.O. Box 5000, Antigonish NS B2G 2W5 Canada. (902)867-3962. **Fax:** (902)867-5563. **E-mail:** tar@stfx.ca. **Website:** www.antigonishreview.com. **Contact:** Bonnie McIsaac, office manager. **100% freelance written.** Quarterly literary magazine for educated and creative readers. *The Antigonish Review*, published quarterly, tries "to produce the kind of literary and visual mosaic that the modern sensibility requires or would respond to." Estab. 1970. Circ. 850. Byline given. Pays on publication. Offers variable kill fee. Publishes ms an average of 8 months after acceptance. Editorial lead time 4 months. Submit seasonal material 4 months in advance. Accepts queries by mail, fax. Responds in 1 month to queries; 6 months to mss. Sample copy for $7 or online. Guidelines for #10 SASE or online.

NONFICTION Needs essays, interview, book reviews/articles. No academic pieces. **Buys 15-20 mss/year.** Query. Length: 1,500-5,000 words **Pays $50 and 2 contributor's copies.**

FICTION Send complete ms. Accepts submissions by fax. Accepts electronic (disk compatible with WordPerfect/IBM and Windows) submissions. Prefers hard copy. Needs literary, translations, contemporary, prose poem. No erotica. **Buys 35-40 mss/year.** Send complete ms. Length: 500-5,000 words. **Pays $50 and 2 contributor's copies for stories.**

POETRY Open to poetry on any subject written from any point of view and in any form. However, writers should expect their work to be considered within the full context of old and new poetry in English and other languages. No more than 6-8 poems should be submitted at any one time. A preferable submission would be 3-4 poems. No previously published poems or simultaneous submissions. Has published poetry by Andy Wainwright, W.J. Keith, Michael Hulse, Jean McNeil, M. Travis Lane, and Douglas Lochhead. Buys 100-125 poems/year. Submit maximum 5 poems. Submit 6-8 poems at a time. Lines/poem: not over 80, i.e., 2 pages. **Pays $10/page to a maximum of $50 and 2 contributor's copies. Acquires first North American serial rights.**

TIPS "Send for guidelines and/or sample copy. Send ms with cover letter and SASE with submission."

ANTIOCH REVIEW

P.O. Box 148, Yellow Springs OH 45387-0148. **E-mail:** mke@antiochreview.org. **Website:** www.antiochreview.org. **Contact:** Robert S. Fogarty, editor; Judith Hall, poetry editor. Quarterly magazine for general, literary, and academic audience. Literary and cultural review of contemporary issues and literature for general readership. *The Antioch Review* "is an independent quarterly of critical and creative thought. For well over 70 years, creative authors, poets, and thinkers have found a friendly reception—regardless of formal reputation. We get far more poetry than we can possibly accept, and the competition is keen. Here, where form and content are so inseparable and reaction is so personal, it is difficult to state requirements or limitations. Studying recent issues of *The Antioch Review* should be helpful." Estab. 1941. Circ. 3,000. Byline given. Pays on publication. Publishes ms an average of 10 months after acceptance. Responds in 3-6 months to mss. Sample copy for $7. Guidelines online.

Work published in *The Antioch Review* has been included frequently in *The Best American Stories, Best American Essays,* and *The Best American Poetry*. Finalist for National Magazine Award for essays in 2009 and 2011, and for fiction in 2010.

NONFICTION Nonfiction submissions are not accepted between June 1-September 1. Length: 2,000-8,000 words. **Pays $20/printed page, plus 2 contributor's copies.**

FICTION Contact: Fiction editor. Quality fiction only, distinctive in style with fresh insights into the human condition. Needs experimental, contemporary. No science fiction, fantasy, or confessions. Send complete ms with SASE, preferably mailed flat. Fiction submissions are not accepted between June 1-September 1. Length: generally under 8,000 words. **Pays $20/printed page, plus 2 contributor's copies.**

POETRY Has published poetry by Richard Howard, Jacqueline Osherow, Alice Fulton, Richard Kenney, and others. Receives about 3,000 submissions/year. Submit 3-6 poems at a time. No previously published poems or simultaneous submissions. Include SASE with all submissions. No light or inspirational verse. Poetry submissions are not accepted between between May 1-September 1. Submit maximum 3-6 poems. **Pays $20/printed page, plus 2 contributor's copies.**

ART TIMES

A Literary Journal and Resource for All the Arts, P.O. Box 730, Mount Marion NY 12456. (845)246-6944. **Fax:** (845)246-6944. **E-mail:** info@ArtTimesJournal. com. **Website:** www.arttimesjournal.com. **Contact:** Raymond J. Steiner, editor. **10% freelance written.** Monthly tabloid covering the arts (visual, theater, dance, music, literary, etc.). "*Art Times* covers the art fields and is distributed in locations most frequented by those enjoying the arts. Our copies are distributed

throughout the lower part of the northeast as well as the metropolitan New York area; locations include theaters, galleries, museums, schools, art clubs, cultural centers, and the like. Our readers are mostly over 40, affluent, art-conscious and sophisticated. Subscribers are located across US and abroad (Italy, France, Germany, Greece, Russia, etc.)." Estab. 1984. Circ. 28,000. Byline given. Pays on publication. Publishes ms an average of 3 years after acceptance. Submit seasonal material 8 months in advance. Accepts simultaneous submissions. Responds in 6 months to queries. Responds in 6 months to mss. Sample copy for sae with 9x12 envelope and 6 first-class stamps. Writer's guidelines for #10 SASE or online.

FICTION Looks for quality short fiction that aspires to be literary. Publishes 1 story each issue. Needs adventure, ethnic, fantasy, historical, humorous, mainstream, science fiction, contemporary. "Nothing violent, sexist, erotic, juvenile, racist, romantic, political, off-beat, or related to sports or juvenile fiction." **Buys 8-10 mss/year.** Send complete ms. Length: up to 1,500 words. **Pays $25 and a 1-year subscription.**

POETRY Needs avant-garde, free verse, haiku, light verse, traditional. Wants "poetry that strives to express genuine observation in unique language. All topics, all forms. We prefer well-crafted 'literary' poems. No excessively sentimental poetry." Publishes 2-3 poems each issue. Buys 30-35 poems/year. Submit maximum 6 poems. Length: no more than 20 lines. **Offers contributor copies and 1 year's free subscription.**

TIPS "Competition is greater (more submissions received), but keep trying. We print new as well as published writers. Be advised that we are presently on an approximate 3-year lead for short stories, 2-year lead for poetry. We are now receiving 300-400 poems and 40-50 short stories per month. Be familiar with *Art Times* and its special audience."

ARTFUL DODGE

Dept. of English, College of Wooster, Wooster OH 44691. (330)263-2577. **E-mail:** artfuldodge@wooster. edu. **Website:** www.wooster.edu/artfuldodge. **Contact:** Daniel Bourne, editor-in-chief; Karin Lin-Greenberg, fiction editor; Marcy Campbell, associate fiction editor; Carolyne Wright, translation editor. *Artful Dodge* is an Ohio-based literary magazine that publishes "work with a strong sense of place and cultural landscape. Besides new American fiction, poetry, and narrative essay, we're also interested in contemporary translation—from all over the globe. There is no theme in this magazine, except literary power. We also have an ongoing interest in translations from Central/Eastern Europe and elsewhere." Estab. 1979. Circ. 1,000. Accepts queries by mail. NoAccepts simultaneous submissions. Responds in 1-6 months to mss. Sample copy for $7. Guidelines for #10 SASE.

NONFICTION Needs narrative essays. Submit with SASE. Length: up to 25 pages. **Pays at least 2 contributor's copies.**

FICTION Contact: Marcy Campbell, fiction editor. Needs experimental, prose poem. "We judge by literary quality, not by genre. We are especially interested in fine English translations of significant prose writers. Translations should be submitted with original texts." **Pays at least 2 contributor's copies.**

POETRY "We are interested in poems that utilize stylistic persuasions both old and new to good effect. We are not afraid of poems which try to deal with large social, political, historical, and even philosophical questions—especially if the poem emerges from one's own life experience and is not the result of armchair pontificating." "We don't want cute, rococo surrealism, someone's warmed-up, left-over notion of an avant-garde that existed 10-100 years ago, or any last bastions of rhymed verse in the civilized world." Buys 20 poems/year. Submit maximum 6 poems. **Pays at least 2 contributor's copies.**

TIPS "Poets may send books for review consideration; however, there is no guarantee we can review them."

BELLINGHAM REVIEW

Mail Stop 9053, Western Washington University, Bellingham WA 98225. (360)650-4863. **E-mail:** bhreview@wwu.edu. **Website:** wwww.bhreview.org. Brenda Miller, editor-in-chief. **Contact:** Lee Olsen, managing editor. **100% freelance written.** Annual small press literary magazine covering poems, stories, and essays. No limitations on form or subject matter. Annual nonprofit magazine published once a year in the spring. Seeks "literature of palpable quality: poems stories and essays so beguiling they invite us to touch their essence. *Bellingham Review* hungers for a kind of writing that nudges the limits of form, or executes traditional forms exquisitely." Estab. 1977. Circ. 2,000. Byline given. Pays on publication when funding allows. Publishes ms an average of 6 months after acceptance. Editorial lead time 6 months. Accepts

simultaneous submissions. Responds in 1-6 months. Sample copy for $12. Guidelines online.

The editors are actively seeking submissions of creative nonfiction, as well as stories that push the boundaries of the form. The Tobias Wolff Award in Fiction Contest runs December 1-March 15; see website for guidelines.

NONFICTION Contact: Nonfiction editors: Chanel Brown and Michelle McMullin. Needs essays, personal experience. Does not want anything nonliterary. Send complete ms. 6,000 words maximum via submittable. **Pays as funds allow, plus contributor copies.**

FICTION Contact: Fiction editors: Zoe Coen, Diane Henderson and Caitlin Morris. Experimental, humor/satire, literary, regional (Northwest). Does not want anything nonliterary. Needs experimental, humorous. **Buys 4-6 mss/year.** Send complete ms. 6,000 words maximum. **Pays as funds allow.**

POETRY Contact: Poetry editors: Jessica Crockett, Jessica Lohafer and Kate Kenney. Needs avant-garde, free verse, traditional. *Bellingham Review*, published twice/year, has no specific preferences as to form. Wants "well-crafted poetry, but are open to all styles." Has published poetry by David Shields, Tess Gallagher, Gary Soto, Jane Hirshfield, Albert Goldbarth, and Rebecca McClanahan. Accepts submissions by postal mail and e-mail. Include SASE. Reads submissions September 15-December 1 only (submissions must be postmarked within this reading period). Responds in 2 months. Will not use light verse. Buys 10-30 poems/year. Submit maximum 3-5/poems at a time. poems. Indicate approximate word count on prose pieces. **Pays contributor's copies, a year's subscription, plus monetary payment (if funding allows).**

TIPS "Open submission period is from Sept. 15-Dec. 1. Mss arriving between December 2 and September 14 will be returned unread. The *Bellingham Review* holds 3 annual contests: the 49th Parallel Award for poetry, the Annie Dillard Award for Nonfiction, and the Tobias Wolff Award for Fiction. Submissions: December 1-March 15. See the individual listings for these contests under Contests & Awards for full details."

BIG PULP

Exter Press, P.O. Box 92, Cumberland MD 21501. **E-mail:** editors@bigpulp.com. **Website:** www.bigpulp.com. **Contact:** Bill Olver, editor. Quarterly literary magazine. Submissions accepted by e-mail only. Defines 'pulp fiction' very broadly: it's lively, challenging, thought-provoking, thrilling and fun, regardless of how many or how few genre elements are packed in. Doesn't subscribe to the theory that genre fiction is disposable; a great deal of literary fiction could easily fall under one of their general categories. Places a higher value on character and story than genre elements. Byline given. Pays on publication. 100% kill fee. Publishes ms 1 year after acceptance. Accepts simultaneous submissions. Responds in 2 months to mss. Sample copy available for $10; excerpts online at no cost. Guidelines online at website.

○ Currently accepting submissions for themed collections only. See website for details on current needs. Submissions are only accepted during certain reading periods; check website to see if magazine is currently open.

FICTION Needs adventure, fantasy, horror, mystery, romance, science fiction, suspense, western, superhero. Does not want generic slice-of-life, memoirs, inspirational, political, pastoral odes. **Buys 70 mss/year.** Submit complete ms. Length: 10,000 words maximum. **Pays $5-25.**

POETRY Needs avant-garde, free verse, haiku, light verse, traditional. All types of poetry are considered, but poems should have a genre connection. Buys 20 poems/year. Submit maximum 5 poems. Length: 100 lines maximum. **Pays $5/poem.**

TIPS "We like to be surprised, and have few boundaries. Fantasy writers may focus on the mundane aspects of a fantastical creature's life, or the magic that can happen in everyday life. Romances do not have to requited, or have happy endings, and the object of one's obsession may not be a person. Mysteries need not focus on 'whodunit?' We're always interested in science or speculative fiction focusing on societal issues, but writers should avoid being partisan or shrill. We also like fiction that crosses genre; for example, a science fiction romance, or fantasy crime story. We have an online archive for fiction and poetry and encourage writers to check it out. That said, *Big Pulp* has a strong editorial bias in favor of stories with monkeys. Especially talking monkeys."

BLACKBIRD

Virginia Commonwealth University Department of English, P.O. Box 843082, Richmond VA 23284. (804)827-4729. **E-mail:** blackbird@vcu.edu. **Website:** www.blackbird.vcu.edu. *Blackbird* is published twice a year. Estab. 2001. Accepts queries by mail, online submission form. Accepts simultaneous submissions. Responds in 6 months. Guidelines online at website.

NONFICTION Needs essays, memoir. No book reviews or criticism. "We primarily look for personal essays, but memoir excerpts are acceptable if self-contained."

FICTION "We primarily look for short stories, but novel excerpts are acceptable if self-contained." Needs novel excerpts, short stories. Submit using online submissions manager or by postal mail. Online submission is preferred.

POETRY Submit 2-6 poems at a time. "If submitting online, put all poems into one document." Submit maximum 6 poems.

TIPS "We like a story that invites us into its world, that engages our senses, soul and mind. We are able to publish long works in all genres, but query *Blackbird* before you send a prose piece over 8,000 words or a poem exceeding 10 pages."

BLACK WARRIOR REVIEW

P.O. Box 862936, Tuscaloosa AL 35486. (205)348-4518. **E-mail:** interns.bwr@gmail.com. **Website:** www.bwr.ua.edu. **Contact:** Kirby Johnson, editor. **90% freelance written.** Semiannual magazine covering fiction, poetry, essays, art, comics, and reviews. "We publish contemporary fiction, poetry, reviews, essays, and art for a literary audience. We publish the freshest work we can find." Estab. 1974. Circ. 2,000. Byline given. Pays on publication. Publishes ms 6 months after acceptance. Accepts queries by online submission form. Accepts simultaneous submissions. Responds in 3-6 months. Sample copy for $10. Guidelines online.

NONFICTION Needs essays, interview, "We are looking for essays that offer a new perspective, an unvoiced thought, an overlooked association—and we hope that you will send us pieces that not only challenge us with their content, but also with their form. We prize the lyric and the language driven, both the sparsely stated and the indulgently ruminative.". **Buys 5 mss/year.** No queries; send complete ms. Length: no more than 7,000 words. "*BWR* **pays a 1-year subscription and a nominal lump-sum fee for all works published."**

FICTION "We are open to good experimental writing and short-short fiction. No genre fiction please. Publishes novel excerpts if under contract to be published." Needs experimental, short stories. **Buys 10 mss/year.** One story/chapter per envelope. Wants work that is conscious of form and well-crafted. Length: no more than 7,000 words. **"*BWR* pays a 1-year subscription and a nominal lump-sum fee for all works published.".**

POETRY "We welcome most styles and forms, and we favor poems that take risks—whether they be quiet or audacious." Submit poems in 1 document. Submit maximum 5 poems. Accepts up to 5 poems per submission at a maximum of 10 pages. **"*BWR* pays a 1-year subscription and a nominal lump-sum fee for all works published.".**

TIPS "We look for attention to language, freshness, honesty, a convincing and sharp voice. Send us a clean, well-printed, proofread ms. Become familiar with the magazine prior to submission."

$$ BOULEVARD

Opojaz, Inc., 6614 Clayton Rd., Box 325, Richmond Heights MO 63117. (314)324-3351. **Fax:** (314)862-2982. **E-mail:** richardburgin@netzero.com; jessicarogen@boulevardmagazine.org. **E-mail:** https://boulevard.submittable.com/submit. **Website:** www.boulevardmagazine.org. **Contact:** Richard Burgin, editor; Jessica Rogen, managing editor. **100% freelance written.** "*Boulevard* is a diverse literary magazine presenting original creative work by well-known authors, as well as by writers of exciting promise." Triannual magazine featuring fiction, poetry, and essays. *Boulevard* is 175-250 pages, digest-sized, flat-spined, with glossy card cover. Receives over 600 unsolicited mss/month. Accepts about 10 mss/issue. Publishes 10 new writers/year. Recently published work by Joyce Carol Oates, Floyd Skloot, John Barth, Stephen Dixon, David Guterson, Albert Goldbarth, Molly Peacock, Bob Hicok, Alice Friman, Dick Allen, and Tom Disch. Sometimes comments on rejected mss. Estab. 1985. Circ. 11,000. Byline given. Pays on publication. Offers Publishes ms an average of 9 months after acceptance. Accepts queries by mail, e-mail. Accepts simultaneous submissions. Responds in 2 weeks to queries; 4-5 months to mss. Subscription: $15 for 3 issues, $27 for 6 issues, $30 for 9 issues. Foreign subscribers, please add $10. Sample copy: $10. Make checks payable to Opojaz, Inc. Subscriptions are online at www.boulevardmagazine.org/subscribe.html. Publishes short fiction, poetry, and nonfiction, including critical and culture essays. Submit by mail or via Submittable. Accepts multiple and simultaneous submissions. Does not accept mss between May 1 and October 1. SASE for reply.

NONFICTION Needs book excerpts, essays, interview, opinion, photo feature. **Buys 10 mss/year.** Length: 8,000 words maximum. **Pays minimum $100, maximum $300.**

FICTION Needs confession, experimental, mainstream, novel excerpts. "We do not want erotica, science fiction, romance, western, horror, or children's stories." **Buys 20 mss/year.** Length: 8,000 words maximum. **Pays $50-500 (sometimes higher) for accepted work.**

POETRY Needs avant-garde, free verse, haiku, traditional. Does not consider book reviews. "Do not send us light verse." Does not want "poetry that is uninspired, formulaic, self-conscious, unoriginal, insipid." Buys 80 poems/year. Submit maximum 5 poems. Length: 200/max lines. **Pays $25-$250.**

TIPS "Read the magazine first. The work *Boulevard* publishes is generally recognized as among the finest in the country. We continue to seek more good literary or cultural essays. Send only your best work."

BURNSIDE REVIEW

P.O. Box 1782, Portland OR 97207. **Website:** www.burnsidereview.org. **Contact:** Dan Kaplan, managing editor. *Burnside Review*, published every 9 months, prints "the best poetry and short fiction we can get our hands on." Each issue includes 1 featured poet with an interview and new poems. "We tend to publish writing that finds beauty in truly unexpected places; that combines urban and natural imagery; that breaks the heart." Estab. 2004. Pays on publication. Publishes ms 9 months after acceptance. Submit seasonal poems 3-6 months in advance. Accepts queries by online submission form. Accepts simultaneous submissions. Responds in 1-6 months. Single copy: $8; subscription: $13. Make checks payable to Burnside Review or order online.

FICTION "Send anything from a group of flash-fiction pieces to a traditional short story, so long as the word count doesn't exceed 5,000 words. We like story. We like character. We don't like hobgoblins. Barthelme, Munro, Carver, and Bender are some of the folks whose work we love." Needs experimental, short stories. Submit 1 short story at a time. Accepts submissions through online submission manager only. **Pays $25 plus 1 contributor's copy.**

POETRY Needs avant-garde, free verse, traditional. Open to all forms. Translations are encouraged. "Would like to see more lyric poetry". Has published poetry by Linda Bierds, Dorianne Laux, Ed Skoog, Campbell McGrath, Paul Guest, and Larissa Szporluk. Reads submissions year-round. "Editors read all work submitted." Seldom comments on rejected work. Submit electronically online. Submit maximum 5 poems. **Pays $25 plus 1 contributor's copy.**

TIPS "*Burnside Review* accepts submissions of poetry and fiction. If you have something else that you think would be a perfect fit for our journal, please query the editor before submitting. We like work that breaks the heart. That leaves us in a place that we don't expect to be. We like the lyric. We like the narrative. We like when the two merge. We like whiskey. We like hourglass figures. We like crying over past mistakes. We like to be surprised. Surprise us."

⊛ BUTTON

P.O. Box 77, Westminster MA 01473. **E-mail:** sally@moonsigns.net. **Website:** www.moonsigns.net. **30% freelance written.** Annual literary magazine. "*Button* is New England's tiniest magazine of poetry, fiction, and gracious living, published once a year. As 'gracious living' is on the cover, we like wit, brevity, cleverly-conceived essays/recipes, poetry that isn't sentimental, or song lyrics. I started *Button* so that a century from now, when people read it in landfills or, preferably, libraries, they'll say, 'Gee, what a great time to have lived. I wish I lived back then." Estab. 1993. Circ. 750. Byline given. Pays on publication. Publishes ms 3-9 months after acceptance. Editorial lead time 6 months. Responds in 1 month to queries. Responds in 2 months to mss. Sometimes comments on rejected mss. Subscription: $5 for 3 issues. Sample copy for $2.50. Guidelines online. "We don't take e-mail submissions, unless you're living overseas, in which case we respond electronically. But we strongly suggest you request writers' guidelines (send an SASE).".

○ Receives 20-40 unsolicited mss/month. Accepts 3-6 mss/issue; 3-6mss/year. *Button* is 16-24 pages, saddle-stapled, with cardstock offset cover with illustrations that incorporate 1 or more buttons. Has published poetry by Amanda Powell, Brendan Galvin, Jean Monahan, Mary Campbell, KevinMcGrath, and Ed Conti.

NONFICTION Needs personal experience, cooking stories. Does not want "the tired, the trite, the sexist, the multiply-folded, the single-spaced, the sentimental, the self-pitying, the swaggering, the infantile (i.e.,

coruscated whimsy and self-conscious quaint), poems about Why You Can't Be Together and stories about How Complicated Am I. Before you send us anything, sit down and read a poem by Stanley Kunitz or a story by Evelyn Waugh, Louisa May Alcott, or anyone who's visited the poles, and if you still think you've written a damn fine thing, have at it. A word count on the top of the page is fine—a copyright or 'all rights reserved' reminder makes you look like a beginner." **Buys 3-6 mss/year.** Length: 300-2,000 words. **Pays small honorarium and copies.**

FICTION Seeks quality fiction. No genre fiction, science fiction, techno-thriller. "Wants more of anything Herman Melville, Henry James, or Betty MacDonald would like to read." **Buys 1-2 mss/year.** Send complete ms with bio, list of publications, and explain how you found the magazine. Include SASE. Length: 300-2,000 words. **Pays honorarium and subscriptions.**

POETRY Needs free verse, traditional. Wants quality poetry; "poetry that incises a perfect figure-8 on the ice, but also cuts beneath that mirrored surface. Minimal use of vertical pronoun. Do not submit more than twice in 1 year." Cover letter is required. Does not want "sentiment; no 'musing' on who or what done ya wrong." Buys 2-4 poems/year. Submit maximum 3 poems. **Pays honorarium and at least 2 contributor's copies.**

TIPS "*Button* writers have been widely published elsewhere, in virtually all the major national magazines. They include Ralph Lombreglia, Lawrence Millman, They Might Be Giants, Combustible Edison, Sven Birkerts, Stephen McCauley, Amanda Powell, Wayne Wilson, David Barber, Romayne Dawnay, Brendan Galvin, and Diana DerHovanessian. Follow the guidelines, make sure you read your work aloud, and don't inflate or deflate your publications and experience. We've published plenty of new folks, but on the merits of the work."

○⊛⊛ THE CAPILANO REVIEW

2055 Purcell Way, North Vancouver BC V7J 3H5 Canada. (604)984-1712. **E-mail:** tcr@capilanou.ca. **Website:** www.thecapilanoreview.ca. **Contact:** Tamara Lee, managing editor. **100% freelance written.** Tri-annual visual and literary arts magazine that "publishes only what the editors consider to be the very best fiction, poetry, drama, or visual art being produced. *TCR* editors are interested in fresh, original work that stimulates and challenges readers. Over the years, the magazine has developed a reputation for pushing beyond the boundaries of traditional art and writing. We are interested in work that is new in concept and in execution." Estab. 1972. Circ. 800. Byline given. Pays on publication. Publishes ms an average of within 1 year after acceptance. Accepts queries by mail. Responds in 4-6 months to mss. Sample copy for $10 (outside of Canada, USD). Guidelines with #10 SASE with IRC or Canadian stamps.

PHOTOS Pays $50 for cover and $50/page to maximum of $200 Canadian. Additional payment for electronic rights; negotiable. Pays on publication. Credit line given.

FICTION Needs experimental, novel concepts, previously unpublished only, literary. No traditional, conventional fiction. Wants to see more innovative, genre-blurring work. **Buys 10-15 mss/year.** Send complete ms with SASE and Canadian postage or IRCs. Does not accept submissions through e-mail or on disks. Length: up to 6,000 words **Pays $50-300.**

POETRY Needs avant-garde, free verse, previously unpublished poetry. Submit up to 8 pages of poetry. Buys 40 poems/year. Submit maximum 8 poems. **Pays $50-300.**

🌐 $ CHAPMAN

Chapman Publishing, 4 Broughton Place, Edinburgh EH1 3RX Scotland. (44)(131)557-2207. **E-mail:** chapman-pub@blueyonder.co.uk. **Website:** www.chapman-pub.co.uk. **Contact:** Joy Hendry, editor. **100% freelance written**. "*Chapman*, Scotland's quality literary magazine, is a dynamic force in Scotland, publishing poetry, fiction, criticism, reviews, and articles on theater, politics, language, and the arts. Our philosophy is to publish new work, from known and unknown writers—mainly Scottish, but also worldwide." Estab. 1970. Circ. 2,000. Pays on publication. Publishes ms an average of 3 months after acceptance. Accepts queries by mail. Sample for £5.75. Guidelines online.

💬 Does not accept e-mail submissions.

NONFICTION Needs essays, expose, general interest, historical, humor, inspirational, interview, personal experience. **Buys 15 mss/year.** Send complete ms. **Pays £8/page (can vary).**

FICTION "Any length, any topic considered—the criterion is quality. Please do not send more than 1 item at a time. We are looking for fiction that is challenging, surprising, different—in some way." Needs experimental, historical, humorous, Scottish/ international. No horror or science fiction. "Submissions should be presented as double-line-spaced typescript, with indented paragraphs. Use double quotes for dialogue and quotations, indicate italics with underscore. Avoid using footnotes—we are not an academic journal." Length: "Any length, but average is 3,000 words. **Negotiates payment individually.**

POETRY Needs avant-garde, free verse, haiku, light verse, traditional. "Submit 4-10 poems laid out so that the shape and structure of the work is shown to best advantage (12 font/15-16 line space ideal). One poem to each sheet." Submit maximum 10 poems.

TIPS "Keep your stories for 6 months and edit carefully. We seek challenging work that attempts to explore difficult/new territory in content and form, but lighter work, if original enough, is welcome. We have no plans at present to publish longer fiction or novels."

THE CHARITON REVIEW

Truman State University Press, 100 E Normal Ave., Kirksville MO 63501. (660)785-8336. **E-mail:** chariton@truman.edu. **Website:** tsup.truman.edu/aboutChariton.asp. **Contact:** James D'Agostino, editor. "*The Chariton Review* is an international literary journal publishing the best in short fiction, essays, poetry, and translations in 2 issues each year. " Estab. 1975. Guidelines online. Send a printout of the submission via snail mail; overseas authors may send submissions as e-mail attachments. See also *The Chariton Review* Short Fiction Prize at tsup.truman.edu/prizes.asp.

💬 James D'Agostino became editor in July 2010. He teaches at Truman State University and is the author of *Nude with Anything.*

POETRY Poetry collections are published through TSUP's annual T.S. Eliot Prize for Poetry. Deadline is October 31 of each year. See competition guidelines at tsup.truman.edu/prizes.asp.

TIPS "TSUP also publishes essay collections. Send mss to: TSUP; 100 E. Normal Ave., Kirksville, MO 63501."

$ $ CHICKEN SOUP FOR THE SOUL PUBLISHING, LLC

Chicken Soup for the Soul Publishing, LLC, **E-mail:** webmaster@chickensoupforthesoul.com (for all inquires). **Website:** www.chickensoup.com. **95% freelance written.** Paperback with 12 publications/year featuring inspirational, heartwarming, uplifting short stories. Estab. 1993. Circ. Over 200 titles; 100 million books in print. Byline given. Pays on publication. Accepts simultaneous submissions. Responds upon consideration. Guidelines online.

Ⓞ "Stories must be written in the first person."

NONFICTION No sermon, essay, eulogy, term paper, journal entry, political, or controversial issues. **Buys 1,000 mss/year.** Send complete ms. Length: 300-1,200 words. **Pays $200.**

POETRY Needs traditional. No controversial poetry.

TIPS "We no longer accept submissions by mail or fax. Stories and poems can only be submitted on our website. Select the 'Submit Your Story' tab on the left toolbar. The submission form can be found there."

COLUMBIA: A JOURNAL OF LITERATURE AND ART

Columbia University, New York NY 10027. **Website:** columbiajournal.org. **Contact:** Laura Standley, managing editor. *"Columbia: A Journal of Literature and Art is an annual publication that features the very best in poetry, fiction, nonfiction, and art. We were founded in 1977 and continue to be one of the few national literary journals entirely edited, designed, and produced by students. You'll find that our minds are open, our interests diverse. We solicit mss from writers we love and select the most exciting finds from our virtual submission box. Above all, our commitment is to our readers—to producing a collection that informs, surprises, challenges, and inspires."* Estab. 1977. Accepts queries by phone. Accepts simultaneous submissions.

Ⓞ Reads submissions March 1-October 31.

NONFICTION Submit using online submissions manager.

FICTION Submit using online submissions manager.

POETRY Submit using online submissions manager.

🟂🟂 CONFRONTATION

English Department, LIU Post, Brookville NY 11548. (516)299-2720. **E-mail:** confrontationmag@gmail.com. **Website:** www.confrontationmagazine.org. **Contact:** Jonna Semeiks, editor-in-chief. **75% freelance written.** Semiannual magazine comprising all forms and genres of stories, poems, essays, memoirs, and plays. A special section contains book reviews. "We also publish the work of 1 visual artist per issue, selected by the editors.". *"Confrontation has been in continuous publication since 1968. Our taste and our magazine is eclectic, but we always look for excellence*

in style, an important theme, a memorable voice. We enjoy discovering and fostering new talent. Each issue contains work by both well-established and new writers. In addition, *Confrontation* often features a thematic special section that 'confronts' a topic. The ensuing confrontation is an attempt to see the many sides of an issue or theme, rather than to present a formed conclusion. We prefer single submissions. Clear copy. No e-mail submissions unless writer resides outside the U.S. Mail submissions with a SASE. We read August 16-May 15. Do not send mss or e-mail submissions between May 16 and August 15. We publish theme issues. Upcoming themes are announced on our website and Facebook and Twitter pages and in our magazine." Estab. 1968. Circ. 2,000. Byline given. Pays on publication. Offers kill fee. Publishes work in the first or second issue after acceptance. Accepts simultaneous submissions. Responds in 8-10 weeks to mss.

Ⓞ *Confrontation* has garnered a long list of awards and honors, including the Editor's Award for Distinguished Achievement from CLMP (given to Martin Tucker, the founding editor of the magazine) and NEA grants. Work from the magazine has appeared in numerous anthologies, including the *Pushcart Prize*, *Best Short Stories* and *The O. Henry Prize Stories.*

NONFICTION Needs essays, personal experience. Special issues: "We publish personal as well as cultural, political and other kinds of essays as well as (self-contained) sections of memoirs.". **Buys 12 mss/year.** Send complete ms. Length: 1,500-5,000 words. **Pays $50-125; more for commissioned work.**

FICTION "We judge on quality of writing and thought or imagination, so we will accept genre fiction. However, it must have literary merit, or it must transcend or challenge genre." Needs experimental as well as more traditional fiction, self-contained novel excerpts, slice-of-life vignettes, lyrical or philosophical fiction. No "proselytizing" literature or conventional genre fiction. **Buys 30-40 mss/year.** Send complete ms. Length: Up to 7,200 words **Pays $50-125; more for commissioned work.**

POETRY Contact: Belinda Kremer, poetry editor. Needs avant-garde or experimental as well as traditional poems (and forms), lyric poems, dramatic monologues, satiric or philosophical poems. In short, a wide range of verse. "*Confrontation* is interested in all poetic forms. Our only criterion is high literary merit. We think of our audience as an educated, lay group of intelligent readers." Has published poetry by David Ray, T. Alan Broughton, David Ignatow, Philip Appleman, Jane Mayhall, and Joseph Brodsky. Submit no more than 12 pages at a time (up to 6 poems). Buys 60 poems per year. *Confrontation* also offers the annual Confrontation Poetry Prize. No sentimental verse. No previously published poems. Lines/poem: Length should generally be kept to 2 pages. **Pays $25-75; more for commissioned work.**

TIPS "We look for literary merit. Keep honing your skills and keep trying."

CONTRARY

PO Box 806363, Chicago IL 60616-3299 (no submissions). **E-mail:** chicago@contrarymagazine.com (no submissions). **Website:** www.contrarymagazine.com. **Contact:** Jeff McMahon, editor. *Contrary* publishes fiction, poetry, literary commentary, and prefers work that combines the virtues of all those categories. Founded at the University of Chicago, it now operates independently and not-for-profit on the South Side of Chicago. "We like work that is not only contrary in content, but contrary in its evasion of the expectations established by its genre. Our fiction defies traditional story form. For example, a story may bring us to closure without ever delivering an ending. We don't insist on the ending, but we do insist on the closure. And we value fiction as poetic as any poem." Quarterly. Member CLMP. Estab. 2003. Circ. 38,000. Pays on publication. Mss published no more than 21 days after acceptance. Responds to queries in 2 weeks; 3 months to mss. Rarely comments on/critiques rejected mss. Guidelines online.

FICTION Contact: Frances Badgett, fiction editor. Needs literary. Accepts submissions through website only: www.contrarymagazine.com/Contrary/Submissions.html. Include estimated word count, brief bio, list of publications. Considers simultaneous submissions. Length: 2,000 words (maximum); average length: 750 words. Publishes short shorts. Average length of short shorts: 750 words. **Pays $20-60.**

POETRY Contact: Shaindel Beers, poetry editor. No mail or e-mail submissions; submit work via the website. Considers simultaneous submissions; no previously published poems. Accepts submissions through online form only. Often comments on rejected poems. Submit maximum 3 poems. **$20 per byline, $60 for featured work.**

TIPS "Beautiful writing catches our eye first. If we realize we're in the presence of unanticipated meaning, that's what clinches the deal. Also, we're not fond of expository fiction. We prefer to be seduced by beauty, profundity, and mystery than to be presented with the obvious."

$ CRAB ORCHARD REVIEW

Dept. of English, Southern Illinois University Carbondale, Faner Hall 2380, Mail Code 4503, 1000 Faner Dr., Carbondale IL 62901. (618)453-6833. **Fax:** (618)453-8224. **Website:** www.craborchardreview.siuc.edu. **Contact:** Jon Tribble, managing editor. "We are a general-interest literary journal published twice/year. We strive to be a journal that writers admire and readers enjoy. We publish fiction, poetry, creative nonfiction, fiction translations, interviews, and reviews." Estab. 1995. Circ. 2,500. Publishes ms an average of 9-12 months after acceptance. Accepts simultaneous submissions. Responds in 3 weeks to queries. Responds in 9 months to mss. Always comments on rejected work. Sample copy for $12. Guidelines online.

💬 Reads submissions February 15-April 30 (Winter/Spring issue) and August 27-November 3 (special Summer/Fall issue).

NONFICTION Send SASE for reply, return of ms. Length: up to 25 pages double-spaced. **Pays $25/published magazine page, $100 minimum, 2 contributor's copies and 1-year subscription.**

FICTION Needs ethnic, excerpted novel. No science fiction, romance, western, horror, gothic, or children's. Wants more novel excerpts that also stand alone as pieces. Send SASE for reply, return of ms. Length: up to 25 pages double-spaced. **Pays $25/published magazine page, $100 minimum, 2 contributor's copies and 1-year subscription.**

POETRY Wants all styles and forms from traditional to experimental. Does not want greeting card verse; literary poetry only. Has published poetry by Luisa A. Igloria, Erinn Batykefer, Jim Daniels, and Bryan Tso Jones. Postal submissions only. Cover letter is preferred. "Indicate stanza breaks on poems of more than 1 page. Poems that are under serious consideration are discussed and decided on by the managing editor and poetry editor." Submit maximum 5 poems. **Pays $25/published magazine page, $50 minimum, 2 contributor's copies and 1-year subscription.**

CRAZYHORSE

College of Charleston, Department of English, 66 George St., Charleston SC 29424. (843)953-4470. E-mail: crazyhorse@cofc.edu. **Website:** crazyhorse.cofc. edu. Semiannual magazine. "We like to print a mix of writing regardless of its form, genre, school, or politics. We're especially on the lookout for original writing that doesn't fit the categories and that engages in the work of honest communication." Estab. 1960. Circ. 1,500. Publishes ms an average of 6-12 months after acceptance. Accepts simultaneous submissions. Responds in 1 week to queries. Responds in 3-4 months to mss. Sample copy for $5. Guidelines for SASE or by e-mail.

○ Reads submissions September 1-May 31.

NONFICTION "*Crazyhorse* publishes 4-6 each year, so we call for the vey best writing, period. We believe literary nonfiction can take any form, from the letter to the list, from the biography to the memoir, from the journal to the obituary. All we call for is precision of word and vision, and that the truth of the matter be the flag of the day." Length: 2,500-8,000 words.

FICTION Accepts all fiction of fine quality, including short shorts and literary essays. **Buys 12-15 mss/year.** Length: 2,500-8,500 words. **Pays 2 contributor's copies and $20 per page.**

POETRY Submit 3-5 poems at a time. No fax, e-mail or disk submissions. Cover letter is preferred. Buys 80 poems/year. Submit maximum 5 poems. **Pays $20-35/ page and 2 contributor's copies.**

TIPS "Write to explore subjects you care about. The subject should be one in which something is at stake. Before sending, ask, 'What's reckoned with that's important for other people to read?'"

CREAM CITY REVIEW

c/o UWM Department of English, P.O. Box 413, Milwaukee WI 53201. **E-mail:** info@creamcityreview.org. **Website:** www.creamcityreview.org. **Contact:** Ching-In Chen, editor-in-chief; Shanae Aurora Martinez, managing editor. Semiannual magazine covering poetry, fiction, and nonfiction by new and established writers. *Cream City Review* publishes "memorable and energetic fiction, poetry, and creative nonfiction. Features reviews of contemporary literature and criticism as well as author interviews and artwork. We are interested in camera-ready art depicting themes appropriate to each issue." Accepts queries by online submission form. Accepts simultaneous submissions.

Responds in 2-8 months to mss. Sample back issues for $7. Guidelines online at www.creamcityreview. org/submit. Check for regular updates at www.facebook.com/creamcityreview. Submit using online submissions manager ONLY.

NONFICTION Contact: nonfiction@creamcityreview.org. Needs essays, (book reviews, 1-10 pp.), interview, personal experience.

PHOTOS Reviews prints, slides.

FICTION Contact: fiction@creamcityreview.org. Needs ethnic, experimental, humorous, literary, regional, flash fiction. "Would like to see more quality fiction. No horror, formulaic, racist, sexist, pornographic, homophobic, science fiction, romance."

POETRY Contact: poetry@creamcityreview.org. Submit maximum 5 poems.

TIPS Please include a few lines about your publication history. *CCR* seeks to publish a broad range of writings and a broad range of writers with diverse backgrounds. We accept submissions for our annual theme issue from August 1-November 1 and general submissions from December 1 April 1. No e-mail submissions, please.

DENVER QUARTERLY

University of Denver, 2000 E. Asbury, Denver CO 80208. (303)871-2892. **Website:** www.denverquarterly.com. **Contact:** Bill Ramke. "We publish fiction, articles, and poetry for a generally well-educated audience, primarily interested in literature and the literary experience. They read *DQ* to find something a little different from a stictly academic quarterly or a creative writing outlet." Quarterly. Reads between September 15 and May 15. Estab. 1996. Circ. 2,000. Publishes ms 1 year after acceptance. Accepts simultaneous submissions. Responds in 3 months. Sample copy for $10.

FICTION "We are interested in experimental fiction (minimalism, magic realism, etc.) as well as in realistic fiction and in writing about fiction. No sentimental, science fiction, romance, or spy thrillers." Submit ms by mail, include SASE. Length: up to 15 pages. **Pays $5/page for fiction and poetry and 2 contributor's copies.**

POETRY Poetry submissions should be comprised of 3-5 poems. Submit ms by mail, include SASE. **Pays $5/page for fiction and poetry and 2 contributor's copies.**

TIPS "We look for serious, realistic, and experimental fiction; stories which appeal to intelligent, demanding readers who are not themselves fiction writers. Nothing so quickly disqualifies a ms as sloppy proofreading and mechanics. Read the magazine before submitting to it. We try to remain eclectic, but the odds for beginners are bound to be small considering the fact that we receive nearly 10,000 mss per year and publish only about 10 short stories."

DESCANT: FORT WORTH'S JOURNAL OF POETRY AND FICTION

TCU Box 298300, Ft. Worth TX 76129. (817)257-5907. **Fax:** (817)257-6239. **E-mail:** descant@tcu.edu. **Website:** www.descant.tcu.edu. **Contact:** Dan Williams, editor. Magazine: 6×9; 120-150 pages; acid-free paper; paper cover. "*descant* seeks high-quality poems and stories in both traditional and innovative form." Member CLMP. Estab. 1956. Circ. 500-750. Pays on publication for one-time rights. Pays 2 contributor's copies; additional copies $6. Accepts simultaneous submissions. Responds in 6-8 weeks to mss. Sample copy for $15. SASE, e-mail, or fax.

Ω Offers 4 cash awards: The $500 Frank O'Connor Award for the best story in an issue; the $250 Gary Wilson Award for an outstanding story in an issue; the $500 Betsy Colquitt Award for the best poem in an issue; and the $250 Baskerville Publishers Award for outstanding poem in an issue. Several stories first published by *descant* have appeared in *Best American Short Stories.*

FICTION Receives 20-30 unsolicited mss/month. Accepts 25-35 mss/year. Publishes ms 1 year after acceptance. Publishes 50% new writers/year. Recently published work by William Harrison, Annette Sanford, Miller Williams, Patricia Chao, Vonesca Stroud, and Walt McDonald. No horror, romance, fantasy, erotica. Send complete ms with cover letter. Include estimated word count and brief bio. Length: 1,000-5,000 words; average length: 2,500 words.

TIPS "We look for character and quality of prose. Send your best short work."

⊙$ DESCANT

P.O. Box 314, Station P, Toronto ON M5S 2S8 Canada. (416)593-2557. **Fax:** (416)593-9362. **E-mail:** info@descant.ca. **E-mail:** submit@descant.ca. **Website:** www.descant.ca. Quarterly journal. Estab. 1970. Circ. 1,200. Pays on publication. Publishes ms an average of 16 months after acceptance. Editorial lead time 1 year. Accepts queries by mail, e-mail, phone. Sample copy for $8.50 plus postage. Guidelines online.

Ω Pays $100 honorarium, plus 1-year's subscription for accepted submissions of any kind.

NONFICTION Needs book excerpts, essays, historical, personal experience, historical.

PHOTOS State availability. Reviews contact sheets, prints. Offers no additional payment for photos accepted with ms.

FICTION Contact: Karen Mulhallen, editor. Short stories or book excerpts. Maximum length 6,000 words; 3,000 words or less preferred. Needs ethnic, experimental, historical, humorous. No erotica, fantasy, gothic, horror, religious, romance, beat. Send complete ms with cover letter. Include estimated word count and brief bio. **Pays $100 (Canadian.**

POETRY Needs free verse, light verse, traditional. "*Descant* seeks high quality poems and stories in both traditional and innovative form." Member CLMP. Literary. Submit maximum 6 poems. **Pays $100.**

TIPS "Familiarize yourself with our magazine before submitting."

DIAGRAM

Department of English, University of Arizona, P.O. Box 210067, Tucson AZ 85721-0067. **E-mail:** editor@thediagram.com. **Website:** www.thediagram.com. Online journal covers poetry, fiction, and nonfiction. Sponsors a yearly chapbook competition. "*DIAGRAM* is an electronic journal of text and art, found and created. We're interested in representations, naming, indicating, schematics, labelling and taxonomy of things; in poems that masquerade as stories; in stories that disguise themselves as indices or obituaries. We specialize in work that pushes the boundaries of traditional genre or work that is in some way schematic. We do publish traditional fiction and poetry, too, but hybrid forms (short stories, prose poems, indexes, tables of contents, etc.) are particularly welcome! We also publish diagrams and schematics (original and found)." Circ. 1,500/day unique visitors online; 300,000+ hits/month. Time between acceptance and publication is 1-10 months. Accepts queries by e-mail. Accepts simultaneous submissions. Responds in 2 weeks to queries; 1-2 months to mss. Often comments on rejected mss. Print-version sample copy: $12 print. Writer's guidelines online.

[O] Publishes 6 new writers/year. Bimonthly. Member CLMP. "We sponsor yearly contests for unpublished hybrid essays and innovative fiction. Guidelines online."

NONFICTION Contact: Nicole Walker, nonfiction editor.

PHOTOS Reviews prints, slides, zip disks, magnetic tapes, DCs, punch cards.

FICTION Receives 100 unsolicited mss/month. Accepts 2-3 mss/issue; 15 mss/year. Needs experimental, literary. "We don't publish genre fiction unless it's exceptional and transcends the genre boundaries." Send complete ms. Accepts submissions by Web submissions manager; no e-mail. If sending by snail mail, send SASE for return of the ms, or send disposable copy of the ms and #10 SASE for reply only. Average length: 250-2,000 words.

POETRY Submit 3-6 poems at a time. Electronic submissions accepted through submissions manager; no e-mail, disk, or fax submissions. Electronic submissions much preferred; print submissions must include SASE if response is expected. Cover letter is preferred. Reads submissions year round. Poems are circulated to an editorial board. Sometimes comments on rejected poems. Sometimes publishes theme issues. Receives about 1,000 poems/year, accepts about 5%. Does not want light verse. Lines/poem: no limit.

TIPS "Submit interesting text, images, sound, and new media. We value the insides of things, vivisection, urgency, risk, elegance, flamboyance, work that moves us, language that does something new, or does something old—well. We like iteration and reiteration. Ruins and ghosts. Mechanical, moving parts, balloons, and frenzy. We want art and writing that demonstrates/interaction; the processes of things; how functions are accomplished; how things become or expire, move or stand. We'll consider anything. We do not consider e-mail submissions but encourage electronic submissions via our submissions manager software. Look at the journal and submissions guidelines before submitting."

$ EPOCH

251 Goldwin Smith Hall, Cornell University, Ithaca NY 14853. (607)255-3385. **Fax:** (607)255-6661. **Website:** english.arts.cornell.edu/publications/epoch. **100% freelance written.** Literary magazine published 3 times/year. Well-written literary fiction, poetry, personal essays. Newcomers welcome. Open to mainstream and avant-garde writing. Estab. 1947. Circ. 1,000. Byline given. Pays on publication. Offers 100% kill fee. Publishes ms an average of 6 months after acceptance. Editorial lead time 6 months. Submit seasonal material 8 months in advance. Accepts queries by mail. Responds in 2 weeks to queries. Responds in 6 weeks to mss. Sometimes comments on rejected mss. Sample copy for $5. Guidelines online and for #10 SASE.

NONFICTION Needs essays, interview. No inspirational. **Buys 6-8 mss/year.** Send complete ms. **Pays $5 and up/printed page.**

PHOTOS Send photos. Reviews contact sheets, transparencies, any size prints. Negotiates payment individually.

FICTION Needs ethnic, experimental, mainstream, novel concepts, literary short stories. No genre fiction. Would like to see more Southern fiction (Southern U.S). **Buys 25-30 mss/year.** Send complete ms. Considers fiction in all forms, short short to novella length. **Pays $5 and up/printed page.**

POETRY Needs avant-garde, free verse, haiku, light verse, traditional. Mss not accompanied by SASE will be discarded unread. Occasionally provides criticism on poems. Considers poetry in all forms. Buys 30-75 poems/year. Submit maximum 5 poems. **Pays $5 and up/printed page.**

TIPS "Tell your story, speak your poem, straight from the heart. We are attracted to language and to good writing, but we are most interested in what the good writing leads us to, or where."

[O] $ $ EVENT

Douglas College, P.O. Box 2503, New Westminster BC V3L 5B2 Canada. (604)527-5293. **Fax:** (604)527-5095. **E-mail:** event@douglascollege.ca. **Website:** www.eventmags.com. **100% freelance written.** Magazine published 3 times/year containing fiction, poetry, creative nonfiction, notes on writing, and reviews. "We are eclectic and always open to content that invites involvement. Generally, we like strong narrative." Estab. 1971. Circ. 1,000. Byline given. Pays on publication. Publishes ms an average of 8 months after acceptance. Accepts queries by mail. Accepts simultaneous submissions. Responds in 1 month to queries. Responds in 6 months to mss. Guidelines online.

[O] *EVENT* does not read mss in July, August, December, and January. No e-mail submissions.

All submissions must include SASE (Canadian postage, or IRCs, or USD $1).

FICTION "We look for readability, style, and writing that invites involvement." Submit maximum 2 stories. Needs contemporary. No technically poor or unoriginal pieces. **Buys 12-15 mss/year.** Send complete ms. Length: 5,000 words maximum. **Pays $25/page up to $500.**

POETRY Needs free verse. "We tend to appreciate the narrative and sometimes the confessional modes." No light verse. Buys 30-40 poems/year. Submit maximum 10 poems. **Pays $25-500.**

TIPS "Write well and read some past issues of *EVENT*."

✪ FICTION

Dept. of English, The City College of New York, 138th St. & Covenant Ave., New York NY 10031. **Website:** www.fictioninc.com. **Contact:** Mark J. Mirsky, editor. "As the name implies, we publish only fiction; we are looking for the best new writing available, leaning toward the unconventional. *Fiction* has traditionally attempted to make accessible the inaccessible, to bring the experimental to a broader audience." Reading period for unsolicited mss is September 15-May 15. Estab. 1972. Circ. 4,000. Publishes ms an average of 1 year after acceptance. Accepts simultaneous submissions. Responds in 3 months to mss. Sample copy for $7. Guidelines online.

O   Stories first published in *Fiction* have been selected for the *Pushcart Prize: Best of the Small Presses*, *O. Henry Prize Stories*, and *Best American Short Stories*.

FICTION Needs experimental, humorous, satire, Also needs contemporary, literary, translations. No romance, science fiction, etc. Submit complete ms via online submissions manager. Length: up to 5,000 words.

TIPS "The guiding principle of *Fiction* has always been to go to terra incognita in the writing of the imagination and to ask that modern fiction set itself serious questions, if often in absurd and comedic voices, interrogating the nature of the real and the fantastic. It represents no particular school of fiction, except the innovative. Its pages have often been a harbor for writers at odds with each other. As a result of its willingness to publish the difficult, experimental, and unusual, while not excluding the well known, *Fiction* has a unique reputation in the US and abroad as a journal of future directions."

☁ THE FIDDLEHEAD

University of New Brunswick, Campus House, 11 Garland Court, Box 4400, Fredericton NB E3B 5A3 Canada. (506)453-3501. **Fax:** (506) 453-5069. **E-mail:** fiddlehd@unb.ca. **Website:** www.thefiddlehead.ca. Mark Anthony Jarman and Gerard Beirne, fiction editors; Sarah Bernstein, Phillip Crymble, Claire Kelly, and Ian LeTourneau, poetry editors. **Contact:** Kathryn Taglia, managing editor. "Canada's longest living literary journal, *The Fiddlehead* is published 4 times/year at the University of New Brunswick, with the generous assistance of the University of New Brunswick, the Canada Council for the Arts, and the Province of New Brunswick. It is experienced; wise enough to recognize excellence; always looking for freshness and surprise. *The Fiddlehead* publishes short stories, poems, book reviews, and a small number of personal essays. Our full-color covers have become collectors' items and feature work by New Brunswick artists and from New Brunswick museums and art galleries. *The Fiddlehead* also sponsors an annual writing contest. The journal is open to good writing in English from all over the world, looking always for freshness and surprise. Our editors are always happy to see new unsolicited works in fiction and poetry. Work is read on an ongoing basis; the acceptance rate is around 1-2%. Apart from our annual contest, we have no deadlines for submissions." Estab. 1945. Circ. 1,500. Pays on publication for first or one-time serial rights. Responds in 3-9 months to mss. Occasionally comments on rejected mss. Sample copy for $15 (U.S.).

FICTION Receives 100-150 unsolicited mss/month. Accepts 4-5 mss/issue; 20-40 mss/year. Agented fiction: small percentage. Publishes high percentage of new writers/year. Needs literary. Send SASE and *Canadian* stamps or IRCs for return of mss. No e-mail, fax, or disc submissions. Simultaneous submissions only if stated on cover letter; must contact immediately if accepted elsewhere. Length: up to 6,000 words. Also publishes short shorts. **Pays up to $40 (Canadian)/published page and 2 contributor's copies.**

POETRY Send SASE and *Canadian* stamps or IRCs for return of mss. No e-mail, fax, or disc submissions. Simultaneous submissions only if stated on cover letter; must contact immediately if accepted elsewhere. Submit maximum 10 poems. **Pays up to $40 (Canadian)/published page and 2 contributor's copies.**

TIPS "If you are serious about submitting to *The Fiddlehead*, you should subscribe or read an issue or 2 to get a sense of the journal. Contact us if you would to order sample back issues ($10-15 plus postage)."

FIELD: CONTEMPORARY POETRY & POETICS

Oberlin College Press, 50 N. Professor St., Oberlin OH 44074-1091. (440)775-8408. **Fax:** (440)775-8124. **E-mail:** oc.press@oberlin.edu. **Website:** www.oberlin.edu/ocpress. **Contact:** managing editor. **60% freelance written.** Biannual magazine of poetry, poetry in translation, and essays on contemporary poetry by poets. *FIELD: Contemporary Poetry and Poetics*, published semiannually in April and October, is a literary journal with "emphasis on poetry, translations, and essays by poets. See electronic submission guidelines." Estab. 1969. Circ. 1,500. Byline given. Pays on publication. Editorial lead time 4 months. Accepts queries by mail, e-mail, fax, phone, online submission form. Responds in 6-8 weeks to mss. Sample copy for $8. Guidelines online and for #10 SASE.

○ *FIELD* is 100 pages, digest-sized, printed on rag stock, flat-spined, with glossy color card cover. Subscription: $16/year, $28 for 2 years. Sample: $8 postpaid. Has published poetry by Michelle Glazer, Tom Lux, Carl Phillips, Betsy Sholl, Charles Simic, Jean Valentine and translations by Marilyn Hacker and Stuart Friebert.

POETRY Needs contemporary, prose poems, free verse, traditional. Submissions are read August 1 through May 31. Submit 3-5 of your best poems. No e-mail submissions. Include cover letter and SASE. Submit using submission manager: www.oberlin.edu/ocpress/submissions.html. Buys 120 poems/year. Submit maximum 5 poems. **Pays $15/page and 2 contributor's copies.**

TIPS "Keep trying!"

FIVE POINTS

Georgia State University, P.O. Box 3999, Atlanta GA 30302-3999. **E-mail:** fivepoints@gsu.edu. **Website:** www.fivepoints.gsu.edu. **Contact:** Megan Sexton. Triannual literary journal publishing short shorts, literary essays, poetry. *"Five Points* is committed to publishing work that compels the imagination through the use of fresh and convincing language." Estab. 1996. Circ. 2,000. Publishes ms an average of 6 months after acceptance. Responds in 1-4 months. Sample copy for $7. Guidelines online.

○ Magazine: 6×9; 200 pages; cotton paper; glossy cover; photos. Has recently published Alice Hoffman, Natasha Tretheway, Pamela Painter, Billy Collins, Philip Levine, George Singleton, Hugh Sheehy, and others.

NONFICTION Reads creative nonfiction January 1-April 1. Include cover letter. Length: up to 7,500 words. **Pays $15/page minimum; $250 maximum, free subscription to magazine and 2 contributor's copies; additional copies $4.**

FICTION Receives 250 unsolicited mss/month. Accepts 4 mss/issue; 15-20 mss/year. Reads fiction January 1-April 1. Publishes 1 new writer/year. Sometimes comments on rejected mss. Sponsors awards/contests. Include cover letter. Average length: 7,500 words. **Pays $15/page minimum; $250 maximum, free subscription to magazine and 2 contributor's copies; additional copies $4.**

POETRY Reads poetry January 1-April 1. Include cover letter with submission. Submit maximum 3 poems. Length: up to 50 lines/poem.

TIPS "We place no limitations on style or content. Our only criteria is excellence. If your writing has an original voice, substance, and significance, send it to us. We will publish distinctive, intelligent writing that has something to say and says it in a way that captures and maintains our attention."

THE FOURTH RIVER

Chatham College, Woodland Rd., Pittsburgh PA 15232. **E-mail:** 4thriver@gmail.com. **Website:** fourthriver.chatham.edu. **Contact:** Sheryl St. Germain, executive editor; Sheila Squillante, editor-in-chief. **100% freelance written.** *The Fourth River*, an annual publication of Chatham University's MFA in Creative Writing Programs, features literature that engages and explores the relationship between humans and their environments. Wants writings that are richly situated at the confluence of place, space, and identity, or that reflect upon or make use of landscape and place in new ways. Estab. 2005. Byline given. Pays with contributor copies only. Publishes mss in 5-8 months after acceptance. Accepts queries by mail. Accepts simultaneous submissions. Responds in 3-5 months to mss. Sample copy for $10. Guidelines online.

○ *The Fourth River* is digest-sized, perfect-bound, with full-color cover by various artists. Accepts about 30-40 poems/year. Press run is 500. Single copy: $10; subscription: $16 for 2 years. Back issues: $5. Make checks payable to Chatham University.

NONFICTION Contact: Sheila Squillante, nonfiction editor. Needs Accepts previously unpublished book excerpts, essays, expose, general interest, historical, humor, opinion, personal experience, travel. Send complete ms. Submit by post or through Submittable. Cover letter is preferred. SASE is required for response. Length: 7,000 maximum (double-spaced).

FICTION Contact: Marc Nieson, fiction editor. Needs previously unpublished adventure, cond novels, confession, ethnic, experimental, fantasy, historical, horror, humorous, mainstream, mystery, novel concepts, romance, science fiction, slice-of-life vignettes, suspense, western, literary. Send complete ms. Submit by post or through Submittable Cover letter is preferred. SASE is required for response. Length: 7,000 words maximum (double-spaced).

POETRY Contact: Heather McNaugher, poetry editor. Needs avant-garde, free verse, haiku, light verse, traditional. No previously published poems. Submit by post or through Submittable. Cover letter is preferred. SASE is required for response. Poems are circulated to an editorial board. Sometimes comments on rejected poems. Sometimes publishes theme issues. Submit maximum 7 poems. Length: 25 pages maximum.

☺ FREEFALL MAGAZINE

Freefall Literary Society of Calgary, 922 Ninth Ave. SE, Calgary AB T2G 0S4 Canada. **E-mail:** editors@ freefallmagazine.ca. **Website:** www.freefallmagazine. ca. **Contact:** Lynn C. Fraser, managing editor. **100% freelance written.** "Magazine published triannually containing fiction, poetry, creative nonfiction, essays on writing, interviews, and reviews. We are looking for exquisite writing with a strong narrative." Estab. 1990. Circ. 1,000. Pays on publication. Accepts queries by e-mail. Guidelines and submission forms online.

NONFICTION Needs essays, interview, creative nonfiction. Submit via e-mail. E-mail subject line should include your name and type of submission (poetry, fiction, nonfiction, creative nonfiction, flash fiction, short fiction, photo, art work, etc.) Include name, contact information, and description of the type of work you are querying about. **Pays $10/printed page in the magazine, to a maximum of $100, and 1 contributor's copy.**

FICTION Submit via website form. Attach submission file (file name format is lastname_firstname_storytitle.doc or .docx or .pdf). Length: no more than 4,000 words. **Pays $10 per printed page in the magazine, to a maximum of $100, and 1 contributor's copy.**

POETRY Submit 2-5 poems via website. Attach submission file (file name format is lastname_firstname_storytitle.doc or .docx or .pdf). Accepts any style of poetry. Submit maximum 5 poems. Length: no more than 6 pages. **Pays $25 per poem and 1 contributor's copy.**

TIPS "Our mission is to encourage the voices of new, emerging, and experienced Canadian writers and provide a platform for their quality work. Although we accept work from all over the world we maintain a commitment to 85% Canadian content."

FUGUE LITERARY MAGAZINE

200 Brink Hall, University of Idaho, P.O. Box 44110, Moscow ID 83844. **E-mail:** fugue@uidaho.edu. **Website:** www.fuguejournal.org. **Contact:** Alexandra Teague, faculty advisor. Biannual literary magazine. "Submissions are accepted online only. Poetry, Fiction, and Nonfiction submissions are accepted September 1-April 1. All material received outside of this period will not be read." $2 submission fee per entry. See website for submission instructions. Estab. 1990. Circ. 500. Accepts queries by online submission form. Accepts simultaneous submissions. Responds in 2-4 months to mss. Sample copies available for $8.00. Guidelines online.

NONFICTION Contact: fugue-prosesubmit@uidaho.edu. Submit 1 essay using online submissions manager. **All contributors receive payment and 2 contributor's copies.**

FICTION Contact: fugue-fiction@uidaho.edu. "Please send no more than 2 short-shorts or 1 story at a time. Submissions in more than 1 genre should be submitted separately. All multiple submissions will be returned unread. Once you have submitted a piece to us, wait for a response on this piece before submitting again." Submit using online submissions manager. **All contributors receive payment and 2 contributor's copies.**

POETRY Contact: fugue-poetry@uidaho.edu. Submit a set of up to 3 poems using online submissions manager. **All contributors receive payment and 2 complimentary copies of the journal.**

TIPS "The best way, of course, to determine what we're looking for is to read the journal. As the name *Fugue* indicates, our goal is to present a wide range of literary perspectives. We like stories that satisfy us both intellectually and emotionally, with fresh language and characters so captivating that they stick with us and invite a second reading. We are also seeking creative literary criticism which illuminates a piece of literature or a specific writer by examining that writer's personal experience."

GARGOYLE

Paycock Press, 3819 N. 13th St., Arlington VA 22201. (703)525-9296. **E-mail:** rchrdpeabody@gmail.com. **E-mail:** gargoyle@gargoylemagazine.com. **Website:** www.gargoylemagazine.com. **Contact:** Richard Peabody, editor, Lucinda Ebersole, co-editor. **75% freelance written.** "*Gargoyle* has always been a scallywag magazine, a maverick magazine, a bit too academic for the underground and way too underground for the academics. We are a writer's magazine in that we are read by other writers and have never worried about reaching the masses." Annual. Wants "edgy realism or experimental works. We run both." Wants to see more Canadian, British, Australian, and Third World fiction. Receives 200 unsolicited mss/week during submission period. Accepts 20-50 mss/issue. Accepts submissions from June 1 until full; in 2013 that was by June 17. Agented fiction 5%. **Publishes 2-3 new writers/year.** Recently published work by Anya Achtenberg, im Agaolu, Nin Andrews, Gary Blankenburg, C.L. Beldsoe, Ann Bogle, Rae Bryant, Patrick Chapman, Nina Corwin, Jim Daniels, Kristina Marie Darling, Sean Thomas Dougherty, Guillermo Fadanelli, Gary Fincke, Rebecca Foust, Stephen Gibson, Maria Gillan, Joe Hall, Michael Hemmingson, Nancy Hightower, David MacLeavey, Kat Meads, Teresa Mibrodt, Leslie F. Miller, Donaji Olmedo, Catherine Owen, David Plumb, Doug Ramspeck, Doug Rice, Kim Roberts, Barry Silesky, Edgar Gabriel Silex, Curtis Smith, Barry Spacks, Susan Tepper, Sue Ellen Thompson, Meredith Trede, Meg Tuite, Sara Uribe, Julie Wakeman-Linn, Vallie Lynn Watson, Brandi Wells, Mary-Sherman Willis, and Bill Wolak. Estab. 1976. Circ. 2,000. Publishes ms 1 year after acceptance. Accepts queries by online submission form. Accepts simultaneous submissions. Responds in 1 month to queries, proposals, and mss. Sample copy for $12.95. Catalog online at FAQ link. "We don't have guidelines; we have never believed in them." Query in an e-mail. "We prefer electronic submissions. Please use submission engine online." For snail mail, send SASE for reply, return of ms or send a disposable copy of ms.

NONFICTION Needs memoir, photo feature, creative nonfiction, literary criticism. **Pays 10% of print run and 50-50 split (after/if we break even). Sends galleys to author.**

FICTION Needs experimental, poetry, literary, short story collections. No romance, horror, science fiction. **Buys 10-15 mss/year.** Length: 1,000-4,500 words.

POETRY Pays contributor's copies.

TIPS "We have to fall in love with a particular fiction."

THE GEORGIA REVIEW

The University of Georgia, Athens GA 30602. (706)542-3481. **Fax:** (706)542-0047. **E-mail:** garev@uga.edu. **Website:** thegeorgiareview.com. **Contact:** Stephen Corey, editor. **99% freelance written.** Quarterly journal. "Our readers are educated, inquisitive people who read a lot of work in the areas we feature, so they expect only the best in our pages. All work submitted should show evidence that the writer is at least as well-educated and well-read as our readers. Essays should be authoritative but accessible to a range of readers." Estab. 1947. Circ. 3,500. Byline given. Pays on publication. Publishes ms an average of 6 months after acceptance. Accepts queries by mail. Responds in 2 weeks to queries. Responds in 2-3 months to mss. Sample copy for $10. Guidelines online.

○ No simultaneous submissions. Electronic submissions available for $3 fee.

NONFICTION Needs essays. **Buys 12-20 mss/year.** For the most part we are not interested in scholarly articles that are narrow in focus and/or overly burdened with footnotes. The ideal essay for *The Georgia Review* is a provocative, thesis-oriented work that can engage both the intelligent general reader and the specialist. Send complete ms. "We do not consider unsolicited mss between May 15-August 15. Submissions received during that period will be returned unread. Work previously published in any form or submitted simultaneously to other journals will not be considered." **Pays $40/published page.**

PHOTOS Send photos. Reviews 5x7 prints or larger. Offers no additional payment for photos accepted with ms.

FICTION "We seek original, excellent writing not bound by type." "Ordinarily we do not publish novel excerpts or works translated into English, and we strongly discourage authors from submitting these."

Buys 12-20 mss/year. Send complete ms. "We do not consider unsolicited mss between May 15-August 15. Submissions received during that period will be returned unread. Work previously published in any form or submitted simultaneously to other journals will not be considered." Open **Pays $50/published page.**

POETRY "We seek original, excellent poetry. Submit 3-5 poems at a time." Buys 60-75 poems/year. Submit maximum 5 poems. **Pays $4/line.**

TIPS "Unsolicited mss will not be considered from May 15-August 15 (annually); all such submissions received during that period will be returned unread. Check website for submission guidelines."

🟢 THE GETTYSBURG REVIEW

Gettysburg College, Gettysburg PA 17325. (717)337-6770. **Fax:** (717)337-6775. **Website:** www.gettysburgreview.com. **Contact:** Peter Stitt, editor. Quarterly magazine. "Our concern is quality. Mss submitted here should be extremely well written. Reading period September 1-May 31." Estab. 1988. Circ. 3,000. Byline given. Pays on publication. Publishes ms an average of 6 months after acceptance. Editorial lead time 1 year. Submit seasonal material 9 months in advance. Accepts queries by mail, fax. Accepts simultaneous submissions. Responds in 1 month to queries. Responds in 3-5 months to mss. Sample copy for $10. Guidelines online.

NONFICTION Needs essays. **Buys 20 mss/year.** Send complete ms. Length: 25 ms pages. **Pays $30/page and 1 contributor's copy.**

FICTION **Contact:** Mark Drew, assisant editor. Wants high quality, literary fiction. Needs experimental, historical, humorous, mainstream, novel concepts, serialized, contemporary. "We require that fiction be intelligent and esthetically written." No genre fiction. **Buys 20 mss/year.** Send complete ms with SASE. Length: 2,000-7,000 words. **Pays $30/page and 1 contributor's copy.**

POETRY Considers "well-written poems of all kinds." Has published poetry by Rita Dove, Alice Friman, Philip Schultz, Michelle Boisseau, Bob Hicok, Linda Pastan, and G.C. Waldrep. Buys 50 poems/year. Submit maximum 5 poems. **Pays $2.50/line and 1 contributor's copy.**

GINOSKO

P.O. Box 246, Fairfax CA 94978. **E-mail:** ginoskoeditor@aol.com. **Website:** www.ginoskoliteraryjournal. com. **Contact:** Robert Paul Cesaretti, editor. "*Ginos ko* (ghin-océ-koe): To perceive, understand, realize, come to know; knowledge that has an inception, a progress, an attainment. The recognition of truth by experience." Accepting short fiction and poetry, creative nonfiction, interviews, social-justice concerns, and spiritual insights for www.GinoskoLiteraryJournal.com. Member CLMP. Estab. 2003. Circ. 9,000+. Website receives 800-1,200 hits/month. Editorial lead time 1-2 months. Accepts queries by mail, e-mail. Accepts simultaneous submissions. Guidelines online at website.

🔵 Reads year round. Length of articles flexible; accepts excerpts. Publishing as semiannual ezine. Check downloadable issues online for tone and style. Downloads free; accepts donations. Also looking for books, art, and music to post online, and links to exchange.

REPRINTS Accepts reprints.

FICTION *Ginosko* Flash Fiction Contest: Deadline is March 1; $5 entry fee; $250 prize.

🟢🟢 GLIMMER TRAIN STORIES

Glimmer Train Press, Inc., P.O. Box 80430, Portland OR 97280. **Fax:** (503)221-0837. **E-mail:** eds@glimmertrain.org. **Website:** www.glimmertrain.org. **90% freelance written.** Triannual magazine of literary short fiction. "We are interested in literary short stories, particularly by new and emerging writers." Estab. 1991. Circ. 12,000. Byline given. Pays on acceptance. Publishes ms an average of 15 months after acceptance. Accepts simultaneous submissions. Responds in 2 months to mss. Sometimes comments on rejected mss. Sample copy for $14 online. Guidelines online.

FICTION Buys 40 mss/year. Submit via the website. "In a pinch, send a hard copy and include SASE for response." Length: 1,200-12,000 words. **Pays $700 for standard submissions, up to $2,500 for contest-winning stories.**

TIPS "In the last 2 years over half of the first-place stories have been their authors' very first publications. See our contest listings in contest and awards section."

🔵 GRAIN

P.O. Box 67, Saskatoon SK S7K 3K1 Canada. (306)244-2828. **Fax:** (306)244-0255. **E-mail:** grainmag@sasktel. net. **Website:** www.grainmagazine.ca. **Contact:** Rilla Friesen, editor. Quarterly magazine covering poetry, fiction, creative nonfiction. "*Grain, The Journal Of Eclectic Writing,* is a literary quarterly that publishes engaging, diverse, and challenging writing and art by some of the best Canadian and international writers and artists. Every issue features superb new writing from both developing and established writers. Each issue also highlights the unique artwork of a different visual artist. *Grain* has garnered national and international recognition for its distinctive, cutting-edge content and design." Estab. 1973. Circ. 1,600. Byline given. Pays on publication for first Canadian serial rights. Typically responds in 3-6 months. Guidelines available by SASE (or SAE and IRC), e-mail, or online.

NONFICTION No academic papers or reportage. "No fax or e-mail submissions; postal submissions only. Send typed, unpublished material only (we consider work published online to be previously published). Please only submit work in 1 genre at 1 time." Length: 5,000 words maximum. **Pays $50-225 CAD (depending on number of pages) and 2 contributor's copies.**

FICTION Needs experimental, literary, mainstream, contemporary. No romance, confession, science fiction, vignettes, mystery. "Submissions must be typed in readable font (ideally 12 point, Times Roman or Courier), free of typos, printed on 1 side only. No staples. Your name and address must be on every page. Pieces of more than 1 page must be numbered. Cover letter with all contact information, title(s), and genre of work is required." Length: 5,000/words max; "stories at the longer end of the word count must be of exceptional quality."

POETRY Needs individual poems, sequences, suites. Wants "High quality, imaginative, well-crafted poetry." Submit up to 12 pages of poetry, typed in readable font on 1 side only. No previously published poems or simultaneous submissions. No fax or e-mail submissions; postal submissions only. Cover letter with all contact information, title(s), and genre of work is required. "No staples. Your name and address must be on every page. Pieces of more than 1 page must be numbered. Please only submit work in one genre at one time." **Pays $50-225 CAD (depending on number of pages) and 2 contributor's copies.**

TIPS "Submissions read September-May only. Mss postmarked between June 1 and August 31 will not be read. Only work of the highest literary quality is accepted. Read several back issues."

ⓢⓢ GUD MAGAZINE

Greatest Uncommon Denominator Publishing, P.O. Box 1537, Laconia NH 03247. **E-mail:** spiderbait1@ gudmagazine.com. **Website:** www.gudmagazine.com. **99% freelance written.** Semiannual magazine covering literary content and art. *"GUD Magazine* transcends and encompasses the audiences of both genre and literary fiction by featuring fiction, art, poetry, essays and reports, comics, and short drama." Estab. 2006. Byline given. Pays on publication. Publishes ms an average of 6-12 months after acceptance. Editorial lead time 6 months. Submit seasonal material 6 months in advance. Accepts queries by online submission form. Accepts simultaneous submissions. Responds in 6 months to mss. Guidelines online.

NONFICTION Needs book excerpts, essays, historical, humor, interview, personal experience, photo feature, travel, interesting event. **Buys 2-4 mss/year.** Submit complete ms using online form. Length: up to 15,000 words. **Pays a minimum of $5/piece, or 3¢/word for longer pieces.**

PHOTOS Send photos and artwork in electronic format. Model releases required for human images. Reviews GIF/JPEG files. Pays $12.

FICTION Needs adventure, erotica, ethnic, experimental, fantasy, horror, humorous, science fiction, suspense. **Buys 40 mss/year.** Submit via online submissions manager. Length: up to 15,000 words. **Pays a minimum of $5/piece, or 3¢/word for longer pieces.**

POETRY Needs avant-garde, free verse, haiku, light verse, traditional. Submit only 1 poem per entry form. Buys 12-20 poems/year. **Pays a minimum of $5/piece, or 3¢/word for longer pieces.**

FILLERS Buys comics. Reviews GIF/JPEG files. **Pays $12.**

TIPS "We publish work in any genre, plus artwork, factual articles, and interviews. We'll publish something as short as 20 words or as long as 15,000, as long as it grabs us. Be warned: We read a lot. We've seen it all before. We are not easy to impress. Is your work original? Does it have something to say? Read it again. If you genuinely believe it to be so, send it. We do accept simultaneous submissions, as well as multiple submissions, but read the guidelines first."

ⓢ GULF COAST: A JOURNAL OF LITERATURE AND FINE ARTS

4800 Calhoun Road, Houston TX 77204-3013. (713)743-3223. **E-mail:** editors@gulfcoastmag.org. **Website:** www.gulfcoastmag.org. **Contact:** Zachary Martin, editor; Karyna McGlynn, managing editor; Michelle Oakes, Justine Post, Patrick James, poetry editors; Julia Brown, Laura Jok, Ashley Wurzbacher, fiction editors; Beth Lyons, Steve Sanders, nonfiction editors. Biannual magazine covering innovative fiction, nonfiction, poetry, visual art, and critical art writing. Estab. 1986. Publishes ms 6 months-1 year after acceptance. Accepts queries by mail, phone. Accepts simultaneous submissions. Responds in 4-6 months to mss. Sometimes comments on rejected mss. Back issue for $8, 7x10 SASE with 4 first-class stamps. Writer's guidelines for #10 SASE or online.

NONFICTION Contact: Nonfiction editor. Needs interview, reviews. *Gulf Coast* reads general submissions, submitted by post or through the online submissions manager, September 1-March 1. Submissions e-mailed directly to the editors or postmarked March 1-September 1 will not be read or responded to. "Please visit our contest page for contest submission guidelines." **Pays $100 per review, and $200 per interview.** Sometimes pays expenses of writers on assignment.

FICTION Contact: Fiction editor. "Please do not send multiple submissions; we will read only 1 submission per author at a given time, except in the case of our annual contests." Needs ethnic, experimental, multicultural, literary, regional, translations, contemporary. No children's, genre, religious/inspirational. *Gulf Coast* reads general submissions, submitted by post or through the online submissions manager September 1-March 1. Submissions e-mailed directly to the editors or postmarked March 1-September 1 will not be read or responded to. "Please visit our contest page for contest submission guidelines." **Pays $50/page.**

POETRY Contact: Poetry editor. Submit up to 5 poems at a time. Considers simultaneous submissions with notification; no previously published poems. Cover letter is required. List previous publications and include a brief bio. Reads submissions September-April. Submit maximum 1-5 poems. **Pays $50/page.**

TIPS "Submit only previously unpublished works. Include a cover letter. Online submissions are strongly preferred. Stories or essays should be typed, double-spaced, and paginated with your name, address, and phone number on the first page, title on subsequent pages. Poems should have your name, address, and phone number on the first page of each." The Annual Gulf Coast Prizes awards publication and $1,500 each in poetry, fiction, and nonfiction; opens in December of each year. Honorable mentions in each category will receive a $250 second prize. Postmark/online entry deadline: March 15 of each year. Winners and honorable mentions will be announced in May. **Entry fee:** $23 (includes 1-year subscription). Make checks payable to *Gulf Coast*. Guidelines online.

HANGING LOOSE

Hanging Loose Press, 231 Wyckoff St., Brooklyn NY 11217. **E-mail:** editor@hangingloosepress.com. **Website:** www.hangingloosepress.com. **Contact:** Robert Hershon, Dick Lourie, and Mark Pawlak, poetry editors. *Hanging Loose*, published in April and October, concentrates on the work of new writers. Wants excellent, energetic poems. Estab. 1966. Responds in 3 months. Sample: $14.

💬 *Hanging Loose* is 120 pages, offset-printed on heavy stock, flat-spined, with 4-color glossy card cover. Considers poetry by teens (one section contains poems by high-school-age poets). Has published poetry by Sherman Alexie, Paul Violi, Donna Brook, Kimiko Hahn, Harvey Shapiro, and Ha Jin.

POETRY Submit up to 6 poems at a time. No fax or e-mail submissions; postal submissions only. No simultaneous submissions. "Would-be contributors should read the magazine first." **Pays small fee and 2 contributor's copies.**

$ HAYDEN'S FERRY REVIEW

C/o Dept. of English, Arizona State University, P.O. Box 870302, Tempe AZ 85287. (480)965-1337. **E-mail:** HFR@asu.edu. **Website:** www.haydensferryreview.org. **Contact:** Sam Martone, editor. **85% freelance written.** Semiannual magazine. "*Hayden's Ferry Review* publishes the best quality fiction, poetry, and creative nonfiction from new, emerging, and established writers." Estab. 1986. Circ. 1,000. Byline given. No honorarium. Publishes ms an average of 6 months after acceptance. Editorial lead time 5 months. Accepts queries by online submission form. Accepts simultaneous submissions. Responds in 1 week or less to e-mail queries. Responds in 3-4 months to mss. Sample copy for $9. Guidelines online.

💬 Work from *Hayden's Ferry Review* has been selected for inclusion in *Pushcart Prize* anthologies and *Best Creative Nonfiction*.

NONFICTION Needs essays, interview, personal experience. **Buys 2 mss/year.** Send complete ms. Word length open **Pays $50.**

PHOTOS Send photos. Reviews slides.

FICTION Contact: Editors change every 1-2 years. Needs ethnic, experimental, humorous, slice-of-life vignettes, contemporary, prose poem. **Buys 10 mss/year.** Send complete ms. Word length open.

POETRY Needs avant-garde, free verse, haiku, light verse, traditional. Buys 60 poems/year. Submit maximum 6 poems. Word length open.

$ THE HOLLINS CRITIC

P.O. Box 9538, Hollins University, Roanoke VA 24020-1538. **E-mail:** acockrell@hollins.edu. **Website:** www.hollins.edu/academics/critic. **Contact:** Cathryn Hankla. **100% freelance written.** Magazine published 5 times/year. Estab. 1964. Circ. 400. Byline given. Pays on publication. Publishes ms an average of 1 year after acceptance. Accepts queries by online submission form. Accepts simultaneous submissions. Responds in 2 months to mss. Sample copy for $3. Guidelines for #10 SASE.

💬 Uses a few short poems in each issue, interesting in form, content, or both. *The Hollins Critic* is 24 pages, magazine-sized. Press run is 500. Subscription: $12/year ($17 outside US). No postal or e-mail submissions. Has published poetry by Natasha Trethewey, Carol Moldaw, David Huddle, Margaret Gibson, and Julia Johnson.

POETRY Needs avant-garde, free verse, traditional. Submit up to 5 poems at a time using the online submission form at www.hollinscriticsubmissions.com, available September 15-December 1. Submissions received at other times will be returned unread. "We read poetry only from September 15-December 15." Publishes 16-20 poems/year. **Pays $25/poem plus 5 contributor's copies.**

TIPS "We accept unsolicited poetry submissions; all other content is by prearrangement."

HUBBUB

5344 SE 38th Ave., Portland OR 97202. **E-mail:** lisa.steinman@reed.edu. **Website:** www.reed.edu/hubbub/. J. Shugrue and Lisa M. Steinman, co-editors. *Hubbub*, published once/year in the spring, is designed "to feature a multitude of voices from interesting contemporary American poets." Wants "poems that are well-crafted, with something to say. We have no single style, subject, or length requirement and in particular will consider long poems." Estab. 1983. Responds in 4 months. Guidelines available for SASE.

POETRY Submit 3-6 typed poems at a time. No previously published poems or simultaneous submissions. Include SASE. "We review 2-4 poetry books/year in short (3-page) reviews; all reviews are solicited. We do, however, list books received/recommended." Send materials for review consideration. Does not want light verse. **Pays $20/poem.**

TIPS Outside judges choose poems from each volume for 3 awards: Vi Gale Award ($500), Stout Award ($75), and Kenneth O. Hanson Award ($100). There are no special submission procedures or entry fees involved.

$ THE HUDSON REVIEW

The Hudson Review, Inc., 684 Park Ave., New York NY 10065. **E-mail:** info@hudsonreview.com. **Website:** www.hudsonreview.com. **Contact:** Paula Deitz, editor. **100% freelance written.** Quarterly magazine publishing fiction, poetry, essays, book reviews; criticism of literature, art, theatre, dance, film and music; and articles on contemporary cultural developments. Estab. 1948. Circ. 2,000. Byline given. Pays on publication. Publishes ms an average of 6 months after acceptance. Editorial lead time 3 months. Accepts queries by mail. Responds in 6 months. Sample copy for $11. Guidelines for #10 SASE or online.

💬 Send with SASE. Mss sent outside accepted reading period will be returned unread if SASE contains sufficient postage.

NONFICTION Contact: Paula Deitz. Needs essays, general interest, historical, opinion, personal experience, travel. **Buys 4-6 mss/year.** Send complete ms between January 1-March 31 only. Length: up to 3,500 words.

FICTION Reads between September 1-November 30 only. **Buys 4 mss/year.** Length: up to 10,000 words.

POETRY Reads poems only between April 1-June 30. Buys 12-20 poems/year. Submit maximum 7 poems.

TIPS "We do not specialize in publishing any particular 'type' of writing; our sole criterion for accepting unsolicited work is literary quality. The best way for you to get an idea of the range of work we publish is to read a current issue. We do not consider simultaneous submissions. Unsolicited mss submitted outside of specified reading times will be returned unread. Do not send submissions via e-mail."

$ HUNGER MOUNTAIN

Vermont College of Fine Arts, 36 College St., Montpelier VT 05602. (802)828-8517. **E-mail:** hungermtn@vcfa.edu. **Website:** www.hungermtn.org. Monthly online publication and annual perfect-bound journal covering high quality fiction, poetry, creative nonfiction, craft essays, writing for children, and artwork. Accepts high quality work from unknown, emerging, or successful writers. No genre fiction, drama, or academic articles, please. *Hunger Mountain* is about 200 pages, 7x10, professionally printed, perfect-bound, with full-bleed color artwork on cover. Press run is 1,000; 10,000 visits online monthly. Single copy: $10; subscription: $12/year, $22 for 2 years. Make checks payable to Vermont College of Fine Arts. Member: CLMP. Estab. 2002. Byline given. Pays on publication. Publishes ms an average of 1 year after acceptance. Submit seasonal material 1 year in advance. Accepts queries by online submission form. NoAccepts simultaneous submissions. Responds in 4 months to mss. Sample copy for $10. Writer's guidelines online.

⬤ Uses online submissions manager.

NONFICTION Needs "We welcome an array of traditional and experimental work, including, but not limited to, personal, lyrical, and meditative essays, memoirs, collages, rants, and humor. The only requirements are recognition of truth, a unique voice with a firm command of language, and an engaging story with multiple pressure points.". No informative or instructive articles, please. Prose for children and young adults is acceptable. Payment varies. Submit complete ms using online submissions manager. Length: no more than 10,000 words.

PHOTOS Send photos. Reviews contact sheets, transparencies, prints, GIF/JPEG files. Slides preferred. Negotiates payment individually.

FICTION "We look for work that is beautifully crafted and tells a good story, with characters that are alive and kicking, storylines that stay with us long after we've finished reading, and sentences that slay us with their precision." Needs adventure, high quality short stories and short shorts. No genre fiction, meaning science fiction, fantasy, horror, erotic, etc. Submit ms using online submissions manager. Length: no more than 10,000 words. **Pays $25-100.**

POETRY Needs avant-garde, free verse, traditional. Submit 3-10 poems at a time. All poems should be in ONE file. "We look for poetry that is as much about the world as about the self, that's an invitation, an opening out, a hand beckoning. We like poems that name or identify something essential that we may have overlooked. We like poetry with acute, precise attention to both content and diction." Submit using

online submissions manager. No light verse, humor/quirky/catchy verse, greeting card verse. Buys 10 poems/year.

TIPS "Mss must be typed, prose double-spaced. Poets submit at least 3 poems. No multiple genre submissions. Fresh viewpoints and human interest are very important, as is originality. We are committed to publishing an outstanding journal of the arts. Do not send entire novels, mss, or short story collections. Do not send previously published work."

💲 INDIANA REVIEW

Ballantine Hall 465, 1020 E. Kirkwood, Indiana University, Bloomington IN 47405. (812)855-3439. **E-mail:** inreview@indiana.edu. **Website:** indianareview. org. **Contact:** Katie Moulton, editor. **100% freelance written.** Biannual magazine. "*Indiana Review*, a non-profit organization run by IU graduate students, is a journal of previously unpublished poetry and fiction. Literary interviews and essays are also considered. We publish innovative fiction, nonfiction, and poetry. We're interested in energy, originality, and careful attention to craft. While we publish many well-known writers, we also welcome new and emerging poets and fiction writers." Estab. 1976. Circ. 5,000. Byline given. Pays on publication. Publishes ms an average of 3-6 months after acceptance. Accepts queries by mail, e-mail. Accepts simultaneous submissions. Responds in 2 or more weeks to queries. Responds in 4 or more months to mss. Sample copy for $12. Guidelines online.

🔑 Break in with 500-1,000 word book reviews of fiction, poetry, nonfiction, and literary criticism published within the last 2 years.

NONFICTION Contact: Justin Wolfe, nonfiction editor. Needs essays, interview, creative nonfiction, reviews. No coming-of-age/slice of life pieces. **Buys 5-7 mss/year.** Send complete ms. Length: up to 8,000. **Pays $5/page ($10 minimum), plus 2 contributor's copies.**

FICTION Contact: Joe Hiland, fiction editor. "We look for daring stories which integrate theme, language, character, and form. We like polished writing, humor, and fiction which has consequence beyond the world of its narrator." Needs ethnic, experimental, mainstream, novel concepts, literary, short fictions, translations. No genre fiction. **Buys 14-18 mss/year.** Send complete ms. Cover letters should be *brief* and demonstrate specific familiarity with the content of a recent issue of *Indiana Review*. Include SASE. Length: up to 8,000 words. **Pays $5/page ($10 minimum), plus 2 contributor's copies**.

POETRY Contact: Michael Mlekoday, poetry editor. "We look for poems that are skillful and bold, exhibiting an inventiveness of language with attention to voice and sonics." Wants experimental, free verse, prose poem, traditional form, lyrical, narrative. Buys 80 poems/year. Submit maximum 6 poems. Length: 5 lines minimum. **Pays $5/page ($10 minimum), plus 2 contributor's copies.**

TIPS "We're always looking for nonfiction essays that go beyond merely autobiographical revelation and utilize sophisticated organization and slightly radical narrative strategies. We want essays that are both lyrical and analytical where confession does not mean nostalgia. Read us before you submit. Often reading is slower in summer and holiday months. Only submit work to journals you would proudly subscribe to, then subscribe to a few. Take care to read the latest 2 issues and specifically mention work you identify with and why. Submit work that `stacks up' with the work we've published. Offers annual poetry, fiction, short-short/prose-poem prizes. See website for full guidelines."

⊙ THE IOWA REVIEW

308 EPB, The University of Iowa, Iowa City IA 52242. (319)335-0462. **Website:** www.iowareview.org. **Contact:** Harilaos Stecopoulos. Triannual magazine. *The Iowa Review*, published 3 times/year, prints fiction, poetry, essays, reviews, and, occasionally, interviews. *The Iowa Review* is 5.5×8.5, approximately 200 pages, professionally printed, flat-spined, first-grade offset paper, Carolina CS1 10-point cover stock. Receives about 5,000 submissions/year, accepts up to 100. Press run is 2,900; 1,500 distributed to stores. Subscription: $25. Stories, essays, and poems for a general readership interested in contemporary literature. Estab. 1970. Circ. 3,500. Pays on publication. Publishes ms an average of 12-18 months after acceptance. Accepts queries by mail. Accepts simultaneous submissions. Responds in 4 months to mss. Sample copy for $9.95 and online. Guidelines online.

○ "This magazine uses the help of colleagues and graduate assistants. Its reading period for unsolicited work is September 1-December 1. From January through April, we read entries to our annual Iowa Awards competition. Check our website for further information."

FICTION "We are open to a range of styles and voices and always hope to be surprised by work we then feel we need." Receives 600 unsolicited mss/month. Accepts 4-6 mss/issue; 12-18 mss/year. Does not read mss January-August. Publishes ms an average of 12-18 months after acceptance. Agented fiction less than 2%. **Publishes some new writers/year.** Recently published work by Jen Fawkes, Chris Offutt, Chinelo Okparanta. Send complete ms with cover letter. "Don't bother with queries." SASE for return of ms. SASE required. Responds in 4 months to mss. Accepts mss by snail mail and online submission form at https://iowareview.submittable.com/submit; no e-mail submissions. Simultaneous submissions accepted. **Pays $.08 per word ($100 minimum), plus 2 contributor's copies.**

POETRY Submit up to 8 pages at a time. Online submissions accepted, but no e-mail submissions. Cover letter (with title of work and genre) is encouraged. SASE required. Reads submissions "only during the fall semester, September through November, and then contest entries in the spring." Time between acceptance and publication is "around a year." Occasionally comments on rejected poems or offers suggestions on accepted poems. Pays $1.50/line of poetry, $40 minimum. "We simply look for poems that, at the time we read and choose, we find we admire. No specifications as to form, length, style, subject matter, or purpose. Though we print work from established writers, we're always delighted when we discover new talent."

TIPS "We publish essays, reviews, novel excerpts, stories, poems, and photography. We have no set guidelines as to content or length but strongly recommend that writers read a sample issue before submitting."

⊙ ⊙ ISLAND

P.O. Box 210, Sandy Bay Tasmania 7006 Australia. (61)(3)6226-2325. **E-mail:** matthew@islandmag.com. **Website:** www.islandmag.com. **Contact:** Matthew Lamb, editor. Quarterly magazine. *Island* seeks quality fiction, poetry, and essays. It is "one of Australia's leading literary magazines, tracing the contours of our national, and international culture, while still retaining a uniquely Tasmanian perspective." Estab. 1979. Circ. 1,500. Accepts queries by e-mail and submissions only online via website. Subscriptions and sample copies available for purchase online. Guidelines online.

○ Only publishes the work of subscribers; you can submit if you are not currently a subscriber, but if your piece is chosen, the subscription will be taken from the fee paid for the piece.

NONFICTION Needs essays. Query first with brief overview of essay and description of why you think it is suitable for *Island*. **Pay varies.**

FICTION Submit 1 piece at a time. **Pay varies.**

POETRY Submit maximum 3 poems. **Pay varies.**

$ THE JOURNAL

The Ohio State University, 164 W. 17th Ave., Columbus OH 43210. (614)292-6065. **Fax:** (614)292-7816. **E-mail:** managingeditor@thejournalmag.org. **Website:** thejournalmag.org. Quarterly magazine. "We are interested in quality fiction, poetry, nonfiction, art, and reviews of new books of poetry, fiction, and nonfiction. We impose no restrictions on category, type, or length of submission for Fiction, Poetry, and Nonfiction. We are happy to consider long stories and self-contained excerpts of novels. Please double-space all prose submissions. Please send 3-5 poems in 1 submission. We only accept online submissions and will not respond to mailed submissions." Estab. 1973. Circ. 1,500. Byline given. Payment for art contributors only. All other contributors receive 2 contributor's copies and a 1-year subscription. Publishes ms an average of 1 year after acceptance. Accepts queries by online submission form. Accepts simultaneous submissions. Responds in 3-4 months to mss. Sample copy for $8 on Submittable or free online spring and fall issues. Guidelines online: thejournalmag.org/submit. Submit online only at thejournal.submittable.com/submit.

💬 "We're open to all forms; we tend to favor work that gives evidence of a mature and sophisticated sense of the language."

NONFICTION Needs essays, interview. Does not accept queries. Send full ms via online submission system at thejournal.submittable.com. Publishes around 8 essays/year.

COLUMNS/DEPARTMENTS Reviews of contemporary poetry, fiction, and nonfiction, 1,500 words maximum. Publishes around 12 reviews/year.

FICTION Needs novel concepts, literary short stories. No romance, science fiction or religious/devotional. Does not accept queries. Send full ms via online submission system at thejournal.submittable.com.

POETRY Needs avant-garde, free verse, traditional. "However else poets train or educate themselves, they must do what they can to know our language. Too much of the writing we see indicates poets do not, in many cases, develop a feel for the possibilities of language, and do not pay attention to craft. Poets should not be in a rush to publish—until they are ready." Publishes about 100 poems/year. Submit maximum 5 poems.

TIPS "Mss are rejected because of lack of understanding of the short story form, shallow plots, undeveloped characters. Cure: Read as much well-written fiction as possible. Our readers prefer 'psychological' fiction rather than stories with intricate plots. Take care to present a clean, well-typed submission."

$ THE KENYON REVIEW

Finn House, 102 W. Wiggin, Gambier OH 43022. (740)427-5208. **Fax:** (740)427-5417. **E-mail:** kenyonreview@kenyon.edu. **Website:** www.kenyonreview.org. **Contact:** Marlene Landefeld. **100% freelance written.** Quarterly magazine covering contemporary literature and criticism. "An international journal of literature, culture, and the arts, dedicated to an inclusive representation of the best in new writing (fiction, poetry, essays, interviews, criticism) from established and emerging writers." Estab. 1939. Circ. 6,000. Byline given. Pays on publication. Publishes ms an average of 1 year after acceptance. Editorial lead time 1 year. Submit seasonal material 1 year in advance. Accepts simultaneous submissions. Responds in 4 months to mss. Sample copy $10, includes postage and handling. Call or e-mail to order. Guidelines online.

💬 *The Kenyon Review* is 180 pages, digest-sized, flat-spined. Receives about 7,000 submissions/year. Also now publishes *KR Online*, a separate and complementary literary magazine.

NONFICTION Needs essays, interview, criticism. Only accepts mss via online submissions program; visit website for instructions. Do not submit via e-mail or snail mail. Receives 130 unsolicited mss/month. Unsolicited mss read September 15-January 15 only. Length: 3-15 typeset pages preferred. **Pays $30/page.**

FICTION Receives 800 unsolicited mss/month. Unsolicited mss read September 15-January 15 only. Recently published work by Alice Hoffman, Beth Ann Fennelly, Romulus Linney, John Koethe, Albert Goldbarth, Erin McGraw. Needs condensed novels, ethnic, experimental, historical, humorous, mainstream, contemporary, excerpts from novels, gay/lesbian, literary, translations. Only accepts mss via online submissions program; visit website for instructions. Do not submit via e-mail or snail mail. Length: 3-15 type-set pages preferred. **Pays $30/page.**

POETRY Features all styles, forms, lengths, and subject matters. Considers translations. Has published poetry by Billy Collins, Diane Ackerman, John Kinsella, Carol Muske-Dukes, Diane di Prima, and Seamus Heaney. Submit up to 6 poems at a time. No previously published poems or simultaneous submissions. Only accepts mss via online submissions program; visit website for instructions. Do not submit via e-mail or snail mail. Reads submissions September 15-January 15. **Pays $40/page.**

TIPS "We no longer accept mailed or e-mailed submissions. Work will only be read if it is submitted through our online program on our website. Reading period is September 15-January 15. We look for strong voice, unusual perspective, and power in the writing."

LITERAL LATTE

200 E. 10th St., Suite 240, New York NY 10003. (212)260-5532. **E-mail:** litlatte@aol.com. **Website:** www.literal-latte.com. **Contact:** Jenine Gordon Bockman. **99% freelance written.** Bimonthly online publication with an annual print anthology featuring the best of the website. "We want great writing in all styles and subjects. A feast is made of a variety of flavors." Estab. 1994. Editorial lead time 3 months. Submit seasonal material 3 months in advance. Accepts queries by mail, e-mail. Accepts simultaneous submissions. Responds in 6 months to mss. Writer's guidelines online, via e-mail, or for #10 SASE.

NONFICTION Contact: Jeff Bockman, editor. Needs essays, personal experience. No scholarly reviews or essays. They must be personal. **Buys 10 mss/year.** Send complete ms. Length: no more than 10,000 words. **Pays minimum of anthology copies and maximum of $1,000.**

FICTION Needs adventure, condensed novels, confessions, erotica, ethnic, experimental, fantasy, historical, horror, humorous, mainstream, mystery, novel excerpts, religious, romance, science fiction, serialized novels, short stories, slice-of-life vignettes, suspense, western. **Buys 12 mss/year.** Send complete ms. Length: no more than 10,000 words. **Pays minimum of anthology copies and maximum of $1,000.**

POETRY "We want any poem that captures the magic of the form." Buys 12 poems/year. Submit maximum 6 poems. Length: no more than 4,000 words.

TIPS "Keeping free thought free and challenging entertainment are not mutually exclusive. Words make a ms stand out, words beautifully woven together in striking and memorable patterns."

⊘⊜⊜ MAISONNEUVE

Maisonneuve Magazine Association, 1051 Boulevard Decarie, P.O. Box 53527, St. Laurent QC H4l 5J9 Canada. (514)482-5089. **Fax:** (514)482-6734. **E-mail:** https://maisonneuvemagazine.submittable.com/submit. **Website:** www.maisonneuve.org. **90% freelance written.** Quarterly magazine covering eclectic curiousity. *Maisonneuve* has been described as a new *New Yorker* for a younger generation, or as *Harper's* meets *Vice*, or as *Vanity Fair* without the vanity—but *Maisonneuve* is its own creature. *Maisonneuve*'s purpose is to keep its readers informed, alert, and entertained, and to dissolve artistic borders between regions, countries, languages, and genres. It does this by providing a diverse range of commentary across the arts, sciences, and daily and social life. The magazine has a balanced perspective, and "brings the news" in a wide variety of ways. Estab. 2002. Circ. under 10,000. Byline given. Pays on publication. Offers 25% kill fee. Publishes ms an average of 4-6 months after acceptance. Editorial lead time 4 months. Submit seasonal material 8 months in advance. Accepts simultaneous submissions. Responds in 2 weeks to queries. Responds in 2 months to mss. Sample copy online. Guidelines online.

> "*Maisonneuve* considers nonfiction writing of all kinds (reporting, essays, memoir, humour, etc.) and visual art (illustration, photography, comics, etc.). To get a sense of the sort of work we publish, please read some back issues."

NONFICTION Needs essays, general interest, historical, humor, interview, personal experience, photo feature. **Buys 20 mss/year.** Query with published clips. Length: 50-5,000 words. **Pays 10¢/word.** Sometimes pays expenses of writers on assignment.

PHOTOS Contact: Contact Jenn McIntyre, art director. State availability. Captions, identification of subjects, model releases required. Reviews GIF/JPEG files. Negotiates payment individually.

COLUMNS/DEPARTMENTS Open House (witty & whimsical), 800-1,200 words; Profiles + Interviews (character insights), 2,000 words; Studio (spotlight on visual artists/trends), 500 words; Manifesto (passionate calls for change), 800 words. **Buys 40-50 mss/year.** Query with published clips. **Pays 10¢/word.**

FICTION "Unfortunately, due to the volume of submissions received and our very small editorial staff, we no longer accept unsolicited submissions of fiction or poetry." Needs adventure, confession, ethnic, experimental, humorous, science fiction, slice-of-life vignettes. **Buys 4 mss/year.** Send complete ms. Length: 1,000-4,000 words. **Pays 10¢/word.**

POETRY Needs avant-garde, free verse, haiku, light verse, traditional. "Unfortunately, due to the volume of submissions received and our very small editorial staff, we no longer accept unsolicited submissions of fiction or poetry." Buys 16-32 poems/year. Submit maximum unlimited poems. **Payment varies.**

FILLERS Needs anecdotes, facts, short humor. **Buys 15 mss/year.** Length: 50-150 words. **Payment varies.**

◐ ⓢ THE MALAHAT REVIEW

The University of Victoria, P.O. Box 1700, STN CSC, Victoria BC V8W 2Y2 Canada. (250)721-8524. **E-mail:** malahat@uvic.ca (for queries only). **Website:** www.malahatreview.ca. **Contact:** John Barton, editor. **100% freelance written. Eager to work with new/unpublished writers**. Quarterly magazine covering poetry, fiction, creative nonfiction, and reviews. "We try to achieve a balance of views and styles in each issue. We strive for a mix of the best writing by both established and new writers." Estab. 1967. Circ. 2,000. Byline given. Pays on acceptance. Publishes ms an average of 6 months after acceptance. Accepts queries by mail. NoAccepts simultaneous submissions. Responds in 2 weeks to queries. Responds in 3-10 months to mss. Sample copy for $16.95 (US). Guidelines online.

NONFICTION Include SASE with Canadian postage or IRCs. **Pays $40/magazine page.**

FICTION Needs general fiction and creative nonfiction. **Buys 12-14 mss/year.** Send complete ms. Length: 8,000 words maximum. **Pays $40/magazine page**.

POETRY Needs avant-garde, free verse, traditional. Buys 100 poems/year. Length: 5-10 pages **Pays $40/magazine page.**

TIPS "Please do not send more than 1 submission at a time: 4-8 poems, 1 piece of creative nonfiction, or 1 short story (do not mix poetry and prose in the same submission). See *The Malahat Review*'s Open Season Awards for poetry and short fiction, creative nonfic-

tion, long poem, and novella contests in the Awards section of our website."

ⓢ ⓢ MANOA

English Dept., University of Hawaii, Honolulu HI 96822. (808)956-3070. **Fax:** (808)956-3083. **E-mail:** mjournal-l@lists.hawaii.edu. **Website:** manoajournal.hawaii.edu. **Contact:** Frank Stewart, editor. Semiannual magazine. *Manoa* is seeking "high-quality literary fiction, poetry, essays, personal narrative. In general, each issue is devoted to new work from Pacific and Asian nations. Our audience is international. US writing need not be confined to Pacific settings or subjects. Please note that we seldom publish unsolicited work." Estab. 1989. Circ. 1,000 print, 10,000 digital. Byline given. Pays on publication. Editorial lead time 9 months. Accepts simultaneous submissions. Responds in 3 weeks to queries. Sample copy for $15 (US). Guidelines online.

◑ *Manoa* has received numerous awards, and work published in the magazine has been selected for prize anthologies. See website for recently published issues.

NONFICTION No Pacific exotica. Query first. Length: 1,000-5,000 words. **Pays $25/printed page.**

FICTION Query first and/or see website. Needs mainstream, contemporary, excerpted novel. No Pacific exotica. **Buys 1-2 in the US (excluding translation) mss/year.** Send complete ms. Length: 1,000-7,500 words. **Pays $100-500 normally ($25 per printed page).**

POETRY No light verse. Buys 10-20 poems/year. Submit maximum 5-6 poems. **Pays $25 per poem.**

TIPS "Not accepting unsolicited mss at this time because of commitments to special projects. Please query before sending mss as e-mail attachments."

ⓢ MICHIGAN QUARTERLY REVIEW

0576 Rackham Bldg., 915 E. Washington, University of Michigan, Ann Arbor MI 48109-1070. (734)764-9265. **E-mail:** mqr@umich.edu. **Website:** www.michiganquarterlyreview.com. **Contact:** Jonathan Freedman, editor; Vicki Lawrence, managing editor. **75% freelance written.** Quarterly journal of literature and the humanities publishing literary essays, fiction, poetry, creative nonfiction, memoir, interviews, and book reviews. "*MQR* is an eclectic interdisciplinary journal of arts and culture that seeks to combine the best of poetry, fiction, and creative nonfiction with outstanding critical essays on literary, cultural, social, and political matters. The flagship journal of the University of Michigan, *MQR* draws on lively minds here and elsewhere, seeking to present accessible work of all varieties for sophisticated readers from within and without the academy." Estab. 1962. Circ. 1,000. Byline given. Pays on publication. Publishes ms an average of 1 year after acceptance. Accepts queries by mail. Responds in 2 months to queries. Responds in 2 months to mss. Sample copy for $4. Guidelines online.

⬤ The Laurence Goldstein Award is a $500 annual award to the best poem published in *MQR* during the previous year. The Lawrence Foundation Award is a $1,000 annual award to the best short story published in *MQR* during the previous year. The Page Davidson Clayton Award for Emerging Poets is a $500 annual award given to the best poet appearing in *MQR* during the previous year who has not yet published a book.

NONFICTION Special issues: Publishes theme issues. Upcoming themes available in magazine and online. **Buys 35 mss/year.** Query. Length: 2,000-5,000 words. **Pays $10/published page.**

FICTION Contact: Fiction Editor. "No restrictions on subject matter or language. We are very selective. We like stories that are unusual in tone and structure, and innovative in language. No genre fiction written for a market. Would like to see more fiction about social, political, cultural matters, not just centered on a love relationship or dysfunctional family." Receives 300 unsolicited mss/month. Accepts 3-4 mss/issue; 12-16 mss/year. Publishes 1-2 new writers/year. Has published work by Rebecca Makkai, Peter Ho Davies, Laura Kasischke, Gerald Shapiro, and Alan Cheuse. Needs literary. **Buys 10 mss/year.** Send complete ms. Length: 1,500-7,000 words; average length: 5,000 words. **Pays $10/published page.**

POETRY No previously published poems or simultaneous submissions. No e-mail submissions. Cover letter is preferred. "It puts a human face on the ms. A few sentences of biography is all I want, nothing lengthy or defensive." Prefers typed mss. Reviews books of poetry. "All reviews are commissioned." **Pays $8-12/published page.**

TIPS "Read the journal and assess the range of contents and the level of writing. We have no guidelines to offer or set expectations; every ms is judged on its unique qualities. On essays—query with a very thorough description of the argument and a copy of the first page. Watch for announcements of special issues, which are usually expanded issues and draw upon a lot of freelance writing. Be aware that this is a university quarterly that publishes a limited amount of fiction and poetry and that it is directed at an educated audience, one that has done a great deal of reading in all types of literature."

💲 MID-AMERICAN REVIEW

Bowling Green State University, Department of English, Bowling Green OH 43403. (419)372-2725. **E-mail:** mar@bgsu.edu. **Website:** www.bgsu.edu/midamericanreview. **Contact:** Abigail Cloud, editor-in-chief. Semiannual magazine of the highest-quality fiction, poetry, and translations of contemporary poetry and fiction. Also publishes creative nonfiction and book reviews of contemporary literature. Reads mss year round. Publishes new and established writers. "We aim to put the best possible work in front of the biggest possible audience. We publish contemporary fiction, poetry, creative nonfiction, translations, and book reviews." Estab. 1981. Circ. 1,500. Byline given. Pays on publication when funding is available. Publishes mss an average of 6 months after acceptance. Accepts queries by online submission form. Responds in 5 months to mss. Sample copy for $9 (current issue); $5 (back issue); $10 (rare back issues). Guidelines online.

⬤ Magazine: 6×9; 208 pages; 60 lb. bond paper; coated cover stock. Contests: The Fineline Competition for Prose Poems, Short Shorts, and Everything In Between (June 1 deadline, $10 per 3 pieces, limit 500 words each); The Sherwood Anderson Fiction Award (November 1 deadline, $10 per piece); and the James Wright Poetry Award (November 1 deadline, $10 per 3 pieces).

NONFICTION Needs creative nonfiction, leaning toward lyrical essays; short book reviews (400-500 words). Submit ms by post with SASE or with online submission manager.

FICTION Contact: Laura Walter, editor. Publishes traditional, character-oriented, literary, experimental, prose poem, and short-short stories. No genre fiction. Submit ms by post with SASE or with online submission manager. Agented fiction 5%. Recently published work by Mollie Ficek and J. David Stevens. Length: 6,000 words maximum.

POETRY Contact: Abigail Cloud, editor. Submit by mail with SASE or with online submission manager. Publishes poems with "textured, evocative images, an awareness of how words sound and mean, and a definite sense of voice. Each line should help carry the poem, and an individual vision must be evident." Recently published work by Mary Ann Samyn, G.C. Waldrep, and Daniel Bourne. Submit maximum 6 poems.

TIPS "We are seeking translations of contemporary authors from all languages into English; submissions must include the original and proof of permission to translate. We would also like to see more creative nonfiction."

🟢 MODERN HAIKU

P.O. Box 930, Portsmouth RI 02871. **E-mail:** modernhaiku@gmail.com. **Website:** modernhaiku.org. **85% freelance written.** Magazine published 3 times/year in February, June, and October covering haiku poetry. *Modern Haiku* is the foremost international journal of English-language haiku and criticism and publishes high-quality material only. Haiku and related genres, articles on haiku, haiku book reviews, and translations comprise its contents. It has an international circulation; subscribers include many university, school, and public libraries. Estab. 1969. Circ. 650. Byline given. Pays on acceptance. Publishes ms an average of 6 months after acceptance. Editorial lead time 4 months. Accepts queries by mail, e-mail. "Now accepts submissions by e-mail; please review submission guidelines policies online.". Responds in 1 week to queries. Responds in 6-8 weeks to mss. Sample copy for $15 in North America, $16 in Canada, $20 in Mexico, $22 overseas. Subscription: $35 ppd by regular mail in the U.S. Payment possible by PayPal on the *Modern Haiku* website. Guidelines available for SASE or online.

💬 Has published haiku by Roberta Beary, Billy Collins, Lawrence Ferlinghetti, Carolyn Hall, Sharon Olds, Gary Snyder, John Stevenson, George Swede, and Cor van den Heuvel. *Modern Haiku* is 140 pages (average), digest-sized, printed on heavy-quality stock, with full-color cover illustrations 4-page full-color art sections. Receives about 15,000 submissions/year, accepts about 1,000. Press run is 700.

NONFICTION Needs essays, anything related to haiku. Send complete ms. **Pays $5/page.**

COLUMNS/DEPARTMENTS Haiku & Senryu; Haibun; Essays (on haiku and related genres); Reviews (books of haiku or related genres). **Buys 40 mss/year.** Send complete ms. **Pays $5/page.**

POETRY Needs haiku, senryu, haibun, haiga. Postal submissions: "Send 5-15 haiku on 1 or 2 letter-sized sheets. Put name and address at the top of each sheet. Include SASE." E-mail submissions: "May be attachments (recommended) or pasted in body of message. Subject line must read: MH Submission. Adhere to guidelines on the website. No payment for haiku sent/accepted by e-mail." Reviews of books of haiku by staff and freelancers by invitation in 350-1,000 words, usually single-book format. Send materials for review consideration with complete ordering information. Does not want "general poetry, tanka, renku, linked-verse forms. No special consideration given to work by children and teens." Buys Publishes 750 poems/year. poems/year. Submit maximum Maximum number of poems: 24. poems. **No payment.**

TIPS "Study the history of haiku, read books about haiku, learn the aesthetics of haiku and methods of composition. Write about your sense perceptions of the suchness of entities; avoid ego-centered interpretations. Be sure the work you send us conforms to the definitions on our website."

MYTHIC DELIRIUM

3514 Signal Hill Ave. NW, Roanoke VA 24017-5148. **E-mail:** mythicdelirium@gmail.com. **Website:** www.mythicdelirium.com. **Contact:** Mike Allen, editor. "*Mythic Delirium* is an online and e-book venue for fiction and poetry that ranges through science fiction, fantasy, horror, interstitial, and cross-genre territory— we love blurred boundaries and tropes turned on their heads. We are interested in work that demonstrates ambition, that defies traditional approaches to genre, that introduces readers to the legends of other cultures, that re-evaluates the myths of old from a modern perspective, that twists reality in unexpected ways. We are committed to diversity and are open to and encourage submissions from people of every race, gender, nationality, sexual orientation, political affiliation and religious belief. We publish 12 short stories and 24 poems a year. Our quarterly ebooks in PDF, EPUB, and MOBI formats, published in July, October, January, and April, will each contain 3 stories and 6 poems. We will also publish 1 story and 2 poems on our website each month." Reading period:

August 1-October 1 annually. Estab. 1998. Responds in 2 months.

FICTION "No unsolicited reprints or multiple submissions. Please use the words 'fiction submission' in the e-mail subject line. Stories should be sent in standard ms format as .rtf or .doc attachments." Length: up to 4,000 words (firm). **Pays 2¢/word.**

POETRY "No unsolicited reprints. Please use the words 'poetry submission' in the e-mail subject line. Poems may be included in the e-mail as .rtf or .doc attachments." Submit maximum 6 poems. Length: open. **Pays $5 flat fee.**

TIPS "*Mythic Delirium* isn't easy to get into, but we publish newcomers in every issue. Show us how ambitious you can be, and don't give up."

NEON MAGAZINE

UK. **E-mail:** info@neonmagazine.co.uk. **Website:** www.neonmagazine.co.uk. **Contact:** Krishan Coupland. Quarterly website and print magazine covering alternative work of any form of poetry and prose, short stories, flash fiction, artwork and reviews. "Genre work is welcome. Experimentation is encouraged. We like stark poetry and weird prose. We seek work that is beautiful, shocking, intense, and memorable. Darker pieces are generally favored over humorous ones." Accepts queries by e-mail. Reports in 1 month. Query if you have received no reply after 6 weeks. Guidelines online.

"Note: *Neon* was previously published as *Four-Volts Magazine.*"

NONFICTION Needs essays, Reviews. No word limit.

FICTION Needs experimental, horror, humorous, science fiction, suspense. "No nonsensical prose; we are not appreciative of sentimentality." **Buys 8-12 mss/year.** No word limit. **Pays royalties.**

POETRY "No nonsensical poetry; we are not appreciative of sentimentality. Rhyming poetry is discouraged." Buys 24-30 poems/year. No word limit. **Pays royalties.**

TIPS "Send several poems, 1 or 2 pieces of prose or several images via form e-mail. Include the word 'submission' in your subject line. Include a short biographical note (up to 100 words). Read submission guidelines before submitting your work."

NEW ENGLAND REVIEW

Middlebury College, Middlebury VT 05753. (802)443-5075. **E-mail:** nereview@middlebury.edu. **E-mail:** Carolyn Kuebler, editor. **Website:** www.nere-

view.com. Quarterly literary magazine. *New England Review* is a prestigious, nationally distributed literary journal. Reads September 1-May 31 (postmarked dates). Estab. 1978. Circ. 2,000. Byline given. Pays on publication. Publishes ms an average of 6 months after acceptance. Accepts simultaneous submissions. Responds in 2 weeks to queries. Responds in 3 months to mss. Sometimes comments on rejected mss. Sample copy for $10 (add $5 for overseas). Guidelines online.

NONFICTION Buys 20-25 mss/year. Send complete ms via online submission manager or postal mail (with SASE). No e-mail submissions. Length: 7,500 words maximum, though exceptions may be made. **Pays $10/page ($20 minimum), and 2 contributor's copies. "For the duration of 2014, *NER* will pay $20/page, courtesy of a year-long NEA grant."**

FICTION Send 1 story at a time, unless it is very short. Serious literary only, novel excerpts. Needs literary. **Buys 25 mss/year.** Send complete ms via online submission manager or postal mail (with SASE). No e-mail submissions. "Will consider simultaneous submissions, but must be stated as such and you must notify us immediately if the ms accepted for publication elsewhere." Prose length: not strict on word count. **Pays $10/page ($20 minimum), and 2 contributor's copies. "For the duration of 2014, *NER* will pay $20/page, courtesy of a year-long NEA grant.".**

POETRY Submit up to 6 poems at a time. No previously published poems or simultaneous submissions. Accepts submissions by postal mail or online submission manager only; accepts questions by e-mail. "Cover letters are useful." Address submissions to "Poetry Editor." Buys 75-90 poems/year. Submit maximum 6 poems. **Pays $10/page ($20 minimum), and 2 contributor's copies. "For the duration of 2014, *NER* will pay $20/page, courtesy of a year-long NEA grant.".**

TIPS "We consider short fiction, including short-shorts, novellas, and self-contained extracts from novels in both traditional and experimental forms. In nonfiction, we consider a variety of general and literary, but not narrowly scholarly essays; we also publish long and short poems, screenplays, graphics, translations, critical reassessments, statements by artists working in various media, testimonies, and letters from abroad. We are committed to exploration of all forms of contemporary cultural expression in the US and abroad. With few exceptions, we print only work not published previously elsewhere."

$ NEW LETTERS

University of Missouri-Kansas City, 5101 Rockhill Rd., Kansas City MO 64110. (816)235-1168. **Fax:** (816)235-2611. **E-mail:** newletters@umkc.edu. **Website:** www.newletters.org. **Contact:** Robert Stewart, editor-in-chief. **100% freelance written.** Quarterly magazine. "*New Letters* continues to seek the best new writing, whether from established writers or those ready and waiting to be discovered. In addition, it supports those writers, readers, and listeners who want to experience the joy of writing that can both surprise and inspire us all." Estab. 1934. Circ. 5,000. Byline given. Pays on publication. Publishes ms an average of 6 months after acceptance. Editorial lead time 6 months. Submit seasonal material 6 months in advance. Accepts queries by mail. Accepts simultaneous submissions. Responds in 1 month to queries; 5 months to mss. Sample copy for $10 or sample articles online. Guidelines online.

💬 Submissions are not read between May 1 and October 1.

NONFICTION Needs essays. No self-help, how-to, or nonliterary work. **Buys 8-10 mss/year.** Send complete ms. 5,000 words maximum. **Pays $40-100.**

PHOTOS Send photos. Reviews contact sheets, 2x4 transparencies, prints. Pays $10-40/photo.

FICTION Contact: Robert Stewart, editor. Needs ethnic, experimental, humorous, mainstream, contemporary. No genre fiction. **Buys 15-20 mss/year.** Send complete ms. 5,000 words maximum. **Pays $30-75.**

POETRY Needs avant-garde, free verse, haiku, traditional. No light verse. Buys 40-50 poems/year. Submit maximum 6 poems. Open. **Pays $10-25.**

TIPS "We aren't interested in essays that are footnoted or essays usually described as scholarly or critical. Our preference is for creative nonfiction or personal essays. We prefer shorter stories and essays to longer ones (an average length is 3,500-4,000 words). We have no rigid preferences as to subject, style, or genre, although commercial efforts tend to put us off. Even so, our only fixed requirement is on good writing."

NEW OHIO REVIEW

English Department, 360 Ellis Hall, Ohio University, Athens OH 45701. (740)597-1360. **E-mail:** noreditors@ohio.edu. **Website:** www.ohiou.edu/nor. **Contact:** Jill Allyn Rosser, editor. *NOR*, published biannually in spring and fall, publishes fiction, nonfiction, and poetry. Single: $9; Subscription: $16. Member: CLMP. Reading period is September 15-December 15 and January 15-April 1. Estab. 2007. Byline given. Accepts queries by mail, e-mail, online submission form. Accepts simultaneous submissions. Responds in 2-4 months. Guidelines online.

NONFICTION Needs essays, humor. Submit complete ms. **Pays minimum of $30 in addition to 2 contributor's copies and 1-year subscription.**

FICTION Needs confessions, experimental, humorous, mainstream. Send complete ms. **Pays $30 minimum in addition to 2 contributor's copies and 1-year subscription.**

POETRY Needs avant-garde, free verse, haiku, light verse, traditional. Submit up to 6 poems at a time. "Do not submit more than once every 6 months. Submit maximum 6 poems.

$ NEW ORLEANS REVIEW

Box 195, Loyola University, New Orleans LA 70118. (504)865-2295. **E-mail:** noreview@loyno.edu. **Website:** neworleansreview.org. **Contact:** Heidi Braden, managing editor. *New Orleans Review* is a biannual journal of contemporary literature and culture, publishing new poetry, fiction, nonfiction, art, photography, film and book reviews. The journal has published an eclectic variety of work by established and emerging writers including Walker Percy, Pablo Neruda, Ellen Gilchrist, Nelson Algren, Hunter S. Thompson, John Kennedy Toole, Richard Brautigan, Barry Spacks, James Sallis, Jack Gilbert, Paul Hoover, Rodney Jones, Annie Dillard, Everette Maddox, Julio Cortazar, Gordon Lish, Robert Walser, Mark Halliday, Jack Butler, Robert Olen Butler, Michael Harper, Angela Ball, Joyce Carol Oates, Diane Wakoski, Dermot Bolger, Roddy Doyle, William Kotzwinkle, Alain Robbe-Grillet, Arnost Lustig, Raymond Queneau, Yusef Komunyakaa, Michael Martone, Tess Gallagher, Matthea Harvey, D. A. Powell, Rikki Ducornet, and Ed Skoog. Estab. 1968. Circ. 1,500. Pays on publication. Accepts queries by online submission form. Accepts simultaneous submissions. Responds in 4 months to mss. Sample copy for $5.

FICTION Contact: Christopher Chambers, editor. Needs "Good writing, from conventional to experimental.". "We are now using an online submission system and require a $3 fee." See website for details. Length: up to 6,500 words. **Pays $25-50 and 2 copies.**

POETRY Submit maximum 3-6 poems.

TIPS "We're looking for dynamic writing that demonstrates attention to the language and a sense of the medium, writing that engages, surprises, moves us. We're not looking for genre fiction or academic articles. We subscribe to the belief that in order to truly write well, one must first master the rudiments: grammar and syntax, punctuation, the sentence, the paragraph, the line, the stanza. We receive about 3,000 mss a year and publish about 3% of them. Check out a recent issue, send us your best, proofread your work, be patient, be persistent."

NEW WELSH REVIEW

P.O. Box 170, Aberystwyth, Ceredigion Wa SY23 1 WZ United Kingdom. 01970-626230. **E-mail:** editor@ newwelshreview.com. **E-mail:** submissions@newwelshreview.com. **Website:** www.newwelshreview. com. **Contact:** Gwen Davies, editor. "*NWR*, a literary quarterly ranked in the top 5 of British literary magazines, publishes stories, poems and critical essays. The best of Welsh writing in English, past and present, is celebrated, discussed, and debated. We seek poems, short stories, reviews, special features/articles, and commentary." Quarterly.

FICTION Send hard copy only with SASE or international money order for return. Outside the UK, submission by e-mail only. **Pays "cheque on publication and one free copy.".**

THE NEW WRITER

the new writer magazine, 1 Vicarage Lane, Stubbington Hampshire PO14 2JU United Kingdom. (44) (158)021-2626. **E-mail:** editor@thenewwriter.com. **Website:** www.thenewwriter.com. **Contact:** Madelaine Smith, editor. Publishes 4 issues/year. Quarterly. "Contemporary writing magazine which publishes the best in fact, fiction and poetry." Estab. 1996. Circ. 1,500. Pays on publication. Publishes ms an average of 1 year after acceptance. Accepts queries by e-mail. Accepts simultaneous submissions. Responds in 4 months to queries. Responds in 6 months to mss.

NONFICTION Query. Length: 1,000-2,000 words. **Pays £20-40.**

FICTION *No unsolicited mss.* Accepts fiction from subscribers only. "We will consider most categories apart from stories written for children. No horror, erotic, or cosy fiction." Query with published clips. Length: 2,000-5,000 words.

POETRY Length: 40 lines maximum.

TIPS "Hone it—always be prepared to improve the story. It's a competitive market."

NINTH LETTER

Department of English, University of Illinois, 608 S. Wright St., Urbana IL 61801. (217)244-3145. **E-mail:** info@ninthletter.com; editor@ninthletter.com. **Website:** www.ninthletter.com. **Contact:** Jodee Stanley, editor. "*Ninth Letter* accepts submissions of fiction, poetry, and essays from September 1-February 28 (postmark dates). *Ninth Letter* is published semi-annually at the University of Illinois, Urbana-Champaign. We are interested in prose and poetry that experiment with form, narrative, and nontraditional subject matter, as well as more traditional literary work." Pays on publication. Accepts queries by mail, online submission form.

NONFICTION Contact: nonfiction@ninthletter. com. "Please send only 1 essay at a time. All mailed submissions must include an SASE for reply." Length: up to 8,000 words. **Pays $25 per printed page and 2 contributor's copies.**

FICTION Contact: fiction@ninthpoetry.com. "Please send only 1 story at a time. All mailed submissions must include an SASE for reply." Length: up to 8,000 words. **Pays $25 per printed page and 2 contributor's copies.**

POETRY Contact: poetry@ninthletter.com. Submit 3-6 poems (no more than 10 pages) at a time. "All mailed submissions must include an SASE for reply." **Pays $25 per printed page and 2 contributor's copies.**

NORTH AMERICAN REVIEW

University of Northern Iowa, 1222 W. 27th St., Cedar Falls IA 50614. (319)273-6455. **Fax:** (319)273-4326. **E-mail:** nar@uni.edu. **Website:** northamericanreview. org. **Contact:** Kim Groninga, nonfiction editor. **90% freelance written.** Published 4 times/year. "The *NAR* is the oldest literary magazine in America and one of the most respected; though we have no prejudices about the subject matter of material sent to us, our first concern is quality." Estab. 1815. Circ. under 5,000. Byline given. Publishes ms an average of 1 year after acceptance. Accepts queries by mail. Responds in 4 months to mss. Sample copy for $7. Guidelines online.

This is the oldest literary magazine in the country and one of the most prestigious. Also one of the most entertaining—and a tough market for the young writer.

NONFICTION Contact: Ron Sandvik, nonfiction editor. Length: Open.

FICTION Open (literary). "No flat narrative stories where the inferiority of the character is the paramount concern." Wants to see more "well-crafted literary stories that emphasize family concerns. We'd also like to see more stories engaged with environmental concerns." Reads fiction mss all year. Publishes ms an average of 1 year after acceptance. **Publishes 2 new writers/year.** Recently published work by Lee Ann Roripaugh, Dick Allen, Rita Welty Bourke. Needs Wants more well-crafted literary stories that emphasize family concerns. No flat narrative stories where the inferiority of the character is the paramount concern. Accepts submissions by USPS mail only. Send complete ms with SASE. Responds in 3 months to queries; 4 months to mss. No simultaneous submissions. Sample copy for $7.

POETRY No restrictions; highest quality only.

TIPS "We like stories that start quickly and have a strong narrative arc. Poems that are passionate about subject, language, and image are welcome, whether they are traditional or experimental, whether in formal or free verse (closed or open form). Nonfiction should combine art and fact with the finest writing. We do not accept simultaneous submissions; these will be returned unread. We read poetry, fiction, and nonfiction year-round."

✪ NORTH CAROLINA LITERARY REVIEW

East Carolina University, Mailstop 555 English, Greenville NC 27858-4353. (252)328-1537. **Fax:** (252)328-4889. **E-mail:** nclrsubmissions@ecu.edu. **Website:** www.nclr.ecu.edu. **Contact:** Gabrielle Freeman. Annual magazine published in summer covering North Carolina writers, literature, culture, history. "Articles should have a North Carolina slant. First consideration is always for quality of work. Although we treat academic and scholarly subjects, we do not wish to see jargon-laden prose; our readers, we hope, are found as often in bookstores and libraries as in academia. We seek to combine the best elements of magazine for serious readers with best of scholarly journal." Estab. 1992. Circ. 750. Byline given. Pays on publication. Publishes ms an average of 1 year after acceptance. Editorial lead time 6 months. Accepts queries by e-mail, online submission form. Responds in 1 month to queries. Responds in 6 months to mss. Sample copy for $10-25. Guidelines online.

○ Uses online submission form.

NONFICTION Needs book excerpts, essays, expose, general interest, historical, humor, interview, opinion, personal experience, photo feature, travel, reviews, short narratives, surveys of archives. No jargon-laden academic articles. **Buys 25-35 mss/year.** Query with published clips. Length: 500-5,000 words. **Pays $50-100 honorarium, extra copies, back issues or subscription (negotiable).**

PHOTOS State availability. True required. Reviews 5x7 or 8x10 prints; snapshot size or photocopy OK. Pays $25-250.

COLUMNS/DEPARTMENTS NC Writers (interviews, biographical/bibliographic essays); Reviews (essay reviews of North Carolina-related fiction, creative nonfiction, or poetry). Query with published clips. **Pays $50-100 honorarium, extra copies, back issues or subscription (negotiable).**

FICTION "Fiction submissions accepted during Doris Betts Prize Competition; see our submission guidelines for detail." Needs experimental, literary, regional. **Buys 3-4 mss/year.** Query electronically using online submission form. Length: no more than 5,000 words. **Pays $50-100 honorarium, extra copies, back issues or subscription (negotiable).**

POETRY *North Carolina poets only.* Submit 3-5 poems at a time. Include cover letter. Buys 5-10 poems/year. Length: 30-150 lines. **Pays $50-100 honorarium, extra copies, back issues or subscription (negotiable).**

FILLERS Buys 2-5 mss/year. Length: 50-500 words. **$50-100 honorarium, extra copies, back issues or subscription (negotiable).**

TIPS "By far the easiest way to break in is with special issue sections. We are especially interested in reports on conferences, readings, meetings that involve North Carolina writers, and personal essays or short narratives with a strong sense of place. See back issues for other departments. Interviews are probably the other easiest place to break in; no discussions of poetics/theory, etc., except in reader-friendly (accessible) language; interviews should be personal, more like conversations, that explore connections between a writer's life and his/her work."

⊘ NORTHWIND

Chain Bridge Press, LLC., 4201 Wilson Blvd., #110, Arlington VA 22203. **E-mail:** info@northwindmagazine.com. **Website:** www.northwindmagazine.com.

Contact: Tom Howard, managing editor. Focus is on originality and provocative, compulsively readable prose and poetry, in any style or genre. Looks for smart, lyrical writing that will appeal to an intelligent and culturally sophisticated audience. *Northwind* is an independent literary magazine published quarterly. Estab. 2011. Byline given. Pays on publication. Publishes ms 2 months after acceptance. Accepts queries by online submission form. Accepts simultaneous submissions. Responds in 8-10 weeks. "If you haven't received a notification e-mail from us after 10 weeks, please feel free to contact us at submissions@northwindmagazine.com." Sample copy online at website. Guidelines online at website.

NONFICTION Needs book excerpts, humor, interview, memoir, personal experience, profile, Want "strong biographical or autobiographical narratives that read like fiction, with clearly defined characters and a compelling story-line.". Does not want essays, reviews, travelogues, or editorials. Submit complete ms using online submission form only. Length: 3,000-8,000 words. **"Pays $150 for the issue's featured story only. All contributors, however, will be provided with a dedicated page on the site for biographical information (including photo), any relevant web site links, and an optional feedback form for readers."**

FICTION "We want the best that you've got. We want crazy beautiful characters, unforced and unsentimental prose, unexpected plots, great opening lines, and edgy dialogue. But mostly we want great, honest stories that move us and leave us shaken through the sheer force of narrative will. Surprise us." Needs erotica, experimental, fantasy, horror, humorous, mainstream, mystery, novel excerpts, science fiction, slice-of-life vignettes, suspense. Does not want flash fiction or micro-fiction. Submit complete ms using online submission form only. Length: 3,000-8,000 words. **"Pays $150 for the issue's featured story only. All contributors, however, will be provided with a dedicated page on the site for biographical information (including photo), any relevant web site links, and an optional feedback form for readers.".**

POETRY Needs Avant-garde, free verse, haiku, traditional. "We accept poetry submissions on any subject and in any style, although we tend to avoid rhyming poetry and prose poems. Read the magazine for excellent examples of what we're seeking. We want compelling ideas, unforced language, and genuine meaning over sentimentality." Submit up to 5 poems at a time, with all pieces in a single file. Submit maximum 5 poems. **"Pays $150 for the issue's featured story only. All contributors, however, will be provided with a dedicated page on the site for biographical information (including photo), any relevant web site links, and an optional feedback form for readers.".**

$ NOTRE DAME REVIEW

University of Notre Dame, 840 Flanner Hall, Notre Dame IN 46556. (574)631-6952. **Fax:** (574)631-4795. **E-mail:** english.ndreview.1@nd.edu. **Website:** ndreview.nd.edu. The *Notre Dame Review* is an indepenent, noncommercial magazine of contemporary American and international fiction, poetry, criticism, and art. Especially interested in work that takes on big issues by making the invisible seen, that gives voice to the voiceless. In addition to showcasing celebrated authors like Seamus Heaney and Czelaw Milosz, the *Notre Dame Review* introduces readers to authors they may have never encountered before, but who are doing innovative and important work. In conjunction with the *Notre Dame Review*, the online companion to the printed magazine, the *nd[re]view* engages readers as a community centered in literary rather than commercial concerns, a community we reach out to through critique and commentary as well as aesthetic experience. Estab. 1995. Circ. 2,000. Pays on publication. Publishes ms an average of 6 months after acceptance. Accepts simultaneous submissions. Responds in 4 or more months to mss. Sample copy for $6. Guidelines online.

💬 Does not accept e-mail submissions. Only reads hardcopy submissions from September through November and from January through March.

FICTION Contact: William O'Rourke, fiction editor. "We're eclectic. Upcoming theme issues planned. List of upcoming themes or editorial calendar available for SASE. Does not read mss May-August." No genre fiction. **Buys 10 mss/year.** Send complete ms with cover letter. Include 4-sentence bio. Send SASE for response, return of ms, or send a disposable copy of ms. Length: 3,000 words. **Pays $5-25.**

POETRY Contact: Orlando Menes, poetry editor. Send complete ms with cover letter. Include 4-sentence bio. Send SASE for response, return of ms, or send a disposable copy of ms. Buys 90 poems/year. Submit maximum 3-5 poems.

TIPS "We're looking for high quality work that takes on big issues in a literary way. Please read our back issues before submitting."

NOW & THEN; THE APPALACHIAN MAGAZINE

East Tennessee State University, Box 70556, Johnson City TN 37614-1707. (423)439-5348. **Fax:** (423)439-6340. **E-mail:** nowandthen@etsu.edu. **E-mail:** sandersr@etsu.edu. **Website:** www.etsu.edu/cass/nowandthen. **Contact:** Fred Sauceman, editor; Randy Sanders, managing editor; Marianne Worthington, poetry editor; Wayne Winkler, music editor; Charlie Warden, photo editor. Literary magazine published twice/year. "*Now & Then* accepts a variety of writing genres: fiction, poetry, nonfiction, essays, interviews, memoirs, and book reviews. All submissions must relate to Appalachia and to the issue's specific theme. Our readership is educated and interested in the region." Estab. 1984. Circ. 1,000. Sample copy available for $8 plus $3 shipping. Guidelines and upcoming themes online.

PHOTOS Photos of environmental, landscapes/scenics, architecture, cities/urban, rural, adventure, performing arts, travel, agriculture, political, disasters. Interested in documentary, fine art, historical/vintage. Photographs must relate to theme of issue. Themes are posted on the website. "We publish photo essays based on the magazine's theme.". Reviews photos with or without a ms. Model/property release preferred. Photo captions preferred, include where the photos was taken. Require images in digital format sent as e-mail attachments as JPEG or TIFF files at 300 dpi minimum.

FICTION Accepts 1-2 mss/issue. Publishes ms 4 months after acceptance. Publishes some new writers/year. Needs adventure, ethnic/multicultural, experimental, fantasy, historical, humor/satire, literary, mainstream, regional, slice-of-life vignettes, excerpted novel, prose poem, "Absolutely has to relate to Appalachian theme. Can be about adjustment to new environment, themes of leaving and returning, for instance. Nothing unrelated to region.". Send complete ms. Accepts submissions by mail, e-mail, with a strong preference for e-mail. Include "information we can use for contributor's note." SASE (or IRC). Responds in 5 months to queries; 5 months to mss. Rarely accepts simultaneous submissions. Writer's guidelines online. Reviews fiction. Length: 1,000-1,500 words. **Pays $50 each accepted article/$25 each accepted poem. Pays on publication.**

POETRY Submit up to 5 poems, with SASE and cover letter including "a few lines about yourself for a contributor's note and whether the work has been published or accepted elsewhere." Will consider simultaneous submissions; occasionally accepts previously published poems. Put name, address and phone number on every poem. Deadlines: last workday in February (spring/summer issue) and August 31 (fall/winter issues). Publishes theme issues.

TIPS "Keep in mind that *Now & Then* only publishes material related to the Appalachian region. Plus we only publish fiction that has some plausible connection to a specific issue's themes. We like to offer first-time publication to promising writers."

$$$ THE PARIS REVIEW

544 West 27th St., New York NY 10001. (212)343-1333. **E-mail:** queries@theparisreview.org. **Website:** www.theparisreview.org. **Contact:** Lorin Stein, editor. Quarterly magazine. "Fiction and poetry of superlative quality, whatever the genre, style or mode. Our contributors include prominent, as well as less well-known and previously unpublished writers. Writers at Work interview series includes important contemporary writers discussing their own work and the craft of writing." Pays on publication. Accepts queries by mail. Accepts simultaneous submissions. Responds in 4 months to mss. Sample copy for $15 (includes postage). Guidelines online.

💬 Address submissions to proper department. Do not make submissions via e-mail.

FICTION Study the publication. Annual Plimpton Prize award of $10,000 given to a new voice published in the magazine. Recently published work by Ottessa Moshfegh, John Jeremiah Sullivan, and Lydia Davis. Send complete ms. Length: no limit. **Pays $1,000-3,000.**

POETRY **Contact:** Robyn Creswell, poetry editor. Submit no more than 6 poems at a time. Poetry can be sent to the poetry editor (please include a self-addressed, stamped envelope). Submit maximum 6 poems. **Pays $75 minimum varies according to length.**

$$ PARNASSUS: POETRY IN REVIEW

Poetry in Review Foundation, 205 W. 89th St., #8F, New York NY 10024. (212)362-3492. **E-mail:** parnew@aol.com. **Website:** www.parnassusreview.com. **Contact:** Herbert Leibowitz, editor and publisher. Annual magazine covering poetry and criticism. "We now publish 1 double issue a year.". *Parnassus: Poetry in Review* provides "a forum where poets, novelists, and critics of all persuasions can gather to review new books of poetry, including translations—international poetries have occupied center stage from our very first issue—with an amplitude and reflectiveness that Sunday book supplements and even the literary quarterlies could not afford. ... Our editorial philosophy is based on the assumption that reviewing is a complex art. Like a poem or a short story, a review essay requires imagination, scrupulous attention to rhythm, pacing, and supple syntax; space in which to build a persuasive, detailed argument; analytical precision and intuitive gambits; verbal play, wit, and metaphor. ... We welcome and vigorously seek out voices that break aesthetic molds and disturb xenophobic habits." Estab. 1972. Circ. 1,800. Byline given. Pays on publication. Publishes ms an average of 12-14 months after acceptance. Accepts queries by mail. Responds in 2 months to mss. Sample copy for $15.

NONFICTION Needs essays. **Buys 30 mss/year.** Query with published clips. Length: 1,500-7,500 words. **Pays $200-750.**

POETRY Needs avant garde, free verse, traditional. Accepts most types of poetry. Buys 3-4 unsolicited poems/year.

TIPS "Be certain you have read the magazine and are aware of the editor's taste. Blind submissions are a waste of everybody's time. We'd like to see more poems that display intellectual acumen and curiosity about history, science, music, etc., and fewer trivial lyrical poems about the self, or critical prose that's academic and dull. Prose should sing."

PEARL

3030 E. Second St., Long Beach CA 90803. (562)434-4523. **E-mail:** pearlmag@aol.com. **Website:** www.pearlmag.com. **Contact:** Joan Jobe Smith and Marilyn Johnson, poetry editors. Biannual magazine featuring poetry, short fiction, and b&w artwork. We also sponsor the Pearl Poetry Prize, an annual contest for a full-length book, as well as the Pearl Short Story Prize. *"Pearl* is an eclectic publication, a place for lively, readable poetry and prose that speaks to real people about real life in direct, living language, profane or sublime." Estab. 1974. Pays with contributor's copy. Publishes ms an average of 6-12 months after accep-

tance. Accepts queries by mail. Accepts simultaneous submissions. Sample copy for $10. Guidelines online.

Submissions are accepted from January-June only. Mss. received between July and Dec. will be returned unread. No e-mail submissions, except from countries outside the U.S. See guidelines.

PHOTOS No photographs. "We only consider camera-ready, b&w spot-art (no shades of gray) that can be reduced without loss of definition or detail. Send clean, high-quality photocopies or original with SASE. Accepted artwork is kept on file and is used as needed.".

FICTION "Our annual fiction issue features the winner of our Pearl Short Story Prize contest as well as shorts shorts and some of the longer stories in our contest. Length: 1,200 words. No obscure, experimental fiction. The winner of the Pearl Short Story Prize receives $250 and 10 copies of the issue the story appears in. Entry fee is $15." Nothing sentimental, obscure, predictable, abstract, or cliché-ridden fiction. Length: 1,200 words. **Short Story Prize of $250, 100 copies of the issue the story appears in.**

POETRY "Our poetry issue contains a 12-15 page section featuring the work of a single poet. Entry fee for the Pearl Poetry Prize is $25." No sentimental, obscure, predictable, abstract or cliché-ridden poetry. Submit maximum 3-5 poems. 40 lines max. Send with cover letter and SASE.

TIPS "We look for vivid, *dramatized* situations and characters, stories written in an original 'voice,' that make sense and follow a clear narrative line. What makes a ms stand out is more elusive, though—more to do with feeling and imagination than anything else."

PLANET-THE WELSH INTERNATIONALIST

P.O. Box 44, Aberystwyth Ceredigion SY23 3ZZ United Kingdom. **E-mail:** emily.trahair@planetmagazine.org.uk. **Website:** www.planetmagazine.org.uk. **Contact:** Emily Trahair, associate editor. Bimonthly journal. A literary/cultural/political journal centered on Welsh affairs but with a strong interest in minority cultures in Europe and elsewhere. *Planet: The Welsh Internationalist*, published quarterly, is a cultural magazine "centered on Wales, but with broader interests in arts, sociology, politics, history, and science." Estab. 1970. Circ. 1,400. Publishes ms 4-6 months after acceptance. Accepts queries by e-mail. Responds in 3 months. Single copy: £6.75; subscription: £22 (£38 overseas). Sample copy for £4. Guidelines online.

FICTION Would like to see more inventive, imaginative fiction that pays attention to language and experiments with form. No magical realism, horror, science fiction. Submit via mail or e-mail (with attachment). No submissions returned unless accompanied by an SASE. Writers submitting from abroad should send at least 3 IRCs for return of typescript; 1 IRC for reply only. E-mail queries accepted. Length: 1,500-4,000 words. **Pays £50/1,000 words.**

POETRY Wants "good poetry in a wide variety of styles. No limitations as to subject matter; length can be a problem." Has published poetry by Nigel Jenkins, Anne Stevenson, and Les Murray. Accepts e-mail (as attachment) and hard copy submissions. SASE or SAE with IRCs essential for reply. Submit maximum 6 poems. **Pays £30/poem.**

TIPS "We do not look for fiction which necessarily has a 'Welsh' connection, which some writers assume from our title. We try to publish a broad range of fiction, and our main criterion is quality. Try to read copies of any magazine you submit to. Don't write out of the blue to a magazine which might be completely inappropriate for your work. Recognize that you are likely to have a high rejection rate, as magazines tend to favor writers from their own countries."

🟢 PLEIADES

Pleiades Press, Department of English, University of Central Missouri, Martin 336, Warrensburg MO 64093. (660)543-8106. **E-mail:** pleiades@ucmo.edu. **Website:** www.ucmo.edu/englphil/pleiades. **Contact:** Kevin Prufer, editor-at-large. **100% freelance written.** Semiannual journal. "We publish contemporary fiction, poetry, interviews, literary essays, special-interest personal essays, and reviews for a general and literary audience from authors from around the world." Reads August 15-May 15. Estab. 1991. Circ. 3,000. Byline given. Pays on publication. Publishes ms an average of 9 months after acceptance. Editorial lead time 9 months. Accepts queries by mail. Accepts simultaneous submissions. Responds in 2 months to queries. Responds in 1-4 months to mss. Sample copy for $5 (back issue); $6 (current issue). Guidelines online. **NONFICTION Contact:** Phong Nguyen, nonfiction editor. Needs book excerpts, essays, interview, reviews. "Nothing pedantic, slick, or shallow." **Buys** 4-6 mss/year. Send complete ms via online submission manager. Length: 2,000-4,000 words. **Pays $10 and contributor's copies.**

FICTION Contact: Phong Nguyen and Matthew Eck, fiction editors. Reads fiction year-round. Needs ethnic, experimental, humorous, mainstream, novel concepts, Also wants magic realism. No science fiction, fantasy, confession, erotica. **Buys 16-20 mss/year.** Send complete ms via online submission manager. Length: 2,000-6,000 words. **Pays $10 and contributor's copies.**

POETRY Contact: Wayne Miller and Kathryn Nuernberger, poetry editors. Needs avant-garde, free verse, haiku, light verse, traditional. Submit 3-5 poems at a time via online submission manager. "Nothing didactic, pretentious, or overly sentimental." Buys 40-50 poems/year. Submit maximum 5 poems. **Pays $3/poem, and contributor copies.**

TIPS "Submit only 1 genre at a time to appropriate editors. Show care for your material and your readers—submit quality work in a professional format. Include cover letter with brief bio and list of publications. Include SASE. Cover art is solicited directly from artists. We accept queries for book reviews."

🟢🟢 PLOUGHSHARES

Emerson College, Ploughshares, 120 Boylston St., Boston MA 02116. **Website:** www.pshares.org. **Contact:** Ladette Randolph, editor-in-chief/executive director; Andrea Martucci, managing editor. *Ploughshares*, published 3 times/year, is "a journal of new writing guest-edited by prominent poets and writers to reflect different and contrasting points of view. Translations are welcome if permission has been granted. Our mission is to present dynamic, contrasting views on what is valid and important in contemporary literature and to discover and advance significant literary talent. Each issue is guest-edited by a different writer. We no longer structure issues around preconceived themes." Editors have included Carolyn Forché, Gerald Stern, Rita Dove, Chase Twichell, and Marilyn Hacker. Has published poetry by Donald Hall, Li-Young Lee, Robert Pinsky, Brenda Hillman, and Thylias Moss. Reads submissions June 1-January 15 (postmark); mss submitted January 16-May 31 will be returned unread. "We do accept electronic submissions—there is a $3 fee per submission, which is waived if you are a subscriber." Estab. 1971. Circ. 6,000. Pays on publication. Publishes ms an average of 6 months after acceptance. Accepts queries by mail, online submission form. Accepts simultaneous submissions. Responds in 3-5 months to mss. Subscription: $30 domestic, $30 plus shipping (see website) foreign. Sample: $14 current issue, $7 back issue, please inquire for shipping rates. Guidelines online.

🔑 A competitive and highly prestigious market. Rotating and guest editors make cracking the line-up even tougher, since it's difficult to know what is appropriate to send.

NONFICTION Needs essays. Submit online or by mail. Length: up to 6,000 words; prefers up to 5,000 words. **Pays $25/printed page; $50 minimum, $250 maximum; 2 contributor's copies; and 1-year subscription.**

FICTION Recently published work by ZZ Packer, Antonya Nelson, and Stuart Dybek. Needs mainstream, literary. "No genre (science fiction, detective, gothic, adventure, etc.), popular formula or commerical fiction whose purpose is to entertain rather than to illuminate." Submit online or by mail. Length: up to 6,000 words; prefers up to 5,000 words. **Pays $25/printed page; $50 minimum, $250 maximum; 2 contributor's copies; and 1-year subscription.**

POETRY Needs avant-garde, free verse, traditional. Submit online or by mail. Submit maximum 5 poems. **Pays $25/printed page; $50 minimum, $250 maximum; 2 contributor's copies; and 1-year subscription.**

TIPS "We no longer structure issues around preconceived themes. If you believe your work is in keeping with our general standards of literary quality and value, submit at any time during our reading period."

$ POETRY

The Poetry Foundation, 61 W. Superior St., Chicago IL 60654. (312)787-7070. **Fax:** (312)787-6650. **E-mail:** editors@poetrymagazine.org. **Website:** www.poetrymagazine.org. Don Share, editor. **Contact:** Valerie Johnson. **100% freelance written.** Monthly magazine. *Poetry*'s website offers featured poems, letters, reviews, interviews, essays, and web-exclusive features. *Poetry*, published monthly by The Poetry Foundation (see separate listing in Organizations), "has no special ms needs and no special requirements as to form: We examine in turn all work received and accept that which seems best." Has published poetry by the major voices of our time as well as new talent. *Poetry* is elegantly printed, flat-spined. Receives 100,000 submissions/year, accepts about 300-350. Press run is 16,000. Single copy: $3.75 current issue, $4.25 back issue; subscription: $35 ($38 for institutions, $47 foreign). Sample: $5.50. Estab. 1912. Circ. 32,500. Byline given. Pays on publication. Publishes ms an average of 9 months after acceptance. Responds in 2 months to mss and queries. Sample copy for $3.75 or online at website. Guidelines online.

NONFICTION Buys 14 mss/year. Query. No length requirements. **Pays $150/page.**

POETRY Accepts all styles and subject matter. Submit no more than 4 poems at a time and less than 10 pages total. No previously published poems. Accepts submissions only at poetry.submittable.com. Reviews books of poetry in multi-book formats of varying lengths. Does not accept unsolicited reviews. Buys 180-250 poems/year. Submit maximum 4 poems. **Pays $150/page ($150 minimum payment).**

🍁 $ THE PRAIRIE JOURNAL

P.O. Box 68073, 28 Crowfoot Terrace NW, Calgary AB Y3G 3N8 Canada. **E-mail:** editor@prairiejournal.org (queries only); prairiejournal@yahoo.com. **Website:** www.prairiejournal.org. **Contact:** A.E. Burke, literary editor. **100% freelance written.** Semiannual magazine publishing quality poetry, short fiction, drama, literary criticism, reviews, bibliography, interviews, profiles, and artwork. "The audience is literary, university, library, scholarly, and creative readers/writers." Estab. 1983. Circ. 650-750. Byline given. Pays on publication. Publishes ms an average of 4-6 months after acceptance. Editorial lead time 2-6 months. Accepts queries by mail, e-mail. Responds in 2 weeks to queries; 2-6 months to mss. Sample copy for $5. Guidelines online.

💬 "Use our mailing address for submissions and queries with samples or for clippings."

NONFICTION Needs essays, humor, interview, literary. No inspirational, news, religious, or travel. **Buys 25-40 mss/year.** Query with published clips. Length: 100-3,000 words. **Pays $50-100, plus contributor's copy.**

PHOTOS State availability. Offers additional payment for photos accepted with ms.

COLUMNS/DEPARTMENTS Reviews (books from small presses publishing poetry, short fiction, essays, and criticism), 200-1,000 words. **Buys 5 mss/year.** Query with published clips. **Pays $10-50.**

FICTION No genre (romance, horror, western—sagebrush or cowboys), erotic, science fiction, or mystery. **Buys 6 mss/year.** Send complete ms. No e-mail submissions. Length: 100-3,000 words. **Pays $10-75.**

POETRY Needs avant-garde, free verse, haiku. *The Prairie Journal*, published twice/year, seeks poetry "of any length; free verse, contemporary themes (feminist, nature, urban, non-political), aesthetic value, a poet's poetry." Does not want to see "most rhymed verse, sentimentality, egotistical ravings. No cowboys or sage brush." Has published poetry by Liliane Welch, Cornelia Hoogland, Sheila Hyland, Zoe Lendale, and Chad Norman. *The Prairie Journal* is 40-60 pages, digest-sized, offset-printed, saddle-stapled, with card cover, includes ads. Receives about 1,000 poems/year, accepts 10%. Press run is 600; the rest are sold on newsstands. Subscription: $10 for individuals, $18 for libraries. Sample: $8 ("use postal money order"). No U.S. stamps. No heroic couplets or greeting card verse. Buys 25-35 poems/year. Submit maximum 6-8 poems. Length: 3-50 lines. **Pays $5-50.**

TIPS "We publish many, many new writers and are always open to unsolicited submissions because we are 100% freelance. Do not send US stamps, always use IRCs. We have poems, interviews, stories, and reviews online (query first)."

[🍁] [$] PRISM INTERNATIONAL

Department of Creative Writing, Buch E462, 1866 Main Mall, University of British Columbia, Vancouver BC V6T 1Z1 Canada. (604)822-2514. **Fax:** (604)822-3616. **E-mail:** prismcirculation@gmail.com. **Website:** www.prismmagazine.ca. **100% freelance written. Works with new/unpublished writers.** A quarterly international journal of contemporary writing—fiction, poetry, drama, creative nonfiction and translation. *PRISM international* is 80 pages, digest-sized, elegantly printed, flat-spined, with original color artwork on a glossy card cover. Readership: public and university libraries, individual subscriptions, bookstores—a world-wide audience concerned with the contemporary in literature. "We have no thematic or stylistic allegiances: Excellence is our main criterion for acceptance of mss." Receives 1,000 submissions/year, accepts about 80. Circulation is for 1,200 subscribers. Subscription: $35/year for Canadian subscriptions, $40/year for US subscriptions, $45/year for international. Sample: $12. Estab. 1959. Circ. 1,200. Pays on publication. Publishes ms an average of 4 months after acceptance. Accepts queries by mail and online. Responds in 4 months to queries. Responds in 3-6 months to mss. Sample copy for $12, more info online. Guidelines online.

NONFICTION No reviews, tracts, or scholarly essays. **Pays $20/printed page, and 1-year subscription.**

FICTION For Drama: one-acts/excerpts of no more than 1500 words preferred. Also interested in seeing dramatic monologues. Needs experimental, novel concepts, traditional. "New writing that is contemporary and literary. Short stories and self-contained novel excerpts. Works of translation are eagerly sought and should be accompanied by a copy of the original. Would like to see more translations. No gothic, confession, religious, romance, pornography, or science fiction." **Buys 12-16 mss/year.** Send complete ms. 25 pages maximum **Pays $20/printed page, and 1-year subscription.**

POETRY Needs avant-garde, traditional. Wants "fresh, distinctive poetry that shows an awareness of traditions old and new. We read everything." Considers poetry by children and teens. "Excellence is the only criterion." Has published poetry by Margaret Avison, Elizabeth Bachinsky, John Pass, Warren Heiti, Don McKay, Bill Bissett, and Stephanie Bolster. Submit maximum 6 poems. **Pays $40/printed page, and 1-year subscription.**

TIPS "We are looking for new and exciting fiction. Excellence is still our No. 1 criterion. As well as poetry, imaginative nonfiction and fiction, we are especially open to translations of all kinds, very short fiction pieces and drama which work well on the page. Translations must come with a copy of the original language work. We pay an additional $10/printed page to selected authors whose work we place on our online version of *PRISM*."

QUARTERLY WEST

University of Utah, 255 S. Central Campus Dr., Room 3500, Salt Lake City UT 84112. **E-mail:** quarterlywest@gmail.com. **Website:** www.quarterlywest.com. **Contact:** Sadie Hoagland and Lillian Bertram, editors. Semiannual magazine. "We publish fiction, poetry, and nonfiction in long and short formats, and will consider experimental as well as traditional works." Estab. 1976. Circ. 1,900. Pays on publication. Publishes ms an average of 6 months after acceptance. Accepts queries by online submission form. Accepts simultaneous submissions. Responds in 6 months to mss. Sample copy for $7.50 or online. Guidelines online.

○ *Quarterly West* was awarded first place for Editorial Content from the American Literary Magazine Awards. Work published in the magazine has been selected for inclusion in the *Pushcart Prize* anthology and *The Best American Short Stories* anthology.

NONFICTION Needs essays, interview, personal experience, travel, book reviews. **Buys 6-8 mss/year.** Send complete ms using online submissions manager only. 10,000 words maximum.

FICTION No preferred lengths; interested in longer, fuller short stories and short shorts. Needs ethnic, experimental, humorous, mainstream, novel concepts, slice-of-life vignettes, short shorts, translations. No detective, science fiction or romance. **Buys 6-10 mss/year.** Send complete ms using online submissions manager only.

POETRY Needs avant-garde, free verse, traditional. Submit 3-5 poems at a time using online submissions manager only. Buys 40-50 poems/year. Submit maximum 5 poems.

TIPS "We publish a special section of short shorts every issue, and we also sponsor a biennial novella contest. We are open to experimental work—potential contributors should read the magazine! Don't send more than 1 story/submission. Biennial novella competition guidelines available upon request with SASE. We prefer work with interesting language and detail—plot or narrative are less important. We don't do Western themes or religious work."

○❸❸ **QUEEN'S QUARTERLY**

144 Barrie St., Queen's University, Kingston ON K7L 3N6 Canada. (613)533-2667. **Fax:** (613)533-6822. **E-mail:** queens.quarterly@queensu.ca. **Website:** www.queensu.ca/quarterly. **Contact:** Joan Harcourt, editor. **95% freelance written.** Quartlery literary magazine. *Queen's Quarterly* is "a general interest intellectual review featuring articles on science, politics, humanities, arts and letters, extensive book reviews, some poetry and fiction." Estab. 1893. Circ. 3,000. Byline given. Pays on publication. Publishes ms on average 6-12 months after acceptance. Accepts queries by e-mail. Responds in 2-3 months to queries. Guidelines online.

○ Digest-sized, 224 pages. Press run is 3,500. Receives about 400 submissions of poetry/year, accepts 40. Has published work by Gail Anderson-Dargatz, Tim Bowling, Emma Donohue, Viktor Carr, Mark Jarman, Rick Bowers, and Dennis Bock. Subscription: $20 Canadian, $25 US for U.S. and foreign subscribers. Sample: $6.50 U.S.

NONFICTION Contact: Boris Castel, editor (articles, essays and reviews).

FICTION Contact: Joan Harcourt, literary editor (fiction and poetry). Needs historical, literary, mainstream, novel excerpts, short stories, women's. "Special emphasis on work by Canadian writers.". Send complete ms with SASE and/or IRC. No reply with insufficient postage. Accepts 2 mss/issue; 8 mss/year. Publishes 5 new writers/year. Length: 2,500-3,000 words. "Submissions over 3,000 words shall not be accepted." **Pays on publication for first North American serial rights. Sends galleys to author.**

POETRY Submit up to 6 poems at a time. No simultaneous submissions. Submissions can be sent on hard copy with a SASE (no replies/returns for foreign submissions unless accompanied by an IRC) or by e-mail and will be responded to by same. Responds in 1 month. "We are especially interested in poetry by Canadian writers. Shorter poems preferred." Has published poetry by Evelyn Lau, Sue Nevill, and Raymond Souster. Each issue contains about 12 pages of poetry. Buys 25 poems/year. **Usually pays $50 (Canadian)/poem (but it varies), plus 2 copies.**

THE RAG

11901 SW 34th Ave., Portland OR 97219. **E-mail:** raglitmag@gmail.com. **E-mail:** submissions@raglitmag.com. **Website:** raglitmag.com. **Contact:** Seth Porter, editor; Dan Reilly, editor. **80% freelance written.** *The Rag* focuses on the grittier genres that tend to fall by the wayside at more traditional literary magazines. *The Rag*'s ultimate goal is to put the literary magazine magazine back into the entertainment market while rekindling the social and cultural value short fiction once held in North American literature. Estab. 2011. Byline given. Pays on acceptance. 100% kill fee for assigned mss that are not posted. Editorial lead time 1-2 months. Accepts queries by e-mail. Accepts simultaneous submissions. Responds in 1 month or less for queries and in 1-2 months for mss.

○ Fee to submit online ($3) is waived if you subscribe or purchase a single issue.

PHOTOS Reviews GIF/JPEG files. Negotiates payment individually.

FICTION Accepts all styles and themes. Needs humorous, transgressive. **Buys 40 mss/year.** Send complete ms. Length: 2,000-10,000 words. **Pays 5¢/word, the average being $250/story.**

POETRY Needs Avant-garde, free verse. Accepts all themes and styles. Submit complete ms. Buys 15-20 poems/year. Submit maximum 5 poems. Length: 5 poems or 2,000 words, whichever occurs first. **Pays $20-100+.**

FILLERS Length: 150-1,000 words. **Pays $20-100.**

TIPS "We like gritty material; material that is psychologically believable and that has some humor in it, dark or otherwise. We like subtle themes, original characters, and sharp wit."

$ RIVER STYX MAGAZINE

Big River Association, 3547 Olive St., Suite 107, St. Louis MO 63103. (314)533-4541. **E-mail:** bigriver@riverstyx.org. **Website:** www.riverstyx.org. **Contact:** Richard Newman, editor. "*River Styx* publishes the highest-quality fiction, poetry, interviews, essays, and visual art. We are an internationally distributed multicultural literary magazine. Mss read May-November." Estab. 1975. Byline given. Pays on publication. Publishes ms an average of 6 months after acceptance. Accepts queries by mail. Accepts simultaneous submissions. Responds in 6 months to mss. Sample copy for $9. Guidelines online.

NONFICTION Needs essays, interview. **Buys 2-5 mss/year.** Send complete ms. **Pays 2 contributor's copies, plus 1-year subscription. Cash payment as funds permit.**

PHOTOS Send photos. Reviews 5x7 or 8x10 b&w and color prints and slides. Pays 2 contributor copies, plus 1-year subscription; plus cash as funds permit.

FICTION Recently published work by George Singleton, Philip Graham, Katherine Min, Richard Burgin, Nancy Zafris, Jacob Appel, and Eric Shade. Needs ethnic, experimental, mainstream, short stories, literary. No genre fiction, less thinly veiled autobiography. **Buys 6-9 mss/year.** Send complete ms with SASE. Length: no more than 23-30 ms pages. **Pays 2 contributor copies, plus 1-year subscription. Cash payment as funds permit.**

POETRY Needs avant-garde, free verse. Wants "excellent poetry—original, energetic, musical, and accessible." Does not want "chopped prose or opaque poetry that isn't about anything." Has published poetry by Jennifer Perrine, Louis Simpson, Molly Peacock, Marilyn Hacker, Yusef Komunyakaa, Andrew Hudgins, and Catie Rosemurgy. Include SASE. No religious. Buys 40-50 poems/year. Submit maximum 3-5 poems. **Pays 2 contributor copies, plus a 1-year subscription. Cash payment as funds permit.**

🌐 $ THE SAVAGE KICK LITERARY MAGAZINE

Murder Slim Press, 29 Alpha Rd., Gorleston Norfolk NR31 0EQ United Kingdom. **E-mail:** moonshine@murderslim.com. **Website:** www.murderslim.com. **100% freelance written.** Semiannual magazine. "*Savage Kick* primarily deals with viewpoints outside the mainstream: honest emotions told in a raw, simplistic way. It is recommended that you are very familiar with the *SK* style before submitting. We have only accepted 8 new writers in 4 years of the magazine. Ensure you have a distinctive voice and story to tell." Estab. 2005. Circ. 500+. Byline given. Pays on acceptance. Publishes ms an average of up to 2 months after acceptance. Accepts queries by mail, e-mail. Accepts simultaneous submissions. Responds in 7-10 days to queries. Guidelines free.

NONFICTION Needs interview, personal experience. **Buys 10-20 mss/year.** Send complete ms. Length: 500-3,000 words. **Pays $25-35.**

COLUMNS/DEPARTMENTS Buys up to 4 mss/year. Query. **Pays $25-35.**

FICTION Needs mystery, slice-of-life vignettes, crime. "Real-life stories are preferred, unless the work is distinctively extreme within the crime genre. No poetry of any kind, no mainstream fiction, Oprah-style fiction, Internet/chat language, teen issues, excessive Shakespearean language, surrealism, overworked irony, or genre fiction (horror, fantasy, science fiction, western, erotica, etc.)." **Buys 10-25 mss/year.** Send complete ms. Length: 500-6,000 words. **Pays $35.**

$ SHENANDOAH

Washington and Lee University, 17 Courthouse Square, Lexington VA 24450. (540)458-8908. **Fax:** (540)458-8461. **E-mail:** shenandoah@wlu.edu. **Website:** shenandoahliterary.org. **Contact:** R.T. Smith, editor. Semiannual digital-only literary journal. For over half a century, *Shenandoah* has been publishing splendid poems, stories, essays, and reviews which display passionate understanding, formal accomplishment and serious mischief. Estab. 1950. Circ. 2,000. Byline given. Pays on publication. Publishes ms an average of 10 months after acceptance. Responds in 3 months to mss. Sample copy for $12. Guidelines online.

💬 Reads submissions September 1-May 15 only. Sponsors the annual James Boatwright III Prize for Poetry, a $1,000 prize awarded to the author of the best poem published in *Shenandoah* during a volume year.

NONFICTION Needs essays, book reviews. **Buys 6 mss/year.** Send complete ms. **Pays $25/page ($250 maximum).**

FICTION Needs mainstream, novel excerpts. No sloppy, hasty, slight fiction. **Buys 15 mss/year.** Send complete ms. **Pays $25/page ($250 maximum).**

POETRY Considers simultaneous submissions "only if we are immediately informed of acceptance elsewhere." No e-mail submissions. All submissions should be typed on 1 side of the paper only, with name and address clearly written on the upper right corner of the ms. Staff reviews books of poetry in 7-10 pages, multibook format. Send materials for review consideration. Most reviews are solicited. "No inspirational, confessional poetry Buys 70 poems/year. Submit maximum 5 poems. **Pays $2.50/line, 1-year subscription, and 1 contributor's copy.**

⊘ SHORT STUFF

Bowman Publications, 2001 I St., #5, Fairbury NE 68352. (402)587-5003. **E-mail:** shortstf89@aol.com. **98% freelance written.** Bimonthly magazine publishing short fiction that is holiday oriented. "We are perhaps an enigma in that we publish only clean stories in any genre. We'll tackle any subject, but don't allow obscene language or pornographic description. Our magazine is for grown-ups, not X-rated 'adult' fare." Estab. 1989. Circ. 5,000. Byline given. Payment and contract upon publication. Editorial lead time 3 months. Submit seasonal material 3 months in advance. Responds in 6 months to mss. Sample copy: send 9x12 SAE with 5 first-class (44¢) stamps. Guidelines for #10 SASE.

NONFICTION Needs humor. Special issues: "We are holiday oriented and each issue reflects the appropriate holidays." Issues are Valentine's (February/March); Easter (April/May); Mom's and Dad's (June/July); Americana (August/September); Halloween (October/November); and Holiday (December/January). **Buys 30 mss/year.** Send complete ms. Include cover letter about the author and synopsis of the story. Length: 500-1,500 words. **Payment varies.**

PHOTOS Send photos. Identification of subjects required. Offers no additional payment for photos accepted with ms.

FICTION Receives 500 unsolicited mss/month. Accepts 9-12 mss/issue; 76 mss/year. Has published work by Bill Hallstead, Dede Hammond, Skye Gibbons. Needs adventure, historical, humorous, mainstream, mystery, romance, science fiction, (seldom), suspense, western. "We want to see more humor—not essay format—real stories with humor; 1,000-word mysteries, modern lifestyles. The 1,000-word pieces have the best chance of publication. No erotica; nothing morbid or pornographic. **Buys 144 mss/year.** Send complete ms. Length: 500-1,500 words. **Payment varies.**

FILLERS Needs anecdotes, short humor. **Buys 200 mss/year.** Length: 20-500 words. **Filler pays variable amount.**

TIPS "We are holiday oriented; mark on outside of envelope if story is for Easter, Mother's Day, etc. We receive 500 mss each month. This is up about 200%. Because of this, I implore writers to send 1 ms at a time. I would not use stories from the same author more than once an issue and this means I might keep the others too long. Please don't e-mail your stories! If you have an e-mail address, please include that with cover letter so we can contact you. If no SASE, we destroy the ms."

$ THE SOUTHERN REVIEW

3990 W. Lakeshore Dr., Baton Rouge LA 70808. (225)578-5108. **Fax:** (225)578-5098. **E-mail:** southernreview@lsu.edu. **Website:** thesouthernreview.org. **Contact:** Jessica Faust, co-editor and poetry editor; Emily Nemens, co-editor and prose editor. **100% freelance written. Works with a moderate number of new/unpublished writers each year; reads unsolicited mss.** Quarterly magazine with emphasis on contemporary literature in the US and abroad. "*The Southern Review* is one of the nation's premiere literary journals. Hailed by *Time* as 'superior to any other journal in the English language,' we have made literary history since our founding in 1935. We publish a diverse array of fiction, nonfiction, and poetry by the country's—and the world's—most respected contemporary writers." Reading period: September1-December 1. All mss submitted during outside the reading period will be recycled. Estab. 1935. Circ. 2,900.

Byline given. Pays on publication. Publishes ms an average of 6 months after acceptance. Accepts queries by mail. Does not accept previously published work.Accepts simultaneous submissions. Responds in 6 months. Sample copy for $12. Guidelines online.

NONFICTION Needs essays. **Buys 25 mss/year.** Submit ms by mail. Length: up to 8,000 words. **Pays $25/ printed page; max $200; 2 contributor's copies and one-year subscription.**

FICTION Wants short stories of lasting literary merit, with emphasis on style and technique; novel excerpts. "We emphasize style and substantial content. No mystery, fantasy or religious mss." Submit 1 ms at a time by mail. "We rarely publish work that is longer than 8,000 words. We consider novel excerpts if they stand alone." Length: up to 8,000 words. **Pays $25/printed page; max $200; 2 contributor's copies and one-year subscription.**

POETRY Submit poems by mail. Submit maximum 5 poems. Length: 1-4 pages. **Pays $25/printed page; max $125; 2 contributor's copies and one-year subscription.**

TIPS "Careful attention to craftsmanship and technique combined with a developed sense of the creation of story will always make us pay attention."

STAND MAGAZINE

School of English, University of Leeds, Leeds LS2 9JT United Kingdom. (44)(113)343-4794. **E-mail:** stand@ leeds.ac.uk. **Website:** www.standmagazine.org. **Contact:** Jon Glover, managing editor. *"Stand Magazine* is concerned with what happens when cultures and literatures meet, with translation in its many guises, with the mechanics of language, with the processes by which the policy receives or disables its cultural makers. *Stand* promotes debate of issues that are of radical concern to the intellectual community worldwide. U.S. submissions can be made through the Virginia office (see separate listing). Estab. 1952. Accepts queries by mail. Guidelines online at website. Submit through postal mail only. Submit complete ms with SASE.

Does not accept e-mail submissions.

FICTION No genre fiction. Up to 3,000 words.

POETRY Submit through postal mail only. Include SASE.

SYCAMORE REVIEW

Purdue University Department of English, 500 Oval Dr., West Lafayette IN 47907. (765) 494-3783. **Fax:** (765) 494-3780. **E-mail:** sycamore@purdue.edu. **Web site:** www.sycamorereview.com. **Contact:** Alisha Karabinus, managing editor; Jessica Jacobs, editor-in-chief. Semiannual magazine publishing poetry, fiction and nonfiction, books reviews and art. *Sycamore Review* is Purdue University's internationally acclaimed literary journal, affiliated with Purdue's College of Liberal Arts and the Dept. of English. Art should present politics in a language that can be felt. Strives to publish the best writing by new and established writers. Looks for well crafted and engaging work, works that illuminate our lives in the collective human search for meaning. Would like to publish more work that takes a reflective look at national identity and how we are perceived by the world. Looks for diversity of voice, pluralistic worldviews, and political and social context. Accepts queries by mail.

NONFICTION Needs essays, humor, memoir, literary memoir, translation, personal. No outside interviews, previously published work (except translations) or genre pieces (conventional sci fi, romance, horror, etc.) No scholarly articles or journalistic pieces. Query for book reviews, brief critical essays as well as all art. **Pays in contributor copies and $50/nonfiction piece.**

FICTION Needs experimental, humorous, mainstream. All prose should be typed, double-spaced, with numbered pages and the author's name and title of the work easily visible on each page. Wait until you have received a response to submit again. **Pays in contributor's copies and $50/short story.**

POETRY Submissions should be typed, double-spaced,with numbered pages and the author's name and the title easily visible on each page. Do not submit more than twice per reading period. Does not publish creative work by any student currently attending Purdue University. Former students should wait one year before submitting. Submit maximum 5 poems. **Pays $25/poem.**

TIPS "We look for originality, brevity, significance, strong dialogue, and vivid detail. We sponsor the Wabash Prize for Poetry (deadline: mid-October) and Fiction (deadline: March 1). $1,000 award for each. All contest submissions will be considered for regular inclusion in the *Sycamore Review.* No e-mail submissions—no exception. Include SASE."

THEMA

Thema Literary Society, P.O. Box 8747, Metairie LA 70011-8747. **E-mail:** thema@cox.net. **Website:** themaliterarysociety.com. **Contact:** Gail Howard, poetry editor. **100% freelance written.** *"THEMA* is designed to stimulate creative thinking by challenging writers with unusual themes, such as 'The Box Under the Bed' and 'Put It In Your Pocket, Lillian.' Appeals to writers, teachers of creative writing, and general reading audience." Estab. 1988. Byline given. Pays on acceptance. Publishes ms, on average, within 6 months after acceptance. Responds in 1 week to queries. Responds in 5 months to mss. Sample $10 U.S./$15 foreign. Upcoming themes and guidelines available in magazine, for SASE, by e-mail, or online.

FICTION Needs adventure, ethnic, experimental, fantasy, historical, humorous, mainstream, mystery, novel concepts, religious, science fiction, slice-of-life vignettes, suspense, western, contemporary, sports, prose poem. No erotica. Send complete ms with SASE, cover letter; include "name and address, brief introduction, specifying the intended target issue for the mss." SASE. Accepts simultaneous, multiple submissions, and reprints. Does not accept e-mailed submissions. **Pays $10-25.**

POETRY Submit up to 3 poems at a time. Include SASE. "All submissions should be typewritten on standard 812x11 paper. Submissions are accepted all year, but evaluated after specified deadlines." Specify target theme. Editor comments on submissions. "Each issue is based on an unusual premise. Please send SASE for guidelines before submitting poetry to find out the upcoming themes." Does not want "scatologic language, alternate lifestyle, explicit love poetry." **Pays $10/poem and 1 contributor's copy.**

THE THREEPENNY REVIEW

P.O. Box 9131, Berkeley CA 94709. (510)849-4545. **E-mail:** wlesser@threepennyreview.com. **Website:** www.threepennyreview.com. Editor: Wendy Lesser. **100% freelance written. Works with small number of new/unpublished writers each year.** Quarterly tabloid. "We are a general-interest, national literary magazine with coverage of politics, the visual arts, and the performing arts." Reading period: January 1-June 30. Estab. 1980. Circ. 9,000. Byline given. Pays on acceptance. Publishes ms an average of 1 year after acceptance. Accepts queries by mail, online submission form. Responds in 1 month to queries; 2 months to mss. Sample copy for $12 or online. Guidelines online.

NONFICTION Needs essays, expose, historical, personal experience, book, film, theater, dance, music,

and art reviews. **Buys 40 mss/year.** Send complete ms. Length: 1,500-4,000 words. **Pays $400.**

FICTION No fragmentary, sentimental fiction. **Buys 10 mss/year.** Send complete ms. Length: 800-4,000 words. **Pays $400 per poem or Table Talk piece.**

POETRY Needs free verse, traditional. No poems without capital letters or poems without a discernible subject. Buys 30 poems/year. Submit maximum 5 poems. Lines/poem: 100 maximum. **Pays $200.**

TIPS Nonfiction (political articles, memoirs, reviews) is most open to freelancers.

TIN HOUSE

McCormack Communications, P.O. Box 10500, Portland OR 97210. (503)219-0622. **Fax:** (503)222-1154. **E-mail:** info@tinhouse.com. **Website:** www.tinhouse.com. **Contact:** Cheston Knapp, managing editor; Holly Macarthur, founding editor. **90% freelance written.** "We are a general interest literary quarterly. Our watchword is quality. Our audience includes people interested in literature in all its aspects, from the mundane to the exalted." Estab. 1998. Circ. 11,000. Byline given. Pays on publication. Publishes ms an average of 6 months after acceptance. Editorial lead time 6 months. Submit seasonal material 6 months in advance. Accepts queries by mail, online submission form. Accepts simultaneous submissions. Responds in 6 weeks to queries. Responds in 3 months to mss. Sample copy for $15. Guidelines online.

Send complete ms September 1-May 31 via regular mail or online submission form. No fax or e-mail submissions.

NONFICTION Needs book excerpts, essays, interview, personal experience. Length: up to 5,000 words. **Pays $50-800 for assigned articles. Pays $50-500 for unsolicited articles.** Sometimes pays expenses of writers on assignment.

COLUMNS/DEPARTMENTS Lost and Found (minireviews of forgotten or underappreciated books), up to 500 words; Readable Feasts (fiction or nonfiction literature with recipes), 2,000-3,000 words; Pilgrimage (journey to a personally significant place, especially literary), 2,000-3,000 words. **Buys 15-20 mss/year.** Send complete ms. **Pays $50-500.**

FICTION Contact: Rob Spillman, fiction editor. Needs experimental, mainstream, novel concepts, literary. **Buys 15-20 mss/year.** Send complete ms September 1-May 31 via regular mail or online submission form. No fax or e-mail submissions. Length up to 5,000 words. **Pays $200-800.**

POETRY Contact: Brenda Shaunessy, poetry editor. Needs avant-garde, free verse, traditional. "No prose masquerading as poetry." Send complete ms September 1-May 31 via regular mail or online submission form. No fax or e-mail submissions. Buys 40 poems/year. Submit maximum 5 poems. **Pays $50-150.**

TIPS "Remember to send an SASE with your submission."

TRIQUARTERLY

School of Continuing Studies, Northwestern University, 339 E. Chicago Ave., Chicago IL 60611. **E-mail:** triquarterly@northwestern.edu. **Website:** www.triquarterly.org. Managing Editor: Matt Carmichael. TriQuarterly welcomes submissions of fiction, creative nonfiction, poetry, short drama, and hybrid work. "We also welcome short-short prose pieces." Reading period: October 16-July 15. Estab. 1964. Accepts queries by online submission form. Accepts simultaneous submissions.

NONFICTION Submit complete ms up to 3,500 words. **Pays honoraria.**

FICTION Submit complete ms up to 3,500 words. **Pays honoraria.**

POETRY Submit maximum 6 poems. **Pays honoraria.**

🍁 VALLUM: CONTEMPORARY POETRY

P.O. Box 598, Victoria Station, Montreal QC H3Z 2Y6 Canada. (514)937-8946. **Fax:** (514)937-8946. **E-mail:** info@vallummag.com. **E-mail:** editors@vallummag.com. **Website:** www.vallummag.com. **Contact:** Joshua Auerbach and Eleni Zisimatos, editors. Poetry/fine arts magazine published twice/year. Publishes exciting interplay of poets and artists. Content for magazine is selected according to themes listed online. Material is not filed but is returned upon request by SASE. E-mail response is preferred. Seeking exciting, unpublished, traditional or avant-garde poetry that reflects contemporary experience. Estab. 2000. Pays on publication. Sample copies available for $10. Guidelines online.

NONFICTION Needs Also publishes reviews, interviews, essays and letters to the editor. Please send queries to editors@vallummag.com before submitting. **Pays $65 for accepted reviews or essays on poetry.**

POETRY Pays honorarium for accepted poems.

⊘ VERSE

English Department, University of Richmond, Richmond VA 23173. **Website:** versemag.blogspot.com; english.richmond.edu/resources/verse.html. **Contact:** Brian Henry, co-editor; Andrew Zawacki, coeditor. *Verse*, published 3 times/year, is an international poetry journal which also publishes interviews with poets, essays on poetry, and book reviews. Wants no specific kind; looks for high-quality, innovative poetry. Focus is not only on American poetry, but on all poetry written in English, as well as translations. Has published poetry by James Tate, John Ashbery, Barbara Guest, Gustaf Sobin, and Rae Armantrout. Estab. 1984. Accepts simultaneous submissions.

NONFICTION Interested in any nonfiction, plus translations, criticisms, interviews, journals/notebooks, etc. Submissions should be chapbook-length (20-40 pages). **Pays $10/page, $250 minimum.**

FICTION Interested in any genre. Submissions should be chapbook-length (20-40 pages). **Pays $10/page, $250 minimum.**

POETRY Submissions should be chapbook-length (20-40 pages). **Pays $10/page, $250 minimum.**

TIPS "Read widely and deeply. Avoid inundating a magazine with submissions; constant exposure will not increase your chances of getting accepted."

$ $ VESTAL REVIEW

127 Kilsyth Road, Apt. 3, Brighton MA 02135. **Website:** www.vestalreview.net. Semi-annual print magazine specializing in flash fiction. *Vestal Review*'s stories have been reprinted in the *Mammoth Book of Miniscule Fiction, Flash Writing, E2Ink Anthologies*, and in the *WW Norton Anthology Flash Fiction Forward*. Circ. 1,500. Pays on publication. Publishes ms an average of 6 months after acceptance. Accepts queries by e-mail. Accepts simultaneous submissions. Responds in 1 week to queries. Responds in 4 months to mss. Guidelines online.

💬 Does not read new submissions in January, June, July, and December. All submissions received during these months will be returned unopened.

FICTION Needs ethnic, horror, mainstream, speculative fiction. "We accept submissions only through our submission manager." Length: 50-500 words. **Pays 3-10¢/word and 1 contributor's copy; additional copies for $10 (plus postage).**

TIPS "We like literary fiction, with a plot, that doesn't waste words. Don't send jokes masked as stories."

THE VIRGINIA QUARTERLY REVIEW

P.O. Box 400223, Charlottesville VA 22904. **E-mail:** vqr@vqronline.org. **Website:** www.vqronline.org. *The Virginia Quarterly Review* is 256 pages, digest-sized, flat-spined. Press run is 7,000. Estab. 1925. Accepts queries by online submission form. Responds in 3 months to mss. Guidelines online.

NONFICTION "We publish literary, art, and cultural criticism; reportage; historical and political analysis; and travel essays. We publish few author interviews or memoirs. In general, we are looking for nonfiction that looks out on the world, rather than within the self." Accepts online submissions only at virginiaquarterlyreview.submittable.com/submit. You can also query via this site. Length: 3,500-10,000 words. **Pays 25¢/word.**

FICTION "We are generally not interested in genre fiction (such as romance, science fiction, or fantasy)." Accepts online submissions only at virginiaquarterlyreview.submittable.com/submit. Length: 2,000-10,000 words. **Pays 25¢/word.**

POETRY *The Virginia Quarterly Review* uses about 45-50 pages of poetry in each issue. No length or subject restrictions. Issues have largely included lyric and narrative free verse, most of which features a strong message or powerful voice. Accepts online submissions only at virginiaquarterlyreview.submittable.com/submit. Submit maximum 5 poems. **Pays $200/poem; for poems longer than 50 lines, the payment is higher.**

⬡ WESTERN HUMANITIES REVIEW

University of Utah, English Department, 255 S. Central Campus Dr., Salt Lake City UT 84112-0494. (801)581-6070. **Fax:** (801)585-5167. **E-mail:** whr@mail.hum.utah.edu. **Website:** ourworld.info/whrweb/. **Contact:** Barry Weller, editor; Nate Liederbach, managing editor. A tri-annual magazine for educated readers. Estab. 1947. Circ. 1,000. Pays in contributor copies. Publishes ms an average of 1 year after acceptance. Accepts simultaneous submissions. Responds in 3-5 months. Sample copy for $10. Guidelines online.

NONFICTION Contact: Stuart Culver, nonfiction editor. **Buys 6-8 unsolicited mss/year.** Send complete ms. **Pays $5/published page.**

FICTION Contact: Michael Mejia, Fiction Editor. Needs experimental, innovative voices. Does not want genre (romance, sci-fi, etc.). **Buys 5-8 mss/year.** Send complete ms. Length: 5,000 words. **Pays $5/published page (when funds available).**

POETRY Contact: Poetry editors: Craig Dworkin, Paisley Rekdal, Tom Stillinger. Considers simultaneous submissions but no more than 5 poems or 25 pages per reading period. No fax or e-mail submissions. Reads submissions October 1-April 1 only. Wants quality poetry of any form, including translations. Has published poetry by Charles Simic, Olena Kalytiak Davis, Ravi Shankar, Karen Volkman, Dan Beachy-Quick, Lucie Brock-Broido, Christine Hume, and Dan Chiasson. Innovative prose poems may be submitted as fiction or nonfiction to the appropriate editor. **Pays 2 contributor's copies.**

TIPS "Because of changes in our editorial staff, we urge familiarity with recent issues of the magazine. We do not publish writer's guidelines because we think that the magazine itself conveys an accurate picture of our requirements. Please, no e-mail submissions."

THE WORCESTER REVIEW

1 Ekman St., Worcester MA 01607. (508)797-4770. **E-mail:** twr.diane@gmail.com. **Website:** www.theworcesterreview.org. **Contact:** Diane Mulligan, managing editor. Annual literary journal covering poetry and short fiction. *The Worcester Review*, published annually by the Worcester County Poetry Association, encourages "critical work with a New England connection; no geographic limitation on poetry and fiction." Wants "work that is crafted, intuitively honest and empathetic. We like high quality, creative poetry, artwork, and fiction. Critical articles should be connected to New England." Estab. 1972. Circ. 500. Publishes ms within 1 year of acceptance. Accepts about 10% unsolicited mss. Agented fiction less than 10%. Accepts simultaneous submissions. Responds in 4-8 months to mss. Sometimes comments on rejected mss. Sample copy: $8. Guidelines available for SASE or online.

NONFICTION Needs critical essays, literary essays, literary criticism. Send complete ms. Length: 1,000-4,000 words. Average length: 2,000 words. **Pays 2 contributor's copies and honorarium if possible.**

FICTION Recently published work by Robert Pinsky, Marge Piercy, Wes McNair, Ed Hirsch. Needs short stories, literary fiction. Send complete ms. "Send only 1 short story—reading editors do not like to read 2 by the same author at the same time. We will use only 1." Length: 1,000-4,000 words. Average length: 2,000 words. **Pays 2 contributor's copies and honorarium if possible.**

POETRY Submit up to 5 poems at a time. Cover letter is optional. Print submissions should be typed on 8.5x11 paper, with poet's name and e-mail address in upper left corner of each page. Include SASE or e-mail for reply. **Pays 2 contributor's copies plus small honorarium.**

TIPS "We generally look for creative work with a blend of craftsmanship, insight and empathy. This does not exclude humor. We won't print work that is shoddy in any of these areas."

💲💲 THE WRITER'S CHRONICLE

Association of Writers & Writing Programs (AWP), Carty House MS 1E3, George Mason University, Fairfax VA 22030-4444. (703)993-4301. **Fax:** (703)993-4302. **E-mail:** chronicle@awpwriter.org. **Website:** www.awpwriter.org. **90% freelance written.** Published 6 times during the academic year; 3 times a semester. Magazine covering the art and craft of writing. "*Writer's Chronicle* strives to: present the best essays on the craft and art of writing poetry, fiction and nonfiction; help overcome the over-specialization of the literary arts by presenting a public forum for the appreciation, debate, and analysis of contemporary literature; present the diversity of accomplishments and points of view within contemporary literature; provide serious and committed writers and students of writing the best advice on how to manage their professional lives; provide writers who teach with new pedagogical approaches for their classrooms; provide the members and subscribers with a literary community as a compensation for a devotion to a difficult and lonely art; provide information on publishing opportunities, grants, and awards; and promote the good works of AWP, its programs, and its individual members." Estab. 1967. Circ. 35,000. Byline given. Pays on publication. Editorial lead time 3 months. Accepts queries by Electronic queries OK but send submissions by postal mail. Accepts simultaneous submissions. Responds in 2 weeks to queries. Sample copy free. Guidelines free and online. Reading period: February 1-August 1.

NONFICTION Needs essays, interview, opinion, (does not mean letters to the editor). No personal essays. **Buys 15-20 mss/year.** Send complete ms. Length: 2,500-7,000 words. **Pays $14 per 100 words for assigned articles.**

TIPS "In general, the editors look for articles that demonstrate an excellent working knowledge of literary issues and a generosity of spirit that esteems the arguments of other writers on similar topics. When writing essays on craft, do not use your own work as an example. Keep in mind that 18,000 of our readers are students or just-emerging writers. They must become good readers before they can become good writers, so we expect essays on craft to show exemplary close readings of a variety of contemporary and older works. Essays must embody erudition, generosity, curiosity, and discernment rather than self-involvement. Writers may refer to their own travails and successes if they do so modestly, in small proportion to the other examples. We look for a generosity of spirit—a general love and command of literature as well as an expert, writerly viewpoint."

💲💲 THE YALE REVIEW

Yale University, P.O. Box 208243, New Haven CT 06520-8243. (203)432-0499. **Fax:** (203)432-0510. **Website:** www.yale.edu/yalereview. **Contact:** J.D. McClatchy, editor. **20% freelance written.** Quarterly magazine. Estab. 1911. Circ. 7,000. Pays prior to publication. Publishes ms an average of 6 months after acceptance. Responds in 1-3 months to mss. Sample copy online. Guidelines online.

NONFICTION Send complete ms with cover letter and SASE. Length: 3,000-5,000 words. **Pays $400-500.**

FICTION Submit complete ms with SASE. All submissions should be sent to the editorial office. **Pays $400-500.**

POETRY Submit with SASE. All submissions should be sent to the editorial office. **Pays $100-250.**

💲 THE YALOBUSHA REVIEW

University of Mississippi, P.O. Box 1848, Dept. of English, University MS 38677. (662)915-3175. **E-mail:** yreditors@gmail.com. **Website:** yr.olemiss. edu/. Annual literary journal seeking quality submissions from around the globe. Reading period is July 15-November 15. Estab. 1995. Circ. 500. Accepts queries by mail. Does not accept previously published workAccepts simultaneous submissions. Responds in 2-4 months to mss. Sample copy for $5. Guidelines for #10 SASE.

NONFICTION Needs essays, memoir, travel, experimental pieces. Does not want sappy confessional or insights into parenthood. Send only 1-page query. Length: 10,000 words. **Pays honorarium when funding available.**

FICTION Needs experimental, historical, humorous, mainstream, novel excerpts, short shorts. **Buys 3-6 mss/year.** Submit "1 short story of traditional length (let's say 8-20 pages), or up to 3 pieces of shorter fiction (less than 5 pages each). If submitting 3 shorter works, please include all piece in 1 file." Use online submissions manager. Length: up to 10,000 words. **Pays honorarium when funding is available.**

POETRY Needs avant-garde, free verse, traditional. Submit 3-5 poems and a brief cover letter. Submit maximum 5 poems. **Pays 2 contributor's copies.**

$$$ ZOETROPE: ALL-STORY

Zoetrope: All-Story, The Sentinel Bldg., 916 Kearny St., San Francisco CA 94133. (415)788-7500. **Website:** www.all-story.com. **Contact:** fiction editor. Quarterly magazine specializing in the best of contemporary short fiction. *Zoetrope: All Story* presents a new generation of classic stories. Estab. 1997. Circ. 20,000. Byline given. Publishes ms an average of 5 months after acceptance. Accepts queries by mail. Accepts simultaneous submissions. Responds in 8 months (if SASE included). Sample copy for $8.00. Guidelines online.

💬 Does not accept submissions September 1-December 31 (with the exception of stories entered in the annual Short Fiction Contest, which are considered for publication in the magazine).

FICTION Buys 25-35 mss/year. "Writers should submit only 1 story at a time and no more than 2 stories a year. We do not accept artwork or design submissions. We do not accept unsolicited revisions nor respond to writers who don't include an SASE." Send complete ms. Length: up to 7,000 words. "Excerpts from larger works, screenplays, treatments, and poetry will be returned unread." **Pays up to $1,000.**

TIPS "Before submitting, nonsubscribers should read several issues of the magazine to determine if their works fit with *All-Story.* Electronic versions of the magazine are available to read, in part, at the website, and print versions are available for purchase by single-issue order and subscription."

$ ZYZZYVA

466 Geary Street, Suite 401, San Francisco CA 94102. (415)440-1510. **E-mail:** editor@zyzzyva.org. **Website:** www.zyzzyva.org. **Contact:** Laura Cogan, editor; Oscar Villalon, managing editor. **100% freelance written. Works with a small number of new/unpublished writers each year.** Magazine published in March, August, and November. "We feature work by writers currently living on the West Coast or in Alaska and Hawaii only. We are essentially a literary magazine but of wide-ranging interests and a strong commitment to nonfiction." Estab. 1985. Circ. 2,500. Byline given. Pays on acceptance. Publishes ms an average of 3 months after acceptance. Accepts queries by mail. Accepts simultaneous submissions. Responds in 1 week to queries. Responds in 1 month to mss. Sample copy for $12 or online. Guidelines online.

💬 Accepts submissions year round. Does not accept online submissions.

NONFICTION Needs book excerpts, general interest, historical, humor, personal experience. **Buys 50 mss/year.** Submit by mail. Include SASE and contact information. Length: no maximum page count. **Pays $50.**

PHOTOS Reviews scans only at 300 dpi, 5.5.

FICTION Needs ethnic, experimental, humorous, mainstream. **Buys 60 mss/year.** Send complete ms by mail. Include SASE and contact information. Length: no maximum word count. **Pays $50.**

POETRY Submit by mail. Include SASE and contact information. Buys 20 poems/year. Submit maximum 5 poems. Length: no maximum page count. **Pays $50.**

TIPS "We are not currently seeking work about any particular theme or topic; that said, reading recent issues is perhaps the best way to develop a sense for the length and quality we are looking for in submissions."

MEN'S

$$$$ ESQUIRE

300 W. 57th St., 21st Floor, New York NY 10019. (212)649-4020. **Website:** www.esquire.com. Monthly magazine covering the ever-changing trends in American culture. *Esquire* is geared toward smart, well-off men. General readership is college educated and sophisticated, between ages 30 and 45. Written mostly by contributing editors on contract. Rarely accepts unsolicited mss. Estab. 1933. Circ. 720,000. Publishes ms an average of 2-6 months after acceptance.

Editorial lead time at least 2 months. Accepts simultaneous submissions. Guidelines online.

NONFICTION Buys 4 features and 12 shorter mss/year. Magazine no longer accepts paper submissions. To submit, use online submission manager at esquiresubmissions.com. Columns average 1,500 words; features average 5,000 words; short front of book pieces average 200-400 words. **Payment varies.**

PHOTOS Uses mostly commissioned photography. Payment depends on size and number of photos.

FICTION "Literary excellence is our only criterion." Needs Needs novel concepts, short stories, memoirs, plays. No pornography, science fiction, or 'true romance' stories. Send complete ms. To submit a story, use online submission manager at esquiresubmissions.com.

TIPS "A writer has the best chance of breaking in at *Esquire* by querying with a specific idea that requires special contacts and expertise. Ideas must be timely and national in scope."

GQ

Conde Nast Publications, Inc., 4 Times Square, New York NY 10036. (212)286-2860. **Fax:** (212)286-7786. **E-mail:** WebLetters@GQ.com. **Website:** www.gq.com. Monthly magazine covering subjects ranging from finance, food, entertainment, technology, celebrity profiles, sports and fashion. *Gentleman's Quarterly* is devoted to men's personal style and taste, from what he wears to the way he lives his life. Estab. 1957. Circ. 964,264.

Query before submitting.

NONFICTION Needs interview, celebrity.

MAXIM

Alpha Media Group, 1040 Avenue of the Americas, 16th Floor, New York NY 10018-3703. (212)302-2626. **Fax:** (212)302-2635. **E-mail:** editors@maximmag.com. **Website:** www.maximonline.com. Monthly magazine covering relationships, sex, women, careers and sports. Written for young, professional men interested in fun and informative articles. Circ. 2.5 million. Editorial lead time 5 months. Sample copy for $3.99 at newstands.

Query before submitting.

MEN'S HEALTH

Rodale, Inc., 33 E. Minor St., Emmaus PA 18098. (212)697-2040. **E-mail:** mhletters@rodale.com. **Website:** www.menshealth.com. **Contact:** Kevin Donahue, senior managing editor. Covers various men's

lifestyles topics, such as fitness, nutrition, fashion, and sexuality. The world's largest men's magazine brand, with 40 editions in 47 countries. Estab. 1987. Circ. 1,918,387.

Query before submitting.

MILITARY

ARMY MAGAZINE

Association of the U.S. Army, 2425 Wilson Blvd., Arlington VA 22201. (800)336-4570. **E-mail:** armymag@ausa.org. **Website:** www.ausa.org. **Contact:** editorial assistant. **70% freelance written. Prefers to work with published/established writers.** Monthly magazine emphasizing military interests. Estab. 1950. Circ. 65,000. Byline given. Pays on publication. Publishes ms an average of 5 months after acceptance. Submit seasonal material 3 months in advance. Accepts queries by mail. Sample copy and writer's guidelines for 9x12 SAE with $1 postage or online.

ARMY Magazine looks for shorter articles; 1,000-1,500 words.

NONFICTION Needs historical, military and original, humor, military feature-length articles and anecdotes, interview, photo feature. Special issues: "We would like to see more pieces about little-known episodes involving interesting military personalities. We especially want material lending itself to heavy, contributor-supplied photographic treatment. The first thing a contributor should recognize is that our readership is very savvy militarily. 'Gee-whiz' personal reminiscences get short shrift, unless they hold their own in a company in which long military service, heroism and unusual experiences are commonplace. At the same time, *ARMY* readers like a well-written story with a fresh slant, whether it is about an experience in a foxhole or the fortunes of a corps in battle.". No rehashed history. No unsolicited book reviews. **Buys 40 mss/year.** Submit complete ms (hard copy and disk). Length: 1,000-1,500 words. **Pays 12-18¢/word.**

PHOTOS Send photos. Captions required. Reviews prints and high resolution digital photos. Pays $50-100 for 8x10 b&w glossy prints; $50-350 for 8x10 color glossy prints and 35mm and high resolution (300 dip JPEGs) digital photos.

SOLDIER OF FORTUNE

2135 11th St., Boulder CO 80302. (303)449-3750. **E-mail:** editorsof@aol.com. **Website:** www.sofmag.com. **Contact:** Lt. Col. Robert A. Brown, editor/publisher.

50% freelance written. Monthly magazine covering military, paramilitary, police, combat subjects, and action/adventure. "We are an action-oriented magazine; we cover combat hot spots around the world. We also provide timely features on state-of-the-art weapons and equipment; elite military and police units; and historical military operations. Readership is primarily active-duty military, veterans, and law enforcement." Estab. 1975. Circ. 60,000. Byline given. Offers 25% kill fee. Responds in 3 weeks to queries. Responds in 1 month to mss. Sample copy for $5. Guidelines with #10 SASE.

NONFICTION Needs expose, general interest, historical, how-to, on weapons and their skilled use, humor, interview, new product, personal experience, photo feature, No. 1 on our list, technical, travel, combat reports, military unit reports, and solid Vietnam and Operation Iraqi Freedom articles. No 'How I won the war' pieces; no op-ed pieces unless they are fully and factually backgrounded; no knife articles (staff assignments only). All submitted articles should have good art; art will sell us on an article. **Buys 75 mss/year.** Query with or without published clips or send complete ms. Send mss to articles editor; queries to managing editor Length: 2,000-3,000 words. **Pays $150-250/page.**

REPRINTS Send disk copy, photocopy of article and information about when and where the material previously appeared. Pays 25% of amount paid for an original article.

PHOTOS Send photos. Captions, identification of subjects required. Reviews contact sheets, transparencies. Pays $500 for cover photo.

FILLERS Contact: Bulletin board editor. Needs newsbreaks, military/paramilitary related has to be documented. Length: 100-250 words. **Pays $50.**

TIPS "Submit a professionally prepared, complete package. All artwork with cutlines, double-spaced typed ms with 5.25 or 3.5 IBM-compatible disk, if available, cover letter including synopsis of article, supporting documentation where applicable, etc. Ms must be factual; writers have to do their homework and get all their facts straight. One error means rejection. Vietnam features, if carefully researched and art heavy, will always get a careful look. Combat reports, again, with good art, are No. 1 in our book and stand the best chance of being accepted. Military unit reports from around the world are well received, as are law-enforcement articles (units, police in action). If you write for us, be complete and factual; pros read *Soldier of Fortune*, and are very quick to let us know if we (and the author) err."

MUSIC CONSUMER

ALARM

Alarm Press, 900 N. Franklin St., Suite 300, Chicago IL 60610. (312)341-1290. **E-mail:** info@alarmpress. com. **Website:** www.alarmpress.com/alarm-magazine. *ALARM*, published 6 times/year, "does one thing, and it does it very well: it publishes the best new music and art in *ALARM* magazine and alarmpress. com. From our headquarters in a small Chicago office, along with a cast of contributing writers spread across the country, we listen to thousands of CDs, view hundreds of gallery openings, and attend lectures and live concerts in order to present inspirational artists who are fueled by an honest and contagious obsession with their art." Accepts queries by mail, e-mail. Only responds if interested. Submit by e-mail with the subject line "ALARM magazine submissions. Please send your work as part of the body of an e-mail; we cannot accept attachments." Alternatively, submissions may be sent by regular mail to Submissions Dept. "*ALARM* is not responsible for the return, loss of, or damage to unsolicited mss, unsolicited artwork, or any other unsolicited materials. Those submitting mss, artwork, or any other materials should not send originals.".

⊛⊛ BLUEGRASS UNLIMITED

Bluegrass Unlimited, Inc., P.O. Box 771, Warrenton VA 20188. (540)349-8181 or (800)BLU-GRAS. **Fax:** (540)341-0011. **E-mail:** editor@bluegrassmusic.com; info@bluegrassmusic.com. **Website:** www.bluegrassmusic.com. **10% freelance written. Prefers to work with published/established writers.** Monthly magazine covering bluegrass, acoustic, and old-time country music. Estab. 1966. Circ. 20,000. Byline given. Pays on publication. Offers negotiated kill fee. Publishes ms an average of 4 months after acceptance. Submit seasonal material 4 months in advance. Accepts queries by mail, e-mail, fax. Responds in 2 weeks to queries. Responds in 2 months to mss. Sample copy free. Guidelines for #10 SASE.

NONFICTION Needs general interest, historical, how-to, interview, personal experience, photo feature, travel. No fan-style articles. **Buys 30-40 mss/year.** Query. Length: Open. **Pays 10-13¢/word.**

REPRINTS Send photocopy with rights for sale noted and information about when and where the material previously appeared. Payment is negotiable.

PHOTOS State availability of or send photos. Identification of subjects required. Reviews 35mm transparencies and 3x5, 5x7, and 8x10 b&w and color prints. Also reviews/prefers digital 300 dpi or better jpg, tif files, index, contact sheet with digital submissions. Pays $50-175 for color; $25-60 for b&w prints; $50-250 for color prints.

FICTION Needs ethnic, humorous. **Buys 3-5 mss/year.** Query. Length: Negotiable. **Pays 10-13¢/word.**

TIPS "We would prefer that articles be informational, based on personal experience, or an interview with lots of quotes from subject, profile, humor, etc. We print less than 10% freelance at this time."

GUITAR WORLD

NewBay Media, LLC, 28 E. 28th St., 12th Floor, New York NY 10016. (212)378-0400. **Fax:** (212)281-4704. **E-mail:** soundingboard@guitarworld.com. **Website:** www.guitarworld.com. Monthly magazine for guitarists. Written for guitar players categorized as either professionals, semi-professionals or amateur players. Every issue offers broad-ranging interviews that cover technique, instruments, and lifestyles. Circ. 150,000. Editorial lead time 2 months.

ROLLING STONE

Wenner Media, 1290 Avenue of the Americas, New York NY 10104. (212)484-1616. **Fax:** (212)484-1664. **E-mail:** rseditors@rollingstone.com; photo@rollingstone.com. **Website:** www.rollingstone.com. **Contact:** Caryn Ganz, editorial director. Biweekly magazine geared towards young adults interested in news of popular music, entertainment and the arts, current news events, politics and American culture. Circ. 1.46 million. Editorial lead time 1 month.

Query before submitting.

SYMPHONY

League of American Orchestras, 33 W. 60th St., Fifth Floor, New York NY 10023. (212)262-5161. **Fax:** (212)262-5198. **E-mail:** clane@americanorchestras.org; jmelick@americanorchestras.org; editor@americanorchestras.org. **Website:** www.symphony.org. **Contact:** Chester Lane, senior editor; Jennifer Melick, managing editor. **50% freelance written.** Quarterly magazine for the orchestra industry and classical music enthusiasts covering classical music, orchestra industry, musicians. *Symphony*, the quarterly magazine of the League of American Orchestras, reports on the critical issues, trends, personalities, and developments of the orchestra world. Every issue includes news, provocative essays, in-depth articles, and cutting-edge research relevant to the entire orchestra field. *Symphony* profiles take readers behind the scenes to meet the people who are making a difference in the orchestra world, while wide-ranging survey articles reveal the strategies and tactics that are helping orchestras meet the challenges of the 21st century. Symphony is a matchless source of meaningful information about orchestras, and serves as an advocate and connector for the orchestra field. Circ. 18,000. Byline given. Pays on acceptance. Publishes ms an average of 10 weeks after acceptance. Editorial lead time 6 months. Submit seasonal material 8 months in advance. Accepts queries by mail, e-mail. Accepts simultaneous submissions. Guidelines online.

NONFICTION Needs book excerpts, essays, inspirational, interview, opinion, personal experience, rare, photo feature, rare, issue features, trend pieces (by assignment only; pitches welcome). Does not want to see reviews, interviews. **Buys 30 mss/year.** Query with published clips. Length: 1,500-3,500 words. **Pays $500-900.** Sometimes pays expenses of writers on assignment.

PHOTOS Rarely commissions photos or illustrations. State availability of or send photos. Captions, identification of subjects required. Reviews contact sheets, negatives, prints, electronic photos (preferred). Offers no additional payment for photos accepted with ms.

COLUMNS/DEPARTMENTS Repertoire (orchestral music—essays); Comment (personal views and opinions); Currents (electronic media developments); In Print (books); On Record (CD, DVD, video), all 1,000-2,500 words. **Buys 12 mss/year.** Query with published clips.

TIPS "We need writing samples before assigning pieces. We prefer to craft the angle with the writer, rather than adapt an existing piece. Pitches and queries should demonstrate a clear relevance to the American orchestra industry and should be timely."

MYSTERY

ELLERY QUEEN'S MYSTERY MAGAZINE

Dell Magazines, 267 Broadway, 4th Floor, New York NY 10017. (212)686-7188. **Fax:** (212)686-7414. **E-mail:**

elleryqueenmm@dellmagazines.com. **Website:** www.themysteryplace.com/eqmm. **Contact:** Jackie Sherbow, assistant editor. **100% freelance written.** Covers mystery fiction. *"Ellery Queen's Mystery Magazine* welcomes submissions from both new and established writers. We publish every kind of mystery short story: the psychological suspense tale, the deductive puzzle, the private eye case—the gamut of crime and detection from the realistic (including the policeman's lot and stories of police procedure) to the more imaginative (including 'locked rooms' and 'impossible crimes'). We look for strong writing, an original and exciting plot, and professional craftsmanship. We encourage writers whose work meets these general criteria to read an issue of *EQMM* before making a submission." Estab. 1941. Circ. 100,000. Byline given. Pays on acceptance. Publishes ms an average of 6-12 months after acceptance. Accepts queries by online submission form. NoAccepts simultaneous submissions. Responds in 3 months to mss. Sample copy for $5.50. Guidelines for SASE or online.

○ Magazine: 5⅞×8⅞, 112 pages with special 192-page combined March/April and September/October issues.

FICTION Contact: Janet Hutchings, editor. "We always need detective stories. Special consideration given to anything timely and original." Needs mystery, suspense. No explicit sex or violence, no gore or horror. Seldom publishes parodies or pastiches. "We do not want true detective or crime stories." **Buys up to 120 mss/year.** *EQMM* uses an online submission system (eqmm.magazinesubmissions.com) that has been designed to streamline our process and improve communication with authors. We ask that all submissions be made electronically, using this system, rather than on paper. All stories should be in standard ms format and submitted in .DOC format. We cannot accept .DOCX, .RTF, or .TXT files at this time. For detailed submission instructions, see eqmm.magazinesubmissions.com or our writers guidelines page (www.themysteryplace.com/eqmm/guidelines). Length: 2,500-8,000 words, but occasionally accepts longer and shorter submissions—including minute mysteries of 250 words, stories up to 12,000 words, and novellas of up to 20,000 words from established authors **Pays 5-8¢/word; occasionally higher for established authors.**

POETRY Wants short mystery verses, limericks. *EQMM* uses an online submission system (eqmm.

magazinesubmissions.com) that has been designed to streamline our process and improve communication with authors. We ask that all submissions be made electronically, using this system, rather than on paper. All stories should be in standard ms format and submitted in .DOC format. We cannot accept .DOCX, .RTF, or .TXT files at this time. For detailed submission instructions, see eqmm.magazinesubmissions.com or our writers guidelines page (www.themysteryplace.com/eqmm/guidelines). Length: 1 page, double spaced maximum.

TIPS "We have a Department of First Stories to encourage writers whose fiction has never before been in print. We publish an average of 10 first stories every year. Mark subject line Attn: Dept. of First Stories."

⊖ HARDBOILED

Gryphon Publications, P.O. Box 209, Brooklyn NY 11228. **Website:** www.gryphonbooks.com. **100% freelance written.** Semiannual book covering crime/mystery fiction and nonfiction. "Hard-hitting crime fiction and private-eye stories—the newest and most cutting-edge work and classic reprints." Estab. 1988. Circ. 1,000. Byline given. Pays on publication. Offers 100% kill fee. Publishes ms an average of 18 months after acceptance. Editorial lead time 1 year. Submit seasonal material 9 months in advance. Accepts queries by mail, fax. Accepts simultaneous submissions. Responds in 2 weeks to queries. Responds in 1 month to mss. Sample copy for $10. Guidelines for #10 SASE.

○ Hardboiled, published 1-2 times/year, is 100 pages with color cover.

NONFICTION Needs book excerpts, essays, expose. **Buys 4-6 mss/year.** Query. Length: 500-3,000 words. **Pays 1 copy.**

REPRINTS Query first.

PHOTOS State availability.

COLUMNS/DEPARTMENTS Occasional review columns/articles on hardboiled writers. **Buys 2-4 mss/year.** Query.

FICTION Contact: Gary Lovisi, editor. Needs mystery, private eye, police procedural, noir, hardboiled crime, and private-eye stories, all on the cutting edge. "No pastiches, violence for the sake of violence." **Buys 40 mss/year.** Query or send complete ms. Length: 500-3,000 words. **Pays $5-50.**

TIPS "Your best bet for breaking in is short hard crime fiction filled with authenticity and brevity. Try a subscription to *Hardboiled* to get the perfect idea of what we are after."

NATURE, CONSERVATION AND ECOLOGY

✪$ ALTERNATIVES JOURNAL

200 University Ave., W, Waterloo ON N2L 3G1 Canada. (519)888-4505. **Fax:** (519)746-0292. **E-mail:** editor@alternativesjournal.ca; marcia@alternativesjournal.ca. **Website:** www.alternativesjournal.ca. **Contact:** Eric Rumble, editor; Marcia Ruby, creative director. **90% freelance written.** Magazine published 6 times/year covering international environmental issues. "*Alternatives Journal*, Canada's national environmental magazine, delivers thoughtful analysis and intelligent debate on Canadian and world environmental issues, the latest news and ideas, as well as profiles of environmental leaders who are making a difference. *A/J* is a bimonthly magazine featuring bright, lively writing by the nation's foremost environmental thinkers and researchers. *A/J* offers a vision of a more sustainable future as well as the tools needed to take us there." Estab. 1971. Circ. 5,000. Byline given. Pays on publication. Offers 50% kill fee. Publishes ms an average of 5 months after acceptance. Editorial lead time 7 months. Submit seasonal material 5 months in advance. Accepts queries by mail, e-mail, fax. Accepts simultaneous submissions. Sample copy free for Canadian writers only. Guidelines online.

NONFICTION Needs book excerpts, essays, expose, humor, interview, opinion. **Buys 50 mss/year.** Query with published clips. Length: 800-3,000 words. **Pays $.10/word (Canadian).** Sometimes pays expenses of writers on assignment.

PHOTOS State availability. Identification of subjects required. Offers $35-75/photo.

TIPS "Before responding to this call for submissions, please read several back issues of the magazine so that you understand the nature of our publication. We also suggest you go through our detailed submission procedures to understand the types and lengths of articles we accept. Queries should explain, in less than 300 words, the content and scope of your article, and should convey your intended approach, tone, and style. Please include a list of people you will interview, potential images or sources for images, and the number of words you propose to write. We would also like to receive a very short bio. And if you have not written for *Alternatives* before, please include other examples of your writing. Articles range from about 500 to 4,000 words in length. Keep in mind that our lead time is several months. Articles should not be so time-bound that they will seem dated once published. Alternatives has a limited budget of $.10 per word for several articles. This stipend is available to professional and amateur writers and students only. Please indicate your interest in this funding in your submission."

ARIZONA WILDLIFE VIEWS

5000 W. Carefee Hwy., Phoenix AZ 85086. (800)777-0015. **E-mail:** awv@azgfd.gov; hrayment@azgfd.gov. **Website:** www.azgfd.gov/magazine. **Contact:** Heidi Rayment. **50% freelance written.** Bimonthly magazine covering Arizona wildlife, wildlife management, and outdoor recreation (specifically hunting, fishing, wildlife watching, boating and off-highway vehicle recreation). "*Arizona Wildlife Views* is a general interest magazine about Arizona wildlife, wildlife management and outdoor recreation. We publish material that conforms to the mission and policies of the Arizona Game and Fish Department. In addition to Arizona wildlife and wildlife management, topics include habitat issues, outdoor recreation involving wildlife, boating, fishing, hunting, bird-watching, animal observation, off-highway vehicle use, etc., and historical articles about wildlife and wildlife management." Circ. 22,000. Byline given. Pays on publication. Publishes ms an average of 10 months after acceptance. Editorial lead time 1 year. Submit seasonal material 2 months in advance. Accepts queries by mail, e-mail (preferred). Accepts simultaneous submissions. Responds in 1 month to queries. Responds in 2 months to mss. Sample copy free. Guidelines online.

NONFICTION Needs general interest, historical, how-to, interview, photo feature, technical, travel, scientific for a popular audience. Does not want "Me and Joe" articles, anthropomorphism of wildlife, or opinionated pieces not based on confirmable facts. **Buys 20 mss/year.** Query. Length: 1,000-2,500 words. **Pays $450-800.**

TIPS "Unsolicited material without proper identification will be returned immediately."

●$ THE BEAR DELUXE MAGAZINE

Orlo, 810 SE Belmont, Studio 5, Portland OR 97214. **E-mail:** bear@orlo.org. **Website:** www.orlo.org. **Contact:** Tom Webb, editor-in-chief; Kristin Rogers

Brown, art director. **80% freelance written.** Covers fiction/essay/poetry/other. 750-4,500 words. Do not combine submissions, rather submit poetry, fiction and essay in separate packages. News essays, on occasion, are assigned out if they have a strong element of reporting. Artists contribute to *The Bear Deluxe* in various ways, including: editorial illustration, editorial photography, spot illustration, independent art, cover art, graphic design, and cartoons. "*The Bear Deluxe Magazine* is a national independent environmental arts magazine publishing significant works of reporting, creative nonfiction, literature, visual art and design. Based in the Pacific Northwest, it reaches across cultural and political divides to engage readers on vital issues effecting the environment. Published twice per year, *The Bear Deluxe* includes a wider array and a higher-percentage of visual artwork and design than many other publications. Artwork is included both as editorial support and as stand alone or independent art. It has included nationally recognized artists as well as emerging artists. As with any publication, artists are encouraged to review a sample copy for a clearer understanding of the magazine's approach. Unsolicited submissions and samples are accepted and encouraged." Estab. 1993. Circ. 19,000. Byline given. Pays on publication. Offers 25% kill fee. Publishes ms an average of 6 months after acceptance. Editorial lead time 6 months. Submit seasonal material 9 months in advance. Accepts queries by mail, e-mail. Accepts simultaneous submissions. Responds in 3-6 months to mail queries. Only responds to e-mail queries if interested. Sample copy for $3. Guidelines for #10 SASE or online.

NONFICTION Needs book excerpts, essays, exposé, general interest, interview, new product, opinion, personal experience, photo feature, travel, artist profiles. Special issues: Publishes 1 theme/2 years. **Buys 40 mss/year.** Query with published clips. Length: 250-4,500 words. Essays: 750-3,000 words. **Pays $25-400, depending on piece.** Sometimes pays expenses.

PHOTOS State availability. Identification of subjects, model releases required. Reviews contact sheets, transparencies, 8x10 prints. Offers $30/photo.

COLUMNS/DEPARTMENTS Reviews (almost anything), 300 words; Front of the Book (mix of short news bits, found writing, quirky tidbits), 300-500 words; Portrait of an Artist (artist profiles), 1,200 words; Back of the Book (creative opinion pieces), 650 words. **Buys 16 mss/year.** Query with published clips. **Pays $25-400, depending on piece.**

FICTION "Stories must have some environmental context, but we view that in a broad sense." Needs adventure, condensed novels, historical, horror, humorous, mystery, novel concepts, western. No detective, children's, or horror. **Buys 8 mss/year.** Query or send complete ms. Length: 750-4,500 words. **Pays free subscription to the magazine, contributor's copies and $25-400, depending on piece; additional copies for postage**.

POETRY Needs avant-garde, free verse, haiku, light verse, traditional. Submit 3-5 poems at a time. Considers previously published poems and simultaneous submissions "so long as noted." Poems are reviewed by a committee of 3-5 people. Publishes 1 theme issue/year. Acquires first or one-time rights. Buys 16-20 poems/year. Submit maximum 3-5 poems. Length: 50 lines maximum. **Pays $20, subscription, and copies.**

FILLERS Needs facts, newsbreaks, short humor. **Buys 10 mss/year.** Length: 100-750 words.

TIPS "Offer to be a stringer for future ideas. Get a copy of the magazine and guidelines, and query us with specific nonfiction ideas and clips. We're looking for original, magazine-style stories, not fluff or PR. Fiction, essay, and poetry writers should know we have an open and blind review policy and should keep sending their best work even if rejected once. Be as specific as possible in queries."

BIRD WATCHER'S DIGEST

P.O. Box 110, Marietta OH 45750. (740)373-5285; (800)879-2473. **Fax:** (740)373-8443. **E-mail:** editor@birdwatchersdigest.com. **E-mail:** submissions@birdwatchersdigest.com. **Website:** www.birdwatchersdigest.com. **Contact:** Bill Thompson III, editor. **60% freelance written.** Bimonthly magazine covering natural history—birds and bird watching. "*BWD* is a nontechnical magazine interpreting ornithological material for amateur observers, including the knowledgeable birder, the serious novice and the backyard bird watcher; we strive to provide good reading and good ornithology. Works with a small number of new/unpublished writers each year." Estab. 1978. Circ. 125,000. Byline given. Pays on publication. Publishes ms an average of 2 years after acceptance. Submit seasonal material 6 months in advance. TrueResponds in 10-12 weeks to queries. Sample copy for $3.99 or access online. Guidelines online.

NONFICTION Needs book excerpts, how-to, relating to birds, feeding and attracting, etc., humor, personal experience, travel. No articles on pet or caged birds, or raising a baby bird. **Buys 45-60 mss/year.** "We gladly accept e-mail queries and ms submissions but aren't not able to respond immediately to most inquiries via e-mail. When submitting by e-mail, please make the subject line read 'Submission—[your topic].' Attach your submission to your e-mail in either MS Word (.doc) or RichText Format (.rtf). Please do not copy and paste your submission into the body of the e-mail. Whether submitting by regular mail or e-mail, please include your full contact information on every page. We ask that you allow 10 to 12 weeks for a response." Length: 600-3,500 words. **Pays from $100.**

PHOTOS Reviews transparencies, prints. Pays $75 minimum for transparencies. "Our payment schedule is $75 per image used regardless of size. Images reused on our table of contents page or on our website will be paid an additional $25. There is no payment or contract for photos used in 'My Way', or for photos that have been loaned for courtesy use.".

TIPS "Obtain a sample copy of *BWD* from us or at your local newsstand, bird store, or bookstore and familiarize yourself with the type of material we regularly publish. We rarely repeat coverage of a topic within a period of 2 to 3 years. We are aimed at an audience ranging from the backyard bird watcher to the very knowledgeable birder; we include in each issue material that will appeal at various levels. We always strive for a good geographical spread, with material from every section of the country. We leave very technical matters to others, but we want facts and accuracy, depth and quality, directed at the veteran bird watcher and at the enthusiastic novice. We stress the joys and pleasures of bird watching, its environmental contribution, and its value for the individual and society."

💲💲 BIRDWATCHING

Madavor Media, LLC, 25 Braintree Hill Office Park, Suite 404, Braintree MA 02184. **Fax:** (262)798-6468. **E-mail:** mail@birdwatchingdaily.com. **Website:** www.birdwatchingdaily.com. Bimonthly magazine for birdwatchers who actively look for wild birds in the field. "*BirdWatching* concentrates on where to find, how to attract, and how to identify wild birds, and on how to understand what they do." Estab. 1987. Circ.

40,000. Byline given. Pays on publication. Accepts queries by mail. Guidelines online.

NONFICTION Needs essays, how-to, attracting birds, interview, personal experience, photo feature, bird photography, travel, birding hotspots in North America and beyond, product reviews/comparisons, bird biology, endangered or threatened birds. No poetry, fiction, or puzzles. **Buys 12 mss/year.** Query with published clips. Length: 500-2,400 words. **Pays $200-400.**

PHOTOS See photo guidelines online. State availability. Identification of subjects required.

💲💲 EARTH ISLAND JOURNAL

Earth Island Institute, 2150 Allston Way, Suite 460, Berkeley CA 94704. **E-mail:** editor@earthisland.org; jmark@earthisland.org. **Website:** www.earthislandjournal.org. **80% freelance written.** Quarterly magazine covering the environment/ecology. Looking for in-depth, vigorously reported stories that reveal the connections between the environment and other contemporary issues. Audience, though modest, includes many of the leaders of the environmental movement. Article pitches should be geared toward this sophisticated audience. Estab. 1985. Circ. 10,000. Byline given. Pays on publication. Publishes ms an average of 4 months after acceptance. Editorial lead time 4 months. Submit seasonal material 4 months in advance. Accepts queries by e-mail. Responds in 4 weeks to queries. Responds in 1 month to mss. Sample copy for $5. Guidelines online.

💭 Does not publish poetry or fiction.

NONFICTION Needs book excerpts, essays, expose, general interest, interview, opinion, personal experience, photo feature. We do not want product pitches, services, or company news. **Buys 20/year mss/year.** Query with published clips. Length: 750-4,000 words. **Pays 25¢ a word for articles.** Sometimes pays expenses of writers on assignment.

PHOTOS Send photos. Reviews contact sheets, GIF/JPEG files. We negotiate payment individually.

COLUMNS/DEPARTMENTS Voices (first person reflection about the environment in a person's life.), 750 words. **Buys 4 mss/year.** Query. **Pays $50.**

TIPS "Given our audience, we are looking for stories that break new ground when it comes to environmental coverage. We are not going to publish a story "about recycling." (I have seriously gotten this pitch.) We MAY, however, be interested in a story about, say, the waste manager in Kansas City, KS, who developed an innovative technology for sorting trash, and how his/her scheme is being copied around the world; that is: we are looking for fresh angles on familiar stories, stories that so far have been overlooked by larger publications."

$$$⊘ NATIONAL PARKS MAGAZINE

National Parks Conservation Association, 777 Sixth St. NW, Suite 700, Washington DC 20001. (202)223-6722; (800)628-7275. **Fax:** (202)454-3333. **E-mail:** npmag@npca.org. **Website:** www.npca.org/magazine/. **Contact:** Scott Kirkwood, editor-in-chief. **60% freelance written. Prefers to work with published/established writers.** Quarterly magazine for a largely unscientific but highly educated audience interested in preservation of National Park System units, natural areas, and protection of wildlife habitat. "*National Parks* magazine publishes articles about areas in the National Park System, proposed new areas, threats to parks or park wildlife, scientific discoveries, legislative issues, and endangered species of plants or animals relevant to national parks. We do not publish articles on general environmental topics, nor do we print articles about land managed by the Fish and Wildlife Service, Bureau of Land Management, or other federal agencies." Estab. 1919. Circ. 340,000. Pays on acceptance. Offers 33% kill fee. Publishes ms an average of 2 months after acceptance. Responds in 3-4 months to queries. Sample copy for $3 and 9x12 SASE or online. Guidelines online.

NONFICTION Needs expose, on threats, wildlife problems in national parks, descriptive articles about new or proposed national parks and wilderness parks. No poetry, philosophical essays, or first-person narratives. No unsolicited mss. Length: 1,500 words. **Pays $1,300 for 1,500-word features and travel articles.**

PHOTOS Not looking for new photographers. Send photos.

TIPS "Articles should have an original slant or news hook and cover a limited subject, rather than attempt to treat a broad subject superficially. Specific examples, descriptive details, and quotes are always preferable to generalized information. The writer must be able to document factual claims, and statements should be clearly substantiated with evidence within the article. *National Parks* does not publish fiction, poetry, personal essays, or 'My trip to...' stories."

$$ NORTHERN WOODLANDS MAGAZINE

Center for Woodlands Education, Inc., 1776 Center Rd., P.O. Box 471, Corinth VT 05039-0471. (802)439-6292; (800)290-5232. **Fax:** (802)368-1053. **E-mail:** dave@northernwoodlands.org. **Website:** www.northernwoodlands.org. **40-60% freelance written.** Quarterly magazine covering natural history, conservation, and forest management in the Northeast. "*Northern Woodlands* strives to inspire landowners' sense of stewardship by increasing their awareness of the natural history and the principles of conservation and forestry that are directly related to their land. We also hope to increase the public's awareness of the social, economic, and environmental benefits of a working forest." Estab. 1994. Circ. 15,000. Byline given. Pays 1 month prior to publication. Publishes ms an average of 6 months after acceptance. Editorial lead time 6 months. Submit seasonal material 6 months in advance. Accepts queries by mail, e-mail. Accepts simultaneous submissions. Responds in 1 month to queries. Responds in 1-2 months to mss. Sample copy and guidelines online.

NONFICTION No product reviews, first-person travelogues, "cute" animal stories, opinion, or advocacy pieces. **Buys 15-20 mss/year.** Query with published clips. Length: 500-3,000 words. **Pay varies per piece.** Sometimes pays expenses of writers on assignment.

PHOTOS State availability. Identification of subjects required. Reviews transparencies, prints, high res digital photos. Offers $35-75/photo.

TIPS "We will work with subject-matter experts to make their work suitable for our audience."

$$ OCEAN MAGAZINE

P.O. Box 84, Rodanthe NC 27968-0084. (252)256-2296. **E-mail:** diane@oceanmagazine.org. **Website:** www.oceanmagazine.org. **100% freelance written.** "*OCEAN* Magazine is a nature magazine. *OCEAN* publishes articles, stories, poems, essays, and photography related to the ocean." Estab. 2004. Circ. 40,000. Byline given. Pays on publication. Publishes ms an average of 2-4 months after acceptance. Editorial lead time 3-6 months. Submit seasonal material 3-6 months in advance. Accepts queries by e-mail. .Accepts simultaneous submissions. Responds in 1 day to 2 months. Sample copy available for $3.25 online, $8.95 print. Guidelines online.

NONFICTION Needs Rarely publishes nonfiction. Accepts book excerpts, essays, general interest, historical, inspirational, interview, opinion, personal experience, photo feature, technical, travel, spiritual. Does not want "poor writing." **Buys 24-36 mss/year.** Query. Length: 75-5,000 words. **Pays $75-250.**

PHOTOS Identification of subjects, model releases required. Reviews 5×7, 8×10, 10×12 JPEG files. Negotiates payment individually. Reviews 5×7, 8×10, 10×12 JPEG files. Negotiates payment individually.

FICTION Needs adventure, fantasy, historical, novel concepts, romance, slice-of-life vignettes. **Buys 1-2 mss/year.** Query. Length: 100-2,000 words. **Pays $75-150.**

POETRY Needs avant-garde, free verse, haiku, light verse, traditional. Buys 12 poems/year. Submit maximum 6 poems. **Pays $25-75.**

FILLERS Needs anecdotes, facts. **Buys reflections mss/year.** Length: 20-100 words. **Pays $25-75.**

TIPS "Submit with a genuine love and concern for the ocean and its creatures."

⊖⊖⊖⊖ SIERRA

85 Second St., 2nd Floor, San Francisco CA 94105. (415)977-5500. **Fax:** (415)977-5799. **E-mail:** sierra. magazine@sierraclub.org; photo.Submissions@sierraclub.org. **Website:** www.sierraclub.org. **Contact:** Tracy Cox, art director. **Works with a small number of new/unpublished writers each year.** Bimonthly magazine emphasizing conservation and environmental politics for people who are well educated, activist, outdoor-oriented, and politically well informed with a dedication to conservation. Estab. 1893. Circ. 695,000. Byline given. Pays on acceptance. Offers negotiable kill fee. Publishes ms an average of 4 months after acceptance. Accepts queries by mail, fax. Responds in 2 months to queries. Sample copy for $3 and SASE, or online. Guidelines online.

○   The editor reports an interest in seeing pieces on environmental heroes, thoughtful features on new developments in solving environmental problems, and outdoor adventure stories with a strong environmental element.

NONFICTION Needs expose, well-documented articles on environmental issues of national importance such as energy, wilderness, forests, etc., general interest, well-researched nontechnical pieces on areas of particular environmental concern, interview, photo feature, photo feature essays on threatened or scenic areas, journalistic treatments of semitechnical topic (energy sources, wildlife management, land use, waste management, etc.). "No 'My trip to ...' or 'Why we must save wildlife/nature' articles; no poetry or general superficial essays on environmentalism; no reporting on purely local environmental issues. **Buys 30-36 mss/year.** Query with published clips. Length: 1,000-3,000 words. **Pays $800-3,000.**

REPRINTS Send photocopy with rights for sale noted and information about when and where the material previously appeared. Payment negotiable.

PHOTOS Publishes photographs pertaining to the natural world and the environment. "We use high-quality, mostly color photographs and prefer digital files. Photographers interested in submitting work to Sierra are encouraged to send a link to their website, along with a stock listing of regions and subjects of specialty for us to review. Please do not send unsolicited transparencies and prints. We review photographers' stock lists (subject matter and locations in photographs) and samples and keep the names of potential contributors on file. Photographers are contacted only when subjects they have in stock are needed. We typically do not post our photo-needs list online or elsewhere. Sierra does not accept responsibility for lost or damaged transparencies sent on spec or for portfolio review. Please e-mail Photo.Submissions@ sierraclub.org.". Send photos. Pays maximum $300 for transparencies; more for cover photos.

COLUMNS/DEPARTMENTS Food for Thought (food's connection to environment); Good Going (adventure journey); Hearth & Home (advice for environmentally sound living); Body Politics (health and the environment); Profiles (biographical look at environmentalists); Hidden Life (exposure of hidden environmental problems in everyday objects); Lay of the Land (national/international concerns), 500-700 words; Mixed Media (essays on environment in the media; book reviews), 200-300 words. **Pays $50-500.**

TIPS Queries should include an outline of how the topic would be covered and a mention of the political appropriateness and timeliness of the article. Statements of the writer's qualifications should be included.

PERSONAL COMPUTERS

WIRED

Condé Nast Publications, 520 Third St., 3rd Floor, San Francisco CA 94107-1815. (415)276-5000. **Fax:**

(415)276-5150. **Website:** www.wired.com/wired. **Contact:** Jacob Young, managing editor. **95% freelance written.** Monthly magazine covering technology and digital culture. Covers the digital revolution and related advances in computers, communications, and lifestyles. Estab. 1993. Circ. 500,000. Byline given. Pays on publication. Offers 25% kill fee. Publishes ms an average of 3 months after acceptance. Editorial lead time 3 months. Accepts queries by e-mail. Responds in 3 weeks to queries. Sample copy for $4.95. Guidelines by e-mail.

Query before submitting.

NONFICTION Needs essays, interview, opinion. No poetry or trade articles. Query. Pays expenses of writers on assignment.

TIPS "Read the magazine. We get too many inappropriate queries. We need quality writers who understand our audience, and who understand how to query."

PHOTOGRAPHY

APOGEE PHOTO MAGAZINE

Jacksonville FL (904)619-2010. **E-mail:** mmeier@ apogeephoto.com. **Website:** apogeephoto.com. **Contact:** Marla Meier, editorial director. "A free online monthly magazine designed to inform, educate and entertain photographers of all ages and levels. Take online photography courses, read photo articles covering a wide range of photo topics and see listings of photo workshops and tours, camera clubs, and books. Submit your articles for publication."

PHOTOS "*Apogee Photo* is interested in providing an electronic forum for high quality work from photographic writers and photographers. We will accept articles up to 1,200 words on any photographic subject geared towards the beginning to advanced photographer. Articles must have a minimum of 4-6 photographs accompanying them. You must hold the copyright and/or have a copyright release from a 3rd party and you must have signed model releases where applicable for any identifiable person or persons which appear in your photographs.". Accepts reviews of new products, 1,000/words max.

TIPS "Please do a search by subject before submitting your article to see if your article covers a new subject or brings a new perspective on a particular subject or theme."

PHOTOGRAPHER'S FORUM MAGAZINE

813 Reddick St., Santa Barbara CA 93103. (805)963-0439, ext. 240. **Fax:** (805)965-0496. **E-mail:** julie@ serbin.com. **Website:** www.pfmagazine.com. **Contact:** Julie Simpson, managing editor. Quarterly magazine for the serious student and emerging professional photographer. Includes feature articles on historic and contemporary photographers, interviews, book reviews, workshop listings, and new products.

NONFICTION Needs historical, interview, new product, photo feature, profile, reviews.

POPULAR PHOTOGRAPHY & IMAGING

Bonnier Corporation, 460 N. Orlando Ave., Suite 200, Winter Park FL 32789. (407)628-4802. **Fax:** (407)628-7061. **E-mail:** mleuchter@hfmus.com; popeditor@hfmus.com. **Website:** www.popularphotography.com. **Contact:** Miriam Leuchter, managing editor. Monthly magazine edited for amateur to professional photographers. Provides incisive instructional articles, authoritative tests of photographic equipment; covers still and digital imaging; travel, color, nature, and large-format columns, plus up-to-date industry information. Estab. 1937. Circ. 450,000. Editorial lead time 2 months.

Query before submitting.

TIPS The Annnual Reader's Picture Contest gives photographers the opportunity to have their work recognized in the largest photo magazine in the world, as well as on PopPhoto.com. See website for submission guidelines, or e-mail acooper@hfmus.com.

POLITICS AND WORLD AFFAIRS

●● THE PROGRESSIVE

409 E. Main St., Madison WI 53703. (608)257-4626. **Fax:** (608)257-3373. **E-mail:** editorial@progressive.org; mattr@progressive.org. **Website:** www.progressive.org. **Contact:** Matthew Rothschild, editor. **75% freelance written.** Monthly magazine of investigative reporting, political commentary, cultural coverage, activism, interviews, poetry, and humor. Estab. 1909. Byline given. Pays on publication. Publishes ms an average of 6 weeks after acceptance. Accepts queries by mail. Responds in 1 month to queries. Sample copy for 9x12 SASE with 4 first-class stamps or sample articles online. Guidelines online.

NONFICTION Query. Length: 500-4,000 words. **Pays $500-1,300.**

POETRY Publishes 1 original poem a month. "We prefer poems that connect up—in 1 fashion or another, however obliquely—with political concerns." **Pays $150.**

TIPS Sought-after topics include electoral coverage, social movement, foreign policy, activism, and book reviews.

THEORIA

Berghahn Books, Inc., c/o Turpin North America, 143 West St., New Milford CT 06776. (860)350-0041. **Fax:** (860)350-0039. **E-mail:** theoriasa@gmail.com; editorial@journals.berghahnbooks.com. **Website:** journals.berghahnbooks.com/th. **Contact:** Chris Allsobrook, managing editor. **100% freelance written.** Academic journal published 4 times/year. "*Theoria* is an engaged, multidisciplinary, peer-reviewed journal of social and political theory. Its purpose is to address—through scholarly debate—the many challenges posed to intellectual life by the major social, political, and economic forces that shape the contemporary world. Thus, it is principally concerned with questions such as how modern systems of power, processes of globalization, and capitalist economic organization bear on matters such as justice, democracy, and truth." Estab. 1947. Circ. 300. Byline sometimes given. Publishes ms an average of 6 months after acceptance. Editorial lead time 3 months. Submit seasonal material 3 months in advance. Accepts queries by mail, e-mail, fax, phone. Responds in 1 week to queries. Responds in 3-4 months to mss. Sample copy free online. Guidelines online or via e-mail.

NONFICTION Needs book excerpts, essays, expose, general interest, historical, interview, review articles, book reviews, theoretical, philosophical, political. **Buys 1 mss/year.** Send complete ms. "Ms must comply with guidelines." Length: 6,000-9,000 words. "Ms must be ready for blind peer review." **No payment.**

PHOTOS State availability. Identification of subjects required. Reviews GIF/JPEG files. Negotiates payment individually.

COLUMNS/DEPARTMENTS Book Reviews, 1,000-1,500 words; Review Articles, 3,000-5,000 words. **Buys 1 mss/year.** Send complete ms.

U.S. NEWS & WORLD REPORT

U.S. News & World Report, Inc., 1050 Thomas Jefferson St. NW, Washington DC 20007. (202)955-2000. **Website:** www.usnews.com. **Contact:** Anne McGrath, managing editor. Weekly magazine devoted largely to reporting and analyzing national and international affairs, politics, business, health, science, technology and social trends. Circ. 2 million. Editorial lead time 10 days.

Query before submitting.

REGIONAL

ALABAMA

◉ ALABAMA LIVING

Alabama Rural Electric Association, 340 TechnaCenter Dr., Montgomery AL 36117. (800)410-2737. **Website:** www.alabamaliving.com. **Contact:** Lenore Vickrey, editor; Michael Cornelison, art director. **80% freelance written.** Monthly magazine covering topics of interest to rural and suburban Alabamians. "Our magazine is an editorially balanced, informational and educational service to members of rural electric cooperatives. Our mix regularly includes Alabama history, Alabama features, gardening, outdoor, and consumer pieces." Estab. 1948. Circ. 400,000. Byline given. Pays on acceptance. Editorial lead time 4 months. Submit seasonal material 4 months in advance. Accepts queries by mail, e-mail. Accepts simultaneous submissions. Responds in 1 month to queries. Sample copy free.

NONFICTION Needs historical, rural-oriented, Alabama slant, Alabama. Special issues: Gardening (March); Travel (April); Home Improvement (May); Holiday Recipes (December). **Buys 20 mss/year.** Send complete ms. Length: 500-750 words. **Pays $250 minimum for assigned articles. Pays $150 minimum for unsolicited articles.**

REPRINTS Send typed ms with rights for sale noted. Pays $100.

PHOTOS Buys 1-3 photos from freelancers/issue; 12-36 photos/year. Pays $100 for color cover; $50 for color inside; $60-75 for photo/text package. **Pays on acceptance.** Credit line given. Buys one-time rights for publication and website; negotiable.

TIPS "Preference given to submissions with accompanying art."

ALASKA

◉◉ ALASKA

301 Arctic Slope Ave., Suite 300, Anchorage AK 99518-3035. (907)272-6070. **Fax:** (907)258-5360. **E-**

mail: editor@alaskamagazine.com; tracy.kalytiak@ alaskamagazine.com. **Website:** www.alaskamagazine. com. **Contact:** Tracy Kalytiak, editor. **70% freelance written. Eager to work with new/unpublished writers.** Magazine published 10 times/year covering topics uniquely Alaskan. Estab. 1935. Circ. 180,000. Byline given. Pays on publication. Publishes ms an average of 6 months after acceptance. Submit seasonal material 1 year in advance. Accepts queries by mail, e-mail. Responds in 2 months to queries and to mss. Sample copy for $4.99 and 9x12 SASE with 7 first-class stamps. Guidelines online.

NONFICTION Needs historical, humor, interview, personal experience, photo feature, travel, adventure, outdoor recreation (including hunting, fishing), Alaska destination stories. No fiction or poetry. **Buys 40 mss/year.** Length: 100-2,000 words **Pays $100-1,250**

PHOTOS *Alaska* is dedicated to depicting life in Alaska through high-quality images of its people, places and wildlife. Color photographs from professional free-lance photographers are used extensively and selected according to their creative and technical merits. Send photos. Captions, identification of subjects required. Reviews 35mm or larger transparencies, slides labeled with your name. Pays $50 maximum for b&w photos; $75-500 for color photos; $300 maximum/day; $2,000 maximum/complete job; $300 maximum/full page; $500 maximum/cover. Buys limited rights, first North American serial rights and electronic rights."Each issue of *Alaska* features a 4, 6 and/or 8-page feature. We're looking for themes and photos to show the best of Alaska. We want sharp, artistically composed pictures. Cover photo always relates to stories inside the issue." Photographers on assignment are paid a competitive day-rate and reimbursed for approved expenses. All assignments are negotiated in advance. Buys first North American publication rights and limited electronic rights and pays upon publication.

TIPS "We're looking for top-notch writing—original, well researched, lively. Subjects must be distinctly Alaskan. A story on a mall in Alaska, for example, won't work for us; every state has malls. If you've got a story about a Juneau mall run by someone who is also a bush pilot and part-time trapper, maybe we'd be interested. The point is *Alaska* stories need to be vivid, focused and unique. Alaska is like nowhere else—we need our stories to be the same way."

ARIZONA

⊖⊖ TUCSON LIFESTYLE

Conley Publishing Group, Ltd., Suite 12, 7000 E. Tanque Verde Rd., Tucson AZ 85715-5318. (520)721-2929. **Fax:** (520)721-8665. **E-mail:** scott@tucsonlifestyle.com. **Contact:** Scott Barker, executive editor. **90% freelance written. Prefers to work with published/established writers.** Monthly magazine covering Southern Arizona-related events and topics. Estab. 1982. Circ. 32,000. Byline given. Pays on acceptance. Publishes ms an average of 6 months after acceptance. Submit seasonal material 1 year in advance. Accepts queries by mail, e-mail. Responds in 2 months to queries. Responds in 3 months to mss. Sample copy for $3.99, plus $3 postage. Guidelines free.

⊶ No fiction, poetry, cartoons, or syndicated columns.

NONFICTION "Avoid obvious tourist attractions and information that most residents of the Southwest are likely to know. No anecdotes masquerading as articles. Not interested in fish-out-of-water, Easterner-visiting-the-Old-West pieces." **Buys 20 mss/ year. Pays $50-500.**

PHOTOS Query about photos before submitting anything.

TIPS "Read the magazine before submitting anything."

CALIFORNIA

⊖⊖ CARLSBAD MAGAZINE

Wheelhouse Media, P.O. Box 2089, Carlsbad CA 92018. (760)729-9099. **Fax:** (760)729-9011. **E-mail:** tim@wheelhousemedia.com. **Website:** www.clickoncarlsbad.com. **Contact:** Tim Wrisley. **80% freelance written.** Bimonthly magazine covering people, places, events, arts in Carlsbad, California. "We are a regional magazine highlighting all things pertaining specifically to Carlsbad. We focus on history, events, people, and places that make Carlsbad interesting and unique. Our audience is both Carlsbad residents and visitors or anyone interested in learning more about Carlsbad. We favor a conversational tone that still adheres to standard rules of writing." Estab. 2004. Circ. 35,000. Byline given. Pays on publication. Publishes ms an average of 6 months after acceptance. Editorial lead time 4 months. Submit seasonal material 6-12 months in advance. Accepts queries by mail, e-mail.

Accepts simultaneous submissions. Responds in 2 months to queries and to mss. Sample copy for $2.31. Guidelines by e-mail.

NONFICTION Needs historical, interview, photo feature, home, garden, arts, events. Does not want self-promoting articles for individuals or businesses, real estate how-to's, advertorials. **Buys 3 mss/year.** Query with published clips. Length: 300-2,700 words. **Pays 20-30¢/word for assigned articles. Pays 20¢/word for unsolicited articles.** Sometimes pays expenses of writers on assignment.

PHOTOS State availability. Reviews GIF/JPEG files. Offers $15-400/photo.

COLUMNS/DEPARTMENTS Carlsbad Arts (people, places or things related to cultural arts in Carlsbad); Happenings (events that take place in Carlsbad); Carlsbad Character (unique Carlsbad residents who have contributed to Carlsbad's character); Commerce (Carlsbad business profiles); Surf Scene (subjects pertaining to the beach/surf in Carlsbad), all 500-700 words. Garden (Carlsbad garden feature); Home (Carlsbad home feature), both 700-1,200 words. **Buys 60 mss/year.** Query with published clips. **Pays $50 flat fee or 20¢/word.**

TIPS "The main thing to remember is that any pitches need to be subjects directly related to Carlsbad. If the subjects focus on surrounding towns, they aren't going to make the cut. We are looking for well-written feature magazine-style articles. E-mail is the preferred method for queries; you will get a response."

😊😊 THE EAST BAY MONTHLY

The Berkeley Monthly, Inc., 1305 Franklin St., Suite 501, Oakland CA 94612. (510)238-9101. **Fax:** (510)238-9163. **Website:** www.themonthly.com. **95% freelance written.** Monthly general interest tabloid covering the San Francisco Bay Area. "We feature distinctive, intelligent articles of interest to *East Bay* readers." Estab. 1970. Circ. 62,000. Byline given. Pays on publication. Editorial lead time 2+ months. Submit seasonal material 3 months in advance. Accepts queries by mail, e-mail. Accepts simultaneous submissions. Responds in 1 month to queries. Responds in 1 month to mss. Sample copy for $3. Writer's guidelines for #10 SASE or by e-mail.

NONFICTION No fiction or poetry. Query with published clips. Length: 1,000-3,000 words. **Pays $100-500.**

REPRINTS Send tearsheet and information about when and where the material previously appeared.

PHOTOS State availability. Identification of subjects required. Negotiates payment individually.

COLUMNS/DEPARTMENTS First Person, 2,000 words. Query with published clips.

SONG OF THE SAN JOAQUIN

P.O. Box 1161, Modesto CA 95353. **E-mail:** cleor36@yahoo.com. **Website:** www.ChaparralPoets.org/SSJ.html. **Contact:** Cleo Griffith, editor. *Song of the San Joaquin*, published quarterly, features "subjects about or pertinent to the San Joaquin Valley of Central California. This is defined geographically as the region from Fresno to Stockton, and from the foothills on the west to those on the east." Wants all forms and styles of poetry. "Keep subject in mind." Does not want "pornographic, demeaning, vague, or trite approaches." Considers poetry by children and teens. Estab. 2003. Publishes ms 3-6 months after acceptance. Submit seasonal poems at least 3 months in advance. Occasionally publishes theme issues. Upcoming themes available for SASE, by e-mail, or online. Responds in up to 3 months.

POETRY This is a quarterly; please keep in mind the seasons of the year. E-mail submissions are preferred; no disk submissions. Cover letter is preferred. "SASE required. All submissions must be typed on 1 side of the page only. Proofread submissions carefully. Name, address, phone number, and e-mail address should appear on all pages. Cover letter should include any awards, honors, and previous publications for each poem, and a biographical sketch of 75 words or less." Reads submissions "periodically throughout the year." Has published poetry by Robert Cooperman, Taylor Graham, Carol Louise Moon, Mimi Moriarty, and Charles Rammelkamp. Submit maximum 3 poems. Length open. **Pays 1 contributor's copy.**

CANADA/INTERNATIONAL

✓😊😊😊 HAMILTON MAGAZINE

Town Media, a division of Sun Media, 1074 Cooke Blvd., Burlington ON L7T 4A8 Canada. (905)634-8003. **Fax:** (905)634-7661. **E-mail:** marc.skulnick@sunmedia.ca; tm.info@sunmedia.ca. **Website:** www.hamiltonmagazine.com. **Contact:** Marc Skulnick, editor; Kate Sharrow, art director. **50% freelance written.** Quarterly magazine devoted to the Greater Hamilton and Golden Horseshoe area (Ontario, Canada).

"Our mandate: to entertain and inform by spotlighting the best of what our city and region has to offer. We invite readers to take part in a vibrant community by supplying them with authoritative and dynamic coverage of local culture, food, fashion, and design. Each story strives to expand your view of the area, every issue an essential resource for exploring, understanding and unlocking the region. Packed with insight, intrigue and suspense, *Hamilton Magazine* delivers the city to your doorstep." Estab. 1978. Byline given. Pays on publication. Offers 50% kill fee. Editorial lead time 2-3 months. Submit seasonal material 2-3 months in advance. Accepts queries by e-mail. Responds in 1 week to queries and to mss. Sample copy with #10 SASE. Guidelines by e-mail.

NONFICTION Needs book excerpts, essays, expose, historical, how-to, humor, inspirational, interview, personal experience, photo feature, religious, travel. Does not want generic articles that could appear in any mass-market publication. Send complete ms. Length: 800-2,000 words. **Pays $200-1,600 for assigned articles; $100-800 for unsolicited articles.** Sometimes pays expenses of writers on assignment.

PHOTOS State availability of or send photos. Identification of subjects required. Reviews 8×10 prints, JPEG files (8×10 at 300dpi). Negotiates payment individually.

COLUMNS/DEPARTMENTS A&E Art, 1,200-2,000 words; A&E Music, 1,200-2,000 words; A&E Books, 1,200-1,400 words. **Buys 12 columns/yr. mss./year.** Send complete ms. **Pays $200-400.**

TIPS "Unique local voices are key and a thorough knowledge of the area's history, politics, and culture is invaluable."

☺❸❸∅ OUTDOOR CANADA MAGAZINE

54 St. Patrick St., Toronto ON M5T 1V1 Canada. (416)599-2000. **E-mail:** editorial@outdoorcanada. ca. **Website:** www.outdoorcanada.ca. **70% freelance written. Works with a small number of new/unpublished writers each year.** Estab. 1972. Circ. 90,000. Byline given. Pays on publication. Publishes ms an average of 8 months after acceptance. Submit seasonal ideas 1 year in advance. Accepts queries by mail, e-mail. Responds in 1 month to queries. Guidelines online.

NONFICTION Needs how-to, fishing, hunting, outdoor issues, outdoor destinations in Canada. **Buys 35-40 mss/year.** Does not accept unsolicited mss. 2,500 words **Pays 75¢ to ¢1 per word.** On a case-by-case basis

REPRINTS Send information about when and where the article previously appeared. Payment varies

PHOTOS Emphasize people in the Canadian outdoors. Captions, model releases required. Fees negotiable.

FILLERS Buys 30-40 mss/year. Length: 100-500 words.

☺ UP HERE

P.O. Box 1350, Yellowknife NT X1A 2N9 Canada. (867)766-6710. **Fax:** (867)873-9876. **E-mail:** matthew@uphere.ca; angela@uphere.ca. **Website:** www. uphere.ca. **Contact:** Matthew Mallon, editor-in-chief; Angela Gzowski, photo editor;. **50% freelance written.** Magazine published 8 times/year covering general interest about Canada's Far North. We publish features, columns, and shorts about people, wildlife, native cultures, travel, and adventure in Yukon, Northwest Territories, and Nunavut. Be informative, but entertaining. Estab. 1984. Circ. 22,000. Byline given. Pays on publication. Offers 50% kill fee. Editorial lead time 6 months. Accepts queries by e-mail. Sample copy for $4.95 (Canadian) and 9x12 SASE.

NONFICTION Needs essays, general interest, how-to, humor, interview, personal experience, photo feature, technical, travel, lifestyle/culture, historical. **Buys 25-30 mss/year.** Query. Length: 1,500-3,000 words. **Fees are negotiable.**

PHOTOS *Please* do not send unsolicited original photos, slides. Send photos. Captions, identification of subjects required. Reviews transparencies, prints.

COLUMNS/DEPARTMENTS Write for updated guidelines, visit website, or e-mail. **Buys 25-30 mss/ year.** Query with published clips.

COLORADO

☺ ARTS PERSPECTIVE MAGAZINE

Shared Vision Publishing, P.O. Box 3042, Durango CO 81302. (970)739-3200. **E-mail:** director@artsperspective.com; denise@sharedvisiononline.com. **Website:** www.artsperspective.com. **100% freelance written.** Quarterly tabloid covering art. "*Arts Perspective Magazine* offers a venue for all of the arts. Artists, writers, musicians, dancers, performers, and galleries are encourage to showcase their work. A resource for supporters of the arts to share a common thread in the continuum of creative expression." Estab. 2004. Circ. 30,000+. Byline given. Pays on publication. Publishes ms an average of 2 months after acceptance. Editorial lead time 2-5 months. Submit seasonal material 2-5 months in advance. Accepts queries by mail, e-mail, phone. Responds in 2 weeks to queries. Responds in 1 month to mss. Sample copy free. Guidelines available at www.artsperspective.com/submissions.php.

PHOTOS Send photos. Identification of subjects, model releases required. Reviews GIF/JPEG files. Offers $15-25 per photo.

POETRY Needs avant-garde, free verse, haiku, light verse, traditional. Buys 4 poems/year. Submit maximum 3 poems. Length: 4-45 lines.

TIPS "Take me to lunch; sense of humor, please."

TELLURIDE MAGAZINE

Big Earth Publishing, Inc., P.O. Box 3488, Telluride CO 81435. (970)728-4245. **Fax:** (866)936-8406. **E-mail:** deb@telluridemagazine.com. **Website:** www.telluridemagazine.com. **Contact:** Deb Dion Kees, editor-in-chief. **75% freelance written.** Telluride: community, events, recreation, ski resort, surrounding region, San Juan Mountains, history, tourism, mountain living. "*Telluride Magazine* speaks specifically to Telluride and the surrounding mountain environment. Telluride is a resort town supported by the ski industry in winter, festivals in summer, outdoor recreation year round, and the unique lifestyle all of that affords. As a National Historic Landmark District with a colorful mining history, it weaves a tale that readers seek out. The local/visitor interaction is key to Telluride's success in making profiles an important part of the content. Telluriders are an environmentally minded and progressive bunch who appreciate efforts toward sustainability and protecting the natural landscape and wilderness that are the region's number one draw." Estab. 1982. Circ. 70,000. Byline given. Pays 60 days from publication. Editorial lead time and advance on seasonal submissions is 6 months. Accepts queries by e-mail. Responds in 2 weeks on queries; 2 months on mss. Sample copy online at website. Guidelines by e-mail.

NONFICTION Needs historical, humor, nostalgic, personal experience, photo feature, travel, recreation, lifestyle. No articles about places or adventures other than Telluride. **Buys 10 mss/year.** Query with published clips. 1,000-2,000 words. **$200-700 for assigned articles; $100-700 for unsolicited articles.** Does not pay expenses.

PHOTOS Send no more than 20 jpeg comps (low-ers) via e-mail or send CD/DVD with submission. Reviews JPEG/TIFF files. Offers $35-300 per photo; negotiates payment individually.

COLUMNS/DEPARTMENTS Telluride Turns (news and current topics); Mountain Health (health issues related to mountain sports, and living at altitude); Nature Notes (explores the flora, fauna, geology and climate of San Juan Mountains); Green Bytes (sustainable & environmentally sound ideas and products for home building), all 500 words. **Buys 40/year mss/year.** Query. **Pays $50-200.**

FICTION "Please contact us; we are very specific about what we will accept." Needs adventure, historical, humorous, slice-of-life vignettes, western, recreation in the mountains. **Buys 2 mss/year.** Query with published clips. 800-1,200 words.

POETRY Needs Any poetry; must reflect mountains or mountain living. Buys 1/year poems/year. Length: 3 lines minimum. **Pays up to to $100.**

FILLERS anecdotes, facts, short humor. **Buys Seldom buys mss/year.** 300-1,000 words. **Pays up to $500.**

FLORIDA

$ FT. MYERS MAGAZINE

15880 Summerlin Rd., Suite 189, Fort Myers FL 33908. (941)433-3884. **E-mail:** ftmyers@optonline.net. **Website:** www.ftmyersmagazine.com. **90% freelance written.** Bimonthly magazine covering regional arts and living for educated, active, successful and creative residents of Lee & Collier counties (FL) and guests at resorts and hotels in Lee County. "Content: Arts, entertainment, media, travel, sports, health, home, garden, environmental issues." Estab. 2001. Circ. 20,000. Byline given. 30 days after publication. Publishes ms an average of 2-6 months after acceptance. Editorial lead time 2-4 months. Submit seasonal material 2-4 months in advance. Accepts queries by e-mail. Accepts simultaneous submissions. Responds in 3 months to queries and to mss. Guidelines online.

NONFICTION Needs essays, general interest, historical, how-to, humor, interview, personal experience, reviews, previews, news, informational. **Buys 10-25 mss/year.** Send complete ms. Length: 750-1,500 words. **Pays $50-150 or approximately 10¢/word.** Sometimes pays expenses of writers on assignment.

PHOTOS State availability of or send photos. Captions, identification of subjects required. Negotiates payment individually; generally offers $25-100/photo or art.

COLUMNS/DEPARTMENTS Media: books, music, video, film, theater, Internet, software (news, previews, reviews, interviews, profiles), 750-1,500 words. Lifestyles: art & design, science & technology, house & garden, health & wellness, sports & recreation, travel & leisure, food & drink (news, interviews, previews, reviews, profiles, advice), 750-1,500 words. **Buys 60 mss/year.** Query with or without published clips or send complete ms. **Pays $50-150.**

❸❸ WHERE (WHERE GUESTBOOK, WHERE MAP, WHERE NEWSLETTER)

Morris Visitor Publications, 699 Broad St., Suite 500, Augusta GA 30901. **Fax:** (305)892-2991. **E-mail:** editorial@wheretraveler.com. **Website:** www.wheretraveler.com. **40% freelance written.** Monthly magazine covering tourism in U.S. cities, certain European cities, and Singapore. Estab. 1936. Circ. 30,000. Byline for features only, but all writers listed on masthead. Pays on publication. Editorial lead time 3 months. Submit seasonal material 3 months in advance. Accepts queries by mail, e-mail. Responds in 1 week to queries Sample copy online. Guidelines by e-mail.
◑ Query before submitting.

NONFICTION Needs new product, photo feature, travel. Query. Length: 500 words.

PHOTOS Send photos. Captions, identification of subjects, model releases required. Reviews GIF/JPEG files. Negotiates payment individually.

COLUMNS/DEPARTMENTS Dining; Entertainment; Museums & Attractions; Art Galleries; Shops & Services; all 50 words. Queries for writer clips only per page of 1 blurbs per page.

TIPS "We look for a new slant on a 'where to go' or 'what to do' in each location."

GENERAL REGIONAL

❸❸ BLUE RIDGE COUNTRY

Leisure Media360, 3424 Brambleton Ave., Roanoke VA 24018. (540)989-6138. **Fax:** (540)989-7603. **E-mail:** krheinheimer@leisuremedia360.com. **Website:** www.blueridgecountry.com. **Contact:** Kurt Rheinheimer, editor. **90% freelance written.** Bimonthly, full-color magazine covering the Blue Ridge region. "The magazine is designed to celebrate the history, heritage and beauty of the Blue Ridge region. It is aimed at adult, upscale readers who enjoy living or traveling in the mountain regions of Virginia, North Carolina, West Virginia, Maryland, Kentucky, Tennessee, South Carolina, Alabama, and Georgia." Estab. 1988. Circ. 425,000. Byline given. Pays on publication. Offers kill fee. Offers $50 kill fee for commissioned pieces only. Publishes ms an average of 8 months after acceptance. Submit seasonal material 6 months in advance. Accepts queries by mail, e-mail, fax; prefer e-mail. Responds in 3-4 months to queries. Responds in 2 months to mss. Sample copy with 9x12 SASE with 6 first-class stamps. Guidelines online.

NONFICTION Needs essays, general interest, historical, personal experience, photo feature, travel. Special issues: "The photo essay will continue to be part of each issue, but for the foreseeable future will be a combination of book and gallery/museum exhibit previews, and also essays of work by talented individual photographers—though we cannot pay, this is a good option for those who are interested in editorial coverage of their work. Those essays will include short profile, web link and contact information, with the idea of getting them, their work and their business directly in front of 425,000 readers' e.". **Buys 25-30 mss/year.** Send complete ms. Length: 200-1,500 words. **Pays $50-250.**

PHOTOS Photos must be shot in region. Outline of region can be found online. Send photos. Identification of subjects required. Reviews transparencies. Pays $40-150 for color inside photo; pays $150 for color or cover. Pays on publication. Credit line given.

COLUMNS/DEPARTMENTS Inns and Getaways (reviews of inns); Mountain Delicacies (cookbooks and recipes); Country Roads (shorts on regional news, people, destinations, events, history, antiques, books); Inns and Getaways (reviews of inns); On the Mountainside (first-person outdoor recreation pieces excluding hikes). **Buys 30-42 mss/year.** Query. **Pays $25-125.**

TIPS "Would like to see more pieces dealing with contemporary history (1940s-70s). Freelancers needed for regional departmental shorts and macro issues affecting whole region. Need field reporters from all areas of Blue Ridge region, especially more from Kentucky, Maryland and South Carolina. We are also looking for updates on the Blue Ridge Parkway, Appalachian Trail, national forests, ecological issues, preservation movements, affordable travel, and interesting short profiles of regional people."

🕙 MIDWEST LIVING

Meredith Corp., 1716 Locust St., Des Moines IA 50309. (515)284-3000. **Fax:** (515)284-3836. **E-mail:** midwestliving@meredith.com. **Website:** www.mid-westliving.com. Bimonthly magazine covering Midwestern families. Regional service magazine that celebrates the interest, values, and lifestyles of Midwestern families. Estab. 1987. Circ. 915,000. Pays on acceptance. Editorial lead time 6 months. Accepts queries by mail, e-mail. Sample copy for $3.95. Guidelines by e-mail.

○ Query before submitting.

NONFICTION Needs general interest, good eating, festivals and fairs, historical, interesting slices of Midwestern history, customs, traditions and the people who preserve them, interview, towns, neighborhoods, families,people whose stories exemplify the Midwest spirit an values, travel, Midwestern destinations with emphasis on the fun and affordable. Query.

PHOTOS State availability.

TIPS "As general rule of thumb, we're looking for stories that are useful to the reader with information of ideas they can act on in their own lives. Most important, we want stories that have direct relevance to our Midwest audience."

⊘ SOUTHCOMM PUBLISHING COMPANY, INC.

541 Buttermilk Pike, Suite 100, Crescent Springs KY 41017. (800)933-3909. **Fax:** (800)488-3101. **E-mail:** cwwalker@southcomm.com. **Website:** southcommpublishing.com. **Contact:** Carolyn Williams-Walker. "Our magazines primarily are used as marketing and economic development pieces, but they are also used as tourism guides and a source of information for newcomers. As such, our editorial supplies entertaining and informative reading for those visiting the communities for the first time, as well as those who have lived in the area for any period of time. We are looking for writers who are interested in writing dynamic copy about Georgia, Tennessee, South Carolina, North Carolina, Alabama, Virginia, Florida, Pennsylvania, Texas, and many other states." Estab. 1985. Byline given. Pays 30 days after acceptance. Publishes ms an average of 1-2 months after acceptance. Accepts queries by mail, e-mail, fax. Sample copy and writer's guidelines free.

NONFICTION "We are not looking for article submissions. We will assign stories to writers in which we're interested. Queries should include samples of published works and biographical information." **Buys 50+ mss/year.** Query or send complete ms. Length: 100-1,000 words. **Pays $25-200.**

TIPS "It is not necessary for writers to live in the areas about which they are writing, but it does sometimes help to be familiar with them. We are not looking for writers to submit articles. We are solely interested in contacting writers for articles that we generate with our clients."

SOUTHERN LIVING

Time Inc. Lifestyle Group, 2100 Lakeshore Dr., Birmingham AL 35209. (205)445-6000. **Fax:** (205)445-6700. **E-mail:** slonline@timeinc.com. **Website:** www.southernliving.com. **Contact:** Claire Machamer, online editor. Monthly magazine covering southern lifestyle. Publication addressing the tastes and interest of contemporary southerners. Estab. 1966. Circ. 2.54 million. Editorial lead time 3 months. Accepts queries by mail. NoSample copy for $4.99 at newsstands. Guidelines by e-mail.

○ Accepts submissions for their Southern Journal column. Article must be southern, commenting on life in this region. "Make it personal, contemporary in the author's point of view; original, not published.

NONFICTION Needs essays. Send ms (typed, double-spaced) by postal mail. Southern Living column: Above all, it must be southern. Need comments on life in this region, written from the standpoint of a person who is intimately familiar with this part of the world. It's personal, almost always involving something that happened to the writer or someone he or she knows very well. Takes special note of stories that are contemporary in their point of view. Length: 500-600 words.

TIPS "The easiest way to break into the magazine for writers new to us is to propose short items."

🕙🕙🕙🕙 SUNSET MAGAZINE

Sunset Publishing Corp., 80 Willow Rd., Menlo Park CA 94025-3691. (650)321-3600. **Fax:** (650)327-7537. **E-mail:** readerletters@sunset.com. **Website:** www.sunset.com. Monthly magazine covering the lifestyle of the Western states. *Sunset* is a Western lifestyle publication for educated, active consumers. Editorial provides localized information on gardening and travel, food and entertainment, home building and remodeling. Byline given. Pays on acceptance. Guidelines online.

NONFICTION Needs travel, in the West. **Buys 50-75 mss/year.** Query before submitting. Freelance articles should be timely and only about the 13 Western states. Garden section accepts queries by mail. Travel section prefers queries by e-mail. Length: 550-750 words. **Pays $1/word.**

COLUMNS/DEPARTMENTS Building & Crafts, Food, Garden, Travel. Travel Guide length: 300-350 words. Direct queries to specific editorial department.

YANKEE

Yankee Publishing, Inc., P.O. Box 520, Dublin NH 03444-0520. (603)563-8111. **Fax:** (603)563-8298. **E-mail:** editors@yankeepub.com. **Website:** www.yankeemagazine.com. **Contact:** Debbie Despres, associate editor; Heather Marcus, photo editor. **60% freelance written.** Monthly magazine covering the New England states of Connecticut, Massachusetts, Maine, New Hampshire, Rhode Island, and Vermont. "Our feature articles, as well as the departments of Home, Food, and Travel, reflect what is happening currently in these New England states. Our mission is to express and perhaps, indirectly, preserve the New England culture—and to do so in an entertaining way. Our audience is national and has 1 thing in common—it loves New England." Estab. 1935. Circ. 317,000. Byline given. Pays on acceptance. Offers kill fee. Editorial lead time 12 months. Submit seasonal material 1 year in advance. Accepts queries by mail, but e-mail queries and submission preferred. Accepts simultaneous submissions. Responds in 2 months to queries. Guidelines online.

NONFICTION Needs essays, general interest, interview. Does not want "good old days" pieces or dialect, humor, or anything outside New England. **Buys 30 mss/year.** Query with published clips and SASE. Length: 2,500 words maximum. **Pays per assignment.** Pays expenses of writers on assignment when appropriate.

PHOTOS All photos and art are assigned to experienced professionals. If interested, send a portfolio with 35mm, 2.25, or 4x5 color transparencies. Do not send any unsolicited original photos or artwork.

TIPS "Submit lots of ideas. Don't censor yourself—let us decide whether an idea is good or bad. We might surprise you. Remember we've been publishing since 1935, so chances are we've already done every 'classic' New England subject. Try to surprise us—it isn't easy. Study the ones we publish—the format should be apparent. It is to your advantage to read several issues of the magazine before sending us a query or a ms. *Yankee* does not publish fiction, poetry, humor, history, memoir, or cartoons as a routine format, nor do we solicit submissions."

GEORGIA

⊜⊜ GEORGIA MAGAZINE

Georgia Electric Membership Corp., P.O. Box 1707, Tucker GA 30085. (770)270-6500. **Fax:** (770)270-6995. **E-mail:** ann.orowski@georgiaemc.com. **Website:** www.georgiamagazine.org. **Contact:** Ann Orowski, editor. **50% freelance written.** We are a monthly magazine for and about Georgians, with a friendly, conversational tone and human interest topics. Estab. 1945. Circ. 516,000. Byline given. Pays on acceptance. Publishes ms an average of 6 months after acceptance. Editorial lead time 2 months. Submit seasonal material 6 months in advance. Accepts simultaneous submissions. Responds in 1 month to subjects of interest. Sample copy for $2. Guidelines for #10 SASE, or by e-mail.

NONFICTION Needs general interest, Georgia-focused, historical, how-to, in the home and garden, humor, inspirational, interview, photo feature, travel. Query with published clips. Length: 1,000-1,200 words; 800 words for smaller features and departments. **Pays $350-500.**

PHOTOS State availability. Identification of subjects, model releases required. Reviews digital images, websites and prints. Negotiates payment individually.

⊜⊜ SAVANNAH MAGAZINE

Morris Publishing Group, P.O. Box 1088, Savannah GA 31402. **Fax:** (912)525-0611. **E-mail:** editor@savannahmagazine.com. **Website:** www.savannahmagazine.com. **Contact:** Annabelle Carr, editor; Amy Paige Condon, associate and digital editor. **95% freelance written.** Bimonthly magazine focusing on homes and entertaining covering coastal lifestyle of Savannah and South Carolina area. "*Savannah Magazine* publishes articles about people, places, and events of interest to the residents of the greater Savannah areas, as well as coastal Georgia and the South Carolina low country. We strive to provide our readers with information that is both useful and entertaining—written in a lively, readable style." Estab. 1990. Circ. 16,000. Byline given. Pays on publication. Offers 20% kill fee. Publishes ms an average of 2 months after acceptance. Editorial lead time 2 months. Submit seasonal material 4 months in advance. Accepts queries by mail, e-mail, fax. Accepts simultaneous submissions. Responds in 4 weeks to queries; 6 weeks to mss. Sample copy free. Guidelines by e-mail.

NONFICTION Needs general interest, historical, humor, interview, travel. Does not want fiction or poetry. Query with published clips. Length: 500-750 words. **Pays $250-450.**

PHOTOS Contact: Contact Michelle Karner, art director. State availability. Reviews GIF/JPEG files. Negotiates payment individually. Offers no additional payment for photos accepted with ms.

IDAHO

$$ SUN VALLEY MAGAZINE

Valley Publishing, LLC, 111 First Ave., N. #1M, Meriwether Building, Hailey ID 83333. (208)788-0770. **Fax:** (208)788-3881. **E-mail:** michael@sunvalleymag.com; julie@sunvalleymag.com. **Website:** www.sunvalleymag.com. **Contact:** Mike McKenna, editor; Julie Molema, art director. **95% freelance written.** Quarterly magazine covering the lifestyle of the Sun Valley area. *Sun Valley Magazine* presents the lifestyle of the Sun Valley area and the Wood River Valley, including recreation, culture, profiles, history and the arts. Estab. 1973. Circ. 17,000. Byline given. Pays on publication. Publishes ms an average of 5 months after acceptance. Editorial lead time 1 year. Submit seasonal material 14 months in advance. Accepts queries by mail. Accepts simultaneous submissions. Responds in 5 weeks to queries. Responds in 2 months to mss. Sample copy for $4.95 and $3 postage. Guidelines for #10 SASE.

NONFICTION Needs historical, interview, photo feature, travel. Special issues: Sun Valley home design and architecture (spring); Sun Valley weddings/wedding planner (summer). Query with published clips. **Pays $40-500.** Sometimes pays expenses of writers on assignment.

REPRINTS Only occasionally purchases reprints.

PHOTOS State availability. Identification of subjects, model releases required. Reviews transparencies. Offers $60-275/photo.

COLUMNS/DEPARTMENTS Conservation issues, winter/summer sports, health and wellness, mountain-related activities and subjects, home (interior design), garden. All columns must have a local slant. Query with published clips. **Pays $40-300.**

TIPS "Most of our writers are locally based. Also, we rarely take submissions that are not specifically assigned, with the exception of fiction. However, we always appreciate queries."

ILLINOIS

$ ILLINOIS ENTERTAINER

4223 W. Lake St., Suite 420, Chicago IL 60624. (773)533-9333. **Fax:** (312)922-9341. **E-mail:** service@illinoisentertainer.com. **Website:** www.illinoisentertainer.com. **80% freelance written.** Monthly free magazine covering popular and alternative music, as well as other entertainment (film, media) in Illinois. Estab. 1974. Circ. 55,000. Byline given. Pays on publication. Offers 50% kill fee. Publishes ms an average of 2 months after acceptance. Editorial lead time 2 months. Submit seasonal material 2 months in advance. Accepts queries by mail. Accepts simultaneous submissions. Responds in 2 months to queries. Sample copy for $5.

NONFICTION Needs expose, how-to, humor, interview, new product, reviews. No personal, confessional, or inspirational articles. **Buys 75 mss/year.** Query with published clips. Length: 600-2,600 words. **Pays $15-160.** Sometimes pays expenses of writers on assignment.

REPRINTS Send typed ms with rights for sale noted and information about when and where the material previously appeared. Pays 100% of amount paid for an original article.

PHOTOS Send photos. Captions, identification of subjects, model releases required. Reviews contact sheets, transparencies, 5x7 prints. Offers $20-200/photo.

COLUMNS/DEPARTMENTS Spins (LP reviews), 100-400 words. **Buys 200-300 mss/year.** Query with published clips. **Pays $8-25.**

TIPS "Send clips, résumé, etc. and be patient. Also, sending queries that show you've seen our magazine and have a feel for it greatly increases your publication chances. Don't send unsolicited material. No e-mail solicitations or queries of any kind."

INDIANA

💲💲💲 INDIANAPOLIS MONTHLY

Emmis Communications, 1 Emmis Plaza, 40 Monument Circle, Suite 100, Indianapolis IN 46204. (317)237-9288. **E-mail:** deborah@emmis.com. **Website:** www.indianapolismonthly.com. **Contact:** Deborah Paul, editorial director. **30% freelance written. Prefers to work with published/established writers.** "*Indianapolis Monthly* attracts and enlightens its upscale, well-educated readership with bright, lively editorial on subjects ranging from personalities to social issues, fashion to food. Its diverse content and attention to service make it the ultimate source by which the Indianapolis area lives." Estab. 1977. Circ. 50,000. Byline given. Pays on publication. Offers kill fee. Offers negotiable kill fee. Publishes ms an average of 2 months after acceptance. Editorial lead time 3 months. Submit seasonal material 3 months in advance. Accepts queries by mail, e-mail. Responds in 6 weeks to queries. Sample copy for $6.10.

○ This magazine is using more first-person essays, but they must have a strong Indianapolis or Indiana tie. It will consider nonfiction book excerpts of material relevant to its readers.

NONFICTION Needs book excerpts by Indiana authors or with strong Indiana ties, essays, expose, general interest, interview, photo feature. "No poetry, fiction, or domestic humor; no 'How Indy Has Changed Since I Left Town', 'An Outsider's View of the 500', or generic material with no or little tie to Indianapolis/Indiana." **Buys 35 mss/year.** Query by mail with published clips. Length: 200-3,000 words. **Pays $50-1,000.**

PHOTOS State availability. Captions, identification of subjects, model releases required. Negotiates payment individually.

TIPS "Our standards are simultaneously broad and narrow: Broad in that we're a general interest magazine spanning a wide spectrum of topics, narrow in that we buy only stories with a heavy emphasis on Indianapolis (and, to a lesser extent, Indiana). Simply inserting an Indy-oriented paragraph into a generic national article won't get it: All stories must pertain primarily to things Hoosier. Once you've cleared that hurdle, however, it's a wide-open field. We've done features on national celebrities—Indianapolis native David Letterman and *Mir* astronaut David Wolf of Indianapolis, to name 2—and we've published 2-paragraph items on such quirky topics as an Indiana gardening supply house that sells insects by mail. Query with clips showing lively writing and solid reporting. No phone queries, please."

KANSAS

💲💲 KANSAS!

1020 S. Kansas Ave, Suite 200, Topeka KS 66612-1354. (785)296-8478. **Fax:** (785)296-6988. **E-mail:** kansas.mag@travelks.com. **Website:** www.kansasmag.com. **90% freelance written.** Quarterly magazine emphasizing Kansas travel attractions and events. Estab. 1945. Circ. 45,000. Byline and courtesy bylines are given to all content. Pays on acceptance. Purchased content will publish an average of 1 year after acceptance. Submit seasonal material 8 months in advance. Accepts queries by mail. Responds in 2 months to queries. Guidelines online.

NONFICTION Needs general interest, photo feature, travel. Query by mail. Length: 750-1,250 words. **Pays $200-350.** Mileage reimbursement is available for writers on assignment in the state of Kansas; TBD by assignment editor.

PHOTOS "We are a full-color photograph/ms publication. Send digital photos (original transparencies only or CD with images available in high resolution) with query.". Captions and location of the image (county and city) are required. Pays $25-75 for gallery images, $150 for cover. Assignments also available, welcome queries.

TIPS "History and nostalgia or essay stories do not fit into our format because they can't be illustrated well with color photos. Submit a query letter describing one appropriate idea with outline for possible article and suggestions for photos. Do not send unsolicited mss."

KENTUCKY

💲💲 KENTUCKY MONTHLY

P.O. Box 559, Frankfort KY 40602-0559. (502)227-0053; (888)329-0053. **Fax:** (502)227-5009. **E-mail:** kymonthly@kentuckymonthly.com; steve@kentuckymonthly.com. **Website:** www.kentuckymonthly.com. **Contact:** Stephen Vest, editor. **50% freelance written.** Monthly magazine. "We publish stories about Kentucky and by Kentuckians, including stories written by those who live elsewhere." Estab. 1998. Circ. 42,000. Byline given. Pays within 3 months of publication. Publishes ms an average of 3 months after acceptance. Editorial lead time 4-12 months. Submit seasonal material 4-10 months in advance. Accepts queries by e-mail. Accepts simultaneous submissions. Responds in 1-3 months to queries. Responds in 1 month to mss. Sample copy and writer's guidelines online.

NONFICTION Needs book excerpts, general interest, historical, how-to, humor, interview, photo feature, religious, travel, all with a Kentucky angle. **Buys 50 mss/year.** Query. Length: 300-2,000 words. **Pays $45-300 for assigned articles. Pays $50-200 for unsolicited articles.**

PHOTOS State availability. Captions required. Reviews negatives.

FICTION Needs adventure, historical, mainstream, novel concepts, all Kentucky-related stories. **Buys 30 mss/year.** Query with published clips. Length: 1,000-5,000 words. **Pays $50-100.**

TIPS "Please read the magazine to get the flavor of what we're publishing each month. We accept articles via e-mail. Approximately 70% of articles are assigned."

MASSACHUSETTS

💲💲 CAPE COD LIFE

13 Steeple St., Suite 204, P.O. Box 1439, Mashpee MA 02649. (508)419-7381. **Fax:** (508)477-1225. **Website:** www.capecodlife.com. **Contact:** Amanda McCole, art director; Patty Dysart, art director. **80% freelance written.** Magazine published 6 times/year focusing on area lifestyle, history and culture, people and places, business and industry, and issues and answers for year-round and summer residents of Cape Cod, Nantucket, and Martha's Vineyard as well as nonresidents who spend their leisure time here. Cape Cod Life Magazine has become the premier lifestyle magazine for the Cape & Islands, featuring topics ranging from arts and events, history and heritage, beaches and boating as well as a comprehensive resource for planning the perfect vacation. Circ. 45,000. Byline given. Pays 90 days after acceptance. Offers 20% kill fee. Submit seasonal material 6 months in advance. Accepts queries by mail. Responds in 3 months to queries. Responds in 3 months to mss. Sample copy for $5. Guidelines for #10 SASE.

NONFICTION Needs book excerpts, general interest, historical, interview, photo feature, travel, outdoors,

gardening, nautical, nature, arts, antiques. **Buys 20 mss/year.** Query. Length: 800-1,500 words. **Pays $200-400.**

PHOTOS Photo guidelines for #10 SASE. Captions, identification of subjects required. Pays $25-225.

TIPS Freelancers submitting *quality* spec articles with a Cape Cod and Islands angle have a good chance at publication. We like to see a wide selection of writer's clips before giving assignments. We also publish *Cape Cod & Islands Home* covering architecture, landscape design, and interior design with a Cape and Islands focus.

MICHIGAN

💲💲 GRAND RAPIDS MAGAZINE

Gemini Publications, 549 Ottawa Ave. NW, Suite 201, Grand Rapids MI 49503. (616)459-4545. **Fax:** (616)459-4800. **E-mail:** cvalade@geminipub.com. **Website:** www.grmag.com. *Grand Rapids* is a general interest life and style magazine designed for those who live in the Grand Rapids metropolitan area or desire to maintain contact with the community. Estab. 1964. Circ. 20,000. Byline given. Pays on publication. Editorial lead time 2 months. Submit seasonal material 2 months in advance. Sample copy for $2 and SASE with $1.50 postage. Guidelines with #10 SASE.

NONFICTION Query. **Pays $25-500.**

MINNESOTA

💲💲 LAKE SUPERIOR MAGAZINE

Lake Superior Port Cities, Inc., P.O. Box 16417, Duluth MN 55816-0417. (218)722-5002. **Fax:** (218)722-4096. **E-mail:** edit@lakesuperior.com. **Website:** www.lakesuperior.com. **Contact:** Konnie LeMay, editor. **40% freelance written. Works with a small number of new/unpublished writers each year. Please include phone number and address with e-mail queries.** Bimonthly magazine covering contemporary and historic people, places and current events around Lake Superior. Estab. 1979. Circ. 20,000. Byline given. Pays on publication. Publishes ms an average of 10 months after acceptance. Submit seasonal material 1 year in advance. Accepts queries by mail, e-mail. Responds in 3 months to queries. Sample copy for $4.95 and 6 first-class stamps. Guidelines online.

NONFICTION Needs book excerpts, general interest, historical, humor, interview, local, personal experience, photo feature, local, travel, local, city profiles, regional business, some investigative. **Buys 15 mss/ year.** Query with published clips. Length: 1,600-2,000 words (features). **Pays $200-400.** Sometimes pays expenses of writers on assignment, with assignments.

PHOTOS Quality photography is our hallmark. Send photos. Captions, identification of subjects, model releases required. Reviews contact sheets, 2x2 and larger transparencies, 4x5 prints. Offers $50/image; $150 for covers.

COLUMNS/DEPARTMENTS Current events and things to do (for Events Calendar section), less than 300 words; Around The Circle (media reviews; short pieces on Lake Superior; Great Lakes environmental issues; themes, letters and short pieces on events and highlights of the Lake Superior Region); Essay (nostalgic lake-specific pieces), up to 1,100 words; Profile (single personality profile with photography), up to 900 words. Other headings include Destinations, Wild Superior, Lake Superior Living, Heritage, Recipe Box. **Buys 20 mss/year.** Query with published clips. **Pays $75-200. Length: 800-1,200 words.**

FICTION Ethnic, historic, humorous, mainstream, novel excerpts, slice-of-life vignettes, ghost stories. Must be targeted regionally. Wants stories that are Lake Superior related. Rarely uses fiction stories. **Buys 2-3 mss/year.** Query with published clips. Length: 300-2,500 words. **Pays $50-125.**

TIPS "Well-researched queries are attended to. We actively seek queries from writers in Lake Superior communities. We prefer mss to queries. Provide enough information on why the subject is important to the region and our readers, or why and how something is unique. We want details. The writer must have a thorough knowledge of the subject and how it relates to our region. We prefer a fresh, unused approach to the subject which provides the reader with an emotional involvement. Almost all of our articles feature quality photography, color or black and white. It is a prerequisite of all nonfiction. All submissions should include a *short* biography of author/photographer; mug shot sometimes used. Blanket submissions need not apply."

MISSOURI

💲💲 MISSOURI LIFE

501 High St., Suite A, Boonville MO 65233. (660)882-9898. **Fax:** (660)882-9899. **E-mail:** dcawthon@missourilife.com. **Website:** www.missourilife.com. **Contact:** David Cawthon, associate editor. **85% freelance written.** Bimonthly magazine covering the state of Missouri. *"Missouri Life's* readers are mostly college-educated people with a wide range of travel and lifestyle interests. Our magazine discovers the people, places, and events—both past and present—that make Missouri a great place to live and/or visit." Estab. 1973. Circ. 96,800. Byline given. Pays on publication. Editorial lead time 6 months. Submit seasonal material 6 months in advance. Accepts queries by mail, e-mail, fax. Responds in approximately 2 months to queries. Sample copy available for $4.95 and SASE with $2.44 first-class postage (or a digital version can be purchased online). Guidelines online.

NONFICTION Needs general interest, historical, travel, all Missouri related. Length: 300-2,000 words. **No set amount per word.**

PHOTOS Contact: Sarah Herrera, associate art director. E-mail: sarah@missourilife.com. (Also contact for art/illustration.). State availability in query; buys all rights nonexclusive. Captions, identification of subjects, model releases required. Offers $50-150/ photo.

COLUMNS/DEPARTMENTS "All Around Missouri (people and places, past and present, written in an almanac style); Missouri Artist (features a Missouri artist), 500 words; Made in Missouri (products and businesses native to Missouri), 500 words. Contact assistant manager for restaurant review queries.

💲💲 RELOCATING TO THE LAKE OF THE OZARKS

Showcase Publishing, 2820 Bagnell Dam Blvd., #1B, Lake Ozark MO 65049. (573)365-2323. **Fax:** (573)365-2351. **E-mail:** spublishingco@msn.com. **Website:** www.relocatingtothelakeoftheozarks.com. **Contact:** Dave Leathers, publisher. Semi-annual relocation guide; free for people moving to the area. Byline given. Pays on publication. Publishes ms an average of 6 months after acceptance. Accepts queries by e-mail. Sample copy for $8.95.

NONFICTION Needs historical, travel, local issues. Length: 600-1,000 words.

PHOTOS Purchases images portraying recreational activities, tourism, nature, business development, cultural events, historical sites, and the people of the lake area. Send color positive film in 35mm or larger format, or send high-resoultion digital images. State

availability of or send photos. Identification of subjects required. Pays $20-300, depending on size.
TIPS "Read the magazine and understand our audience."

NEVADA

💲💲 NEVADA MAGAZINE

401 N. Carson St., Carson City NV 89701. (775)687-5416. **Fax:** (775)687-6159. **E-mail:** editor@nevadamagazine.com. **Website:** www.nevadamagazine.com. **25% freelance written. Works with a small number of new/unpublished writers each year.** Bimonthly magazine published by the state of Nevada to promote tourism. Estab. 1936. Circ. 20,000. Byline given. Pays on publication. Publishes ms an average of 6 months after acceptance. Submit seasonal material 6 months in advance. Accepts queries by e-mail (preferred). Responds in 1 month to queries.
NONFICTION Length: 700-1,000 words. **Pays $50-250.**
PHOTOS Contact: Query art director Sean Nebeker (snebeker@nevadamagazine.com). Reviews digital images. Pays $25-250; cover, $250.
TIPS "Keep in mind the magazine's purpose is to promote Nevada tourism."

NEW MEXICO

💲💲 NEW MEXICO MAGAZINE

Lew Wallace Bldg., 495 Old Santa Fe Trail, Santa Fe NM 87501-2750. (505)827-7447. **E-mail:** letters@nmmagazine.com. **E-mail:** queries@nmmagazine.com; artdirector@nmmagazine.com. **Website:** www.nmmagazine.com. **70% freelance written.** Covers areas throughout the state. "We want to publish a lively editorial mix, covering both the down-home (like a diner in Tucumcari) and the upscale (a new bistro in world-class Santa Fe)." Explore the gamut of the Old West and the New Age. "Our magazine is about the power of place—in particular more than 120,000 square miles of mountains, desert, grasslands, and forest inhabited by a culturally rich mix of individuals. It is an enterprise of the New Mexico Tourism Department, which strives to make potential visitors aware of our state's multicultural heritage, climate, environment, and uniqueness." Estab. 1923. Circ. 100,000. Pays on acceptance. 20% kill fee. Publishes ms an average of 3 months after acceptance. Submit seasonal material 1

year in advance. Accepts queries by mail, e-mail (preferred). Does not accept previously published submissions.Responds to queries if interested. Sample copy for $5. Guidelines online.
💿 No unsolicited mss. Does not return unsolicited material.
NONFICTION "Submit your story idea along with a working head and subhead and a paragraph synopsis. Include published clips and a short sum-up about your strengths as a writer. We will consider your proposal as well as your potential to write stories we've conceptualized."
REPRINTS Rarely publishes reprints, but sometimes publishes excerpts from novels and nonfiction books.
PHOTOS "Purchased as portfolio or on assignment. Photographers interested in photo assignments should reference submission guidelines on the contributors' page of our website.".

NEW YORK

💲💲 ADIRONDACK LIFE

P.O. Box 410, Route 9N, Jay NY 12941-0410. (518)946-2191. **Fax:** (518)946-7461. **E-mail:** aledit@adirondacklife.com; astoltie@adirondacklife.com; alprod@adirondacklife.com. **Website:** www.adirondacklife.com. **Contact:** Annie Stoltie, editor; Kelly Hofschneider, photo editor. **70% freelance written. Prefers to work with published/established writers.** Magazine published 8 issues/year, including special Annual Outdoor Guide, emphasizes the Adirondack region and the North Country of New York State in articles covering outdoor activities, history, and natural history directly related to the Adirondacks. Estab. 1970. Circ. 50,000. Byline given. Pays 30 days after publication. Publishes ms an average of 10 months after acceptance. Submit seasonal material 1 year in advance. Accepts queries by mail, e-mail. Does not accept previously published work.Sample copy for $3 and 9x12 SAE. Guidelines online.
NONFICTION Special issues: Outdoors (May); Single-topic Collector's issue (September). **Buys 20-25 unsolicited mss/year.** Query with published clips. Accepts queries, but not unsolicited mss, via e-mail. Length: 1,000-4,000 words. **Pays 30¢/word.** Sometimes pays expenses of writers on assignment.
PHOTOS "All photos must have been taken in the Adirondacks. Each issue contains a photo feature. Purchased with or without ms on assignment. All photos

must be individually identified as to the subject or locale and must bear the photographer's name.". Send photos. Reviews color transparencies, b&w prints. Pays $150 for full page, b&w, or color; $400 for cover (color only,vertical in format). Credit line given.

COLUMNS/DEPARTMENTS Special Places (unique spots in the Adirondack Park); Watercraft; Barkeater (personal essays); Wilderness (environmental issues); Working (careers in the Adirondacks); Home; teryears; Kitchen; Profile; Historical Preservation; Sporting Scene. Length: 1,200-2,100 words. Query with published clips. **Pays 30¢/word.**

FICTION Considers first-serial novel excerpts in its subject matter and region.

TIPS "Do not send a personal essay about your meaningful moment in the mountains. We need factual pieces about regional history, sports, culture, and business. We are looking for clear, concise, well-organized mss that are strictly Adirondack in subject. Check back issues to be sure we haven't already covered your topic. Check out our guidelines online."

CITY LIMITS

Community Service Society of New York, 105 E. 22nd St., Floor 3, New York NY 10010. (212)614-5397. **E-mail:** editor@citylimits.org. **Website:** www.citylimits.org. **Contact:** Jarrett Murphy, executive editor. **50% freelance written.** Monthly magazine covering urban politics and policy in New York City. "*City Limits* is a nonprofit online magazine focusing on issues facing New York City and its neighborhoods, particularly low-income communities. The magazine is strongly committed to investigative journalism, in-depth policy analysis, hard-hitting profiles, and investigation of pressing civic issues in New York City. Driven by a mission to inform public discourse, the magazine provides the factual reporting, human faces, data, history, and breadth of knowledge necessary to understanding the nuances, complexities, and hard truths of the city, its politics, and its people." Estab. 1976. Byline given. Pays on publication. Offers 50% kill fee. Publishes ms an average of 3 months after acceptance. Editorial lead time 2 months. Accepts queries by mail, e-mail, fax. Accepts simultaneous submissions. Responds in 1 month. Sample copy for $2.95. Guidelines free.

NONFICTION Needs book excerpts, exposé, humor, interview, opinion, photo feature. No essays, polemics. **Buys 25 mss/year.** Query with published clips. Length: 400-3,500 words. **Pays $150-2,000 for assigned articles. Pays $100-800 for unsolicited articles.** Pays expenses of writers on assignment.

PHOTOS State availability. Model release required for children. Reviews contact sheets, negatives, transparencies. Buys 20 photos from freelancers/issue; 200 photos/year. Pays $100 for color cover; $50-100 for b&w inside. Pays on publication. Credit line given. Buys rights for use in *City Limits* in print and online; higher rate given for online use.

COLUMNS/DEPARTMENTS Making Change (nonprofit business), Big Idea (policy news), Book Review—all 800 words; Urban Legend (profile), First Hand (Q&A)—both 350 words. **Buys 15 mss/year.** Query with published clips.

TIPS "Our specialty is covering low-income communities. We want to report untold stories about news affecting neighborhoods at the grassroots. We're looking for stories about housing, health care, criminal justice, child welfare, education, economic development, welfare reform, politics, and government. We need good photojournalists who can capture the emotion of a scene. We offer huge pay for great photos."

OHIO

$$ AKRON LIFE

Baker Media Group, 1653 Merriman Rd., Suite 116, Akron OH 44313. (330)253-0056. **Fax:** (330)253-5868. **E-mail:** info@bakermediagroup.com. **E-mail:** editor@bakermediagroup.com; acymerman@bakermediagroup.com. **Website:** www.akronlife.com. **Contact:** Abby Cymerman, managing editor. **10% freelance written.** Monthly regional magazine covering Summit, Stark, Portage and Medina counties. "*Akron Life* is a monthly lifestyles publication committed to providing information that enhances and enriches the experience of living in or visiting Akron and the surrounding region of Summit, Portage, Medina and Stark counties. Each colorful, thoughtfully designed issue profiles interesting places, personalities and events in the arts, sports, entertainment, business, politics and social scene. We cover issues important to the Greater Akron area and significant trends affecting the lives of those who live here." Estab. 2002. Circ. 15,000. Byline given. Pays on publication. Offers 50% kill fee. Publishes ms an average of 4-6 months after acceptance. Editorial lead time 2+ months. Submit seasonal material 6 months in advance. Accepts queries by mail, e-mail, fax. Sample copy free. Guidelines free.

NONFICTION Needs essays, general interest, historical, how-to, humor, interview, photo feature, travel. Query with published clips. Length: 300-2,000 words. **Pays $0.10 max/word for assigned and unsolicited articles.**

PHOTOS State availability. Captions, identification of subjects, model releases required. Reviews GIF/JPEG files. Negotiates payment individually.

TIPS "It's best to submit a detailed query along with samples of previously published works. Include why you think the story is of interest to our readers, and be sure to have a fresh approach."

💲💲💲 CLEVELAND MAGAZINE

City Magazines, Inc., 1422 Euclid Ave., Suite 730, Cleveland OH 44115. (216)771-2833. **Fax:** (216)781-6318. **E-mail:** gleydura@clevelandmagazine.com; miller@clevelandmagazine.com. **Website:** www.clevelandmagazine.com. **Contact:** Kristen Miller, design director; Steve Gleydura, editor. **60% freelance written. Mostly by assignment.** Monthly magazine with a strong Cleveland/Northeast Ohio angle. Estab. 1972. Circ. 50,000. Byline given. Pays on publication. Publishes ms an average of 3 months after acceptance. Editorial lead time 6 months. Submit seasonal material 8 months in advance. Accepts queries by mail, e-mail, fax. Accepts simultaneous submissions. Responds in 2 months to queries.

NONFICTION Needs general interest, historical, humor, interview, travel, home and garden. Query with published clips. Length: 800-4,000 words. **Pays $250-1,200.**

PHOTOS Buys an average of 50 photos from freelancers/issue; 600 photos/year. Model release required for portraits; property release required for individual homes. Photo captions required; include names, date, location, event, phone. Pays on publication. Credit line given. Buys one-time publication, electronic and promotional rights.

COLUMNS/DEPARTMENTS Talking Points (opinion or observation-driven essay), approximately 1,000 words. Query with published clips. **Pays $300.**

💲💲💲 OHIO MAGAZINE

Great Lakes Publishing Co., 1422 Euclid Ave., Suite 730, Cleveland OH 44115. (216)771-2833. **E-mail:** lblake@ohiomagazine.com. **Website:** www.ohiomagazine.com. **Contact:** Lesley Blake, art director. **50%**

freelance written. "*Ohio Magazine* serves energetic and involved Ohioans by providing award-winning stories and pictures of Ohio's most interesting people, arts, entertainment, history, homes, dining, family life, festivals and regional travel. We capture the beauty, the adventure and the fun of life in the Buckeye State.". Estab. 1978. Circ. 40,000. Byline given. Pays on publication. 20% kill fee. Publishes ms an average of 6 months after acceptance. Submit seasonal material 6 months in advance. Accepts queries by mail, e-mail. Responds in 3 months to queries. Responds in 3 months to mss. Sample copy for $3.95 and 9x12 SAE or online. Guidelines online.

NONFICTION Query with résumé and at least 3 published clips. Length: 1,000-3,000 words. **Pays $300-1,200.** Sometimes pays expenses of writers on assignment.

REPRINTS Contact Emily Vanuch, advertising coordinator. Pays 50% of amount paid for an original article.

PHOTOS Rate negotiable.

COLUMNS/DEPARTMENTS **Buys minimum 5 unsolicited mss/year. Pays $100-600.**

TIPS "Freelancers should send all queries in writing (either by mail or e-mail), not by telephone. Successful queries demonstrate an intimate knowledge of the publication. We are looking to increase our circle of writers who can write about the state in an informative and upbeat style. Strong reporting skills are highly valued."

OKLAHOMA

💲💲 OKLAHOMA TODAY

P.O. Box 1468, Oklahoma City OK 73101-1468. (405)230-8450. **Fax:** (405)230-8650. **E-mail:** megan.rossman@travelok.com. **Website:** www.oklahomatoday.com. **Contact:** Megan Rossman, photography editor. **80% freelance written. Works with approximately 25 new/unpublished writers each year.** Bimonthly magazine covering people, places, and things of Oklahoma. "We are interested in showing off the best Oklahoma has to offer; we're pretty serious about our travel slant but regularly run history, nature, and personality profiles." Estab. 1956. Circ. 45,000. Byline given. Pays on publication. Publishes ms an average of 6 months after acceptance. Submit seasonal material 1 year in advance. Accepts queries by mail, e-mail. Responds in 4 months to queries. Sample copy for $4.95 and 9x12 SASE or online. Guidelines online.

NONFICTION Needs book excerpts, on Oklahoma topics, historical, Oklahoma only, interview, Oklahomans only, photo feature, in Oklahoma, travel, in Oklahoma. No phone queries. **Buys 20-40 mss/year.** Query with published clips. Length: 250-3,000 words. **Pays $25-750.**

PHOTOS "We are especially interested in developing contacts with photographers who live in Oklahoma or have shot here. Send samples. Photo guidelines with SASE.". Captions, identification of subjects required.

TIPS "The best way to become a regular contributor to *Oklahoma Today* is to query us with 1 or more story ideas, each developed to give us an idea of your proposed slant. We're looking for lively, concise, well-researched and reported stories, stories that don't need to be heavily edited and are not newspaper style. We have a 3-person full-time editorial staff, and freelancers who can write and have done their homework get called again and again."

OREGON

$$ OREGON COAST

4969 Hwy. 101 N, Suite 2, Florence OR 97439. (800)348-8401. **E-mail:** Alicia@nwmags.com. **Website:** www.northwestmagazines.com. **Contact:** Alicia Spooner. **65% freelance written.** Bimonthly magazine covering the Oregon Coast. Estab. 1982. Circ. 50,000. Byline given. Pays after publication. Offers 33% (on assigned stories only, not on stories accepted on spec) kill fee. Publishes ms an average of up to 1 year after acceptance. Submit seasonal material 6 months in advance. Accepts queries by mail, e-mail. Responds in 3 months to queries. Sample copy for $4.50. Guidelines online.

NONFICTION **Buys 55 mss/year.** Query with published clips. Length: 500-1,500 words. **Pays $75-350, plus 2 contributor copies.**

REPRINTS Send tearsheet or photocopy and information about when and where the material previously appeared. Pays an average of 60% of the amount paid for an original article.

PHOTOS Photo submissions with no ms or stand alone or cover photos. Send photos. Captions, identification of subjects, True required. Slides or high-resolution digital.

TIPS "Slant article for readers who do not live at the Oregon Coast. At least 1 historical article is used in each issue. Ms/photo packages are preferred over mss with no photos. List photo credits and captions for each photo. Check all facts, proper names, and numbers carefully in photo/ms packages. Must pertain to Oregon Coast somehow.

PENNSYLVANIA

$$ PENNSYLVANIA

Pennsylvania Magazine Co., P.O. Box 755, Camp Hill PA 17001-0755. (717)697-4660. **E-mail:** editor@pa-mag.com. **Website:** www.pa-mag.com. **90% freelance written.** Bimonthly magazine covering people, places, events, and history in Pennsylvania. Estab. 1981. Circ. 33,000. Byline given. Pays on acceptance except for articles (by authors unknown to us) sent on speculation. Offers 25% kill fee for assigned articles. Publishes ms an average of 9 months after acceptance. Submit seasonal material 9 months in advance. Accepts queries by mail, e-mail. Responds in 4-6 weeks to queries. Sample copy free. Guidelines for #10 SASE or by e-mail.

NONFICTION Nothing on Amish topics, hunting, or skiing. **Buys 75-120 mss/year.** Query. Length: 750-2,500 words. **Pays 15¢/word.**

REPRINTS Send photocopy with rights for sale noted and information about when and where the material previously appeared. Pays 5¢/word.

PHOTOS "Contact editor via e-mail for photography instructions. We work primarily with digital images and prefer raw when possible." Photography Essay (highlights annual photo essay contest entries and showcases individual photographers). Captions required. Digital photos (send printouts and CD OR DVD or contact to upload to Dropbox folder. Pays $25-35 for inside photos; $150 for covers.

COLUMNS/DEPARTMENTS Round Up (short items about people, unusual events, museums, historical topics/events, family and individually owned consumer-related businesses), 250-1,300 words; Town and Country (items about people or events illustrated with photos or commissioned art), 500 words. Include SASE. Query. **Pays 15¢/word.**

TIPS "Our publication depends upon freelance work—send queries. Remember that a subject isn't an idea. Send the topic and your approach to the topic when you query. Answer the question: Would this be interesting to someone across the state? Find things that interest you enough that you'd travel 30-50 miles in a car to see/do/explore it, and send a query on that."

$$ PHILADELPHIA STYLE

Philadelphia Style Magazine, LLC, 141 League St., Philadelphia PA 19147. (215)468-6670. **Fax:** (215)223-3095. **E-mail:** info@phillystylemag.com. **Website:** www.phillystylemag.com. **Contact:** Kristin Detterline-Munro. **50% freelance written.** "Bimonthly magazine covering upscale living in the Philadelphia region. Topics include: celebrity interviews, fashion (men's and women's), food, home and design, real estate, dining, beauty, travel, arts and entertainment, and more. Our magazine is a positive look at the best ways to live in the Philadelphia region. Submitted articles should speak to an upscale, educated audience of professionals that live in the Delaware Valley." Estab. 1999. Circ. 60,000. Byline given. Pays on publication. Offers 25% kill fee. Publishes ms an average of 3 months after acceptance. Editorial lead time 2-4 months. Submit seasonal material 6 months in advance. Accepts queries by mail, e-mail, fax.

NONFICTION Needs general interest, interview, travel, region-specific articles. "We are not looking for articles that do not have a regional spin." **Buys 100+ mss/year.** Send complete ms. Length: 300-2,500 words. **Pays $50-500.**

COLUMNS/DEPARTMENTS Declarations (celebrity interviews and celebrity contributors); Currents (fashion news); Manor (home and design news); Liberties (beauty and travel news); Dish (dining news); Life in the City (fresh, quirky, regional reporting on books, real estate, art, retail, dining, events, and little-known stories/facts about the region), 100-500 words; Vanguard (people on the forefront of Philadelphia's arts, media, fashion, business, and social scene), 500-700 words; In the Neighborhood (reader-friendly reporting on up-and-coming areas of the region including dining, shopping, attractions, and recreation), 2,000-2,500 words. Query with published clips or send complete ms. **Pays $50-500.**

TIPS "Mail queries with clips or mss. Articles should speak to a stylish, educated audience."

$$$$ PITTSBURGH MAGAZINE

WiesnerMedia, Washington's Landing, 600 Waterfront Dr., Suite 100, Pittsburgh PA 15222-4795. (412)304-0900. **Fax:** (412)304-0938. **E-mail:** editors@pittsburghmagazine.com. **Website:** www.pittsburghmag.com. **Contact:** Cindi Lash, editor-in-chief; Betsy Benson, publisher and vice president. **70% freelance written.** Monthly magazine covering the Pittsburgh metropolitan area. *Pittsburgh* presents issues, analyzes problems, and strives to encourage a better understanding of the community. Region is Western Pennsylvania, Eastern Ohio, Northern West Virginia, and Western Maryland. Estab. 1970. Circ. 75,000. Byline given. Pays on publication. Offers kill fee. Publishes ms an average of 2 months after acceptance. Submit seasonal material 6 months in advance. Accepts queries by mail. Responds in 2 months to queries. Sample copy for $2 (old back issues). Guidelines online at www.pittsburghmagazine.com/Pittsburgh-Magazine/Writers-Guidelines, or via SASE.

💬 The editor reports a need for more hard news, analysis, and stories targeting readers in their 30s and 40s, especially those with young families. Prefers to work with published/established writers with knowledge of and contacts in Western Pennsylvania. The monthly magazine is purchased on newsstands and by subscription.

NONFICTION Needs expose, lifestyle, sports, informational, service, business, medical, profile. "We have minimal interest in historical articles and we do not publish fiction, poetry, advocacy, or personal reminiscence pieces." Query in writing with outline and clips. Length: 1,200-4,000 words. **Pays $300-1,500+.**

PHOTOS Query. Model releases required. Pays pre-negotiated expenses of writer on assignment.

TIPS "Best bet to break in is through hard news with a region-wide impact or service pieces or profiles with a regional interest. The point is that we want more stories that reflect our region, not just a tiny part. And we *never* consider any story without a strong regional focus."

$ SUSQUEHANNA LIFE

217 Market St., Lewisburg PA 17837. (800)232-1670. **Fax:** (570)524-7796. **E-mail:** susquehannalife@gmail.com. **Website:** www.susquehannalife.com. **80% freelance written.** Quarterly magazine covering Central Pennsylvania lifestyle. Estab. 1993. Circ. 45,000. Byline given. Pays on publication. Offers 50% kill fee. Publishes ms an average of 6-9 months after acceptance. Editorial lead time 3-6 months. Submit seasonal material 4-6 months in advance. Accepts queries by e-mail. Responds in 4-6 weeks to queries. Responds

in 1-3 months to mss. Sample copy for $4.95, plus 5 first-class stamps. Guidelines for #10 SASE.

NONFICTION Needs book excerpts, general interest, historical, how-to, inspirational, related to the region, interview, photo feature, travel. Does not want fiction. **Buys 30-40 mss/year.** Query or send complete ms. Length: 800-1,200 words. **Pays $75-125.** Sometimes pays expenses of writers on assignment.

PHOTOS Send photos. Captions, identification of subjects, model releases required. Reviews contact sheets, prints, GIF/JPEG files. Offers $20-25/photo; $100+ for cover photos.

POETRY Must have a Central Pennsylvania angle.

TIPS "When you query, do not address letter to 'Dear Sir'; address the letter to the name of the publisher/editor. Demonstrate your ability to write. You need to be familiar with the type of articles we use and the particular flavor of the region. Only accepts submissions with a Central Pennsylvania angle."

SOUTH CAROLINA

🌕🌕 HILTON HEAD MONTHLY

P.O. Box 5926, Hilton Head Island SC 29938. **Fax:** (843)842-5743. **E-mail:** editor@hiltonheadmonthly.com. **Website:** www.hiltonheadmonthly.com. **Contact:** Barry Kaufman, editor. **75% freelance written.** Monthly magazine covering the people, business, community, environment, and lifestyle of Hilton Head, SC, and the surrounding Lowcountry. "Our mission is to offer lively, fresh writing about Hilton Head Island, an upscale, environmentally conscious and intensely pro-active resort community on the coast of South Carolina." Circ. 35,000. Byline given. Pays on publication. Offers 50% kill fee. Publishes ms an average of 6 months after acceptance. Editorial lead time 3 months. Submit seasonal material 4 months in advance. Accepts queries by mail, e-mail, . NoAccepts simultaneous submissions. Responds in 1 week to queries. Responds in 4 months to mss. Sample copy for $3.

NONFICTION Needs general interest, historical, history only, how-to, home related, humor, interview, Hilton Head residents only, opinion, general humor or Hilton Head Island community affairs, personal experience, travel. "Everything is local, local, local, so we're especially interested in profiles of notable residents (or those with Lowcountry ties) and original takes on home design/maintenance, environmen-

tal issues, entrepreneurship, health, sports, arts and entertainment, humor, travel and volunteerism. We like to see how national trends/issues play out on a local level." **Buys 225-250 mss/year.** Query with published clips.

PHOTOS State availability. Reviews contact sheets, prints, digital samples. Negotiates payment individually.

COLUMNS/DEPARTMENTS News; Business; Lifestyles (hobbies, health, sports, etc.); Home; Around Town (local events, charities and personalities); People (profiles, weddings, etc.). Query with synopsis. **Pays 20¢/word.**

TIPS "Sure, Hilton Head is known primarily as an affluent resort island, but there's plenty more going on than just golf and tennis; this is a lively community with a strong sense of identity and decades-long tradition of community, volunteerism, and environmental preservation. We don't need any more tales of why you chose to retire here or how you fell in love with the beaches, herons, or salt marshes. Seek out lively, surprising characters—there are plenty—and offer fresh (but not trendy) takes on local personalities, Southern living, and green issues."

TEXAS

🌕 HILL COUNTRY SUN

T.D. Austin Lane, Inc., 100 Commons Rd., Suite 7, #319, Dripping Springs TX 78620. (512)484-9716. **E-mail:** melissa@hillcountrysun.com. **Website:** www.hillcountrysun.com. **75% freelance written.** Monthly tabloid covering traveling in the Central Texas Hill Country. Publishes stories of interesting people, places and events in the Central Texas Hill Country. Estab. 1990. Circ. 34,000. Byline given. Pays on acceptance. Publishes ms an average of 2 months after acceptance. Editorial lead time 1 month. Submit seasonal material 2 months in advance. Accepts queries by mail and e-mail. Responds in 1 week to queries. Sample copy free. Guidelines online.

NONFICTION Needs interview, travel. No first person articles. **Buys 50 mss/year.** Query. Length: 600-800 words. **Pays $60 or more.**

PHOTOS State availability of or send photos. Identification of subjects required. No additional payment for photos accepted with ms.

TIPS "Writers must be familiar with both the magazine's style and the Texas Hill Country."

☺☺☺ TEXAS HIGHWAYS

P.O. Box 141009, Austin TX 78714-1009. (800)839-4997. **Website:** www.texashighways.com. **70% freelance written.** Monthly magazine encourages travel within the state and tells the Texas story to readers around the world. Estab. 1974. Circ. 250,000. Pays on acceptance. Publishes ms an average of 1 year after acceptance. Accepts queries by mail. Responds in 2 months to queries. Guidelines online.

NONFICTION Query with description, published clips, additional background materials (charts, maps, etc.) and SASE. Length: 1,200-1,500 words. **Pays 40-50¢/word.**

TIPS "We like strong leads that draw in the reader immediately and clear, concise writing. Be specific and avoid superlatives. Avoid overused words. Don't forget the basics—who, what, where, when, why, and how."

☺☺☺☺ TEXAS MONTHLY

Emmis Publishing LP, P.O. Box 1569, Austin TX 78767. (512)320-6900. **Fax:** (512)476-9007. **E-mail:** lbaldwin@texasmonthly.com. **Website:** www.texasmonthly.com. **Contact:** Jake Silverstein, editor; Leslie Baldwin, photo editor; Andi Beierman, deputy art director. **10% freelance written.** Monthly magazine covering Texas. Estab. 1973. Circ. 300,000. Byline given. Pays on acceptance, $1/word and writer's expenses. Publishes ms an average of 1-3 months after acceptance. Editorial lead time 2 months. Submit seasonal material 3 months in advance. Accepts queries by mail, e-mail, fax. Responds in 6-8 weeks to queries and mss. Guidelines online.

NONFICTION Contact: John Broders, associate editor (jbroders@texasmonthly.com). Needs book excerpts, essays, expose, general interest, interview, personal experience, photo feature, travel. Does not want articles without a Texas connection. Query. Length: 2,000-5,000 words.

PHOTOS Contact: Leslie Baldwin (lbaldwin@texasmonthly.com).

TIPS "Stories must appeal to an educated Texas audience. *Texas Monthly* covers the state's politics, sports, business, culture and changing lifestyles. We like solidly researched reporting that uncovers issues of public concern, reveals offbeat and previously unreported topics, or uses a novel approach to familiar topics. It contains lengthly features, interviews, essays, book excerpts, and reviews of books and movies.

Does not want articles without a Texas connection. Any issue of the magazine would be a helpful guide; sample copy for $7."

☺☺ TEXAS PARKS & WILDLIFE

4200 Smith School Rd., Bldg. D, Austin TX 78744. (800)937-9393. **Fax:** (512)389-8397. **E-mail:** magazine@tpwd.state.tx.us. **Website:** www.tpwmagazine.com. **20% freelance written.** Monthly magazine featuring articles about "Texas hunting, fishing, birding, outdoor recreation, game and nongame wildlife, state parks, environmental issues." All articles must be about Texas. Estab. 1942. Circ. 150,000. Byline given. Pays on acceptance. Offers kill fee. Kill fee determined by contract, usually $200-250. Publishes ms an average of 4 months after acceptance. Accepts queries by mail. Responds in 1 month to queries; 3 months to mss. Sample copy and guidelines online.

○ *Texas Parks & Wildlife* needs more short items for front-of-the-book scout section and wildlife articles written from a natural history perspective (not for hunters).

NONFICTION Needs general interest (Texas only), how-to, outdoor activities, photo feature, travel, state parks, and small towns. **Buys 20 mss/year.** Query with published clips; follow up by e-mail 1 month after submitting query. Length: 500-2,500 words. **Pays per article content.** Sometimes pays expenses of writers on assignment, but must be approved in advance.

PHOTOS Send photos to photo editor. Captions, identification of subjects required. Reviews transparencies. Offers $65-500/photo.

TIPS "Queries with a strong seasonal peg are preferred. Our planning progress begins 7-8 months before the date of publication. That means you have to think ahead: *What will Texas outdoor enthusiasts want to read about 7 months from today?*"

VERMONT

☺☺ VERMONT LIFE MAGAZINE

One National Life Dr., 6th Fl, Montpelier VT 05620. (802)828-3241. **Fax:** (802)828-3366. **E-mail:** editors@vtlife.com. **Website:** www.vermontlife.com. **Contact:** Bill Anderson, managing editor. **90% freelance written. Prefers to work with published/established writers.** Quarterly magazine. "We read all story ideas submitted, but we cannot reply individually to each one. If we want to pursue a given ms or idea, we will contact you within 30 days of receiving it. Please bear in mind that *Vermont Life* produces pages as much as 6 months in advance of publication and may require photographs to be taken a year ahead of publication. We seek stories that have to do with contemporary Vermont culture and the Vermont way of life. As the state magazine, we are most interested in ideas that present positive aspects of life in Vermont. However, while we are nonpartisan, we have no rules about avoiding controversy when the presentation of the subject can illustrate some aspect of Vermont's unique character. We prefer reporting and journalism built around original ideas and insights, emerging trends, and thought-provoking connections in a Vermont context." Estab. 1946. Circ. 53,000. Byline given. Publishes ms an average of 9 months after acceptance. Submit seasonal material 1 year in advance. Accepts queries by e-mail only; no phone queries. Responds in 1 month to queries. "Read online guidelines before submitting: www.vermontlife.com/guidelines-for-contributors.".

❖➥ "We are generally not in the market for op-ed opinion pieces, first-person accounts, memoirs, poetry, historical reconstructions, stories with anniversary pegs, or 'one thing' stories that promote an individual business, event, service organization, or the like. In assessing story ideas, we ask ourselves: 'Who would be happier to see this, the people it is about, or the reader?'"

PHOTOS Buys seasonal photographs. Gives assignments but only with experienced photographers. Query via e-mail only. Original digital photos from cameras of at least 6 megapixels. Photographs should be current (taken within the last 3 years). Metadata for each image must include captions; photographer's name, the location from which the photo was taken, especially the town; identification of subjects and important landmarks; date; model releases required. Pays $75-200 inside color; $500 for cover.

TIPS "Review online guidelines before submitting queries or photography."

VIRGINIA

❂❂ THE ROANOKER

Leisure Publishing Co., 3424 Brambleton Ave., Roanoke VA 24018. (540)989-6138; (800)548-1672. **Fax:** (540)989-7603. **E-mail:** jwood@leisurepublishing.com; krheinheimer@leisurepublishing.com. **Web**site: www.theroanoker.com. **Contact:** Kurt Rheinheimer, editor; Austin Clark, creative director; Patty Jackson, production director. **75% freelance written. Works with a small number of new/unpublished writers each year.** Magazine published 6 times/year. "*The Roanoker* is a general interest city magazine for the people of Roanoke, Virginia and the surrounding area. Our readers are primarily upper-income, well-educated professionals between the ages of 35 and 60. Coverage ranges from hard news and consumer information to restaurant reviews and local history." Estab. 1974. Circ. 10,000. Byline given. Pays on publication. Publishes ms an average of 4 months after acceptance. Submit seasonal material 4 months in advance. Accepts queries by mail, e-mail, fax. Responds in 2 months to queries. Sample copy for $2 with 9x12 SASE and 5 first-class stamps or online.

NONFICTION Needs exposé, historical, how-to, live better in western Virginia, interview, of well-known area personalities, photo feature, travel, Virginia and surrounding states, periodic special sections on fashion, real estate, media, banking, investing. **Buys 30 mss/year.** Send complete ms. 1,400 words maximum. **Pays $35-200.**

PHOTOS Send photos. Captions, model releases required. Reviews color transparencies, digital submissions. Pays $25-50/published photograph.

COLUMNS/DEPARTMENTS Skinny (shorts on people, Roanoke-related books, local issues, events, arts and culture).

TIPS "We're looking for more pieces on contemporary history (1930s-70s). It helps if freelancer lives in the area. The most frequent mistake made by writers in completing an article for us is not having enough Roanoke-area focus: use of area experts, sources, slants, etc."

❂❂ VIRGINIA LIVING

Cape Fear Publishing, 109 E. Cary St., Richmond VA 23219. (804)343-7539. **Fax:** (804)649-0306. **E-mail:** ErinParkhurst@CapeFear.com. **Website:** www.virginialiving.com. **Contact:** Erin Parkhurst, editor. **80% freelance written.** Bimonthly magazine covering life and lifestyle in Virginia. "We are a large-format (10x13) glossy magazine covering life in Virginia, from food, architecture, and gardening, to issues, profiles, and travel." Estab. 2002. Circ. 70,000. Byline given. Pays on publication. Publishes ms an average of 4-6 months after acceptance. Editorial lead time

2-6 months. Submit seasonal material 1 year in advance. Accepts queries by mail. NoAccepts simultaneous submissions. Responds in 1-3 month to queries. Sample copy for $5.

NONFICTION Needs book excerpts, essays, expose, general interest, historical, interview, new product, personal experience, photo feature, travel, architecture, design. No fiction, poetry, previously published articles, or stories with a firm grasp of the obvious. **Buys 180 mss/year.** Query with published clips or send complete ms. Length: 300-3,000 words. **Pays 50¢/word.**

PHOTOS Contact: Sonda Andersson Pappan, art director. Captions, identification of subjects, model releases required. Reviews contact sheets, 6x7 transparencies, 8x10 prints, GIF/JPEG files. Negotiates payment individually.

COLUMNS/DEPARTMENTS Beauty; Travel; Books; Events; Sports (all with a unique Virginia slant), all 1,000-1,500 words. **Buys 50 mss/year.** Send complete ms. **Pays $120-200.**

TIPS "Queries should be about fresh subjects in Virginia. Avoid stories about Williamsburg, Chincoteague ponies, Monticello, the Civil War, and other press release-type topics. We prefer to introduce new subjects, faces, and ideas, and get beyond the many clichés of Virginia. Freelancers would also do well to think about what time of the year they are pitching stories for, as well as art possibilities. We are a large-format magazine, so photography is a key component to our stories."

WISCONSIN

⊖⊖ MADISON MAGAZINE

Morgan Murphy Media, 7025 Raymond Rd., Madison WI 53719. (608)270-3600. **Fax:** (608)270-3636. **E-mail:** bnardi@madisonmagazine.com. **Website:** www.madisonmagazine.com. **Contact:** Brennan Nardi, editor. **75% freelance written.** Monthly magazine covering life in the greater Madison, Wisconsin, area. Estab. 1978. Byline given. Pays on publication. Offers 33% kill fee. Publishes ms an average of 2 months after acceptance. Editorial lead time 3 months. Submit seasonal material 3-4 months in advance. Accepts queries by mail, e-mail. Accepts simultaneous submissions. Responds in 3 weeks to queries. Responds in 3 weeks to mss. Sample copy free. Guidelines available.

NONFICTION Needs book excerpts, essays, expose, general interest, historical, how-to, humor, inspirational, interview, new product, opinion, personal experience, photo feature, religious, technical, travel.

PHOTOS State availability. Reviews contact sheets. Negotiates payment individually.

COLUMNS/DEPARTMENTS Your Town (local events) and OverTones (local arts/entertainment), both 300 words; Habitat (local house/garden) and Business (local business), both 800 words. **Buys 120 mss/year.** Query with published clips. **Pays variable amount.**

FILLERS Needs anecdotes, facts, gags, newsbreaks, short humor. Length: 100 words. **Pays 20-30¢/word.**

TIPS "Our magazine is local, so only articles pertaining to Madison, Wisconsin, are considered. Specific queries are heavily appreciated. We like fresh, new content taken in a local perspective. Show us what you're like to write for us."

WYOMING

⊖ WYOMING RURAL ELECTRIC NEWS (WREN)

2710 Thomas Ave., Cheyenne WY 82001. (307)772-1986. **Fax:** (307)634-0728. **E-mail:** wren@wyomingrea.org. **Website:** www.wyomingrea.org/community/wren-magazine.php. **40% freelance written.** Monthly magazine (except in January) for audience of small town residents, vacation-home owners, farmers, and ranchers. Estab. 1954. Circ. 39,100. Byline given. Pays on acceptance. Publishes ms an average of 2 months after acceptance. Submit seasonal material 2 months in advance. Accepts queries by mail, e-mail. Responds in 1 month to queries. Sample copy for $2.50 and 9x12 SASE. Guidelines for #10 SASE.

NONFICTION No nostalgia, sarcasm, or tongue-in-cheek. **Buys 4-10 mss/year.** Send complete ms. Length: 600-800 words. **Pays up to $150, plus 3 copies.**

REPRINTS Send tearsheet or photocopy and information about when and where the material previously appeared.

PHOTOS Color only.

TIPS "Always looking for fresh, new writers. Submit entire ms. Don't submit a regionally set story from some other part of the country. Photos and illustrations (if appropriate) are always welcomed. We want factual articles that are blunt, to the point, accurate."

RELIGIOUS

ALIVE NOW

1908 Grand Ave., P.O. Box 340004, Nashville TN 37203. (615)340-7254. **Fax:** (615)340-7267. **E-mail:** alivenow@upperroom.org. **Website:** www.alivenow.org; www.upperroom.org. **Contact:** Beth A. Richardson, editor. *Alive Now*, published bimonthly, is a devotional magazine that invites readers to enter an ever-deepening relationship with God. "*Alive Now* seeks to nourish people who are hungry for a sacred way of living. Submissions should invite readers to see God in the midst of daily life by exploring how contemporary issues impact their faith lives. Each word must be vivid and dynamic and contribute to the whole. We make selections based on a list of upcoming themes. Mss which do not fit a theme will be returned." *Alive Now* is 48 pages. Estab. 1971. Circ. 70,000. Pays on acceptance. Accepts queries by mail, e-mail. Subscription: $17.95/year (6 issues); $26.95 for 2 years (12 issues). Additional subscription information, including foreign rates, online. Guidelines online at website. Submissions should invite readers to seek God in the midst of daily life by exploring how contemporary issues impact their faith lives. If ms does not fit a theme, it will not be considered. Themes can be found online. Prefers electronic submissions attached as Word document. Postal submissions should include SASE. Include name, address, theme on each sheet. Payment will be made at the time of acceptance for publication. "We will notify contributors of ms status when we make final decisions for an issue, approximately 2 months before the issue date.".

FICTION Pays $35 or more on acceptance.

POETRY Pays $35 or more on acceptance.

ANCIENT PATHS

P.O. Box 7505, Fairfax Station VA 22039. **E-mail:** sklyarburris@yahoo.com. **Website:** www.editor-skylar.com/magazine/table.html. **Contact:** Skylar H. Burris, Editor. *Ancient Paths*, published biennially in odd-numbered years, provides "a forum for quality Christian poetry. All works should have a spiritual theme. The theme may be explicitly Christian or broadly religious. Works published in *Ancient Paths* explore themes such as redemption, sin, forgiveness, doubt, faith, gratitude for the ordinary blessings of life, spiritual struggle, and spiritual growth. Please, no overly didactic works. Subtlety is preferred." Estab. 1998. Responds in 3-4 weeks "if rejected; longer if being seriously considered." Single copy: $5 for new e-book format; $10 for hard copy back issues. Make checks payable to Skylar Burris. Guidelines available for SASE or online.

FICTION E-mail submissions only. Paste flash fiction directly in e-mail message. Use the subject heading "AP Online Submission (title of your work)." Include name and e-mail address at top of e-mail. Previously published works accepted, provided they are not currently online. Please indicate if your work has been published elsewhere." Needs flash fiction. Length: no more than 900 words. **"Payment for online publication will be $1.25 for the first work and $0.75 for each additional work accepted.".**

POETRY E-mail all submissions. Paste poems in e-mail message. Use the subject heading "AP Online Submission (title of your work)." Include your name and e-mail address at the top of your e-mail. Poems may be rhymed, unrhymed, free verse, or formal. Does not want 'preachy' poetry, inconsistent meter, or forced rhyme; no stream of conscious or avant-garde work; no esoteric academic poetry. Length: no more than 40 lines. **"Payment for online publication will be $1.25 for the first work and $0.75 for each additional work accepted." Published poets and authors will also receive discount code for $3 off 2 past printed issues.**

TIPS "Read the great religious poets: John Donne, George Herbert, T.S. Eliot, Lord Tennyson. Remember not to preach. This is a literary magazine, not a pulpit. This does not mean you do not communicate morals or celebrate God. It means you are not overbearing or simplistic when you do so."

⊛⊛ CATHOLIC FORESTER

Catholic Order of Foresters, 355 Shuman Blvd., P.O. Box 3012, Naperville IL 60566-7012. **Fax:** (630)983-3384. **E-mail:** magazine@catholicforester.org. **Website:** www.catholicforester.org. **Contact:** Editor; art director. **5% freelance written.** Quarterly magazine for members of the Catholic Order of Foresters, a fraternal insurance benefit society. "*Catholic Forester* is a quarterly magazine filled with product features, member stories, and articles affirming fraternalism, unity, friendship, and true Christian charity among members. Although a portion of each issue is devoted to the organization and its members, a few freelance pieces are published in most issues. These articles cover varied topics to create a balanced issue for the purpose of informing, educating, and entertaining our readers." Estab. 1883. Circ. 77,000. Pays on acceptance. Editorial lead time 6 months. Submit seasonal material 6 months in advance. TrueResponds in 3 months to mss. Sample copy for 9x12 SAE and 4 first-class stamps. Guidelines online.

NONFICTION Needs health and wellness, money management and budgeting, parenting and family life, insurance, nostalgia, humor, inspirational, religious, Will consider previously published work. **Buys 1-5 mss/year.** Send complete ms by mail, fax, or e-mail. Rejected material will not be returned without accompanying SASE. Length: 500-1,000 words. **Pays 50¢/word.**

PHOTOS State availability. Negotiates payment individually.

FICTION Needs humorous, religious, inspirational. 1-5 Length: 500-1,500 words. **Pays 50¢/word.**

POETRY Needs light verse, traditional. Buys 3 poems/year. Length: 15 lines maximum. **Pays 30¢/word.**

TIPS "Our audience includes a broad age spectrum, ranging from youth to seniors. A good children's story with a positive lesson or message would rate high on our list."

🟢🟢 CHRISTIAN HOME & SCHOOL

Christian Schools International, 3350 E. Paris Ave. SE, Grand Rapids MI 49512. (616)957-1070, ext. 240. **Fax:** (616)957-5022. **E-mail:** rheyboer@csionline.org. **Website:** www.csionline.org/christian_home_and_school. **30% freelance written. Works with a small number of new/unpublished writers each year.** Magazine published 2 times/year during the school year covering family life and Christian education. In addition, a special high school issue is published each spring. *Christian Home & School* is designed for parents in the United States and Canada who send their children to Christian schools and are concerned about the challenges facing Christian families today. These readers expect a mature, Biblical perspective in the articles, not just a Bible verse tacked onto the end. Estab. 1922. Circ. 66,000. Byline given. Pays on publication. Publishes ms an average of 4 months after acceptance. Submit material 4 months in advance. Accepts queries by mail, e-mail. Responds in 1 month to queries. Sample copy for 9x12 SAE with 4 first-class stamps. Guidelines only for #10 SASE or online. For article topics, refer to the editorial calendar online.

🗨 The editor reports an interest in seeing articles on how to experience and express forgiveness in your home, help your child make good choices, and raise kids who are opposites, and promote good educational practices in Christian schools and current education issues.

NONFICTION Needs book excerpts, interview, opinion, personal experience, articles on parenting and school life. **Buys 30 mss/year.** Send complete ms as a Word document. Length: 1,000-2,000 words. **Pays $175-250.**

TIPS "Features are the area most open to freelancers. We are publishing articles that deal with contemporary issues that affect parents. Use an informal easy-to-read style rather than a philosophical, academic tone. Try to incorporate vivid imagery and concrete, practical examples from real life. We look for mss with a mature Christian perspective."

COLUMBIA

1 Columbus Plaza, New Haven CT 06510. (203)752-4398. **Fax:** (203)752-4109. **E-mail:** columbia@kofc.org. **Website:** www.kofc.org/columbia. **Contact:** Alton Pelowski, editor. Monthly magazine for Catholic families. Caters primarily to members of the Knights of Columbus. Estab. 1921. Circ. 1,500,000. Pays on acceptance. Accepts queries by mail, e-mail. Sample copy and writer's guidelines online.

NONFICTION No reprints, poetry, cartoons, puzzles, short stories/fiction. Query with SASE or by e-mail. Length: 750-1,500 words. **Payment varies.**

CONSCIENCE

Catholics for Choice, 1436 U St. NW, Suite 301, Washington D.C. 20009. (202)986-6093. **E-mail:** conscience@catholicsforchoice.org. **Website:** www.catholicsforchoice.org. **Contact:** Jon O'Brien, executive editor. **80% written by nonstaff writers. Publishes 40 freelance submissions yearly; 10% by unpublished writers, 50% by authors who are new to the magazine, 70% by experts.** "Conscience offers in-depth coverage of a range of topics, including contemporary politics, Catholicism, women's rights in society and in religions, U.S. politics, reproductive rights, sexuality and gender, ethics and bioethics, feminist theology, social justice, church and state issues, and the role of religion in formulating public policy." Estab. 1980. Circ. 12,000. Byline given. Pays on publication. Publishes ms an average of 2 months after acceptance. Accepts queries by mail, e-mail. Responds in 4 months to queries. Sample copy free with 9x12 envelope and $1.85 postage. Guidelines with #10 SASE.

NONFICTION Needs book excerpts, interview, opinion, personal experience, a small amount, issue analysis. **Buys 4-8 mss/year.** Send complete ms. Length: 1,500-3,500 words. **Pays $200 negotiable.**

REPRINTS Send typed ms with rights for sale noted and information about when and where the material previously appeared. Pays 20-30% of amount paid for an original article.

PHOTOS Sample copies available. Buys up to 25 photos/year. Model/property release preferred. Photo captions preferred; include title, subject, photographer's name. Reviews photos with or without a ms. Pays $300 maximum for color cover; $50 maximum for b&w inside. Pays on publication. Credit line given.

COLUMNS/DEPARTMENTS Book Reviews, 600-1,200 words. **Buys 4-8 mss/year. Pays $75.**

TIPS "Our readership includes national and international opinion leaders and policymakers, librarians, members of the clergy and the press, and leaders in the fields of theology, ethics, and women's studies. Articles should be written for a diverse and educated audience."

EVANGEL

Light and Life Communications, 770 N. High School Rd., Indianapolis IN 46214. (317)244-3660. **Contact:** Julie Innes, editor. *Evangel,* published quarterly, is an adult Sunday School paper. "Devotional in nature, it lifts up Christ as the source of salvation and hope. The mission of *Evangel* is to increase the reader's understanding of the nature and character of God and the nature of a life lived for Christ. Material that fits this mission and isn't longer than 1 page will be considered." Estab. 1897 by free Methodist denomination. Circ. less than 10,000. Pays on publication. Publishes ms 18-36 months after acceptance. Submit seasonal poems 1 year in advance. Responds in 4-6 weeks to submissions. Responds in up to 2 months to poems. Seldom comments on rejected poems. Sample copy and writer's guidelines for #10 SASE. "Write 'guidelines request' on your envelope to separate it from the submissions.".

○ *Evangel* is 8 pages, 5.5 x 8.5, printed in 4-color, unbound, color and b&w photos. Weekly distribution. Press run is about 10,000. Subscription: $2.59/quarter (13 weeks).

FICTION Fiction involves people coping with everday crises, making decisions that show spiritual growth. Accepts 3-4 mss/issue; 156-200 mss/year. Publishes 7 new writers/year. Needs true religious/inspirational. "No fiction without any semblance of Christian message or where the message clobbers the reader. Looking for devotional-style short pieces, 500 words or less." Send complete ms. Accepts multiple submissions. **Pays 5¢/word and 2 contributor's copies.**

POETRY Submit no more than 5 poems at a time. Considers simultaneous submissions. Cover letter is preferred. "Poetry must be typed on 8.5x11 white paper. In the upper left-hand corner of each page, include your name, address, and phone number. In the upper right-hand corner of cover page, specify what rights you are offering. One-eighth of the way down the page, give the title. All subsequent material must be double-spaced with 1-inch margins." Accepts about 5% of poetry received. Rarely uses rhyming work. **Pays $10 plus 2 contributor's copies.**

TIPS Desires concise, tight writing that supports a solid thesis and fits the mission expressed in the guidelines.

☯ ❸ ❺ FAITH TODAY

Evangelical Fellowship of Canada, P.O. Box 5885, West Beaver Creek Post Office, Richmond Hill ON L4B 0B8 Canada. (905)479-5885. **Fax:** (905)479-4742. **Website:** www.faithtoday.ca. Bimonthly magazine. "*FT* is the magazine of an association of more than 40 evangelical denominations, but serves evangelicals in all denominations. It focuses on church issues, social issues, and personal faith as they are tied to the Canadian context. Writing should explicitly acknowledge that Canadian evangelical context." Estab. 1983. Circ. 20,000. Byline given. Pays on publication. Offers 30-50% kill fee. Publishes ms an average of 4 months after acceptance. Editorial lead time 4 months. Accepts queries by mail, e-mail, fax. Responds in 6 weeks to queries. Sample copy for SASE in Canadian postage. Guidelines online at www.faithtoday.ca/writers. "View complete back issues at www.faithtoday.ca/digital. Or download 1 of our free apps from www.faithtoday.ca.".

NONFICTION Needs book excerpts, Canadian authors only, essays, Canadian authors only, interview, Canadian subjects only, opinion, religious, news feature. **Buys 75 mss/year.** Query. Length: 400-2,000 words. **Pays $100-500 Canadian.** Sometimes pays expenses of writers on assignment.

REPRINTS Send photocopy. Rarely used. Pays 50% of amount paid for an original article.

PHOTOS State availability. True required. Reviews contact sheets.

TIPS "Query should include brief outline and names of the sources you plan to interview in your research. Use Canadian postage on SASE."

⊘ ⊛ FCA MAGAZINE

Fellowship of Christian Athletes, 8701 Leeds Rd., Kansas City MO 64129. (816)921-0909; (800)289-0909. **Fax:** (816)921-8755. **E-mail:** mag@fca.org. **Website:** www.fca.org/mag. **Contact:** Clay Meyer, editor; Matheau Casner, creative director. **50% freelance written. Prefers to work with published/established writers, but works with a growing number of new/unpublished writers each year.** Published 6 times/year. "We seek to serve as a ministry tool of the Fellowship of Christian Athletes by informing, inspiring, and involving coaches, athletes, and all whom they influence, that they may make an impact for Jesus Christ." Estab. 1959. Circ. 80,000. Byline given. Pays on publication. Publishes ms an average of 4 months after acceptance. Submit seasonal material 6 months in advance. Responds to queries/mss in 3 months. Sample copy for $2 and 9x12 SASE with 3 first-class stamps. Guidelines available at www.fca.org/mag/media-kit.

NONFICTION Needs inspirational, interview (with name athletes and coaches solid in their faith), personal experience, photo feature. **Buys 5-20 mss/year.** "Articles should be accompanied by at least 3 quality photos." Query. Considers electronic submissions via e-mail. Length: 1,000-2,000 words. **Pays $150-400 for assigned and unsolicited articles.**

PHOTOS State availability. Reviews contact sheets. Payment based on size of photo.

TIPS "Profiles and interviews of particular interest to coed athlete, primarily high school and college age. Our graphics and editorial content appeal to youth. The area most open to freelancers is profiles on or interviews with well-known athletes or coaches (male, female, minorities) who have been or are involved in some capacity with FCA."

⊘ ⊛ GUIDEPOSTS MAGAZINE

110 William St., Suite 901, New York NY 10038. **E-mail:** submissions@guidepostsmag.com. **Website:** www.guideposts.com. **40% freelance written. Works with a small number of new/unpublished writers each year.** Monthly magazine featuring personal inspirational stories. *Guideposts* is an inspirational monthly magazine for people of all faiths, in which men and women from all walks of life tell in true, first-person narrative how they overcame obstacles, rose above failures, handled sorrow, gained new spiritual insight, and became more effective people through faith in God. Estab. 1945. Pays on publication. Offers kill fee. Offers 20% kill fee on assigned stories, but not to first-time freelancers. Publishes ms an average of several months after acceptance. Guidelines online.

◗ "Many of our stories are ghosted articles, so the writer would not get a byline unless it was his/her own story. Because of the high volume of mail the magazine receives, we regret we *cannot* return mss, and will contact writers only if their material can be used."

NONFICTION Buys 40-60 unsolicited mss/year. Length: 250-1,500 words. **Pays $100-500.** Pays expenses of writers on assignment.

TIPS "Study the magazine before you try to write for it. Each story must make a single spiritual point that readers can apply to their own daily lives. And it may be easier to just sit down and write them than to have to go through the process of preparing a query. They should be warm, well written, intelligent, and upbeat. We require personal narratives that are true and have some spiritual aspect, but the religious element can be subtle and should *not* be sermonic. A writer succeeds with us if he or she can write a true article using short-story techniques with scenes, drama, tension, and a resolution of the problem presented."

HIGHWAY NEWS

Transport For Christ, P.O. Box 117, 1525 River Rd., Marietta PA 17547. (717)426-9977. **Fax:** (717)426-9980. **E-mail:** editor@transportforchrist.org. **Website:** www.transportforchrist.org. **Contact:** Inge Koenig. **50% freelance written.** Monthly magazine covering trucking and Christianity. "We publish human interest stories, testimonials, and teachings that have a foundation in Biblical/Christian values. Since truck drivers and their families are our primary readers, we publish works that they will find edifying and helpful." Estab. 1957. Circ. 20,000. Byline given. Publishes ms an average of 1 year after acceptance. Submit seasonal material 1 year in advance. Accepts queries by mail, e-mail, fax, if permission is granted by the publisherAccepts simultaneous submissions. Responds in 1 month to queries. Responds in 2 months to mss. Sample copy free. Writer's guidelines by e-mail. ◑ Does not pay writers.

NONFICTION Needs trucking-related essays, general interest, humor, inspirational, interview, personal experience, photo feature, religious, trucking. No sermons full of personal opinions. Nothing of political nature. Send complete ms. Length: 600-800 words.

PHOTOS Send photos. Captions, identification of subjects, model releases required. Reviews prints, GIF/JPEG files. Does not pay for photos.

COLUMNS/DEPARTMENTS From the Road (stories by truckers on the road); Devotionals with Trucking theme; both 600 words. Send complete ms.

FILLERS Needs anecdotes, facts, short humor. Length: 20-200 words.

TIPS "We are especially interested in human interest stories about truck drivers. Find a trucker doing something unusual or good and write a story about him or her. Be sure to send pictures."

HOLINESS TODAY

Nazarene Global Ministry Center, 17001 Prairie Star Pkwy., Lenexa KS 66220. (913)577-0500. **E-mail:** holinesstoday@nazarene.org. **Website:** www.holinesstoday.org. **Contact:** Carmen J. Ringhiser, managing editor; Frank M. Moore, editor-in-chief. *Holiness Today*, published bimonthly online and in print, is the primary print voice of the Church of the Nazarene, with articles geared to enhance holiness living by connecting Nazarenes with our heritage, vision, and mission through real life stories of God at work in the world. *Holiness Today* (print) is 40 pages. Subscription: $12/year U.S. Circ. 20,000.

◕ HORIZONS

100 Witherspoon St., Louisville KY 40202-1396. (502)569-5897. **Fax:** (502)569-8085. **E-mail:** yvonne.hileman@pcusa.org. **Website:** www.pcusa.org/horizons. **Contact:** Yvonne Hileman, assistant editor. Bimonthly. "Magazine owned and operated by Presbyterian Women in the PC(USA), Inc. offering information and inspiration for Presbyterian women by addressing current issues facing the church and the world." Estab. 1988. Circ. 20,000. Pays on publication. Publishes ms an average of 4 months after acceptance. Accepts queries by mail, e-mail, fax. Sample copy for

$4 and 9x12 SAE. Guidelines for writers are on the *Horizons* website.

NONFICTION Needs essays, "Accepts nonfiction articles and essays only, on theme.". Send complete ms by mail, e-mail, or fax. Include contact information. Length: 600-1,800 words. **Pays "an honorarium of no less than $50 per page printed in the magazine—amount will vary depending on time and research required for writing the article."**

FICTION Submit queries and/or complete ms by mail, e-mail, or fax. Include contact information. Length: 600-1,800 words. **Pays an honorarium of no less than $50 per page printed in the magazine—amount will vary depending on time and research required for writing the article.**

◕◕ LIGUORIAN

One Liguori Dr., Liguori MO 63057. (636)223-1538. **Fax:** (636)223-1595. **E-mail:** liguorianeditor@liguori.org. **Website:** www.liguorian.org. **Contact:** Elizabeth Herzing, managing editor. **25% freelance written. Prefers to work with published/established writers.** Magazine published 10 times/year for Catholics. "Our purpose is to lead our readers to a fuller Christian life by helping them better understand the teachings of the gospel and the church and by illustrating how these teachings apply to life and the problems confronting them as members of families, the church, and society." Estab. 1913. Circ. 60,000. Pays on acceptance. Submit seasonal material 8 months in advance. Accepts queries by mail, e-mail, fax. Responds in 3 months to mss. Sample copy for 9x12 SAE with 3 first-class stamps or online. Guidelines for #10 SASE and online.

NONFICTION "No travelogue approach or unresearched ventures into controversial areas. Also, no material found in secular publications—fad subjects that already get enough press, pop psychology, or negative articles. *Liguorian* does not consider *retold* Bible stories." Buys 30-40 unsolicited mss/year. Length: 400-2,200 words. **Pays 12-15¢/word and 5 contributor's copies.**

PHOTOS Photographs on assignment only unless submitted with and specific to article.

FICTION Needs religious, inspirational, senior citizen/retirement. Send complete ms. Length: 1,500-2,200 words. **Pays 12-15¢/word and 5 contributor's copies.**

TIPS "First read several issues containing short stories. We look for originality and creative input in each story we read. Consideration requires the author studies the target market and presents a carefully polished ms. We publish 1 fiction story per issue. Compare this with the 25 or more we receive over the transom each month. We believe fiction is a highly effective mode for transmitting the Christian message; however, many fiction pieces are written without a specific goal or thrust—an interesting incident that goes nowhere is not a story."

⊖⊕ THE LOOKOUT

Standard Publishing, 8805 Governor's Hill Dr., Suite 400, Cincinnati OH 45249. (513)931-4050. **Fax:** (513)931-0950. **E-mail:** lookout@standardpub.com. **Website:** www.lookoutmag.com. **Contact:** Shawn McMullen, editor. **50% freelance written.** Weekly magazine for Christian adults, with emphasis on spiritual growth, family life, and topical issues. "Our purpose is to provide Christian adults with practical, Biblical teaching and current information that will help them mature as believers." Estab. 1894. Circ. 38,000. Byline given. Pays on acceptance. Offers 33% kill fee. Publishes ms an average of 1 year after acceptance. Editorial lead time 9 months. Submit seasonal material 1 year in advance. Accepts queries by mail, e-mail. No previously published materialAccepts simultaneous submissions. Responds in 10 weeks to queries and mss. Sample copy for $1. Guidelines by e-mail or online.

○   Audience is mainly conservative Christians. Mss only accepted by mail.

NONFICTION Needs inspirational, interview, opinion, personal experience, religious. No fiction or poetry. **Buys 100 mss/year.** Send complete ms. Length: 1,200-1,400 words. **Pays 11-17¢/word.**

PHOTOS State availability. Identification of subjects required. Offers no additional payment for photos accepted with ms.

TIPS "*The Lookout* publishes from a theologically conservative, nondenominational, and noncharismatic perspective. We aim primarily for those aged 30-55. Most readers are married and have elementary to young adult children. Our emphasis is on the needs of ordinary Christians who want to grow in their faith. We value well-informed articles that offer lively and clear writing as well as strong application. We often address tough issues and seek to explore fresh ideas or recent developments affecting today's Christians."

THE MENNONITE

718 N. Main St., Newton KS 67114-1703. (866)866-2872 ext. 34398. **Fax:** (316)283-0454. **E-mail:** gordonh@themennonite.org. **Website:** www.themennonite.org. **Contact:** Gordon Houser, associate editor. *The Mennonite*, published monthly, seeks "to help readers glorify God, grow in faith and become agents of healing and hope in the world. Our readers are primarily people in Mennonite churches." Single copy: $3; subscription: $46 U.S. Estab. 1998. Circ. 8,000. Publishes ms up to 1 year after acceptance. Responds in 2 weeks. Guidelines online.

NONFICTION Needs general interest, religious, Bible study, prayer, environment, aging, death/dying, Christmas, Easter, children, parenting, marriage, singleness, racism, peace and justice, worship, health issues, arts, personal stories of Mennonites exercising their faith. Query via e-mail (preferred). Include name, address, phone number, 1-sentence summary of the article and "3 catchy, creative titles. Illustrations, charts, graphs, and photos (in color) to go with the article are welcome." If sending by regular mail, also include an SASE. Length: 1,200-1,500 words for feature articles. **Payment varies. We only pay for solicited articles.**

TIPS "Writing should be concise, accessible to the general reader, and with strong lead paragraphs. This last point cannot be overemphasized. The lead paragraph is the foundation of a good article. It should provide a summary of the article. We are especially interested in personal stories of Mennonites exercising their faith."

MESSAGE OF THE OPEN BIBLE

Open Bible Churches, 2020 Bell Ave., Des Moines IA 50315-1096. (515)288-6761. **Fax:** (515)288-2510. **E-mail:** andrea@openbible.org. **Website:** www.openbible.org. **5% freelance written.** "*The Message of the Open Bible* is the official bimonthly publication of Open Bible Churches. Its readership consists mostly of people affiliated with Open Bible." Estab. 1932. Circ. 2,700. Byline given. Publishes ms an average of 4-6 months after acceptance. Editorial lead time 6 months. Submit seasonal material 6 months in advance. Accepts queries by mail, e-mail. Responds in 1 month to queries. Responds in 2 months to mss. Sample copy for SAE with 9x12 envelope and 3 first-class stamps.

Writer's guidelines for #10 SASE or by e-mail (message@openbible.org).

◯ Does not pay for articles.

NONFICTION Needs inspirational, teachings or challenges, interview, personal experience, religious, testimonies, news. No sermons. Send complete ms. Length: 650 words maximum.

PHOTOS State availability. Reviews 5x7 prints, GIF/ JPEG files. Does not pay for photos.

⊕⊝ MY DAILY VISITOR

Our Sunday Visitor, Inc., Publishing Division, 200 Noll Plaza, Huntington IN 46750. (260)356-8400. **Fax:** (260)356-8472. **E-mail:** mdvisitor@osv.com; mhogan@osv.com. **Website:** www.osv.com. **Contact:** Michelle Hogan, executive assistant. **99% freelance written.** Bimonthly magazine of scripture meditations based on the day's Catholic Mass readings. Circ. 33,000. Byline given. Pays on acceptance. Publishes ms an average of 6 months after acceptance. Accepts queries by mail, e-mail. Responds in 2 months to queries. Sample copy and writer's guidelines for #10 SAE with 3 first-class stamps.

◯ Sample meditations and guidelines online. Each writer does 1 full month of meditations on assignment basis only.

NONFICTION Needs inspirational, personal experience, religious. **Buys 12 mss/year.** Query with published clips. Length: 130-140 words times the number of days in month. **Pays $500 for 1 month (28-31) of meditations and 5 free copies.**

TIPS "Previous experience in writing scripture-based Catholic meditations or essays is helpful."

⊕⊝ ONE

Catholic Near East Welfare Association, 1011 First Ave., New York NY 10022-4195. (212)826-1480. **Fax:** (212)838-1344. **E-mail:** cnewa@cnewa.org. **Website:** www.cnewa.org. **Contact:** Deacon Greg Kandra, executive editor. **75% freelance written.** Bimonthly magazine for a Catholic audience with interest in the Near East, particularly its current religious, cultural and political aspects. Estab. 1974. Circ. 100,000. Byline given. Pays on publication. Publishes ms an average of 6 months after acceptance. Accepts queries by mail, fax. Responds in 1 month to queries. Sample copy and writer's guidelines for 7 1/2 x 10 1/2 SAE with 2 first-class stamps.

NONFICTION Length: 1,200-1,800 words. **Pays 20¢/ edited word.**

PHOTOS "Photographs to accompany ms are welcome; they should illustrate the people, places, ceremonies, etc. which are described in the article. We prefer color transparencies but occasionally use b&w.". Pay varies depending on use—scale from $50-300.

TIPS "We are interested in current events in the Near East as they affect the cultural, political, and religious lives of the people."

⊕⊝ POINT

Converge Worldwide (Baptist General Conference), Mail Code 200, 11002 Lake Hart Dr., Orlando FL 32832. **Fax:** (866)990-8980. **E-mail:** bob.putman@ convergeww.org. **Website:** www.convergeworldwide.org. **15% freelance written.** Nonprofit, religious, evangelical Christian magazine published 4 times/year covering Converge Worldwide. *Point* is the official magazine of Converge Worldwide (BCG). Almost exclusively uses articles related to Converge, their churches, or by/about Converge people. Circ. 43,000. Byline given. Pays on publication. Offers 50% kill fee. Editorial lead time 6 months. Submit seasonal material 6 months in advance. Accepts queries by e-mail. Responds in 1 month to queries. Responds in 3 months to mss. Sample copy for #10 SASE. Guidelines available free.

NONFICTION Buys 10-15 mss/year. Query with published clips. Wnats "articles about our people, churches, missions. View online at: www.convergeworldwide.org. before sending anything." Length: 300-1,500 words. **Pays $60-280.** Sometimes pays expenses of writers on assignment.

PHOTOS State availability. Captions, identification of subjects, model releases required. Reviews prints, some high-resolution digital. Offers $15-60/photo.

COLUMNS/DEPARTMENTS Converge Connection (blurbs of news happening in Converge Worldwide), 50-150 words. Send complete ms and photos. **Pays $30.**

TIPS "Please study the magazine and the denomination. We will send sample copies to interested freelancers and give further information about our publication needs upon request. Freelancers from our churches who are interested in working on assignment are especially welcome."

⊝⊝ PRAIRIE MESSENGER

Benedictine Monks of St. Peter's Abbey, P.O. Box 190, Muenster SK S0K 2Y0 Canada. (306)682-1772. **Fax:** (306)682-5285. **E-mail:** pm.canadian@stpeterspress.ca. **Website:** www.prairiemessenger.ca. **Contact:** Maureen Weber, associate editor. **10% Freelance written.** Weekly Catholic publication published by the Benedictine Monks of St. Peter's Abbey. Has a strong focus on ecumenism, social justice, interfaith relations, aboriginal issues, arts and culture. Estab. 1904. Circ. 5,000. Byline given. Pays on publication. Publishes ms an average of 4 months after acceptance. Submit seasonal material 3 months in advance. Accepts queries by mail, e-mail, fax, phone. Accepts simultaneous submissions. Responds only if interested; send nonreturnable samples. Sample copy for 9x12 SASE with $1 Canadian postage or IRCs. Guidelines online. "Because of government subsidy regulations, we are no longer able to accept non-Canadian freelance material.".

NONFICTION Needs interview, opinion, religious. "No articles on abortion." **Buys 15 mss/year.** Send complete ms. Length: 500-800 words. **Pays $60/article.** Sometimes pays expenses of writers on assignment.

PHOTOS Send photos. Captions required. Reviews 3x5 prints. Offers $25/photo.

❷❸ PRESBYTERIANS TODAY

Presbyterian Church (U.S.A.), 100 Witherspoon St., Louisville KY 40202-1396. (502)569-5520. **Fax:** (502)569-8887. **E-mail:** today@pcusa.org. **Website:** www.pcusa.org/today. **Contact:** Patrick David Heery, editor. **25% freelance written. Prefers to work with published/established writers.** Denominational magazine published 11 times/year covering religion, denominational activities, and public issues for members of the Presbyterian Church (U.S.A.). "The magazine's purpose is to increase understanding and appreciation of what the church and its members are doing to live out their Christian faith." Estab. 1867. Circ. 40,000. Byline given. Pays on acceptance. Offers 50% kill fee. Publishes ms an average of 6 months after acceptance. Editorial lead time 3 months. Submit seasonal material 3 months in advance. Accepts queries by e-mail. Responds in 2 weeks to queries. Sample copy free. Guidelines online.

NONFICTION Needs how-to, inspirational, Presbyterian programs, everyday Christian issues. **Buys 20 mss/year.** Send complete ms. Length: 1,000-1,800 words. **Pays $300 maximum for assigned articles; $75-300 for unsolicited articles.**

PHOTOS State availability. Identification of subjects required. Reviews contact sheets, transparencies, color prints, digital images. Negotiates payment individually.

❸ PURPOSE

1582 Falcon, Hillsboro KS 67063. **E-mail:** CarolD@MennoMedia.org. **Website:** www.mennomedia.org. **Contact:** Carol Duerksen, editor. **75% freelance written.** Magazine focuses on Christian discipleship—how to be a faithful Christian in the midst of everyday life situations. Uses personal story form to present models and examples to encourage Christians in living a life of faithful discipleship. *Purpose*, published monthly by Faith & Life Resources, an imprint of the Mennonite Publishing Network (the official publisher for the Mennonite Church in the US and Canada), is a "religious young adult/adult monthly." Focuses on "action-oriented, discipleship living." Estab. 1968. Circ. 8,500. Pays on acceptance. Publishes ms an average of 18 months after acceptance. Submit seasonal material 1 year in advance. Accepts queries by e-mail. Accepts simultaneous submissions. Responds in 3 months to queries, responds in 6 months to mss. Sample (with guidelines): $2 and 9x12 SAE. Guidelines online: www.faithandliferesources.org/periodicals/purpose.

○ *Purpose* is digest-sized with 4-color printing throughout. Receives about 2,000 poems/year, accepts 150.

NONFICTION Special issues: Needs short, personal true anecdotal stories. Must meet monthly themes (see website). **Buys 140 mss/year.** E-mail submissions preferred. Length: 350-600 words. **Pays $25-50.**

PHOTOS Photos purchased with ms must be sharp enough for reproduction; requires prints in all cases. Captions required.

POETRY Needs free verse, light verse, traditional. Prefers e-mail submissions. Postal submissions should be double-spaced, typed on 1 side of sheet only. Buys 140 poems/year. Length: 12 lines maximum. **Pays $10-20/poem depending on length and quality, plus 2 contributor's copies.**

FILLERS 6¢/word maximum.

TIPS "Many stories are situational, how to respond to dilemmas. Looking for first-person storylines. The story form is an excellent literary device to help readers explore discipleship issues. The first 2 paragraphs are crucial in establishing the mood/issue to be resolved in the story. Work hard on the development of these."

REFORM JUDAISM

633 Third Ave., New York NY 10017-6778. (212)650-4240. **Fax:** (212)650-4249. **E-mail:** rjmagazine@urj.org. **Website:** www.reformjudaismmag.org. **Contact:** Joy Weinberg, managing editor. **30% freelance written.** Quarterly magazine of Jewish issues for contemporary Jews. "*Reform Judaism* is the official voice of the Union for Reform Judaism, linking the institutions and affiliates of Reform Judaism with every Reform Jew. *RJ* covers developments within the movement while interpreting events and Jewish tradition from a Reform perspective." Estab. 1972. Circ. 310,000. Byline given. Pays on publication. Offers kill fee for commissioned articles. Publishes ms an average of 3 months after acceptance. Submit seasonal material 6 months in advance. Accepts simultaneous submissions. Responds in 2 months to queries and to mss. Sample copy for $3.50. Guidelines online.

NONFICTION Buys 30 mss/year. Submit complete ms. SASE is preferable and will elicit a faster response. Cover stories: 2,500-3,500 words; major feature: 1,800-2,500 words; secondary feature: 1,200-1,500 words; department (e.g., travel): 1,200 words. **Pays 30¢/published word.** Sometimes pays expenses of writers on assignment.

REPRINTS Send tearsheet, photocopy or typed ms with rights for sale and information about when and where the material previously appeared. Usually doesn't publish reprints.

PHOTOS Send photos. Identification of subjects required. Reviews 8x10/color or slides, b&w prints, and printouts of electronic images. Payment varies.

FICTION Needs humorous, religious, sophisticated, cutting-edge, superb writing. **Buys 4 mss/year.** Send complete ms. Length: 600-2,500 words. **Pays 30¢/published word.**

TIPS "We prefer a stamped postcard including the following information/checklist: __, we are interested in publishing; __No, unfortunately the submission doesn't meet our needs; __Maybe, we'd like to hold on to the article for now. Submissions sent this way will receive a faster response."

THE SECRET PLACE

American Baptist Home Mission Societies, ABC/USA, P.O. Box 851, Valley Forge PA 19482. (610)768-2434. **E-mail:** thesecretplace@abc-usa.org. **100% freelance written.** Quarterly devotional covering Christian daily devotions. Estab. 1937. Circ. 250,000. Byline given. Pays on acceptance. Editorial lead time 1 year. Submit seasonal material 9 months in advance. For free sample and guidelines, send 6x9 SASE.

NONFICTION Needs inspirational. **Buys about 400 mss/year.** Send complete ms. Length: 100-200 words. **Pays $20.**

POETRY Needs avant-garde, free verse, light verse, traditional. Buys Publishes 12-15 poems/year. poems/year. Submit maximum Maximum number of poems: 6. poems. Length: 4-30 lines. **Pays $20.**

TIPS "Prefers submissions via e-mail."

SEEK

8805 Governor's Hill Dr., Suite 400, Cincinnati OH 45239. (513)931-4050, ext. 351. **E-mail:** seek@standardpub.com. **Website:** www.standardpub.com. "Inspirational stories of faith-in-action for Christian adults; a Sunday School take-home paper." Quarterly. Religious/inspirational, religious fiction and religiously slanted historical and humorous fiction. No poetry. List of upcoming themes online. Accepts 150 mss/year. Send complete ms. Prefers submissions by e-mail. "*SEEK* corresponds to the topics of Standard Publishing's adult curriculum line and is designed to further apply these topics to everyday life. Unsolicited mss must be written to a theme list. Estab. 1970. Circ. 27,000. Byline given. Pays on acceptance. Acceptance to publishing time is 1 year. Accepts queries by e-mail. Writer's guidelines online.

Magazine: 5.5×8.5; 8 pages; newsprint paper; art and photo in each issue.

NONFICTION Send complete ms. **Pays 7 cents/word for first rights; 5 cents/word for reprint rights.**

REPRINTS Reprints pay 5 cents/word.

FICTION Needs religious/inspirational, religious fiction and religiously slanted historical and humorous fiction. Send complete ms. Prefers submissions by e-mail. **Pays 7¢/word.**

TIPS "Write a credible story with a Christian slant—no preachments; avoid overworked themes such as joy in suffering, generation gaps, etc. Most mss are rejected by us because of irrelevant topic or message, unrealistic story, or poor character and/or plot development. We use fiction stories that are believable."

ST. ANTHONY MESSENGER

Franciscan Media, 28 W. Liberty St., Cincinnati OH 45202-6498. (513)241-5615. **Fax:** (513)241-0399. **E-**

mail: mageditors@franciscanmedia.org. **Website:** www.stanthonymessenger.org. **Contact:** John Feister, editor. **55% freelance written.** Monthly general-interest magazine for a national readership of Catholic families, most of which have children or grandchildren in grade school, high school, or college. "*St. Anthony Messenger* is a Catholic family magazine which aims to help its readers lead more fully human and Christian lives. We publish articles that report on a changing church and world, opinion pieces written from the perspective of Christian faith and values, personality profiles, and fiction which entertains and informs." Estab. 1893. Circ. 105,000. Byline given. Pays on acceptance. Publishes ms within an average of 1 year after acceptance. Submit seasonal material 6 months in advance. Accepts queries by mail, e-mail, fax. Responds in 3 weeks to queries. Responds in 2 months to mss. Sample copy for 9x12 SAE with 4 first-class stamps. Please study writers' guidelines at StAnthonyMessenger.org.

NONFICTION Needs how-to, on psychological and spiritual growth, problems of parenting/better parenting, marriage problems/marriage enrichment, humor, inspirational, interview, opinion, limited use; writer must have special qualifications for topic, personal experience, if pertinent to our purpose, photo feature, informational, social issues. **Buys 35-50 mss/year.** Query with published clips. Length: 2,000-2,500 words. **Pays 20¢/word.** Sometimes pays expenses of writers on assignment.

FICTION Needs mainstream, religious, senior citizen/retirement. "We do not want mawkishly sentimental or preachy fiction. Stories are most often rejected for poor plotting and characterization, bad dialogue (listen to how people talk), and inadequate motivation. Many stories say nothing, are 'happenings' rather than stories. No fetal journals, no rewritten Bible stories." **Buys 12 mss/year.** Send complete ms. Length: 2,000-2,500 words. **Pays 20¢/word maximum and 2 contributor's copies; $1 charge for extras.**

POETRY Contact: Poetry Editor. Submit a few poems at a time. "Please include your phone number and a SASE with your submission. Do not send us your entire collection of poetry. Poems must be original." Submit seasonal poems several months in advance. "Our poetry needs are very limited." Submit maximum 4-5 poems. Length: up to 20-25 lines; "the shorter, the better." **Pays $2/line; $20 minimum.**

TIPS "The freelancer should consider why his or her proposed article would be appropriate for us, rather than for *Redbook* or *Saturday Review*. We treat human problems of all kinds, but from a religious perspective. Articles should reflect Catholic theology, spirituality, and employ a Catholic terminology and vocabulary. We need more articles on prayer, scripture, Catholic worship. Get authoritative information (not merely library research); we want interviews with experts. Write in popular style; use lots of examples, stories, and personal quotes. Word length is an important consideration."

TRICYCLE

1115 Broadway Suite 1113, New York NY 10010. (646)461-9847. **E-mail:** editorial@tricycle.com. **Website:** www.tricycle.com. **80% freelance written.** Quarterly magazine providing a unique and independent public forum for exploring Buddhist teachings and practices, establishing a dialogue between Buddhism and the broader culture, and introducing Buddhist thinking to Western disciplines. "*Tricycle* readers tend to be well educated and open minded." Estab. 1991. Circ. 50,000. Byline given. Pays on publication. Offers 25% kill fee. Editorial lead time 3 months. Accepts queries by mail, e-mail (preferable). Accepts simultaneous submissions. Responds in 3 months to queries and mss. Sample copy for $7.95 or online at website. Guidelines online.

NONFICTION Needs book excerpts, essays, general interest, historical, humor, inspirational, interview, personal experience, photo feature, religious, travel. **Buys 4-6 mss/year.** Length: 1,000-5,000 words.

PHOTOS State availability. Captions, identification of subjects required. Reviews contact sheets. Negotiates payment individually.

COLUMNS/DEPARTMENTS Reviews (film, books, tapes), 600 words; Science and Gen Next, both 700 words. **Buys 6-8 mss/year.** Query.

TIPS "For your submission to be considered, we ask that you first send us a 1-page query outlining your idea, relevant information about your writing background and any Buddhist background, your familiarity with the subject of your proposal, and so on. If you have clips or writing samples, please send these along with your proposal."

🌓 💲 U.S. CATHOLIC

Claretian Publications, 205 W. Monroe St., Chicago IL 60606. (312)236-7782. **Fax:** (312)236-8207. **E-**

mail: editors@uscatholic.org. **E-mail:** submissions@ uscatholic.org. **Website:** www.uscatholic.org. **Mostly freelance written.** Monthly magazine covering contemporary issues from a Catholic perspective. "*U.S. Catholic* is dedicated to the belief that it makes a difference whether you're Catholic. We invite and help our readers explore the wisdom of their faith tradition and apply their faith to the challenges of the 21st century." Estab. 1935. Circ. 25,000. Byline given. Pays on acceptance. Publishes ms an average of 6 months after acceptance. Editorial lead time 8 months. Submit seasonal material 6 months in advance. Accepts queries by mail, e-mail. Responds in 1 month to queries. Responds in 2 months to mss. Guidelines online.

🖋 Please include SASE with written ms.

NONFICTION Needs essays, inspirational, opinion, personal experience, religious. **Buys 100 mss/year.** Send complete ms. Length: 700-1,400 words. **Pays minimum $200.**

PHOTOS State availability.

FICTION Contact: Caitlyn Schmid. Accepts short stories. "Topics vary, but unpublished fiction should be no longer than 1,800 words and should include strong characters and cause readers to stop for a moment and consider their relationships with others, the world, and/or God. Specifically religious themes are not required; subject matter is not restricted. E-mail submissions@uscatholic.org. Usually responds in 8-10 weeks. Minimum payment is $200." Needs ethnic, mainstream, religious, slice-of-life vignettes. **Buys 4-6 mss/year.** Send complete ms. Length: 700-1,800 words.

POETRY Contact: Caitlyn Schmid. Needs free verse. Submit 3-5 poems at a time. Lines/poem: 50 maximum. Considers simultaneous submissions; no previously published poems. Accepts e-mail submissions (pasted into body of message; no attachments). Cover letter is preferred. No light verse. Buys 12 poems/year. Submit maximum 5 poems. Length: 50 lines. **Pays $75.**

🌐💲 WOMAN ALIVE

Christian Publishing and Outreach, Garcia Estate, Canterbury Rd., Worthing West Sussex BN13 1BW United Kingdom. (44)(1903) 60-4352. **E-mail:** womanalive@cpo.org.uk. **Website:** www.womanalive. co.uk. **Contact:** Jackie Harris, editor; Wendy Longhurst, editorial assistant. *Woman Alive* is a Christian magazine geared specifically toward women. It cov-

ers all denominations and seeks to inspire, encourage, and provide resources to women in their faith, helping them to grow in their relationship with God and providing practical help and biblical perspective on the issues impacting their lives. Pays on publication. Accepts queries by mail, e-mail. Sample copy for £1.50, plus postage. Guidelines online.

NONFICTION Needs how-to, personal experience, travel; also, building life skills and discipleship, interviews with Christian women in prominent positions or who are making a difference in their communities/jobs, women facing difficult challenges or taking on new challenges, affordable holiday destinations written from a Christian perspective. Submit clips, bio, article summary, ms, SASE. Length: 750-850 words/1-page article; 1,200-1,500 words/2-page article; 1,600-1,800 words/3-page article. **Pays £75/1-page article; £100/2-page article; £130/3-page article.**

PHOTOS Send photos. Reviews 300 dpi digital images.

RETIREMENT

AARP BULLETIN

AARP, 601 E. Street NW, Washington DC 20049. **E-mail:** member@aarp.org. **Website:** www.aarp.org/bulletin. *AARP Bulletin* provides timely insights and news on health, healthy policy, Social Security, consumer protection, and more from an award-winning source.

🖋 Query before submitting. Does not accept unsolicited mss. Difficult market to break into.

💲💲💲💲 AARP THE MAGAZINE

AARP, c/o Editorial Submissions, 601 E. St. NW, Washington DC 20049. **E-mail:** aarpmagazine@aarp.org. **Website:** www.aarp.org/magazine. **50% freelance written. Prefers to work with published/established writers.** Bimonthly magazine covering issues that affect people over the age of 50. *AARP The Magazine* is devoted to the varied needs and active life interests of AARP members, age 50 and over, covering such topics as financial planning, travel, health, careers, retirement, relationships, and social and cultural change. Its editorial content serves the mission of AARP seeking through education, advocacy, and service to enhance the quality of life for all by promoting independence, dignity, and purpose. Circ. 22,721,661. Byline given. Pays on acceptance. Offers 25% kill fee. Publishes ms an average of 6 months after acceptance. Submit seasonal material 6 months in advance. Accepts queries by mail, e-mail only. Responds in 3 months to queries. Sample copy free. Guidelines online.

NONFICTION No previously published articles. Query with published clips. *No unsolicited mss.* Features and departments cover the following categories: finance, health and fitness, food and nutrition, travel, consumerism, general interest, and relationships. Length: Up to 2,000 words. **Pays $1/word.** Sometimes pays expenses of writers on assignment.

PHOTOS Photos purchased with or without accompanying mss. Pays $250 and up for color; $150 and up for b&w.

TIPS "The most frequent mistake made by writers in completing an article for us is poor follow-through with basic research. The outline is often more interesting than the finished piece. We do not accept unsolicited mss."

$ MATURE YEARS

The United Methodist Publishing House, 201 Eighth Ave. S., P.O. Box 801, Nashville TN 37202-0801. (615)749-6292. **Fax:** (615)749-6512. **E-mail:** matureyears@umpublishing.org. **80% freelance written. Prefers to work with published/established writers.** Quarterly magazine designed to help persons in and nearing the retirement years understand and appropriate the resources of the Christian faith in dealing with specific problems and opportunities related to aging. Estab. 1954. Circ. 55,000. Pays on acceptance. Publishes ms an average of 1 year after acceptance. Submit seasonal material 14 months in advance. Responds in 2 weeks to queries. Responds in 2 months to mss. Sample copy for $6 and 9x12 SAE. Writer's guidelines for #10 SASE or by e-mail.

NONFICTION Needs how-to, hobbies, inspirational, religious, travel, special guidelines, older adult health, finance issues. **Buys 75-80 mss/year.** Send complete ms; e-mail submissions preferred. Length: 900-2,000 words. **Pays $45-125.** Sometimes pays expenses of writers on assignment.

REPRINTS Send tearsheet, photocopy, or typed ms with rights for sale noted and information about when and where the material previously appeared. Pays at same rate as for previously unpublished material.

PHOTOS Send photos. Captions, model releases required. Negotiates pay individually.

COLUMNS/DEPARTMENTS Health Hints (retirement, health), 900-1,500 words; Going Places (travel, pilgrimage), 1,000-1,500 words; Fragments of Life (personal inspiration), 250-600 words; Modern Revelations (religious/inspirational), 900-1,500 words; Money Matters (personal finance), 1,200-1,800 words; Merry-Go-Round (cartoons, jokes, 4-6 line humorous verse); Puzzle Time (religious puzzles, crosswords). **Buys 4 mss/year.** Send complete ms. **Pays $25-45.**

POETRY Needs free verse, haiku, light verse, traditional. Submit seasonal and nature poems for spring from December through February; for summer, March through May; for fall, June through August; and for winter, September through November. Accepts fax and e-mail submissions (e-mail preferred). Buys 24 poems/year. Submit maximum 6 poems. Length: 3-16 lines of up to 50 characters maximum. **Pays $5-20.**

TIPS "Practice writing dialogue! Listen to people talk; take notes; master dialogue writing! Not easy, but well worth it! Most inquiry letters are far too long. If you can't sell me an idea in a brief paragraph, you're not going to sell the reader on reading your finished article or story."

RURAL

COUNTRY

The Reader's Digest Association, 5400 S. 60th St., Greendale WI 53129. **E-mail:** editors@country-magazine.com. **Website:** www.country-magazine.com. *Country* celebrates the breathtaking beauty, engaging people, enduring values, and spirutally rewarding lifestyle of the American countryside. Pays on acceptance. Guidelines online.

NONFICTION All stories are considered on speculation, do not send a query. Submit via mail or e-mail. Photos and mss submitted through the mail will not be returned. E-mailed stories should be included in the body of an e-mail or in an attached .doc, .docx, .rtf, or .odt file. Word length usually runs 400-500 words for a 1-page story. **Pays $250 for story submissions that run a page or more.**

PHOTOS To e-mail photos, attach them as a high-res JPG file (at least 1800 x 1200 pixels or 1 MB file size). Requires caption information.

😊😊 HOBBY FARMS

I-5 Publishing, P.O. Box 12106, Lexington KY 40580. **Fax:** (859)243-3699. **E-mail:** hobbyfarms@i5publishing.com. **Website:** www.hobbyfarms.com. **75% freelance written.** Bimonthly magazine covering small farms and rural lifestyle. "*Hobby Farms* is the magazine for rural enthusiasts. Whether you have a small garden or 100 acres, there is something in *Hobby Farms* to educate, enlighten, or inspire you." Estab. 2001. Circ. 252,801. Byline given. Pays on publication. Publishes ms an average of 6 months after acceptance. Editorial lead time 4 months. Submit seasonal material 6 months in advance. Accepts queries by mail, e-mail. Responds in 2 months to queries. Responds in 2 months to mss. Guidelines free.

O   "Writing tone should be conversational, but authoritative."

NONFICTION Needs historical, how-to, farm or livestock management, equipment, etc., interview, personal experience, technical, breed or crop profiles. **Buys 10 mss/year.** Send complete ms. Length: 1,500-2,500 words. Sometimes pays expenses of writers on assignment. Limit agreed upon in advance.

PHOTOS State availability of or send photos. Identification of subjects, model releases required. Reviews GIF/JPEG files. Negotiates payment individually.

TIPS "Please state your specific experience with any aspect of farming (livestock, gardening, equipment, marketing, etc)."

MONADNOCK TABLE: THE GUIDE TO OUR REGION'S FOOD, FARMS, & COMMUNITY

60 West Street, Keene NH 03431. (603)369-2525. **E-mail:** marcia@monadnocktable.com; info@monadnocktable.com. **Website:** www.monadnocktable.com. **Contact:** Marcia Passos Duffy, editor. Quarterly magazine for local food/farms in the Monadnock Region of New Hampshire. Estab. 2010. Circ. 10,000. Byline given. Pays on publication. 25% kill fee. Publishes ms 3 months after acceptance. Editorial lead time 3 months. Submit seasonal material 3 months in advance. Accepts queries by e-mail. Reports in 1 month to queries and mss. Sample copy online. Guidelines are online.

O   "Must be about trends, profiles, etc., of local food and farms in the Monadnock Region of New Hampshire."

NONFICTION Needs book excerpts, essays, how-to, interview, opinion, personal experience. Length: 500-1,000 words. **Pays $75 for profile stories up to 600 words and $125 for features up to 1,200 words.** Sometimes pays expenses of writers on assignment. (limit agreed upon in advance)

PHOTOS Freelancers should state of photos with submission. Captions required. Reviews GIF/JPEG files. Offers no additional payment for photos accepted with ms.

COLUMNS/DEPARTMENTS Local Farmer (profile of local farmer in Monadnock Region), up to 600 words; Local Eats (profile of local chef and/or restaurant using local food), up to 600 words; Feature (how-to or "think" piece about local foods), up 1,000; Books/Opinion/Commentary (review of books, book excerpt, commentary, opinion pieces about local food), up to 500 words. **Buys 10 mss/year.** Query.

TIPS "Please query first with your qualifications. Please read magazine first for style (magazines online). Must have a local (Monadnock Region, New Hampshire) angle."

😊😊 RANGE MAGAZINE

Purple Coyote Corp., 106 E. Adams St., Suite 201, Carson City NV 89706. (775)884-2200. **Fax:** (775)884-2213. **E-mail:** edit@rangemagazine.com. **Website:** www.rangemagazine.com. **Contact:** C.J. Hadley, editor/publisher. **70% freelance written.** Award-winning quarterly magazine covering ranching, farming, and the issues that affect agriculture. *RANGE* magazine is devoted to the issues that threaten the West, its people, lifestyles, lands and wildlife. No stranger to controversy, *RANGE* is the leading forum for opposing viewpoints in the search for solutions that will halt the deletion of a national resource, the American rancher. Estab. 1991. Pays on publication. Publishes ms an average of 3-6 months after acceptance. Accepts queries by e-mail. Responds in 4-8 weeks to queries. Responds in 1-4 months to mss. Sample copy for $2. Guidelines online.

NONFICTION Needs major ranch features in American West, issues that affect ranchers, profiles, short book excerpts that suit range, humor, photo essays. No sports or events. No book reviews. Writer must be familiar with *RANGE*. Query. Length: 500-2,000 words. **Pays $50-500.**

PHOTOS Contact: C.J. Hadley, editor/publisher. State availability of photography. Captions and identification must be included with all photos. Reviews high-res digitals on disk or flash drive with contact sheets. FTP site available. Slides and prints also reviewed. Pays $25-75, $100 for cover.

$ RURAL HERITAGE

P.O. Box 2067, Cedar Rapids IA 52406. (319)362-3027. **E-mail:** info@ruralheritage.com. **Website:** www.ruralheritage.com. **Contact:** Joe Mischka, editor. **98% freelance written. Willing to work with a small number of new/unpublished writers.** Bimonthly magazine devoted to the training and care of draft animals. Estab. 1976. Circ. 9,500. Byline given. Pays on publication. Publishes ms an average of 6 months after acceptance. Submit seasonal material 6 months in advance. Accepts queries by mail, e-mail. Responds in 3 months to queries. Sample copy for $8. Guidelines online.

NONFICTION Needs how-to, farming with draft animals, interview, people using draft animals, photo feature. No articles on *mechanized* farming. **Buys 200 mss/year.** Query or send complete ms. Length: 1,200-1,500 words. **Pays 5¢/word.**

PHOTOS 6 covers/year, animals in harness $200. Photo guidelines with #10 SASE or online. Captions, identification of subjects required. Pays $10.

POETRY Needs traditional. **Pays $5-25.**

TIPS "Thoroughly understand our subject: working draft animals in harness. We'd like more pieces on plans and instructions for constructing various horse-drawn implements and vehicles. Always welcome are: 1.) Detailed descriptions and photos of horse-drawn implements, 2.) Prices and other details of draft animal and implement auctions and sales."

$$ RURALITE

P.O. Box 558, Forest Grove OR 97116-0558. (503)357-2105. **Fax:** (503)357-8615. **E-mail:** editor@ruralite.org. **E-mail:** curtisc@ruralite.org. **Website:** www.ruralite.org. **Contact:** Curtis Condon, editor. **80% freelance written. Works with new, unpublished writers.** Monthly magazine aimed at members of consumer-owned electric utilities throughout 7 western states. General-interest publication used by 48 rural electric cooperatives and PUDs. Readers are predominantly rural and small-town residents interested in stories about people and issues that affect Northwest lifestyles. Estab. 1954. Circ. 330,000. Byline given. Pays on acceptance. Accepts queries by mail. Responds in 1 month to queries. Sample copy for 9x12 SAE with $1.61 of postage affixed. Guidelines online.

NONFICTION Buys 50-60 mss/year. Query. Length: 100-2,000 words. **Pays $50-500.**

REPRINTS Send typed ms with rights for sale noted and information about when and where the material previously appeared.

PHOTOS Illustrated stories are the key to a sale. Stories without art rarely make it. Color prints/negatives, color slides, all formats accepted. No black & white. Inside color is $25-100; cover photo is $250-350.

TIPS "Study recent issues. Follow directions when given an assignment. Be able to deliver a complete package (story and photos). We're looking for regular contributors to whom we can assign topics from our story list after they've proven their ability to deliver quality mss."

SCIENCE

$$$$ AMERICAN ARCHAEOLOGY

The Archaeological Conservancy, 5301 Central Ave. NE, #902, Albuquerque NM 87108. (505)266-9668. **Fax:** (505)266-0311. **E-mail:** tacmag@nm.net. **Website:** www.americanarchaeology.org. **Contact:** Michael Bawaya, editor; Vicki Singer, art director. **60% freelance written.** Quarterly magazine. "We're a popular archaeology magazine. Our readers are very interested in this science. Our features cover important digs, prominent archaeologists, and most any aspect of the science. We only cover North America." Estab. 1997. Circ. 35,000. Byline given. Pays on acceptance. Offers 20% kill fee. Publishes ms an average of 3 months after acceptance. Editorial lead time 3 months. Accepts queries by mail, e-mail, fax. Responds in 3 weeks to queries. Responds in 1 month to mss

NONFICTION No fiction, poetry, humor. **Buys 15 mss/year.** Query with published clips. Length: 1,500-3,000 words. **Pays $1,000-2,000.** Pays expenses of writers on assignment.

PHOTOS State availability. Identification of subjects required. Reviews transparencies, prints. Pays $50 and up for occasional stock images; assigns work by project (pay varies); negotiable. **Pays on acceptance.** Credit line given. Buys one-time rights. Offers $400-600/photo shoot. Negotiates payment individually.

TIPS "Read the magazine. Features must have a considerable amount of archaeological detail."

$$$$ ARCHAEOLOGY

Archaeological Institute of America, 36-36 33rd St., Long Island NY 11106. (718)472-3050. **Fax:** (718)472-

3051. **E-mail:** cvalentino@archaeology.org. **E-mail:** editorial@archaeology.org. **Website:** www.archaeology.org. **Contact:** Editor-in-chief. **50% freelance written.** *ARCHAEOLOGY* combines worldwide archaeological findings with photography, specially rendered maps, drawings, and charts. Covers current excavations and recent discoveries, and includes personality profiles, technology updates, adventure, travel and studies of ancient cultures. "*ARCHAEOLOGY* magazine is a publication of the Archaeological Institute of America, a 130-year-old nonprofit organization. The magazine has been published continuously for more than 60 years. We have a total audience of nearly 750,000, mostly in the United States and Canada. Our readership is a combination of the general public, enthusiastic amateurs, and scholars in the field. Publishing bimonthly, we bring our readers all the exciting aspects of archaeology: adventure, discovery, culture, history, technology, and travel. Authors include both professional journalists and professional archaeologists. If you are a scientist interested in writing about your research for *ARCHAEOLOGY*, see tips and suggestions on writing for a general audience online." Estab. 1948. Circ. 750,000. Byline given. Pays on acceptance. Offers 25% kill fee. Submit seasonal material 6 months in advance. Accepts queries by mail, e-mail, fax. Accepts simultaneous submissions. Sample copy and writer's guidelines free. Guidelines online. Request photographer's sample copy for $6 through paypal to scribblesbyshannon@yahoo.com.

NONFICTION Needs essays, general interest. "Our reviews department looks for short (250- to 500-word) articles on museums, books, television shows, movies, websites, and games of interest to our readers. While the material reviewed may not be purely archaeological in nature, it should have a strong archaeological element to it. Reviews should not simply summarize the material, but provide a critical evaluation.". **Buys 6 mss/year.** Query preferred. "Preliminary queries should be no more than 1 or 2 pages (500 words max.) in length and may be sent to the Editor-in-Chief by mail or via e-mail to editorial@archaeology.org. We do not accept telephone queries. Check our online index and search to make sure that we have not already published a similar article. Your query should tell us the following: who you are, why you are qualified to cover the subject, how you will cover the subject (with an emphasis on narrative structure, new knowledge, etc.), and why our readers would be interested in the subject." Length: 1,000-3,000 words. **Pays $2,000 maximum.** Sometimes pays expenses of writers on assignment.

PHOTOS Clips and credentials are helpful. While illustrations are not the sole responsibility of the author, it helps to give us a sense of how the article could be illustrated; if possible, e-mail an example of 2 or 3 images that might accompany the article (noting where and from whom such images may be obtained). Please do not e-mail unusually large images or too many images at a time; we will request additional ones if needed. Please do not mail us unsolicited CDs, transparencies, or slides as they will not be returned. If you do not have access to images, referrals to professional photographers with relevant material are appreciated. Send photos. Identification of subjects, True required. Reviews 4x5 color transparencies, 35mm color slides.

COLUMNS/DEPARTMENTS Insider is a piece of about 2,500 words dealing with subject matter with which the author has an intimate, personal interest. **Conversation** is a one-page interview in a Q&A format with someone who has made a considerable impact on the field of archaeology or has done something unusual or intriguing. **Letter From...** is an account of a personal experience involving a particular topic or site. "Letters" have included a visit to an alien-archaeology theme park, the account of an archaeologist caught in a civil war, and an overnight stay with the guards at Angkor Wat. "Letters" are usually about 2,500 to 3,000 words in length. **Artifact** is the last editorial page of the magazine. Its purpose is to introduce the reader to a single artifact that reveals something surprising about a site or an historical event. Unusual artifacts recently excavated are preferred and visuals must be of the highest quality. The writer must explain the archaeological context, date, site found, etc., as well as summarize the artifact's importance in about 200 words or less. First person accounts by the actual excavators or specialists are preferred, although exceptions are be made.

TIPS "We reach nonspecialist readers interested in art, science, history, and culture. Our reports, regional commentaries, and feature-length articles introduce readers to recent developments in archaeology worldwide."

⊖⊖ ASTRONOMY

Kalmbach Publishing, 21027 Crossroads Circle, P.O. Box 1612, Waukesha WI 53187-1612. (800)533-6644.

Fax: (262)798-6468. **Website:** www.astronomy.com. David J. Eicher, editor. **Contact:** LuAnn Williams Belter, art director (for art and photography). **50% of articles submitted and written by science writers; includes commissioned and unsolicited.** Monthly magazine covering the science and hobby of astronomy. "Half of our magazine is for hobbyists (who are active observers of the sky); the other half is directed toward armchair astronomers who are intrigued by the science." Estab. 1973. Circ. 108,000. Byline given. Pays on acceptance. Does pay a kill fee, although rarely used. Responds in 1 month to queries. Responds in 3 months to mss. online.

NONFICTION Needs book excerpts, new product, announcements, photo feature, technical, space, astronomy. **Buys 75 mss/year.** Please query on all article ideas Length: 500-3,000 words. **Pays $100-1,000.**

TIPS "Submitting to *Astronomy* could be tough—take a look at how technical astronomy is. But if someone is a physics teacher or an amateur astronomer, he or she might want to study the magazine for a year to see the sorts of subjects and approaches we use, and then submit a proposal. Submission guidelines online."

CHEMMATTERS

1155 16th St., NW, Washington DC 20036. (202)872-6164. **Fax:** (202)833-7732. **E-mail:** chemmatters@acs.org. **Website:** www.acs.org/chemmatters. **Contact:** Patrice Pages, editor; Cornithia Harris, art director. Covers content covered in a standard high school chemistry textbook. Estab. 1983. Pays on acceptance. Publishes ms 6 months after acceptance. Accepts queries by mail, e-mail. Accepts simultaneous submissions. Responds to queries/mss in 4 weeks. Sample copies free for 10x13 SASE and 3 first-class stamps. Writer's guidelines free for SASE (available as e-mail attachment upon request).

NONFICTION Query with published clips. **Pays $500-1,000 for article. Additional payment for mss/illustration packages and for photos accompanying articles.**

TIPS "Be aware of the content covered in a standard high school chemistry textbook. Choose themes and topics that are timely, interesting, fun, *and* that relate to the content and concepts of the first-year chemistry course. Articles should describe real people involved with real science. Best articles feature young people making a difference or solving a problem."

POPULAR SCIENCE

Bonnier Corporation, 2 Park Ave., 9th Floor, New York NY 10016. **Website:** www.popsci.com. **Contact:** Jill C. Shomer, managing editor. **50% freelance written.** Monthly magazine for the well-educated adult, interested in science, technology, new products. *Popular Science* is devoted to exploring (and explaining) to a nontechnical, but knowledgeable, readership the technical world around us. Covers all of the sciences, engineering, and technology, and above all, products. Especially focused on the new, the ingenious, and the useful. Contributors should be as alert to the possibility of selling pictures and short features as they are to major articles. Estab. 1872. Circ. 1,450,000. Byline given. Pays on acceptance. Offers 25% kill fee. Editorial lead time 3 months. Accepts queries by mail, e-mail, fax. Responds in 1 month to queries. Guidelines online.

NONFICTION *Popular Science* welcomes pitches from writers who want to tell amazing stories about scientific and technological advances in every realm. Query should include a brief summary of the proposed article and provide some indication of a plan to execute the reporting. Links to past work might also be helpful. Reads every query but will respond only to those that are under serious consideration.

TIPS "Probably the easiest way to break in here is by covering a news story in science and technology that we haven't heard about yet. We need people to be acting as scouts for us out there, and we are willing to give the most leeway on these performances. We are interested in good, sharply focused ideas in all areas we cover. We prefer a vivid, journalistic style of writing, with the writer taking the reader along with him, showing the reader what he saw, through words."

❸❸❸❸ SCIENTIFIC AMERICAN

75 Varick St., 9th Floor, New York NY 10013-1917. (212)451-8200. **E-mail:** editors@sciam.com. **Website:** www.sciam.com. **Contact:** Mariette DiChristina, editor-in-chief. Monthly magazine covering developments and topics of interest in the world of science. "*Scientific American* brings its readers directly to the wellspring of exploration and technological innovation. The magazine specializes in first-hand accounts by the people who actually do the work. Their personal experience provides an authoritative perspective on future growth. Over 100 of our authors have won Nobel Prizes. Complementing those articles

are regular departments written by *Scientific American*'s staff of professional journalists, all specialists in their fields. *Scientific American* is the authoritative source of advance information. Authors are the first to report on important breakthroughs, because they're the people who make them. It all goes back to *Scientific American*'s corporate mission: to link those who use knowledge with those who create it." Estab. 1845. Circ. 710,000. Byline given. Pays on publication. Guidelines online.

NONFICTION Query before submitting. **Pays $1/word average.** Pays expenses of writers on assignment.

SCIENCE FICTION, FANTASY AND HORROR

ANALOG SCIENCE FICTION & FACT

Dell Magazines, 267 Broadway, 4th Floor, New York NY 10007-2352. (212)686-7188. **Fax:** (212)686-7414. **E-mail:** analog@dellmagazines.com. **Website:** www.analogsf.com. **Contact:** Dr. Stanley Schmidt, editor. **100% freelance written. Eager to work with new/unpublished writers.** *Analog* seeks "solidly entertaining stories exploring solidly thought-out speculative ideas. But the ideas, and consequently the stories, are always new. Real science and technology have always been important in *ASF,* not only as the foundation of its fiction, but as the subject of articles about real research with big implications for the future." Estab. 1930. Circ. 50,000. Byline given. Pays on acceptance. Publishes ms an average of 10 months after acceptance. Accepts queries by mail. Responds to mss in 2-3 months. Sample copy for $5 and SASE. Guidelines online.

💬 Fiction published in *Analog* has won numerous Nebula and Hugo Awards.

NONFICTION Needs fact articles. **Buys 11 mss/year.** Send complete ms. Submit via online submissions manager (preferred) or postal mail. Does not accept e-mail submissions. Length: up to 5,000 words. **Pays 7¢/word.**

FICTION Wants "science fiction stories. That is, stories in which some aspect of future science or technology is so integral to the plot that, if that aspect were removed, the story would collapse. The science can be physical, sociological, or psychological. The technology can be anything from electronic engineering to biogenetic engineering. But the stories must be strong and realistic, with believable people doing believable things—no matter how fantastic the background might be." Submit via online submissions manager (preferred) or postal mail. Does not accept e-mail submissions. Needs science fiction, hard science/technological, soft/sociological. No fantasy or stories in which the scientific background is implausible or plays no essential role. **Buys 60-100 unsolicited mss/year.** Submit via online submissions manager. Prefers lengths between 2,000-7,000 words for shorts, 10,000-20,000 words for novelettes, and 40,000-80,000 for serials. **Analog pays 7-9¢/word for short stories up to 7,500 words, $525-675 for stories between 7,500 and 10,000 words, and 7-7.5¢/word for longer material.**

TIPS "I'm looking for irresistibly entertaining stories that make me think about things in ways I've never done before. Read several issues to get a broad feel for our tastes, but don't try to imitate what you read."

$ APEX MAGAZINE

Apex Publications, LLC, P.O. Box 24323, Lexington KY 40524. (859)312-3974. **E-mail:** jason@apexbookcompany.com. **Website:** www.apexbookcompany.com. **100% freelance written.** Monthly e-zine publishing dark speculative fiction. "An elite repository for new and seasoned authors with an other-worldly interest in the unquestioned and slightly bizarre parts of the universe." Estab. 2004. Circ. 13,000 unique visits per month. Byline given. Pays on publication. Offers 30% kill fee. Publishes ms an average of 2 months after acceptance. Editorial lead time 2 months. Submit seasonal material 2 months in advance. Accepts queries by e-mail. Responds in 20-30 days to queries and to mss. Sample copy online. Guidelines online.

💬 "We want science fiction, fantasy, horror, and mash-ups of all three of the dark, weird stuff down at the bottom of your little literary heart." Monthly e-zine publishing dark speculative fiction. Circ. 10,000 unique visits per month. Nonfiction Pays writer expenses: No. Buys 24 mss/year. Send complete ms. Length: 100-7,500 words. Pays $0.05/word.

FICTION Needs science fiction. **Buys 24 mss/year.** Send complete ms. Length: 100-7,500 words. **Pays 5¢/word.**

$ ASIMOV'S SCIENCE FICTION

Dell Magazine Fiction Group, 267 Broadway, 4th Floor, New York NY 10007. (212)686-7188. **Fax:** (212)686-7414. **E-mail:** asimovssf@dellmagazines.com. **Website:** www.asimovs.com. **Contact:** Sheila

Williams, editor; Victoria Green, senior art director. **98% freelance written. Works with a small number of new/unpublished writers each year.** *Asimov's*, published 10 times/year, including 2 double issues, is 5.875x8.625 (trim size); 112 pages; 30 lb. newspaper; 70 lb. to 8 pt. C1S cover stock; illustrations; rarely photos. "Magazine consists of science fiction and fantasy stories for adults and young adults. Publishes the best short science fiction available." Estab. 1977. Circ. 50,000. Pays on acceptance. Publishes ms an average of 6-12 months after acceptance. Accepts queries by mail. Responds in 2 months to queries. Responds in 3 months to mss. Sample copy for $5. Guidelines for #10 SASE or online.

💬 Named for a science fiction "legend," *Asimov's* regularly receives Hugo and Nebula Awards. Editor Gardner Dozois has received several awards for editing including Hugos and those from *Locus* magazine.

FICTION Wants "science fiction primarily. Some fantasy and humor. It is best to read a great deal of material in the genre to avoid the use of some very old ideas." Submit ms via online submissions manager or postal mail; no e-mail submissions. Needs fantasy, science fiction, hard science, soft sociological. No horror or psychic/supernatural, sword and sorcery, explicit sex or violence that isn't integral to the story. Would like to see more hard science fiction. **Buys 10 mss/issue mss/year.** Length: 750-15,000 words. **Pays 7-9¢/word for short stories up to 7,500 words; 7-7.5¢/word for longer material. Works between 7,500-10,000 words by authors who make more than 7¢/word for short stories will receive a flat rate that will be no less than the payment would be for a shorter story.).**

POETRY Submit ms via online submissions manager or postal mail; no e-mail submissions. Recently published poetry by PMF Johnson, Suzanne Palmer, Robert Borksi, and Geoffrey A. Landis. Length: 40 lines maximum. **Pays $1/line.**

TIPS "In general, we're looking for 'character-oriented' stories, those in which the characters, rather than the science, provide the main focus for the reader's interest. Serious, thoughtful, yet accessible fiction will constitute the majority of our purchases, but there's always room for the humorous as well."

$ LEADING EDGE

4087 JKB, Provo UT 84602. **E-mail:** editor@leadingedgemagazine.com; fiction@leadingedgemagazine.com; art@leadingedgemagazine.com. **Website:** www.leadingedgemagazine.com. **Contact:** Diane Cardon, senior editor. **90% freelance written.** Semiannual magazine covering science fiction and fantasy. "We strive to encourage developing and established talent and provide high-quality speculative fiction to our readers." Does not accept mss with sex, excessive violence, or profanity. "*Leading Edge* is a magazine dedicated to new and upcoming talent in the fields of science fiction and fantasy." Estab. 1981. Circ. 200. Byline given. Pays on publication. Publishes ms an average of 2-4 months after acceptance. Responds in 2-4 months to mss. Single copy: $5.95. "We no longer provide subscriptions, but *Leading Edge* is now available on Amazon Kindle, as well as print-on-demand.". Guidelines online at website.

💬 Accepts unsolicited submissions.

FICTION Needs fantasy, science fiction. **Buys 14-16 mss/year.** Send complete ms with cover letter and SASE. Include estimated word count. Length: 15,000 words maximum. **Pays 1¢/word; $10 minimum.**

POETRY Needs avant-garde, haiku, light verse, traditional. "Publishes 2-4 poems per issue. Poetry should reflect both literary value and popular appeal and should deal with science fiction- or fantasy-related themes." Submit 1 or more poems at a time. No e-mail submissions. Cover letter is preferred. Include name, address, phone number, length of poem, title, and type of poem at the top of each page. Please include SASE with every submission." Submit maximum 10 poems. Pays $10 for first 4 pages; $1.50/each subsequent page.

TIPS "Buy a sample issue to know what is currently selling in our magazine. Also, make sure to follow the writer's guidelines when submitting."

THE MAGAZINE OF FANTASY & SCIENCE FICTION

P.O. Box 3447, Hoboken NJ 07030. (201) 876-2551. **E-mail:** fandsf@aol.com. **Website:** www.fandsf.com. **Contact:** Gordon Van Gelder, editor. **100% freelance written.** "*The Magazine of Fantasy and Science Fiction* publishes various types of science fiction and fantasy short stories and novellas, making up about 80% of each issue. The balance of each issue is devoted to articles about science fiction, a science column, book and film reviews, cartoons, and competitions." Bimonthly. Estab. 1949. Circ. 40,000. Byline given. Pays on acceptance. Publishes ms an average of 9-12 months after acceptance. Submit seasonal material 8 months in advance. Responds in 2 months to queries. Sample copy for $6. Guidelines for SASE, by e-mail or website.

COLUMNS/DEPARTMENTS Curiosities (reviews of odd and obscure books), 270 words max. Accepts 6 mss/year. Query. **Pays $50.**

FICTION Contact: Gordon Van Gelder, Editor. "Prefers character-oriented stories. We receive a lot of fantasy fiction, but never enough science fiction." Needs adventure, fantasy, horror, space fantasy, sword & sorcery, dark fantasy, futuristic, psychological, supernatural, science fiction, hard science/technological, soft/sociological. **Buys Accepts 60-90/mss. mss/year.** No electronic submissions. Send complete ms. Length: up to 25,000 words **Pays 7-10¢/word**.

POETRY Wants only poetry that deals with the fantastic or the science fictional. Has published poetry by Rebecca Kavaler, Elizabeth Bear, Sophie M. White, and Robert Frazier. "I buy poems very infrequently—just when one hits me right." **Pays $50/poem and 2 contributor's copies.**

TIPS "Good storytelling makes a submission stand out. Regarding mss, a well-prepared ms (i.e., one that follows the traditional format, like that described here: www.sfwa.org/writing/vonda/vonda.htm) stands out more than any gimmicks. Read an issue of the magazine before submitting. New writers should keep their submissions under 15,000 words—we rarely publish novellas by new writers."

ON SPEC

P.O. Box 4727, Station South, Edmonton AB T6E 5G6 Canada. (780)628-7121. **E-mail:** onspec@onspec.ca. **E-mail:** onspecmag@gmail.com. **Website:** www.onspec.ca. **95% freelance written.** Quarterly magazine covering Canadian science fiction, fantasy, and horror. "We publish speculative fiction and poetry by new and established writers, with a strong preference for Canadian-authored works." Estab. 1989. Circ. 2,000. Byline given. Pays on acceptance. Publishes ms an average of 6-18 months after acceptance. Editorial lead time 6 months. Accepts queries by mail. Accepts simultaneous submissions. Responds in 2 weeks to queries; 6 months after deadline to mss. Sample copy for $8. Guidelines for #10 SASE or online.

See website guidelines for submission announcements. "Please refer to website for information regarding submissions, as we are not open year-round."

FICTION Needs fantasy, horror, science fiction, magic realism, ghost stories, fairy stories. No media tie-in or shaggy-alien stories. No condensed or excerpted novels, religious/inspirational stories, fairy tales. **Buys 50 mss/year.** Send complete ms. Electronic submissions preferred. Length: 1,000-6,000 words.

POETRY Needs avant-garde, free verse. No rhyming or religious material. Buys 6 poems/year. Submit maximum 10 poems. Length: 4-100 lines. **Pays $50 and 1 contributor's copy.**

TIPS "We want to see stories with plausible characters, a well-constructed, consistent, and vividly described setting, a strong plot and believable emotions; characters must show us (not tell us) their emotional responses to each other and to the situation and/or challenge they face. Also: Don't send us stories written for television. We don't like media tie-ins, so don't watch TV for inspiration! Read instead! Strong preference given to submissions by Canadians."

SCIFAIKUEST

P.O. Box 782, Cedar Rapids IA 52406. **E-mail:** gatrix65@yahoo.com. **Website:** albanlake.com/scifaikuest. **Contact:** Tyree Campbell, managing editor; Teri Santitoro, editor. *Scifaikuest*, published quarterly both online and in print, features "science fiction/fantasy/horror minimalist poetry, especially scifaiku, and related forms. We also publish articles about various poetic forms and reviews of poetry collections. The online and print versions of *Scifaikuest* are different." Wants "artwork, scifaiku, and speculative minimalist forms such as tanka, haibun, ghazals, senryu. No 'traditional' poetry." Has published poetry by Tom Brinck, Oino Sakai, Deborah P. Kolodji, Aurelio Rico Lopez III, Joanne Morcom, and John Dunphy. *Scifaikuest* (print edition) is 32 pages, digest-sized, offset-printed, perfect-bound, with color cardstock cover, includes ads. Receives about 500 poems/year, accepts about 160 (32%). Press run is 100/issue; 5 distributed free to reviewers. Single copy: $7; subscription: $20/year, $37 for 2 years. Make checks payable to Tyree Campbell/Alban Lake Publishing. Member: The Speculative Literature Foundation. *Scifaikuest* was voted #1 poetry magazine in the 2004 Preditors & Editors poll. Estab. 2003. Responds in 6-8 weeks. Guidelines online.

POETRY Submit 5 poems at a time. Accepts e-mail submissions (pasted into body of message). No disk submissions; artwork as e-mail attachment or inserted body of e-mail. "Submission should include snail-mail address and a short (1-2 lines) bio." Reads submissions year round. Submit seasonal poems 6 months in advance. Time between acceptance and publication is 1-2 months. "Editor Teri Santitoro makes all decisions regarding acceptances." Often comments on rejected poems. Lines/poem: varies, depending on poem type. **Pays $1/poem, $4/review or article, and 1 contributor's copy.**

SUSPENSE MAGAZINE

JRSR Ventures, 26500 W. Agoura Rd., Suite 102-474, Calabasas CA 91302. **Fax:** (310)626-9670. **E-mail:** editor@suspensemagazine.com; john@suspensemagazine.com. **Website:** www.suspensemagazine.com. **Contact:** John Raab, publisher/CEO/editor-in-chief. **100% freelance written.** Monthly consumer magazine covering suspense, mystery, thriller, and horror genre. Estab. 2007. Pays on acceptance. Pays 100% kill fee. Publishes ms 6-9 months after acceptance. Editorial lead time is 6-9 months. Accepts queries by e-mail. Responds in 1-2 weeks to queries; 2-3 months to mss.

NONFICTION Needs true crime. Query. Length: 1,000-3,000 words. **Pays commissions only, by assignment only.**

COLUMNS/DEPARTMENTS Book Reviews (reviews for newly released fiction); Graphic Novel Reviews (reviews for comic books/graphic novels), 250-1,000 words. **Buys 6-12 mss/year.** Query. **Pays by assignment only**

FICTION Needs horror, mystery, suspense, thrillers. No explicit scenes. **Buys 15-30 mss/year.** Query. Length: 500-5,000 words.

TIPS "Unpublished writers are welcome and encouraged to query. Our emphasis is on horror, suspense, thriller, and mystery."

$ TALES OF THE TALISMAN

Hadrosaur Productions, P.O. Box 2194, Mesilla Park NM 88047-2194. **E-mail:** hadrosaur@zianet.com. **Website:** www.talesofthetalisman.com. **Contact:** David Lee Summers, editor. **95% freelance written.** Quarterly magazine covering science fiction and fantasy. "*Tales of the Talisman* is a literary science fiction and fantasy magazine. We publish short stories, poetry, and articles with themes related to science fiction and fantasy. Above all, we are looking for thought-provoking ideas and good writing. Speculative fiction set in the past, present, and future is welcome. Likewise, contemporary or historical fiction is welcome as long as it has a mythic or science fictional element. Our target audience includes adult fans of the science fiction and fantasy genres along with anyone else who enjoys thought-provoking and entertaining writing." Estab. 1995. Circ. 200. Byline given. Pays on acceptance. Offers 100% kill fee. Publishes ms an average of 9 months after acceptance. Editorial lead time 9-12 months. Submit seasonal material 1 year in advance. Accepts queries by mail, e-mail. Responds in 1 week to queries. Responds in 1 month to mss. Sample copy for $8. Guidelines online.

💬 Fiction and poetry submissions are limited to reading periods of January 1-February 15 and July 1-August 15.

NONFICTION Needs interview, technical, articles on the craft of writing. "We do not want to see unsolicited articles—please query first if you have an idea that you think would be suitable for *Tales of the Talisman*'s audience. We do not want to see negative or derogatory articles." **Buys 1-3 mss/year.** Query. Length: 1,000-3,000 words. **Pays $10 for assigned articles.**

FICTION Contact: David L. Summers, editor. Needs fantasy, space fantasy, sword and sorcery, horror, science fiction, hard science/technological, soft/sociological. "We do not want to see stories with graphic violence. Do not send 'mainstream' fiction with no science fictional or fantastic elements. Do not send stories with copyrighted characters, unless you're the copyright holder." **Buys 25-30 mss/year.** Send complete ms. Length: 1,000-6,000 words. **Pays $6-10.**

POETRY Needs avant-garde, free verse, haiku, light verse, traditional. "Do not send 'mainstream' poetry with no science fictional or fantastic elements. Do not send poems featuring copyrighted characters, unless you're the copyright holder." Buys 24-30 poems/year. Submit maximum 5 poems. Length: 3-50 lines.

TIPS "Let your imagination soar to its greatest heights and write down the results. Above all, we are looking for thought-provoking ideas and good writing. Our emphasis is on character-oriented science fiction and fantasy. If we don't believe in the people living the story, we generally won't believe in the story itself."

SEX

$$$$⊘ PENTHOUSE

General Media Communications, 2 Penn Plaza, 11th Floor, New York NY 10121. (212)702-6000. **Fax:** (212)702-6279. **E-mail:** pbloch@pmgi.com. **Website:**

www.penthouse.com. Monthly magazine. *Penthouse* is for the sophisticated male. Its editorial scope ranges from outspoken contemporary comment to photography essays of beautiful women. *Penthouse* features interviews with personalities, sociological studies, humor, travel, food and wine, and fashion and grooming for men. Estab. 1969. Circ. 640,000. Byline given. Pays 2 months after acceptance. Offers 25% kill fee. Editorial lead time 3 months. Accepts simultaneous submissions. Guidelines for #10 SASE.

NONFICTION Needs expose, general interest, to men, interview. **Buys 50 mss/year.** Send complete ms. Length: 4,000-6,000 words. **Pays $3,000.**

COLUMNS/DEPARTMENTS Length: 1,000 words. **Buys 25 mss/year.** Query with published clips or send complete ms. **Pays $500.**

TIPS "Because of our long lead time, writers should think at least 6 months ahead. We take chances. Go against the grain; we like writers who look under rocks and see what hides there."

PLAYBOY MAGAZINE

9346 Civic Center Dr., #200, Beverly Hills CA 90210. (310)264-6600, **Fax:** (310)786-7440. **Website:** www.playboy.com. Monthly magazine. The preeminent entertainment magazine for the sophisticated urban male. This legendary brand continues to produce top-tier literature and journalism while maintaining its legacy as the industry's most artful and provocative image maker. Estab. 1953.

Query before submitting.

✚ TALENT DRIPS EROTIC LITERARY EZINE

Cleveland OH 44102. (216)799-9775. **E-mail:** talentdripseroticpublishing@yahoo.com. **Website:** eroticatalentdrips.wordpress.com. **Contact:** Kimberly Steele, founder. *Talent Drips*, published monthly online, focuses solely on showcasing new erotic fiction. Estab. 2007. Time between acceptance and publication is 2 months. Accepts queries by e-mail. Accepts previously published material and poetryAccepts simultaneous submissions. Responds in 3 weeks. Guidelines online.

FICTION Needs erotic short stories. Submit short stories between 5,000 and 10,000 words by e-mail to talentdripseroticpublishing@yahoo.com. Stories should be pasted into body of message. Reads submissions during publication months only. **Pays $15 for each accepted short story.**

POETRY Needs erotic. Submit 2-3 poems at a time, maximum 30 lines each by e-mail to talentdripseroticpublishing@yahoo.com. Considers previously published and simultaneous submissions. Accepts e-mail pasted into body of message. Reads submissions during publication months only. **Pays $10 for each accepted poem.**

TIPS "Please read our take on the difference between *erotica* and *pornography;* it's on the website. *Talent Drips* does not accept pornography. And please keep poetry 30 lines or less."

SPORTS

ARCHERY AND BOWHUNTING

⊝⊝ BOW & ARROW HUNTING

Beckett Media LLC, 22840 Savi Ranch Pkwy., Suite 200, Yorba Linda CA 92887. (714)200-1900. **Fax:** (800)249-7761. **E-mail:** JBell@Beckett.com; editorial@bowandarrowhunting.com. **Website:** www.bowandarrowhunting.com. **70% freelance written.** Magazine published 9 times/year covering bowhunting. Dedicated to serve the serious bowhunting enthusiast. Writers must be willing to share their secrets so readers can become better bowhunters. Estab. 1962. Circ. 90,000. Byline given. Pays on publication. Publishes ms an average of 2 months after acceptance. Submit seasonal material 6 months in advance. Accepts queries by mail, e-mail. Accepts simultaneous submissions. Responds in 1 month to queries; 6 weeks to mss. Sample copy and writer's guidelines free.

NONFICTION Needs how-to, humor, interview, opinion, personal experience, technical. **Buys 60 mss/year.** Send complete ms. Length: 1,700-3,000 words. **Pays $200-450.**

PHOTOS Send photos. Captions required. Reviews contact sheets, digital images only; no slides or prints accepted. Offers no additional payment for photos accepted with ms.

FILLERS Needs facts, newsbreaks. **Buys 12 mss/year.** Length: 500 words. **Pays $20-100.**

TIPS "Inform readers how they can become better at the sport, but don't forget to keep it fun! Sidebars are recommended with every submission."

⊖⊖ BOWHUNTER

InterMedia Outdoors, 6385 Flank Dr., Suite 800, Harrisburg PA 17112. (717)695-8085. **Fax:** (717)545-2527. **E-mail:** curt.wells@imoutdoors.com. **Website:** www.bowhunter.com. Mark Olszewski, art director; Jeff Waring, publisher. **Contact:** Curt Wells, editor. **50% freelance written.** Bimonthly magazine covering hunting big and small game with bow and arrow. "We are a special-interest publication, produced by bowhunters for bowhunters, covering all aspects of the sport. Material included in each issue is designed to entertain and inform readers, making them better bowhunters." Estab. 1971. Circ. 126,480. Byline given. Pays on acceptance. Submit seasonal material 8 months in advance. Accepts queries by mail, e-mail, fax. Responds in 1 month to queries. Responds in 2 months to mss. Sample copy for $2 and 8 1/2x11 SASE with appropriate postage. Guidelines for #10 SASE or online.

NONFICTION Needs general interest, how-to, interview, opinion, personal experience, photo feature. **Buys 60-plus mss/year.** Query. Length: 250-2,000 words. **Pays $500 maximum for assigned articles. Pays $100-400 for unsolicited articles.** Sometimes pays expenses of writers on assignment.

PHOTOS Send photos. Captions required. Reviews high-res digital images. Reviews photos with or without a ms. Offers $50-300/photo. Pays $50-125 for b&w inside; $75-300 for color inside; $600 for cover, "occasionally more if photo warrants it." **Pays on acceptance.** Credit line given. Buys one-time publication rights.

TIPS "A writer must know bowhunting and be willing to share that knowledge. Writers should anticipate *all* questions a reader might ask, then answer them in the article itself or in an appropriate sidebar. Articles should be written with the reader foremost in mind; we won't be impressed by writers seeking to prove how good they are—either as writers or bowhunters. We care about the reader and don't need writers with 'I' trouble. Features are a good bet because most of our material comes from freelancers. The best advice is: Be yourself. Tell your story the same as if sharing the experience around a campfire. Don't try to write like you think a writer writes."

⊖⊖ BOWHUNTING WORLD

Grand View Media Group, 6121 Baker Rd., Suite 101, Minnetonka MN 55345. (888)431-2877. **E-mail:** mo-lis@grandviewmedia.com. **Website:** www.bowhunt-ingworld.com. **Contact:** Mark Olis. **50% freelance written.** Bimonthly magazine with 3 additional issues for bowhunting and archery enthusiasts who participate in the sport year-round. Estab. 1952. Circ. 95,000. Byline given. Pays on acceptance. Publishes ms an average of 5 months after acceptance. Responds in 1 week (e-mail queries). Responds in 6 weeks to mss. Sample copy for $3 and 9x12 SASE with 10 first-class stamps. Guidelines with #10 SASE.

◯ Accepts queries by mail, but prefers e-mail.

NONFICTION Buys 60 mss/year. Send complete ms. Length: 1,500-2,500 words. **Pays $350-600.**

PHOTOS "We are seeking cover photos that depict specific behavioral traits of the more common big game animals (scraping whitetails, bugling elk, etc.) and well-equipped bowhunters in action. Must include return postage.".

TIPS "Writers are strongly advised to adhere to guidelines and become familiar with our format, as our needs are very specific. Writers are urged to query by e-mail. We prefer detailed outlines of 6 or so article ideas/query. Assignments are made for the next 18 months."

BICYCLING

⊖⊖⊖ ADVENTURE CYCLIST

Adventure Cycling Assn., Box 8308, Missoula MT 59807. (406)721-1776, ext. 222. **Fax:** (406)721-8754. **E-mail:** magazine@adventurecycling.org. **Website:** www.adventurecycling.org/adventure-cyclist. **Contact:** Greg Siple, art director; Michael Deme, editor. **75% freelance written.** Published 9 times/year for Adventure Cycling Association members, emphasizing bicycle tourism and travel. Estab. 1975. Circ. 45,500. Byline given. Pays on publication. Kill fee 25%. Submit seasonal material 12 months in advance. Sample copy and guidelines for 9x12 SAE with 4 first-class stamps. Info available at www.adventurecycling.org/adventure-cyclist/adventure-cyclist-submissions.

NONFICTION Needs first-person bike-travel accounts (U.S. and worldwide), essays, how-to, profiles, photo feature, technical, U.S. or foreign tour accounts. **Buys 20-25 mss/year.** Send complete ms. Length: 1,400-3,500 words. **Inquiries requested prior to complete mss. Pays sliding scale per word.**

PHOTOS State availability.

⊖⊖ CYCLE CALIFORNIA! MAGAZINE

1702-L Meridian Ave. #289, San Jose CA 95125. (408)924-0270. **Fax:** (408)292-3005. **E-mail:** tcorral@cyclecalifornia.com; BMack@cyclecalifornia.com. **Website:** www.cyclecalifornia.com. **Contact:** Tracy L. Corral; Bob Mack, publisher. **75% freelance written.** Magazine published 11 times/year covering Northern California bicycling events, races, people. Issues (topics) covered include bicycle commuting, bicycle politics, touring, racing, nostalgia, history—anything at all to do with riding a bike. Estab. 1995. Circ. 32,000 print; 40,000 digital. Byline given. Pays on publication. Publishes ms an average of 3 months after acceptance. Editorial lead time 6 weeks. Submit seasonal material 6 weeks in advance. Accepts queries by e-mail. Accepts simultaneous submissions. Responds in 1 month to queries. Sample copy with 9x12 SASE and $1.39 first-class postage. Guidelines with #10 SASE.

NONFICTION Needs historical, how-to, interview, opinion, personal experience, technical, travel. Special issues: Bicycle Tour & Travel (January/February). No articles about any sport that doesn't relate to bicycling. No product reviews. **Buys 36 mss/year.** Query. Length: 500-1,500 words. **Pays 10-15¢/word.**

PHOTOS Send photos. Identification of subjects preferred. Negotiates payment individually.

COLUMNS/DEPARTMENTS Buys 2-3 mss/year. Query with published clips. **Pays 10-15¢/word.**

TIPS "E-mail us with good ideas. While we don't exclude writers from other parts of the country, articles really should reflect a Northern California slant, or be of general interest to bicyclists. We prefer stories written by people who like and use their bikes."

⊖⊖ VELONEWS

Inside Communications, Inc., 3002 Sterling Circle, Suite 100, Boulder CO 80301. (303)440-0601. **Fax:** (303)444-6788. **E-mail:** webletters@competitorgroup.com. **E-mail:** nrogers@competitorgroup.com. **Website:** www.velonews.com. **Contact:** Neal Rogers, editor-in-chief. **40% freelance written.** Monthly tabloid covering bicycle racing. Estab. 1972. Circ. 48,000. Byline given. Pays on publication. Publishes ms an average of 1 month after acceptance. Responds in 3 weeks to queries.

NONFICTION Buys 80 mss/year. Query. Length: 300-1,200 words. **Pays $100-400.**

REPRINTS Send typed ms with rights for sale noted and information about when and where the material previously appeared.

PHOTOS State availability. Captions, identification of subjects required.

BOATING

⊖⊖⊖ CANOE & KAYAK

GrindMedia, LLC, 236 Avenida Fabricante, Suite 201, San Clemente CA 92672. (425)827-6363. **E-mail:** jeff@canoekayak.com; joe@canoekayak.com; dave@canoekayak.com. **Website:** www.canoekayak.com. **Contact:** Jeff Moag, editor-in-chief; Joe Carberry, managing editor; Dave Shively, associate editor. **75% freelance written.** Bimonthly magazine covering paddlesports. "*Canoe & Kayak* is North America's No. 1 paddlesports resource. Our readers include flatwater and whitewater canoeists and kayakers of all skill levels. We provide comprehensive information on destinations, technique and equipment. Beyond that, we cover canoe and kayak camping, safety, the environment, and the history of boats and sport." Estab. 1972. Circ. 70,000. Byline given. Pays on publication. Publishes ms an average of 6 months after acceptance. Editorial lead time 6 months. Submit seasonal material 8 months in advance. Accepts queries by mail, e-mail. Responds in 2 months to queries. Sample copy and writer's guidelines for 9x12 SAE with 7 first-class stamps.

NONFICTION Needs historical, how-to, canoe, kayak camp, load boats, paddle whitewater, etc., personal experience, photo feature, technical, travel. Special issues: Whitewater Paddling; Beginner's Guide; Kayak Touring; Canoe Journal. No cartoons, poems, stories in which bad judgement is portrayed or 'Me and Molly' articles. **Buys 25 mss/year.** Send complete ms. Length: 400-2,500 words. **Pays $100-800 for assigned articles. Pays $100-500 for unsolicited articles.**

PHOTOS "Some activities we cover are canoeing, kayaking, canoe fishing, camping, canoe sailing or poling, backpacking (when compatible with the main activity) and occasionally inflatable boats. We are not interested in groups of people in rafts, photos showing disregard for the environment or personal safety, gasoline-powered engines unless appropriate to the discussion, or unskilled persons taking extraordinary risks.". State availability. Captions, identification of subjects, model releases required. Reviews 35mm transparencies, 4x6 prints. Offers $75-500/photo.

COLUMNS/DEPARTMENTS Put In (environment, conservation, events), 500 words; Destinations (canoe and kayak destinations in US, Canada), 1,500 words; Essays, 750 words. **Buys 40 mss/year.** Send complete ms. **Pays $100-350.**

FILLERS Needs anecdotes, facts, newsbreaks. **Buys 20 mss/year.** Length: 200-500 words. **Pays $25-50.**

TIPS "Start with Put-In articles (short featurettes) or short, unique equipment reviews. Or give us the best, most exciting article we've ever seen—with great photos. Read the magazine before submitting."

⊛⊛⊛ CHESAPEAKE BAY MAGAZINE

1819 Bay Ridge Ave., Annapolis MD 21403. (410)263-2662, ext. 32. **Fax:** (410)267-6924. **E-mail:** editor@chesapeakeboating.net. **Website:** www.chesapeakeboating.net. **Contact:** Ann Levelle, managing editor; T.F. Sayles, editor. **60% freelance written.** Monthly magazine covering boating and the Chesapeake Bay. "Our readers are boaters. Our writers should know boats and boating. Read the magazine before submitting." Estab. 1972. Circ. 46,000. Byline given. Pays within 2 months after acceptance. Publishes ms an average of 1 year after acceptance. Editorial lead time 1 year. Submit seasonal material 1 year in advance. Accepts queries by mail, e-mail, fax, phone. Accepts simultaneous submissions. Responds in 2 months to queries. Responds in 3 months to mss. Sample copy for $5.19 prepaid and SASE.

NONFICTION **Buys 30 mss/year.** Query with published clips. Length: 300-3,000 words. **Pays $100-1,000.** Pays expenses of writers on assignment.

PHOTOS Captions, identification of subjects required. Offers $75-250/photo, $400/day rate for assignment photography. Pays $400 for color cover; $75-250 for color *stock* inside, depending on size; $200-1,200 for *assigned* photo package. Pays on publication. Credit line given. Buys one-time rights.

TIPS "Send us unedited writing samples (not clips) that show the writer can write, not just string words together. We look for well-organized, lucid, lively, intelligent writing."

⊛⊛ COAST&KAYAK MAGAZINE

Wild Coast Publishing, P.O. Box 24 Stn. A, Nanaimo BC V9R 5K4 Canada. (250)244-6437; (866)984-6437. **Fax:** (866)654-1937. **E-mail:** editor@coastandkayak.com. **Website:** www.coastandkayak.com. **Contact:**

John Kimantas, editor. **75% freelance written.** Quarterly magazine with a major focus on paddling the Pacific coast. "We promote safe paddling, guide paddlers to useful products and services, and explore coastal environmental issues." Estab. 1991. Circ. 65,000 print and electronic readers. Byline given. Pays on publication. Publishes ms an average of 4 months after acceptance. Editorial lead time 4 months. Submit seasonal material 4 months in advance. Accepts queries by mail, e-mail. Sample copy and guidelines online.

NONFICTION Needs how-to, paddle, travel, humor, new product, personal experience, technical, travel, trips. **Buys 25 mss/year.** Query. Length: 1,000-1,500 words. **Pays $50-75.**

PHOTOS State availability. Captions, identification of subjects required. Reviews low-res JPEGs. Offers $25-50/photo.

TIPS "You must know paddling—though novice paddlers are welcome. A strong environmental or wilderness appreciation component is advisable. We are willing to help refine work with flexible people. E-mail queries preferred. Check out our editorial calendar for our upcoming features."

⊛⊛⊛⊛ CRUISING WORLD

The Sailing Co., 55 Hammarlund Way, Middletown RI 02842. (401)845-5100. **Fax:** (401)845-5180. **E-mail:** cw.mss@gmail.com; elaine.lembo@cruisingworld.com; bill.roche@bonniercorp.com. **Website:** www.cruisingworld.com. **Contact:** Elaine Lembo, deputy editor; Bill Roche, art director. **60% freelance written.** Monthly magazine covering sailing, cruising/adventuring, do-it-yourself boat improvements. "*Cruising World* is a publication by and for sailboat owners who spend time in home waters as well as voyaging the world. Its readership is extremely loyal, savvy, and driven by independent thinking." Estab. 1974. Circ. 155,000. Byline given. **Pays on acceptance for articles;** on publication for photography. Publishes ms an average of 18 months after acceptance. Editorial lead time 3 months. Submit seasonal material 1 year in advance. Accepts queries by mail. Responds in 2 months to queries. Responds in 4 months to mss. Sample copy free. Guidelines online.

NONFICTION Needs book excerpts, essays, expose, general interest, historical, how-to, humor, interview, new product, opinion, personal experience, photo feature, technical, travel. No travel articles that have nothing to do with cruising aboard sailboats from 20-

50 feet in length. **Buys dozens mss/year.** Send complete ms. **Pays $50-1,500 for assigned articles. Pays $50-1,000 for unsolicited articles.** Sometimes pays expenses of writers on assignment.

PHOTOS Send high-res (minimum 300 DPI) images on CD. Send photos. Captions required. Reviews negatives, transparencies, color slides preferred. Payment upon publication. Also buys stand-alone photos.

COLUMNS/DEPARTMENTS Shoreline (sailing news, people, and short features; contact Elaine Lembo), 300 words maximum; Hands-on Sailor (refit, voyaging, seamanship, how-to), 1,000-1,500 words. **Buys dozens mss/year.** Query with or without published clips or send complete ms.

TIPS "*Cruising World's* readers know exactly what they want to read, so our best advice to freelancers is to carefully read the magazine and envision which exact section or department would be the appropriate place for proposed submissions."

GOOD OLD BOAT

Partnership for Excellence, Inc., 7340 Niagara Lane N., Maple Grove MN 55311. (763)494-0314. **E-mail:** karen@goodoldboat.com. **Website:** www.goodoldboat.com. **Contact:** Karen Larson, editor. **90% freelance written.** Bimonthly magazine covering sailing. *Good Old Boat* magazine focuses on maintaining, upgrading, and loving fiberglass cruising sailboats from the 1960s and well into the 2000s. Readers see themselves as part of a community of sailors who share similar maintenance and replacement concerns not generally addressed in the other sailing publications. Readers do much of the writing about projects they have done on their boats and the joy they receive from sailing them. Estab. 1998. Circ. 30,000. Pays 2 months in advance of publication. Publishes ms an average of 12-18 months after acceptance. Editorial lead time 4 months. Submit seasonal material 12-15 months in advance. Accepts queries by mail, e-mail. Accepts simultaneous submissions. Responds in 1-2 weeks to queries. Responds in 2-6 months to mss. Downloadable sample copy free. Guidelines online.

NONFICTION Needs general interest, historical, how-to, interview, personal experience, photo feature, technical. "Articles written by non-sailors serve no purpose for us." **Buys 150 mss/year.** Query or send complete ms. **Payment varies; refer to published rates online.**

PHOTOS State availability of or send photos. "We do not pay additional fees for photos except when they run as covers, or are specifically requested to support an article.".

TIPS "Our shorter pieces are the best way to break into our magazine. We publish many Simple Solutions and Quick & Easy pieces. These are how-to tips that have worked for sailors on their boats. In addition, our readers send lists of projects which they've done on their boats and which they could write for publication. We respond to these queries with a thumbs up or down by project. Articles are submitted on speculation, but they have a better chance of being accepted once we have approved of the suggested topic."

$ $ HEARTLAND BOATING

The Waterways Journal, Inc., 319 N. Fourth St., Suite 650, St. Louis MO 63102. (314)241-4310. **Fax:** (314)241-4207. **E-mail:** brad@heartlandboating.com. **Website:** www.heartlandboating.com. **Contact:** Brad Kovach, editor. **75% freelance written.** Magazine published 7 times/year covering recreational boating on the inland waterways of mid-America, from the Great Lakes south to the Gulf of Mexico. "Our writers must have experience with, and a great interest in, boating in mid-America. *Heartland Boating's* content is both informative and humorous—describing boating life as the heartland boater knows it. The content reflects the challenge, joy, and excitement of our way of life. We are devoted to both power and sailboating enthusiasts throughout middle America; houseboats are included. The focus is on the freshwater inland rivers and lakes of the heartland, primarily the waters of the Arkansas, Tennessee, Cumberland, Ohio, Missouri, Illinois, and Mississippi rivers, the Tennessee-Tombigbee Waterway, The Gulf Intracoastal Waterway, and the lakes along these waterways." Estab. 1989. Circ. 10,000. Byline given. Pays on publication. Editorial lead time 3 months. Accepts queries by mail. Responds only if interested. Sample copy upon request. Guidelines for #10 SASE.

NONFICTION Needs how-to, articles about navigation, maintenance, upkeep, or making time spent aboard easier and more comfortable, humor, personal experience, technical, Great Loop legs, trips along waterways and on-land stops. Special issues: Annual houseboat issue in March looks at what is coming out on the houseboat market for the coming year. **Buys 100 mss/year.** Send complete ms. Length: 850-1,500 words. **Pays $150-250.**

REPRINTS Send tearsheet, photocopy or typed ms and information about when and where the material previously appeared.

PHOTOS Magazine published 8 times/year covering recreational boating on the inland waterways of mid-America, from the Great Lakes south to the Gulf of Mexico and over to the east. Send photos. Model release is required, property release is preferred, photo captions are required. Include names and locations. Reviews prints, digital images. Offers no additional payment for photos accepted with ms.

COLUMNS/DEPARTMENTS Books Aboard (assigned book reviews), 400 words. Buys 8-10 mss/year. Pays $40. Handy Hints (boat improvement or safety projects), 1,000 words. Buys 8 mss/year. Pays $180. Heartland Haunts (waterside restaurants, bars or B&Bs), 1,000 words. Buys 16 mss/year. Pays $160. Query with published clips or send complete ms.

TIPS "We begin planning the next year's schedule starting in August. So submitting material between August 1 and October 15 is the best way to proceed."

⊘❸❸ HOUSEBOAT MAGAZINE

Harris Publishing, Inc., 360 B St., Idaho Falls ID 83402. **Fax:** (208)522-5241. **E-mail:** blk@houseboatmagazine.com. **Website:** www.houseboatmagazine.com. **Contact:** Brady L. Kay, executive editor. **35% freelance written.** Quarterly magazine for houseboaters who enjoy reading everything that reflects the unique houseboating lifestyle. If it is not a houseboat-specific article, please do not query. Estab. 1990. Circ. 25,000. Byline given. Pays on acceptance. Offers 25% kill fee. Publishes ms an average of 3 months after acceptance. Editorial lead time 6 months. Submit seasonal material 6 months in advance. Accepts simultaneous submissions. Responds in 1 month to queries. Sample copy for $5. Guidelines by e-mail.

○ No unsolicited mss. Accepts queries by mail and fax, but e-mail strongly preferred.

NONFICTION Needs how-to, interview, new product, personal experience, travel. **Buys 36 mss/year.** Query before submitting. Length: 1,500-2,200 words. **Pays $200-500.**

PHOTOS Often required as part of submission package. Color prints discouraged. Digital prints are unacceptable. Seldom purchases photos without ms, but occasionally buys cover photos. Captions, model releases required. Reviews transparencies, high-resolution electronic images. Offers no additional payment for photos accepted with ms.

COLUMNS/DEPARTMENTS Pays $150-300.

TIPS "As a general rule, how-to articles are always in demand. So are stories on unique houseboats or houseboaters. You are less likely to break in with a travel piece that does not revolve around specific people or groups. Personality profile pieces with excellent supporting photography are your best bet."

❷❸❸ PACIFIC YACHTING

OP Publishing, Ltd., 1166 Alberni St, Suite 802, Vancouver BC V6E 3Z3 Canada. (604)428-0259. **Fax:** (604)620-0425. **E-mail:** editor@pacificyachting.com; ayates@oppublishing.com. **Website:** www.pacificyachting.com. **Contact:** Dale Miller, editor; Arran Yates, art director. **90% freelance written.** Monthly magazine covering all aspects of recreational boating in the Pacific Northwest. "The bulk of our writers and photographers not only come from the local boating community, many of them were long-time *PY* readers before coming aboard as a contributor. The *PY* reader buys the magazine to read about new destinations or changes to old haunts on the British Columbia coast and the Pacific Northwest and to learn the latest about boats and gear." Estab. 1968. Circ. 19,000. Byline given. Pays on publication. Publishes ms an average of 6 months after acceptance. Editorial lead time 4 months. Submit seasonal material 6 months in advance. Accepts queries by mail, e-mail, fax. Sample copy for $6.95, plus postage charged to credit card. Guidelines online.

NONFICTION Needs historical, British Columbia coast only, how-to, humor, interview, personal experience, technical, boating related, travel, cruising, and destination on the British Columbia coast. "No articles from writers who are obviously not boaters!" Query. Length: 800-2,000 words. **Pays $150-500. Pays some expenses of writers on assignment for unsolicited articles.** Pays expenses of writers on assignment.

PHOTOS Send photos. Identification of subjects required. Reviews digital photos transparencies, 4 x 6 prints, and slides. Offers no additional payment for photos accepted with ms. Offers $25-400 for photos accepted alone.

COLUMNS/DEPARTMENTS Currents (current events, trade and people news, boat gatherings, and festivities), 50-250 words. Reflections; Cruising, both 800-1,000 words. Query. **Pay varies.**

TIPS "Our reader wants you to balance important navigation details with first-person observations, blending the practical with the romantic. Write tight, write short, write with the reader in mind, write to inform, write to entertain. Be specific, accurate, and historic."

🅢🅢 PONTOON & DECK BOAT

Harris Publishing, Inc., 360 B. St., Idaho Falls ID 83402. (208)524-7000. **Fax:** (208)522-5241. **E-mail:** blk@pdbmagazine.com. **Website:** www.pdbmagazine.com. **Contact:** Brady L. Kay, editor. **15% freelance written.** Magazine published 11 times/year covering boating. A boating niche publication geared toward the pontoon and deck boating lifestyle and consumer market. Audience is comprised of people who utilize these boats for varied family activities and fishing. Magazine is promotional of the PDB industry and its major players. Seeks to give the reader a twofold reason to read publication: to celebrate the lifestyle, and to do it aboard a first-class craft. Estab. 1995. Circ. 84,000. Byline given. Pays on publication. Editorial lead time 2 months. Submit seasonal material 3 months in advance. Accepts simultaneous submissions. Responds in 6 weeks to queries. Responds in 3 months to mss. Sample copy and writer's guidelines free.

NONFICTION Needs how-to, personal experience, technical, remodeling, rebuilding. "We are saturated with travel pieces; no general boating, humor, fiction, or poetry." **Buys 15 mss/year.** Send complete ms. Length: 600-2,000 words. **Pays $50-300.** Sometimes pays expenses of writers on assignment.

PHOTOS State availability. Captions, model releases required. Reviews transparencies.

COLUMNS/DEPARTMENTS No Wake Zone (short, fun quips); Better Boater (how-to). **Buys 6-12 mss/year.** Query with published clips. **Pays $50-150.**

TIPS "Be specific to pontoon and deck boats. Any general boating material goes to the slush pile. The more you can tie together the lifestyle, attitudes, and the PDB industry, the more interest we'll take in what you send us."

🅢🅢🅢 POWER & MOTORYACHT

10 Bokum Rd., Essex CT 06426. (860)767-3200. **E-mail:** jwood@aimmedia.com; cwhite@aimmedia.com. **Website:** www.powerandmotoryacht.com. Erin Kenney, creative director. **Contact:** Jason Y. Wood, editor-in-chief; Chris White, managing editor. **25% freelance written.** Monthly magazine covering powerboats 24 feet and larger with special emphasis on the 35-foot-

plus market. "Readers have an average of 33 years experience boating, and we give them accurate advice on how to choose, operate, and maintain their boats as well as what electronics and gear will help them pursue their favorite pastime. In addition, since powerboating is truly a lifestyle and not just a hobby for them, *Power & Motoryacht* reports on a host of other topics that affect their enjoyment of the water: chartering, sportfishing, and the environment, among others. Articles must therefore be clear, concise, and authoritative; knowledge of the marine industry is mandatory. Include personal experience and information for marine industry experts where appropriate." Estab. 1985. Circ. 157,000. Byline given. Pays on acceptance. Offers 33% kill fee. Publishes ms an average of 4-6 months after acceptance. Editorial lead time 4-6 months. Submit seasonal material 4-6 months in advance. Accepts queries by mail, e-mail. Responds in 1 month to queries. Sample copy with 10x12 SASE. Guidelines with #10 SASE or via e-mail.

NONFICTION Needs how-to, interview, personal experience, photo feature, travel. No unsolicited mss or articles about sailboats and/or sailing yachts (including motorsailers or cruise ships). **Buys 20-25 mss/year.** Query with published clips. Length: 800-1,500 words. **Pays $500-1,000 for assigned articles.** Sometimes pays expenses of writers on assignment.

PHOTOS State availability. Captions, identification of subjects required. Reviews 8x10 transparencies, GIF/JPEG files (minimum 300 dpi). Offers no additional payment for photos accepted with ms.

TIPS "Take a clever or even unique approach to a subject, particularly if the topic is dry/technical. Pitch us on yacht cruises you've taken, particularly if they're in off-the-beaten-path locations."

🅢🅢🅢 SAIL

180 Canal St., Suite 301, Boston MA 02114. (617)720-8600. **Fax:** (617)723-0912. **E-mail:** sailmail@sailmagazine.com. **Website:** www.sailmagazine.com. **Contact:** Peter Nielsen, editor-in-chief. **30% freelance written.** Monthly magazine written and edited for everyone who sails—aboard a coastal or bluewater cruiser, trailerable, one-design or offshore racer, or daysailer. How-to and technical articles concentrate on techniques of sailing and aspects of design and construction, boat systems, and gear; the feature section emphasizes the fun and rewards of sailing in a practical and instructive way. Estab. 1970. Circ. 180,000. Byline given. Pays

on acceptance. Publishes ms an average of 1 year after acceptance. Accepts queries by mail, e-mail, fax. Responds in 3 months to queries. Guidelines with SASE or online (download).

NONFICTION Needs how-to, personal experience, technical, distance cruising, destinations. Special issues: Cruising, chartering, commissioning, fitting-out, special race (e.g., America's Cup), Top 10 Boats. **Buys 50 mss/year.** Query. Length: 1,500-3,000 words. **Pays $200-800.** Sometimes pays expenses of writers on assignment.

PHOTOS Prefers transparencies. High-res digital photos (300 dpi) are also accepted, as are high-quality color prints (preferably with negatives attached). Captions, identification of subjects, True required. Payment varies, up to $1,000 if photo used on cover.

COLUMNS/DEPARTMENTS Sailing Memories (short essay); Sailing News (cruising, racing, legal, political, environmental); Under Sail (human interest). Query. **Pays $50-400.**

TIPS "Request an articles' specification sheet. We look for unique ways of viewing sailing. Skim old issues of *Sail* for ideas about the types of articles we publish. Always remember that *Sail* is a sailing magazine. Stay away from gloomy articles detailing all the things that went wrong on your boat. Think constructively and write about how to avoid certain problems. You should focus on a theme or choose some aspect of sailing and discuss a personal attitude or new philosophical approach to the subject. Notice that we have certain issues devoted to special themes—for example, chartering, electronics, commissioning, and the like. Stay away from pieces that chronicle your journey in the day-by-day style of a logbook. These are generally dull and uninteresting. Select specific actions or events (preferably sailing events, not shorebound activities), and build your articles around them. Emphasize the sailing."

⊛⊛⊛ SAILING MAGAZINE

125 E. Main St., P.O. Box 249, Port Washington WI 53074. (262)284-3494. **Fax:** (262)284-7764. **E-mail:** editorial@sailingmagazine.net. **Website:** www.sailingmagazine.net. **Contact:** Greta Schanen, managing editor. Monthly magazine for the experienced sailor. Estab. 1966. Circ. 45,000. Pays after publication. Accepts queries by mail, e-mail. Responds in 2 months to queries.

NONFICTION Needs book excerpts, how-to, tech pieces on boats and gear, interview, personal experience, travel by sail. **Buys 15-20 mss/year.** Send com-

plete ms. Prefers text in Word on disk for Mac or to e-mail address. Length: 750-2,500 words. **Pays $100-800.**

PHOTOS Captions required. Reviews color transparencies. Pays $50-400.

⊛⊛ SAILING WORLD

Bonnier Corporation, 55 Hammarlund Way, Middletown RI 02842. (401)845-5100. **Fax:** (401)845-5180. **E-mail:** editor@sailingworld.com. **Website:** www.sailingworld.com. **Contact:** Dave Reed, editor. **40% freelance written.** Magazine published 10 times/year covering performance sailing. Estab. 1962. Circ. 65,000. Byline given. Pays on publication. Publishes ms an average of 4 months after acceptance. Responds in 1 month to queries. Sample copy for $5. Guidelines online.

NONFICTION Needs how-to, for racing and performance-oriented sailors, interview, photo feature, Regatta sports and charter. No travelogs. **Buys 5-10 unsolicited mss/year.** "Prospective contributors to Sailing World should study recent issues of the magazine to determine appropriate subject matter. The emphasis here is on performance sailing: keep in mind that the Sailing World readership is relatively educated about the sport. Unless you are dealing with a totally new aspect of sailing, you can and should discuss ideas on an advanced technical level; however, extensive formulae and graphs don't play well to our audience. When in doubt as to the suitability of an article or idea, submit a written query before time and energy are misdirected. (Because of the volume of queries received, editors cannot accept phone calls.)" Length: 400-1,500 words. **Pays $400 for up to 2,000 words.** Does not pay expenses of writers on assignment unless pre-approved.

TIPS "Send query with outline and include your experience. Prospective contributors should study recent issues of the magazine to determine appropriate subject matter. The emphasis here is on performance sailing: keep in mind that the *Sailing World* readership is relatively educated about the sport. Unless you are dealing with a totally new aspect of sailing, you can and should discuss ideas on an advanced technical level. 'Gee-whiz' impressions from beginning sailors are generally not accepted."

⊛⊛⊛⊛ SHOWBOATS INTERNATIONAL

Boat International Media, 41-47 Hartfield Rd., London SW19 3RQ United Kingdom. (954)522-2628 (U.S. number). **Fax:** (954)522-2240. **E-mail:** marilyn.mower@boatinternationalmedia.com. **Website:** www.boat-international.com. **Contact:** Marilyn Mower, editorial director. **70% freelance written.** Magazine published 10 times/year covering luxury superyacht industry. Estab. 1995. Circ. 50,000. Byline given. Pays on publication. Offers 30% kill fee. Editorial lead time 2 months. Submit seasonal material 4 months in advance. Accepts queries by e-mail. Responds in 2 months to mss. Sample copy for $6.00. Guidelines free.

NONFICTION Travel/destination pieces that are superyacht related. **Buys 6/year mss/year.** Query. Length: 700-2,500 words. **Pays $300 minimum, $2,000 maximum for assigned articles.** Generally

PHOTOS State availability. Captions required. Reviews contact sheets, GIF/JPEG files. negotiates payment individually.

FICTION NONE

🄺🄢 SOUTHERN BOATING

Southern Boating & Yachting, Inc., 330 N. Andrews Ave., Ft. Lauderdale FL 33301. (954)522-5515. **Fax:** (954)522-2260. **E-mail:** liz@southernboating.com; john@southernboating.com. **Website:** www.southernboating.com. **Contact:** Liz Pasch, editorial director; John Lambert, art director. **50% freelance written.** Monthly boating magazine. Upscale monthly yachting magazine focusing on the Southeast U.S., Bahamas, Caribbean, and Gulf of Mexico. Estab. 1972. Circ. 40,000. Byline given. Pays within 30 days of publication. Publishes ms an average of 3 months after acceptance. Editorial lead time 3 months. Submit seasonal material 3 months in advance. Accepts queries by e-mail.

NONFICTION Needs how-to, boat maintenance, travel, boating related, destination pieces. **Buys 50 mss/year.** Query. Length: 900-1,200 words. **Pays $500-600 with art.**

PHOTOS State availability of or send photos. Captions, identification of subjects, model releases required. Reviews digital files.

COLUMNS/DEPARTMENTS Weekend Workshop (how-to/maintenance), 900 words; What's New in Electronics (electronics), 900 words; Engine Room (new developments), 900 words. **Buys 24 mss/year.** Query first; see media kit for special issue focus.

🄺🄢 WATERWAY GUIDE

P.O. Box 1125, 16273 General Puller Hwy., Deltaville VA 23043. (804)776-8999. **Fax:** (804)776-6111. **E-mail:** joan@waterwayguide.com. **Website:** www.waterwayguide.com. **Contact:** Tom Hale, editor. **90% freelance written.** Annual magazine covering intracoastal waterway travel for recreational boats. Six editions cover coastal waters from Maine to Florida, the Bahamas, the Gulf of Mexico, the Great Lakes, and the Great Loop Cruise of America's inland waterways. "Writer must be knowledgeable about navigation and the areas covered by the guide." Estab. 1947. Circ. 30,000. Byline given. Pays on publication. Publishes ms an average of 3 months after acceptance. Editorial lead time 4 months. Submit seasonal material 3 months in advance. Accepts queries by mail, phone. Responds in 6 weeks to queries. Responds in 2 months to mss. Sample copy for $39.95 with $3 postage.

NONFICTION Needs essays, historical, how-to, photo feature, technical, travel. **Buys 6 mss/year.** Send complete ms. Length: 250-5,000 words. **Pays $50-500.**

PHOTOS Send photos. Captions, identification of subjects required. Reviews transparencies, 3 x 5 prints. Offers $25-50/photo.

TIPS "Must have on-the-water experience and be able to provide new and accurate information on geographic areas covered by *Waterway Guide*."

🄢 WATERWAYS WORLD

Waterways World, Ltd, 151 Station St., Burton-on-Trent Staffordshire DE14 1BG United Kingdom. 01283 742950. **E-mail:** editorial@waterwaysworld.com. **Website:** www.waterwaysworld.com. **Contact:** Bobby Cowling, editor. Monthly magazine publishing news, photographs, and illustrated articles on all aspects of inland waterways in Britain, and on limited aspects of waterways abroad. Estab. 1972. Pays on publication. Editorial lead time 2 months. Accepts queries by mail, e-mail. NoGuidelines by e-mail.

NONFICTION Does not want poetry or fiction. Submit query letter or complete ms, SAE.

PHOTOS Captions required. Reviews transparencies, gloss prints, 300 dpi digital images, maps/diagrams.

GENERAL INTEREST

ESPN THE MAGAZINE

ESPN Inc. (The Walt Disney Company/Hearst Corporation), 19 E. 34th St., New York NY 10016. **E-mail:** post@espnmag.com. **Website:** www.espn.go.com/magazine. **Contact:** Craig Winston, managing editor. Bi-weekly sports magazine published by ESPN. *ESPN The Magazine* covers Major League Baseball, National Basketball Association, National Football League, National Hockey League, college basketball, and college football. The magazine typically takes a more light-hearted and humorous approach to sporting news. Estab. 1998. Circ. 2.1 million.

⬤ Query before submitting. Difficult market to break into.

SPORTS ILLUSTRATED

Time, Inc., 1271 Avenue of the Americas, New York NY 10020. (212)522-1212. **E-mail:** story_queries@si-mail.com. **Website:** www.si.com. Weekly magazine covering sports. *Sports Illustrated* reports and interprets the world of sport, recreation, and active leisure. It previews, analyzes, and comments upon major games and events, as well as those noteworthy for character and spirit alone. It features individuals connected to sport and evaluates trends concerning the part sport plays in contemporary life. In addition, the magazine has articles on such subjects as sports gear and swim suits. Special departments deal with sports equipment, books, and statistics. Estab. 1954. Circ. 3.3 million. Accepts queries by mail. Responds in 4-6 weeks to queries.

⬤ Query before submitting. Do not send photos or graphics. Include a SASE for return of materials.

NONFICTION Query.

GOLF

💲💲 AFRICAN AMERICAN GOLFER'S DIGEST

80 Wall St., Suite 720, New York NY 10005. (212)571-6559. **E-mail:** debertcook@aol.com. **Website:** www.africanamericangolfersdigest.com. **Contact:** Debert Cook, managing editor. **100% freelance written.** Quarterly. Covering golf lifestyle, health, travel destinations and reviews, golf equipment, golfer profiles. "Editorial should focus on interests of our market demographic of African Americans with historical, artistic, musical, educational (higher learning), automotive, sports, fashion, entertainment, and other categories of high interest to them." Estab. 2003. Circ. 20,000. Byline given. Publishes ms an average of 3 months after acceptance. Editorial lead time 3-6 months. Submit seasonal material 3-6 months in advance. Accepts queries by e-mail. Accepts simultaneous submissions. Responds in 3 weeks to queries. Responds in 3 months to mss. Sample copy for $6. Guidelines by e-mail.

NONFICTION Needs how-to, interview, new product, personal experience, photo feature, technical, travel., golf-related. **Buys 3 mss/year.** Query. Length: 250-1,500 words. **Pays 10-50¢/word.**

PHOTOS State availability. Captions, identification of subjects, model releases required. Reviews GIF/JPEG files (300 dpi or higher at 4x6). Negotiates payment individually. Credit line given.

COLUMNS/DEPARTMENTS Profiles (celebrities, national leaders, entertainers, corporate leaders, etc., who golf); Travel (destination/golf course reviews); Golf Fashion (jewelry, clothing, accessories). **Buys 3 mss/year.** Query. **Pays 10-50¢/word.**

FILLERS Needs anecdotes, facts, gags, newsbreaks, short humor. **Buys 3 mss/year.** Length: 20-125 words. **Pays 10-50¢/word.**

TIPS "Emphasize golf and African American appeal."

💲💲💲💲💲 GOLF CANADA

Chill Media Inc., 482 S. Service Rd. E., Suite 103, Oakville ON L6J 2X6 Canada. (905)337-1886. **Fax:** (905)337-1887. **E-mail:** scotty@ichill.ca; alison@ichill.ca. **Website:** www.golfcanada.ca. Alison King, managing editor. **Contact:** Scott Stevenson, publisher. **80% freelance written.** Magazine published 4 times/year covering Canadian golf. *Golf Canada* is the official magazine of the Royal Canadian Golf Association, published to entertain and enlighten members about RCGA-related activities and to generally support and promote amateur golf in Canada. Estab. 1994. Circ. 159,000. Byline given. Pays 30 days after publication. Offers 25% kill fee. Editorial lead time 3 months. Submit seasonal material 6 months in advance. Accepts queries by mail, e-mail, fax, phone. Sample copy free.

NONFICTION Needs historical, interview, new product, opinion, photo feature, travel. Query with published clips. Length: word counts vary. **Rates are negotiated upon agreement.** Sometimes pays expenses of writers on assignment.

PHOTOS State availability. Captions required. Reviews contact sheets, negatives, transparencies, prints. Rates negotiated upon agreement.

COLUMNS/DEPARTMENTS Guest Column (focus on issues surrounding the Canadian golf community), 700 words. Query. **Rates are negotiated upon agreement.**

TIPS "Keep story ideas focused on Canadian competitive golf."

GOLF DIGEST

The Golf Digest Companies, 4 Times Square, 14th Floor, New York NY 10036. (212)286-2860. **Fax:** (212)286-3147. **E-mail:** editor@golfdigest.com. **Website:** www.golfdigest.com. Monthly magazine covering the sport of golf. Written for all golf enthusiasts, whether recreational, amateur, or professional player. Estab. 1950. Circ. 1,660,022. Editorial lead time 6 months. Accepts queries by mail. Sample copy for $3.95.

💬 Query before submitting.

NONFICTION Query.

GOLF MAGAZINE

Time4 Media, Inc., 1271 Avenue of the Americas, New York NY 10020. (212)779-5000. **Fax:** (212)779-5522. **E-mail:** editor@golf.com. **Website:** www.golfonline.com. Monthly magazine written for all levels of golf enthusiasts, including beginners, experts and pros. Estab. 1954. Circ. 1,403,685. Editorial lead time 6 weeks.

💬 Query before submitting.

$$$ GOLF TIPS

Werner Publishing Corp., 12121 Wilshire Blvd., 12th Floor, Los Angeles CA 90025-1176. (310)820-1500. **Fax:** (310)826-5008. **E-mail:** editors@golftipsmag.com. **Website:** www.golftipsmag.com. **95% freelance written.** Magazine published 9 times/year covering golf instruction and equipment. "We provide mostly concise, very clear golf instruction pieces for the serious golfer." Estab. 1986. Circ. 300,000. Byline given. Pays on publication. Offers 33% kill fee. Publishes ms an average of 2 months after acceptance. Editorial lead time 3 months. Submit seasonal material 4 months in advance. Responds in 1 month to queries. Sample copy free. Guidelines online.

NONFICTION Needs book excerpts, how-to, interview, new product, photo feature, technical, travel: all golf related. "Generally, golf essays rarely make it." **Buys 125 mss/year.** Send complete ms. Length: 250-2,000 words. **Pays $300-1,000 for assigned articles. Pays $300-800 for unsolicited articles.** Sometimes pays expenses of writers on assignment.

PHOTOS State availability. Captions, identification of subjects required. Reviews 2x2 transparencies. Negotiates payment individually.

COLUMNS/DEPARTMENTS Stroke Saver (very clear, concise instruction), 350 words; Lesson Library (book excerpts—usually in a series), 1,000 words; Travel Tips (formatted golf travel), 2,500 words. **Buys 40 mss/year.** Query with or without published clips or send complete ms. **Pays $300-850.**

TIPS "Contact a respected PGA professional and find out if they're interested in being published. A good writer can turn an interview into a decent instruction piece."

GUNS

AMERICAN RIFLEMAN

National Rifle Association, 11250 Waples Mill Rd., Fairfax VA 22030-9400. **E-mail:** publications@nrahq.org. **E-mail:** armedcitizen@nrahq.org. **Website:** www.americanrifleman.org. Monthly magazine. *American Rifleman* is a shooting and firearms interest publication, owned by the National Rifle Association. Estab. 1923. Circ. 1.9 million.

💬 Query before submitting for anything other than the Armed Citizen column.

COLUMNS/DEPARTMENTS Accepts articles for the Armed Citizen column. Send via e-mail.

$$ GUN DIGEST THE MAGAZINE

F+W Media, 700 E. State St., Iola WI 54990. (715)445-2214. **Fax:** (715)445-4087. **E-mail:** gundigestonline@fwmedia.com. **Website:** www.gundigest.com. **Uses 90% freelancers.** Bimonthly magazine covering firearms. "*Gun Digest the Magazine* covers all aspects of the firearms community, from collectible guns to tactical gear to reloading and accessories. We also publish gun reviews and tests of new and collectible firearms and news features about firearms legislation. We are 100 percent pro-gun, fully support the NRA, and make no bones about our support of Constitutional freedoms." Byline given. Pays on publication. Publishes ms 2 months after acceptance. Editorial lead time 3 months. Accepts queries by e-mail. Responds in 3 weeks on queries; 1 month on mss. Free sample copy. Guidelines available via e-mail.

NONFICTION Needs general interest (firearms related), historical, how-to, interview, new product, nostalgic, profile, technical, All submissions must focus on firearms, accessories, or the firearms industry and legislation. Stories that include hunting reference must have as their focus the firearms or ammunition used. The hunting should be secondary. Special issues: *Gun Digest* magazine also publishes an annual gear guide. "We do not publish 'Me and Joe' hunting stories." **Buys 50-75 mss/year.** Query. 500-3,500 max. **$175-500 for assigned and for unsolicited articles. Does not pay in contributor copies.** Does not pay expenses.

PHOTOS Send photos with submission. Requires captions, identification of subjects. Reviews GIF/JPEG files (and TIF files); 300 DPI submitted on a CD (size). Offers no additional payment for photos accepted with ms.

TIPS "Be an expert in your field. Submit clear copy using the AP stylebook as your guide."

😊😊 MUZZLE BLASTS

P.O. Box 67, Friendship IN 47021. (812)667-5131. **Fax:** (812)667-5136. **E-mail:** mblastdop@seidata.com. **Website:** www.nmlra.org. **65% freelance written.** Monthly magazine. "Articles must relate to muzzleloading or the muzzleloading era of American history." Estab. 1939. Circ. 17,500. Byline given. Pays on publication. Offers $50 kill fee. Publishes ms an average of 6 months after acceptance. Editorial lead time 4 months. Submit seasonal material 6 months in advance. Responds in 1 month to mss. Sample copy and writer's guidelines free.

NONFICTION Needs book excerpts, general interest, historical, how-to, humor, interview, new product, personal experience, photo feature, technical, travel. No subjects that do not pertain to muzzleloading. **Buys 80 mss/year.** Query. Length: 2,000-2,500 words. **Pays $150 minimum for assigned articles. Pays $50 minimum for unsolicited articles.**

PHOTOS Send photos. Captions, model releases required. Reviews prints and digital images. Negotiates payment individually.

COLUMNS/DEPARTMENTS Buys 96 mss/year. Query. **Pays $50-200.**

FICTION Must pertain to muzzleloading. Needs adventure, historical, humorous. **Buys 6 mss/year.** Query. Length: 2,500 words. **Pays $50-300.**

FILLERS Needs facts. **Pays $50.**

😊😊 SHOTGUN SPORTS MAGAZINE

P.O. Box 6810, Auburn CA 95604. (530)889-2220. **Fax:** (530)889-9106. **E-mail:** shotgun@shotgunsportsmagazine.com. **Website:** www.shotgunsportsmagazine.com. **Contact:** Johnny Cantu, editor-in-chief. **50% freelance written. Welcomes new writers.** Monthly magazine covering all the shotgun sports and shotgun hunting—sporting clays, trap, skeet, hunting, gunsmithing, shotshell patterning, shotsell reloading, mental training for the shotgun sports, shotgun tests, anything shotgun. Pays on publication. Publishes ms an average of 1-6 months after acceptance. Sample copy and writer's guidelines available on the website.

💬 Responds within 3 weeks. Subscription: $32.95 (U.S.); $49.95 (Canada); $79.95 (foreign).

NONFICTION Needs Currently needs anything with a 'shotgun' subject. Think pieces, roundups, historical, interviews, etc. No articles promoting a specific club or sponsored hunting trip, etc. Submit complete ms with photos by mail with SASE. Can submit by e mail. Make Length: 1,500-3,000 words. **Pays $50-150.**

REPRINTS Photo

PHOTOS 5x7 or 8x10 b&w or 4-color with appropriate captions. On disk or e-mailed at least 5-inches and 300 dpi (contact Graphics Artist for details). Reviews transparencies (35 mm or larger), b&w, or 4-color. Send photos.

TIPS "Do not fax ms. Send good photos. Take a fresh approach. Create a professional, yet friendly article. Send diagrams, maps, and photos of unique details, if needed. For interviews, more interested in 'words of wisdom' than a list of accomplishments. Reloading articles must include source information and backup data. Check your facts and data! If you can't think of a fresh approach, don't bother. If it's not about shotguns or shotgunners, don't send it. Never say, 'You don't need to check my data; I never make mistakes.'"

HIKING AND BACKPACKING

😊😊😊😊 BACKPACKER MAGAZINE

Cruz Bay Publishing, Inc., an Active Interest Media Co., 5720 Flatiron Parkway, Boulder CO 80301. **E-mail:** gfullerton@backpacker.com (senior associate photo editor). **Website:** www.backpacker.com. Dennis Lewon, editor-in-chief (features & people), dlewon@backpacker.com; Rachel Zurer, senior editor, (destinations & heroes), rzurer@backpacker.com; Casey Lyons, senior editor (skills & survival), caseylyons@aimmedia.com; Maren Kasselik, assistant editor (destinations), mkasselik@aimmedia.com; Kristin Hostetter, gear editor, khostetter1@gmail.com. **50% freelance written.** Magazine published 9 times/year covering wilderness travel for backpackers. Estab. 1973. Circ. 340,000. Byline given. Pays on acceptance. 25% kill fee. 6 months. Accepts queries by mail (include SASE for returns), e-mail (preferred,with attachments and web links). Responds in 2-4 weeks to queries. Free sample copy. Guidelines online.

NONFICTION Needs Primarily service based, *Backpacker* needs how-to, inspirational, interview, new product, personal experience, technical, travel., Occasionally accepts feature essays, expose and historical stories from proven freelancers. *Backpacker* primarily covers hiking. When warranted, we cover canoeing, kayaking, snowshoeing, cross-country skiing, and other human-powered modes of travel. Wilderness or backcountry: The true backpacking experience means getting away from the trailhead and into the wilds. Whether a dayhike or a weeklong trip, out-of-the-way, unusual destinations are what we're looking for. No step-by-step accounts of what you did on your summer vacation—stories that chronicle every rest stop and gulp of water. Query with published clips before sending complete ms. Length: 150-3,000 words. **Pays 10¢-$1/word.**

PHOTOS Buys 80 photos from freelancers/issue; 720 photos/year. Needs transparencies or hi-res digital of people backpacking, camping, landscapes/scenics. Reviews photos with or without a ms. Model/property release required (if necessary). Accepts images in digital format. Send via ZIP, e-mail as JPEG files at 72 dpi for review (300 dpi needed to print). State availability. Payment varies.

COLUMNS/DEPARTMENTS Life List (personal essay telling a story about a premier wilderness destination or experience) 400 words; Top 3 (great hiking destinations around a theme), 350 words; Rip & Go (weekend backpacking destinations) 400 words; Trail Mix (themed local hikes e.g. 'See This Now,' 'Braggin' Rights,' and 'Secrets of a Ranger') 50-200 words; Master Class (expert-based skills blowout, organized by beginner, intermediate and expert, on a hiking-specific theme) 900 words; Test Kitchen (food-related field test and recipes) 500 words; Out Alive (first-person, skills-based survival account) 900 words; Troubleshoot This (skills to face a specific hazard) 200 words; Chart of Death (infographic presentation of skills related to a particular survival hazard), research-based, 300-500 words; Field Notes (first-person reviews of new gear) 150 words. **Buys 50-75 mss/year.**

TIPS Our best advice is to read the publication—most freelancers don't know the magazine at all. The best way to break in is with an article for the Top 3, Rip & Go, Heroes, Trail Mix, Troubleshoot This or Out Alive departments. The ability/willingness to provide web content (GPS tracks, how-to video, audio, slideshows) may also help land an assignment.

HORSE RACING

AMERICAN TURF MONTHLY

747 Middle Neck Rd., Great Neck NY 11024. (516)773-4075. **Fax:** (516)773-2944. **E-mail:** jcorbett@americanturf.com; editor@americanturf.com. **Website:** www.americanturf.com. **Contact:** Joe Girardi, editor. **90% freelance written.** Monthly magazine squarely focused on Thoroughbred racing, handicapping and wagering. *ATM* is a magazine for horseplayers, not owners, breeders, or 12-year-old girls enthralled with ponies. Estab. 1946. Circ. 30,000. Byline given. Pays on publication. Publishes ms an average of 4 months after acceptance. Editorial lead time 2 months. Submit seasonal material 2 months in advance. Accepts queries by mail, e-mail. Responds in 1 month to queries. Sample copy and writer's guidelines free.

○ "*American Turf Monthly*, the only handicapping magazine sold on news stands within the U.S. and Canada, has been entertaining horse racing enthusiasts since 1946. Each issue draws the reader into the exhilarating world of horse racing with features written by premier handicapping authors in the sport. The photography and creative design capture the spellbinding highlights of the race tracks to satiate the thrill seeking desire of the wagering player."

NONFICTION Needs No historical essays, bilious 'guest editorials,' saccharine poetry, fiction. Special issues: Triple Crown/Kentucky Derby (May); Saratoga/Del Mar (August); Breeder's Cup (November). **Buys Length: 800-2,000 words. Pays $75-300 for assigned articles. Pays $100-500 for unsolicited articles. mss/year.** Query. Length: 800-2,000 words. **Pays $75-300 for assigned articles. Pays $100-500 for unsolicited articles.** No.

PHOTOS Send photos. Identification of subjects required. Reviews 3 x 5 transparencies, prints, 300 dpi TIFF images on CD. Offers $25 for b&w or color interior; $150 min. for color cover. Pays on publication. Credit line given.

FILLERS newsbreaks, short humor Needs newsbreaks, short humor. **Buys 5 mss/year.** Length: 400 words. **Pays $25.**

TIPS "Like horses and horse racing."

⊙⊙ HOOF BEATS

750 Michigan Ave., Columbus OH 43215. **E-mail:** hoofbeats@ustrotting.com. **Website:** www.hoofbeatsmagazine.com. **60% freelance written.** Monthly magazine covering harness racing and standardbred horses. "Articles and photos must relate to harness racing or standardbreds. We do not accept any topics that do not touch on these subjects." Estab. 1933. Circ. 10,000. Byline given. Pays on publication. Offers 25% kill fee. Publishes ms an average of 2-4 months after acceptance. Editorial lead time 6 months. Submit seasonal material

6 months in advance. Accepts queries by mail, e-mail, fax. Accepts simultaneous submissions. Responds in 2 weeks to queries. Responds in 1 month to mss. Sample copy online. Guidelines free.

NONFICTION Needs general interest, how-to, interview, personal experience, photo feature, technical. "We do not want any fiction or poetry." **Buys 48-72 mss/year.** Query. Length: 750-3,000 words. **Pays $100-500. Pays $100-500 for unsolicited articles.**

PHOTOS State availability. Identification of subjects required. Reviews contact sheets. We offer $25-100 per photo.

COLUMNS/DEPARTMENTS Equine Clinic (standardbreds who overcame major health issues), 900-1,200 words; Profiles (short profiles on people or horses in harness racing), 600-1,000 words; Industry Trends (issues impacting standardbreds & harness racing), 1,000-2,000 words. **Buys 60 mss/year.** Query. **Pays $100-500.**

TIPS "We welcome new writers who know about harness racing or are willing to learn about it. Make sure to read *Hoof Beats* before querying to see our slant & style. We look for informative/promotional stories on harness racing—not exposés on the sport."

HUNTING AND FISHING

🖲🖲 AMERICAN ANGLER

735 Broad St., Augusta GA 30904. (706)828-3971. **E-mail:** steve.walburn@morris.com; wayne.knight@morris.com. **Website:** www.americanangler.com. **Contact:** Steve Walburn, editor; Wayne Knight, art director. **95% freelance written.** Bimonthly magazine covering fly fishing. "*American Angler* is devoted exclusively to fly fishing. We focus mainly on coldwater fly fishing for trout, steelhead, and salmon, but we also run articles about warmwater and saltwater fly fishing. Our mission is to supply our readers with well-written, accurate articles on every aspect of the sport—angling techniques and methods, reading water, finding fish, selecting flies, tying flies, fish behavior, places to fish, casting, managing line, rigging, tackle, accessories, entomology, and any other relevant topics. Each submission should present specific, useful information that will increase our readers' enjoyment of the sport and help them catch more fish." Estab. 1976. Circ. 35,000. Byline given. Pays on publication. Publishes ms an average of 6 months after acceptance. Editorial lead time 3 months. Submit seasonal material 5 months in advance.

Accepts queries by e-mail only to steve.walburn@morris.com. Accepts simultaneous submissions. Responds in 6 weeks to queries. Responds in 2 months to mss.

NONFICTION Needs how-to, most important, personal experience, photo feature, seldom, technical. No superficial, broad-brush coverage of subjects. **Buys 45-60 mss/year.** Query with published clips. Length: 800-2,200 words. **Pays $200-600.**

REPRINTS Send information about when and where the material previously appeared. Pay negotiable.

PHOTOS "How-to pieces—those that deal with tactics, rigging, fly tying, and the like—must be accompanied by appropriate photography or rough sketches for our illustrator. Naturally, where-to stories must be illustrated with shots of scenery, people fishing, anglers holding fish, and other pictures that help flesh out the story and paint the local color. Do not bother sending sub-par photographs. We only accept photos that are well lit, tack sharp, and correctly framed. A fly-tying submission should always include samples of flies to send to our staff photographer, even if photos of the flies are included.". Send photos. Captions, identification of subjects required. Digital photos only. Offers no additional payment for photos accepted with ms. Pays $600-700 for color cover; $30-350 for color inside. Pays on publication. Credit line given. Buys one-time rights, first rights for covers. "Payment is made just prior to publication. "We don't pay by the word, and length is only one of the variables considered. The quality and completeness of a submission may be more important than its length in determining rates, and articles that include good photography are usually worth more. As a guideline, the following rates generally apply: Feature articles pay $450 (and perhaps a bit more if we're impressed), while short features pay $200 to $400. Generally, these rates assume that useful photos, drawings, or sketches accompany the words.

COLUMNS/DEPARTMENTS One-page shorts (problem solvers), 350-750 words. Query with published clips. **Pays $100-300.**

TIPS "If you are submitting for the first time, please submit complete queries."

🖲🖲🖲 AMERICAN HUNTER

National Rifle Association, 11250 Waples Mill Rd., Fairfax VA 22030-9400. (703)267-1336. **Fax:** (703)267-3971. **E-mail:** publications@nrahq.org; americanhunter@nrahq.org; lcromwell@nrahq.org. **Website:** www.americanhunter.org. **Contact:** J. Scott Olmsted, editor-in-chief. Monthly magazine for hunters who are members of the National Rifle Association (NRA). *American Hunter* contains articles dealing with various sport hunting and related activities both at home and abroad. With the encouragement of the sport as a prime game management tool, emphasis is on technique, sportsmanship and safety. In each issue hunting equipment and firearms are evaluated, legislative happenings affecting the sport are reported, lore and legend are retold and the business of the Association is recorded in the Official Journal section. Circ. 1,000,000. Byline given. Pays on publication. Accepts queries by mail, e-mail. Responds in 6 months to queries. Guidelines with #10 SASE.

NONFICTION Special issues: Pheasants, whitetail tactics, black bear feed areas, mule deer, duck hunters' transport by land and sea, tech topics to be decided; rut strategies, muzzleloader moose and elk, fall turkeys, staying warm, goose talk, long-range muzzleloading. Not interested in material on fishing, camping, or firearms knowledge. Query. Length: 1,800-2,000 words. **Pays up to $1,000.**

REPRINTS Copies for author will be provided upon publication. No reprints possible.

PHOTOS Captions preferred. Accepts images in digital format only, no slides. Model release required "for every recognizable human face in a photo.". Pays $125-600/image; $1,000 for color cover; $400-1,400 for text/photo package. Pays on publication. Credit line given. No additional payment made for photos used with ms. Photos purchased with or without accompanying mss.

COLUMNS/DEPARTMENTS Hunting Guns, Hunting Loads, destination and adventure, and Public Hunting Grounds. Study back issues for appropriate subject matter and style. Length: 800-1,500 words. **Pays $300-800.**

TIPS "Although unsolicited mss are accepted, detailed query letters outlining the proposed topic and approach are appreciated and will save both writers and editors a considerable amount of time. If we like your story idea, you will be contacted by mail or phone and given direction on how we'd like the topic covered. NRA Publications accept all mss and photographs for consideration on a speculation basis only. Story angles should be narrow, but coverage must have depth. How-to articles are popular with readers and might range from methods for hunting to techniques on making gear used on successful hunts. Where-to articles should contain contacts and information needed to arrange a similar hunt. All submissions are judged on three criteria: Story angle (it should be fresh, interesting, and informative); quality of writing (clear and lively—capable of holding the readers' attention throughout); and quality and quantity of accompanying photos (sharpness, reproducability, and connection to text are most important.)"

⊘⑤⑤ BC OUTDOORS HUNTING AND SHOOTING

Outdoor Group Media, #201a-7261 River Place, Mission BC V4S 0A2 Canada. (604)820-3400. **Fax:** (604)820-3477. **E-mail:** info@outdoorgroupmedia.com; mmitchell@outdoorgroupmedia.com; production@outdoorgroupmedia.com. **Website:** www.bcoutdoorsmagazine.com. **Contact:** Mike Mitchell, editor. **80% freelance written.** Biannual magazine covering hunting, shooting, camping, and backroads in British Columbia, Canada. "*BC Outdoors Magazine* publishes 7 sport fishing issues a year with 2 hunting and shooting supplement issues each summer and fall. Our magazine is about the best outdoor experiences in BC. Whether you're camping on an ocean shore, hiking into your favorite lake, or learning how to fly-fish on your favourite river, we want to showcase what our province has to offer to sport fishing and outdoor enthusiasts. *BC Outdoors Hunting and Shooting* provides trusted editorial for trapping, deer hunting, big buck, bowhunting, bag limits, baitling, decoys, calling, camouflage, tracking, trophy hunting, pheasant hunting, goose hunting, hunting regulations, duck hunting, whitetail hunting, hunting regulations, hunting trips, and mule deer hunting." Estab. 1945. Circ. 30,000. Byline given. Pays on publication. Offers kill fee. Publishes ms an average of 3 months after acceptance. Accepts queries by e-mail. Guidelines for 8x10 SASE with 7 Canadian first-class stamps.

NONFICTION Needs how-to, new or innovative articles on hunting subjects, personal experience, outdoor adventure, outdoor topics specific to British Columbia. **Buys 50 mss/year.** "Please query the publication before submitting. Please do not send unsolicited mss or photos. Your pitch should be no more than 100-words outlining exactly what your story will be. You should be able to encapsulate the essence of your story and show us why our readers would be interested in reading or knowing what you are writing about. Queries need to be clear, succinct and straight to the point. Show us why we should publish your article in 150 words or less." Length: 1,700-2,000 words. **Pays $300-500.**

PHOTOS Biannual magazine emphasizing hunting, RV camping, canoeing, wildlife and management issues in British Columbia only. Sample copy available for $4.95 Canadian. Family oriented. "By far, most photos accompany mss. We are always on the lookout for good covers—wildlife, recreational activities, people in the outdoors—of British Columbia, vertical and square format. Photos with mss must, of course, illustrate the story. There should, as far as possible, be something happening. Photos generally dominate lead spread of each story. They are used in everything from double-page bleeds to thumbnails.". State availability. Model/property release preferred. Photo captions or at least full identification required.

COLUMNS/DEPARTMENTS Column needs basically supplied in-house.

TIPS "Send us material on fishing and hunting. We generally just send back nonrelated work. We want in-depth information and professional writing only. Emphasis on environmental issues. Those pieces with a conservation component have a better chance of being published. Subject must be specific to British Columbia. We receive many mss written by people who obviously do not know the magazine or market. The writer has a better chance of breaking in with short, lesser-paying articles and fillers, because we have a stable of regular writers who produce most main features."

⊖⊙ DEER & DEER HUNTING

F+W Media, Inc., 700 E. State St., Iola WI 54990. (715)445-2214. **E-mail:** Outdoorsfw@gmail.com. **Website:** www.deeranddeerhunting.com. **Contact:** Dan Schmidt, editor-in-chief. **95% freelance written.** Magazine published 10 times/year covering white-tailed deer. "Readers include a cross section of the deer hunting population—individuals who hunt with bow, gun, or camera. The editorial content of the magazine focuses on white-tailed deer biology and behavior, management principle and practices, habitat requirements, natural history of deer, hunting techniques, and hunting ethics. We also publish a wide range of how-to articles designed to help hunters locate and get close to deer at all times of the year. The majority of our readership consists of 2-season hunters (bow & gun) and approximately one-third camera hunt." Estab. 1977. Circ. 200,000. Byline given. Pays on acceptance. Publishes ms an average of 18 months after acceptance. Edito-

rial lead time 6 months. Submit seasonal material 12 months in advance. Accepts queries by mail, e-mail. Responds in 1 month to queries. Responds in 2 months to mss. Sample copy for 9x12 SASE. Guidelines online.

NONFICTION Needs general interest, historical, how-to, photo feature, technical. No "Joe and me" articles. **Buys 100 mss/year.** Send complete ms. Length: 1,000-2,000 words. **Pays $150-600 for assigned articles. Pays $150-400 for unsolicited articles.** Sometimes pays expenses of writers on assignment.

PHOTOS Send photos. Captions required. Reviews transparencies. Offers $25-200/photo; $500 for cover photos.

COLUMNS/DEPARTMENTS Deer Browse (odd occurrences), 500 words. **Buys 10 mss/year.** Query. **Pays $25-250.**

FICTION Mood deer hunting pieces. **Buys 9 mss/year.** Send complete ms.

FILLERS Needs facts, newsbreaks. **Buys 40-50 mss/year.** Length: 100-500 words. **Pays $15-150.**

TIPS "Feature articles dealing with deer biology or behavior should be documented by scientific research (the author's or that of others) as opposed to a limited number of personal observations."

⊖⊙ THE DRAKE MAGAZINE

P.O. Box 11546, Denver CO 80211. (720)638-3114. **E-mail:** info@drakemag.com. **Website:** www.drakemag.com. **70% freelance written.** Quarterly magazine for people who love flyfishing. Estab. 1998. Byline given. Pays 1 month after publication. Publishes ms an average of 1 year after acceptance. Editorial lead time 1 year. Submit seasonal material 1 year in advance. Accepts queries by e-mail. Responds in 6 months to mss. Guidelines online.

NONFICTION Needs flyfishing news items from your local area, historical, humor, opinion, personal experience, photo feature, short essays, travel, flyfishing related. **Buys 20-30 mss/year.** Query. Length: 650-2,000 words. **Pays 25¢/word, "depending on the amount of work we have to put into the piece."**

PHOTOS State availability. Offers $50-200/photo.

⊖⊙⊙ FIELD & STREAM

2 Park Ave., New York NY 10016. (212)779-5296. **Fax:** (212)779-5114. **E-mail:** fsletters@bonniercorp.com. **Website:** www.fieldandstream.com. **50% freelance written.** Broad-based monthly service magazine for the hunter and fisherman. Editorial content consists of articles of penetrating depth about national hunt-

ing, fishing, and related activities. Also humor, personal essays, profiles on outdoor people, conservation, sportsmen's insider secrets, tactics and techniques, and adventures. Estab. 1895. Circ. 1,500,000. Byline given. Pays on acceptance for most articles. Accepts queries by mail. Responds in 1 month to queries. Guidelines online.

PHOTOS Contact: Photo editor. Send photos. Reviews slides (prefers color). When purchased separately, pays $450 minimum for color.

TIPS "Writers are encouraged to submit queries on article ideas. These should be no more than a paragraph or 2, and should include a summary of the idea, including the angle you will hang the story on, and a sense of what makes this piece different from all others on the same or a similar subject. Many queries are turned down because we have no idea what the writer is getting at. Be sure that your letter is absolutely clear. We've found that if you can't sum up the point of the article in a sentence or 2, the article doesn't have a point. Pieces that depend on writing style, such as humor, mood, and nostalgia or essays often can't be queried and may be submitted in ms form. The same is true of short tips. All submissions to *Field & Stream* are on an on-spec basis. Before submitting anything, however, we encourage you to *study*, not simply read, the magazine. Many pieces are rejected because they do not fit the tone or style of the magazine, or fail to match the subject of the article with the overall subject matter of *Field & Stream*."

😊😊 FLORIDA SPORTSMAN

Wickstrom Communications, Intermedia Outdoors, 2700 S. Kanner Hwy., Stuart FL 34994. (772)219-7400. **Fax:** (772)219-6900. **E-mail:** editor@floridasportsman.com. **Website:** www.floridasportsman.com. **30% freelance written.** Monthly magazine covering fishing, boating, hunting, and related sports—Florida and Caribbean only. Edited for the boatowner and offshore, coastal, and fresh water fisherman. It provides a how, when, and where approach in its articles, which also includes occasional camping, diving, and hunting stories—plus ecology; in-depth articles and editorials attempting to protect Florida's wilderness, wetlands, and natural beauty. Circ. 115,000. Byline given. Pays on acceptance. Publishes ms an average of 6 months after acceptance. Submit seasonal material 6 months in advance. Accepts queries by mail, e-mail. Responds within 1 month to query by mail or e-mail. Sample copy free. E-mail editor for submission guidelines.

NONFICTION Needs essays, environment or nature, how-to, fishing, hunting, boating, humor, outdoors angle, personal experience, in fishing, etc., technical, boats, tackle, etc., as particularly suitable for Florida specialties. **Buys 20-40 mss/year.** Query. Length: 1,500-2,500 words. **Pays $475.**

PHOTOS High-res digital images on CD preferred. Reviews 35mm transparencies, 4×5 and larger prints. Offers no additional payment for photos accepted with ms. Pays up to $750 for cover photos.

TIPS "Feature articles are sometimes open to freelancers; however there is little chance of acceptance unless contributor is an accomplished and avid outdoorsman *and* a competent writer-photographer with considerable experience in Florida."

😊😊 FUR-FISH-GAME

2878 E. Main St., Columbus OH 43209-9947. **E-mail:** ffgcox@ameritech.net. **Website:** www.furfishgame.com. **Contact:** Mitch Cox, editor. **65% freelance written.** Monthly magazine for outdoorsmen of all ages who are interested in hunting, fishing, trapping, dogs, camping, conservation, and related topics. Estab. 1900. Circ. 118,000. Byline given. Pays on acceptance. Publishes ms an average of 4 months after acceptance. Responds in 2 months to queries. Sample copy for $1 and 9x12 SASE. Guidelines with #10 SASE.

NONFICTION Query. Length: 500-3,000 words. **Pays $50-250 or more for features depending upon quality, photo support, and importance to magazine.**

PHOTOS Send photos. Captions, True required. Reviews transparencies, color 5×7 or 8×10 prints, digital photos on CD only with thumbnail sheet of small images and a numbered caption sheet. Pays $35 for separate freelance photos.

TIPS "We are always looking for quality how-to articles about fish, game animals, or birds that are popular with everyday outdoorsmen but often overlooked in other publications, such as catfish, bluegill, crappie, squirrel, rabbit, crows, etc. We also use articles on standard seasonal subjects such as deer and pheasant, but like to see a fresh approach or new technique. Instructional trapping articles are useful all year. Articles on gun dogs, ginseng, and do-it-yourself projects are also popular with our readers. An assortment of photos and/or sketches greatly enhances any ms, and sidebars, where applicable, can also help. No phone queries, please."

⊛⊛ GAME & FISH

P.O. Box 420235, Palm Coast FL 32142-0235. (770)953-9222. **Fax:** (678)279-7512. **E-mail:** ken.dunwoody@imoutdoors.com. **Website:** www.gameandfishmag.com. **Contact:** Ken Dunwoody, editorial director; Ron Sinfelt, photo editor; Allen Hansen, graphic artist. **90% freelance written.** Publishes 28 different monthly outdoor magazines, each one covering the fishing and hunting opportunities in a particular state or region (see individual titles to contact editors). Estab. 1975. Circ. 570,000 for 28 state-specific magazines. Byline given. Pays 3 months prior to cover date of issue. Offers negotiable kill fee. Publishes ms an average of 7 months after acceptance. Submit seasonal material 8 months in advance. Accepts queries by mail, e-mail, fax. Responds in 3 months to queries. Sample copy for $3.50 and 9x12 SASE. Guidelines for #10 SASE.

○ "To query information regarding writing guidelines and submissions for any of our *Game & Fish* magazines, please contact Ken Dunwoody, editorial director of *Game & Fish*."

NONFICTION Length: 1,500-2,400 words. **Pays $150-300; additional payment made for electronic rights.**
PHOTOS Captions, identification of subjects required. Reviews transparencies, prints, digital images. Cover photos $250, inside color $75, and b&w $25.
TIPS "Our readers are experienced anglers and hunters, and we try to provide them with useful, specific articles about where, when, and how to enjoy the best hunting and fishing in their state or region. We also cover topics concerning game and fish management. Most articles should be tightly focused and aimed at outdoorsmen in 1 particular state. After familiarizing themselves with our magazine(s), writers should query the appropriate state editor (see individual listings) or send to Ken Dunwoody."

⊛⊛⊛ GRAY'S SPORTING JOURNAL

Morris Communications Corp., 735 Broad St., Augusta GA 30901. (706)724-0851. **E-mail:** editorgsj@gmail.com. **Website:** www.grayssportingjournal.com. **Contact:** James R. Babb, editor. **75% freelance written.** 7 issues per year magazine High-end hunting and fishing—think *Field & Stream* meets *The New Yorker.* "We expect competent, vividly written prose—fact or fiction—that has high entertainment value for a very sophisticated audience of experienced hunters and anglers. We do not consider previously published material. We do, however, occasionally run prepublication book excerpts. To get a feel for what Gray's publishes, review several back issues. Note that we do not, as a rule, publish 'how-to' articles; this is the province of our regular columnists." Estab. 1975. Circ. 32,000. Byline given. Pays on publication. Publishes ms an average of 1 year after acceptance. Editorial lead time 14 months. Submit seasonal material 16 months in advance. Accepts simultaneous submissions. Responds in 3 months to mss. Guidelines online.

NONFICTION Needs essays, historical, humor, personal experience, photo feature, travel. Special issues: Gray's publishes three themed issues each year: August is always entirely devoted to upland birdhunting; April to fly fishing; December to sporting travel. All other issues—February, May, September, November—focus on seasonally appropriate themes. Each issue always features a travel piece, from exotic destinations to right around the corner. We publish no how-to of any kind. **Buys 20-30 mss/year.** Send complete ms via e-mail. Length: 1,500-12,000 words. **Pays $600-1,000 for unsolicited articles.**
PHOTOS State availability. Reviews contact sheets, GIF/JPEG files. We negotiate payment individually.
FICTION Accepts quality fiction with some aspect of hunting or fishing at the core. Needs adventure, experimental, historical, humorous, slice-of-life vignettes. If some aspect of hunting or fishing isn't at the core of the story, it has zero chance of interesting *Gray's.* **Buys 20 mss/year.** Send complete ms. Length: 1,500-12,000 words. **Pays $600-1,000.**
POETRY Needs avant-garde, haiku, light verse, traditional. Buys 7/year poems/year. Submit maximum 3 poems. Length: 10-40 lines.
TIPS "Write something different, write something well—fiction or nonfiction—write something that goes to the heart of hunting or fishing more elegantly, more inspirationally, than the 1,500 or so other unsolicited mss we review each year. For best results, submit by e-mail. Mail submissions can take weeks longer to hear back."

⊛⊛ MARLIN

P.O. Box 8500, Winter Park FL 32790. (407)628-4802. **Fax:** (407)628-7061. **E-mail:** editor@marlinmag.com. **Website:** www.marlinmag.com. **90% freelance written.** Magazine published 8 times/year covering the sport of big game fishing (billfish, tuna, dorado, and wahoo). "Our readers are sophisticated, affluent, and serious about their sport—they expect a high-class, well-written magazine that provides information and practical advice." Estab. 1982. Circ. 50,000. Byline given. Pays on acceptance. Publishes ms an average of 3 months after acceptance. Submit seasonal material 3 months in advance. Sample copy free with SASE. Guidelines online.

NONFICTION Needs general interest, how-to, bait-rigging, tackle maintenance, etc., new product, personal experience, photo feature, technical, travel. No freshwater fishing stories. No 'Me & Joe went fishing' stories. **Buys 30-50 mss/year.** Query with published clips. Length: 800-3,000 words. **Pays $250-500.**

REPRINTS Send photocopy and information about when and where the material previously appeared. Pays 50-75% of amount paid for original article.

PHOTOS State availability. Reviews original slides. Offers $50-300 for inside use, $1,000 for a cover.

COLUMNS/DEPARTMENTS Tournament Reports (reports on winners of major big game fishing tournaments), 200-400 words; Blue Water Currents (news features), 100-400 words. **Buys 25 mss/year.** Query. **Pays $75-250.**

TIPS "Tournament reports are a good way to break in to *Marlin*. Make them short but accurate, and provide photos of fishing action or winners' award shots (*not* dead fish hanging up at the docks). We always need how-tos and news items. Our destination pieces (travel stories) emphasize where and when to fish, but also include information on where to stay. For features: Crisp, high-action stories with emphasis on exotic nature, adventure, personality, etc.—nothing flowery or academic. Technical/how-to: concise and informational—specific details. News: Again, concise with good details—watch for legislation affecting big game fishing, outstanding catches, new clubs and organizations, new trends, and conservation issues."

$ MICHIGAN OUT-OF-DOORS

P.O. Box 30235, Lansing MI 48912. (517)371-1041. **Fax:** (517)371-1505. **E-mail:** thansen@mucc.org; magazine@mucc.org. **Website:** www.michiganoutofdoors.com. **Contact:** Tony Hansen, editor. **75% freelance written.** Monthly magazine emphasizing Michigan hunting and fishing with associated conservation issues. Estab. 1947. Circ. 40,000. Byline given. Pays on acceptance. Publishes ms an average of 6 months after acceptance. Submit seasonal material 6 months in advance. Accepts queries by e-mail only. Responds in 1 month to queries. Sample copy for $3.50. Guidelines for free.

NONFICTION Needs expose, historical, how-to, interview, opinion, personal experience, photo feature. All topics must pertain to hunting and fishing topics in Michigan. Special issues: Archery Deer and Small Game Hunting (October); Firearm Deer Hunting (November); Cross-country Skiing and Early-ice Lake Fishing (December or January); Camping/Hiking (May); Family Fishing (June). No humor or poetry. **Buys 96 mss/year.** Send complete ms. Length: 1,000-2,000 words. **Pays $150 minimum for feature stories. Photos must be included with story.**

PHOTOS Captions required. Offers no additional payment for photos accepted with ms; others $20-175.

TIPS "Top priority is placed on queries that offer new ideas on hard-core hunting and fishing topics. Submit seasonal material 6 months in advance. Wants to see new approaches to subject matter."

$$ MUSKY HUNTER MAGAZINE

P.O. Box 340, 7978 Hwy. 70 E., St. Germain WI 54558. (715)477-2178. **Fax:** (715)477-8858. **E-mail:** editor@muskyhunter.com. **Website:** www.muskyhunter.com. **Contact:** Jim Saric, editor. **90% freelance written.** Bimonthly magazine on musky fishing. Serves the vertical market of musky fishing enthusiasts. "We're interested in how-to, where-to articles." Estab. 1988. Circ. 37,000. Byline given. Pays on publication. Publishes ms an average of 4 months after acceptance. Submit seasonal material 4 months in advance. Responds in 2 months to queries. Sample copy with 9x12 SASE and $2.79 postage. Guidelines with #10 SASE.

NONFICTION Needs historical, related only to musky fishing, how-to, catch muskies, modify lures, boats, and tackle for musky fishing, personal experience (must be musky fishing experience), technical, fishing equipment, travel, to lakes and areas for musky fishing. **Buys 50 mss/year.** Send complete ms. Length: 1,000-2,500 words. **Pays $100-300 for assigned articles. Pays $50-300 for unsolicited articles.**

PHOTOS Send photos. Identification of subjects required. Reviews 35mm transparencies, 3x5 prints, high-res digital images preferred. Offers no additional payment for photos accepted with ms.

$$ RACK MAGAZINE

Buckmasters, Ltd., 10350 U.S. Hwy. 80 E., Montgomery AL 36117. (800)240-3337. **Fax:** (334)215-3535. **E-mail:** mhandley@buckmasters.com. **Website:** www.buckmasters.com. **50% freelance written.** Monthly (July-December) magazine covering big game hunting. "All features are either first- or third-person narratives detailing the successful hunts for world-class, big game animals—mostly white-tailed deer and other North American species." Estab. 1998. Circ. 75,000. Byline given. Pays on publication. Publishes ms an average of 9 months after acceptance. Editorial lead time 9-12 months. Submit seasonal material 9 months in advance. Accepts queries by e-mail. Accepts simultaneous submissions. Responds in 1 month to queries. Responds in 2 months to mss. Sample copy free. Guidelines free.

NONFICTION Needs personal experience. "We're interested only in articles chronicling successful hunts." **Buys 40-50 mss/year.** Query. Length: 1,000 words. **Pays $100-325 for assigned and unsolicited articles.**

PHOTOS Send photos. Captions, identification of subjects required. Reviews transparencies, prints, GIF/JPEG files.

TIPS "Ask for and read the writer's guidelines."

$$ SALT WATER SPORTSMAN

Bonnier Corporation, 460 N. Orlando Ave., Suite 200, Winter Park FL 32789. (407)628-4802. **E-mail:** editor@saltwatersportsman.com. **Website:** www.saltwatersportsman.com. **Contact:** Glenn Law, editor. **85% freelance written.** Monthly magazine covering saltwater sport fishing. *Salt Water Sportsman* is edited for serious marine sport fishermen whose lifestyle includes the pursuit of game fish in U.S. waters and around the world. It provides information on fishing trends, techniques, and destinations, both local and international. Each issue reviews offshore and inshore fishing boats, high-tech electronics, innovative tackle, engines, and other new products. Coverage also focuses on sound fisheries management and conservation. Circ. 170,000. Byline given. Pays on acceptance. Offers kill fee. Publishes ms an average of 5 months after acceptance. Submit seasonal material 8 months in advance. Accepts queries by mail, e-mail. Responds in 1 month to queries. Guidelines available by request.

NONFICTION Needs how-to, personal experience, technical, travel, to fishing areas. **Buys 100 mss/year.** Query. Length: 1,200-1,500 words. **Pays $300-750.**

PHOTOS Captions required. Reviews low res digital files, requires RAW files for publication. Pays $1,500 minimum for cover.

COLUMNS/DEPARTMENTS Sportsman's Tips (short, how-to tips and techniques on salt water fishing, emphasis is on building, repairing, or reconditioning specific items or gear). Send complete ms.

TIPS "There are a lot of knowledgeable fishermen/budding writers out there who could be valuable to us with a little coaching. Many don't think they can write a story for us, but they'd be surprised. We work with writers. Shorter articles that get to the point which are accompanied by good, sharp photos are hard for us to turn down. Having to delete unnecessary wordage—conversation, clichés, etc.—that writers feel is mandatory is annoying. Often they don't devote enough attention to specific fishing information."

$$$$ SPORT FISHING

Bonnier Corporation, 460 N. Orlando Ave., Suite 200, Winter Park FL 32789. (407)628-4802. **Fax:** (407)628-7061. **E-mail:** Editor@sportfishingmag.com. **Website:** www.sportfishingmag.com. **50% freelance written.** Magazine published 10 times/year covering saltwater angling, saltwater fish and fisheries. "*Sport Fishing*'s readers are middle-aged, affluent, mostly male, who are generally proficient in and very educated to their sport. We are about fishing from boats, not from surf or jetties." Estab. 1985. Circ. 250,000. Byline given. Pays on acceptance. Offers 25% kill fee. Publishes ms an average of 6-12 months after acceptance. Editorial lead time 2-12 months. Submit seasonal material 1 year in advance. Accepts queries by e-mail. Responds in 1 week to queries. Responds in 1 month to mss. Sample copy with #10 SASE. Guidelines online.

NONFICTION Needs general interest, how-to. Query. Length: 2,500-3,000 words. **Pays $500-750 for text only; $1,500+ possible for complete package with photos.** Answer.

PHOTOS State availability. Reviews GIF/JPEG files. Offers $75-400/photo.

TIPS "Queries please; no over-the-transom submissions. Meet or beat deadlines. Include quality photos when you can. Quote the experts. Balance information with readability. Include sidebars."

$$$ SPORTS AFIELD

Field Sports Publishing, 15621 Chemical Ln., Huntington Beach CA 92649. (714)373-4910. **E-mail:** letters@sportsafield.com. **Website:** www.sportsafield.com. **Contact:** Jerry Gutierrez, art director. **60% freelance written**. Magazine published 6 times/year covering big game hunting. "We cater to the upscale hunting market, especially hunters who travel to exotic destinations like Alaska and Africa. We are not a deer hunting magazine, and we do not cover fishing." Estab. 1887. Circ. 50,000. Byline given. Pays 1 month prior to publication. Publishes ms an average of 6 months after acceptance. Editorial lead time 4 months. Submit seasonal material 5 months in advance. Accepts queries by mail, e-mail. Responds in 2 months to queries and to mss Sample copy for $7.99. Guidelines online.

NONFICTION Needs personal experience, travel. **Buys 6-8 mss/year.** Query. Length: 1,500-2,500 words. **Pays $500-800.**

PHOTOS State availability. Captions, model releases required. Reviews 35mm slides transparencies, TIFF/JPEG files. Offers no additional payment for photos accepted with ms.

FILLERS Needs newsbreaks. **Buys 30 mss/year.** Length: 200-500 words. **Pays $75-150.**

☺☺ TRAPPER & PREDATOR CALLER

F+W Media, Inc., 700 E. State St., Iola WI 54990. (715)445-2214. **E-mail:** jared.blohm@fwmedia.com. **Website:** www.trapperpredatorcaller.com. **75% freelance written.** Tabloid published 10 times/year covering trapping and predator calling, fur trade. "Our editorial goal is to inform, educate and entertain our readers with articles, photographs and illustrations that promote trapping and predator calling." Must have mid-level to advanced knowledge, because *T&PC* is heavily how-to focused. Estab. 1975. Circ. 42,000. Byline given. Pays within 45 days of publication. Publishes ms an average of 6 months after acceptance. Editorial lead time 1 year. Submit seasonal material 1 year in advance. Accepts queries by e-mail.

NONFICTION Needs how-to, interview, personal experience, travel. **Buys 100 mss/year.** Query or send complete ms via e-mail. Length: 1,500-2,500 words. **Pays $250 for assigned articles.**

PHOTOS Send photos. Reviews high-resolution digital photos, slides, prints. Digital photos should be saved as TIFF or JPEG files. Minimum 300 dpi.

TIPS "Check your facts. An error in fact reduces the credibility of the magazine and hurts your relationship with us. Please double check spelling, dates, proper names, etc."

☺☺ TURKEY COUNTRY

National Wild Turkey Federation, P.O. Box 530, Edgefield SC 29824-0530. (803)637-3106. **Fax:** (803)637-0034. **E-mail:** info@nwtf.net; turkeycountry@nwtf.net. **E-mail:** klee@nwtf.net. **Website:** www.turkeycountrymagazine.com. **Contact:** Karen Lee, editor; Gregg Powers, managing editor; P.J. Perea, senior editor; Matt Lindler, photo editor. **50-60% freelance written.** Bimonthly educational magazine for members of the National Wild Turkey Federation. Topics covered include hunting, history, restoration, management, biology, and distribution of wild turkey. Estab. 1973. Circ. 180,000. Byline given. Pays on acceptance. Publishes ms an average of 6 months after acceptance. Editorial lead time 1 year. Accepts queries by mail, e-mail. Responds in 2 months to queries Sample copy for $3 and 9x12 SAE. Guidelines online. ◑ Submit queries by June 1 of each year.

NONFICTION Query (preferred) or send complete ms. Length: 500-1,200 words. **Pays $250-550.**

PHOTOS "We want quality photos submitted with features. Illustrations also acceptable. We are using more and more inside color illustrations. No typical hunter-holding-dead-turkey photos or setups using mounted birds or domestic turkeys. Photos with how-to stories must make the techniques clear (i.e., how to make a turkey call; how to sculpt or carve a bird in wood).". Identification of subjects, model releases required. Reviews transparencies, high resolution digital images.

FICTION Must contribute to the education, enlightenment, or entertainment of readers in some special way.

TIPS "The writer should simply keep in mind that the audience is 'expert' on wild turkey management, hunting, life history, and restoration/conservation history. He/she must know the subject. We are buying more third person, more fiction, more humor—in an attempt to avoid the 'predictability trap' of a single subject magazine."

◐ WESTERN SPORTSMAN

202-9644 54 Ave., Edmonton AB T6E 5V1 Canada. (780)643-3963. **Fax:** (780)643-3960. **E-mail:** editor@westernsportsman.com. **Website:** www.westernsportsman.com. **90% freelance written.** Bimonthly magazine for anglers and hunters. Main coverage area is Alberta, Saskatchewan, Manitoba, and the Northern Territories. Occasionally publishes adventure destination stories that cover parts of the country as well. Short news items pertaining to all provinces/territories are also accepted. Tries to include as much information as possible on all subjects in each edition. Estab. 1968. Circ. 35,000. Byline given. Pays on publication. Accepts queries by e-mail. Responds in 1 month to queries. Guidelines available for free only online, or by e-mail.

○ Familiarize yourself with the magazine and query before submitting. Queries accepted April 1 to May 30.

NONFICTION Buys 60 mss/year. Length: 1,500-2,000 words for features; 600-1,000 words for columns; 150-300 words for news items. **Payment is negotiable.**

PHOTOS No additional payment for photos with ms. Also purchased without ms. Pays up to $200 for front cover.

MARTIAL ARTS

◎◎ JOURNAL OF ASIAN MARTIAL ARTS

Via Media Publishing Co., 941 Calle Mejia, #822, Santa Fe NM 87501. (505)983-1919. **E-mail:** md@journalofasianmartialarts.com. **Website:** www.goviamedia.com. **90% freelance written.** "Quarterly magazine covering all historical and cultural aspects related to Asian martial arts, offering a mature, well-rounded view of this uniquely fascinating subject. Although the journal treats the subject with academic accuracy (references at end), writing need not lose the reader!". Estab. 1991. Circ. 10,000. Byline given. Pays on publication. Publishes ms an average of 1 year after acceptance. Submit seasonal material 6 months in advance. Responds in 1 month to queries. Responds in 2 months to mss. Sample copy for $10. Guidelines with #10 SASE or online.

NONFICTION Needs essays, expose, historical, how-to, martial art techniques and materials, e.g., weapons, interview, personal experience, photo feature, place or person, religious, technical, travel. No articles overburdened with technical/foreign/scholarly vocabulary, or material slanted as indirect advertising or for personal aggrandizement. **Buys 30 mss/year.** Query with short background and martial arts experience. Length: 1,000-10,000 words. **Pays $150-500.**

PHOTOS State availability. Identification of subjects, model releases required. Reviews contact sheets, negatives, transparencies, prints. Offers no additional payment for photos accepted with ms.

COLUMNS/DEPARTMENTS Location (city, area, specific site, Asian or non-Asian, showing value for martial arts, researchers, history); Media Review (film, book, video, museum for aspects of academic and artistic interest). Length: 1,000-2,500 words. **Buys 16 mss/year.** Query. **Pays $50-200.**

FICTION Needs adventure, historical, humorous, slice-of-life vignettes, translation. No material that does not focus on martial arts culture. **Buys 1 mss/year.** Query. Length: 1,000-10,000 words. **Pays $50-500, or copies.**

POETRY Needs avant-garde, free verse, haiku, light verse, traditional. No poetry that does not focus on martial arts culture. Buys 2 poems/year. Submit maximum 10 poems. **Pays $10-100, or copies.**

FILLERS Needs anecdotes, facts, gags, newsbreaks, short humor. **Buys 2 mss/year.** Length: 25-500 words. **Pays $1-50, or copies.**

TIPS "Always query before sending a ms. We are open to varied types of articles; most however require a strong academic grasp of Asian culture. For those not having this background, we suggest trying a museum review, or interview, where authorities can be questioned, quoted, and provide supportive illustrations. We especially desire articles/reports from Asia, with photo illustrations, particularly of a martial art style, so readers can visually understand the unique attributes of that style, its applications, evolution, etc. Location and media reports are special areas that writers may consider, especially if they live in a location of martial art significance."

◎ KUNG FU TAI CHI

Pacific Rim Publishing, 40748 Encyclopedia Circle, Fremont CA 94538. (510)656-5100. **Fax:** (510)656-8844. **E-mail:** gene@kungfumagazine.com. **Website:** www.kungfumagazine.com. **70% freelance written.** Bimonthly magazine covering Chinese martial arts and culture. *Kung Fu Tai Chi* covers the full range of Kung Fu culture, including healing, philosophy, meditation, Fengshui, Buddhism, Taoism, history, and the latest events in art and culture, plus insightful features on the martial arts. Circ. 15,000. Byline given. Pays on publication. Editorial lead time 4 months. Submit seasonal material 4 months in advance. Accepts queries by mail, e-mail, fax, phone. Responds in 2 months to queries. Responds in 3 months to mss. Sample copy for $4.99 or online. Guidelines online.

NONFICTION Needs general interest, historical, interview, personal experience, religious, technical, travel, cultural perspectives. No poetry or fiction. **Buys 70 mss/year.** Query. Length: 500-2,500 words. **Pays $35-125.**

PHOTOS Send photos. Captions, identification of subjects required. Reviews 5x7 prints, GIF/JPEG files. Offers no additional payment for photos accepted with ms.

TIPS "Check out our website and get an idea of past articles."

⊛⊛ T'AI CHI

Wayfarer Publications, P.O. Box 39938, Los Angeles CA 90039. (323)665-7773. **Fax:** (323)665-1627. **E-mail:** taichi@tai-chi.com. **Website:** www.tai-chi.com. **Contact:** Marvin Smalheiser, editor. **90% freelance written.** Quarterly magazine covering T'ai Chi Ch'uan as a martial art and for health and fitness. "Covers T'ai Chi Ch'uan and other internal martial arts, plus qigong and Chinese health, nutrition, and philosophical disciplines. Readers are practitioners or laymen interested in developing skills and insight for self-defense, health, and self-improvement." Estab. 1977. Circ. 50,000. Byline given. Pays on publication. Publishes ms an average of 3 months after acceptance. Editorial lead time 3 months. Submit seasonal material 6 months in advance. Accepts queries by mail, e-mail, fax. Responds in 3 weeks to queries. Responds in 3 months to mss. Sample copy for $5.99. Guidelines online.

NONFICTION Needs essays, how-to, on T'ai Chi Ch'uan, qigong, and related Chinese disciplines, interview, personal experience. "Do not want articles promoting an individual, system, or school." Send complete ms. Length: 1,200-4,500 words. **Pays $75-500.**

PHOTOS Send photos. Captions, identification of subjects, model releases required. Reviews color or b&w 4x6 or 5x7 prints, digital files suitable for print production. "Offers no additional payment for photos accepted with ms, but overall payment takes into consideration the number and quality of photos.".

TIPS "Think and write for practitioners and laymen who want information and insight, and who are trying to work through problems to improve skills and their health. No promotional material."

MISCELLANEOUS SPORTS

⊛ LACROSSE MAGAZINE

113 W. University Pkwy., Baltimore MD 21210. (410)235-6882. **Fax:** (410)366-6735. **E-mail:** feedback@ laxmagazine.com. **Website:** www.laxmagazine.com; www.uslacrosse.org. **Contact:** Matt DaSilva, editor; Gabriella O'Brien, art director;. **60% freelance written.** Monthly magazine covering the sport of lacrosse. "*Lacrosse* is the only national feature publication devoted to the sport of lacrosse. It is a benefit of membership in U.S. Lacrosse, a nonprofit organization devoted to promoting the growth of lacrosse and preserving its history. U.S. Lacrosse maintains *Lacrosse Magazine Online* (LMO) at www.laxmagazine.com. *LMO* fea-

tures daily lacrosse news and scores directly from lacrosse-playing colleges. *LMO* also includes originally-produced features and news briefs covering all levels of play. Occasional feature articles printed in *Lacrosse* are re-published at *LMO*, and vice versa. The online component of *Lacrosse* will do things that a printed publication can't—provide news, scores and information in a timely manner." Estab. 1978. Circ. 235,000. Byline given. Pays on publication. Publishes ms an average of 2 months after acceptance. Editorial lead time 2 months. Submit seasonal material 2 months in advance. Sample copy free. Guidelines at www.uslacrosse.org.

NONFICTION Needs book excerpts, general interest, historical, how-to, drills, conditioning, x's and o's, etc., interview, new product, opinion, personal experience, photo feature, technical. **Buys 30-40 mss/year.** Length: 500-1,750 words. **Payment negotiable.** Sometimes pays expenses of writers on assignment.

PHOTOS State availability. Captions, identification of subjects required. Reviews contact sheets, 4x6 prints. Negotiates payment individually.

COLUMNS/DEPARTMENTS First Person (personal experience), 1,000 words; Fitness (conditioning/strength/exercise), 500-1,000 words; How-to, 500-1,000 words. **Buys 10-15 mss/year. Payment negotiable.**

TIPS "As the national development center of lacrosse, we are particularly interested in stories about the growth of the sport in non-traditional areas of the U.S. and abroad, written for an audience already knowledgeable about the game."

⊛ SKYDIVING

1665 Lexington Ave., Suite 102, DeLand FL 32724. (386)736-9779. **Fax:** (386)736-9786. **E-mail:** sue@skydivingmagazine.com; mike@skydivingmagazine.com. **Website:** www.skydivingmagazine.com. **Contact:** Sue Clifton, editor; Mike Truffer, publisher. **25% freelance written.** Monthly tabloid featuring skydiving for sport parachutists, worldwide dealers and equipment manufacturers. "*Skydiving* is a news magazine. Its purpose is to deliver timely, useful and interesting information about the equipment, techniques, events, people and places of parachuting. Our scope is national. *Skydiving*'s audience spans the entire spectrum of jumpers, from first-jump students to veterans with thousands of skydives. Some readers are riggers with a keen interest in the technical aspects of parachutes, while others are weekend 'fun' jumpers who want information to help them make travel plans and equipment purchases." Estab. 1979. Circ. 14,200. Byline given. Pays on publication. Publishes ms an average of 3 months after acceptance. Accepts simultaneous submissions. Responds in 1 month to queries. Sample copy for $2. Guidelines online.

NONFICTION No personal experience or human interest articles. Query. Length: 500-1,000 words. **Pays $25-100.** Sometimes pays expenses of writers on assignment.

PHOTOS State availability. Captions required. Reviews 5x7 and larger b&w glossy prints. Offers no additional payment for photos accepted with ms.

FILLERS Needs newsbreaks. Length: 100-200 words. **Pays $25 minimum.**

TIPS "The most frequent mistake made by writers in completing articles for us is that the writer isn't knowledgeable about the sport of parachuting. Articles about events are especially time-sensitive so yours must be submitted quickly. We welcome contributions about equipment. Even short, 'quick look' articles about new products are appropriate for *Skydiving*. If you know of a drop zone or other place that jumpers would like to visit, write an article describing its features and tell them why you liked it and what they can expect to find if they visit it. Avoid first-person articles."

RUNNING

⊖⊖ RUNNING TIMES

Rodale, Inc., 400 S. 10th St., Emmaus PA 18098-0099. (610)967-5171. **Fax:** (610)967-8964. **E-mail:** editor@runningtimes.com. **Website:** www.runningtimes.com. **Contact:** Jonathan Beverly, editor-in-chief. **40% freelance written**. Magazine published 10 times/year covering distance running and racing. "*Running Times* is the national magazine for the experienced running participant and fan. Our audience is knowledgeable about the sport and active in running and racing. All editorial relates specifically to running: improving performance, enhancing enjoyment, or exploring events, places, and people in the sport." Estab. 1977. Circ. 125,000. Byline given. Pays on publication. Publishes ms an average of 3 months after acceptance. Editorial lead time 4-6 months. Submit seasonal material 6 months in advance. Accepts queries by mail, e-mail. Responds in 1 month to queries. Responds in 2 months to mss. Sample copy for $8. Guidelines online.

NONFICTION Needs book excerpts, essays, historical, how-to, training, humor, inspirational, interview, new product, opinion, personal experience, with theme, purpose, evidence of additional research and/or special expertise, photo feature, news, reports. No basic, beginner how-to, generic fitness/nutrition, or generic first-person accounts. **Buys 35 mss/year.** Query. Length: 1,500-3,000 words. **Pays $600-2,500 for assigned articles. Pays $500-2,000 for unsolicited articles.** Sometimes pays expenses of writers on assignment.

PHOTOS State availability. Identification of subjects required. Negotiates payment individually.

COLUMNS/DEPARTMENTS Training (short topics related to enhancing performance), 1,000 words; Sports-Med (application of medical knowledge to running), 1,000 words; Nutrition (application of nutritional principles to running performance), 1,000 words. **Buys 10 mss/year.** Query. **Pays $200-400.**

FICTION Any genre, with running-related theme or characters. Buys 1 ms/year. Send complete ms. Length: 1,500-3,000 words. **Pays $100-500.**

TIPS "Thoroughly get to know runners and the running culture, both at the participant level and the professional, elite level."

⊖⊖ TRAIL RUNNER

Big Stone Publishing, 2567 Dolores Way, Carbondale CO 81623. (970)704-1442. **Fax:** (970)963-4965. **E-mail:** ywinn@bigstonepub.com; mbenge@bigstonepub.com. **Website:** www.trailrunnermag.com. **Contact:** Michael Benge, editor; Yitka Winn, associate editor. **80% freelance written**. Magazine published 8x year, covering trail runing, ultratanning, fastpacking, adventure racing, and snowshoeing. Covers all aspects of off-road running. "North America's only magazine dedicated to trail running. In-depth editorial and compelling photography informs, entertains and inspires readers of all ages and abilities to enjoy the outdoors and to improve their health and fitness through the sport of trail running." Estab. 1999. Circ. 31,000. Byline given. Pays 30 days post-publication Publishes ms an average of 2 months after acceptance. Editorial lead time is 3 months. Submit seasonal material 5 months in advance. Accepts queries by e-mail. Accepts simultaneous submissions. Responds in 4 weeks to queries. Sample copy for $5. Guidelines online at trailrunnermag.com/contributors.

◗   "Your well-written query should present a clear, original and provocative story angle, not merely a topic or idea, and should reflect your thorough knowledge of the magazine's content, editorial style and tone."

NONFICTION Needs expose, historical, how-to, humor, inspirational, interview, personal experience, technical, travel, racing. Does not want "My first trail race." **Buys 30-40 mss/year.** Query with one or two writing samples (preferably previously published articles), including your name, phone number and e-mail address. Identify which department your story would be best suited for. **Pays 25¢/word for assigned and unsolicited articles.**

PHOTOS "*Trail Runner* regularly features stunning photography of trail running destinations, races, adventures and faces of the sport.". State availability of photos with submission. Captions, identification of subjects. Reviews GIF/JPEG files. Offers $50-250/photo.

COLUMNS/DEPARTMENTS Contact: Michael Benge, editor, or Yitka Winn, associate editor. Making Tracks (news, race reports, athlete Q&A), 300-800 words; Trail Tips, Training , Trail Rx (injury prevention/treatment, recovery), Take Your Mark (race previews); Nutrition (sports nutrition, health news), 800-1,000 words; Adventure, Great Escapes (running destinations/trails), Faces (athlete profiles), 1,200 words **Buys 40 mss/year.** Query with published clips. **Pays 25 cents/word.**

FILLERS Needs anecdotes, facts, newsbreaks, short humor. **Buys 10 mss/year.** Length: 75-400 words. **Pays 30 cents/word.**

TIPS "Demonstrate familiarity with the sport. Best way to break in is with interesting and unique news, stories, insights. Submit thoughtful, detailed queries, not just vague story ideas."

SKIING AND SNOW SPORTS

⊘❸❸❸ SKIING MAGAZINE

Bonnier Corp., 5720 Flatiron Pkwy., Boulder CO 80301. (303)253-6300. **Fax:** (303)448-7638. **E-mail:** editor@ skiingmag.com. **Website:** www.skinet.com/skiing. **60% freelance written.** Magazine published 8 times/ year. *Skiing Magazine* is an online ski-lifestyle publication written and edited for recreational skiers. Its content is intended to help them ski better (technique), buy better (equipment and skiwear), and introduce them to new experiences, people, and adventures. Estab. 1936. Circ. 430,000. Byline given. Pays on acceptance. Offers 15% kill fee. Publishes ms an average of 3 months after

acceptance. Submit seasonal material 8 months in advance. Accepts queries by mail, e-mail. Sample copy with 9 x 12 SASE and 5 first-class stamps.

O   Does not accept unsolicited mss, and assumes no responsibility for their return.

NONFICTION Needs essays, historical, how-to, humor, interview, personal experience. **Buys 5-10 mss/ year.** Send complete ms. Length: 1,000-3,500 words. **Pays $500-1,000 for assigned articles. Pays $300-700 for unsolicited articles.** Pays expenses of writers on assignment.

PHOTOS Sponsors 12-week-long internship based at editorial headquarters in Boulder, CO. Intern workload includes: assisting in our photo studio and on assignment, photo retouching, coordinating photography, working with our art department to build cohesive features, invoicing, production workflow, and participating in staff meetings. "We try to keep the grunt work to a minimum. *Skiing Magazine* is a small staff (4 editors and 2 art directors), so interns work closely with staffers. Interns should be dedicated, hard-working, conscientious, and fun-loving, with a career interest in photography. A very strong foundation in the CS3 Creative Suite, as well as previous journalism or photography experience is required. A passion for the sport of skiing helps." All internships are unpaid. E-mail résumé, cover letter, and portfolio to: Niall@skiingmag. com. Send photos. Captions, identification of subjects, model releases required. Offers $75-300/photo.

FILLERS Needs facts, short humor. **Buys 10 mss/year.** Length: 60-75 words. **Pays $50-75.**

TIPS "Writers must have an extensive familiarity with the sport and know what concerns, interests, and amuses skiers. Start with short pieces ('hometown hills,' 'dining out,' 'sleeping in'). Columns are most open to freelancers."

WATER SPORTS

◔❸ DIVER

216 East Esplanade, North Vancouver BC V7L 1A3 Canada. (604)988-0711. **Fax:** (604)988-0747. **E-mail:** editor@divermag.com. **Website:** www.divermag.com. Magazine published 8 times/year emphasizing sport SCUBA diving, ocean science, and technology for a well-educated, active readership across North America and around the world. Circ. 30,000. Accepts queries by e-mail.

NONFICTION Query first. Length: 500-3,000 words. **Pays 12.5 cents/word.**

PHOTOS Captions, identification of subjects required. Reviews JPEG/TIFF files (300 dpi), slides, maps, drawings. $100 full page, $50 half page, $25 quarter page or smaller photos inside, $350 for cover photo.

$ THE WATER SKIER

1251 Holy Cow Rd., Polk City FL 33868. (863)324-4341. **Fax:** (863)325-8259. **E-mail:** satkinson@usawaterski.org. **Website:** www.usawaterski.org. **Contact:** Scott Atkinson, editor. **10-20% freelance written.** Magazine published 6 times/year. *The Water Skier* is the membership magazine of USA Water Ski, the national governing body for organized water skiing in the United States. The magazine has a controlled circulation and is available only to USA Water Ski's membership, which is made up of 17,000 active competitive water skiers. The editorial content of the magazine features distinctive and informative writing about the sport of water skiing and wakeboarding. Estab. 1951. Circ. 20,000. Byline given. Editorial lead time 4 months. Submit seasonal material 6 months in advance. Responds in 2 weeks to queries. Sample copy for $3.50. Guidelines with #10 SASE.

NONFICTION Buys 10-15 mss/year. Query. Length: 1,500-3,000 words. **Pays $100-150.**

REPRINTS Send photocopy. Payment negotiable.

PHOTOS State availability. Captions, identification of subjects required. Reviews contact sheets. Negotiates payment individually.

COLUMNS/DEPARTMENTS The Water Skier News (small news items about people and events in the sport), 400-500 words. Other topics include safety, training (3-event, barefoot, disabled, show ski, ski race, kneeboard, and wakeboard); champions on their way; new products. Query. **Pays $50-100.**

TIPS "Contact the editor through a query letter (please, no phone calls) with an idea. Avoid instruction, these articles are written by professionals. Concentrate on articles about the people of the sport. We are always looking for interesting stories about people in the sport."

TEEN AND YOUNG ADULT

$$ CICADA MAGAZINE

Cricket Magazine Group, 70 E. Lake St., Suite 800, Chicago IL 60601. **E-mail:** cicada@cicadamag.com. **Website:** www.cricketmag.com/cicada. **Contact:** Submissions editor. Bimonthly literary magazine for ages 14 and up. Publishes 6 issues per year. Estab. 1998. Circ. 10,000. Pays after publication. Accepts simultaneous submissions. Responds in 3-6 months to mss. Guidelines online at submittable.cricketmag.com or www.cricketmag.com/submissions.

NONFICTION Needs essays, personal experience, First-person experiences of interest to teens and young adult readers. submittable.cricketmag.com; www.cricketmag.com/submissions Length: 5,000 words maximum; **Pays up to 25¢/word.**

REPRINTS Payment varies.

FICTION Needs Realistic, contemporary and historical fiction as well as humor, mysteries, fantasy and science fiction. Length: 9,000 words maximum **Pays up to 25¢/word.**

POETRY Needs free verse, light verse, traditional. Reviews serious, humorous, free verse, rhyming. Length: 25 lines maximum. **Pays up to $3/line ($25 minimum).**

TIPS "Quality writing, good literary style, genuine teen sensibility, depth, humor, good character development, avoidance of stereotypes. Read several issues to familiarize yourself with our style."

$$$$ SEVENTEEN

300 W. 57th St., 17th Floor, New York NY 10019. (917)934-6500. **Fax:** (917)934-6574. **E-mail:** mail@seventeen.com. **Website:** www.seventeen.com. **20% freelance written.** Monthly magazine. *Seventeen* is a young woman's first fashion and beauty magazine. Tailored for young women in their teens and early twenties, *Seventeen* covers fashion, beauty, health, fitness, food, college, entertainment, fiction, plus crucial personal and global issues. Estab. 1944. Circ. 2.4 million. Byline given. Pays on acceptance. Offers 25% kill fee. Publishes ms an average of 6 months after acceptance. Accepts queries by mail. Responds in 3 months to queries.

💬 Query before submitting.

NONFICTION Length: 1,200-2,500 words. **Pays $1/word, occasionally more.** Pays expenses of writers on assignment.

PHOTOS Photos usually by assignment only.

TIPS "Writers have to ask themselves whether or not they feel they can find the right tone for a *Seventeen* article—a tone which is empathetic, yet never patronizing; lively, yet not superficial. Not all writers feel comfortable with, understand, or like teenagers. If you don't like them, *Seventeen* is the wrong market for you. An excellent way to break in to the magazine is by con-

CONSUMER MAGAZINES

tributing ideas for quizzes or the 'My Story' (personal essay) column."

TEEN VOGUE

Condé Nast Publications, 4 Times Square, 10th Floor, New York NY 10036. (212)286-2860. **Fax:** (212)286-2378. **Website:** www.teenvogue.com. Magazine published 10 times/year. Written for sophisticated teenage girls age 12-17 years old. Circ. 450,000. Editorial lead time 2 months.

○ Query before submitting.

❂❸❺ WHAT'S HERS/WHAT'S HIS MAGAZINES

(formerly *What Magazine*), What! Publishers Inc., 108-93 Lombard Ave., Winnipeg MB R3B 3B1 Canada. (204)985-8160. **Fax:** (204)957-5638. **E-mail:** letters@whatshers.com; letters@whatshis.com. **40% freelance written**. Magazine published 5 times during the school year covering teen issues and pop culture. *What's HERS* and *What's HIS* magazines are distributed to high school students across Canada. We produce 2 gender specific magazines that are empowering, interactive and entertaining. We respect the reader— today's teens are smart and creative (and critical). Estab. 1987. Circ. 280,000 (180,000 HERS; 100,000 HIS). Byline given. Pays 1 month after publication. Offers negotiable kill fee. Publishes ms an average of 3 months after acceptance. Editorial lead time 5 months. Submit seasonal material 5 months in advance. Accepts queries by mail, e-mail, fax. Responds in 2 months to queries. Responds in 1 month to mss. Sample copy for 9 x 12 SAE with Canadian postage. Guidelines for #10 SAE with Canadian postage.

NONFICTION Needs general interest, interview, issue-oriented features. No clichÃ´ teen material. **Buys 6-10 mss/year.** Query with published clips. Length: 500-1,800 words. **Pays $150-400 (Canadian).** Sometimes pays expenses of writers on assignment.

PHOTOS Send photos. Identification of subjects required. Reviews transparencies, 4x6 prints. Negotiates payment individually.

TIPS We have an immediate need for savvy freelancers to contribute features, short articles, interviews, and reviews that speak to our intelligent teen audience. Looking for fresh talent and new ideas in the areas of entertainment, gaming, pop culture, teen issues, international events as they relate to readers, celebs and 'real people' profiles, lifestyle articles, extreme sports and any other stories of relevance to today's Canadian teen.

❸❺ YOUNG SALVATIONIST

The Salvation Army, P.O. Box 269, Alexandria VA 22313-0269. (703)684-5500. **Fax:** (703)684-5539. **E-mail:** ys@usn.salvationarmy.org. **Website:** www.use. salvationarmy.org. **Contact:** Major Amy Reardon. **10% freelance written**. Monthly magazine for high school and early college youth. "*Young Salvationist* provides young people with biblically based inspiration and resources to develop their spirituality. Only material with Christian perspective with practical real-life application will be considered." Circ. 48,000. Byline given. Pays on printing. Publishes ms an average of 6 months after acceptance. Submit seasonal material 6 months in advance. Accepts queries by Accepts complete mss by mail and e-mail. Responds in 2 months to mss. Sample copy for 9x12 SAE with 3 first-class stamps or online. Writer's guidelines and theme list for #10 SASE or online.

○ "Works with a small number of new/unpublished writers each year."

NONFICTION Needs how-to, humor, inspirational, interview, personal experience, photo feature, religious. **Buys 10 mss/year.** Send complete ms. Length: 700-900 words. **Pays 25¢/word for first rights.**

REPRINTS Send tearsheet, photocopy, or typed ms with rights for sale noted and information about when and where the material previously appeared. Pays 10¢/word for reprints.

TIPS "Study magazine, familiarize yourself with the unique 'Salvationist' perspective of *Young Salvationist*; learn a little about the Salvation Army; media, sports, sex, and dating are strongest appeal."

TRAVEL, CAMPING AND TRAILER

❸❺ AAA MIDWEST TRAVELER

AAA Auto Club of Missouri, 12901 N. 40 Dr., St. Louis MO 63141. (314)523-7350 ext. 6301. **Fax:** (314)523-6982. **E-mail:** dreinhardt@aaamissouri.com. **Website:** www. aaa.com/traveler. **Contact:** Deborah Reinhardt, managing editor. **80% freelance written.** Bimonthly magazine covering travel and automotive safety. "We provide members with useful information on travel, auto safety and related topics." Estab. 1901. Circ. 500,000. Byline given. Pays on acceptance. Offers $50 kill fee. Editorial lead time 1 year. Submit seasonal material 6 months in advance. Accepts queries by mail, e-mail, fax. Accepts simultaneous submissions. Responds in 1 month to queries. Responds in 1 month to mss. Sample copy with 10x13 SASE and 4 First-Class stamps. Guidelines with #10 SASE.

NONFICTION Needs travel. No humor, fiction, poetry or cartoons. **Buys 20-30 mss/year.** Query; query with published clips the first time. Length: 800-1,200 words. **Pays $400.**

PHOTOS State availability. Captions required. Reviews transparencies, prints. Offers no additional payment for photos accepted with ms.

TIPS "Send queries between December and February, as we plan our calendar for the following year. Request a copy. Serious writers ask for media kit to help them target their piece. Send a SASE or download online. Travel destinations and tips are most open to freelancers; all departments and auto-related news handled by staff. We see too many `Here's a recount of our family vacation' mss. Go easy on first-person accounts."

BACKROADS

P.O. Box 317, Branchville NJ 07826. (973)948-4176. **Fax:** (973)948-0823. **E-mail:** editor@backroadsusa.com. **Website:** www.backroadsusa.com. **50% freelance written.** Monthly tabloid covering motorcycle touring. "*Backroads* is a motorcycle tour magazine geared toward getting motorcyclists on the road and traveling. We provide interesting destinations, unique roadside attractions and eateries, plus Rip & Ride Route Sheets. We cater to all brands. Although *Backroads* is geared towards the motorcycling population, it is not by any means limited to just motorcycle riders. Non-motorcyclists enjoy great destinations, too. As time has gone by, *Backroads* has developed more and more into a cutting-edge touring publication. We like to see submissions that give the reader the distinct impression of being part of the ride they're reading. Words describing the feelings and emotions brought on by partaking in this great and exciting lifestyle are encouraged." Estab. 1995. Circ. 50,000. Byline given. Pays 1 month after publication. Editorial lead time 1 month. Submit seasonal material 3 months in advance. Accepts queries by mail, e-mail. Responds in 1 month. Sample copy for $4. Guidelines online at website.

NONFICTION "What *Backroads* does not want is any 'us vs. them' submissions. We are decidedly nonpolitical and secular. *Backroads* is about getting out and riding, not getting down on any particular group, nor do we feel this paper should be a pulpit for a writer's beliefs ...

be they religious, political, or personal." Query. Needs travel Features: "This type of story offers a good opportunity for prospective contributors. They MUST feature spectacular photography, color preferably, and may be used as a cover story, if of acceptable quality. **All submissions must be accompanied by images**, with an SASE of adequate size (10x13) to return all material sent as well as a copy of the issue in which they were published, and a hard copy printout of the article, including your name, address, and phone number. If none is enclosed, the materials will not be returned. Text submissions are accepted via US mail or e-mail. We can usually convert most any file type, although it is easier to submit in plain text format, sometimes called ASCII." **Pays $75 and up; varies.**

PHOTOS Digital photos may be sent via US mail on CD or via e-mail if they are in a stuffed file. All images must be no smaller then 300 dpi and at least 4x6. If you are sending images at 72 dpi. We do not accept photographs, slides, or negatives. Send photos. Offers no additional payment for photos accepted with ms.

COLUMNS/DEPARTMENTS We're Outta Here (weekend destinations), 500-750 words; Great All-American Diner Run (good eateries with great location), 500-750 words; Thoughts from the Road (personal opinion/insights), 400-600 words; Mysterious America (unique and obscure sights), 500-750 words; Big City Getaway (day trips), 500-750 words. **Buys 20-24 mss/year.** Query. **Pays $75/article.**

⊙ CAMPING TODAY

126 Hermitage Rd., Butler PA 16001-0720. (724)283-7401; (412)629-0918. **E-mail:** d_johnston01@msn.com. **Website:** www.fcrv.org. **Contact:** DeWayne Johnston & June Johnston, editors. **30% freelance written.** Bimonthly official membership publication of the FCRV. *Camping Today* is the member magazine forFamily Campers & RVers, a non-profit camping and RV organization with over4,200 families in the U.S. and Canada. The majority of members are retired. Sometake grandchildren camping. Working families with kids travel and camp whentime permits. FCRV has local clubs or chapters in almost every state andprovince. 70% of content is about member activities. Estab. 1983. Circ. 10,000. Byline given. Pays on publication. Publishes ms an average of 6 months after acceptance. Editorial lead time: 3 months. Submit seasonal material 3 months in advance. Accepts simultaneous submissions. Responds in 2 months to queries and mss. Sample copy

and guidelines for 3 first-class stamps. Guidelines for #10 SASE.

NONFICTION Needs humor, camping or travel related, interview, interesting campers, new product, technical, RVs related, travel, interesting places to visit by RV, camping. **Buys 5-10 mss/year.** Query by mail or e-mail or send complete ms with photos. Length: 700-2,000 words. **Pays $50-150.**

REPRINTS Send typed ms with rights for sale noted and information about when and where the material previously appeared. Pays 35-50% of amount paid for original article.

PHOTOS Need b&w or sharp color prints. Send photos. Captions required.

TIPS "Freelance material on RV travel, RV maintenance/safety, and items of general camping interest throughout the U.S. and Canada will receive special attention. Good photos increase your chances. See website."

CONDE NAST TRAVELER

Condé Nast, 4 Times Square, 14th Floor, New York NY 10036. (212)286-2860. **Fax:** (212)286-2258. **E-mail:** web@condenasttraveler.com; letters@condenasttraveler.com. **Website:** www.cntraveler.com. **Contact:** Laura Garvey and Maeve Nicholson, editorial assistants; Greg Ferro, managing editor. Monthly magazine. Condé Nast Traveler is a luxury and lifestyle magazine. Estab. 1987. Circ. 800,000.

Query before submitting. Difficult market to break into.

PHOTOS Contact: Leonor Mamanna, senior photo editor.

ESCAPEES MAGAZINE

Sharing the RV Lifestyle, Roving Press, 100 Rainbow Dr., Livingston TX 77351. (888)757-2582. **Fax:** (409)327-4388. **E-mail:** editor@escapees.com. **Website:** escapees.com. **Contact:** Allyssa Dyson, editorial assistant. *Escapees* magazine's contributors are RVers interested in sharing the RV lifestyle. Audience includes full-time RVers, snowbirds, and those looking forward to traveling extensively. Escapees members have varying levels of experience; therefore, the magazine looks for a wide variety of material, beyond what is found in conventional RV magazines, and welcomes submissions on all phases of RV life, especially relevant mechanical/technical information. About 85% of the club members are retired, over 98% travel without children, and about 50% live in their motorhomes,

fifth-wheels, or travel trailers on a full-time basis. A bimonthly magazine that provides a total support network to RVers and shares the RV lifestyle. Estab. 1979. Circ. 25,000. Byline given. Pays on publication. Publishes ms an average of 3-6 months after acceptance. Editorial lead time: 3 months. Submit season material 6 months in advance. Accepts simultaneous submissions. Responds in 2 weeks to queries. Responds in 3 months to ms. Sample copy available for free for #10 SASE. Guidelines online and by e-mail at departmentseditor@escapees.com. Editor does not accept articles based on queries alone. Decisions for use of material are based on the full article with any accompanying photos, graphics, or diagrams. Only complete articles will be considered.

NONFICTION Needs general interest, historical, how-to, humor, inspirational, interview, nostalgic, personal experience, photo feature, profile, technical, travel. Do not send anything religious, political or unrelated to RVs. Submit complete ms. When submitting an article via e-mail as an attachment, please include the text in the body of the e-mail. Word length: between 300-1,400 words. Please include word count on first page of article. **Pays between $50-150 for unsolicited articles.** Publication sometimes "pays" writers with contributor copies rather than a cash payment, often in exchange for company bio/company product themeed photos.

PHOTOS Contact: Cole Carter, graphic artist. Freelancers should send photos with submissions. Captions, model releases, and identification of subjects are all required. Reviews GIF/JPEG files. Negotiates payment individually.

COLUMNS/DEPARTMENTS Contact: Allyssa Dyson, editorial assistant. One column, "SKP Stops," featuring short blurbs with photos on unique travel destination stops for RVers. Averages 300-500 words. **Buys 10-15 mss/year.** Submit complete ms. **Pays $25-75 for columns.**

TIPS "Use an engaging, conversational tone. Well-placed humor is refreshing. Eliminate any fluff and verbosity. Avoid colloquialisms."

FAMILY MOTOR COACHING

8291 Clough Pike, Cincinnati OH 45244. (513)474-3622; (800)543-3622. **Fax:** (513)388-5286. **E-mail:** rgould@fmca.com; magazine@fmca.com. **Website:** www.fmca.com. **Contact:** Robbin Gould, editor. **80% freelance written. We prefer that writers be experienced RVers.** Monthly magazine emphasizing travel by motorhome, motorhome mechanics, maintenance, and other technical information. *"Family Motor Coaching* magazine is edited for the members and prospective members of the Family Motor Coach Association who own or are about to purchase self-contained, motorized recreational vehicles known as motorhomes. Featured are articles on travel and recreation, association news and activities, plus articles on new products and motorhome maintenance and repair. Approximately 1/3 of editorial content is devoted to travel and entertainment, 1/3 to association news, and 1/3 to new products, industry news, and motorhome maintenance." Estab. 1963. Circ. 140,000. Byline given. Pays on acceptance. Publishes ms an average of 8 months after acceptance. Submit seasonal material 4 months in advance. Accepts queries by mail, e-mail, fax. Responds in 3 months to queries. Sample copy for $3.99; $5 if paying by credit card. Guidelines with #10 SASE or request PDF by e-mail.

NONFICTION Needs how-to, do-it-yourself motorhome projects and modifications, humor, interview, new product, technical, motorhome travel (various areas of North America accessible by motorhome), bus conversions, nostalgia. **Buys 50-75 mss/year.** Query with published clips. Length: 1,000-2,000 words. **Pays $100-500, depending on article category.**

PHOTOS State availability. Captions, model releases, True required. Offers no additional payment for b&w contact sheets, 35mm 21/4x21/4 color transparencies, or high-res electronic images (300 dpi and at least 4x6 in size).

TIPS "The greatest number of contributions we receive are travel; therefore, that area is the most competitive. However, it also represents the easiest way to break into our publication. Articles should be written for those traveling by self-contained motorhome. The destinations must be accessible to motorhome travelers and any peculiar road conditions should be mentioned."

⊙⊙ HIGHWAYS

Affinity Group, Inc., 2575 Vista Del Mar Dr., Ventura CA 93001. (805)667-4100. **E-mail:** highways@goodsamclub.com. **Website:** www.goodsamclub.com/highways. Monthly magazine covering recreational vehicle lifestyle. "All of our readers own some type of RV—a motorhome, trailer, pop-up, tent—so our stories need to include places that you can go with large vehicles, and campgrounds in and around the area where they can spend the night." Estab. 1966. Circ. 975,000.

Byline given. Pays on acceptance. Offers 50% kill fee. Publishes ms an average of 6 months after acceptance. Accepts queries by e-mail. Responds in 2 weeks to queries. Sample copy and writer's guidelines free or online.

NONFICTION Needs how-to, repair/replace something on an RV, humor, technical, travel, all RV related. **Buys 15-20 mss/year.** Query. Length: 800-1,100 words.

COLUMNS/DEPARTMENTS On the Road (issue related); RV Insight (for people new to the RV lifestyle); Action Line (consumer help); Tech Topics (tech Q&A); Camp Cuisine (cooking in an RV); Product Previews (new products). No plans on adding new columns/departments.

TIPS "Know something about RVing. People who drive motorhomes or pull trailers have unique needs that have to be incorporated into our stories. We're looking for well-written, first-person stories that convey the fun of this lifestyle and way to travel."

JOURNEY MAGAZINE

AAA, 1745 114th Ave., SE, Bellevue WA 98004. (800)562-2582. **E-mail:** sueboylan@aaawin.com; robbhatt@aaawin.com. **Website:** www.aaajourney.com/magazine. **Contact:** Susan Boylan, art director. Bimonthly magazine. For members of AAA Washington; reaches readers in Washington and northern Idaho. Our goal is to present readers with lively and informative stories on lifestyle, travel and automotive topics that encourage them to discover and explore the Northwest and beyond. Articles range from 500 to 1,800 words. We assign stories based on writers' proposals, and rarely accept completed mss. We look for writers who combine sound research and reporting skills with a strong voice and excellent storytelling ability. We adhere to AP style. A solid knowledge of the Pacific Northwest is also required. We create our editorial calendar in the spring for the following calendar year. We encourage you to read several issues of *Journey* to familiarize yourself with our publication before you submit article ideas. *Journey* pays up to $1 per word upon acceptance for first North American rights. Some stories run alternatively in our Western and Puget Sound editions and may also be published on the Website. We run all articles with high-quality photographs and illustrations. If you are a published photographer, let us know but please do not submit any photos unless requested. To be considered for an assignment, mail a query along with three samples of published work. Circ. 550,000. Pays on acceptance Responds within 3 months with SASE.

PILOT GETAWAYS MAGAZINE

Airventure Publishing LLC, P.O. Box 550, Glendale CA 91209. (818)241-1890; (877)745-6849. **Fax:** (818)241-1895. **E-mail:** info@pilotgetaways.com; editor@pilot-getaways.com. **Website:** www.pilotgetaways.com. **Contact:** John T. Kounis, editor. **90% freelance written.** Bimonthly magazine covering aviation travel for private pilots. *Pilot Getaways* is a travel magazine for private pilots. Our articles cover destinations that are easily accessible by private aircraft, including details such as airport transportation, convenient hotels, and attractions. Other regular features include fly-in dining, flying tips, and bush flying. Estab. 1999. Circ. 25,000. Byline given. Pays on publication. Editorial lead time 4 months. Submit seasonal material 9 months in advance. Accepts queries by mail, e-mail, fax, phone. Accepts simultaneous submissions. Responds in 2 weeks to queries; 2 months to mss. Sample copy and writer's guidelines free.

NONFICTION Needs travel, specifically travel guide articles. "We rarely publish articles about events that have already occurred, such as travel logs about trips the authors have taken or air show reports." **Buys 30 mss/year.** Query. Length: 1,000-3,500 words. **Pays $100-500.**

PHOTOS State availability. Captions, identification of subjects required. Reviews contact sheets, negatives, 35mm transparencies, prints, GIF/JPEG/TIFF files. Negotiates payment individually.

COLUMNS/DEPARTMENTS Weekend Getaways (short fly-in getaways), 2,000 words; Fly-in Dining (reviews of airport restaurants), 1,200 words; Flying Tips (tips and pointers on flying technique), 1,000 words; Bush Flying (getaways to unpaved destinations), 1,500 words. **Buys 20 mss/year.** Query. **Pays $100-500.**

TIPS *Pilot Getaways* follows a specific format, which is factual and informative. We rarely publish travel logs that chronicle a particular journey. Rather, we prefer travel guides with phone numbers, addresses, prices, etc., so that our readers can plan their own trips. The exact format is described in our writer's guidelines.

TIMES OF THE ISLANDS

Times Publications, Ltd., P.O. Box 234, Lucille Lightbourne Bldg., #7, Providenciales Turks & Caicos Islands British West Indies. (649)946-4788. **Fax:** (649)946-4788. **E-mail:** timespub@tciway.tc. **Website:** www.timespub.tc. **60% freelance written.** Quarterly magazine covering the Turks & Caicos Islands. "*Times of the Islands* is used by the public and private sector to inform visitors and potential investors/developers about the Islands. It goes beyond a superficial overview of tourist attractions with in-depth articles about natural history, island heritage, local personalities, new development, offshore finance, sporting activities, visitors' experiences, and Caribbean fiction." Estab. 1988. Circ. 10,000. Byline given. Pays on publication. Publishes ms an average of 6 months after acceptance. Editorial lead time 4 months. Submit seasonal material at least 4 months in advance. Accepts queries by e-mail. Accepts simultaneous submissions. Responds in 6 weeks to queries. Responds in 2 months to mss. Sample copy for $6. Guidelines online.

NONFICTION Needs book excerpts, essays, general interest, Caribbean art, culture, cooking, crafts, historical, humor, interview, locals, personal experience, trips to the Islands, photo feature, technical, island businesses, travel, book reviews, nature, ecology, business (offshore finance), watersports. **Buys 20 mss/year.** Query. Length: 500-3,000 words. **Pays $150-500.**

REPRINTS Send photocopy and information about when and where the material previously appeared. Payment varies

PHOTOS Send photos. Identification of subjects required. Reviews digital photos. Pays $15-150/photo.

COLUMNS/DEPARTMENTS On Holiday (unique experiences of visitors to Turks & Caicos), 500-1,500 words. **Buys 4 mss/year.** Query. **Pays $150.**

FICTION Needs adventure, sailing, diving, ethnic, Caribbean, historical, Caribbean, humorous, travel-related, mystery, novel concepts. **Buys 2-3 mss/year.** Query. Length: 1,000-3,000 words. **Pays $250-400.**

TIPS "Make sure that the query/article specifically relates to the Turks and Caicos Islands. The theme can be general (ecotourism, for instance), but the ms should contain specific and current references to the Islands. We're a high-quality magazine, with a small budget and staff, and are very open-minded to ideas (and mss). Writers who have visited the Islands at least once would probably have a better perspective from which to write."

TRAVEL + LEISURE

American Express Publishing Corp., 1120 Avenue of the Americas, 9th Floor, New York NY 10036. (212)382-5600. **Website:** www.travelandleisure.com. **Contact:** Laura Teusink, managing editor. **95% freelance writ-**

ten. *Travel + Leisure* is a monthly magazine edited for affluent travelers. It explores the latest resorts, hotels, fashions, foods, and drinks, as well as political, cultural, and economic issues affecting travelers. Circ. 950,000. Byline given. Pays on acceptance. Offers 25% kill fee. Accepts queries by mail, online submission form. Responds in 6 weeks to queries and mss. Sample copy for $5.50 from (800)888-8728. Guidelines online.

NONFICTION Needs travel. **Buys 40-50 feature (3,000-5,000 words) and 200 short (125-500 words) mss/year.** Query online or by postal mail. An online query will receive a faster response. Editors are looking for a compelling reason to assign an article: a specific angle, news that makes the subject fresh, a writer's enthusiasm for and familiarity with the topic. **Pays $4,000-6,000/feature; $100-500/short piece.** Pays expenses of writers on assignment.

PHOTOS Contact: Photo Dept. Discourages submission of unsolicited transparencies. Captions required. Payment varies.

COLUMNS/DEPARTMENTS Length: 2,500-3,500 words. **Buys 125-150 mss/year. Pays $2,000-3,500.**

TIPS "Queries should not be generic, but should specify what is new or previously uncovered in a destination or travel-related subject area."

WOMEN'S

ALLURE

Conde Nast Publications, 4 Times Square, 10th Floor, New York NY 10036. (212)286-2860. **Fax:** (212)286-4654. **E-mail:** alluremag@aol.com. **Website:** www.allure.com. Monthly magazine covering fashion, beauty, fitness, etc. Geared toward the professional modern woman, offering the most comprehensive understanding of trends, science, and service information, as well as the most valued product recommendations in the field. Circ. 1,108,256.

Query before submitting.

ALL YOU

Time Inc., 135 W. 50th St., 2nd Floor, New York NY 10020. **E-mail:** realitycheckers@allyou.com. **Website:** www.allyou.com. Monthly magazine that focuses on realistic and affordable ideas, budget-friendly recipes, candid health information, smart shopping strategies, high-value coupons on products, hair and beauty ideas, fashion for real women's bodies, and real-life advice for women from women. *All You* speaks directly to value-minded women helping them to live well for less

in every area of their life. Mission is to help readers save money, save time, get food on the table faster, and prepare for the holidays with ease.

Query before submitting.

CHATELAINE

One Mount Pleasant Rd., 8th Floor, Toronto ON M4Y 2Y5 Canada. (416)764-2890. **Fax:** (416)764-2891. **E-mail:** storyideas@chatelaine.rogers.com. **Website:** www.chatelaine.com. **Contact:** Carly Deziel, assistant to the editor-in-chief. Monthly magazine covering Canadian women's lifestyles. "*Chatelaine* is edited for Canadian women ages 25-49, their changing attitudes and lifestyles. Key editorial ingredients include health, finance, social issues, and trends, as well as fashion, beauty, food, and home decor. Regular departments include Health pages, Entertainment, Money, Home, Humour, and How-to." Byline given. Pays on acceptance. Offers 25-50% kill fee. Accepts queries by mail, e-mail (preferred). Responds in 4-6 weeks to queries; up to 2 months to proposals. Guidelines online.

Does not accept unsolicited mss. Submit story ideas online.

NONFICTION Query. **Pays $1/word.**

COSMOPOLITAN

Hearst Corporation, 300 W. 57th St., New York NY 10019-3791. (212)649-2000. **E-mail:** cosmo@hearst.com; youtellcosmo@hearst.com. **Website:** www.cosmopolitan.com. Monthly magazine that includes articles on women's issues, relationships, sex, health, careers, self-improvement, celebrities, fashion, and beauty. *Cosmopolitan* is an international magazine for women. Estab. 1886. Circ. 3 million. Accepts queries by mail, e-mail.

Difficult market to break into.

NONFICTION *Cosmopolitan* is the largest magazine in the world and does not consider itself a starting point for writers. If you have a good set of published clips and a strong idea that you think would fit in Cosmo, e-mail your query, with "Story Pitch" in the subject line. An editor will then get in touch if they are interested in the idea. Consider using the masthead to get in touch with the editor most appropriate for your query.

COUNTRY WOMAN

Reiman Publications, 5400 S. 60th St., Greendale WI 53129. (414)423-0100. **E-mail:** editors@countrywomanmagazine.com. **Website:** www.countrywomanmagazine.com. **Contact:** Lori Lau Grzybowski, editor. **75-85% freelance written.** Bimonthly magazine.

Country Woman is for contemporary rural women of all ages and backgrounds and from all over the U.S. and Canada. It includes a sampling of the diversity that makes up rural women's lives—love of home, family, farm, ranch, community, hobbies, enduring values, humor, attaining new skills and appreciating present, past and future all within the context of the lifestyle that surrounds country living. Estab. 1970. Byline given. Pays on acceptance. Submit seasonal material 5 months in advance. Accepts queries by mail. Accepts simultaneous submissions. Responds in 2 months to queries. Responds in 3 months to mss. Sample copy for $2 and SASE. Guidelines with #10 SASE.

NONFICTION Needs general interest, historical, how-to, crafts, community projects, decorative, antiquing, etc., humor, inspirational, interview, personal experience, photo feature, packages profiling interesting country women-all pertaining to rural women's interests. Query. 1,000 words maximum.

REPRINTS Send typed ms with rights for sale noted and information about when and where the material previously appeared. Payment varies

PHOTOS Uses only excellent quality color photos. No b&w. We pay for photo/feature packages. State availability of or send photos. Captions, identification of subjects, model releases required. Reviews 35mm or 2.25 transparencies, excellent-quality color prints.

COLUMNS/DEPARTMENTS Why Farm Wives Age Fast (humor), I Remember When (nostalgia), and Country Decorating. Length: 500-1,000 words. **Buys 10-12 mss/year.** Query or send ms.

FICTION Contact: Kathleen Anderson, managing editor. Main character *must* be a country woman. All fiction must have a country setting. Fiction must have a positive, upbeat message. Includes fiction in every issue. Would buy more fiction if stories suitable for our audience were sent our way. No contemporary, urban pieces that deal with divorce, drugs, etc. Send complete ms. Length: 750-1,000 words.

POETRY Needs light verse, traditional. Poetry must have rhythm and rhyme. It must be country-related, positive, and upbeat. Always looking for seasonal poetry. Buys 6-12 poems/year. Submit maximum 6 poems. Length: 4-24 lines. **Pays $10-25/poem plus one contribtor's copy.**

TIPS "We have broadened our focus to include country women, not just women on farms and ranches but also women who live in a small town or country home and/or simply have an interest in country-oriented top-ics. This allows freelancers a wider scope in material. Write as clearly and with as much zest and enthusiasm as possible. We love good quotes, supporting materials (names, places, etc.) and strong leads and closings. Readers relate strongly to where they live and the lifestyle they've chosen. They want to be informed and entertained, and that's just exactly why they subscribe. Readers are busy—not too busy to read—but when they do sit down, they want good writing, reliable information and something that feels like a reward. How-to, humor, personal experience and nostalgia are areas most open to freelancers. Profiles, to a certain degree, are also open. Be accurate and fresh in approach."

🟢🟢🟢🟢 ELLE

Hachette Filipacchi Media U.S., Inc., 300 W. 57th St., 24th Floor, New York NY 10019. (212)903-5000. **Website:** www.elle.com. Monthly magazine. Edited for the modern, sophisticated, affluent, well-traveled woman in her twenties to early thirties. Circ. 1,100,000. Editorial lead time 3 months.

Query before submitting.

ESSENCE

135 W. 50th St., New York NY 10020. **Website:** www.essence.com. Monthly magazine. *Essence* is the magazine for today's black women. Edited for career-minded, sophisticated and independent achievers, *Essence*'s editorial is dedicated to helping its readers attain their maximum potential in various lifestyles and roles. The editorial content includes career and educational opportunities; fashion and beauty; investing and money management; health and fitness; parenting; information on home decorating and food; travel; cultural reviews; fiction; and profiles of achievers and celebrities. Estab. 1970. Circ. 1 million. Byline given. Pays on acceptance. Offers 25% kill fee. Editorial lead time 6 months. Submit seasonal material 6 months in advance. Accepts queries by mail, fax. Responds in 2 months to queries. Responds in 2 months to mss. Sample copy for $3.25. Guidelines online.

NONFICTION Needs book excerpts, novel excerpts. **Buys 200 mss/year.** Query with a letter that explains story concept, proposed story length, possible experts, and why this idea would appeal to the *Essence* reader. Query letters should be no longer than 1 page and should address a specific editor. Departments include: Arts and Entertainment (Cori Murray), Books and Poetry (Patrik Henry Bass), Beauty (Corynne Corbett), Health, Relationships, and Food (Sharon Boone), Personal Essays (Rosemarie Robotham), News (Wendy Wilson), Work and Wealth (Tanisha Sykes), and Feature Articles/Personal Growth (Teresa Wiltz and Rosemarie Robotham). Length will be given upon assignment. **Pays by the word.**

REPRINTS Send tearsheet and information about when and where the material previously appeared. Pays 50% of the amount paid for the original article.

PHOTOS Would like to see photographs for our travel section that feature Black travelers. State availability. Model releases required. Pays from $200 up depending on the size of the image.

TIPS Please note that *Essence* no longer accepts unsolicited mss for fiction or nonfiction, except for the Brothers, Where There's a Will, Making Love Work, Our World, Back Talk and Interiors columns. So please only send query letters for nonfiction story ideas.

🌀🌀🌀 FAMILY CIRCLE

Meredith Corporation, 805 Third Ave., 24th Floor, New York NY 10022. **Website:** www.familycircle.com. Lisa Kelsey, art director. **Contact:** Cassie Kreitner, editorial assistant. **80% freelance written.** Magazine published every 3 weeks. A national women's service magazine which covers many stages of a woman's life, along with her everyday concerns about social, family, and health issues. Submissions should focus on families with children ages 8-16. Estab. 1932. Circ. 4,200,000. Byline given. Offers 20% kill fee. Editorial lead time 4 months. Submit seasonal material 4 months in advance. Responds in 2 months to queries. Responds in 2 months to mss. For back issues, send $6.95 to P.O. Box 3156, Harlan IA 51537. Guidelines online.

NONFICTION Needs essays, opinion, personal experience, women's interest subjects such as family and personal relationships, children, physical and mental health, nutrition and self-improvement. No fiction or poetry. **Buys 200 mss/year.** Submit detailed outline, 2 clips, cover letter describing your publishing history, SASE or IRCs. Length: 1,000-2,500 words. **Pays $1/ word.**

TIPS "Query letters should be concise and to the point. Also, writers should keep close tabs on *Family Circle* and other women's magazines to avoid submitting recently run subject matter."

FIRST FOR WOMEN

Bauer Media Group, 270 Sylvan Ave., Englewood Cliffs NJ 07632. (201)569-6699. **E-mail:** contactus@firstfor-women.com. **Website:** www.firstforwomen.com. *First*

for Women, published 17 times/year, covers everything from beauty, health, nutrition, cooking, decor, and fun. Every issue also includes a 24-page cookbook that pulls out from the center of the magazine. Magazine is visual with a lot of quick tips. Estab. 1989. Circ. 1.3 million.

◖ Query before submitting. Difficult market to break into.

🌀🌀🌀🌀 GLAMOUR

Conde Nast Publications, Inc., 4 Times Square, 16th Floor, New York NY 10036. (212)286-2860. **Fax:** (212)286-8336. **Website:** www.glamour.com. **Contact:** Cynthia Leive, editor-in-chief. Monthly magazine covering subjects ranging from fashion, beauty and health, personal relationships, career, travel, food and entertainment. *Glamour* is edited for the contemporary woman, and informs her of the trends and recommends how she can adapt them to her needs, and motivates her to take action. Estab. 1939. Circ. 2,374,170. Accepts queries by mail.

⚿ Query before submitting.

NONFICTION Needs personal experience, relationships, travel.

PHOTOS Only uses professional photographers.

🌀🌀🌀 GOOD HOUSEKEEPING

Hearst Corp., 300 W. 57th St., 28th Floor, New York NY 10019. (212)649-2200. **Website:** www.goodhousekeeping.com. Monthly magazine covering women's interests. *Good Housekeeping* is edited for the new traditionalist. Articles which focus on food, fitness, beauty, and childcare draw upon the resources of the Good Housekeeping Institute. Editorial includes human interest stories, articles that focus on social issues, money management, health news, and travel. Circ. 4,000,000. Byline given. Pays on acceptance. Offers 25% kill fee. Submit seasonal material 6 months in advance. Responds in 2-3 months to queries. Responds in 2-3 months to mss. Call for a sample copy. Guidelines online.

NONFICTION Buys 4-6 mss/year. Query. Length: 500 words. Pays expenses of writers on assignment.

PHOTOS Photos purchased mostly on assignment. State availability. Model releases required. Pays $100-350 for b&w; $200-400 for color photos.

COLUMNS/DEPARTMENTS Profiles (inspirational, activist or heroic women), 400-600 words. Query with published clips. **Pays $1/word for items 300-600 words.**

TIPS "Always send an SASE and clips. We prefer to see a query first. Do not send material on subjects already covered in-house by the Good Housekeeping Institute—these include food, beauty, needlework and crafts."

⊜⊜ GRACE ORMONDE WEDDING STYLE

Elegant Publishing, Inc., P.O. Box 89, Barrington RI 02806. (401)245-9726. **Fax:** (401)245-5371. **E-mail:** contact@weddingstylemagazine.com. **Website:** www.weddingstylemagazine.com. **Contact:** Human Resources. **90% freelance written.** Monthly digital and print magazine covering weddings for the affluent bride. Estab. 1997. Circ. 400,000. Pays on publication. Publishes ms an average of 4 months after acceptance. Editorial lead time 6 months. Guidelines by e-mail.

◑   Does not accept queries.

PHOTOS State availability. Reviews transparencies. Negotiates payment individually.

TIPS E-mail résumé and 5 clips/samples in any area of writing.

INSTYLE

Time, Inc., 1271 Avenue of the Americas, 18th Floor, New York NY 10020. (212)522-1212. **Fax:** (212)522-0867. **E-mail:** letters@instylemag.com. **Website:** www.instyle.com. **Contact:** Angela Matusik, executive editor. Monthly magazine. Written to be the most trusted style adviser and lifestyle resource for women. Circ. 1,670,000. Editorial lead time 4 months.

◑   Query before submitting.

MARIE CLAIRE

Hearst Corporation, 300 West 57th St., 34th Floor, New York NY 10019-1497. **Website:** www.marieclaire.com. Monthly women's magazine focusing on women around the world and worldwide issues. Also covers health, beauty, and fashion topics. Estab. 1937. Circ. 950,000. Accepts queries by mail. Responds in 4-6 weeks. Guidelines online.

NONFICTION Prefers story proposals, rather than completed mss. Send query letter detailing idea via postal mail. If the editors find the subject suitable, they will respond. Enclose clips of previously published materials. Materials will not be returned.

MORE

Meredith Corporation, 125 Park Ave., New York NY 10017. **E-mail:** more@meredith.com. **Website:** www.more.com. **Contact:** Ila Stanger, managing editor. Magazine published 10 times/year. *More* celebrates women of style and substance. The magazine is the leading voice for the woman who lives in a constant state of possibility. Estab. 1998. Circ. 1.8 million. Byline given. Lead time is 4 months. Accepts queries by mail. Guidelines online.

◑   Query before submitting.

NONFICTION *More* only accepts queries, before submissions. Keep query brief (1-2 pages), citing lead and describing how you will research and develop story. Be specific, and direct query to the appropriate editor, as listed on the masthead of the magazine. Send published clips, credits, and a résumé. Does not respond unless a SASE is enclosed. Word length is discussed upon assignment. Average story length is 2,000 words. **Payment is discussed upon assignment.**

⊜⊜⊜⊜ MS. MAGAZINE

433 S. Beverly Dr., Beverly Hills CA 90212. (310)556-2515. **Fax:** (310)556-2514. **E-mail:** mkort@msmagazine.com. **Website:** www.msmagazine.com. **Contact:** Michele Kort, senior editor. **80-90% freelance written.** Quarterly magazine on women's issues and news. Estab. 1972. Circ. 150,000. Byline given. Offers 25% kill fee. Responds in 3 months to queries. Responds in 3 months to mss. Sample copy for $9. Guidelines online.

NONFICTION Needs international and national women's news, investigative reporting, personal narratives of prize-winning journalists and feminist thinkers. **Buys 4-5 feature (2,000-3,000 words) and 4-5 short (500 words) mss/year.** Query with published clips. Length: 300-3,500 words. **Pays $1/word; 50¢/word for news stories and book reviews.**

COLUMNS/DEPARTMENTS Buys 6-10 mss/year. **Pays $1/word.**

FICTION "*Ms.* welcomes the highest-quality original fiction and poetry, but is publishing these infrequently as of late."

⊜⊜ NA'AMAT WOMAN

505 Eighth Ave., Suite 2302, New York NY 10018. (212)563-5222. **Fax:** (212)563-5710. **E-mail:** naamat@naamat.org; judith@naamat.org. **Website:** www.naamat.org. **Contact:** Judith Sokoloff, editor. **80% freelance written.** Quarterly magazine covering Jewish issues/subjects. "We cover issues and topics of interest to the Jewish community in the U.S., Israel, and the rest of the world with emphasis on Jewish women's issues." Estab. 1926. Circ. 12,000. Byline given. Pays on publication. Publishes ms an average of 6 months after acceptance. Submit seasonal material 6 months in advance. Accepts queries by mail, e-mail. Accepts simultaneous submissions. Responds in 4 weeks to que-

ries. Responds in 3 months to mss. Sample copy for $2. Guidelines by e-mail.

NONFICTION Needs book excerpts, essays, historical, interview, personal experience, photo feature, travel, Jewish topics & issues, political & social issues & women's issues. **Buys 16-20 mss/year.** Send complete ms. **Pays 10-20¢/word for assigned and unsolicited articles.** Some

PHOTOS State availability. Reviews GIF/JPEG files. Negotiates payment individually.

FICTION "We want serious fiction, with insight, reflection and consciousness." Needs novel excerpts, literary with Jewish content. "We do not want fiction that is mostly dialogue. No corny Jewish humor. No Holocaust fiction." **Buys 1-2 mss/year.** Query with published clips or send complete ms. Length: 2,000-3,000 words. **Pays 10-20¢/word for assigned articles and for unsolicited articles.**

TIPS "No maudlin nostalgia or romance; no hackneyed Jewish humor."

RO, THE OPRAH MAGAZINE

Hearst Corp., 1700 Broadway, 38th Floor, New York NY 10019-5905. (212)903-5187. **Fax:** (212)977-1947. **Website:** www.oprah.com. Monthly magazine founded by Oprah Winfrey and Hearst Corporation, primarily marketed at women. Circ. 2.4 million. Guidelines available.

🖛 Query before submitting.

🟂🟂🟂🟂 PREGNANCY

Pregnancy Magazine Group, **E-mail:** editors@pregnancymagazine.com. **Website:** www.pregnancymagazine.com. **Contact:** Paul Banas, publisher. **90% freelance written.** Magazine covering products, wellness, technology, fashion, and beauty for pregnant women and products, health, and child care for babies up to 12 months old. 11 issues including annual buyers' guide. "Most of our audience are first-time moms who seek advice and information about health, relationships, diet, celebrities, fashion, and green living for pregnant women and babies up to 12 months old. Our readers are first-time and experienced moms (and dads) who want articles that are relevant to their modern lives. Our goal is to help our readers feel confident and prepared for pregnancy and parenthood by providing the best information for today's parents." Estab. 2000. Circ. Digital edition: 30,000; Buyers' Guide: 250,000. Offers kill fee. Editorial lead time 5 months. Submit seasonal

material 5-6 months in advance. Guidelines available at www.pregnancymagazine.com/writers.

NONFICTION Buys very few mss/year. Length: 350-2,000 words.

TIPS "Interested freelancers should first read *Pregnancy*'s Writer's Guidelines, which are available at www.pregnancymagazine.com/writers. When sending pitch ideas, be sure to follow those guidelines carefully."

EAL SIMPLE

Time Inc., 1271 Avenue of the Americas, New York NY 10020. (212)522-1212. **Fax:** (212)467-1392. **Website:** www.realsimple.com. *Real Simple* is a monthly women's interest magazine. *Real Simple* features articles and information related to homekeeping, childcare, cooking, and emotional wellbeing. The magazine is distinguished by its clean, uncluttered style of layout and photos. Estab. 2000. Circ. 1.97 million.

🖛 Query before submitting.

🟂🟂🟂 REDBOOK MAGAZINE

Hearst Corp., Articles Department, Redbook, 300 W. 57th St., 22nd Floor, New York NY 10019. **Website:** www.redbookmag.com. Monthly magazine covering women's issues. *Redbook* is targeted to women between the ages of 25-45 who define themselves as smart, capable, and happy with their lives. Many, but not all, of readers are going through 1 of 2 key life transitions: single to married and married to mom. Each issue is a provocative mix of features geared to entertain and inform them, including: News stories on contemporary issues that are relevant to the reader's life and experience, and explore the emotional ramifications of cultural and social changes; girst-person essays about dramatic pivotal moments in a woman's life; marriage articles with an emphasis on strengthening the relationship; short parenting features on how to deal with universal health and behavioral issues; reporting on exciting trends in women's lives. Estab. 1903. Circ. 2,200,000. Pays on acceptance. Publishes ms an average of 6 months after acceptance. Responds in 3 months to queries. Responds in 3 months to mss. Guidelines online.

NONFICTION Query with published clips and SASE. Length: 2,500-3,000 words/features; 1,000-1,500 words/short articles.

TIPS "Most *Redbook* articles require solid research, well-developed anecdotes from on-the-record sources, and fresh, insightful quotes from established experts in a field that pass our 'reality check' test. Articles must apply to women in our demographics. Writers are advised to read at least the last 6 issues of the magazine (available in most libraries) to get a better understanding of appropriate subject matter and treatment. We prefer to see detailed queries rather than completed mss, and suggest that you provide us with some ideas for sources/experts. Please enclose 2 or more samples of your writing, as well as a SASE."

☺☺☺☺ SELF

Conde Nast, 4 Times Square, New York NY 10036. (212)286-2860. **Fax:** (212)286-6174. **E-mail:** comments@self.com. **Website:** www.self.com. Monthly magazine for women ages 20-45. Self-confidence, self-assurance, and a healthy, happy lifestyle are pivotal to *Self* readers. This healthy lifestyle magazine delivers by addressing real-life issues from the inside out, with unparalleled energy and authority. From beauty, fitness, health and nutrition to personal style, finance, and happiness, the path to total well-being begins with *Self*. Circ. 1.3 million. Byline given on features and most short items. Pays on acceptance. Accepts queries by online submission form. Accepts simultaneous submissions. Responds in 1 month to queries. Guidelines for #10 SASE.

Query before submitting.

NONFICTION **Buys 40 mss/year.** Query with published clips. Length: 1,500-5,000 words. **Pays $1-2/word.**

COLUMNS/DEPARTMENTS Uses short, news-driven items on health, fitness, nutrition, money, jobs, love/sex, psychology and happiness, travel. Length: 300-1,000 words. **Buys 50 mss/year.** Query with published clips. **Pays $1-2/word.**

☺☺ SKIRT!

Morris Communications, 1 Henrietta St., First Floor, Charleston SC 29403. (843)958-0027. **Fax:** (843)958-0029. **E-mail:** submissions@skirt.com; digitalmedia@skirt.com. **Website:** www.skirt.com. **Contact:** Nikki Hardin, publisher. **50% freelance written.** Monthly magazine covering women's interest. *Skirt!* is all about women—their work, play, families, creativity, style, health, wealth, bodies, and souls. The magazine's attitude is spirited, independent, outspoken, serious, playful, irreverent, sometimes controversial, and always passionate. Estab. 1994. Circ. 285,000. Byline given. Pays on publication. Publishes ms an average of 2 months after acceptance. Editorial lead time 2-3 months. Submit seasonal material 2-3 months in advance. Accepts queries by e-mail (preferred). Accepts

simultaneous submissions. Responds in 6-8 weeks to queries. Responds in 1-2 months to mss. Guidelines online.

NONFICTION Needs essays, humor, personal experience. "Do not send feature articles. We only accept submissions of completed personal essays that will work with our monthly themes online." **Buys 100+ mss/year.** Send complete ms via e-mail. Length: 900-1,200 words. **Pays $150-200.**

TIPS "Surprise and charm us. We look for fearless essays that take chances with content and subject. *Skirt!* is not your average women's magazine. We push the envelope and select content that makes our readers think. Please review guidelines and themes online before submitting."

☺☺☺☺ VOGUE

Condé Nast, 4 Times Square, 12th Floor, New York NY 10036-6518. (212)286-2860. **Website:** www.vogue.com. Monthly magazine. *Vogue* mirrors the changing roles and concerns of women, covering not only evolutions in fashion, beauty and style, but the important issues and ideas of the arts, health care, politics, and world affairs. Estab. 1892. Circ. 1.1 million. Byline sometimes given. Pays on acceptance. Offers 25% kill fee. Responds in 3 months to queries. Guidelines for #10 SASE.

Query before submitting.

NONFICTION Query with published clips. 2,500 words maximum. **Pays $1-2/word.**

TIPS "Sophisticated, surprising and compelling writing a must. Please note: *Vogue* accepts *very* few unsolicited mss. Most stories are generated in-house and are written by staff."

WOMAN'S DAY

Hearst Communications, Inc., 300 W. 57th St., 28th Floor, New York NY 10019. (212)649-2000. **E-mail:** womansday@hearst.com. **Website:** www.womansday.com. **Contact:** Sue Kakstys, managing editor. Monthly magazine. Woman's Day is a women's magazine that covers such topics as homemaking, food, nutrition, physical fitness, physical attractiveness, and fashion. Estab. 1937. Circ. 3.3 million. Accepts queries by e-mail. Guidelines online.

NONFICTION Editors work almost exclusively with experienced writers who have clips from major national magazines. Accepts unsolicited mss only from writers with such credentials. There are no exceptions. E-mail an idea or mss that might be of interest and include recent, published clips. Will respond only if interested. Does not accept hard copy submissions.

☺☺☺ WOMAN'S WORLD

Bauer Publishing Co., 270 Sylvan Ave., Englewood Cliffs NJ 07632. (201)569-6699. **Fax:** (201)569-3584. **E-mail:** dearww@bauerpublishing.com; dearww@aol.com. **Website:** winit.womansworldmag.com. **Contact:** Stephanie Saible, editor-in-chief. Weekly magazine covering human interest and service pieces of interest to family-oriented women across the nation. *Woman's World* is a women's service magazine. It offers a blend of fashion, food, parenting, beauty, and relationship features coupled with the true-life human interest stories. Publishes short romances and mini-mysteries for all women, ages 18-68. Estab. 1980. Circ. 1.6 million. Pays on acceptance. Publishes ms an average of 4 months after acceptance. Submit seasonal material 4 months in advance. Accepts queries by mail. Responds in 2 months to mss. Guidelines for #10 SASE.

○ *Woman's World* is not looking for freelancers to take assigments generated by the staff, but it will assign stories to writers who have made a successful pitch.

FICTION Contact: Johnene Granger, fiction editor. Looking for short story, romance, and mainstream of 800 words and mini-mysteries of 1,000 words. Each of story should have a light romantic theme and can be written from either a masculine or feminine point of view. Women characters may be single, married, or divorced. Plots must be fast moving with vivid dialogue and action. The problems and dilemmas inherent in them should be contemporary and realistic, handled with warmth and feeling. The stories must have a positive resolution. Specify Fiction on envelope. Always enclose SASE. Responds in 4 months. No phone or fax queries. Pays $1,000 for romances on acceptance for North American serial rights for 6 months. The 1,000 word mini-mysteries may feature either a "whodunnit" or "howdunnit" theme. The mystery may revolve around anything from a theft to murder. Not interested in sordid or grotesque crimes. Emphasis should be on intricacies of plot rather than gratuitous violence. The story must include a resolution that clearly states the villain is getting his or her come-uppance. Submit complete mss. Specify Mini-Mystery on envelope. Enclose SASE. No phone queries. Needs mystery, romance, contemporary. Not interested in science fiction, fantasy, historical romance, or foreign locales. No explicit sex, graphic language, or seamy settings. Send complete ms. Romances: 800 words; mysteries: 1,000 words.

TIPS The whole story should be sent when submitting fiction. Stories slanted for a particular holiday should be sent at least 6 months in advance. "Familiarize yourself totally with our format and style. Read at least a year's worth of *Woman's World* fiction. Analyze and dissect it. Regarding romances, scrutinize them not only for content but tone, mood and sensibility."

TRADE JOURNALS

Many writers who pick up *Writer's Market* for the first time do so with the hope of selling an article to one of the popular, high-profile consumer magazines found on newsstands and in bookstores. Many of those writers are surprised to find an entire world of magazine publishing exists outside the realm of commercial magazines—trade journals. Writers who have discovered trade journals have found a market that offers the chance to publish regularly in subject areas they find interesting, editors who are typically more accessible than their commercial counterparts, and pay rates that rival those of the big-name magazines. [Note: All of the magazines listed in the Trade Journals section are paying markets. However, some of the magazines are not identified by payment rates ($) because the magazines preferred not to disclose specific payment information.]

Trade journal is the general term for any publication focusing on a particular occupation or industry. Other terms used to describe the different types of trade publications are business, technical, and professional journals. They are read by truck drivers, bricklayers, farmers, fishermen, heart surgeons, and just about everyone else working in a trade or profession. Trade periodicals are sharply angled to the specifics of the professions on which they report. They offer business-related news, features, and service articles that will foster their readers' professional development.

Editors at trade journals tell us their audience is made up of knowledgeable and highly interested readers. Writers for trade journals have to either possess knowledge about the field in question or be able to report it accurately from interviews with those who do. Writers who have or can develop a good grasp of a specialized body of knowledge will find trade magazine editors who are eager to hear from them.

An ideal way to begin your foray into trade journals is to write for those that report on your present profession. Whether you've been teaching dance, farming, or working as a paralegal, begin by familiarizing yourself with the magazines that serve your occupation. After you've read enough issues to have a feel for the kinds of pieces the magazines run, approach the editors with your own article ideas. If you don't have experience in a profession but can demonstrate an ability to understand (and write about) the intricacies and issues of a particular trade that interests you, editors will still be willing to hear from you.

ADVERTISING, MARKETING AND PR

◎◎◎ BRAND PACKAGING

BNP Media, 2401 W. Big Beaver Rd., Suite 700, Troy MI 48084. (248)786-1680. **Fax:** (847)405-4100. **E-mail:** zielinskil@bnpmedia.com. **Website:** www.brandpackaging.com. **Contact:** Laura Zielinski, editor-in-chief. **15% freelance written.** Magazine published 10 times/year covering how packaging can be a marketing tool. Publishes strategies and tactics to make products stand out on the shelf. Market is brand managers who are marketers but need to know something about packaging. Estab. 1997. Circ. 33,000. Byline given. Pays on acceptance. Publishes ms an average of 2 months after acceptance. Editorial lead time 3 months. Submit seasonal material 3 months in advance. Accepts queries by mail, fax. Sample copy free. Guidelines online.

NONFICTION Needs how-to, interview, new product. **Buys 10 mss/year.** Send complete ms. Length: 600-2,400 words. **Pays 40-50¢/word.**

PHOTOS State availability. Identification of subjects required. Reviews contact sheets, 35mm transparencies, 4x5 prints. Negotiates payment individually.

COLUMNS/DEPARTMENTS Emerging Technology (new packaging technology), 600 words. **Buys 10 mss/year.** Query. **Pays $150-300.**

TIPS "Be knowledgeable on marketing techniques and be able to grasp packaging techniques. Be sure you focus on packaging as a marketing tool. Use concrete examples. We are not seeking case histories at this time."

◎ DECA DIMENSIONS

1908 Association Dr., Reston VA 20191. (703)860-5000. **Fax:** (703)860-4013. **E-mail:** publications@deca.org; communications@deca.org. **E-mail:** christopher_young@deca.org. **Website:** www.deca.org. **Contact:** Christopher Young. **30% freelance written.** Quarterly magazine covering marketing, professional development, business, career training during school year (no issues published May-August). *DECA Dimensions* is the membership magazine for DECA—The Association of Marketing Students, primarily ages 15-19 in all 50 states, the U.S. territories, Germany, and Canada. The magazine is delivered through the classroom. Students are interested in developing professional, leadership, and career skills. Estab. 1947. Circ.

160,000. Byline given. Pays on publication. No kill fee. Editorial lead time 3 months. Submit seasonal material 4 months in advance. Accepts queries by mail, e-mail, fax, phone. Accepts simultaneous submissions. Sample copy free.

NONFICTION Needs essays, general interest, how-to, get jobs, start business, plan for college, etc., interview, business leads, personal experience, working, leadership development. **Buys 10 mss/year.** Submit a paragraph description of your article. Length: 500-1,000 words. **Pays $125 for assigned articles. Pays $100 for unsolicited articles.**

REPRINTS Send typed ms and information about when and where the material previously appeared. Pays 85% of amount paid for an original article.

COLUMNS/DEPARTMENTS Professional Development; Leadership, 500-1,000 words. **Buys 6 mss/year.** Send complete ms. **Pays $ 75-100.**

TIPS "Articles can be theme specific, but we accept a variety of articles that are appropriate for our readership on topics such as community service, leadership development, or professionalism. The primary readership of the magazine is compromised of high school students, and articles should be relevant to their needs and interests. In most cases, articles should not promote the products or services of a specific company or organization; however, you may use examples to convey concepts or principles."

◎◎ O'DWYER'S PR REPORT

271 Madison Ave., #600, New York NY 10016. (212)679-2471; (866)395-7710. **Fax:** (212)683-2750. **E-mail:** john@odwyerpr.com. **Website:** www.odwyerpr.com. **Contact:** John O'Dwyer, associate publisher/editor. Monthly magazine providing PR articles. *O'Dwyer's* has been covering public relations, marketing communications, and related fields for over 40 years. The company provides the latest news and information about PR firms and professionals, the media, corporations, legal issues, jobs, technology, and much more through its website, weekly newsletter, monthly magazine, directories, and guides. Many of the contributors are PR people publicizing themselves while analyzing something. Byline given. No kill fee. Accepts queries by mail.

NONFICTION Needs opinion. Query. **Pays $250.**

◎◎◎ PROMO MAGAZINE

Access Intelligence, (203)899-8442. **E-mail:** podell@accessintel.com. **Website:** www.chiefmarketer.com/

promotional-marketing. **Contact:** Patricia Odell, executive editor. **5% freelance written.** Monthly magazine covering promotion marketing. *Promo* serves marketers, and stories must be informative, well written, and familiar with the subject matter. Estab. 1987. Circ. 25,000. Byline given. Pays on publication. Offers 25% kill fee. Publishes ms an average of 2 months after acceptance. Editorial lead time 3 months. Submit seasonal material 3 months in advance. Responds in 1 month to queries. Sample copy for $5.

NONFICTION Needs exposè, general interest, how-to, marketing programs, interview, new product, promotion. No general marketing stories not heavily involved in promotions. Generally does not accept unsolicited mss; query first. **Buys 6-10 mss/year.** Query with published clips. **Pays $1,000 maximum for assigned articles. Pays $500 maximum for unsolicited articles.** Sometimes pays expenses of writers on assignment.

PHOTOS State availability. Captions, identification of subjects, model releases required. Reviews contact sheets, negatives. Negotiates payment individually.

TIPS "Understand that our stories aim to teach marketing professionals about successful promotion strategies. Case studies or new promos have the best chance."

SHOPPER MARKETING

Path to Purchase Institute, 8550 W. Bryn Mawr Ave., Suite 200, Chicago IL 60631. (773)992-4450. **Fax:** (773)992-4455. **E-mail:** shoppermarketing@p2pi.org. **Website:** www.shoppermarketingmag.com. **80% freelance written.** Monthly publication covering advertising and primarily the shopper marketing industry. Covers how brands market to the shopper at retail, what insights/research they gathered to reach that shopper and how they activated the program at retail. Writes case studies on shopper marketing campaigns, displays, packaging, retail media, and events. Writes major category reports, company profiles, trends features, and more. Readers are marketers and retailers, and a small selection of P-O-P producers (the guys that build the displays). Estab. 1988. Circ. 18,000. Byline given. Pays on acceptance. Offers no kill fee. Editorial lead time 2 months. Submit seasonal material 3 months in advance. Accepts queries by e-mail. Accepts simultaneous submissions. Responds in 1 month to queries. Sample copy and guidelines free.

$$ SIGN BUILDER ILLUSTRATED

Simmons-Boardman Publishing Corp., 55 Broad St., 26th Floor, New York NY 10004. (252)355-5806. **E-mail:** jwooten@sbpub.com; abray@sbpub.com. **Website:** www.signshop.com. **Contact:** Jeff Wooten, editor; Ashley Bray, associate editor. **40% freelance written.** Monthly magazine covering sign and graphic industry. *Sign Builder Illustrated* targets sign professionals where they work: on the shop floor. Topics cover the broadest spectrum of the sign industry, from design to fabrication, installation, maintenance, and repair. Readers own a similarly wide range of shops, including commercial, vinyl, sign erection and maintenance, electrical and neon, architectural, and awnings. Estab. 1987. Circ. 14,500. Byline given. Pays on acceptance. Offers 10% kill fee. Publishes ms an average of 3 months after acceptance. Editorial lead time 3 months. Submit seasonal material 4 months in advance. Accepts queries by mail, e-mail, fax, phone. Accepts simultaneous submissions. Responds in 1 month to queries. Sample copy and writer's guidelines free.

NONFICTION Needs historical, how-to, humor, interview, photo feature, technical. **Buys 50-60 mss/year.** Query. Length: 1,000-1,500 words. **Pays $250-550 for assigned articles.**

PHOTOS Send photos. Captions, identification of subjects required. Reviews 3x5 prints. Negotiates payment individually,.

TIPS "Be very knowledgeable about a portion of the sign industry you are covering. We want our readers to come away from each article with at least 1 good idea, 1 new technique, or 1 more 'trick of the trade.' At the same time, we don't want a purely textbook listing of 'do this, do that.' Our readers enjoy *Sign Builder Illustrated* because the publication speaks to them in a clear and lively fashion, from 1 sign professional to another. We want to engage the reader who has been in the business for some time. While there might be a place for basic instruction in new techniques, our average paid subscriber has been in business over 20 years, employs over 7 people, and averages $800,000 in annual sales. These people aren't neophytes content with retread articles they can find anywhere. It's important for our writers to use anecdotes and examples drawn from the daily sign business."

⊙⊙ SIGNCRAFT

SignCraft Publishing Co., Inc., P.O. Box 60031, Fort Myers FL 33906. (239)939-4644. **Fax:** (239)939-0607. **E-mail:** signcraft@signcraft.com. **Website:** www. signcraft.com. **10% freelance written.** Bimonthly magazine covering the sign industry. Estab. 1980. Circ. 14,000. Byline given. Pays on publication. Offers negotiable kill fee. Publishes ms an average of 6 months after acceptance. Accepts queries by mail, e-mail, fax. Responds in 1 month to queries. Sample copy and writer's guidelines for $3.

NONFICTION Needs interview. **Buys 10 mss/year.** Query. Length: 500-2,000 words.

TIPS "Like any trade magazine, we need material of direct benefit to our readers. We can't afford space for material of marginal interest."

⊙⊙⊙ SOCAL MEETINGS + EVENTS MAGAZINE

Tiger Oak Publications, One Tiger Oak Plaza, 900 S. Third St., Minneapolis MN 55415. **Fax:** (612)338-0532. **E-mail:** bobby.hart@tigeroak.com. **Website:** meetingsmags.com. **Contact:** Bobby Hart, managing editor. **80% freelance written.** Meetings + Events Media Group, including Minnesota Meetings + Events, Illinois Meetings + Events, Colorado Meetings & Events, Michigan Meetings + Events, California Meetings + Events, Texas Meetings + Events, Northwest Meetings + Events, Mountain Meetings, Pennsylvania Meetings + Evens and New Jersey Meetings + Events is a group of premier quarterly trade magazines for meetings planners and hospitality service providers throughout the US. Thesemagazines aim to report on and promote businesses involved in the meetings and events industry, covering current and emerging trends, people and venues in the meetings and events industry in their respective regions. Estab. 1993. Circ. approximately 20,000 per title. Byline given. Pays on acceptance. Offers 20% kill fee. Publishes ms an average of 4 months after acceptance. Editorial lead time 4-6 months. Submit seasonal material 6 months in advance. Accepts queries by mail. Accepts simultaneous submissions. Responds in 1-2 weeks to queries.

NONFICTION Needs general interest, historical, interview, new product, opinion, personal experience, photo feature, technical, travel. **Buys 30 mss/year.** "Each query should tell us: What the story will be about; how you will tell the story (what sources you will use, how you will conduct research, etc.); why is the story pertinent to the market audience. Please also attach PDFs of 3 published magazine articles." Length: 600-1,500 words. **The average department length story (4-700 words) pays about $2-300 and the average feature length story (1,000-1,200 words) pays up to $800, depending on the story. These rates are not guaranteed and vary.**

PHOTOS State availability. Identification of subjects, model releases required. Negotiates payment individually.

COLUMNS/DEPARTMENTS Meet + Eat (restaurant reviews); Facility Focus (venue reviews); Regional Spotlight (city review), 1,000 words. **Buys 30 mss/year.** Query with published clips. **Pays $400-600.**

TIPS "Familiarization with the meetings and events industry is critical, as well as knowing how to write for a trade magazine. Writers experienced in writing for the trade magazine business industry are preferred."

⊙⊙⊙ TEXAS MEETINGS + EVENTS

Tiger Oak Publications, One Tiger Oak Plaza, 900 S. 3rd St., Minneapolis MN 55401. (612)548-3180. **Fax:** (612)548-3181. **E-mail:** bobby.hart@tigeroak.com. **Website:** tx.meetingsmags.com. **Contact:** Bobby Hart, managing editor. **80% freelance written.** Quarterly magazine covering meetings and events industry. *Texas Meetings & Events* magazine is the premier trade publication for meetings planners and hospitality service providers in the state. This magazine aims to report on and promote businesses involved in the meetings and events industry. The magazine covers current and emerging trends, people and venues in the meetings and events industry in the state. Estab. 1993. Circ. 20,000. Byline given. Pays on acceptance. Offers 20% kill fee. Publishes ms an average of 4 months after acceptance. Editorial lead time 4-6 months. Submit seasonal material 6 months in advance. Accepts queries by mail. Accepts simultaneous submissions. Responds in 1-2 weeks to queries. Guidelines online.

NONFICTION Needs general interest, historical, interview, new product, opinion, personal experience, photo feature, technical, travel. **Buys 30 mss/year.** Query with published clips of 3 magazine articles. Length: 600-1,500 words. **Pays $400-800.**

PHOTOS State availability. Identification of subjects, model releases required. Negotiates payment individually.

COLUMNS/DEPARTMENTS Meet + Eat (restaurant reviews); Facility Focus (venue reviews); Regional Spotlight (city review), 1,000 words. **Buys 30 mss/year.** Query with published clips. **Pays $400-600.**
TIPS "Familiarization with the meetings and events industry is critical, as well as knowing how to write for a trade magazine. Writers experienced in writing for the trade magazine business industry are preferred."

ART, DESIGN AND COLLECTIBLES

⊛⊛ AIRBRUSH ACTION MAGAZINE

Action, Inc., P.O. Box 438, Allenwood NJ 08720. (732)223-7878; (800)876-2472. **Fax:** (732)223-2855. **E-mail:** ceo@airbrushaction.com. **Website:** www.airbrushaction.com. **Contact:** Cliff Stieglitz, publisher. **80% freelance written.** Bimonthly magazine covering the spectrum of airbrush applications: automotive and custom paint applications, illustration, T-shirt airbrushing, fine art, automotive and sign painting, hobby/craft applications, wall murals, fingernails, temporary tattoos, artist profiles, reviews, and more. Estab. 1985. Circ. 35,000. Byline given. Pays 1 month after publication. Publishes ms an average of 6 months after acceptance. Editorial lead time 6 months. Submit seasonal material 6 months in advance. Accepts queries by mail, e-mail, fax. Accepts simultaneous submissions.
NONFICTION Needs how-to, humor, inspirational, interview, new product, personal experience, technical. Doesn't want anything unrelated to airbrush. Query with published clips. **Pays 15¢/word.** Sometimes pays expenses of writers on assignment.
PHOTOS Digital images preferred. Send photos. Captions, identification of subjects, model releases required. Negotiates payment individually.
COLUMNS/DEPARTMENTS Query with published clips.
TIPS "Send bio and writing samples. Send well-written technical information pertaining to airbrush art. We publish a lot of artist profiles—they all sound the same. Looking for new pizzazz!"

⊛⊛ ANTIQUEWEEK

MidCountry Media, 27 N. Jefferson St., P.O. Box 90, Knightstown IN 46148. (800)876-5133. **Fax:** (800)345-3398. **E-mail:** davidb@antiqueweek.com; tony@antiqueweek.com. **Website:** www.antiqueweek.com. **Contact:** David Blower, Jr., senior editor; Tony Gregory, publisher. **80% freelance written.** Weekly tabloid covering antiques and collectibles with 3 editions: Eastern, Central, and National, plus the monthly *AntiqueWest*. *AntiqueWeek* has a wide range of readership from dealers and auctioneers to collectors, both advanced and novice. Readers demand accurate information presented in an entertaining style. Estab. 1968. Circ. 50,000. Byline given. Pays on publication. Offers 10% kill fee or $25. Submit seasonal material 1 month in advance. Accepts queries by mail, e-mail. Sample copy free. Guidelines by e-mail.
NONFICTION Needs historical, how-to, interview, opinion, personal experience, antique show and auction reports, feature articles on particular types of antiques and collectibles. **Buys 400-500 mss/year.** Query. Length: 1,000-2,000 words. **Pays $50-250.**
REPRINTS Send electronic copy with rights for sale noted and information about when and where the material previously appeared.
PHOTOS All material must be submitted electronically via e-mail or on CD. Send photos. Identification of subjects required.
TIPS "Writers should know their topics thoroughly. Feature articles must be well researched and clearly written. An interview and profile article with a knowledgeable collector might be the break for a first-time contributor. We seek a balanced mix of information on traditional antiques and 20th century collectibles."

⊛ THE APPRAISERS STANDARD

New England Appraisers Association, 6973 Crestridge Dr., Memphis TN 38119. (901)758-2659. **E-mail:** ETuten551@aol.com. **Website:** www.newenglandappraisers.org. **Contact:** Edward Tuten, editor. **50% freelance written. Works with a small number of new/unpublished writers each year.** Quarterly publication covering the appraisals of antiques, art, collectibles, jewelry, coins, stamps, and real estate. Estab. 1980. Circ. 1,000. Short bio and byline given. Pays on publication. No kill fee. Publishes ms an average of 1 year after acceptance. Submit seasonal material 2 months in advance. Accepts queries by mail, e-mail. Accepts simultaneous submissions. Responds in 1 month to queries. Responds in 2 months to mss. Sample copy for 9x12 SAE with $1 postage. Guidelines for #10 SASE.

NONFICTION Needs interview, personal experience, technical, travel. Send complete ms. Length: 700 words. **Pays $60.**

REPRINTS "Send typed ms with rights for sale noted and information about when and where the material previously appeared."

PHOTOS Send photos. Identification of subjects required. Reviews negatives, prints. Offers no additional payment for photos accepted with ms.

TIPS "Interviewing members of the association for articles, reviewing, shows, and large auctions are all ways for writers who are not in the field to write articles for us. Articles should be geared to provide information which will help the appraisers with ascertaining value, detecting forgeries or reproductions, or simply providing advice on appraising the articles. I would like writers to focus on particular types of antiques: i.e. types of furniture, glass, artwork, etc., giving information on the history of this type of antique, good photos, recent sale prices, etc."

ARCHITECTURAL RECORD

McGraw-Hill, 2 Penn Plaza, 9th Floor, New York NY 10121. (212)904-2594. **Fax:** (212)904-4256. **Website:** www.architecturalrecord.com. **Contact:** Elisabeth Broome, managing editor. **50% freelance written.** Monthly magazine covering architecture and design. Magazine for architects, designers, and other related fields. Several available categories for submission; see website and "Call for Entries" tab for specific details. Estab. 1891. Circ. 110,000. Byline given. Pays on publication. Offers 25% kill fee. Publishes ms an average of 2 months after acceptance. Editorial lead time 2 months. Submit seasonal material 2 months in advance. Accepts queries by mail. Responds in 2 weeks to queries. Responds in 2 months to mss. Sample copy and writer's guidelines online.

NONFICTION Query before submitting. Pitch the project. Does not accept unsolicited mss.

TIPS "First read the magazine and study its various parts, so you understand what kinds of stories we run. We recommend reading a year's worth of issues since many special sections and themed issues occur on a semi-annual or annual basis. If you wish your project to be evaluated as a general feature, make sure it ranks among those you've seen in recent issues of RECORD. Keep in mind that internationally only 100 projects per year make it to the pages of Architectural Record.

It is better to be realistic at the outset than disappointed by unfounded expectations."

ARCHITECTURE NEW ZEALAND

AGM, Private Bag 99915, Newmarket Auckland 1031 New Zealand. (64)(9)846-4068; or 09 847 9320. **Website:** www.agm.co.nz. **Contact:** Nathan Inkpen, publisher. Bimonthly magazine covering issues relating to building design, construction, and management. This is the official magazine of the New Zealand Institute of Architects. It provides national coverage of the best residential, commercial, and institutional architecture, plus constructive criticism and issues of professional practice. No kill fee.

NONFICTION Query before submitting.

ART MATERIALS RETAILER

Fahy-Williams Publishing, Inc., 171 Reed St., P.O. Box 1080, Geneva NY 14456. (315)789-0458. **Fax:** (315)789-4263. **E-mail:** tmanzer@fwpi.com. **Website:** www.artmaterialsretailer.com. J. Kevin Fahy, publisher (kfahy@fwpi.com). **Contact:** Tina Manzer, editorial director. **10% freelance written.** Quarterly magazine covering retail stores that sell art materials. Offers book reviews, retailer-recommended products, and profiles of stores from around the country. Estab. 1998. Byline given. Pays on publication. No kill fee. Editorial lead time 2 months. Submit seasonal material 3 months in advance. Accepts simultaneous submissions. Responds in 3 weeks to queries. Responds in 3 months to mss. Sample copy and writer's guidelines free.

NONFICTION Needs book excerpts, how-to, interview, personal experience. **Buys 2 mss/year.** Send complete ms. Length: 1,500-3,000 words. **Pays $50-250.** Sometimes pays expenses of writers on assignment.

PHOTOS State availability. Identification of subjects required. Reviews transparencies. Offers no additional payment for photos accepted with ms.

FILLERS Needs anecdotes, facts, newsbreaks. **Buys 5 mss/year.** Length: 500-1,500 words. **Pays $50-125.**

TIPS "We like to review mss rather than queries. Artwork (photos, drawings, etc.) is a real plus. We (and our readers) enjoy practical, nuts-and-bolts, news-you-can-use articles."

FAITH + FORM

47 Grandview Terrace, Essex CT 06426. (860)575-4702. **E-mail:** mcrosbie@faithandform.com. **Website:**

www.faithandform.com. **Contact:** Michael J. Crosbie, editor-in-chief. **50% freelance written.** Quarterly magazine covering relgious buildings and art. *Faith + Form*, devoted to religious art and architecture, is read by artists, designers, architects, clergy, congregations, and all who care about environments for worship. Writers must be knowledgeable about environments for worship, or able to explain them. Estab. 1967. Circ. 4,500. Byline given. Publishes ms an average of 6 months after acceptance. Editorial lead time 6 months. Submit seasonal material 6 months in advance. Accepts queries by online submission form. YesAccepts simultaneous submissions. Responds in 2 weeks to queries. Responds in 1 month to mss. Sample copy online. Guidelines available.

NONFICTION Needs book excerpts, essays, how-to, inspirational, interview, opinion, personal experience, photo feature, religious, technical. **Buys 6 mss/year.** Query. Submit via online submission form, in Microsoft Word or Rich Text format. Length: 500-2,500 words.

PHOTOS Photos must be scanned at a size no smaller than 5x7, at 300 dpi. State availability. Captions required. Reviews Photoshop or TIFF files. Offers no additional payment for photos accepted with ms.

COLUMNS/DEPARTMENTS News, 250-750 words; Book Reviews, 250-500 words. **Buys 3 mss/year.** Query.

$$$ HOW

F+W Media, Inc., 10151 Carver Rd., Suite 200, Blue Ash OH 45242. (513)531-2690. **Fax:** (513)531-2902. **E-mail:** editorial@howdesign.com. **Website:** www.howdesign.com. **75% freelance written.** Bi-monthly magazine covering graphic design profession. *HOW: Design Ideas at Work* strives to serve the business, technological and creative needs of graphic-design professionals. The magazine provides a practical mix of essential business information, up-to-date technological tips, the creative whys and hows behind noteworthy projects, and profiles of professionals who are impacting design. The ultimate goal of *HOW* is to help designers, whether they work for a design firm or for an inhouse design department, run successful, creative, profitable studios. Estab. 1985. Circ. 40,000. Byline given. Pays on acceptance. No kill fee. Responds in 6 weeks to queries.

🔑 The HOW brand now extends beyond the print magazine to annual events for design professionals, yearly design competitions, digital products and books.

NONFICTION Special issues: Self-Promotion Annual (September/October); Business Annual (November/December); In-House Design Annual (January/February); International Annual of Design (March/April); Creativity/Paper/Stock Photography (May/June); Digital Design Annual (July/August). No how-to articles for beginning artists or fine-art-oriented articles. **Buys 40 mss/year.** Query with published clips and samples of subject's work, artwork, or design. Length: 1,500-2,000 words. **Pays $700-900.** Sometimes pays expenses of writers on assignment.

PHOTOS State availability. Captions required. Reviews information updated and verified.

COLUMNS/DEPARTMENTS Creativity (focuses on creative exercises and inspiration) 1,200-1,500 words. In-House Issues (focuses on business and creativity issues for corporate design groups), 1,200-1,500 words. Business (focuses on business issue for design firm owners), 1,200-1, 500 words. **Buys Number of columns: 35. mss/year.** Query with published clips. **Pays $250-400.**

TIPS "We look for writers who can recognize graphic designers on the cutting-edge of their industry, both creatively and business-wise. Writers must have an eye for detail, and be able to relay *HOW*'s editorial style in an interesting, concise manner—without omitting any details. Showing you've done your homework on a subject—and that you can go beyond asking those same old questions—will give you a big advantage."

$$ THE PASTEL JOURNAL

F+W Media, Inc., 10151 Carver Rd., Suite #200, Cincinnati OH 45242. (513)531-2690. **Fax:** (513)891-7153. **E-mail:** pjedit@fwmedia.com. **Website:** www.pasteljournal.com. **Contact:** Anne Hevener, editor; Jessica Canterbury, managing editor. Bimonthly magazine covering pastel art. *The Pastel Journal* is the only national magazine devoted to the medium of pastel. Addressing the working professional as well as passionate amateurs, *The Pastel Journal* offers inspiration, information, and instruction to our readers. Estab. 1999. Circ. 22,000. Byline given. Pays on acceptance. Offers 25% kill fee. Publishes ms an average of 3-6 months after acceptance. Editorial lead time 6 months. Submit seasonal material 6 months in advance. Accepts queries by mail. Accepts simultaneous submissions. Responds in 4-6 weeks to queries. Guidelines online. **NONFICTION** Needs how-to, interview, new product, profile. Does not want articles that aren't art-related. Review magazine before submitting. Query with or without published clips. Length: 500-2,000 words. **Payment does not exceed $600.**

PHOTOS State availability of or send photos. Captions required. Reviews transparencies, prints, GIF/JPEG files. Offers no additional payment for photos accepted with ms.

🟢🟢🟢 PRINT

F+W Media, Inc., 10151 Carver Rd., Suite 200, Blue Ash OH 45242. (513)531-2690. **E-mail:** info@printmag.com. **Website:** www.printmag.com. **75% freelance written.** Bimonthly magazine covering graphic design and visual culture. *PRINT*'s articles, written by design specialists and cultural critics, focus on the social, political, and historical context of graphic design, and on the places where consumer culture and popular culture meet. Aims to produce a general interest magazine for professionals with engagingly written text and lavish illustrations. By covering a broad spectrum of topics, both international and local, *Print* tries to demonstrate the significance of design in the world at large. Estab. 1940. Circ. 45,000. Byline given. Pays on acceptance. Offers 25% kill fee. Publishes ms an average of 3 months after acceptance. Editorial lead time 3 months. Submit seasonal material 3 months in advance. Accepts queries by e-mail. Responds in 2 weeks to queries. Responds in 1 month to mss.

NONFICTION Needs essays, interview, opinion. **Buys 35-40 mss/year.** Query with published clips. Length: 1,000-2,500 words. **Pays $1,250.** Sometimes pays expenses of writers on assignment.

COLUMNS/DEPARTMENTS Query with published clips. **Pays $800.**

TIPS "Be well versed in issues related to the field of graphic design; don't submit ideas that are too general or geared to nonprofessionals."

🟢🟢 PROFESSIONAL ARTIST

Turnstile Publishing, 1500 Park Center Dr., Orlando FL 32835. (407)563-7000. **Fax:** (407)563-7099. **E-mail:** jandreasson@professionalartistmag.com. **Website:** www.professionalartistmag.com. **Contact:** Jenny Andreasson, assistant editor. **75% freelance written.** Monthly magazine. Professional Artist is dedicated

to providing independent visual artists from all backgrounds with the insights, encouragement and business strategies they need to make a living with their artwork. Estab. 1986. Circ. 20,000. Pays on publication. No kill fee. YesSample print copy for $5. Guidelines online.

💬 Welcomes nuts-and-bolts, practical articles of interest to professional visual artists, emerging or professional. Examples: How-to's, first-person stories on how an artist has built his career or an aspect of it, interviews with artists (business/career-building emphasis), web strategies, and pieces on business practices and other topics of use to artists. The tone of magazine is practical, and uplifting.

NONFICTION Needs essays, the psychology of creativity, how-to, interview, successful artists with a focus on what made them successful, networking articles, marketing topics, technical articles (new equipment, new media, computer software, Internet marketing.), cartoons, art law, including pending legislation that affects artists (copyright law, Internet regulations, etc.). Does not run reviews or art historical pieces, nor writing characterized by "critic-speak," philosophical hyperbole, psychological arrogance, politics, or New Age religion. Also, does not condone a get-rich-quick attitude. Send complete ms. **Pays $250.**

REPRINTS Send photocopy or typed ms and information about when and where the material previously appeared. Pays $50.

PHOTOS Reviews b&w glossy or color prints. Pays $25.

COLUMNS/DEPARTMENTS "If an artist or freelancer sends us good articles regularly, and based on results we feel that he is able to produce a column at least 3 times per year, we will invite him to be a contributing writer. If a gifted artist-writer can commit to producing an article on a monthly basis, we will offer him a regular column and the title contributing editor." Send complete ms.

TIPS "We strongly suggest that you read a copy of the publication before submitting a proposal. Most queries are rejected because they are too general for our audience."

🟢 TEXAS ARCHITECT

Texas Society of Architects, 500 Chicon St., Austin TX 78702. (512)478-7386. **Fax:** (512)478-0528. **Web-**

site: www.texasarchitect.org. **Contact:** Catherine Gavin, editor. **30% freelance written. Mostly written by unpaid members of the professional society.** Bimonthly journal covering architecture and architects of Texas. *Texas Architect* is a highly visually-oriented look at Texas architecture, design, and urban planning. Articles cover varied subtopics within architecture. Readers are mostly architects and related building professionals. Estab. 1951. Circ. 12,500. Byline given. Pays on publication. No kill fee. Publishes ms an average of 3 months after acceptance. Submit seasonal material 4 months in advance. Accepts queries by mail, e-mail. Responds in 6 weeks to queries. Guidelines online.

NONFICTION Needs interview, photo feature, technical, book reviews. Query with published clips. Length: 100-2,000 words. **Pays $50-100 for assigned articles.**

PHOTOS Send photos. Identification of subjects required. Reviews contact sheets, 35mm or 4x5 transparencies, 4x5 prints. Offers no additional payment for photos accepted with ms.

COLUMNS/DEPARTMENTS News (timely reports on architectural issues, projects, and people), 100-500 words. **Buys 10 articles/year mss/year.** Query with published clips. **Pays $50-100.**

⊙⊙ WATERCOLOR ARTIST

F+W Media, Inc., 10151 Carver Rd., Suite #200, Blue Ash OH 45242. (513)531-2690. **Fax:** (513)891-7153. **Website:** www.watercolorartistmagazine.com. **Contact:** Jennifer Hoffman, art director; Kelly Kane, editor. Bimonthly magazine covering water media arts. Estab. 1984. Circ. 44,000. Byline given. Pays on acceptance. Publishes ms an average of 3-6 months after acceptance. Editorial lead time 6 months. Submit seasonal material 6 months in advance. Accepts queries by mail. Accepts simultaneous submissions. Writer's guidelines available at www.artistsnetwork.com/contactus.

○ "*Watercolor Artist* is the definitive source of how-to instruction and creative inspiration for artists working in water-based media."

NONFICTION Needs book excerpts, essays, how-to, inspirational, interview, new product, personal experience. Does not want articles that aren't art-related. Review magazine before submitting. **Buys 36 mss/year.** Send query letter with images. Length: 350-2,500 words. **Pays $150-600.**

PHOTOS State availability of or send photos. Captions required. Reviews transparencies, prints, slides, GIF/JPEG files.

AUTO AND TRUCK

AFTERMARKET BUSINESS WORLD

Advanstar Communications, 24950 Country Club Blvd., Suite 200, North Olmsted OH 44070. (440)891-2746. **Fax:** (440)891-2675. **E-mail:** kmcnamara@advanstar.com. **Website:** www.aftermarketbusiness.com. **Contact:** Krista McNamara, managing editor. The mission of *Aftermarket Business World* (formerly *Aftermarket Business*) involves satisfying the needs of U.S. readers who want to do business here and elsewhere and helping readers in other countries who want to do business with U.S. companies. Editorial material for *Aftermarket Business World* focuses on news, trends, and analysis about the international automotive aftermarket. Written for corporate executives and key decision makers responsible for buying automotive products (parts, accessories, chemicals) and other services sold at retail to consumers and professional installers, it's the oldest continuously published business magazine covering the retail automotive aftermarket, and is the only publication dedicated to the specialized needs of this industry. Estab. 1936. Circ. 120,000. Byline given. "Corporate policy requires all freelancers to sign a print and online usage contract for stories." Pays on publication. Payment is negotiable. Sample copies available; call (888)527-7008 for rates.

TIPS "We can't stress enough the importance of knowing our audience. We are not a magazine aimed at car dealers or consumers. Our readers are auto parts distributors. Looking through sample issues will show you a lot about what we need."

⊘⊛ AUSTRALASIAN PAINT & PANEL

Yaffa Publishing, 17-21 Bellevue St., Surry Hills NSW 2010 Australia. (61)(2)9281-2333. **Fax:** (61)(2)9281-2750. **E-mail:** samstreet@yaffa.com.au. **Website:** www.paintandpanel.com.au. Bimonthly magazine for the entire smash repair industry in Australia. Read by business owners, tradespeople, equipment suppliers, training organizations, industry associations, and insurance industry. Query before submitting.

⊗⊗ AUTOINC.

Automotive Service Association, P.O. Box 929, Bedford TX 76095-0929. (800)272-7467. **Fax:** (817)685-0225. **E-mail:** editor@asashop.org. **Website:** www.autoinc.org. **10% freelance written.** Monthly magazine covering independent automotive repair. The mission of *AutoInc.*, ASA's official publication, is to be the informational authority for ASA and industry members nationwide. Its purpose is to enhance the professionalism of these members through management, technical and legislative articles, researched and written with the highest regard for accuracy, quality, and integrity. Estab. 1952. Circ. 14,000. Byline given. Pays on publication. No kill fee. Publishes ms an average of 3 months after acceptance. Editorial lead time 2 months. Accepts queries by mail, e-mail, fax. Accepts simultaneous submissions. Responds in 6 weeks to queries. Responds in 2 months to mss. Sample copy for $5 or online. Guidelines online.

NONFICTION Needs how-to, automotive repair, technical. No coverage of staff moves or financial reports. **Buys 6 mss/year.** Query with published clips. Length: 1,200 words. **Pays $300.** Sometimes pays phone expenses of writers on assignment.

PHOTOS State availability of or send photos. Captions, identification of subjects, model releases required. Reviews 2×3 transparencies, 3×5 prints, high resolution digital images. Negotiates payment individually.

TIPS "Learn about the automotive repair industry, specifically the independent shop segment. Understand the high-tech requirements needed to succeed today. We target professional repair shop owners rather than consumers."

⊗ AUTO RESTORER

BowTie, Inc., 3 Burroughs, Irvine CA 92618. (213)385-2222. **Fax:** (213)385-8565. **E-mail:** tkade@bowtieinc.com. **Website:** www.autorestorermagazine.com. **Contact:** Ted Kade, editor. **85% freelance written.** Monthly magazine covering auto restoration. "Our readers own old cars and they work on them. We help our readers by providing as much practical, how-to information as we can about restoration and old cars." Estab. 1989. Circ. 60,000. Pays on publication. Publishes mss 3 months after acceptance. Submit seasonal material 4 months in advance. Accepts queries by mail, e-mail, fax. Responds in 2 months to queries. Sample copy for $7. Guidelines free.

⌐☞ Areas most open to freelance work are technical illustrations for feature articles and renderings of classic cars for various sections.

NONFICTION Needs how-to, auto restoration, new product, photo feature, technical product evaluation. **Buys 60 mss/year.** Query first. Length: 250-2,000/words. **Pays $150/published page, including photos and illustrations.**

PHOTOS Emphasizes restoration of collector cars and trucks. Readers are 98% male, professional/technical/managerial, ages 35-65. Buys 47 photos from freelancers/issue; 564 photos/year. Send photos. Model/property release preferred. Photo captions required; include year, make and model of car; identification of people in photo. Reviews photos with accompanying ms only. Reviews contact sheets, transparencies, 5x7 prints. Looks for "technically proficient or dramatic photos of various automotive subjects, auto portraits, detail shots, action photos, good angles, composition and lighting. We're also looking for photos to illustrate how-to articles such as how to repair a damaged fender or how to repair a carburetor.". Pays $50 for b&w cover; $35 for b&w inside. Pays on publication. Credit line given.

TIPS "Interview the owner of a restored car. Present advice to others on how to do a similar restoration. Seek advice from experts. Go light on history and nonspecific details. Make it something that the magazine regularly uses. Do automotive how-tos."

⊗⊗ BUSINESS FLEET

Bobit Publishing, 3520 Challenger St., Torrance CA 90501. (310)533-2400. **E-mail:** chris.brown@bobit.com. **Website:** www.businessfleet.com. **Contact:** Chris Brown, executive editor. **10% freelance written.** Bimonthly magazine covering businesses which operate 10-50 company vehicles. Estab. 2000. Circ. 100,000. Byline given. Pays on publication. Offers 25% kill fee. Publishes ms an average of 3 months after acceptance. Editorial lead time 2 months. Submit seasonal material 2 months in advance. Accepts queries by mail, e-mail, fax. Responds in 3 weeks to queries. Responds in 2 months to mss. Sample copy and writer's guidelines free.

⬤ While it is a trade publication aimed at a business audience, *Business Fleet* has a lively, conversational style. The best way to get a feel for their "slant" is to read the magazine.

NONFICTION Needs how-to, interview, new product, personal experience, photo feature, technical. **Buys 16 mss/year.** Query with published clips. Length: 500-2,000 words. **Pays $100-400.** Sometimes pays expenses of writers on assignment.

PHOTOS State availability. Captions required. Reviews 3x5 prints. Negotiates payment individually.

TIPS "Our mission is to educate our target audience on more economical and efficient ways of operating company vehicles, and to inform the audience of the latest vehicles, products, and services available to small commercial companies. Be knowledgeable about automotive and fleet-oriented subjects."

$ $ FENDERBENDER

DeWitt Publishing, 1043 Grand Ave. #372, St. Paul MN 55105. (651)224-6207. **Fax:** (651)224-6212. **E-mail:** news@fenderbender.com; jweyer@fenderbender.com. **Website:** www.fenderbender.com. **Contact:** Jake Weyer, editor. **50% freelance written.** Monthly magazine covering automotive collision repair. Estab. 1999. Circ. 58,000. Byline given. Pays on publication. Offers 20% kill fee. Publishes ms an average of 2 months after acceptance. Editorial lead time 3 months. Submit seasonal material 6 months in advance. Accepts queries by e-mail. Accepts simultaneous submissions. Responds in 1-2 months to queries. Responds in 2-3 months to mss. Sample copy for SAE with 10x13 envelope and 6 first-class stamps. Guidelines online.

NONFICTION Needs exposè, how-to, inspirational, interview, technical. Does not want personal narratives or any other first-person stories. No poems or creative writing mss. Query with published clips. Length: 1,800-2,500 words. **Pays 25-60¢/word.** Sometimes pays expenses of writers on assignment.

PHOTOS Send photos. Captions, identification of subjects, model releases required. Reviews PDF, GIF/JPEG files. Offers no additional payment for photos accepted with ms.

COLUMNS/DEPARTMENTS Q&A, 600 words; Shakes, Rattles & Rollovers; Rearview Mirror. Query with published clips. **Pays 25-35¢/word.**

TIPS "Potential writers need to be knowledgeable about the auto collision repair industry. They should also know standard business practices and be able to explain to shop owners how they can run their businesses better."

$ $ FLEETSOLUTIONS

NAFA Fleet Management Association, 125 Village Blvd., Suite 200, Princeton NJ 08540. (609)986-1053; (609)720-0882. **Fax:** (609)720-0881; (609)452-8004. **E-mail:** publications@nafa.org; info@nafa.org. **Website:** www.nafa.org. **10% freelance written.** Magazine published 6 times/year covering automotive fleet management. Generally focuses on car, van, and light-duty truck management in US and Canadian corporations, government agencies, and utilities. Editorial emphasis is on general automotive issues; improving jobs skills, productivity, and professionalism; legislation and regulation; alternative fuels; safety; interviews with prominent industry personalities; technology; association news; public service fleet management; and light-duty truck fleet management. Estab. 1957. Circ. 4,000. Bylines provided. Pays on publication. No kill fee. Publishes ms an average of 4 months after acceptance. Editorial lead time 2 months. Accepts queries by mail. Accepts simultaneous submissions. Responds in 1 month to queries. Sample copy online. Guidelines free.

NONFICTION Needs interview, technical. **Buys 24 mss/year.** Query with published clips. Length: 500-3,000 words. **Pays $500 maximum.**

PHOTOS State availability. Reviews electronic images.

OLD CARS WEEKLY

F+W Media, Inc., 700 E. State St., Iola WI 54990-0001. (715)445-4612. **Fax:** (715)445-2214. **E-mail:** angelo.vanbogart@fwmedia.com. **Website:** www.oldcarsweekly.com. **Contact:** Angelo Van Bogart, editor. **30% freelance written.** Weekly tabloid for anyone restoring, selling, or driving an old car. Estab. 1971. Circ. 55,000. Byline given. Pays within 3 months after publication date. No kill fee. Publishes ms an average of 6 months after acceptance. Call circulation department for sample copy. Guidelines for #10 SASE.

NONFICTION Needs how-to, technical, auction prices realized lists. No "Grandpa's Car," "My First Car," or "My Car" themes from freelance contributors. **Buys 1,000 mss/year.** Send complete ms. Length: 400-1,600 words. **Payment varies.**

PHOTOS Send photos. Captions, identification of subjects required. **Pays $5/photo.** Offers no additional payment for photos accepted with ms.

TIPS "Seventy-five percent of our freelance material is done by a small group of regular contributors.

Many new writers break in here, but we are usually overstocked with material and rarely seek nostalgic or historical pieces from new authors. We are searching for news stories and in-depth historical features that fit the needs of a nostalgic, car-oriented audience. Authors with good skills can work up to longer stories. The best queries are *checklists* where we can quickly mark a *yes* or *no* to article ideas."

☺☺☺ OVERDRIVE

Randall-Reilly Publishing, 3200 Rice Mine Rd. NE, Tuscaloosa AL 35406. (205)349-2990. **Fax:** (205)750-8070. **E-mail:** mheine@rrpub.com; jcrissey@rrpub.com. **Website:** www.etrucker.com. **Contact:** Max Heine, editorial director; Jeff Crissey, editor. **5% freelance written.** Monthly magazine for independent truckers. Estab. 1961. Circ. 100,000. Byline given. Pays on publication. Offers 10% kill fee. Publishes ms an average of 2 months after acceptance. Responds in 2 months to queries. Sample copy for 9x12 SASE. Digital copy online.

NONFICTION Needs essays, exposè, how-to, truck maintenance and operation, interview, successful independent truckers, personal experience, photo feature, technical. Send complete ms. Length: 500-2,500 words. **Pays $300-1,500 for assigned articles.**

PHOTOS Photo fees negotiable.

TIPS "Talk to independent truckers. Develop a good knowledge of their concerns as small-business owners, truck drivers, and individuals. We prefer articles that quote experts, people in the industry, and truckers, to first-person expositions on a subject. Get straight facts. Look for good material on truck safety, on effects of government regulations, and on rates and business relationships between independent truckers, brokers, carriers, and shippers."

☺☺☺ TIRE NEWS

Rousseau Automotive Communication, 455, Notre-Dame East, Suite 311, Montreal QC H2Y 1C9 Canada. (514)289-0888; 1-877-989-0888. **Fax:** (514)289-5151. **E-mail:** administration@autosphere.ca. **Website:** www.autosphere.ca. **Contact:** Luc Champagne, editor-in-chief. Bimonthly magazine covering the Canadian tire industry. *Tire News* focuses on education/training, industry image, management, new tires, new techniques, marketing, HR, etc. Estab. 2004. Circ. 18,725. Byline given. Pays on publication. Publishes ms an average of 2 months after acceptance. Editorial lead time 2 months. Submit seasonal material 2

months in advance. YesAccepts simultaneous submissions. Responds in 2 weeks to queries. Responds in 2 months to mss. Sample copy free. Guidelines by e-mail.

NONFICTION Needs general interest, how-to, inspirational, interview, new product, technical. Does not want opinion pieces. **Buys 5 mss/year.** Query with published clips. Length: 550-610 words. **Pays up to $200 (Canadian).**

PHOTOS Send photos. Captions required. Reviews GIF/JPEG files. Offers no additional payment for photos accepted with ms.

FILLERS Needs facts. **Buys 2 mss/year.** Length: 550-610 words. **Pays $0-200.**

☺☺ TOWING & RECOVERY FOOTNOTES

Dominion Enterprises, 2484 Windy Pines Bend, Virginia Beach VA 23456. (757)351-8633. **Fax:** (757)233-7047. **E-mail:** david@trfootnotes.com; heidi@trfootnotes.com. **Website:** www.trfootnotes.com. **100% freelance written.** Monthly trade newspaper and marketplace for the nation's towing and recovery industry. Estab. 1991. Circ. 25,000. Byline given. Pays within 2-3 weeks of acceptance. No kill fee. Publishes ms an average of 2-3 months after acceptance. Editorial lead time 2 months. Submit seasonal material 2 months in advance. Accepts queries by mail, e-mail, phone. YesResponds in 2 weeks to queries. Responds in 1 month to mss. Sample copy free. Guidelines free.

NONFICTION Needs historical, how-to, humor, interview, new product, opinion, personal experience, photo feature, technical. **Buys 500 mss/year.** Query with published clips. Length: 800-2,000 words. **Pays $200-$600 for assigned articles.**

PHOTOS Send photos. Captions, identification of subjects required. Reviews GIF/JPEG files. Negotiates payment individually.

COLUMNS/DEPARTMENTS Columns vary from issue to issue; no regular departments available to freelancers; columns are given names appropriate to topic, and often repeat no matter who the author is. **Buys 250 mss/year.** Query with published clips.

☺☺☺ WESTERN CANADA HIGHWAY NEWS

Craig Kelman & Associates, 2020 Portage Ave., 3rd Floor, Winnipeg MB R3J 0K4 Canada. (204)985-9785. **Fax:** (204)985-9795. **E-mail:** terry@kelman.ca. **Website:** highwaynews.ca. **Contact:** Terry Ross, editor. **30% freelance written.** Quarterly magazine covering trucking. The official magazine of the Alberta, Saskatchewan, and Manitoba trucking associations. As the official magazine of the trucking associations in Alberta, Saskatchewan and Manitoba, *Western Canada Highway News* is committed to providing leading edge, timely information on business practices, technology, trends, new products/services, legal and legislative issues that affect professionals in Western Canada's trucking industry. Estab. 1995. Circ. 4,500. Byline given. Pays on publication. No kill fee. Publishes ms an average of 2 months after acceptance. Editorial lead time 3 months. Submit seasonal material 3 months in advance. Accepts simultaneous submissions. Responds in 1 month to queries and mss. Sample copy for 10x13 SAE with 1 IRC. Guidelines for #10 SASE.

NONFICTION Needs essays, general interest, how-to, run a trucking business, interview, new product, opinion, personal experience, photo feature, technical, profiles in excellence (bios of trucking or associate firms enjoying success). **Buys 8-10 mss/year.** Query. Length: 500-3,000 words. **Pays 18-25¢/word.** Sometimes pays expenses of writers on assignment.

PHOTOS State availability. Identification of subjects required. Reviews 4x6 prints.

COLUMNS/DEPARTMENTS Safety (new safety innovation/products), 500 words; Trade Talk (new products), 300 words. Query. **Pays 18-25¢/word.**

TIPS "Our publication is fairly time sensitive regarding issues affecting the trucking industry in Western Canada. Current 'hot' topics are international trucking, security, driver fatigue, health and safety, emissions control, and national/international highway systems."

AVIATION AND SPACE

💲💲 AEROSAFETY WORLD MAGAZINE

Flight Safety Foundation, 801 N. Fairfax St., Suite 400, Alexandria VA 22314-1774. (703)739-6700. **Fax:** (703)739-6708. **E-mail:** jackman@flightsafety.org. **Website:** www.flightsafety.org. **Contact:** Frank Jackman, director of publications. Monthly newsletter covering safety aspects of airport operations. Full-color monthly magazine offers in-depth analysis of important safety issues facing the industry, with emphasis on timely news coverage in a convenient format and eye-catching contemporary design. Estab.

1974. Pays on publication. Accepts queries by mail, e-mail. "Generally, the ms must be unpublished and must not be under consideration for publication elsewhere. In some circumstances, the Foundation may consider a previously published ms if it has been rewritten and adapted for Foundation readers. If your ms has been copyrighted, a copyright transfer may be required before your ms will be published by the Foundation."Catalog online. Guidelines online.

NONFICTION Needs technical. Query. **Pays $300-1,500.**

PHOTOS Pays $75 for each piece of original art.

TIPS "Few aviation topics are outside its scope."

💲💲 AIRCRAFT MAINTENANCE TECHNOLOGY

Cygnus Business Media, 1233 Janesville Ave., Fort Atkinson WI 53538. (920)563-6388. **Fax:** (920)569-4603. **E-mail:** barb.zuehlke@AviationPros.com. **Website:** www.amtonline.com. **Contact:** Barb Zuehlke, senior editor. **10% freelance written.** Magazine published 10 times/year covering aircraft maintenance. *Aircraft Maintenance Technology* provides aircraft maintenance professionals worldwide with a curriculum of technical, professional, and managerial development information that enables them to more efficiently and effectively perform their jobs. Estab. 1989. Circ. 41,500 worldwide. Byline given. Pays on publication. No kill fee. Publishes ms an average of 2 months after acceptance. Editorial lead time 3 months. Submit seasonal material 6 months in advance. Accepts queries by online submission form. Accepts simultaneous submissions. Responds in 2 weeks to queries. Responds in 1 month to mss. Sample copy free. Guidelines for #10 SASE or by e-mail.

NONFICTION Needs how-to, technical, safety. Special issues: Aviation career issue (August). No travel/pilot-oriented pieces. **Buys 10-12 mss/year.** Query with published clips. Please use the online form to contact us. 600-1,500 words, technical articles 2,000 words **Pays $200.**

PHOTOS State availability. Captions, identification of subjects, model releases required. Offers no additional payment for photos accepted with ms.

COLUMNS/DEPARTMENTS Professionalism, 1,000-1,500 words; Safety Matters, 600-1,000 words; Human Factors, 600-1,000 words. **Buys 10-12 mss/year.** Query with published clips. **Pays $200**

TIPS "This is a technical magazine approved by the FAA and Transport Canada for recurrency training for technicians. Freelancers should have a strong background in aviation, particularly maintenance, to be considered for technical articles. Columns/Departments: Freelancers still should have a strong knowledge of aviation to slant professionalism, safety, and human factors pieces to that audience."

⊙⊙ AVIATION INTERNATIONAL NEWS

The Convention News Co., 214 Franklin Ave., Midland Park NJ 07432. (201)444-5075. **Fax:** (201)444-4647. **E-mail:** nmoll@ainonline.com; editor@ainonline.com; ayannaco@ainonline.com. **Website:** www.ainonline.com. **Contact:** Nigel Moll, editor; Annmarie Yannaco, managing editor. **30-40% freelance written.** Monthly magazine, with daily onsite issues published at 3 conventions and 2 international air shows each year, and twice-weekly AINalerts via e-mail covering business and commercial aviation with news features, special reports, aircraft evaluations, and surveys on business aviation worldwide, written for business pilots and industry professionals. "While the heartbeat of *AIN* is driven by the news it carries, the human touch is not neglected. We pride ourselves on our people stories about the industry's 'movers and shakers' and others in aviation who make a difference." Estab. 1972. Circ. 40,000. Byline given. Pays on acceptance and upon receipt of writer's invoice. Offers variable kill fee. Publishes ms an average of 2 months after acceptance. Editorial lead time 2 months. Submit seasonal material 3 months in advance. Accepts queries by mail, e-mail, fax. Responds in 6 weeks to queries. Responds in 2 months to mss. Sample copy for $10. Writer's guidelines for 9x12 SAE with 3 first-class stamps.

NONFICTION Needs how-to, aviation, interview, new product, opinion, personal experience, photo feature, technical. Does not puff pieces. "Our readers expect serious, real news. We don't pull any punches. *AIN* is not a 'good news' publication; it tells the story, both good and bad." **Buys 150-200 mss/year.** Query with published clips. Do not send mss by e-mail unless requested. Length: 200-3,000 words. **Pays 40¢/word to first timers, higher rates to proven** *AIN* **freelancers.** Pays expenses of writers on assignment.

PHOTOS Send photos. Captions required. Reviews contact sheets, transparencies, prints, TIFF files (300 dpi). Negotiates payment individually.

TIPS "Our core freelancers are professional pilots with good writing skills, or good journalists and reporters with an interest in aviation (some with pilot licenses) or technical experts in the aviation industry. The ideal *AIN* writer has an intense interest in and strong knowledge of aviation, a talent for writing news stories, and journalistic cussedness. Hit me with a strong news story relating to business aviation that takes me by surprise—something from your local area or area of expertise. Make it readable, fact-filled, and in the inverted pyramid style. Double-check facts and names. Interview the right people. Send me good, clear photos and illustrations. Send me well-written, logically ordered copy. Do this for me consistently and we may take you along on our staff to 1 of the conventions in the US or an airshow in Paris, Singapore, London, or Dubai."

⊙⊙ GROUND SUPPORT WORLDWIDE MAGAZINE

Cygnus Business Media, 1233 Janesville Ave., Fort Atkinson WI 53538. (920)563-1644. **Fax:** (920)563-1699. **E-mail:** steve.smith@AviationPros.com. **Website:** www.aviationpros.com/magazine/gsm. **Contact:** Steve Smith, editor. **20% freelance written.** Magazine published 10 times/year. Readers are those aviation professionals who are involved in ground support: the equipment manufacturers, the suppliers, the ramp operators, ground handlers, and airport and airline managers. Covesr issues of interest to this community: deicing, ramp safety, equipment technology, pollution, etc. Estab. 1993. Circ. 15,000+. Pays on publication. No kill fee. Publishes ms an average of 2 months after acceptance. Editorial lead time 2 months. Accepts queries by mail, e-mail, fax. Responds in 3 weeks to queries; 3 months to mss. Sample copy for SAE with 9x11 envelope and 5 first-class stamps.

NONFICTION Needs how-to, use or maintain certain equipment, interview, new product, opinion, photo feature, technical aspects of ground support and issues, industry events, meetings, new rules and regulations. **Buys 12-20 mss/year.** Send complete ms. Length: 500-2,000 words. **Pays $100-300.**

PHOTOS Send photos. Identification of subjects required. Reviews 35mm prints, electronic preferred, slides. Offers additional payment for photos accepted with ms.

TIPS "Write about subjects that relate to ground services. Write in clear and simple terms—personal experience is always welcome. If you have an aviation background or ground support experience, let us know."

☉☉☉ PROFESSIONAL PILOT

Queensmith Communications Corp., 30 S. Quaker Lane, Suite 300, Alexandria VA 22314. (703)370-0606. **Fax:** (703)370-7082. **E-mail:** editor@propilotmag. com; jcohen@propilotmag.com; editorial@propilot-mag.com. **Website:** www.propilotmag.com. **Contact:** Murray Smith, editor/publisher; Jessica Cohen, associate editor. **75% freelance written.** Monthly magazine covering corporate, noncombat government, law enforcement, and various other types of professional aviation. The typical reader of *Professional Pilot* has a sophisticated grasp of piloting/aviation knowledge and is interested in articles that help him/her do the job better or more efficiently. Estab. 1967. Circ. 40,000. Byline given. Pays on publication. Offers kill fee. Kill fee negotiable. Publishes ms an average of 2-3 months after acceptance. Accepts queries by mail, e-mail.

NONFICTION Buys 40 mss/year. Query. Length: 750-2,500 words. **Pays $200-1,000, depending on length. A fee for the article will be established at the time of assignment.** Sometimes pays expenses of writers on assignment.

PHOTOS Prefers transparencies or high resolution 300 JPEG digital images. Send photos. Captions, identification of subjects required. Additional payment for photos negotiable.

TIPS "Query first. Freelancer should be a professional pilot or have background in aviation. Authors should indicate relevant aviation experience and pilot credentials (certificates, ratings and hours). We place a greater emphasis on corporate operations and pilot concerns."

BEAUTY AND SALON

AQUA MAGAZINE

22 E. Mifflin St., Suite 910, Madison WI 53703. (608)249-0186. **E-mail:** scott@aquamagazine.com. **Website:** www.aquamagazine.com. **Contact:** Scott Webb, executive editor; Eric Herman, senior editor; Cailley Hammel, associate editor; Scott Maurer, art director. *AQUA Magazine* is a print and online publication dedicated to the pool and spa industry. AQUA provides the industry's top decision-makers with the timely, critical information they need to be successful in their jobs. Every month thousands of spa and pool professionals turn to the online and print pages of *AQUA* for its valuable mix of editorial. Estab. 1976. Circ. 15,000.

COLUMNS/DEPARTMENTS Columns include: product features, industry issue stories, business columns, reader profiles, industry news.

TIPS Wants to see "visually arresting, architectural images, high quality, multiple angles, day/night lighting situations. Photos including people are rarely published."

☉☉ BEAUTY STORE BUSINESS

Creative Age Communications, 7628 Densmore Ave., Van Nuys CA 91406. (818)782-7328, ext. 353; (800)442-5667. **Fax:** (818)782-7450. **E-mail:** mbat-ist@creativeage.com; mbirenbaum@creativeage.com; skelly@creativeage.com. **Website:** www.beautystore-business.com. Shelley Moench-Kelly, managing editor. **Contact:** Manyesha Batist, editor/online editor. **50% freelance written.** Monthly magazine covering beauty store business management, news, and beauty products. The primary readers of the publication are owners, managers, and buyers at open-to-the-public beauty stores, including general-market and multicultural market-oriented ones with or without salon services. Secondary readers are those at beauty stores only open to salon industry professionals. Also goes to beauty distributors. Estab. 1994. Circ. 15,000. Byline given. Pays on acceptance. Offers kill fee. Offers negotiable kill fee. Publishes ms an average of 3 months after acceptance. Editorial lead time 3 months. Submit seasonal material 4 months in advance. Accepts queries by mail, e-mail, fax. Responds in 1 week to queries. Responds in 2 weeks, if interested. Sample copy free.

NONFICTION Needs how-to, business management, merchandising, e-commerce, retailing, interview, industry leaders/beauty store owners. **Buys 20-30 mss/year.** Query. Length: 1,800-2,200 words. **Pays $250-525 for assigned articles.** Sometimes pays expenses of writers on assignment.

PHOTOS Do not send computer art electronically. State availability. Captions, identification of subjects required. Reviews transparencies, computer art (artists work on Macs, request 300 dpi, on CD or Zip disk, saved as JPEG, TIFF, or EPS). Negotiates payment individually.

☉☉☉ COSMETICS

Rogers Publishing Limited, One Mount Pleasant Rd., 8th Floor, Toronto ON M4Y 2Y5 Canada. (416)764-

1680. **Fax:** (416)764-1704. **E-mail:** kristen.vinakmens@ cosmetics.rogers.com. **Website:** www.cosmeticsmag. com. **Contact:** Kristen Vinakmens, editor-in-chief. **10% freelance written.** Bimonthly magazine covering cosmetics for industry professionals. Estab. 1972. Circ. 13,000. Byline given. Pays on acceptance. Offers 50% kill fee. Publishes ms an average of 3 months after acceptance. Editorial lead time 4 months. Submit seasonal material 4 months in advance. Accepts queries by mail. Responds in 1 month to queries. Sample copy for $6 (Canadian) and 8% GST.

○ Main reader segment is the retail trade—department stores, drugstores, salons, estheticians— owners and cosmeticians/beauty advisors; plus manufacturers, distributors, agents, and suppliers to the industry.

NONFICTION Needs general interest, interview, photo feature. **Buys 1 mss/year.** Query. Length: 250-1,200 words. **Pays 25¢/word.** Sometimes pays expenses of writers on assignment.

PHOTOS Send photos. Captions, identification of subjects, model releases required. Reviews 2 1/2 up to 8x10 transparencies, 4x6 up to 8x10 prints, 35mm slides; e-mail pictures in 300 dpi JPEG format. Offers no additional payment for photos accepted with ms.

COLUMNS/DEPARTMENTS "All articles assigned on a regular basis from correspondents and columnists that we know personally from the industry."

TIPS "Must have broad knowledge of the Canadian cosmetics, fragrance, and toiletries industry and retail business. 99.9% of freelance articles are assigned by the editor to writers involved with the Canadian cosmetics business."

⊙⊙ DAYSPA

Creative Age Publications, 7628 Densmore Ave., Van Nuys CA 91406. (818)782-7328, ext. 301. **Fax:** (818)782-7450. **Website:** www.dayspamagazine.com. **Contact:** Linda Kossoff, executive editor. **50% freelance written.** Monthly magazine covering the business of day spas, multi-service/skincare salons, and resort/hotel spas. *Dayspa* includes only well-targeted business and trend articles directed at the owners and managers. It serves to enrich, enlighten, and empower spa/salon professionals. Estab. 1996. Circ. 31,000. Byline given. Pays on acceptance. No kill fee. Publishes ms an average of 4 months after acceptance. Editorial lead time 4 months. Submit seasonal material 4 months in advance. Accepts queries by mail, e-mail, fax, phone, on-

line submission form. Responds in 2 months to queries. Sample copy for $5.

NONFICTION Buys 40 mss/year. Query. Length: 1,500-1,800 words. **Pays $150-500.**

PHOTOS Send photos. Identification of subjects, model releases required. Negotiates payment individually.

COLUMNS/DEPARTMENTS Legal Pad (legal issues affecting salons/spas); Money Matters (financial issues); Management Workshop (spa management issues); Health Wise (wellness trends), all 1,200-1,500 words. **Buys 20 mss/year.** Query. **Pays $150-400.**

DERMASCOPE MAGAZINE

Aesthetics International Association, 310 E. Interstate 30, Suite B107, Garland TX 75043. (469)429-9300. **Fax:** (469)429-9301. **E-mail:** press@dermascope.com. **Website:** www.dermascope.com. **Contact:** Amanda Strunk-Miller, managing editor. Monthly magazine covering aesthetics (skin care) and body and spa therapy. Magazine is a source of practical advice and continuing education for skin care, body, and spa therapy professionals. Main readers are salon, day spa, and destination spa owners, managers, or technicians and aesthetics students. Estab. 1978. Circ. 16,000. No byline given. No kill fee. Publishes ms an average of 6 months after acceptance. Editorial lead time 3 months. Submit seasonal material 6 months in advance. Accepts queries by mail, e-mail, fax. Responds in 4-6 months. Sample copy available by phone. Guidelines online.

○ A copyright waiver must be signed guaranteeing article has not been submitted elsewhere. Does not pay for articles.

NONFICTION Needs book excerpts, general interest, historical, how-to, inspirational, personal experience, photo feature, technical. Query with published clips. Include biography, along with contact info for readers; a professional headshot; a 1-2 sentence quote/tease about the article; and 3-5 review questions. How-tos, skin therapy, body therapy, diet, nutrition, spa, equipment, medical procedures, makeup, and business articles should be approximately 1,500-2,000 words. Feature stories should be 1,800-2,500 words. Sidebars are a plus. Stories exceeding 2,500 may be printed in part and run in concurrent issues.

REPRINTS Does not accept reprints.

MASSAGE & BODYWORK

Associated Bodywork & Massage Professionals, 25188 Genesee Trail Rd., Suite 200, Golden CO 80401 (303)674-8478 or (800)458-2267. **Fax:** (303)674-0859.

E-mail: editor@abmp.com. **Website:** www.massage-andbodywork.com. **85% freelance written.** Bimonthly magazine covering therapeutic massage/bodywork. A trade publication for the massage therapist, and bodyworker. An all-inclusive publication encompassing everything from traditional Swedish massage to energy work to other complementary therapies (i.e., homeopathy, herbs, aromatherapy, etc.). Pays on acceptance. No kill fee. Publishes ms an average of 6 months after acceptance. Editorial lead time 6 months. Submit seasonal material 6 months in advance. Accepts queries by e-mail. Responds in 60 days to queries. Guidelines online.

NONFICTION Needs how-to, technique/modality, interview, opinion, personal experience, technical. No fiction. **Buys 60-75 mss/year.** Query with published clips. Length: 1,000-3,000 words.

PHOTOS Not interested in photo submissions separate from feature queries. State availability. Captions, identification of subjects, model releases required. Reviews digital images (300 dpi). Negotiates payment individually.

COLUMNS/DEPARTMENTS Buys 20 mss/year.

TIPS "Know your topic. Offer suggestions for art to accompany your submission. *Massage & Bodywork* looks for interesting, tightly focused stories concerning a particular modality or technique of massage, bodywork, and somatic therapies. The editorial staff welcomes the opportunity to review mss which may be relevant to the field of massage and bodywork in addition to more general pieces pertaining to complementary and alternative medicine. This would include the widely varying modalities of massage and bodywork (from Swedish massage to Polarity therapy), specific technical or ancillary therapies, including such topics as biomagnetics, aromatherapy, and facial rejuvenation. Reference lists relating to technical articles should include the author, title, publisher, and publication date of works cited according to Chicago Manual of Style. Word count: 1,500-3,000 words; longer articles negotiable."

🔾🔾 MASSAGE MAGAZINE

5150 Palm Valley Rd., Suite 103, Ponte Vedra Beach FL 32082. (904)285-6020. **Fax:** (904)285-9944. **E-mail:** kmenehan@massagemag.com. **Website:** www.massagemag.com. **60% freelance written.** Magazine about massage and other touch therapies published 10-12 times/year. Readers are professional therapists

who have been in practice for several years. About 80% are self-employed; 95% live in the United States. The vast majority of readers have completed formal training in massage therapy. The techniques they practice include Swedish, sports and geriatric massage, energy work and myotherapy, among many others. Readers work in settings ranging from home-based studios to spas to integrated clinics. Estab. 1985. Circ. 50,000. Byline given. Pays on publication. Publishes ms an average of 2 months-24 months after acceptance. Accepts queries by e-mail. Responds in 2 months to queries. Responds in 3 months to mss. Sample copy for $6.95. Guidelines online.

NONFICTION Needs book excerpts, essays, general interest, how-to, interview, personal experience, photo feature, technical, experiential. No multiple submissions. Length: 1,500-3,000 words. **Pays $50-400.**

REPRINTS Send tearsheet of article and electronic ms with rights for sale noted and information about when and where the material previously appeared. Pays 50-75% of amount paid for an original article

PHOTOS Send photos with submission via e-mail. Identification of subjects, True required. Offers $15-40/photo; $40-100/illustration.

COLUMNS/DEPARTMENTS Profiles; News and Current Events; Practice Building (business); Technique; Mind/Body/Spirit. Length: anywhere from 200-2,500 words. See website for details. **Pays $75-300 for assigned articles.**

FILLERS Needs facts, newsbreaks. Length: 100-800 words. **Pays $125 maximum.**

TIPS "Our readers seek practical information on how to help their clients, improve their techniques, and/or make their businesses more successful, as well as feature articles that place massage therapy in a positive or inspiring light. Since most of our readers are professional therapists, we do not publish articles on topics like 'How Massage Can Help You Relax.' Please study a few back issues so you know what types of topics and tone we're looking for."

🔾🔾 NAILPRO

Creative Age Publications, 7628 Densmore Ave., Van Nuys CA 91406. (800) 442-5667; (818)782-7328. **Fax:** (818)782-7450. **E-mail:** nailpro@creativeage.com. **Website:** www.nailpro.com. **Contact:** Stephanie Yaggy, executive editor. **75% freelance written.** Monthly magazine written for manicurists and nail technicians working in a full-service salon or nails-only salons. Estab. 1989. Circ. 65,000. Byline given. Pays on acceptance. No kill fee. Publishes ms an average of 6 months after acceptance. Editorial lead time 3 months. Submit seasonal material 3 months in advance. Accepts queries by mail, e-mail, fax. Accepts simultaneous submissions. Responds in 6 weeks to queries. Sample copy for $2 and 9x12 SASE.

○ "*Nailpro* covers technical and business aspects of working in a salon and operating nailcare services, as well as the nailcare industry in general."

NONFICTION Needs book excerpts, how-to, humor, inspirational, interview, personal experience, photo feature, technical. No general interest articles or business articles not geared to the nail-care industry. **Buys 50 mss/year.** Query. Length: 1,000-3,000 words. **Pays $150-450.**

REPRINTS Send typed ms with rights for sale noted and information about when and where the material previously appeared. Pays 25-50% of amount paid for an original article.

PHOTOS Send photos. Identification of subjects, model releases required. Reviews transparencies, prints. Negotiates payment individually. Pays on acceptance.

COLUMNS/DEPARTMENTS All Business (articles on building salon business, marketing and advertising, dealing with employees), 1,500-2,000 words; Attitudes (aspects of operating a nail salon and trends in the nail industry), 1,200-2,000 words. **Buys 50 mss/year.** Query. **Pays $250-350.**

⊘⊖⊖ NAILS

Bobit Business Media, 3520 Challenger St., Torrance CA 90503. (310)533-2457. **Fax:** (310)533-2507. **E-mail:** judy.lessin@bobit.com. **Website:** www.nailsmag.com. **Contact:** Judy Lessin, features editor. **10% freelance written**. Monthly magazine. *NAILS* seeks to educate its readers on new techniques and products, nail anatomy and health, customer relations, working safely with chemicals, salon sanitation, and the business aspects of running a salon. Estab. 1983. Circ. 55,000. Byline given. Pays on acceptance. No kill fee. Submit seasonal material 4 months in advance. Accepts queries by mail, e-mail. Responds in 1 month to queries. Visit website to view past issues.

NONFICTION Needs historical, how-to, inspirational, interview, personal experience, photo feature, technical. No articles on 1 particular product, company profiles, or articles slanted toward a particular company or manufacturer. **Buys 20 mss/year.** Query with published clips. Length: 1,200-2,000 words. **Pays $200-400.** Sometimes pays expenses of writers on assignment.

PHOTOS State availability. Captions, identification of subjects, model releases required. Reviews contact sheets, transparencies, prints (any standard size acceptable). Offers $50-200/photo.

TIPS "Send clips and query; *do not send unsolicited mss.* We would like to see ideas for articles on a unique salon or a business article that focuses on a specific aspect or problem encountered when working in a salon. The Salon Profile section, which profiles nail salons and full-service salons, is most open to freelancers. Focus on an innovative business idea or unique point of view. Articles from experts on specific business issues—insurance, handling difficult employees, cultivating clients—are encouraged."

⊖⊖ PULSE MAGAZINE

HOST Communications Inc., 2365 Harrodsburg Rd., Suite A325, Lexington KY 40504. (859)226-4326. **Fax:** (859)226-4445. **E-mail:** mae.manacap-johnson@ ispastaff.com. **Website:** www.experienceispa.com/ media/pulse-magazine. **Contact:** Mae Manacap-Johnson, editor. **20% freelance written.** Magazine published 10 times/year covering spa industry. *Pulse* is the magazine for the spa professional. As the official publication of the International SPA Association, its purpose is to advance the business of the spa professionals by informing them of the latest trends and practices and promoting the wellness aspects of spa. *Pulse* connects people, nurtures their personal and professional growth, and enhances their ability to network and succeed in the spa industry. Estab. 1991. Circ. 5,300. Byline given. Pays on publication. Publishes ms an average of 1 month after acceptance. Editorial lead time 3 months. Submit seasonal material 4 months in advance. Accepts queries by e-mail. Sample copy for #10 SASE. Guidelines by e-mail.

NONFICTION Needs general interest, how-to, interview, new product. Does not want articles focused on spas that are not members of ISPA, consumer-focused articles (market is the spa industry professional), or features on hot tubs ("not *that* spa industry"). **Buys 8-10 mss/year.** Query with published clips. Length: 800-2,000 words. **Pays $250-500.** Sometimes pays expenses of writers on assignment.

PHOTOS Send photos. Captions required. Reviews GIF/JPEG files. Negotiates payment individually.

TIPS "Understand the nuances of association publishing (different than consumer and B2B). Send published clips, not Word documents. Experience in writing for health and wellness market is helpful. Only feature ISPA member companies in the magazine; visit our website to learn more about our industry and to see if your pitch includes member companies before making contact."

⊛⊛ SKIN DEEP

Associated Skin Care Professionals, 25188 Genesee Trail Rd., Suite 200, Golden CO 80401. (800)789-0411. **E-mail:** editor@ascpskincare.com; getconnected@ascpskincare.com. **Website:** www.ascpskincare.com. **Contact:** Carrie Patrick, editor. **80% freelance written.** Bimonthly magazine covering technical, educational, and business information for estheticians with an emphasis on solo practitioners and spa/salon employees or independent contractors. Audience is the U.S. individual skin care practitioner who may work on her own and/or in a spa or salon setting. Magazine keeps her up to date on skin care trends and techniques and ways to earn more income doing waxing, facials, peels, microdermabrasion, body wraps and other skin treatments. Product-neutral stories may include novel spa treatments within the esthetician scope of practice. Does not cover mass-market retail products, hair care, nail care, makeup, physician only treatments/products, cosmetic surgery, or invasive treatments like colonics or ear candling. Successful stories have included how-tos on paraffin facials, aromatherapy body wraps, waxing tips, how to read ingredient labels, how to improve word-of-mouth advertising, and how to choose an online scheduling software package. Estab. 2003. Circ. 12,000+. Byline given. Pays on acceptance. No kill fee. Publishes ms an average of 4-6 months after acceptance. Editorial lead time 4-5 months. Submit seasonal material 7 months in advance. Accepts queries by e-mail. Responds in 2 weeks to queries.

NONFICTION "We don't run general consumer beauty material or products that are very rarely run a new product that is available through retail outlets. 'New' products means introduced in the last 12 months. We do not run industry personnel announcements or stories on individual spas/salons or getaways. We don't cover hair or nails." **Buys 12 mss/year.** Query. Length: 1,200-1,600 words. **Pays $75-300 for assigned articles.**

TIPS "Visit website to read previous issues and learn about what we do. Submit a brief query with an idea to determine if you are on the right track. State specifically what value this has to estheticians and their work/income. Please note that we do not publish fashion, cosmetics, hair, or consumer-focused articles."

⊛⊛ SKIN INC. MAGAZINE

Allured Business Media, 336 Gundersen Dr., Suite A, Carol Stream IL 60188. (630)653-2155. **Fax:** (630)653-2192. **E-mail:** cchristensen@allured.com. **Website:** www.skininc.com. **Contact:** Cathy Christensen, senior editor. **30% freelance written.** Magazine published 12 times/year as an educational resource for skin care professionals interested in business solutions, treatment techniques, and skin science. Estab. 1988. Circ. 30,000. Byline given. Pays on publication. No kill fee. Publishes ms an average of 6 months after acceptance. Editorial lead time 6 months. Submit seasonal material 1 year in advance. Accepts queries by mail, e-mail, fax, phone. Responds in 3 weeks to queries. Responds in 1 month to mss. Sample copy and writer's guidelines free.

NONFICTION Needs general interest, how-to, interview, personal experience, technical. **Buys 6 mss/year.** Query with published clips. Length: 2,000 words. **Pays $100-300 for assigned articles. Pays $50-200 for unsolicited articles.**

PHOTOS State availability. Captions, identification of subjects, model releases required. Reviews 3x5 prints. Offers no additional payment for photos accepted with ms.

COLUMNS/DEPARTMENTS Finance (tips and solutions for managing money), 2,000-2,500 words; Personnel (managing personnel), 2,000-2,500 words; Marketing (marketing tips for salon owners), 2,000-2,500 words; Retail (retailing products and services in the salon environment), 2,000-2,500 words. Query with published clips. **Pays $50-200.**

FILLERS Needs facts, newsbreaks. **Buys 6 mss/year.** Length: 250-500 words. **Pays $50-100.**

TIPS "Have an understanding of the professional spa industry."

BEVERAGES AND BOTTLING

AMERICAN BAR ASSOCIATION JOURNAL

321 N. Clark St., 20th Floor, Chicago IL 60654. (312)988-5822. **E-mail:** debora.clark@americanbar.org. **Website:** www.abajournal.com. **Contact:** Debora Clark, deputy design director. Monthly membership

magazine of the American Bar Association. Emphasizes law and the legal profession. Readers are lawyers. Estab. 1915. Circ. 330,000.

⚪❸❺ BAR & BEVERAGE BUSINESS MAGAZINE

Mercury Publications, 1740 Wellington Ave., Winnipeg MB R3H 0E8 Canada. (204)954-2085. **Fax:** (204)954-2057. **E-mail:** edufault@mercurypublications.ca; editorial@mercurypublications.ca. **Website:** www.barandbeverage.com. **Contact:** Elaine Dufault, associate publisher and national account manager. **33% freelance written.** Bimonthly magazine providing information on the latest trends, happenings, buying-selling of beverages and product merchandising. Estab. 1998. Circ. 16,077. Byline given. Pays 30-45 days from receipt of invoice. Offers 33% kill fee. Submit seasonal material 3 months in advance. Accepts simultaneous submissions. Sample copy and writer's guidelines free or by e-mail.

🅞 Does not accept queries for specific stories. Assigns stories to Canadian writers.

NONFICTION Needs how-to, making a good drink, training staff, etc., interview. Industry reports, profiles on companies. Query with published clips. Length: 500-9,000 words. **Pays 25-35¢/word.** Sometimes pays expenses of writers on assignment.

PHOTOS State availability. Captions required. Reviews negatives, transparencies, 3-5 prints, JPEG, EPS or TIFF files. Negotiates payment individually.

COLUMNS/DEPARTMENTS Out There (bar and beverage news in various parts of the country), 100-500 words. Query. **Pays $0-100.**

❸❺ MICHIGAN HOSPITALITY REVIEW

Michigan Licensed Beverage Association, 920 N. Fairview, Lansing MI 48912. (800)292-2896. **Fax:** (517)374-1165. **E-mail:** editor@mlba.org; info@mlba.org. **Website:** www.mlba.org. **Contact:** Nicole Jones, editor. **40-50% freelance written.** Monthly trade magazine devoted to the beer, wine, and spirits industry in Michigan. It is dedicated to serving those who make their living serving the public and the state through the orderly and responsible sale of beverages. Estab. 1983. Circ. 4,200. Pays on publication. No kill fee. Editorial lead time 3 months. Submit seasonal material 3 months in advance. Accepts queries by mail, e-mail. Responds in 2 weeks to queries. Responds in 1 month to mss. Sample copy for $5 or online.

NONFICTION Needs essays, general interest, historical, how-to, make a drink, human resources, tips, etc, humor, interview, new product, opinion, personal experience, photo feature, technical. **Buys 24 mss/year.** Send complete ms. Length: 1,000 words. **Pays $20-200.**

COLUMNS/DEPARTMENTS Open to essay content ideas. Interviews (legislators, others), 750-1,000 words; personal experience (waitstaff, customer, bartenders), 500 words. **Buys 12 mss/year.** Send complete ms. **Pays $25-100.**

TIPS "We are particularly interested in nonfiction concerning responsible consumption/serving of alcohol. We are looking for product reviews, company profiles, personal experiences, and news articles that would benefit our audience. Our audience is a busy group of business owners and hospitality professionals striving to obtain pertinent information that is not too wordy."

❸❺❺ VINEYARD & WINERY MANAGEMENT

P.O. Box 14459, Santa Rosa CA 95402-6459. (707)577-7700. **Fax:** (707)577-7705. **E-mail:** tcaputo@vwm-media.com. **Website:** www.vwmmedia.com. **Contact:** Tina Caputo, editor-in-chief. **80% freelance written.** Bimonthly magazine of professional importance to grape growers, winemakers, and winery sales and business people. Headquartered in Sonoma County, California, *Vineyard & Winery Management* proudly remains a leading independent wine trade magazine serving all of North America. Estab. 1975. Circ. 6,500. Byline given. Pays on publication. 20% kill fee. Accepts queries by e-mail. Responds in 3 weeks to queries. Responds in 1 month to mss. Sample copy free. Guidelines for by e-mail.

🅞 Focuses on the management of people and process in the areas of viticulture, enology, winery marketing and finance. Articles are written with a high degree of technical expertise by a team of wine industry professionals and top-notch journalists. Timely articles and columns keep subscribers poised for excellence and success.

NONFICTION Needs how-to, interview, new product, technical. **Buys 30 mss/year.** Query. Length: 1,500-2,000 words. **Pays approximately $500/feature.** Sometimes pays expenses of writers on assignment.

PHOTOS State availability. Captions, identification of subjects required. Digital photos preferred, JPEG or TIFF files 300 pixels/inch resolution at print size. Pays $20/each photo published.

TIPS "We're looking for long-term relationships with authors who know the business and write well. Electronic submissions required; query for formats."

💲💲 WINES & VINES

Wine Communications Group, 65 Mitchell Blvd., Suite A, San Rafael CA 94903. (415)453-9700; (866)453-9701. **Fax:** (415)453-2517. **E-mail:** edit@winesandvines. com; info@winesandvines.com. **Website:** www. winesandvines.com. **Contact:** Jim Gordon, editor; Kate Lavin, managing editor. **50% freelance written.** Monthly magazine covering the North American winegrape and winemaking industry. "Since 1919, *Wines & Vines Magazine* has been the authoritative voice of the wine and grape industry—from prohibition to phylloxera, we have covered it all. Our paid circulation reaches all 50 states and many foreign countries. Because we are intended for the trade—including growers, winemakers, winery owners, wholesalers, restauranteurs, and serious amateurs—we accept more technical, informative articles. We do not accept wine reviews, wine country tours, or anything of a wine consumer nature." Estab. 1919. Circ. 5,000. Byline given. Pays 30 days after acceptance. No kill fee. Publishes ms an average of 3 months after acceptance. Editorial lead time 2 months. Submit seasonal material 4 months in advance. Accepts queries by e-mail. Responds in 2-3 weeks to queries. Sample copy for $5. Guidelines free.

NONFICTION Needs interview, new product, technical. "No wine reviews, wine country travelogues, 'lifestyle' pieces, or anything aimed at wine consumers. Our readers are professionals in the field." **Buys 60 mss/year.** Query with published clips. Length: 1,000-2,000 words. **Pays flat fee of $500 for assigned articles.**

PHOTOS Prefers JPEG files (JPEG, 300 dpi minimum). Can use high-quality prints. State availability of or send photos. Captions, identification of subjects required. Does not pay for photos submitted by author, but will give photo credit.

BOOK AND BOOKSTORE

💲 THE BLOOMSBURY REVIEW

1553 Platte St., Suite 206, Denver CO 80202. (303)455-3123. **Fax:** (303)455-7039. **E-mail:** info@bloomsburyreview.com. **E-mail:** editors@bloomsburyreview.

com. **Website:** www.bloomsburyreview.com. **Contact:** Marilyn Auer, editor-in-chief/publisher. **75% freelance written.** Quarterly tabloid covering books and book-related matters. Publishes book reviews, interviews with writers and poets, literary essays, and original poetry. Audience consists of educated, literate, nonspecialized readers. Estab. 1980. Circ. 35,000. Byline given. Pays on publication. No kill fee. Publishes ms an average of 4-6 months after acceptance. Accepts queries by mail. Responds in 4 months to queries. Sample copy for $5 and 9x12 SASE. Guidelines for #10 SASE or online.

NONFICTION Needs essays, interview, book reviews. **Buys 60 mss/year.** Send complete ms. Length: 100-1,000 words. **Pays $10-20. Sometimes pays writers with contributor copies or other premiums if writer agrees.**

PHOTOS State availability of photos. Reviews prints. Offers no additional payment for photos accepted with ms.

COLUMNS/DEPARTMENTS Book reviews and essays, 500-1,500 words. **Buys 6 mss/year.** Query with published clips or send complete ms. **Pays $10-20.**

POETRY Contact: Ray Gonzalez, poetry editor. Needs Needs avant-garde, free verse, haiku, traditional. Buys 20 poems/year. Submit maximum 5 poems. **Pays $5-10.**

TIPS "We appreciate receiving published clips and/or completed mss. Please, no rough drafts. Book reviews should be of new books (within 6 months of publication)."

💲💲 FOREWORD REVIEWS

425 Boardman Ave., Suite B, Traverse City MI 49684. (231)933-3699. **Fax:** (231)933-3899. **E-mail:** howard@forewordreviews.com; victoria@forewordreviews. com. **Website:** www.forewordreviews.com. **Contact:** Howard Lovy, book review editor; Victoria Sutherland, publisher. **95% freelance written.** Bimonthly magazine covering reviews of good books independently published. In each issue of the magazine, there are 3 to 4 feature *ForeSight* articles focusing on trends in popular categories. These are in addition to the 75 or more critical reviews of forthcoming titles from independent presses in the *Review* section. Look online for review submission guidelines or view editorial calendar. Estab. 1998. Circ. 16,000 (about 80% librarians, 10% bookstores, 10% publishing professionals). Byline given. Pays 2 months after publication. No kill

fee. Publishes ms an average of 2-3 months after acceptance. Editorial lead time 3-4 months. Submit seasonal material 5 months in advance. Accepts queries by mail, e-mail. Responds in 1 month to queries. Responds in 1 month to mss. Sample copy for $10 and 8 ½ x11 SASE with $1.50 postage.

NONFICTION Query with published clips. All review submissions should be sent to the book review editor. Submissions should include a fact sheet or press release. Length: 400-1,500 words. **Pays $25-200 for assigned articles.**

TIPS "Be knowledgeable about the needs of booksellers and librarians—remember we are an industry trade journal, not a how-to or consumer publication. We review books prior to publication, so book reviews are always assigned—but send us a note telling subjects you wish to review, as well as a résumé."

THE HORN BOOK MAGAZINE

The Horn Book, Inc., 56 Roland St., Suite 200, Boston MA 02129. (617)628-0225. **Fax:** (617)628-0882. **Website:** www.hbook.com. **Contact:** Cynthia Ritter, assistant editor. **75% freelance written. Prefers to work with published/established writers.** Bimonthly magazine covering children's literature for librarians, booksellers, professors, teachers and students of children's literature. Estab. 1924. Circ. 8,000. Byline given. Pays on publication. No kill fee. Publishes ms an average of 4 months after acceptance. Submit seasonal material 6 months in advance. Accepts queries by mail, e-mail, fax. Accepts simultaneous submissions. Responds in 3 months to queries. Sample copy and writer's guidelines online.

NONFICTION Needs , interviews with children's book authors and illustrators, topics of interest to the children's book world. **Buys 20 mss/year.** Query or send complete ms. Preferred length: 1,000-2,000 words. **Pays honorarium upon publication.**

TIPS "Writers have a better chance of breaking into our publication with a query letter on a specific article they want to write."

VIDEO LIBRARIAN

3435 NE Nine Boulder Dr., Poulsbo WA 98370. (360)626-1259. **Fax:** (360)626-1260. **E-mail:** vidlib@videolibrarian.com. **Website:** www.videolibrarian.com. **75% freelance written.** Bimonthly magazine covering DVD reviews for librarians. "*Video Librarian* reviews approximately 225 titles in each issue: children's, documentaries, how-to's, movies, TV,

music and anime." Estab. 1986. Circ. 2,000. Byline given. Pays on publication. Publishes ms an average of 2 months after acceptance. Editorial lead time 2 months. Accepts queries by e-mail. YesAccepts simultaneous submissions. Responds in 1 week to queries. Sample copy for $11.

NONFICTION **Buys 500+ mss/year.** Query with published clips. Length: 200-300 words. **Pays $10-20/review.**

TIPS "We are looking for DVD reviewers with a wide range of interests, good critical eye, and strong writing skills."

BRICK, GLASS AND CERAMICS

STAINED GLASS

Stained Glass Association of America, 9313 East 63rd St., Raytown MO 64133. (800)438-9581. **Fax:** (816)737-2801. **E-mail:** stainedglassquarterly@gmail.com. **Website:** www.stainedglassquarterly.com. **Contact:** Richard Gross, editor and media director. **70% freelance written.** Quarterly magazine. *Stained Glass* is the official voice of the Stained Glass Association of America. As the oldest, most respected stained glass publication in North America, *Stained Glass* preserves the techniques of the past as well as illustrates the trends of the future. This vital information, of significant value to the professional stained glass studio, is also of interest to those for whom stained glass is an avocation or hobby. Estab. 1906. Circ. 8,000. Byline given. Pays on publication. No kill fee. Publishes ms an average of 1 year after acceptance. Editorial lead time 6 months. Submit seasonal material 8 months in advance. Accepts queries by mail, e-mail, fax. Responds in 3 months to queries. Sample copy free. Guidelines online.

NONFICTION Needs how-to, humor, interview, new product, opinion, photo feature, technical. **Buys 9 mss/year.** Query or send complete ms, but must include photos or slides—very heavy on photos. Length: 2,500-3,500 words. **Pays $125/illustrated article; $75/nonillustrated.**

REPRINTS Accepts previously published submissions from stained glass publications only. Send tearsheet of article. Payment negotiable.

PHOTOS Send photos. Identification of subjects required. Reviews 4x5 transparencies, send slides with submission. Pays $75 for non-illustrated. Pays $125, plus 3 copies for line art or photography.

COLUMNS/DEPARTMENTS Columns must be illustrated. Teknixs (technical, how-to, stained and glass art), word length varies by subject. **Buys 4 mss/year.** Query or send complete ms, but must be illustrated.

TIPS "We need more technical articles. Writers should be extremely well versed in the glass arts. Photographs are extremely important and must be of very high quality. Submissions without photographs or illustrations are seldom considered unless something special and writer states that photos are available. However, prefer to see with submission."

US GLASS, METAL & GLAZING

Key Communications, Inc., P.O. Box 569, Garrisonville VA 22463. (540)720-5584, ext.114. **Fax:** (540)720-5687. **E-mail:** info@glass.com; erogers@glass.com. **Website:** www.usglassmag.com. **Contact:** Ellen Rogers, editor. **25% freelance written.** Monthly magazine for companies involved in the flat glass trades. Estab. 1966. Circ. 27,000. Byline given. Pays on publication. No kill fee. Publishes ms an average of 3 months after acceptance. Editorial lead time 3 months. Submit seasonal material 2 months in advance. Accepts queries by mail, e-mail. Accepts simultaneous submissions. Responds in 1 month to queries. Responds in 2 months to mss. Sample copy online.

NONFICTION **Buys 12 mss/year.** Query with published clips. **Pays $300-600 for assigned articles.** Sometimes pays expenses of writers on assignment.

PHOTOS State availability. Captions, identification of subjects required. Reviews contact sheets. Offers no additional payment for photos accepted with ms.

BUILDING INTERIORS

FABRICS + FURNISHINGS INTERNATIONAL

SIPCO Publications + Events, 3 Island Ave., Suite 6i, Miami Beach FL 33139. **E-mail:** eric@sipco.net. **Website:** www.fandfi.com. **Contact:** Eric Schneider, editor/publisher. **10% freelance written.** Bimonthly magazine covering commercial, hospitality interior design, and manufacturing. *F+FI* covers news from vendors who supply the hospitality interiors industry. Estab. 1990. Circ. 11,000+. Byline given. Pays on publication. Offers $100 kill fee. Editorial lead time 3 months. Submit seasonal material 3 months in advance. Accepts queries by e-mail. Accepts simultaneous submissions. Sample copy online.

NONFICTION Needs interview, technical. Does not want opinion or consumer pieces. Readers must learn something from our stories. Query with published clips. Length: 500-1,000 words. **Pays $250-350.**

PHOTOS Send photos. Captions, identification of subjects required. Reviews GIF/JPEG files. Offers no additional payment for photos accepted with ms.

TIPS "Give us a lead on a new project that we haven't heard about. Have pictures of space and ability to interview designer on how they made it work."

KITCHEN & BATH DESIGN NEWS

Cygnus Business Media, 3 Huntington Quadrangle, Suite 301N, Melville NY 11747. **Fax:** (631)845-7218. **E-mail:** janice.costa@cygnuspub.com. **Website:** www.forresidentialpros.com. **15% freelance written.** Monthly tabloid for kitchen and bath dealers and design professionals, offering design, business and marketing advice to help our readers be more successful. It is not a consumer publication about design, a book for do-it-yourselfers, or a magazine created to showcase pretty pictures of kitchens and baths. Rather, the magazine covers the professional kitchen and bath design industry in depth, looking at the specific challenges facing these professionals, and how they address these challenges. Estab. 1983. Circ. 51,000. Byline given. Pays on publication. Publishes ms an average of 2-3 months after acceptance. Editorial lead time 2 months. Accepts queries by mail, e-mail, fax. Responds in 2-4 weeks to queries. Sample copy online. Guidelines by e-mail.

NONFICTION Needs how-to, interview. Does not want consumer stories, generic business stories, or "I remodeled my kitchen and it's so beautiful" stories. This is a magazine for trade professionals, so stories need to be both slanted for these professionals, as well as sophisticated enough so that people who have been working in the field 30 years can still learn something from them. **Buys 16 mss/year.** Query with published clips. Length: 1,100-3,000 words. **Pays $200-650.** Sometimes pays expenses of writers on assignment.

PHOTOS Send photos. Identification of subjects required. Offers no additional payment for photos accepted with ms.

TIPS "This is a trade magazine for kitchen and bath dealers and designers, so trade experience and knowledge of the industry are essential. We look for writers who already know the unique challenges facing this industry, as well as the major players, acronyms, etc. This is not a market for beginners, and the vast majority of our freelancers are either design professionals, or experienced in the industry."

$$ QUALIFIED REMODELER

Cygnus Business Media, 1233 Janesville Ave., Fort Atkinson WI 53538. **E-mail:** Rob.Heselbarth@cygnus.com. **Website:** www.forresidentialpros.com. **Contact:** Rob Heselbarth, editorial director. **5% freelance written.** Monthly magazine covering residential remodeling. Estab. 1975. Circ. 83,500. Byline given. Pays on acceptance. No kill fee. Publishes ms an average of 1 month after acceptance. Editorial lead time 3 months. Submit seasonal material 2 months in advance. Accepts queries by mail, e-mail, fax, phone. Sample copy online.

NONFICTION Needs how-to, business management, new product, photo feature, best practices articles, innovative design. **Buys 12 mss/year.** Query with published clips. Length: 1,200-2,500 words. **Pays $300-600 for assigned articles. Pays $200-400 for unsolicited articles.** Sometimes pays expenses of writers on assignment.

PHOTOS Send photos. Reviews negatives, transparencies. Negotiates payment individually.

COLUMNS/DEPARTMENTS Query with published clips. **Pays $400**

TIPS "We focus on business management issues faced by remodeling contractors. For example, sales, marketing, liability, taxes, and just about any matter addressing small business operation."

$$$$ REMODELING

HanleyWood, LLC, One Thomas Circle NW, Suite 600, Washington DC 20005. (202)452-0800. **Fax:** (202)785-1974. **E-mail:** salfano@hanleywood.com; ibush@hanleywood.com; sbell@hanleywood.com. **Website:** www.remodelingmagazine.com. **Contact:** Sal Alfano, editorial director; Ingrid Bush, managing editor; Sarah Bell, art director. **10% freelance written.** Monthly magazine covering residential and light commercial remodeling. "We cover the best new ideas in remodeling design, business, construction and products." Estab. 1985. Circ. 80,000. Byline given. Pays on publication. Offers 5¢/word kill fee. Publishes ms an average of 3 months after acceptance. Accepts queries by mail, e-mail, fax. Sample copy free.

NONFICTION Needs interview, new product, technical, small business trends. **Buys 6 mss/year.** Query with published clips. Length: 250-1,000 words. **Pays $1/word.** Sometimes pays expenses of writers on assignment.

PHOTOS State availability. Captions, identification of subjects, model releases required. Reviews 4x5 transparencies, slides, 8x10 prints. Offers $25-125/photo.

TIPS "We specialize in service journalism for remodeling contractors. Knowledge of the industry is essential."

$$ WALLS & CEILINGS

2401 W. Big Beaver Rd., Suite 700, Troy MI 48084. (313)894-7380. **Fax:** (248)362-5103. **E-mail:** wyattj@bnpmedia.com; mark@wwcca.org. **Website:** www.wconline.com. **Contact:** John Wyatt, editor; Mark Fowler, editorial director. **20% freelance written.** Monthly magazine for contractors involved in lathing and plastering, drywall, acoustics, fireproofing, curtain walls, and movable partitions, together with manufacturers, dealers, and architects. Estab. 1938. Circ. 30,000. Byline given. Pays on publication. No kill fee. Publishes ms an average of 6 months after acceptance. Submit seasonal material 4 months in advance. Accepts queries by mail, e-mail. Accepts simultaneous submissions. Responds in 6 months to queries. Sample copy for 9x12 SAE with $2 postage. Guidelines for #10 SASE.

NONFICTION Needs how-to, drywall and plaster construction and business management, technical. **Buys 20 mss/year.** Query or send complete ms. Length: 1,000-1,500 words. **Pays $50-500.** Sometimes pays expenses of writers on assignment.

REPRINTS Send tearsheet or photocopy with rights for sale noted and information about when and where the material previously appeared. Pays 50% of the amount paid for an original article.

PHOTOS Send photos. Captions, identification of subjects required. Reviews contact sheets, negatives, transparencies, prints.

BUSINESS MANAGEMENT

$$$$$ BEDTIMES

International Sleep Products Association, 501 Wythe St., Alexandria VA 22314. (703)683-8371. **E-mail:** jkitchen@sleepproducts.org. **Website:** www.bedtimesmagazine.com; www.sleepproducts.org. **Con-**

tact: Jane Kitchen, editor-in-chief. **20-40% freelance written.** Monthly magazine covering the mattress manufacturing industry. Estab. 1917. Circ. 3,800. Byline given. Pays on acceptance. No kill fee. Publishes ms an average of 3 months after acceptance. Editorial lead time 2 months. Accepts queries by e-mail. Accepts simultaneous submissions. Responds in 1 month to queries. Sample copy for $4. Guidelines by e-mail.

NONFICTION No pieces that do not relate to business in general or mattress industry in particular. **Buys 15-25/year mss/year.** Query with published clips. Length: 500-2,500 words. **Pays 50-$1/word for short features; $2,000 for cover story.**

PHOTOS State availability. Identification of subjects required. Negotiates payment individually.

TIPS "Cover topics have included: annual industry forecast; e-commerce; flammability and home furnishings; the risks and rewards of marketing overseas; the evolving family business; the shifting workplace environment; and what do consumers really want? Our news and features are straightforward—we are not a lobbying vehicle for our association. No special slant."

💲💲💲 BUSINESS TRAVEL EXECUTIVE

5768 Remington Dr., Winston-Salem NC 27104. (336)766-1961. **E-mail:** dbooth@askbte.com. **Website:** www.askbte.com. **Contact:** Dan Booth, managing editor. **90% freelance written.** Monthly magazine covering corporate procurement of travel services. Byline given. Pays on publication. No kill fee. Publishes ms an average of 2 months after acceptance. Editorial lead time 0-3 months. Accepts queries by e-mail.

NONFICTION Needs how-to, technical. **Buys 48 mss/year.** Please send unsolicited submissions, at your own risk. Please enclose a SASE for return of material. Submission of letters implies the right to edit and publish all or in part. Length: 800-2,000 words. **Pays $200-800.**

COLUMNS/DEPARTMENTS Meeting Place (meeting planning and management); Hotel Pulse (hotel negotiations, contracting and compliance); Security Watch (travel safety); all 1,000 words. **Buys 24 mss/year.** Query. **Pays $200-400.**

TIPS "We are not a travel magazine. We publish articles designed to help corporate purchasers of travel negotiate contracts, enforce policy, select automated services, track business travelers, and account for their safety and expenditures, understand changes in the various industries associated with travel. Do not submit mss without an assignment. Look at the website for an idea of what we publish."

💲💲 CBA RETAILERS + RESOURCES

CBA, the Association for Christian Retail, 9240 Explorer Dr., Suite 200, Colorado Springs CO 80920. **Fax:** (719)272-3510. **E-mail:** ksamuelson@cbaonline. org; info@cbaonline.org. **Website:** www.cbaonline. org. **30% freelance written.** Monthly magazine covering the Christian retail industry. Writers must have knowledge of and direct experience in the Christian retail industry. Subject matter must specifically pertain to the Christian retail audience. Estab. 1968. Byline given. Pays on publication. No kill fee. Publishes ms an average of 3 months after acceptance. Editorial lead time 3 months. Submit seasonal material 6 months in advance. Accepts queries by e-mail. Responds in 2 months to queries. Sample copy for $9.50 or online.

NONFICTION Buys 24 mss/year. Query. Length: 750-1,500 words. **Pays 30¢/word upon publication.**

TIPS "Only experts on Christian retail industry, completely familiar with retail audience and their needs and considerations, should submit a query. Do not submit articles unless requested."

💲💲 CONTRACTING PROFITS

Trade Press Publishing, 2100 W. Florist Ave., Milwaukee WI 53209. (414)228-7701; (800)727-7995. **Fax:** (414)228-1134. **E-mail:** dan.weltin@tradepress.com. **Website:** www.cleanlink.com/cp. **Contact:** Dan Weltin, editor-in-chief. **40% freelance written.** Magazine published 10 times/year covering building service contracting and business management advice. The pocket MBA for this industry—focusing not only on cleaning-specific topics, but also discussing how to run businesses better and increase profits through a variety of management articles. Estab. 1995. Circ. 32,000. Byline given. Pays within 30 days of acceptance. No kill fee. Editorial lead time 2 months. Submit seasonal material 3 months in advance. Accepts queries by mail, e-mail. Responds in weeks to queries. Sample copy online. Guidelines free.

NONFICTION Needs expose, how-to, interview, technical. No product-related reviews or testimonials. **Buys 30 mss/year.** Query with published clips. Length: 1,000-1,500 words. **Pays $100-500.** Sometimes pays expenses of writers on assignment.

COLUMNS/DEPARTMENTS Query with published clips.

TIPS "Read back issues on our website and be able to understand some of those topics prior to calling."

CONTRACT MANAGEMENT

National Contract Management Association, 21740 Beaumeade Circle, Suite 125, Ashburn VA 20147. (571)382-0082. **Fax:** (703)448-0939. **E-mail:** khansen@ncmahq.org. **Website:** www.ncmahq.org. **Contact:** Kerry McKinnon Hansen, director of publications and editor-in-chief. **10% freelance written.** Monthly magazine covering contract and business management. Most of the articles published in *Contract Management (CM)* are written by NCMA members, although one does not have to be an NCMA member to be published in the magazine. Articles should concern some aspect of the contract management profession, whether at the level of a beginner or that of the advanced practitioner. Estab. 1960. Circ. 23,000. Byline given. Pays on publication. No kill fee. Publishes ms an average of 3 months after acceptance. Editorial lead time 10 weeks. Submit seasonal material 3 months in advance. Accepts queries by mail, e-mail, fax, phone. YesAccepts simultaneous submissions. Responds in 2 weeks to queries. Responds in 1 month to mss. Sample copy and writer's guidelines online.

NONFICTION Needs essays, general interest, how-to, humor, inspirational, new product, opinion, technical. No company or CEO profiles. Read a copy of publication before submitting. **Buys 6-10 mss/year.** Query with published clips. Send an inquiry including a brief summary (150 words) of the proposed article to the managing editor before writing the article. Length: 1,800-4,000 words. **Pays $300.**

PHOTOS State availability. Captions, identification of subjects required. Offers no additional payment for photos accepted with ms.

COLUMNS/DEPARTMENTS Professional Development (self-improvement in business), 1,000-1,500 words; Back to Basics (basic how-tos and discussions), 1,500-2,000 words. **Buys 2 mss/year.** Query with published clips. **Pays $300.**

TIPS "Query and read at least 1 issue. Visit website to better understand our audience."

EXPANSION MANAGEMENT

Penton Media, Inc., 1300 E. 9th St., Cleveland OH 44114. (216)931-9252. **E-mail:** aselko@industryweek.

com. **Website:** www.industryweek.com/expansion-management. **Contact:** Adrienne Selko, senior editor. **50% freelance written.** Monthly magazine covering economic development. Estab. 1986. Circ. 45,000. Byline given. Pays on acceptance. No kill fee. Publishes ms an average of 1 month after acceptance. Editorial lead time 2 months. Sample copy for $7. Guidelines free.

Part of *Industry Week* magazine.

NONFICTION Buys 120 mss/year. Query with published clips. Length: 800-1,200 words. **Pays $200-400 for assigned articles.** Sometimes pays expenses of writers on assignment.

PHOTOS Send photos. Captions required. Offers no additional payment for photos accepted with ms.

TIPS "Send clips first, then call."

EXPO

Red 7 Media, 10 Norden Place, Norwalk CT 06855. (203)899-8428. **E-mail:** mrondon@accessintel.com; mhart@accessintel.com. **E-mail:** tsilber@accessintel.com. **Website:** www.expoweb.com. **Contact:** Tony Silber, general manager; Michael Rondon, associate editor; Michael Hart, editor. **80% freelance written.** Magazine covering expositions. *EXPO* is published 10 times a year. It includes sales- and marketing-focused features about destinations, case studies and revenue-generating ideas, as well as coverage of new products and services for its audience—show organizers and their managers. Byline given. Pays on publication. Offers 50% kill fee. Editorial lead time 3 months. Accepts queries by mail, e-mail, fax. Responds in 3 weeks to queries. Sample copy and guidelines free.

NONFICTION Needs how-to, interview. Query with published clips. Length: 600-2,400 words. **Pays 50¢/word.** Pays expenses of writers on assignment.

PHOTOS State availability.

COLUMNS/DEPARTMENTS Profile (personality profile), 650 words; Exhibitor Matters (exhibitor issues) and EXPOTech (technology), both 600-1,300 words. **Buys 10 mss/year.** Query with published clips.

TIPS "*EXPO* offers shorter features and departments, while continuing to offer in-depth reporting. Editorial is more concise, using synopsis, bullets, and tidbits whenever possible. Every article needs sidebars, call-outs, graphs, charts, etc., to create entry points for readers. Headlines and leads are more provocative. And writers should elevate the level of shop talk, demonstrating that *EXPO* is the leader in the industry. We plan our editorial calendar about 1 year in advance, but we are always open to new ideas. Please query before submitting a story to *EXPO*. Tell us about your idea and what our readers would learn. Include your qualifications to write about the subject and the sources you plan to contact."

💲💲 INTENTS

Industrial Fabrics Association International, 1801 County Rd. B W, Roseville MN 55113. (651)225-2508; (800)-225-4324. **Fax:** (651)631-9334. **E-mail:** editorial@ifai.com; srniemi@ifai.com; jclafferty@ifai.com. **Website:** www.ifai.com/publications/intents; intentsmag.com. **Contact:** Susan R. Niemi, publisher; Jill C. Lafferty, editor. **50% freelance written.** Bimonthly magazine covering tent-rental and special-event industries. *InTents* is the official publication of IFAI's Tent Rental Division, delivering "the total tent experience." *InTents* offers focused, credible information needed to stage and host safe, successful tented events. Issues of the magazine include news, trends and behind-the-scenes coverage of the latest events in tents. Estab. 1995. Circ. 12,000. Byline given. Pays on acceptance. No kill fee. Publishes ms an average of 2 months after acceptance. Editorial lead time 3 months. Accepts queries by mail, e-mail, fax. Sample copy and writer's guidelines free.

NONFICTION Needs how-to, interview, new product, photo feature, technical. **Buys 12-18 mss/year.** Query. Length: 800-2,000 words. **Pays $300-500.** Sometimes pays expenses of writers on assignment.

PHOTOS State availability. Captions, identification of subjects, model releases required. Reviews contact sheets, negatives, prints, digital images. Negotiates payment individually.

TIPS "We look for lively, intelligent writing that makes technical subjects come alive."

💲💲 MAINEBIZ

Mainebiz Publications, Inc., 48 Free St., Portland ME 04101. (207)761-8379. **Fax:** (207)761-0732. **E-mail:** ccoultas@mainebiz.biz; editorial@mainebiz.biz. **Website:** www.mainebiz.biz. **Contact:** Carol Coultas, editor. **25% freelance written.** Biweekly tabloid covering business in Maine. *Mainebiz* is read by business decision makers across the state. Readers look to the publication for business news and analysis. Estab. 1994. Circ. 13,000. Byline given. Pays on publication. Offers 10% kill fee. Publishes ms an average of 1 month after acceptance. Editorial lead time 1 month.

Submit seasonal material 2 months in advance. Accepts queries by mail, e-mail. Responds in 3 weeks to queries. Sample copy online.

NONFICTION Needs essays, expose, interview, business trends. Special issues: See website for editorial calendar. **Buys 50+ mss/year.** Query with published clips. Length: 500-2,500 words. **Pays $50-250.** Pays expenses of writers on assignment.

PHOTOS State availability. Identification of subjects required. Reviews GIF/JPEG files. Negotiates payment individually.

TIPS "If you wish to contribute, please spend some time familiarizing yourself with *Mainebiz*. Tell us a little about yourself, your experience and background as a writer and qualifications for writing a particular story. If you have clips you can send us via e-mail, or web addresses of pages that contain your work, please send us a representative sampling (no more than 3 or 4, please). Stories should be well thought out with specific relevance to Maine. Arts and culture-related queries are welcome, as long as there is a business angle. We appreciate unusual angles on business stories and regularly work with new freelancers. Send the text of your query or submission in plain text in the body of your e-mail, rather than as an attached file, as we may not be able to read the format of your file. We do our best to respond to all inquiries, but be aware that we are sometimes inundated."

💲💲💲💲 NATIONAL BLACK MBA MAGAZINE

1 E. Wacker, Suite 3500, Chicago IL 60601. (312)236-2622. **Fax:** (312)236-0390. **E-mail:** elaine@naylor.com. **Website:** www.nbmbaa.org. **80% freelance written.** Online magazine covering business career strategy, economic development, and financial management. Estab. 1997. Circ. 45,000. Byline given. Pays after publication. Offers 10-20% or $500 kill fee. Publishes ms an average of 1 month after acceptance. Editorial lead time 2-3 months. Submit seasonal material 3-4 months in advance. Accepts queries by mail, e-mail, fax. No

PHOTOS State availability of or send photos. Identification of subjects required. Reviews ZIP disk. Offers no additional payment for photos accepted with ms.

COLUMNS/DEPARTMENTS Management Strategies (leadership development), 1,200-1,700 words; Features (business management, entreprenuerial finance); Finance; Technology. Send complete ms. **Pays $500-1,000.**

RETAIL INFO SYSTEMS NEWS

Edgell Communications, 4 Middlebury Blvd., Randolph NJ 07869. (973)607-1300. **Fax:** (973)607-1395. **E-mail:** ablair@edgellmail.com; jskorupa@edgellmail.com. **Website:** www.risnews.com. **Contact:** Adam Blair, editor; Joe Skorupa, group editor-in-chief. **65% freelance written.** Monthly magazine covering retail technology. Estab. 1988. Circ. 22,000. Byline sometimes given. Pays on publication. No kill fee. Publishes ms an average of 2 months after acceptance. Editorial lead time 3 months. Submit seasonal material 3 months in advance. Accepts queries by mail. Sample copy online.

O   Readers are functional managers/executives in all types of retail and consumer goods firms. They are making major improvements in company operations and in alliances with customers/suppliers.

NONFICTION Needs essays, exposè, how-to, humor, interview, technical. **Buys 80 mss/year.** Query with published clips. Length: 700-1,900 words. **Pays $600-1,200 for assigned articles.** Sometimes pays expenses of writers on assignment.

PHOTOS State availability of or send photos. Identification of subjects required. Negotiates payment individually.

COLUMNS/DEPARTMENTS News/trends (analysis of current events), 150-300 words. **Buys 4 articles/year mss/year.** Query with published clips. **Pays $100-300.**

TIPS "Case histories about companies achieving substantial results using advanced management practices and/or advanced technology are best."

RTOHQ: THE MAGAZINE

1504 Robin Hood Trail, Austin TX 78703. (800)204-2776. **Fax:** (512)794-0097. **E-mail:** nferguson@rtohq.org; bkeese@rtohq.org. **Website:** www.rtohq.org. **Contact:** Neil Ferguson, art director; Bill Keese, executive editor. **50% freelance written.** Bimonthly magazine covering the rent-to-own industry. *RTOHQ: The Magazine* is the only publication representing the rent-to-own industry and members of APRO. The magazine covers timely news and features affecting the industry, association activities, and member profiles. Awarded best 4-color magazine by the American Society of Association Executives in 1999. Estab. 1980.

Circ. 5,500. Byline given. Pays on acceptance. Offers 25% kill fee. Publishes ms an average of 2 months after acceptance. Editorial lead time 2 months. Submit seasonal material 4 months in advance. Accepts queries by mail, e-mail, fax, phone, online submission form. Accepts simultaneous submissions. Responds in 1 month to queries. Responds in 2 months to mss. Sample copy free.

NONFICTION Needs expose, general interest, how-to, inspirational, interview, technical, industry features. **Buys 12 mss/year.** Query with published clips. Length: 1,200-2,500 words. **Pays $150-700.** Sometimes pays expenses of writers on assignment.

SECURITY DEALER & INTEGRATOR

Cygnus Business Media, 12735 Morris Rd., Bldg. 200, Suite 180, Alpharetta GA 30004. (800)547-7377, ext 2226. **E-mail:** paul.rothman@cygnus.com. **Website:** www.securityinfowatch.com/magazine. **Contact:** Paul Rothman, editor-in-chief. **25% freelance written.** Circ. 25,000. Byline sometimes given. Pays 3 weeks after publication. No kill fee. Publishes ms an average of 3 months after acceptance. Accepts queries by e-mail. Accepts simultaneous submissions.

O   "*Security Dealer & Integrator* magazine is a leading voice for security resellers and the related security service community, covering business intelligence and technology solutions that effectively mitigate a wide variety of security risks faced by commercial, industrial, government, and residential resellers. Content includes vertical market and industry specific needs; new technologies and their impact on the market; business issues including operations, business development, funding, mergers and acquisitions; and in-depth coverage of the market's vendors."

NONFICTION Needs how-to, interview, technical. No consumer pieces. Query by e-mail. Length: 1,000-3,000 words. **Pays $300 for assigned articles; $100-200 for unsolicited articles.** Sometimes pays expenses of writers on assignment.

PHOTOS State availability. Captions, identification of subjects required. Reviews contact sheets, transparencies. Offers $25 additional payment for photos accepted with ms.

COLUMNS/DEPARTMENTS Closed Circuit TV, Access Control (both on application, installation, new products), 500-1,000 words. **Buys 25 mss/year.** Query by mail only. **Pays $100-150.**

TIPS "The areas of our publication most open to freelancers are technical innovations, trends in the alarm industry, and crime patterns as related to the business as well as business finance and management pieces."

SMART BUSINESS

Smart Business Network, Inc., 835 Sharon Dr., Suite 200, Cleveland OH 44145. (440)250-7000. **Fax:** (440)250-7001. **E-mail:** tshryock@sbnonline. com. **Website:** www.sbnonline.com. **Contact:** Todd Shryock, managing editor. **5% freelance written.** Monthly business magazine with an audience made up of business owners and top decision makers. *Smart Business* is one of the fastest growing national chains of regional management journals for corporate executives. Every issue delves into the minds of the most innovative executives in each of our regions to report on how market leaders got to the top and what strategies they use to stay there. Estab. 1989. Byline given. Pays on publication. Offers 50% kill fee. Publishes ms an average of 2 months after acceptance. Editorial lead time 3 months. Submit seasonal material 3 months in advance. Accepts queries by mail, e-mail. Responds in 2 weeks to queries. Responds in 1 month to mss. Sample copy online. Guidelines by e-mail.

- Publishes local editions in Dallas, Houston, St. Louis, Northern California, San Diego, Orange County, Tampa Bay/St. Petersburg, Miami, Philadelphia, Cincinnati, Detroit, Los Angeles, Broward/Palm Beach, Cleveland, Akron/Canton, Columbus, Pittsburgh, Atlanta, Chicago, and Indianapolis.

NONFICTION Needs how-to, interview. No breaking news or news features. **Buys 10-12 mss/year.** Query with published clips. Length: 1,150-2,000 words. **Pays $200-500.** Sometimes pays expenses of writers on assignment.

PHOTOS State availability. Identification of subjects required. Reviews negatives, prints. Offers no additional payment for photos accepted with ms.

TIPS "The best way to submit to *Smart Business* is to read us—either online or in print. Remember, our audience is made up of top level business executives and owners."

THE STATE JOURNAL

WorldNow, P.O. Box 11848, Charleston WV 25339. (304)395-1313. **E-mail:** aali@wowktv.com. **Website:**

www.statejournal.com. **Contact:** Ann Ali, managing editor. **30% freelance written.** Weekly journal dedicated to providing stories of interest to the business community in West Virginia. Estab. 1984. Circ. 10,000. Byline given. Pays on publication. No kill fee. Publishes ms an average of 3 weeks after acceptance. Submit seasonal material 4 months in advance. Accepts queries by mail, e-mail, fax. Sample copy and writer's guidelines for #10 SASE.

NONFICTION Needs general interest, interview, new product, (all business related). **Buys 400 mss/year.** Query. Length: 250-1,500 words. **Pays $50.** Sometimes pays expenses of writers on assignment.

PHOTOS State availability. Captions required. Reviews contact sheets. Offers $15/photo.

TIPS "Localize your work—mention West Virginia specifically in the article; or talk to business people in West Virginia."

VENECONOMY/VENECONOMA

VenEconomia, Edificio Gran Sabana, Piso 1, Ave. Abraham Lincoln, No. 174, Blvd. de Sabana Grande, Caracas Venezuela. (58)(212)761-8121. **Fax:** (58)(212)762-8160. **E-mail:** mercadeo@veneconomia.com. **Website:** www.veneconomia.com; www.veneconomy. com. **70% freelance written.** Monthly business magazine covering business, political, and social issues in Venezuela. *VenEconomy*'s subscribers are mostly business people, both Venezuelans and foreigners doing business in Venezuela. Some academics and diplomats also read our magazine. The magazine is published monthly both in English and Spanish. Freelancers may query in either language. Slant is decidedly pro-business, but not dogmatically conservative. Development, human rights, political, and environmental issues are covered from a business-friendly angle. Estab. 1983. Byline given. Pays on publication. Offers 50% kill fee. Publishes ms an average of 1 month after acceptance. Editorial lead time 1-2 months. Submit seasonal material 1 month in advance. Accepts queries by e-mail. Accepts simultaneous submissions. Responds in 2 weeks to queries. Responds in 4 months to mss. Sample copy by e-mail.

NONFICTION **Contact:** Francisco Toro, political editor. Needs essays, expose, interview, new product, opinion. No first-person stories or travel articles. **Buys 50 mss/year.** Query. Length: 1,100-3,200 words. **Pays 10-15¢/word for assigned articles.** Sometimes pays expenses of writers on assignment.

TIPS "A Venezuela tie-in is absolutely indispensable. While most of our readers are business people, *VenEconomy* does not limit itself strictly to business-magazine fare. Our aim is to give our readers a sophisticated understanding of the main issues affecting the country as a whole. Stories about successful Venezuelan companies, or foreign companies doing business successfully with Venezuela, are particularly welcome. Stories about the oil-sector, especially as it relates to Venezuela, are useful. Other promising topics for freelancers outside Venezuela include international trade and trade negotiations, US-Venezuela bilateral diplomatic relations, international investors' perceptions of business prospects in Venezuela, and international organizations' assessments of environmental, human rights, or democracy and development issues in Venezuela, etc. Both straight reportage and somewhat more opinionated pieces are acceptable, articles that straddle the borderline between reportage and opinion are best. Before querying, ask yourself: Would this be of interest to me if I was doing business in or with Venezuela?"

$$$ WORLD TRADE

2401 W. Big Beaver Rd., Suite 700, Troy MI 48084. (216)280-4467. **Fax:** (248)502-1060. **E-mail:** toscanoc@bnpmedia.com. **Website:** www.worldtradewt100.com. **Contact:** Cristina Toscano. **50% freelance written.** Monthly magazine covering international business. Estab. 1988. Circ. 75,000. Byline given. Pays on publication. No kill fee. Publishes ms an average of 1 month after acceptance. Editorial lead time 3 months. Accepts queries by mail, fax.

NONFICTION Needs interview, technical, market reports, finance, logistics. **Buys 40-50 mss/year.** Query with published clips. Length: 450-1,500 words. **Pays 50¢/word.**

PHOTOS State availability. Identification of subjects required. Reviews transparencies, prints. Negotiates payment individually.

COLUMNS/DEPARTMENTS International Business Services, 800 words; Shipping, Supply Chain Management, Logistics, 800 words; Software & Technology, 800 words; Economic Development (US, International), 800 words. **Buys 40-50 mss/year. Pays 50¢/word.**

TIPS "We seek writers with expertise in their subject areas, as well as solid researching and writing skills. We want analysts more than reporters. We don't accept unsolicited mss, and we don't want phone calls. Please read *World Trade* before sending a query."

CHURCH ADMINISTRATION AND MINISTRY

$ CHRISTIAN COMMUNICATOR

9118 W. Elmwood Dr., Suite 1G, Niles IL 60714-5820. (847)296-3964. **Fax:** (847)296-0754. **E-mail:** ljohnson@wordprocommunications.com. **Website:** acwriters.com. **Contact:** Lin Johnson, managing editor. **50% freelance written.** Monthly magazine covering Christian writing and speaking. Circ. 3,000. Byline given. Pays on publication. No kill fee. Publishes ms an average of 6-12 months after acceptance. Editorial lead time 3 months. Submit seasonal material 9 months in advance. Accepts queries by e-mail. Responds in 6-8 weeks to queries. Responds in 8-12 weeks to mss. Sample copy for SAE and 5 first-class stamps. Writer's guidelines by e-mail or online.

NONFICTION Needs how-to, interview, "Articles on writing nonfiction, research, creativity.". **Buys 90 mss/year.** Query or send complete ms only by e-mail. Length: 650-1,000 words. **Pays $10. $5 for reviews. ACW CD for anecdotes.**

POETRY Contact: Sally Miller (sallymiller@ameritech.net). Needs free verse, light verse, traditional. Buys Publishes 22 poems/year. poems/year. Submit maximum Maximum number of poems: 3. poems. Length: 4-20 lines. **Pays $5.**

FILLERS Needs anecdotes, short humor. **Buys 10-30 mss/year.** Length: 75-300 words. **Pays CD.**

TIPS "We primarily use how-to articles and profiles of editors. However, we're willing to look at any other pieces geared to the writing life."

THE CHRISTIAN LIBRARIAN

Association of Christian Librarians, P.O. Box 4, Cedarville OH 45314. **E-mail:** info@acl.org. **E-mail:** trobinson@whitworth.edu. **Website:** www.acl.org. **Contact:** Tami Robinson, managing editor. **80% freelance written.** Magazine published twice a year covering Christian librarianship in higher education. *The Christian Librarian* is directed to Christian librarians in institutions of higher learning and publishes articles on Christian interpretation of librarianship, theory and practice of library science, scholarly studies, bibliographic essays, reviews, and human-interest articles relating to books and libraries. Estab.

1956. Circ. 800. Byline given. No kill fee. Editorial lead time 3 months. Accepts queries by e-mail to editor-in-chief, apowell@pointloma.edu. Responds in 1 month to mss. Sample copy for $5. Guidelines may be found online at www.acl.org/index.cfm/the-christian-librarian.

NONFICTION Needs how-to, librarianship, technical, bibliographic essays. No articles on faith outside the realm of librarianship or articles based on specific church denomination. Includes peer reviewed content. Do not send book reviews that haven't been requested by the Review Editor. Send complete ms. Deadlines are: February 15, August 15. Length: 1,000-5,00 words for mss; no more than 500 words for reviews.

CREATOR MAGAZINE

P.O. Box 3538, Pismo Beach CA 93448. (800)777-6713. **E-mail:** customerservice@creatormagazine.com. **Website:** www.creatormagazine.com. **Contact:** Bob Burroughs, editor. **35% freelance written.** Bimonthly magazine. Most readers are church music directors and worship leaders. Content focuses on the spectrum of worship styles from praise and worship to traditional to liturgical. All denominations subscribe. Articles on worship, choir rehearsal, handbells, children's/youth choirs, technique, relationships, etc. Estab. 1978. Circ. 6,000. Byline given. Pays on publication. No kill fee. Publishes ms an average of 3 months after acceptance. Editorial lead time 3 months. Submit seasonal material 4 months in advance. Accepts queries by mail. Accepts simultaneous submissions. Sample copy for SAE with 9x12 envelope and 5 first-class stamps. Guidelines free.

> "Dedicated to 'Balanced Music Ministry,' *Creator* does not espouse denominational or other agendas. Issues are full of timely how-to articles, reviews of new publications, thought-provoking essays, and our famous Clip Art."

NONFICTION Needs essays, how-to, be a better church musician, choir director, rehearsal technician, etc., humor, short personal perspectives, inspirational, interview, call first, new product, call first, opinion, personal experience, photo feature, religious, technical, choral technique. Special issues: July/August is directed toward adult choir members, rather than directors. **Buys 20 mss/year.** Query or send complete ms. Length: 1,000-10,000 words. **Pays $30-75 for assigned articles. Pays $30-60 for un-**solicited articles. Pays expenses of writers on assignment.

PHOTOS State availability of or send photos. Captions required. Reviews negatives, 8x10 prints. Offers no additional payment for photos accepted with ms.

COLUMNS/DEPARTMENTS Hints & Humor (music ministry short ideas, cute anecdotes, ministry experience), 75-250 words; Inspiration (motivational ministry stories), 200-500 words; Children/Youth (articles about specific choirs), 1,000-5,000 words. **Buys 15 mss/year.** Query or send complete ms. **Pays $20-60.**

TIPS "Request guidelines and stick to them. If theme is relevant and guidelines are followed, we'll probably publish your article."

GROUP MAGAZINE

Simply Youth Ministry, 1515 Cascade Ave., Loveland CO 80538. (970)669-3836. **E-mail:** sfirestone@group.com. **Website:** www.youthministry.com/group-magazine. **Contact:** Scott Firestone IV, associate editor. **50% freelance written.** Bimonthly magazine for Christian youth workers. *Group* is the interdenominational magazine for leaders of Christian youth groups. *Group's* purpose is to supply ideas, practical help, inspiration, and training for youth leaders. Estab. 1974. Circ. 55,000. Byline sometimes given. Pays on acceptance. No kill fee. Editorial lead time 4 months. Submit seasonal material 5 months in advance. Accepts queries by mail, e-mail, fax. Responds in 8-10 weeks to queries. Responds in 2 months to mss. Sample copy for $2, plus 10x12 SAE and 3 first-class stamps.

NONFICTION Needs inspirational, personal experience, religious. No fiction, prose, or poetry. **Buys 30 mss/year.** Query. Submit online, through website. Length: 200-2,000 words. **Pays $50-250.** Sometimes pays expenses of writers on assignment.

COLUMNS/DEPARTMENTS "Try This One" section needs short ideas (100-250 words) for youth group use. These include games, fundraisers, crowdbreakers, Bible studies, helpful hints, outreach ideas, and discussion starters. "Hands-on Help" section needs mini-articles (100-350 words) that feature practical tips for youth leaders on working with students, adult leaders, and parents. **Pays $50.**

TIPS "We are always looking for submissions for short, novel, practical ideas that have worked in actual youth ministry settings. It's best to familiarize yourself with *Group Magazine* before sending in ideas for our departments."

💲💲 THE JOURNAL OF ADVENTIST EDUCATION

General Conference of SDA, 12501 Old Columbia Pike, Silver Spring MD 20904. (301)680-5069. **Fax:** (301)622-9627. **E-mail:** rumbleb@gc.adventist.org; goffc@gc.adventist.org. **Website:** jae.adventist.org. Chandra Goff. **Contact:** Beverly J. Robinson-Rumble, editor. Bimonthly (except skips issue in summer) professional journal covering teachers and administrators in Seventh Day Adventist school systems. Published 5 times/year in English, 2 times/year in French, Spanish, and Portuguese. Emphasizes procedures, philosophy and subject matter of Christian education. Estab. 1939. Circ. 14,000 in English; 13,000 in other languages. Byline given. Pays on publication. No kill fee. Publishes ms an average of 1 year after acceptance. Editorial lead time 1 year. Accepts queries by mail, e-mail, fax, phone. Responds in 6 weeks to queries. Responds in 4 months to mss. Sample copy for sae with 10x12 envelope and 5 first-class stamps. Guidelines online.

NONFICTION Needs book excerpts, essays, how-to, education-related, personal experience, photo feature, religious, education. "No brief first-person stories about Sunday Schools." Query. All articles must be submitted in electronic format. Store in Word or .rtf format. If you submit a CD, include a printed copy of the article with the CD. Articles should be 6-8 pages long, with a max of 10 pages, including references. Two-part articles will be considered. Length: 1,000-1,500 words. **Pays $25-300.**

REPRINTS Send tearsheet or photocopy and information about when and where the material previously appeared.

PHOTOS Buys 5-15 photos from freelancers/issue; up to 75 photos/year. Photos of children/teens, multicultural, parents, education, religious, health/fitness, technology/computers with people, committees, offices, school photos of teachers, students, parents, activities at all levels, elementary though graduate school. Reviews photos with or without a ms. Model release preferred. Photo captions preferred. Uses mostly digital color images but also accepts color prints; 35mm, 21/4x21/4, 4x5 transparencies. Send digital photos via ZIP, CD, or DVD (preferred); e-mail as TIFF, GIF, JPEG files at 300 DPI. Do not send large numbers of photos as e-mail attachments. Send query letter with prints, photocopies, transparencies. Provide self-promotion piece to be kept on file for possible future assignments. Responds in 1 month to queries. Simultaneous submissions and previously published work OK. State availability of or send photos. Pays $100-350 for color cover; $50-100 for color inside. Willing to negotiate on electronic usage of photos. Pays on publication. Credit line given.

TIPS "Articles may deal with educational theory or practice, although the *Journal* seeks to emphasize the practical. Articles dealing with the creative and effective use of methods to enhance teaching skills or learning in the classroom are especially welcome. Whether theoretical or practical, such essays should demonstrate the skillful integration of Seventh-day Adventist faith/values and learning."

💲 KIDS' MINISTRY IDEAS

Review and Herald Publishing Association, 55 W. Oak Ridge Dr., Hagerstown MD 21740. (301)393-3178. **Fax:** (301)393-3209. **E-mail:** kidsmin@rhpa.org. **Website:** www.kidsministryideas.org. **Contact:** Editor. **95% freelance written.** A quarterly resource for children's leaders, those involved in Vacation Bible School and Story Hours, home school teachers, etc., *Kids' Ministry Ideas* provides affirmation, pertinent and informative articles, program ideas, resource suggestions, and answers to questions from a Seventh-day Adventist Christian perspective. Estab. 1991. Circ. 3,000. Byline given. Pays on acceptance. Publishes ms an average of 3 months after acceptance. Editorial lead time 3 months. Submit seasonal material 6 months to 1 year in advance. Accepts queries by mail, e-mail, fax. Responds in 3 weeks to queries. Responds in 3 months to mss. Sample copy free. Writer's guidelines online.

NONFICTION Needs inspirational, new products related to children's ministry, articles fitting the mission of *Kids' Ministry Ideas*. **Buys 40-60 mss/year.** Send complete ms. Articles generally cover a 2-page spread and should be no more than 800 words. One-page articles should be 300 words. Queries are welcome. Length: 300-800 words. **Pays $20-100 for assigned articles. Pays $20-70 for unsolicited articles. Writers can expect payment within 5-6 weeks of acceptance. Upon publication, authors are sent 1 complimentary copy of the issue in which their material appears.**

PHOTOS State availability. Captions required.

COLUMNS/DEPARTMENTS Buys 20-30 mss/year. Query. **Pays $20-100.**

TIPS "*Kids' Ministry Ideas* is a resource that is practical. Material needs to provide specific, helpful how-to's for children's leaders. Articles on a wide range of subjects appear in *KMI*, but they generally have 1 thing in common—practical ideas and easy-to-understand instructions that people can implement in their area of ministry. Use of sidebars, boxes, and lists of information is encouraged, as this dilutes copy intensity and makes articles more readable."

$$ LEADERSHIP JOURNAL

Christianity Today International, 465 Gundersen Dr., Carol Stream IL 60188. (630)260-6200. **Fax:** (630)260-0114. **E-mail:** ljeditor@leadershipjournal.net. **Website:** www.christianitytoday.com/le. Skye Jethani, managing editor. **Contact:** Marshall Shelley, editor-in-chief. **75% freelance written. Works with a small number of new/unpublished writers each year.** Quarterly magazine. Writers must have a knowledge of and sympathy for the unique expectations placed on pastors and local church leaders. Each article must support points by illustrating from real life experiences in local churches. Estab. 1980. Circ. 48,000. Byline given. Pays on acceptance. Offers 33% kill fee. Publishes ms an average of 6 months after acceptance. Editorial lead time 6 months. Submit seasonal material 6 months in advance. Accepts queries by mail, e-mail, fax. Responds in 2 weeks to queries. Responds in 2 months to mss. Sample copy for free or online.

NONFICTION Needs how-to, humor, interview, personal experience, sermon illustrations. No articles from writers who have never read our journal. No unsolicited ms. **Buys 60 mss/year.** Query with proposal. Send a brief query letter describing your idea and how you plan to develop it. Length: 300-3,000 words. **Pays $35-400.** Sometimes pays expenses of writers on assignment.

COLUMNS/DEPARTMENTS Contact: Skye Jethanis, managing editor. Toolkit (book/software reviews), 500 words. **Buys 8 mss/year.** Query.

TIPS "Every article in *Leadership* must provide practical help for problems that church leaders face. *Leadership* articles are not essays expounding a topic or editorials arguing a position or homilies explaining Biblical principles. They are how-to articles, based on first-person accounts of real-life experiences in ministry. They allow our readers to see `over the shoulder' of a colleague in ministry who then reflects on those experiences and identifies the lessons learned. As you know, a magazine's slant is a specific personality that readers expect (and it's what they've sent us their subscription money to provide). Our style is that of friendly conversation rather than directive discourse—what I learned about local church ministry rather than what you need to do."

$ MOMENTUM

National Catholic Educational Association, 1005 N. Glebe Rd., Suite 525, Arlington VA 22201. (800)711-6232. **Fax:** (703)243-0025. **E-mail:** momentum@ncea.org. **Website:** www.ncea.org/publications/momentum. **Contact:** Brian E. Gray, editor. **65% freelance written.** Quarterly educational journal covering educational issues in Catholic schools and parishes. *Momentum* is a membership journal of the National Catholic Educational Association. The audience is educators and administrators in Catholic schools K-12, and parish programs. Estab. 1970. Circ. 19,000. Byline given. Pays on publication. No kill fee. Publishes ms an average of 3 months after acceptance. Accepts queries by e-mail. Sample copy for $5 SASE and 8 first-class stamps. Guidelines online.

NONFICTION No articles unrelated to educational and catechesis issues. **Buys 40-60 mss/year.** Query and send complete ms. Length: 1,500 words for feature articles; 700-1,000 words for columns, "From the Field," and opinion pieces or essays; 500-750 words for book reviews. **Pays $75 maximum.**

PHOTOS State availability of photos. Captions, identification of subjects required. Reviews prints. Offers no additional payment for photos accepted with ms.

COLUMNS/DEPARTMENTS : From the Field (practical application in classroom); DRE Directions (parish catechesis), both 700 words. **Buys 10 columns. mss/year.** Query and send complete ms. **Pays $50.**

$$ THE PRIEST

Our Sunday Visitor, Inc., 200 Noll Plaza, Huntington IN 46750. (800)348-2440. **Fax:** (260)359-9117. **E-mail:** tpriest@osv.com. **Website:** www.osv.com. **Contact:** Editorial Department. **40% freelance written.** Monthly magazine that publishes articles to aid priests in their day-to-day parish ministry. Includes items on spirituality, counseling, administration, theology, personalities, the saints, etc. Byline given.

Pays on acceptance. No kill fee. Editorial lead time 3 months. Submit seasonal material 4 months in advance. Accepts queries by mail, e-mail, fax, phone. Responds in 5 weeks to queries. Responds in 3 months to mss. Sample copy free. Guidelines online.

NONFICTION Needs essays, historical/nostalgic, humor, inspirational, interview/profile, opinion, personal experience, photo feature, religious. **Buys 96 mss/year.** Send complete ms. Length: 1,500 words maximum. **Pays $200 minimum for assigned articles. Pays $50 minimum for unsolicited articles.**

PHOTOS Send photos. Captions, identification of subjects required. Reviews prints. Negotiates payment individually.

TIPS "Please do not stray from the magisterium of the Catholic Church."

$ RTJ'S CREATIVE CATECHIST

Twenty-Third Publications, P.O. Box 6015, New London CT 06320. (800)321-0411, ext. 188. **Fax:** (860)437-6246. **E-mail:** creativesubs@rtjscreativecatechist.com; editor@rtjscreativecatechist.com. **Website:** www.rtjscreativecatechist.com. **Contact:** Robyn Lee, editor. Monthly magazine for Catholic catechists and religion teachers. The mission of *RTJ's Creative Catechist* is to encourage and assist Catholic DREs and catechists in their vocation to proclaim the gospel message and lead others to the joy of following Jesus Christ. *RTJ* provides professional support, theological content, age appropriate methodology, and teaching tools. Estab. 1966. Circ. 30,000. Byline given. Pays on acceptance. Publishes ms an average of 3-20 months after acceptance. Editorial lead time 4 months. Submit seasonal material 6 months in advance. Accepts queries by mail, e-mail. Accepts simultaneous submissions. Responds in 1-2 weeks to queries. Responds in 1-2 months to mss. Sample copy for SAE with 9x12 envelope and 3 first-class stamps. Guidelines free.

NONFICTION Needs how-to, inspirational, personal experience, religious, articles on celebrating church seasons, sacraments, on morality, on prayer, on saints. Special issues: Sacraments; Prayer; Advent/Christmas; Lent/Easter. All should be written by people who have experience in religious education, or a good background in Catholic faith. Does not want fiction, poems, plays, articles written for Catholic school teachers (i.e., math, English, etc.), or articles that are academic rather than catechetical in nature. **Buys 35-40 mss/year.** Send complete ms. Length: 600-1,300 words. **Pays $100-125 for assigned articles. Pays $75-125 for unsolicited articles.**

COLUMNS/DEPARTMENTS Catechist to Catechist (brief articles on crafts, games, etc., for religion lessons); Faith and Fun (full-page religious word games, puzzles, mazes, etc., for children). **Buys 30 mss/year.** Send complete ms. **Pays $20-125.**

TIPS "We look for clear, concise articles written from experience. Articles should help readers move from theory/doctrine to concrete application. Unsolicited mss not returned without SASE. No fancy formatting; no handwritten mss. Author should be able to furnish article on disk or via e-mail if possible."

$$ TODAY'S CATHOLIC TEACHER

Peter Li Education Group, 2621 Dryden Rd., Suite 300, Dayton OH 45439. (937)293-1415; (800)523-4625, x1139. **Fax:** (937)293-1310. **E-mail:** bshepard@peterli.com. **E-mail:** bshepard@peterli.com. **Website:** www.catholicteacher.com. **Contact:** Elizabeth Shepard, editor. **60% freelance written.** Magazine published 6 times/year during school year covering Catholic education for grades K-12. Looks for topics of interest and practical help to teachers in Catholic elementary schools in all curriculum areas including religion technology, discipline, and motivation. Estab. 1972. Circ. 50,000. Byline given. Pays on publication. No kill fee. Publishes ms an average of 2 months after acceptance. Editorial lead time 3 months. Submit seasonal material 6 months in advance. Accepts queries by mail, e-mail, fax. Accepts simultaneous submissions. Responds in 1 month to queries. Responds in 3 months to mss. Sample copy for $3 or online. Guidelines online.

NONFICTION Needs essays, how-to, humor, interview, personal experience. No articles pertaining to public education. **Buys 15 mss/year.** Query or send complete ms. Query letters are encouraged. E-mail, write, call, or fax the editor for editorial calendar. Articles may be submitted as hard copy; submission by e-mail with accompanying hard copy is appreciated. Length: 600-1,500 words. **Pays $100-250.** Sometimes pays expenses of writers on assignment.

PHOTOS State availability. Captions, identification of subjects, model releases required. Reviews transparencies, prints. Offers $20-50/photo.

TIPS "Although our readership is primarily classroom teachers, *Today's Catholic Teacher* is also read by principals, supervisors, superintendents, boards of education, pastors, and parents. *Today's Catholic Teacher* aims to be for Catholic educators a source of information not available elsewhere. The focus of articles should span the interests of teachers from early childhood through junior high. Articles may be directed to just 1 age group, yet have wider implications. Preference is given to material directed to teachers in grades 4-8. The desired magazine style is direct, concise, informative, and accurate. Writing should be enjoyable to read, informal rather than scholarly, lively, and free of educational jargon."

☺☺☺ WORSHIP LEADER MAGAZINE

32234 Paseo Adelanto, Suite A, San Juan Capistrano CA 92675. (949)240-9339. **Fax:** (949)240-0038. **Website:** www.worshipleader.com. **Contact:** Jeremy Armstrong, managing editor. **80% freelance written.** Bimonthly magazine covering all aspects of Christian worship. *Worship Leader Magazine* exists to challenge, serve, equip, and train those involved in leading the 21st century church in worship. The intended readership is the worship team (all those who plan and lead) of the local church. Estab. 1990. Circ. 40,000. Byline given. Pays on publication. Offers 50% kill fee. Editorial lead time 3 months. Submit seasonal material 6 months in advance. Accepts queries by online submission form. Responds in 6 weeks to queries. Responds in 3 months to mss. Sample copy for $5.

NONFICTION Needs general interest, how-to, related to purpose/audience, inspirational, interview, opinion. **Buys 15-30 mss/year.** Unsolicited articles are only accepted for the web and should be between 700 and 900 words. Web articles are published on a gratis basis and are often the first step in creating a relationship with *Worship Leader Magazine* and its readers, which could lead to more involvement as a writer. Length: 700-900 words. **Pays $200-800 for assigned articles. Pays $200-500 for unsolicited articles.** Sometimes pays expenses of writers on assignment.

PHOTOS State availability. Identification of subjects required. Negotiate payment individually.

TIPS "Our goal has been and is to provide the tools and information pastors, worship leaders, and ministers of music, youth, and the arts need to facilitate and enhance worship in their churches. In achieving this goal, we strive to maintain high journalistic standards, Biblical soundness, and theological neutrality. Our intent is to present the philosophical, scholarly insight on worship, as well as the day-to-day, 'putting it all together' side of worship, while celebrating our unity and diversity."

☺☺ YOUTHWORKER JOURNAL

Salem Publishing/CCM Communications, 402 BNA Dr., Suite 400, Nashville TN 37217-2509. **E-mail:** articles@youthworker.com. **E-mail:** ALee@Salem-Publishing.com. **Website:** www.youthworker.com. **Contact:** Steve Rabey, editor; Amy L. Lee, managing editor. **100% freelance written.** Website and bimonthly magazine covering professional youth ministry in the church and parachurch. Estab. 1984. Circ. 20,000. Byline given. Pays on publication. No kill fee. Publishes ms an average of 3 months after acceptance for print; immediately online. Editorial lead time 6 months for print; immediately online. Submit seasonal material 6 months in advance for print. Accepts queries by e-mail, online submission form. Responds within 6 weeks to queries. Sample copy for $5. Guidelines online.

NONFICTION Needs essays, new product, youth ministry books only, personal experience, photo feature, religious. Special issues: See website for themes in upcoming issues. Query. Length: 250-3,000 words. **Pays $15-200.**

PHOTOS Send photos. Reviews GIF/JPEG files. Negotiates payment individually.

TIPS "We exist to help meet the personal and professional needs of career, Christian youth workers in the church and parachurch. Proposals accepted on the posted theme, according to the writer's guidelines on our website. It's not enough to write well—you must know youth ministry."

CLOTHING

APPAREL

801 Gervais St., Suite 101, Columbia SC 29201. (803)771-7500. **Fax:** (803)799-1461. **E-mail:** jspeer@apparelmag.com. **Website:** www.apparelmag.com. **Contact:** Jordan Speer, editor-in-chief. **25% freelance written.** Monthly magazine for CEO's and top management in apparel and soft goods businesses including manufacturers and retailers. Circ. 18,000. Byline given. Pays on receipt of article. No kill fee. Responds in 2 weeks to queries. Sample copy free. Guidelines free.

COLUMNS/DEPARTMENTS Columns: R Winning Strategies; International Watch; Best Practices; Retail Strategies; Production Solutions.

TIPS "Articles should be written in a style appealing to busy top managers and should in some way foster thought or new ideas, or present solutions/alternatives to common industry problems/concerns. CEOs are most interested in quick read pieces that are also informative and substantive. Articles should not be based on opinions but should be developed through interviews with industry manufacturers, retailers, or other experts, etc. Sidebars may be included to expand upon certain aspects within the article. If available, illustrations, graphs/charts, or photographs should accompany the article."

💲💲💲 FOOTWEAR PLUS

9 Threads, 36 Cooper Square, 4th Floor, New York NY 10003. (646)278-1550. **Fax:** (646)278-1553. **E-mail:** editorialrequests@9threads.com. **Website:** www.footwearplusmagazine.com. **Contact:** Brittany Leitner, assistant editor. **20% freelance written.** Monthly magazine covering footwear fashion and business. A business to-business publication targeted at footwear retailers. Covers all categories of footwear and age ranges with a focus on new trends, brands and consumer buying habits, as well as retailer advice on operating the store more effectively. Estab. 1990. Circ. 18,000. Byline given. Pays on publication. No kill fee. Publishes ms an average of 1-2 months after acceptance. Editorial lead time 1-2 months. Sample copy for $5.

NONFICTION Needs interview, new product, technical. Does not want pieces unrelated to footwear/fashion industry. **Buys 10-20 mss/year.** Query. Length: 500-2,500 words. **Pays $1,000 maximum.** Sometimes pays expenses of writers on assignment.

💲💲 MADE TO MEASURE

The Uniform Magazine, UniformMartket LLC, 633 Skokie Blvd., Suite 490, Northbrook IL 60062. (224)406-8840. **Fax:** (224)406-8850. **E-mail:** news@uniformmarket.com. **Website:** www.madetomeasuremag.com; www.uniformmarketnews.com. **Contact:** Rick Levine, editor. **50% freelance written.** Semi-annual magazine covering uniforms and career apparel. A semi-annual magazine/buyers' reference containing leading sources of supply, equipment, and services of every description related to the Uniform, Career Apparel, and allied trades, throughout the en-tire US. Estab. 1930. Circ. 25,000. Byline given. Pays on acceptance. No kill fee. Publishes ms an average of 2 months after acceptance. Editorial lead time 4 months. Submit seasonal material 4 months in advance. Accepts queries by mail, e-mail. Accepts simultaneous submissions. Responds in 3 weeks to queries. Sample copy online.

NONFICTION Needs interview, new product, personal experience, photo feature, technical. **Buys 6-8 mss/year.** Query with published clips. Length: 1,000-3,000 words. Sometimes pays expenses of writers on assignment.

PHOTOS State availability. Reviews contact sheets, any prints. Negotiates payment individually.

TIPS "We look for features about large and small companies who wear uniforms (restaurants, hotels, industrial, medical, public safety, etc.)."

💲💲 TEXTILE WORLD

Billian Publishing Co., 2100 RiverEdge Pkwy., Suite 1200, Atlanta GA 30328. (770)955-5656. **Fax:** (770)952-0669. **E-mail:** editor@textileworld.com. **Website:** www.textileworld.com. **Contact:** James Borneman, editor-in-chief. **5% freelance written.** Bimonthly magazine covering the business of textile, apparel, and fiber industries with considerable technical focus on products and processes. Estab. 1868. Byline given. Pays on publication. No kill fee.

NONFICTION Needs business, technical. No puff pieces pushing a particular product. **Buys 10 mss/year.** Query. Length: 500 words minimum. **Pays $200/published page.**

PHOTOS Send photos. Captions required. Reviews prints. Offers no additional payment for photos accepted with ms.

CONSTRUCTION AND CONTRACTING

💲💲 AUTOMATED BUILDER

CMN Associates, Inc., 2401 Grapevine Dr., Oxnard CA 93036. (805)351-5931. **Fax:** (805)351-5755. **E-mail:** cms03@pacbell.net. **Website:** www.automatedbuilder.com. **Contact:** Don O. Carlson, editor/publisher. **5% freelance written.** "*Automated Builder* covers management, production and marketing information on all 7 segments of home, apartment and commercial construction. These include: (1) production (site) builders, (2) panelized home manufacturers, (3)

HUD-code (mobile) home manufacturers, (4) modular home manufacturers, (5) component manufacturers, (6) special unit (commercial) manufacturers, and (7) all types of builders and builders/dealers. The in-plant material is technical in content and covers new machine technologies and improved methods for in-plant building and erecting. Home and commercial buyers will see the latest in homes and commercial structures." Estab. 1964. Circ. 75,000 when printed. Byline given if desired. Pays on acceptance. Publishes ms an average of 2 months after acceptance. Editorial lead time 2 months. Accepts queries by mail, e-mail, fax. Responds in 2 weeks to queries.

NONFICTION "No fiction and no planned 'dreams.' Housing projects must be built or under construction. Same for commercial structures" **Buys 6-8 mss/year.** Phone queries OK. Length: 500-750 words. **Pays $250 for stories including photos.**

PHOTOS Captions are required for each photo. Offers no additional payment for photos accepted with ms. Payment is on acceptance.

TIPS "Stories often are too long, too loose; we prefer 500-750 words plus captions. We prefer a phone query on feature articles. If accepted on query, articles will rarely be rejected later. It is required that every story and photos are cleared with the source before sending to *Automated Builder.* At-Home segment will contain details and photos of newest residential and commercial buildings sold or ready for sale. At-Home segment also will welcome stories and photos of new units added to existing homes or commercial structures. Ideal layout would be one page of photos with exterior and/or interior photos of the structures and an adjoining page for text."

$$$ THE CONCRETE PRODUCER

Hanley-Wood, LLC, 8725 W. Higgins Rd., Suite 600, Chicago IL 60631. (773)824-2400; (773)824-2496. **E-mail:** tbagsarian@hanleywood.com; ryelton@hanleywood.com; TCPeditor@hanleywood.com. **Website:** www.theconcreteproducer.com. **Contact:** Tom Bagsarian group managing ditor; Richard Yelton, editor-at-large. **25% freelance written.** Monthly magazine covering concrete production. Audience consists of producers who have succeeded in making concrete the preferred building material through management, operating, quality control, use of the latest technology, or use of superior materials. Estab. 1982. Circ. 18,000. Byline given. Pays on acceptance. No kill fee. Publishes ms an average of 2 months after acceptance. Editorial lead time 4 months. Accepts queries by mail, e-mail, fax, phone. Responds in 1 week to queries. Responds in 2 months to mss. Sample copy for $4. Guidelines free.

NONFICTION Needs how-to, promote concrete, new product, technical. **Buys 10 mss/year.** Send complete ms. Length: 500-2,000 words. **Pays $200-1,000.** Sometimes pays expenses of writers on assignment.

PHOTOS Scan photos at 300 dpi. State availability. Captions, identification of subjects required. Reviews transparencies, prints. Offers no additional payment for photos accepted with ms.

$ HARD HAT NEWS

Lee Publications, Inc., P.O. Box 121, Palatine Bridge NY 13428. (518)673-3763; (800)218-5586. **Fax:** (518)673-2381. **E-mail:** jcasey@leepub.com. **Website:** www.hardhat.com. **Contact:** Jon Casey, editor. **50% freelance written.** Biweekly tabloid covering heavy construction, equipment, road, and bridge work. "Our readers are contractors and heavy construction workers involved in excavation, highways, bridges, utility construction, and underground construction." Estab. 1980. Circ. 15,000. Byline given. No kill fee. Editorial lead time 2 weeks. Submit seasonal material 2 weeks in advance. Accepts queries by mail, e-mail, fax, phone. Sample copy and writer's guidelines free.

NONFICTION Needs interview, new product, opinion, photo feature, technical. Send complete ms. Length: 800-2,000 words. **Pays $2.50/inch.** Sometimes pays expenses of writers on assignment.

PHOTOS Send photos. Captions, identification of subjects required. Reviews prints, digital preferred. Offers $15/photo.

COLUMNS/DEPARTMENTS Association News; Parts and Repairs; Attachments; Trucks and Trailers; People on the Move.

TIPS "Every issue has a focus—see our editorial calendar. Special consideration is given to a story that coincides with the focus. A color photo is necessary for the front page. Vertical shots work best. We need more writers in metro New York area. Also, we are expanding our distribution into the Mid-Atlantic states and need writers in New York, Massachusetts, Vermont, Connecticut, and New Hampshire."

$$ HOME ENERGY MAGAZINE

Home Energy Magazine, 1250 Addison St., Suite 211B, Berkeley CA 94702. (510)524-5405. **Fax:** (510)981-

1406. **E-mail:** contact@homeenergy.org; jpgunshinan@homeenergy.org. **Website:** www.homeenergy.org. **Contact:** Jim Gunshinan, managing editor. **10% freelance written.** Bimonthly magazine covering green home building and renovation. Readers are building contractors, energy auditors, and weatherization professionals. They expect technical detail, accuracy, and brevity. Estab. 1984. Circ. 5,000. Byline given. Pays on publication. Offers 10% kill fee. Publishes ms an average of 4 months after acceptance. Editorial lead time 4 months. Accepts queries by e-mail. Responds in 2 weeks to queries. Responds in 2 months to mss. Guidelines available by online or by e-mail.

NONFICTION Needs interview, technical. Does not want articles for consumers/general public. **Buys 6 mss/year.** Query with published clips. Submit article via e-mail. Length: 900-3,500 words. **Pays 20¢/word; $500 maximum for both assigned and unsolicited articles.**

COLUMNS/DEPARTMENTS "Trends" are short stories explaining a single advance or research result (400-1,800 words). "Features" are longer pieces that provide more in-depth information (1,800-3,500 words). "Field Notes" provide readers with first-person testimonials (1,500-3,000 words). "Columns" provide readers with direct answers to their specific questions (400-1,500 words). Submit columns via e-mail. Accepts Word, RTF documents, Text documents, and other common formats.

$$$ INTERIOR CONSTRUCTION

Ceilings & Interior Systems Construction Association, 1010 Jorie Blvd., Suite 30, Oak Brook IL 60523. (630)584-1919. **Fax:** (866)560-8537. **E-mail:** rmgi@comcast.net; cisca@cisca.org. **Website:** www.cisca.org. **Contact:** Rick Reuland, managing editor. Quarterly magazine on acoustics and commercial specialty ceiling construction. The resource for the Ceilings & Interior Systems Construction Industry. Features examine leading industry issues and trends like specialty ceilings, LEED, acoustics, and more. Each issue features industry news, new products, columns from industry experts, and CISCA news and initiatives. Estab. 1950. Circ. 3,000. Byline given. Pays on publication. No kill fee. Publishes ms an average of 1 1/2 months after acceptance. Editorial lead time 2-3 months. Accepts queries by e-mail. Sample copy by e-mail. Guidelines available.

NONFICTION Needs new product, technical. Query with published clips. Publishes 1-2 features per issue. Length: 700-1,700 words. **Pays $400 minimum, $800 maximum for assigned articles.**

$$ METAL ROOFING MAGAZINE

a Division of F+W Media, Inc., 700 E. Iola St., Iola WI 54990-0001. (715)445-4612. **Fax:** (715)445-4087. **Website:** www.constructionmagnet.com/metal-roofing. **10% freelance written.** Bimonthly magazine covering roofing. *Metal Roofing Magazine* offers contractors, designers, suppliers, architects, and others in the construction industry a wealth of information on metal roofing—a growing segment of the roofing trade. Estab. 2000. Circ. 26,000. Byline given. Pays on publication. Publishes ms an average of 3 months after acceptance. Editorial lead time 3 months. Submit seasonal material 3 months in advance. Accepts queries by mail. Accepts simultaneous submissions. Sample copy free.

NONFICTION Needs book excerpts, historical, how-to, interview, new product, opinion, photo feature, technical. No advertorials. **Buys 15 mss/year.** Query with published clips. Length: 750 words minimum. **Pays $100-500 for assigned articles.**

PHOTOS Send photos. Captions, identification of subjects required. Reviews GIF/JPEG files. Negotiates payment individually.

COLUMNS/DEPARTMENTS Gutter Opportunities; Stay Cool; Metal Roofing Details; Spec It. **Buys 15 mss/year.** Send complete ms. **Pays $0-500.**

TIPS "Read our magazine online for a sense of our typical subject matter and audience. Contact by regular mail is best."

$$$ NETCOMPOSITES

4a Broom Business Park, Bridge Way Chesterfield S41 9QG UK. **E-mail:** info@netcomposites.com. **Website:** www.netcomposites.com. **1% freelance written.** Bimonthly newsletter covering advanced materials and fiber-reinforced polymer composites, plus a weekly electronic version called *Composite eNews. Advanced Materials & Composites News* covers markets, applications, materials, processes, and organizations for all sectors of the global hi-tech materials world. Audience is management, academics, researchers, government, suppliers, and fabricators. Focus on news about growth opportunities. Estab. 1978. Circ. 15,000+. Byline sometimes given. Pays on publication. No kill fee. Publishes ms an average of 1 month after acceptance.

TRADE JOURNALS

Editorial lead time 2 weeks. Submit seasonal material 1 month in advance. Accepts queries by e-mail. Responds in 1 week to queries. Responds in 1 month to mss. Sample copy for #10 SASE.

NONFICTION Needs new product, technical, industry information. **Buys 4-6 mss/year.** Query. 300 words. **Pays $200/final printed page.**

PHOTOS State availability. Captions, identification of subjects, model releases required. Reviews 4x5 transparencies, prints, 35mm slides, JPEGs (much preferred). Offers no additional payment for photos accepted with ms.

POB MAGAZINE

BNP Media, 2401 W. Big Beaver Rd., Suite 700, Troy MI 48084. (248)362-3700. **E-mail:** mehtab@bnpmedia.com. **Website:** www.pobonline.com. **Contact:** Benita Mehta, managing editor. **5% freelance written,**. Monthly magazine covering surveying, mapping, and geomatics. Estab. 1975. Circ. 39,000. Byline given. Pays on publication. Publishes ms an average of 3 months after acceptance. Editorial lead time 3 months. Accepts queries by e-mail, phone. Sample copy and guidelines online.

NONFICTION Query. Document should be saved in Microsoft Word or text-only format. Also include an author byline and biography. Length: 1,700-2,200 words, with 2 graphics included. **Pays $400.**

PHOTOS State availability. Captions, identification of subjects required. Reviews GIF/JPEG files. Offers no additional payment for photos accepted with ms.

TIPS "Authors must know our profession and industry."

PRECAST INC./MC MAGAZINE

National Precast Concrete Association, 1320 City Center Dr., Suite 200, Carmel IN 46032. (317)571-9500. **Fax:** (317)571-0041. **E-mail:** rhyink@precast.org. **Website:** www.precast.org. **Contact:** Ron Hyink, managing editor. **75% freelance written.** Bimonthly magazine covering manufactured concrete products. *Precast Inc.* is a publication for owners and managers of factory-produced concrete products used in construction. Publishes business articles, technical articles, company profiles, safety articles, and project profiles, with the intent of educating our readers in order to increase the quality and use of precast concrete. Estab. 1995. Circ. 8,500. Byline given. Pays on acceptance. No kill fee. Publishes ms an average of 6 months after acceptance. Editorial lead time 3 months.

Accepts queries by mail, e-mail, fax. Accepts simultaneous submissions. Responds in 1 month to queries. Responds in 2 months to mss. Sample copy online. Guidelines online.

NONFICTION Needs how-to, business, interview, technical, concrete manufacturing. No humor, essays, fiction, or fillers. **Buys 8-14 mss/year.** Query or send complete ms. Length: 1,500-2,500 words. **Pays $250-750.** Sometimes pays expenses of writers on assignment.

PHOTOS State availability. Captions required. Offers no additional payment for photos accepted with ms.

TIPS "Understanding audience interests and needs is important and expressing a willingness to tailor a subject to get the right slant is critical. Our primary freelance needs are about general business or technology topics. Of course, if you are an engineer or a writer specializing in industry, construction, or manufacturing technology, other possibilities may exist. Writing style should be concise, yet lively and entertaining. Avoid clichès. We require a third-person perspective, and encourage a positive tone and active voice. For stylistic matters, follow the *AP Style Book*."

RURAL BUILDER

a Division of F+W Media, Inc., 700 E. State St., Iola WI 54990-0001. (715)445-4612, ext. 13644. **Fax:** (715)445-4087. **E-mail:** sharon.thatcher@fwmedia.com. **Website:** www.ruralbuilder.com. **10% freelance written**. Magazine published 8 times/year covering rural building. *"Rural Builder* serves diversified town and country builders, offering them help managing their businesses through editorial and advertising material about metal, wood, post-frame, and masonry construction." Estab. 1967. Circ. 30,000. Byline given. Pays on publication. Publishes ms an average of 3 months after acceptance. Editorial lead time 3 months. Submit seasonal material 3 months in advance. Accepts queries by mail, e-mail. Accepts simultaneous submissions. Sample copy free.

NONFICTION Needs how-to, new product, opinion, photo feature, technical. No advertorials. **Buys 10 mss/year.** Query with published clips. 750 words minimum. **Pays $100-300.**

PHOTOS Send photos. Captions, identification of subjects required. Reviews GIF/JPEG files. Negotiates payment individually.

COLUMNS/DEPARTMENTS Money Talk (taxes for business); Tech Talk (computers for builders); Tool

Talk (tools); Management Insights (business management); all 1,000 words. **Buys 10 mss/year.** Send complete ms. **Pays $0-250.**

TIPS "Read our magazine online for a sense of our typical subject matter and audience. Contact by e-mail is best. No advertorials, please."

⊛⊛ UNDERGROUND CONSTRUCTION

Oildom Publishing Company of Texas, Inc., P.O. Box 941669, Houston TX 77094-8669. (281)558-6930, ext. 220. **Fax:** (281)558-7029. **E-mail:** rcarpenter@oildom.com; oklinger@oildom.com; ebailey@oildom.com. **Website:** www.undergroundconstructionmagazine.com. **Contact:** Robert Carpenter, editor; Oliver Klinger, publisher; Elizabeth Bailey, art director. **35% freelance written.** Monthly magazine covering underground oil and gas pipeline, water and sewer pipeline, cable construction for contractors, and owning companies. Circ. 38,000. No kill fee. Publishes ms an average of 6 months after acceptance. Accepts queries by mail, e-mail, fax, phone. Responds in 1 month to mss. Sample copy for SAE.

NONFICTION Needs how-to, , job stories and industry issues. Query with published clips. Length: 1,000-2,000 words. **Pays $3-500.** Sometimes pays expenses of writers on assignment.

PHOTOS Send photos. Captions required. Reviews color prints and slides.

DECORATED APPAREL AND IMPRINTED INDUSTRY

⊛⊛ IMPRESSIONS

Nielsen Business Media, 1145 Sanctuary Pkwy., Suite 355, Alpharetta GA 30009-4772. (800)241-9034. **Fax:** (770)777-8733. **E-mail:** mderryberry@impressionsmag.com; jlaster@impressionsmag.com; michelle.havich@emeraldexpo.com. **Website:** www.impressionsmag.com. **Contact:** Marcia Derryberry, editor-in-chief; Jamar Laster, senior editor; Michelle Havich, managing editor. **30% freelance written.** Magazine, published 13 times/year, covering computerized embroidery and digitizing design. Authoritative, up-to-date information on screen printing, embroidery, heat-applied graphics and inkjet-to-garment printing. Readable, practical business and/or technical articles that show readers how to succeed in their profession. Estab. 1994. Circ. 20,000. Byline given. Pays on publication. No kill fee. Publishes ms an average of 3 months after acceptance. Editorial lead time 3 months. Submit seasonal material 6 months in advance. Accepts queries by mail, e-mail. Accepts simultaneous submissions. Sample copy for $10.

NONFICTION Needs how-to, embroidery, sales, marketing, design, general business info, interview, new product, photo feature, technical, computerized embroidery. **Buys 40 mss/year.** Query. Length: 800-2,000 words. **Pays $200 and up for assigned articles.**

PHOTOS Send photos. Reviews transparencies, prints. Negotiates payment individually.

TIPS "Show us you have specified knowledge, experience, or contacts in the embroidery industry or a related field."

DRUGS, HEALTH CARE AND MEDICAL PRODUCTS

⊛⊛⊛⊛⊘ ACP INTERNIST/ACP HOSPITALIST

American College of Physicians, 191 N. Independence Mall W., Philadelphia PA 19106-1572. (215)351-2400. **E-mail:** acpinternist@acponline.org; acphospitalist@acponline.org. **Website:** www.acpinternist.org; www.acphospitalist.org. **Contact:** Jennifer Kearney-Strouse, editor of *ACP Internist*; Jessica Berthold, editor of *ACP Hospitalist*. **40% freelance written.** Monthly magazine covering internal medicine/hospital medicine. Writes for specialists in internal medicine, not a consumer audience. Topics include clinical medicine, practice management, health information technology, and Medicare issues. Estab. 1981. Circ. 85,000 (*Internist*), 24,000 (*Hospitalist*). Byline given. Offers kill fee. Negotiable. Publishes ms an average of 2 months after acceptance. Editorial lead time 4 months. Submit seasonal material 6 months in advance. Accepts queries by e-mail. Sample copy online. Guidelines free.

NONFICTION Needs interview. Query with published clips. Length: 700-2,000 words. **Pays $500-2,000 for assigned articles.** Pays expenses of writers on assignment.

PHOTOS Contact: Ryan Dubosar, senior editor. State availability. Reviews TIFF/JPEG files. Negotiates payment individually.

⊛ AUSTRALIAN HEALTH REVIEW

CSIRO Publishing, 150 Oxford St., Collingwood VIC 3066 Australia. (61)(3)9662-7616. **Fax:** (61)(3)9662-7611. **E-mail:** publishing.ahr@csiro.au. **Website:**

www.publish.csiro.au/journals/ahr. Published 5 times a year on behalf of the Australian Healthcare and Hospitals Association. *AHR* provides information for decision makers in the health care industry and is read by health care professionals, managers, planners, and policy makers throughout Australia and the region. Byline given. Guidelines online.

NONFICTION Needs opinion, feature articles, research notes, case studies, book reviews, editorials. Send complete ms. Length: 500-5,000 words.

PHOTOS Send photos. Offers no additional payment for photos accepted with ms.

$$ LABTALK

P.O. Box 593, Big Bear City CA 92314. (909)547-2234. **E-mail:** cwalker@jobson.com. **Website:** www.LabTalkOnline.com. **Contact:** Christie Walker, editor. **20% freelance written.** Magazine published 6 times/year for the eye wear industry. Estab. 1970. Accepts simultaneous submissions.

TIPS "Write for the optical laboratory owner and manager."

$$$ VALIDATION TIMES

Washington Information Source Co., 19-B Wirt St. SW, Leesburg VA 20175. (703)779-8777. **Fax:** (703)779-2508. **E-mail:** rmashaw@fdainfo.com. **Website:** www.fdainfo.com. **Contact:** Rebecca Masahw, managing editor. Monthly newsletters covering regulation of pharmaceutical and medical devices. Writes to executives who have to keep up on changing FDA policies and regulations, and on what their competitors are doing at the agency. Estab. 1999. Byline given. Pays on publication. No kill fee. Publishes ms an average of 1 month after acceptance. Editorial lead time 1 month. Submit seasonal material 1 month in advance. Accepts queries by mail. Responds in 1 month to queries. Sample copy and writer's guidelines free.

NONFICTION Needs how-to, technical, regulatory. No lay interest pieces. **Buys 50-100 mss/year.** Query. Length: 600-1,500 words. **Pays $100/half day; $200 full day to cover meetings and same rate for writing.** Sometimes pays expenses of writers on assignment.

TIPS "If you're covering a conference for non-competing publications, call me with a drug or device regulatory angle."

EDUCATION AND COUNSELING

$ ARTS & ACTIVITIES

Publishers' Development Corp., 12345 World Trade Dr., San Diego CA 92128. (858)605-0242. **Fax:** (858)605-0247. **E-mail:** ed@artsandactivities.com. **Website:** www.artsandactivities.com. **Contact:** Maryellen Bridge, editor-in-chief. **95% freelance written. Eager to work with new/unpublished writers.** Monthly (except July and August) magazine covering art education at levels from preschool through college for educators and therapists engaged in arts and crafts education and training. Estab. 1932. Circ. 20,000. Byline given. Pays on publication. No kill fee. Publishes ms 6 months to 3 years after acceptance. Submit seasonal material 6 months in advance. Accepts queries by mail, e-mail. Responds in 3 months to queries. Sample copy for SAE with 9x12 envelope and 8 first-class stamps. Guidelines online.

NONFICTION Needs historical, arts, activities, history, how-to, classroom art experiences, artists' techniques, interviews of artists, opinion on arts activities curriculum, ideas of how-to do things better, philosophy of art education, personal experience (ties in with the how-to) articles of exceptional art programs. **Buys 80-100 mss/year.** Length: 500-1,500 words. **Pays $35-150.**

TIPS "Frequently in unsolicited mss, writers obviously have not studied the magazine to see what style of articles we publish. Send for a sample copy to familiarize yourself with our style and needs. The best way to find out if his/her writing style suits our needs is for the author to submit a ms on speculation. We prefer an anecdotal style of writing so that readers will feel as though they are there in the art room as the lesson/project is taking place. Also, good quality photographs of student artwork are important. We are a visual art magazine!"

⊙$ THE ATA MAGAZINE

11010 142nd St. NW, Edmonton AB T5N 2R1 Canada. (780)447-9400. **Fax:** (780)455-6481. **E-mail:** government@teachers.ab.ca. **Website:** www.teachers.ab.ca. Quarterly magazine covering education. Estab. 1920. Circ. 42,100. Byline given. Pays on publication. No kill fee. Publishes ms an average of 4 months after acceptance. Editorial lead time 2 months. Submit seasonal material 2 months in advance. Accepts queries by mail, e-mail, fax, phone. Accepts simultaneous submissions. Responds in 2 months to queries. Sample copy free. Guidelines online.

NONFICTION Query with published clips. Length: 500-1,500 words. **Pays $75 (Canadian).**

PHOTOS Send photos. Captions required. Reviews 4x6 prints. Negotiates payment individually.

AUSTRALASIAN JOURNAL OF EARLY CHILDHOOD

Early Childhood Australia, P.O. Box 86, Deakin West ACT 2600 Australia. (61)(2)6242-1800. **Fax:** (61)(2)6242-1818. **E-mail:** publishing@earlychildhood.org.au. **Website:** www.earlychildhoodaustralia.org.au. **Contact:** Chris Jones, publishing manager. Nonprofit early childhood advocacy organization, acting in the interests of young children aged from birth to 8 years of age, their families and those in the early childhood field. Specialist publisher of early childhood magazines, journals, and booklets. Guidelines online.

NONFICTION Needs essays. Send complete ms. Length: Magazine articles, 600-1,000 words; research-based papers, 3,000-6,500 words; submissions for booklets, approximately 5,000 words.

COLLEGEXPRESS MAGAZINE

Carnegie Communications, LLC, 2 LAN Dr., Suite 100, Westford MA 01886. **E-mail:** info@carnegiecomm.com. **Website:** www.collegexpress.com. *CollegeXpress Magazine*, formerly *Careers and Colleges*, provides juniors and seniors in high school with editorial, tips, trends, and websites to assist them in the transition to college, career, young adulthood, and independence. Byline given. Pays on acceptance plus 45 days. Accepts queries by mail, e-mail. Responds to queries in 6 weeks. Contributor's guidelines available electronically.

  Distributed to 760,000 homes of 15- to 17-year-olds and college-bound high school graduates, and 10,000 high schools.

NONFICTION Needs Young adults/teens: careers, college, health, how-to, humorous, interview/profile, personal development, problem-solving, social issues, sports, travel. **Buys 10-20 mss/year.** Query. Length: 1,000-1,500 words.

TIPS "Articles with great quotes, good reporting, good writing. Rich with examples and anecdotes. Must tie in with the objective to help teenaged readers plan for their futures. Current trends, policy changes

and information regarding college admissions, financial aid, and career opportunities."

THE FORENSIC TEACHER MAGAZINE

Wide Open Minds Educational Services, P.O. Box 5263, Wilmington DE 19808. **E-mail:** admin@theforensicteacher.com. **Website:** www.theforensicteacher.com. **Contact:** Dr. Mark R. Feil, editor. **70% freelance written.** Quarterly magazine covering forensic education. Readers are middle, high and post-secondary teachers who are looking for better, easier and more engaging ways to teach forensics as well as law enforcement and scientific forensic experts. Writers understand this and are writing from a forensic or educational background, or both. Prefers a first-person writing style. Estab. 2006. Circ. 30,000. Byline given. Pays 60 days after publication. No kill fee. Publishes ms an average of 6 months after acceptance. Editorial lead time 6 months. Submit seasonal material 6 months in advance. Accepts queries by e-mail. Accepts simultaneous submissions. Responds in 2 weeks to queries; 2 months to mss. Sample copy available at website. Guidelines online.

NONFICTION Needs how-to, personal experience, photo feature, technical, lesson plans. Does not want poetry, fiction or anything unrelated to medicine, law, forensics or teaching. **Buys 18 mss/year.** Send complete ms. Length: 400-2,000 words. **Pays 2¢/word.**

PHOTOS State availability. Captions required. Reviews GIF/JPEG files/pdf. Send photos separately in e-mail, not in the article. Negotiates payment individually.

COLUMNS/DEPARTMENTS Needs lesson experiences or ideas, personal or professional experiences with a branch of forensics. "If you've done it in your classroom please share it with us. Also, if you're a professional, please tell our readers how they can duplicate the lesson/demo/experiment in their classrooms. Please share what you know."

FILLERS Needs : facts, newsbreaks. **Buys 15 fillers/year. mss/year.** Length: 50-200 words. **Pays 2¢/word.**

TIPS "Your article will benefit forensics teachers and their students. It should inform, entertain and enlighten the teacher and the students. Would you read it if you were a busy forensics teacher? Also, don't send a rèsumè and tell us how much experience you have and ask for an assignment; query via e-mail with an outline of your proposed piece."

$$ THE HISPANIC OUTLOOK IN HIGHER EDUCATION

220 Kinderkamack Rd., Westwood NJ 07675. (800)549-8280. **Fax:** (201)587-9105. **Website:** www.hispanicoutlook.com. **50% freelance written.** Biweekly magazine (except during the summer) covering higher education of Hispanics. Looking for higher education story articles, with a focus on Hispanics and the advancements made by and for Hispanics in higher education. Circ. 28,000. Byline given. Pays on publication. No kill fee. Publishes ms an average of 2 months after acceptance. Editorial lead time 2 months. Submit seasonal material 3 months in advance. Accepts queries by mail, e-mail, fax. Accepts simultaneous submissions. Sample copy free.

NONFICTION Needs historical, interview of academic or scholar, opinion on higher education, personal experience egarding higher education only. **Buys 20-25 mss/year.** Query with published clips. Length: 1,800-2,200 words. **Pays $400 minimum for print articles, and $300 for online articles when accepted.** Pays expenses of writers on assignment.

PHOTOS Send photos. Reviews color or b&w prints, digital images must be 300 dpi (call for e-mail photo address). Offers no additional payment for photos accepted with ms.

TIPS "Articles explore the Hispanic experience in higher education. Special theme issues address sports, law, health, corporations, heritage, women, and a wide range of similar issues; however, articles need not fall under those umbrellas."

$$ PTO TODAY

PTO Today, Inc., 100 Stonewall Blvd., Suite 3, Wrentham MA 02093. (800)644-3561. **Fax:** (508)384-6108. **E-mail:** editor@ptotoday.com. **Website:** www.ptotoday.com. **Contact:** Craig Bystrynski, editor-in-chief. **50% freelance written.** Magazine published 6 times during the school year covering the work of school parent-teacher groups. Celebrates the work of school parent volunteers and provide resources to help them do that work more effectively. Estab. 1999. Circ. 80,000. Byline given. Pays on acceptance. Offers 30% kill fee. Publishes ms an average of 4-6 months after acceptance. Editorial lead time 4 months. Submit seasonal material 4 months in advance. Accepts queries by e-mail. Guidelines by e-mail.

NONFICTION Needs general interest, how-to, interview, personal experience. **Buys 20 mss/year.** Query. "We review but do not encourage unsolicited submissions." Features are roughly 1,200-2,200 words. Average assignment is 1,200 words. Department pieces are 600-1,200 words. **Payment depends on the difficulty of the topic and the experience of the writer. "We pay by the assignment, not by the word; our pay scale ranges from $200 to $700 for features and $150 to $400 for departments. We occasionally pay more for high-impact stories and highly experienced writers. We buy all rights, and we pay on acceptance (within 30 days of invoice)."** Sometimes pays expenses of writers on assignment.

PHOTOS State availability. Identification of subjects required. Negotiates payment individually.

TIPS "It's difficult for us to find talented writers with strong experience with parent groups. This experience is a big plus. Also, it helps to review our writer's guidelines before querying. All queries must have a strong parent group angle."

READING TODAY

800 Barksdale Rd., P.O. Box 8139, Newark DE 19714-8139. (800)336-7323. **Fax:** (302)731-1057. **E-mail:** readingtoday@reading.org. **Website:** www.reading.org. Bimonthly magazine covering teaching literacy, children's and young adult's literature, and reading education. *Reading Today* is the membership magazine of the International Reading Association (IRA). Emphasizes reading education. Readers are educators who belong to the IRA. Estab. 1983. Circ. 70,000. Byline given. Pays on acceptance. Responds in 1 month. Simultaneous submissions and previously published work OK. Sample copy and guidelines online.

NONFICTION Send complete mss. "Use the IRA Style Guide at www.reading.org/styleguide.aspx. Consider inserting short section headers every 3 or 4 paragraphs. Include captions for photos. You can include references, but keep them to a minimum (this is a magazine, not a journal). Include a short bio: 'Name is position at organization, e-mail@e-mail.com.'" Length: 300-1,500 words.

$ SCHOOLARTS MAGAZINE

Davis Art, 50 Portland St., Worcester MA 01608. **E-mail:** jgothing@davisart.com. **E-mail:** sasubmissions@davisart.com. **Website:** www.davisart.com. **Contact:** Jackie Gothing. **85% freelance written.** Monthly magazine (August/September-May/June), serving arts and craft education profession, K-12, higher education, and museum education programs written by and for art teachers. Estab. 1901. Pays on publication (honorarium and 4 copies). No kill fee. Publishes ms an average of 24 months after acceptance. Accepts queries by mail. Responds in 2-4 months to queries. Guidelines online.

Ⓠ Each issue of the volume year revolves around a theme that focuses on the human side of the studio art projects, i.e., story, play, meaning. The editor determines which issue/theme is the best fit for articles, so don't worry about fitting a theme. It is more important to be passionate about your lesson, idea, or concept. Look online for upcoming themes.

NONFICTION Query or send complete ms and SASE. E-mail submissions are also accepted. See website for details. Length: 800 words maximum. **Pays $30-150.**

TIPS "We prefer articles on actual art projects or techniques done by students in actual classroom situations. Philosophical and theoretical aspects of art and art education are usually handled by our contributing editors. Our articles are reviewed and accepted on merit and each is tailored to meet our needs. Keep in mind that art teachers want practical tips above all—more hands-on information than academic theory. Write your article with the accompanying photographs in hand. The most frequent mistakes made by writers are bad visual material (photographs, drawings) submitted with articles, a lack of complete descriptions of art processes, and no rationale behind programs or activities. Familiarity with the field of art education is essential. Review recent issues of *SchoolArts*."

🎬 SCREEN EDUCATION

P.O. Box 2040, St. Kilda West VIC 3182 Australia. (61)(3)9525-5302. **Fax:** (61)(3)9537-2325. **E-mail:** screen_ed@atom.org.au. **Website:** www.screeneducation.com.au. Quarterly magazine written by and for teachers and students in secondary and primary schools, covering media education across all curriculum areas. Guidelines online.

NONFICTION Needs general interest, interview, reviews, classroom activities. E-mail proposals or complete article. Length: 1,000-3,000 words.

PHOTOS Reviews TIFF/JPEG files.

TEACHERS & WRITERS MAGAZINE

Teachers & Writers Collaborative, 520 Eighth Ave., Suite 2020, New York NY 10018. (212)691-6590. **Fax:** (212)675-0171. **E-mail:** editors@twc.org. **Website:** www.twc.org/magazine. **75% freelance written.** Quarterly magazine covering how to teach creative writing (kindergarten through university). *Teachers & Writers Magazine* covers a cross-section of contemporary issues and innovations in education and writing, and engages writers, educators, critics, and students in a conversation on the nature of creativity and the imagination. Estab. 1967. Circ. 5,000. Byline given. Pays on publication. No kill fee. Publishes ms an average of 4-6 months after acceptance. Editorial lead time 4 months. Submit seasonal material 4-6 months in advance. Accepts queries by e-mail, as an attachment (preferred). Accepts simultaneous submissions. Responds in 4-8 weeks to queries. Responds in 3-6 months to mss. Sample copy for $5. Guidelines by e-mail.

NONFICTION Needs book excerpts, on creative writing education, essays, interview, opinion, personal experience, creative writing exercises. Length: 500-2,500 words.

🌱 TEACHERS OF VISION

A Publication of Christian Educators Association, 227 N. Magnolia Ave., Suite 2, Anaheim CA 92801. (714)761-1476. **E-mail:** TOV@ceai.org. **Website:** www.ceai.org. **70% freelance written.** Magazine published 4 times/year for Christians in public education. *Teachers of Vision*'s articles inspire, inform, and equip teachers and administrators in the educational arena. Readers look for teacher tips, integrating faith and work, and general interest education articles. Topics include subject matter, religious expression and activity in public schools, and legal rights of Christian educators. Audience is primarily public school educators. Other readers include teachers in private schools, university professors, school administrators, parents, and school board members. Estab. 1953. Circ. 10,000. Byline given. Pays on publication. No kill fee. Publishes ms an average of 6 months after acceptance. Editorial lead time 4 months. Submit seasonal material 4 months in advance. Accepts queries by mail, e-mail. Accepts simultaneous submissions. Responds in 1 month to queries; 3-4 months to mss. Sample copy for SAE with 9x12 envelope and 4 first-class stamps. Guidelines online.

NONFICTION Needs how-to, humor, inspirational, interview, opinion, personal experience, religious. No preaching. **Buys 50-60 mss/year.** Query or send complete ms if 2,000 words or less. Length: 1,500 words. **Pays $40-50.**

REPRINTS Buys reprints.

PHOTOS State availability of photos. Offers no additional payment for photos accepted with ms.

COLUMNS/DEPARTMENTS Query. **Pays $10-40.**

POETRY Will accept poetry if pertains to public schools.

FILLERS Send with SASE—must relate to public education.

TIPS "We are looking for material on living out one's faith in appropriate, legal ways in the public school setting."

TEACHING MUSIC

MENC: The National Association for Music Education, 1806 Robert Fulton Dr., Reston VA 20191. **E-mail:** carolinea@nafme.org. **Website:** www.musiced. nafme.org. **Contact:** Caroline Arlington. Journal covering music education issued 6 times a year. *Teaching Music* offers music educators a forum for the exchange of practical ideas that will help them become more effective teachers. Written in an easy-to-read, conversational style, the magazine includes timely information to interest, inform, and inspire music teachers and those who support their work. Byline given. *Does not pay writers at this time.* No kill fee. Publishes ms an average of 24 months after acceptance. Editorial lead time 12-18 months. Accepts queries by e-mail (preferably in Word). Responds in 2 weeks to queries. Responds in 3 months to mss. Guidelines online.

NONFICTION Needs how-to, inspirational, personal experience, lesson plan(s), classroom management, student recruitment and retention, students with special needs, conducting techniques, cross-curricular integration, multicultural music, assessment. Send complete ms. Length: 1,300-1,600 words.

PHOTOS Send in color photographs or other graphics that illustrate the main points of their articles. Photographers should obtain permission from the parents/guardians of minors whose photographs are submitted. Release form is online. Send photos after ms accepted.

⊖⊖ TEACHING THEATRE

Educational Theatre Association, 2343 Auburn Ave., Cincinnati OH 45219-2815. (513)421-3900. **E-mail:** jpalmarini@schooltheatre.org. **Website:** www. schooltheatre.org. **Contact:** James Palmarini, editor. **65% freelance written.** Quarterly magazine covering education theater K-12; primary emphasis on middle and secondary level education. Estab. 1989. Circ. 5,000. Byline given. Pays on acceptance. No kill fee. Publishes ms an average of 3 months after acceptance. Editorial lead time 2 months. Accepts queries by mail, e-mail. YesAccepts simultaneous submissions. Responds in 4-6 weeks to queries. Responds in 3 months to mss. Sample copy online. Guidelines available by request.

○ *Teaching Theatre* emphasizes the teaching, theory, philosophy issues that are of concern to teachers at the elementary, secondary, and— as they relate to teaching K-12 theater—college levels. A typical issue includes an article on acting, directing, playwriting, or technical theatre; a profile of an outstanding educational theatre program; a piece on curriculum design, assessment, or teaching methodology; and a report on current trends or issues in the field, such as funding, standards, or certification.

NONFICTION Needs book excerpts, essays, how-to, interview, opinion, technical theater. **Buys 12-15 mss/ year.** Query. A typical issue might include: an article on theatre curriculum development; a profile of an exemplary theatre education program; a how-to teach piece on acting, directing, or playwriting; and a news story or 2 about pertinent educational theatre issues and events. Once articles are accepted, authors are asked to supply their work electronically via e-mail. Length: 750-4,000 words **Pays $50-350.**

PHOTOS State availability. Reviews digital images (300 dpi minimum), prints. Unless other arrangements are made, payment for articles includes payment for the photos and illustrations.

TIPS Wants "articles that address the needs of the busy but experienced high school theater educators. Fundamental pieces on the value of theater education are not of value to us—our readers already know that."

⊖⊖⊖⊖ TEACHING TOLERANCE

A Project of The Southern Poverty Law Center, 400 Washington Ave., Montgomery AL 36104. (334)956-8374. **Fax:** (334)956-8488. **E-mail:** editor@teachingtolerance.org. **Website:** www.teachingtolerance.org. **30% freelance written.** Semiannual magazine. Estab. 1991. Circ. 400,000. Byline given. Pays on acceptance. No kill fee. Editorial lead time 6 months. Submit seasonal material 6 months in advance. Accepts queries by mail, fax, online submission form. Sample copy avialble online. Guidelines availabel online.

"*Teaching Tolerance* is dedicated to helping K-12 teachers promote tolerance and understanding between widely diverse groups of students. Includes articles, teaching ideas, and reviews of other resources available to educators."

NONFICTION Needs essays, how-to, classroom techniques, personal experience, classroom, photo feature. No jargon, rhetoric or academic analysis. No theoretical discussions on the pros/cons of multicultural education. **Buys 2-4 mss/year.** Submit outlines or complete mss. Length: 400-1,600 words. **Pays $1/ word.** Pays expenses of writers on assignment.

PHOTOS State availability. Captions, identification of subjects required. Reviews contact sheets, transparencies.

COLUMNS/DEPARTMENTS Features (stories and issues related to anti-bias education), 800-1,600 words; Why I Teach (personal reflections about life in the classroom), 600 words or less; Story Corner (designed to be read by or to students and must cover topics that are appealing to children), 600 words; Activity Exchange (brief descriptions of classroom lesson plans, special projects or other school activities that can be used by others to promote tolerance), 400 words. **Buys 8-12 mss/year.** Query with published clips. Does not accept unsolicited mss. **Pays $1/ word or $250/submission, pending.**

TIPS "We want lively, simple, concise writing. Be descriptive and reflective, showing the strength of programs dealing successfully with diversity by employing clear descriptions of real scenes and interactions, and by using quotes from teachers and students. Study previous issues of the magazine before submitting. Most open to articles that have a strong classroom focus. We are interested in approaches to teaching tolerance and promoting understanding that really work that we might not have heard of. We want to inform, inspire and encourage our readers. We know what's happening nationally; we want to know what's happening in your neighborhood classroom."

$ TECH DIRECTIONS

Prakken Publications, Inc., P.O. Box 8623, P, Ann Arbor MI 48107-8623. (734)975-2800. **Fax:** (734)975-2787. **E-mail:** susanne@techdirections.com. **Website:** www.techdirections.com. **Contact:** Susanne Peckham, managing editor. **100% freelance written. Eager to work with new/unpublished writers.** Monthly (except June and July) magazine covering issues, trends, and activities of interest to science, technical, and technology educators at the elementary through post-secondary school levels. Estab. 1934. Circ. 40,000. Byline given. Pays on publication. No kill fee. Publishes ms an average of 1 year after acceptance. Responds in 1 month to queries. Sample copy for $5. Guidelines online.

NONFICTION Needs general interest, how-to, personal experience, technical, think pieces. **Buys 50 unsolicited mss/year.** Length: 2,000-3,000 words. **Pays $50-150.**

PHOTOS Send photos. Reviews color prints. Payment for photos included in payment for ms. Will accept electronic art as well.

COLUMNS/DEPARTMENTS Direct from Washington (education news from Washington, DC); Technology Today (new products under development); Technologies Past (profiles the inventors of last century); Mastering Computers, Technology Concepts (project orientation).

TIPS "We are mostly interested in articles written by technology and science educators about their class projects and their ideas about the field. We need more and more technology-related articles, especially written for the community college level."

ELECTRONICS AND COMMUNICATION

$$ THE ACUTA JOURNAL

Information Communications Technology in Higher Education, ACUTA, 152 W. Zandale Dr., Suite 200, Lexington KY 40503. (859)278-3338. **Fax:** (859)278-3268. **E-mail:** aburton@acuta.org; pscott@acuta.org. **Website:** www.acuta.org. **Contact:** Amy Burton, director of strategic relationships; Patricia Scott, director of communications. **20% freelance written.** Quarterly professional association journal covering information communications technology (ICT) in higher education. Audience includes, primarily, middle to upper management in the IT/telecommunications department on college/university campuses. They are highly skilled, technology-oriented professionals who provide data, voice, and video communications services for residential and academic purposes. Estab. 1997. Circ. 2,200. Byline given. Pays on publication. No kill fee. Publishes ms an average of 6 months after acceptance. Editorial lead time 6 months. Accepts queries by mail, e-mail, fax, phone. Responds in 1 month to queries. Responds in 2 months to mss. Sample copy for SAE with 9x12 envelope and 6 first-class stamps. Guidelines free.

NONFICTION Needs how-to, ICT, technical, technology, case study, college/university application of technology. **Buys 6-8 mss/year.** Query. Length: 1,200-4,000 words. **Pays 8-10¢/word.** Sometimes pays expenses of writers on assignment.

PHOTOS State availability. Captions, model releases required. Reviews prints. Offers no additional payment for photos accepted with ms.

TIPS "Our audience expects every article to be relevant to information communications technology on the college/university campus, whether it is related to technology, facilities, or management. Writers must read back issues to understand this focus and the level of technicality we expect."

DIGITAL OUTPUT

Rockport Custom Publishing, LLC, 100 Cummings Center, Suite 321E, Beverly MA 01915. (978)921-7850, ext. 13. **E-mail:** mdonovan@rdigitaloutput.net; edit@rockportpubs.com. **Website:** www.digitaloutput.net. **Contact:** Melissa Donovan, editor. **70% freelance written.** Monthly magazine covering electronic pre-press, desktop publishing, and digital imaging, with articles ranging from digital capture and design to electronic prepress and digital printing. *Digital Output* is a national business publication for electronic publishers and digital imagers, providing monthly articles which examine the latest technologies and digital methods and discuss how to profit from them. Readers include service bureaus, prepress and reprographic houses, designers, commercial printers, wide-format printers, ad agencies, corporate communications, sign shops, and others. Estab. 1994. Circ. 25,000. Byline given. Pays on publication. Offers 10-20% kill fee. Publishes ms an average of 2 months after acceptance. Editorial lead time 3 months. Submit seasonal material 3 months in advance. Accepts queries by mail, e-mail. Responds in 3 weeks to queries. Responds in 1 month to mss. Sample copy for $4.50 or online.

NONFICTION Needs how-to, interview, technical, case studies. **Buys 36 mss/year.** Query with published clips or hyperlinks to posted clips. Length: 1,500-4,000 words. **Pays $250-600.**

PHOTOS Send photos.

TIPS "Our readers are graphic arts professionals. The freelance writers we use are deeply immersed in the technology of commercial printing, desktop publishing, digital imaging, color management, PDF workflow, inkjet printing, and similar topics."

SOUND & VIDEO CONTRACTOR

NewBay Media, LLC, 28 E. 28th St., 12th Floor, New York NY 10016. (818)236-3667. **Fax:** (913)514-3683. **E-mail:** cwisehart@nbmedia.com; jgutierrez@nbmedia.com. **Website:** www.svconline.com. Cynthia Wisehart, editor. **Contact:** Cynthia Wisehart, editor; Jessaca Gutierrez, managing and online editor. **60% freelance written.** Monthly magazine covering professional audio, video, security, acoustical design, sales, and marketing. Estab. 1983. Circ. 24,000. Byline given. Pays on acceptance. No kill fee. Publishes ms an average of 3 months after acceptance. Editorial lead time 3 months. Accepts queries by mail, e-mail, fax, phone. Accepts simultaneous submissions. Responds ASAP to queries. Sample copy and writer's guidelines free.

NONFICTION Needs historical, how-to, photo feature, technical, professional audio/video applications, installations, product reviews. No opinion pieces, advertorial, interview/profile, expose/gossip. **Buys 60 mss/year.** Query. Length: 1,000-2,500 words. **Pays $200-1,200 for assigned articles. Pays $200-650 for unsolicited articles.**

REPRINTS Accepts previously published submissions.

PHOTOS Send photos. Identification of subjects required. Reviews transparencies, prints. Offers no additional payment for photos accepted with ms.

COLUMNS/DEPARTMENTS Security Technology Review (technical install information); Sales & Marketing (techniques for installation industry); Video Happenings (Pro video/projection/storage technical info), all 1,500 words. **Buys 30 mss/year.** Query. **Pays $200-350.**

TIPS "We want materials and subject matter that would be of interest to audio/video/security/low-voltage product installers/contractors/designers professionals. If the piece allows our readers to save time, money and/or increases their revenues, then we have reached our goals. Highly technical is desirable."

SQL SERVER MAGAZINE

Penton Media, 221 E. 29th St., Loveland CO 80538. (970)663-4700. **Fax:** (970)667-2321. **E-mail:** articles@

sqlmag.com. **Website:** www.sqlmag.com. **Contact:** Lavon Peters, managing editor. **35% freelance written.** Monthly magazine covering Microsoft SQL Server. *SQL Server Magazine* is the only magazine completely devoted to helping developers and DBAs master new and emerging SQL Server technologies and issues. It provides practical advice and lots of code examples for SQL Server developers and administrators, and includes how-to articles, tips, tricks, and programming techniques offered by SQL Server experts. Estab. 1999. Circ. 20,000. Byline given. "Penton Media pays for articles upon publication. Payment rates are based on the author's writing experience and the quality of the article submitted. We will discuss the payment rate for your article when we notify you of its acceptance." Offers $100 kill fee. Publishes ms an average of 6 months after acceptance. Editorial lead time 4+ months. Accepts queries by mail, e-mail. Responds in 6 weeks to queries. Responds in 2-3 months to mss. Sample copy online. Guidelines online.

NONFICTION Needs how-to, technical, SQL Server administration and programming. Nothing promoting third party products or companies. **Buys 25-35 mss/year.** Send complete ms. Length: 1,800-2,500 words. **Pays $200 for feature articles; $500 for Focus articles.**

COLUMNS/DEPARTMENTS Contact: R2R Editor. Reader to Reader (helpful SQL Server hints and tips from readers), 200-400 words. **Buys 6-12 mss/year.** Send complete ms. **Pays $50**

TIPS "Read back issues and make sure that your proposed article doesn't overlap previous coverage. When proposing articles, state specifically how your article would contain new information compared to previously published information, and what benefit your information would be to *SQL Server Magazine*'s readership."

ENERGY AND UTILITIES

⊜⊜ ELECTRICAL APPARATUS

Barks Publications, Inc., Suite 901, 500 N. Michigan Ave., Chicago IL 60611. (312)321-9440. **Fax:** (312)321-1288. **E-mail:** eamagazine@barks.com. **Website:** www.barks.com/eacurr.html. **Contact:** Elsie Dickson, acting publisher; Kevin N. Jones, senior editor. Monthly magazine for persons working in electrical and electronic maintenance, in industrial plants and service and sales centers, who install and service

electric motors, transformers, generators, controls, and related equipment. Contact staff members by telephone for their preferred e-mail addresses. Estab. 1967. Circ. 16,000. Byline given. Pays on publication. No kill fee. Publishes ms an average of 1 month after acceptance. Accepts queries by mail, fax. Responds in 1 week to queries. Responds in 2 weeks to mss.

NONFICTION Needs technical. Length: 1,500-2,500 words. **Pays $250-500 for assigned articles.**

TIPS "All feature articles are assigned to staff and contributing editors and correspondents. Professionals interested in appointments as contributing editors and correspondents should submit résumé and article outlines, including illustration suggestions. Writers should be competent with a camera, which should be described in résumé. Technical expertise is absolutely necessary, preferably an E.E. degree, or practical experience. We are also book publishers and some of the material in *EA* is now in book form, bringing the authors royalties. Also publishes an annual directory, subtitled *ElectroMechanical Bench Reference*."

✪⊜⊜ ELECTRICAL BUSINESS

CLB Media, Inc., 222 Edward St., Aurora ON L4G 1W6 Canada. (905)727-0077; (905)713-4391. **Fax:** (905)727-0017. **E-mail:** acapkun@annexweb.com. **Website:** www.ebmag.com. **Contact:** Anthony Capkun, editor. **35% freelance written.** Tabloid published 10 times/year covering the Canadian electrical industry. *Electrical Business* targets electrical contractors and electricians. It provides practical information readers can use right away in their work and for running their business and assets. Estab. 1964. Circ. 18,097. Byline given. Pays on acceptance. Offers 50% kill fee. Publishes ms an average of 1-2 months after acceptance. Editorial lead time 3 months. Submit seasonal material 6 months in advance. Accepts queries by e-mail, phone. Accepts simultaneous submissions. Responds in 1 month to queries. Responds in 1 month to mss. Sample copy online. Guidelines free.

NONFICTION Needs how-to, technical. Special issues: Summer Blockbuster issue (June/July); Special Homebuilders' issue (November/December). **Buys 15 mss/year.** Query. Length: 800-1,200 words. **Pays 40¢/word.** Sometimes pays expenses of writers on assignment.

PHOTOS State availability. Captions, identification of subjects, model releases required. Reviews GIF/JPEG files. Negotiates payment individually.

COLUMNS/DEPARTMENTS Atlantic Focus (stories from Atlantic Canada); Western Focus (stories from Western Canada, including Manitoba); Trucks for the Trade (articles pertaining to the vehicles used by electrical contractors); Tools for the Trade (articles pertaining to tools used by contractors); all 800 words. **Buys 6 mss/year.** Query. **Pays 40¢/word.**

TIPS "Call me, and we'll talk about what I need, and how you can provide it. Stories must have Canadian content."

PIPELINE & GAS JOURNAL

Oildom Publishing, 1160 Dairy Ashford, Suite 610, Houston TX 77079. (281)558-6930. **Fax:** (281)558-7029. **E-mail:** rtubb@oildom.com. **Website:** www.pgjonline.com; www.oildompublishing.com. Rita Tubb, man. ed. **Contact:** Rita Tubb, managing editor; Jeff Share, editor. **15% freelance written.** Covers pipeline operations worldwide. Edited for personnel engaged in energy pipeline design construction operations, as well as marketing, storage, supply, risk management and regulatory affairs, natural gas transmission and distribution companies. Estab. 1859. Circ. 29,000. Byline given. Pays on publication. Publishes mss 2 months after acceptance. Editorial lead time 1 month. Accepts queries by e-mail to jshare@oildom.com. Responds in 2-3 weeks to queries; 1-2 months to mss. Sample copy free. Guidelines online at pgjonline.com.

NONFICTION Contact: Editor. Needs interview, new product, travel, case studies. Query. Length: 2,000-3,000 words.

COLUMNS/DEPARTMENTS Contact: Senior editor: lbullion@oildom.com. What's New: Product type items, 100 words; New Products: Product items, 50-100 words; Business New: Personnel Change, 25-35 words; Company New: 35-50 words.

$$ PUBLIC POWER

1875 Connecticut Ave. NW, Suite 1200, Washington DC 20009-5715. (202)467-2900. **Fax:** (202)467-2910. **E-mail:** magazine@publicpower.org; dblaylock@publicpower.org; rthomas@PublicPower.org. **Website:** www.publicpowermedia.org. **Contact:** David L. Blaylock, editor; Robert Thomas, art director. **60% freelance written. Prefers to work with published/established writers.** Publication of the American Public Power Association, published 8 times a year. Emphasizes electric power provided by cities, towns, and utility districts. Estab. 1942. Byline given. Pays on acceptance. No kill fee. Publishes ms an average of 3 months after acceptance. Accepts queries by mail, e-mail, fax. Responds in 6 months to queries. Sample copy and writer's guidelines free.

NONFICTION Pays $500 and up.

PHOTOS Reviews electronic photos (minimum 300 dpi at reproduction size).

TIPS "We look for writers who are familiar with energy policy issues."

$$ SOLAR INDUSTRY

Zackin Publications, Inc., P.O. Box 2180, Waterbury CT 06722. (800)325-6745. **Fax:** (203)262-4680. **E-mail:** mputtre@solarindustrymag.com. **Website:** www.solarindustrymag.com. **Contact:** Michael Puttrè, editor. **5% freelance written. Prefers to work with published/established writers.** *Solar Industry* magazine is a monthly trade publication serving professionals in the solar energy industry. Estab. 1980. Circ. 10,000. Pays on publication. No kill fee. Publishes ms an average of 2 months after acceptance. Submit seasonal material 4 months in advance. Accepts queries by mail, e-mail, fax, phone. Responds in 2 weeks to queries. Sample copies online. Guidelines online.

NONFICTION Needs how-to, improve retail profits and business know-how, interview, of successful retailers in this field. No general business articles not adapted to this industry. **Buys 10 mss/year.** Query. Length: 1,500-2,000 words. **Pay varies.**

PHOTOS State availability. Identification of subjects required. Reviews color transparencies. Pays $25-125 maximum for 5x7 b&w prints.

TIPS "A freelancer can best break into our publication with features about readers (retailers). Stick to details about what has made this person a success."

$$$ TEXAS CO-OP POWER

Texas Electric Cooperatives, Inc., 1122 Colorado St., 24th Floor, Austin TX 78701. (512)486-6242. **E-mail:** editor@texas-ec.org. **Website:** www.texascooppower.com. **60% freelance written.** Monthly magazine covering rural and suburban Texas life, people, and places. *Texas Co-op Power* provides more than 1 million households and businesses educational and technical information about electric cooperatives in a high-quality and entertaining format to promote the general welfare of cooperatives, their member-owners, and the areas in which they serve. *Texas Co-op Power* is published by your electric cooperative to enhance the quality of life of its member-customers in an educational and entertaining format. Estab. 1948. Circ. 1.3 million. Byline given. Pays after any necessary rewrites. No kill fee. Publishes ms an average of 6 months after acceptance. Editorial lead time 4-5 months. Submit seasonal material 6 months in advance. Accepts queries by mail, e-mail, fax, online submission form. Accepts simultaneous submissions. Responds in 1 month to queries. Responds in 3 months to mss. Sample copy online. Guidelines for #10 SASE.

NONFICTION Needs general interest, historical, interview, photo feature, travel. **Buys 30 mss/year.** Query with published clips. Length: 800-1,200 words. **Pays $500-1,200.** Sometimes pays expenses of writers on assignment.

PHOTOS State availability. Identification of subjects, model releases required. Reviews transparencies, prints. Negotiates payment individually.

TIPS "We're looking for Texas-related, rural-based articles, often first-person, always lively and interesting."

ENGINEERING AND TECHNOLOGY

❂❸❸❸ CANADIAN CONSULTING ENGINEER

Business Information Group, 80 Valleybrook Dr., Toronto ON M3B 2S9 Canada. (416)510-5119. **Fax:** (416)510-5134. **E-mail:** bparsons@ccemag.com. **Website:** www.canadianconsultingengineer.com. **Contact:** Bronwen Parsons, editor. **20%% freelance written. Freelancers must sign a copyright agreement.** Bimonthly magazine covering consulting engineering in private practice. Estab. 1958. Circ. 8,900. Byline given depending on length of story. Pays on publication. Offers 50% kill fee. Publishes ms an average of 4 months after acceptance. Editorial lead time 6 months. Responds in 3 months to mss. Sample copy free.

❂   Canadian content only. Impartial editorial required.

NONFICTION Needs historical, new product, technical, engineering/construction projects, environmental/construction issues. **Buys 8-10 mss/year.** Length: 300-1,500 words. **Pays $200-1,000 (Canadian).** Sometimes pays expenses of writers on assignment.

PHOTOS State availability. Negotiates payment individually.

COLUMNS/DEPARTMENTS Export (selling consulting engineering services abroad); Management (managing consulting engineering businesses); On-Line (trends in CAD systems); Employment; Business; Construction and Environmental Law (Canada); all 800 words. **Buys 4 mss/year.** Query with published clips. **Pays $250-400.**

❸❸ COMPOSITES MANUFACTURING MAGAZINE

(formerly *Composites Fabrication Magazine*), American Composites Manufacturers Association, 3033 Wilson Blvd., Suite 420, Arlington VA 22201. (703)525-0511. **E-mail:** communications@acma-net.org; info@acmanet.org. **Website:** www.acmanet.org. Monthly magazine covering any industry that uses reinforced composites: marine, aerospace, infrastructure, automotive, transportation, corrosion, architecture, tub and shower, sports, and recreation. Primarily publishes educational pieces, the how-to of the shop environment. Also publishes marketing, business trends, and economic forecasts relevant to the composites industry. Estab. 1979. Circ. 12,000. Byline given. Pays on acceptance. No kill fee. Publishes ms an average of 2-3 months after acceptance. Editorial lead time 2 months. Accepts queries by e-mail. YesAccepts simultaneous submissions. Responds in 1 week to queries. Responds in 1 month to mss. Sample copy free. Guidelines by e-mail and online. Specific details on submission types online.

NONFICTION Needs how-to, composites manufacturing, new product, technical, marketing, related business trends and forecasts. Special issues: "Each January we publish a World Market Report where we cover all niche markets and all geographic areas relevant to the composites industry. Freelance material will be considered strongly for this issue.". No need to query company or personal profiles unless there is an extremely unique or novel angle. **Buys 5-10 mss/year.** Query. *Composites Manufacturing* invites freelance feature submissions, all of which should be sent via e-mail as a Microsoft Word attachment. A query letter is required. Length: 1,500-2,000 words. **Pays 20-40¢/word (negotiable).** Sometimes pays expenses of writers on assignment.

COLUMNS/DEPARTMENTS "We publish columns on HR, relevant government legislation, industry lessons learned, regulatory affairs, and technology. Average word length for columns is 500 words. We would entertain any new column idea that hits hard on industry matters." Query. **Pays $300-350.**

TIPS "The best way to break into the magazine is to empathize with the entrepreneurial and technical background of readership, and come up with an exclusive, original, creative story idea. We pride ourselves on not looking or acting like any other trade publication (composites industry or otherwise). Our editor is very open to suggestions, but they must be unique. Don't waste his time with canned articles dressed up to look exclusive. This is the best way to get on the 'immediate rejection list.'"

✪⊛⊛⊛ CONNECTIONS+

The Magazine for ICT Professionals, Business Information Group, 80 Valleybrook Dr., Toronto ON M3B 2S9 Canada. (416)510-6752. **Fax:** (416)510-5134. **E-mail:** pbarker@connectionsplus.ca. **Website:** www.connectionsplus.ca. **Contact:** Paul Barker, editor. **50% freelance written.** Magazine published 6 times/year covering the structured cabling/telecommunications industry. Estab. 1998. Circ. 15,000 print; 45,000 electronic. Byline given. Pays on publication. No kill fee. Publishes ms an average of 1 month after acceptance. Editorial lead time 3 months. Submit seasonal material 1 month in advance. Accepts queries by mail, e-mail, phone. Accepts simultaneous submissions. Sample copy online. Guidelines free.

◯   *Connections+* is written for engineers, designers, contractors, and end users who design, specify, purchase, install, test, and maintain structured cabling and telecommunications products and systems.

NONFICTION Needs technical, case studies, features. No reprints or previously written articles. All articles are assigned by editor based on query or need of publication. **Buys 12 mss/year.** Query with published clips. Length: 1,500-2,500 words. **Pays 40-50¢/word.** Sometimes pays expenses of writers on assignment.

PHOTOS State availability. Captions, identification of subjects required. Reviews contact sheets, prints. Negotiates payment individually.

COLUMNS/DEPARTMENTS Focus on Engineering/Design; Focus on Installation; Focus on Maintenance/Testing; all 1,500 words. **Buys 7 mss/year.** Query with published clips. **Pays 40-50¢/word.**

TIPS "Visit our website to see back issues, and visit links on our website for background."

EMBEDDED TECHNOLOGY

Tech Briefs Media Group, 261 Fifth Ave., Suite 1901, New York NY 10016. (212)490-3999. **E-mail:** bruce@abpi.net. **Website:** www.embeddedtechmag.com. **Contact:** Bruce Bennett. **100% freelance written.** Bimonthly magazine covering embedded, industrial, and COTS computers. *Embedded Technology*'s audience consists of computer and electronics engineers, designers, scientists, technicians, and systems integrators. Articles tend to be highly technical in nature and cover everything from the latest ASICs and FPGAs to single board computers and data transfer protocols. Estab. 2005. Circ. 71,000. Byline given. No monetary payment. No kill fee. Publishes ms an average of 3-6 months after acceptance. Editorial lead time 3-6 months. Accepts queries by e-mail. Sample copy and guidelines online.

NONFICTION Contact: Bruce A. Bennett. Needs technical. "We don't want anything non-technical." Query. Length: 1,200-1,500 words.

TIPS "Our authors tend to work in the embedded computing industry and have solid academic and professional credentials. They're writing for professional and peer recognition, not monetary reward."

⊛⊛⊛ ENTERPRISE MINNESOTA MAGAZINE

Enterprise Minnesota, Inc., 310 4th Ave. S., Suite 7050, Minneapolis MN 55415. (612)373-2900; (800)325-3073. **Fax:** (612)373-2901. **E-mail:** editor@enterpriseminnesota.org. **Website:** www.enterpriseminnesota.org. **Contact:** Tom Mason, editor. **90% freelance written.** Magazine published 5 times/year. *Minnesota Technology* is for the owners and top management of Minnesota's technology and manufacturing companies. The magazine covers technology trends and issues, global trade, management techniques, and finance. Profile new and growing companies, new products, and the innovators and entrepreneurs of Minnesota's technology sector. Estab. 1991. Circ. 16,000. Byline given. Pays on publication. Offers 10% kill fee. Publishes ms an average of 3 months after acceptance. Editorial lead time 1 month. Submit seasonal material 1 year in advance. Accepts queries by mail, e-mail. Guidelines free.

NONFICTION Needs general interest, how-to, interview. **Buys 60 mss/year.** Query with published clips. **Pays $150-1,000.**

COLUMNS/DEPARTMENTS Feature Well (Q&A format, provocative ideas from Minnesota business and industry leaders), 2,000 words; Up Front (mini profiles, anecdotal news items), 250-500 words. Query with published clips.

🟢🟢 LD+A

Illuminating Engineering Society of North America, 120 Wall St., 17th Floor, New York NY 10005-4001. (212)248-5000, ext. 108. **Fax:** (212)248-5017. **E-mail:** ptarricone@ies.org; ies@ies.org. **Website:** www.ies.org. **Contact:** Paul Tarricone, editor/associate publisher. **10% freelance written.** Monthly magazine. *LD+A* is geared to professionals in lighting design and the lighting field in architecture, retail, entertainment, etc. Estab. 1971. Circ. 10,000. Byline given. Pays on acceptance. No kill fee. Publishes ms an average of 4 months after acceptance. Editorial lead time 2 months. Submit seasonal material 4 months in advance. Accepts queries by mail, e-mail, fax, phone. Accepts simultaneous submissions. Responds in 2 weeks to queries. Sample copy free. Guidelines online.

NONFICTION Needs historical, how-to, opinion, personal experience, photo feature, technical. No articles blatantly promoting a product, company, or individual. **Buys 6-10 mss/year.** Query. Length: 1,500-2,000 words.

PHOTOS Send photos. Captions required. Reviews JPEG/TIFF files. Offers no additional payment for photos accepted with ms.

COLUMNS/DEPARTMENTS Essay by Invitation (industry trends), 1,200 words. Query. **Does not pay for columns.**

TIPS "Most of our features detail the ins and outs of a specific lighting project. From museums to stadiums and highways, *LD+A* gives its readers an indepth look at how the designer(s) reached their goals."

🟢🟢 MFRTECH EJOURNAL

Manufacturers Group Inc., P.O. Box 4310, Lexington KY 40544. **E-mail:** editor@mfrtech.com. **Website:** www.mfrtech.com. **40% freelance written.** Magazine published daily online covering manufacturing and technology from news throughout the U.S. Editorial includes anufacturing news, expansions, acquisition white papers, case histories, new product announcements, feature submissions, book synopsis. Estab. 1976 (print). Circ. 60,000+ weekly subscribers (e-mail); 750,000 monthly online visitors. Byline given. 30 days followiong publication. Offers 25% kill fee. Publishes ms 3-4 days after acceptance. Editorial lead time 2 weeks. Submit seasonal material 2 weeks in advance. Sample copy online. Guidelines by e-mail.

NONFICTION Needs new product, opinion, technical. General interest, inspirational, personal, travel, book excerpts. Length: 750-1,500 words; byline: 75 words. **Pays $0.20/word published.**

PHOTOS Up to 3 photo or graphic images permitted; must come as an attachment to ms submissions via e-mail as JPEGs and no larger than 300x300 pixels each.

COLUMNS/DEPARTMENTS New Plant Announcement, Acquisitions, Expansions, New Technology, Federal, Case Histories, Human Resources, Marketing. Query. **Pays $0.20/word.**

🟢🟢 MINORITY ENGINEER

Equal Opportunity Publications, Inc., 445 Broad Hollow Rd., Suite 425, Melville NY 11747. (631)421-9421. **Fax:** (516)421-0359. **E-mail:** jschneider@eop.com; info@eop.com. **Website:** www.eop.com. **Contact:** James Schneider, director, editorial and production. **60% freelance written. Prefers to work with published/established writers.** Triannual magazine covering career guidance for minority engineering students and minority professional engineers. Estab. 1969. Circ. 15,000. Byline given. Pays on publication. No kill fee. Publishes ms an average of 3 months after acceptance. Editorial lead time 3 months. Accepts queries by mail, e-mail, fax, phone. Accepts simultaneous submissions. Responds in 2 weeks to queries. Responds in 2 months to mss. Sample copy and writer's guidelines for 9x12 SAE with 5 first-class stamps. Guidelines free.

NONFICTION Needs book excerpts, general interest, on specific minority engineering concerns, how-to, land a job, keep a job, etc., interview, minority engineer role models, opinion, problems of ethnic minorities, personal experience, student and career experiences, technical, on career fields offering opportunities for minority engineers, articles on job search techniques, role models. No general information. Query. Length: 1,500-2,500 words. **Pays $350 for assigned articles.** Sometimes pays expenses of writers on assignment.

REPRINTS Send typed ms with rights for sale noted and information about when and where the material previously appeared. Pays 100% of amount paid for an original article.

PHOTOS State availability.

TIPS Articles should focus on career guidance, role model and industry prospects for minority engineers. Prefers articles related to careers, not politically or socially sensitive.

PHOTONICS TECH BRIEFS

Tech Briefs Media Group, 261 5th Ave., Suite 1901, New York NY 10016. (212)490-3999. **E-mail:** bruce@abpi.net. **Website:** www.techbriefsmediagroup.com. **Contact:** Bruce Bennett, editor. **100% freelance written.** Magazine published 6 times/year covering lasers, optics, and photonic systems. *Photonics Tech Briefs'* audience consists of engineers, designers, scientists, and technicians working in all aspects of the laser, optics, and photonics industries. Articles tend to be highly technical in nature and cover everything from lasers, fiber optics and infrared technology to biophotonics, photovoltaics, and digital imaging systems. Circ. 102,698. Byline given. No monetary payment. No kill fee. Publishes ms an average of 3-6 months after acceptance. Editorial lead time 3-6 months. Accepts queries by e-mail. Sample copy and guidelines online.

NONFICTION Needs technical. Does not want anything non-technical. Query without published clips or send complete ms. Length: 1,200-1,500 words.

TIPS "Our authors tend to work in the photonics/optics industry and have solid academic and professional credentials. They're writing for professional and peer recognition, not monetary reward."

⊕⊕⊕⊕ RAILWAY TRACK AND STRUCTURES

Simmons-Boardman Publishing, 55 Broad St., 26th Floor, New York NY 10004. (212)620-7200. **Fax:** (212)633-1165. **E-mail:** Mischa@sbpub-chicago.com; Jnunez@sbpub-chicago.com. **Website:** www.rtands.com. **Contact:** Mischa Wanek-Libman, editor; Jennifer Nunez, assistant editor. **1% freelance written.** Monthly magazine covering railroad civil engineering. *RT&S* is a nuts-and-bolts journal to help railroad civil engineers do their jobs better. Estab. 1904. Circ. 9,500. Byline given. Pays on publication. Offers 90% kill fee. Publishes ms an average of 1 month after acceptance. Editorial lead time 2 months. Submit seasonal material 3 months in advance. Accepts queries by mail, fax, phone. YesAccepts simultaneous submissions. Responds in 1 month to queries and to mss. Sample copy online.

NONFICTION Needs how-to, new product, technical. Does not want nostalgia or "railroadiana." **Buys 1 mss/year.** Query. Length: 900-2,000 words. **Pays $500-1,000.** Sometimes pays expenses of writers on assignment.

PHOTOS State availability. Captions, identification of subjects, model releases required. Reviews GIF/JPEG files. Negotiates payment individually.

TIPS "We prefer writers with a civil engineering background and railroad experience."

⊕⊕ WOMAN ENGINEER

Equal Opportunity Publications, Inc., 445 Broad Hollow Rd., Suite 425, Melville NY 11747. (631)421-9421. **Fax:** (631)421-1352. **E-mail:** info@eop.com; jschneider@eop.com. **Website:** www.eop.com. **Contact:** James Schneider, editor. **60% freelance written. Works with a small number of new/unpublished writers each year.** Triannual magazine aimed at advancing the careers of women engineering students and professional women engineers. Estab. 1968. Circ. 16,000. Byline given. Pays on publication. No kill fee. Publishes ms an average of 3 months after acceptance. Editorial lead time 3 months. Accepts queries by mail, e-mail, fax, phone. Responds in 2 weeks to queries. Responds in 2 months to mss. Sample copy and writer's guidelines free.

NONFICTION Needs how-to, find jobs, interview, personal experience. Query. Length: 1,500-2,500 words. **Pays $350 for assigned articles.**

PHOTOS Captions, identification of subjects required. Reviews color slides but will accept b&w.

TIPS "We are looking for first-person 'As I See It' personal perspectives. Gear it to our audience."

ENTERTAINMENT AND THE ARTS

⊕⊕⊕ AMERICAN CINEMATOGRAPHER

American Society of Cinematographers, 1782 N. Orange Dr., Hollywood CA 90028. (800)448-0145; outside US: (323)969-4333. **Fax:** (323)876-4973. **E-mail:** stephen@ascmag.com. **Website:** www.theasc.com. **Contact:** Stephen Pizzello, executive editor. **90% freelance written.** Monthly magazine covering cinematography (motion picture, TV, music video, commercial). "*American Cinematographer* is a trade publication devoted to the art and craft of cinematography. Our readers are predominantly film industry professionals." Estab. 1919. Circ. 45,000. Byline given. Pays on publication. Offers 50% kill fee. Publishes ms an average of 2-3 months after acceptance. Editorial lead time 2 months. Submit seasonal material 3 months in advance. Accepts queries by mail, e-mail, phone. Responds in 2 weeks to queries; 2 months to mss. Sample copy and writer's guidelines free.

NONFICTION Contact: Stephen Pizzello, editor. Needs interview, new product, technical. No reviews or opinion pieces. **Buys 20-25 mss/year.** Query with published clips. Length: 1,000-4,000 words. **Pays $400-1,500.** Sometimes pays expenses of writers on assignment.

TIPS "Familiarity with the technical side of film production and the ability to present that information in an articulate fashion to our audience are crucial."

AMERICAN THEATRE

Theatre Communications Group, 520 8th Ave., 24th Floor, New York NY 10018. (212)609-5900. **E-mail:** jim@tcg.org. **Website:** www.tcg.org. **Contact:** Jim O'Quinn, editor-in-chief. **60% freelance written.** Monthly magazine covering theatre. Focus is on American regional nonprofit theatre. *American Theatre* typically publishes 2 or 3 features and 4-6 back-of-the-book articles covering trends and events in all types of theatre, as well as economic and legislative developments affecting the arts. *American Theatre* covers trends and events in all types of theatre, as well as economic and legislative developments affecting the arts. *American Theatre* rarely publishes articles about commercial, amateur or university theatre, nor about works that would widely be classified as dance or opera, except at the editors' discretion. While significant productions may be highlighted in the Critic's Notebook section, *American Theatre* does not review productions (but does review theatre-related books). Estab. 1982. Circ. 100,000. Byline given. Pays on publication. Editorial lead time 2 months. Submit seasonal material 3 months in advance. Accepts queries by mail, e-mail, online submission form. YesAccepts simultaneous submissions. Responds in 2 months to queries. Sample copy and guidelines online.

Writers wishing to submit articles to *American Theatre* should mail or e-mail a query to editor-in-chief Jim O'Quinn outlining a particular proposal; unsolicited material is rarely accepted. Include a brief rèsumè and sample clips. Planning of major articles usually occurs at least 3 months in advance of publication. All mss are subject to editing.

NONFICTION Needs book excerpts, essays, exposè, general interest, historical, how-to, humor, inspirational, interview, opinion, personal experience, photo feature, travel. Special issues: Training (January); International (May/June); Season Preview (October). No unsolicited submissions (rarely accepted). No reviews. Query with outlined proposal and published clips. Include brief rèsumè and SASE. Length: 200-2,000 words. **"While fees are negotiated per ms, we pay an average of $350 for full-length (2,500-3,500 words) features, and less for shorter pieces."**

PHOTOS Contact: Kitty Suen, creative director: atphoto@tcg.com. Send photos. Captions required. Reviews JPEG files. Negotiates payment individually.

TIPS "The main focus is on professional American nonprofit theatre. Don't pitch music or film festivals. Must be about theatre."

BOXOFFICE MAGAZINE

Boxoffice Media, LLC, 9107 Wilshire Blvd., Ste. 450, Beverly Hills CA 90210. (310) 876-9090. **E-mail:** ken@boxoffice.com. **Website:** www.BoxOffice.com. **15% freelance written.** Providing news and numbers to the film industry since 1920. Magazine about the motion picture industry for executives and managers working in the film business, including movie theater owners and operators, Hollywood studio personnel and leaders in allied industries. Estab. 1920. Circ. 6,000. Byline given. Pays on publication. No kill fee. Publishes ms an average of 3 months after acceptance. Submit seasonal material 5 months in advance. Accepts queries by mail, e-mail, fax. Sample copy for $5 in US; $10 outside U.S.

"*BOXOFFICE* Magazine has been the premier trade magazine covering The Business of Movies for industry insiders. In November 2010, we began publishing our new fan magazine, available at a theater near you. If you love the movies, you'll love The New *BOXOFFICE* Magazine. Check out our online edition. In addition to the fastest and most accurate box office on the Internet, we review more than 600 movies a year—every theatrical release in the US and major festival screenings from around the world as well as exclusive features and interviews with top filmmakers and industry executives and the latest news from Hollywood.

If you're a film aficionado (for love or money), check out our sister site, www.boxofficemaga-zine.com for all the latest on your favorite films and filmmakers."

NONFICTION Needs book excerpts, essays, interview, new product, personal experience, photo feature, technical, investigative all regarding movie theatre business. Query with published clips. Length: 800-2,500 words. **Pays 10¢/word.**

PHOTOS Uses 4×5, 8×10 glossy color or b&w prints; 35mm, 21/4×21/4, 4×5 transparencies. Accepts images in digital format. State availability. Captions required. Reviews prints, slides and JPEG files. Pays $10/printed photo. Pays on publication. Credit line sometimes given.

TIPS "Purchase a sample copy and read it. Then, write a clear, comprehensive outline of the proposed story, and enclose a résumé and published clips to the managing editor."

DANCE TEACHER

McFadden Performing Arts Media, 333 Seventh Ave., 11th Floor, New York NY 10001. **Fax:** (646)459-4000. **E-mail:** khildebrand@dancemedia.com. **Website:** www.dance-teacher.com. **Contact:** Karen Hildebrand, editor-in-chief; Joe Sullivan, managing editor. **60% freelance written.** Monthly magazine. Estab. 1979. Circ. 25,000. Byline given. Pays on publication. No kill fee. Publishes ms an average of 3 months after acceptance. Submit seasonal material 6 months in advance. Accepts queries by mail, e-mail, fax, phone, online submission form. Responds in 3 months to mss. Sample copy for SAE with 9x12 envelope and 6 first-class stamps. Guidelines available for free.

NONFICTION Needs how-to, teach, health, business, legal. Special issues: Summer Programs (January); Music & More (May); Costumes and Production Preview (November); College/Training Schools (December). No PR or puff pieces. All articles must be well researched. **Buys 50 mss/year.** Query. Length: 700-2,000 words. **Pays $100-300.**

PHOTOS Send photos. Reviews contact sheets, negatives, transparencies, prints. Limited photo budget.

TIPS "Read several issues—particularly seasonal. Stay within writer's guidelines."

DRAMATICS MAGAZINE

Educational Theatre Association, 2343 Auburn Ave., Cincinnati OH 45219. (513)421-3900. **E-mail:** dcorathers@schooltheatre.org. **Website:** schoolthe-atre.org. **Contact:** Don Corathers, editor. *Dramatics* is for students (mainly high school age) and teachers of theater. Mix includes how-to (tech theater, acting, directing, etc.), informational, interview, photo feature, humorous, profile, technical. *Dramatics* wants student readers to grow as theater artists and become a more discerning and appreciative audience. Material is directed to both theater students and their teachers, with strong student slant. Tries to portray the theater community in all its diversity. Estab. 1929. Circ. 35,000. Byline given. Pays on acceptance. Publishes ms 3 months after acceptance. TrueAccepts simultaneous submissions. Sample copy available for 9x12 SAE with 4-ounce first-class postage. Guidelines available for SASE.

NONFICTION Needs Young adults: arts/crafts, careers, how-to, interview/profile, multicultural (all theater-related). Does not want to see academic treatises. **Buys 50 mss/year.** Submit complete ms. Length: 750-3,000 words. **Pays $50-500 for articles.**

FICTION Young adults: drama (one-act and full-length plays). "We prefer unpublished scripts that have been produced at least once." Does not want to see plays that show no understanding of the conventions of the theater. No plays for children, no Christmas or didactic "message" plays. Submit complete ms. Buys 5-9 plays/year. Emerging playwrights have better chances with résumé of credits. Length: 750-3,000 words. **Pays $100-500 for plays.**

TIPS "Obtain our writer's guidelines and look at recent back issues. The best way to break in is to know our audience—drama students, teachers, and others interested in theater—and write for them. Writers who have some practical experience in theater, especially in technical areas, have an advantage, but we'll work with anybody who has a good idea. Some freelancers have become regular contributors."

EMMY MAGAZINE

Academy of Television Arts & Sciences, 5220 Lankershim Blvd., North Hollywood CA 91601. **E-mail:** emmymag@emmys.org. **Website:** www.emmymagazine.com; www.emmys.tv/emmy-magazine. **Contact:** Juan Morales, editor-in-chief; Gail Polevoi, editor. **90% freelance written. Prefers to work with published/established writers.** Bimonthly magazine on television for TV professionals. Circ. 14,000. Byline given. Pays on publication or within 6 months. Offers 25% kill fee. Publishes ms an average of 4 months after acceptance. Accepts queries by mail. Responds in 1 month to queries. Sample copy for sae with 9x12 envelope and 6 first-class stamps. Guidelines online. **NONFICTION** Query with published clips. Length: 1,500-2,000 words. **Pays $1,000-1,200.**

COLUMNS/DEPARTMENTS Mostly written by regular contributors, but newcomers can break in with filler items with In the Mix or short profiles in Labors of Love. Length: 250-500 words, depending on department. Query with published clips. **Pays $250-500.**

TIPS "Please review recent issues before querying us. Query with published, television related clips. No fanzine, academic, or nostalgic approaches, please. Demonstrate experience in covering the business of television and your ability to write in a lively and compelling manner about programming trends and new technology. Identify fascinating people behind the scenes, not just in the executive suites, but in all ranks of the industry."

MAKE-UP ARTIST MAGAZINE

12808 NE 95th St., Vancouver WA 98682. (360)882-3488. **E-mail:** heatherw@kpgmedia.com. **Website:** www.makeupmag.com; www.makeup411.com; www.imats.net. **Contact:** Heather Wisner, managing editor; Michael Key, publisher/editor-in-chief. **90% freelance written.** Bimonthly magazine covering all types of professional make-up artistry. Audience is a mixture of high-level make-up artists, make-up students, and movie buffs. Writers should be comfortable with technical writing, and should have substantial knowledge of at least 1 area of makeup, such as effects or fashion. This is an entertainment-industry magazine, so writing should have an element of fun and storytelling. Good interview skills required. Estab. 1996. Circ. 16,000. Byline given. Pays within 30 days of publication. No kill fee. Editorial lead time 6 weeks. Submit seasonal material 2 months in advance. Accepts queries by e-mail. Accepts simultaneous submissions. Sample copy for $7. Guidelines available via e-mail. **NONFICTION** Needs features, how-to, new products, photo features, profile. "Does not want fluff pieces about consumer beauty products." **Buys 20+ mss/year.** Query with published clips. Length: 500-3,000 words. **Pays 20-50¢/word.** Sometimes pays expenses of writers on assignment.

PHOTOS Send photos. Captions, identification of subjects required. Reviews prints, GIF/JPEG files. Negotiates payment individually.

COLUMNS/DEPARTMENTS Cameo (short yet thorough look at a make-up artist not covered in a feature story), 800 words (15 photos); Lab Tech (how-to advice for effects artists, usually written by a current make-up artist working in a lab), 800 words (3 photos); Backstage (analysis, interview, tips, and behind the scenes info on a theatrical production's make-up), 800 words (3 photos). **Buys 30 columns/year. mss/year.** Query with published clips. **Pays $100.**

TIPS "Read books about professional make-up artistry (see makeupmag.com/shop). Read online interviews with make-up artists. Read make-up oriented mainstream magazines, such as *Allure*. Read *Cinefex* and other film-industry publications. Meet and talk to make-up artists and make-up students."

SCREEN MAGAZINE

Screen Enterprises, Inc., 676 N. LaSalle Blvd., #501, Chicago IL 60654. (312)640-0800. **Fax:** (312)640-1928. **E-mail:** editor@screenmag.com. **Website:** www.screenmag.com. **Contact:** Andrew Schneider, editor. **5% freelance written.** Biweekly Chicago-based trade magazine covering advertising and film production in the Midwest and national markets. *Screen* is written for Midwest producers (and other creatives involved) of commercials, AV, features, independent corporate, and multimedia. Estab. 1979. Circ. 15,000. Byline given. Pays on publication. No kill fee. Accepts queries by e-mail. Responds in 3 weeks to queries. Sample copy online.

NONFICTION Needs interview, new product, technical. No general AV; nothing specific to other markets; no no-brainers or opinion. **Buys 26 mss/year.** Query with published clips. Length: 750-1,500 words. **Pays $50.**

PHOTOS Send photos. Captions required. Reviews prints. Offers no additional payment for photos accepted with ms.

TIPS "Our readers want to know facts and figures. They want to know the news about a company or an individual. We provide exclusive news of this market, in as much depth as space allows without being boring, with lots of specific information and details. We write knowledgably about the market we serve. We recognize the film/video-making process is a difficult one because it 1) is often technical, 2) has implications not immediately discerned."

TRADE JOURNALS

$ SOUTHERN THEATRE

Southeastern Theatre Conference, P.O. Box 9868, 3309 Northampton Dr., Greensboro NC 27429-0868. (336)292-6041. **E-mail:** deanna@setc.org. **Website:** www.setc.org/southern-theatre. **Contact:** Deanna Thompson, editor. **100% freelance written.** Quarterly magazine covering all aspects of theater in the Southeast, from innovative theater companies, to important trends, to people making a difference in the region. All stories must be written in a popular magazine style but with subject matter appropriate for theater professionals (not the general public). The audience includes members of the Southeastern Theatre Conference, founded in 1949 and the nation's largest regional theater organization. These members include individuals involved in professional, community, college/university, children's, and secondary school theater. The magazine also is purchased by more than 100 libraries. Estab. 1962. Circ. 4,200. Byline given. Pays on publication. No kill fee. Publishes ms an average of 3 months after acceptance. Editorial lead time 3 months. Submit seasonal material 6 months in advance. Accepts queries by mail, e-mail. Responds in 3 months to queries. Responds in 6 months to mss. Sample copy for $10. Guidelines online.

NONFICTION Needs general interest, innovative theaters and theater programs, trend stories, interview, people making a difference in Southeastern theater. Special issues: Playwriting (Fall issue, all stories submitted by January 1). No scholarly articles. **Buys 15-20 mss/year.** Send complete ms. Length: 1,000-3,000 words. **Pays $50 for feature stories.**

PHOTOS State availability of or send photos. Captions, identification of subjects, model releases required. Reviews transparencies, prints. Offers no additional payment for photos accepted with ms.

COLUMNS/DEPARTMENTS *Outside the Box* (innovative solutions to problems faced by designers and technicians), 800-1,000 words; *400 Words* (column where the theater professionals can sound off on issues), 400 words; 800-1,000 words; *Words, Words, Words* (reviews of books on theater), 400 words. Query or send complete ms **No payment for columns.**

TIPS "Look for a theater or theater person in your area that is doing something different or innovative that would be of interest to others in the profession, then write about that theater or person in a compelling way. We also are looking for well-written trend stories (talk to theaters in your area about trends that are affecting them), and we especially like stories that help our readers do their jobs more effectively. Send an e-mail detailing a well-developed story idea, and ask if we're interested."

FARM

AGRICULTURAL EQUIPMENT

$ AG WEEKLY

Lee Agri-Media, P.O. Box 918, Bismarck ND 58501. (701)255-4905. **Fax:** (701)255-2312. **E-mail:** mark.conlon@lee.net. **Website:** www.agweekly.com. **Contact:** Mark Conlon, editor. **40% freelance written.** *Ag Weekly* is an agricultural publication covering production, markets, regulation, politics. Writers need to be familiar with Idaho agricultural commodities. No printed component; website with 6,000 monthly unique visitors; weekly e-mail newsletter with 3,000 subscribers. Byline given. Pays on publication. Publishes ms an average of 1 month after acceptance. Editorial lead time 1 month. Submit seasonal material 1 month in advance. Accepts queries by e-mail. YesAccepts simultaneous submissions. Responds in 2 weeks to queries. Responds in 1 month to mss. Sample copy online. Guidelines with #10 SASE.

NONFICTION Needs interview, new product, opinion, travel, ag-related. Does not want anything other than local/regional ag-related articles. No cowboy poetry. **Buys 100 mss/year.** Query. Length: 250-700 words. **Pays $40-70.**

PHOTOS State availability. Captions required. Reviews GIF/JPEG files. Offers $10/photo.

$$ IMPLEMENT & TRACTOR

Farm Journal, 222 S. Jefferson St., Mexico MO 65265. (573)581-9641. **E-mail:** meckelkamp@farmjournal.com; editors@agweb.com. **Website:** www.implementandtractor.com. **Contact:** Margy Eckelkamp. **10% freelance written.** Bimonthly magazine covering the agricultural equipment industry. *Implement & Tractor* offers equipment reviews and business news for agricultural equipment dealers, ag equipment manufacturers, distributors, and aftermarket suppliers. Estab. 1895. Circ. 5,000. Byline given. Pays on publication. No kill fee. Publishes ms an average of 3-4 months after acceptance. Editorial lead time 2 months. Accepts queries by mail, e-mail. Responds in 2 months to queries. Sample copy for $6.

CROPS AND SOIL MANAGEMENT

⚠️💲 AMERICAN/WESTERN GROWER

Meister Media Worldwide, 37733 Euclid Ave., Willoughby OH 44094. (440)942-2000. **E-mail:** bdsparks@meistermedia.com; deddy@meistermedia.com. **Website:** www.fruitgrower.com. **Contact:** Brian Sparks, editor; David Eddy, editor. **3% freelance written.** Annual magazines covering commercial fruit growing. Estab. 1880. Circ. 44,000. Byline given. Pays on publication. No kill fee. Publishes ms an average of 4 months after acceptance. Editorial lead time 2 months. Submit seasonal material 4 months in advance. Accepts queries by mail, e-mail, fax, phone. Responds in 2 weeks to queries. Responds in 2 months to mss. Sample copy and writer's guidelines free.

NONFICTION Needs how-to, better grow fruit crops. **Buys 6-10 mss/year.** Send complete ms. Length: 800-1,200 words. **Pays $200-250.** Sometimes pays expenses of writers on assignment.

PHOTOS Send photos. Reviews prints, slides. Negotiates payment individually.

TIPS "How-to articles are best."

⚠️💲 COTTON GROWER MAGAZINE

Meister Media Worldwide, Cotton Media Group, 8000 Centerview Pkwy., Suite 114, Cordova TN 38018-4246. (901)756-8822. **E-mail:** mccue@meistermedia.com. **Website:** www.cotton247.com. **Contact:** Mike McCue, editor. **5% freelance written.** Monthly magazine covering cotton production, cotton markets, and related subjects. Circ. 43,000. Byline given. Pays on acceptance. No kill fee. Publishes ms an average of 2 months after acceptance. Editorial lead time 2 months. Submit seasonal material 2 months in advance. Accepts queries by mail, e-mail, fax, phone. Accepts simultaneous submissions. Sample copy free.

○ Readers are mostly cotton producers who seek information on production practices, equipment, and products related to cotton.

NONFICTION Needs interview, new product, photo feature, technical. No fiction or humorous pieces. **Buys 5-10 mss/year.** Query with published clips. Length: 500-800 words. **Pays $200-400.** Sometimes pays expenses of writers on assignment.

PHOTOS State availability. Captions, identification of subjects required. Reviews transparencies. Offers no additional payment for photos accepted with ms.

💲 FRUIT GROWERS NEWS

Great American Publishing, P.O. Box 128, Sparta MI 49345. (616)887-9008. **Fax:** (616)887-2666. **E-mail:** fgnedit@fruitgrowersnews.com. **Website:** www.fruitgrowersnews.com. **Contact:** Matt Milkovich, managing editor; Lee Dean, editorial director. **10% freelance written.** Monthly tabloid covering agriculture. "Our objective is to provide commercial fruit growers of all sizes with information to help them succeed." Estab. 1961. Circ. 16,429. Pays on publication. No kill fee. Publishes ms an average of 2 months after acceptance. Editorial lead time 1-2 months. Submit seasonal material 3 months in advance. Accepts queries by mail, e-mail, fax. Accepts simultaneous submissions. Responds in 2 weeks to queries. Responds in 1 month to mss. Sample copy free.

NONFICTION Needs general interest, interview, new product. No advertorials or other puff pieces. **Buys 25 mss/year.** Query with published clips and résumé. Length: 600-1,000 words. **Pays $150-250.** Sometimes pays expenses of writers on assignment.

PHOTOS Send photos. Captions required. Reviews prints. Offers $15/photo.

⚠️💲 GOOD FRUIT GROWER

Washington State Fruit Commission, 105 S. 18th St., #217, Yakima WA 98901. (509)575-2315. **E-mail:** casey.corr@goodfruit.com. **Website:** www.goodfruit.com. **Contact:** O. Casey Corr, managing editor. **10% freelance written.** Semi-monthly magazine covering tree fruit/grape growing. Estab. 1946. Circ. 11,000. Byline given. Pays on acceptance. Publishes ms an average of 2 months after acceptance. Accepts queries by mail, e-mail. Accepts simultaneous submissions. Responds in 1 week to queries. Responds in 1 month to mss. Sample copy free. Guidelines free.

NONFICTION Buys 20 mss/year. Query. Length: 500-1,500 words. **Pays 40-50¢/word.** Sometimes pays expenses of writers on assignment.

PHOTOS Contact: Jim Black. Reviews GIF/JPEG files. Negotiates payment individually.

TIPS "We want well-written, accurate information. We deal with our writers honestly and expect the same in return."

💲 GRAIN JOURNAL

Country Journal Publishing Co., 3065 Pershing Court, Decatur IL 62526. (800)728-7511. **E-mail:** ed@grainnet.com. **Website:** www.grainnet.com. **Contact:** Ed Zdrojewski, editor. **5% freelance written.** Bimonthly

try. The *Bulletin* is mailed free to commercial cattlemen who have purchased an Angus bull and had the registration transferred to them and to others who sign a request card. Estab. 1985. Circ. 65,000-70,000. Byline given. Pays on publication. No kill fee. Publishes ms an average of 3 months after acceptance. Editorial lead time 3 months. Submit seasonal material 3 months in advance. Accepts queries by mail, e-mail. Accepts simultaneous submissions. Responds in 3 weeks to queries. Responds in 3 months to mss. Sample copy for $5. Guidelines for #10 SASE.

NONFICTION Needs how-to, cattle production, interview, technical, cattle production. **Buys 10 mss/year.** Query with published clips. Length: 800-2,500 words. **Pays $50-600.** Pays expenses of writers on assignment.

PHOTOS Send photos. Identification of subjects required. Reviews 5×7 transparencies, 5×7 glossy prints. Offers $25/photo.

TIPS Read the publication and have a firm grasp of the commercial cattle industry and how the Angus breed fits in that industry.

$$$ ANGUS JOURNAL

Angus Productions, Inc., 3201 Frederick Ave., St. Joseph MO 64506-2997. (816)383-5270. **Fax:** (816)233-6575. **E-mail:** shermel@angusjournal.com. **Website:** www.angusjournal.com. **40% freelance written.** Monthly magazine covering Angus cattle. The *Angus Journal* is the official magazine of the American Angus Association. Its primary function as such is to report to the membership association activities and information pertinent to raising Angus cattle. Estab. 1919. Circ. 13,500. Byline given. Pays on publication. No kill fee. Publishes ms an average of 3 months after acceptance. Editorial lead time 2 months. Submit seasonal material 3 months in advance. Accepts queries by mail, e-mail, fax. Accepts simultaneous submissions. Responds in 3 weeks to queries. Responds in 2 months to mss. Sample copy for $5. Guidelines with #10 SASE.

NONFICTION Needs how-to, cattle production, interview, technical, related to cattle. **Buys 20-30 mss/year.** Query with published clips. Length: 800-3,500 words. **Pays $50-1,000.** Pays expenses of writers on assignment.

PHOTOS Send photos. Identification of subjects required. Reviews 5×7 glossy prints. Offers $25-400/photo.

TIPS "Have a firm grasp of the cattle industry."

BACKYARD POULTRY

Countryside Publications, Ltd., 145 Industrial Dr., Medford WI 54451. (715)785-7979. **Fax:** (715)785-7414. **E-mail:** byp@tds.net; customerservice@backyardpoultrymag.com. **Website:** www.backyardpoultrymag.com. **Contact:** Ryan Slabaugh, editor. Bimonthly magazine covering breed selection, housing, management, health and nutrition, and other topics of interest to promote more and better raising of small-scale poultry. Query first.

$$ THE BRAHMAN JOURNAL

Carl and Victoria Lambert, 915 12th St., Hempstead TX 77445. (979)826-4347. **Fax:** (979)826-2007. **E-mail:** info@brahmanjournal.com; vlambert@brahmanjournal.com. **Website:** www.brahmanjournal.com. **Contact:** Victoria Lambert, editor. **10% freelance written.** Monthly magazine promoting, supporting, and informing the owners and admirers of American Brahman Cattle through honest and forthright journalism. *The Brahman Journal* provides timely and useful information about one of the largest and most dynamic breeds of beef cattle in the world. In each issue, *The Brahman Journal* reports on Brahman shows, events, and sales as well as technical articles and the latest research as it pertains to the Brahman Breed. Estab. 1971. Circ. 4,000. Byline given. Pays on publication. No kill fee. Publishes ms an average of 2 months after acceptance. Submit seasonal material 3 months in advance. Sample copy for SAE with 9x12 envelope and 5 first-class stamps.

NONFICTION Needs general interest, historical, interview. Special issues: See the Calendar online for special issues. **Buys 3-4 mss/year.** Query with published clips. Length: 1,200-3,000 words. **Pays $100-250.**

REPRINTS Send typed ms with rights for sale noted. Pays 50% of amount paid for an original article.

PHOTOS Photos needed for article purchase. Send photos. Captions required. Reviews 4x5 prints. Offers no additional payment for photos accepted with ms.

TIPS "Since *The Brahman Journal* is read around the world, being sent to 48 different countries, it is important that the magazine contain a wide variety of information. *The Brahman Journal* is read by seed stock producers, show ring competitors, F-1 breeders and Brahman lovers from around the world."

$$ THE CATTLEMAN

Texas and Southwestern Cattle Raisers Association, 1301 W. Seventh St., Suite 201, Fort Worth TX 76102. **E-mail:** ehbrisendine@tscra.org. **Website:** www.thecattlemanmagazine.com. **Contact:** Ellen H. Brisendine, editor. **25% freelance written.** Monthly magazine covering the Texas/Oklahoma beef cattle industry. Specializes in in-depth, management-type articles related to range and pasture, beef cattle production, animal health, nutrition, and marketing. Wants "how-to" articles. Estab. 1914. Circ. 15,400. Byline given. Pays on acceptance. No kill fee. Publishes ms an average of 2 months after acceptance. Editorial lead time 2 months. Submit seasonal material 6 months in advance. Accepts queries by mail, e-mail. Sample copy free. Guidelines online.

NONFICTION Needs how-to, interview, new product, personal experience, technical, ag research. Special issues: Editorial calendar themes include: Horses (January); Range and Pasture (February); Livestock Marketing (July); Hereford and Wildlife (August); Feedlots (September); Bull Buyers (October); Ranch Safety (December). Does not want to see anything not specifically related to beef production in the Southwest. **Buys 20 mss/year.** Query with published clips. Length: 1,500-2,000 words. **Pays $200-350 for assigned articles. Pays $100-350 for unsolicited articles.** Sometimes pays expenses of writers on assignment.

PHOTOS Identification of subjects required. Reviews transparencies, prints, digital files. Offers no additional payment for photos accepted with ms.

TIPS "Subscribers said they were most interested in the following topics in this order: range/pasture, property rights, animal health, water, new innovations, and marketing. *The Cattleman* prefers to work on an assignment basis. However, prospective contributors are urged to write the managing editor of the magazine to inquire of interest on a proposed subject. Occasionally, the editor will return a ms to a potential contributor for cutting, polishing, checking, rewriting, or condensing. Be able to demonstrate background/knowledge in this field. Include tearsheets from similar magazines."

$$ FEED LOT MAGAZINE

Feed Lot Magazine, Inc., P.O. Box 850, Dighton KS 67839. (620)397-2838. **Fax:** (620)397-2839. **E-mail:** feedlot@st-tcl.net. **Website:** www.feedlotmagazine.com. **60% freelance written.** Bimonthly magazine that provides readers with the most up-to-date information on the beef industry in concise, easy-to-read articles designed to increase overall awareness among the feedlot community. "The editorial information content fits a dual role: large feedlots and their related cow/calf operations, and large 500pl cow/calf, 100pl stocker operations. The information covers all phases of production from breeding, genetics, animal health, nutrition, equipment design, research through finishing fat cattle. *Feed Lot* publishes a mix of new information and timely articles which directly affect the cattle industry." Estab. 1992. Circ. 12,000. Byline given. Pays on publication. Offers 50% kill fee. Publishes ms an average of 2 months after acceptance. Editorial lead time 2 months. Submit seasonal material 6 months in advance. Accepts queries by mail, e-mail, fax. Responds in 1 month to queries. Sample copy and writer's guidelines e-mailed.

NONFICTION Needs interview, new product, cattle-related, photo feature. Send complete ms; original material only. Length: 100-700 words. **Pays 30¢/word.**

PHOTOS State availability of or send photos. Captions, model releases required. Reviews contact sheets. Negotiates payment individually.

TIPS "Know what you are writing about—have a good knowledge of the subject."

$ SHEEP! MAGAZINE

Countryside Publications, Ltd., 145 Industrial Dr., Medford WI 54451. (715)785-7979; (800)551-5691. **Fax:** (715)785-7414. **E-mail:** sheepmag@tds.net; singersol@countrysidemag.com. **Website:** www.sheepmagazine.com. **Contact:** Nathan Griffith, editor. **35% freelance written. Prefers to work with published/established writers.** Bimonthly magazine published in north-central Wisconsin. Estab. 1980. Circ. 11,000. Byline given. Pays on publication. Offers $30 kill fee. Submit seasonal material 3 months in advance.

💬 Looking for clear, concise, useful information for sheep raisers who have a few sheep to a 1,000 ewe flock.

NONFICTION Needs book excerpts, how-to, on innovative lamb and wool marketing and promotion techniques, efficient record-keeping systems, or specific aspects of health and husbandry, interview, on experienced sheep producers who detail the economics and management of their operation, new product, of value to sheep producers; should be written by someone who has used them, technical, on genetics health and nutrition. **Buys 80 mss/year.** Send complete ms. Length: 750-2,500 words. **Pays $45-150.**

PHOTOS Color photos (vertical compositions of sheep and/or people) for cover. 35mm photos or other visuals improve chances of a sale. Identification of subjects required.

TIPS "Send us your best ideas and photos! We love good writing!"

MANAGEMENT

$ AG JOURNAL

Arkansas Valley Publishing, 422 Colorado Ave., (P.O. Box 500), La Junta CO 81050. (719)384-1453. **E-mail:** publisher@ljtdmail.com; bcd@ljtdmail.com. **Website:** www.agjournalonline.com. **Contact:** Candi Hill, publisher/editor; Jennifer Justice, assistant editor. **20% freelance written.** Weekly journal covering agriculture. Estab. 1949. Circ. 11,000. Byline given. Pays on publication. No kill fee. Publishes ms an average of 2 weeks after acceptance. Editorial lead time 1 month. Submit seasonal material 1 month in advance. Accepts queries by e-mail. YesResponds in 2 weeks to queries. Sample copy and writer's guidelines free.

💬 The *Ag Journal* covers people, issues, and events relevant to agriculture producers in a 7-state region (Colorado, Kansas, Oklahoma, Texas, Wyoming, Nebraska, New Mexico).

NONFICTION Needs how-to, interview, new product, opinion, photo feature, technical. Query by e-mail only. **Pays 4¢/word.** Sometimes pays expenses of writers on assignment.

PHOTOS State availability. Captions, identification of subjects required. Offers $8/photo.

🌐 $ SMALLHOLDER MAGAZINE

Newsquest Media Group, 3 Falmouth Business Park, Bickland Water Rd., Falmouth Cornwall TR11 4SZ United Kingdom. (01)326-213338. **Fax:** (01)326-212084. **E-mail:** editorial@smallholder.co.uk. **Website:** www.smallholder.co.uk. **Contact:** Graham Smith. Smallholder magazine is the leading monthly publication for the small producer and self-reliant household and has a publishing history spanning more than 100 years. The magazine has a reputation for quality and informed editorial content, and back issues are highly collectable. It is available nationally, through newsagent sales, specialist retail outlets and by subscription. No kill fee. Accepts queries by e-mail. Sample copy online. Guidelines by e-mail.

NONFICTION Length: 700-1,400 words. **Pays 4£/word.**

PHOTOS Send photos. Reviews 300 dpi digital images. Pays £5-50.

MISCELLANEOUS FARM

$ $ ACRES U.S.A.

P.O. Box 301209, Austin TX 78703. (512)892-4400. **Fax:** (512)892-4448. **E-mail:** editor@acresusa.com. **Website:** www.acresusa.com. "Monthly trade journal written by people who have a sincere interest in the principles of organic and sustainable agriculture." Estab. 1970. Circ. 20,000. Byline given. Pays on publication. No kill fee. Editorial lead time 3 months. Submit seasonal material 6 months in advance. Accepts queries by mail, e-mail, fax. Accepts simultaneous submissions. Sample copy and writer's guidelines free.

NONFICTION Needs expose, how-to, personal experience. Special issues: Seeds (January), Poultry (March), Certified Organic (May), Livestock (June), Homesteading (August), Soil Fertility & Testing (October). Does not want poetry, fillers, product profiles, or anything with a promotional tone. **Buys about 50 mss/year.** Send complete ms. Length: 1,000-2,500 words. **Pays 10¢/word**

PHOTOS State availability of or send photos. Captions, identification of subjects required. Reviews GIF/JPEG/TIF files. Negotiates payment individually.

$ $ BEE CULTURE

P.O. Box 706, Medina OH 44256-0706. (330)725-6677; (800)289-7668. **Fax:** (330)725-5624. **E-mail:** kim@beeculture.com. **Website:** www.beeculture.com. **Contact:** Mr. Kim Flottum, editor. **50% freelance written.** Covers the natural science of honey bees. "Monthly magazine for beekeepers and those interested in the natural science of honey bees, with environmentally-oriented articles relating to honey bees or pollination." Estab. 1873. Pays on publication. No kill fee. Publishes ms an average of 4 months after acceptance. Accepts queries by mail, e-mail, fax, phone. Responds in 1 month to mss. Sample copy with 9x12 SASE and 5 first-class stamps. Guidelines and sample copy online.

NONFICTION Needs interview, personal experience, photo feature. No "How I Began Beekeeping" articles. Highly advanced, technical, and scientific abstracts accepted for review for quarterly Refered section. Length: 2,000 words average. **Pays $200-250.**

REPRINTS Send photocopy and information about when and where the material previously appeared. Pays about the same as for an original article, on negotiation.

PHOTOS Color prints, 5x7 standard, but 3x5 are OK. Electronic images encouraged. Digital JPEG, color only, at 300 dpi best, prints acceptable. Model release required. Photo captions preferred. Pays $50 for cover photos. Photos payment included with article payment.

TIPS "Do an interview story on commercial beekeepers who are cooperative enough to furnish accurate, factual information on their operations. Frequent mistakes made by writers in completing articles are that they are too general in nature and lack management knowledge."

🌑🌑🌑 PRODUCE BUSINESS

Phoenix Media Network Inc., P.O. Box 810425, Boca Raton FL 33481. (561)994-1118. **E-mail:** kwhitacre@ phoenixmedianet.com; info@producebusiness.com. **Website:** www.producebusiness.com. **Contact:** Ken Whitacre, publisher/editorial director. **90% freelance written.** Monthly magazine covering produce and floral marketing. Addresses the buying end of the produce/floral industry, concentrating on supermarkets, chain restaurants, etc. Estab. 1985. Circ. 16,000. Byline given. Pays 30 days after publication. Offers $50 kill fee. Editorial lead time 2 months. Accepts queries by e-mail. NoSample copy and guidelines free.

NONFICTION Does not want unsolicited articles. **Buys 150 mss/year.** Query with published clips. Length: 1,200-10,000 words. **Pays $240-1,200.** Pays expenses of writers on assignment.

REGIONAL FARM

🌑🌑 AMERICAN AGRICULTURIST

5227 Baltimore Pike, Littlestown PA 17340. (717)359-0150. **Fax:** (717)359-0250. **E-mail:** jvogel@farm-progress.com. **Website:** www.farmprogress.com. **20% freelance written.** Monthly magazine covering cutting-edge technology and news to help farmers improve their operations. Publishes cutting-edge technology with ready on-farm application. Estab. 1842. Circ. 32,000. Pays on publication. No kill fee. Publishes ms an average of 3 months after acceptance. Editorial lead time 3 months. Submit seasonal material

3 months in advance. Accepts queries by e-mail, fax. Responds in 2 weeks to queries. Responds in 1 month to mss. Guidelines for #10 SASE.

NONFICTION Needs how-to, humor, inspirational, interview, new product, technical, No stories without a strong tie to Mid-Atlantic farming. **Buys 20 mss/ year.** Query. Length: 500-1,000 words. **Pays $250-500.** Sometimes pays expenses of writers on assignment.

PHOTOS Send photos. Captions, identification of subjects, model releases required. Reviews transparencies, JPEG files. Offers $75-200/photo.

COLUMNS/DEPARTMENTS Country Air (humor, nostalgia, inspirational), 300-400 words. **Buys 12 mss/year.** Send complete ms. **Pays $100.**

🌑🌑 FLORIDA GROWER

Meister Media Worldwide, 37733 Euclid Ave., Willoughby OH 44094. (440)942-2000. **E-mail:** fgiles@ meistermedia.com; pprusnak@meistermedia.com. **Website:** www.growingproduce.com/floridagrower; www.meistermedia.com/publications/florida-grower. **Contact:** Frank Giles, editor; Paul Rusnak, managing editor. **10% freelance written.** Monthly magazine edited for the Florida farmer with commercial production interest primarily in citrus, vegetables, and other ag endeavors. Goal is to provide articles that update and inform on such areas as production, ag financing, farm labor relations, technology, safety, education, and regulation. Estab. 1907. Circ. 12,200. Byline given. Pays on publication. No kill fee. Editorial lead time 2 months. Submit seasonal material 3 months in advance. Accepts queries by mail, e-mail, fax, phone. Responds in 1 month to queries. Sample copy for SAE with 9x12 envelope and 5 First-Class stamps. Guidelines free.

NONFICTION Needs interview, photo feature, technical. Query with published clips. Length: 700-1,000 words. **Pays $150-250.**

PHOTOS Send photos.

🌑 THE LAND

Free Press Co., P.O. Box 3169, Mankato MN 56002-3169. (507)345-4523. **E-mail:** editor@thelandonline. com. **Website:** www.thelandonline.com. **40% freelance written.** Weekly tabloid covering farming and rural life in Minnesota and Northern Iowa. "Although we're not tightly focused on any one type of farming, our articles must be of interest to farmers. In other words, will your article topic have an impact on people who live and work in rural areas? Prefers to work with Minnesota or Iowa writers." Estab. 1976. Circ. 33,000. Byline given. Pays on acceptance. No kill fee. Publishes ms an average of 2 months after acceptance. Editorial lead time 2 months. Submit seasonal material 2 months in advance. Accepts queries by mail, e-mail. Responds in 3 weeks to queries. Responds in 2 months to mss. Sample copy free. Guidelines with #10 SASE.

NONFICTION Needs general interest, ag, how-to, crop, livestock production, marketing. **Buys 80 mss/year.** Query. Length: 500-750 words. **Pays $50-70 for assigned articles.**

PHOTOS Send photos. Reviews contact sheets. Negotiates payment individually.

COLUMNS/DEPARTMENTS Query. **Pays $10-50.**

TIPS "Be enthused about rural Minnesota and Iowa life and agriculture, and be willing to work with our editors. We try to stress relevance. When sending me a query, convince me the story belongs in a Minnesota farm publication."

FINANCE

⊙❸❸❸ ADVISOR'S EDGE

Rogers Media, Inc., 333 Bloor St. E., 6th Floor, Toronto ON M4W 1G6 Canada. **E-mail:** philip.porado@rci.rogers.com. **Website:** www.advisor.ca. **Contact:** Philip Porado, executive editor. Monthly magazine covering the financial industry (financial advisors and investment advisors). *Advisor's Edge* focuses on sales and marketing opportunities for the financial advisor (how they can build their business and improve relationships with clients). Estab. 1998. Circ. 36,000. Byline given. Pays on publication. Offers 25% kill fee. Publishes ms an average of 3 months after acceptance. Editorial lead time 3 months. Accepts queries by e-mail. Sample copy online.

NONFICTION Needs how-to, interview. No articles that aren't relevant to how a financial advisor does his/her job. **Buys 12 mss/year.** Query with published clips. Length: 1,500-2,000 words. **Pays $900 (Canadian).**

⊙❸❸❸❸ AFP EXCHANGE

Association for Financial Professionals, 4520 East-West Hwy., Suite 750, Bethesda MD 20814. (301)907-2862. **E-mail:** exchange@afponline.org. **Website:** www.afponline.org/exchange. **20% freelance written.** Monthly magazine covering corporate treasury, corporate finance, B2B payments issues, corporate risk management, accounting and regulatory issues from the perspective of corporations. Welcomes interviews with CFOs and senior level practitioners. Best practices and practical information for corporate CFOs and treasurers. Tone is professional, intended to appeal to financial professionals on the job. Most accepted articles are written by professional journalists and editors, many featuring high-level AFP members in profile and case studies. Estab. 1979. Circ. 25,000. Byline given. Pays on publication. Offers kill fee. Pays negotiable kill fee in advance. Editorial lead time 2 months. Submit seasonal material 3 months in advance. Accepts queries by e-mail. Responds in 1 week to queries. Responds in 1 month to mss.

NONFICTION Needs book excerpts, how-to, interview, personal experience, technical. No PR-type articles pointing to any type of product or solution. **Buys 3-4 mss/year.** Query. Length: 1,100-1,800 words. **Pays 75¢-$1 for assigned articles.**

COLUMNS/DEPARTMENTS Cash Flow Forecasting (practical tips for treasurers, CFOs); Financial Reporting (insight, practical tips); Risk Management (practical tips for treasurers, CFOs); Corporate Payments (practical tips for treasurers), all 1,000-1,300 words; Professional Development (success stories, career related, about high level financial professionals), 1,100 words. **Buys 10 mss/year.** Query. **Pays $75¢-$1/word.**

FILLERS Needs anecdotes. Length: 400-700 words. **Pays 75¢/word.**

TIPS "Accepted submissions deal with high-level issues relevant to today's corporate CFO or treasurer, including issues of global trade, global finance, accounting, M&A, risk management, corporate cash management, international regulatory issues, communications issues with corporate boards and shareholders, and especially new issues on the horizon. Preference given to articles by or about corporate practitioners in the finance function of mid-to large-size corporations in the U.S. or abroad. Also purchase articles by accomplished financial writers. Cannot accept content that points to any product, 'solution' or that promotes any vendor. Should not be considered a PR outlet. Authors may be required to sign agreement."

BAI BANKING STRATEGIES ONLINE

Bank Administration Institute (BAI), 115 S. LaSalle St., Suite 3300, Chicago IL 60606. (770)394-8615. **E-mail:** kcline@bai.org. **Website:** www.bai.org/bankingstrategies. **Contact:** Kenneth Cline, managing editor. **70% freelance written**. Magazine covering banking and financial services. Online magazine covers banking from a strategic and managerial perspective for its senior financial executive audience. Each issue includes in-depth trend articles and interviews with influential executives. Accepts queries by e-mail. Responds almost immediately. Guidelines online.

NONFICTION Needs how-to, articles that help institutions be more effective and competitive in the marketplace, interview, executive interviews. No topic queries, we assign stories to freelancers. I'm looking for qualifications as opposed to topic queries. I need experienced writers/reporters. **Buys 30 mss/year.** E-queries preferred. First send a one-page synopsis. Length: 600-1,000 words **Does not pay.**

TIPS Demonstrate ability and financial services expertise. I'm looking for freelancers who can write according to our standards, which are quite high.

$$$ COLLECTIONS & CREDIT RISK

SourceMedia, One State St. Plaza, 27th Floor, New York NY 10004. (212)803-8200. **Fax:** (212)843-9600. **E-mail:** darren.waggoner@sourcemedia.com. **Website:** www.collectionscreditrisk.com. **Contact:** Darren Waggoner, chief editor. **33% freelance written.** Monthly journal covering debt collections and credit risk management. *Collections & Credit Risk* is the only magazine that brings news and trends of strategic and competitive importance to collections and credit-policy executives who are driving the collections industry's growth and diversification in both commercial and consumer credit. These executives work for financial institutions, insurance companies, collections agencies, law firms and attorney networks, health-care providers, retailers, telecoms and utility companies, manufacturers, wholesalers, and government agencies. Estab. 1996. Circ. 30,000. Byline given. Pays on acceptance. Offers kill fee. Kill fee determined case by case. Publishes ms an average of 3 months after acceptance. Editorial lead time 3 months. Accepts queries by mail. Sample copy free or online.

NONFICTION Needs interview, technical, business news and analysis. No unsolicited submissions accepted—freelancers work on assignment only. **Buys 30-40 mss/year.** Query with published clips. Length: 1,000-2,500 words. **Pays $800-1,000.** Sometimes pays expenses of writers on assignment.

TIPS "This is a business news and analysis magazine focused on events and trends affecting the credit-risk management and collections professions. Our editorial approach is modeled after *Business Week, Forbes, Fortune, Wall Street Journal.* No fluff accepted."

$$$ CREDIT TODAY

P.O. Box 720, Roanoke VA 24004. (540)343-7500. **E-mail:** robl@credittoday.net; editor@credittoday.net. **Website:** www.credittoday.net. **Contact:** Rob Lawson, publisher. **10% freelance written.** Web-based publication covering business or trade credit. Estab. 1997. No byline given. Pays on acceptance. Publishes ms an average of 1 week after acceptance. Editorial lead time 1-2 months. Accepts queries by e-mail. NoSample copy free. Guidelines free.

NONFICTION Needs how-to, interview, technical. Does not want "puff" pieces promoting a particular product or vendor. **Buys 20 mss/year.** Send complete ms. Length: 700-1,800 words. **Pays $200-1,400.**

TIPS "Make pieces actionable, personable, and a quick read."

$$ CREDIT UNION MANAGEMENT

Credit Union Executives Society, 5510 Research Park Dr., Madison WI 53711. (608)271-2664. **E-mail:** lisa@cues.org; cues@cues.org. **Website:** www.cumanagement.org. **Contact:** Lisa Hochgraf, editor. **44% freelance written.** Monthly magazine covering credit union, banking trends, management, HR, and marketing issues. "Our philosophy mirrors the credit union industry of cooperative financial services." Estab. 1978. Circ. 7,413. Pays on acceptance. No kill fee. Publishes ms an average of 2 months after acceptance. Editorial lead time 3 months. Submit seasonal material 4 months in advance. Accepts queries by mail. Accepts simultaneous submissions. Responds in 2 weeks to queries; 1 month to mss. Sample copy and writer's guidelines free.

NONFICTION Needs book excerpts, how-to, be a good mentor/leader, recruit, etc., interview, technical. **Buys 74 mss/year.** Query with published clips. Length: 700-2,400 words. **$250-350 for assigned features.** Phone expenses only

COLUMNS/DEPARTMENTS Management Network (book/Web reviews, briefs), 300 words; e-marketing, 700 words; Point of Law, 700 words; Best Practices (new technology/operations trends), 700 words. Query with published clips.

TIPS "The best way is to e-mail an editor; include rèsumè, cover letter and clips. Knowledge of financial services is very helpful."

💲💲💲 THE FEDERAL CREDIT UNION

National Association of Federal Credit Unions, 3138 10th St. N., Arlington VA 22201. (703)522-4770; (800)336-4644. **Fax:** (703)524-1082. **E-mail:** msc@nafcu.org; sbroaddus@nafcu.org. **Website:** www.nafcu.org/tfcuonline. **Contact:** Susan Broaddus, managing editor. **30% freelance written.** Published bimonthly, *The Federal Credit Union* is the official publication of the National Association of Federal Credit Unions. The magazine is dedicated to providing credit union management, staff, and volunteers with in-depth information (HR, technology, security, board management, etc.) they can use to fulfill their duties and better serve their members. The editorial focus includes coverage of management issues, operations, and technology as well as volunteer-related issues. Looking for writers with financial, banking, or credit union experience, but will work with inexperienced (unpublished) writers based on writing skill. Estab. 1967. Circ. 8,000. Byline given. Pays on publication. No kill fee. Publishes ms an average of 3 months after acceptance. Submit seasonal material 5 months in advance. Accepts queries by mail, e-mail, fax. Accepts simultaneous submissions. Responds in 2 months to queries. Sample copy for SAE with 10x13 envelope and 5 first-class stamps. Guidelines for #10 SASE.

NONFICTION Needs humor, inspirational, interview. Query with published clips and SASE. Length: 1,200-2,000 words. **Pays $400-1,000.**

PHOTOS Send photos. Identification of subjects, model releases required. Reviews 35mm transparencies, 5x7 prints, high-resolution photos. Offers no additional payment for photos accepted with ms. Pays $50-500.

TIPS "We would like more articles on how credit unions are using technology to serve their members and more articles on leading-edge technologies they can use in their operations. If you can write on current trends in technology, human resources, or strategic planning, you stand a better chance of being published than if you wrote on other topics."

💲💲 SERVICING MANAGEMENT

Zackin Publications, P.O. Box 2180, Waterbury CT 06722. (800)325-6745. **Fax:** (203)262-4680. **E-mail:** pbarnard@sm-online.com. **Website:** www.sm-online.com. **Contact:** Patrick Barnard, editor. **15% freelance written.** Monthly magazine covering residential mortgage servicing. Estab. 1989. Circ. 20,000. Byline given. Pays on acceptance. No kill fee. Publishes ms an average of 2 months after acceptance. Accepts queries by mail, e-mail, fax, phone. Responds in 2 weeks to queries. Sample copy free. Guidelines online.

NONFICTION Needs how-to, interview, new product, technical. **Buys 10 mss/year.** Query. Length: 1,500-2,500 words.

PHOTOS State availability. Identification of subjects required. Reviews contact sheets. Offers no additional payment for photos accepted with ms.

COLUMNS/DEPARTMENTS Buys 5 mss/year. Query. **Pays $200.**

💲💲💲💲 USAA MAGAZINE

USAA, 9800 Fredericksburg Rd., San Antonio TX 78288. **E-mail:** usaamagazine@usaa.com. **Website:** www.usaa.com/maglinks. **80% freelance written.** Quarterly magazine covering financial security for USAA members. Conservative, common-sense approach to personal finance issues. Especially interested in how-to articles and pieces with actionable tips. Estab. 1970. Circ. 5.1 million. Byline given. Pays on acceptance. Offers 25% kill fee. Publishes ms an average of 4 months after acceptance. Editorial lead time 6 months. Submit seasonal material 6 months in advance. Accepts queries by e-mail. Responds in 6-8 weeks to queries. No mss accepted. Sample copy online. Guidelines by e-mail.

NONFICTION Needs general interest, (finance), historical, (military), how-to, (personal finance), interview, (military/financial), personal experience, (finance). No poetry, photos, lifestyle unrelated to military or personal finance. **Buys 20 mss/year.** Submit a detailed query letter explaining story idea and listing possible sources. Does not accept unsolicited mss. Length: 600-1,500 words. **Pays $750-1,500 for assigned articles.** Sometimes pays expenses of writers on assignment.

TIPS "Story must take a unique or innovative approach to the personal finance topic. Piece must be actionable and useful. (Not philosophical or academic.)"

FLORIST, NURSERIES AND LANDSCAPERS

💲💲 DIGGER

Oregon Association of Nurseries, 29751 S.W. Town Center Loop W., Wilsonville OR 97070. (503)682-

5089; (800) 342-6401. **Fax:** (503)682-5099. **E-mail:** ckipp@oan.org; info@oan.org. **Website:** www.oan. org. **Contact:** Curt Kipp, publications manager. **50% freelance written.** Monthly magazine covering nursery and greenhouse industry. *Digger* is a monthly magazine that focuses on industry trends, regulations, research, marketing, and membership activities. In August the magazine becomes *Digger Farwest Edition*, with all the features of *Digger* plus a complete guide to the annual Farwest Show, one of North America's top-attended nursery industry trade shows. Circ. 8,000. Byline given. Pays on receipt of copy. Offers 100% kill fee. Publishes ms an average of 2 months after acceptance. Editorial lead time 6 weeks. Submit seasonal material 2 months in advance. Accepts queries by mail, e-mail, fax, phone. Sample copy and writer's guidelines free.

NONFICTION Needs general interest, how-to, propagation techniques, other crop-growing tips, interview, personal experience, technical. Special issues: Farwest Edition (August): this is a triple-size issue that runs in tandem with our annual trade show (14,500 circulation for this issue). No articles not related or pertinent to nursery and greenhouse industry. **Buys 20-30 mss/year.** Query. Length: 800-2,000 words. **Pays $125-400 for assigned articles. Pays $100-300 for unsolicited articles.** Sometimes pays expenses of writers on assignment.

PHOTOS State availability. Captions, identification of subjects required. Reviews high-res digital images sent by e-mail or on CD preferred. Offers $25-150/ photo.

TIPS "Our best freelancers are familiar with or have experience in the horticultural industry. Some 'green' knowledge is a definite advantage. Our readers are mainly nursery and greenhouse operators and owners who propagate nursery stock/crops, so we write with them in mind."

❸ GROWERTALKS

Ball Publishing, 622 Town Rd., P.O. Box 1660, West Chicago IL 60186. (630)231-3675; (630)588-3401. **Fax:** (630)231-5254. **E-mail:** info@ballpublishing.com; jzurko@ballpublishing.com; cbeytes@growertalks. com. **Website:** www.growertalks.com. **Contact:** Jen Zurko, managing editor; Chris Beytes, editor. **50% freelance written.** Monthly magazine covering horticulture. *GrowerTalks* serves the commercial greenhouse grower. Editorial emphasis is on floricultural

crops: bedding plants, potted floral crops, foliage, and fresh cut flowers. Readers are growers, managers, and owners. Looking for writers who've had experience in the greenhouse industry. Estab. 1937. Circ. 9,500. Byline given. Pays on publication. No kill fee. Publishes ms an average of 3 months after acceptance. Editorial lead time 4 months. Submit seasonal material 3 months in advance. Accepts queries by mail, e-mail, fax. Responds in 1 month to queries. Sample copy and writer's guidelines free.

NONFICTION Needs how-to, time- or money-saving projects for professional flower/plant growers, interview, ornamental horticulture growers, personal experience, of a grower, technical, about growing process in greenhouse setting. No articles that promote only 1 product. **Buys 36 mss/year.** Query. Length: 1,200-1,600 words. **Pays $125 minimum for assigned articles. Pays $75 minimum for unsolicited articles.**

PHOTOS State availability. Captions, identification of subjects, model releases required. Reviews 2 1/2x2 1/2 slides and 3x5 prints. Negotiates payment individually.

TIPS "Discuss magazine with ornamental horticulture growers to find out what topics that have or haven't appeared in the magazine interest them."

❸❸ TREE CARE INDUSTRY MAGAZINE

Tree Care Industry Association, 136 Harvey Rd., Suite 101, Londonderry NH 03053. (800)733-2622 or (603)314-5380. **Fax:** (603)314-5386. **E-mail:** editor@ tcia.org. **Website:** www.tcia.org. **Contact:** Don Staruk, editor. **50% freelance written.** Monthly magazine covering tree care and landscape maintenance. Estab. 1990. Circ. 24,000. Byline given. Pays within 1 month of publication. No kill fee. Publishes mss an average of 3 months after acceptance. Editorial lead time 10 weeks. Submit seasonal material 3 months in advance. Accepts queries by e-mail. Responds within 2 days to queries. Responds in 2 months to mss. Sample copies: View digital version online. Guidelines free.

NONFICTION Needs book excerpts, historical, interview, new product, technical. **Buys 60 mss/year.** Query with published clips. Length: 900-3,500 words. **Pays negotiable rate.**

PHOTOS Send photos with submission by e-mail or FTP site. Captions, identification of subjects required. Reviews prints. Negotiate payment individually.

COLUMNS/DEPARTMENTS Buys 40 mss/year. Send complete ms. **Pays $100 and up.**

TIPS "Preference is given to writers with background and knowledge of the tree care industry; our focus is relatively narrow."

GOVERNMENT AND PUBLIC SERVICE

💲 AMPC TODAY

Associated Mail and Parcel Centers (AMPC), 5411 E. State St., #599, Rockford IL 61108. **Fax:** (815)316-8256. **E-mail:** hello@ampc.org; ellen.peters@ampc.org. **Website:** www.ampc.org. **Contact:** Jim Kitzmiller, executive director; Ellen Peters, editor. **85% freelance articles.** Bimonthly magazine covering mail and parcel industry/retail shipping stores. Readers are the owners and operators of retail shipping and business service stores. These are convenience stores for packing, shipping, and other services including mailbox rental and mail forwarding. The stores are both independent and franchise operated; they are small and generally family or owner operated. The biggest obstacle to success is for the owner to leave the store for training, networking, planning, managing, and sales. Estab. 1984. Circ. 2,400. Byline given. Pays on publication. 3 months from acceptance to publication. Editorial lead time: 3 months. Accepts queries by mail, e-mail. Accepts previously published submissions. Accepts simultaneous submissions. Sample copy online at website.

NONFICTION Needs essays, how-to, inspirational, interview, new product, technical, typical topics can be: packing, shipping, mailbox rentals, freight shipping, UPS, FedEx, DHL, USPS, bulk mailing, copy service, binding, laminating, retail fill items, packaging supplies, custom boxes, customer service, store profiles, and diversified profit centers. Send complete ms. Length: 500-2,000/words. **Pays $50-150 for assigned articles and for unsolicited articles.** Pays expenses sometimes (limit agreed upon in advance). Does not pay with contributor copies or other premiums rather than cash.

PHOTOS Send photos with submission. Requires identification of subjects. Review GIF/JPEG files. Offers no additional payment for photos accepted with ms.

COLUMNS/DEPARTMENTS Column pays $50-150.

TIPS "It is important that you be very knowledgeable about the subject of the mail and parcel industry along with retail you are covering. Our articles are usually written by store owners or vendors to the industry, but that is not a requirement. Our readers run the gamut of new store owners to 30-year veterans and the articles can be geared to anywhere in between, but must be accurate and engaging. Although best practices of store operations is important, our mission is to help our members become more successful, more profitable, and the articles should support that."

💲💲 AMERICAN CITY & COUNTY

Penton Media, 6151 Powers Ferry Rd. NW, Suite 200, Atlanta GA 30339. (770)618-0199. **Fax:** (770)618-0349. **E-mail:** bill.wolpin@penton.com; erin.greer@penton.com. **Website:** www.americancityandcounty.com. **Contact:** Bill Wolpin, editorial director; Erin Greer, managing editor. **40% freelance written.** Monthly magazine covering local and state government in the U.S. Estab. 1909. Circ. 65,000. Byline given. Pays on publication. Offers 25% kill fee. Publishes ms an average of 2 months after acceptance. Editorial lead time 3 months. Accepts queries by e-mail. Accepts simultaneous submissions. Sample copy online. Guidelines by e-mail.

🗨 *American City & County* is received by elected and appointed local and state government officials and public and private engineers. Included in the circulation list are administrators, supervisors and department heads of municipal, county, township, state, and special district governments. The magazine maintains its leadership position by providing these readers with news, government trends, policy alternatives, and operational solutions.

NONFICTION Needs new product, local and state government news analysis. **Buys 36 mss/year.** Query. Length: 600-2,000 words. **Pays 30¢/published word.** Sometimes pays expenses of writers on assignment.

PHOTOS State availability. Captions required. Reviews GIF/JPEG files. Negotiates payment individually.

COLUMNS/DEPARTMENTS Issues & Trends (local and state government news analysis), 500-700 words. **Buys 24 ms/year. mss/year.** Query. **Pays $150-250.**

TIPS "We use only third-person articles. We do not tell the reader what to do; we offer the facts and assume the reader will make his or her own informed decision. We cover city and county government and state highway departments. We do not cover state legislatures or the federal government, except as they affect local government."

AUSTRALASIAN PARKS AND LEISURE

P.O. Box 210, Bendigo Central VIC 3552 Australia. **E-mail:** journal@parkleisure.com.au. **Website:** www.parksleisure.com.au/journal. Quarterly magazine including general professional articles, notes, announcements, photographic features, refereed academic articles and more. *Australasian Parks and Leisure*'s major function is to provide a professional service to members of the 2 organizations and to provide opportunities for the dissemination of information and ideas in the field of parks and leisure. Guidelines online.

NONFICTION Needs general interest, how-to, technical. Query. Length: 1,000-1,500 words.

PHOTOS Captions, identification of subjects required. Reviews JPEG files (300 dpi).

TIPS "Articles should be written in direct, informative style, avoiding jargon and too much abstract material."

BLUE LINE MAGAZINE

12A-4981 Highway 7 East, Suite 254, Markham ON L3R 1N1 Canada. (905)640-3048. **Fax:** (905)640-7547. **E-mail:** blueline@blueline.ca. **Website:** www.blueline.ca. Monthly magazine keeping readers on the leading edge of law enforcement information, whether it be case law, training issues or technology trends. Estab. 1989. Circ. 12,000.

NONFICTION Needs general interest, how-to, interview, new product. Query.

COUNTY

Texas Association of Counties, 1210 San Antonio St., Austin TX 78701. (512)478-8753. **Fax:** (512)481-1240. **E-mail:** marias@county.org. **Website:** www.county.org. **Contact:** Maria Sprow, managing editor. **15% freelance written.** Bimonthly magazine covering county and state government in Texas. Provides elected and appointed county officials with insights and information that help them do their jobs and enhances communications among the independent office-holders in the courthouse. Estab. 1988. Circ. 5,500. Byline given. Pays on acceptance. No kill fee. Publishes ms an average of 2 months after acceptance. Editorial lead time 2 months. Submit seasonal material 4 months in advance. Accepts queries by mail, e-mail, phone. Responds in 2 weeks to queries. Responds in 1 month to mss. Sample copy and writer's guidelines for 8x10 SAE with 3 first-class stamps.

NONFICTION Needs historical, photo feature, government innovations. **Buys 5 mss/year.** Query with published clips. Length: 1,000-3,000 words. **Pays $500-700.** Sometimes pays expenses of writers on assignment.

PHOTOS State availability. Captions, identification of subjects, model releases required. Negotiates payment individually.

COLUMNS/DEPARTMENTS Safety; Human Resources; Risk Management (all directed toward education of Texas county officials), maximum length 1,000 words. **Buys 2 mss/year.** Query with published clips. **Pays $500.**

TIPS "Identify innovative practices or developing trends that affect Texas county officials, and have the basic journalism skills to write a multi-sourced, informative feature."

EVIDENCE TECHNOLOGY MAGAZINE

P.O. Box 555, Kearney MO 64060. **E-mail:** kmayo@evidencemagazine.com. **Website:** www.evidencemagazine.com. **Contact:** Kristi Mayo, editor. Bimonthly magazine providing news and information relating to the collection, processing, and preservation of evidence. This is a business-to-business publication, not a peer reviewed journal. Looks for mainstream pieces. Readers want general crime scenes and forensic science articles. Accepts queries by e-mail. Guidelines online.

NONFICTION Needs general interest, how-to, interview, new product, technical. Query. **Pays 2 contributor copies.**

PHOTOS Provide photos and/or illustrations. Reviews JPEG files (300 dpi or larger).

TIPS "Opening a dialogue with the editor will give you the opportunity to get guidelines on length, style, and deadlines."

FIRE APPARATUS & EMERGENCY EQUIPMENT

21-00 Rt. 208 South, Fair Lawn NJ 07410. (973)251-5050. **Fax:** (973)251-5065. **E-mail:** news@firemagazine.com. **Website:** www.fireapparatus.com. **Contact:** Robert Halton, editor-in-chief. Monthly magazine focused on fire trucks, tools, and new technology. Publishes the only monthly magazine devoted exclusively to the trucks, tools, equipment, and gear firefighters and emergency medical and rescue crews use. Pays on publication.

NONFICTION Needs general interest, how-to, new product, technical. Query. Send submissions written in Microsoft Word by e-mail as attachments. Length: Up to 2,000 words.

PHOTOS Most features are accompanied with photos and graphics. Photos should be high-res, generally 300 dpi, with a minimum requirement of 266 dpi at 9.75 inches wide.

TIPS "Most of our authors and photographers work or have backgrounds in emergency services or are associated with companies in the industry. We will consider unsolicited material, but it is best to query us if you have an idea before you start writing."

😊😊 FIRE CHIEF

Primedia Business, 330 N. Wabash Ave., Suite 2300, Chicago IL 60611. (312)595-1080. **Fax:** (312)595-0295. **E-mail:** lisa@firechief.com; sundee@firechief.com. **Website:** www.firechief.com. **Contact:** Lisa Allegretti, editor; Sundee Koffarnus; art director. **60% freelance written.** Monthly magazine covering the fire chief occupation. "*Fire Chief* is the management magazine of the fire service, addressing the administrative, personnel, training, prevention/education, professional development, and operational issues faced by chiefs and other fire officers, whether in paid, volunteer, or combination departments. We're potentially interested in any article that can help them do their jobs better, whether that's as incident commanders, financial managers, supervisors, leaders, trainers, planners, or ambassadors to municipal officials or the public." Estab. 1956. Circ. 53,000. Byline given. Pays on publication. Offers kill fee. Kill fee negotiable. Publishes ms an average of 6 months after acceptance. Editorial lead time 2 months. Submit seasonal material 4 months in advance. Accepts queries by mail, e-mail, fax. Responds in 1 month to queries. Responds in 2 months to mss. Sample copy and submission guidelines free.

NONFICTION Needs how-to, technical. "We do not publish fiction, poetry, or historical articles. We also aren't interested in straightforward accounts of fires or other incidents, unless there are one or more specific lessons to be drawn from a particular incident, especially lessons that are applicable to a large number of departments." **Buys 50-60 mss/year.** Query first with published clips. Length: 1,000-10,000 words.

Pays \$50-400. Sometimes pays expenses of writers on assignment.

PHOTOS State availability. Captions, identification of subjects required. Reviews transparencies, prints.

COLUMNS/DEPARTMENTS Training Perspectives; EMS Viewpoints; Sound Off; Volunteer Voice; all 1,000-1,800 words.

TIPS "Writers who are unfamiliar with the fire service are very unlikely to place anything with us. Many pieces that we reject are either too unfocused or too abstract. We want articles that help keep fire chiefs well informed and effective at their jobs."

FIRE ENGINEERING

PennWell Corporation, 21-00 Rt. 208 S., Fair Lawn NJ 07410-2602. (800)962-6484, ext. 5047. **E-mail:** dianer@pennwell.com. **Website:** www.fireengineering.com. **Contact:** Diane Rothschild, executive editor. Monthly magazine covering issues of importance to firefighters. Estab. 1877. Accepts queries by mail, e-mail. Responds in 2-3 months to mss. Guidelines online.

NONFICTION Needs how-to, new product, incident reports, training. Send complete ms.

PHOTOS Reviews electronic format only: JPEG/TIFF/EPS files (300 dpi).

COLUMNS/DEPARTMENTS Volunteers Corner; Training Notebook; Rescue Company; The Engine Company; The Truck Company; Fire Prevention Bureau; Apparatus; The Shops; Fire Service EMS; Fire Service Court; Speaking of Safety; Fire Commentary; Technology Today; and Innovations: Homegrown. Send complete ms.

😊😊 FIREHOUSE MAGAZINE

Cygnus Business Media, 1233 Janesville Ave., Fort Atkinson WI 53538. (800)547-7377. **E-mail:** lizfn@cygnuspub.com. **Website:** www.firehouse.com. **Contact:** Elizabeth Friszell-Nerouslas, managing editor. **85% freelance written. Works with a small number of new/unpublished writers each year.** Monthly magazine. *Firehouse* covers major fires nationwide, controversial issues and trends in the fire service, the latest firefighting equipment and methods of firefighting, historical fires, firefighting history and memorabilia. Fire-related books, fire safety education, hazardous-materials incidents, and the emergency medical services are also covered. Estab. 1976. Circ. 83,538 (print). Byline given. Pays on publication. No kill fee. Accepts queries by mail, e-mail, fax, online submission form.

Sample copy for SAE with 9x12 envelope and 8 first-class stamps.

○ "Our primary editorial objectives are to educate, inform and entertain our audience of 1.5 million career and volunteer firefighters and thousands of fire buffs."

NONFICTION Needs book excerpts, of recent books on fire, EMS, and hazardous materials, historical, great fires in history, fire collectibles, the fire service of yesteryear, how-to, fight certain kinds of fires, buy and maintain equipment, run a fire department, technical on almost any phase of firefighting, techniques, equipment, training, administration, trends in the fire service. No profiles of people or departments that are not unusual or innovative, reports of nonmajor fires, articles not slanted toward firefighters' interests. No poetry. **Buys 100 mss/year.** Query. "If you have any story ideas, questions, hints, tips, etc., please do not hesitate to call." Length: 500-3,000 words. The average length of each article is between 2-3 pages, including visuals. **Pays $50-400 for assigned articles.**

PHOTOS *Firehouse* is a visually-oriented publication. Please include photographs (color preferred) with captions (or a description of what is taking place in the photo), illustrations, charts or diagrams that support your ms. The highest priority is given to those submissions that are received as a complete package. Pays $25-200 for transparencies and color prints. Cannot accept negatives.

COLUMNS/DEPARTMENTS Training (effective methods); Book Reviews; Fire Safety (how departments teach fire safety to the public); Communicating (PR, dispatching); Arson (efforts to combat it). Length: 750-1,000 words. **Buys 50 mss/year.** Query or send complete ms. **Pays $100-300.**

TIPS "Have excellent fire service credentials and be able to offer our readers new information. Read the magazine to get a full understanding of the subject matter, the writing style, and the readers before sending a query or ms. Indicate sources for photos. Be sure to focus articles on firefighters."

FIRE PROTECTION CONTRACTOR

550 High St., Suite 220, Auburn CA 95603. (530)823-0706. **Fax:** (530)823-6937. **E-mail:** info@fpcmag.com. **Website:** www.fpcmag.com. **Contact:** Brant Brumbeloe, editor. Monthly magazine for the benefit of fire protection contractors, engineers, designers, sprinkler fitters, apprentices, fabricators, manufacturers, and distributors of fire protection products used in automatic fire sprinkler systems. Estab. 1978. Guidelines online.

NONFICTION Needs general interest, how-to, interview, new product, technical. Query. E-mail articles in Word or WordPerfect format, or as an attachment in an e-mail. Length: 800 words.

FIRERESCUE

4180 La Jolla Village Dr., Suite 260, La Jolla CA 92037. (800)266-5367. **E-mail:** frm.editor@pennwell.com. **Website:** www.firefighternation.com. **Contact:** editor. "FireRescue covers the fire and rescue markets. Our 'Read It Today, Use It Tomorrow' mission weaves through every article and image we publish. Our readers consist of fire chiefs, company officers, training officers, firefighters, and technical rescue personnel." Estab. 1997. Circ. 50,000. Pays on publication. Accepts queries by mail, e-mail. Responds in 1 month to mss. Guidelines online.

NONFICTION Needs general interest, how-to, interview, new product, technical. "All story ideas must be submitted with a cover letter that outlines your qualifications and includes your name, full address, phone, and e-mail address. We accept story submissions in 1 of the following 2 formats: query letters and mss." Length: 800-2,200 words. **Pays $100—$200 for features.**

PHOTOS Looks for "photographs that show firefighters in action, using proper techniques and wearing the proper equipment. Submit timely photographs that show the technical aspects of firefighting and rescue. ". Digital images in JPEG, TIFF, or EPS format at 72 dpi for initial review. We require 300 dpi resolution for publication. If you send images as attachments via e-mail, compress your files first.

TIPS "Read back issues of the magazine to learn our style. Research back issues to ensure we haven't covered your topic within the past three years. Read and follow the instructions on our guidelines page."

⊛⊛ LAW ENFORCEMENT TECHNOLOGY MAGAZINE

Cygnus Business Media, 1233 Janesville Ave., Fort Atkinson WI 53538. (800)547-7377. **E-mail:** officer@corp.officer.com; jonathan.kozlowski@cygnusb2b.com; news@corp.officer.com. **Website:** www.officer.com. **Contact:** Jonathan Kozlowski, editor. **40% freelance written.** Monthly magazine covering police management and technology. Estab. 1974. Circ.

30,000. Byline given. Pays on publication. No kill fee. Publishes ms an average of 4 months after acceptance. Editorial lead time 6 months. Responds in 1 month to queries. Responds in 2 months to mss. Guidelines free. **NONFICTION** Needs how-to, interview, photo feature, police management and training. **Buys 30 mss/year.** Query. Length: 1,200-2,000 words. **Pays $75-400 for assigned articles.**

REPRINTS Send typed ms with rights for sale noted and information about when and where the material previously appeared. Payment negotiable.

PHOTOS Send photos. Captions required. Reviews contact sheets, negatives, 5x7 or 8x10 prints. Offers no additional payment for photos accepted with ms.

TIPS "Writer should have background in police work or currently work for a police agency. Most of our articles are technical or supervisory in nature. Please query first after looking at a sample copy. Prefers mss, queries, and images be submitted electronically."

⊖⊖ PLANNING

American Planning Association, 205 N. Michigan Ave., Suite 1200, Chicago IL 60601. (312)431-9100. **Fax:** (312)786-6700. **E-mail:** slewis@planning.org. **Website:** www.planning.org. **Contact:** Sylvia Lewis, editor; Joan Cairney, art director. **30% freelance written.** Monthly magazine emphasizing urban planning for adult, college-educated readers who are regional and urban planners in city, state, or federal agencies or in private business, or university faculty or students. Estab. 1972. Circ. 44,000. Byline given. Pays on publication. No kill fee. Publishes ms an average of 2 months after acceptance. Accepts queries by mail, e-mail, fax. Responds in 5 weeks to queries. Guidelines online.

NONFICTION Special issues: Transportation Issue. Also needs news stories up to 500 words. **Buys 44 features and 33 news story mss/year.** Length: 500-3,000 words. **Pays $150-1,500.**

PHOTOS "We prefer authors supply their own photos, but we sometimes take our own or arrange for them in other ways.". State availability. Captions required. Pays $100 minimum for photos used on inside pages and $300 for cover photos.

⊖⊖ POLICE AND SECURITY NEWS

DAYS Communications, Inc., 1208 Juniper St., Quakertown PA 18951-1520. (215)538-1240. **Fax:** (215)538-1208. **E-mail:** dyaw@policeandsecuritynews.com. **Website:** www.policeandsecuritynews.com. **Contact:** David Yaw, publisher. **40% freelance written.**

Bimonthly periodical on public law enforcement and Homeland Security. "Our publication is designed to provide educational and entertaining information directed toward management level. Technical information written for the expert in a manner the nonexpert can understand." Estab. 1984. Circ. 24,000. Byline given. Pays on publication. No kill fee. Publishes ms an average of 2 months after acceptance. Accepts queries by mail, e-mail, fax, phone, online submission form. Accepts simultaneous submissions. Sample copy and writer's guidelines with 10x13 SASE with $2.53 postage.

NONFICTION Contact: Al Menear, articles editor. Needs exposè, historical, how-to, humor, interview, opinion, personal experience, photo feature, technical. **Buys 12 mss/year.** Query. Length: 200-2,500 words. **Pays 10¢/word. Sometimes pays in trade-out of services.**

REPRINTS Send tearsheet, photocopy or typed ms with rights for sale noted and information about when and where the material previously appeared.

PHOTOS State availability. Reviews 3x5 prints. Offers $10-50/photo.

FILLERS Needs facts, newsbreaks, short humor. **Buys 6 mss/year.** Length: 200-2,000 words. **10¢/word.**

THE POLICE CHIEF

International Association of Chiefs of Police, 44 Canal Center Plaza, Suite 200, Alexandria VA 22314. (703)836-6767. **Fax:** (703)836-4543. **E-mail:** dgudakunst@theiacp.org. **E-mail:** submissions@theiacp.org. **Website:** www.policechiefmagazine.org. **Contact:** Danielle Gudakunst, managing editor. Monthly magazine covering law enforcement issues. Articles are contributed by practitioners in law enforcement or related fields. Mss must be original work, previously unpublished and not simultaneously submitted to another publisher. No word rate is paid or other remuneration given. Contributors' opinions and statements are not purported to define official IACP policy or imply IACP endorsement. Byline given. Responds in 3-6 months Guidelines online at website.

NONFICTION Needs general interest, administration, innovative techniques, new technological developments/applications, success stories, operational procedures, research, and other topics of interest to law enforcement administrators and practitioners. Authors are encouraged to submit via e-mail. Brief biographical sketch of each author containing author's name, position title, agency, and complete mailing address must

accompany mss. 2,000-4,000/words. **Byline credit and 5 complimentary copies of issue with your article.**
PHOTOS Photos encouraged.

$$$$ YOUTH TODAY

Kennesaw State University, 1000 Chastain Rd., MD 2212, Bldg. 22, Kennesaw GA 30144. (678)797-2899. **E-mail:** jfleming@youthtoday.org. **Website:** www.youthtoday.org. **Contact:** John Fleming, editor. **50% freelance written.** Bi-monthly newspaper covering businesses that provide services to youth. Audience is people who run youth programs—mostly nonprofits and government agencies—who want help in providing services and getting funding. Estab. 1994. Circ. 9,000. Byline given. Pays on publication. Offers $200 kill fee for features. Editorial lead time 2 months. Accepts queries by mail, e-mail, or disk. Accepts simultaneous submissions. Responds in 2 weeks to queries. Responds in 1 month to mss. Sample copy for $5. Guidelines online.

💬 "Our freelance writers work for or have worked for daily newspapers, or have extensive experience writing for newspapers and magazines."

NONFICTION Needs exposè, general interest, technical. "No feel-good stories about do-gooders. We examine the business of youth work." **Buys 5 mss/year.** Query. Send rèsumè, short cover letter, clips. Length: 600-2,500 words. **Pays $150-2,000 for assigned articles.** Pays expenses of writers on assignment.
PHOTOS Identification of subjects required. Offers no additional payment for photos accepted with ms.
COLUMNS/DEPARTMENTS "*Youth Today* also publishes 750-word guest columns, called Viewpoints. These pieces can be based on the writer's own experiences or based on research, but they must deal with an issue of interest to our readership and must soundly argue an opinion, or advocate for a change in thinking or action within the youth field."
TIPS "Business writers have the best shot. Focus on evaluations of programs, or why a program succeeds or fails. Please visit online."

GROCERIES AND FOOD PRODUCTS

$$$ CONVENIENCE DISTRIBUTION

American Wholesale Marketers Association, 2750 Prosperity Ave., Suite 530, Fairfax VA 22031. (703)208-3358. **Fax:** (703)573-5738. **E-mail:** info@awmanet.org; joanf@awmanet.org. **Website:** www.awmanet.org. **Contact:** Joan Fay, associate publisher and editor. **70% freelance written.** Magazine published 10 times/year. See website for editorial calendar. Covers trends in candy, tobacco, groceries, beverages, snacks, and other product categories found in convenience stores, grocery stores, and drugstores, plus distribution topics. Contributors should have prior experience writing about the food, retail, and/or distribution industries. Editorial includes a mix of columns, departments, and features (2-6 pages). Also covers AWMA programs. Estab. 1948. Circ. 11,000. Byline given. Pays on acceptance. No kill fee. Publishes ms an average of 2 months after acceptance. Editorial lead time 3-4 months. Accepts queries by e-mail only. Guidelines online.
NONFICTION Needs how-to, technical, industry trends, also profiles of distribution firms. No comics, jokes, poems, or other fillers. **Buys 40 mss/year.** Query with published clips. Length: 1,200-3,600 words. **Pays 50¢/word.** Pays expenses of writers on assignment.
PHOTOS Authors must provide artwork (with captions) with articles.
TIPS "We're looking for reliable, accurate freelancers with whom we can establish a long-term working relationship. We need writers who understand this industry. We accept very few articles on speculation. Most are assigned. To consider a new writer for an assignment, we must first receive his or her résumé , at least 2 writing samples, and references."

$$$$ FOOD PRODUCT DESIGN MAGAZINE

P.O. Box 3439, Northbrook IL 60065-3439. (480)990-1101 ext. 1241; (800)581-1811. **E-mail:** lkuntz@vpico.com. **Website:** www.foodproductdesign.com. **Contact:** Lynn A. Kuntz, editor-in-chief. **50% freelance written.** Monthly magazine covering food processing industry. Written for food technologists by food technologists. No food service/restaurant, consumer, or recipe development. Official media for SupplySide, *Food Product Design* delivers practical, use-it-now, take-it-to-the-bench editorial for product development professionals, as well as market intelligence and analysis of industry news for the executive-level reader. *Food Product Design* is the industry's leading product development content and information source. Estab. 1991. Circ. 30,000. Byline given. Pays on acceptance. Publishes ms an average of 2 months after acceptance. Editorial lead time 4 months. Sample copy for SAE with 9x12 envelope and 5 first-class stamps.

NONFICTION Needs technical. **Buys 30 mss/year.** Length: 1,500-7,000 words. **Pays $100-1,500.** Sometimes pays expenses of writers on assignment.

REPRINTS Accepts previously published submissions, depending on where it was published.

PHOTOS State availability. Captions required. Reviews transparencies, prints. Offers no additional payment for photos accepted with ms.

COLUMNS/DEPARTMENTS Pays $100-500.

TIPS "If you haven't worked in the food industry in research and development, or QA/QC, don't bother to call us. If you can't communicate technical information in a way that is clear, easy-to-understand, and well organized, don't bother to call us. While perfect grammar is not expected, good grammar and organization is."

$ FRESH CUT MAGAZINE

Great American Publishing, P.O. Box 128, 75 Applewood Dr., Suite A, Sparta MI 49345. (616)887-9008. **Fax:** (616)887-2666. **E-mail:** fcedit@freshcut.com. **Website:** www.freshcut.com. **Contact:** Lee Dean, editorial director. **20% freelance written.** Monthly magazine covering the value-added and pre-cut fruit and vegetable industry. Interested in articles that focus on what different fresh-cut processors are doing. Estab. 1993. Circ. 16,000. Byline given. Pays on publication. No kill fee. Publishes ms an average of 2 months after acceptance. Editorial lead time 2 months. Accepts queries by mail, e-mail, fax, phone, online submission form. Responds in 1 month to queries. Responds in 2 months to mss. Sample copy for SAE with 9x12 envelope. Guidelines for #10 SASE.

NONFICTION Needs historical, new product, opinion, technical. **Buys 2-4 mss/year.** Query with published clips.

REPRINTS Send tearsheet with rights for sale noted and information about when and where the material previously appeared. Pays 50% of amount paid for an original article.

PHOTOS Send photos. Identification of subjects required. Reviews transparencies. Offers no additional payment for photos accepted with ms.

COLUMNS/DEPARTMENTS Packaging; Food Safety; Processing/Engineering. **Buys 20 mss/year.** Query. **Pays $125-200.**

$$ THE PRODUCE NEWS

800 Kinderkamack Rd., Suite 100, Oradell NJ 07649. (201)986-7990. **Fax:** (201)986-7996. **E-mail:** groh@theproducenews.com. **Website:** www.theproducenews.com. **Contact:** John Groh, editor/publisher. **10% freelance written. Works with a small number of new/unpublished writers each year.** Weekly magazine for commercial growers and shippers, receivers, and distributors of fresh fruits and vegetables, including chain store produce buyers and merchandisers. Estab. 1897. Pays on publication. No kill fee. Publishes ms an average of 2 weeks after acceptance. Accepts queries by mail, e-mail. Responds in 1 month to queries. Sample copy and writer's guidelines for 10x13 SAE and 4 first-class stamps.

NONFICTION Query. **Pays $1/column inch minimum.** Sometimes pays expenses of writers on assignment.

PHOTOS B&W glossies or color prints. Pays $8-10/photo.

TIPS "Stories should be trade oriented, not consumer oriented. As our circulation grows, we are interested in stories and news articles from all fresh-fruit-growing areas of the country."

$$ PRODUCE RETAILER

Vance Publishing Corp., 10901 West 84th Ter. Suite 200, Lenexa KS 66214. (913) 438-0603; (512)906-0733. **E-mail:** pamelar@produceretailer.com; treyes@produceretailer.com. **Website:** produceretailer.com. **Contact:** Pamela Riemenschneider, editor; Tony Reyes, art director. **10% freelance written.** Monthly magazine. "*Produce Merchandising* is the only monthly journal on the market that is dedicated solely to produce merchandising information for retailers. Our purpose is to provide information about promotions, merchandising, and operations in the form of ideas and examples." Estab. 1988. Circ. 12,000. Byline given. Pays on acceptance. No kill fee. Publishes ms an average of 3 months after acceptance. Editorial lead time 3 months. Accepts queries by mail. Responds in 2 weeks to queries. Sample copy free.

NONFICTION Needs how-to, interview, new product, photo feature, technical, contact the editor for a specific assignment. **Buys 48 mss/year.** Query with published clips. Length: 1,000-1,500 words. **Pays $200-600.** Pays expenses.

PHOTOS State availability of or send photos. Captions, identification of subjects, model releases required. Reviews color slides and 3x5 or larger prints. Offers no additional payment for photos accepted with ms.

COLUMNS/DEPARTMENTS Contact: Contact editor for a specific assignment. **Buys 30 mss/year.** Query with published clips. **Pays $200-450.**

TIPS Send in clips and contact the editor with specific story ideas. Story topics are typically outlined up to a year in advance.

✪$$ WESTERN GROCER MAGAZINE

Mercury Publications Ltd., 1740 Wellington Ave., Winnipeg MB R3H 0E8 Canada. (204)954-2085, ext. 291; (800)337-6372. **Fax:** (204)954-2057. **E-mail:** rbradley@mercurypublications.ca. **Website:** www.westerngrocer.com. **Contact:** Robin Bradley, associate publisher and national account manager. **75% freelance written.** Bimonthly magazine covering the grocery industry. Reports for the Western Canadian grocery, allied non-food and institutional industries. Each issue features a selection of relevant trade news and event coverage from the West and around the world. Feature reports offer market analysis, trend views, and insightful interviews from a wide variety of industry leaders. *The Western Grocer* target audience is independent retail food stores, supermarkets, manufacturers and food brokers, distributors and wholesalers of food, and allied non-food products, as well as bakers, specialty and health food stores, and convenience outlets. Estab. 1916. Circ. 15,500. Byline given. Pays 30-45 days from receipt of invoice. Offers 33% kill fee. Submit seasonal material 3 months in advance. Sample copy and writer's guidelines free.

Ⓞ Assigns stories to Canadian writers based on editorial needs of publication.

NONFICTION Needs how-to, interview. Does not want industry reports and profiles on companies. Query with published clips. Length: 500-9,000 words. **Pays 25-35¢/word.** Sometimes pays expenses of writers on assignment.

PHOTOS State availability. Captions required. Reviews negatives, transparencies, 3x5 prints, JPEG, EPS, or TIF files. Negotiates payment individually.

TIPS "E-mail, fax, or mail a query outlining your experience, interest, and pay expectations. Include clippings."

HOME FURNISHINGS AND HOUSEHOLD GOODS

ENLIGHTENMENT

Bravo Integrated Media, 620 W. Germantown Pike, Suite 440, Plymouth Meeting PA 19462. (800)774-9861. **E-mail:** news@enlightenmentmag.com. **Website:** www.enlightenmentmag.com. **Contact:** Linda Longo, editorial director. **25% freelance written. Prefers to work with published/established writers.** Monthly magazine for lighting showrooms/department stores. Estab. 1923. Circ. 10,000. Pays on publication. No kill fee. Publishes ms an average of 6 months after acceptance. Submit seasonal material 6 months in advance. Accepts queries by mail. Responds in 2 months to queries. Sample copy for SAE with 9x12 envelope and 4 first-class stamps.

NONFICTION Needs interview, with lighting retailers, personal experience, as a businessperson involved with lighting, technical, concerning lighting or lighting design, profile (of a successful lighting retailer/lamp buyer). **Buys less than 10 mss/year.** Query.

REPRINTS Send tearsheet and information about when and where the material previously appeared.

PHOTOS State availability. Captions required.

TIPS "Have a unique perspective on retailing lamps and lighting fixtures. We often use freelancers located in a part of the country where we'd like to profile a specific business or person. Anyone who has published an article dealing with any aspect of home furnishings will have high priority."

HOSPITALS, NURSING AND NURSING HOMES

ALZHEIMER'S CARE GUIDE

Freiberg Press Inc., P.O. Box 612, Cedar Falls IA 50613. (319)553-0642. **Fax:** (319)553-0644. **E-mail:** kfreiberg@cfu.net. **Website:** www.care4elders.com. **25% freelance written**. Bimonthly magazine covering Alzheimer's care. Aimed at caregivers of Alzheimer's patients. Interested in either inspirational first-person type stories or features/articles involving authoritative advice or caregiving tips. Estab. 1992. Circ. 10,000. Byline sometimes given. Pays on acceptance. No kill fee. Accepts queries by e-mail.

Ⓞ Query first. Only pays for assigned articles.

NONFICTION Needs book excerpts, interview, personal experience, technical. **Buys 50 mss/year.** Query. Length: 500-2,000 words.

☺☺ CURRENT NURSING IN GERIATRIC CARE

Freiberg Press Inc., P.O. Box 612, Cedar Falls IA 50613. (319)553-0642; (800)354-3371. **Fax:** (319)553-0644. **E-mail:** bfreiberg@cfu.net. **Website:** www.care4elders.com. **Contact:** Bill Freiberg. **25% freelance written.** Bimonthly trade journal covering medical information and new developments in research for geriatric nurses and other practitioners. Estab. 2006. Byline sometimes given. Pays on acceptance. No kill fee. Accepts queries by e-mail. Sample copy free; send e-mail to Kathy Freiberg at kfreiberg@cfu.net.

NONFICTION Query. Length: 500-1,500 words. **Pays 15¢/word for assigned articles.**

PHOTOS State availability.

☺☺☺ HOSPITALS & HEALTH NETWORKS

Health Forum Inc., 155 N. Wacker Dr., Suite 400, Chicago IL 60606. (312)893-6800. **Fax:** (312)422-4500. **E-mail:** rhill@healthforum.com; bsantamour@healthforum.com. **Website:** www.hhnmag.com. **Contact:** Richard Hill, editor; Bill Santamour, managing editor. **25% freelance written.** Monthly magazine covering hospitals. Online business publication for hospital and health system executives. Uses only writers who are thoroughly familiar with the hospital field. Potential articles should focus on a critical aspect of health care leadership and, if possible, should address the future of health care. Estab. 1926. Circ. 88,000. Byline given. Pays on acceptance. Offers variable kill fee. Publishes ms an average of 3 months after acceptance. Editorial lead time 6-7 months. Accepts queries by e-mail. Responds in 2-4 months to queries. Guidelines online.

NONFICTION Needs interview, technical. Query editor with a working title, a 50-100 word abstract, and a short biographical sketch. Length: 800-1,200 words.

TIPS "All articles must appeal to an executive-level audience in hospitals and health systems. We particularly seek articles that: Provide a new or cutting-edge angle on leadership in the changing health care environment; promote community health improvement and cross-sector collaboration; stimulate teamwork and integrated approaches to health care delivery; inspire new ways of thinking about health care services and related social issues; offer strategies and insights from industries outside of health care; engage our readers in creative or unexpected ways."

☺☺☺ LONG TERM CARE

Ontario Long Term Care Association, 345 Renfrew Dr., Third Floor, Markham ON L3R 9S9 Canada. (905)470-8995. **Fax:** (905)470-9595. **E-mail:** info@oltca.com; klucchetta@oltca.com. **Website:** www.oltca.com. **Contact:** Kim Lucchetta. Quarterly magazine covering professional issues and practical articles of interest to staff working in a long-term care setting (nursing home, retirement home). Information must be applicable to a Canadian setting; focus should be on staff and on resident well-being. Estab. 1990. Circ. 6,000. Byline given. Pays on publication. No kill fee. Publishes ms an average of 4 months after acceptance. Editorial lead time 3 months. Submit seasonal material 5 months in advance. Responds in 3 months to queries. Sample copy online.

NONFICTION Needs general interest, how-to, practical, of use to long term care practitioners, inspirational, interview. No product-oriented articles. Query with published clips. Electronic versions in either Wordperfect or MS Word are preferred. Length: 400-2,500 words. **Pays up to $500 (Canadian).**

PHOTOS Send photos. Captions, model releases required. Reviews contact sheets, 5x5 prints. Offers no additional payment for photos accepted with ms.

COLUMNS/DEPARTMENTS Query with published clips. **Pays up to $500 (Canadian).**

TIPS "Articles must be positive, upbeat, and contain helpful information that staff and managers working in the long-term care field can use. Focus should be on staff and resident well being. Articles that highlight new ways of doing things are particularly useful. Please call the editor to discuss ideas. Must be applicable to Canadian settings."

☺☺☺ NURSEWEEK

Gannett Healthcare Group, 1721 Moon Lake Blvd., Suite 540, Hoffman Estates IL 60169. **E-mail:** editor@nurse.com. **Website:** www.nurse.com. **Contact:** Nick Hut, editor. **98% freelance written.** Biweekly magazine covering nursing news. Covers nursing news about people, practice, and the profession. Review several issues for content and style. Also consider e-mailing your idea to the editorial director in your region (see list online). The editorial director can help you with the story's focus or angle, along with the organization and development of ideas. Estab. 1999. Circ. 155,000. Byline given. Pays on publication. Offers $200 kill fee. Publishes ms an average of 2 months after acceptance. Editorial lead time 2-3 months. Submit seasonal material 4 months in advance. Accepts queries by e-mail. Accepts simultaneous submissions. Sample copy free. Guidelines online.

NONFICTION Needs interview, personal experience, , articles on innovative approaches to clinical care and evidence-based nursing practice, health-related legislation and regulation, community health programs, healthcare delivery systems, and professional development and management, advances in nursing specialties such as critical care, geriatrics, perioperative care, women's health, home care, long-term care, emergency care, med/surg, pediatrics, advanced practice, education, and staff development. **Buys 20 mss/year.** Query with a 50-word summary of story and a list of RN experts you plan to interview. Length: 900 words. **Pays $200-800 for assigned or unsolicited articles.**

PHOTOS Send photos. Captions, model releases required. Reviews contact sheets, GIF/JPEG files. Offers no additional payment for photos accepted with ms.

TIPS "Pitch us nursing news, AP style, minimum 3 sources, incorporate references. The stories we publish are short and written in a conversational, magazine-style rather than a scholarly tone. In keeping with any article appearing in a nursing publication, clinical accuracy is essential."

⊖⊖ NURSING

(formerly *Nursing2012*), Lippincott Williams & Wilkins, 323 Norristown Rd., Suite 200, Ambler PA 19002-2758. (215)646-8700. **Fax:** (215)654-1328. **E-mail:** nursingeditor@wolterskluwer.com. **Website:** journals.lww.com/nursing/pages/default.aspx. **Contact:** Linda Laskowski-Jones, RN, ACNS-BC, CCRN, CEN, MS, FAWM. **100% freelance written.** Monthly magazine written by nurses for nurses. Looks for practical advice for the direct caregiver that reflects the author's experience. Any form acceptable, but focus must be nursing. Published monthly, *Nursing2014* is widely regarded as offering current, practical contents to its readers, and has won many editorial awards testifying to the quality of its copy and graphics. The editorial and clinical staff, a 18-member editorial board of distinguished clinicians and prac-

titioners, and over 100 invited reviewers help ensure the quality of this publication. Estab. 1971. Circ. over 300,000. Byline given. Pays on publication. Offers 50% kill fee. Publishes ms an average of 18 months after acceptance. Submit seasonal material 8 months in advance. Responds in 2 weeks to queries. Responds in 3 months to mss. Sample copy for $5. Guidelines online.

NONFICTION Needs book excerpts, exposè, how-to, specifically as applies to nursing field, inspirational, opinion, personal experience, photo feature. No articles from patients' point of view, poetry, etc. **Buys 100 mss/year.** Query. All mss can be submitted online through the journal's submissionline. Using this process will expedite review and feedback, and allows the the author to see where the ms is in the editorial process at any time after it's accepted. Encourages authors to register there and follow the directions. Length: 3,500 words (continuing ed feature); 2,100 words (features); short features/departments, 700 words. **Pays $50-400 for assigned articles.**

REPRINTS Send photocopy and information about when and where the material previously appeared. Pays 50% of amount paid for an original articles.

PHOTOS State availability. Model releases required. Offers no additional payment for photos accepted with ms.

TIPS "Basically, *Nursing2013* is a how-to journal, full of hands-on, practical articles. We look for the voice of experience from authors and for articles that help our readers deal with problems they face. We're always interested in taking a look at mss that fall into the following categories: clinical articles, drug articles, charting/documentation, emotional problems, legal problems, ethical dilemmas, and difficult or challenging cases."

⊖ SCHOOL NURSE NEWS

Franklin Communications, Inc., 71 Redner Rd., Morristown NJ 07960. (973)644-4003. **Fax:** (973)644-4062. **E-mail:** editor@schoolnursenews.org. **Website:** www.schoolnursenews.org. **Contact:** Deb Ilardi. **10% freelance written.** Magazine published 5 times/year covering school nursing. *School Nurse News* focuses on topics related to the health issues of school-aged children and adolescents (grades K-12), as well as the health and professional issues that concern school nurses. This is an excellent opportunity for both new and experienced writers. *School Nurse News* publishes feature articles as well as news articles and regular departments, such as Asthma & Allergy Watch, Career & Salary Survey, Oral Health, Nursing Currents, and Sights & Sounds. Estab. 1982. Circ. 7,500. Byline given. Pays on publication. Publishes ms an average of 3-6 months after acceptance. Editorial lead time 3-6 months. Submit seasonal material 6 months in advance. Accepts queries by e-mail, fax, phone. Sample copy free. Guidelines online.

NONFICTION Needs how-to, interview, new product, personal experience. **Buys 1-2 mss/year.** Query. Send via e-mail or forward ms with disk. Mss can include case histories, scenarios of health office situations, updates on diseases, reporting of research, and discussion of procedures and techniques, among others. The author is responsible for the accuracy of content. References should be complete, accurate, and in APA format. Tables, charts and photographs are welcome. Authors are responsible for obtaining permission to reproduce any material that has a pre-existing copyright. The feature article, references, tables, and charts should total 8-10 typewritten pages, double-spaced. The author's name should be included only on the top sheet. The top sheet should also include the title of the article, the author's credentials, current position, address, and phone. **Pays $100.**

HOTELS, MOTELS, CLUBS, RESORTS AND RESTAURANTS

⊙⊙ BARTENDER MAGAZINE

Foley Publishing, P.O. Box 158, Liberty Corner NJ 07938. (908)766-6006. **Fax:** (908)766-6607. **E-mail:** barmag@aol.com. **Website:** www.bartender.com. **Contact:** Jackie Foley, editor. **100% freelance written. Prefers to work with published/established writers; eager to work with new/unpublished writers.** Quarterly magazine emphasizing liquor and bartending for bartenders, tavern owners, and owners of restaurants with full-service liquor licenses. Estab. 1979. Circ. 150,000. Byline given. Pays on publication. No kill fee. Publishes ms an average of 3 months after acceptance. Submit seasonal material 3 months in advance. Accepts simultaneous submissions. Responds in 2 months to mss. Sample copy with 9x12 SAE and 4 first-class stamps.

NONFICTION Needs general interest, historical, how-to, humor, interview with famous bartenders or ex-bartenders, new product, opinion, personal experience, photo feature, travel, nostalgia, unique bars, new techniques, new drinking trends, bar sports, bar magic tricks. Special issues: Special issues: Annual Calendar and Daily Cocktail Recipe Guide. Send complete ms and SASE. Length: 100-1,000 words.

REPRINTS Send tearsheet and information about when and where the material previously appeared. Pays 25% of amount paid for an original article.

PHOTOS Send photos. Captions, model releases required. Pays $7.50-50 for 8x10 b&w glossy prints; $10-75 for 8x10 color glossy prints.

COLUMNS/DEPARTMENTS Bar of the Month; Bartender of the Month; Creative Cocktails; Bar Sports; Quiz; Bar Art; Wine Cellar; Tips from the Top (from prominent figures in the liquor industry); One For the Road (travel); Collectors (bar or liquor-related items); Photo Essays. Length: 200-1,000 words. Query by mail only with SASE. **Pays $50-200.**

FILLERS Needs anecdotes, newsbreaks, short humor, clippings, jokes, gags. Length: 25-100 words. **Pays $5-25.**

TIPS "To break in, absolutely make sure your work will be of interest to all bartenders across the country. Your style of writing should reflect the audience you are addressing. The most frequent mistake made by writers in completing an article for us is using the wrong subject."

⊙⊙ EL RESTAURANTE (FORMERLY EL RESTAURANTE MEXICANO)

P.O. Box 2249, Oak Park IL 60303-2249. (708)267-0023. **E-mail:** kfurore@comcast.net. **Website:** www.restmex.com. **Contact:** Kathleen Furore, editor. Bi-monthly magazine covering Mexican and other Latin cuisines. "*el Restaurante* offers features and business-related articles that are geared specifically to owners and operators of Mexican, Tex-Mex, Southwestern, and Latin cuisine restaurants and other foodservice establishments that want to add that type of cuisine." Estab. 1997. Circ. 25,000. Byline given. Pays on publication. No kill fee. Publishes ms an average of 3 months after acceptance. Responds in 2 months to queries. Sample copy free.

NONFICTION "No specific knowledge of food or restaurants is needed; the key qualification is to be a good reporter who knows how to slant a story toward the Mexican restaurant operator." **Buys 2-4 mss/year.**

Query with published clips. Length: 800-1,200 words. **Pays $250-300.**

TIPS "Query with a story idea, and tell how it pertains to Mexican restaurants."

⊘ⓈⓈⓈⓈ HOSPITALITY TECHNOLOGY

Edgell Communications, 4 Middlebury Blvd., Randolph NJ 07869. (973)607-1300. **E-mail:** alorden@edgellmail.com; dcreamer@edgellmail.com. **Website:** www.htmagazine.com. **Contact:** Abigail Lorden, editor-in-chief; Dorothy Creamer, managing editor. **70% freelance written.** Magazine published 9 times/year covering restaurant and lodging executives who manage hotels, casinos, cruise lines, quick service restaurants, etc. Covers the technology used in foodservice and lodging. Readers are the operators, who have significant IT responsibilities. Estab. 1996. Circ. 16,000. Byline given. Pays on acceptance. No kill fee. Publishes ms an average of 1 month after acceptance. Editorial lead time 2 months. Accepts queries by mail, e-mail. Responds in 2 weeks to queries.

○   This publication will not respond to all inquiries, due to the number of submissions—only those that are of particular interest to the editor.

NONFICTION Needs how-to, interview, new product, technical. Special issues: Publishes 2 studies each year: the Restaurant Industry Technology Study and the Lodging Industry Technology Study. No unsolicited mss. **Buys 40 mss/year.** Query with published clips. Length: 800-1,200 words. **Pays $1/word.** Sometimes pays expenses of writers on assignment.

◐ⓈⓈ HOTELIER

Kostuch Media Ltd., 101-23 Lesmill Rd., Toronto ON M3B 3P6 Canada. (416)447-0888. **Fax:** (416)447-5333. **E-mail:** rcaira@foodservice.ca. **Website:** www.hoteliermagazine.com. **Contact:** Rosanna Caira, editor & publisher. **40% freelance written.** Magazine published 8 times/year covering the Canadian hotel industry. Canada's leading hotel publication. Provides comprehensive and insightful content focusing on business developments, trend analysis, and profiles of the industry's movers and shakers. Estab. 1989. Circ. 9,000. Byline given. Pays on publication. No kill fee. Editorial lead time 3 months. Submit seasonal material 2 months in advance. Accepts queries by mail, fax. Query for free sample copy. Query for free guidelines.

NONFICTION Needs how-to, new product. No case studies. **Buys 30-50 mss/year.** Query. Length: 700-1,500 words. **Pays 35¢/word (Canadian) for assigned articles.** Sometimes pays expenses of writers on assignment.

PHOTOS Send photos. Offers $30-75/photo.

ⓈⓈ INSITE

Christian Camp and Conference Association, P.O. Box 62189, Colorado Springs CO 80962-2189. (719)260-9400. **Fax:** (719)260-6398. **E-mail:** editor@ccca.org; info@ccca.org. **Website:** www.ccca.org. **75% freelance written. Prefers to work with published/established writers.** Bimonthly magazine emphasizing the broad scope of organized camping with emphasis on Christian camps and conference centers. All who work in youth camps and adult conferences read *InSite* for inspiration and to get practical help in ways to serve in their operations. Estab. 1963. Circ. 8,500. Byline given. Pays on publication. No kill fee. Publishes ms an average of 4 months after acceptance. Accepts queries by mail, e-mail. Responds in 1 month to queries. Sample copy for $4.99 plus 9x12 SASE. Guidelines online.

NONFICTION Needs general interest, trends in organized camping in general (Christian camping in particular), how-to, anything involved with organized camping (including motivating staff, programming, healthcare, maintenance, and camper follow-up), inspirational, profiles and practical applications of Scriptural principles to everyday situations in camping, interviews with movers and shakers in Christian camping. **Buys 15-20 mss/year.** Query required. Length: Features: 1,200-1,500 words; How-To: 1,000-1,200 words; Sidebars: 250-500 words. **Pays 20¢/word.**

REPRINTS Send photocopy and information about when and where the material previously appeared. Pays 50% of amount paid for an original article. Quotes are subject to change.

PHOTOS Price negotiable for 35mm color transparencies and high-quality digital photos.

TIPS "The most frequent mistake made by writers is that they send articles unrelated to our readers. Review our publication guidelines first. Interviews are the best bet for freelancers."

ⓈⓈⓈ PIZZA TODAY

Macfadden Protech, LLC, 908 S. 8th St., Suite 200, Louisville KY 40203. (502)736-9500. **Fax:** (502)736-

magazine covering grain handling and merchandising. *Grain Journal* serves the North American grain industry, from the smallest country grain elevators and feed mills to major export terminals. Estab. 1972. Circ. 12,000. Byline sometimes given. Pays on publication. No kill fee. Publishes ms an average of 2 months after acceptance. Editorial lead time 2 months. Submit seasonal material 2 months in advance. Accepts simultaneous submissions. Sample copy free.

NONFICTION Needs how-to, interview, new product, technical. Query. 750 words maximum. **Pays $100.**

PHOTOS Send photos. Captions, identification of subjects required. Reviews contact sheets, negatives, transparencies, 3x5 prints, electronic files. Offers $50-100/photo.

TIPS "Call with your idea. We'll let you know if it is suitable for our publication."

$ ONION WORLD

Columbia Publishing, 8405 Ahtanum Rd., Yakima WA 98903. (509)949-0550. **Fax:** (509)248-4056. **E-mail:** dbrent@columbiapublications.com. **Website:** www.onionworld.net. **Contact:** Brent Clement, managing editor/publisher. **25% freelance written.** Monthly magazine covering the world of onion production and marketing for onion growers and shippers. Estab. 1985. Circ. 5,500. Byline given. Pays on publication. No kill fee. Publishes ms an average of 1 month after acceptance. Submit seasonal material 1 month in advance. Accepts queries by e-mail or phone. Accepts simultaneous submissions. Responds in 1 month to queries. Sample copy for SAE with 9x12 envelope and 5 first-class stamps.

NONFICTION Needs general interest, historical, interview. Special issues: Editorial calendar online. **Buys 30 mss/year.** Query. Length: 1,200-1,250 words. **Pays $100-250 per article, depending upon length. Mileage paid, but query first.**

REPRINTS Send photocopy and information about when and where the material previously appeared. Pays 50% of amount paid for an original article.

PHOTOS Send photos. Captions, identification of subjects required. Offers no additional payment for photos accepted with ms, unless it's a cover shot.

TIPS "Writers should be familiar with growing and marketing onions. We use a lot of feature stories on growers, shippers, and others in the onion trade—what they are doing, varieties grown, their problems, solutions, marketing plans, etc."

$ SPUDMAN

Great American Publishing, P.O. Box 128, Sparta MI 49345. (616)887-9008. **Fax:** (616)887-2666. **E-mail:** bills@spudman.com; spudedit@spudman.com. **Website:** www.spudman.com. **Contact:** Bill Schaefer, managing editor. **10% freelance written.** Monthly magazine covering potato industry's growing, packing, processing, and chipping. Estab. 1964. Circ. 10,000. Byline given. Pays on publication. Offers $75 kill fee. Publishes ms an average of 2 months after acceptance. Editorial lead time 2 months. Submit seasonal material 4 months in advance. Accepts queries by mail, e-mail. YesResponds in 2-3 weeks to queries. Sample copy for SAE with 8½ x 11 envelope and 3 first-class stamps. Guidelines for #10 SASE.

$ THE VEGETABLE GROWERS NEWS

Great American Publishing, P.O. Box 128, Sparta MI 49345. (616)887-9008, ext. 102. **Fax:** (616)887-2666. **E-mail:** vgnedit@vegetablegrowersnews.com. **Website:** www.vegetablegrowersnews.com. **Contact:** Matt Milkovich, managing editor. **10% freelance written.** Monthly tabloid covering agriculture. Estab. 1970. Circ. 16,000. Pays on publication. No kill fee. Publishes ms an average of 2 months after acceptance. Editorial lead time 1-2 months. Submit seasonal material 3 months in advance. Accepts queries by mail, e-mail, fax. Accepts simultaneous submissions. Responds in 2 weeks to queries. Responds in 1 month to mss. Sample copy free.

NONFICTION Needs general interest, interview, new product. No advertorials, other puff pieces. **Buys 25 mss/year.** Query with published clips and résumé. Length: 800-1,200 words. **Pays $100-125.** Sometimes pays expenses of writers on assignment.

PHOTOS Send photos. Captions required. Reviews prints. Offers $15/photo.

LIVESTOCK

$$ ANGUS BEEF BULLETIN

Angus Productions, Inc., 3201 Frederick Ave., St. Joseph MO 64506-2997. (816)383-5270. **Fax:** (816)233-6575. **E-mail:** shermel@angusjournal.com. **Website:** www.angusbeefbulletin.com. **Contact:** Shauna Rose Hermel, editor. **45% freelance written.** Tabloid published 5 times/year covering commercial cattle indus-

9502. **E-mail:** jwhite@pizzatoday.com. **Website:** www.pizzatoday.com. **Contact:** Jeremy White, editor-in-chief. **30% freelance written. Works with published/established writers; occasionally works with new writers.** Monthly magazine for the pizza industry, covering trends, features of successful pizza operators, business and management advice, etc. Estab. 1984. Circ. 44,000. Byline given. Pays on acceptance. No kill fee. Publishes ms an average of 2 months after acceptance. Submit seasonal material 3 months in advance. Accepts queries by mail, e-mail, fax. Responds in 2 months to queries. Responds in 3 weeks to mss. Sample copy for sae with 10x13 envelope and 6 first-class stamps. Guidelines for #10 SASE and online.

O Offer solid information and creative solutions to specific management problems. Strive to present an "insider's view." Every story published in *Pizza Today* should be crammed with tips for operating a better business. Complex or technical concepts should be presented in a manner that's clear to the lay reader contemplating entry into the pizza foodservice industry, but not so basic that experienced veterans are turned off.

NONFICTION Needs interview, entrepreneurial slants, pizza production and delivery, employee training, hiring, marketing, and business management. No fillers, humor, or poetry. **Buys 85 mss/year.** Length: 1,000 words. **Pays 50¢/word, occasionally more.** Sometimes pays expenses of writers on assignment.

PHOTOS Captions required. Reviews contact sheets, negatives, transparencies, color slides, 5x7 prints.

TIPS "Our most pressing need is for articles that would fall within our Front of the House section. Review the magazine before sending in your query."

⊖⊖⊖ SANTÉ MAGAZINE

On-Premise Communications, 160 Benmont Ave., Suite 92, Third Floor, West Wing, Bennington VT 05201. (802)442-6771. **Fax:** (802)442-6859. **E-mail:** mvaughan@santemagazine.com. **Website:** www.isantemagazine.com. **Contact:** Mark Vaughan, editor. **75% freelance written.** Four-issues-per-year magazine covering food, wine, spirits, and management topics for restaurant professionals. Information and specific advice for restaurant professionals on operating a profitable food and beverage program. Writers should "speak" to readers on a professional-to-professional basis. Estab. 1996. Circ. 45,000. By-

line given. Pays on publication. Offers 50% kill fee. Publishes ms an average of 2 months after acceptance. Editorial lead time 3 months. Submit seasonal material 6 months in advance. Accepts queries by e-mail. Responds in 2 weeks to queries. Does not accept mss. Sample copy available. Guidelines by e-mail.

O "Articles should be concise and to the point and should closely adhere to the assigned word count. Our readers will only read articles that provide useful information in a readily accessible format. Where possible, articles should be broken into stand-alone sections that can be boxed or otherwise highlighted."

NONFICTION Needs interview, restaurant business news. Does not want consumer-focused pieces. **Buys 20 mss/year.** Query with published clips. Length: 650-1,800 words. Sometimes pays expenses of writers on assignment.

PHOTOS State availability. Captions required. Reviews PDF/GIF/JPEG files 500kb-10mb. Offers no additional payment for photos accepted.

COLUMNS/DEPARTMENTS Due to a Redesign, 650 words; Bar Tab (focuses on 1 bar's unique strategy for success), 1,000 words; Restaurant Profile (a business-related look at what qualities make 1 restaurant successful), 1,000 words; Maximizing Profits (covers 1 great profit-maximizing strategy per issue from several sources), Signature Dish (highlights 1 chef's background and favorite dish with recipe), Sommeliers Choice (6 top wine managers recommend favorite wines; with brief profiles of each manager), Distillations (6 bar professionals offer their favorite drink for a particular type of spirit; with brief profiles of each manager), 1,500 words; Provisions (like The Goods only longer; an in-depth look at a special ingredient), 1,500 words. **Buys 20 mss/year.** Query with published clips. **Pays $300-800.**

TIPS "Present 2 or 3 of your best ideas via e-mail. Include a brief statement of your qualifications. Attach your resumè and 3 electronic clips. The same format may be used to query via postal mail if necessary."

⊘⊖⊖ WESTERN HOTELIER MAGAZINE

Mercury Publications, Ltd., 1740 Wellington Ave., Winnipeg MB R3H 0E8 Canada. (204)954-2085. **Fax:** (204)954-2057. **E-mail:** dbastable@mercurypublications.ca. **Website:** www.westernhotelier.com. **Contact:** David Bastable, associate publisher and national accounts manager. **33% freelance written.** Quarterly magazine covering the hotel industry. *Western Hotelier* is dedicated to the accommodation industry in Western Canada and U.S. western border states. *WH* offers the West's best mix of news and feature reports geared to hotel management. Feature reports are written on a sector basis and are created to help generate enhanced profitability and better understanding. Circ. 4,342. Byline given. Pays 30-45 days from receipt of invoice. Offers 33% kill fee. Submit seasonal material 3 months in advance. Accepts queries by mail, fax. Accepts simultaneous submissions. Responds in 2 weeks to queries. Sample copy and writer's guidelines free.

NONFICTION Needs how-to, train staff, interview. Industry reports and profiles on companies. Query with published clips. Length: 500-9,000 words. **Pays 25-35¢/word.** Sometimes pays expenses of writers on assignment.

PHOTOS State availability. Captions required. Reviews negatives, transparencies, 3x5 prints, JPEG, EPS, or TIF files. Negotiates payment individually.

TIPS "E-mail, fax, or mail a query outlining your experience, interests, and pay expectations. Include clippings."

🍁$$ WESTERN RESTAURANT NEWS

Mercury Publications, Ltd., 1740 Wellington Ave., Winnipeg MB R3H 0E8 Canada. (204)954-2085. **Fax:** (204)954-2057. **E-mail:** editorial@mercury.mb.ca. **Website:** www.westernrestaurantnews.com; www.mercury.mb.ca. **Contact:** Nicole Sherwood, editorial coordinator. **20% freelance written.** Bimonthly magazine covering the restaurant trade in Western Canada. Reports profiles and industry reports on associations, regional business developments, etc. *Western Restaurant News* is the authoritative voice of the foodservice industry in Western Canada. Offering a total package to readers, *WRN* delivers concise news articles, new product news, and coverage of the leading trade events in the West, across the country, and around the world. Estab. 1994. Circ. 14,532. Byline given. Pays 30-45 days from receipt of invoice. Offers 33% kill fee. Submit seasonal material 3 months in advance. Accepts queries by mail, fax. Accepts simultaneous submissions. Sample copy and writer's guidelines free.

NONFICTION Needs how-to, interview. Industry reports and profiles on companies. Query with published clips. "E-mail, fax, or mail a query outlining your experience, interests, and pay expectations. Include clippings." Length: 500-9,000 words. **Pays 25-35¢/word.** Sometimes pays expenses of writers on assignment.

PHOTOS State availability. Captions required. Reviews negatives, transparencies, 3x5 prints, JPEG, EPS, or TIFF files. Negotiates payment individually.

INDUSTRIAL OPERATIONS

🍁$$ COMMERCE & INDUSTRY

Mercury Publications, Ltd., 1740 Wellington Ave., Winnipeg MB R3H 0E8 Canada. (204)954-2085. **Fax:** (204)954-2057. **E-mail:** editorial@mercury.mb.ca. **Website:** www.commerceindustry.ca. **Contact:** Nicole Sherwood, editorial coordinator. **75% freelance written.** Bimonthly magazine covering the business and industrial sectors. Offers new product news, industry event coverage, and breaking trade specific business stories. Industry reports and company profiles provide readers with an in-depth insight into key areas of interest in their profession. Estab. 1948. Circ. 18,876. Byline given. Pays 30-45 days from receipt of invoice. Offers 33% kill fee. Submit seasonal material 3 months in advance. Accepts queries by mail, e-mail, fax. Accepts simultaneous submissions. Responds in 2 weeks to queries. Sample copy and writer's guidelines free or by e-mail.

NONFICTION Needs how-to, interview. Industry reports and profiles on companies. Query with published clips. Length: 500-9,000 words. **Pays 25-35¢/word.** Sometimes pays expenses of writers on assignment.

PHOTOS State availability. Captions required. Reviews negatives, transparencies, 3x5 prints, JPEG, EPS or TIF files. Negotiates payment individually.

TIPS "E-mail, fax, or mail a query outlining your experience, interests and pay expectations. Include clippings."

$$ INDUSTRIAL WEIGH & MEASURE

WAM Publishing Co., P.O. Box 2247, Hendersonville TN 37077. (615)239-8087. **E-mail:** dave.mathieu@comcast.net. **Website:** www.weighproducts.com. **Contact:** David M. Mathieu, publisher. Bimonthly magazine for users of industrial scales; covers material handling and logistics industries. Estab. 1914. Circ. 13,900. Byline given. Pays on acceptance. Offers 20% kill fee. Accepts queries by mail, e-mail, phone. Responds in 2 weeks to queries. Sample copy online.

NONFICTION Needs interview with presidents of companies, personal experience, guest editorials on government involvement in business, technical, profilse (about users of weighing and measurement equipment). **Buys 15 mss/year.** Query on technical articles; submit complete ms for general interest material. Length: 1,000-2,500 words. **Pays $175-300.**

⬡⬡ MODERN MATERIALS HANDLING

Peerless Media, 111 Speen St., Suite 200, Framingham MA 01701. (508)663-1500. **E-mail:** mlevans@ehpub.com; robert.trebilcock@myfairpoint.net. **Website:** www.mmh.com. **Contact:** Michael Levans, editorial director. **40% freelance written.** Magazine published 13 times/year covering warehousing, distribution centers, and inventory. *Modern Materials Handling* is a national magazine read by managers of warehouses and distribution centers. Focuses on lively, well-written articles telling readers how they can achieve maximum facility productivity and efficiency. Covers technology, too. Estab. 1945. Circ. 81,000. Byline given. Pays on acceptance (allow 4-6 weeks for invoice processing). No kill fee. Publishes ms an average of 1 month after acceptance. Editorial lead time 3 months. Accepts queries by mail, e-mail, fax. Sample copy and guidelines free.

NONFICTION Needs how-to, new product, technical. Special issues: State-of-the-Industry Report, Peak Performer, Salary and Wage survey, Warehouse of the Year. Doesn't want anything that doesn't deal with the topic of warehousing. No general-interest profiles or interviews. **Buys 25 mss/year.** Query with published clips. **Pays $300-650.**

PHOTOS State availability. Captions, identification of subjects required. Reviews negatives, transparencies, prints. Offers no additional payment for photos accepted with ms.

TIPS "Learn a little about warehousing and distributors, and write well. We typically don't accept specific article queries, but welcome introductory letters from journalists to whom we can assign articles. But authors are welcome to request an editorial calendar and develop article queries from it."

♻⬡⬡⬡⬡ PEM PLANT ENGINEERING & MAINTENANCE

CLB Media, Inc., 222 Edward St., Aurora ON L4G 1W6 Canada. (905)727-0077. **Fax:** (905)727-0017. **E-mail:** rbegg@annexweb.com. **Website:** www.pem-mag.com. **Contact:** Rehana Begg, editor. **30% free-**

lance written. Bimonthly magazine looking for informative articles on issues that affect plant floor operations and maintenance. Estab. 1977. Circ. 18,500. Byline given. Pays on publication. No kill fee. Publishes ms an average of 3 months after acceptance. Editorial lead time 4 months. Submit seasonal material 4 months in advance. Accepts simultaneous submissions. Responds in 3 weeks to queries. Responds in 1 month to mss. Sample copy free. Guidelines available.

NONFICTION Needs how-to, keep production downtime to a minimum, better operate an industrial operation, new product, technical. **Buys 6 mss/year.** Query with published clips. Length: 750-4,000 words. **Pays $500-1,400 (Canadian).** Sometimes pays expenses of writers on assignment.

PHOTOS State availability. Captions required. Reviews transparencies, prints. Negotiates payment individually.

TIPS "Information can be found at our website. Call us for sample issues, ideas, etc."

INFORMATION SYSTEMS

⬡⬡⬡ DESKTOP ENGINEERING

Level 5 Communications, Inc., 1283 Main St., P.O. Box 1039, Dublin NH 03444. (603)563-1631. **Fax:** (603)563-8192. **E-mail:** jgooch@deskeng.com. **E-mail:** de-editors@deskeng.com. **Website:** www.deskeng.com. **Contact:** Jamie Gooch, managing editor. **90% freelance written.** Monthly magazine covering computer hardware/software for hands-on design and mechanical engineers, analysis engineers, and engineering management. Ten special supplements/year. Estab. 1995. Circ. 63,000. Byline given. Pays in month of publication. Kill fee for assigned story. Publishes ms an average of 2 months after acceptance. Editorial lead time 3 months. Accepts queries by mail, e-mail, phone. Responds in 2 weeks to queries; 1 month to mss. Sample copy for free with 8x10 SASE. Guidelines online.

NONFICTION Needs how-to, new product, reviews, technical, design. No fluff. **Buys 50-70 mss/year.** Query. Submit outline before you write an article. Length: 800-1,200 word articles (plus artwork) presenting tutorials, application stories, product reviews or other features; 500-700 word guest commentaries for almost any topic related to desktop engineering. **Pays per project. Pay negotiable for unsolicited articles.** Sometimes pays expenses of writers on assignment.

PHOTOS "No matter what type of article you write, it must be supported and enhanced visually. Visual information can include screen shots, photos, schematics, tables, charts, checklists, time lines, reading lists, and program code. The exact mix will depend on your particular article, but each of these items must be accompanied by specific, detailed captions.". Send photos. Captions required. Negotiates payment individually.

COLUMNS/DEPARTMENTS Product Briefs (new products), 50-100 words; Reviews (software, hardware), 500-1,500 words.

$ JOURNAL OF INFORMATION ETHICS

McFarland & Co., Inc., Publishers, P.O. Box 611, Jefferson NC 28640. (336)246-4460. **E-mail:** hauptman@stcloudstate.edu. **90% freelance written.** Semiannual scholarly journal covering all of the information sciences. Addresses ethical issues in all of the information sciences with a deliberately interdisciplinary approach. Topics range from electronic mail monitoring to library acquisition of controversial material to archival ethics. The *Journal*'s aim is to present thoughtful considerations of ethical dilemmas that arise in a rapidly evolving system of information exchange and dissemination. Estab. 1992. Byline given. Pays on publication. No kill fee. Publishes ms an average of 2 years after acceptance. Submit seasonal material 8 months in advance. Accepts queries by mail, e-mail, phone. Sample copy for $30. Guidelines free.

NONFICTION Needs essays, opinion, book reviews. **Buys 10-12 mss/year.** Send complete ms. Length: 500-3,500 words. **Pays $25-50, depending on length.**

TIPS "Familiarize yourself with the many areas subsumed under the rubric of information ethics, e.g., privacy, scholarly communication, errors, peer review, confidentiality, e-mail, etc. Present a well-rounded discussion of any fresh, current, or evolving ethical topic within the information sciences or involving real-world information collection/exchange."

$$$$ TECHNOLOGY REVIEW

MIT, One Main St., 13th Floor, Cambridge MA 02142. (617)475-8000. **Fax:** (617)475-8042. **E-mail:** jason.pontin@technologyreview.com; david.rotman@technologyreview.com. **Website:** www.technologyreview.com. **Contact:** Jason Pontin, editor-in-chief; David Rotman, editor. Magazine published 10 times/year covering information technology, biotech, material science, and nanotechnology. *Technology Review* promotes the understanding of emerging technologies and their impact. Estab. 1899. Circ. 310,000. Byline given. Pays on acceptance. Accepts queries by mail, e-mail.

NONFICTION Query with a pitch via online contact form. Length: 2,000-4,000 words. **Pays $1-3/word.**

FILLERS Short tidbits that relate laboratory prototypes on their way to market in 1-5 years. Length: 150-250 words. **Pays $1-3/word.**

INSURANCE

$$$$ ADVISOR TODAY

NAIFA, 2901 Telestar Court, Falls Church VA 22042. (703)770-8204. **E-mail:** amseka@naifa.org. **Website:** www.advisortoday.com. **Contact:** Ayo Mseka, editor-in-chief. **25% freelance written.** Monthly magazine covering life insurance and financial planning. Writers must demonstrate an understanding at what insurance agents and financial advisors do to earn business and serve their clients. Estab. 1906. Circ. 110,000. Pays on acceptance or publication (by mutual agreement with editor). No kill fee. Publishes ms an average of 3 months after acceptance. Editorial lead time: 3 months. Submit seasonal material 6 months in advance. Accepts queries by mail, e-mail, fax, phone. Accepts simultaneous submissions. Sample copy free. Guidelines online at www.advisortoday.com/about/contribute.cfm.

NONFICTION Buys 8 mss/year. "We prefer e-mail submissions in Microsoft Word format. For other formats and submission methods, please query first. For all articles and queries, contact Ayo Mseka. Web articles should cover the same subject matter covered in the magazine. The articles can be between 300-800 words and should be submitted to Ayo Mseka. Please indicate where a story has been previously published articles have been accepted." Length: 2,300 words for cover articles; 1,000 words for feature articles; 650-700 words for columns and speciality articles; 300-800 words for web articles. **Pays $800-2,000.**

JEWELRY

$$ THE ENGRAVERS JOURNAL

P.O. Box 318, Brighton MI 48116. (810)229-5725. **Fax:** (810)229-8320. **E-mail:** editor@engraversjournal.com. **Website:** www.engraversjournal.com. **Contact:** Managing editor. **70% freelance written.** Monthly magazine covering the recognition and identification industry (engraving, marking devices, awards, jewelry, and signage). "We provide practical information for the education and advancement of our readers, mainly retail business owners." Estab. 1975. Byline given. Pays on acceptance. No kill fee. Publishes ms an average of 3-9 months after acceptance. Accepts queries by mail, e-mail, fax. Responds in 2 weeks to mss. Sample copy free. Guidelines free.

NONFICTION Needs general interest, industry related, how-to, small business subjects, increase sales, develop new markets, use new sales techniques, etc., technical. No general overviews of the industry. Length: 1,000-5,000 words. **Pays $200 and up.**

REPRINTS Send tearsheet, photocopy or typed ms with rights for sale noted, and information about when and where the material previously appeared. Pays 50-100% of amount paid for original article.

PHOTOS Send photos. Captions, identification of subjects, model releases required. Pays variable rate.

TIPS "Articles should always be down to earth, practical, and thoroughly cover the subject with authority. We do not want the 'textbook' writing approach, vagueness, or theory—our readers look to us for sound, practical information. We use an educational slant, publishing both trade-oriented articles and general business topics of interest to a small retail-oriented readership."

JOURNALISM AND WRITING

$$$$ AMERICAN JOURNALISM REVIEW

University of Maryland Foundation, Knight Hall, University of Maryland, College Park MD 20742. (301)405-8805. **Fax:** (301)405-8323. **E-mail:** editor@ajr.umd.edu. **Website:** www.ajr.org. **Contact:** Lucy Dalglish, dean and publisher. **80% freelance written.** Bimonthly magazine covering print, broadcast, and online journalism. American Journalism Review covers ethical issues, trends in the industry, and coverage that falls short. Circ. 25,000. Byline given. Pays within 1 month after publication. Offers 25% kill fee. Publishes ms an average of 2 months after acceptance. Editorial lead time 1 month. Accepts queries by mail, e-mail. Responds in 1 month to queries and unsolicited mss. Sample copy for $4.95 pre-paid or online. Guidelines online.

NONFICTION Needs expose, personal experience, ethical issues. **Buys many mss/year.** Send complete ms. Length: 2,000-4,000 words. **Pays $1,500-2,000.** Pays expenses of writers on assignment.

FILLERS Needs anecdotes, facts, short humor, short pieces. Length: 150-1,000 words. **Pays $100-250.**

TIPS "Write a short story for the front-of-the-book section. We prefer queries to completed articles. Include in a page what you'd like to write about, who you'll interview, why it's important, and why you should write it."

$ AUTHORSHIP

National Writers Association, 10940 S. Parker Rd., #508, Parker CO 80134. (303)841-0246. **E-mail:** natlwritersassn@hotmail.com. **Website:** www.nationalwriters.com. Quarterly magazine covering writing articles only. "Association magazine targeted to beginning and professional writers. Covers how-to, humor, marketing issues. Disk and e-mail submissions preferred." Estab. 1950s. Circ. 4,000. Byline given. Pays on acceptance. No kill fee. Editorial lead time 3 months. Submit seasonal material 6 months in advance. Accepts simultaneous submissions. Responds in 2 months to queries. Sample copy for stamped, self-addressed, 8½x11 envelope.

NONFICTION **Buys 25 mss/year.** Query or send complete ms. Length: 1,200 words. **Pays $10, or discount on memberships and copies.**

PHOTOS State availability. Identification of subjects, model releases required. Reviews 5x7 prints. Offers no additional payment for photos accepted with ms.

TIPS "Members of National Writers Association are given preference."

$ BOOK DEALERS WORLD

North American Bookdealers Exchange, P.O. Box 606, Cottage Grove OR 97424. (541)942-7455. **Fax:** (541)942-7455. **E-mail:** nabe@bookmarketingprofits.com. **Website:** www.bookmarketingprofits.com. **50% freelance written.** Quarterly magazine covering writing, self-publishing, and marketing books by mail. Circ. 20,000. Byline given. Pays on publication. No kill fee. Publishes ms an average of 3 months after acceptance. Accepts simultaneous submissions. Responds in 1 month to queries. Sample copy for $3.

NONFICTION Needs book excerpts, writing, mail order, direct mail, publishing, how-to, home business by mail, advertising, interview, of successful self-publishers, positive articles on self-publishing, new writing angles, marketing. **Buys 10 mss/year.** Send complete ms. Length: 1,000-1,500 words. **Pays $25-50.**

REPRINTS Send typed ms with rights for sale noted and information about when and where the material previously appeared. Pays 80% of amount paid for an original article.

COLUMNS/DEPARTMENTS Publisher Profile (on successful self-publishers and their marketing strategy). Length: 250-1,000 words. **Buys 20 mss/year.** Send complete ms. **Pays $5-20.**

FILLERS Fillers concerning writing, publishing, or books. **Buys 6 mss/year.** Length: 100-250 words. **Pays $3-10.**

TIPS "Query first. Get a sample copy of the magazine."

○●● CANADIAN SCREENWRITER

Writers Guild of Canada, 366 Adelaide St. W., Suite 401, Toronto ON M5V 1R9 Canada. (416)979-7907. **Fax:** (416)979-9273. **E-mail:** info@wgc.ca; m.parker@wgc.ca. **Website:** www.wgc.ca. **Contact:** Maureen Parker, executive director. **80% freelance written.** Magazine published 3 times/year covering Canadian screenwriting for television, film, radio, and digital media. *Canadian Screenwriter* profiles Canadian screenwriters, provides industry news, and offers practical writing tips for screenwriters. Estab. 1998. Circ. 4,000. Byline given. Pays on acceptance. Offers 50% kill fee. Publishes ms an average of 1 month after acceptance. Editorial lead time 2 months. Submit seasonal material 2 months in advance. Accepts queries by e-mail. YesResponds in 1 week to queries. Responds in 1 month to mss. Sample copy free. Guidelines by e-mail.

NONFICTION Needs how-to, humor, interview. Does not want writing on foreign screenwriters; the focus is on Canadian-resident screenwriters. **Buys 12 mss/year.** Query with published clips. Length: 750-2,200 words. **Pays 50¢/word.** Sometimes pays expenses of writers on assignment.

PHOTOS State availability. Identification of subjects required. Reviews GIF/JPEG files. Negotiates payment individually.

TIPS "Read other Canadian film and television publications."

○● CANADIAN WRITER'S JOURNAL

Box 1178, New Liskeard ON P0J 1P0 Canada. (705)647-5424. **Fax:** (705)647-8366. **E-mail:** editor@cwj.ca. **Website:** www.cwj.ca. **Contact:** Deborah Ranchuk, editor. **75% freelance written.** Bimonthly magazine for writers. Digest-size magazine for writers emphasizing short "how-to" articles, which convey easily understood information useful to both apprentice and professional writers. General policy and postal subsidies require that the magazine must carry a substantial Canadian content. We try for about 90% Canadian content, but prefer good material over country of origin, or how well you're known. Writers may query, but unsolicited mss are welcome. Estab. 1984. Circ. 350. Byline given. Pays on publication. No kill fee. Publishes ms an average of 2-9 months after acceptance. Accepts queries by mail, e-mail, fax, phone; preference will be given to the article that can be submitted electronically. Responds in 2 months to queries. Sample copy for $8, including postage. Guidelines online.

NONFICTION Needs how-to, articles for writers, , humorous and seasonal items. **Buys 200 mss/year.** Query optional. 400-2,500/words for articles; 250-500/words for book reviews **Pays $7.50/published magazine page (approx. 450 words), plus 1 complimentary copy. A $2 premium is paid for electronic submissions.**

REPRINTS Send typed ms with rights for sale noted and information about when and where the material previously appeared.

FICTION Fiction is published only through semi-annual short fiction contest with April 30 deadline. Send SASE for rules, or see guidelines online. Does not want gratuitous violence or sex subject matters. Accepts submissions by e-mail. Responds in 2 months to queries. Pays on publication for one-time rights.

POETRY Poetry must be unpublished elsewhere; short poems or extracts used as part of articles on the writing of poetry. Submit up to 5 poems at a time. No previously published poems. Accepts e-mail submissions (pasted into body of message, with 'Submission' in the subject line). Include SASE with postal submissions. "U.S. postage accepted; do not affix to envelope. Poems should be titled." Responds in 3-6 months. **Pays $2-5 per poem published (depending on length) and 1 contributor's copy. SASE required for response and payment.**

TIPS "We prefer short, tightly written, informative how-to articles. US writers: note that US postage cannot be used to mail from Canada. Obtain Canadian stamps, use IRCs, or send small amounts in cash."

⊛⊛⊛ ECONTENT MAGAZINE

Information Today, Inc., 143 Old Marlton Pike, Medford NJ 08055. (609)654-6266. **Fax:** (609)654-4309. **E-mail:** theresa.cramer@infotoday.com. **Website:** www.econtentmag.com. **Contact:** Theresa Cramer, editor. **90% freelance written.** Monthly magazine covering digital content trends, strategies, etc. *EContent* is a business publication. Readers need to stay on top of industry trends and developments. Estab. 1979. Circ. 12,000. Byline given. Pays within 1 month of publication. Editorial lead time 3-4 months. Accepts queries by e-mail. Responds in 3 weeks to queries. Responds in 1 month to mss. Sample copy and writer's guidelines online.

NONFICTION Needs expose, how-to, interview, new product, opinion, technical, news features, strategic and solution-oriented features. No academic or straight Q&A. **Buys 48 mss/year.** Query with published clips. Submit electronically as e-mail attachment. Length: 1,000 words. **Pays 40-50¢/word.** Sometimes pays expenses of writers on assignment.

PHOTOS State availability. Captions required. Negotiates payment individually.

COLUMNS/DEPARTMENTS Profiles (short profile of unique company, person or product), 1,200 words; New Features (breaking news of content-related topics), 500 words maximum. **Buys 40 mss/year.** Query with published clips. **Pays 30-40¢/word.**

TIPS "Take a look at the website. Most of the time, an e-mail query with specific article ideas works well. A general outline of talking points is good, too. State prior experience."

⊙⊛ FELLOWSCRIPT

InScribe Christian Writers' Fellowship, P.O. Box 6201, Wetaskiwin AB T9A 2E9 Canada. **E-mail:** fellowscripteditor@gmail.com. **Website:** www.inscribe.org. **Contact:** Pam Myrtroen, acquisitions editor. **100% freelance written.** Quarterly writers' newsletter featuring Christian writing. Readers are Christians with a commitment to writing. Among readership are best-selling authors and unpublished beginning writers. Submissions should include practical information, something the reader can immediately put into practice. Estab. 1983. Circ. 200. Byline given. Pays on publication. No kill fee. Publishes ms an average of 6-12 months after acceptance. Editorial lead time 3 months. Submit seasonal material 4 months in advance. Accepts queries by e-mail, prefers full ms by e-mail; postal submissions only accepted from In-Scribe members. Accepts simultaneous submissions. Responds in 1 month to queries and mss. Sample copy for $5, 9x12 SAE, and 3 first-class stamps (Canadian) or IRCs. Guidelines online.

NONFICTION Needs essays, exposè, how-to, for writers, interview, new product. Does not want poetry, fiction, personal experience, testimony or think piece, commentary articles. **Buys 30-45 mss/year.** Send complete ms attached in rtf or doc format. Length: 750-1,000 words. **Pays 2 1/2¢/word (first rights); 1 1/2¢/word reprints (Canadian funds).**

COLUMNS/DEPARTMENTS Book reviews, 150-300 words; Market Updates, 50-300 words. **Buys 1-3. mss/year.** Send complete ms. **Pays 1 contributor's copy.**

FILLERS Needs facts, newsbreaks. **Buys 5-10 mss/year.** Length: 25-300 words. **Pays 1 contributor's copy.**

TIPS "Send your complete ms by e-mail (pasted into the message, no attachments). E-mail is preferred. Tell us a bit about yourself. Write in a casual, first-person, anecdotal style. Be sure your article is full of practical material, something that can be applied. Most of our accepted freelance submissions fall into the 'how-to' category, and involve tasks, crafts, or procedures common to writers. Please do not send inspirational articles (i.e., 'How I sold My First Story')."

⊙⊛ FREELANCE MARKET NEWS

The Writers Bureau Ltd., 8-10 Dutton St., Manchester M3 1LE England. (44)(161)819-9922. **Fax:** (44)(161)819-2842. **E-mail:** fmn@writersbureau.com. **Website:** www.freelancemarketnews.com. **15% freelance written.** Monthly newsletter covering freelance writing. For all writers, established and new, *Freelance Market News* is an excellent source for the most up to date information about the publishing world. It is packed with news, views and the latest advice about new publications, plus the trends and developments in established markets, in the UK and around the world. Informs readers about publications that are looking for new writers and even warn about those writers should avoid. Estab. 1968. Byline given. Pays on acceptance. No kill fee. Publishes ms an average of 3 months after acceptance. Editorial lead time 3 months. Submit seasonal material 3 months in advance. Accepts queries by mail, e-mail, fax. YesSample copy and guidelines online.

○ Prefers to receive a complete ms rather than a query.

NONFICTION Needs how-to sell your writing/improve your writing. **Buys 12 mss/year.** Length: 1,00 words. **Pays £50/1,000 words.**

COLUMNS/DEPARTMENTS New Markets (magazines which have recently been published); Fillers & Letters; Overseas Markets (obviously only English-language publications); Market Notes (established publications accepting articles, fiction, reviews, or poetry). All should be between 40 and 200 words. **Pays £40/1,000 words.**

⊕⊕ FREELANCE WRITER'S REPORT

CNW Publishing, Inc., 45 Main St., P.O. Box A, North Stratford NH 03590-0167. (603)922-8338. **E-mail:** fwrwm@writers-editors.com. **Website:** www.writers-editors.com. **25% freelance written.** Monthly newsletter covering the business of freelance writing. *FWR* covers the marketing and business/office management aspects of running a freelance writing business. Articles must be of value to the established freelancer; nothing basic. Estab. 1982. Byline given. Pays on publication. No kill fee. Publishes ms an average of 12 months after acceptance. Editorial lead time 2 months. Submit seasonal material 2 months in advance. Accepts simultaneous submissions. Responds in 1 week to queries. Responds in 2 weeks to mss. Sample copy for 6x9 SAE with 2 first-class stamps (for back copy); $4 for current copy. Guidelines and sample copy online.

NONFICTION Needs book excerpts, how-to (market, increase income or profits). Does not want articles about the basics of freelancing. **Buys 15 mss/year.** Send complete ms by e-mail. Length: up to 900 words. **Pays 10¢/word.**

TIPS "Write in a terse, newsletter style."

⊕⊕⊕ MSLEXIA

Mslexia Publications Ltd., P.O. Box 656, Newcastle upon Tyne NE99 1PZ United Kingdom. (44)(191)204-8860. **E-mail:** submissions@mslexia.co.uk; postbag@mslexia.co.uk. **Website:** www.mslexia.co.uk. **Contact:** Debbie Taylor, editorial director. **60% freelance written.** Quarterly magazine offering advice and publishing opportunities for women writers, plus poetry and prose submissions on a different theme each issue. "*Mslexia* tells you all you need to know about exploring your creativity and getting into print. No other magazine provides *Mslexia*'s unique mix of advice and inspiration; news, reviews, interviews; competitions, events,

grants; all served up with a challenging selection of new poetry and prose. *Mslexia* is read by authors and absolute beginners. A quarterly master class in the business and psychology of writing, it's the essential magazine for women who write." Estab. 1998. Circ. 9,000. Byline given. Pays on publication. Offers 50% kill fee. Publishes ms an average of 1 month after acceptance. Editorial lead time 3 months. Submit seasonal material 3 months in advance. Accepts queries by mail, e-mail, phone. Accepts simultaneous submissions. Responds in 3 months to mss. Sample copy online. Writer's guidelines online or by e-mail.

○ This publication accepts e-mail submissions except from UK writers submitting to New Writing themed writing.

NONFICTION Needs how-to, interview, opinion, personal experience. No general items about women or academic features. "We are only interested in features (for tertiary-educated readership) about women's writing and literature." **Buys 40 mss/year.** Query with published clips. Length: 500-2,200 words. **Pays $70-400 for assigned articles. Pays $70-300 for unsolicited articles.** Sometimes pays expenses of writers on assignment.

COLUMNS/DEPARTMENTS "We are open to suggestions, but would only commission 1 new column/year, probably from a UK-based writer." **Buys 12 mss/year.** Query with published clips.

FICTION See guidelines online. "Submissions not on 1 of our current themes will be returned (if submitted with a SASE) or destroyed." **Buys 30 mss/year.** Send complete ms. Length: 50-2,200 words. **Pays £15 per 1,000 words prose plus contributor's copies.**

POETRY Needs avant-garde, free verse, haiku, traditional. Buys 40 poems/year. Submit maximum 4 poems. **Pays £25 per poem plus contributor's copies.**

TIPS "Read the magazine; subscribe if you can afford it. *Mslexia* has a particular style and relationship with its readers which is hard to assess at a quick glance. The majority of our readers live in the UK, so feature pitches should be aware of this. We never commission work without seeing a written sample first. We rarely accept unsolicited mss, but prefer a short letter suggesting a feature, plus a brief bio and writing sample."

⊕⊕ NOVEL & SHORT STORY WRITER'S MARKET

F+W Media, Inc., 10151 Carver Rd., Suite 200, Blue Ash OH 45242. (513)531-2690. **Fax:** (513)531-2686. **E-**

mail: marketbookupdates@fwmedia.com. **Website:** www.writersmarket.com. **Contact:** Rachel Randall, managing editor. **85% freelance written.** Annual resource book covering the fiction market. In addition to thousands of listings for places to get fiction published, *NSSWM*'s feature articles on the craft and business of fiction writing, as well as interviews with successful fiction writers, editors, and agents. Articles are unique in that they always offer an actionable takeaway. In other words, readers must learn something immediately useful about the creation or marketing of fiction. Estab. 1981. Byline given. Pays on acceptance plus 45 days. Offers 25% kill fee. Accepts queries by e-mail only. Include "NSSWM Query" in the subject line. Responds in 4 weeks to queries.

Accepts proposals during the summer.

NONFICTION Needs how-to, write, sell and promote fiction; find an agent; etc., interview, personal experience. **Buys 12-15 mss/year.** Length: 1,500-2,500 words. **Pays $400-700.**

PHOTOS Send photos. Identification of subjects required. Reviews prints, GIF/JPEG files (hi-res). Offers no additional payment for photos accepted with ms.

TIPS "The best way to break into this book is to review the last few years' editions and look for aspects of the fiction industry that we haven't covered recently. Send a specific, detailed pitch stating the topic, angle, and 'take-away' of the piece, what sources you intend to use, and what qualifies you to write this article. Freelancers who have published fiction and/or have contacts in the industry have an advantage."

POETS & WRITERS MAGAZINE

90 Broad St., Suite 2100, New York NY 10004. (212)226-3586. **E-mail:** editor@pw.org. **Website:** www.pw.org/magazine. **Contact:** Kevin Larimer, editor. **95% freelance written.** Bimonthly professional trade journal for poets and fiction writers and creative nonfiction writers. Estab. 1987. Circ. 60,000. Byline given. Pays on publication. Offers 25% kill fee. Publishes ms an average of 4 months after acceptance. Submit seasonal material 4 months in advance. Accepts queries by mail, e-mail. Responds in 2 months to mss. Sample copy for $5.95. Guidelines online.

No poetry or fiction submissions.

NONFICTION Needs how-to, craft of poetry, fiction or creative nonfiction writing, interviews, with poets or writers of fiction and creative nonfiction, personal essays about literature, regional reports of literary activity, reports on small presses, service pieces about publishing trends. **Buys 35 mss/year.** Send complete ms. Length: 700-3,000 (depending on topic) words.

PHOTOS State availability. Reviews color prints. Offers no additional payment for photos accepted with ms.

COLUMNS/DEPARTMENTS Literary and Publishing News, 700-1,000 words; Profiles of Emerging and Established Poets, Fiction Writers and Creative Nonfiction Writers, 2,000-3,000 words; Craft Essays and Publishing Advice, 2,000-2,500 words. Query with published clips or send complete ms. **Pays $225-500.**

TIPS "We typically assign profiles to coincide with an author's forthcoming book publication. We are not looking for the Get Rich Quick or 10 Easy Steps variety of writing and publishing advice."

QUILL & SCROLL MAGAZINE

Quill and Scroll International Honorary Society for High School Journalists, University of Iowa, School of Journalism and Mass Communication, 100 Adler Journalism Bldg., Iowa City IA 52242. (319)335-3457. **Fax:** (319)335-3989. **E-mail:** quill-scroll@uiowa.edu. **Website:** www.quillandscroll.org. **Contact:** Vanessa Shelton, executive director. **20% freelance written.** Fall and spring issues covering scholastic journalism-related topics during school year. Primary audience is high school journalism students working on and studying topics related to newspapers, yearbooks, radio, television, and online media; secondary audience is their teachers and others interested in this topic. Invites journalism students and advisers to submit mss about important lessons learned or obstacles overcome. Estab. 1926. Circ. 10,000. Byline given. Pays on acceptance and publication. No kill fee. Publishes ms an average of 4 months after acceptance. Editorial lead time 2 months. Accepts queries by mail, e-mail. Accepts simultaneous submissions. Responds in 2 weeks to queries. Guidelines available.

NONFICTION Needs essays, how-to, humor, interview, new product, opinion, personal experience, photo feature, technical, travel, types on topic. Does not want articles not pertinent to high school student journalists. Query with your submission. Length: 600-1,000 words. **Pays $100-500 for assigned articles. Pays complementary copy and $200 maximum for unsolicited articles.** Sometimes pays expenses of writers on assignment.

PHOTOS State availability. Reviews GIF/JPEG files. Offers no additional payment for photos accepted with ms.

⊕⊕⊕ QUILL MAGAZINE

Society of Professional Journalists, 3909 N. Meridian St., Indianapolis IN 46208. **Fax:** (317)920-4789. **E-mail:** sleadingham@spj.org; quill@spj.org. **Website:** www.spj.org/quill.asp. **Contact:** Scott Leadingham, editor. **75% freelance written.** Monthly magazine covering journalism and the media industry. *Quill* is a how-to magazine written by journalists. Focuses on the industry's biggest issues while providing tips on how to become better journalists. Estab. 1912. Circ. 10,000. Byline given. Pays on acceptance. Offers 25% kill fee. Publishes ms an average of 2 months after acceptance. Editorial lead time 2-3 months. Submit seasonal material 2-3 months in advance. Accepts queries by e-mail. YesAccepts simultaneous submissions. Sample copy online.

NONFICTION Needs general interest, how-to, technical. Does not want personality profiles and straight research pieces. **Buys 12 mss/year.** Query. Length: 800-2,500 words. **Pays $150-800.**

⊕⊕⊕ WRITER'S DIGEST

F+W Media, Inc., 10151 Carver Rd., Suite #200, Blue Ash OH 45242. (513)531-2690. **E-mail:** wdsubmissions@fwmedia.com. **Website:** www.writersdigest.com. **75% freelance written.** Magazine for those who want to write better, get published and participate in the vibrant culture of writers. Readers look for specific ideas and tips that will help them succeed, whether success means getting into print, finding personal fulfillment through writing, or building and maintaining a thriving writing career and network. *Writer's Digest*, the No. 1 magazine for writers, celebrates the writing life, and what it means to be a writer in today's publishing environment. Estab. 1920. Byline given. Pays on acceptance. Offers 25% kill fee. Publishes ms an average of 6-9 months after acceptance. Accepts queries by e-mail only. Responds in 2-4 months to queries and mss. Guidelines and editorial calendar online (writersdigest.com/submission-guidelines).

○ The magazine does not accept or read e-queries with attachments.

NONFICTION Needs essays, how-to, humor, inspirational, interviews, profiles. Does not accept phone, snail mail, or fax queries. Does not buy newspaper clippings or reprints of articles previously published in other writing magazines. Book and software reviews are handled in-house, as are most *WD* interviews. **Buys 40 mss/year.** A query should include a thorough outline that introduces your article proposal and highlights each of the points you intend to make. Your query should discuss how the article will benefit readers, why the topic is timely, and why you're the appropriate writer to discuss the topic. Please include your publishing credential related to your topic with your submission. Do not send attachments. Length: 800-1,500 words. **Pays 30-50¢/word.**

TIPS "*InkWell* is the best place for new writers to break in. We recommend you consult our editorial calendar before pitching feature-length articles. Check our writer's guidelines for more details."

⊕ WRITER'S WEB WATCH

Communications Concepts, Inc., 7481 Huntsman Blvd., #720, Springfield VA 22153-1648. (703)643-2200. **Website:** www.writerswebwatch.com. Monthly newsletter on business writing and communications. Readers are company writers, editors, communicators, and executives. They need specific, practical advice on how to write well as part of their job. Estab. 1983. Byline sometimes given. Pays within 45 days of acceptance. No kill fee. Publishes ms an average of 3 months after acceptance. Editorial lead time 3 months. Accepts queries by mail, e-mail, online submission form. Responds in 1 month to queries. Sample copy online.

NONFICTION Needs how-to. **Buys 90 mss/year.** Accepts electronic final mss. E-mail attached word processing files. Length: 100-600 words. **Pays $35-150.**

COLUMNS/DEPARTMENTS Writing Techniques (how-to business writing advice); Style Matters (grammar, usage, and editing); Online Publishing (writing, editing, and publishing for the Web); Managing Publications; PR & Marketing (writing).

FILLERS Short tips on writing or editing. Mini-reviews of communications websites for business writers, editors, and communicators. Length: 100-250 words. **Pays $35.**

TIPS "We do not use material on how to get published or how to conduct a freelancing business. Format your copy to follow *Writer's Web Watch* style. Include postal and e-mail addresses, phone numbers, website URLs, and prices for products/services mentioned in articles."

🖐🖐🖐🖐 WRITTEN BY

7000 W. Third St., Los Angeles CA 90048. (323)782-4699. **Fax:** (323)782-4800. **Website:** www.wga.org/writtenby/writtenby.aspx. **40% freelance written.** Magazine published 9 times/year. *Written By* is the premier magazine written by and for America's screen and TV writers. Focuses on the craft of screenwriting and covers all aspects of the entertainment industry from the perspective of the writer. Audience is screenwriters and most entertainment executives. Estab. 1987. Circ. 12,000. Byline given. Pays on acceptance. Offers 10% kill fee. Publishes ms an average of 2 months after acceptance. Editorial lead time 4 months. Submit seasonal material 4 months in advance. Accepts queries by mail, e-mail, fax, phone, online submission form. Guidelines for #10 SASE.

🖵 Guidelines are currently being rewritten. Contact via phone or online contact form to pitch a story idea.

NONFICTION Needs book excerpts, essays, historical, humor, interview, opinion, personal experience, photo feature, technical, software. No beginner pieces on how to break into Hollywood, or how to write scripts. **Buys 20 mss/year.** Query with published clips. Length: 500-3,500 words. **Pays $500-3,500 for assigned articles.** Sometimes pays expenses of writers on assignment.

PHOTOS State availability. Captions, identification of subjects, model releases required. Reviews transparencies. Offers no additional payment for photos accepted with ms.

COLUMNS/DEPARTMENTS Pays $1,000 maximum.

TIPS "We are looking for more theoretical essays on screenwriting past and/or present. Also, the writer must always keep in mind that our audience is made up primarily of working writers who are inside the business; therefore all articles need to have an 'insider' feel and not be written for those who are still trying to break in to Hollywood. We prefer a hard copy of submission or e-mail."

LAW

🖐🖐🖐🖐 ABA JOURNAL

American Bar Association, 321 N. Clark St., 20th Floor, Chicago IL 60654. (312)988-6018. **Fax:** (312)988-6014. **E-mail:** releases@americanbar.org. **Website:** www.abajournal.com. **Contact:** Allen Pusey, editor and publisher. **10% freelance written.** Monthly magazine covering the trends, people and finances of the legal profession from Wall Street to Main Street to Pennsylvania Avenue. The *ABA Journal* is an independent, thoughtful, and inquiring observer of the law and the legal profession. The magazine is edited for members of the American Bar Association. Circ. 380,000. Byline given. Pays on acceptance. No kill fee. Accepts queries by e-mail, fax. Sample copy free. Guidelines online.

NONFICTION "We don't want anything that does not have a legal theme. No poetry or fiction." **Buys 5 mss/year.** "We use freelancers with experience reporting for legal or consumer publications; most have law degrees. If you are interested in freelancing for the *Journal*, we urge you to include your résumé and published clips when you contact us with story ideas." Length: 500-3,500 words. **Pays $300-2,000 for assigned articles.**

COLUMNS/DEPARTMENTS The National Pulse/Ideas from the Front (reports on legal news and trends), 650 words; eReport (reports on legal news and trends), 500-1,500 words. "The *ABA Journal eReport* is our weekly online newsletter sent out to members." **Buys 25 mss/year.** Query with published clips. **Pays $300, regardless of story length.**

🟠 ALTERNATIVE LAW JOURNAL

The Legal Service Bulletin Co-operative, Ltd., Law Faculty, Monash University VIC 3800 Australia. 61 3 9544 0974. **Fax:** 61 3 9905 5305. **E-mail:** altlj.org@monash.edu; deb.candy@monash.edu. **Website:** www.altlj.org. **Contact:** Deb Candy, managing editor. Quarterly magazine covering the promotion of social justice issues, legal system, development of alternative practice, community legal education and support of law reform activity. The *Alternative Law Journal* is a quaterly, refereed law journal published by the Legal Service Bulletin Co-operative Ltd in Melbourne, Australia. Guidelines online.

NONFICTION Needs general interest, interview. Send complete ms. Length: Varies. Articles up to 4,000 words, with preference given to shorter articles. Briefs around 1,000-1,500 words. Law and culture reviews up to 800 words. Mentions 100-150 words.

COLUMNS/DEPARTMENTS Legal Studies, Asia-Pacific, "Sit-Down Girlie," Sport and Law, DownUnderAllOver. See website for details on column editors. E-mail article to the journal.

FILLERS Length: 100-150 words.

TIPS Heavy, scholarly or overly legalistic articles are not encouraged. We particularly discourage excessive footnotes.

💲💲💲 BENCH & BAR OF MINNESOTA

Minnesota State Bar Association, 600 Nicollet Mall #380, Minneapolis MN 55402. (612)333-1183; 800-882-6722. **Fax:** (612)333-4927. **E-mail:** jhaverkamp@mnbar.org. **Website:** www.mnbar.org. **Contact:** Judson Haverkamp, editor. **5% freelance written.** Magazine published 11 times/year. *Bench & Bar* seeks reportage, analysis, and commentary on changes in the law, trends and issues in the law and the legal profession, especially in Minnesota. Preference to items of practical/professional human interest to lawyers and judges. Audience is mostly Minnesota lawyers. Estab. 1931. Circ. 17,000. Byline given. Pays on acceptance. No kill fee. Publishes ms an average of 3 months after acceptance. Responds in 1 month to queries. Guidelines for free online or by mail.

NONFICTION Needs analysis and exposition of current trends, developments and issues in law, legal profession, especially in Minnesota. Balanced commentary and "how-to" considered. Does not want one-sided opinion pieces or advertorial. **Buys 2-3 mss/year.** Send query or complete ms. Length: 1,000-3,500 words. **Pays $500-1,500.** Some expenses of writers on assignment.

PHOTOS State availability. Identification of subjects, model releases required. Reviews 5x7 prints. Pays $25-100 upon publication.

💲💲💲💲 CALIFORNIA LAWYER

Daily Journal Corp., 44 Montgomery St., Suite 250, San Francisco CA 94104. (415)296-2400. **Fax:** (415)296-2440. **E-mail:** bo_links@dailyjournal.com. **Website:** www.callawyer.com. **Contact:** Bo Links, legal editor. **30% freelance written.** Monthly magazine of law-related articles and general-interest subjects of appeal to lawyers and judges. Primary mission is to cover the news of the world as it affects the law and lawyers, helping readers better comprehend the issues of the day and to cover changes and trends in the legal profession. Readers are all California lawyers, plus judges, legislators, and corporate executives. Although the magazine focuses on California and the West, they have subscribers in every state. *California Lawyer* is a general interest magazine for people interested in law. Estab. 1981. Circ. 140,000. Byline giv-

en. Pays on acceptance. Offers 25% kill fee. Publishes ms an average of 3 months after acceptance. Editorial lead time 3 months. Accepts queries by e-mail. No previously published articles.Sample copy and writer's guidelines for #10 SASE.

NONFICTION Needs essays, general interest, interview, news and feature articles on law-related topics. **Buys 12 mss/year.** Send complete ms. "We are interested in concise, well-written and well-researched articles on issues of current concern, as well as well-told feature narratives with a legal focus. We would like to see a description or outline of your proposed idea, including a list of possible sources." Length: 500-5,000 words. **Pays $50-2,000.** Pays expenses of writers on assignment.

PHOTOS **Contact:** Marsha Sessa, art director. State availability. Identification of subjects, model releases required. Reviews prints.

COLUMNS/DEPARTMENTS California Esq. (current legal trends), 300 words. **Buys 6 mss/year.** Query with or without published clips. **Pays $50-250.**

💲💲💲💲 INSIDECOUNSEL

222 S. Riverside Plaza, Suite 620, Chicago IL 60606. (312)654-3500. **E-mail:** rsteeves@insidecounsel.com. **Website:** www.insidecounsel.com. **Contact:** Rich Steeves, managing editor. **50% freelance written.** Monthly tabloid covering legal information for attorneys. *InsideCounsel* is a monthly national magazine that gives general counsel and inhouse attorneys information on legal and business issues to help them better manage corporate law departments. It routinely addresses changes and trends in law departments, litigation management, legal technology, corporate governance and inhouse careers. Law areas covered monthly include: intellectual property, international, technology, project finance, e-commerce, and litigation. All articles need to be geared toward the inhouse attorney's perspective. Estab. 1991. Circ. 45,000. Byline given. Pays on publication. No kill fee. Publishes ms an average of 3 months after acceptance. Editorial lead time 3 months. Submit seasonal material 3 months in advance. Accepts queries by mail, e-mail. Responds in 3 weeks to queries. Sample copy for $17. Guidelines online.

🖸　　Formerly *Corporate Legal Times.*

NONFICTION Needs interview, news about legal aspects of business issues and events. **Buys 12-25 mss/**

year. Query with published clips. Length: 500-3,000 words. **Pays $500-2,000.**

PHOTOS Freelancers should state availability of photos with submission. Identification of subjects required. Reviews color transparencies, b&w prints. Offers $25-150/photo.

TIPS "Our publication targets general counsel and in-house lawyers. All articles need to speak to them, not to the general attorney population. Query with clips and a list of potential in-house sources."

⊖⊖⊖ JCR

National Court Reporters Association, 8224 Old Courthouse Rd., Vienna VA 22180. (800)272-6272, ext. 164. **E-mail:** jschmidt@ncra.org. **Website:** www.theJCR.com. **Contact:** Jacqueline Schmidt, editor. **10% freelance written.** Monthly, except bimonthly November/December, magazine covering court reporting, captioning, and CART provision. "The *JCR* has 2 complementary purposes: to communicate the activities, goals, and mission of its publisher, the National Court Reporters Association; and, simultaneously, to seek out and publish diverse information and views on matters significantly related to the court reporting and captioning professions." Estab. 1899. Circ. 18,000. Byline sometimes given. Pays on acceptance. No kill fee. Publishes ms an average of 4-5 months after acceptance. Editorial lead time 4 months. Submit seasonal material 4 months in advance. Accepts queries by mail, e-mail. Sample copy free. Ms guidelines are available on www.NCRA.org under "Submit content.".

NONFICTION Needs book excerpts, how-to, interview, technical, legal issues. **Buys 6-10 mss/year.** Query. Length: 1,200-2,500 words. **Pays $1,000 maximum for assigned articles. Pays $100 maximum for unsolicited articles.** Sometimes pays expenses of writers on assignment.

COLUMNS/DEPARTMENTS Language (proper punctuation, grammar, dealing with verbatim materials); Technical (new technologies, using mobile technology, using technology for work); Book excerpts (language, crime, legal issues)—all 1,000 words.

⊖⊖⊖ JOURNAL OF COURT REPORTING

National Court Reporters Association, 8224 Old Courthouse Rd., Vienna VA 22180. (800)272-6272, ext. 164. **E-mail:** jschmidt@ncrahq.org. **Website:** www.ncraonline.org. **Contact:** Jacqueline Schmidt,

editor. **10% freelance written.** Monthly (bimonthly July/August and November/December) magazine. The *Journal of Court Reporting* has 2 complementary purposes: to communicate the activities, goals and mission of its publisher, the National Court Reporters Association; and, simultaneously, to seek out and publish diverse information and views on matters significantly related to the court reporting and captioning professions. Estab. 1899. Circ. 20,000. Byline sometimes given. Pays on acceptance. No kill fee. Publishes ms an average of 4-5 months after acceptance. Editorial lead time 4 months. Submit seasonal material 4 months in advance. Accepts queries by mail, e-mail. Accepts simultaneous submissions. Sample copy free. Guidelines online.

NONFICTION Needs book excerpts, how-to, interview, technical, legal issues. **Buys 10 mss/year.** Query. Length: no more than 1,000 words. Sometimes pays expenses of writers on assignment.

COLUMNS/DEPARTMENTS Language (proper punctuation, grammar, dealing with verbatim materials); Technical (new technologies, using mobile technology, using technology for work); Book excerpts (language, crime, legal issues), all 1,000 words; Puzzles (any, but especially word-related games). **Pays $100.**

⊕⊖⊖⊖⊖ NATIONAL

The Canadian Bar Association, 500-865 Carling Ave., Ottawa ON K1S 5S8 Canada. (613)237-2925. **Fax:** (613)237-0185. **E-mail:** beverleys@cba.org; national@cba.org. **Website:** www.nationalmagazine.ca. **Contact:** Beverley Spencer editor-in-chief. **90% freelance written.** Magazine published 8 times/year covering practice trends and business developments in the law, with a focus on technology, innovation, practice management, and client relations. Estab. 1993. Circ. 37,000. Byline given. Pays on acceptance. Offers 50% kill fee. Publishes ms an average of 2 months after acceptance. Editorial lead time 2 months. Accepts queries by e-mail. Sample copy free.

NONFICTION Buys 25 mss/year. Query with published clips. Length: 1,000-2,500 words. **Pays $1/word.** Sometimes pays expenses of writers on assignment.

⊖⊖ THE NATIONAL JURIST AND PRE LAW

Cypress Magazines, 7670 Opportunity Rd #105, San Diego CA 92111. (858)300-3201; (800)296-9656. **Fax:** (858)503-7588. **E-mail:** jack@cypressmagazines.com;

callahan@cypressmagazines.com. **Website:** www.nationaljurist.com. **Contact:** Jack Crittenden, editor-in-chief. **25% freelance written.** Bimonthly magazine covering law students and issues of interest to law students. Estab. 1991. Circ. 145,000. Pays on publication. No kill fee. Accepts queries by mail, e-mail.

NONFICTION Needs general interest, how-to, humor, interview. **Buys 4 mss/year.** Query. Length: 750-3,000 words. **Pays $100-500.**

PHOTOS State availability. Reviews contact sheets. Negotiates payment individually.

COLUMNS/DEPARTMENTS Pays $100-500.

$ PARALEGAL TODAY

Conexion International Media, Inc., 6030 Marshalee Dr., Elkridge MD 21075-5935. (443)445-3057. **Fax:** (443)445-3257. **E-mail:** pinfanti@connexionmedia.com. **Website:** www.paralegaltoday.com. **Contact:** Patricia E. Infanti, editor-in-chief; Charles Buckwalter, publisher. Quarterly magazine geared toward all legal assistants/paralegals throughout the U.S. and Canada, regardless of specialty (litigation, corporate, bankruptcy, environmental law, etc.). How-to articles to help paralegals perform their jobs more effectively are most in demand, as are career and salary information, technolgoy tips, and trends pieces. Estab. 1983. Circ. 8,000. Byline given. Pays on publication. Offers kill fee ($25-50 standard rate). Editorial lead time is 10 weeks. Submit seasonal material 3 months in advance. Accepts queries by mail, e-mail, fax, online submission form. Accepts simultaneous submissions. Responds in 2 months to mss. Sample copy online. Guidelines online.

NONFICTION Needs interview, unique and interesting paralegals in unique and particular work-related situations, news (brief, hard news topics regarding paralegals), features (present information to help paralegals advance their careers). Send query letter first; if electronic, send submission as attachment. **Pays $75-300.**

PHOTOS Send photos.

TIPS "Query editor first. Features run 1,500-2,500 words with sidebars. Writers must understand our audience. There is some opportunity for investigative journalism as well as the usual features, profiles, and columns. How-to articles are especially desired. If you are a great writer who can interview effectively and really dig into the topic to grab readers' attention, we need you."

$$ THE PENNSYLVANIA LAWYER

Pennsylvania Bar Association, 100 South St., P.O. Box 186, Harrisburg PA 17108. **E-mail:** editor@pabar.org; palawyer@editorialenterprises.com. **Website:** www.pabar.org. **Contact:** Donald C. Sarvey, editorial director. **25% freelance written. Prefers to work with published/established writers.** Bimonthly magazine published as a service to the legal profession and the members of the Pennsylvania Bar Association. Estab. 1979. Circ. 30,000. Byline given. Pays on acceptance. No kill fee. Publishes ms an average of 6 months after acceptance. Submit seasonal material 6 months in advance. Accepts queries by mail, e-mail, online submission form. Responds in 2 months to queries and mss. Sample copy for $2. Writer's guidelines for #10 SASE or by e-mail.

NONFICTION Needs how-to, interview, law-practice management, technology. **Buys 8-10 mss/year.** Query. Length: 1,200-1,500 words. **Pays $50 for book reviews; $75-400 for assigned articles; $150 for unsolicited articles.** Sometimes pays expenses of writers on assignment.

PHOTOS State availability. Identification of subjects required. Reviews contact sheets. Negotiates payment individually.

THE PUBLIC LAWYER

American Bar Association Government and Public Sector Lawyers Division, ABA Government and Public Sector Lawyers Division, 321 N. Clark St., MS 19.1, Chicago IL 60610. (312)988-5809. **Fax:** (312)988-5271. **E-mail:** katherine.mikkelson@americanbar.org. **Website:** www.governmentlawyer.org. **60% freelance written.** Biiannual magazine covering government attorneys and the legal issues that pertain to them. The mission of *The Public Lawyer* is to provide timely, practical information useful to all public lawyers regardless of practice setting. Publishes articles covering topics that are of universal interest to a diverse audience of public lawyers, such as public law office management, dealing with the media, politically motivated personnel decisions, etc. Articles must be national in scope. Estab. 1993. Circ. 6,500. Byline given. Publishes ms an average of 4 months after acceptance. Editorial lead time 6 months. Accepts queries by e-mail. Accepts simultaneous submissions. Responds in 1 month to queries. Responds in 2 months to mss. Sample copy free. Guidelines online.

NONFICTION Needs interview, opinion, technical, book reviews. Does not want "pieces that do not relate to the status of government lawyers or that are not legal issues exclusive to government lawyers. We accept very few articles written by private practice attorneys." **Buys 6-8 mss/year.** Query. Length: 2,000-5,000 words. **Pays contributor copies.**

PHOTOS State availability. Identification of subjects, model releases required. Reviews GIF/JPEG files. Offers no additional payment for photos accepted with ms.

TIPS "Articles stand a better chance of acceptance if they include one or more sidebars. Examples of sidebars include pieces explaining how government and public sector lawyers could use suggestions from the main article in their own practice, checklists, or other reference sources."

STUDENT LAWYER

ABA Publishing, Law Student Division, American Bar Association, 321 N. Clark St., Chicago IL 60654. (312)988-6049. **Fax:** (312)988-6081. **Website:** www.abanet.org/lsd/studentlawyer. **Contact:** Barry Malone, editor. **Works with a small number of new writers each year.** Monthly trade journal (September-May), 4-color, emphasizing legal education and social/legal issues. "*Student Lawyer* is a legal affairs magazine published by the Law Student Division of the American Bar Association. It is not a legal journal. It is a features magazine, competing for a share of law students' limited spare time—so the articles we publish must be informative, lively, good reads. We have no interest whatsoever in anything that resembles a footnoted, academic article. We are interested in professional and legal education issues, sociolegal phenomena, legal career features, and profiles of lawyers who are making an impact on the profession." Original artwork is returned to the artist after publication. Estab. 1972. Circ. 32,000. Byline given. No kill fee. Editorial lead time 4-6 months. Accepts queries by e-mail. Guidelines online.

NONFICTION No fiction; no footnoted academic articles or briefs. Query with published clips. Submit by MS Word attachment. Length: 2,000-2,500 words.

TIPS "We are not a law review; we are a features magazine with law school (in the broadest sense) as the common denominator. Write clearly and well. Expect to work with the editor to polish mss to perfection. We do not make assignments to writers with whose work we are not familiar. If you're interested in writing for us, send a detailed, thought-out query with 3 previously published clips. We are always willing to look at material on spec. Sorry, we don't return mss."

💲💲💲💲 **SUPER LAWYERS**

Thomson Reuters, 610 Opperman Dr., Eagan MN 55123. (877)787-5290. **Website:** www.superlawyers.com. **Contact:** Erik Lundegaard, editor. **100% freelance written.** Monthly magazine covering law and politics. Publishes glossy magazines in every region of the country; all serve a legal audience and have a storytelling sensibility. Writes profiles of interesting attorneys exclusively. Estab. 1990. Byline given. Pays on acceptance. Offers 25% kill fee. Publishes ms an average of 1 month after acceptance. Editorial lead time 6 months. Submit seasonal material 6 months in advance. Accepts queries by phone, online submission form. Accepts simultaneous submissions. Sample copy free. Guidelines free.

NONFICTION Needs general interest, historical. Query. Length: 500-2,000 words. **Pays 50¢-$1.50/ word.**

LUMBER

💲💲 **PALLET ENTERPRISE**

Industrial Reporting, Inc., 10244 Timber Ridge Dr., Ashland VA 23005. (804)550-0323. **Fax:** (804)550-2181. **E-mail:** edb@ireporting.com; chaille@ireporting.com. **Website:** www.palletenterprise.com. **Contact:** Edward C. Brindley, Jr., Ph.D., publisher; Chaille Brindley, assistant publisher. **40% freelance written.** Monthly magazine covering lumber and pallet operations. The *Pallet Enterprise* is a monthly trade magazine for the sawmill, pallet, remanufacturing, and wood processing industries. Articles should offer technical, solution-oriented information. Anti-forest articles are not accepted. Articles should focus on machinery and unique ways to improve profitability/make money. Estab. 1981. Circ. 14,500. Pays on publication. Editorial lead time 2 months. Submit seasonal material 2 months in advance. Accepts queries by mail, e-mail, fax, phone. YesAccepts simultaneous submissions. Sample copy online. Guidelines free.

NONFICTION Needs interview, new product, opinion, technical, industry news, environmental, forests operation/plant features. No lifestyle, humor, general news, etc. **Buys 20 mss/year.** Query with published clips. Length: 1,000-3,000 words. **Pays $200-400 for**

assigned articles. **Pays $100-400 for unsolicited articles.** Sometimes pays expenses of writers on assignment.

PHOTOS State availability. Captions, identification of subjects required. Reviews 3x5 prints. Negotiates payment individually.

COLUMNS/DEPARTMENTS Green Watch (environmental news/opinion affecting US forests), 1,500 words. **Buys 12 mss/year.** Query with published clips. **Pays $200-400.**

TIPS "Provide unique environmental or industry-oriented articles. Many of our freelance articles are company features of sawmills, pallet manufacturers, pallet recyclers, and wood waste processors."

💲💲 TIMBERLINE

Industrial Reporting, Inc., 10244 Timber Ridge Dr., Ashland VA 23005. (804)550-0323. **Fax:** (804)550-2181. **E-mail:** chaille@ireporting.com. **Website:** www.timberlinemag.com. **Contact:** Chaille Brindley, assistant publisher. **50% freelance written.** Monthly tabloid covering the forest products industry. Estab. 1994. Circ. 30,000. Byline given. Pays on publication. Editorial lead time 2 months. Submit seasonal material 2 months in advance. Accepts queries by mail, e-mail, fax. YesAccepts simultaneous submissions. Sample copy online. Guidelines free.

⭕ Articles should offer technical, solution-oriented information. Anti-forest products, industry articles are not accepted. Articles should focus on machinery and unique ways to improve profitability and make money.

NONFICTION Contact: Tim Cox, editor. Needs historical, interview, new product, opinion, technical, industry news, environmental operation/plant features. No lifestyles, humor, general news, etc. **Buys 25 mss/year.** Query with published clips. Length: 1,000-3,000 words. **Pays $200-400 for assigned articles. Pays $100-400 for unsolicited articles.** Sometimes pays expenses of writers on assignment.

PHOTOS State availability. Captions, identification of subjects required. Reviews 3x5 prints. Negotiates payment individually.

COLUMNS/DEPARTMENTS Contact: Tim Cox, editor. From the Hill (legislative news impacting the forest products industry), 1,800 words; Green Watch (environmental news/opinion affecting U.S. forests), 1,500 words. **Buys 12 mss/year.** Query with published clips. **Pays $200-400.**

TIPS "Provide unique environmental or industry-oriented articles. Many of our freelance articles are company features of logging operations or sawmills."

💲💲 TIMBERWEST

TimberWest Publications, LLC, P.O. Box 610, Edmonds WA 98020. (425)778-3388. **Fax:** (425)771-3623. **E-mail:** timberwest@forestnet.com; diane@forestnet.com. **Website:** www.forestnet.com. **Contact:** Diane Mettler, managing editor. **75% freelance written.** Monthly magazine covering logging and lumber segment of the forestry industry in the Northwest. Publishes primarily profiles on loggers and their operations—with an emphasis on the machinery—in Washington, Oregon, Idaho, Montana, Northern California, and Alaska. Some timber issues are highly controversial, and although the magazine will report on the issues, this is a pro-logging publication. Does not publish articles with a negative slant on the timber industry. Estab. 1975. Circ. 10,000. Byline given. Pays on acceptance. No kill fee. Editorial lead time 3 months. Accepts queries by mail, fax. Responds in 3 weeks to queries. Sample copy for $2. Guidelines for #10 sase.

NONFICTION Needs historical, interview, new product. No articles that put the timber industry in a bad light, such as environmental articles against logging." **Buys 50 mss/year.** Query with published clips. Length: 1,100-1,500 words. **Pays $350.** Pays expenses of writers on assignment.

PHOTOS Send photos. Captions, identification of subjects required. Reviews contact sheets, transparencies, prints, GIF/JPEG files. Offers no additional payment for photos accepted with ms.

FILLERS Needs facts, newsbreaks. **Buys 10 mss/year.** Length: 400-800 words. **Pays $100-250.**

TIPS "We are always interested in profiles of loggers and their operations in Alaska, Oregon, Washington, Montana, and Northern California. We also want articles pertaining to current industry topics, such as fire abatement, sustainable forests, or new technology. Read an issue to get a clear idea of the type of material *TimberWest* publishes. The audience is primarily loggers and topics that focus on an 'evolving' timber industry versus a 'dying' industry will find a place in the magazine. When querying, a clear overview of the article will enhance acceptance."

MACHINERY AND METAL

🟢🟢🟢 AMERICANMACHINIST.COM

Penton Media, 1300 E. 9th St., Cleveland OH 44114. (216)931-9464. **Fax:** (913)514-6386. **E-mail:** robert.brooks@penton.com. **Website:** www.americanmachinist.com. **Contact:** Robert Brooks, editor-in-chief. **10% freelance written.** Monthly online website covering all forms of metalworking covering all forms of metalworking. Accepts contributed features and articles. *American Machinist* is an essential online source dedicated to metalworking in the United States. Readers are the owners and managers of metalworking shops. Publishes articles that provide the managers and owners of job shops, contract shops, and captive shops the information they need to make their operations more efficient, more productive, and more profitable. Articles are technical in nature and must be focused on technology that will help these shops to become more competitive on a global basis. Readers are skilled machinists. This is not the place for lightweight items about manufacturing. Not interested in articles on management theories. Estab. 1877. Circ. 80,000. Byline sometimes given. Offers 20% kill fee. Publishes ms an average of 1-2 months after acceptance. Editorial lead time 3-6 months. Submit seasonal material 4-6 months in advance. Accepts queries by mail, e-mail, phone. Responds in 1-2 weeks to queries. Responds in 1 month to mss. Sample copy online.

NONFICTION Needs general interest, how-to, new product, opinion, personal experience, photo feature, technical. Query with published clips. Length: 600-2,400 words. **Pays $300-1,200.** Sometimes pays expenses of writers on assignment.

PHOTOS State availability. Captions, identification of subjects, model releases required. Reviews GIF/JPEG files. Negotiates payment individually.

FILLERS Needs anecdotes, facts, gags, newsbreaks, short humor. **Buys 12-18 mss/year.** Length: 50-200 words. **Pays $25-100.**

TIPS "With our exacting audience, a writer would do well to have some background working with machine tools."

🟢🟢🟢 CUTTING TOOL ENGINEERING

CTE Publications, Inc., 1 Northfield Plaza, Suite 240, Northfield IL 60093. (847)714-0175. **Fax:** (847)559-4444. **E-mail:** alanr@jwr.com. **Website:** www.ctemag.com. **Contact:** Alan Richter, editor. **40% freelance written.** Monthly magazine covering industrial metal cutting tools and metal cutting operations. *Cutting Tool Engineering* serves owners, managers, and engineers who work in manufacturing, specifically manufacturing that involves cutting or grinding metal or other materials. Writing should be geared toward improving manufacturing processes. Circ. 48,000. Byline given. Pays on publication. Offers 50% kill fee. Publishes ms an average of 2 months after acceptance. Editorial lead time 2 months. Accepts queries by mail, fax. Responds in 2 months to mss. Sample copy and writers guidelines free.

NONFICTION Needs how-to, opinion, personal experience, technical. Does not want fiction or articles that don't relate to manufacturing. **Buys 10 mss/year.** Length: 1,500-3,000 words. **Pays $750-1,500.** Pays expenses of writers on assignment.

PHOTOS State availability. Captions required. Reviews transparencies, prints. Negotiates payment individually.

TIPS "For queries, write 2 clear paragraphs about how the proposed article will play out. Include sources that would be in the article."

🟢🟢🟢 EQUIPMENT JOURNAL

Pace Publishing, 5160 Explorer Dr., Unit 6, Mississauga ON L4W 4T7 Canada. (416)459-5163. **E-mail:** editor@equipmentjournal.com. **Website:** www.equipmentjournal.com. Canada's national heavy equipment newspaper. Focuses on the construction, material handling, mining, forestry and on-highway transportation industries." Estab. 1964. Circ. 23,000 subscriber. Byline given. Pays on publication. No kill fee. Publishes ms an average of 1-2 months after acceptance. Editorial lead time 2-3 months. Accepts queries by mail. YesAccepts simultaneous submissions. Sample copy and guidelines free.

NONFICTION Needs how-to, interview, new product, photo feature, technical. No material that falls outside of *EJ*'s mandate—the Canadian equipment industry. **Buys 15 mss/year.** Send complete ms. "We prefer electronic submissions. We do not accept unsolicited freelance submissions." Length: 500-1,500 words. **$250-400 for assigned and unsolicited articles.** Sometimes pays expenses of writers on assignment.

PHOTOS Contact: Nathan Medcalf, editor. State availability. Identification of subjects required. 4 x 6 prints. Negotiates payment individually.

TIPS "Please pitch a story, instead of asking for an assignment. We are looking for stories of construction sites."

⊜⊜⊜ THE FABRICATOR

833 Featherstone Rd., Rockford IL 61107. (815)399-8700. **Fax:** (815)381-1370. **E-mail:** timh@thefabricator.com. **Website:** www.thefabricator.com; www.fmacommunications.com. **Contact:** Dan Davis, editor-in-chief; Tim Heston, senior editor. **15% freelance written.** Monthly magazine covering metal forming and fabricating. Purpose is to disseminate information about modern metal forming and fabricating techniques, machinery, tooling, and management concepts for the metal fabricator. Estab. 1971. Circ. 58,000. Byline given. Pays on publication. No kill fee. Editorial lead time 6 months. Accepts queries by mail, e-mail. Responds in 2 weeks to queries. Responds in 1 month to mss. Sample copy free.

NONFICTION Needs how-to, technical, company profile. Query with published clips. Length: 1,200-2,000 words. **Pays 40-80¢/word.**

PHOTOS Request guidelines for digital images. State availability. Captions, identification of subjects required. Reviews transparencies, prints. Negotiates payment individually.

MACHINE DESIGN

Penton Media, Penton Media Bldg., 1300 E. 9th St., Cleveland OH 44114. (216)931-9412. **Fax:** (216)621-8469. **E-mail:** mdeditor@penton.com. **Website:** www.machinedesign.com. Semimonthly magazine covering machine design. Covers the design engineering of manufactured products across the entire spectrum of the industry for people who perform design engineering functions. Circ. 134,000. No kill fee. Editorial lead time 10 weeks. Accepts queries by mail, e-mail. No

NONFICTION Needs how-to, new product, technical. Send complete ms.

COLUMNS/DEPARTMENTS Query with or without published clips, or send complete ms.

⊜⊜ SPRINGS

Spring Manufacturers Institute, 2001 Midwest Rd., Suite 106, Oak Brook IL 60523-1335. (630)495-8588. **Fax:** (630)495-8595. **E-mail:** lynne@smihq.org. **Website:** www.smihq.org. **Contact:** Lynne Carr, general manager. **10% freelance written.** Quarterly magazine covering precision mechanical spring manufacture. Articles should be aimed at spring manufacturers. Estab. 1962. Circ. 10,800. Byline given. Pays on pub-

lication. No kill fee. Publishes ms an average of 3-6 months after acceptance. Editorial lead time 4 months. Accepts simultaneous submissions. Sample copy free. Guidelines online.

NONFICTION Needs general interest, how-to, interview, opinion, personal experience, technical. **Buys 4-6 mss/year.** Length: 2,000-10,000 words. **Pays $100-600 for assigned articles.**

PHOTOS State availability. Captions required. Reviews prints, digital photos. Offers no additional payment for photos accepted with ms.

TIPS "In analyzing all contributions, *Springs* looks for information that will help our readers run their businesses more effectively. We are far more interested in comprehensive detail than flashy writing. In fact, we like to develop a 'partnership in expertise' with our authors; you provide the technical knowledge and we assist you with communications and presentation skills. Thus, once your article is accepted for publication, you should expect the editor to be in touch regarding the edited version of your ms. All authors receive edited copy before publication so they can verify the factual accuracy of the reworked piece."

⊜⊜⊜ STAMPING JOURNAL

Fabricators & Manufacturers Association (FMA), 833 Featherstone Rd., Rockford IL 61107. (815)399-8700. **Fax:** (815)381-1370. **E-mail:** dand@thefabricator.com; timh@thefabricator.com. **Website:** www.thefabricator.com. **Contact:** Dan Davis, editor-in-chief; Tim Heston, senior editor. **15% freelance written.** Bimonthly magazine covering metal stamping. Looks for how-to and educational articles—nonpromotional. Estab. 1989. Circ. 35,000. Byline given. Pays on publication. No kill fee. Editorial lead time 6 months. Accepts queries by mail, e-mail, phone. Responds in 2 weeks to queries. Sample copy and writer's guidelines free.

NONFICTION **Pays 40-80¢/word.** Sometimes pays expenses of writers on assignment.

PHOTOS State availability. Captions, identification of subjects required. Negotiates payment individually.

TIPS "Articles should be impartial and should not describe the benefits of certain products available from certain companies. They should not be biased toward the author's or against a competitor's products or technologies. The publisher may refuse any article that does not conform to this guideline."

$ $ $ $ TODAY'S MACHINING WORLD

Screw Machine World, Inc., 4235 W. 166th St., Oak Forest IL 60452. (708)535-2237. **Fax:** (708)850-1334. **E-mail:** emily@todaysmachiningworld.com; noah@todaysmachiningworld.com. **Website:** www.todaysmachiningworld.com. **Contact:** Emily Halgrimson, managing editor; Noah Graff, writer/website editor. **40% freelance written.** Online magazine covering metal turned parts manufacturing in the US and worldwide. Hire writers to tell a success story or challenge regarding our industry. Estab. 2001. Byline given. Pays on publication. Publishes ms an average of 2 months after acceptance. Editorial lead time 2-4 months. Submit seasonal material 2 months in advance. Responds in 1 month to mss. Guidelines free.

NONFICTION Needs general interest, how-to. **Buys 12-15 mss/year.** Query. Do not send unsolicited mss. Length: 1,500-2,500 words.

PHOTOS State availability. Captions required. Reviews GIF/JPEG files. Negotiates payment individually.

COLUMNS/DEPARTMENTS Shop Doc (manufacturing problem/solution), 500 words. Query.

TIPS "You may submit an idea related to manufacturing that would be of interest to our readers. If you pitch it, we'll respond!"

THE WORLD OF WELDING

Hobart Institute of Welding Technology, 400 Trade Square E, Troy OH 45373. (937)332-5603. **Fax:** (937)332-5220. **E-mail:** hiwt@welding.org. **Website:** www.worldofwelding.org. **10% freelance written.** Quarterly magazine covering welding training and education. Estab. 1930. Circ. 6,500. Byline given. Publishes ms an average of 3 months after acceptance. Editorial lead time 3 months. Submit seasonal material 3 months in advance. Accepts queries by mail, e-mail, fax. Accepts simultaneous submissions. Responds in 1 week to queries. Responds in 3 months to mss. Sample copy and guidelines free.

O The content must be educational and must contain welding topic information.

NONFICTION Needs general interest, historical, how-to, interview, personal experience, photo feature, technical, welding topics. Query with published clips.

PHOTOS Send photos. Captions, identification of subjects, model releases required. Reviews GIF/JPEG files. Offers no additional payment for photos accepted with ms.

FILLERS Needs facts, newsbreaks. Query.

TIPS "Writers must be willing to donate material on welding and metallurgy related topics, welded art/sculpture, personal welding experiences. An editorial committee reviews submissions and determines acceptance."

MAINTENANCE AND SAFETY

$ $ AMERICAN WINDOW CLEANER MAGAZINE

12 Publishing Corp., 750-B NW Broad St., Southern Pines NC 28387. (910)693-2644. **Fax:** (910)246-1681. **E-mail:** info@awcmag.com; karen@awcmag.com. **Website:** www.awcmag.com. **Contact:** Karen Grinter, creative director. **20% freelance written.** Bimonthly magazine on window cleaning. Produces articles to help window cleaners become more profitable, safe, professional, and feel good about what they do. Estab. 1986. Circ. 8,000. Byline given. Pays on acceptance. Offers 33% kill fee. Publishes ms an average of 4-8 months after acceptance. Editorial lead time 2 months. Submit seasonal material 3 months in advance. Responds in 2 weeks to queries. Responds in 1 month to mss. Sample copy free.

NONFICTION Needs how-to, humor, inspirational, interview, personal experience, photo feature, technical, add-on business. "We do not want PR-driven pieces. We want to educate—not push a particular product." **Buys 20 mss/year.** Query. Length: 500-5,000 words. **Pays $50-250.**

PHOTOS State availability. Captions required. Reviews contact sheets, transparencies, 4x6 prints. Offers $10 per photo.

COLUMNS/DEPARTMENTS Window Cleaning Tips (tricks of the trade); 1,000-2,000 words; Humor-anecdotes-feel good-abouts (window cleaning industry); Computer High-Tech (tips on new technology), all 1,000 words **Buys 12 mss/year.** Query. **Pays $50-100.**

TIPS "*American Window Cleaner Magazine* covers an unusual niche that gets people's curiosity. Articles that are technical in nature and emphasize practical tips or safety, and how to work more efficiently, have the best chances of being published. Articles include: window cleaning unusual buildings, landmarks; working for well-known people/celebrities; window cleaning in resorts/casinos/unusual cities; humor or satire about our industry or the public's perception of it. At some point, we make phone contact and chat to see if our interests are compatible."

$ $ EXECUTIVE HOUSEKEEPING TODAY

The International Executive Housekeepers Association, 1001 Eastwind Dr., Suite 301, Westerville OH 43081-3361. (614)895-7166. **Fax:** (614)895-1248. **E-mail:** ldriscoll@ieha.org; excel@ieha.org. **Website:** www.ieha.org. **Contact:** Leah Driscoll, editor. **50% freelance written.** Monthly magazine for nearly 5,000 decision makers responsible for housekeeping management (cleaning, grounds maintenance, laundry, linen, pest control, waste management, regulatory compliance, training) for a variety of institutions: hospitality, healthcare, education, retail, government. Estab. 1930. Circ. 5,500. Byline given. No kill fee. Publishes ms an average of 6 months after acceptance. Editorial lead time 2 months. Submit seasonal material 3 months in advance. Accepts queries by mail, e-mail, fax, phone.

NONFICTION Needs general interest, interview, new product, related to magazine's scope, personal experience, in housekeeping profession, technical. **Buys 30 mss/year.** Query with published clips. Length: 1,500-2,000 words.

PHOTOS State availability. Identification of subjects required. Offers no additional payment for photos accepted with ms.

COLUMNS/DEPARTMENTS Federal Report (OSHA/EPA requirements), 1,000 words; Industry News; Management Perspectives (industry specific), 1,500-2,000 words. Query with published clips.

TIPS "Have a background in the industry or personal experience with any aspect of it."

MANAGEMENT AND SUPERVISION

APICS MAGAZINE

APICS The Association for Operations Management, 8430 W. Bryn Mawr Ave., Suite 1000, Chicago IL 60631. (773)867-1777. **E-mail:** editorial@apics.org. **Website:** www.apics.org. **Contact:** Elizabeth Rennie, managing editor. **15% freelance written.** Bimonthly magazine covering operations management, enterprise, supply chain, production and inventory management, warehousing and logistics. *APICS* is an award-winning publication featuring in-novative ideas and real-world strategies for inventory, materials, production, and supply chain management; planning and scheduling; purchasing; logistics; warehousing; transportation and logistics; and more. Estab. 1987. Circ. 45,000. Byline given. Pays on acceptance. Offers 50% kill fee. Publishes ms an average of 2 months after acceptance. Editorial lead time 3-4 months. Submit seasonal material 3-4 months in advance. Accepts queries by e-mail. Accepts simultaneous submissions.

NONFICTION Needs technical, General research/reporting. Does not want vendor-driven articles. **Buys 3-5 mss/year.** Query. Length: 1,750-2,250 words.

$ $ $ HUMAN RESOURCE EXECUTIVE

LRP Publications Magazine Group, P.O. Box 980, Horsham PA 19044-0980. (215)784-0910. **Fax:** (215)784-0275. **E-mail:** kfrasch@lrp.com. **E-mail:** tgarrison@lrp.com. **Website:** www.hronline.com. **Contact:** Kristen B. Frasch, managing editor; Terri Garrison, editorial assistant. **30% freelance written.** Magazine published 16 times/year serving the information needs of chief human resource professionals/executives in companies, government agencies, and nonprofit institutions with 500 or more employees. Estab. 1987. Circ. 75,000. Byline given. Pays on acceptance. Offers kill fee. Pays 50% kill fee on assigned stories. Publishes ms an average of 2 months after acceptance. Accepts queries by mail, e-mail, fax. Responds in 1 month to mss. Guidelines online.

NONFICTION Needs book excerpts, interview. **Buys 16 mss/year.** Query with published clips. Length: 1,800 words. **Pays $200-1,000.** Sometimes pays expenses of writers on assignment.

PHOTOS State availability. Identification of subjects required. Reviews contact sheets. Offers no additional payment for photos accepted with ms.

$ $ INCENTIVE

Northstar Travel Media LLC, 100 Lighting Way, Secaucus NJ 07094. (201)902-2000; (201)902-1975. **E-mail:** lcioffi@ntmllc.com; dting@ntmllc.com. **Website:** www.incentivemag.com. **Contact:** Lori Cioffi, editorial director; Deanna Ting, managing editor. Monthly magazine covering sales promotion and employee motivation: managing and marketing through motivation. Estab. 1905. Circ. 41,000. Byline given. Pays on acceptance. No kill fee. Publishes ms an average of 3 months after acceptance. Accepts queries by mail, e-mail, fax. Responds in 1 month to queries.

Responds in 2 months to mss. Sample copy for SAE with 9x12 envelope.

NONFICTION Needs general interest, motivation, demographics, how-to, types of sales promotion, buying product categories, using destinations, interview, sales promotion executives, travel, incentive-oriented, corporate case studies. **Buys 48 mss/year.** Query with published clips. Length: 1,000-2,000 words. **Pays $250-700 for assigned articles. Does not pay for unsolicited articles.** Pays expenses of writers on assignment.

REPRINTS Send tearsheet and information about when and where the material previously appeared. Pays 50% of the amount paid for an original article.

PHOTOS Send photos. Identification of subjects required. Reviews contact sheets, transparencies. Offers some additional payment for photos accepted with ms.

TIPS "Read the publication, then query."

$$ PLAYGROUND MAGAZINE

Harris Publishing, 360 B St., Idaho Falls ID 83402. (208)652-3683. **Fax:** (208)652-7856. **Website:** www.playgroundmag.com. **25% freelance written.** Magazine published quarterly covering playgrounds, play-related issues, equipment, and industry trends. *Playground Magazine* targets park and recreation management, elementary school teachers and administrators, child care facilities, and parent-group leader readership. Articles should focus on play and the playground market as a whole, including aquatic play and surfacing. Estab. 2000. Circ. 35,000. Byline given. Pays on publication. No kill fee. Publishes ms an average of 6 months after acceptance. Editorial lead time 2 months. Submit seasonal material 1 year in advance. Accepts queries by mail, e-mail. Accepts simultaneous submissions. Responds in 1 month to queries. Responds in 2 months to mss. Sample copy for $5. Guidelines for #10 SASE.

NONFICTION Needs how-to, interview, new product, opinion, personal experience, photo feature, technical, travel. *Playground Magazine* does not publish any articles that do not directly relate to play and the playground industry. **Buys 4-6 mss/year.** Query. Length: 800-1,500 words. **Pays $50-300 for assigned articles.** Sometimes pays expenses of writers on assignment.

PHOTOS State availability of or send photos. Captions, identification of subjects, model releases required. Reviews 35mm transparencies, GIF/JPEG files (350 dpi or better). Offers no additional payment for photos accepted with ms.

COLUMNS/DEPARTMENTS Dream Spaces (an article that profiles a unique play area and focuses on community involvement, unique design, or human interest), 800-1,200 words. **Buys 2 mss/year.** Query. **Pays $100-300.**

TIPS "We are looking for articles that managers can use as a resource when considering playground construction, management, safety, installation, maintenance, etc. Writers should find unique angles to playground-related features such as current trends in the industry, the value of play, natural play, the need for recess, etc. We are a trade journal that offers up-to-date industry news and features that promote play and the playground industry."

MARINE AND MARITIME INDUSTRIES

$ AUSMARINE

Baird Publications, Suite 3, 20 Cato St., Hawthorne East 3123 Australia. (61)(3)9824-6055. **Fax:** (61)(3)9824-6588. **E-mail:** marinfo@baird.com.au; ausmarine@baird.com.au. **Website:** www.bairdmaritime.com. Monthly magazine covering the Australian commercial fishing and government marine industry. *Ausmarine* offers its readers information and ideas as to how to improve the efficiency and profitability of their business operations through the adoption of new technology and equipment, improved operational techniques and systems, and by simply providing them with the information required to make the right business decisions. Estab. 1978.

NONFICTION Query for submission info.

$$ CURRENTS

Marine Technology Society, 1100 H St. NW, Suite LL-100, Washington DC 20005. (202)717-8705. **Fax:** (202)347-4302. **E-mail:** publications@mtsociety.org. **Website:** www.mtsociety.org. **Contact:** Mary Beth Loutinsky, communications manager. Bimonthly newsletter covering commercial, academic, scientific marine technology. Readers are engineers and technologists who design, develop ,and maintain the equipment and instruments used to understand and explore the oceans. The newsletter covers society news, industry news, science and technology news, and similar news. Estab. 1963. Circ. 3,200. Byline giv-

TRADE JOURNALS

en. Pays on acceptance. No kill fee. Editorial lead time 1-2 months. Accepts queries by e-mail. YesAccepts simultaneous submissions. Responds in 4 weeks to queries Sample copy free.

NONFICTION Needs interview, technical. **Buys 1-6 mss/year.** Query. Length: 250-500 words. **Pays $100-500 for assigned articles.** Sometimes pays expenses of writers on assignment.

🌐🟢 PROFESSIONAL MARINER

Navigator Publishing, P.O. Box 569, Portland ME 04112. (207)772-2466. **Fax:** (207)772-2879. **E-mail:** dyanchunas@professionalmariner.com. **Website:** www.professionalmariner.com. **Contact:** Dom Yanchunas, editor. **75% freelance written.** Bimonthly magazine covering professional seamanship and maritime industry news. Estab. 1993. Circ. 29,000. Byline given. Pays on publication. No kill fee. Editorial lead time 3 months. Accepts queries by mail, e-mail. Accepts simultaneous submissions.

NONFICTION **Buys 15 mss/year.** Query. Length: varies; short clips to long profiles/features. **Pays 25¢/word.** Sometimes pays expenses of writers on assignment.

PHOTOS Send photos. Captions, identification of subjects required. Reviews prints, slides. Negotiates payment individually.

TIPS "Remember that our audience comprises maritime industry professionals. Stories must be written at a level that will benefit this group."

🟢 WORK BOAT WORLD

Baird Maritime, Suite 3, 20 Cato St., Hawthorn East Victoria 3123 Australia. (61)(3)9824-6055. **Fax:** (61)(3)9824-6588. **E-mail:** marinfo@baird.com.au; editor@baird.com.au. **Website:** www.bairdmaritime.com. Monthly magazine covering all types of commercial, military, and government vessels to around 130 meters in length. Maintaining close contact with ship builders, designers, owners and operators, suppliers of vessel equipment and suppliers of services on a worldwide basis, the editors and journalists of *Work Boat World* seek always to be informative. They constantly put themselves in the shoes of readers so as to produce editorial matter that interests, educates, informs, and entertains. Estab. 1982.

NONFICTION Needs general interest, how-to, interview, new product. Query. See website for info on upcoming editorial material.

MEDICAL

🌐 ADVANCE FOR RESPIRATORY CARE & SLEEP MEDICINE

Merion Publications, Inc., 2900 Horizon Dr., Box 61556, King of Prussia PA 19406. (800)355-5627, ext. 1324. **Fax:** (610)278-1425. **E-mail:** ptarapchak@advanceweb.com. **Website:** respiratory-care-sleep-medicine.advanceweb.com; www.advanceweb.com. **Contact:** Pamela Tarapchak, editor. **50% freelance written.** Biweekly magazine covering clinical, technical and business management trends for professionals in pulmonary, respiratory care, and sleep. *ADVANCE for Respiratory Care & Sleep Medicine* welcomes original articles, on speculation, from members of the respiratory care and sleep professions. Once accepted, mss become the property of *ADVANCE for Respiratory Care & Sleep Medicine* and cannot be reproduced elsewhere without permission from the editor. An honorarium is paid for published articles. Estab. 1988. Circ. 45,500. Byline given. Pays on publication. Offers 75% kill fee. Publishes ms an average of 6 months after acceptance. Editorial lead time 1 month. Submit seasonal material 3 months in advance. Accepts queries by mail, e-mail. Accepts simultaneous submissions. Responds in 2 weeks to queries. Responds in up to 6 months to mss. Sample copy online. Guidelines online for download.

NONFICTION Needs technical. "We do not want to get general information articles about specific respiratory care related diseases. For example, our audience is all too familiar with cystic fibrosis, asthma, COPD, bronchitis, Alpha 1 Antitrypsin Defiency, pulmonary hypertension and the like." **Buys 2-3 mss/year.** Query. E-mail article and send printout by mail. Length: 1,500-2,000/words; double-spaced, 4-7 pages. **Pays honorarium.** Sometimes pays expenses of writers on assignment.

PHOTOS State availability. Captions, identification of subjects, model releases required. Reviews GIF/JPEG files. Negotiates payment individually.

TIPS "The only way to truly break into the market for this publication on a freelance basis is to have a background in health care. All of our columnists are caregivers; most of our freelancers are caregivers. Any materials that come in of a general nature like 'contact me for freelance writing assignments or photography' are discarded."

$ ADVANCE NEWSMAGAZINES

Merion Publications Inc., 2900 Horizon Dr., King of Prussia PA 19406. (800)355-5627, ext. 1229. **Fax:** (610)278-1425. **E-mail:** advance@merion.com. **Website:** www.advanceweb.com. More than 30 magazines covering allied health fields, nursing, age management, long-term care, and more. Byline given. Pays on publication. Editorial lead time 3 months. Accepts queries by e-mail only.

NONFICTION Needs interview, new product, personal experience, technical. Query with published clips. Include name, and phone and fax number for verification. Length: 2,000 words.

COLUMNS/DEPARTMENTS Phlebotomy Focus, Safety Solutions, Technology Trends, POL Perspectives, Performance in POCT, Eye on Education.

$$$ AHIP COVERAGE

America's Health Insurance Plans, 601 Pennsylvania Ave. NW, South Bldg., Suite 500, Washington DC 20004. (202)778-8493. **Fax:** (202)331-7487. **E-mail:** ahip@ahip.org. **Website:** www.ahip.org. **75% freelance written.** Bimonthly magazine geared toward administrators in America's health insurance companies. Articles should inform and generate interest and discussion about topics on anything from patient care to regulatory issues. Estab. 1990. Circ. 12,000. Byline given. Pays within 30 days of acceptance of article in final form. Offers 30% kill fee. Publishes ms an average of 2 months after acceptance. Editorial lead time 2 months. Submit seasonal material 4 months in advance. Accepts queries by mail, e-mail, fax. Accepts simultaneous submissions. Sample copy free.

NONFICTION Needs book excerpts, how-to, how industry professionals can better operate their health plans, opinion. "We do not accept stories that promote products." Send complete ms. Length: 1,800-2,500 words. **Pays 65¢/word minimum.** Pays phone expenses of writers on assignment.

TIPS "Look for health plan success stories in your community; we like to include case studies on a variety of topics—including patient care, provider relations, regulatory issues—so that our readers can learn from their colleagues. Our readers are members of our trade association and look for advice and news. Topics relating to the quality of health plans are the ones more frequently assigned to writers, whether a feature or department. We also welcome story ideas. Just send us a letter with the details."

AMERICA'S PHARMACIST

National Community Pharmacists Association, 100 Daingerfield Rd., Suite 205, Alexandria VA 22314-2885. (800)544-7447. **Fax:** (703)683-3619. **E-mail:** mike.conlan@ncpanet.org. **Website:** www.americaspharmacist.net. **Contact:** Michael F. Conlan, vice president; Chris Linville, managing editor. **10% freelance written.** Monthly magazine. *America's Pharmacist* publishes business and management information and personal profiles of independent community pharmacists, the magazine's principal readers. Articles feature the very latest in successful business strategies, specialty pharmacy services, medication safety, consumer advice, continuing education, legislation, and regulation. Estab. 1904. Circ. 25,000. Byline given. Pays on publication. No kill fee. Publishes ms an average of 3 months after acceptance. Editorial lead time 3 months. Submit seasonal material 3 months in advance. Accepts queries by mail, e-mail, fax. Accepts simultaneous submissions. Responds in 1 week to queries. Responds in 2 weeks to mss. Sample copy free.

NONFICTION Needs interview, business information. **Buys 3 mss/year.** Query. Length: 1,500-2,500 words.

PHOTOS State availability. Captions, identification of subjects, model releases required. Reviews contact sheets. Negotiates payment individually.

$ AT THE CENTER

Right Ideas, Inc., P.O. Box 309, Fleetwood PA 19522. (800)588-7744. **Fax:** (800)588-7744. **E-mail:** info@atcmag.com. **Website:** www.atcmag.com. **20% freelance written.** Webzine published 4 times/year that provides encouragement and education to the staff, volunteers, and board members working in crisis pregnancy centers. Estab. 2000. Circ. 30,000. Byline given. Pays on publication. No kill fee. Publishes ms an average of 1 year after acceptance. Editorial lead time 6 months. Submit seasonal material 1 year in advance. Accepts queries by mail, e-mail, fax. Accepts simultaneous submissions. Responds in 1 month to queries. Responds in 3-4 months to mss. Sample copy online. Guidelines for #10 SASE or by e-mail.

NONFICTION **Buys about 12 mss/year.** Query. Length: 800-1,200 words. **Pays $150 for assigned articles. Pays $50-150 for unsolicited articles.**

TIPS "Generally, we don't have enough space to print personal stories. If your story is relevant to the things you want to share with staff and volunteers of the centers, your best chance to get it published is to keep it brief (a couple paragraphs). Any scripture references should be quoted from KJV or ESV."

EMERGENCY MEDICINE NEWS

Lippincott Williams & Wilkins, Wolters Kluwer Health, 333 7th Ave., 19th Floor, New York NY 10001. **E-mail:** emn@lww.com. **Website:** www.em-news. com. **100% freelance written.** Monthly publication covering emergency medicine only, not emergency nursing, EMTs, PAs. *Emergency Medicine News* provides breaking coverage of advances, trends and issues within the field, as well as clinical commentary with a CME activity by Editorial Board Chairman James R. Roberts, MD, a leader in the field. Estab. 1978. Circ. 34,000. Byline given. Pays on acceptance. Editorial lead time 2 months. Submit seasonal material 4 months in advance. Accepts queries by e-mail. Responds in 2 weeks to queries. Responds in 1 month to mss. Sample copy online.

NONFICTION Query.

TIPS "Best way to break in is to read publication online and pitch unique idea. No queries just touting experience or looking for assignment."

⊖⊖ JEMS

PennWell Corporation, 525 B St., Suite 1800, San Diego CA 92101. (800)266-5367. **E-mail:** rkelley@ pennwell.com. **Website:** www.jems.com. **Contact:** Ryan Kelley, senior editor. **95% freelance written.** Monthly magazine directed to personnel who serve the pre-hospital emergency medicine industry: paramedics, EMTs, emergency physicians and nurses, administrators, EMS consultants, etc. Estab. 1980. Circ. 45,000. Byline given. Pays on publication. No kill fee. Publishes ms an average of 6 months after acceptance. Submit seasonal material 6 months in advance. Accepts queries by e-mail. Responds in 2-3 months to queries. Sample copy free. Guidelines available at www.jems.com/about/author-guidelines.

NONFICTION Needs essays, expose, general interest, how-to, humor, interview, new product, opinion, personal experience, photo feature, technical; continuing education. **Buys 50 mss/year.** Query Ryan Kelley with contact information, suggested title, ms document (can be an outline), a summary, a general ms classification, and photos or figures to be considered with the ms. **Pays $100-350.**

PHOTOS State availability. Identification of subjects, model releases required. Reviews 4x6 prints, digital images. Offers $25 minimum per photo.

COLUMNS/DEPARTMENTS Length: 850 words maximum. Query with or without published clips. **Pays $50-250.**

TIPS "Please submit a 1-page cover letter with your ms. Your letter should answer these questions: 1) What specifically are you going to tell *JEMS* readers about pre-hospital medical care? 2) Why do *JEMS* readers need to know this? 3) How will you make your case (i.e., literature review, original research, interviews, personal experience, observation)? Your query should explain your qualifications, as well as include previous writing samples."

⊖⊖⊖ MANAGED CARE

780 Township Line Rd., Yardley PA 19067. (267)685-2788. **Fax:** (267)685-2966. **E-mail:** jmarcille@managedcaremag.com. **Website:** www.managedcaremag. com. **Contact:** John Marcille, editor. **75% freelance written.** Monthly magazine that delivers high-interest, full-length articles and shorter features on clinical and business aspects of the health care industry. Emphasizes practical, usable information that helps HMO medical directors and pharmacy directors cope with the options, challenges, and hazards in the rapidly changing health care industry. Estab. 1992. Circ. 44,000. Byline given. Pays on acceptance. Offers 20% kill fee. Publishes ms an average of 6 weeks after acceptance. Editorial lead time 3 months. Submit seasonal material 4 months in advance. Accepts queries by mail, e-mail, fax. Responds in 3 weeks to queries. Responds in 2 months to mss. Sample copy free. Guidelines online.

NONFICTION Needs book excerpts, general interest, trends in health-care delivery and financing, quality of care, and employee concerns, how-to, deal with requisites of managed care, such as contracts with health plans, affiliation arrangements, accreditation, computer needs, etc., original research and review articles that examine the relationship between health care delivery and financing. Also considered occasionally are personal experience, opinion, interview/profile, and humor pieces, but these must have a strong managed care angle and draw upon the insights of (if they are not written by) a knowledgeable managed care professional. **Buys 40 mss/year.** Query with published clips.

Length: 1,000-3,000 words. **Pays 75¢/word.** Pays expenses of writers on assignment.

PHOTOS State availability. Reviews contact sheets, negatives, transparencies, prints. Negotiates payment individually.

TIPS "Know our audience (health plan executives) and their needs. Study our website to see what we cover."

MEDESTHETICS

Creative Age Communications, 7628 Densmore Ave., Van Nuys CA 91406. **E-mail:** ihansen@creativeage. com. **Website:** www.medestheticsmagazine.com. **Contact:** Inga Hansen, associate publisher/executive editor. **50% freelance written.** Bimonthly magazine covering noninvasive medical aesthetic services such as laser hair removal, skin rejuvenation, injectable fillers, and neurotoxins. *MedEsthetics* is a business-to-business magazine written for and distributed to dermatologists, plastic surgeons, and other physicians offering noninvasive medical aesthetic services. Covers the latest equipment and products as well as legal and management issues specific to medspas, laser centers, and other medical aesthetic practices. Estab. 2005. Circ. 20,000. Byline given. Pays on acceptance. Publishes ms an average of 3 months after acceptance. Editorial lead time 3 months. Submit seasonal material 3 months in advance. Accepts queries by e-mail. Responds in 1 month to queries.

NONFICTION Needs new product, technical. Does not want articles directed at consumers. **Buys 25 mss/year.** Query.

PHOTOS State availability. Identification of subjects, model releases required. Reviews transparencies, prints. Negotiates payment individually.

TIPS "We work strictly on assignment. Query with article ideas; do not send mss. We respond to queries with article assignments that specify article requirements."

MIDWIFERY TODAY

P.O Box 2672, Eugene OR 97402. (541)344-7438. **Fax:** (541)344-1422. **E-mail:** editorial@midwiferytoday. com and jan@midwiferytoday.com (editorial only); layout@midwiferytoday.com (photography). **Website:** www.midwiferytoday.com. **Contact:** Jan Tritten, editor-in-chief and publisher. **95% freelance written.** Quarterly magazine. Through networking and education, *Midwifery Today*'s mission is to return midwifery to its rightful position in the family; to make mid-

wifery care the norm throughout the world; and to redefine midwifery as a vital partnership with women. Estab. 1986. Circ. 3,000. Byline given. No kill fee. Publishes ms an average of 5 months after acceptance. Editorial lead time 3-9 months. Submit seasonal material 6 months in advance. Accepts queries by e-mail. Accepts simultaneous submissions. Responds in 2 weeks to queries. Responds in 1 month to mss. Sample copy online. Guidelines online.

NONFICTION Needs book excerpts, essays, how-to, humor, inspirational, interview, opinion, personal experience, photo feature, clinical research, herbal articles, birth stories, business advice. **Buys 60 mss/year.** Send complete ms. Length: 300-3,000 words.

PHOTOS State availability. Model releases required. Reviews prints, GIF/JPEG files. $15-$50 per photo.

COLUMNS/DEPARTMENTS News: "In My Opinion" (150-750 words). **Buys 8 columns/year. mss/year.** Send complete ms.

POETRY Needs avant-garde, haiku, light verse, traditional. Accepts e-mail submissions (pasted into body of message or as attachment). Cover letter is required. Does not want poetry unrelated to pregnancy or birth. Does not want poetry that is "off subject or puts down the subject." Buys 4/year poems/year. Maximum line length: 25. **Pays 2 contributor's copies. Acquires first rights.**

FILLERS Needs Needs anecdotes, facts, newsbreaks. Length: 100-600 words.

TIPS "Use Chicago Manual of Style formatting."

⊛⊛⊛⊛ MODERN PHYSICIAN

Crain Communications, 360 N. Michigan Ave., Chicago IL 60601-3806. (312)649-5439. **Fax:** (312)280-3183. **E-mail:** mgoozner@modernhealthcare.com; hmeyer@modernhealthcare.com. **Website:** www. modernhealthcare.com. **Contact:** Merrill Goozner, editor; Harris Meyer. **10% freelance written.** Monthly magazine covering business and management news for doctors. *Modern Physician* offers timely topical news features with lots of business information: revenues, earnings, financial data, etc. Estab. 1997. Circ. 24,000. Byline given. Pays on acceptance. No kill fee. Publishes ms an average of 2 months after acceptance. Editorial lead time 2 months. Accepts queries by mail, e-mail. Responds in 6 weeks to queries. Sample copy free. Writer's guidelines sent after query.

NONFICTION Length: 750-1,000 words. **Pays 75¢-$1/word. (Does not pay for Guest Commentaries.)**

TIPS "Read the publication, know our audience, and come up with a good story idea that we haven't thought of yet."

🖤 THE NEW ZEALAND JOURNAL OF PHYSIOTHERAPY

New Zealand Society of Physiotherapists, P.O. Box 27386, Wellington New Zealand. (64)(4)801-6500. **Fax:** (64)(4)801-5571. **E-mail:** nzsp@physiotherapy. org.nz; pnz@physiotherapy.org.nz. **Website:** www. physiotheraphy.org.nz. Acadmic journal publishing papers relevant to the theory and practice of physiotheraphy. No kill fee. NoGuidelines online.

NONFICTION Send complete ms.

🖤 THE NEW ZEALAND MEDICAL JOURNAL

NZMJ, c/o Sharon Cuzens, NZMA, P.O. Box 156, Wellington 6140 New Zealand. (027)446-3326. **E-mail:** nzmj@nzma.org.nz. **Website:** www.nzma.org. nz/journal. **Contact:** Frank Frizelle, professor. No kill fee. Accepts queries by online submission form. NoGuidelines online.

🖥 Only accepts submissions via online submissions manager.

NONFICTION Send complete ms.

☺💲💲 OPTICAL PRISM

250 The East Mall, Suite 1113, Toronto ON M9B 6L3 Canada. (416)233-2487. **Fax:** (416)233-1746. **E-mail:** info@opticalprism.ca. **Website:** www.opticalprism.ca. **30% freelance written.** Magazine published 10 times/ year. Covers the health, fashion, and business aspects of the optical industry in Canada. Estab. 1982. Circ. 10,000. Byline given. Pays on publication. Publishes ms an average of 2 months after acceptance. Editorial lead time 3 months. Submit seasonal material 3 months in advance. Accepts queries by mail, e-mail. YesAccepts simultaneous submissions. Digital copy online.

NONFICTION Needs interview, related to optical industry. Special issues: Editorial themes and feature topics online in media kit. Query. Length: 1,000-1,600 words. **Pays 40¢/word (Canadian).** Sometimes pays expenses of writers on assignment.

COLUMNS/DEPARTMENTS Insight (profiles on people in the eyewear industry—also sometimes schools and businesses), 700-1,000 words. **Buys 5 mss/year.** Query. **Pays 40¢/word.**

TIPS "Please look at our editorial themes, which are on our website, and pitch articles that are related to the themes for each issue."

💲💲 PHYSICIAN MAGAZINE

Physicians News Network, 707 Wilshire Blvd., Suite 3800, Los Angeles CA 90017. (760)805-5040. **E-mail:** sheri@physiciansnetwork.com; editors@physiciansnewsnetwork.com. **Website:** www.physiciansnewsnetwork.com. **Contact:** Sheri Carr, COO/editor. **25% freelance written.** Monthly magazine covering non-technical articles of relevance to physicians. Estab. 1908. Circ. 18,000. Byline given. Pays on acceptance. Offers 10% kill fee. Publishes ms an average of 2-3 months after acceptance. Editorial lead time 2-3 months. Accepts queries by e-mail. Accepts simultaneous submissions. Responds in 4 weeks to queries. Responds in 2 months to mss. Sample copy online.

NONFICTION Needs general interest. **Buys 12-24 mss/year.** Query with published clips. Length: 600-3,000 words. **Pays $200-600 for assigned articles.**

PHOTOS State availability.

COLUMNS/DEPARTMENTS Medical World (tips/ how-to's), 800-900 words. Query with published clips. **Pays $$200-$600.**

TIPS "We want professional, well-researched articles covering policy, issues, and other concerns of physicians. No personal anecdotes or patient viewpoints."

💲💲 PLASTIC SURGERY NEWS

American Society of Plastic Surgeons, 444 E. Algonquin Rd., Arlington Heights IL 60005. **Fax:** (847)981-5458. **E-mail:** mss@plasticsurgery.org. **Website:** www. plasticsurgery.org. **Contact:** Mike Stokes, managing editor. **15% freelance written.** Monthly tabloid covering plastic surgery. *Plastic Surgery News* readership is comprised primarily of plastic surgeons and those involved with the specialty (nurses, techs, industry). The magazine is distributed via subscription and to all members of the American Society of Plastic Surgeons. The magazine covers a variety of specialty-specific news and features, including trends, legislation, and clinical information. Estab. 1960. Circ. 6,000. Byline given. Pays on acceptance. Offers 25% kill fee. Publishes ms an average of 1-2 months after acceptance. Editorial lead time 1-3 months. Accepts queries by e-mail. Accepts simultaneous submissions. Responds in 2 weeks to queries. Responds in 3 months to mss. Sample copy for 10 first-class stamps. Guidelines by e-mail.

NONFICTION Needs expose, how-to, new product, technical. Does not want celebrity or entertainment based pieces. **Buys 20 mss/year.** Query with published clips. Length: 1,000-3,500 words. **Pays 20-40¢/word.** Sometimes pays expenses of writers on assignment.

COLUMNS/DEPARTMENTS Digital Plastic Surgeon (technology), 1,500-1,700 words.

⊖⊜ PODIATRY MANAGEMENT

Kane Communications, Inc., P.O. Box 750129, Forest Hills NY 11375. (718)897-9700. **Fax:** (718)896-5747. **E-mail:** bblock@podiatrym.com. **Website:** www.podiatrym.com. Magazine published 9 times/year for practicing podiatrists. Aims to help the doctor of podiatric medicine to build a bigger, more successful practice, to conserve and invest his money, to keep him posted on the economic, legal, and sociological changes that affect him. Estab. 1982. Circ. 16,500. Byline given. Pays on publication. $75 kill fee. Submit seasonal material 4 months in advance. Accepts queries by e-mail. Accepts simultaneous submissions. Responds in 2 weeks to queries. Sample copy for $5 and 9x12 SAE. Guidelines for #10 SASE.

NONFICTION Buys 35 mss/year. Length: 1,500-3,000 words. **Pays $350-600.**

REPRINTS Send photocopy. Pays 33% of amount paid for an original article.

PHOTOS State availability. Pays $15 for b&w contact sheet.

TIPS "Articles should be tailored to podiatrists, and preferably should contain quotes from podiatrists."

⊖⊜ PRIMARY CARE OPTOMETRY NEWS

SLACK Inc., 6900 Grove Rd., Thorofare NJ 08086-9447. (856)848-1000. **Fax:** (856)848-5991. **E-mail:** editor@healio.com; optometry@healio.com. **Website:** www.healio.com/optometry. **Contact:** Michael D. DePaolis, editor. **5% freelance written.** Monthly tabloid covering optometry. *Primary Care Optometry News* strives to be the optometric professional's definitive information source by delivering timely, accurate, authoritative and balanced reports on clinical issues, socioeconomic and legislative affairs, ophthalmic industry, and research developments, as well as updates on diagnostic and thereapeutic regimens and techniques to enhance the quality of patient care. Estab. 1996. Circ. 39,000. Byline given. Pays on publication. Offers 50% kill fee. Publishes ms an average of 2 months after acceptance. Editorial lead time 2

months. Accepts queries by mail, e-mail, fax, phone. Responds in 2 weeks to queries. Sample copy online. Guidelines by e-mail.

NONFICTION Needs how-to, interview, new product, opinion, technical. **Buys 20 mss/year.** Query. Length: 800-1,000 words. **Pays $350-500.** Sometimes pays expenses of writers on assignment.

PHOTOS State availability. Captions, model releases required. Reviews GIF/JPEG files. Offers no additional payment for photos accepted with ms.

COLUMNS/DEPARTMENTS What's Your Diagnosis (case presentation), 800 words. **Buys 40 mss/year.** Query. **Pays $100-500.**

TIPS "Either e-mail or call the editor with questions or story ideas."

⊘⊖⊜ STRATEGIC HEALTH CARE MARKETING

Health Care Communications, 11 Heritage Lane, P.O. Box 594, Rye NY 10580. (914)967-6741. **Fax:** (914)967-3054. **E-mail:** healthcomm@aol.com. **Website:** www.strategichealthcare.com. **Contact:** Michele von Dambrowski, editor and publisher. **90% freelance written.** Monthly newsletter covering health care marketing and management in a wide range of settings, including hospitals, medical group practices, home health services, and managed care organizations. Emphasis is on strategies and techniques employed within the health care field and relevant applications from other service industries. Works with published/established writers only. *Strategic Health Care Marketing* is specifically seeking writers with expertise/contacts in managed care, patient satisfaction, and e-health. Estab. 1984. Byline given. Pays on publication. Offers 25% kill fee. Publishes ms an average of 2 months after acceptance. Accepts queries by mail, e-mail. Responds in 1 month to queries. Sample copy for SAE with 9x12 envelope and 3 first-class stamps. Guidelines sent with sample copy only.

NONFICTION Needs how-to, interview, new product, technical. **Buys 50 mss/year.** Query. Length: 1,000-1,800 words. **Pays $100-500.** Sometimes pays expenses of writers on assignment with prior authorization.

PHOTOS Photos, unless necessary for subject explanation, are rarely used. State availability. Captions, model releases required. Reviews contact sheets. Offers $10-30/photo.

TIPS "Writers with prior experience on the business beat for newspapers or newsletters will do well. We require a sophisticated, in-depth knowledge of health care and business. This is not a consumer publication—the writer with knowledge of both health care and marketing will excel. Absolutely no unsolicited mss; any received will be returned or discarded unread."

MUSIC TRADE

$ CLASSICAL SINGER MAGAZINE

Classical Publications, Inc., P.O. Box 1710, Draper UT 84020. (801)254-1025, ext. 14. **Fax:** (801)254-3139. **E-mail:** editorial@classicalsinger.com. **Website:** www.classicalsinger.com. **Contact:** Sara Thomas. Monthly magazine covering classical singers. Estab. 1988. Circ. 7,000. Byline given, plus bio and contact info. Pays on publication. No kill fee. Publishes ms an average of 3 months after acceptance. Editorial lead time 3 months. Submit seasonal material 3 months in advance. Accepts queries by e-mail. TrueResponds in 1 month to queries. Potential writers will be given password to website version of magazine and writer's guidelines online.

NONFICTION Needs book excerpts, expose, carefully done, how-to, humor, interview, new product, personal experience, photo feature, religious, technical, travel, , crossword puzzles on opera theme. Does not want reviews unless they are assigned. Query with published clips. Length: 500-3,000 words. **Pays 5¢/word ($50 minimum). Writers also receive 10 contributor's copies.** Pays telephone expenses of writers with assignments when Xerox copy of bill submitted.

PHOTOS Send photos. Captions required.

TIPS "*Classical Singer Magazine* has a full-color glossy cover and glossy b&w and color pages inside. It ranges in size from 56 pages during the summer to 120 pages in September. Articles need to meet this mission statement: 'Information for a classical singer's career, support for a classical singer's life, and enlightenment for a classical singer's art.'"

⊘$ INTERNATIONAL BLUEGRASS

International Bluegrass Music Association, 608 W. Iris Dr., Nashville TN 37204. (615)256-3222. **Fax:** (615)256-0450. **E-mail:** info@ibma.org. **Website:** www.ibma.org. **10% freelance written.** Bimonthly newsletter of the International Bluegrass Music Association. *International Bluegrass* is the business publication for the bluegrass music industry. Interested in hard news and features concerning how to reach that potential and how to conduct business more effectively. Estab. 1985. Circ. 4,500. Byline given. Pays on publication. No kill fee. Publishes ms an average of 2 months after acceptance. Submit seasonal material 4 months in advance. Accepts queries by mail, e-mail, phone. Accepts simultaneous submissions. Responds in 1 month to queries. Sample copy for SAE with 6x9 envelope and 2 first-class stamps.

NONFICTION Needs book excerpts, essays, how-to, conduct business effectively within bluegrass music, new product, opinion. No interview/profiles/feature stories of performers (rare exceptions) or fans. **Buys 6 mss/year.** Query. Length: 1,000-1,200 words. **Pays up to $150/article for assigned articles.**

REPRINTS Send photocopy of article and information about when and where the article previously appeared. Does not pay for reprints.

PHOTOS Send photos. Captions, identification of subjects, True required. Offers no additional payment for photos accepted with ms.

COLUMNS/DEPARTMENTS Staff written.

TIPS "We're interested in a slant strongly toward the business end of bluegrass music. We're especially looking for material dealing with audience development and how to book bluegrass bands outside of the existing market."

$$ THE MUSIC & SOUND RETAILER

Testa Communications, 25 Willowdale Ave., Port Washington NY 11050. (516)767-2500. **E-mail:** dferrisi@testa.com. **Website:** www.msretailer.com. **Contact:** Dan Ferrisi, editor. **10% freelance written.** Monthly magazine covering business to business publication for music instrument products. *The Music & Sound Retailer* covers the music instrument industry and is sent to all dealers of these products, including Guitar Center, Sam Ash, and all small independent stores. Estab. 1983. Circ. 11,700. Byline given. Pays on publication. Offers $100 kill fee. Editorial lead time 1 month. Submit seasonal material 2 months in advance. Accepts queries by e-mail. Accepts simultaneous submissions. Responds in 2 weeks to queries. Responds in 1 month to mss. Sample copy for #10 SASE. Guidelines free.

NONFICTION Needs how-to, new product, opinion, (does not mean letters to the editor), personal experience. Concert and CD reviews are never published; neiter are interviews with musicians. **Buys 25 mss/year.** Query with published clips. Length: 1,000-2,000 words. **Pays $300-400 for assigned and unsolicited**

articles. Sometimes pays expenses of writers on assignment.

PHOTOS Send photos. Captions required. Reviews GIF/JPEG files. Offers no additional payment for photos accepted with ms.

MUSIC CONNECTION

Music Connection, Inc., 14654 Victory Blvd., 1st Floor, Encino CA 91436. (818)995-0101. **Fax:** (818)995-9235. **E-mail:** markn@musicconnection.com; contactmc@musicconnection.com. **Website:** www.musicconnection.com. **Contact:** Mark Nardone, associate publisher. **40% freelance written.** Monthly magazine geared toward working musicians and/or other industry professionals, including producers/engineers/studio staff, managers, agents, publicists, music publishers, record company staff, concert promoters/bookers, etc. Found in select major booksellers and all Guitar Centers in America. Estab. 1977. Circ. 75,000. Byline given. Pays after publication. Kill fee varies. Publishes ms an average of 2 months after acceptance. Editorial lead time 2 months. Submit seasonal material 2 months in advance. Sample copy for $5. Online copy also available.

NONFICTION Needs how-to, music industry related, interview, new product, technical. Query with published clips. Length: 1,000-5,000 words. **Payment varies.** Sometimes pays expenses of writers on assignment.

TIPS "Articles must be informative 'how-to' music/music industry-related pieces, geared toward a trade-reading audience comprised mainly of musicians. No fluff."

❸❸❸ OPERA NEWS

Metropolitan Opera Guild, Inc., 70 Lincoln Center Plaza, 6th Floor, New York NY 10023. **E-mail:** info@operanews.com. **Website:** www.operanews.com. **Contact:** Kitty March. **75% freelance written.** Monthly magazine for people interested in opera—the opera professional as well as the opera audience. Estab. 1936. Circ. 105,000. Byline given. Pays on publication. No kill fee. Publishes ms an average of 4 months after acceptance. Editorial lead time 4 months. Accepts queries by e-mail. Sample copy for $5.

NONFICTION Needs historical, interview, informational, think pieces, opera, and CD, DVD and book reviews. Does not accept works of fiction or personal remembrances. Send unsolicited mss, article proposals and queries, along with several published clips. Length: 1,500-2,800 words. **Pays $450-1,200.** Sometimes pays expenses of writers on assignment.

PHOTOS State availability.

COLUMNS/DEPARTMENTS Buys 24 mss/year.

❸ OVERTONES

Handbell Musicians of America, P.O. Box 1765, Findlay OH 45839-1765. **E-mail:** jrsmith@handbellmusicians.org. **Website:** handbellmusicians.org/music-resources/overtones. **Contact:** J.R. Smith, publications director. **80% freelance written.** Bimonthly magazine covering English handbell ringing and conducting. *Overtones* is a 48-page magazine with extensive educational articles, photos, advertisements, and graphic work. Handbell Musicians of America is dedicated to advancing the musical art of handbell/handchime ringing through education, community, and communication. The purpose of *Overtones* is to provide a printed resource to support that mission. Offers how-to articles, inspirational stories, and interviews with well-known people and unique ensembles. Estab. 1954. Circ. 8,000. Byline given. Pays on publication. No kill fee. Publishes ms an average of 4 months after acceptance. Editorial lead time 4 months. Submit seasonal material 4 months in advance. Accepts queries by mail, e-mail. YesResponds in 1 month to queries and to mss. Sample copy available by e-mail. Guidelines online. Style guideline should follow *The Chicago Manual of Style.*

NONFICTION Needs essays, general interest, historical, how-to, inspirational, interview, religious, technical. Does not want product news or promotional material. **Buys 8-12 mss/year.** Send complete ms via e-mail, CD, DVD, or hard copy. Length: 1,200-2,000 words. **Pays $120.** Sometimes pays expenses of writers on assignment.

PHOTOS State availability of or send photos. Captions required. Reviews 8x10 prints, JPEG/TIFF files. Offers no additional payment for photos accepted with ms.

COLUMNS/DEPARTMENTS Handbells in Education (topics covering the use of handbells in school setting, teaching techniques, etc.); Handbells in Worship (topics and ideas for using handbells in a church setting); Tips & Tools (variety of topics from ringing and conducting techniques to score study to maintenance); Community Connections (topics covering issues relating to the operation/administration/techniques for community groups); Music Reviews (recommendations and descriptions of music following particular themes, i.e., youth music, difficult music, seasonal, etc.). Length should be 800-1,200 words. Query. **Pays $80.**

TIPS "When writing profiles/interviews, try to determine what is especially unique or inspiring about the individual or ensemble and write from that viewpoint. Please have some expertise in handbells, education, or church music to write department articles."

$$ VENUES TODAY

18350 Mt. Langley, Suite 201, Fountain Valley CA 92708. (714)378-5400. **Fax:** (714)378-0040. **E-mail:** linda@venuestoday.com; dave@venuestoday.com. **Website:** www.venuestoday.com. **Contact:** Linda Deckard, publisher and editor-in-chief; Dave Broks, senior writer and assignment editor. **70% freelance written.** Weekly magazine covering the live entertainment industry and the buildings that host shows and sports. Needs writers who can cover an exciting industry from the business side, not the consumer side. Readers are venue managers, concert promoters, those in the concert and sports business, not the audience for concerts and sports. Need business journalists who can cover the latest news and trends in the market. Estab. 2002. Byline given. Pays on publication. Publishes ms an average of 1 month after acceptance. Editorial lead time 1-2 months. Submit seasonal material 1-2 months in advance. Accepts queries by mail, e-mail, fax. Accepts simultaneous submissions. Responds in 1 week to queries. Sample copy online. Guidelines free.

NONFICTION Needs interview, photo feature, technical, travel. Does not want customer slant, marketing pieces. Query with published clips. Length: 500-1,500 words. **Pays $100-250.** Pays expenses of writers on assignment.

PHOTOS State availability. Captions, identification of subjects required. Reviews GIF/JPEG files. Negotiates payment individually.

COLUMNS/DEPARTMENTS Venue News (new buildings, trend features, etc.); Bookings (show tours, business side); Marketing (of shows, sports, convention centers); Concessions (food, drink, merchandise). Length: 500-1,200 words. **Buys 250 mss/year.** Query with published clips. **Pays $100-250.**

FILLERS Needs gags. **Buys 6 mss/year. Pays $100-300.**

PAPER

$$ THE PAPER STOCK REPORT

McEntee Media Corp., 9815 Hazelwood Ave., Strongsville OH 44149. (440)238-6603. **Fax:** (440)238-6712. **E-mail:** ken@recycle.cc; psr@recycle.cc. **Website:** www.recycle.cc/psrpage.htm. **Contact:** Ken McEntee, editor/publisher. Bimonthly newsletter covering market trends and news in the paper recycling industry. Audience is interested in new innovative markets, applications for recovered scrap paper, as well as new laws and regulations impacting recycling. Estab. 1990. Circ. 2,000. Byline given. Pays on publication. No kill fee. Publishes ms an average of 1 month after acceptance. Editorial lead time 2 months. Submit seasonal material 2 months in advance. Accepts queries by mail, e-mail, fax, phone. Accepts simultaneous submissions. Responds in 1 month to queries. Sample copy for #10 SAE with 55¢ postage.

NONFICTION Needs book excerpts, essays, expose, general interest, historical, interview, new product, opinion, photo feature, technical, all related to paper recycling. **Buys 0-13 mss/year.** Send complete ms. Length: 250-1,000 words. **Pays $50-250 for assigned articles. Pays $25-250 for unsolicited articles.** Pays expenses of writers on assignment.

PHOTOS State availability. Identification of subjects required. Reviews contact sheets. Negotiates payment individually.

TIPS "Articles must be valuable to readers in terms of presenting new market opportunities or cost-saving measures."

$$ RECYCLED PAPER NEWS

McEntee Media Corp., 9815 Hazelwood Ave., Strongsville OH 44149. (440)238-6603. **Fax:** (440)238-6712. **E-mail:** ken@recycle.cc. **Website:** www.recycle.cc. **Contact:** Ken McEntee, owner. **10% freelance written.** Monthly newsletter covering the recycling and composting industries. Interested in any news impacting the paper recycling industry, as well as other environmental issues in the paper industry, i.e., water/air pollution, chlorine-free paper, forest conservation, etc., with special emphasis on new laws and regulations. Estab. 1990. Pays on publication. No kill fee. Publishes ms an average of 2 months after acceptance. Editorial lead time 1 month. Submit seasonal material 1 month in advance. Accepts queries by mail, e-mail, fax, phone. Accepts simultaneous submissions. Responds in 2 months to queries. Sample copy for 9x12 SAE and 55¢ postage. Guidelines for #10 SASE.

NONFICTION Needs book excerpts, essays, how-to, interview, new product, opinion, personal experience, photo feature, technical, new business, legislation, regulation, business expansion. **Buys 0-5 mss/year.** Query with published clips. **Pays $10-500.**

COLUMNS/DEPARTMENTS Query with published clips. **Pays $10-500.**

TIPS "We appreciate leads on local news regarding recycling or composting, i.e., new facilities or businesses, new laws and regulations, unique programs, situations that impact supply and demand for recyclables, etc. International developments are also of interest."

PETS

💲💲 PET AGE

Journal Multimedia, 220 Davidson Ave., Suite 302, Somerset NJ 08873. (732)246-5722. **Website:** www. petage.com. **Contact:** Michelle Maskaly, editor-in-chief. **90% freelance written.** Monthly magazine for pet/pet supplies retailers, covering the complete pet industry. Estab. 1971. Circ. 23,022. Byline given. Pays on acceptance. No kill fee. Publishes ms an average of 3 months after acceptance. Sample copy and writer's guidelines available.

○ Prefers to work with published/established writers. Will consider new writers.

NONFICTION No profiles of industry members and/or retail establishments or consumer-oriented pet articles. **Buys 80 mss/year.** Query with published clips. Length: 1,500-2,200 words. **Pays 15¢/word for assigned articles.** Pays documented telephone expenses.

PHOTOS Captions, identification of subjects required. Reviews transparencies, slides, and 5x7 glossy prints.

TIPS "This is a business publication for busy people, and must be very informative in easy-to-read, concise style. Articles about animal care or business practices should have the pet-retail angle or cover issues specific to this industry."

💲💲 PET PRODUCT NEWS INTERNATIONAL

I-5 Publishing, LLC, P.O. Box 6050, Mission Viejo CA 92690. (949)855-8822. **Fax:** (949)855-3045. **E-mail:** ppneditor@i5publishing.com; erothrock@i5publishing.com. **Website:** www.petproductnews.com. **Contact:** Ellyce Rothrock, editor. **70% freelance written.** Monthly magazine. *Pet Product News* covers business/legal and economic issues of importance to pet product retailers, suppliers, and distributors, as well as product information and animal care issues. Looking for straightforward articles on the proper care of dogs, cats, birds, fish, and exotics (reptiles, hamsters, etc.) as information the retailers can pass on to new pet owners. Estab. 1947. Circ. 26,000. Byline given. Pays on publication. Offers $50 kill fee. Editorial lead time 3 months. Submit seasonal material 4 months in advance. Accepts queries by mail, fax. Responds in 2 weeks to queries. Sample copy for $5.50. Guidelines for #10 SASE.

NONFICTION Needs general interest, interview, new product, photo feature, technical. No "cute" animal stories or those directed at the pet owner. **Buys 150 mss/year.** Query. Length: 500-1,500 words. **Pays $175-350.**

COLUMNS/DEPARTMENTS The Pet Dealer News™ (timely news stories about business issues affecting pet retailers), 800-1,000 words; Industry News (news articles representing coverage of pet product suppliers, manufacturers, distributors, and associations), 800-1,000 words; Pet Health News™ (pet health and articles relevant to pet retailers); Dog & Cat (products and care of), 1,000-1,500 words; Fish & Bird (products and care of), 1,000-1,500 words; Small Mammals (products and care of), 1,000-1,500 words; Pond/Water Garden (products and care of), 1,000-1,500 words. **Buys 120 mss/year.** Query. **Pays $150-300.**

TIPS "Be more than just an animal lover. You have to know about health, nutrition, and care. Product and business articles are told in both an informative and entertaining style. Talk to pet store owners and see what they need to know to be better business people in general, who have to deal with everything from balancing the books and free trade agreements to animal rights activists. All sections are open, but you have to be knowledgeable on the topic, be it taxes, management, profit building, products, nutrition, animal care, or marketing."

PLUMBING, HEATING, AIR CONDITIONING AND REFRIGERATION

♻💲💲 HPAC: HEATING PLUMBING AIR CONDITIONING

80 Valleybrook Dr., Toronto ON M3B 2S9 Canada. (416)442-5600. **Fax:** (416)510-5140. **E-mail:** smacisaac@hpacmag.com; kturner@hpacmag.com. **E-mail:** smacisaac@hpacmag.com. **Website:** www. hpacmag.com. **Contact:** Sandy MacIsaac, art director; Kerry Turner, editor. **20% freelance written.** Monthly magazine. For a prompt reply, enclose a sheet on which is typed a statement either approving or rejecting the suggested article which can either be checked off, or a quick answer written in and signed and returned. Estab. 1923. Circ. 16,500. Pays on publication. No kill fee. Publishes ms an average of 3 months after acceptance.

Accepts queries by mail, e-mail, phone. Responds in 2 months to queries.

🎤 "We primarily want articles that show *HPAC* readers how they can increase their sales and business step-by-step based on specific examples of what others have done."

NONFICTION Needs how-to, technical. Length: 1,000-1,500 words. **Pays 25¢/word.** Sometimes pays expenses of writers on assignment.

REPRINTS Send tearsheet or photocopy with rights for sale noted and information about when and where the material previously appeared.

PHOTOS Prefers 4x5 or 5x7 glossies, high-res JPEGs. Photos purchased with ms.

TIPS "Topics must relate directly to the day-to-day activities of *HPAC* readers in Canada. Must be detailed, with specific examples, quotes from specific people or authorities—show depth. We specifically want material from other parts of Canada besides southern Ontario. U.S. material must relate to Canadian readers' concerns."

💲💲 SNIPS MAGAZINE

BNP Media, 2401 W. Big Beaver Rd., Suite 700, Troy MI 48084. (248)244-6416. **Fax:** (248)362-0317. **E-mail:** mcconnellm@bnpmedia.com. **Website:** www.snipsmag.com. **Contact:** Michael McConnell. **2% freelance written.** Monthly magazine for sheet metal, heating, ventilation, air conditioning, and metal roofing contractors. Estab. 1932. No kill fee. Publishes ms an average of 3 months after acceptance. Accepts queries by mail, e-mail, fax, phone. Call for writer's guidelines.

NONFICTION Length: under 1,000 words unless on special assignment. **Pays $200-300.**

PHOTOS Negotiable.

PRINTING

💲💲 THE BIG PICTURE

ST Media Group International, 11262 Cornell Park Dr., Cincinnati OH 45242. (513)421-2050. **E-mail:** gregory.sharpless@stmediagroup.com. **Website:** bigpicture.net. **Contact:** Gregory Sharpless, editor-in-chief. **20% freelance written.** Magazine published 9 times/year covering wide-format digital printing. *The Big Picture* covers wide-format printing as well as digital workflow, finishing, display, capture, and other related topics. Readers include digital print providers, sign shops, commercial printers, in-house print operations, and other

print providers across the country. Primarily interested in the technology and work processes behind wide-format printing, but also run trend features on segments of the industry (innovations in point-of-purchase displays, floor graphics, fine-art printing, vehicle wrapping, textile printing, etc.). Estab. 1996. Circ. 21,500 controlled. Byline given. Pays on publication. Offers 20% kill fee. Publishes ms an average of 2 months after acceptance. Editorial lead time 2 months. Accepts queries by e-mail. YesAccepts simultaneous submissions. Responds in 2 weeks to queries. Responds in 1 month to mss. Sample copy online. Guidelines available.

NONFICTION Needs how-to, interview, new product, technical. Does not want broad consumer-oriented pieces that do not speak to the business and technical aspects of producing print for pay. **Buys 15-20 mss/year.** Query with published clips. Length: 1,500-2,500 words. **Pays $500-700 for assigned articles.**

PHOTOS Send photos. Reviews GIF/JPEG files hires. Offers no additonal payment for photos accepted with ms.

TIPS "Interest in and knowledge of the digital printing industry will position you well to break into this market. You have to be willing to drill down into the production aspects of digital printing to write for us."

💲💲 IN-PLANT GRAPHICS

North American Publishing Co., 1500 Spring Garden St., 12th Floor, Philadelphia PA 19130. (215)238-5321. **Fax:** (215)238-5457. **E-mail:** bobneubauer@napco.com. **Website:** www.ipgonline.com. **Contact:** Bob Neubauer, editor. **40% freelance written.** *In-Plant Graphics* features articles designed to help in-house printing departments increase productivity, save money, and stay competitive. *IPG* features advances in graphic arts technology and shows inplants how to put this technology to use. Audience consists of print shop managers working for (non-print related) corporations (i.e., hospitals, insurance companies, publishers, nonprofits), universities, and government departments. They often oversee graphic design, prepress, printing, bindery, and mailing departments. Estab. 1951. Circ. 23,100. Byline given. Pays on publication. No kill fee. Publishes ms an average of 3 months after acceptance. Editorial lead time 2 months. Submit seasonal material 3 months in advance. Accepts queries by mail, e-mail, fax. Guidelines online.

NONFICTION Needs new product, graphic arts, technical, graphic arts/printing/prepress. No articles on desktop publishing software or design software. No Internet publishing articles. **Buys 5 mss/year.** Query with published clips. Length: 800-1,500 words. **Pays $350-500.**

PHOTOS Photos should be at least 266 dpi. State availability. Captions, identification of subjects required. Reviews transparencies, prints. Negotiates payment individually.

TIPS "To get published in *IPG*, writers must contact the editor with an idea in the form of a query letter that includes published writing samples. Writers who have covered the graphic arts in the past may be assigned stories for an agreed-upon fee. We don't want stories that tout only 1 vendor's products and serve as glorified commercials. All profiles must be well balanced, covering a variety of issues. If you can tell us about an in-house printing operation is doing innovative things, we will be interested."

◎◎ SCREEN PRINTING

ST Media Group International, 11262 Cornell Park Dr., Cincinnati OH 45242. (513)421-2050, ext. 331. **Fax:** (513)421-5144. **E-mail:** gregory.sharpless@st-mediagroup.com. **Website:** www.screenweb.com. **Contact:** Gregory Sharpless. **30% freelance written.** Monthly magazine for the screen printing industry, including screen printers (commercial, industrial, and captive shops), suppliers and manufacturers, ad agencies, and allied profession. Estab. 1953. Circ. 17,500. Byline given. Pays on publication. No kill fee. Publishes ms an average of 3 months after acceptance. Accepts queries by mail, e-mail, fax. Sample copy available. Guidelines for #10 SASE.

○ Works with a small number of new/unpublished writers each year.

NONFICTION Buys 10-15 mss/year. Query. Unsolicited mss not returned. **Pays $400 minimum for major features.**

PHOTOS Cover photos negotiable; b&w or color. Published material becomes the property of the magazine.

TIPS "Be an expert in the screen-printing industry with supreme or special knowledge of a particular screen-printing process, or have special knowledge of a field or issue of particular interest to screen-

printers. If the author has a working knowledge of screen printing, assignments are more readily available. General management articles are rarely used."

PROFESSIONAL PHOTOGRAPHY

◎◎ NEWS PHOTOGRAPHER

National Press Photographers Association, Inc., 6677 Whitemarsh Valley Walk, Austin TX 78746-6367. **E-mail:** magazine@nppa.org; info@nppa.org. **Website:** www.nppa.org. **Contact:** Donald R. Winslow, editor. Magazine on photojournalism published 10 times/year. *News Photographer* magazine is dedicated to the advancement of still and television news photography. The magazine presents articles, interviews, profiles, history, new products, electronic imaging, and news related to the practice of photojournalism. Estab. 1946. Circ. 11,000. Byline given. Pays on acceptance. Offers 100% kill fee. Publishes ms an average of 4 months after acceptance. Editorial lead time 2 months. Submit seasonal material 2 months in advance. Accepts queries by mail, e-mail, fax, phone. YesAccepts simultaneous submissions. Responds in 1 month to queries. Sample copy for SAE with 9x12 envelope and 3 first-class stamps. Guidelines free.

NONFICTION Needs historical, how-to, interview, new product, opinion, personal experience, photo feature, technical. **Buys 10 mss/year.** Query. Length: 1,500 words. **Pays $300.** Pays expenses of writers on assignment.

PHOTOS State availability. Captions, identification of subjects required. Reviews high resolution, digital images only. Negotiates payment individually.

COLUMNS/DEPARTMENTS Query.

◎◎ THE PHOTO REVIEW

140 E. Richardson Ave., Suite 301, Langhorne PA 19047. (215)891-0214. **Fax:** (215)891-9358. **E-mail:** info@photoreview.org. **Website:** www.photoreview.org. **50% freelance written.** Quarterly magazine covering art photography and criticism. "*The Photo Review* publishes critical reviews of photography exhibitions and books, critical essays, and interviews. We do not publish how-to or technical articles." Estab. 1976. Circ. 2,000. Byline given. Pays on publication. No kill fee. Publishes ms an average of 9-12 months after acceptance. Editorial lead time 3 months. Submit seasonal material 6 months in advance. Accepts queries by

mail. Accepts simultaneous submissions. Responds in 2 months to queries. Responds in 3 months to mss. Sample copy for $7. Guidelines for #10 SASE.

NONFICTION Needs interview, photography essay, critical review. No how-to articles. **Buys 20 mss/year.** Send complete ms. 2-20 typed pages **Pays $10-250.**

REPRINTS "Send tearsheet, photocopy, or typed ms with rights for sale noted and information about when and where the material previously appeared." Payment varies.

PHOTOS Send photos. Captions required. Reviews contact sheets, transparencies, prints. Offers no additional payment for photos accepted with ms.

SHUTTERBUG

Source Interlink Media, 1415 Chaffee Dr., Suite 1, Titusville FL 32780. **Fax:** (321)225-3149. **E-mail:** editorial@shutterbug.com. **Website:** www.shutterbug.com. **90% freelance written.** Monthly covering photography and digial imaging. Written for the avid amateur, part-time, and full-time professional photographers. Covers equipment techniques, profiles, technology, and news in photography. Estab. 1972. Circ. 90,000. Byline given. Pays on publication. Editorial lead time minimum 3 months. Submit seasonal material 6 months in advance. Accepts queries by mail, e-mail. Responds in 1 month to queries. Responds in 1 month to mss.

NONFICTION Query. Does not accept unsolicited mss. Length: Depends on subject matter and content. **Payment rate is on published page including photographs.**

PHOTOS Send photos. Captions, model releases required. Reviews contact sheets, transparencies, CD-ROMs. Offers no additional payment for photos, except for cover shot.

TIPS "Write first for submission requirements and please be familiar with a few months of the magazine's content before submitting. No over the transom material, photos or mss, accepted."

REAL ESTATE

😊😊 AREA DEVELOPMENT ONLINE

Halcyon Business Publications, Inc., 400 Post Ave., Westbury NY 11590. (516)338-0900, ext. 211. **Fax:** (516)338-0100. **E-mail:** gerri@areadevelopment.com. **Website:** www.areadevelopment.com. **Contact:** Geraldine Gambale, editor. **80% freelance written. Prefers to work with published/established writers.** Quarterly magazine covering corporate facility planning and site selection for industrial chief executives worldwide. Estab. 1965. Circ. 60,000. Byline given. Pays on publication. No kill fee. Publishes ms an average of 2 months after acceptance. Accepts queries by mail, e-mail, fax. Responds in 3 months to queries. Sample copy free. Guidelines for #10 sase.

NONFICTION Needs historical, if it deals with corporate facility planning, how-to, experiences in site selection and all other aspects of corporate facility planning, interview, corporate executives and industrial developers. **Buys 75 mss/year.** Query. Length: 1,500-2,000 words. **Pays 40¢/word.** Sometimes pays expenses of writers on assignment.

PHOTOS State availability. Captions, identification of subjects required. Reviews JPEGS of at least 300 dpi. Negotiates payment individually.

✪😊😊😊 CANADIAN PROPERTY MANAGEMENT

Media Edge, 5255 Yonge St., Suite 1000, Toronto ON M2N 2P4 Canada. (416)512-8186. **Fax:** (416)512-8344. **E-mail:** barbc@mediaedge.ca. **Website:** www.remi-network.com/canadian-property-management/home/. **Contact:** Barbara Carss, editor-in-chief. **10% freelance written.** Magazine published 8 times/year covering Canadian commercial, industrial, institutional (medical and educational), and residential properties. *Canadian Property Management* magazine is a trade journal supplying building owners and property managers with Canadian industry news, case law reviews, technical updates for building operations and events listings. Building and professional profile articles are regular features. Estab. 1985. Circ. 12,500. Byline given. Pays on publication. No kill fee. Publishes ms an average of 3 months after acceptance. Editorial lead time 2 months. Submit seasonal material 2 months in advance. Accepts queries by mail, e-mail, fax, phone. Accepts simultaneous submissions. Responds in 3 weeks to queries. Responds in 2 months to mss. Sample copy for $5, subject to availability. Guidelines free.

NONFICTION Needs interview, technical. No promotional articles (i.e., marketing a product or service geared to this industry). Query with published clips. Length: 700-1,200 words. **Pays 35¢/word.**

PHOTOS State availability. Captions, identification of subjects, model releases required. Reviews transparencies, 3x5 prints, digital (at least 300 dpi). Offers no additional payment for photos accepted with ms.

TIPS "We do not accept promotional articles serving companies or their products. Freelance articles that are strong, information-based pieces that serve the interests and needs of property managers and building owners stand a better chance of being published. Proposals and inquiries with article ideas are appreciated the most. A good understanding of the real estate industry (management structure) is also helpful for the writer."

⊕⊛ THE COOPERATOR

Yale Robbins, Inc., 102 Madison Ave., 5th Floor, New York NY 10016. (212)683-5700. **Fax:** (212)545-0764. **E-mail:** editorial@cooperator.com. **Website:** www.cooperator.com. **70% freelance written.** Monthly tabloid covering real estate in the New York City metro area. *The Cooperator* covers condominium and cooperative issues in New York and beyond. It is read by condo unit owners and co-op shareholders, real estate professionals, board members and managing agents, and other service professionals. Estab. 1980. Circ. 40,000. Byline given. Pays on publication. No kill fee. Publishes ms an average of 3 months after acceptance. Submit seasonal material 3 months in advance. Accepts queries by mail, e-mail, fax. Responds in 1 month to queries. Sample copy and writer's guidelines free.

NONFICTION Needs interview, new product, personal experience. No submissions without queries. Query with published clips. Length: 1,500-2,000 words. **Pays $325-425.** Sometimes pays expenses of writers on assignment.

PHOTOS State availability.

COLUMNS/DEPARTMENTS Profiles of co-op/condo-related businesses with something unique; Building Finance (investment and financing issues); Buying and Selling (market issues, etc.); Design (architectural and interior/exterior design, lobby renovation, etc.); Building Maintenance (issues related to maintaining interior/exterior, facades, lobbies, elevators, etc.); Legal Issues Related to Co-Ops/Condos; Real Estate Trends, all 1,500 words. **Buys 100 mss/year.** Query with published clips.

TIPS "You must have experience in business, legal, or financial. Must have published clips to send in with résumè and query."

⊕⊛ FLORIDA REALTOR MAGAZINE

Florida Association of Realtors, 7025 Augusta National Dr., Orlando FL 32822. (407)438-1400. **Fax:** (407)438-1411. **E-mail:** flrealtor@floridarealtors.org. **Website:** www.floridarealtormagazine.com. **Contact:** Doug Damerst, editor-in-chief. **70% freelance written.** Journal published 10 times/year covering the Florida real estate profession. "As the official publication of the Florida Association of Realtors, we provide helpful articles for our 125,000 members. We report new practices that lead to successful real estate careers and stay up on the trends and issues that affect business in Florida's real estate market." Estab. 1925. Circ. 114,592. Byline given. Pays on publication. No kill fee. Publishes ms an average of 2 months after acceptance. Editorial lead time 3 months. Accepts queries by mail, e-mail, fax. Sample copy online.

NONFICTION No fiction or poetry. **Buys varying number of mss/year.** Query with published clips. Length: 800-1,500 words. **Pays $500-700.** Sometimes pays expenses of writers on assignment.

PHOTOS State availability of photos. Captions, identification of subjects, model releases required. Negotiates payment individually.

COLUMNS/DEPARTMENTS Some written in-house: Law & Ethics, 900 words; Market It, 600 words; Technology & You, 800 words; ManageIt, 600 words. **Buys varying number of mss/year. Payment varies.**

TIPS "Build a solid reputation for specializing in real estate business writing in state/national publications. Read the magazine online at floridarealtors.org/magazine. Query with specific article ideas."

⊕⊛ OFFICE BUILDINGS MAGAZINE

Yale Robbins, Inc., 102 Madison Ave., New York NY 10016. (212)683-5700. **Fax:** (212)497-0017. **E-mail:** mrosupport@mrofficespace.com. **Website:** marketing.yrpubs.com/officebuildings. **15% freelance written.** Annual magazine published in 12 separate editions covering market statistics, trends, and thinking of area professionals on the current and future state of the real estate market. Estab. 1987. Circ. 10,500. Byline sometimes given. Pays 1 month after publication. Offers kill fee. Editorial lead time 2 months. Accepts queries by mail, e-mail. Sample copy and writer's guidelines free.

NONFICTION **Buys 15-20 mss/year.** Query with published clips. Length: 1,500-2,000 words. **Pays $600-700.** Sometimes pays expenses of writers on assignment.

⊕⊛ PROPERTIES MAGAZINE

Properties Magazine, Inc., 3826 W. 158th St., Cleveland OH 44111. (216)251-2655. **Fax:** (216)251-0064. **E-mail:** mwatt@propertiesmag.com. **Website:** www.propertiesmag.com. **Contact:** Mark Watt, managing editor/

art director. **25% freelance written.** Monthly magazine covering real estate, residential, commerical construction. *Properties Magazine* is published for executives in the real estate, building, banking, design, architectural, property management, tax, and law community—busy people who need the facts presented in an interesting and informative format. Estab. 1946. Circ. over 10,000. Byline given. Pays on publication. No kill fee. Publishes ms an average of 2 months after acceptance. Editorial lead time 2 months. Submit seasonal material 2 months in advance. Accepts queries by mail, fax. Responds in 3 weeks to queries. Sample copy for $3.95.

NONFICTION Needs general interest, how-to, humor, new product. Special issues: Environmental issues (September); Security/Fire Protection (October); Tax Issues (November); Computers In Real Estate (December). **Buys 30 mss/year.** Send complete ms. Length: 500-2,000 words. **Pays 50¢/column line.** Sometimes pays expenses of writers on assignment.

PHOTOS Send photos. Captions required. Reviews prints. Offers no additional payment for photos accepted with ms. Negotiates payment individually.

COLUMNS/DEPARTMENTS Buys 25 mss/year. Query or send complete ms. **Pays 50¢/column line.**

☺☯☯ REM

2255B Queen St. E., Suite #1178, Toronto ON M4E 1G3 Canada. (416)425-3504. **E-mail:** jim@remonline.com. **Website:** www.remonline.com. **Contact:** Jim Adair, managing editor. **35% freelance written.** Monthly Canadian trade journal covering real estate. "*REM* provides Canadian real estate agents and brokers with news and opinions they can't get anywhere else. It is an independent publication and not affiliated with any real estate board, association, or company." Estab. 1989. Circ. 28,000. Pays on acceptance. Offers 25% kill fee. Publishes ms an average of 2 months after acceptance. Editorial lead time 3 months. Submit seasonal material 3 months in advance. Accepts queries by mail, e-mail. YesAccepts simultaneous submissions. Sample copy free.

NONFICTION Needs book excerpts, expose, inspirational, interview, new product, personal experience. "No articles geared to consumers about market conditions or how to choose a realtor. Must have Canadian content." **Buys 60 mss/year.** Query. Length: 500-1,500 words. **Pays $200-400.**

PHOTOS Send photos. Captions, identification of subjects required. Reviews transparencies, prints, GIF/JPEG files. Offers $25/photo.

TIPS "Stories must be of interest or practical use for Canadian realtors. Check out our website to see the types of stories we require."

☯☯ ZONING PRACTICE

American Planning Association, 205 N. Michigan Ave., Suite 1200, Chicago IL 60601. (312)431-9100. **Fax:** (312)786-6700. **E-mail:** zoningpractice@planning.org. **Website:** www.planning.org/zoningpractice/index.htm. **90% freelance written.** Monthly newsletter covering land-use regulations including zoning. Publication is aimed at practicing urban planners and those involved in land-use decisions, such as zoning administrators and officials, planning commissioners, zoning boards of adjustment, land-use attorneys, developers, and others interested in this field. The material published comes from writers knowledgeable about zoning and subdivision regulations, preferably with practical experience in the field. Anything published needs to be of practical value to our audience in their everyday work. Estab. 1984. Circ. 2,000. Byline given. Pays on publication. Offers 50% kill fee. Publishes ms an average of 3 months after acceptance. Editorial lead time 6 months. Accepts queries by mail, e-mail, fax, phone. Responds in 2 weeks to queries. Responds in 1 month to mss. Sample copy free. Guidelines available atwww.planning.org/zoningpractice/contrib-guidelines.htm.

NONFICTION Needs technical. See description. We do not need general or consumer-interest articles about zoning because this publication is aimed at practitioners. **Buys 12 mss/year.** Query. Length: 3,000-5,000 words. **Pays $300 minimum for assigned articles.** Sometimes pays expenses of writers on assignment.

PHOTOS State availability. Captions required. Reviews GIF/JPEG files. Negotiates payment individually.

TIPS "Breaking in is easy if you know the subject matter and can write in plain English for practicing planners. We are always interested in finding new authors. We generally expect authors will earn another $200 premium for participating in an online forum called Ask the Author, in which they respond to questions from readers about their article. This requires a deep practical sense of how to make things work with regard to your topic."

RESOURCES AND WASTE REDUCTION

$$ COMPOSTING NEWS

McEntee Media Corp., 9815 Hazelwood Ave., Strongsville OH 44149. (440)238-6603. **Fax:** (440)238-6712. **E-mail:** ken@recycle.cc. **Website:** www.compostingnews.com. **Contact:** Ken McEntee, editor. **5% freelance written.** Monthly newsletter about the composting industry. *Composting News* features the latest news and vital issues of concern to the producers, marketers, and end-users of compost, mulch and other organic waste-based products. Estab. 1992. Circ. 1,000. Pays on publication. No kill fee. Publishes ms an average of 1 month after acceptance. Editorial lead time 1 month. Submit seasonal material 1 month in advance. Accepts queries by mail, e-mail, fax, phone. YesAccepts simultaneous submissions. Responds in 2 months to queries. Sample copy for 9x12 SAE and 55¢ postage. Guidelines for #10 SASE.

NONFICTION Needs book excerpts, essays, general interest, how-to, interview, new product, opinion, personal experience, photo feature, technical, new business, legislation, regulation, business expansion. **Buys 0-5 mss/year.** Query with published clips. Length: 100-5,000 words. **Pays $10-500.**

COLUMNS/DEPARTMENTS Query with published clips. **Pays $10-500.**

TIPS "We appreciate leads on local news regarding composting, i.e., new facilities or business, new laws and regulations, unique programs, situations that impact supply and demand for composting. International developments are also of interest."

$$$ EROSION CONTROL

Forester Media Inc., 2946 De La Vina St., Santa Barbara CA 93105. (805)682-1300. **Fax:** (805)682-0200. **E-mail:** eceditor@forester.net. **Website:** www.erosioncontrol.com. **Contact:** Janice Kaspersen, editor. **60% freelance written.** Magazine published 7 times/year covering all aspects of erosion prevention and sediment control. *Erosion Control* is a practical, hands-on, how-to professional journal. Readers are civil engineers, landscape architects, builders, developers, public works officials, road and highway construction officials and engineers, soils specialists, farmers, landscape contractors, and others involved with any activity that disturbs significant areas of surface vegetation. Estab. 1994. Circ. 23,000. Byline given. Pays 1 month after acceptance. No kill fee. Publishes ms an average of 3 months after acceptance. Editorial lead time 4 months. Submit seasonal material 4 months in advance. Accepts queries by mail, e-mail, fax, phone. Responds in 3 weeks to queries. Sample copy and writer's guidelines free.

NONFICTION Needs photo feature, technical. **Buys 15 mss/year.** Query with published clips. Length: 3,000-4,000 words. **Pays $700-850.** Sometimes pays expenses of writers on assignment.

PHOTOS Send photos. Captions, identification of subjects, model releases required. Reviews transparencies, prints. Offers no additional payment for photos accepted with ms.

TIPS "Writers should have a good grasp of technology involved and good writing and communication skills. Most of our freelance articles include extensive interviews with engineers, contractors, developers, or project owners, and we often provide contact names for articles we assign."

$$ MSW MANAGEMENT

Forester Media Inc., P.O. Box 3100, Santa Barbara CA 93130. (805)682-1300. **Fax:** (805)682-0200. **E-mail:** jtrotti@forester.net. **Website:** www.mswmanagement.com. **Contact:** John Trotti, group editor. **70% freelance written.** Bimonthly magazine. *MSW Management* is written for public sector solid waste professionals—the people working for the local counties, cities, towns, boroughs, and provinces. They run the landfills, recycling programs, composting, and incineration. They are responsible for all aspects of garbage collection and disposal; buying and maintaining the associated equipment; and designing, engineering, and building the waste processing facilities, transfer stations, and landfills. Estab. 1991. Circ. 25,000. Byline given. Pays 30 days after acceptance. No kill fee. Editorial lead time 4 months. Submit seasonal material 4 months in advance. Accepts queries by mail, e-mail, fax, phone. Accepts simultaneous submissions. Responds in 6 weeks to queries. Responds in 2 months to mss. Sample copy and writer's guidelines free.

NONFICTION Needs photo feature, technical. No rudimentary, basic articles written for the average person on the street. Readers are experienced professionals with years of practical, in-the-field experience. Any material submitted that is too fundamental will be rejected. **Buys 15 mss/year.** Query. Length: 3,000-

4,000 words. **Pays $350-750.** Sometimes pays expenses of writers on assignment.

PHOTOS Send photos. Captions, identification of subjects, model releases required. Reviews transparencies, prints. Offers no additional payment for photos accepted with ms.

TIPS "We're a small company, easy to reach. We're open to any and all ideas as to possible editorial topics. We endeavor to provide the reader with usable material, and present it in full color with graphic embellishment whenever possible. Dry, highly technical material is edited to make it more palatable and concise. Most of our feature articles come from freelancers. Interviews and quotes should be from public sector solid waste managers and engineers, not PR people, not manufacturers. Strive to write material that is 'over the heads' of our readers. If anything, attempt to make them 'reach.' Anything submitted that is too basic, elementary, fundamental, rudimentary, etc., cannot be accepted for publication."

$$$ STORMWATER

Forester Media Inc., 2946 De La Vina St., Santa Barbara CA 93105. (805)682-1300. **Fax:** (805)682-0200. **E-mail:** sweditor@forester.net. **Website:** www.stormh2o.com. **Contact:** Janice Kaspersen, editor. **10% freelance written.** Magazine published 8 times/year covering stormwater issues. *Stormwater* is a practical business journal for professionals involved with surface water quality issues, protection, projects, and programs. Readers are municipal employees, regulators, engineers, and consultants concerned with stormwater management. Estab. 2000. Circ. 20,000. Byline given. Pays 1 month after acceptance. No kill fee. Publishes ms an average of 3 months after acceptance. Editorial lead time 4 months. Submit seasonal material 4 months in advance. Accepts queries by mail, e-mail. Responds in 3 weeks to queries. Guidelines free.

NONFICTION Needs technical. **Buys 8-10 mss/year.** Query with published clips. Length: 3,000-4,000 words. **Pays $500-900.** Sometimes pays expenses of writers on assignment.

PHOTOS Send photos. Captions, identification of subjects, model releases required. Offers no additional payment for photos accepted with ms.

TIPS "Writers should have a good grasp of the technology and regulations involved in stormwater management and good interviewing skills. Our freelance articles include extensive interviews with engineers, stormwater managers, and project owners, and we often provide contact names for articles we assign. See past editorial content online."

$$ WATER WELL JOURNAL

National Ground Water Association, 601 Dempsey Rd., Westerville OH 43081. **Fax:** (614)898-7786. **E-mail:** tplumley@ngwa.org. **Website:** www.waterwelljournal.org. **Contact:** Thad Plumley, director of publications; Mike Price, associate editor. Each month the *Water Well Journal* covers the topics of drilling, rigs and heavy equipment, pumping systems, water quality, business management, water supply, on-site waste water treatment, and diversification opportunities, including geothermal installations, environmental remediation, irrigation, dewatering, and foundation installation. It also offers updates on regulatory issues that impact the ground water industry. Circ. 24,000. Byline given. Pays on publication. Publishes ms an average of 3 months after acceptance. Editorial lead time 6 weeks. Submit seasonal material 3 months in advance. Accepts queries by mail. Responds in 2 weeks to queries. Responds in 1 month to mss. Guidelines free.

NONFICTION Needs essays, sometimes, historical, sometimes, how-to, recent examples include how-to chlorinate a well; how-to buy a used rig; how-to do bill collections, interview, new product, personal experience, photo feature, technical, business management. No company profiles or extended product releases. **Buys up to 30 mss/year.** Query with published clips. Length: 1,000-3,000 words. **Pays $150-400.**

PHOTOS State availability. Captions, identification of subjects required. Offers $50-250/photo.

TIPS "Some previous experience or knowledge in groundwater/drilling/construction industry helpful. Published clips are a must."

SELLING AND MERCHANDISING

$ THE AMERICAN SALESMAN

National Research Bureau, 320 Valley St., Burlington IA 52601. (319)752-5415. **E-mail:** contact@salestrainingandtechniques.com. **E-mail:** articles@salestrainingandtechniques.com. **Website:** www.salestrainingandtechniques.com. **80% freelance written.** Monthly magazine covering sales and marketing. *The American Salesman Magazine* is designed for sales professionals. Its primary objective is to provide informative articles which develop the attitudes, skills, and personal and professional qualities of sales representatives, allowing them to use more of their potential to increase productivity and achieve goals. Byline given. Publishes ms an average of 1 month after acceptance. Editorial lead time 1 month. Submit seasonal material 2 months in advance. Accepts queries by e-mail. Sample copy free. Guidelines by e-mail.

NONFICTION Needs personal experience. **Buys 24 mss/year.** Send complete ms. Length: 500-1,000 words. **Pays 4¢/word.**

🌐🌐 BALLOONS & PARTIES MAGAZINE

PartiLife Publications, 65 Sussex St., Hackensack NJ 07601. (201)441-4224. **Fax:** (201)342-8118. **E-mail:** mark@balloonsandparties.com. **Website:** www.balloonsandparties.com. **Contact:** Mark Zettler, publisher. **10% freelance written.** International trade journal published bi-monthly for professional party decorators and gift delivery businesses. *BALLOONS & Parties Magazine* is published 6 times a year by PartiLife Publications, L.L.C., for the balloon, party and event fields. New product data, letters, mss, and photographs should be sent as "Attention: Editor" and should include sender's full name, address, and telephone number. SASE required on all editorial submissions. All submissions considered for publication unless otherwise noted. Unsolicited materials are submitted at sender's risk and *BALLOONS & Parties*/PartiLife Publications, L.L.C., assumes no responsibility for unsolicited materials. Estab. 1986. Circ. 7,000. Byline given. Pays on publication. No kill fee. Publishes ms an average of 3 months after acceptance. Submit seasonal material 6 months in advance. Accepts queries by mail, e-mail, fax, phone. Responds in 6 weeks to queries. Sample copy for SAE with 9x12 envelope.

NONFICTION Needs essays, how-to, interview, new product, personal experience, photo feature, technical, craft. **Buys 12 mss/year.** Send complete ms. Length: 500-1,500 words. **Pays $100-300 for assigned articles. Pays $50-200 for unsolicited articles.** Sometimes pays expenses of writers on assignment.

REPRINTS Send typed ms with rights for sale noted and information about when and where the material previously appeared. Length: up to 2,500 words. Pays 10¢/word.

PHOTOS Send photos. Captions, identification of subjects, model releases required. Reviews 2x2 transparencies, 3x 5 prints.

COLUMNS/DEPARTMENTS Problem Solver (small business issues); Recipes That Cook (centerpiece ideas with detailed how-to); 400-1,000 words. Send complete ms with photos.

TIPS "Show unusual, lavish, and outstanding examples of balloon sculpture, design and decorating, and other craft projects. Offer specific how-to information. Be positive and motivational in style."

🌐 C&I RETAILING

Convenience & Impulse Retailing; Berg Bennett, Pty Ltd., Suite 6, The Atrium, 340 Darling St., Balmain NSW 2041 Australia. (61)(2)9555-1355. **Fax:** (61)(2)9555-1434. **E-mail:** magazine@c-store.com.au. **Website:** www.c-store.com.au. Bimonthly magazine covering retail store layout, consumer packaged goods, forecourt, impulse retailing as well as convenience food. Circ. 25,250.

NONFICTION Needs general interest, how-to, new product, Also industry news. Query.

🌐🌐 CASUAL LIVING MAGAZINE

Progresive Business Media/Today Group, 7025 Albert Pick Rd., Suite 200, Greensboro NC 27409. (336)605-1122. **Fax:** (336)605-1143. **E-mail:** cingram@casualliving.com. **Website:** www.casualliving.com. **Contact:** Cinde Ingram, editor-in-chief. **10% freelance written.** Monthly magazine covering outdoor furniture and accessories, barbecue grills, spas, and more. *Casual Living* is a trade only publication for the casual furnishings and related industries, published monthly. Writes about new products, trends, and casual furniture retailers, plus industry news. Estab. 1958. Circ. 10,000. Pays on publication. Publishes ms an average of 1-2 months after acceptance. Editorial lead time 1-2 months. Submit seasonal material 2 months in advance. Accepts queries by mail, e-mail. Responds in 2 weeks to queries. Sample copy online.

NONFICTION Needs how-to, interview. **Buys 20 mss/year.** Query with published clips. Length: 300-1,000 words. **Pays $300-700.** Sometimes pays expenses of writers on assignment.

PHOTOS Contact: Alexa Boschini, editorial assistant. Identification of subjects required. Reviews GIF/JPEG files. Negotiates payment individually.

🌐🌐🌐 CONSUMER GOODS TECHNOLOGY

Edgell Communications, 4 Middlebury Blvd., Randolph NJ 07869. (973)607-1300. **Fax:** (973)607-1395. **E-mail:** aackerman@edgellmail.com. **Website:** www.

consumergoods.edgl.com. **Contact:** Alliston Ackerman, editor. **40% freelance written.** Monthly tabloid benchmarking business technology performance. Estab. 1987. Circ. 25,000. Byline given. Pays on publication. No kill fee. Publishes ms an average of 2 months after acceptance. Editorial lead time 3 months. Accepts queries by e-mail. Sample copy online. Guidelines by e-mail.

NONFICTION Needs essays, expose, interview. **Buys 60 mss/year.** Query with published clips. Length: 700-1,900 words. **Pays $600-1,200.** Sometimes pays expenses of writers on assignment.

PHOTOS Identification of subjects, model releases required. Negotiates payment individually.

COLUMNS/DEPARTMENTS Columns 400-750 words—featured columnists. **Buys 4 mss/year.** Query with published clips. **Pays 75¢-$1/word.**

TIPS "All stories in *Consumer Goods Technology* are told through the voice of the consumer goods executive. We only quote VP-level or C-level CG executives. No vendor quotes. We're always on the lookout for freelance talent. We look in particular for writers with an in-depth understanding of the business issues faced by consumer goods firms and the technologies that are used by the industry to address those issues successfully. 'Bits and bytes' tech writing is not sought; our focus is on benchmarking the business technology performance of CG firms, CG executives, CG vendors, and CG vendor products. Our target reader is tech-savvy, CG C-level decision maker. We write to, and about, our target reader."

⊗⊗ NICHE

The Rosen Group, 3000 Chestnut Ave., Suite 300, Baltimore MD 21211. (410)889-3093, ext. 231. **Fax:** (410)243-7089. **E-mail:** hoped@rosengrp.com. **Website:** www.nichemagazine.com. **Contact:** Hope Daniels, editorial director. **80% freelance written.** Quarterly trade magazine for the progressive craft gallery retailer. Each issue includes retail gallery profiles, store design trends, management techniques, financial information, and merchandising strategies for small business owners, as well as articles about craft artists and craft mediums. Estab. 1988. Circ. 25,000. Byline given. Pays on publication. No kill fee. Publishes ms an average of 6-9 months after acceptance. Editorial lead time 9 months. Submit queries for seasonal material 1 year in advance. Accepts queries by e-mail. Responds in 4-6 weeks to queries. Responds in 3 months to mss. Sample copy for $3.

NONFICTION Needs interview, photo feature, articles targeted to independent retailers and small business owners. **Buys 15-20 mss/year.** Query with published clips. **Pays $300-700.** Sometimes pays expenses of writers on assignment.

PHOTOS Send photos. Captions required. Reviews e-images only. Negotiates payment individually.

COLUMNS/DEPARTMENTS Retail Details (short items at the front of the book, general retail information); Artist Profiles (short biographies of American Craft Artists); Retail Resources (including book/video/seminar reviews and educational opportunities pertaining to retailers). Query with published clips. **Pays $25-100 per item.**

⊗ O&A MARKETING NEWS

KAL Publications, Inc., 559 S. Harbor Blvd., Suite A, Anaheim CA 92805-4525. (714)563-9300. **Fax:** (714)563-9310. **E-mail:** kathy@kalpub.com. **Website:** www.kalpub.com. **3% freelance written.** Bimonthly tabloid. *O&A Marketing News* is editorially directed to people engaged in the distribution, merchandising, installation, and servicing of gasoline, oil, TBA, quick lube, carwash, convenience store, alternative fuel, and automotive aftermarket products in the 13 Western states. Estab. 1966. Circ. 7,500. Byline sometimes given. Pays on publication. No kill fee. Publishes ms an average of 2 months after acceptance. Editorial lead time 1 month. Submit seasonal material 1 month in advance. Accepts queries by mail, e-mail, fax. Accepts simultaneous submissions. Responds in 2 months to queries. Responds in 2 months to mss. Sample copy for SASE with 9x13 envelope and 10 first-class stamps.

NONFICTION Needs interview, photo feature, industry news. Does not want anything that doesn't pertain to the petroleum marketing industry in the 13 Western states. **Buys 35 mss/year.** Send complete ms. Length: 100-500 words. **Pays $1.25/column inch.**

PHOTOS State availability of or send photos. Captions, identification of subjects required. Reviews contact sheets, 4x6 prints, digital images. Offers $5/photo.

COLUMNS/DEPARTMENTS Oregon News (petroleum marketing news in state of Oregon). **Buys 7 mss/year.** Send complete ms. **Pays $1.25/column inch.**

FILLERS Needs gags, short humor. **Buys 7 fillers/year mss/year.** Length: 1-200 words. **Pays per column inch.**

TIPS "Seeking Western industry news pertaining to the petroleum marketing industry. It can be something simple—like a new gas station or quick lube opening.

News from 'outlying' states such as Montana, Idaho, Wyoming, New Mexico, and Hawaii is always needed—but any timely, topical news-oriented stories will also be considered."

💲💲 SMART RETAILER

Emmis Communications, P.O. Box 5000, N7528 Aanstad Rd., Iola WI 54945. (800)331-0038. **Fax:** (715)445-4053. **E-mail:** jonespublishingeditor@yahoo.com; carief@smart-retailer.com. **Website:** www.smart-retailer.com. **Contact:** Carie Ferg, publisher. **50% freelance written.** Magazine published 7 times/year covering independent retail, gift, and home decor. *Smart Retailer* is a trade publication for independent retailers of gifts and home accents. Estab. 1993. Circ. 32,000. Byline given. Pays 1 month after acceptance of final ms. Offers $50 kill fee. Publishes ms an average of 4-6 months after acceptance. Editorial lead time 4-6 months. Submit seasonal material 8-10 months in advance. Accepts queries by mail, e-mail, fax. YesAccepts simultaneous submissions. Usually responds in 4-6 weeks (only if accepted). Sample articles are online. Guidelines by e-mail.

NONFICTION Needs how-to, pertaining to retail, interview, new product, finance, legal, marketing, small business. No fiction, poetry, fillers, photos, artwork, or profiles of businesses, unless queried and first assigned. **Buys 20 mss/year.** Send complete ms, with résumé and published clips to: Writers Query, *Smart Retailer*. Length: 1,000-2,500 words. **Pays $275-500 for assigned articles. Pays $200-350 for unsolicited articles.** Sometimes pays expenses of writers on assignment. Limit agreed upon in advance.

COLUMNS/DEPARTMENTS Display & Design (store design and product display), 1,500 words; Retailer Profile (profile of retailer, assigned only), 1,800 words; Vendor Profile (profile of manufacturer, assigned only), 1,200 words; Technology (Internet, computer-related articles as applies to small retailers), 1,500 words; Marketing (marketing ideas and advice as applies to small retailers), 1,500 words; Finance (financial tips and advice as applies to small retailers), 1,500 words; Legal (legal tips and advice as applies to small retailers), 1,500 words; Employees (tips and advice on hiring, firing, and working with employees as applies to small retailers), 1,500 words. **Buys 15 mss/year.** Query with published clips or send complete ms. **Pays $250-350.**

💲💲 TRAVEL GOODS SHOWCASE

Travel Goods Association, 301 North Harrison St., #412, Princeton NJ 08540. (877)842-1938. **Fax:** (877)842-1938. **E-mail:** info@travel-goods.org; cathy@travel-goods.org. **Website:** www.travel-goods.org. **Contact:** Cathy Hays. **5-10% freelance written.** Magazine published quarterly. *Travel Goods Showcase*, the largest trade magazine devoted to travel products, contains articles for retailers, dealers, manufacturers, and suppliers about luggage, business cases, personal leather goods, handbags, and accessories. Special articles report on trends in fashion, promotions, selling and marketing techniques, industry statistics, and other educational and promotional improvements and advancements. Estab. 1975. Circ. 21,000. Byline given. Pays on acceptance. Offers $50 kill fee. Publishes ms an average of 2 months after acceptance. Editorial lead time 3 months. Submit seasonal material 2 months in advance. Accepts queries by mail, e-mail. Responds in 2 weeks to queries. Responds in 1 month to mss. Sample copy and writer's guidelines free.

NONFICTION Needs interview, new product, technical, travel, retailer profiles with photos. No manufacturer profiles. **Buys 3 mss/year.** Query with published clips. Length: 1,200-1,600 words. **Pays $200-400.**

💲💲💲 VERTICAL SYSTEMS RESELLER

Edgell Communications, Inc., 4 Middlebury Blvd., Randolph NJ 07869. (973)607-1300. **Fax:** (973)607-1395. **E-mail:** gkoroneos@edgellmail.com. **Website:** www.vsr.edgl.com. **Contact:** George L. Koroneos, editor-in-chief. **60% freelance written.** Monthly journal covering channel strategies that build business. Estab. 1992. Circ. 30,000. Byline given. Pays on acceptance. No kill fee. Publishes ms an average of 2 months after acceptance. Editorial lead time 3 months. Accepts queries by mail, e-mail, fax. Accepts simultaneous submissions. Responds in 2 weeks to queries. Responds in 2 months to mss. Sample copy online.

NONFICTION Needs interview, opinion, technical, technology/channel issues. **Buys 36 mss/year.** Query with published clips. Editorial calendar online with lead-generation opportunities. Length: 1,000-1,700 words. **Pays $200-800 for assigned articles.** Sometimes pays expenses of writers on assignment.

PHOTOS Send photos. Identification of subjects, model releases required. Offers no additional payment for photos accepted with ms.

$$$ VM+SD

ST Media Group International, 11262 Cornell Park Dr., Cincinnati OH 45242. (513)421-2050. **Fax:** (513)421-5144. **E-mail:** robin.donovan@stmediagroup.com; VMSD@halldata.com. **Website:** www.vmsd.com. **Contact:** Robin Donovan, managing editor. **10% freelance written.** Monthly magazine covering retailing store design, store planning, visual merchandising, brand marketing. Estab. 1872. Circ. 20,000. Byline given. Pays on acceptance. Offers $100 kill fee. Publishes ms an average of 1-2 months after acceptance. Editorial lead time 2-3 months. Submit seasonal material 3-4 months in advance. Accepts queries by e-mail. Sample copy free. Guidelines free.

NONFICTION Buys 2-3 mss/year. Query with details of project, including a press release if available, high-resolution, professional photos, the date the store opened, and any other information available. Length: 500-1,000 words. **Pays $400-1,000.**

PHOTOS Send photos. Reviews GIF/JPEG files. Negotiates payment individually.

COLUMNS/DEPARTMENTS Editorial calendar online. **Buys 5-6 mss/year.** Query. **Pays $500-750.**

TIPS "We need to see a demonstrated understanding of our industry, its issues and major players; strong reporting and interviewing skills are also important. Merely facile writing is not enough for us."

SPORT TRADE

$$ AQUATICS INTERNATIONAL

Hanley Wood, LLC, 6222 Wilshire Blvd., Suite 600, Los Angeles CA 90048. **Fax:** (323)801-4972. **E-mail:** etaylor@hanleywood.com. **Website:** www.aquaticsintl.com. **Contact:** Erika Taylor, editor. Magazine published 10 times/year covering public swimming pools and waterparks. Devoted to the commercial and public swimming pool industries. The magazine provides detailed information on designing, building, maintaining, promoting, managing, programming, and outfitting aquatics facilities. Estab. 1989. Circ. 30,000. Byline given. Pays on publication. No kill fee. Publishes ms an average of 3 months after acceptance. Editorial lead time 3 months. Responds in 1 month to queries. Sample copy for $10.50.

NONFICTION Needs how-to, interview, technical. **Buys 6 mss/year.** Send query letter with published clips/samples. Length: 1,500-2,500 words. **Pays $525 for assigned articles.**

COLUMNS/DEPARTMENTS Pays $250.

$$ ARROWTRADE MAGAZINE

Arrow Trade Publishing Corp., 3479 409th Ave. NW, Braham MN 55006. (320)396-3473. **Fax:** (320)396-3206. **E-mail:** timdehn@arrowtrademag.com. **Website:** www.arrowtrademag.com. **80% freelance written.** Bimonthly magazine covering the archery industry. Readers are interested in articles that help them operate their businesses better. They are primarily owners or managers of sporting goods stores and archery pro shops. Estab. 1996. Circ. 13,000. Byline given. Pays on publication. No kill fee. Publishes ms an average of 2 months after acceptance. Editorial lead time 2 months. Accepts queries by mail, e-mail, fax. Responds in 2 weeks to queries. Responds in 2 weeks to mss. Sample copy for SAE with 9x12 envelope and 10 First-Class stamps.

NONFICTION Needs interview, new product. "Generic business articles won't work for our highly specialized audience." **Buys 24 mss/year.** Query with published clips. Length: 3,400-4,800 words. **Pays $350-550.** Sometimes pays expenses of writers on assignment.

PHOTOS Send photos. Captions required. Must provide digital photos on CD or DVD or sent to FTP site. Offers no additional payment for photos accepted with ms.

TIPS "Our readers are hungry for articles that help them decide what to stock and how to do a better job selling or servicing it. Articles needed typically fall into 1 of these categories: business profiles on outstanding retailers, manufacturers, or distributors; equipment articles that cover categories of gear, citing trends in the market, and detailing why products have been designed a certain way and what type of use they're best suited for; basic business articles that help dealers do a better job of promoting their business, managing their inventory, training their staff, etc. Good interviewing skills are a must, as especially in the equipment articles we like to see a minimum of 6 sources."

$$ BOATING INDUSTRY

EPG Media, 3300 Fernbrook Lane N., Suite 200, Plymouth MN 55447. (763)383-4400. **E-mail:** jonathan.sweet@boatingindustry.com. **Website:** www.boatingindustry.com. **Contact:** Jonathan Sweet, editor-in-chief. **Less than 10% freelance written.** Bimonthly magazine covering recreational marine industry management. "We write for those in the industry—not the consumer. Our subject is the business of boating. All of our articles must be analytical and predictive, telling our readers where the industry is going, rather than where it's been." Estab. 1929. Circ. 23,000. Byline given. Pays on publication. Offers 50% kill fee. Publishes ms an average of 2 months after acceptance. Editorial lead time 2 months. Submit seasonal material 2 months in advance. Accepts queries by mail, e-mail. Responds in 1 month to queries. Sample copy online. Guidelines free.

NONFICTION Needs technical, business. **Buys 30 mss/year.** Query with published clips. Length: 250-2,500 words. **Pays $25-250.** Sometimes pays expenses of writers on assignment.

PHOTOS State availability. Captions, identification of subjects required. Reviews 2x2 transparencies, 4x6 prints. Negotiates payment individually.

💲💲 BOWLING CENTER MANAGEMENT

Luby Publishing, 122 S. Michigan Ave., Suite 1806, Chicago IL 60603. (312)341-1110. **Fax:** (312)341-1180. **E-mail:** mikem@lubypublishing.com. **Website:** www.bcmmag.com. **Contact:** Michael Mazek, editor. **50% freelance written.** Monthly magazine covering bowling centers, family entertainment. *Bowling Center Management* is the industry's leading business publication and offical trade magazien of the Bowling Proprietor's Association of America. Readers are looking for novel ways to draw more customers. Accordingly, the magazine looks for articles that effectively present such ideas. Estab. 1995. Circ. 12,000. Byline given. Pays on acceptance. Publishes ms an average of 3 months after acceptance. Editorial lead time 3 months. Submit seasonal material 6 months in advance. Accepts queries by e-mail. YesAccepts simultaneous submissions. Responds in 2-3 weeks to queries. Sample copy for $10.

NONFICTION Needs how-to, interview. **Buys 10-20 mss/year.** Query. Length: 750-1,500 words. **Pays $150-350.**

TIPS "Send a solid, clever query by e-mail with knowledge and interest in an industry trend."

💲💲 GOLF COURSE MANAGEMENT

Golf Course Superintendents Association of America, 1421 Research Park Dr., Lawrence KS 66049. (800)472-7878. **Fax:** (785)832-3643. **E-mail:** shollister@gcsaa.org; bsmith@gcsaa.org; tcarson@gcsaa.org. **Website:** www.gcsaa.org. **Contact:** Scott Hollister, editor-in-chief; Bunny Smith, senior managing editor; Teresa Carson, senior science editor. **50% freelance written.** Monthly magazine covering the golf course superintendent. *GCM* helps the golf course superin-

tendent become more efficient in all aspects of their job. Estab. 1924. Circ. 40,000. Byline given. Pays on acceptance. No kill fee. Publishes ms an average of 6 months after acceptance. Editorial lead time 6 months. Submit seasonal material 6 months in advance. Accepts simultaneous submissions. Responds in 3 weeks to queries. Responds in 1 month to mss. Sample copy free. Guidelines available at www2.gcsaa.org/gcm/ed_features.asp and www2.gcsaa.org/gcm/ed_research.asp.

NONFICTION Needs how-to, interview. No articles about playing golf. **Buys 40 mss/year.** Query for either feature, research, or superintendent article. Submit electronically, preferably as e-mail attachment. Send 1-page synopsis or query for feature article to Scott Hollister. For research articles, submit to Teresa Carson. If you are a superintendent, contact Bunny Smith. Length: 1,500-2,000 words. **Pays $400-600.** Sometimes pays expenses of writers on assignment.

PHOTOS Send photos. Identification of subjects required. Offers no additional payment for photos accepted with ms.

TIPS "Writers should have prior knowledge of golf course maintenance, agronomy and turfgrass science, and the overall profession of the golf course superintendent."

💲💲 INTERNATIONAL BOWLING INDUSTRY

B2B Media, Inc., 12655 Ventura Blvd., Studio City CA 91604. (818)789-2695. **Fax:** (818)789-2812. **E-mail:** info@bowlingindustry.com. **Website:** www.bowlingindustry.com. **40% freelance written.** Online monthly magazine covering ownership and management of bowling centers (alleys) and pro shops. *IBI* publishes articles in all phases of bowling center and bowling pro shop ownership and management, among them finance, promotion, customer service, relevant technology, architecture, and capital improvement. The magazine also covers the operational areas of bowling centers and pro shops such as human resources, food and beverage, corporate and birthday parties, ancillary attractions (go-karts, gaming and the like), and retailing. Articles must have strong how-to emphasis. They must be written specifically in terms of the bowling industry, although content may be applicable more widely. Estab. 1993. Circ. 10,200. Byline given. Pays on acceptance. Offers $50 kill fee. Publishes ms an average of 3 months after acceptance. Submit seasonal material 3 months in advance. Accepts queries by mail, e-mail, fax. Accepts simultaneous submissions. Responds in 2 weeks to queries. Responds in 1 month to mss. Sample copy for #10 SASE. Guidelines free.

NONFICTION Needs how-to, interview, new product, technical. **Buys 40 mss/year.** Send complete ms. Length: 1,100-1,400 words. **Pays $250.** Sometimes pays expenses of writers on assignment.

PHOTOS State availability. Identification of subjects required. Reviews JPEG photos. Offers no additional payment for photos accepted with ms.

TIPS "Please supply writing samples, applicable list of credits, and bio."

POOL & SPA NEWS

Hanley Wood, LLC, 6222 Wilshire Blvd., Suite 600, Los Angeles CA 90048. (323)801-4972. **Fax:** (323)801-4986. **E-mail:** etaylor@hanleywood.com; jmcclain@hanleywood.com. **Website:** poolspanews.com. **Contact:** Erika Taylor, editorial director; Joanne McClain, managing editor. **15% freelance written.** Semimonthly magazine covering the swimming pool and spa industry for builders, retail stores, and service firms. Estab. 1960. Circ. 16,300. Pays on publication. No kill fee. Publishes ms an average of 2 months after acceptance. Accepts queries by mail, e-mail. Responds in 1 month to queries. Sample copy for $5 and 9x12 SAE and 11 first-class stamps.

NONFICTION Needs interview, technical. Send résumé with published clips. Length: 500-2,000 words. **Pays $150-550.** Pays expenses of writers on assignment.

REPRINTS Send typed ms with rights for sale noted and information about when and where the material previously appeared. Payment varies.

PHOTOS Payment varies.

COLUMNS/DEPARTMENTS Payment varies.

REFEREE

Referee Enterprises, Inc., 2017 Lathrop Ave., Racine WI 53405. (800)733-6100. **Fax:** (262)632-5460. **E-mail:** submissions@referee.com. **Website:** www.referee.com. **Contact:** Julie Sternberg, managing editor. **75% freelance written.** Monthly magazine covering sports officiating. *Referee* is a magazine for and read by sports officials of all kinds with a focus on baseball, basketball, football, softball, and soccer officiating. Estab. 1976. Circ. 40,000. Byline given. Pays on acceptance. Offers kill fee. Kill fee negotiable. Publishes ms an average of 6 months after acceptance. Editorial lead time 6 months. Accepts queries by mail, e-mail. Responds in 2 weeks to queries. Responds in 1 month to mss. Sample copy with #10 SASE. Guidelines available at www.referee.com/index.php/referee-magazine/writers-guidlines.

NONFICTION Needs book excerpts, essays, historical, how-to, sports officiating related, humor, interview, opinion, photo feature, technical, as it relates to sports officiating. "We don't want to see articles with themes not relating to sport officiating. General sports articles, although of interest to us, will not be published." **Buys 40 mss/year.** Query with published clips. Length: 500-3,500 words. **Pays $50-400.** Sometimes pays expenses of writers on assignment.

PHOTOS State availability. Identification of subjects required. Reviews photos mailed on CD or DVD. Offers $35-40 per photo.

TIPS "Query first and be persistent. We may not like your idea, but that doesn't mean we won't like your next one. Professionalism pays off."

SKI AREA MANAGEMENT

Beardsley Publications, 84 Cross Brook Rd., P.O. Box 644, Woodbury CT 06798. (203)263-0888. **Fax:** (203)266-0452. **E-mail:** donna@saminfo.com; jenn@saminfo.com. **Website:** www.saminfo.com. **Contact:** Donna Jacobs. **85% freelance written.** Bimonthly magazine covering everything involving the management and development of ski resorts. Report on new ideas, developments, marketing, and regulations with regard to ski and snowboard resorts. Estab. 1962. Circ. 4,500. Byline given. Pays on publication. Offers kill fee. Offers kill fee. Editorial lead time 2 months. Submit seasonal material 3 months in advance. Accepts queries by mail, e-mail. Responds in 2 weeks to queries. Sample copy for 9x12 SAE with $3 postage or online. Guidelines for #10 SASE.

NONFICTION Needs historical, how-to, interview, new product, opinion, personal experience, technical. Does not want anything that does not specifically pertain to resort operations, management, or financing. **Buys 25-40 mss/year.** Query. Length: 500-2,500 words. **Pays $50-400.**

PHOTOS Send photos. Identification of subjects required. Reviews transparencies, prints. Offers no additional payment for photos accepted with ms.

TIPS "Know what you are writing about. We are read by people dedicated to skiing and snowboarding and to making the resort experience the best possible for their customers. It is a trade publication read by professionals."

STONE, QUARRY AND MINING

♻$$ CANADIAN MINING JOURNAL

Business Information Group, 80 Valleybrook Dr., Toronto ON M3B 2S9 Canada. (416)510-6742. **Fax:** (416)510-5138. **E-mail:** rnoble@canadianminingjournal.com. **Website:** www.canadianminingjournal.com. **Contact:** Russell Noble, editor. **5% freelance written.** Magazine covering mining and mineral exploration by Canadian companies. *Canadian Mining Journal* provides articles and information of practical use to those who work in the technical, administrative, and supervisory aspects of exploration, mining, and processing in the Canadian mineral exploration and mining industry. Estab. 1882. Circ. 11,000. Byline given. Pays on publication. No kill fee. Publishes ms an average of 3 months after acceptance. Submit seasonal material 3 months in advance. Accepts queries by mail, e-mail, fax, phone. Responds in 1 week to queries. Responds in 1 month to mss.

NONFICTION Needs opinion, technical, operation descriptions. **Buys 6 mss/year.** Query with published clips. Length: 500-1,400 words. **Pays $100-600.** Pays expenses of writers on assignment.

PHOTOS State availability. Photos require caption, identification of subjects. Reviews 4x6 prints or high-resolution files. Negotiates payment individually.

COLUMNS/DEPARTMENTS Guest editorial (opinion on controversial subject related to mining industry), 600 words. **Buys 3 mss/year.** Query with published clips. **Pays $150.**

TIPS "We need articles about mine sites that would be expensive/difficult for me to reach. We also need to know the writer is competent to understand and describe the technology in an interesting way."

⊕ CONTEMPORARY STONE & TILE DESIGN

Business News Publishing Media, 210 Route 4 East, Suite 203, Paramus NJ 07652. (201)291-9001, ext. 8611. **Fax:** (201)291-9002. **E-mail:** jennifer@stoneworld.com. **Website:** www.stoneworld.com. **Contact:** Jennifer Adams, editor. Quarterly magazine covering the full range of stone and tile design and architecture—from classic and historic spaces to current projects. Estab. 1995. Circ. 21,000. Byline given. Pays on publication. No kill fee. Publishes ms an average of 3 months after acceptance. Submit seasonal material 6 months in advance. Responds in 3 weeks to queries. Sample copy for $10.

NONFICTION Needs interview, prominent architect/designer or firm, photo feature, technical, architectural design. **Buys 8 mss/year.** Query with published clips. Length: 1,500-3,000 words. **Pays $6/column inch.** Pays expenses of writers on assignment.

PHOTOS State availability. Captions, identification of subjects required. Reviews transparencies, prints. Pays $10/photo accepted with ms.

COLUMNS/DEPARTMENTS Upcoming Events (for the architecture and design community); Stone Classics (featuring historic architecture); question and answer session with a prominent architect or designer. Length: 1,500-2,000 words. **Pays $6/inch.**

TIPS "The visual aspect of the magazine is key, so architectural photography is a must for any story. Cover the entire project, but focus on the stonework or tile work and how it relates to the rest of the space. Architects are very helpful in describing their work and often provide excellent quotes. As a relatively new magazine, we are looking for freelance submissions and are open to new feature topics. This is a narrow subject, however, so it's a good idea to speak with an editor before submitting anything."

$$ PIT & QUARRY

Questex Media Group, 1360 E. Ninth St., Suite 1070, Cleveland OH 44114. (216)706-3711; (216)706-3747. **Fax:** (216)706-3710. **E-mail:** info@pitandquarry.com; kyanik@northcoastmedia.net. **Website:** www.pitandquarry.com. **Contact:** Kevin Yanik, managing editor. **10-20% freelance written.** Monthly magazine covering nonmetallic minerals, mining, and crushed stone. Audience has knowledge of construction-related markets, mining, minerals processing, etc. Estab. 1916. Circ. 23,000. Byline given. Pays on acceptance. No kill fee. Publishes ms an average of 2 months after acceptance. Editorial lead time 2 months. Accepts queries by e-mail. Accepts simultaneous submissions. Responds in 1 month to queries. Responds in 4 months to mss.

NONFICTION Needs how-to, interview, new product, technical. No humor or inspirational articles. **Buys 3-4 mss/year.** Query. Length: 2,000-2,500 words. **Pays $250-500 for assigned articles. Does not pay for unsolicited articles.** Sometimes pays expenses of writers on assignment.

PHOTOS State availability. Identification of subjects, model releases required. Offers no additional payment for photos accepted with ms.

COLUMNS/DEPARTMENTS Brand New; Techwatch; E-business; Software Corner; Equipment Showcase. Length: 250-750 words. **Buys 5-6 mss/year.** Query. **Pays $250-300.**

TIPS "Be familiar with quarry operations (crushed stone or sand and gravel), as opposed to coal or metallic minerals mining. Know construction markets. We always need equipment-focused features on specific quarry operations."

$ STONE WORLD

BNP Media, 2401 W. Big Beaver Rd., Suite 700, Troy MI 48084. (201)291-9001. **Fax:** (201)291-9002. **E-mail:** jennifer@stoneworld.com. **Website:** www.stoneworld.com. **Contact:** Jennifer Adams, editor. Monthly magazine on natural building stone for producers and users of granite, marble, limestone, slate, sandstone, onyx, and other natural stone products. Estab. 1984. Circ. 21,000. Byline given. Pays on publication. No kill fee. Publishes ms an average of 4 months after acceptance. Submit seasonal material 6 months in advance. Responds in 2 months to queries. Sample copy for $10.

NONFICTION Needs how-to, fabricate and/or install natural building stone, interview, photo feature, technical, architectural design, artistic stone uses, statistics, factory profile, equipment profile, trade show review. **Buys 10 mss/year.** Send complete ms. Length: 600-3,000 words. **Pays $6/column inch.** Pays expenses of writers on assignment.

REPRINTS Send photocopy with rights for sale noted and information about when and where the material previously appeared. Pays 50% of amount paid for an original article.

PHOTOS State availability. Captions, identification of subjects required. Reviews transparencies, prints, slides, digital images. Pays $10/photo accepted with ms.

COLUMNS/DEPARTMENTS News (pertaining to stone or design community); New Literature (brochures, catalogs, books, videos, etc., about stone); New Products (stone products); New Equipment (equipment and machinery for working with stone); Calendar (dates and locations of events in stone and design communities). Query or send complete ms. Length 300-600 words. **Pays $6/inch.**

TIPS "Articles about architectural stone design accompanied by professional color photographs and quotes from designing firms are often published, especially when 1 unique aspect of the stone selection or installation is highlighted. We are also interested in articles about new techniques of quarrying and/or fabricating natural building stone."

TOY, NOVELTY AND HOBBY

$$ MODEL RETAILER

Kalmach Publishing Co., 21027 Crossroads Circle, Waukesha WI 53187. (262)796-8776. **E-mail:** jreich@kalmbach.com. **E-mail:** editor@modelretailer.com. **Website:** www.modelretailer.com. **Contact:** Jeff Reich, editor. **20% freelance written.** Monthly magazine. *Model Retailer* covers the business of hobby retailing, from financial and store management issues to product and industry trends. Goal is to provide owners and managers with the tools and information they need to be successful retailers. Estab. 1987. Circ. 6,000. Byline given. Pays on acceptance. Kill fee: 25%. Publishes ms an average of 2 months after acceptance. Editorial lead time 3 months. Submit seasonal material 6 months in advance. Accepts queries by mail, e-mail. Sample copy free. Guidelines online.

NONFICTION Needs how-to, business, new product. No articles that do not have a strong hobby or small retail component. **Buys 24-36 mss/year.** Query with published clips. "We welcome queries for feature articles and columns and the submission of articles sent on speculation. Queries and submissions accepted by e-mail only." Length: 800-1,600 words. **Pays $100-450.** Sometimes pays expenses of writers on assignment.

PHOTOS State availability. Captions, identification of subjects required. Reviews digital images. Negotiates payment individually.

PEN WORLD

Masterpiece Litho, Inc., P.O. Box 550246, Houston TX 77255-0246. (713)869-9997. **Fax:** (713)869-9993. **E-mail:** editor@penworld.com. **Website:** www.penworld.com. **Contact:** Laura Chandler, editor. Magazine published 6 times/year covering fine writing instruments. Published for writing instrument enthusiasts—new pens at all price points, vintage pens, fine papers, inks, accessories, reviews, how-tos. Circ. 30,000. No kill fee.

TRANSPORTATION

BUS CONVERSIONS

Bus Conversion Magazine, 9852 Katella Ave., #361, Anaheim CA 92804. (657)221-0432. **E-mail:** editor@busconversions.com. **Website:** www.busconversions.com. **Contact:** Mike Sullivan, editor. **95% freelance written.** Monthly magazine covering the bus conversion industry. *Bus Conversion Magazine* is the go-to resource for RV bus conversion enthusiasts. Each monthly issue contains detailed how-to articles on a wide range of bus conversion and updating projects. Estab. 1992. Circ. 10,000. Pays on publication. No kill fee. Accepts queries by mail, e-mail.

NONFICTION Needs how-to, articles on the electrical, plumbing, mechanical, decorative, and structural aspects of bus conversions; buses that are converted into RVs.

PHOTOS Submit phots online using e-mail or dropbox. Comercially printed photos (glossy) also accepted with submission. Photos not returned unless SASE is included.

COLUMNS/DEPARTMENTS Industry Update; Products of Interest; Ask the Experts; One For the Road; Road Fix.

TIPS "Most of our writers are our readers. Knowledge of bus conversions and the associated lifestyle is a prerequisite."

LIMOUSINE DIGEST

(*Limousine Digest*), Digest Publications, 3 Reeves Station Rd., Medford NJ 08055. (609)953-4900. **Fax:** (609)953-4905. **E-mail:** info@limodigest.com. **Website:** www.limodigest.com. **Contact:** Dawn Sheldon, assistant publisher. **10% freelance written.** Monthly magazine covering ground transportation. *Limousine Digest* is the voice of the luxury ground transportation industry. Covers all aspects of ground transportation, from vehicles to operators, safety issues, and political involvement. Estab. 1990. Circ. 10,000. Byline given. Pays on publication. No kill fee. Publishes ms an average of 3 months after acceptance. Editorial lead time 1 year. Submit seasonal material 3 months in advance. Accepts queries by mail, e-mail, fax. Accepts simultaneous submissions. Sample copy free.

NONFICTION Needs historical, how-to, start a company, market your product, humor, inspirational, interview, new product, personal experience, photo feature, technical, travel, industry news, business. **Buys** 7-9 mss/year. Send complete ms. Length: Minimum of 600 words. **Negotiates flat-fee and per-word rates individually. Will pay authors in advertising trade-outs.**

PHOTOS Must include photos to be considered. Send photos. Captions, identification of subjects, model releases required. Reviews negatives. Negotiates payment individually.

COLUMNS/DEPARTMENTS New Model Showcase (new limousines, sedans, buses), 1,000 words; Player Profile (industry members profiled), 700 words; Hall of Fame (unique vehicles featured), 500-700 words. **Buys 5 mss/year.** Query. **Negotiates flat-fee and per-word rates individually. Will pay authors in advertising trade-outs.**

☺☺ METRO MAGAZINE (CALIFORNIA)

Bobit Business Media, 3520 Challenger St., Torrance CA 90503. (310)533-2400. **Fax:** (310)533-2502. **E-mail:** info@metro-magazine.com. **E-mail:** alex.roman@bobit.com. **Website:** www.metro-magazine.com. **Contact:** Alex Roman, managing editor. **10% freelance written.** Magazine published 10 times/year covering transit bus, passenger rail, and motorcoach operations. METRO's coverage includes both public transit systems and private bus operators, addressing topics such as funding mechanisms, procurement, rolling stock maintenance, privatization, risk management, and sustainability. *Metro Magazine* delivers business, government policy, and technology developments that are *industry specific* to public transportation. Estab. 1904. Circ. 20,500. Byline given. Pays on acceptance. Offers 10% kill fee. Publishes ms an average of 2 months after acceptance. Editorial lead time 3 months. Submit seasonal material 3 months in advance. Accepts queries by e-mail. Responds in 2 weeks to queries. Responds in 1 month to mss. Sample copy for $8. Guidelines by e-mail.

NONFICTION Needs how-to, interview, of industry figures, new product, related to transit—bus and rail—private bus, technical. **Buys 6-10 mss/year.** Query. Length: 400-1,500 words. **Pays $80-400.**

PHOTOS State availability. Captions, identification of subjects, model releases required. Negotiates payment individually.

COLUMNS/DEPARTMENTS Query. **Pays 20¢/word.**

☺☺⊘ SCHOOL BUS FLEET

Bobit Business Media, 3520 Challenger St., Torrance CA 90503. (310)533-2400. **Fax:** (310)533-2512. **E-mail:** sbf@bobit.com. **Website:** www.schoolbusfleet.com.

Magazine covering school transportation of K-12 population. Most readers are school bus operators, public and private. Estab. 1956. Circ. 24,000. Byline given. Pays on acceptance. Offers 25% kill fee or $50. Publishes ms an average of 3 months after acceptance. Editorial lead time 3 months. Submit seasonal material 3 months in advance. Accepts queries by mail, e-mail, fax. Responds in 1 month to queries. Sample copy free. *Not currently accepting submissions.* Query first.

TRAVEL TRADE

⊛⊛ CRUISE INDUSTRY NEWS

441 Lexington Ave., Suite 809, New York NY 10017. (212)986-1025. **Fax:** (212)986-1033. **E-mail:** oivind@cruiseindustrynews.com. **Website:** www.cruiseindustrynews.com. **Contact:** Oivind Mathisen, editor. **20% freelance written.** Quarterly magazine covering cruise shipping. Magazine about the business of cruise shipping for the industry, including cruise lines, shipyards, financial analysts, etc. Estab. 1991. Circ. 10,000. Byline given. Pays on acceptance or on publication. Offers 25% kill fee. Publishes ms an average of 4 months after acceptance. Editorial lead time 3 months. Accepts queries by mail. Reponse time varies. Sample copy for $15. Guidelines for #10 SASE.

NONFICTION Needs interview, new product, photo feature, business. No travel stories. **Buys more than 20 mss/year.** Query with published clips. Length: 500-1,500 words. **Pays $.50/word published.** Sometimes pays expenses of writers on assignment.

PHOTOS State availability. Pays $25-50/photo.

⊛⊛ LEISURE GROUP TRAVEL

Premier Tourism Marketing, 621 Plainfield Rd., Suite 406, Willowbrook IL 60527. (630)794-0696. **Fax:** (630)794-0652. **E-mail:** randy@ptmgroups.com. **E-mail:** editor@ptmgroups.com. **Website:** www.leisuregrouptravel.com. **Contact:** Randy Mink, managing editor. **35% freelance written.** Bimonthly magazine covering group travel. Covers destinations and editorial relevant to the group travel market. Estab. 1994. Circ. 15,012. Byline given. Pays on publication. No kill fee. Editorial lead time 6 months. Submit seasonal material 6 months in advance. Accepts queries by mail, e-mail. Sample copy online.

NONFICTION Needs travel. **Buys 75 mss/year.** Query with published clips. Length: 1,200-3,000 words. **Pays $0-1,000.**

⊛ LL&A MAGAZINE

Media Diversified, Inc., 96 Karma Rd., Markham ON L3R 4Y3 Canada. (905)944-0265. **Fax:** (416)296-0994. **E-mail:** info@mediadiversified.com. **Website:** www.llanda.com. **5% freelance written.** Quarterly magazine for the travel, business, and fashion accessory market. Estab. 1966. Circ. 7,000. Byline given. Pays on publication. No kill fee. Editorial lead time 6 weeks. Accepts queries by e-mail. Sample copy and guidelines free.

NONFICTION Needs general interest, how-to, new product, technical.

⊛⊛ MIDWEST MEETINGS®

Hennen Publishing, 302 Sixth St. W, Brookings SD 57006. (605)692-9559. **Fax:** (605)692-9031. **E-mail:** info@midwestmeetings.com; editor@midwestmeetings.com. **Website:** www.midwestmeetings.com. **Contact:** Randy Hennen. **20% freelance written.** Quarterly magazine covering meetings/conventions industry. We provide information and resources to meeting/convention planners with a Midwest focus. Estab. 1996. Circ. 28,500. Byline given. Pays on acceptance. Publishes ms an average of 5 months after acceptance. Editorial lead time 3 months. Submit seasonal material 3 months in advance. Accepts queries by e-mail. Sample copy free. Guidelines by e-mail.

NONFICTION Needs essays, general interest, historical, how-to, humor, interview, personal experience, travel. Does not want marketing pieces related to specific hotels/meeting facilities. **Buys 15-20 mss/year.** Send complete ms. Length: 500-1,000 words. **Pays 5-50¢/word.**

PHOTOS Send photos. Captions, identification of subjects and permission statements/photo releases required. Reviews JPEG/EPS/TIF files (300 dpi). Offers no additional payment for photos accepted with ms.

TIPS If you were a meeting/event planner, what information would help you to perform your job better? We like lots of quotes from industry experts, insider tips, personal experience stories, etc. If you're not sure, e-mail the editor.

⊛⊛⊛ RV BUSINESS

G&G Media Group, 2901 E. Bristol St., Suite B, Elkhart IN 46514. (574)266-7980, ext. 13. **Fax:** (574)266-7984. **E-mail:** bhampson@rvbusiness.com; bhampson@g-gmediagroup.com. **Website:** www.rvbusiness.com. **Contact:** Bruce Hampson, editor. **50% freelance written.** Bimonthly magazine. *RV Business* caters to a specific audience of people who manufacture, sell, market, insure, finance, service and supply, components for recreational vehicles. Estab. 1972. Circ. 21,000. Byline given. Pays on acceptance. Offers kill fee. Publishes ms an average of 2 months after acceptance. Editorial lead time 2 months. Accepts queries by e-mail only. Sample copy free.

NONFICTION Needs new product, photo feature, industry news and features. No general articles without specific application to market. **Buys 50 mss/year.** Query with published clips. Length: 125-2,200 words. **Pays $50-1,000.** Sometimes pays expenses of writers on assignment.

COLUMNS/DEPARTMENTS Top of the News (RV industry news), 75-400 words; Business Profiles, 400-500 words; Features (indepth industry features), 800-2,000 words. **Buys 300 mss/year.** Query. **Pays $50-1,000.**

TIPS "Query. Send 1 or several ideas and a few lines letting us know how you plan to treat it/them. We are always looking for good authors knowledgeable in the RV industry or related industries. We need more articles that are brief, factual, hard hitting, and business oriented. Review other publications in the field, including enthusiast magazines."

$$ SCHOOL TRANSPORTATION NEWS

STN Media Co., P.O. Box 789, Redondo Beach CA 90277. (310)792-2226. **Fax:** (310)792-2231. **E-mail:** ryan@stnonline.com; sylvia@stonline.com. **Website:** www.stnonline.com. **Contact:** Ryan Gray, editor-in-chief; Sylvia Arroyo, managing editor. **20% freelance written.** Monthly magazine covering school bus and pupil transportation industries in North America. Contributors to *School Transportation News* must have a basic understanding of K-12 education and automotive fleets and specifically of school buses. Articles cover such topics as manufacturing, operations, maintenance and routing software, GPS, security and legislative affairs. A familiarity with these principles is preferred. Additional industry information is online. New writers must perform some research of the industry or exhibit core competencies in the subject matter. Estab. 1991. Circ. 24,000. Byline given. Pays on publication. No kill fee. Editorial lead time 1-2 months. Submit seasonal material 3 months in advance. Accepts queries by e-mail. Accepts simultaneous submissions. Sample copy free. Guidelines free.

NONFICTION Needs book excerpts, general interest, historical, humor, inspirational, interview, new product, personal experience, photo feature, technical. Does not want strictly localized editorial. Wants articles that put into perspective the issues of the day. Query with published clips. Length: 600-1,200 words. **Pays $150-300.** Sometimes pays expenses of writers on assignment.

PHOTOS Contact: Sylvia Arroyo, managing editor. No Answer. Captions, model releases required. Reviews GIF/JPEG files. Offers $150-200/photo.

COLUMNS/DEPARTMENTS Creative Special Report, Cover Story, Top Story; Book/Video Reviews (new programs/publications/training for pupil transporters), both 600 words. **Buys 40 mss/year.** Query with published clips. **Pays $150.**

TIPS "Potential freelancers should exhibit a basic proficiency in understanding school bus issues and demonstrate the ability to report on education, legislative and business affairs, as well as a talent with feature writing. It would be helpful if the writer has previous contacts within the industry. Article pitches should be e-mailed only."

$$ SPECIALTY TRAVEL INDEX

Alpine Hansen, P.O. Box 458, San Anselmo CA 94979. (415)455-1643. **E-mail:** info@specialtytravel.com. **Website:** www.specialtytravel.com. **90% freelance written.** Semiannual magazine covering adventure and special interest travel. Estab. 1980. Circ. 35,000. Byline given. Pays on receipt and acceptance of all materials. No kill fee. Editorial lead time 3 month. Submit seasonal material 3 months in advance. Accepts queries by mail, e-mail. Writer's guidelines on request.

NONFICTION Needs how-to, personal experience, photo feature, travel. **Buys 15 mss/year.** Query. Length: 1,250 words. **Pays $300 minimum.**

REPRINTS Send tearsheet. Pays 100% of amount paid for an original article.

PHOTOS State availability. Captions, identification of subjects required. Reviews EPS/TIFF files. Negotiates payment individually.

TIPS "Write about group travel and be both creative and factual. The articles should relate to both the travel agent booking the tour and the client who is traveling."

$ TRAVEL42

NORTHSTAR Travel Media, 331 High St., Winston-Salem NC 27101. (855)872-8542. **Fax:** (336)714-3168. **E-mail:** csheaffer@ntmllc.com. **Website:** www.travel-42.com. **Contact:** Cindy Sheaffer, editorial director. Worldwide guide to destinations, accommodations, and cruise ships, sold to travel professionals on subscription basis. Estab. 2011. No byline given. Pays 1 month after acceptance. No kill fee. Accepts queries by e-mail preferred.

TIPS "We may require sample hotel or cruise reports on facilities near freelancer's hometown before giving the first assignment. No byline because of sensitive nature of reviews."

VETERINARY

ANIMAL SHELTERING

Animal Sheltering Magazine, PO Box 15276, North Hollywood CA 91615. (800)565-9226. **E-mail:** asm@ humanesociety.org. **Website:** www.animalsheltering. org. **Contact:** Shevaun Brannigan, production/marketing manager; Carrie Allan, editor. **20% freelance written.** Magazine for animal care professionals and volunteers, dealing with animal welfare issues faced by animal shelters, animal control agencies, and rescue groups. Emphasis on news for the field and professional, hands-on work. Readers are shelter and animal control directors, kennel staff, field officers, humane investigators, animal control officers, animal rescuers, foster care volunteers, general volunteers, shelter veterinarians, and anyone concerned with local animal welfare issues. Estab. 1978. Circ. 6,000. Sample copies are free; contact Shevaun Brannigan at sbrannigan@hsus.org. Guidelines available by e-mail.

NONFICTION Approximately 6-10 submissions published each year from non-staff writers; of those submissions, 50% are from writers new to the publication. **"Payment varies depending on length and complexity of piece. Longer features generally $400–600; short news pieces generally $200. We rarely take unsolicited work, so it's best to contact the editor with story ideas."**

REPRINTS "Aquires first publication rights. We also grant permission, with a credit to the magazine and writer, to readers who want to use the materials to educate their supporters, staff and volunteers. Contact asm@humanesociety.org for writers' guidelines."

PHOTOS Pays $150 for cover; $75 for inside.

TIPS "We almost always need good photos of people working with animals in an animal shelter or in the field. We do not use photos of individual dogs, cats, and other companion animals as often as we use photos of people working to protect, rescue or care for dogs, cats, and other companion animals."

VETERINARY ECONOMICS

8033 Flint St., Lenexa KS 66214. (800)255-6864. **Fax:** (913)871-3808. **E-mail:** ve@advanstar.com. **Website:** veterinarybusiness.dvm360.com. **20% freelance written.** Monthly magazine covering veterinary practice management. "We address the business concerns and management needs of practicing veterinarians." Estab. 1960. Circ. 54,000. Byline given. Pays on publication. No kill fee. Publishes ms an average of 6 months after acceptance. Editorial lead time 3 months. Submit seasonal material 3 months in advance. Accepts queries by mail, e-mail. Accepts simultaneous submissions. Responds in 3 months to queries. Sample copy free. Guidelines online.

NONFICTION Needs how-to, interview, personal experience. **Buys 24 mss/year.** Send complete ms. Length: 1,000-2,000 words. **Pays $40-350.**

PHOTOS Send photos. Captions, identification of subjects required. Reviews transparencies, prints. Offers no additional payment for photos accepted with ms.

COLUMNS/DEPARTMENTS Practice Tips (easy, unique business tips), 250 words or fewer. Send complete ms. **Pays $40.**

TIPS "Among the topics we cover: veterinary hospital design, client relations, contractual and legal matters, investments, day-to-day management, marketing, personal finances, practice finances, personnel, collections, and taxes. We also cover news and issues within the veterinary profession; for example, articles might cover the effectiveness of Yellow Pages advertising, the growing number of women veterinarians, restrictive-covenant cases, and so on. Freelance writers are encouraged to submit proposals or outlines for articles on these topics."

CONTESTS & AWARDS

//

The contests and awards listed in this section are arranged by subject. Nonfiction writers can turn immediately to nonfiction awards listed alphabetically by the name of the contest or award. The same is true for fiction writers, poets, playwrights and screenwriters, journalists, children's writers, and translators. You'll also find general book awards, fellowships offered by arts councils and foundations, and multiple category contests.

To make sure you have all the information you need about a particular contest, always check the official website or contact the contest director before entering a contest. The listings in this section are brief, and many contests have lengthy, specific rules and requirements that we could not include in our limited space. Often a specific entry form must accompany your submission.

When you receive a set of guidelines, you will see that some contests are not applicable to all writers. The writer's age, previous publication, geographic location, and length of the work are common matters of eligibility. Read the requirements carefully to ensure you don't enter a contest for which you are not qualified. You should also be aware that every year, more and more contests, especially those sponsored by "little" literary magazines, are charging entry fees.

Winning a contest or award can launch a successful writing career. Take a professional approach by doing a little extra research. Find out who the previous winner of the award was by investing in a sample copy of the magazine in which the prize-winning article, poem, or short story appeared. Attend the staged reading of an award-winning play. Your extra effort will be to your advantage in competing with writers who simply submit blindly.

PLAYWRITING & SCRIPTWRITING

10 MINUTE PLAY CONTEST & FESTIVAL

Weathervane Playhouse, 1301 Weathervane Lane, Akron OH 44313. (330)836-2626. **E-mail:** 10minuteplay@weathervaneplayhouse.com. **Website:** www.weathervaneplayhouse.com. **Contact:** Eileen Moushey. Annual 8x10 TheatreFest. Must be US citizen 18 years or older. All rights remain with writers. Each year there is a special prop that must be incorporated into that year's plays. See website for details. All entries must be sent electronically, as attachments. Printed plays will not be considered. Guidelines online. The mission of the Weathervane Playhouse 8x10 TheatreFest is to promote the art of play writing, present new works, and introduce area audiences to the short play form. The competition will provide Weathervane with recognition for quality and innovative theatre. Deadline: May 16. Submission period begins December 1. Prize: Prizes: Each of 8 finalists receive full productions of their plays during TheatreFest, held in mid-July. 1st Place: $350; 2nd Place: $250; Audience Favorite: $150; 5 runners-up: $50 each. First round judges include individuals with experience in every area of stagecraft, including tech designers, actors, directors, stage managers, and playwrights.

THE ACADEMY NICHOLL FELLOWSHIP IN SCREENWRITING

1313 Vine St., Hollywood CA 90028-8107. (310)247-3010. **E-mail:** nicholl@oscars.org. **Website:** www.oscars.org/nicholl/index.html. An entrant's total earnings for motion picture and television writing may not exceed $25,000 before the end of the competition. This limit applies to compensation for motion picture and television writing services as well as for the sale of (or sale of an option on) screenplays, teleplays, stage plays, books, treatments, stories, premises and any other source material. Members and employees of the Academy of Motion Picture Arts and Sciences and their immediate families are not eligible, nor are competition judges and their immediate families. Deadline: April 10. The first and quarterfinal rounds are judged by industry professionals who are not members of the Academy. The semifinal round is judged by Academy members drawn from across the spectrum of the motion picture industry. The finalist scripts are judged by the Academy Nicholl Committee.

ACCLAIM FILM AND TV SCRIPT CONTESTS

Acclaim Scripts, 300 Central Ave, Suite 501, St. Petersburg FL 33701. (727)502-9049. **E-mail:** info@acclaimscripts.com. **Website:** www.acclaimtv.netfirms.com. Annual contest for TV and film scripts. Open to all writers worldwide. Work must be original material of the author(s). Must not be sold or optioned at time of submission. Multiple entries may be submitted (include separate entry form for each submission). Two categories for TV: comedy and drama. Deadline: February 7 (early); March 7 (regular); April 11 (late). Prize: TV: Winner of each category receives $500. Film: 1st Place: $1,000. All winners and finalists may receive consideration by established production companies and agencies.

ACCOLADE COMPETITION

7946 Ivanhoe Ave., Suite 201, La Jolla CA 92037. (858)454-9868. **E-mail:** info@accoladecompetition.org. **Website:** www.accoladecompetition.org. The Accolade Competition has been a showcase for cinematic gems and unique voices for 10 years. International awards competition, not a traditional film festival. Submissions in other than English must be subtitled or include transcript. Multiple entries are allowed and each entry may be entered in multiple categories. Submit on DVD in NTSC or PAL format. Entries will not be returned. Deadline: March 7. Prize: Awards include: Annual Humanitarian Award, Fast Focus Short Film Award, $4,800 Post-Production Award, and $1,500 Studio Award. See website for details on these awards. Also recognizes: Best of Show, Awards of Excellence, & Award of Merit. Best of Show honors are granted only if worthy productions are discovered. No more than 15% of entries are granted Awards of Excellence. Notable artistic and technical productions are recognized at the Award Of Merit award level. Judged by in-house staff.

AFC STORYTELLING INTERNATIONAL SCREENWRITING COMPETITION

African Film Commission, 1801 Century Park E., Suite 2400, Los Angeles CA 90067. (310)556-9661. **Fax:** (310)277-1278. **E-mail:** africafilmcommission@gmail.org. **Website:** www.africafilmcommission.org. Conceived to promote understanding of African life through screenplays and documentary projects and to create greater international cooperation in bringing African subject matters and locales to the screen. Scripts must have African content and themes. Three categories have been created for writers to compete: Africa—African Diaspora: Focused on the stories and people of Africa, this category seeks projects with a distinctly African point of view that enlightens, challenges, and informs the reader; Go Green—Sustainability: This subject matter deals with the growing concerns about the state of the self, immediate relationships, the environment, and the planet; International—All Stories: This category has no limits on subject matter or content, but simply seeks to reward the most compelling, well-crafted stories of shared humanity from around the world. Early Bird Deadline: October 2. Regular Deadline: November 20. Final Deadline: December 30. Contest begins September 2. Prize: Prizes vary based on awards. Visit website for application and details. Judged by a panel of entertainment industry professionals.

☯ ALBERTA PLAYWRITING COMPETITION

Alberta Playwrights' Network, 2633 Hochwald Ave. SW, Calgary AB T3E 7K2 Canada. (403)269-8564. **Fax:** (403)265-6773. **Website:** www.albertaplaywrights.com. Offered annually for unproduced scripts with full-length and discovery categories. Discovery is open only to previously unproduced playwrights (intended for emerging playwrights). Open only to residents of Alberta. Guidelines and rules online. Deadline: March 1. Prize: Grand Prize Category: $3,500 (CAD); Discovery Prize Category: $1,500 (CAD).

ALL ACCESS SCREENWRITING COMPETITION

SellAScript.com, 6506 Green Valley Circle, #313, Culver City CA 90230. (310)577-3181. **Website:** www.sellascript.com. Contest to provide winners with exclusive access to Hollywood. Electronic and mail submissions are both accepted. Script may not be under option at the time of entry nor at the time the material is chosen as a finalist or a winner. Deadline: December 15. Prize: 1st Place: $2,000; 2nd Place: $300; 3rd Place: $100. Each of the 3 winners also receives industry exposure and access, including: screenplay synopsis submitted to 29 participating companies, a free 6-month subscription to the Writer's Rolodex, and more. See website for additional details on prize package. Five finalists are also awarded prizes. Judged by Paul Harvey and Donna Milazzo

ALLIANCE OF WOMEN FILMMAKERS SCRIPT COMPETITION

Alliance of Women Filmmakers, 1317 N. San Fernando Blvd. #340, Burbank CA 91504. (818)749-6162. **E-mail:** info@womenfilmmakersalliance.org. **E-mail:** dmeans25@yahoo.com. **Website:** www.lawomensfest.com. Empowers women filmmakers to make culturally diverse contributions through film to Los Angeles Communities, as well as educate and inform audiences of social, political, and health issues impacting women globally. Early deadline: September 1. Regular Deadline: September 15. Late deadline: October 1. Prize: Prizes are sponsored and vary from year to year.

ANNUAL AUSTIN FILM FESTIVAL SCREENPLAY & TELEPLAY COMPETITION

Austin Film Festival, 1801 Salina St., Austin TX 78702. (512)478-4795. **Fax:** (512)478-6205. **E-mail:** screenplaydirector@austinfilmfestival.com; info@austinfilmfestival.com. **Website:** www.austinfilmfestival.com. **Contact:** Matt Dy, screenplay competition director. The Austin Film Festival, held annually in late October, is looking for quality screenplays and teleplays which will be read by industry professionals. AFF provides 'Readers' notes' to all Second Rounders (top 10%) and higher for no charge. Two main categories: Drama Category and Comedy Category. Two optional Award Categories (additional entry of $20 per category); Latitude Productions Award and Dark Hero Studios Sci-Fi Award. Teleplay Competition: The teleplay competition is now open to pilots as well as spec scripts. Two main categories: Half-hour Sitcom and One-Hour Drama/Comedy. Deadline: Screenplay: April 30. Late Screenplay: May 31. Telplay: April 30. Prize: $5,000 in Comedy and Drama; $2,500 for Sponsored Award and Sci-Fi Award.

THE ANNUAL BLANK THEATRE YOUNG PLAYWRIGHTS FESTIVAL

The Blank Theatre Co., P.O. Box 1094, Los Angeles CA 90078-1094. (323)871-8018. **E-mail:** submissions@youngplaywrights.com. **Website:** www.youngplaywrights.com. Offered annually for unpublished work to encourage young writers to write for the theater by presenting their work as well as through our mentoring programs. Open to all writers 19 or younger on the submission date. Deadline: March 15. Prize: Winning plays will be performed in the Festival in Los Angeles in June. Accomplished professional writers make up a team of mentors who help winning playwrights prepare their work for public performance. Experienced directors and mentors work closely with playwrights during the rehearsal process.

THE ANNUAL CONTEST OF CONTEST WINNERS™ COMPETITION

ScriptDoctor.com, 3661 N. Campbell Ave., Suite 222, Tucson AZ 85719. **E-mail:** thedoc@scriptdoctor.com. **Website:** www.scriptdoctor.com. **Contact:** Howard Allen. Must be at least 18 years of age. No entry may have earned money or other consideration for more than $5,000. "Winners must have placed in a competition on our list or approved by us."

ANNUAL NATIONAL PLAYWRITING COMPETITION

Wichita State University, School of Performing Arts, 1845 Fairmount, Box 153, Wichita KS 67260. (316)978-3646. **Fax:** (316)978-3202. **E-mail:** bret.jones@wichita.edu. **Contact:** Bret Jones, director of theatre. The contest will be open to all undergraduate and graduate students enrolled at any college or university in the United States. Please indicate school affiliation. All submissions must be original, unpublished and un-produced. Both full-length and one-act plays may be submitted. Full-length plays in 1 or more acts should be a minimum of 90 minutes playing time. Two or 3 short plays on related themes by the same author will be judged as 1 entry. The total playing time should be a minimum of 90 minutes. One-act plays should be a minimum of 30 minutes playing time to a maximum of 60 minutes playing time. Musicals should be a minimum of 90 minutes playing time and must include a CD of the accompanying music. Scripts should contain no more than 4-6 characters and setting must be suitable for an 85-seat Black box theatre. Eligible playwrights may submit up to 2 entries per contest year. One typewritten, bound copy should be submitted. Scripts must be typed and arranged in professional play script format. See information provided in *The Dramatist's Sourcebook* or the following website (www.pubinfo.vcu.edu/artweb/playwriting/format.html) for instruction on use of professional format. Two title pages must be included: 1 bound and the other unbound. The unbound title page should display the author's name, address, telephone number, and e-mail address if applicable. The bound title page should only display the name of the script; do not include any personal identifying information on the bound title page. Scripts may be submitted via e-mail. Submit in PDF format. Include all information requested for mail in scripts with electronic submission. Deadline: January 16. Prize: Production by the Wichita State University Theatre. Winner will be announced after March 15. No entry may be withdrawn after March 1. Judged by a panel of 3 or more selected from the school faculty. May also include up to 3 experienced, faculty approved WSU School of Performing Arts students.

A+ PLAYWRITING CONTEST FOR TEACHERS

Pioneer Drama Service, Inc., P.O. Box 4267, Englewood CO 80155. (303)779-4035. **Fax:** (303)779-4315. **E-mail:** editors@pioneerdrama.com. **E-mail:** submissions@pioneerdrama.com. **Website:** www.pioneerdrama.com. **Contact:** Lori Conary, submissions editor. Playwright must be a current or retired faculty member at an accredited K-12 public or private school in the US or Canada. All plays submitted through this contest must have been produced within the last 2 years at the school where the playwright teaches. Rules and guidelines online. Encourages the development of quality plays written specifically by teachers and other educators. All qualifying mss accepted for publication will be considered contest finalists. Deadline: Submissions will be accepted on an on-going basis with a June 30 cutoff each year. Prize: $500 royalty advance and a one-time $500 donation to the school theatre program where the play was first produced. Judged by editors.

APPALACHIAN FESTIVAL OF PLAYS & PLAYWRIGHTS

Barter Theatre, Box 867, Abingdon VA 24212-0867. (276)619-3316. **Fax:** (276)619-3335. **E-mail:** apfestival@bartertheatre.com. **Website:** www.bartertheatre.com/festival. **Contact:** Nick Piper, associate director/director, New Play Development. With the annual Appalachian Festival of New Plays & Playwrights, Barter Theatre wishes to celebrate new, previously unpublished/unproduced plays by playwrights from the Appalachian region. If the playwrights are not from Appalachia, the plays themselves must be about the region. Deadline: March 1. Prize: $250, a staged reading performed at Barter's Stage II theater, and some transportation compensation and housing during the time of the festival. There may be an additional award for the best staged readings.

BAY AREA PLAYWRIGHTS FESTIVAL

Produced by Playwrights Foundation, 1616 16th Street, Suite 350, San Francisco CA 94103. **E-mail:** literary@playwrightsfoundation.org. **Website:** www.playwrightsfoundation.org. **Contact:** Margot Manburg. Offered annually for unpublished plays by established and emerging theater writers to support and encourage development of a new work. Unproduced full-length plays only. Guidelines online. Submissions only accepted as PDFs. Deadline: Mid-July through mid-September. Prize: Small stipend and in-depth development process with dramaturg and director, and a professionally staged reading in San Francisco.

BEVERLY HILLS FILM FESTIVAL SCREENPLAY COMPETITION

Beverly Hills Film Festival, 9663 Santa Monica Blvd, Suite 777, Beverly Hills CA 90210. (310)779-1206. **E-mail:** info@beverlyhillsfilmfestival.com. **Website:** www.beverlyhillsfilmfestival.com/. Annual film festival that strives to bring creative new talent to the forefront and make dreams a reality. Selects feature-length and short-length screenplays for competition that will grab the reader and audience passionately and captivate them, whether the characters are likeable or not. Please indicate if the submission is complete, or work in progress. Include a cover page that has the title, writer(s) name, genre, and total number of pages; indicate if the submission is complete, or a work-in-progress; a brief statement from the writer regarding the script; a brieg biography of the writer; and any accompanying artwork. Deadline: August 17 (earlybird), November 17 (regular), January 17, February 15 (extended).

TIPS "The BHFF looks for the heart of the story, the driving force; we want to see what's at stake and feel so compelled with the story that it's hard to put the screenplay down."

BIG BEAR LAKE SCREENWRITING COMPETITION

P.O. Box 1981, Big Bear Lake CA 92315-1981. (909)866-3433. **E-mail:** BigBearFilmFest@aol.com. **Website:** www.bigbearfilmfestival.com. Deadline: April 1. Prize: No confirmed money prizes, but winners receive software and their script submitted to studios.

BIG BREAK INTERNATIONAL SCREENWRITING COMPETITION

Final Draft, Inc., 26707 W. Agoura Rd., Suite 205, Calabasas CA 91302. (818)995-8995. **E-mail:** bigbreak@finaldraft.com. **Website:** www.finaldraft.com/bigbreak. **Contact:** Shelly Mellott, VP events and services. Big Break is an annual, global screenwriting contest designed to launch the careers of aspiring writers with over $80,000 in cash and prizes, as well as A-list executive meetings. Winners and finalists alike have had their screenplays optioned and produced and have secured high-profile representation as well as lucrative writing deals. No rights to submitted materials are acquired or purchased. Contest is open to any writer. Guidelines and rules online. No paper submissions. Submissions must be unpublished. Enter online. Deadline: April 30 (early bird), July 15 (standard), July 31 (extended). Prize: Prizes: 1st Place prizes: $15,000 total cash, plus finalist prizes, airfare to L.A., 3-night hotel stay (unless winner resides in or around L.A.), lunch with executives. 2nd Place prizes: $4,000 total cash, plus finalist prizes, airfare to L.A., 3-night hotel stay (unless winner resides in or around L.A.), lunch with executives. 3rd Place prizes: $2,000 total cash, plus finalist prizes, airfare to L.A., 3-night hotel stay (unless winner resides in or around L.A.), lunch with executives. 4th and 5th Place prizes: $250 total cash, plus finalist prizes. See 6th through 20th Place Finalist Prizes online. Judged by industry readers in first 2 rounds. A panel of notable industry professionals conducts the final judging. Information on previous judges can be found online.

CALIFORNIA YOUNG PLAYWRIGHTS CONTEST

Playwrights Project, 3675 Ruffin Rd., Suite 330, San Diego CA 92123-1870. (858)384-2970. **Fax:** (858)384-2974. **E-mail:** write@playwrightsproject.org. **Website:** www.playwrightsproject.org. **Contact:** Cecelia Kouma, executive director. Annual contest open to Californians under age 19. Annual contest. "Our organization and the contest is designed to nurture promising young writers. We hope to develop playwrights and audiences for live theater. We also teach playwriting." Submissions are required to be unpublished and not produced professionally. Submissions made by the author. SASE for contest rules and entry form. Scripts must be a minimum of 10 standard typewritten pages; send 2 copies. Scripts will *not* be returned. If requested, entrants receive detailed evaluation letter. Guidelines online. Deadline: June 1. Prize: Scripts will be produced in spring at a professional theatre in San Diego. Writers submitting scripts of 10 or more pages receive a detailed script evaluation letter upon request. Judged by professionals in the theater community, a committee of 5-7; changes somewhat each year.

THE CLAYMORE AWARD

Killer Nashville, P.O. Box 680759, Franklin TN 37068-0759. (615)599-4032. **E-mail:** claymore@killernashville.com. **Website:** www.claymoreaward.com and www.killernashville.com. **Contact:** Clay Stafford, Event Founder. "Although anyone with an unpublished ms is eligible to submit, the award would best benefit authors who have not been previously published, and published authors who are between publishers and would like to get some buzz about their new works. We don't want to exclude anyone, though, so if you're a published author with an unpublished ms not under contract, you'd like to enter, please be our guest." The Claymore Award is Killer Nashville's award for the best opening for an unpublished ms submitted to the judging committee. Deadline: May 31. The Award will be presented at the Killer Nashville Thriller, Mystery, and Crime Literature Conference held annually on the weekend surrounding the fourth Saturday in August. Prize: An engraved dagger award and consideration for publication by the judging publisher. Judged by a committee of experienced readers and writers will review all submissions in a blind judging process. They will recommend and submit 10 mss to the sponsor publisher, whose editors will make the final decision and award the Claymore Award to the winning author. All decisions are final and at the sole discretion of the publisher.

COE COLLEGE PLAYWRITING FESTIVAL

Coe College, 1220 First Ave. NE, Cedar Rapids IA 52402-5092. (319)399-8624. **Fax:** (319)399-8557. **E-mail:** swolvert@coe.edu. **Website:** www.theatre.coe.edu. **Contact:** Susan Wolverton. Offered biennially for a new, full-length, original, unproduced and unpublished play in its final stages of development that would benefit from a week-long workshop at Coe. No musicals, adaptations, translations or collaborations will be considered. Open to any writer. One clean, bound script; a resume; the play's development history; and a statement of development goals for your play (one page). Deadline: November 1 (even years). Submission period begins October 1. Prize: $500, plus 1-week residency as guest artist with airfare, room and board provided. Residency occurs in April (odd years).

CREATIVE WORLD AWARDS (CWA) INTERNATIONAL SCREENWRITING COMPETITION

4712 Admiralty Way #268, Marina del Rey CA 90292. **E-mail:** info@creativeworldawards.com. **Website:** www.creativeworldawards.com. **Contact:** Marlene Neubauer/Heather Waters. CWA's professionalism, industry innovation, and exclusive company list make this competition a leader in the industry. CWA offers the grand prize winner a production opportunity and has helped many past entrants get optioned and representation. CWA accepts all genres of features, shorts, and television. Check out the website for more details. All screenplays must be in English and in standard spec screenplay format. See website's FAQ page for more detailed information. Deadline: See website. Prize: Over $30,000 in cash and prizes awarded in 10 categories.

DRURY UNIVERSITY ONE-ACT PLAY CONTEST

Drury University, 900 N. Benton Ave., Springfield MO 65802-3344. **E-mail:** msokol@drury.edu. **Contact:** Mick Sokol. Offered in even-numbered years for unpublished and professionally unproduced plays. One play per playwright. Guidelines for SASE or by e-mail. Deadline: December 1. Prize: 1st Place: $300; Honorable Mention: $150.

DUBUQUE FINE ARTS PLAYERS ANNUAL ONE-ACT PLAY CONTEST

Dubuque Fine Arts Players, PO Box 1160, Dubuque IA 52004-1160. **E-mail:** contact@dbqoneacts.org. **Website:** www.dbqoneacts.org. Annual competition that selects 3 one-act plays each year, awards cash prizes and produces the winning plays in October. Plays for submission must be unpublished and unproduced. Applications may be submitted online or by US mail, as listed online. Deadline: January 31. Prize: Prizes: 1st Place: $600; 2nd Place: $300; 3rd Place: $200. All plays are read at least twice and as many as 6 times by community readers. Final judging is done by a group of 3 directors and 2 other qualified judges.

EERIE HORROR FILM FESTIVAL SCREENPLAY COMPETITION

P.O. Box 98, Edinboro PA 16412. (814)873-2483. E-mail: greg@eeriehorrorfest.com; info@eeriehorrorfest.com. **Website:** www.eeriehorrorfilmfestival.com/. Horror film festival that provides more opportunities and exposure for filmmakers, screenwriters, and video game developers working within the horror, science fiction, and suspense genres, as well as to draw more attention to the Northwestern Pennsylvania region. See website for details as the next festival approaches in October.

ESSENTIAL THEATRE PLAYWRITING AWARD

The Essential Theatre, 1414 Foxhall Ln., #10, Atlanta GA 30316. (404) 212-0815. **E-mail:** pmhardy@aol.com. **Website:** www.essentialtheatre.com. **Contact:** Peter Hardy. Offered annually for unproduced, full-length plays by Georgia resident writers. No limitations as to style or subject matter. Submissions can be e-mailed in PDF or Word Documents, or sent by postal mail. See website for full guidelines. Deadline: April 23. Prize: $600 and full production.

SHUBERT FENDRICH MEMORIAL PLAYWRITING CONTEST

Pioneer Drama Service, Inc., P.O. Box 4267, Englewood CO 80155. (303)779-4035. **Fax:** (303)779-4315. **E-mail:** editors@pioneerdrama.com. **E-mail:** submissions@pioneerdrama.com. **Website:** www.pioneerdrama.com. **Contact:** Lori Conary, submissions editor. Previously unpublished submissions only. Open to all writers not currently published by Pioneer Drama Service. SASE for contest rules and guidelines or view online. No entry fee. Cover letter, SASE for return of ms, and proof of production or staged reading must accompany all submissions. Encourages the development of quality theatrical material for educational and family theater. Deadline: Ongoing contest; a winner is selected by June 1 each year from all submissions received the previous year. Prize: $1,000 royalty advance in addition to publication. Judged by editors.

FESTIVAL OF NEW AMERICAN PLAYS

Firehouse Theatre Project, 1609 W. Broad St., Richmond VA 23220. (804)355-2001. **E-mail:** jase@firehousetheatre.org. **Website:** www.firehousetheatre.org. **Contact:** Jase Smith, artistic director. Annual contest designed to support new and emerging American playwrights. Scripts must be full-length and previously unpublished/unproduced. Submissions should be mailed in standard ms form with no fancy binding. Scripts should be secured simply with a binder clip only. All author information must be on a title page separate from the body of the ms and no reference to the author is permitted in the body of the script. Scripts must be accompanied by a letter of recommendation from a theater company or individual familiar with your work. Letters of recommendation do not need to be specific to the play submitted; they may be general recommendations of the playwright's work. All letters must be received with the script, not under separate cover. Scripts received without a letter will not be considered. Due to the volume of mail, mss cannot be returned. All American playwrights welcome to submit their work. Deadline: September 1. Prize: 1st Place: $1,000 and a staged reading; 2nd Place: $500 and a staged reading. Judged by a panel of individuals with experience in playwriting and literature.

FLICKERS: SCREENPLAY COMPETITION

FLICKERS: Rhode Island International Film Festival, P.O. Box 162, Newport RI 02840. (401)861-4445. **Fax:** (401)490-6735. **E-mail:** info@film-festival.org. **Website:** www.film-festival.org/enterascreenplay.php. Annual screenplay contest for all genres. Screenplays must have been written in the past 2 years. Full-length scripts, no more than 130 pages. Half-hour shorts or teleplays, no more than 40 pages. Submissions must be in English. Submissions must use 12-point Courier font. Pages should be numbered. 3-hole punch and brads with front and back cover for non-digital files. No promotional material. No shooting scripts. See website for more details. The purpose of the contest is to promote, embolden and cultivate screenwriters in their quest for opportunities within the industry. Deadline: July 15. Prize: The Grand Prize winner will become a central focus during ScriptBiz™ the screenplay pitch forum held during the Festival. The Grand Prize winner will also receive prizes valued at over $10,000. This includes travel, up to four nights accommodations, Final Draft software and screenplay promotions. Judged by a distinguished panel of industry professionals, educators, peers, and film fans. Screenplays will be judged on creativity, innovation, vision, originality and the use of language. The key element is that of communication and how it complements and is transformed by the language of film.

JOHN GASSNER MEMORIAL PLAYWRITING COMPETITION

New England Theatre Conference, 215 Knob Hill Dr., Hamden CT 06158. **Fax:** (203)288-5938. **E-mail:** mail@netconline.org. **Website:** www.netconline.org. Annually seeks unpublished full-length plays and scripts. Open to all. Playwrights living outside New England may participate. Deadline: April 15. Prize: 1st Place: $1,000; 2nd Place: $500.

⚓ GOVERNOR GENERAL'S LITERARY AWARD FOR DRAMA

Canada Council for the Arts, 150 Elgin St., P.O. Box 1047, Ottawa ON K1P 5V8 Canada. (613)566-4414, ext. 5573. **Website:** www.canadacouncil.ca/prizes/ggla. Offered for the best English-language and the best French-language work of drama by a Canadian. Publishers submit titles for consideration. Deadline: Depends on the book's publication date. Books in English: March 15, June 1 or August 7. Books in French: March 15 or July 15. Prize: Each laureate receives $25,000; non-winning finalists receive $1,000.

THE MARILYN HALL AWARDS FOR YOUTH THEATRE

P.O. Box 148, Beverly Hills CA 90213. **Website:** www. beverlyhillstheatreguild.com. **Contact:** Candace Coster, competition coordinator. The Marilyn Hall Awards consist of 2 monetary prizes for plays suitable for grades 6-8 (middle school) or for plays suitable for grades 9-12 (high school). The 2prizes will be awarded on the merits of the play scripts, which includes its suitability for the intended audience. The plays should be approximately 45-75 minutes in length. There is no production connected to any of the prizes, though a staged reading is optional at the discretion of the BHTG. Unpublished submissions only. Authors must be U.S. citizens or legal residents and must sign entry form personally. Deadline: Postmarked between January 15 and the last day of February. Prize: 1st Prize: $700; 2nd Prize: $300.

AURAND HARRIS MEMORIAL PLAYWRITING AWARD

The New England Theatre Conference, Inc., 215 Knob Hill Dr., Hamden CT 06518. **Fax:** (203)288-5938. **E-mail:** mail@netconline.org. **Website:** www.netconline.org. Offered annually for an unpublished full-length play for young audiences. Guidelines online

or for SASE. Open to all. Deadline: May 1. Prize: 1st Place: $1,000; 2nd Place: $500

HENRICO THEATRE COMPANY ONE-ACT PLAYWRITING COMPETITION

P.O. Box 90775, Henrico VA 23273. (804)501-5138. **Fax:** (804)501-5284. **E-mail:** per22@co.henrico.va.us. **Contact:** Amy A. Perdue, cultural arts senior coordinator. Offered annually for previously unpublished or unproduced plays or musicals to produce new dramatic works in one-act form. Scripts with small casts and simpler sets given preference. Controversial themes and excessive language should be avoided. Only one-act plays or musicals will be considered. The ms should be a one-act original (not an adaptation), unpublished, and unproduced, free of royalty and copyright restrictions. Scripts with smaller casts and simpler sets may be given preference. Controversial themes and excessive language should be avoided. Standard play script form should be used. All plays will be judged anonymously; therefore, there should be two title pages; the first must contain the play's title and the author's complete address and telephone number. The second title page must contain only the play's title. The playwright must submit two excellent quality copies. Receipt of all scripts will be acknowledged by mail. Scripts will be returned if SASE is included. No scripts will be returned until after the winner is announced. The HTC does not assume responsibility for loss, damage or return of scripts. All reasonable care will be taken. Deadline: July 1. Prize: Prizes: $300 prize. $200 to runner-up. Winning entries may be produced; videotape sent to author.

HOLIDAY SCREENPLAY CONTEST

P.O. Box 450, Boulder CO 80306. (303)629-3072. **E-mail:** Cherubfilm@aol.com. **Website:** www.Holiday-ScreenplayContest.com. Scripts must be centered around 1 holiday (New Year's Day, President's Day, Valentine's Day, St. Patrick's Day, April Fool's Day, Easter, 4th of July, Halloween, Thanksgiving, Hanukkah, Christmas, Kwanzaa, or any other world holiday you would like to feature). This contest is limited to the first 400 entries. Screenplays must be in English. Screenplays must not have been previously optioned, produced, or purchased prior to submission. Multiple submissions are accepted, but each submission requires a separate online entry and separate fee. Screenplays must be between 90-125 pages. Deadline: November 30. Prize: Up to $500.

HORROR SCREENPLAY CONTEST

Cherub Productions, P.O. Box 540, Boulder Co 80306. (303)629-3072. **E-mail:** Cherubfilm@aol.com. **Website:** www.horrorscreenplaycontest.com. Annual contest that accepts horror scripts. Contest limited to the first 600 entries. Screenplays must be between 90-125 pages. Deadline: July 20. Prize: More than $5,000 in cash and prizes.

THE KILLER NASHVILLE SILVER FALCHION AWARD

Killer Nashville, P.O. Box 680759, Franklin TN 37068-0750. (615)599-4032. **E-mail:** contact@killernashville.com. **Website:** www.killernashville.com. **Contact:** Clay Stafford. Any fiction or nonfiction book-length work published for the first time in the past year, in which a crime drives the storyline, may be nominated by either the publisher or author of the book. Four copies of the work being nominated must be submitted with entry forms to be considered. Deadline: January 15. Entries will be evaluated by judges, who will choose five finalists from the following categories: Best Novel, Best First Novel, Best Paperback, Best e-Book Original, Best Nonfiction, Best Juvenile, Best Young Adult, and Best Anthology. Winners chosen by the Killer Nashville Writers' Conference attendees.

L.A. DESIGNERS' THEATRE-COMMISSIONS

L.A. Designers' Theatre, P.O. Box 1883, Studio City CA 91614. (323)650-9600 or (323)654-2700 T.D.D. **Fax:** (323)654-3210. **E-mail:** ladesigners@gmail.com. **Contact:** Richard Niederberg, artistic director. "Quarterly contest to promote new work andpush it through a Theatrical Production onto the conveyor belt toFilmed or Digital Origination entertainment. All submissions must beregistered with the copyright office and be unpublished. Material willnot be returned. Do not submit any proposal that will not fit in a #10envelope. No rules, guidelines, fees, or entry forms. Just present anidea that can be commissioned into a full work. Proposals for as ofyet un-completed works are encouraged. Unpopular political, religious,social, or other themes are encouraged; 'street' language and nudityare acceptable. Open to any writer." Deadline: March 15, June 15, September 15, December 15. Prize: production or publication of the work in the Los Angeles market. "We only want 'first refusal' for the Rights and a License that is clear of any legal, stated, unstated or implied obligation to any other person or entity. You continue to OWN your work."

NATIONAL ONE-ACT PLAYWRITING COMPETITION (CANADA)

Ottawa Little Theatre, 400 King Edward Ave., Ottawa ON K1N 7M7 Canada. (613)233-8948. **Fax:** (613)233-8027. **Website:** www.ottawalittletheatre.com. **Contact:** Lynn McGuigan, executive director. Encourages literary and dramatic talent in Canada. Guidelines online. Deadline: October 15. Prize: 1st Place: $1,000; 2nd Place: $700; 3rd Place: $500; Sybil Cooke Award for a Play Written for Children or Young People: $500.

NEVADA FILM OFFICE SCREENWRITER'S COMPETITION

6655 W. Sahara Ave., Suite C-106, Las Vegas NV 89101. 1-877-NEV-FILM. **E-mail:** lvnfo@nevadafilm.com. **E-mail:** screenwriters@nevadafilm.com. **Website:** www.nevadafilm.com/screenwriting-competition. Competition open to all unsold screenwriters. At least 75% of the locations in the script must be filmable in Nevada. See website for guidelines Deadline: August 31. Prize: Winning script will be eligible for consideration to be pitched to production companies willing to read the winning script. Winner will also receive a complimentary posting of logline, synopsis and full script on the premier screenwriting marketplace InkTip.com, 2 complimentary roundtrip tickets on Southwest Airlines and a complimentary 3 day/ 2 night hotel stay at The D hotel in downtown Las Vegas. Judged by experienced, professional writers and story analysts from a script service company.

NEW WORKS FOR THE STAGE

COE College Theatre Arts Department, 1220 First Ave. NE, Cedar Rapids IA 52402. (319)399-8624. **Fax:** (319)399-8557. **E-mail:** swolvert@coe.edu. **Website:** www.public.coe.edu/departments/theatre. **Contact:** Susan Wolverton. Offered in odd-numbered years to encourage new work, to provide an interdisciplinary forum for the discussion of issues found in new work, and to offer playwright contact with theater professionals who can provide response to new work. Full-length, original, unpublished and unproduced scripts only. No musicals, adaptations, translations, or collaborations. Submit 1-page synopsis, résumé, and SASE if the script is to be returned. Deadline: November 1 even years. Prize: $500, plus travel, room and board for residency at the college.

ONE IN TEN SCREENPLAY CONTEST

Cherub Productions, P.O. Box 540, Boulder CO 80306. **E-mail:** Cherubfilm@aol.com. **Website:** www.OneIn-TenScreenplayContest.com. Scripts that provide a positive potrayal of gays and lesbians. "A requirement of the competition is that at least one of the primary characters in the screenplay be gay or lesbian (bisexual, transgender, questioning, and the like) and that gay and lesbian characters must be portrayed positively. All writers are encouraged to enter!" Deadline: September 1. Prize: $1,000.

THE PAGE INTERNATIONAL SCREENWRITING AWARDS

The PAGE Awards Committee, 7510 Sunset Blvd., #610, Hollywood CA 90046-3408. **E-mail:** info@PAGEawards.com. **Website:** www.PAGEawards.com. **Contact:** Zoe Simmons, Contest Coordinator. Annual competition to discover the most talented new screenwriters from across the country and around the world. Each year, awards are presented to 31 screenwriters in 10 different genre categories: action/adventure, comedy, drama, family film, historical film, science fiction, thriller/horror, short film script, TV drama pilot, and TV comedypilot. Guidelines and entry forms are online. The contest is open to all writers 18 years of age and older who have not previously earned more than $25,000 writing for film and/or television. Please visit contest website for a complete list of rules and regulations. Deadline: January 15 (early); February 15 (regular); March 15 (late); April 15 (last minute). Prize: Prizes: Over $50,000 in cash and prizes, including a $25,000 grand prize, plus gold, silver, and bronze prizes in all 10 categories. Most importantly, the award-winning writers receive extensive publicity and industry exposure. Judging is done entirely by Hollywood professionals, including industry script readers, consultants, agents, managers, producers, and development executives.

SCRIPTAPALOOZA SCREENPLAY COMPETITION

Endorsed by Write Brothers and Robert McKee, 7775 Sunset Blvd., #200, Hollywood CA 90046. (310)801-5366. **E-mail:** info@scriptapalooza.com. **Website:** www.scriptapalooza.com. "From choosing our judges to creating opportunities, our top priority has always been the writer. We surround ourselves with reputable and successful companies, including many producers, literary agents, and managers who read your scripts. Our past winners have won Emmy's, been signed by agents, managers, had their scripts optioned, and even made into movies. Scriptapalooza will promote, pitch and push the semifinalists and higher for a full year." Deadline: January 6, March 3, April 14, and April 21. Prize: 1st Place: $10,000; over $50,00 in prizes for the entire competition. The top 100 scripts will be considered by over 95 production companies.

SCRIPTAPALOOZA TELEVISION WRITING COMPETITION

7775 Sunset Blvd., Suite #200, Hollywood CA 90046. (310)801-5366. **E-mail:** info@scriptapalooza.com. **Website:** www.scriptapaloozatv.com. Biannual competition accepting entries in 4 categories: Reality shows, sitcoms, original pilots, and 1-hour dramas. There are more than 25 producers, agents, and managers reading the winning scripts. Two past winners won Emmys because of Scriptapalooza and 1 past entrant now writes for Comedy Central. Winners announced February 15 and August 30. For contest results, visit website. Length: Standard television format whether 1 hour, 1-half hour, or pilot. Open to any writer 18 or older. Guidelines online. Accepts inquiries by e-mail or phone. Deadline: October 1 and April 15. Prize: 1st Place: $500; 2nd Place: $200; 3rd Place: $100 (in each category); production company consideration.

TIPS Pilots should be fresh and new and easy to visualize. Spec scripts should stay current with the shows, up-to-date story lines, characters, etc.

SCRIPT PIPELINE SCREENWRITING COMPETITION

1304 N. Highland, #272, Hollywood CA 90028. (323)424-4243. **E-mail:** entry@scriptpipeline.com. **Website:** scriptpipeline.com. **Contact:** Matt Misetich, general manager. The Script Pipeline Annual Screenwriting and Annual TV Writing Competitions continue a long tradition of discovering up-and-coming creative talent and connecting them with top producers, agencies, and managers across both studio and independent markets. This is an international competition open to all original feature film screenplays that have yet to be produced, optioned, or sold. Open to writers 18 years and older. All genres, styles, and formats accepted. Over 200 companies review the finalists, and numerous contest alumni have caught the attention of major agencies, including WME, Paradigm, and CAA. The result: $5 million in specs sold from Pipeline competition finalists and "recommend" writers since 2003. Early deadline: March 1. Regular deadline: May 1. Prize: $20,000 in cash for the winners; $100,000 in prizes to anyone who enters.

"SET IN PHILADELPHIA" SCREENWRITING COMPETITION

Greater Philadelphia Film Office, 1515 Arch St., 11th Floor, Philadelphia PA 19102. (215)686-2668. **Fax:** (215)686-3659. **Website:** www.film.org. Screenplays must be "shootable" primarily in the Greater Philadelphia area (includes the surrounding counties). All genres and storytelling approaches are acceptable. Feature length screenplays must be between 85-130 pages in length. TV pilot scripts must be 35-70 pages. There are 4 different awards, such as an award for best TV pilot, as well as the best script from a regional writer, and best script from a student. See the website for full details. Prize: $10,000 grand prize, with other prizes offered.

SOUTHEASTERN THEATRE CONFERENCE HIGH SCHOOL NEW PLAY CONTEST

SETC, 1175 Revolution Mill Dr., Suite 14, Greensboro NC 27405. **E-mail:** setc_hs_new_plays@Yahoo.com. **Website:** www.setc.org. **Contact:** Meredith Levy. Annual contest for one-act plays (no musicals, adaptations, or collaborations) on any subject. The script should be a one-act play that has not been published or professionally produced. Each applicant may submit one play only. E-mail play as a PDF and application form to setc_hs_new_plays@Yahoo.com. Visit website for additional details and required application form. High school student playwrights who currently reside in 1 of the 10 states in the SETC region are eligible. These states include Alabama, Florida, Georgia, Kentucky, Mississippi, North Carolina, South Carolina, Tennessee, Virginia, and West Virginia. Deadline: Submit October 1-December 1. Prize: $250, subsidy to attend the annual SETC convention in March with an adult chaperone, and a staged reading followed by a talkback.

SOUTHERN PLAYWRIGHTS COMPETITION

Jacksonville State University, Department of English, 700 Pelham Rd. N., Jacksonville AL 36265-1602. (256)782-5498. **Fax:** (256)782-5441. **E-mail:** smoersch@jsu.edu. **E-mail:** swhitton@jsu.edu. **Website:** www.jsu.edu/depart/english/southpla.htm. **Contact:** Sarah Moersch. Competition for playwrights native

to or a resident of Alabama, Arkansas, Florida, Georgia, Kentucky, Louisiana, Mississippi, North Carolina, South Carolina, Tennessee, Texas, Virginia, or West Virginia. Plays must deal with the Southern experience. Entries must be original, full-length plays. No musicals or adaptations will be accepted. The playwright may submit only one play. All entries must be typed, securely bound, and clearly identified. Synopsis of script must be included. Legal clearance of all materials not in the public domain will be the responsibility of the playwright. The Southern Playwrights Competition seeks to identify and encourage the best of Southern playwriting. Deadline: January 15. Prize: $1,000 and production of the play.

SOUTHWEST WRITERS

3200 Carlisle Blvd., NE Suite #114, Albuquerque NM 87110. (505)830-6034. **E-mail:** swwriters@juno.com. **Website:** www.southwestwriters.com. The Southwest Writers Writing Contest encourages and honors excellence in writing. In addition to competing for cash prizes and the coveted Storyteller Award, contest entrants may receive an optional written critique of their entry from a qualified contest critiquer. Non-profit organization dedicated to helping members of all levels in their writing. Members enjoy perks such as networking with professional and aspiring writers; substantial discounts on mini-conferences, workshops, writing classes, and annual and quarterly SWW writing contest; monthly newsletter; two writing programs per month; critique groups, critique service (also for nonmembers); discounts at bookstores and other businesses; and website linking. Deadline: May 1 (up to May 15 with a late fee). Submissions begin March 1. Prize: A 1st, 2nd, and 3rd place winner will be judged in each of the 12 categories. 1st place: $200; 2nd place: $150; 3rd place: $100. $1,500 for the Storyteller Award, the entry judged the best of all entries in all categories. Judged by a panel; the top 10 in each category will be sent to appropriate editors or literary agents to determine the final top 3 places.

TELEVISION OUTREACH PROGRAM (TOP)

The Scriptwriters Network (SWN), P.O. Box 642806, Los Angeles CA 90064. **E-mail:** info@scriptwritersnetwork.org. **E-mail:** top@scriptwritersnetwork.org. **Website:** www.scriptwritersnetwork.org. **Contact:** Hoda Shoukry and Mark Litton, co-directors. TOP is open to both SWN members and non-members who are 18 years of age or older. Spec scripts for half-hour or one-hour network or cable series in production as of the entry deadline are eligible. Pilot scripts for original series are also eligible. All scripts must be wholly original works of the writer or writing team. Electronic submissions must be posted by midnight on the entry deadline. Submit online. Do not put name or contact information anywhere on the submitted script or title page. Personal information should only be included in the entry form so that scripts remain anonymous. Please check website for complete, detailed entry submission directions. Deadline: July. Two readers will evaluate script and provide written feedback, analyzing structure, story development, characterization, dialogue, format, as well as overall impressions. If recommended by two readers, the script will advance to Phase Two.

TENNESSEE SCREENWRITING ASSOCIATION SCRIPT COMPETITION

2298 Rosa L. Parks Blvd., Nashville TN 37228. (615)316-9448. **E-mail:** info@tennscreen.com. **Website:** www.tennscreen.com. Competition for the best low- or micro-budget scripts. Seeks to promote writers with the potential for investors, crowd-funding proposals, and many other tools. Deadline: February 28. Prize: The grand prize winner will receive notes from professional Hollywood screenwriter Robert Orr, production notes from independent Hollywood producer Guilia Prenna, an estimated budget breakdown for the script, and much more. See website for complete prize package details.

THEATRE CONSPIRACY ANNUAL NEW PLAY CONTEST

Theatre Conspiracy, 10091 McGregor Blvd., Ft. Myers FL 33919. (239)936-3239. **E-mail:** info@theatreconspiracy.org. **Website:** theatreconspiracy.org. **Contact:** Bill Taylor, producing artistic director. Offered annually for full-length plays that are unproduced. Work submitted to the contest must be a full length play with eight characters or less and have simple to moderate technical demands. Plays having up to three previous productions are welcome. No musicals. Deadline: March 30. Prize: $700 and full production. Judged by a panel of qualified theatre teachers, directors and performers.

YOUNG PLAYWRIGHTS FESTIVAL NATIONAL PLAYWRITING COMPETITION

Young Playwrights, Inc., P.O. Box 5134, New York NY 10185. (212)594-5440. **Fax:** (212)594-5441. **E-mail:** literary@youngplaywrights.org. **Website:** youngplaywrights.org. **Contact:** Literary Manager. The Young Playwrights Inc. Festival National Playwriting Competition is offered annually to identify talented American playwrights aged 18 or younger. Please include your address, phone number, e-mail address, and date of birth on the title page. Open to US residents only. Deadline: January 2 (postmarked). Prize: Winners receive an invitation to New York City for the annual Young Playwrights, Inc. Writers Conference and a professionally staged reading of their play. Entrants retain all rights to their work.

YOUNG PLAYWRIGHTS INC. WRITE A PLAY! NYC COMPETITION

Young Playwrights, Inc., Young Playwrights Inc. NYC, P.O. Box 5134, New York NY 10185. (212)594-5440. **Fax:** (212)684-4902. **E-mail:** literary@youngplaywrights.org. **Website:** www.youngplaywrights.org. **Contact:** Literary Manager. Offered annually for stage plays of any length (no musicals, screenplays, or adaptations) by NYC elementary, middle, and high school students only. Play must be submitted by students, not teachers. There are no restrictions on length, style, or subject, but collaborations of more than 3 writers will not be accepted. Screenplays and musicals are not eligible, nor are adaptations. Scripts should be typed and stapled, and pages must be numbered. Scripts must have a cover page with title of play, playwright's name, home address (with apartment number and zip code), phone number, school, grade, and date of birth. Submit a copy of your play and keep the original; scripts will not be returned. Deadline: postmarked on or before March 1. Prize: Prize varies.

ANNA ZORNIO MEMORIAL CHILDREN'S THEATRE PLAYWRITING COMPETITION

University of New Hampshire, Department of Theatre and Dance, PCAC, 30 Academic Way, Durham NH 03824. (603)862-3038. **Fax:** (603)862-0298. **E-mail:** mike.wood@unh.edu. **Website:** cola.unh.edu/theatre-dance/resource/zornio. **Contact:** Michael Wood. Offered every 4 years for unpublished well-written plays or musicals appropriate for young audiences with a maximum length of 60 minutes. May submit more than 1 play, but not more than 3. Honors the late Anna Zornio, an alumna of The University of New Hampshire, for dedication to and inspiration of playwriting for young people, K-12th grade. Deadline: March of 2016. Prize: $500.

ARTS COUNCILS & FELLOWSHIPS

$50,000 GIFT OF FREEDOM

A Room of Her Own Foundation, P.O. Box 778, Placitas NM 87043. **E-mail:** info@aroomofherownfoundation.org. **Website:** www.aroomofherownfoundation.org. **Contact:** Tracey Cravens-Gras, associate director. The publicly funded award provides very practical help—both materially and in professional guidance and moral support with mentors and advisory council—to assist women in making their creative contribution to the world. The Gift of Freedom competition will determine superior finalists from each of 3 genres: Creative nonfiction, fiction, and poetry. Open to female residents of the US. Award application cycle dates are yet to be determined. Visit website at www.aroho.org for more information about the next application window. Prize: One genre finalist will be awarded the $50,000 Gift of Freedom grant, distributed over 2 years in support of the completion of a particular creative project. The 2 remaining genre finalists will each receive a $5,000 prize.

☯ ADVANCED ARTIST AWARD

Government of Yukon, P.O. Box 2703, (L-3), Whitehorse YT Y1A 2C6 Canada. (867)667-8789. **Fax:** (867)393-6456. **E-mail:** artsfund@gov.yk.ca. **Website:** www.tc.gov.yk.ca/arts.html. The Advanced Artist Award (AAA) assists individual Yukon visual, literary and performing artists practicing at a senior level with innovative projects, travel, or educational pursuits that contribute to their personal artistic development and to their community. The intended results and outcomes of the Advanced Artist Award are to encourage artistic creativity, to enable artists to develop their skills, and to improve the ability of artists to promote their works or talents. Deadlines: April 1 and October 1. Prize: Prizes: Level A artists: up to $5,000; Level B artists: up to $2,500. Judged by peer assessment (made up of senior Yukon artists representing the various disciplines seen in applicants for that round).

AKC GAZETTE ANNUAL FICTION CONTEST

260 Madison Ave., New York NY 10016. (212)696-8333. The *Gazette* sponsors an annual fiction contest for short short stories under 2,000 words on some subject relating to purebred or mixed breed dogs. Fic-

tion for magazine needs a slant toward the serious fancier with real insight into the human/dog bond and breed-specific purebred behavior. Contest requirements available for SASE or online. Deadline: January 31. Prize: 1st Place: $500; 2nd Place: $250; 3rd Place: $100. AKC retains the right to publish the three prize-winning entries. Judges by panel selected by AKC Publications. Winner will be chose based on style, content, originality, and the appeal of the story.

ALABAMA STATE COUNCIL ON THE ARTS INDIVIDUAL ARTIST FELLOWSHIP

201 Monroe St., Montgomery AL 36130. (334)242-4076, ext. 236. **Fax:** (334)240-3269. **E-mail:** anne.kimzey@arts.alabama.gov. **Website:** www.arts.state.al.us. **Contact:** Anne Kimzey, literature program manager. Must be a legal resident of Alabama who has lived in the state for 2 years prior to application. Competition receives 25 submissions annually. Accepts inquiries by e-mail and phone. The following should be submitted: a résumé and a list of published works with reviews, if available; and a minimum of 10 pages of poetry or prose, but no more than 20 pages. Please label each page with title, artist's name, and date. If published, indicate where and the date of publication. Please do not submit bound material. Guidelines available in January online. Recognizes the achievements and potential of Alabama writers. Deadline: March 1. Applications must be submitted online by eGRANT. Judged by independent peer panel. Winners notified by mail and announced online in June.

ALASKA STATE COUNCIL ON THE ARTS CAREER OPPORTUNITY GRANT AWARD

Alaska State Council on the Arts, 161 Klevin St., Suite 102, Anchorage AK 99508-1506. (907)269-6610. **Fax:** (907)269-6601. **E-mail:** andrea.noble@alaska.gov. **Website:** www.eed.state.ak.us/aksca. **Contact:** Andrea Noble, visual & literary arts program director. Grants designed to provide financial assistance to professional artists for travel to in-state, national, or international events, programs or seminars and for other activities that will contribute to the strength of the artist's professional standing or skill. These cash awards help professional artists take advantage of impending, concrete opportunities that will significantly advance their work or careers. The awards are for unique, short-term opportunities that do not constitute routine completion of work in progress. Check website for information and details on applying. Deadline: Applications accepted quarterly. Prize: Applicants may request grants in variable amounts from $100 to $1,000 rounded to the nearest $100. Career Opportunity Grants will not exceed $1,000.

TIPS "Guidelines online. Accepts inquiries by fax, phone and e-mail."

GEORGE BENNETT FELLOWSHIP

Phillips Exeter Academy, 20 Main St., Exeter NH 03833. **E-mail:** teaching_opportunities@exeter.edu. **Website:** www.exeter.edu/fellowships. Annual award for fellow and family to provide time and freedom from material considerations to a person seriously contemplating or pursuing a career as a writer. Applicants should have a ms in progress which they intend to complete during the fellowship period. Ms should be fiction, nonfiction, novel, short stories, or poetry. Duties: To be in residency at the Academy for the academic year; to make oneself available informally to students interested in writing. Committee favors writers who have not yet published a book with a major publisher. Deadline for application: December 2. A choice will be made, and all entrants notified in mid-April. Prize: Cash stipend (currently $14,626), room and board. Judged by committee of the English department.

CHLA RESEARCH GRANTS

Children's Literature Association, 1301 W. 22nd Street, Suite 202, Oak Brook IL 60523. (630)571-4520. **Fax:** (708)876-5598. **E-mail:** info@childlitassn. org. **Website:** www.childlitassn.org. **Contact:** ChLA Grants Chair. Offered annually. Three types of grants are available: Faculty Research Grants, Beiter Graduate Student Research Grants, and Diversity Research Grant. The grants are awarded for proposals dealing with criticism or original scholarship with the expectation that the undertaking will lead to publication (or a conference presentation for student awards) and make a significant contribution to the field of children's literature in the area of scholarship or criticism. Funds are not intended for work leading to the completion of a professional degree. Guidelines online. Deadline: February 1. Prize: $500-1,500. Judged by the ChLA Grants Committee and Diversity Committee, respectively.

CREATIVE & PERFORMING ARTISTS & WRITERS FELLOWSHIP

American Antiquarian Society, 185 Salisbury St., Worcester MA 01609. (508)755-5221. **Fax:** (508)753-3311. **Website:** www.americanantiquarian.org. **Contact:** James David Moran. Annual fellowship for creative and performing artists, writers, filmmakers, journalists, and other persons whose goals are to produce imaginative, non-formulaic works dealing with pre-20th century American history.c Application instructions online. Deadline: October 5. Prize: The stipend will be $1,350 for fellows residing on campus (rent-free) in the society's scholars' housing, located next to the main library building. The stipend will be $1,850 for fellows residing off campus. Fellows will not be paid a travel allowance. Judged by AAS staff and outside reviewers.

TIPS "Successful applicants are those whose work is for the general public rather than for academic or educational audiences."

DELAWARE DIVISION OF THE ARTS

820 N. French St., Wilmington DE 19801. (302)577-8278. **Fax:** (302)577-6561. **E-mail:** kristin.pleasanton@state.de.us. **Website:** www.artsdel.org. **Contact:** Kristin Pleasanton, coordinator. Award to help further careers of emerging and established professional artists. For Delaware residents only. Guidelines available after May 1 online. Accepts inquiries by e-mail, phone. Results announced in December. Winners notified by mail. Results online. Open to any Delaware writer over 18 years of ages and not in a degree-granting program. Deadline: August 1. Prize: $10,000 for masters; $6,000 for established professionals; $3,000 for emerging professionals. Judged by out-of-state, nationally recognized professionals in each artistic discipline.

TIPS "Follow all instructions and choose your best work sample."

DOBIE PAISANO WRITER'S FELLOWSHIP

The Graduate School, The University of Texas at Austin, Attn: Dobie Paisano Program, 110 Inner Campus Drive Stop G0400, Austin TX 78712-0531. (512)232-3609. **Fax:** (512)471-7620. **E-mail:** gbarton@austin. utexas.edu. **Website:** www.utexas.edu/ogs/Paisano. **Contact:** Gwen Barton. Sponsored by the Graduate School at The University of Texas at Austin and the Texas Institute of Letters, the Dobie Paisano Fellowship Program provides solitude, time, and a comfortable place for Texas writers or writers who have written significantly about Texas. At the time of the application, the applicant must meet one of the following requirements: (1) be a native Texan, (2) have resided in Texas at least three years at some time, or (3) have published significant work with a Texas subject. Those who meet requirement 1 or 2 do not have to meet the Texas subject matter restriction. Deadline: January 15. Prize: The Ralph A. Johnston memorial Fellowship is for a period of 4 months with a stipend of $5,000 per month. It is aimed at writers who have already demonstrated some publishing and critical success. The Jesse H. Jones Writing Fellowship is for a period of approximately 6 months with a stipend of $3,000 per month. It is aimed at, but not limited to, writers who are early in their careers.

TIPS "Three sets of each complete application must be submitted. Electronic submissions are not allowed. Guidelines and application forms are on the website or may be requested by sending a SASE (3-ounce postage) to the above address and attention of 'Dobie Paisano Fellowship Project.'"

JOSEPH R. DUNLAP FELLOWSHIP

William Morris Society in the US, Washington D.C., Department of English, University of California-Davis, Davis CA 95616. **E-mail:** us@morrissociety.org. **E-mail:** ecmille1@gmail.com. **Website:** www.morrissociety.org. **Contact:** Prof. Elizabeth Miller, university of California-Davis. Offered annually to promote study of the life and work of William Morris (1834-96), British poet, designer, and socialist. Award may be for research, a creative project, or a translation. Curriculum vitae, 1-page proposal, and 2 letters of recommendation required for application. Applicants must be US citizens or permanent residents. Deadline: December 15 of the year before the award is to be applied. Prize: Up to $1,000; multiple and partial awards possible.

GAP (GRANTS FOR ARTIST PROJECTS) PROGRAM

Artist Trust, 1835 12th Ave., Seattle WA 98122. (206)467-8734. **Fax:** (866)218-7878. **E-mail:** miguel@artisttrust.org; info@artisttrust.org. **Website:** www.artisttrust.org. **Contact:** Miguel Guillén, program manager. The GAP grant is awarded annually to 60 Washington state artists of all disciplines. Artist projects may include (but are not limited to): The development, completion or presentation of new work; publication; travel for artistic research or to present or complete work; documentation of work; and advanced workshops for professional development. Full-time students are not eligible. Applicationswill be posted online in March. Applicants must be a practicing artist, 18 years of age or older by application deadline date, a generative artist, and a resident of Washington state at the time of application and when the award is granted. Deadline: April. Prize: Up to $1,500 for artist-generated projects.

⬤ THE HODDER FELLOWSHIP

Lewis Center for the Arts, 185 Nassau St., Princeton NJ 08544. (609)258-1500. **E-mail:** anikolop@princeton.edu. **Website:** www.princeton.edu/arts/lewis_center/society_of_fellows. **Contact:** Angelo Nikolopoulos, program assistant, Creative Writing. Preference is given to applicants outside academia. Candidates for the Ph.D. are not eligible. Submit a resume, sample of previous work (10 pages maximum, not returnable), and a project proposal of 2-3 pages. Guidelines online. Princeton University is an equal opportunity employer and complies with applicable EEO and affirmative action regulations. Apply online. The Hodder Fellowship will be given to writers of exceptional promise to pursue independent projects at Princeton University during the current academic year. Typically the fellows are poets, playwrights, novelists, creative nonfiction writers and translators who have published one highly acclaimed work and are undertaking a significant new project that might not be possible without the "studious leisure" afforded by the fellowship. Deadline: October 1. Prize: $75,000 stipend.

MARILYN HOLINSHEAD VISITING SCHOLARS FELLOWSHIP

University of Minnesota, 113 Anderson Library, 222 21st Ave. South, Minneapolis MN 55455. **Website:** www.lib.umn.edu/clrc/awards-grants-and-fellowships. Marilyn Hollinshead Visiting Scholars Fund for Travel to the Kerlan Collection will be available for research study in 2014. Applicants may request up to $1,500. Send a letter with the proposed purpose and plan to use specific research materials (mss and art), dates, and budget (including airfare and per diem). Travel and a written report on the project must be completed and submitted in 2014. Deadline: January 30.

MASSACHUSETTS CULTURAL COUNCIL ARTIST FELLOWSHIP PROGRAM

Massachusetts Cultural Council, 10 St. James Ave., 3rd Floor, Boston MA 02116-3803. (617)727-3668. **Fax:** (617)727-0044. **E-mail:** mcc@art.state.ma.us.

Website: www.massculturalcouncil.org; artsake. massculturalcouncil.org. **Contact:** Dan Blask, program officer. Awards in poetry, fiction/creative nonfiction, and dramatic writing (among other discipline categories) are given in recognition of exceptional original work (check website for award amount). Accepts inquiries by fax, e-mail and phone. Must be 18 years or older and a legal residents of Massachusetts for the last 2 years and at time of award. This excludes students in directly-related degree programs and grant recipients within the last 3 years. Looking to award artistic excellence and creative ability, based on work submitted for review. Judged by independent peer panels composed of artists and arts professionals. **TIPS** "Send in your best work and follow guidelines (online)."

JENNY MCKEAN MOORE VISITING WRITER

English Department, George Washington University, Rome Hall, 801 22nd St. NW, Suite 760, Washington DC 20052. (202)994-6180. **Fax:** (202)994-7915. **E-mail:** tvmallon@gwu.edu. **Website:** columbian.gwu. edu/departmentsprograms/english/creativewriting/ activitiesevents. **Contact:** Lisa Page, Acting Director of Creative Writing. The position is filled annually, bringing a visiting writer to The George Washington University. During each semester the Writer teaches 1 creative-writing course at the university as well as a community workshop. Seeks someone specializing in a different genre each year—fiction, poetry, creative nonfiction. For the 2013-14 academic year looking for a creative nonfiction writer. Guidelines for application will be announced in *The Writer's Chronicle*. Annual stipend between $50,000 and $60,000, plus reduced-rent townhouse on campus (not guaranteed). Application Deadline: November 25. Prize: Annual stipend varies, depending on endowment performance; most recently, stipend was $58,000, plus reduced-rent townhouse (not guaranteed).

NEBRASKA ARTS COUNCIL INDIVIDUAL ARTISTS FELLOWSHIPS

Nebraska Arts Council, 1004 Farnam St., Plaza Level, Omaha NE 68102. (402)595-2122. **Fax:** (402)595-2334. **E-mail:** nac.info@nebraska.gov. **Website:** www.nebraskaartscouncil.org. Offered every 3 years (literature alternates with other disciplines) to recognize exemplary achievements by originating artists in their fields of endeavor and support the contributions made by Nebraska artists to the quality of life in Nebraska. Funds available are announced in September prior to the deadline. Must be a resident of Nebraska for at least 2 years prior to submission date; 18 years of age; and not enrolled in an undergraduate, graduate, or certificate-granting program in English, creative writing, literature, or related field. Deadline: November 15. Prize: Distinguished achievement awards are $5,000 and merit awards are $1,000-2,000.

NORTH CAROLINA ARTS COUNCIL REGIONAL ARTIST PROJECT GRANTS

North Carolina Arts Council, Dept. of Cultural Resources, MSC #4632, Raleigh NC 27699-4634. (919)807-6500. **Fax:** (919)807-6532. **E-mail:** david. potorti@ncdcr.gov. **Website:** www.ncarts.org. **Contact:** David Potorti, literature director. See website for contact information for the local arts councils that distribute these grants. Open to any writer living in North Carolina. Deadline: Late summer/early fall. Prize: $500-3,000 awarded to writers to pursue projects that further their artistic development.

OREGON LITERARY FELLOWSHIPS

925 S.W. Washington, Portland OR 97205. (503)227-2583. **E-mail:** susan@literary-arts.org. **Website:** www. literary-arts.org. **Contact:** Susan Denning, director of programs and events. Annual fellowships for writers of fiction, poetry, literary nonfiction, young readers and drama. Guidelines available in February for SASE. Accepts inquiries by e-mail, phone. Oregon residents only. Recipients announced in January. Deadline: Last Friday in June. Prize: $2,500 minimum award, for approximately 10 writers and 2 publishers. Judged by out-of-state writers

SCREENPLAY FESTIVAL

15021 Ventura Blvd., #523, Sherman Oaks CA 91403. (424)248-9221. **Fax:** (866)770-2994. **E-mail:** info@ screenplayfestival.com. **Website:** www.screenplay-festival.com. This festival is an opportunity to give all scriptwriters a chance to be noticed and have their work read by the power players. Entries in the feature-length competition must be more than 60 pages; entries in the short screenplay contest must be fewer than 60 pages. The Screenplay Festival was established to solve two major problems. One, it is simply too difficult for talented writers who have no "connections" to gain recognition and get their material read by legitimate agents, producers, directors and investors. Two, agents, producers, directors, and investors complain that they cannot find any great material, but they will generally not accept "unsolicited material." This means that unless the script comes from a source that is known to them, they will not read it. Screenplay Festival was established to help eliminate this "chicken and egg" problem. By accepting all submitted screenplays and judging them based upon their quality—not their source or their standardized formatting or the quality of the brads holding them together—Screenplay Festival looks to give undiscovered screenwriters an opportunity to rise above the crowd. Deadline: September 1. Prize: $1,000 in all categories.

WALLACE E. STEGNER FELLOWSHIPS

Creative Writing Program, Stanford University, Stanford CA 94305-2087. (650)723-0011. **Fax:** (650)723-3679. **E-mail:** stegnerfellowship@stanford.edu. **Website:** www.stanford.edu/group/creativewriting/stegner. Offers 5 fellowships in poetry and 5 in fiction for promising writers who can benefit from 2 years of instruction and participation in the program. Online application preferred. "We do not require a degree for admission. No school of writing is favored over any other. Chronological age is not a consideration." Deadline: September 1-December 1. Prize: Fellowships of $26,000 plus tuition of over $7,000/year.

TENNESSEE ARTS COMMISSION LITERARY FELLOWSHIP

Tennessee Arts Commission, 401 Charlotte Ave., Nashville TN 37243-0780. **Fax:** (615)741-8559. **E-mail:** lee.baird@state.tn.us. **Website:** tn.gov/arts. **Contact:** Lee Baird, director of literary programs. Awarded annually in recognition of professional Tennessee artists, i.e., individuals who have received financial compensation for their work as professional writers. Applicants must have a publication history other than vanity press. Three fellowships awarded annually to outstanding literary artists who live and work in Tennessee. Categories are in fiction, creative nonfiction, and poetry. Deadline: January 27. Prize: $5,000 Judged by an out-of-state adjudicator.

WISCONSIN INSTITUTE FOR CREATIVE WRITING FELLOWSHIP

6195B H.C. White Hall, 600 N. Park St., Madison WI 53706. **E-mail:** rfkuka@wisc.edu. **Website:** www.wisc.edu/english/cw. **Contact:** Sean Bishop, graduate coordinator. Fellowship provides time, space and an intellectual community for writers working on first books. Receives approximately 300 applicants a year for each genre. Judged by English Department faculty and current fellows. Candidates can have up to one published book in the genre for which they are applying. Open to any writer with either an M.F.A. or Ph.D. in creative writing. Please enclose a SASE for notification of results. Results announced online by May 1. Applicants should submit up to 10 pages of poetry or one story or excerpt of up to 30 pages and a résumé or vita directly to the program during the month of February. See instructions online for submitting online. An applicant's name must not appear on the writing sample (which must be in ms form) but rather on a separate sheet along with address, social security number, phone number, e-mail address and title(s) of submission(s). Candidates should also supply the names and phone numbers of two references. Accepts inquiries by e-mail and phone. Deadline: Last day of February. Prize: $27,000 for a 9-month appointment. **TIPS** "Send your best work. Stories seem to have a small advantage over novel excerpts."

FICTION

24-HOUR SHORT STORY CONTEST

WritersWeekly.com, 5726 Cortez Rd. W., #349, Bradenton FL 34210. **E-mail:** writersweekly@writersweekly.com. **Website:** www.writersweekly.com/misc/contest.php. **Contact:** Angela Hoy. Quarterly contest in which registered entrants receive a topic at start time (usually noon Central Time) and have 24 hours to write a story on that topic. All submissions must be returned via e-mail. Each contest is limited to 500 people. Upon entry, entrant will receive guidelines and details on competition, including submission process. Deadline: Quarterly—see website for dates. Prize: 1st Place: $300; 2nd Place: $250; 3rd Place: $200. There are also 20 honorable mentions and 60 door prizes (randomly drawn from all participants). The top 3 winners' entries are posted on WritersWeekly.com (non-exclusive electronic rights only) and receive a Freelance Income Kit. Writers retain all rights to their work. See website for full details on prizes. Judged by Angela Hoy (publisher of WritersWeekly.com and Booklocker.com).

THE SHERWOOD ANDERSON FOUNDATION FICTION AWARD

12330 Ashton Mill Terrace, Glen Allen VA 23059. **E-mail:** sherwoodandersonfoundation@gmail.com. **Website:** sherwoodandersonfoundation.org. **Con-**

tact: Anna McKean, foundation president. Contest is to honor, preserve and celebrate the memory and literary work of Sherwood Anderson, American realist for the first half of the 20th century. Annual award supports developing writers of short stories and novels. Entrants must have published at least one book of fiction or have had several short stories published in major literary and/or commercial publication. Self-published stories do not qualify. Send a detailed résumé that includes a bibliography of your publications. Include a cover letter that provides a history of your writing experience and your plans for writing projects. Also, submit 2 or 3 examples of what you consider to be your best work. Do not send mss by e-mail. Only mss in English will be accepted. Open to any writer who meets the qualifications listed above. Accepts inquiries by e-mail. Mail your application to the above address. No mss or publications will be returned. Deadline: April 1. Prize: $20,000 grant award.

SHERWOOD ANDERSON SHORT FICTION AWARD

Mid-American Review, Mid-American Review, Dept. of English, Box WM, BGSU, Bowling Green OH 43403. (419)372-2725. **Fax:** (419)372-4642. **E-mail:** mar@bgsu.edu. **Website:** www.bgsu.edu/midamericanreview. **Contact:** Katrin Tschirgi, managing editor. Offered annually for unpublished mss (6,000 word limit). Contest is open to all writers not associated with a judge or *Mid-American Review*. Guidelines online or for SASE. Deadline: November 1. Prize: $1,000, plus publication in the spring issue of *Mid-American Review.* Four Finalists: Notation, possible publication Judged by editors and a well-known writer, i.e., Aimee Bender or Anthony Doerr. 2013-14 Judge: Lance Olsen.

THE BALTIMORE REVIEW CONTESTS

The Baltimore Review, 6514 Maplewood Rd., Baltimore MD 21212. **Website:** www.baltimorereview.org. **Contact:** Barbara Westwood Diehl, senior editor. Each summer and winter issue includes a contest theme (see submissions guidelines for theme). Prizes are awarded for first, second, and third place among all categories—poetry, short stories, and creative nonfiction. All entries are considered for publication. Open to all writers. Only unpublished work will be considered. Asks only for the right to publish the work for the first time. Deadline: May 31 and November 30. Prize: 1st Place: $500; 2nd Place: $200; 3rd Place: $100.

Most winning works are published. Judged by the editors of *The Baltimore Review*.

BARD FICTION PRIZE

Bard College, P.O. Box 5000, Annandale-on-Hudson NY 12504-5000. (845)758-7087. **E-mail:** bfp@bard.edu. **Website:** www.bard.edu/bfp. The Bard Fiction Prize is intended to encourage and support young writers of fiction to pursue their creative goals and to provide an opportunity to work in a fertile and intellectual environment. Prize: $30,000 cash award and appointment as writer-in-residence at Bard College for 1 semester. Judged by committee of 5 judges (authors associated with Bard College). No entry fee. Cover letter should include name, address, phone, e-mail and name of publisher where book was previously published. Guidelines available by SASE, fax, phone, e-mail, or online. Deadline: July 15. Entries must be previously published. Open to U.S. citizens aged 39 and below. Results announced by October 15. Winners notified by phone. For contest results, e-mail, or visit website. **Contact:** Irene Zedlacher. Open to younger American writers. Cover letter should include name, address, phone, e-mail and name of publisher where book was previously published. Entries must be previously published. Open to U.S. citizens aged 39 and below. Guidelines available by SASE, fax, phone, e-mail, or online. Results announced by October 15. Winners notified by phone. For contest results, e-mail, or visit website. The Bard Fiction Prize is intended to encourage and support young writers of fiction to pursue their creative goals and to provide an opportunity to work in a fertile and intellectual environment. Deadline: July 15. Prize: $30,000 and appointment as writer-in-residence at Bard College for 1 semester. Judged by a committee of 5 judges (authors associated with Bard College).

BELLEVUE LITERARY REVIEW GOLDENBERG PRIZE FOR FICTION

Bellevue Literary Review, NYU Dept of Medicine, 550 First Ave., OBV-A612, New York NY 10016. (212)263-3973. **E-mail:** info@blreview.org; stacy@blreview.org. **Website:** www.blreview.org. **Contact:** Stacy Bodziak, managing editor. The BLR prizes award outstanding writing related to themes of health, healing, illness, the mind and the body. Annual competition/award for short stories. Receives about 200-300 entries per category. Send credit card information or make checks payable to Bellevue Literary Review.

Guidelines available in February. Accepts inquiries by e-mail, phone, mail. Submissions open in February. Results announced in December and made available to entrants with SASE, by e-mail, online. Winners notified by mail, by e-mail. Entries should be unpublished. Anyone may enter contest. Length: No minimum; maximum of 5,000 words. Writers may submit own work. Deadline: July 1. Prize: $1,000 and publication in *The Bellevue Literary Review*. BLR editors select semi-finalists to be read by an independent judge who chooses the winner. Previous judges include Amy Hempel, Rick Moody, Rosellen Brown, and Andre Dubus III.

BEST LESBIAN EROTICA

BLE 2013, 31-64 21st St., #319, Long Island City NY 11106. **E-mail:** kwarnockble@gmail.com. **Website:** www.kathleenwarnock.com/best-lesbian-erotica. html. **Contact:** Kathleen Warnock, series editor. Call for submissions for *Best Lesbian Erotica*, an annual collection. Categories include: novel excerpts, short stories; poetry will be considered but is not encouraged. Accepts both previously published and unpublished material; will accept submissions that have appeared in other themed anthologies. Open to any writer. All submissions must include an e-mail address for response. No mss will be returned, so please do not include SASE. Include cover page with author's name/pen name if using one, title of submission(s), address, phone, e-mail. All submissions must be typed and double-spaced. Submit double-sided copies. Length: 5,000 words. Submit 2 different pieces of work. Submit 2 hard copies of each submission. "Will only accept e-mail copies if the following conditions apply: You live outside of North America or Europe; the cost of postage would be prohibitive from your home country; the post office system in your country is dreadful (US does not count); the content of your submission may be illegal to send via postal mail in your home country." Deadline: April 1. Prize: $100 for each published story, plus 2 copies of the anthology.

BINGHAMTON UNIVERSITY JOHN GARDNER FICTION BOOK AWARD

Creative Writing Program, Binghamton University, Binghamton University, Department of English, General Literature, and Rhetoric, Library North Room 1149, P.O. Box 6000, Binghamton NY 13902-6000. (607)777-2713. **E-mail:** cwpro@binghamton.edu. **Website:** binghamton.edu/english/creative-writing/.

Contact: Maria Mazziotti Gillan, director. Contest offered annually for a novel or collection of fiction published in previous year in a press run of 500 copies or more. Each book submitted must be accompanied by an application form. Publisher may submit more than 1 book for prize consideration. Send 3 copies of each book. Guidelines online. Author or publisher may submit. Deadline: March 1. Prize: $1,000. Judged by a professional writer not on Binghamton University faculty.

BOULEVARD SHORT FICTION CONTEST FOR EMERGING WRITERS

Boulevard Magazine, 6614 Clayton Rd., PMB #325, Richmond Heights MO 63117. (314)862-2643. **Website:** www.richardburgin.net/boulevard. **Contact:** Jessica Rogen, managing editor. Offered annually for unpublished short fiction to a writer who has not yet published a book of fiction, poetry, or creative nonfiction with a nationally distributed press. Holds first North American rights on anything not previously published. Open to any writer with no previous publication by a nationally known press. Guidelines for SASE or online. Accepts works up to 8,000 words. Simultaneous submissions are allowed, but previously accepted or published work is ineligible. Entries will be judged by the editors of *Boulevard Magazine*. Send typed, double-spaced ms(s) and SAS post card for acknowledgement of receipt. Deadline: December 31. Prize: $1,500, and publication in 1 of the next year's issues.

CANADIAN AUTHORS ASSOCIATION FICTION AWARD

6 West St. N, Suite 203, Orillia ON L3V 5B8 Canada. (705)325-3926 or (866)216-6222. **E-mail:** admin@canauthors.org. **Website:** www.canauthors.org. **Contact:** Courtney Thompson. Offered annually for a full-length novel by a Canadian citizen or permanent immigrant. Entry form required. Obtain entry form by e-mail or from website. Deadline: January 15. Prize: $2,000 and a silver medal

CANADIAN SHORT STORY COMPETITION

Red Tuque Books, Unit #6, 477 Martin St., Penticton BC V2A 5L2 Canada. (778)476-5750. **Fax:** (778)476-5750. **E-mail:** dave@redtuquebooks.ca. **Website:** www.redtuquebooks.ca. **Contact:** David Korinetz, contest director. Offered annually for unpublished works. Purpose of award is to promote Canada and

Canadian publishing. Stories require a Canadian element. There are three ways to qualify. They can be written by a Canadian, written about Canadians, or take place somewhere in Canada. Deadline: December 31. Prize: 1st Place: $500; 2nd Place: $150; 3rd Place: $100; and 10 prizes of $25 will be given to honorable mentions. All 13 winners will be published in an anthology. They will each receive a complimentary copy. Judged by Canadian authors in the fantasy/sci-fi/horror field. Acquires first print rights. Contest open to anyone.

TIPS "The 2013 contest, 'Candian Tales of the Fantastic,' will be looking for the fantastic (Sci-Fi/Fantasy/Horror). The 2014 contest, 'Candian Tales of the Mysterious,' will be looking for stories that have an element of Mystery (Mystery/Detective/Ghost Story). The 2015 contest, 'Candian Tales of the Heart,' will be looking for stories that elicit strong emotion (Romance/Humour/Contemporary)."

THE ALEXANDER PATTERSON CAPPON FICTION AWARD

New Letters, University of Missouri-Kansas City, 5101 Rockhill Rd., Kansas City MO 64110-2499. (816)235-1168. **Fax:** (816)235-2611. **E-mail:** newletters@umkc.edu. **Website:** www.newletters.org. **Contact:** Ashley Kaine. Offered annually for the best short story to discover and reward new and upcoming writers. Buys first North American serial rights. Open to any writer. Deadline: May 18. Prize: 1st Place: $1,500 and publication in a volume of *New Letters*. All entries will be given consideration for publication in future issues of *New Letters*.

⊕ CASCADE WRITING CONTEST & AWARDS

Oregon Christian Writers, 1075 Willow Lake Road N., Keizer Oregon 97303. **E-mail:** cascade@oregonchristianwriters.org. **Website:** oregonchristianwriters.org/ocw-cascade-writing-contest/. **Contact:** Marilyn Rhoads and Julie McDonald Zander. The Cascade Awards are presented at the annual Oregon Christian Writers Summer Conference (held at the Red Lion on the River in Portland, Oregon each August) attended by national editors, agents, and professional authors. Award given for each of the following categories: Published Fiction Book, Unpublished Fiction Book, Nonfiction/Memoir, Poetry, Devotional Books, Young Adult Novels, Middle Grade Fiction Book and Middle Grade Nonfiction Book, Children's Fiction and Nonfiction Book, and Short Entries, including: Articles, Stories, and Published Blog. Two additional special Cascade Awards are presented each year, the Trailblazer Award to a writer who has distinguished him/herself in the field of Christian writing and a Writer of Promise Award for a writer who demonstrates unusual promise in the field of Christian writing. For a full list of categories, entry rules, and scoring elements, visit website. Guidelines and rules available on the website. Entry forms will be available on the first day for entry. Annual multi-genre competition to encourage both published and emerging writers in the field of Christian writing. Deadline: February 14-March 31. Prize: Award certificate presented at the Cascade Awards ceremony during the Oregon Christian Writers Annual Summer Conference. Finalists are listed in the conference notebook and winners are listed online. Cascade Trophies are awarded to the recipients of the Trailblazer and Writer of Promise Awards. Judged by published authors, editors, librarians, and retail book store owners and employees. Final judging by editors, agents, and published authors from the Christian publishing industry.

KAY CATTARULLA AWARD FOR BEST SHORT STORY

Texas Institute of Letters, P.O. Box 609, Round Rock TX 78680. **E-mail:** tilsecretary@yahoo.com. **Website:** texasinstituteofletters.org. Offered annually for work published January 1-December 31 of previous year to recognize the best short story. The story submitted must have appeared in print for the first time to be eligible. Writers must have been born in Texas, must have lived in Texas for at least 2 consecutive years, or the subject matter of the work must be associated with Texas. See website for guidelines. See website for details and instructions on entering the competition. Deadline: January 10. Prize: $1,000.

G. S. SHARAT CHANDRA PRIZE FOR SHORT FICTION

BkMk Press, University House, 5101 Rockhill Rd., Kansas City MO 64110-2499. (816)235-2558. **Fax:** (816)235-2611. **E-mail:** bkmk@umkc.edu; newletters@umkc.edu. **Website:** www.newletters.org. Offered annually for the best book-length ms collection (unpublished) of short fiction in English by a living author. Translations are not eligible. Initial judging is done by a network of published writers. Final judging is done by a writer of national reputation. Guidelines for SASE, by e-mail, or online. Short fiction collections should be approximately 125 pages minimum, 300 pages maximum, double spaced. Deadline: January 15. Prize: $1,000, plus book publication by BkMk Press.

➕💬 PEGGY CHAPMAN-ANDREWS FIRST NOVEL AWARD

P.O. Box 6910, Dorset DT6 9QB United Kingdom. **E-mail:** info@bridportprize.org.uk. **Website:** www.bridportprize.org.uk. **Contact:** Frances Everitt, administrator. Award to promote literary excellence and new writers. Enter first chapters of novel, up to 8,000 words plus 300 word synopsis. Send SASE for entry form or enter online. Deadline: May 31. Prize: 1st Prize: £1,000 plus mentoring & possible publication. Judged by Alison Moore, The Literary Consultancy & A.M. Heath Literary Agents.

THE CHARITON REVIEW SHORT FICTION PRIZE

Truman State University Press, 100 East Normal Ave., Kirksville MO 63501-4221. **Website:** tsup.truman.edu. An annual award for the best unpublished short fiction on any theme up to 5,000 words in English. Mss must be double-spaced on standard paper and bound only with a clip. Electronic submissions are not allowed. Include 2 title pages: 1 with the ms title and the author's contact information (name, address, phone, e-mail), and the other with only the ms title. (The author's name must not appear on or within the ms.) Enclose a SASE for notification when your ms is received. Mss will not be returned. Current Truman State University faculty, staff, or students are not eligible to compete. Deadline: September 30. Prize: $1,000 and publication in *The Chariton Review* for the winner. Three finalists will also be published in the Spring issue. The final judge will be announced after the finalists have been selected in January.

COPTALES CONTEST

Sponsored by Oak Tree Press, 140 E. Palmer St., Taylorville IL 62568. **E-mail:** publisher@oaktreebooks.com. **E-mail:** CT-ContestAdmin@oaktreebooks.com. **Website:** www.oaktreebooks.com. **Contact:** Billie Johnson, publisher. Open to novels and true stories that feature a law enforcement main character. Word count should range from 60,000-80,000 words. Text must be presented in a rich text format and double-spaced. Ms cover page must list author e-mail address and estimated word count. Guidelines

and entry forms are available for SASE or online. The goal of the CopTales Contest is to discover and publish new authors, or authors shifting to a new genre. This annual contest is open to writers who have not published in the mystery genre in the past three years, as well as completely unpublished authors. Deadline: September 1. Prize: Publishing contract, book published in trade paperback and e-book formats with a professionally designed, four-color cover. See website for details. Judged by a select panel of editors and professional crime writers.

➕ CRITIQUE MY NOVEL WRITING CONTEST

Critique My Novel, 2408 W. 8th, Amarillo TX 79106. **E-mail:** contest@critiquemynovel.com. **Website:** critiquemynovel.com/2014_writing_contest. **Contact:** Catherine York, contest/award director. Annual contest new and emerging writers. Send the first 10,000 words of a novel (must be unpublished, self-published, or published through a vanity/independent press). Include a cover sheet that contains the following information: novel title, genre, word count of full ms, e-mail address. Do not put name on submission. See website for full details and guidelines. The main purpose is to help new writers. The focus is on feedback on all entries, and prizes for the best. Deadline: March 1-April 30 (early bird), May 1-June 30 (regular deadline). Prize: Personal feedback from 4 judges for every entrant; cash prize, set of writing resources for top 4 novels; final 3 novels also receive a voucher and are sent to agents for feedback and consideration; 10 round-2 novels and author websites listed on Critique My Novel. Judges listed online. Includes guest judges from literary agencies who help in the final deliberations.

DARK OAK MYSTERY CONTEST

Oak Tree Press, 140 E. Palmer St., Taylorville IL 62568. (217)824-6500. **E-mail:** oaktreepub@aol.com. **E-mail:** DO-ContestAdmin@oaktreebooks.com. **Website:** www.oaktreebooks.com. Offered annually for an unpublished mystery ms (up to 80,000 words) of any sort from police procedurals to amateur sleuth novels. Acquires first North American, audio and film rights to winning entry. Open to authors not published in the past 3 years. Deadline: September 1. Prize: Publishing Agreement, and launch of the title. Judged by a select panel of editors and professional mystery writers.

DEAD OF WINTER

E-mail: editors@toasted-cheese.com. **Website:** www. toasted-cheese.com. **Contact:** Stephanie Lenz, editor. The contest is a winter-themed horror fiction contest with a new topic each year. Topic and word limit announced October 1. The topic is usually geared toward a supernatural theme. Entries must be unpublished. Accepts inquiries by e-mail. Cover letter should include name, address, e-mail, word count, and title. Word limit varies each year. Open to any writer. Guidelines available in October online. Deadline: December 21. Results announced January 31. Winners notified by e-mail. List of winners online. Prize: Amazon gift certificates and publication in *Toasted Cheese*. Also offers honorable mention. Judged by 2 *Toasted Cheese* editors who blind judge each contest. Each judge uses her own criteria to rate entries.
TIPS "Follow online submission guidelines."

WILLIAM F. DEECK MALICE DOMESTIC GRANTS FOR UNPUBLISHED WRITERS

Malice Domestic, P.O. Box 8007, Gaithersburg MD 20898-8007. **E-mail:** grants@malicedomestic.org. **Website:** www.malicedomestic.org. **Contact:** Harriette Sackler. Offered annually for unpublished work in the mystery field. Malice awards up to 2 grants to unpublished writers in the Malice Domestic genre at its annual convention in May. The competition is designed to help the next generation of Malice authors get their first work published and to foster quality Malice literature. Malice Domestic literature is loosely described as mystery stories of the Agatha Christie type, i.e., traditional mysteries. These works usually feature no excessive gore, gratuitous violence, or explicit sex. Writers who have been published previously in the mystery field, including publication of a mystery novel, short story, or dramatic work, are ineligible to apply. Members of the Malice Domestic Board of Directors and their families are ineligible to apply. Malice encourages applications from minority candidates. Guidelines online. Deadline: November 15. Prize: $1,500, plus a comprehensive registration to the following year's convention and two nights' lodging at the convention hotel.

JACK DYER FICTION PRIZE

Crab Orchard Review, Department of English, Mail Code 4503, Faner Hall 2380, Southern Illinois University at Carbondale, 1000 Faner Drive, Carbondale IL 62901. **E-mail:** jtribble@siu.edu. **Website:** www.

craborchardreview.siu.edu. **Contact:** Jon C. Tribble, man. editor. Offered annually for unpublished short fiction. *Crab Orchard Review* acquires first North American serial rights to all submitted work. One winner and at least 2 finalists will be chosen. Entries must be unpublished. Length: 6,000 words maximum. Please note that no stories will be returned. Results announced by end of August. Guidelines online. Deadline: April 21. Submissions period begins February 21. Prize: $2,000, publication and 1-year subscription to *Crab Orchard Review*. Finalists are offered $500 and publication. Judged by editorial staff (pre-screening); winner chosen by genre editor.
TIPS "Carefully read directions for entering and follow them exactly. Send us your best work. Note that simultaneous submissions are accepted for this prize, but the winning entry must NOT be accepted elsewhere. No electronic submissions."

MARY KENNEDY EASTHAM FLASH FICTION PRIZE

Category in the Soul-Making Keats Literary Competition, The Webhallow House, 1544 Sweetwood Dr., Broadmoor Village CA 94015-2029. **E-mail:** Eileen-Malone@comcast.net. **Website:** www.soulmaking-contest.us. **Contact:** Eileen Malone. Keep each story under 500 words. Three stories per entry. One story per page, typed, double-spaced, and unidentified. Deadline: November 30. Prize: Prizes: 1st Place: $100; 2nd Place: $50; 3rd Place: $25.
TIPS "Send me your best stuff but more than that make my heart beat faster. Surprise me. Read great writing daily and WRITE. WRITE. WRITE. To be successful you need to do your best every day for a very long time."

⊕ FABLERS MONTHLY CONTEST

818 Los Arboles Lane, Santa Fe NM 87501. **Website:** www.fablers.net. **Contact:** W.B. Scott. Monthly contest for previously unpublished writers to help develop amateur writers. Guidelines posted online. No entry fee. Open to any writer. Deadline: 14th of each month. Prize: $100. Judged by members of website.

☾ THE FAR HORIZONS AWARD FOR SHORT FICTION

The Malahat Review, University of Victoria, P.O. Box 1700, Stn CSC, Victoria BC V8W 2Y2 Canada. (250)721-8524. **Fax:** (250)472-5051. **E-mail:** mala-hat@uvic.ca. **E-mail:** horizons@uvic.ca. **Website:** www.malahatreview.ca. **Contact:** John Barton, editor. Submissions must be unpublished. No simultaneous submissions. Submit 1 piece of short fiction, 3,500 words maximum; no restrictions on subject matter or aesthetic approach. Include separate page with author's name, address, e-mail, and title; no identifying information on mss pages. E-mail submissions are accepted. Do not include SASE for results; mss will not be returned. Guidelines online. Winner and finalists contacted by e-mail. Open to "emerging short fiction writers from Canada, the US, and elsewhere" who have not yet published their fiction in a full-length book (48 pages or more). 2011 winner: Zoey Peterson; 2013 winner: Kerry-Lee Powell. Deadline: May 1 (odd-numbered years). Prize: $1,000 CAD, publication in fall issue of *The Malahat Review* (see separate listing in Magazines/Journals). Announced in fall online, Facebook page, and in quarterly e-newsletter, *Malahat Lite*.

FIRSTWRITER.COM INTERNATIONAL SHORT STORY CONTEST

firstwriter.com, United Kingdom. **Website:** www.firstwriter.com. **Contact:** J. Paul Dyson, managing editor. Accepts short stories up to 3,000 words on any subject and in any style. Deadline: April 1. Prize: Totals about $300. Ten special commendations will also be awarded and all the winners will be published in *firstwriter* magazine and receive a $36 subscription voucher, allowing an annual subscription to be taken out for free. All submissions are automatically considered for publication in *firstwriter* magazine and may be published there online. Judged by *firstwriter* magazine editors.

FISH PUBLISHING FLASH FICTION COMPETITION

Durrus, Bantry, County Cork Ireland. **E-mail:** info@fishpublishing.com. **Website:** www.fishpublishing.com. Annual prize awarding flash fiction. Max length: 300 words. You may enter as many times as you wish. See website for details and rules. "This is an opportunity to attempt what is one of the most difficult and rewarding tasks—to create, in a tiny fragment, a completely resolved and compelling story in 300 words or less." Deadline: February 28. Prize: First Prize: €1,000 ($1,200). The 10 published authors will receive 5 copies of the Anthology and will be invited to read at the launch during the West Cork Literary Festival in July. 2013 competition judged by Glenn Patterson.

FISH SHORT STORY PRIZE

Durrus, Bantry Co. Cork Ireland. **E-mail:** info@fishpublishing.com. **Website:** www.fishpublishing.com. Annual worldwide competition to recognize the best short stories. Entries must not have been published before. Entry online or by post. See website for full details of competitions, and information on the Fish Editorial and Critique Services, and the Fish Online Writing Courses. Deadline: November 30. Prize: Overall prize fund: €5,000. 1st prize: €3,000. 2nd Prize: 1 week at Anam Cara Writers Retreat in West Cork and €300. 3rd Prize: €300. Closing date 30th November. The best 10 will be published in the Fish Anthology, launched in July at the West Cork Literary Festival. Winners announced 17 March.

H.E. FRANCIS SHORT STORY COMPETITION

Ruth Hindman Foundation, University of Alabama in Huntsville, Department of English, Morton Hall Room 222, Huntsville AL 35899. **Website:** www.hefranciscompetition.com. Offered annually for unpublished work, not to exceed 5,000 words. Acquires first-time publication rights. Using the electronic submission system or by mail, submit a story of up to 5,000 words. If submitting by mail, include three copies of the story. Send an SASE or visit the website for complete guidelines. Deadline: December 31. Prize: $2,000. Judged by a panel of nationally recognized, award-winning authors, directors of creative writing programs, and editors of literary journals.

GIVAL PRESS NOVEL AWARD

Gival Press, LLC, P.O. Box 3812, Arlington VA 22203. (703)351-0079. **E-mail:** givalpress@yahoo.com. **Website:** www.givalpress.com. **Contact:** Robert L. Giron. Offered annually for a previously unpublished original novel (not a translation). Guidelines by phone, online, via e-mail, or by mail with SASE. Results announced late fall of same year. Winners notified by phone. Results made available to entrants with SASE, by e-mail, online. Open to any author who writes original work in English. Length: 30,000-100,000 words. Cover letter should include name, address, phone, e-mail, word count, novel title; include a short bio and short synopsis. Only the title and word count should appear on the actual ms. Writers may submit own work. "To award the best literary novel." Deadline: May 30. Prize: $3,000, plus publication of book with a standard contract and author's copies. Final judge is announced after winner is chosen. Entries read anonymously.

TIPS "Review the types of mss Gival Press has published. We stress literary works."

GIVAL PRESS SHORT STORY AWARD

Gival Press, P.O. Box 3812, Arlington VA 22203. (703)351-0079. **E-mail:** givalpress@yahoo.com. **Website:** www.givalpress.com. **Contact:** Robert L. Giron, publisher. Annual literary, short story contest. Entries must be unpublished. Open to anyone who writes original short stories, which are not a chapter of a novel, in English. Receives about 100-150 entries per category. Guidelines online, via e-mail, or by mail. Results announced in the fall of the same year. Winners notified by phone. Results available with SASE, by e-mail, and online. Length: 5,000-15,000 words. Include name, address, phone, e-mail, word count, title on cover letter; include short bio. Only the title and word count should be found on ms. Writers may submit their own ficiton. Recognizes the best literary short story. Deadline: August 8. Prize: $1,000 and publication online. Judged anonymously.

GLIMMER TRAIN'S FAMILY MATTERS CONTEST

Glimmer Train, 4763 SW Maplewood Rd., P.O. Box 80430, Portland OR 97280. (503)221-0836. **Fax:** (503)221-0837. **E-mail:** eds@glimmertrain.org. **Website:** www.glimmertrain.org. **Contact:** Susan Burmeister-Brown. This contest is now held twice a year, during the months of April and October. Winners are contacted 2 months after the close of each contest, and results officially announced one week later. Submit online. The word count for this contest generaly ranges from 1,500 to 5,000 words, though up 12,000 words is fine. See complete guidelines online. Deadline: April 30 and October 31. Prize: 1st Place: $1,500, publication in *Glimmer Train Stories*, and 20 copies of that issue; 2nd Place: $500 and consideration for publication; 3rd Place: $300 and consideration for publication.

TIPS "We are looking for stories about families of all configurations. It's fine to draw heavily on real life experiences, but the work must read like fiction and all stories accepted for publication will be presented as fiction."

GLIMMER TRAIN'S FICTION OPEN

Glimmer Train, Inc., Glimmer Train Press, Inc., 4763 SW Maplewood Rd., P.O. Box 80430, Portland OR 97280. (503)221-0836. **Fax:** (503)221-0837. **E-mail:** eds@glimmertrain.org. **Website:** www.glimmertrain. org. **Contact:** Linda Swanson-Davies. Submissions to this category generally range from 2,000-8,000 words, but up to 20,000 is fine. Held twice a year. Submit online. Winners will be called 2 months after the close of the contest. Deadline: June 30 and December 31. Prize: 1st Place $2,500, publication in *Glimmer Train Stories*, and 20 copies of that issue; 2nd Place $1,000 and consideration for publication; 3rd Place: $600 and consideration for publication.

GLIMMER TRAIN'S SHORT-STORY AWARD FOR NEW WRITERS

Glimmer Train Press, Inc., 4763 SW Maplewood Rd., P.O. Box 80430, Portland OR 97280. (503)221-0836. **Fax:** (503)221-0837. **E-mail:** eds@glimmertrain.org. **Website:** www.glimmertrain.org. **Contact:** Linda Swanson-Davies. Offered for any writer whose fiction hasn't appeared in a nationally distributed print publication with a circulation over 5,000. Submissions to this category generally range from 1,500-6,000 words, but up to 12,000 is fine. Held quarterly. Submit online. Winners will be called 2 months after the close of the contest. Deadline: February 28, May 31, August 31, and November 30. Prize: 1st Place: $1,500, publication in *Glimmer Train Stories*, and 20 copies of that issue; 2nd Place: $500 and consideration for publication; 3rd Place: $300 and consideration for publication.

TIPS "This contest is now held quarterly. In a recent edition of *Best American Short Stories*, of the top '100 Distinguished Short Stories,' 10 appeared in *Glimmer Train Stories*, more than any other publication in the country, including *The New Yorker*. Of those 10, 3 were those authors' first stories accepted for publication."

GLIMMER TRAIN'S VERY SHORT FICTION CONTEST

Glimmer Train Press, Inc., 4763 SW Maplewood Rd., P.O. Box 80430, Portland OR 97280. (503)221-0836. **Fax:** (503)221-0837. **E-mail:** eds@glimmertrain.org. **Website:** www.glimmertrain.org. **Contact:** Susan Burmeister-Brown. Offered to encourage the art of the very short story. Word count: 3,000 maximum. Held quarterly. Submit online. Results announced 2 months after the close of the contest. Deadline: January 31, April 30, July 31, and October 31. Prize: 1st Place: $1,500, publication in *Glimmer Train Stories*, and 20 copies of that issue; 2nd Place: $500 and con-

---

sideration for publication; 3rd Place: $300 and consideration for publication.

TIPS "There is no minimum word count, though it is rare for a piece under 500 words to read as a full story."

GOVERNOR GENERAL'S LITERARY AWARD FOR FICTION

Canada Council for the Arts, 150 Elgin St., P.O. Box 1047, Ottawa ON K1P 5V8 Canada. (613)566-4414, ext. 5573. **Fax:** (613)566-4410. **Website:** www.canadacouncil.ca/prizes/ggla. Offered annually for the best English-language and the best French-language work of fiction by a Canadian. Publishers submit titles for consideration. Deadline: Depends on the book's publication date. Books in English: March 15, June 1 or August 7. Books in French: March 15 or July 15. Prize: Each laureate receives $25,000; non-winning finalists receive $1,000.

THE GOVER PRIZE

Best New Writing, P.O. Box 11, Titusville NJ 08530. **Fax:** (609)968-1718. **E-mail:** submissions@bestnewwriting.com. **Website:** www.bestnewwriting.com/BNWgover.html. **Contact:** Christopher Klim, senior editor. Open to all writers. Submissions msut be previously unpublished. Guidelines online. Entries limited to 500 words or less. The Gover Prize, named after groundbreaking author Robert Gover, awards an annual prize and publication in *Best New Writing* for the best short fiction and creative nonfiction. Deadline: September 15-January 10. Prize: $250 grand prize; publication in *Best New Writing* for finalists (approximately 12), holds 6-month world exclusive rights. Judged by *Best New Writing* editorial staff.

LYNDALL HADOW/DONALD STUART SHORT STORY COMPETITION

Fellowship of Australian Writers (WA), P.O. Box 6180, Swanbourne WA 6910 Australia. (61)(8)9384-4771. **Fax:** (61)(8)9384-4854. **E-mail:** admin@fawwa.org.au. **Website:** www.fawwa.org.au. Annual contest for unpublished short stories (maximum 3,000 words). Reserves the right to publish entries in a FAWWA publication or online. Guidelines online or for SASE. Deadline: June 1. Prize: 1st Place: $400; 2nd Place; $100; Highly Commended: $50.

DRUE HEINZ LITERATURE PRIZE

University of Pittsburgh Press, Eureka Building, 5th Floor, 3400 Forbes Ave., Eureka Bldg., 5th Floor, Pittsburgh PA 15260. (412)383-2492. **Fax:** (412)383-2466. **Website:** www.upress.pitt.edu. Offered annually to writers who have published a book-length collection of fiction or a minimum of 3 short stories or novellas in commercial magazines or literary journals of national distribution. Does not return mss. Deadline: Submit May 1- June 30 only. Prize: $15,000. Judged by anonymous nationally known writers such as Robert Penn Warren, Joyce Carol Oates, and Margaret Atwood.

LORIAN HEMINGWAY SHORT STORY COMPETITION

Hemingway Days Festival, P.O. Box 993, Key West FL 33041. **E-mail:** shortstorykw@gmail.com. **Website:** www.shortstorycompetition.com. **Contact:** Eva Eliot, editorial assistant. Offered annually for unpublished short stories up to 3,500 words. Guidelines available via mail, e-mail, or online. Accepts inquiries by SASE, e-mail, or visit website. Entries must be unpublished. Open to all writers whose work has not appeared in a nationally distributed publication with a circulation of 5,000 or more. Looking for excellence, pure and simple—no genre restrictions, no theme restrictions. We seek a writer's voice that cannot be ignored. All entrants will receive a letter from Lorian Hemingway and a list of winners, via mail or e-mail, by October 1. Results announced at the end of July during Hemingway Days festival. Winners notified by phone prior to announcement. Award to encourage literary excellence and the efforts of writers whose voices have yet to be heard. Deadline: May 15. Prize: Prizes: 1st Place: $1,500, plus publication of his or her winning story in *Cutthroat: A Journal of the Arts*; 2nd-3rd Place: $500; honorable mentions will also be awarded. Judged by a panel of writers, editors, and literary scholars selected by author Lorian Hemingway. (Lorian Hemingway is the competition's final judge.)

TONY HILLERMAN PRIZE

Wordharvest, 1063 Willow Way, Santa Fe NM 87507. (505)471-1565. **E-mail:** wordharvest@wordharvest.com. **Website:** www.wordharvest.com. **Contact:** Anne Hillerman and Jean Schaumberg, co-organizers. Awarded annually for the best first mystery set in the Southwest. Murder or another serious crime or crimes must be at the heart of the story, with the emphasis on the solution rather than the details of the crime. Multiple entries accepted. Accepts inquiries by e-mail, phone. Entries should be unpublished; self-published work is generally accepted. Length: no less than 220 type written pages, or approximately 60,000 words. Cover letter should include name, address, phone, e-mail, list of publishing credits. Please include SASE for response. Writers may submit their own work. Honors the contributions made by Tony Hillerman to the art and craft of the mystery. Deadline: June 1. Prize: $10,000 advance and publication by St. Martin's Press. Nominees will be selected by judges chosen by the editorial staff of St. Martin's Press, with the assistance of independent judges selected by organizers of the Tony Hillerman Writers Conference (Wordharvest), and the winner will be chosen by St. Martin's editors.

TOM HOWARD/JOHN H. REID FICTION & ESSAY CONTEST

c/o Winning Writers, 351 Pleasant St., PMB 222, Northampton MA 01060-3961. (866)946-9748. **Fax:** (413)280-0539. **E-mail:** adam@winningwriters.com. **Website:** www.winningwriters.com. **Contact:** Adam Cohen, President. Now in its 22nd year. Open to all writers. Submit any type of short story, essay or other work of prose. Both published and unpublished works are welcome. In the case of published work, the contestant must own the online publication rights. Submit online. Contest sponsored by Winning Writers. Guidelines online in September. Early submission encouraged. Prefers inquiries by e-mail. Length: 6,000 words max per entry. Cover letter should include name, address, phone, e-mail, story title, and place(s) where story was previously published (if any). Only the title should be on the actual ms. Writers may submit own work. Winners notifed by e-mail. Results made available to entrants online. Deadline: April 30. Prize: Prizes: Two 1st prizes of $1,000 will be awarded, plus 10 honorable mentions of $100 each. Judged by Arthur Powers.

L. RON HUBBARD'S WRITERS OF THE FUTURE CONTEST

P.O. Box 1630, Los Angeles CA 90078. (323)466-3310. **Fax:** (323)466-6474. **E-mail:** contests@authorservicesinc.com. **Website:** www.writersofthefuture.com. **Contact:** Joni Labaqui, contest director. Foremost competition for new and amateur writers of unpublished science fiction or fantasy short stories or novelettes. Offered to find, reward and publicize new speculative fiction writers so they may more easily attain professional writing careers. Open to writers who have not professionally published a novel or short

novel, more than 1 novelette, or more than 3 short stories. Entries must be unpublished. Limit 1 entry per quarter. Open to any writer. Results announced quarterly in e-newsletter. Winners notified by phone. Contest has 4 quarters. There shall be 3 cash prizes in each quarter. In addition, at the end of the year, the 4 first-place, quarterly winners will have their entries rejudged, and a grand prize winner shall be determined. Eligible entries are previously unpublished short stories or novelettes (under 17,000 words) of science fiction or fantasy. Guidelines for SASE or online. Accepts inquiries by fax, e-mail, phone. Mss: White paper, black ink; double-spaced; typed; each page appropriately numbered with title, no author name. Include cover page with author's name, address, phone number, e-mail address (if available), as well as estimated word count and the title of the work. Online submissions are accepted. Hard copy submissions will not be returned. Deadline: December 31, March 31, June 30, September 30. Prize: Prize (awards quarterly): 1st Place: $1,000; 2nd Place: $750; and 3rd Place: $500. Annual grand prize: $5,000. Judged by Dave Wolverton (initial judge), then by a panel of 4 professional authors.

INDIANA REVIEW FICTION CONTEST

Ballantine Hall 465, Indiana University, 1020 E. Kirkwood Ave., Bloomington IN 47405-7103. (812)855-3439. **Fax:** (812)855-4253. **E-mail:** inreview@indiana.edu. **Website:** indianareview.org. **Contact:** Katie Moulton, editor. Contest for fiction in any style and on any subject. Open to any writer. Mss will not be returned. No works forthcoming elsewhere, are eligible. Simultaneous submissions accepted, but in the event of entrant withdrawal, contest fee will not be refunded. Maximum length: 8,000 words. Deadline: October 31. Submission period begins September 1. Prize: $1,000, publication in the Indiana Review and contributor's copies. Judged by guest judges.

TIPS "We look for a command of language and structure, as well as a facility with compelling and unusual subject matter. It's a good idea to obtain copies of issues featuring past winners to get a more concrete idea of what we are looking for."

✆ INTERNATIONAL 3-DAY NOVEL CONTEST

Box 2106 Station Terminal, Vancouver BC V6B 3T5 Canada. **E-mail:** info@3daynovel.com. **Website:** www.3daynovel.com. **Contact:** Melissa Edwards, managing editor. "Can you produce a masterwork of fiction in three short days? The 3-Day Novel Contest is your chance to find out. For more than 30 years, hundreds of writers step up to the challenge each Labour Day weekend, fuelled by nothing but adrenaline and the desire for spontaneous literary nirvana. It's a thrill, a grind, a 72-hour kick in the pants and an awesome creative experience. How many crazed plotlines, coffee-stained pages, pangs of doubt and moments of genius will next year's contest bring forth? And what will you think up under pressure?" Entrants write in whatever setting they wish, in whatever genre they wish, anywhere in the world. Entrants may start writing as of midnight on Friday night, and must stop by midnight on Monday night. Then they print entry and mail it in to the contest for judging. Deadline: Friday before Labor Day weekend. Prize: 1st place receives publication; 2nd place receives $500; 3rd place receives $100.

THE IOWA SHORT FICTION AWARD

Iowa Writers' Workshop, 507 N. Clinton St., 102 Dey House, Iowa City IA 52242-1000. **Website:** www.uiowapress.org. **Contact:** Jim McCoy, director. Annual award to give exposure to promising writers who have not yet published a book of prose. Open to any writer. Current University of Iowa students are not eligible. No application forms are necessary. Announcement of winners made early in year following competition. Winners notified by phone. No application forms are necessary. Do not send original ms. Include SASE for return of ms. Entries must be unpublished, but stories previously published in periodicals are eligible for inclusion. The ms must be a collection of short stories of at least 150 word-processed, double-spaced pages. Deadline: September 30. Submission period: August 1-September 30. Packages must be postmarked by September 30. Prize: publication by University of Iowa Press Judged by senior Iowa Writers' Workshop members who screen mss; published fiction author of note makes final selections.

JERRY JAZZ MUSICIAN NEW SHORT FICTION AWARD

Jerry Jazz Musician, 2207 NE Broadway, Portland OR 97232. **E-mail:** jm@jerryjazz.com. **Website:** www.jerryjazz.com. Three times a year, *Jerry Jazz Musician* awards a writer who submits the best original, previously unpublished work of approximately 3,000-5,000 words. The winner will be announced via a mailing of the *Jerry Jazz* newsletter. Publishers, artists, musicians, and interested readers are among those who subscribe to the newsletter. Additionally, the work will be published on the home page of *Jerry Jazz Musician* and featured there for at least 4 weeks. The *Jerry Jazz Musician* reader tends to have interests in music, history, literature, art, film, and theater—particularly that of the counter-culture of mid-20th century America. Guidelines online. Deadline: September, January, and May. See website for specific dates. Prize: $100. Judged by the editors of *Jerry Jazz Musician*.

JESSE H. JONES AWARD FOR BEST WORK OF FICTION

P.O. Box 609, Round Rock TX 78680. **E-mail:** tilsecretary@yahoo.com. **Website:** texasinstituteofletters.org. Offered annually by Texas Institute of Letters for work published January 1-December 31 of year before award is given to recognize the writer of the best book of fiction entered in the competition. Writers must have been born in Texas, have lived in the state for at least 2 consecutive years at some time, or the subject matter of the work should be associated with the state. See website for details and information on submitting. Deadline: January 10. Prize: $6,000.

JAMES JONES FIRST NOVEL FELLOWSHIP

Wilkes University, Creative Writing Department, Wilkes University, 84 West South Street, Wilkes-Barre PA 18766. (570)408-4547. **Fax:** (570)408-3333. **E-mail:** Jamesjonesfirstnovel@wilkes.edu. **Website:** www.wilkes.edu/pages/1159.asp. Offered annually for unpublished novels, novellas, and closely-linked short stories (all works in progress). This competition is open to all American writers who have not previously published novels. Submit a 2-page (maximum) outline of the entire novel and the first 50 pages of the novel-in-progress are to be submitted. The ms must be typed and double-spaced; outline may be single-spaced. Entrants submitting via snail mail should include their name, address, telephone number and e-mail address (if available) on the title page, but nowhere else on the ms. For those entrants submitting online, name, address, telephone number and e-mail address should not appear anywhere on the ms. Pages should be numbered. The award is intended to honor the spirit of unblinking honesty, determination, and insight into modern culture exemplified by the late James Jones. Deadline: March 1. Submission period begins October 1. Prize: $10,000; 2 runners-up get $1,000 honorarium.

LITERAL LATTÉ FICTION AWARD

Literal Latté, 200 E. 10th St., Suite 240, New York NY 10003. (212)260-5532. **E-mail:** litlatte@aol.com. **Website:** www.literal-latte.com. **Contact:** Edward Estlin, contributing editor. Award to provide talented writers with 3 essential tools for continued success: money, publication, and recognition. Offered annually for unpublished fiction (maximum 10,000 words). Guidelines online. Open to any writer. Winners notified by phone. Winners announced in April. All winners published in *Literal Latté*. Deadline: January 15. Prize: 1st Place: $1,000 and publication in *Literal Latté*; 2nd Place: $300; 3rd Place: $200; also up to 7 honorable mentions.

LITERAL LATTE SHORT SHORTS CONTEST

Literal Latte, 200 E. 10th St., Suite 240, New York NY 10003. (212)260-5532. **E-mail:** litlatte@aol.com. **Website:** www.literal-latte.com. **Contact:** Jenine Gordon Bockman, editor. Annual contest. Send unpublished shorts. 2,000 words max. All styles welcome. Name, address, phone number, e-mail address (optional) on cover page only. Include SASE or e-mail address for reply. All entries considered for publication Deadline: June 30. Prize: $500. Judged by the editors.

THE MARY MACKEY SHORT STORY PRIZE CATEGORY

Soul-Making Keats Literary Competition, The Webhallow House, 1544 Sweetwood Dr., Broadmoor Village CA 94015. **E-mail:** SoulKeats@mail.com. **Website:** www.soulmakingcontest.us. **Contact:** Eileen Malone. Open annually to any writer. One story/entry, up to 5,000 words. All prose works must be typed, page numbered, and double-spaced. Identify only with 3x5 card. Deadline: November 30. Prize: Cash prizes.

THE MALAHAT REVIEW NOVELLA PRIZE

The Malahat Review, University of Victoria, P.O. Box 1700 STN CSC, Victoria BC V8W 2Y2 Canada. (250)721-8524. **E-mail:** malahat@uvic.ca. **E-mail:** novella@uvic.ca. **Website:** malahatreview.ca. **Contact:** John Barton, editor. Held in alternate years with the Long Poem Prize. Submit novellas between 10,000 and 20,000 words in length. Include separate page with author's name, address, e-mail, and novella ti-

tle; no identifying information on mss. pages. E-mail submissions are now accepted. Do not include SASE for results; mss will not be returned. Guidelines online.2010 winner was Tony Tulathimutte, 2012 winner was Naben Ruthnum. Winner and finalists contacted by e-mail. Offered to promote unpublished novellas. Obtains first world rights. After publication rights revert to the author. Open to any writer. Deadline: February 1 (even years). Prize: $1,500 CAD and one year's subscription. Winner published in summer issue of *The Malahat Review* and announced online, Facebook page, and in quarterly e-newsletter, *Malahat Lite*.

MARY MCCARTHY PRIZE IN SHORT FICTION

Sarabande Books, P.O. Box 4456, Louisville KY 40204. (502)458-4028. **Fax:** (502)458-4065. **E-mail:** info@sarabandebooks.org. **Website:** www.sarabandebooks.org. **Contact:** Kirby Gann, managing editor. Offered annually to publish an outstanding collection of stories, novellas, or a short novel (less than 250 pages). All finalists considered for publication. Deadline: January 1-February 14. Prize: $2,000 and publication (standard royalty contract).

MARJORIE GRABER MCINNIS SHORT STORY AWARD

ACT Writers Centre, Gorman House Arts Centre, Ainslie Ave., Braddon ACT 2612 Australia. (61)(2)6262-9191. **Fax:** (61)(2)6262-9191. **E-mail:** admin@actwriters.org.au. **Website:** www.actwriters.org.au. Open theme for a short story with 1,500-3,000 words. Guidelines online. Open only to unpublished emerging writers residing within the ACT or region. Deadline: September 25. Prize: $600 and publication. Five runners-up receive book prizes. All winners may be published in the ACT writers centre newsletter and on the ACT writers centre website.

DAVID NATHAN MEYERSON PRIZE FOR FICTION

Southwest Review, P.O. Box 750374, Dallas TX 75275-0374. (214) 768-1037. **Fax:** (214) 768-1408. **E-mail:** swr@smu.edu. **Website:** www.smu.edu/southwestreview. **Contact:** Jennifer Cranfill, senior editor. Annual award given to a writer who has not published a first book of fiction, either a novel or collection of stories. All contest entrants will receive a copy of the issue in which the winning piece appears. Submissions must be no longer than 8,000 words. Work should be printed without the author's name. Name and address should appear only on the cover letter. Submissions will not be returned. Deadline: May 1 (postmarked). Prize: $1,000 and publication in the *Southwest Review*. **TIPS** "A cover letter with name, address, and other relevant information may accompany the piece which must be printed without any identifying information. Get guidelines for SASE or online."

NATIONAL WRITERS ASSOCIATION NOVEL WRITING CONTEST

The National Writers Association, 10940 S. Parker Rd. #508, Parker CO 80134. (303)841-0246. **E-mail:** natlwritersassn@hotmail.com. **Website:** www.nationalwriters.com. **Contact:** Sandy Whelchel, director. Open to any genre or category. Contest begins December 1. Open to any writer. Entries must be unpublished. Length: 20,000-100,000 words. Contest forms are available on the NWA website or an attachment will be sent upon request via e-mail or with an SASE. Annual contest to help develop creative skills, to recognize and reward outstanding ability, and to increase the opportunity for the marketing and subsequent publication of novel mss. Deadline: April 1. Prize: 1st Place: $500; 2nd Place: $250; 3rd Place: $150. Judged by editors and agents.

NATIONAL WRITERS ASSOCIATION SHORT STORY CONTEST

10940 S. Parker Rd., #508, Parker CO 80134. (303)841-0246. **E-mail:** natlwritersassn@hotmail.com. **Website:** www.nationalwriters.com. Opens April 1. Any genre of short story ms may be entered. All entries must be postmarked by July 1. Only unpublished works may be submitted. All mss must be typed, double-spaced, in the English language. Maximum length is 5,000 words. Those unsure of proper ms format should request Research Report #35. The entry must be accompanied by an entry form (photocopies are acceptable) and return SASE if you wish the material and rating sheets returned. Submissions will be destroyed, otherwise. The U.S. Postal Service will not allow us to use your metered postage unless it is undated. Receipt of entry will not be acknowledged without a return postcard. Author's name and address must appear on the first page. Entries remain the property of the author and may be submitted during the contest as long as they are not published before the final notification of winners. Final prizes will be awarded at the NWAF Workshop in June. The purpose of the National Writers Assn. Short Story Contest is to encourage the development of creative skills, recognize and reward outstanding ability in the area of short story writing. Prize: 1st - 5th place awards will be presented at the NWAF Conference. 1st Prize: $250; 2nd Prize: $100; 3rd Prize: $50; 4th - 10th places will receive a book. 1st - 3rd place winners may be asked to grant one-time rights for publication in *Authorship* magazine. Honorable Mentions receive a certificate. Judging will be based on originality, marketability, research, and reader interest. Copies of the judges evaluation sheets will be sent to entrants furnishing an SASE with their entry.

THE NELLIGAN PRIZE FOR SHORT FICTION

Colorado Review/Center for Literary Publishing, 9105 Campus Delivery, Dept. of English, Colorado State University, Ft. Collins CO 80523-9105. (970)491-5449. **E-mail:** creview@colostate.edu. **Website:** nelliganprize.colostate.edu. **Contact:** Stephanie G'Schwind, editor. Annual competition/award for short stories. Receives approximately 900 stories. All entries are read blind by Colorado Review's editorial staff. 10-15 entries are selected to be sent on to a final judge. "The Nelligan Prize for Short Fiction was established in memory of Liza Nelligan, a writer, editor, and friend of many in Colorado State University's English Department, where she received her master's degree in literature in 1992. By giving an award to the author of an outstanding short story each year, we hope to honor Liza Nelligan's life, her passion for writing, and her love of fiction." Deadline: March 12. Prize: $2,000 and publication of story in *Colorado Review*.

FRANK O'CONNOR AWARD FOR SHORT FICTION

descant, Texas Christian University's literary journal, TCU Box 298300, Fort Worth TX 76129. (817)257-5907. **Fax:** (817)257-6239. **E-mail:** descant@tcu.edu. **Website:** www.descant.tcu.edu. **Contact:** Dan Williams and Alex Lemon, editors. Offered annually for unpublished short stories. Publication retains copyright but will transfer it to the author upon request. Deadline: September-March. Prize: $500.

THE FLANNERY O'CONNOR AWARD FOR SHORT FICTION

The University of Georgia Press, Main Library, 3rd Floor, 320 S. Jackson St., Athens GA 30602. (706)369-6130. **Fax:** (706)369-6131. **Website:** www.ugapress.org. This competition welcomes short story or novella collections. Stories may have been published singly, but should not have appeared in a book-length collection of the author's own work. Length: 40,000-75,000 words. Accepts electronic submissions via website. Accepts multiple submissions, and simultaneous submissions, if identified. Title, author's name, and contact information should appear on a top cover sheet only. Include a table of contents. All submissions and announcement of winners and finalists will be confirmed via e-mail. Deadline: April 1-May 31. Prize: 2 winners receive $1,000 and book contracts from the University of Georgia Press.

ON THE PREMISES CONTEST

On The Premises, LLC, 4323 Gingham Court, Alexandria VA 22310. (202) 262-2168. **E-mail:** questions@onthepremises.com. **Website:** www.onthepremises.com. **Contact:** Tarl Roger Kudrick or Bethany Granger, copublishers. *On the Premises* aims to promote newer and/or relatively unknown writers who can write creative, compelling stories told in effective, uncluttered and evocative prose. Each contest challenges writers to produce a great story based on a broad premise that the editors supply as part of the contest. Submissions are accepted via the web, only. Entries should be unpublished. Length: minimum 1,000 words; maximum 5,000. No name or contact info should be in ms. Writers may submit own work. Check website for details on the specific premise that writers should incorporate into their story. Results announced within 2 weeks of contest deadline. Winners notified via newsletter and with publication of *On the Premises.* Results made available to entrants online and in publication. Deadline: Contests held every four months, check website for exact dates. Prize: 1st Prize: $180; 2nd Prize: $140; 3rd Prize: $100; Honorable Mentions recieve $40. All prize winners are published in *On the Premises* magazine in HTML and PDF format. Judged by a panel of judges with professional editing and writing experience.
TIPS "Write something compelling, creative, and well-crafted. Above all, clearly use the contest premise."

✚ KENNETH PATCHEN AWARD FOR THE INNOVATIVE NOVEL

Eckhard Gerdes Publishing, 12 Simpson Street, Apt. D, Geneva IL 60134. **E-mail:** egerdes@experimentalfiction.com. **Website:** www.experimentalfiction.com. **Contact:** Eckhard Gerdes. This award will honor the most innovative novel submitted during the previous calendar year. Kenneth Patchen is celebrated for being among the greatest innovators of American fiction, incorporating strategies of concretism, asemic writing, digression, and verbal juxtaposition into his writing long before such strategies were popularized during the height of American postmodernist experimentation in the 1970s. See guidelines and application form online at website. Deadline: All submissions must be postmarked between January 1 and July 31. Prize: $1,000, 20 complimentary copies. Judged by novelist James Chapman.

THE PATERSON FICTION PRIZE

The Poetry Center at Passaic Community College, One College Blvd., Paterson NJ 07505. (973)684-6555. **Fax:** (973)523-6085. **E-mail:** mgillan@pccc.edu. **Website:** www.pccc.edu/poetry. **Contact:** Maria Mazziotti Gillan, executive director. Offered annually for a novel or collection of short fiction published the previous calendar year. For more information, visit the website or send SASE. Deadline: April 1. Prize: $1,000.

PEARL SHORT STORY PRIZE

3030 E. Second St., Long Beach CA 90803. (562)434-4523. **E-mail:** Pearlmag@aol.com. **Website:** www.pearlmag.com. **Contact:** Marilyn Johnson, fiction editor. Award to provide a larger forum and help widen publishing opportunities for fiction writers in the small press and to help support the continuing publication of *Pearl*. Include a brief bio and SASE for reply or return of mss. Accepts simultaneous submissions, but asks to be notified if story is accepted elsewhere. Entries must be unpublished. Length: 4,000 words maximum. Open to any writer. Guidelines for SASE or online. Accepts queries by e-mail or fax. Results announced in September. Winners notified by mail. For contest results, send SASE, e-mail, or visit website. Submission period: April 1-May 31. Prize: $250, publication in *Pearl* and 10 copies of the journal. Judged by the editors of *Pearl*: Marilyn Johnson and Joan Jobe Smith.
TIPS "Although we are open to all types of fiction, we look most favorably on coherent, well-crafted narratives containing interesting, believable characters in meaningful situations."

WILLIAM PEDEN PRIZE IN FICTION

The Missouri Review, 357 McReynolds Hall, Columbia MO 65211. (573)882-4474. **Fax:** (573)884-4671. **E-mail:** mutmrcontestquestion@moreview.com. **Web-**

site: www.missourireview.com. **Contact:** Michael Nye, managing editor. Offered annually for the best story published in the past volume year of the magazine. All stories published in *The Missouri Review* are automatically considered. Guidelines online or for SASE. Prize: $1,000 and a reading/reception.

EDGAR ALLAN POE AWARD

1140 Broadway, Suite 1507, New York NY 10001. (212)888-8171. **Fax:** (212)888-8107. **E-mail:** mwa@mysterywriters.org. **Website:** www.mysterywriters.org. Mystery Writers of America is the leading association for professional crime writers in the United States. Members of MWA include most major writers of crime fiction and nonfiction, as well as screenwriters, dramatists, editors, publishers, and other professionals in the field. Purpose of the award: Honor authors of distinguished works in the mystery field. Previously published submissions only. Submissions made by the author, author's agent; "normally by the publisher." Work must be published/produced the year of the contest. Deadline: November 30. Prize: Awards ceramic bust of "Edgar" for winner; scrolls for all nominees. Judged by professional members of Mystery Writers of America (writers).

THE KATHERINE ANNE PORTER PRIZE FOR FICTION

Nimrod International Journal, The University of Tulsa, 800 S. Tucker Dr., Tulsa OK 74104. (918)631-3080. **Fax:** (918)631-3033. **E-mail:** nimrod@utulsa.edu. **Website:** www.utulsa.edu/nimrod. **Contact:** Eilis O'Neal. Submissions must be unpublished. Work must be in English or translated by original author. Author's name must not appear on ms. Include cover sheet with title, author's name, address, phone number, and e-mail address (author must have a US address by October of contest year to enter). Mark "Contest Entry" on submission envelop and cover sheet. Include SASE for results only; mss will not be returned. Guidelines available for #10 SASE or online. 7,500-word maximum for short stories. Deadline: April 30. Prize: Prizes: 1st Place: $2,000 and publication; 2nd Place: $1,000 and publication. Judged by the *Nimrod* editors, who select the finalists and a recognized author, who selects the winners.

⊕ PRESS 53 AWARD FOR SHORT FICTION

Press 53, 411 W. Fourth St., Suite 101A, Winston-Salem NC 27101. **E-mail:** kevin@press53.com. **Website:** www.press53.com. **Contact:** Kevin Morgan Watson, publisher. Awarded to an outstanding, unpublished collection of short stories. Details and guidelines online. Deadline: December 31. Submission period begins September 1. Finalists announced March 1. Winner announced on May 3. Publication in October. Prize: Publication of winning short story collection, $1,000 cash advance, travel expenses and lodging for a special reading and book signing in Winston-Salem, NC, attendance as special guest to the Press 53/*Prime Number Magazine* Gathering of Writers, and 10 copies of the book. Judged by publisher Kevin Morgan and fiction editor Christine Norris.

○ THOMAS H. RADDALL ATLANTIC FICTION AWARD

Writers' Federation of Nova Scotia, 1113 Marginal Rd., Halifax NS B3H 4P7 Canada. (902)423-8116. **Fax:** (902)422-0881. **E-mail:** director@writers.ns.ca. **Website:** www.writers.ns.ca. **Contact:** Nate Crawford, executive director. The Thomas Head Raddall Atlantic Fiction Award is awarded for a novel or a book of short fiction by a full-time resident of Atlantic Canada. Detailed guidelines and eligibility criteria online. Deadline: First Friday in December. Prize: Valued at $25,000 for winning title.

HAROLD U. RIBALOW PRIZE

Hadassah WZOA, 50 W. 58th St., New York NY 10019. (212)451-6286. **Fax:** (212)451-6257. **E-mail:** magtemp3@hadassah.org; atigay@hadassah.org. **Website:** www.hadassah.org/. **Contact:** Deb Meisels, coordinator. Offered annually for English-language books of fiction (novel or short stories) on a Jewish theme published the previous year. Books should be submitted by the publisher. Administered annually by *Hadassah Magazine*. Deadline: Aoril 1. Prize: $3,000. The official announcement of the winner will be made in thefall.

○ THE ROGERS WRITERS' TRUST FICTION PRIZE

The Writers' Trust of Canada, 460 Richmond St. W., Suite 600, Toronto ON M5V 1Y1 Canada. (416)504-8222. **Fax:** (416)504-9090. **E-mail:** info@writerstrust.com. **Website:** www.writerstrust.com. **Contact:** Amanda Hopkins. Awarded annually for a distinguished work of fiction—either a novel or short story collection—published within the previous year. Presented at the Writers' Trust Awards event held in Toronto each fall. Open to Canadian citizens and permanent residents only. Deadline: August. Prize: $25,000 and $2,500 to 4 finalists.

JOANNA CATHERINE SCOTT NOVEL EXCERPT PRIZE CATEGORY

Soul-Making Keats Literary Competition Category, The Webhallow House, 1544 Sweetwood Dr., Broadmoor Village CA 94015-2029. **E-mail:** soulkeats@mail.com. **Website:** www.soulmakingcontest.us. **Contact:** Eileen Malone. Open annually to any writer. Send first chapter or the first 20 pages, whichever comes first. Include a 1-page synopsis indicating category at top of page. Identify with 3x5 card only. Deadline: November 30. Prize: 1st Place: $100; 2nd Place: $50; 3rd Place: $25.

✛ SCREAMINMAMAS MAGICAL FICTION CONTEST

1911 Cleveland St., Hollywood FL 33020. **E-mail:** screaminmamas@gmail.com. **Website:** www.screaminmamas.com/contests. **Contact:** Darlene Pistocchi, editor/managing director. "The contest celebrates moms and the magical spirit of the holidays. If you had an opportunity to be anything you wanted to be, what would you be? Transport yourself! Become that character and write a short story around that character. Can be any genre." Length: 800-3,000 words. Open only to moms. Deadline: June 30. Prize: $40, publication.

✛ SCREAMINMAMAS MAGICAL FICTION CONTEST

1911 Cleveland St., Hollywood FL 33020. **E-mail:** screaminmamas@gmail.com. **Website:** www.screaminmamas.com/contests. **Contact:** Darlene Pistocchi, editor/managing director. "Looking for light romantic comedy. Can be historical or contemporary—something to lift the spirits and celebrate the gift of innocent romance that might be found in the everyday life of a busy mom." Length: 800-2,000 words. Open only to moms. Deadline: June 30. Prize: $40, publication.

MICHAEL SHAARA AWARD FOR EXCELLENCE IN CIVIL WAR FICTION

Civil War Institute at Gettysburg College, 300 N. Washington St., Campus Box 435, Gettysburg PA 17325. (717)337-6574. **Fax:** (717)337-6596. **E-mail:** civilwar@gettysburg.edu. **Website:** www.gettysburg.edu/cwi. **Contact:** Diane Brennan, administrative assistant. Offered annually for fiction published for the first time, in January 1-December 31 of the year of the award, to encourage examination of the Civil War from unique perspectives or by taking an unusual approach. All Civil War novels are eligible. To nominate a novel, send 4 copies of the novel to the address above with a cover letter. Nominations should be made by publishers, but authors and critics can nominate as well. Any novel about the Civil War published (for the first time) in the current calendar year to "encourage fresh approaches to Civil War fiction" is eligible. Self-published books are not eligible. This includes books printed and bound by a company hired and paid by the author to publish his/her work in book form. Deadline: December 31. Prize: $5,000.

THREE CHEERS AND A TIGER

E-mail: editors@toasted-cheese.com. **Website:** www.toasted-cheese.com. **Contact:** Stephanie Lenz, editor. Contestants are to write a short story (following a specific theme) within 48 hours. Contests are held first weekend in spring (mystery) and first weekend in fall (sf/f). Word limit announced at the start of the contest. Contest-specific information is announced 48 hours before the contest submission deadline. Results announced in April and October. Winners notified by e-mail. List of winners online. Entries must be unpublished. Open to any writer. Accepts inquiries by e-mail. Cover letter should include name, address, e-mail, word count and title. Information should be in the body of the e-mail. It will be removed before the judging begins. Prize: Amazon gift certificates and publication. Blind-judged by 2 *Toasted Cheese* editors. Each judge uses his or her own criteria to choose entries.

TIPS "Follow the theme, word count and other contest rules. We have more suggestions at our website."

WASSNODE SHORT FICTION PRIZE

Passages North, Department of English, Northern Michigan University, 1401 Presque Isle Ave., Marquette MI 49855. (906)227-1203. **Fax:** (906)227-1096. **E-mail:** passages@nmu.edu. **Website:** www.passagesnorth.com. **Contact:** Jennifer Howard. Offered every 2 years to publish new voices in literary fiction (maximum 7,500 words). Guidelines for SASE or online. Submissions accepted online Deadline: February 15. Submission period begins January 15. Prize: $1,000 and publication for winner; 2 honorable mentions are also published; all entrants receive a copy of *Passages North*.

GARY WILSON SHORT FICTION AWARD

descant, Texas Christian University's literary journal, TCU, TCU Box 298300, Fort Worth TX 76129. (817)257-5907. **Fax:** (817)257-6239. **E-mail:** descant@tcu.edu. **Website:** www.descant.tcu.edu. **Contact:** Dan Williams and Alex Lemon, editors. Offered annually for an outstanding story in an issue. Prize: $250.

TOBIAS WOLFF AWARD IN FICTION

Bellingham Review, Mail Stop 9053, Western Washington University, Bellingham WA 98225. (360)650-4863. **E-mail:** bhreview@wwu.edu. **Website:** www.bhreview.org. **Contact:** Brenda Miller. Offered annually for unpublished work. Guidelines online; online submissions only. Categories: novel exceprts and short stories. Entries must be unpublished. Length: 6,000 words or less per story or chapter. Open to any writer. Electronic submissions only. Enter submissions through Submittable, a link to which is available on the website. Winner announced in August and notified by e-mail. Deadline: Contest runs December 1 - March 15. Prize: $1,000, plus publication and subscription.

WORLD FANTASY AWARDS

P.O. Box 43, Mukilteo WA 98275. **E-mail:** sfexecsec@gmail.com. **Website:** www.worldfantasy.org. **Contact:** Peter Dennis Pautz, president. Offered annually for previously published work in several categories, including life achievement, novel, novella, short story, anthology, collection, artist, special award-pro and special award-nonpro. Works are recommended by attendees of current and previous 2 years' conventions and a panel of judges. Entries must be previously published. Published submissions from previous calendar year. Word length: 10,000-40,000 for novella, 10,000 for short story. All fantasy is eligible, from supernatural horror to Tolkien-esque to sword and sorcery to the occult, and beyond. Cover letter should include name, address, phone, e-mail, word count, title, and publications where submission was previously published, submitted to the address above and the panel of judges when they appear on the website. Results announced November 1 at annual convention. For contest results, visit website. Guidelines available in December for SASE or online. Awards to recognize excellence in fantasy literature worldwide. Deadline: June 1. Prize: Bust of H.P. Lovecraft. Judged by panel.

WOW! WOMEN ON WRITING QUARTERLY FLASH FICTION CONTEST

WOW! Women on Writing, P.O. Box 41104, Long Beach CA 90853. **E-mail:** contestinfo@wow-womenonwriting.com. **Website:** www.wow-womenonwriting.com/contest.php. **Contact:** Angela Mackintosh, editor. Contest offered quarterly. "We are open to all themes and genres, although we do encourage writers to take a close look at our literary agent guest judge for the season if you are serious about winning." Entries must be 250-750 words. Deadline: August 31, November 30, February 28, May 31. Prize: **1st place:** $350 cash prize, $25 Amazon gift certificate, book from sponsor, story published on WOW! Women On Writing, interview on blog; **2nd place:** $250 cash prize, $25 Amazon gift certificate, book our sponsor, story published on WOW! Women On Writing, interview on blog; **3rd place:** $150 cash prize, $25 Amazon gift certificate, book from sponsor, story published on WOW! Women On Writing, interview on blog; **7 runners up:** $25 Amazon gift certificate, book from sponsor, story published on WOW! Women on Writing, interview on blog; **10 honorable mentions:** $20 gift certificate from Amazon, book our sponsor, story title and name published on WOW!Women On Writing.

WRITER'S DIGEST SHORT SHORT STORY COMPETITION

Writer's Digest, 10151 Carver Road, Suite 200, Blue Ash OH 45242. (715)445-4612; ext. 13430. **E-mail:** WritersDigestShortShortStoryCompetition@fwmedia.com. **Website:** www.writersdigest.com. **Contact:** Nicole Howard. Looking for fiction that's bold, brilliant, and brief. Send your best in 1,500 words or fewer. All entries must be original, unpublished, and not submitted elsewhere at the time of submission. *Writer's Digest* reserves one-time publication rights to the 1st-25th winning entries. Winners will be notified by Feb. 28. Early bird deadline: November 17. Extended deadline: December 15. Prize: 1st Place: $3,000 and a trip to Writer's Digest Conference; 2nd Place: $1,500; 3rd Place: $500; 4th-10th Place: $100; 11th-25th Place: $50 gift certificate for Writer's Digest Books.

NONFICTION

AMERICA & ME ESSAY CONTEST

P.O. Box 30400, 7373 W. Saginaw Hwy., Lansing MI 48917. **E-mail:** lfedewa@fbinsmi.com. **Website:** https://www.farmbureauinsurance-mi.com/About_

Us/Corporate_And_Social_Responsibility/America_And_Me/. Focuses on encouraging students to write about their personal Michigan heroes: someone they know personally who has encouraged them and inspired them to want to live better and achieve more. Open to Michigan eighth graders. Contest rules and entry form online. Encourages Michigan youth to explore their roles in America's future. Deadline: November 15. Prize: $1,000, plaque, and medallion for top 10 winners.

ANTHEM ESSAY CONTEST

The Ayn Rand Institute, P.O. Box 57044, Irvine CA 92619-7044. (949)222-6550. **Fax:** (949)222-6558. **E-mail:** essay@aynrand.org. **Website:** www.aynrand.org/contests. Offered annually to encourage analytical thinking and excellence in writing (600-1,200 word essay), and to expose students to the philosophic ideas of Ayn Rand. "For information contact your English teacher or guidance counselor or visit our website." Open to 8th, 9th and 10th graders. Deadline: March 20. Prize: 1st Place: $2,000; 2nd Place (5): $500; 3rd Place (10): $200; Finalist (45): $50; Semifinalist (175): $30.

THE ASCAP DEEMS TAYLOR AWARDS

American Society of Composers, Authors & Publishers, One Lincoln Plaza, New York NY 10023. (212)621-6318. **E-mail:** jsteinblatt@ascap.com. **Website:** www.ascap.com. **Contact:** Jim Steinblatt. The ASCAP Deems Taylor Awards program recognizes books, articles, broadcasts, and websites on the subject of music selected for their excellence. Written works must be published in the U.S. in English, during the calendar year of the awards. The subject matter may be biographical or critical, reportorial or historical—almost any form of nonfiction prose about music and/or its creators. However, instructional textbooks, how-to-guides, or works of fiction will not be accepted. Honors the memory of composer/critic/commentator Deems Taylor. Deadline: May 31. Submission period begins February 1. Prize: Several categories of cash prizes are presented to writers of award-winning books and newspaper, journal, or magazine articles (includes program notes, liner notes and on-line publications). Awards are also presented to the authors and journalists as well as to their respective publishers.

ATLAS SHRUGGED ESSAY CONTEST

The Ayn Rand Institute, P.O. Box 57044, Irvine CA 92619-7044. (949)222-6550, ext. 247. **Fax:** (949)222-6558. **E-mail:** essay@aynrand.org. **Website:** www.aynrand.org/contests. Offered annually to encourage analytical thinking and excellence in writing, and to expose students to the philosophic ideas of Ayn Rand. Open to 12th graders and college undergraduate and graduate students. Essay length: 800-1,600 words. Essays are judged both on style and content. Guidelines on the website. The winning applicant will be judged on both style and content. Judges will look for writing that is clear, articulate and logically organized. Winning essays must demonstrate an outstanding grasp of the philosophic meaning of *Atlas Shrugged*. Essay submissions are evaluated in a fair and unbiased four-round judging process. Judges are individually selected by the Ayn Rand Institute based on a demonstrated knowledge and understanding of Ayn Rand's works. Deadline: October 24. Prize: Prizes: 1st Place: $10,000; 2nd Place (3 awards): $2,000; 3rd Place (5 awards): $1,000; Finalists (25 awards): $100; Semifinalists (50 awards): $50.

BANCROFT PRIZE

Columbia University, c/o Office of the University Librarian, 517 Butter Library, Mail Code 1101, 535 W. 114th St., New York NY 10027. (212)854-7309. **Fax:** (212)854-9099. **Website:** library.columbia.edu/subject-guides/amerihist/bancroft.html. **Contact:** Bancroft Prize Committee. The Bancroft Prizes are awarded annually by Columbia University in the City of New York. Two annual prizes are awarded to the authors of distinguished works in either or both of the following categories: American History (including biography) and Diplomacy. Awards are for books published in the previous year. Send 4 copies, 3 for the members of the jury on the award and 1 for the Libraries of Columbia University. Deadline: November 1. Prize: $10,000 for the winning entry in each category.

🔄 BRITISH CZECH AND SLOVAK ASSOCIATION WRITING COMPETITION

24 Ferndale, Tunbridge Wells Kent TN2 3NS England. **E-mail:** prize@bcsa.co.uk. **Website:** www.bcsa.co.uk/specials.html. Annual contest for original writing (1,500-2,000 words) in English on the links between Britain and the Czech/Slovak Republics, or describing society in transition in the Republics since 1989. Entries can be fact or fiction. Topics can include his-

tory, politics, the sciences, economics, the arts, or literature. Deadline: June 30. Winners announced in November. Prize: 1st Place: £300; 2nd Place: £100.

CANADIAN AUTHORS ASSOCIATION AWARD FOR CANADIAN HISTORY

6 West St. N, Suite 203, Orillia ON L3V 5B8 Canada. (705)325-3926. **E-mail:** admin@canadianauthors.org. **Website:** www.canadianauthors.org. **Contact:** Anita Purcell. Offered annually for a work of historical nonfiction on a Canadian topic by a Canadian author. Entry form required. Obtain entry form from contact name or download from website. Deadline: January 15. Prize: $2,000 and a silver medal. The CAA Awards Chair appoints a trustee for this award. That trustee selects two judges. The identities of the trustee and judges are confidential throughout the judging process. Decisions of the trustee and judges are final, and they may choose not to award a prize. A shortlist of the best three entries in each category is announced in June. The winners are announced at the gala awards banquet during the annual CanWrite! conference in June.

CANADIAN LIBRARY ASSOCIATION STUDENT ARTICLE CONTEST

Canadian Library Association, 1150 Morrison Dr., Suite 400, Ottawa ON K2H 8S9 Canada. (613)232-9625, ext. 322. **Fax:** (613)563-9895. **E-mail:** info@cla.ca. **Website:** www.cla.ca. **Contact:** Judy Green. Offered annually to unpublished articles discussing, analyzing, or evaluating timely issues in librarianship or information science. Open to all students registered in or recently graduated from a Canadian library school, a library techniques program, or faculty of education library program. Submissions may be in English or French. Deadline: March 31. Prize: $200 and the winning article will be published in *Feliciter*, the magazine of the Canadian Library Association.

THE DOROTHY CHURCHILL CAPPON CREATIVE NONFICTION AWARD

New Letters, University of Missouri-Kansas City, 5101 Rockhill Rd., Kansas City MO 64110. (816)235-1168. **Fax:** (816)235-2611. **E-mail:** newletters@umkc.edu. **Website:** www.newsletters.org. **Contact:** Ashley Kaine. Contest is offered annually for unpublished work to discover and reward emerging writers and to give experienced writers a place to try new genres. Acquires first North American serial rights. Open to any writer. Guidelines by SASE or online. Deadline:

May 18. Prize: 1st Place: $1,500 and publication in a volume of *New Letters*; runner-up will receive a copy of a recent book of poetry or fiction courtesy of BkMk Press. All entries will receive consideration for publication in future editions of *New Letters*.

MORTON N. COHEN AWARD

Modern Language Association of America, 26 Broadway, 3rd Floor, New York NY 10004-1789. (646)576-5141. **Fax:** (646)458-0030. **E-mail:** awards@mla.org. **Website:** www.mla.org. **Contact:** Coordinator of Book Prizes. Awarded in odd-numbered years for a distinguished collection of letters. At least 1 volume of the edition must have been published during the previous 2 years. Editors need not be members of the MLA. Under the terms of the award, the winning collection will be one that provides readers with a clear, accurate, and readable text; necessary background information; and succinct and eloquent introductory material and annotations. The edited collection should be in itself a work of literature. Deadline: May 1. Prize: A cash award and a certificate to be presented at the Modern Language Association's annual convention in January.

THE SHAUGHNESSY COHEN PRIZE FOR POLITICAL WRITING

The Writers' Trust of Canada, 460 Richmond St. W., Suite 600, Toronto ON M5V 1Y1 Canada. (416)504-8222. **Fax:** (416)504-9090. **E-mail:** info@writerstrust.com. **Website:** www.writerstrust.com. **Contact:** Amanda Hopkins. Awarded annually for a nonfiction book of outstanding literary merit that enlarges understanding of contemporary Canadian political and social issues. Presented at the Politics & the Pen event each spring in Ottawa. Open to Canadian citizens and permanent residents only. Prize: $25,000 and $2,500 to 4 finalists.

CARR P. COLLINS AWARD FOR NONFICTION

The Texas Institute of Letters, P.O. Box 609, Round Rock TX 78680. **E-mail:** tilsecretary@yahoo.com. **Website:** texasinstituteofletters.org/. Offered annually for work published January 1-December 31 of the previous year to recognize the best nonfiction book by a writer who was born in Texas, who has lived in the state for at least 2 consecutive years at one point, or a writer whose work has some notable connection with Texas. See website for guidelines and instructions on submitting. Deadline: January 10. Prize: $5,000.

☺ CREATIVE NONFICTION CONTEST

PRISM international, Creative Writing Program, UBC, Buch E462—1866 Main Mall, Vancouver BC V6T 1Z1 Canada. **E-mail:** prismwritingcontest@gmail.com. **Website:** www.prismmagazine.ca. Offered annually for published and unpublished writers to promote and reward excellence in literary nonfiction writing. *PRISM* buys first North American serial rights upon publication. Also buys limited Web rights for pieces selected for the website. Open to anyone except students and faculty of the Creative Writing Program at UBC or people who have taken a creative writing course at UBC in the 2 years prior to contest deadline. All entrants receive a 1-year subscription to *PRISM*. Guidelines for SASE (Canadian postage only), via e-mail, or visit the website. Deadline: November 28. Prize: $1,500 grand prize, $300 runner-up, and $200 second runner-up.

DIAGRAM ESSAY CONTEST

Department of English, University of Arizona, P.O. Box 210067, Tucson AZ 85721-0067. **E-mail:** nmp@thediagram.com; editor@thediagram.com. **Website:** www.thediagram.com/contest.html. **Contact:** Ander Monson, editor. Contest for essays up to 10,000 words. Deadline: End of October. Check website for more details. Prize: $1,000 and publication. Finalist essay also published. Judged by Ander Monson and Nicole Walker.

GORDON W. DILLON/RICHARD C. PETERSON MEMORIAL ESSAY PRIZE

American Orchid Society, Inc., American Orchid Society, 10901 Old Cutler Rd., Coral Gables FL 33156. (305)740-2010. **Fax:** (305)740-2011. **E-mail:** theaos@aos.org. **E-mail:** rmchatton@aos.org. **Website:** www.aos.org. **Contact:** Jim Watson, Editor, *Orchids*. The Gordon W. Dillon\Richard C. Peterson Memorial Essay Prize is an annual writing competition. Open to amateur and professional writers. The theme is announced each May in *Orchids* magazine. All themes deal with an aspect of orchids. Acquires one-time rights. The essay must be an original, unpublished article. Submissions must be no more than 5,000 words in length. Submissions will be judged without knowledge of the identity of the author. Established to honor the memory of two former editors of the *AOS Bulletin* (now *Orchids*). Deadline: November 30. Prize: Cash award and a certificate. Winning entry usually published in the June issue of *Orchids* magazine.

☺ THE DONNER PRIZE

The Award for Best Book on Public Policy by a Canadian, The Donner Canadian Foundation, 400 Logan Ave., Toronto ON M4M 2N9 Canada. (416)368-8253. **E-mail:** sherry@naylorandassociates.com. **Website:** www.donnerbookprize.com. **Contact:** Sherry Naylor. Offered annually for nonfiction published January 1-December 31 that highlights the importance of public policy and to reward excellent work in this field. Entries must be published in either English or French. Open to Canadian citizens. Deadline: November 30. Prize: Winning book receives $50,000; shortlisted titles get $7,500 each.

EDUCATOR'S AWARD

The Delta Kappa Gamma Society International, P.O. Box 1589, Austin TX 78767-1589. (888)762-4685. **Fax:** (512)478-3961. **Website:** www.dkg.org. **Contact:** Kathy Flynn, chair; Dr. Linda Eller, society headquarters. Offered annually for quality research and nonfiction published January-December of previous year. This award recognizes educational research and writings of female authors whose work may influence the direction of thought and action necessary to meet the needs of today's complex society. The book must be written by 1 or 2 women who are citizens of any country in which The Delta Kappa Gamma Society International is organized: Canada, Costa Rica, Denmark, Estonia, Finland, Germany, Great Britain, Guatemala, Iceland, Mexico, The Netherlands, Norway, Puerto Rico, Sweden, US, Panama. Guidelines (required) for SASE. The Educators Award Committee is charged with the responsibility of selecting an appropriate book as winner of the annual Educator's Award. Committee members read and evaluate books submitted by publishers that meet the criteria of having been written by women and whose content may influence the direction of thought and action necessary to meet the needs of today's complex society; furthermore, the content must be of more than local interest with relationship, direct or implied, to education everywhere. Deadline: February 1. Prize: $2,500. Judged by Educators Award Committee.

EVANS BIOGRAPHY & HANDCART AWARDS

Mountain West Center for Regional Studies, Room 339, Old Main, 0735 Old Main Hill, Utah State University, Logan UT 84322-0735. (435)797-0299. **Fax:** (435)797-1092. **E-mail:** mwc@usu.edu. **Website:**

mountainwest.usu.edu/evans.aspx. **Contact:** Patricia Lambert, director. The Evans Biography and Handcart Awards encourage the best in research and writing about the Interior West through the giving of two annual prizes for excellence in biography. The Evans Biography Award is given to the best biography of a person who lived a significant portion of his or her life in the Interior West, or, in the words of the awards' founders, "Mormon Country" - that region historically influenced by Mormon institutions and social practices. The Evans Handcart Award is given to a biography addressing similar subjects as the Evans Biography Award, but often by an emerging author or written as a family history. Send 6 copies of the book and one copy of the author's resume. See website for details. Deadline: January 1 for books published in the previous calendar years. Prize: $10,000 for the Evans Biography Award; and $2,500 for the Evans Handcart Award. Judged by a local jury of five scholars and book experts.

☼ EVENT NONFICTION CONTEST

EVENT, Poetry and Prose., P.O. Box 2503, New Westminster BC V3L 5B2 Canada. (604)527-5293. **Fax:** (604)527-5095. **E-mail:** event@douglascollege. ca. **Website:** eventmags.com. Offered annually for unpublished creative nonfiction. Maximum length: 5,000 words. Acquires first North American serial print rights and limited non-exclusive digital rights for the winning entries. Open to any writer, except Douglas College employees and students. Previously published material, including that which has appeared online or has been accepted for publication elsewhere, cannot be considered. No simultaneous submissions. The writer should not be identified on the entry. Include separate cover sheet with name, address, phone number/e-mail, and title(s). Enter online or send to address above. Multiple entries are allowed; however, each entry must be accompanied by its own entry fee. Pay online or make check or international money order payable to EVENT. Deadline: April 15. Prize: Judges reserve the right to award 2 or 3 prizes: 3 at $500 or 2 at $750, plus publication payment.

DINA FEITELSON RESEARCH AWARD

International Reading Association, Division of Research & Policy, 800 Barksdale Rd., Newark DE 19714-8139. (302)731-1600, ext. 423. **Fax:** (302)731-1057. **E-mail:** research@reading.org. **Website:** www.reading. org. **Contact:** Marcella Moore. This is an award for an exemplary work published in English in a refereed journal that reports on an empirical study investigating aspects of literacy acquisition, such as phonemic awareness, the alphabetic principle, bilingualism, or cross-cultural studies of beginning reading. Articles may be submitted for consideration by researchers, authors, et al. Copies of the applications and guidelines can be downloaded in PDF format from the website. Deadline: September 1. Prize: Monetary award and recognition at the International Reading Association's annual convention.

☼ GOVERNOR GENERAL'S LITERARY AWARD FOR LITERARY NONFICTION

Canada Council for the Arts, 150 Elgin St., P.O. Box 1047, Ottawa ON K1P 5V8 Canada. (613)566-4414, ext. 5573. **Website:** www.canadacouncil.ca/prizes/ ggla. **Contact:** Lori Knoll. Offered annually for the best English-language and the best French-language work of literary nonfiction by a Canadian. Deadline: Depends on the book's publication date: Books in English: March 15, June 1 or August 7. Books in French: March 15 or July 15. Prize: Each laureate receives $25,000; non-winning finalists receive $1,000.

JOHN GUYON LITERARY NONFICTION PRIZE

Crab Orchard Review, Department of English, Fane Hall 2380 - Mail Code 4503, 1000 Faner Drive, Carbondale IL 62901. **E-mail:** jtribble@siu.edu. **Website:** www.craborchardreview.siu.edu. **Contact:** Jon C. Tribble, managing editor. Offered annually for excellence in the writing of creative nonfiction. Not a prize for academic essays. *Crab Orchard Review* acquires first North American serial rights to submitted works. Open to US citizens only. See website for guidelines and details. Deadline: April 21. Submission period begins February 21. Prize: $2,000 and publication. At least 2 finalists are each offered $500 and publication.

ALBERT J. HARRIS AWARD

International Reading Association, Division of Research and Policy, 800 Barksdale Rd., Newark DE 19714-8139. (302)731-1600, ext. 423; (800)336-7323. **Fax:** (302)731-1057. **E-mail:** research@reading.org. **Website:** www.reading.org. **Contact:** Marcella Moore. Offered annually to recognize outstanding published works focused on the identification, prevention, assessment, or instruction of learners experiencing difficulty learning to read. Articles may be nominated by researchers, authors, and others. Copies of the applications and guidelines can be downloaded in PDF format from the website. Deadline: September 1. Prize: Monetary award and recognition at the International Reading Association's annual convention.

HENDRICKS AWARD

The New Netherland Institute, Cultural Education Center, Room 10D45, 222 Madison Ave., Albany NY 12230. **Fax:** (518)473-0472. **E-mail:** nyslfnn@mail. nysed.gov. **Website:** www.newnetherlandinstitute. org. Given annually to the best book or book-length ms relating to any aspect of New Netherland and its legacy. Two categories of submissions will be considered in alternate years :(1) recently completed dissertations and unpublished book-length mss, and (2) recently published books. If there is no suitable winner in the designated category in any particular year, submissions from the alternate category will be considered. In addition, submissions from previous years will be reconsidered for the Award. Entries must be based on research completed or published within three years prior to the deadline for submission. Entries may deal with any aspect of New Netherland and its legacy. Biographies of individuals whose careers illuminate aspects of the history of New Netherland and its legacy are eligible, as are mss dealing with literature and the arts, provided that the methodology is historical. Deadline: February 1. Prize: $5,000. Judged by a 5-member panel of scholars.

THOMAS J. HRUSKA MEMORIAL PRIZE IN NONFICTION

Passages North, Department of English, Northern Michigan University, 1401 Presque Isle Ave., Marquette MI 49855. (906) 227-1203. **Fax:** (906) 227-1096. **Website:** www.passagesnorth.com. **Contact:** Kate Myers Hanson, acquisitions. Contest for nonfiction. *Passages North* also offers poetry and fiction contests. Send SASE for announcement of winners. Author's name may appear anywhere on ms or cover letter. Mss will not be returned. All entrants receive a contest issue. Honorable mentions will also be chosen for each contest and may or may not be published according to the needs of the editors. Deadline: February 15. Prize: $1,000 1st Place prize and publication.

THE HUNGER MOUNTAIN CREATIVE NONFICTION PRIZE

Vermont College, 36 College St., Montpelier VT 05602. (802)828-8517. **E-mail:** hungermtn@vcfa.edu. **Website:** www.hungermtn.org. **Contact:** Miciah Bay Gault,

editor. Annual contest for the best writing in creative nonfiction. Submit essays under 10,000 words. Guidelines online. Accepts entries online or via mail. Deadline: September 10. Prize: $1,000 and publication. Two honorable mentions receive $100 each.

IRA OUTSTANDING DISSERTATION OF THE YEAR AWARD

International Reading Association, 800 Barksdale Rd., P.O. Box 8139, Newark DE 19714-8139. (302)731-1600. **Fax:** (302)731-1057. **E-mail:** research@reading.org. **Website:** www.reading.org. **Contact:** Marcella Moore, project manager. Dissertations in reading or related fields are eligible for the competition. Studies using any research approach (ethnographic, experimental, historical, survey, etc.) are encouraged. Each study is assessed in the light of this approach, the scholarly qualification of its report, and its significant contributions to knowledge within the reading field. The application process is open to those who have completed dissertations in any aspect of the field of reading or literacy between May 15 and May 14 of the calendar year. A routine check is made with the home university of the applicant to protect all applicants, their universities, and the International Reading Association from false claims. Studies may use any research approach (ethnographic, experimental, historical, survey, etc.). Each study will be assessed in light of its approach, its scholarship, and its significant contributions to knowledge within the reading/literacy field. Deadline: October 1. Prize: $1,000.

TILIA KLEBENOV JACOBS RELIGIOUS ESSAY PRIZE CATEGORY

Soul Making Keats Literary Competition, The Webhallow House, 1544 Sweetwood Dr., Broadmoor Village CA 94015-2029. **E-mail:** SoulKeats@mail.com. **Website:** www.soulmakingcontest.us. **Contact:** Eileen Malone. Call for thoughtful writings of up to 3,000 words. "No preaching, no proselytizing." Open annually to any writer. Previously published material is accepted. Indicate category on cover page and on identifying 3x5 card. Up to 3,000 words, double-spaced. See website for more details. Deadline: November 30. Prize: 1st Place: $100; 2nd Place $50; 3rd Place $25.

KATHERINE SINGER KOVACS PRIZE

Modern Language Association of America, 26 Broadway, 3rd Floor, New York NY 10004-1789. (646)576-5141. **Fax:** (646)458-0030. **E-mail:** awards@mla.org. v

LITERAL LATTÉ ESSAY AWARD

Literal Latté, 200 E. 10th St., Suite 240, New York NY 10003. (212)260-5532. **E-mail:** litlatte@aol.com. **Website:** www.literal-latte.com. **Contact:** Jenine Gordon Bockman. Open to any writer. Send previously unpublished personal essays, 10,000 words max. All topics accepted. Include e-mail address for reply. Acquires first rights. Visit website for guidelines and tastes. Deadline: September 30. Prize: 1st Place: $1,000; 2nd Place: $300; 3rd Place: $200. Judged by the editors.

☻ TONY LOTHIAN PRIZE

Under the auspices of the Biographers' Club, 79 Arlington Ave., London N1 7BA United Kingdom. (44) (20)7 359 7769. **E-mail:** ariane.bankes@gmail.com. **Website:** www.biographersclub.co.uk. **Contact:** Ariane Banks, prize administrator. "Entries should consist of a 10-page synopsis and 10 pages of a sample chapter for a proposed biography, plus cv, sources and a note on the market for the book. Open to any writer who has not previously been published or commissioned or written a biography." Deadline: August 1. Prize: £2,000. Judges have included Michael Holroyd, Victoria Glendinning, Selina Hastings, Frances Spalding, Lyndall Gordon, Anne de Courcy, Nigel Hamilton, Anthony Sampson, and Mary Lovell. **TIPS** "Further details at www.biographersclub.co.uk."

JAMES RUSSELL LOWELL PRIZE

Modern Language Association of America, 26 Broadway, 3rd Floor, New York NY 10004-1789. (646)576-5141. **Fax:** (646)458-0030. **E-mail:** awards@mla.org. **Website:** www.mla.org. **Contact:** Coordinator of Book Prizes. For an outstanding literary or linguistic study, a critical edition of an important work, or a critical biography. Open to studies dealing with literary theory, media, cultural history, or interdisciplinary topics. Books must be published in the previous year. Authors must be current members of the MLA. Send 6 copies of the book. Deadline: March 1. Prize: A cash award and a certificate to be presented at the Modern Language Association's annual convention in January.

RICHARD J. MARGOLIS AWARD

c/o Margolis & Bloom, LLP, 535 Boylston St., 8th Floor, Boston MA 02116. (617)267-9700, ext. 517. **Fax:** (617)267-3166. **E-mail:** hsm@margolis.com. **Website:** www.margolis.com/award. **Contact:** Harry S. Margolis. Sponsored by the Blue Mountain Center, this annual award is given to a promising new journalist or essayist whose work combines warmth, humor, wisdom, and concern with social justice. Applicants should be aware that this award is for nonfiction reporting and commentary, not for creative nonfiction, fiction, or poetry. Applications should include at least two examples of the your work (published or unpublished, 30 pages maximum) and a short biographical note including a description of your current and anticipated work. Also please indicate what you will work on while attending the Blue Mountain residency. Please send three copies of these writing samples. Samples will not be returned. Deadline: July 1. Prize: $5,000.

HOWARD R. MARRARO PRIZE

Modern Language Association of America, 26 Broadway, 3rd Floor, New York NY 10004-1789. (646)576-5141. **Fax:** (646)458-0030. **E-mail:** awards@mla.org. **Website:** www.mla.org. **Contact:** Coordinator of Book Prizes. Offered in even-numbered years for an outstanding scholarly work on any phase of Italian literature or comparative literature involving Italian. Books must have been published in the previous year. Authors must be members of the MLA. Requires 4 copies of the book. Deadline: May 1. Prize: A cash award and a certificate to be presented at the Modern Language Association's annual convention in January.

KENNETH W. MILDENBERGER PRIZE

Modern Language Association of America, 26 Broadway, 3rd Floor, New York NY 10004-1789. (646)576-5141. **Fax:** (646)458-0030. **E-mail:** awards@mla.org. **Website:** www.mla.org. **Contact:** Coordinator of Book Prizes. Offered in odd-numbered years for a publication from the previous year in the field of language, culture, literacy, or literature with a strong application to the teaching of languages other than English. Author need not be a member of the MLA. Books must have been published in the previous 2 years. Requires 4 copies of the book. Deadline: May 1. Prize: A cash award, and a certificate, to be presented at the Modern Language Association's annual convention in January, and a year's membership in the MLA.

C. WRIGHT MILLS AWARD

The Society for the Study of Social Problems, 901 McClung Tower, University of Tennessee, Knoxville TN 37996-0490. (865)689-1531. **Fax:** (865)689-1534. **E-mail:** mkoontz3@utk.edu. **Website:** www.sssp1.org. **Contact:** Michele Smith Koontz, Administrative Officer and Meeting Manager. Offered annually for a book published the previous year that most effectively critically addresses an issue of contemporary public importance; brings to the topic a fresh, imaginative perspective; advances social scientific understanding of the topic; displays a theoretically informed view and empirical orientation; evinces quality in style of writing; and explicitly or implicitly contains implications for courses of action. Self-nominations are acceptable. Edited volumes, textbooks, fiction, and self published works are not eligible. Deadline: December 15. Prize: $500 stipend.

MLA PRIZE FOR A BIBLIOGRAPHY, ARCHIVE, OR DIGITAL PROJECT

Modern Language Association of America, 26 Broadway, 3rd Floor, New York NY 10004-1789. (646)576-5141. **Fax:** (646)458-0030. **E-mail:** awards@mla.org. **Website:** www.mla.org. **Contact:** Coordinator of Book Prizes. Offered in even-numbered years for an outstanding enumerative or descriptive bibliography, archive, or digital project. Open to any writer or publisher. At least 1 volume must have been published in the previous 2 years. Editors need not be members of the MLA. Criteria for determining excellence include evidence of analytical rigor, meticulous scholarship, intellectual creativity, and subject range and depth. Deadline: May 1. Prize: A cash prize and a certificate to be presented at the Modern Language Association's annual convention in January.

MLA PRIZE FOR A FIRST BOOK

Modern Language Association of America, 26 Broadway, 3rd Floor, New York NY 10004-1789. (646)576-5141. **Fax:** (646)458-0030. **E-mail:** awards@mla.org. **Website:** www.mla.org. **Contact:** Coordinator of Book Prizes. Offered annually for the first book-length scholarly publication by a current member of the association. To qualify, a book must be a literary or linguistic study, a critical edition of an important work, or a critical biography. Studies dealing with literary theory, media, cultural history, and interdisciplinary topics are eligible; books that are primarily translations will not be considered. See listing for James Russell Lowe Prize—prize offered for same criteria. Deadline: April 1. Prize: A cash award and a certificate to be presented at the Modern Language Association's annual convention in January.

MLA PRIZE FOR A SCHOLARLY EDITION

Modern Language Association of America, 26 Broadway, 3rd Floor, New York NY 10004. (646)576-5141. **Fax:** (646)458-0030. **E-mail:** awards@mla.org. **Website:** www.mla.org. Offered in odd-numbered years for an outstanding scholarly edition. Editions may be in single or multiple volumes. At least one volume must have been published in the 2 years prior to the award deadline. Editors need not be members of the MLA. To qualify for the award, an edition should be based on an examination of all available relevant textual sources; the source texts and the edited text's deviations from them should be fully described; the edition should employ editorial principles appropriate to the materials edited, and those principles should be clearly articulated in the volume; the text should be accompanied by appropriate textual and other historical contextual information; the edition should exhibit the highest standards of accuracy in the presentation of its text and apparatus; and the text and apparatus should be presented as accessibly and elegantly as possible. Deadline: May 1. Prize: A cash award and a certificate to be presented at the Modern Language Association's annual convention in January.

MLA PRIZE FOR INDEPENDENT SCHOLARS

Modern Language Association of America, 26 Broadway, 3rd Floor, New York NY 10004. (646)576-5141. **Fax:** (646)458-0030. **E-mail:** awards@mla.org. **Website:** www.mla.org. Offered in even-numbered years for a scholarly book in the field of English or other modern languages and literatures. Book must have been published within the 2 years prior to prize deadline. At the time of publication of the book, author must not be enrolled in a program leading to an academic degree or hold a tenured, tenure-accruing, or tenure-track position in postsecondary education. Authors need not be members of the MLA. Requires 6 copies of the book and a completed application. Deadline: May 1. Prize: A cash award, a certificate, and a year's membership in the MLA.

LINDA JOY MYERS MEMOIR VIGNETTE PRIZE CATEGORY

Soul-Making Keats Literary Competition, Webhallow House, 1544 Sweetwood Dr., Broadmoor Village CA 94015-2029. **E-mail:** soulkeats@mail.com. **Website:** www.soulmakingcontest.us. **Contact:** Eileen Malone. Open annually to any writer. One memoir/entry, up to 1,500 words, double spaced. Previously published material is acceptable. Indicate category on first page. Identify only with 3x5 card. Deadline: November 30. Prize: 1st Place: $100; 2nd Place: $50; 3rd Place: $25.

◑ NATIONAL BUSINESS BOOK AWARD

PwC and BMO Financial Group, 121 Richmond St. W., Suite 605, Toronto ON M5H 2K1 Canada. (416)868-1500. **Fax:** (416)868-1502. **Website:** www.nbbaward.com. Offered annually for books published January 1-December 31 to recognize excellence in business writing in Canada. Publishers nominate books. Deadline: December 31. Prize: $20,000 (CAN).

NATIONAL WRITERS ASSOCIATION NONFICTION CONTEST

The National Writers Association, 10940 S. Parker Rd., #508, Parker CO 80134. (303)841-0246. **E-mail:** natlwritersassn@hotmail.com. **Website:** www.nationalwriters.com. Only unpublished works may be submitted. Judging of entries will not begin until the contest ends. Nonfiction in the following areas will be accepted: articles—submission should include query letter, 1st page of ms, separate sheet citing 5 possible markets; essay—the complete essay and 5 possible markets on separate sheet; nonfiction book proposal including query letter, chapter by chapter outline, first chapter, bio and market analysis. Those unsure of proper ms format should request Research Report #35. The purpose of the National Writers Association Nonfiction Contest is to encourage the writing of nonfiction and recognize those who excel in this field. Deadline: December 31. Prize: 1st - 5th place awards will be presented at the NWAF Conference. Other winners will be notified by March 31st. 1st Prize: $200 and Clearinghouse representation if winner is book proposal; 2nd Prize: $100; 3rd Prize: $50; 4th - 10th places will receive a book. Honorable Mentions receive a certificate. Judging will be based on originality, marketability, research, and reader interest. Copies of the judges evaluation sheets will be sent to entrants furnishing an SASE with their entry.

THE PHI BETA KAPPA AWARD IN SCIENCE

The Phi Beta Kappa Society, 1606 New Hampshire Ave. NW, Washington DC 20009. (202)265-3808. **Fax:** (202)986-1601. **E-mail:** awards@pbk.org. **Website:** www.pbk.org/bookawards. **Contact:** Awards Coordinator. Offered annually for outstanding contributions by scientists to the literature of science. To be eligible, biographies of scientists must have a substantial critical emphasis on their scientific research. Entries must have been published May 1-April 30. Entries must be submitted by the publisher. Entries must be preceded by a letter certifying that the book(s) conforms to all the conditions of eligibility and stating the publication date of each entry. If accepted, 6 copies of each entry are required. Ineligible entries will be returned by Phi Beta Kappa. Books will not be entered officially in the competition until all copies and the letter of certification have been received. Open only to original works in English and authors of US residency and publication. The intent of the award is to encourage literate and scholarly interpretations of the physical and biological sciences and mathematics; monographs and compendiums are not eligible. Deadline: February 14. Prize: $10,000.

PRESERVATION FOUNDATION CONTESTS

The Preservation Foundation, Inc., 2313 Pennington Bend, Nashville TN 37214. **E-mail:** preserve@storyhouse.org. **Website:** www.storyhouse.org. **Contact:** Richard Loller, publisher. Three contests offered annually for unpublished nonfiction. Biography/Autobiography (1,500-10,000 words)—a true story of an individual(s) personally known to the author. Or, it may be the true story of the author's life, the whole or an episode. General nonfiction (1,500-5,000 words)—any appropriate nonfiction topic. Travel nonfiction (1,500-5,000 words)—must be true story of trip by author or someone known personally by author. Open to any previously unpublished writer. Defined as having earned no more than $750 by creative writing in any previous year. Stories must be submitted by e-mail or as electronic files by regular mail. No paper mss can be considered. No story may be entered in more than one contest. See website for contest details. Deadline: August 31. Prize: 1st Place: $100 in each category; certificates for finalists.

◑ EVELYN RICHARDSON NONFICTION AWARD

Writers' Federation of Nova Scotia, 1113 Marginal Rd., Halifax NS B3H 4P7 Canada. (902)423-8116. **Fax:** (902)422-0881. **E-mail:** director@writers.ns.ca. **Website:** www.writers.ns.ca. The Evelyn Richardson Memorial Nonfiction Award is awarded for a book of creative nonfiction by a resident of Nova Scotia. Detailed guidelines and eligibility criteria online. Deadline: First Friday in December. Prize: Vaulted at $2,000 for the winning title.

ALDO AND JEANNE SCAGLIONE PRIZE FOR COMPARATIVE LITERARY STUDIES

Modern Language Association of America, 26 Broadway, 3rd Floor, New York NY 10004-1789. (646)576-5141. **Fax:** (646)458-0030. **E-mail:** awards@mla.org. **Website:** www.mla.org. **Contact:** Coordinator of Book Prizes. Offered annually for outstanding scholarly work in comparative literary studies involving at least 2 literatures. Works of literary history, literary criticism, philology, and literary theory are eligible, as are works dealing with literature and other arts and disciplines, including cinema; books that are primarily translations will not be considered. Books must have been published in the past calendar year. Authors must be current members of the MLA. Requires 4 copies of the book. Deadline: May 1. Prize: A cash award and a certificate to be presented at the Modern Language Association's annual convention in January.

ALDO AND JEANNE SCAGLIONE PRIZE FOR FRENCH AND FRANCOPHONE STUDIES

Modern Language Association of America, 26 Broadway, 3rd Floor, New York NY 10004. (646)576-5141. **Fax:** (646)458-0030. **E-mail:** awards@mla.org. **Website:** www.mla.org. Offered annually for an outstanding scholarly work in French or francophone linguistics or literary studies. Works of literary history, literary criticism, philology, and literary theory are eligible for consideration; books that are primarily translations will not be considered. Books must have been published in the previous year. Authors must be current members of the MLA. Requires 4 copies of the book. Deadline: May 1. Prize: A cash award and a certificate to be presented at the Modern Language Association's annual convention in January.

ALDO AND JEANNE SCAGLIONE PRIZE FOR ITALIAN STUDIES

Modern Language Association of America, 26 Broadway, 3rd Floor, New York NY 10004-1789. (646)576-5141. **Fax:** (646)458-0030. **E-mail:** awards@mla.org. **Website:** www.mla.org. **Contact:** Coordinator of Book Prizes. Offered in odd-number years for an outstanding scholarly work on any phase of Italian literature or culture or comparative literature involving Italian. This shall include works that study literary or cultural theory, science, history, art, music, society, politics, cinema, and linguistics, preferably but not necessarily relating other disciplines to literature.

Books must have been published in the previous year. Authors must be members of the MLA. Requires 4 copies of the book. Deadline: May 1. Prize: A cash award and a certificate to be presented at the Modern Language Association's annual convention in January.

ALDO AND JEANNE SCAGLIONE PRIZE FOR STUDIES IN GERMANIC LANGUAGES & LITERATURE

Modern Language Association of America, 26 Broadway, 3rd Floor, New York NY 10004. (646)576-5141. **Fax:** (646)458-0030. **E-mail:** awards@mla.org. **Website:** www.mla.org. Offered in even-numbered years for an outstanding scholarly work on the linguistics or literatures of any of the Germanic languages (Danish, Dutch, German, Norwegian, Swedish, Yiddish). Works of literary history, literary criticism, philology, and literary theory are eligible for consideration; books that are primarily translations will not be considered. Books must have been published in the previous 2 years. Authors must be members of the MLA. Requires 4 copies of the book. Deadline: May 1. Prize: A cash award, and a certificate to be presented at the Modern Language Association's annual convention in January.

ALDO AND JEANNE SCAGLIONE PUBLICATION AWARD FOR A MS IN ITALIAN LITERARY STUDIES

Modern Language Association, 26 Broadway, 3rd Floor, New York NY 10004-1789. (646)576-5141. **Fax:** (646)458-0030. **E-mail:** awards@mla.org. **Website:** www.mla.org. **Contact:** Coordinator of Book Prizes. Offerred annualy for an outstanding ms dealing with any aspect of the languages and literatures of Italy, including medieval Latin and comparative studies or intellectual history if the work's main thrust is clearly related to the humanities. Materials from ancient Rome are eligible if related to postclassical developments. Also eligible are translations of classical works of prose and poetry produced in Italy prior to 1900 in any language (e.g., neo-Latin, Greek) or in a dialect of Italian (e.g., Neapolitan, Roman, Sicilian). Eligible are book mss in English or Italian that are ready for submission or already submitted to a press. Mss must be approved or ready for publication before award deadline. Authors must be current members of the MLA, residing in the United States or Canada. Requires 4 copies, plus contact and biographical information. Deadline: August 1. Prize: A cash award and a certificate to be presented at the Modern Language Association's annual convention in January.

WILLIAM SANDERS SCARBOROUGH PRIZE

Modern Language Association of America, 26 Broadway, 3rd Floor, New York NY 10004-1789. (646)576-5141. **Fax:** (646)458-0030. **E-mail:** awards@mla.org. **Website:** www.mla.org. **Contact:** Coordinator of book prizes. Offered annually for an outstanding study of black American literature or culture. Books must have been published in the previous year. Authors need not be members of the MLA. Requires 4 copies of the book. Deadline: May 1. Prize: A cash award, and a certificate to be presented at the Modern Language Association's annual convention in January.

⊕ SCREAMINMAMAS CREATIVE NONFICTION CONTEST

1911 Cleveland St., Hollywood FL 33020. **E-mail:** screaminmamas@gmail.com. **Website:** www.screaminmamas.com/contests. **Contact:** Darlene Pistocchi, editor/managing director. "Looking for stories that revolve around the kids and/or pets. Must be true! Take an incident or scene that is embedded in your brain and share it with us. Story can be dramatic or humorous, happy or sad. Looking for the real deal." Stories should be 600-1,500 words. Open only to moms. Deadline: March 31. Prize: $40, publication.

MINA P. SHAUGHNESSY PRIZE

Modern Language Association of America, 26 Broadway, 3rd Floor, New York NY 10004-1789. (646)576-5141. **Fax:** (646)458-0030. **E-mail:** awards@mla.org. **Website:** www.mla.org. **Contact:** Coordinator of Book Prizes. Offered in even-numbered years for a work in the fields of language, culture, literacy, or literature with strong application to the teaching of English. Books must have been published in the previous 2 years. Authors need not be members of the MLA. Requires 4 copies of the book. Deadline: May 1. Prize: A cash prize, a certificate, to be presented at the Modern Language Association's annual convention in January, and a 1-year membership in the MLA.

VFW VOICE OF DEMOCRACY

Veterans of Foreign Wars of the U.S., National Headquarters, 406 W. 34th St., Kansas City MO 64111. (816)968-1117. **E-mail:** kharmer@vfw.org. **Website:** www.vfw.org/Community/Voice-of-Democracy/. The Voice of Democracy Program is open to students in grades 9-12 (on the Nov. 1 deadline), who are enrolled in a public, private or parochial high school or home study program in the United States and its territories. Contact your local VFW Post to enter (entry must not be mailed to the VFW National Headquarters, only to a local, participating VFW Post. Purpose is to give high school students the opportunity to voice their opinions about their responsibility to our country and to convey those opinions via the broadcast media to all of America. Deadline: November 1. Prize: Winners receive awards ranging from $1,000-30,000.

WESTERN WRITERS OF AMERICA

271CR 219, Encampment WY 82325. (307)329-8942. **Fax:** (307)327-5465 (call first). **E-mail:** wwa.moulton@gmail.com. **Website:** www.westernwriters.org. **Contact:** Candy Moulton, executive director. 17 Spur Award categories in various aspects of the American West. Send entry form with your published work. Accepts multiple submissions, each with its own entry form. The nonprofit Western Writers of America has promoted and honored the best in Western literature with the annual Spur Awards, selected by panels of judges. Awards, for material published last year, are given for works whose inspirations, image and literary excellence best represent the reality and spirit of the American West.

↻ THE HILARY WESTON WRITERS' TRUST PRIZE FOR NONFICTION

The Writers' Trust of Canada, 460 Richmond St. W., Suite 600, Toronto ON M5V 1Y1 Canada. (416)504-8222. **Fax:** (416)504-9090. **E-mail:** info@writerstrust.com. **Website:** www.writerstrust.com. **Contact:** Amanda Hopkins. Offered annually for a work of nonfiction published in the previous year. Award presented at a a gala event held in Toronto each fall. Open to Canadian citizens and permanent residents only. Deadline: August. Prize: $60,000 and $5,000 to 4 finalists.

THE ELIE WIESEL PRIZE IN ETHICS ESSAY CONTEST

The Elie Wiesel Foundation for Humanity, 555 Madison Ave., 20th Floor, New York NY 10022. **Fax:** (212)490-6006. **Website:** www.eliewieselfoundation.org. **Contact:** Leslie Meyers. This annual competition is intended to challenge undergraduate juniors and seniors in colleges and universities throughout the US to analyze ethical questions and concerns facing them in today's complex society. All students are encouraged to write thought-provoking, personal essays.

Deadline: Early December. Prize: 1st Prize: $5,000; 2nd Prize: $2,500; 3rd Prize: $1,500; Honorable Mentions (2): $500. Judged by a distinguished panel of readers who evaluate all contest entries. A jury, including Elie Wiesel, chooses the winners.

WRITING CONFERENCE WRITING CONTESTS

P.O. Box 664, Ottawa KS 66067-0664. (785)242-1995. **Fax:** (785)242-1995. **E-mail:** jbushman@writingconference.com. **E-mail:** support@studentq.com. **Website:** www.writingconference.com. **Contact:** John H. Bushman, contest director. Unpublished submissions only. Submissions made by the author or teacher. Purpose of contest: To further writing by students with awards for narration, exposition and poetry at the elementary, middle school and high school levels. Deadline: January 8. Prize: Awards plaque and publication of winning entry in The Writers' Slate online, April issue. Judged by a panel of teachers.

YEARBOOK EXCELLENCE CONTEST

100 Adler Journalism Building, Iowa City IA 52242-2004. (319)335-3457. **Fax:** (319)335-3989. **E-mail:** quill-scroll@uiowa.edu. **Website:** www.quillandscroll.org. **Contact:** Vanessa Shelton, executive director. High school students who are contributors to or staff members of a student yearbook at any public or private high school are invited to enter the competition. Awards will be made in each of the 18 divisions. There are two enrollment categories: Class A: more than 750 students; Class B: 749 or less. Winners will receive Quill and Scroll's National Award Gold Key and, if seniors, are eligible to apply for one of the Edward J. Nell Memorial or George and Ophelia Gallup scholarships. Open to students whose schools have Quill and Scroll charters. Previously published submissions only. Submissions made by the author or school yearbook adviser. Must be published in the 12-month span prior to contest deadline. Visit website for list of current and previous winners. Purpose is to recognize and reward student journalists for their work in yearbooks and to provide student winners an opportunity to apply for a scholarship to be used freshman year in college for students planning to major in journalism. Deadline: November 1.

LAMAR YORK PRIZE FOR NONFICTION CONTEST

The Chattahoochee Review, Georgia Perimeter College, 2101 Womack Rd., Dunwoody GA 30338-4497.

(770)274-5479. **E-mail:** gpccr@gpc.edu. **Website:** thechattahoocheereview.gpc.edu. **Contact:** Anna Schachner, Editor. Offered annually for unpublished creative nonfiction and nonscholarly essays up to 5,000 words. *The Chattahoochee Review* buys first rights only for winning essay/ms for the purpose of publication in the summer issue. Entries should be submitted via Submittable. See website for details and guidelines. Deadline: January 31. Submission period begins October 1. Prize: 2 prizes of $1,000 each, plus publication. Judged by the editorial staff of *The Chattahoochee Review*.

WRITING FOR CHILDREN & YOUNG ADULTS

AMERICAN ASSOCIATION OF UNIVERSITY WOMEN AWARD IN JUVENILE LITERATURE

4610 Mail Service Center, Raleigh NC 27699-4610. (919)807-7290. **E-mail:** michael.hill@ncdcr.gov. **Contact:** Michael Hill, awards coordinator. Annual award. Book must be published during the year ending June 30. Submissions made by author, author's agent or publisher. SASE for contest rules. Author must have maintained either legal residence or actual physical residence, or a combination of both, in the state of North Carolina for 3 years immediately preceding the close of the contest period. Only published work (books) eligible. Recognizes the year's best work of juvenile literature by a North Carolina resident. Deadline: July 15. Prize: Awards a cup to the winner and winner's name inscribed on a plaque displayed within the North Carolina Office of Archives and History. Judged by three-judge panel.

◐ HANS CHRISTIAN ANDERSEN AWARD

Nonnenweg 12, Postfach Ba CH-4003 Switzerland. **E-mail:** liz.page@ibby.org. **E-mail:** ibby@ibby.org. **Website:** www.ibby.org. **Contact:** Liz Page, director. The Hans Christian Andersen Award, awarded every two years by the International Board on Books for Young People (IBBY), is the highest international recognition given to an author and an illustrator of children's books. The Author's Award has been given since 1956, the Illustrator's Award since 1966. Her Majesty Queen Margrethe II of Denmark is the Patron of the Hans Christian Andersen Awards. The awards are presented at the biennial congresses of IBBY. Awarded to an author and to an illustrator, living at the time of the nomination, who by the outstanding value of their work are judged to have made a lasting contribution to literature for children and young people. The complete works of the author and of the illustrator will be taken into consideration in awarding the medal, which will be accompanied by a diploma. Candidates are nominated by National Sections of IBBY in good standing. Prize: Awards medals according to literary and artistic criteria. Judged by the Hans Christian Andersen Jury.

☻ MARILYN BAILLIE PICTURE BOOK AWARD

The Canadian Children's Book Centre, 40 Orchard View Blvd., Suite 217, Toronto ON M4R 1B9 Canada. (416)975-0010, ext. 222. **Fax:** (416)975-8970. **E-mail:** meghan@bookcentre.ca. **Website:** www.bookcentre. ca. **Contact:** Meghan Howe. The Marilyn Baillie Picture Book Award honors excellence in the illustrated picture book format. To be eligible, the book must be an original work in English, aimed at children ages 3-8, written and illustrated by Canadians and first published in Canada. Eligible genres include fiction, nonfiction and poetry. Books must be published between Jan. 1 and Dec. 31 of the previous calendar year. New editions or re-issues of previously published books are not eligible for submission. Deadline: December 20. Prize: $20,000.

TIPS "Please visit website for submission guidelines and eligibility criteria."

JOHN AND PATRICIA BEATTY AWARD

2471 Flores St., San Mateo CA 94403. (650)376-0886. **Fax:** (650)539-2341. **E-mail:** bartlett@scfl.lib.ca.us. **Website:** www.cla-net.org. **Contact:** Diane Bartlett, award chair. The California Library Association's John and Patricia Beatty Award, sponsored by Baker & Taylor, honors the author of a distinguished book for children or young adults that best promotes an awareness of California and its people. Must be a children's or young adult books published in the previous year, set in California, and highlight California's cultural heritage or future. Send title suggestiosn to the committee members. Deadline: January 31. Prize: $500 and an engraved plaque. Judged by a committee of CLA members, who select the winning title from books published in the United States during the preceding year.

☻ THE GEOFFREY BILSON AWARD FOR HISTORICAL FICTION FOR YOUNG PEOPLE

The Canadian Children's Book Centre, 40 Orchard View Blvd., Suite 217, Toronto ON M4R 1B9 Canada. (416)975-0010, ext. 222. **Fax:** (416)975-8970. **Website:** www.bookcentre.ca. **Contact:** Meghan Howe. Awarded annually to reward excellence in the writing of an outstanding work of historical fiction for young readers, by a Canadian author, published in the previous calendar year. Open to Canadian citizens and residents of Canada for at least 2 years. Books must be published between January 1 and December 31 of the previous year. Books must be first foreign or first Canadian editions. Autobiographies are not eligible. Jury members will consider the following: historical setting and accuracy, strong character and plot development, well-told, original story, and stability of book for its intended age group. Deadline: December 20. Prize: $5,000.

THE IRMA S. AND JAMES H. BLACK AWARD

Bank Street College of Education, 610 W. 112th St., New York NY 10025-1898. (212)875-4458. **Fax:** (212)875-4558. **E-mail:** kfreda@bankstreet.edu; apryce@bankstreet.edu. **Website:** bankstreet.edu/center-childrens-literature/irma-black-award/. **Contact:** Kristin Freda. Award give to an outstanding book for young children—a book in which text and illustrations are inseparable, each enhancing and enlarging on the other to produce a singular whole. Entries must have been published during the previous calendar year. Publishers submit books. Submit only one copy of each book. Does not accept unpublished mss. Deadline: mid-December. Prize: A scroll with the recipient's name and a gold seal designed by Maurice Sendak. Judged by a committee of older children and children's literature professionals. Final judges are first-, second-, and third-grade classes at a number of cooperating schools.

BOSTON GLOBE-HORN BOOK AWARDS

The Boston Globe, Horn Book, Inc., 56 Roland St., Suite 200, Boston MA 02129. (617)628-0225. **Fax:** (617)628-0882. **E-mail:** info@hbook.com; khedeen@hbook.com. **Website:** hbook.com/bghb/. **Contact:** Katrina Hedeen. Offered annually for excellence in literature for children and young adults (published June 1-May 31). Categories: picture book, fiction and poetry, nonfiction. Judges may also name up to 2 honor books in each category. Books must be published in the US, but may be written or illustrated by citizens of any country. The Horn Book Magazine publishes speeches given at awards ceremonies. Guidelines for SASE or online. Submit a book directly to each of the judges. See website for details on submitting, as well as contest guidelines. Deadline: May 15. Prize: $500 and an engraved silver bowl; honor book recipients receive an engraved silver plate. Judged by a panel of 3 judges selected each year.

CHILDREN'S AFRICANA BOOK AWARD

Outreach Council of the African Studies Association, c/o Rutgers University, 132 George St., New Brunswick NJ 08901. (732)932-8173; (301)585-9136. **Fax:** (732)932-3394. **E-mail:** africaaccess@aol.com. **E-mail:** harrietmcguire@earthlink.net. **Website:** www.africaaccessreview.org. **Contact:** Brenda Randolph, chairperson. The Children's Africana Book Awards are presented annually to the authors and illustrators of the best books on Africa for children and young people published or republished in the U.S. The awards were created by the Outreach Council of the African Studies Association (ASA) to dispel stereotypes and encourage the publication and use of accurate, balanced children's materials about Africa. The awards are presented in 2 categories: Young Children and Older Readers. Entries must have been published in the calendar year previous to the award. Work submitted for awards must be suitable for children ages 4-18; a significant portion of books' content must be about Africa; must by copyrighted in the calendar year prior to award year; must be published or republished in the US. Books should be suitable for children and young adults, ages 4-18. A significant portion of the book's content should be about Africa. Books must be copyrighted the previous year to be eligible for the awards. Judged by African Studies and Children's Literature scholars. Nominated titles are read by committee members and reviewed by external African Studies scholars with specialized academic training.

CHILDREN'S BOOK GUILD AWARD FOR NONFICTION

E-mail: theguild@childrensbookguild.org. **Website:** www.childrensbookguild.org. Annual award. "One doesn't enter. One is selected. Our jury annually selects one author for the award." Honors an author or illustrator whose total work has contributed significantly to the quality of nonfiction for children. Prize: Cash and an engraved crystal paperweight. Judged by a jury of Children's Book Guild specialists, authors, and illustrators.

MARGARET A. EDWARDS AWARD

50 East Huron St., Chicago IL 60611-2795. (312)280-4390 or (800)545-2433. **Fax:** (312)280-5276. **E-mail:** yalsa@ala.org; noconnor@ala.org. **Website:** www.ala.org/yalsa/edwards. **Contact:** Nichole O'Connor. Annual award administered by the Young Adult Library Services Association (YALSA) of the American Library Association (ALA) and sponsored by *School Library Journal* magazine. Awarded to an author whose book or books, over a period of time, have been accepted by young adults as an authentic voice that continues to illuminate their experiences and emotions, giving insight into their lives. The book or books should enable them to understand themselves, the world in which they live, and their relationship with others and with society. The book or books must be in print at the time of the nomination. Submissions must be previously published no less than 5years prior to the first meeting of the current Margaret A. Edwards Award Committee at Midwinter Meeting. Nomination form is available on the YALSA website. Deadline: December 1. Prize: $2,000. Judged by members of the Young Adult Library Services Association.

DOROTHY CANFIELD FISHER CHILDREN'S BOOK AWARD

Midstate Library Service Center, 578 Paine Tpke. N., Berlin VT 05602. (802)828-6954. **E-mail:** grace.greene@state.vt.us. **Website:** www.dcfaward.org. **Contact:** Mary Linney, chair. Annual award to encourage Vermont children to become enthusiastic and discriminating readers by providing them with books of good quality by living American or Canadian authors published in the current year. E-mail for entry rules. Titles must be original work, published in the U.S., and be appropriate to children in grades 4-8. The book must be copyrighted in the current year. It must be written by an American author living in the U.S. or Canada, or a Canadian author living in Canada or the U.S. Deadline: December of year book was published. Prize: Awards a scroll presented to the winning author at an award ceremony. Judged by children, grades 4-8, who vote for their favorite book.

⊕ THE NORMA FLECK AWARD FOR CANADIAN CHILDREN'S NONFICTION

The Canadian Children's Book Centre, 40 Orchard View Blvd., Suite 217, Toronto ON M4R 1B9 Canada. (416)975-0010 ext. 222. **Fax:** (416)975-8970. **E-mail:** meghan@bookcentre.ca. **Website:** www.bookcentre.ca. **Contact:** Meghan Howe, library coordinator. The Norma Fleck Award was established by the Fleck Family Foundation to recognize and raise the profile of exceptional nonfiction books for young people. Offered annually for books published between January 1 and December 31 of the previous calendar year. Open to Canadian citizens or landed immigrants. Books must be first foreign or first Canadian editions. Nonfiction books in the following categories are eligible: culture and the arts, science, biography, history, geography, reference, sports, activities, and pastimes. Deadline: December 20. Prize: $10,000. The award will go to the author unless 40% or more of the text area is composed of original illustrations, in which case the award will be divided equally between author and illustrator. Judged by at least 3 of the following: a teacher, a librarian, a bookseller, and a reviewer. A judge will have a deep understanding of, and some involvement with, Canadian children's books.

GOLDEN KITE AWARDS

Society of Children's Book Writers and Illustrators (SCBWI), SCBWI Golden Kite Awards, 8271 Beverly Blvd., Los Angeles CA 90048-4515. (323)782-1010. **E-mail:** sararutenberg@scbwi.org. **Website:** www.scbwi.org. Society of Children's Book Writers and Illustrators, 8271 Beverly Blvd.Los Angeles CA 90048. (323)782-1010. **E-mail:** scbwi@scbwi.org. **Website:** www.scbwi.org. **Contact:** SCBWI Golden Kite Coordinator. Annual award. Estab. 1973. "The works chosen will be those that the judges feel exhibit excellence in writing, and in the case of the picture-illustrated books—in illustration, and genuinely appeal to the interests and concerns of children. For the fiction and nonfiction awards, original works and single author collections of stories or poems of which at least half are new and never before published in book form are eligible—anthologies and translations are not. For the picture-illustration awards, the art or photographs must be original works (the texts—which may be fiction or nonfiction—may be original, public domain or previously published). Deadline for entries: December 15. SASE for award rules. No entry fee. Awards, in addition to statuettes and plaques, the four winners receive $2,500 cash award plus trip to LA SCBWI Conference. The panel of judges will consist of professional authors, illustrators, editors or agents." Requirements for entrants: "must be a member of SCBWI and books must be published in that year." Winning books will be displayed at national conference in August. Books to be entered, as well as further inquiries, should be submitted to: The Society of Children's Book Writers and Illustrators, above address. Given annually to recognize excellence in children's literature in 4 categories: fiction, nonfiction, picture book text, and picture book illustration. Books submitted must be published in the previous calendar year. Both individuals and publishers may submit. Submit 4 copies of book. Submit to one category only, except in the case of picture books. Deadline: December 1. Prize: One Golden Kite Award Winner and one Honor Book will be chosen per category. Winners and Honorees will receive a commemorative poster also sent to publishers, bookstores, libraries, and schools; a press release; an announcement on the SCBWI website; and on SCBWI Social Networks. Also receive an expense-paid trip to Los Angeles to attend the award ceremony.

⊕ GOVERNOR GENERAL'S LITERARY AWARD FOR CHILDREN'S LITERATURE

Canada Council for the Arts, 150 Elgin St., P.O. Box 1047, Ottawa ON K1P 5V8 Canada. (613)566-4414, ext. 5573. **Website:** www.canadacouncil.ca/prizes/ggla. Offered for the best English-language and the best French-language works of children's literature by a Canadian in 2 categories: text and illustration. Publishers submit titles for consideration. Deadline: Depends on the book's publication date. Books in English: March 15, June 1, or August 7. Books in French: March 15 or July 15. Prize: Each laureate receives $25,000; non-winning finalists receive $1,000.

CAROL OTIS HURST CHILDREN'S BOOK PRIZE

Westfield Athenaeum, 6 Elm St., Westfield MA 01085. (413)568-7833. **Website:** www.westath.org. The Carol Otis Hurst Children's Book Prize honors outstanding works of fiction and nonfiction written for children and young adults through the age of 18. For a work to be considered, the writer must either be a native or a current resident of New England. While the prize is presented annually to an author whose work best exemplifies the highest standards of writing for this age group regardless of genre or topic or geographical setting, the prize committee is especially interested in those books that treat life in the region. Further, entries will be judged on how well they succeed in portraying one or more of the following elements: childhood, adolescence, family life, schooling, social and political developments, fine and performing artistic expression, domestic arts, environmental issues, transportation and communication, changing technology, military experience at home and abroad, business and manufacturing, workers and the labor movement, agriculture and its transformation, racial and ethnic diversity, religious life and institutions, immigration and adjustment, sports at all levels, and the evolution of popular entertainment. Books must have been copyrighted in their original format during the calendar year, January 1 to December 31, of the year preceding the year in which the prize is awarded. Any individual, publisher, or organization may nominate a book. See website for details and guidelines. Prize: $500.

EZRA JACK KEATS/KERLAN MEMORIAL FELLOWSHIP

113 Elmer L. Andersen Library, 222 21st Ave. S., University of Minnesota, Minneapolis MN 55455. E-mail: clrc@umn.edu. Website: https://www.lib.umn.edu/clrc/awards-grants-and-fellowships. Contact: Lisa Von Drasek, curator. This fellowship from the Ezra Jack Keats Foundation will provide $1,500 to a talented writer and/or illustrator of children's books who wishes to use the Kerlan Collection for the furtherance of his or her artistic development. Special consideration will be given to someone who would find it difficult to finance a visit to the Kerlan Collection. The Ezra Jack Keats Fellowship recipient will receive transportation costs and a per diem allotment. See website for application deadline and for digital application materials. Winner will be notified in February. Study and written report must be completed within the calendar year. Deadline: January 30.

KENTUCKY BLUEGRASS AWARD

Northern Kentucky University, 405 Steely Library, Nunn Drive, Highland Heights KY 41099. (859)572-6620. E-mail: smithjen@nku.edu. Website: kba.nku.edu. The Kentucky Bluegrass Award is a student choice program. The KBA promotes and encourages Kentucky students in kindergarten through grade 12 to read a variety of quality literature. Each year, a KBA committee for each grade category chooses the books for the four Master Lists (K-2, 3-5, 6-8 and 9-12). All Kentucky public and private schools, as well as public libraries, are welcome to participate in the program. To nominate a book, see the website for form and details. Deadline: March 1. Judged by students who read books and choose their favorite.

☺ THE VICKY METCALF AWARD FOR CHILDREN'S LITERATURE

The Writers' Trust of Canada, 460 Richmond St. W., Suite 600, Toronto ON M5V 1Y1 Canada. (416)504-8222. E-mail: info@writerstrust.com. Website: www.writerstrust.com. Contact: Amanda Hopkins. The Metcalf Award is presented to a Canadian writer for a body of work in children's literature at The Writers' Trust Awards event held in Toronto each Fall. Open to Canadian citizens and permanent residents only.

NEW ENGLAND BOOK AWARDS

1955 Massachusetts Ave., #2, Cambridge MA 02140. (617)547-3642. Fax: (617)547-3759. E-mail: nan@neba.org. Website: www.newenglandbooks.org/BookAwards. Contact: Nan Sorenson, assistant executive director. Annual award. Previously published submissions only. Submissions made by New England booksellers; publishers. Submit written nominations only; actual books should not be sent. Member bookstores receive materials to display winners' books. Award is given to a specific title, fiction, nonfiction, children's. The titles must be either about New England, set in New England or by an author residing in the New England. The titles must be hardcover, paperback orginal or reissue that was published between September 1 and August 31. Entries must be still in print and available. Deadline: June 13. Judged by NEIBA membership.

HELEN KEATING OTT AWARD FOR OUTSTANDING CONTRIBUTION TO CHILDREN'S LITERATURE

10157 SW Barbur Blvd. #102C, Portland OR 97219. (503)244-6919. Fax: (503)977-3734. E-mail: csla@worldaccessnet.com. Website: www.cslainfo.org. Contact: Glenda Strombom; Judy Janzen, administrator of CSLA. Annual award given to a person or organization that has made a significant contribution to promoting high moral and ethical values through children's literature. Recipient is honored in July during the conference. Awards certificate of recognition, the awards banquet, and one-night's stay in the hotel. A nomination for an award may be made by anyone. An application form is available by contacting Judy Janzen. Elements of creativity and innovation will be given high priority by the judges. A detailed description of the reasons for the nomination should be given, accompanied by documentary evidence of accomplishment. The nominator should give his or her name, address, telephone number, e-mail address, and a brief explanation of his or her knowledge of the individual's efforts. Elements of creativity and innovation will be given high priority. Applications should include at least 2 examples of your work (published or unpublished, 30 pages maximum) and a short biographical note including a description of your current and anticipated work. Also, indicate what you will work on while attending the Blue Mountain residency. Send three copies of these writing samples. Samples will not be returned.

PATERSON PRIZE FOR BOOKS FOR YOUNG PEOPLE

The Poetry Center at Passaic County Community College, One College Blvd., Paterson NJ 07505. (973)684-6555. **Fax:** (973)523-6085. **E-mail:** mgillan@pccc.edu. **Website:** www.pccc.edu/poetry. **Contact:** Maria Mazziotti Gillan, executive director. Award for a book published in the previous year in each age category (Pre-K-Grade 3, Grades 4-6, Grades 7-12). Deadline: March 15. Prize: $500.

PENNSYLVANIA YOUNG READERS' CHOICE AWARDS PROGRAM

148 S. Bethelehem Pike, Ambler PA 19002-5822. (215)643-5048. **E-mail:** bellavance@verizon.net. **Website:** www.psla.org. **Contact:** Jean B. Bellavance, coordinator. Submissions nominated by a person or group. Must be published within 5 years of the award—for example, books published in 2010 to present are eligible for the 2014-2015 award. SASE for contest rules and entry forms or check the Program wiki at pyrca.wikispaces.com. View information at the Pennsylvania School Librarians' website or the Program wiki. Must be currently living in North America. The purpose of the Pennsylvania Young Reader's Choice Awards Program is to promote the reading of quality books by young people in the Commonwealth of Pennsylvania, to encourage teacher and librarian collaboration and involvement in children's literature, and to honor authors whose works have been recognized by the students of Pennsylvania. Deadline:

September 1. Prize: Framed certificate to winning authors. Four awards are given, one for each of the following grade level divisions: K-3, 3-6, 6-8, YA. Judged by children of Pennsylvania (they vote).

POCKETS FICTION-WRITING CONTEST

P.O. Box 340004, Nashville TN 37203-0004. (615)340-7333. **Fax:** (615)340-7267. **E-mail:** pockets@upperroom.org. **Website:** www.pockets.upperroom.org. **Contact:** Lynn W. Gilliam, senior editor. Designed for 6- to 12-year-olds, *Pockets* magazine offers wholesome devotional readings that teach about God's love and presence in life. The content includes fiction, scripture stories, puzzles and games, poems, recipes, colorful pictures, activities, and scripture readings. Freelance submissions of stories, poems, recipes, puzzles and games, and activities are welcome. Stories should be 750-1,000 words. Multiple submissions are permitted. Past winners are ineligible. The primary purpose of *Pockets* is to help children grow in their relationship with God and to claim the good news of the gospel of Jesus Christ by applying it to their daily lives. *Pockets* espouses respect for all human beings and for God's creation. It regards a child's faith journey as an integral part of all of life and sees prayer as undergirding that journey. Deadline: Entries are received beginning March 1 and must be postmarked no later than August 15. Prize: $500 and publication in magazine.

PURPLE DRAGONFLY BOOK AWARDS

4696 W. Tyson St., Chandler AZ 85226-2903. (480)940-8182. **Fax:** (480)940-8787. **E-mail:** cristy@fivestarpublications.com. **Website:** www.purpledragonflybookawards.com; www.fivestarpublications.com; www.fivestarbookawards.com. **Contact:** Cristy Bertini, contest coordinator. Five Star Publications presents the Purple Dragonfly Book Awards, which were conceived and designed with children in mind. "Not only do we want to recognize and honor accomplished authors in the field of children's literature, but we also want to highlight and reward up-and-coming, newly published authors and younger published writers." The Purple Dragonfly Book Awards are divided into 3 distinct subject categories, ranging from books on the environment and cooking to sports and family issues. (Click on the "Categories" tab on the website for a complete list.) The Purple Dragonfly Book Awards are geared toward stories that appeal to children of all ages. Looking for stories that inspire, inform, teach or entertain. "A Purple Dragonfly seal on your book's cover tells parents, grandparents, educators and caregivers they are giving children the very best in reading excellence." Being honored with a Purple Dragonfly Award confers credibility upon the winner, as well as provides positive publicity to further their success. The goal of these awards is to give published authors the recognition they deserve and provide a helping hand to further their careers. The awards are open to books published in any calendar year and in any country that are available for purchase. Books entered must be printed in English. Traditionally published, partnership published and self-published books are permitted, as long as they fit the above criteria. Deadline: May 1 (postmarked). Submissions postmarked March 1 or earlier that meet all submission requirements are eligible for the Early Bird reward: A free copy of *The Economical Guide to Self-Publishing* or *Promote Like a Pro: Small Budget, Big Show*. Prize: Grand Prize winner will receive a $300 cash prize, 100 foil award seals (more can be ordered for an extra charge), 1 hour of marketing consultation from Five Star Publications, and $100 worth of Five Star Publications' titles, as well as publicity on Five Star Publications' websites and inclusion in a winners' news release sent to a comprehensive list of media outlets. The Grand Prize winner will also be placed in the Five Star Dragonfly Book Awards virtual bookstore with a thumbnail of the book's cover, price, 1-sentence description and link to Amazon.com for purchasing purposes, if applicable. 1st Place: All first-place winners of categories will be put into a drawing for a $100 prize. In addition, each first-place winner in each category receives a certificate commemorating their accomplishment, 25 foil award seals (more can be ordered for an extra charge) and mention on Five Star Publications' websites. Judged by industry experts with specific knowledge about the categories over which they preside.

QUILL AND SCROLL INTERNATIONAL WRITING AND PHOTO CONTEST, AND BLOGGING COMPETITION

School of Journalism, Univ. of Iowa, 100 Adler Journalism Bldg., Iowa City IA 52242-2004. (319)335-3457. **Fax:** (319)335-3989. **E-mail:** quill-scroll@uiowa.edu. **E-mail:** vanessa-shelton@uiowa.edu. **Website:** quillandscroll.org. **Contact:** Vanessa Shelton, contest director. Entries must have been published in a high school or profesional newspaper or website during the previous year, and must be the work of a currently enrolled high school student, when published. Open to students. Annual contest. Previously published submissions only. Submissions made by the author or school media adviser. Deadline: February 5. Prize: Winners will receive *Quill and Scroll*'s National Award Gold Key and, if seniors, are eligible to apply for one of the scholarships offered by *Quill and Scroll*. All winning entries are automatically eligible for the International Writing and Photo Sweepstakes Awards. Engraved plaque awarded to sweepstakes winners.

TOMÁS RIVERA MEXICAN AMERICAN CHILDREN'S BOOK AWARD

Dr. Jesse Gainer, Texas State University, 601 University Drive, San Marcos TX 78666-4613. (512)245-2357. **Website:** riverabookaward.org. **Contact:** Dr. Jesse Gainer, award director. Texas State University College of Education developed the Tomas Rivera Mexican American Children's Book Award to honor authors and illustrators who create literature that depicts the Mexican American experience. The award was established in 1995 and was named in honor of Dr. Tomas Rivera, a distinguished alumnus of Texas State University. The book will be written for children and young adults (0-16 years). The text and illustrations will be of highest quality. The portrayal/representations of Mexican Americans will be accurate and engaging, avoid stereotypes, and reflect rich characterization. The book may be fiction or non- fiction. See website for more details and directions. Deadline: November 1.

SCBWI MAGAZINE MERIT AWARDS

8271 Beverly Blvd., Los Angeles CA 90048. **Website:** www.scbwi.org. **Contact:** Stephanie Gordon, award coordinator. The SCBWI is a professional organization of writers and illustrators and others interested in children's literature. Membership is open to the general public at large. All magazine work for young people by an SCBWI member—writer, artist or photographer—is eligible during the year of original publication. In the case of co-authored work, both authors must be SCBWI members. Members must submit their own work. Requirements for entrants: 4 copies each of the published work and proof of publication (may be contents page) showing the name of the magazine and the date of issue.Previously published submissions only. For rules and procedures see website. Must be a SCBWI member. Recognizes outstanding original magazine work for young people published during that year, and having been written or illustrated by members of SCBWI. Deadline: January 1-December 15 of the year of publication. Prize: Awards plaques and honor certificates for each of 4 categories (fiction, nonfiction, illustration and poetry). Judged by a magazine editor and two "full" SCBWI members.

☯ TD CANADIAN CHILDREN'S LITERATURE AWARD

The Canadian Children's Book Centre, 40 Orchard View Blvd., Suite 217, Toronto ON M4R 1B9 Canada. (416)975-0010, ext. 222. **Fax:** (416)975-8970. **Website:** www.bookcentre.ca. **Contact:** Meghan Howe. The TD Canadian Children's Literature Award is for the most distinguished book of the year. All books, in any genre, written and illustrated by Canadians and for children ages 1-12 are eligible. Only books first published in Canada are eligible for submission. Books must be published between January 1 and December 31 of the previous calendar year. Open to Canadian citizens and/or permanent residents of Canada. Submission deadline: December 20. Prize: Prizes: Two prizes of $30,000, 1 for English, 1 for French. $10,000 will be divided among the Honour Book English titles and Honour Book French titles, to a maximum of 4; $2,500 shall go to each of the publishers of the English and French grand-prize winning books for promotion and publicity.

TIPS "Please visit website for submission guidelines and eligibility criteria, as well as specific submission deadline."

VEGETARIAN ESSAY CONTEST

The Vegetarian Resource Group, P.O. Box 1463, Baltimore MD 21203. (410)366-VEGE. **Fax:** (410)366-8804. **E-mail:** vrg@vrg.org. **Website:** www.vrg.org. A 2-3 page essay on any aspect of vegetarianism. Entrants should base their paper on interviewing, research, and/or personal opinon. You need not be a vegetarian to enter. Three different entry categories: age 14-18; age 9-13; and age 8 and under. Prize: $50.

RITA WILLIAMS YOUNG ADULT PROSE PRIZE CATEGORY

Soul-Making Keats Literary Competition, The Webhallow House, 1544 Sweetwood Drive, Broadmoor Village CA 94015-2029. **E-mail:** pennobhill@aol.com. **Website:** www.soulmakingcontest.us. **Contact:** Eileen Malone. Grades 9-12 or equivalent age. Up to 3,000 words in story, essay, journal entry, creative

nonfiction or memoir. Complete rules and guidelines online. Deadline: November 30 (postmarked). Prize: $100 for first place; $50 for second place; $25 for third place. Judged by Rita Wiliams, an Emmy-award winning investigative reporter with KTVU-TV in Oakland, California.

TIPS "This contest is for young adult writers, high school age writers; no adults writing for children."

WORK-IN-PROGRESS GRANT

Society of Children's Book Writers and Illustrators (SCBWI), 8271 Beverly Blvd., Los Angeles CA 90048. (323)782-1010. **E-mail:** scbwi@scbwi.org. **Website:** www.scbwi.org. Four grants—one designated specifically for a contemporary novel for young people, one for nonfiction, one for an unpublished writer, one general fiction—to assist SCBWI members in the completion of a specific project. Open to SCBWI members only. Deadline: February 15-March 15.

GENERAL

⊘♥ AUSTRALIAN CHRISTIAN BOOK OF THE YEAR AWARD

Australian Christian Literature Society, P.O. Box 198, Forest Hill Victoria 3131 Australia. **E-mail:** admin@sparklit.org. **Website:** www.sparklit.org. **Contact:** The Awards Coordinator. The Australian Christian Book of the Year Award is given annually to an original book written by an Australian citizen normally resident in Australia and published by an Australian publisher. The award recognizes and encourages excellence in Australian Christian writing. Entries must be published by April 1 of the year prior to competition. Deadline: March 31. Prize: $2,500 (AUD) and a framed certificate.

JAMIE CAT CALLAN HUMOR PRIZE

Category in the Soul-Making Keats Literary Competition, The Webhallow House, 1544 Sweetwood Dr., Broadmoor Village CA 94015-2029. **E-mail:** SoulKeats@mail.com. **Website:** www.soulmaking-contest.us. **Contact:** Eileen Malone. Any form, 2,500 words or less. One piece per entry. Previously published material is accepted. Open annually to any writer. Deadline: November 30. Prize: First Place: $100; Second Place: $50; Third Place: $25. Judged by Jamie Cat Callan.

TIPS "Make me laugh out loud."

♻ DAFOE BOOK PRIZE

J.W. Dafoe Foundation, 351 University College, University of Manitoba, Winnipeg MB R3T 2M8 Canada. **E-mail:** ferguss@cc.umanitoba.ca. **Contact:** Dr. James Fergusson. The Dafoe Book Prize was established to honor John Dafoe, editor of the *Winnipeg Free Press* from 1900 to 1944, and is awarded each year for distinguished writing by Canadians or authors in resident in Canada that contributes to the understanding of Canada, Canadians, and/or Canada's place in the world. Books must be published January-December of previous publishing year—i.e., 2014 Award is for books published in 2013. Co-authored books are eligible, but not edited books consisting of chapters from many different authors. Submit 4 copies of book. Deadline: December 6. Prize: $10,000. Judged by board members and academics.

● THE DEBUT DAGGER

Crime Writers' Association, New Writing Competition, P.O. Box 3408, Norwich NR3 3WE England. **E-mail:** director@thecwa.co.uk. **Website:** www.thecwa.co.uk. **Contact:** Mary Andrea Clarke. Annual competition for unpublished crime writers. Submit the opening 3,000 words of a crime novel, plus a 500-1,000 word synopsis of its continuance. Open to any writer who has not had a novel commercially published in any genre. Only accepts entries in Microsoft Word Document or PDF form. Submissions should not include entrant's name anywhere on the documents. See website for details on guidelines and submitting. Deadline: January 31. Submission period begins November 1. Prize: 1st Prize: £700. All shortlisted entrants will receive a professional assessment of their entries. Judged by a panel of top crime editors and agents, and the shortlisted entries are sent to publishers and agents.

THE FOUNTAINHEAD ESSAY CONTEST

The Ayn Rand Institute, P.O. Box 57044, Irvine CA 92619-7044. **E-mail:** essay@aynrand.org. **Website:** www.aynrand.org/contests. Offered annually to encourage analytical thinking and excellence in writing, and to expose students to the philosophic ideas of Ayn Rand. "For information contact your English teacher or guidance counselor, or visit our website." Length: 800-1,600 words. Open to 11th and 12th graders. Deadline: April 26. Prize: Prizes: 1st Place: $10,000; 2nd Place (5): $2,000; 3rd Place (10): $1,000; Finalist (45): $100; Semifinalist (175): $50.

THE GLENNA LUSCHEI PRAIRIE SCHOONER AWARDS

Prairie Schooner, 123 Andrews Hall, P.O. Box 880334, Lincoln NE 68588-0334. (402)472-0911. **Fax:** (402)472-9771. **E-mail:** prairieschooner@unl.edu; psbookprize@unl.edu. **Website:** prairieschooner.unl.edu/. **Contact:** Kwame Dawes. Annual awards for work published in *Prairie Schooner* in the previous year. Offers one large prize and 10 smaller awards. See website for more details. Contact *Prairie Schooner* for further information. Prize: One award of $1,500 and 10 awards of $250 each.

INDEPENDENT PUBLISHER BOOK AWARDS

Jenkins Group/Independent Publisher Online, 1129 Woodmere Ave., Ste. B, Traverse City MI 49686. (231)933-4954, ext. 1011. **Fax:** (231)933-0448. **E-mail:** jimb@bookpublishing.com. **Website:** www.independentpublisher.com. **Contact:** Jim Barnes. Honors the year's best independently published titles from around the world. The IPPY Awards reward those who exhibit the courage, innovation, and creativity to bring about change in the world of publishing. Independent spirit and expertise comes from publishers of all areas and budgets, and we judge books with that in mind. Entries will be accepted in over 70 categories, visit website to see details. Open to any published writer. Accepts books published within the past 2 years. See website for guidelines and details. Deadline: March 16. Price of submission rises after January 25. Prize: Gold, silver and bronze medals for each category; foil seals available to all. Judged by a panel of experts representing the fields of design, writing, bookselling, library, and reviewing.

DOROTHEA LANGE—PAUL TAYLOR PRIZE

Center for Documentary Studies, 1317 W. Pettigrew St., Duke University, Durham NC 27705. (919)660-3662. **Fax:** (919)681-7600. **E-mail:** alexad@duke.edu. **Website:** documentarystudies.duke.edu/awards/dorothea-lange-paul-taylor-prize. **Contact:** Alexa Dilworth. Award from the Center for Documentary Studies at Duke University, supporting documentary artists, working alone or in teams, who are involved in extended, on-going fieldwork projects that rely on and exploit the interplay of words and images. More information online. First announced a year after the Center for Documentary Studies' founding at Duke University, the prize was created to encourage a collaboration between documentary writers and photographers in the tradition of the acclaimed photographer Dorothea Lange and writer and social scientist Paul Taylor. Deadline: May 7. Submissions accepted starting in February.

MLA PRIZE IN UNITED STATES LATINA & LATINO AND CHICANA & CHICANO LITERARY AND CULTURAL STUDIES

Modern Language Association of America, 26 Broadway, 3rd Floor, New York NY 10004-1789. (646)576-5141. **Fax:** (646)458-0030. **E-mail:** awards@mla.org. **Website:** www.mla.org. **Contact:** Coordinator of Book Prizes. Offered in odd-numbered years for an outstanding scholarly study in any language of United States Latina and Latino or Chicana and Chicano literature or culture. Books must have been published in the two previous years before the award. Authors must be current members of the MLA. Requires 4 copies of the book. Deadline: May 1. Prize: A cash award, and a certificate to be presented at the Modern Language Association's annual convention in January.

NACUSA YOUNG COMPOSERS' COMPETITION

Box 49256 Barrington Station, Los Angeles CA 90049. (541)765-2406. **E-mail:** nacusa@music-usa.org. **Website:** www.music-usa.org/nacusa. **Contact:** Greg Steinke. Send for application. Samples are not required. Encourages the composition of new American concert hall music. Deadline: October 30. Prize: Prizes: 1st Prize: $400; 2nd Prize: $100; and possible Los Angeles performances. Applications are judged by a committee of experienced NACUSA composer members.

OHIOANA WALTER RUMSEY MARVIN GRANT

Ohioana Library Association, 274 E. First Ave., Suite 300, Columbus OH 43201. (614)466-3831. **Fax:** (614)728-6974. **E-mail:** ohioana@ohioana.org. **Website:** www.ohioana.org. **Contact:** David Weaver, executive director. Open to unpublished authors born in Ohio or who have lived in Ohio for a minimum of 5 years. Must be 30 years of age or younger. Guidelines for SASE or online. Winner notified in early summer. Up to 6 pieces of prose may be submitted; maximum 60 pages, minimum 10 pages double-spaced, 12-point type. Entries must be unpublished. Award to encourage young, unpublished writers 30 years of age or younger. Competition for short stories or novels in progress. Deadline: January 31. Prize: $1,000.

DAVID RAFFELOCK AWARD FOR PUBLISHING EXCELLENCE

National Writers Association, 10940 S. Parker Rd., #508, Parker CO 80134. (303)841-0246. **E-mail:** natlwritersassn@hotmail.com. **Website:** www.national-writers.com. **Contact:** Sandy Whelchel. Contest is offered annually for books published the previous year. Published works only. Open to any writer. Guidelines for SASE, by e-mail or online. Winners announced in June at the NWAF conference and notified by mail or phone. List of winners available for SASE or visit website. Purpose is to assist published authors in marketing their works and to reward outstanding published works. Deadline: May 15. Prize: Publicity tour, including airfare, valued at $5,000.

BYRON CALDWELL SMITH BOOK AWARD

The University of Kansas, Hall Center for the Humanities, 900 Sunnyside Ave., Lawrence KS 66045. (785)864-4798. **E-mail:** vbailey@ku.edu. **Website:** www.hallcenter.ku.edu. **Contact:** Victor Bailey, director. Offered in odd years. To qualify, applicants must live or be employed in Kansas and have written an outstanding book published within the previous 2 calendar years. Translations are eligible. Guidelines for SASE or online. Deadline: March 1. Prize: $1,500.

FRED WHITEHEAD AWARD FOR DESIGN OF A TRADE BOOK

Texas Institute of Letters, P.O. Box 609, Round Rock TX 78680. **E-mail:** tilsecretary@yahoo.com. **Website:** www.texasinstituteofletters.org. Offered annually for the best design for a trade book. Open to Texas residents or those who have lived in Texas for 2 consecutive years. See website for guidelines. **Deadline: early January**; see website for exact date. Prize: $750.

◎ THE WRITERS' TRUST ENGEL/FINDLEY AWARD

The Writers' Trust of Canada, 460 Richmond St. W., Suite 600, Toronto ON M5V 1Y1 Canada. (416)504-8222. **Fax:** (416)504-9090. **E-mail:** info@writerstrust.com. **Website:** www.writerstrust.com. **Contact:** Amanda Hopkins. The Writers' Trust Engel/Findley Award is presented annually at The Writers' Trust Awards Event, held in Toronto each fall, to a Canadian writer for a body of work in hope of continued contribution to the richness of Canadian literature.

Open to Canadian citizens and permanent residents only. Prize: $25,000.

JOURNALISM

AAAS KAVLI SCIENCE JOURNALISM AWARDS

American Association for the Advancement of Science, Office of News and Information, 1200 New York Ave. NW, Washington DC 20005. **Website:** www.aaas.org/SJAwards. **Contact:** Awards Coordinator. Offered annually to recognize scientists, journalists, and public servants for significant contributions to science and to the public's understanding of science. Entries are submitted online, only. Enter e-mail address in online contact form to be alerted when entry forms are available. See website for guidelines and details. Deadline: August 1. Prize: $3,000 and a trip to AAAS Annual Meeting (travel and hotel expenses will be reimbursed). Judged by committees of reporters and editors.

THE AMERICAN LEGION FOURTH ESTATE AWARD

The American Legion, The American Legion, 700 N. Pennsylvania St., Indianapolis IN 46204. (317)630-1253. **E-mail:** pr@legion.org. **Website:** www.legion.org/presscenter/fourthestate. Offered annually for journalistic works published the previous calendar year. Subject matter must deal with a topic or issue of national interest or concern. Entry must include cover letter explaining entry, and any documentation or evidence of the entry's impact on the community, state, or nation. No printed entry form. Guidelines available by SASE or online. Deadline: February 18. Prize: $2,000 stipend to defray expenses of recipient accepting the award at The American Legion National Convention in August. Judged by members of The National Public Relations Commission of The American Legion.

FRANK LUTHER MOTT-KAPPA TAU ALPHA RESEARCH AWARD IN JOURNALISM

University of Missouri School of Journalism, 76 Gannett Hall, Columbia MO 65211-1200. (573)882-7685. **E-mail:** umcjourkta@missouri.edu. **Website:** www.kappataualpha.org. **Contact:** Dr. Keith Sanders, exec. dir., Kappa Tau Alpha. Offered annually for best researched book in mass communication. Submit 6 copies; no forms required. Deadline: Decem-

ber 9. Prize: $1,000. Judged by a panel of university professors of journalism and mass communication and national officers of Kappa Tau Alpha.

INVESTIGATIVE JOURNALISM GRANT

Fund For Investigative Journalism, Fund for Investigative Journalism, 529 14th Street NW, 13th Floor, Washington DC 20045. (202662-7564. **E-mail:** fundfij@gmail.com. **Website:** www.fij.org. **Contact:** Sandy Bergo, Executive Director. Offered 3 times/year for original investigative newspaper and magazine stories, radio and TV documentaries, and books. Guidelines online. See website for details on applying for a grant. Deadlines: Vary. Check website. Prize: Grants of $500-10,000. (Average Grant: $5,000.)

SCIENCE IN SOCIETY AWARDS

National Association of Science Writers, Inc., P.O. Box 7905, Berkeley CA 94707. (510)647-9500. **E-mail:** director@nasw.org. **Website:** www.nasw.org. **Contact:** Tinsley Davis. Offered annually for investigative or interpretive reporting about the sciences and their impact on society. Categories: books, commentary and opinions, longformat science reporting, and science reporting for a local or regional market. Material may be a single article or broadcast, or a series. Works must have been first published or broadcast in North America between January 1 and December 31 of the previous year. Deadline: February 1. Prize: $2,500, and a certificate of recognition in each category.

TRANSLATION

ALTA NATIONAL TRANSLATION AWARD

American Literary Translators Association, The University of Texas at Dallas, 800 W. Campbell Rd., JO51, Richardson TX 75080-3021. (972)883-2093. **Fax:** (972)883-6303. **E-mail:** maria.suarez@utdallas.edu. **Website:** www.literarytranslators.org. **Contact:** Jeffrey Green. Awarded annualy for the best book-length translation of a work into English. Winner announced each year at ALTA's annual conference. To be eligible, the translation must be by an American citizen or U.S. resident, from any language into English, of a book-length work of fiction, poetry, drama, or creative nonfiction (literary criticism, philosophy, and biographies are not eligible), and published anywhere in the world during the previous year. Honors the translator whose work, by virtue of both its quality and significance, has made the most valuable contribution to literary translation in the preceding calendar year. Deadline: March 31. Prize: $5,000; winner announced and featured at annual ALTA conference in the fall; press release distributed to major publications. Judged by a panel of translators.

AMERICAN-SCANDINAVIAN FOUNDATION TRANSLATION PRIZE

The American-Scandinavian Foundation, 58 Park Ave., New York NY 10016. (212)779-3587. **E-mail:** grants@amscan.org. **Website:** www.amscan.org. **Contact:** Matthew Walters, director of fellowships & grants. The annual ASF translation competition is awarded for the most outstanding translations of poetry, fiction, drama, or literary prose written by a Scandinavian author born after 1800. Accepts inquiries by e-mail, or through online application. Instructions an application online. Entries must be unpublished. Length: No more than 50 pages for drama and fiction; no more than 35 pages for poetry. Open to any writer. Results announced in November. Winners notified by e-mail. Results available on the ASF website. Guidelines online. Deadline: June 1. Prize: The Nadia Christensen Prize includes a $2000 award, publication of an excerpt in Scandinavian Review, and a commemorative bronze medallion; The Leif and Inger Sjöberg Award, given to an individual whose literature translations have not previously been published, includes a $1,000 award, publication of an excerpt in Scandinavian Review, and a commemorative bronze medallion.

DER-HOVANESSIAN PRIZE

New England Poetry Club, 376 School St., Watertown MA 02472. **E-mail:** contests@nepoetryclub.org. **Website:** www.nepoetryclub.org. **Contact:** Audrey Kalajin. For a translation from any language into English. Send a copy of the original. Funded by John Mahtesian. Contest open to members and nonmembers. Poems should be typed and submitted in duplicate with author's name, address, phone, and e-mail address of writer on only 1 copy. Label poems with contest name. Entries should be sent by regular mail only. Entries should be original, unpublished poems in English. No poem should be entered in more than 1 contest, nor have won a previous contest. Deadline:

May 31. Prize: $200. Judges are well-known poets and sometimes winners of previous NEPC contests.

SOEURETTE DIEHL FRASER AWARD FOR BEST TRANSLATION OF A BOOK

P.O. Box 609, Round Rock TX 78680. **E-mail:** tilsecretary@yahoo.com. **Website:** texasinstituteofletters.org. Offered every 2 years to recognize the best translation of a literary book into English. Translator must have been born in Texas or have lived in the state for at least 2 consecutive years at some time. Check website for guidelines and instructions on submitting. Deadline: January 10. Prize: $1,000.

THE FRENCH-AMERICAN AND THE FLORENCE GOULD FOUNDATIONS TRANSLATION PRIZES

28 W. 44th St., Suite 1420, New York NY 10036. (646)588-6786. **E-mail:** ebriet@frenchamerican.org. **Website:** www.frenchamerican.org. **Contact:** Eugenie Briet. Annual contest to promote French literature in the United States by extending its reach beyond the first language and giving translators and their craft greater visibility among publishers and readers alike. The prize also seeks to increase the visibility of the publishers who bring these important French works of literature, in translation of exceptional quality, to the American market by publicizing the titles and giving more visibility to the books they publish. Entries must have been published for the first time in the United States between January 1 and December 31, of the previous year. Deadline: December 31. Prize: $10,000 award. Jury committee made up of translators, writers, and scholars in French literature and culture.

⟳ GOVERNOR GENERAL'S LITERARY AWARD FOR TRANSLATION

Canada Council for the Arts, 150 Elgin St., P.O. Box 1047, Ottawa ON K1P 5V8 Canada. (613)566-4414, ext. 5573. **Fax:** (613)566-4410. **Website:** www.canadacouncil.ca/prizes/ggla. Offered for the best English-language and the best French-language work of translation by a Canadian. Publishers submit titles for consideration Deadline: Depends on the book's publication date. Books in English: March 15, June 1, or August 7. Books in French: March 15 or July 15. Prize: Each laureate receives $25,000; non-winning finalists receive $1,000.

CONTESTS & AWARDS

THE HAROLD MORTON LANDON TRANSLATION AWARD

Academy of American Poets, 75 Maiden Lane, Suite 901, New York NY 10038. (212)274-0343. **Fax:** (212)274-9427. **E-mail:** awards@poets.org. **Website:** www.poets.org. **Contact:** Awards Coordinator. Offered annually to recognize a published translation of poetry from any language into English. Open to living US citizens. Deadline: February 15. Prize: $1,000.

FENIA AND YAAKOV LEVIANT MEMORIAL PRIZE IN YIDDISH STUDIES

Modern Language Association of America, 26 Broadway, 3rd Floor, New York NY 10004-1789. (646)576-5141. **Fax:** (646)458-0030. **E-mail:** awards@mla.org. **Website:** www.mla.org. **Contact:** Coordinator of book prizes. Offered in even-numbered years for an outstanding English translation of a Yiddish literary work. Cultural studies, critical biographies, or edited works in the field of Yiddish folklore or linguistic studies are eligible to compete. Books must have been published within the past 4 years. Authors need not be members of the MLA. Requires 4 copies of the book. Deadline: May 1. Prize: A cash prize, and a certificate, to be presented at the Modern Language Association's annual convention in January.

LOIS ROTH AWARD

Modern Language Association, 26 Broadway, 3rd Floor, New York NY 10004. (646)576-5141. **Fax:** (646)458-0030. **E-mail:** awards@mla.org. **Website:** www.mla.org. Offered in odd-numbered years for an outstanding translation into English of a book-length literary work. Translators need not be members of the MLA. Translations must have been published in the previous calendar year. Requires 6 copies, plus 12-15 pages of text in the original language. Deadline: April 1. Prize: A cash award and a certificate to be presented at the Modern Language Association's annual convention in January.

ALDO AND JEANNE SCAGLIONE PRIZE FOR A TRANSLATION OF A LITERARY WORK

Modern Language Association, 26 Broadway, 3rd Floor, New York NY 10004-1789. (646)576-5141. **Fax:** (646)458-0030. **E-mail:** awards@mla.org. **Website:** www.mla.org. **Contact:** Coordinator of Book Prizes. Offered in even-numbered years for an outstanding translation into English of a book-length literary work. Translations must have been published in the

previous calendar year. Translators need not be members of the MLA. Requires 6 copies of the book, plus 12-15 pages of text in the original language. Deadline: April 1. Prize: A cash award and a certificate to be presented at the Modern Language Association's annual convention in January.

ALDO AND JEANNE SCAGLIONE PRIZE FOR A TRANSLATION OF A SCHOLARLY STUDY OF LITERATURE

Modern Language Association of America, 26 Broadway, 3rd Floor, New York NY 10004-1789. (646)576-5141. **Fax:** (646)458-0030. **E-mail:** awards@mla.org. **Website:** www.mla.org. **Contact:** Coordinator of Book Prizes. Offered in odd-numbered years for an outstanding translation into English of a book-length work of literary history, literary criticism, philology, or literary theory. Translators need not be members of the MLA. Books must have been published in the previous 2 years. Requires 4 copies of the book. Deadline: May 1. Prize: A cash award and a certificate to be presented at the Modern Language Association's annual convention in January.

POETRY

✪ ACORN-PLANTOS AWARD FOR PEOPLES POETRY

Acorn-Plantos Award Committee, 36 Sunset Ave., Hamilton ON L8R 1V6 Canada. **E-mail:** jeffseff@allstream.net. **Contact:** Jeff Seffinga. Annual contest for work that appeared in print in the previous calender year. This award is given to the Canadian poet who best (through the publication of a book of poems) exemplifies populist or peoples poetry in the tradition of Milton Acorn, Ted Plantos, et al. Work may be entered by the poet or the publisher; the award goes to the poet. Entrants must submit 5 copies of each title. Poet must be a citizen of Canada or a landed immigrant. Publisher need not be Canadian. Deadline: June 30. Prize: $500 (CDN) and a medal. Judged by a panel of poets in the tradition who are not entered in the current year.

AKRON POETRY PRIZE

The University of Akron Press, 120 E. Mill St., Suite 415, Akron OH 44308. (330)972-5342. **Fax:** (330)972-8364. **E-mail:** uapress@uakron.edu; marybid@uakron.edu. **Website:** www3.uakron.edu/uapress/poetryprize.html. **Contact:** Mary Biddinger, editor/award director. Submissions must be unpublished. Considers simultaneous submissions (with notification of acceptance elsewhere). Submit 48 or more pages, typed, single-spaced; optional self-addressed postcard for confirmation. Mss will not be returned. Do not send mss bound or enclosed in covers. See website for complete guidelines. Competition receives 500+ entries. 2013 winner was John Repp for *Fat Jersey Blues*. Winner posted online by September 30. Intimate friends, relatives, current and former students of the final judge (students in an academic, degree-conferring program or its equivalent) and current faculty, staff, students, and alumni of the University of Akron or the Northeast Ohio MFA Program (NEOMFA) are not eligible to enter the Akron Poetry Prize competition. **Deadline:** April 15-June 15. **Prize:** $1,500, plus publication of a book-length ms.

THE AMERICAN POETRY JOURNAL BOOK PRIZE

P.O. Box 2080, Aptos CA 95001-2080. **E-mail:** editor@americanpoetryjournal.com. **Website:** www.americanpoetryjournal.com. Both free and formal verse styles are welcome. Multiple submissions are acceptable. Submit 50-65 paginated pages of poetry, table of contents, acknowledgments, bio, and e-mail address (for results). No SASE required; mss will be recycled. Guidelines online. The American Poetry Journal Book Prize Awards $1,000 and publication. Winners of previous contests were Mark Conway, Quinn Latimer and Jennifer Moss. **Deadline:** February 28 for snail mail postmarks, five days later for electronic submissions. **Prize:** $1,000 and 20 published copies. All entries will be considered for publication.

THE ANHINGA PRESS-ROBERT DANA PRIZE FOR POETRY

Anhinga Press, P.O. Box 3665, Tallahassee FL 32315. (850)577-0745. **Fax:** (850)577-0745. **E-mail:** info@anhinga.org. **Website:** www.anhinga.org. **Contact:** Rick Campbell, poetry editor. Offered annually for a book-length collection of poetry by an author writing in English. Guidelines for SASE or online. Past winners include Frank X. Gaspar, Earl S. Braggs, Julia Levine, Keith Ratzlaff, and Lynn Aarti Chandhok, and Rhett Iseman Trull. Mss must be 48-80 pages, excluding front matter. **Deadline:** Submissions will be accepted from February 15-May 15. **Prize:** $2,000, a reading tour of selected Florida colleges and uninversities, and the winning ms will be published. Past judges

include Donald Hall, Joy Harjo, Robert Dana, Mark Jarman, and Tony Hoagland.

ANNUAL GIVAL PRESS OSCAR WILDE AWARD

Gival Press, LLC, P.O. Box 3812, Arlington VA 22203. (703)351-0079. **E-mail:** givalpress@yahoo.com. **Website:** www.givalpress.com. **Contact:** Robert L. Giron. Award given to the best previously unpublished original poem—written in English of any length, in any style, typed, double-spaced on 1 side only—which best relates gay/lesbian/bisexual/transgendered life, by a poet who is 18 years or older. Entrants are asked to submit their poems without any kind of identification (with the exception of titles) and with a separate cover page with the following information: name, address (street, city, and state with zip code), telephone number, e-mail address (if available), and a list of poems by title. Checks drawn on American banks should be made out to Gival Press, LLC. **Deadline:** June 27 (postmarked). **Prize:** $100 and the poem, along with information about the poet, will be published on the Gival Press website.

☺ ANNUAL VENTURA COUNTY WRITERS CLUB POETRY CONTEST

Ventura County Writers Club Poetry Contest, P.O. Box 3373, Thousand Oaks CA 91362. (805)524-6970. **E-mail:** poetrycontest@venturacountywriters.com; website@venturacountywriters.com. **Website:** www.venturacountywriters.com. **Contact:** Kate Sexton, president. Annual poetry contest. Holds 2 youth categories for poets under 18: Division A is open to entrants ages 13 to 18; and, Division B is open to poets ages 12 and under. Poets 18 and older are invited to enter in the Adult category. The contest is open to poets worldwide as long as the poem is in English. For both print and electronic entries, checks should be made payable to Ventura County Writers Club or VCWC. E-mail with "Poetry Contest" in the subject line. Send one poem per attachment. Send cover sheet in separate attachment with information as shown above. Include a cover sheet copy with your entry fee(s). **Deadline:** February 15. **Prize:** The adult and A/V categories will award $100 for first place, $75 for second and $50 for third place. The two youth categories will award $50 for first place, $35 for second and $25 for third place.

ANNUAL WORLD HAIKU COMPETITION & ANNUAL WORLD TANKA CONTEST

P.O. Box 17331, Arlington VA 22216. **E-mail:** LPEzineSubmissions@gmail.com. **Website:** lyricalpassionpoetry.yolasite.com. **Contact:** Raquel D. Bailey. Contest is open to all writers. Requires first rights for all previously unpublished works. Only e-mail entries accepted for contests. Promotes Japanese short form poetry. Deadline: See website for details. Prize: Monetary compensation and publication. Judged by experienced editors and award-winning writers from the contemporary writing community.

ART AFFAIR POETRY CONTEST

P.O. Box 54302, Oklahoma City OK 73154. **E-mail:** okpoets@aol.com. **Website:** www.shadetreecreations.com. **Contact:** Barbara Shepherd, acquisitions. The annual Art Affair Poetry Contest is open to any poet. Multiple entries accepted with entry fee for each and may be mailed in the same packet. Guidelines online. Winners' list will be published on the Art Affair website in December. Poems must be unpublished. Submit original poems on any subject, in any style, no more than 60 lines (put line count in the upper right-hand corner of first page). Include cover page with poet's name, address, phone number, and title of poem. Do not include SASE; poems will not be returned. Deadline: October 1. Prize: Prizes: 1st Prize: $40 and certificate; 2nd Prize: $25 and certificate; and 3rd Prize: $15 and certificate. Honorable Mention certificates will be awarded at the discretion of the judges.

ATLANTIC POETRY PRIZE

Writers' Federation of Nova Scotia, 1113 Marginal Rd., Halifax NS B3H 4P7 Canada. (902)423-8116. **Fax:** (902)422-0881. **E-mail:** director@writers.ns.ca. **Website:** www.writers.ns.ca. The Atlantic Poetry Prize is an annual award designed to honor the best book of poetry by a resident of Atlantic Canada. Detailed guidelines and eligibility criteria online. Deadline: First Friday in December. Prize: Valued at $2,000 for the winning title.

ELINOR BENEDICT POETRY PRIZE

Passages North, Northern Michigan University, 1401 Presque Isle Ave., Marquette MI 49855. **E-mail:** passages@nmu.edu. **Website:** passagesnorth.com/contests/. **Contact:** Jennifer A. Howard, Editor-in-Chief. Prize given biennially for a poem or a group of poems. Deadline: March 22. Submission period begins January 15. Prize: $1,000 and publication for winner; 2 honorable mentions are also published; all entrants receive a copy of *Passages North*. Judged by Aimee Nezhukumatathil.

THE PATRICIA BIBBY FIRST BOOK AWARD

Patricia Bibby Award, Tebot Bach, P.O. Box 7887, Huntington Beach CA 92615-7887. **E-mail:** mifanwy@tebotbach.org; info@tebotbach.org. **Website:** www.tebotbach.org. **Contact:** Mifanwy Kaiser. Annual competition open to all poets writing in English who have not committed to publishing collections of poetry of 36 poems or more in editions of over 400 copies. Offers award and publication of a book-length poetry ms by Tebot Bach. Complete guidelines available by e-mail or online. Deadline: October 31. Prize: $1,000 and book will be published. Judged by Dorothy Barresi.

BINGHAMTON UNIVERSITY MILT KESSLER POETRY BOOK AWARD

Binghamton University Creative Writing Program, Department of English, General Literature, and Rhetoric, Library North Room 1149, Vestal Parkway East, P.O. Box 6000, Binghamton NY 13902-6000. (607)777-2713. **Fax:** (607)777-2408. **E-mail:** cwpro@binghamton.edu. **Website:** www2.binghamton.edu/english/creative-writing/binghamton-center-for-writers. **Contact:** Maria Mazziotti Gillan, creative writing program director. Annual award for a book of poems written in English, 48 pages or more in length, selected by judges as the strongest collection of poems published in that year. Print on demand is acceptable but no self-published or vanity press work will be considered. Each book submitted must be accompanied by an application form online. Poet or publisher may submit more than 1 book for prize consideration. Send 3 copies of each book. Deadline: March 1. Prize: $1,000.

THE BITTER OLEANDER PRESS LIBRARY OF POETRY BOOK AWARD

The Bitter Oleander Press, 4983 Tall Oaks Dr., Fayetteville NY 13066-9776. (315)637-3047. **Fax:** (315)637-5056. **E-mail:** info@bitteroleander.com. **Website:** www.bitteroleander.com. **Contact:** Paul B. Roth. The Bitter Oleander Press Library of Poetry Book Award replaces the 15-year long run of the Frances Locke Memorial Poetry Award. Guidelines online Entrants must have had at least 1 standard edition of poetry published previously, not self-published, not a chapbook. Mss must be 48-80 pages of poetry in length, legibly typed or computer generated, with 2 cover sheets: 1 with title and author's contact information; the other having the title only. No e-mail submissions will be allowed. Winning ms to be published the following year. Deadline: May 1-June 15 (postmarked). Early or late entries will be disqualified. Prize: $1,000, plus book publication of the winning ms.

BLUE MOUNTAIN ARTS/SPS STUDIOS POETRY CARD CONTEST

P.O. Box 1007, Boulder CO 80306. (303)449-0536. **Fax:** (303)447-0939. **E-mail:** poetrycontest@sps.com. **E-mail:** editorial@sps.com. **Website:** www.sps.com. Biannual poetry card contest. All entries msut be the original creation of the submitting author. Looking for original poetry that is rhyming or non-rhyming, although non-rhyming poetry reads better. Poems may also be considered for possible publication on greeting cards or in book anthologies. Guidelines online. Deadline: December 31 and June 30. Prize: 1st Place: $300; 2nd Place: $150; 3rd Place: $50. Blue Mountain Arts editorial staff.

TIPS "We suggest that you write about real emotions and feelings and that you have some special person or occasion in mind as you write."

THE FREDERICK BOCK PRIZE

Poetry, 61 W. Superior St., Chicago IL 60654. (312)787-7070. **Fax:** (312)787-6650. **E-mail:** editors@poetry-magazine.org. **Website:** www.poetryfoundation.org. Several prizes are awarded annually for the best work printed in *Poetry* during the preceding year. Only poems already published in the magazine are eligible for consideration, and no formal application is necessary. The winners are announced in the November issue. Upon acceptance, *Poetry* licenses exclusive worldwide first serial rights, including electronic rights, for publication, as well as non-exclusive rights to reprint, reuse, and archive the work, in any format, in perpetuity. Copyright reverts to author upon first publication. Any writer may submit poems to *Poetry*. Prize: $500.

THE BOSTON REVIEW ANNUAL POETRY CONTEST

Boston Review, P.O. Box 425786, Cambridge MA 02142. (617)324-1360. **Fax:** (617)452-3356. **E-mail:** review@bostonreview.net. **Website:** www.bostonreview. net. Offers $1,500 and publication in *Boston Review* (see separate listing in Magazines/Journals). Any poet writing in English is eligible, unless he or she is a current student, former student, or close personal friend of the judge. Submissions must be unpublished. Submit up to 5 poems, no more than 10 pages total, in duplicate. Include cover sheet with poet's name, address, and phone number; no identifying information on the poems themselves. No cover note is necessary for online submissions. No mss will be returned. Guidelines available for SASE or online. Deadline: June 1. Winner announced in early November online.

BOULEVARD EMERGING POETS CONTEST

PMB 325, 6614 Clayton Rd., Richmond Heights MO 63117. **E-mail:** richardburgin@att.net; jessicarogen@boulevardmagazine.org. **Website:** www.boulevard-magazine.org. **Contact:** Jessica Rogen, managing editor. Annual Emerging Poets Contest offers $1,000 and publication in *Boulevard* (see separate listing in Magazines/Journals) for the best group of 3 poems by a poet who has not yet published a book of poetry with a nationally distributed press. All entries will be considered for publication and payment at regular rates. Submissions must be unpublished. Considers simultaneous submissions. Submit 3 poems, typed; may be a sequence or unrelated. On page one of first poem type poet's name, address, phone number, and titles of the 3 poems. Deadline: June 1. Prize: $1,000 and publication.

BARBARA BRADLEY PRIZE

New England Poetry Club, 376 School St., Watertown MA 02472 . **E-mail:** contests@nepoetryclub. org. **Website:** www.nepoetryclub.org. **Contact:** Audrey Kalajin. For a lyric poem under 20 lines, written by a woman. Contest open to members and nonmembers. Poems should be typed and submitted in duplicate with author's name, address, phone, and e-mail address of writer on only 1 copy. (Judges receive copies without names.) Copy only. Label poems with contest name. Entries should be sent by regular mail only. Special delivery or signature required mail will be returned by the post office. Entries should be original, unpublished poems in English. No poem should be entered in more than 1 contest, nor have won a previous contest. No entries will be returned. NEPC will not engage in correspondence regarding poems or contest decisions. Deadline: May 31. Prize: $200. Judged by well-known poets and sometimes winners of previous NEPC contests.

BRICK ROAD POETRY BOOK CONTEST

Brick Road Poetry Press, Inc., P.O. Box 751, Columbus GA 31902. (706)649-3080. **Fax:** (706)649-3094. **E-mail:** editor@brickroadpoetrypress.com. **Website:** www.brickroadpoetrypress.com. **Contact:** Ron Self and Keith Badowski, co-editors/founders. Annual competition for an original collection of 50-100 pages of poetery. Book-length poetry mss only. Simultaneous submissions accepted. Single sideded, single spaced only. No more than one poem per page. Electronic submissions are accepted, see website for details. Include a cover letter with poetry publication/recognition highlights. Deadline: November 1. Submission period begins August 1. Prize: $1,000, publication in both print and e-book formats, and 25 copies of the book. May also offer publication contracts to the top finalists.

TIPS "The best way to discover all that poetry can be and to expand the limits of your own poetry is to read expansively."

BRIGHT HILL PRESS POETRY CHAPBOOK COMPETITION

Bright Press Hill & Literary Center, P.O. Box 193, 94 Church St., Treadwell NY 13846. (607)829-5055. **E-mail:** brighthillpress@stny.rr.com. **Website:** www.brighthillpress.org. The annual Bright Hill Press Chapbook Award recognizes an outstanding collection of poetry. Guidelines available for SASE, by e-mail, or online. Collection of original poetry, 48-64 pages, single spaced, one poem to a page (no name) with table of contents. Ms must be submitted in Times New Roman, 12 pt. type only. No illustrations, no cover suggestions. Bio and acknowledgments of poems that have been previously published should be included in Comments Box. See website for more details, and information on submitting a hard copy. Deadline: November 30. Submission period begins October 25. Prize: A publication contract with Bright Hill Press and $1,000, publication in print format, and 30 copies of the printed book. Judged by a nationally-known poet.

TIPS "Publish your poems in literary magazines before trying to get a whole ms published. Publishing individual poems is the best way to hone your complete ms."

BRITTINGHAM PRIZE IN POETRY; FELIX POLLAK PRIZE IN POETRY

University of Wisconsin Press, Department of English, 600 N. Park St., University of Wisconsin, Madison WI 53706. **E-mail:** rwallace@wisc.edu. **Website:** www.wisc.edu/wisconsinpress/poetryguide.html.

Contact: Ronald Wallace, contest director. The annual Brittingham Prize in Poetry is 1 of 2 prizes awarded by The University of Wisconsin Press (see separate listing for the Felix Pollak Prize in Poetry in this section). Submissions must be unpublished as a collection, but individual poems may have been published elsewhere (publication must be acknowledged). Considers simultaneous submissions if notified of selection elsewhere. Submit 60-90 unbound ms pages, typed single-spaced (with double spaces between stanzas). Clean photocopies are acceptable. Include 1 title page with poet's name, address, and telephone number and 1 with title only. No translations. Strongly encourages electronic submissions via website. SASE required for postal submissions. Will return results only; mss will not be returned. Guidelines online. Deadline: Submit August 15 - September 15. Prize: $1,000, plus publication. Judged by a distinguished poet who will remain anonymous until the winners are announced in mid-February.

GERALD CABLE BOOK AWARD

Silverfish Review Press, P.O. Box 3541, Eugene OR 97403. (541)344-5060. **E-mail:** sfrpress@earthlink.net. **Website:** www.silverfishreviewpress.com. **Contact:** Rodger Moody, editor. Awarded annually to a book-length ms of original poetry by an author who has not yet published a full-length collection. There are no restrictions on the kind of poetry or subject matter; translations are not acceptable. Mss should be at least 48 pages in length. Clean photo copies are acceptable. The poet's name should not appear on the ms. Include a separate title page with name, address, and phone number. Poems may have appeared in periodicals, chapbooks, or anthologies, but should not be acknowledged. Simultaneous submissions are accepted. Accepts e-mail submissions. See website for more details and guidelines. Deadline: October 15. Prize: $1,000, publication, and 25 copies of the book. The winner will be announced in March.

CAKETRAIN CHAPBOOK COMPETITION

P.O. Box 82588, Pittsburgh PA 15218. **E-mail:** editors@caketrain.org. **Website:** www.caketrain.org/competitions. Deadline: October 1. Prize: $250 cash and 25 copies of their chapbook.

⊕ CHRISTMAS POETRY CONTEST

P.O. Box 1001, Reynoldsburg OH 43068. **E-mail:** dianaperry@DianaPerryBooks.com. **Website:** dianaperrybooks.com. **Contact:** Diana Perry. Purpose: "To give exposure to beginning poets trying to break in to the business and get noticed." Deadline: October 31. Prize: 1st Place: $200, trophy, mention online, t-shirt, press releases in your local newspapers; 2nd Place: $150, trophy, mention online, t-shirt, press releases in your local newspapers; 3rd Place: $100, trophy, mention online, t-shirt, press releases in your local newspapers; 4th/5th places: $50/$25, plaque, mention online, t-shirt, press releases in your local newspapers. "We also list names of next 25 honorable mentions online. Contest guidelines and entry form online. CHECK WEBSITE FOR GUEST JUDGES. Mail entry form, your poem, and a $15 money order only to Christmas Poetry Contest at above address postmarked no earlier than September 1 and no later October 31. Winners announced both online and via snail mail December 1. Prizes mailed within 10 days of announcement. Judged by Diana Perry and guest judge.

THE CENTER FOR BOOK ARTS POETRY CHAPBOOK COMPETITION

The Center for Book Arts, 28 W. 27th St., 3rd Floor, New York NY 10001. (212)481-0295. **Fax:** (866)708-8994. **E-mail:** info@centerforbookarts.org. **Website:** www.centerforbookarts.org. Annual competition for unpublished collections of poetry. Individual poems may have been previously published. Collection must not exceed 500 lines or 24 pages (does not include cover page, title pages, table of contents, or acknowledgements pages). Copies of winning chapbooks available through website. The cover page should contain, on a single detachable page, the ms title and author's name, along with address, phone number, and e-mail. The author's name should not appear anywhere else. A second title page should be provided without the author's name or other identification. Please provide a table of contents and a separate acknowledgements page containing prior magazine or anthology publication of individual poems. Mss should be bound with a simple spring clip. Poems may have appeared in journals or anthologies but not as part of a book-length collection. Competition is open to all poets writing in English who have published no more than 2 full-length books. Poets may not have studied with either judge in a degree-granting program for the last 5 years. Deadline: December 1. Prize: $500 award, $500 honorarium for a reading, publication, and 10 copies of chapbook. Judged by David St. John and Sharon Dolin.

⊕ CHRISTMAS POETRY CONTEST

P.O. Box 1001, Reynoldsburg OH 43068. **E-mail:** dianaperry@DianaPerryBooks.com. **Website:** dianaperrybooks.com. **Contact:** Diana Perry. Purpose: "To give exposure to beginning poets trying to break in to the business and get noticed." Deadline: October 31. Prize: 1st Place: $200, trophy, mention online, t-shirt, press releases in your local newspapers; 2nd Place: $150, trophy, mention online, t-shirt, press releases in your local newspapers; 3rd Place: $100, trophy, mention online, t-shirt, press releases in your local newspapers; 4th/5th places: $50/$25, plaque, mention online, t-shirt, press releases in your local newspapers. "We also list names of next 25 honorable mentions online. Contest guidelines and entry form online. CHECK WEBSITE FOR GUEST JUDGES. Mail entry form, your poem, and a $15 money order only to Christmas Poetry Contest at above address postmarked no earlier than September 1 and no later October 31. Winners announced both online and via snail mail December 1. Prizes mailed within 10 days of announcement. Judged by Diana Perry and guest judge.

JOHN CIARDI PRIZE FOR POETRY

BkMk Press, University of Missouri-Kansas City, 5100 Rockhill Rd., Kansas City MO 02903-1803. (816)235-2558. **E-mail:** bkmk@umkc.edu. **Website:** www.umkc.edu/bkmk. Offered annually for the best book-length collection (unpublished) of poetry in English by a living author. Translations are not eligible. Guidelines for SASE, by e-mail, or online. Deadline: January 15. Prize: $1,000, plus book publication by BkMk Press. Judged by a network of published writers. Final judging is done by a writer of national reputation.

CIDER PRESS REVIEW BOOK AWARD

P.O. Box 33384, San Diego CA 92163. **E-mail:** editor@ciderpressreview.com. **Website:** ciderpressreview.com/bookaward. Annual award from *Cider Press Review*. Submissions must be unpublished as a collection, but individual poems may have been previously published elsewhere. Submit book-length ms of 48-80 pages. Submissions can be made online using the submission form on the website or by mail. If sending by mail, include 2 cover sheets—1 with title, author's name, and complete contact information; and 1 with title only, all bound with a spring clip. Does not require SASE; notification via e-mail and on the website, only. Mss cannot be returned. Online submissions must be in Word for PC or PDF format, and should not include title page with author's name. The editors strongly urge contestants to use online delivery if possible. Review the complete submission guidelines and learn more online at website. Deadline: Submit September 1-November 30. Prize: $1,500, publication, and 25 author's copies of a book length collection of poetry. Author receives a standard publishing contract. Initial print run is not less than 1,000 copies. CPR acquires first publication rights. Judged by Jeffrey Harrison in 2014. Previous judge was Charles Harper Webb.

CLEVELAND STATE UNIVERSITY POETRY CENTER PRIZES

Cleveland State University Poetry Center, Cleveland State University Poetry Center Prizes, Department of English, 2121 Euclid Avenue, Cleveland OH 44115-2214. (216)687-3986. **Fax:** (216)687-6943. **E-mail:** poetrycenter@csuohio.edu. **Website:** www.csuohio.edu/poetrycenter. **Contact:** Frank Giampietro. Ms should contain a minimum of 48 and a maximum of 100 pages of poetry. See website for specific details and rules. Offered annually to identify, reward, and publish the best unpublished book-length poetry ms (minimum 48 pages) in 2 categories: First Book Award and Open Competition (for poets who have published at least one collection with a press run of 500). Deadline: March 13. Prize: First Book and Open Book Competitions awards publication and a $1000 advance against royalties for an original ms of poetry in each category

CLOCKWISE CHAPBOOK COMPETITION

Tebot Bach, Tebot Bach, Clockwise, P.O. Box 7887, Huntington Beach CA 92615. (714)968-0905. **Fax:** (714)968-4677. **E-mail:** mifanwy@tebotbach.org. **Website:** www.tebotbach.org/clockwise.html. Annual competition for a collection of poetry. Submit 24-32 pages of original poetry in English. Must be previously unpublished poetry for the full collection; individual poems may have been published. Full guidelines, including submission info, online. Deadline: April 15. Prize: $500 and a book publication in Perfect Bound Editions. Winner announced in September with publication the following April. Judged by Gail Wronsky.

CLOUDBANK CONTEST

P.O. Box 610, Corvallis OR 97339. **E-mail:** michael@cloudbankbooks.com. **Website:** www.cloudbankbooks.com. **Contact:** Michael Malan, poetry and short fiction. For contest submissions, the writer's name, address, e-

mail, and the titles of the poems/flash fiction pieces being submitted should be typed on a cover sheet only, not on the pages of poems or flash fiction. No electronic submissions. Send no more than 5 poems or short prose pieces (500 words or less) for the contest or for regular submissions. Prize: $200 and publication, plus an extra copy of the issue in which the winning poem appears. Two contributors' copies will be sent to writers whose work appears in the magazine. Judged by Michael Malan and Peter Sears.

🌑 TOM COLLINS POETRY PRIZE

Fellowship of Australian Writers (WA), P.O. Box 6180, Swanbourne WA 6910 Australia. (61)(8)9384-4771. **Fax:** (61)(8)9384-4854. **E-mail:** admin@fawwa.org.au. **Website:** www.fawwa.org.au. Annual contest for unpublished poems maximum 60 lines. Reserves the right to publish entries in a FAWWA publication or on its website. Guidelines online or for SASE. See website for details, guidelines, and entry form. Deadline: December 15. Submission period begins September 1. Prize: 1st Place: $1,000; 2nd Place; $400; 4 Highly Commended: $150 each.

THE COLORADO PRIZE FOR POETRY

Colorado Review/Center for Literary Publishing, Department of English, Colorado State University, 9105 Campus Delivery, Ft. Collins CO 80523. (970)491-5449. **E-mail:** creview@colostate.edu. **Website:** coloradoprize.colostate.edu. **Contact:** Stephanie G'Schwind, editor. Submission must be unpublished as a collection, but individual poems may have been published elsewhere. Submit mss of 48-100 pages of poetry on any subject, in any form, double- or single-spaced. Include 2 titles pages: 1 with ms title only, the other with ms title and poet's name, address, and phone number. Enclose SASP for notification of receipt and SASE for results; mss will not be returned. Guidelines available for SASE or by e-mail. Guidelines available for SASE or online at website. Poets can also submit online via our online submission manager through our website. Deadline: Early January. Check website for exact deadline. Prize: $2,000 and publication of a book-length ms.

CONCRETE WOLF POETRY CHAPBOOK CONTEST

P.O. Box 1808, Kingston WA 98346. **E-mail:** concretewolf@yahoo.com. **Website:** concretewolf.com. "We prefer chapbooks that have a theme, either obvious (i.e., chapbook about a divorce) or understated (i.e., all the poems mention the color blue). We like a collection that feels more like a whole than a sampling of work. We have no preference as to formal or free verse. We probably slightly favor lyric and narrative poetry to language and concrete, but excellent examples of any style get our attention." Considers simultaneous submissions if notified of acceptance elsewhere. Submit up to 26 pages of poetry, paginated. Include table of contents and acknowledgments page. Include 2 cover sheets: 1 with ms title, poet's name, address, phone number, and e-mail; 1 without poet's identification. Include SASE for results; mss will not be returned. Send 10x12 envelope stamped with $2.65 for copy of winning chapbook. Guidelines online. Deadline: November 30. Prize: Publication and 100 author copies of a perfectly-bound chapbook.

CPR EDITOR'S PRIZE FIRST OR SECOND BOOK AWARD

P.O. Box 33384, San Diego CA 92163. **E-mail:** editor@ ciderpressreview.com. **Website:** ciderpressreview. com/bookaward. Annual award from *Cider Press Review*. Submissions must be unpublished as a collection, but individual poems may have been previously published elsewhere. Submit book-length ms of 48-80 pages. Submissions can be made online using the submission form on the website or by mail. If sending by mail, include 2 cover sheets—1 with title, author's name, and complete contact information; and 1 with title only, all bound with a spring clip. Check website for change of address coming in the future. Include SASE for results only if no e-mail address included; notification via e-mail and on the website; mss cannot be returned. Online submissions must be in Word for PC or PDF format, and should not include title page with author's name. The editors strongly urge contestants to use online delivery if possible. Review the complete submission guidelines and learn more online at website. Deadline: submit between April 1-June 30. Prize: $1,000, publication, and 25 author's copies of a book length collection of poetry. Author receives a standard publishing contract. Initial print run is not less than 1,000 copies. CPR acquires first publication rights. Judged by *Cider Press Review* editors.

CRAB ORCHARD SERIES IN POETRY FIRST BOOK AWARD

First Book Award, Dept. of English, Mail Code 4503, Southern Illinois University Carbondale, 1000 Faner Drive, Carbondale IL 62901. (618)453-6833. **E-mail:** jtribble@siu.edu. **Website:** www.craborchardreview. siu.edu. **Contact:** Jon Tribble, series editor. Annual award that selects a first book of poems for publication from an open competition of mss, in English, by a U.S. citizen or permanent resident who has neither published, nor committed to publish, a volume of poetry 48 pages or more in length in an edition of over 500 copies (individual poems may have been previously published; for the purposes of the Crab Orchard Series in Poetry, a ms which was in whole or in part submitted as a thesis or dissertation as a requirement for the completion of a degree is considered unpublished and is eligible). See website for complete formatting instructions. Guidelines available for SASE or online. Deadline: July 8. Submission period begins May 10. Prize: Offers $3,500 ($2,000 prize plus $1,500 honorarium for a reading at Southern Illinois University Carbondale) and a publication contract.

CRAB ORCHARD SERIES IN POETRY OPEN COMPETITION AWARDS

Department of English, Mail Code 4503, Faner Hall 2380, Southern Illinois University at Carbondale, Carbondale IL 62901. **E-mail:** jtribble@siu.edu. **Website:** www.craborchardreview.siu.edu. **Contact:** Jon Tribble, series editor. Annual competition to award unpublished, original collections of poems written in English by United States citizens and permanent residents (individual poems may have been previously published). Two volumes of poems will be selected from the open competition of mss. Considers simultaneous submissions, but series editor must be informed immediately upon acceptance. Mss should be typewritten or computer-generated (letter quality only; no dot matrix), single-spaced; clean photocopy is recommended as mss are not returned. See guidelines for complete formatting instructions. Guidelines available for SASE or online. Deadline: November 18. Submission period begins October 1. Prize: Both winners will be awarded a $2500 prize and $1500 as an honorarium for a reading at Southern Illinois University Carbondale. Both readings will follow the publication of the poets' collections by Southern Illinois University Press.

DANCING POETRY CONTEST

AEI Contest Chair, Judy Cheung, 704 Brigham Ave., Santa Rosa CA 95404-5245. (707)528-0912. **E-mail:** jhcheung@comcast.net. **Website:** www.dancingpoetry.com. **Contact:** Judy Cheung, contest chair. Line Limit: 40 lines maximum each poem. No limit on number of entries. Send two typed, clear copies of each entry. Show name, address, telephone number, e-mail and how you heard about the contest on one copy only. Poems must be in English or include English translation Deadline: May 15. Prize: Prizes: Three Grand Prizes will receive $100 each plus the poems will be danced and videotaped at this year's Dancing Poetry Festival; six First Prizes will receive $50 each; twelve Second Prizes will receive $25 each; and thirty Third Prizes will receive $10 each.

TIPS "We always look for something new and different including new twists to old themes, different looks at common situations, inovative concepts for dynamic, thought provoking entertainment."

DREAM HORSE PRESS NATIONAL POETRY CHAPBOOK PRIZE

P.O. Box 2080, Felton CA 95001-2080. **E-mail:** dreamhorsepress@yahoo.com. **Website:** www.dreamhorsepress.com. **Contact:** J.P. Dancing Bear, Editor/Publisher. All entries will be considered for publication. Submissions may be previously published in magazines/journals but not in books or chapbooks. Considers simultaneous submissions with notification. Submit 20-28 pages of poetry in a readable font with table of contents, acknowledgments, bio, e-mail address for results, and entry fee. Poet's name should not appear anywhere on the ms. Accepts multiple submissions (with separate fee for each entry). Mss will be recycled after judging. Guidelines online. Make checks/money orders made payable to Dream Horse Press. Recent previous winners include M.R.B. Chelko, Cynthia Arrieu-King, and Ariana-Sophia Kartsonis. Deadline: June 30. Prize: $500, publication, and 25 copies of a handsomely printed chapbook. Judged by C.J. Sage.

T.S. ELIOT PRIZE FOR POETRY

Truman State University Press, 100 E. Normal Ave., Kirksville MO 63501. (660)785-7336. **Fax:** (660)785-4480. **E-mail:** tsup@truman.edu. **Website:** tsup.truman.edu. **Contact:** Nancy Rediger. The ms may include individual poems previously published in journals or anthologies, but may not include a significant number of poems from a published chapbook or self-published book. Submit 60-100 pages. Include 2 title pages: 1 with poet's name, address, e-mail address, phone number, and ms title; the other with ms title only. Include SASE for acknowledgment of ms receipt only; mss will not be returned. Guidelines available for SASE or online. Deadline: October 31. Prize:

$2,000 and publication. Judge announced after close of competition.

JANICE FARRELL POETRY PRIZE CATEGORY

Soul-Making Keats Literary Competition, The Webhallow House, 1544 Sweetwood Dr., Broadmoor Village CA 94015. **E-mail:** SoulKeats@mail.com. **Website:** www.soulmakingcontest.us. **Contact:** Eileen Malone. Previously published okay. Poetry may be double- or single-spaced. One-page poems only, and only 1 poem/page. All poems must be titled. Three poems/entry. Indicate category on each poem. Identify with 3x5 card only. Open to all writers. Deadline: November 30. Prize: Cash prizes. Judged by a local San Francisco successfully published poet.

THE JEAN FELDMAN POETRY PRIZE

Washington Writers' Publishing House, P.O. Box 15271, Washington DC 20003. **E-mail:** wwphpress@gmail.com. **Website:** www.washingtonwriters.org. Poets living within 75 miles of the Capitol are invited to submit a ms of either a novel or a collection of short stories. Ms should be 50-70 pages, single spaced. Author's name should not appear on the ms. The title page of each copy should contain the title only. Provide name, address, telephone number, e-mail address, and title on a separate cover sheet accompanying the submission. A separate page for acknowledgments may be included for stories or excerpts previously published in journals and anthologies. Submit an electronic copy via e-mail or send 2 copies of the ms via mail. Deadline: November 1. Submission period begins July 1. Prize: $500 and 50 copies of the book.

FIELD POETRY PRIZE

Oberlin College Press/FIELD, 50 N. Professor St., Oberlin OH 44074-1095. (440)775-8408. **Fax:** (440)775-8124. **E-mail:** oc.press@oberlin.edu. **Website:** www.oberlin.edu/ocpress/prize.htm. **Contact:** Marco Wilkinson, managing editor. Offered annually for an unpublished book-length collection of poetry (mss of 50-80 pages). Contest seeks to encourage the finest in contemporary poetry writing. Open to any writer. Deadline: Submit in May only. Prize: $1,000 and the book is published in Oberlin College Press's FIELD Poetry Series.

FISH POETRY PRIZE

Durrus, Bantry Co. Cork Ireland. **E-mail:** info@fishpublishing.com. **Website:** www.fishpublishing.

com. For poems up to 200 words. Age Range: Adult. The best 10 will be published in the Fish Anthology, launched in July at the West Cork Literary Festival. Entries must not have been published before. Entry on-line or by post. See website for full details of competitions, and information on the Fish Editorial and Critique Services, and the Fish Online Writing Courses. Do not put your name or address or any other details on the poem, use a separate sheet. Receipt of entry will be acknowledged by e-mail. Poems will not be returned. Maximum words for each poem is 200, and you may enter as many as you wish, provided there is an entry fee for each one. Full details and rules are online. Entry is deemed to be acceptance of these rules. Publishing rights of the 10 winning poems are held by Fish Publishing for one year after the publication of the Anthology. The aim of the competition is to discover and publish new writers. Deadline: March 30. Prize: €1,000 ($1,200). Results announced April 30. Judged by Ruth Padel.

FIVE POINTS JAMES DICKEY PRIZE FOR POETRY

Five Points, Georgia State University, P.O. Box 3999, Atlanta GA 30302-3999. (404)413-5812. **Website:** www.fivepoints.gsu.edu. Offered annually for unpublished poetry. Enter online or send 3 unpublished poems, no longer than 50 lines each, name and address on each poem, SASE for receipt and notification of winner. Winner announced in Spring issue. Deadline: December 1. Prize: $1,000, plus publication.

FOOD VERSE CONTEST

Literal Latte, 200 East 10th St., Suite 240, New York NY 10003. (212)260-5532. **E-mail:** litlatte@aol.com. **Website:** www.literal-latte.com. **Contact:** Jenine Gordon Bockman, editor. Open to any writer. Poems should have food as an ingredient. Submissions required to be unpublished. Guidelines online at website. Literal Latte acquires first rights. Annual contest to give support and exposure to great writing. Deadline: January 31. Prize: $500 Judged by the Editors.

⊕ FORT WORTH HAIKU SOCIETY'S QUARTERLY CONTEST

Fort Worth Haiku Society, 5008 Flagstone Dr., Ft. Worth TX 76114. (817)624-8803. **E-mail:** vanpire13@aol.com. **Website:** cliffordroberts.tripod.com/fwha. **Contact:** Cliff "Kawazu" Roberts. Offered quarterly. Guidelines and entry forms are available for SASE. Holds one time publication rights to winner; all rights revert to author after publication the following year. To encourage the appreciation and knowledge of the English language and Japanese style poetry (haiku and senryu). Deadline: January 15, May 15, July 15, and October 15. Prize: $15 first place, plus publication; $10 second place; $5 third place. Judged by members of FWHS or guest judges from the Haiku Society of America.

TIPS Entries must have strong seasonal Kigo and be 17 syllables or less. No titles or capitalization except for proper names and no punctuation other than those necessary to identify phrase from fragment.

GERTRUDE PRESS POETRY CHAPBOOK CONTEST

P.O. Box 28281, Portland OR 97228. **E-mail:** editor@gertrudepress.org; poetry@gertrudepress.org. **Website:** www.gertrudepress.org. Annual chapbook contest for 25-30 pages of poetry. Individual poems may have been previously published; unpublished poems are welcome. Poetry may be of any subject matter, and writers from all backgrounds are encouraged to submit. Include list of acknowledgments and cover letter indicating how poet learned of the contest. Include 1 title page with identifying information and 1 without. Guidelines available in *Gertrude* (see separate listing in Magazines/Journals), for SASE, by e-mail, or online. Deadline: May 15. Submission period begins September 15. Prize: $100, publication, and 50 complimentary copies of the chapbook.

ALLEN GINSBERG POETRY AWARDS

The Poetry Center at Passaic County Community College, One College Blvd., Paterson NJ 07505. (973)684-6555. Fax: (973)523-6085. **E-mail:** mgillan@pccc.edu. **Website:** www.pccc.edu/poetry. **Contact:** Maria Mazziotti Gillan, executive director. All winning poems, honorable mentions, and editor's choice poems will be published in *Paterson Literary Review*. Winners will be asked to participate in a reading that will be held in the Paterson Historic District. Submissions must be unpublished. Submit up to 5 poems (no poem more than 2 pages long). Send 4 copies of each poem entered. Include cover sheet with poet's name, address, phone number, e-mail address and poem titles. Poet's name should not appear on poems. Include SASE for results only; poems will not be returned. Guidelines available for SASE or online. Deadline: April 1 (postmark). Prize: 1st Prize: $1,000; 2nd Prize: $200; 3rd Prize: $100.

GIVAL PRESS POETRY AWARD

Gival Press, LLC, P.O. Box 3812, Arlington VA 22203. (703)351-0079. **E-mail:** givalpress@yahoo.com. **Website:** www.givalpress.com. **Contact:** Robert L. Giron, editor. Offered annually for a previously unpublished poetry collection as a complete ms, which may include previously published poems; previously published poems must be acknowledged, and poet must hold rights. Guidelines for SASE, by e-mail, or online. Open to any writer, as long as the work is original, not a translation, and is written in English. The copyright remains in the author's name; certain rights fall to the publisher per the contract. Must be at least 45 typed pages of poetry, on one side only. Entrants are asked to submit their poems without any kind of identification (with the exception of the titles) and with a separate cover page with the following information: Name, address (street, city, state, and zip code), telephone number, e-mail address (if available), short bio, and a list of the poems by title. Checks drawn on American banks should be made out to Gival Press, LLC. The competition seeks to award well-written, origional poetry in English on any topic, in any style. Deadline: December 15 (postmarked). Prize: $1,000, publication, and 20 copies of the publication. The editor narrows entries to the top 10; previous winner selects top 5 and chooses the winner—all done anonymously.

GOLDEN ROSE AWARD

New England Poetry Club, 654 Green St., No. 2, Cambridge MA 02139. **Website:** www.nepoetryclub.org. **Contact:** NEPC contest coordinator. Given annually to the poet, who by their poetry and inspiration to and encouragement of other writers, has made a significant mark on American poetry. Traditionally given to a poet with some ties to New England so that a public reading may take place. Contest open to members and nonmembers. Poems should be typed and submitted in duplicate with author's name, address, phone, and e-mail address of writer on only 1 copy. (Judges receive copies without names.) Copy only. Label poems with contest name. Entries should be sent by regular mail only. Special delivery or signature required mail will be returned by the post office. Entries should be original, unpublished poems in English. No poem should be entered in more than 1 contest, nor have won a previous contest. No entries will be returned. NEPC will not engage in correspondence regarding poems or contest decisions. Deadline: May 31. Judged by well-known poets and sometimes winners of previous NEPC contests.

◐ GOVERNOR GENERAL'S LITERARY AWARD FOR POETRY

Canada Council for the Arts, 150 Elgin St., P.O. Box 1047, Ottawa ON K1P 5V8 Canada. (613)566-4414, ext. 5573. **Fax:** (613)566-4410. **Website:** www.canadacouncil.ca/prizes/ggla. Offered for the best English-language and the best French-language work of poetry by a Canadian. Publishers submit titles for consideration. Deadline: Depends on the book's publication date. Books in English: March 15, June 1, or August 7. Books in French: March 15 or July 15. Prize: Each laureate receives $25,000; non-winning finalists receive $1,000.

THE GREEN ROSE PRIZE IN POETRY

New Issues Poetry & Prose, Deptartment of English, Western Michigan University, 1903 W. Michigan Ave., Kalamazoo MI 49008-5331. (269)387-8185. **Fax:** (269)387-2562. **Website:** www.wmich.edu/new-issues. Offered annually for unpublished poetry. The university will publish a book of poems by a poet writing in English who has published 1 or more full-length collections of poetry. *New Issues* may publish as many as 3 additional mss from this competition. Guidelines for SASE or online. *New Issues Poetry & Prose* obtains rights for first publication. Book is copyrighted in the author's name. Considers simultaneous submissions, but *New Issues* must be notified of acceptance elsewhere. Submit a ms of at least 48 pages, typed; single-spaced preferred. Clean photocopies acceptable. Do not bind; use manila folder or metal clasp. Include cover page with poet's name, address, phone number, and title of the ms. Also include brief bio, table of contents, and acknowledgments page. Submissions are also welcome through the online submission manager www.newissuespoetryprose.submittable.com. For hardcopy mss only, you may include SASP for notification of receipt of ms and SASE for results only; mss will be recycled. Guidelines available for SASE, by fax, e-mail, or online. Winner is announced in January or February online. The winning ms will be published in spring of following year. 2013 winner was Ralph Angel (*Your Moon*). Deadline: Submit May 1-September

30. Winner is announced in January or February online. Prize: $2,000 and publication of a book of poems.

☺ THE GRIFFIN POETRY PRIZE

The Griffin Trust for Excellence in Poetry, 363 Parkridge Crescent, Oakville ON L6M 1A8 Canada. (905)618-0420. **E-mail:** info@griffinpoetryprize.com. **Website:** www.griffinpoetryprize.com. **Contact:** Ruth Smith. The Griffin Poetry Prize is Canada's most generous poetry award. The awards go to one Canadian and one international poet who writes in the English language. Submissions must come from publishers. A book of poetry must be a first-edition collection. Must have been published in the previous calendar year. Deadline: December 31. Prize: Two $65,000 (CAD) prizes. One prize will go to a living Canadian poet or translator, the other to a living poet or translator from any country, which may include Canada. An additional $10,000 (CAD) goes to each shortlisted poet. Judged by a panel of qualified English-speaking judges of stature. Judges are chosen by the Trustees of The Griffin Trust For Excellence in Poetry.

GREG GRUMMER POETRY AWARD

Phoebe, MSN 2C5, George Mason University, 4400 University Dr., Fairfax VA 22030. **E-mail:** phoebeliterature@gmail.com. **Website:** www.phoebejournal.com. **Contact:** Darby Price, poetry editor. Offered annually for unpublished work. Submit up to 4 poems, no more than 10 pages total. Guidelines online. Requests first serial rights, if work is to be published. The purpose of the award is to recognize new and exciting poetry. Deadline: March 8. Prize: $1,000 and publication in the *Phoebe* and a 1-year subscription. Judged by a recognized poet.

KATHRYN HANDLEY PROSE POEM PRIZE CATEGORY

Soul-Making Keats Literary Competition, The Webhallow House, 1544 Sweetwood Dr., Broadmoor Village CA 94015-2029. **E-mail:** SoulKeats@mail.com. **Website:** www.soulmakingcontest.us. **Contact:** Eileen Malone. Open annually to all writers. Poetry may be double- or single-spaced. 1-page prose poems only, and only 1 prose poem/page. Three poems/entry. Indicate category on each poem. Identify only with 3x5 card. Deadline: November 30. Prize: 1st Place: $100; 2nd Place: $50; 3rd Place: $25.

THE BESS HOKIN PRIZE

Poetry, 61 W. Superior St., Chicago IL 60654. (312)787-7070. **Fax:** (312)787-6650. **E-mail:** editors@poetrymagazine.org. **Website:** www.poetrymagazine.org. Offered annually for poems published in *Poetry* during the preceding year (October-September). Upon acceptance, *Poetry* licenses exclusive worldwide first serial rights, including electronic rights, for publication, as well as non-exclusive rights to reprint, reuse, and archive the work, in any format, in perpetuity. Copyright reverts to author upon first publication. "Established in 1947 through the generosity of our late friend and guarantor, Mrs. David Hokin, and is given annually in her memory." Prize: $1,000.

FIRMAN HOUGHTON PRIZE

New England Poetry Club, 376 School St., Watertown MA 02472. **E-mail:** contests@nepoetryclug.org. **Website:** www.nepoetryclub.org. **Contact:** Audrey Kalajin. For a lyric poem in honor of the former president of NEPC. Deadline: May 31. Prize: $250. Judged by well-known poets and sometimes winners of previous NEPC contests.

TOM HOWARD/MARGARET REID POETRY CONTEST

Tom Howard Books, Tom Howard Books, c/o Winning Writers, 351 Pleasant St., PMB 222, Northampton MA 01060-3961. **E-mail:** adam@winningwriters.com. **Website:** www.winningwriters.com. **Contact:** Adam Cohen. Offers annual awards of Tom Howard Prize, for a poem in any style or genre, and Margaret Reid Prize, for a poem that rhymes or has a traditional style. All entries that win cash prizes will be published on the Winning Writers website. Submissions maybe published or unpublished, may have won prizes elsewhere, and may be entered in other contests. No limit on number of lines per poem or number of poems submitted. See complete guidelines online. Deadline: September 30. Submission period begins April 15. Prize: Prizes: Each prize is $1,000, with 10 Honorable Mentions of $100 each (any style).

THE LYNDA HULL MEMORIAL POETRY PRIZE

Crazyhorse, Department of English, College of Charleston, 66 George St., Charleston SC 29424. (843)953-4470. **E-mail:** crazyhorse@cofc.edu. **Website:** crazyhorse.cofc.edu. **Contact:** Prize Director. The annual Lynda Hull Memorial Poetry Prize for a single poem. All entries will be considered for publication.

Submissions must be unpublished. Submit online or by mail up to 3 original poems (no more than 10 pages). Include cover page (placed on top of ms) with poet's name, address, e-mail, and telephone number; no identifying information on mss (blind judging). Accepts multiple submissions with separate fee for each. Include SASP for notification of receipt of ms and SASE for results only; mss will not be returned. Guidelines available for SASE or online. Deadline: January 31. Prize: $2,000 and publication in *Crazyhorse*.

⊘ ILLINOIS STATE POETRY SOCIETY ANNUAL CONTEST

Illinois State Poetry Society, 6455 Big Bear Dr., Indian Head Park IL 60525. **Website:** illinoispoets.org. **Contact:** Susan T. Moss, president. Annual contest to encourage the crafting of excellent poetry. Guidelines and entry forms available for SASE. Deadline: September 30. Prize: Cash prizes of $50, $30, and $10. Three Honorable Mentions. Poet retains all rights. Judged by out-of-state professionals.

INDIANA REVIEW POETRY PRIZE

Indiana Review, Poetry Prize, Indiana Review, Ballantine Hall 465, 1020 E. Kirkwood Ave., Bloomington IN 47405-7103. (812)855-3439. **Fax:** (812)855-9535. **E-mail:** inreview@indiana.edu. **Website:** www.indianareview.org. **Contact:** Michael Mlekoday, Poetry Editor. Offered annually for unpublished work. Open to any writer. Send no more than 3 poems per entry. Guidelines online and with SASE request. Send no more than 3 poems per entry, 8 pages maximum. Each fee entitles entrant to a 1-year subscription. Deadline: April 1. Prize: $1,000 honorarium and publication. Judged by Nikky Finney in 2013.

IOWA POETRY PRIZES

University of Iowa Press, 119 West Park Rd., 100 Kuhl House, Iowa City IA 52242. (319)335-2000. **Fax:** (319)335-2055. **E-mail:** uipress@uiowa.edu. **Website:** www.uiowapress.org. Offered annually to encourage poets and their work. Submissions must be postmarked during the month of April; put name on title page only. This page will be removed before ms is judged. Open to writers of English (US citizens or not). Mss will not be returned. Previous winners are not eligible. Deadline: April 30. Prize: Publication under standard royalty agreement.

RANDALL JARRELL POETRY COMPETITION

North Carolina Writers' Network, Terry L. Kennedy, MFA Writing Program, 3302 MHRA Building, UNC Greensboro, Greensboro NC 27402-6170. **E-mail:** tlkenned@uncg.edu. **Website:** www.ncwriters.org. **Contact:** Terry L. Kennedy. Offered annually for unpublished work to honor Randall Jarrell and his life at UNC Greensboro, by recognizing the best poetry submitted. The competition is open to any writer who is a legal resident of North Carolina or a member of the North Carolina Writers' Network. Submissions should be one poem only (40-line limit). Poem must be typed (single-spaced) and stapled in the left-hand corner. Author's name should not appear on the poem. Instead, include a separate cover sheet with author's name, address, e-mail address, phone number, and poem title. Poem will not be returned. Include a self-addressed stamped envelope for a list of winner and finalists. The winner and finalists will be announced in May. Deadline: March 1. Prize: $200 and publication at *storySouth* (www.storysouth.com).

THE ROBINSON JEFFERS TOR HOUSE PRIZE FOR POETRY

The Robinson Jeffers Tor House Foundation, 26304 Ocean View Ave., Carmel CA 93923. (831)624-1813. **Fax:** (831)624-3696. **E-mail:** thf@torhouse.org. **Website:** www.torhouse.org. "The annual Prize for Poetry is a living memorial to American poet Robinson Jeffers (1887-1962). Open to well-crafted poetry in all styles, ranging from experimental work to traditional forms, including short narrative poems. Each poem should be typed on 8 1/2" by 11" paper, and no longer than three pages. On a cover sheet only, include: name, mailing address, telephone number and e-mail; titles of poems; bio optional. Multiple and simultaneous submissions welcome. $10 for first 3 poems, $15 for up to 6 poems; $2.50 for each additional poem. Checks and money orders should be made out to Tor House Foundation. Send poems, fee and SASE to Poetry Prize Coordinator, Tor House Foundation, P.O. Box 223240, Carmel, CA 93922. The annual Tor House Prize for Poetry is a living memorial to American poet Robinson Jeffers (1887-1962). Deadline: March 15. Prize: $1,000 honorarium for award-winning poem; $200 for up to 4 Honorable Mentions. Poems must be original and unpublished. Final judging by Ellen Bass." **Contact:** Eliot Ruchowitz-Roberts, Poetry Prize Coordinator. The annual Prize for Poetry is a living memorial to American poet Robinson Jeffers (1887-1962). Open to well-crafted poetry in all styles, ranging from experimental work to traditional forms, including short narrative poems. Poems must be original and unpublished. Each poem should be typed on 8 1/2" by 11" paper, and no longer than three pages. On a cover sheet only, include: name, mailing address, telephone number and e-mail; titles of poems; bio optional. Multiple and simultaneous submissions welcome. Deadline: March 15. Prize: $1,000 honorarium for award-winning poem; $200 for up to four Honorable Mentions.

JUNIPER PRIZE FOR POETRY

University of Massachusetts Press, Amherst MA 01003. (413)545-2217. **Fax:** (413)545-1226. **E-mail:** info@umpress.umass.edu. **Website:** www.umass.edu/umpress. **Contact:** Karen Fisk. The University of Massachusetts Press offers the annual Juniper Prize for Poetry, awarded in alternate years for the first and subsequent books. Considers simultaneous submissions, but if accepted for publication elsewhere, please notify immediately. Mss by more than 1 author, entries of more than 1 mss simultaneously or within the same year, and translations are not eligible. Submit paginated ms of 50-70 pages of poetry, with paginated contents page, credits page, and information on previously published books. Include 2 cover sheets: 1 with contract information, 1 without. Mss will not be returned. Guidelilnes available for SASE or online. Deadline: August 1-September 29. Winners announced online in April on the press website. Prize: Publication and $1,500 in addition to royalties.

BARBARA MANDIGO KELLY PEACE POETRY AWARDS

Nuclear Age Peace Foundation, PMB 121, 1187 Coast Village Rd., Suite 1, Santa Barbara CA 93108-2794. (805)965-3443. **Fax:** (805)568-0466. **E-mail:** wagingpeace@napf.org. **Website:** www.wagingpeace.org. Offers an annual series of awards "to encourage poets to explore and illuminate positive visions of peace and the human spirit." Awards $1,000 to adult contestants, $200 to youth in each 2 categories (13-18 and 12 and under), plus Honorable Mentions in each category. Submissions must be unpublished. Submit up to 3 poems in any form, unpublished and in English; maximum 30 lines/poem. Send 2 copies; put name, address, e-mail, phone number, and age (for youth) in upper right-hand corner of 1 copy of each poem.

Title each poem; do not staple individual poems together. "Any entry that does not adhere to ALL of the contest rules will not be considered for a prize. Poets should keep copies of all entries as we will be unable to return them." Guidelines available for SASE or online. **Entry fee:** Adult: $15 for up to 3 poems; 13-18: $5 for up to 3 poems; no fee for 12 and under. **Deadline:** July 1 (postmark). Judges: a committee of poets selected by the Nuclear Age Peace Foundation. Winners will be announced by October 1 by mail and online. Winning poems from current and past contests are posted on the Foundation's website. "The Nuclear Age Peace Foundation reserves the right to publish and distribute the award-winning poems, including Honorable Mentions." The Barbara Mandigo Kelly Peace Poetry Contest was created to encourage poets to explore and illuminate positive visions of peace and the human spirit. The annual contest honors the late Barbara Kelly, a Santa Barbara poet and longtime supporter of peace issues. Awards are given in 3 categories: adult (over 18 years), youth between 12 and 18 years, and youth under 12. All submitted poems should be unpublished. Deadline: July 1 (postmarked). Prize: Adult: $1,000; Youth (13-18): $200; Youth (12 and under): $200. Honorable Mentions may also be awarded. Judged by a committee of poets selected by the Nuclear Age Peace Foundation. The foundation reserves the right to publish and distribute the award-winning poems, including honorable mentions. **TIPS** "Poets should keep copies of all entries as we will be unable to return them. Copies of the winning poems from the 2003 Awards will be posted on the Nuclear Age Peace Foundationline after October 1, 2009."

LEVIS READING PRIZE

Virginia Commonwealth University, Department of English, Levis Reading Prize, VCU Department of English, 900 Park Avenue, Hibbs Hall, Room 306, P.O. Box 842005, Richmond VA 23284-2005. (804)828-1329. **Fax:** (804)828-8684. **E-mail:** mosesschmitl@vcu.edu. **E-mail:** englishgrad@vcu.edu. **Website:** www.has.vcu.edu/eng/resources/levis_prize/levis_prize.htm. **Contact:** Lena Moses-Schmitt, Levis Fellow. Offered annually for books of poetry published in the previous year to encourage poets early in their careers. The entry must be the writer's first or second published book of poetry. Previously published books in other genres, or previously published chapbooks or self-published material, do not count as books for this purpose. Entries may be submitted by either author or publisher, and must include three copies of the book (48 pages or more), a cover letter, and a brief biography of the author including previous publications. (Entries from vanity presses are not eligible.) The book must have been published in the previous calendar year. Entrants wishing acknowledgment of receipt must include a self-addressed stamped postcard. Deadline: January 15. Prize: $2,000 and an expense-paid trip to Richmond to present a public reading.

THE RUTH LILLY POETRY PRIZE

Poetry, 61 W. Superior St., Chicago IL 60654. (312)787-7070. **Fax:** (312)787-6650. **E-mail:** editors@poetry-magazine.org. **Website:** www.poetrymagazine.org. Awarded annually, the $100,000 Ruth Lilly Poetry Prize honors a living U.S. poet whose lifetime accomplishments warrant extraordinary recognition. Established in 1986 by Ruth Lilly, the Prize is one of the most prestigious awards given to American poets and is one of the largest literary honors for work in the English language. Deadline: No submissions or nominations considered. Prize: $100,000.

LITERAL LATTÉ POETRY AWARD

Literal Latté, 200 E. 10th St., Suite 240, New York NY 10003. (212)260-5532. **E-mail:** LitLatte@aol.com. **Website:** www.literal-latte.com. **Contact:** Jenine Gordon Bockman, editor. Offered annually to any writer for unpublished poetry (maximum 2,000 words per poem). All styles welcome. Winners published in *Literal Latté*. Acquires first rights. Deadline: Postmark by July 15. Prize: 1st Place: $1,000; 2nd Place: $300; 3rd Place: $200. Judged by the editors.

THE MACGUFFIN NATIONAL POET HUNT CONTEST

The MacGuffin, The MacGuffin, Schoolcraft College, 18600 Haggerty Rd., Livonia MI 48152. (734)462-4400, ext. 5327. **Fax:** (734)462-4679. **E-mail:** macguffin@schoolcraft.edu. **Website:** www.macguffin.org. **Contact:** Gordon Krupsky, managing editor. *The MacGuffin*, established in 1984, is a national literary magazine from Schoolcraft College in Livonia, Michigan. An entry consists of three poems. Poems must not be previously published, and must be the original work of the contestant. See website for additional details. The mission of The MacGuffin is to encourage, support, and enhance the literary arts in the Schoolcraft College community, the region, the state, and the nation. Deadline: Must be postmarked

between April 1 and June 3. Prize: $500. Recent judges include: Terry Blackhawk, Dorianne Laux, Philip Levine, and Carl Dennis.

NAOMI LONG MADGETT POETRY AWARD

Lotus Press, Inc., P.O. Box 21607, Detroit MI 48221. **E-mail:** lotuspress@comcast.net. **Website:** www.lotuspress.org. **Contact:** Constance Withers. Offered annually to recognize an unpublished book-length poetry ms by an African American. Guidelines for SASE, by e-mail, or online. Deadline: January 2-March 1. Prize: $500 and publication by Lotus Press.

☉ THE MALAHAT REVIEW LONG POEM PRIZE

The Malahat Review, Box 1700 STN CSC, Victoria BC V8W 2Y2 Canada. **E-mail:** malahat@uvic.ca. **Website:** www.malahatreview.ca. **Contact:** John Barton, editor. Long Poem Prize offered in alternate years with the Novella Contest. Open to any writer. Offers 2 awards of $1,000 CAD each for a long poem or cycle (10-20 printed pages). Includes publication in *The Malahat Review* and a 1-year subscription. Open to entries from Canadian, American, and overseas authors. Obtains first world rights. Publication rights after revert to the author. Submissions must be unpublished. No simultaneous submissions. Submit a single poem or cycle of poems, 10-20 published pages (a published page equals 32 lines or less, including breaks between stanzas); no restrictions on subject matter or aesthetic approach. Include separate page with poet's name, address, e-mail, and title; no identifying information on mss pages. Do not include SASE for results; mss will not be returned. Guidelines online. Deadline: February 1 (odd-numbered years). Prize: Two $1,000 prizes. Winners published in the summer issue of *The Malahat Review*, announced in summer online, Facebook page, and in quarterly e-newsletter *Malahat lite*. Judged by 3 recognized poets. Preliminary readings by editorial board.

THE MORTON MARR POETRY PRIZE

Southwest Review, Southern Methodist University, P.O. Box 750374, Dallas TX 75275. (214)768-1037. **Fax:** (214)768-1408. **E-mail:** swr@mail.smu.edu. **Website:** www.smu.edu/southwestreview. **Contact:** Prize coordinator. Annual award for poem(s) by a writer who has not yet published a book of poetry. Submit no more than 6 poems in a "traditional" form (e.g., sonnet, sestine, villanelle, rhymed stanzas, blank verse, et al.). Submissions will not be returned. All entrants will receive a copy of the issue in which the winning poems appear. Deadline: September 30. Prize: Prizes: $1,000 for 1st place; $500 for 2nd place; plus publication in the Southwest Review.

KATHLEEN MCCLUNG SONNET PRIZE CATEGORY

Soul-Making Keats Literary Competition, The Webhallow House, 1544 Sweetwood Dr., Broadmoor Village CA 94015-2029. **E-mail:** soulkeats@mail.com. **Website:** www.soulmakingcontest.us. **Contact:** Eileen Malone. Call for Shakespearean and Petrarchan sonnets on the theme of the "beloved." Previously published material is accepted. Indicate category on cover page and on identifying 3x5 card. Open annually to any writer. Deadline: November 3. Prize:1st Place: $100; 2nd Place: $50; 3rd Place: $25.

VASSAR MILLER PRIZE IN POETRY

University of North Texas Press, 1155 Union Circle, #311336, Denton TX 76203. (940)565-2142. **Fax:** (940)565-4590. **Website:** untpress.unt.edu. **Contact:** John Poch. Annual prize awarded to a collection of poetry. No limitations to entrants. In years when the judge is announced, we ask that students of the judge not enter to avoid a perceived conflict. All entries should contain identifying material only on the one cover sheet. Entries are read anonymously. Deadline: Mss may be submitted between 9 A.M. on September 1 and 5 P.M. on October 31, through online submissions manager only. Prize: $,1000 and publication by University of North Texas Press. Judged by a different eminent writer selected each year. Some prefer to remain anonymous until the end of the contest.

SHEILA MARGARET MOTTON PRIZE

New England Poetry Club, 2 Farrar St., Cambridge MA 02138. (617)744-6034. **E-mail:** info@nepoetryclub.org. **Website:** www.nepoetryclub.org. **Contact:** Audrey Kalajin. Book prize for a book of poetry published in the last 2 years. Send 2 copies of book of poetry published in the last 2 years. Contest open to members and nonmembers. Poems should be typed and submitted in duplicate with author's name, address, phone, and e-mail address of writer on only 1 copy. (Judges receive copies without names.) Copy only. Label poems with contest name. Entries should be sent by regular mail only. Special delivery or signature required mail will be returned by the post office. Entries should be original, unpublished poems in English. No poem should be entered in more than

1 contest, nor have won a previous contest. No entries will be returned. NEPC will not engage in correspondence regarding poems or contest decisions. Deadline: May 31. Prize: $500. Judged by well-known poets and sometimes winners of previous NEPC contests.

ERIKA MUMFORD PRIZE

New England Poetry Club, 376 School St., Watertown MA 02472. **E-mail:** contests@nepoetryclub.org. **Website:** www.nepoetryclub.org/contests.htm. **Contact:** Audrey Kalajin. Offered annually for a poem in any form about foreign culture or travel. Funded by Erika Mumford's family and friends. Contest open to members and nonmembers. Deadline: May 31. Prize: $250. Judged by well-known poets and sometimes winners of previous NEPC contests.

NATIONAL WRITERS ASSOCIATION POETRY CONTEST

The National Writers Association, 10940 S. Parker Rd. #508, Parker CO 80134. (303)841-0246. **E-mail:** natlwritersassn@hotmail.com. **Website:** www.nationalwriters.com. **Contact:** Sandy Whelchel, director. Annual contest to encourage the writing of poetry, an important form of individual expression but with a limited commercial market. Deadline: October 1. Prize: 1st Place: $100; 2nd Place: $50; 3rd Place: $25.

THE PABLO NERUDA PRIZE FOR POETRY

Nimrod International Journal, 800 S. Tucker Dr., Tulsa OK 74104. (918)631-3080. **Fax:** (918)631-3033. **E-mail:** nimrod@utulsa.edu. **Website:** www.utulsa.edu/nimrod. **Contact:** Eilis O'Neal. Annual award to discover new writers of vigor and talent. Open to US residents only. Submissions must be unpublished. Work must be in English or translated by original author. Submit 3-10 pages of poetry (1 long poem or several short poems). Poet's name must not appear on ms. Include cover sheet with poem title(s), poet's name, address, phone and fax numbers, and e-mail address (poet must have a US address by October of contest year to enter). Mark "Contest Entry" on submission envelope and cover sheet. Include SASE for results only; mss will not be returned. Guidelines available for #10 SASE or online. Winners will be announced on *Nimrod*'s website. Submissions must be unpublished. Work must be in English or translated by original author. Submit 3-10 pages of poetry (1 long poem or several short poems). Poet's name must not appear on ms. Include cover sheet with poem title(s), poet's name, address, phone and fax numbers, and e-

CONTESTS & AWARDS

mail address (poet must have a US address by October of contest year to enter). Mark "Contest Entry" on submission envelope and cover sheet. Include SASE for results only; mss will not be returned. Guidelines available for #10 SASE or online. Deadline: April 30. Prize: Prizes: 1st Place: $2,000 and publication; 2nd Place: $1,000 and publication. Judged by the *Nimrod* editors (finalists). A recognized author selects the winners.

THE NEW ISSUES POETRY PRIZE

New Issues Poetry & Prose, New Issues Poetry & Prose, Department of English, Western Michigan University, 1903 W. Michigan Ave., Kalamazoo MI 49008-5331. (269)387-8185. **Fax:** (269)387-2562. **E-mail:** new-issues@wmich.edu. **Website:** www.wmich.edu/newissues. Offered annually for publication of a first book of poems by a poet writing in English who has not previously published a full-length collection of poems in an edition of 500 or more copies. *New Issues Poetry & Prose* obtains rights for first publication. Book is copyrighted in author's name. Guidelines for SASE or online. Additional mss will be considered from those submitted to the competition for publication. Considers simultaneous submissions, but *New Issues* must be notified of acceptance elsewhere. Submit ms of at least 48 pages, typed, single-spaced preferred. Clean photocopies acceptable. Do not bind; use manila folder or metal clasp. Include cover page with poet's name, address, phone number, and title of the ms. Also include brief bio and acknowledgments page. Submissions are also welcome through the online submission manager www.newissuespoetryprose.submittable.com. For hardcopy submissions only, you may include SASP for notification of receipt of ms and SASE for results only; no mss will be returned. Winning ms will be named in May and published in the next spring. Deadline: November 30. Prize: $2,000, plus publication of a book-length ms. A national judge selects the prize winner and recommends other mss. The editors decide on the other books considering the judge's recommendation, but are not bound by it. 2014 judge: Fanny Howe; 2015 judge: TBD.

THE ORPHIC PRIZE FOR POETRY

Dream Horse Press, P.O. Box 2080, Aptos CA 95001-2080. **E-mail:** dreamhorsepress@yahoo.com. **Website:** www.dreamhorsepress.com. **Contact:** J.P. Dancing Bear, Editor/Publisher. The Orphic Prize for Poetry is an annual award offered by Dream Horse Press.

All entries will be considered for publication. Both free verse and formal verse styles are welcome. Submissions may be entered in other contests, "but if your ms is accepted for publication elsewhere, you must notify Dream Horse Press immediately." Submit 48-80 pages of poetry, paginated, with table of contents, acknowledgments, and bio. Include separate cover letter with poet's name, biographical information, and e-mail address (when available). Poet's name should not appear anywhere on the ms. Mss will be recycled after judging. Guidelines online. Recent winners include: Sheila Black and Ash Bowen. Deadline: October 31. Five day extended deadline for electronic submissions. Prize: $1,000 and publication of a book-length ms by Dream Horse Press. Judging is anonymous.

THE PATERSON POETRY PRIZE

The Poetry Center at Passaic County Community College, One College Blvd., Paterson NJ 07505. (973)684-6555. **Fax:** (973)523-6085. **E-mail:** mgillan@pccc.edu. **Website:** www.pccc.edu/poetry. **Contact:** Maria Mazziotti Gillan, executive director. The Paterson Poetry Prize offers an annual award for the strongest book of poems (48 or more pages) published in the previous year. The winner will be asked to participate in an awards ceremony and to give a reading at The Poetry Center. Minimum press run: 500 copies. Publishers may submit more than 1 title for prize consideration; 3 copies of each book must be submitted. Include SASE for results; books will not be returned (all entries will be donated to The Poetry Center Library). Guidelines and application form (required) available for SASE or online. Deadline: February 1. Prize: $1,000.

PEARL POETRY PRIZE

Pearl Editions, 3030 E. Second St., Long Beach CA 90803. (562)434-4523. **Fax:** (562)434-4523. **E-mail:** pearlmag@aol.com. **Website:** www.pearlmag.com. **Contact:** Marilyn Johnson, editor/publisher. Offered annually to provide poets with further opportunity to publish their poetry in book-form and find a larger audience for their work. Guidelines available for SASE or online. Mss must be original works written in English. Open to all writers. Submit May 1-June 30, only. Prize: $1,000. publication by Pearl Editions, and 25 author's copies for a book-length ms.

JEAN PEDRICK PRIZE

New England Poetry Club, 2 Farrar St., Cambridge MA 02138. **E-mail:** contests@nepoetryclub.org. **Web-**

site: www.nepoetryclub.org. **Contact:** Audrey Kala-jin. Prize for a chapbook published in the last two years. Send 2 chabooks. Deadline: May 31. Prize: $100. Judged by well-known poets and sometimes winners of previous NEPC contests.

PERUGIA PRESS PRIZE

Perugia Press, P.O. Box 60364, Florence MA 01062. **Website:** www.perugiapress.com. **Contact:** Susan Kan. Submissions must be unpublished as a collection, but individual poems may have been previously published in journals, chapbooks, and anthologies. Considers simultaneous submissions if notified of acceptance elsewhere. Follow online guidelines carefully. Electronic submissions available through website. No translations or self-published books. Multiple submissions accepted if accompanied by separate entry fee for each. Use USPS or electronic submission, not FedEx or UPS. Winner announced by April 1 by e-mail or SASE (if included with entry). The Perugia Press Prize is for a first or second poetry book by a woman. Poet must have no more than 1 previously published book of poems (chapbooks don't count). Deadline: Submit August 1-November 15. Prize: $1,000 and publication. Judged by panel of Perugia authors, booksellers, scholars, etc.

➕ PRESS 53 AWARD FOR POETRY

Press 53, 411 W. Fourth St., Suite 101A, Winston-Salem NC 27101. **E-mail:** kevin@press53.com. **Website:** www.press53.com. **Contact:** Kevin Morgan Watson, publisher. Awarded to an outstanding, unpublished collection of poetry. Details and guidelines online. Deadline: July 31. Submission period begins April 1. Finalists announced October 1. Winner announced on December 1. Publication in April. Prize: Publication of winning poetry collection as a Tom Lombardo Poetry Selection, $1,000 cash advance, travel expenses and lodging for a special reading and book signing in Winston-Salem, NC, attendance as special guest to the Press 53/*Prime Number Magazine* Gathering of Writers, and 10 copies of the book. Judged by Press 53 poetry series editor Tom Lombardo.

➕ RHINO FOUNDERS' PRIZE

RHINO, The Poetry Forum, P.O. Box 591, Evanston IL 60204. **E-mail:** editors@rhinopoetry.org. **Website:** rhinopoetry.org. **Contact:** Editors. Send best, unpublished poetry, translations, and flash fiction (750 words max). Visit website for previous winners and more information. Submit online or by mail. Include a cover letter listing your name, address, e-mail, and/or telephone number, titles of poems, how you learned about RHINO, and fee. Mss will not be returned. Deadline: April 1-October 31. Prize: $300, publication, featured online, and nominated for a Pushcart Prize. Two runners-ups will receive $50, publication, and will be featured online. Occasionally nominates runner-up for a Pushcart Prize.

TIPS "RHINO values original voice, musicality, fresh language, and respect for the reader."

ROANOKE-CHOWAN POETRY AWARD

The North Carolina Literary & Historical Assoc., 4610 Mail Service Center, Raleigh NC 27699-4610. (919)807-7290. **Fax:** (919)733-8807. **E-mail:** michael. hill@ncdcr.gov. **Website:** www.history.ncdcr.gov/affiliates/lit-hist/awards/awards.htm. **Contact:** Michael Hill, awards coordinator. Offers annual award for an original volume of poetry published during the 12 months ending June 30 of the year for which the award is given. Open to authors who have maintained legal or physical residence, or a combination of both, in North Carolina for the 3 years preceding the close of the contest period. Submit 3 copies of each entry. Guidelines available for SASE or by fax or e-mail. Winner announced October 15. Deadline: July 15.

ERNEST SANDEEN PRIZE IN POETRY AND THE RICHARD SULLIVAN PRIZE IN SHORT FICTION

University of Notre Dame, Dept. of English, 356 O'Shaughnessy Hall, Notre Dame IN 46556-5639. (574)631-7526. **Fax:** (574)631-4795. **E-mail:** creative-writing@nd.edu. **Website:** english.nd.edu/creative-writing/publications/sandeen-sullivan-prizes. **Contact:** Director of Creative Writing. The Sandeen/Sullivan Prize in Poetry and Short Fiction is awarded to the author who has published at least one volume of short fiction or one volume of poetry. Awarded bi-annually, but judged quadrennially. Though the Sandeen Prize is open to any author, with the exception of graduates of the University of Notre Dame, who has published at least one volume of short stories (Sullivan) or one collection of poetry (Sandeen), judges pay special attention to second volumes. Please include a vita and/or a biographical statement which includes your publishing history. Will also see a selection of reviews of the earlier collection. Please submit two copies of mss and inform if the mss is available on computer disk. Include an SASE for acknowledgment of receipt of your submission. If you would like your ms returned, please send an SASE. Mss will not otherwise be returned. Submissions Period: May 1 - September 1. Prize: $1,000, a $500 award and a $500 advance against royalties from the Notre Dame Press.

✚ SCREAMINMAMAS MOTHER'S DAY POETRY CONTEST

1911 Cleveland St., Hollywood FL 33020. **E-mail:** screaminmamas@gmail.com. **Website:** www.screaminmamas.com/contests. **Contact:** Darlene Pistocchi, editor/managing director. "What does it mean to be a mom? There is so much to being a mom—get deep, get creative! We challenge you to explore different types of poetry: descriptive, reflective, narrative, lyric, sonnet, ballad, limerick... you can even go epic!" Open only to moms. Poems should be 20-60 lines. Deadline: December 31. Prize: $40, publication.

✪ SHORT GRAIN CONTEST

Box 67, Saskatoon SK S7K 3K1 Canada. (306)244-2828. **E-mail:** grainmag@sasktel.net. **Website:** www.grainmagazine.ca/contest.html. **Contact:** Sarah Taggart, business administrator (inquiries only). The annual Short Grain Contest includes a category for poetry of any style up to 100 lines and fiction of any style up to 2,500 words, offering 3 prizes. Each entry must be original, unpublished, not submitted elsewhere for publication or broadcast, nor accepted elsewhere for publication or broadcast, nor entered simultaneously in any other contest or competition for which it is also eligible to win a prize. Entries must be typed on 8½x11 paper. It must be legible. No simultaneous submissions. A separate covering page must be attached to the text of your entry, and must provide the following information: Poet's name, complete mailing address, telephone number, e-mail address, entry title, category name, and line count. Accepts online submissions, see website for details. An absolutely accurate word or line count is required. No identifying information on the text pages. Entries will not be returned. Names of the winners and titles of the winning entries will be posted on the *Grain Magazine* website in August; only the winners will be notified. Deadline: April 1. Prize: $1,000, plus publication in *Grain Magazine*.

SLIPSTREAM ANNUAL POETRY CHAPBOOK CONTEST

Slipstream, Slipstream Poetry Contest, Dept. W-1, P.O. Box 2071, Niagara Falls NY 14301. **E-mail:** editors@slipstreampress.org. **Website:** www.slipstream-press.org. **Contact:** Dan Sicoli, co-editor. Slipstream Magazine is a yearly anthology of some of the best poetry you'll find today in the American small press. Send up to 40 pages of poetry: any style, format, or theme (or no theme). Send only copies of your poems, not originals. Mss will no longer be returned. See website for specific details. Offered annually to help promote a poet whose work is often overlooked or ignored. Open to any writer. Deadline: December 1. Prize: $1,000 plus 50 professionally-printed copies of your book.

HELEN C. SMITH MEMORIAL AWARD FOR POETRY

The Texas Institute of Letters, P.O. Box 609, Round Rock TX 78680. **E-mail:** tilsecretary@yahoo.com. **Website:** texasinstituteofletters.org/. Offered annually for the best book of poems published January 1-December 31 of previous year. Poet must have been born in Texas, have lived in the state at some time for at least 2 consecutive years, or the subject matter must be associated with the state. See website for submission details and information. Deadline: January 10. Prize: $1,200.

THE SOW'S EAR POETRY COMPETITION

The Sow's Ear Poetry Review, P.O. Box 127, Millwood VA 22646. **E-mail:** rglesman@gmail.com. **Website:** www.sows-ear.kitenet.net. **Contact:** Robert G. Lesman, managing editor. Open to adults. Send unpublished poems to the address above. Please do not put your name on poems. Include a separate sheet with poem titles, name, address, phone, and e-mail address if available, or a SASE for notification of results. No length limit on poems. Simultaneous submission acceptable (checks with finalists before sending to final judge). Send poems in September or October. Deadline: November 1. Prize: $1,000, publication, and the option of publication for approximately twenty finalists.

SPARK QUARTERLY WRITING CONTEST

Spark: A Creative Anthology (Empire & Great Jones Creative Arts Foundation), 13024 S. 3100 W, Riverton UT 84065. **E-mail:** editor@sparkanthology.org. **Website:** www.SparkAnthology.org/contests. **Contact:** Brian Lewis, contest director. This contest is open to any writer without restriction on age, location, genre, or previous publication credits. Encourages both established and emerging writers to participate. Submissions must be unpublished. Entries are accepted and managed online. Writers can view their work's status on the submission site, and winners will be posted at SparkAnthology.org/contests/winners. Prizes are awarded for excellent poetry and excellent prose, with no regard to the entrant's previous publication experience. Prose includes both fiction and nonfiction, and poetry includes all forms and meters. Prize: Grand Prize (one each for Poetry and Prose) always includes cash and publication. Judged by staff of *Spark: A Creative Anthology,* plus two previously-published professional writers as guest judges who are not on Spark staff. Guest judges change with each contest.

⊕ SPORTS FICTION AND ESSAY CONTEST

Winning Writers, 351 Pleasant St., PMB 222, Northampton MA 01060-3961. (866)946-9748. **Fax:** (413)280-0539. **E-mail:** adam@winningwriters.com. **Website:** www.winningwriters.com. **Contact:** Adam Cohen. Now in its 3rd year. Submit stories and essays with sports-related themes. Winners announced on WinningWriters.com and in free e-mail newsletter. Entrants who provided vaild e-mail addresses will also receive notifcation. See separate listing for the Wergle Flomp Humor Poetry Contest in this section. Submissions may be published or unpublished. Considers simultaneous submissions. Multiple entries also accepted. Submit online. Guidelines online. Submission Period: November 15 - May 31. Prize: Offers two 1st prizes of $1,000 each, plus 10 honorable mentions of $100 each. All prize winners receive online publication at WinningWriters.com. Judged by award-winning poet Jendi Reiter.

TIPS "Whether you're a player or a fan, or the kid who counted the minutes till gym class was over, sports can bring out the best and the worst in human nature. In this arena, teamwork, loyalty, courage, disappointment, failure, fame (and shame), and second chances are regularly on display. Sports can reinforce bullying and social dominance, or offer personal empowerment to an underdog. Yet stories and essays about sports are too often dismissed as 'genre writing'. This contest aims to bridge the gap between the worlds of physical culture and literary culture. We'd like to see the jocks and the writers sit down at the same lunchroom table and discover that they're both on a journey of self-transformation through disciplined risk-taking...and that they both really, really like to win."

THE EDWARD STANLEY AWARD

Prairie Schooner, 123 Andrews Hall, P.O. Box 880334, Lincoln NE 68588-0334. (402)472-0911. **Fax:** (402)472-9771. **E-mail:** prairieschooner@unl.edu. **Website:** www.prairieschooner.unl.edu. **Contact:** Editor in Chief. Offered annually for poetry published in *Prairie Schooner* in the previous year. Prize: $1,000.

THE ELIZABETH MATCHETT STOVER MEMORIAL AWARD

Southwest Review, Southern Methodist University, P.O. Box 750374, Dallas TX 75275-0374. (214)768-1037. **Fax:** (214)768-1408. **E-mail:** swr@mail.smu.edu. **Website:** www.smu.edu/southwestreview. **Contact:** Jennifer Cranfill, senior editor, and Willard Spiegelman, editor-in-chief. Offered annually to the best works of poetry that have appeared in the magazine in the previous year. Please note that mss are submitted for publication, not for the prizes themselves. Guidelines for SASE and online. Prize: $300. Judged by Jennifer Cranfill and Willard Spiegelman.

TIPS "Not an open contest. Annual prize in which winners are chosen from published pieces during the preceding year."

○ UTMOST CHRISTIAN POETRY CONTEST

Utmost Christian Writers Foundation, 121 Morin Maze, Edmonton Alberta T6K 1V1 Canada. (780)265-4650. **E-mail:** nnharms@telusplanet.net. **Website:** www.utmostchristianwriters.com. **Contact:** Nathan Harms, executive director. Utmost is founded on—and supported by—the dreams, interests and aspirates of individual people. Contest is only open to Christians. Poems may be rhymed or free verse, up to 60 lines, but must not have been published previously or have won any prize in any previous competition of any kind. Deadline: February 28. Prize: Prizes: 1st Place: $1,000; 2nd Place: $500; 10 prizes of $100 are offered for honorable mention; $300 for best rhyming poem and $200 for an honorable mention rhyming poem. Judged by a committee of the Directors of Utmost Christian Writers Foundation (who work under the direction of Barbara Mitchell, chief judge).

TIPS "Besides providing numerous resources for Christian writers and poets, Utmost also provides a marketplace where Christian writers and poets can sell their work. Please follow our guidelines. We receive numerous unsuitable submissions from writers. We encourage writers to submit suitable material. The best way to do this is to read the guidelines specific to your project—poetry, book reviews, articles—and then take time to look at the material we have already published in that area. The final step is to evaluate your proposed submission in comparison to the material we have used previously. If you complete these steps and strongly feel that your material is appropriate for us, we encourage you to submit it."

DANIEL VAROUJAN AWARD

New England Poetry Club, 376 School St., Watertown MA 02472. **E-mail:** contests@nepoetryclub.org. **Website:** www.nepoetryclub.org. **Contact:** Audrey Kalajin. For a poem on any subject, worthy of poet Daniel Varoujan who was executed by the Ottoman Turks in the 1915 genocide of the Armenian population. Jailed while awaiting execution, he finished a ms of sweet pastoral poems. Send entry in duplicate, one without name and address of writer. Deadline: May 31. Prize: $1,000. Judged by well-known poets and sometimes winners of previous NEPC contests.

THE WASHINGTON PRIZE

Dearlove Hall, Adirondack Community College, 640 Bay Rd., Queensbury NY 12804. **E-mail:** editor@wordworksdc.com. **Website:** www.wordworksdc.com. **Contact:** Nancy White, Washington Prize administrator. Sponsors an ongoing poetry reading series, educational programs, and and three additional imprints: The Tenth Gate, International Editions, and the Hilary Tham Capital Collection. Sponsors The Washington Prize, one of the older ms publishing prizes, and The Jacklyn Potter Young Poets Competition. Additional information online. Winners announced in August. Book publication planned for January of the following year. Submit a ms of 48-64 pages. Submit online, or if on paper, include 2 title pages, 1 with and 1 without author information, an acknowledgments page, a table of contents and a cover letter containing a brief bio. Electronic submissions are also accepted at www.wordworksbooks.org. Deadline: Submit January 15-March 15 (postmark). Prize: $1,500 and publication of a book-length ms of original poetry in English by a living American poet (US or Canadian citizen or resident).

WERGLE FLOMP HUMOR POETRY CONTEST

Winning Writers, 351 Pleasant St., PMB 222, Northampton MA 01060. (866)946-9748. **Fax:** (413)280-0539. **E-mail:** adam@winningwriters.com.

Website: www.winningwriters.com. **Contact:** Adam Cohen. This annual contest seeks today's best humor poems. One poem of any length should be submitted. Poem may be published or unpublished. The poem should be in English. Inspired gibberish is also accepted. See website for guidelines, examples, and to submit your poem. Nonexclusive right to publish submissions on WinningWriters.com, in e-mail newsletter, and in press releases. Submit one humor poem online. No length limit. Deadline: April 1. Prize: 1st prize of $1,000, plus 10 honorable mentions of $100 each. Judged by Jendi Reiter (final).

WHITE PINE PRESS POETRY PRIZE

White Pine Press, P.O. Box 236, Buffalo NY 14201. **E-mail:** wpine@whitepine.org. **Website:** www.whitepine.org. **Contact:** Dennis Maloney, editor. Offered annually for previously published or unpublished poets. Ms: Up to 80 pages of original work; translations are not eligible. Poems may have appeared in magazines or limited-edition chapbooks. Open to any US citizen. Deadline: November 30 (postmarked). Prize: $1,000 and publication. Final Judge is a poet of national reputation. All entries are screened by the editorial staff of White Pine Press.

THE J. HOWARD AND BARBARA M.J. WOOD PRIZE

Poetry, 61 W. Superior St., Chicago IL 60654. (312)787-7070. **Fax:** (312)787-6650. **E-mail:** editors@poetrymagazine.org. **Website:** www.poetrymagazine.org. Offered annually for poems published in *Poetry* during the preceding year (October-September). Upon acceptance, *Poetry* licenses exclusive worldwide first serial rights, including electronic rights, for publication, as well as non-exclusive rights to reprint, reuse, and archive the work, in any format, in perpetuity. Copyright reverts to author upon first publication. Prize: $5,000.

WORKING PEOPLE'S POETRY COMPETITION

Blue Collar Review, P.O. Box 11417, Norfolk VA 23517. **E-mail:** red-ink@earthlink.net. **Website:** www.partisanpress.org. Poetry should be typed as you would like to see it published, with your name and address on each page. Include cover letter with entry." Guidelines online. Deadline: May 15. Prize: $100, 1-year subscription to *Blue Collar Review* (see separate listing in Magazines/Journals) and 1-year posting of winning poem to website.

JAMES WRIGHT POETRY AWARD

Mid-American Review, Dept. of English, Bowling Green State University, Bowling Green OH 43403. (419)372-2725. **Fax:** (419)372-4642. **E-mail:** clouda@bgsu.edu. **Website:** www.bgsu.edu/midamerican-review. **Contact:** Abigail Cloud, editor. Offered annually for unpublished poetry. Open to all writers not associated with *Mid-American Review* or judge. Guidelines online or for SASE. Deadline: November 1. Prize: $1,000 and publication in spring issue of *Mid-American Review*. Judged by editors and a well known writer, i.e., Kathy Fagan, Bob Hicok, Michelle Boisseau. 2013-14 judge: Benjamin Grossberg.

THE YALE SERIES OF YOUNGER POETS

Yale University Press, P.O. Box 209040, New Haven CT 06520. **Website:** yalepress.yale.edu/yupbooks/youngerpoets.asp. The Yale Series of Younger Poets offers publication and royalties to 1 winning book-length ms. Open to U.S. citizens under age 40 at the time of entry who have not published a volume of poetry; poets may have published a limited edition chapbook of 300 copies or less. Poems may have been previously published in newspapers and periodicals and used in the book ms if so identified. No translations. Submit 48-64 pages of poetry, paginated, printed single-sided, with each new poem starting on a new page. Do not bind or staple ms; loose sheets may be placed in an envelope of appropriate size. Include 2 cover sheets: 1 showing ms title, poet's name, address, telephone number, e-mail address, and page count; the second with ms title only. Also include TOC and acknowledgments page, as well as a brief bio at the end of ms (optional). Include SASP for notification of receipt of ms and SASE for results; mss will not be returned. No e-mail submissions. Guidelines (with additional submission details) online. Deadline: November 15.

MULTIPLE WRITING AREAS

🌑 ADELAIDE FESTIVAL AWARDS FOR LITERATURE

Arts SA, GPO Box 2308, Adelaide SA 5001 Australia. (61)(8)8463-5444. **Fax:** (61)(8)8463-5420. **E-mail:** artssa@dpc.sa.gov.au. **Website:** www.arts.sa.gov.au. Introduced by the South Australia Government, the awards celebrate Australia's writing culture by offering national and State-based literary prizes, as well as fellowships for South Australian writers. Award categories: Premier's Award, Children's Literature, Fiction, John Bray Poetry, Nonfiction, Young Adult Fiction, Jill Blewett Playwright's and Wakefield Press Unpublished Ms. Prize: $10,000-25,000 for each award.

🌑 AESTHETICA CREATIVE WORKS COMPETITION

P.O. Box 371, York YO23 1WL United Kingdom. **E-mail:** cherie@aestheticamagazine.com; info@aestheticamagazine.com. **E-mail:** submissions@aestheticamagazine.com. **Website:** www.aestheticamagazine.com. The Aesthetica Creative Works Competition represents the scope of creative activity today, and provides an opportunity for both new and established artists to nurture their reputations on an international scale. There are three categories: Short Film Festival, Art Prize, and Creative Writing. Art Prize has four sub-categories, Creative writing has two. See website for guidelines and more details. The Aesthetica Creative Works Competition represents the scope of creative activity today, and provides an opportunity for both new and established artists to nurture their reputations on an international scale. There are three categories: Artwork & Photography, Fiction and Poetry. See guidelines online. The Aesthetica Creative Works Competition is looking to discover talented artists and writers. The editor of Aesthetica is a Fellow of the Royal Society of Arts. See guidelines online. Works should be completed in English Deadline: August 31. Prize: £500-1,000, Each winner will receive an additional prize from our competition partners. Winners will be published in the Aesthetica Creative Works Annual. Winners will receive a complimentary copy of the Aesthetica Creative Works Annual and publication of the work in their creative section (3 winners). **TIPS** "You will be notified by Oct. 31, 2011; please do not contact us beforehand. For further equeries, visit our FAQ page online at website."

ALLIGATOR JUNIPER AWARD

Alligator Juniper/Prescott College, 220 Grove Ave., Prescott AZ 86301. (928)350-2012. **Fax:** (928)776-5102. **E-mail:** alligatorjuniper@prescott.edu. **Website:** www.prescott.edu/alligatorjuniper/national-contest/index.html. **Contact:** Skye Anicca, managing editor. Annual contest for unpublished fiction, creative nonfiction, and poetry. Open to all age levels. Each entrant receives a personal letter from staff regarding the status of their submission, as well as minor feedback on the piece. Accepts simultaneous submissions, but inform on cover letter and contact immediately, should work be selected elsewhere. Maximum length: 30 pages or 5 poems. Deadline: October 1. Prize: $1,000 plus publication in all three categories. Finalists in each genre are recognized as such, published, and paid in copies. Judged by the distinguished writers in each genre and Prescott College writing students enrolled in the Literary Journal Practicum course.

THE AMERICAN GEM LITERARY FESTIVAL

Film*Makers* Magazine/Write Brothers, **E-mail:** info@filmmakers.com. **Website:** www.filmmakers.com/contests/short/. **Contact:** Jennifer Brooks. Worldwide contest to recognize excellent short screenplays and short stories. Ms submissions must be between 3-45 pages (there is an extra fee for anything between 46-65 pages) and up to industry standards. See website for more details. Must not have been previously optioned or sold to market or to a film producer. Preferable that the ms has not yet been adapted to a screenplay. Short stories should be no more than 50 pages, double-spaced, to a maximum of 12,500 words. Must not have been previously published. Deadlines: November 30 (early bird), January 30 (regular), March 15 (late), April 30 (final). Prize: Short Script: 1st Place: $1,000, pitches script to producers, free admission pass to the Great American Pitch Fest, and more; 2nd Place: $250; 3rd Place: $150; 4th Place: $100; 5th Place: $50. Top 3 win screenwriting software from Write Brothers. Top 25 scripts receive a certificate of achievement award. Short Story: 1st Place: $250. Top 3 win receive screenwriting software from Write Brothers.

AMERICAN LITERARY REVIEW CONTESTS

American Literary Review, P.O. Box 311307, University of North Texas, Denton TX 76203-1307. (940)565-2755. **E-mail:** americanliteraryreview@gmail.com. **Website:** english.unt.edu/alr. Contest to award excellence in short fiction, creative nonfiction, and poetry. Multiple entries are acceptable, but each entry must be accompanied with a reading fee. Do not put any identifying information in the file itself; include the author's name, title(s), address, e-mail address, and phone number in the boxes provided in the online submissions manager. Short fiction: Limit 8,000 words per work. Creative nonfiction: Limit 6,500 words per work. Deadline: October 1. Submission period begins June 1. Prize: $1,000 prize for each category, along with publication in the Spring online issue of the *American Literary Review*.

AMERICAS AWARD

Consortium of Latin American Studies Program, University of Wisconsin-Milwaukee, P.O. Box 413, Milwaukee WI 53201. **Website:** claspprograms.org/americasaward. **Contact:** Claire Gonzalez. The Américas Award encourages andc ommends authors, illustrators, and publishers who produce quality children's and young adult books that portray Latin America the Caribbean, or Latinos in the United States. Up to 2 awards (for primary and secondary reading levels) are given in recognition of US published works of fiction, poetry, folklore, or selected nonfiction (from picture books to works for young adults). The award winners and commended titles are selected for their (1) distinctive literary quality; (2) cultural contextualization; (3) exceptional integration of text, illustration and design; and (4) potential for classroom use. To nominate a copyright title from the previous year, publishers are invited to submit review copies to the committee members listed on the website. Publishers should send 8 copies of the nominated book. Deadline: January 18. Prize: $500, plaque and a formal presentation at the Library of Congress, Washington DC.

A MIDSUMMER TALE

E-mail: editors@toasted-cheese.com. **Website:** www.toasted-cheese.com. **Contact:** Theryn Fleming, editor. A Midsummer Tale is open to non-genre fiction and creative nonfiction. There is a different theme each year. Entries must be unpublished. Accepts inquiries by e-mail. Cover letter should include name, address, e-mail, word count, and title. Length: 1,000-5,000 words. Open to any writer. Guidelines available in April online. Deadline: June 21. Results announced on July 31. Winners notified by e-mail. List of winners online. Prize: Amazon gift certificates and publication in Toasted Cheese. Entries are blind-judged.

ANNUAL WRITING CONTEST

Lumina, the literary journal of Sarah Lawrence College, Sarah Lawrence College Slonim House, One Mead Way, Bronxville NY 10708. **E-mail:** lumina@gm.slc.edu. **Website:** www.luminajournal.com/contest. Annual writing contest in poetry, fiction, or creative nonfiction (varies by year). Please visit website in late August for complete and updated contest rules. Typical reading period: Sept. 1 - Nov. 15. Electronic submissions only. Deadline: October 15. Prize: 1st Place: $500.

ARIZONA AUTHORS' ASSOCIATION ANNUAL NATIONAL LITERARY CONTEST AND BOOK AWARDS

Arizona Authors' Association, 6145 W. Echo Ln., Glendale AZ 85302. (623)847-9343. **E-mail:** info@azauthors.com. **Website:** www.azauthors.com. Offered annually for previously unpublished poetry, short stories, essays, novels, and articles. Awards for published books in fiction, nonfiction, and children's. Winners announced at an award banquet in Glendale in November, and short pieces and excerpts published in *Arizona Literary Magazine*. Open to all writers anywhere in the world. Guidelines for unpublished and published categories vary, see website for guidelines. Deadline: July 1. Prize: First Prize: $100 and publication, and/or feature in the *Arizona Literary Magazine*. Additional prizes awarded in all categories and individual, specific categories.

ART AFFAIR SHORT STORY AND WESTERN SHORT STORY CONTESTS

Art Affair - Contest, P.O. Box 54302, Oklahoma City OK 73154. **E-mail:** artaffair@aol.com. **Website:** www.shadetreecreations.com. The annual Art Affair Writing Contests include (General) Short Story and Western Short Story categories. See separate listing for Poetry contest. Open to any writer. All short stories must be unpublished. Multiple entries accepted in both categories with separate entry fees for each. Submit original stories on any subject and timeframe for general Short Story category, and submit original western stories for Western Short Story—word limit for all entries is 5,000 words. Guidelines online. Put word count in the upper right-hand corner of first page; mark "Western" on western short stories. All ms. must be double-spaced on 8.5x11 white paper. Type title of short story on first page and headers on following pages. Include cover page with writer's name, address, phone number, and ms title. Deadline: October 1. Prize: Prize (in both categories): 1st Place: $50; 2nd Place: $25; 3rd Place: $15.

ARTIST TRUST FELLOWSHIP AWARD

1835 12th Ave., Seattle WA 98122. (209)467-8734 ext. 11. **Fax:** (866)218-7878. **E-mail:** info@artisttrust.org. **Website:** www.artisttrust.org. **Contact:** Miguel Guillen, Program Manager. Fellowships award $7,500 to practicing professional artists of exceptional talent and demonstrated ability. The Fellowship is a merit-based, not a project-based award. Recipients present a Meet the Artist Event to a community in Washington State that has little or no access to the artist and their work. Awards 14 fellowships of $7,500 and 2 residencies with $1,000 stipends at the Millay Colony. Artist Trust Fellowships are awarded in two-year cycles. Applicants must be 18 years of age or older, Washington State residents at the time of application and payment, and generative artists. Deadline: January 13. Applications available December 3. Prize: $7,500.

� ATLANTIC WRITING COMPETITION FOR UNPUBLISHED MSS

Writers' Federation of Nova Scotia, 1113 Marginal Rd., Halifax NS B3H 4P7. (902)423-8116. **Fax:** (902)422-0881. **E-mail:** programs@writers.ns.ca. **Website:** www.writers.ns.ca. **Contact:** Hillary Titley. Annual program designed to honor work by unpublished writers in all 4 Atlantic Provinces. Entry is open to writers unpublished in the category of writing they wish to enter. Prizes are presented in the fall of each year. Categories include: adult novel, writing for children, poetry, short story, juvenile/young adult novel, creative nonfiction, and play. Judges return written comments when competition is concluded. Page lengths and rules vary based on categories. See website for details. Anyone resident in the Atlantic Provinces since September 1st immediately prior to the deadline date is eligible to enter. Only one entry per category is allowed. Each entry requires its own entry form and registration fee. Deadline: February 3. Prize: Prizes vary based on categories. See website for details.

AUTUMN HOUSE POETRY, FICTION, AND NONFICTION PRIZES

P.O. Box 60100, Pittsburgh PA 15211. (412)381-4261. **E-mail:** gcerto@autumhouse.org; info@autumnhouse.org. **E-mail:** autumnh420@gmail.com. **Website:** autumnhouse.org. **Contact:** Giuliana Certo, managing editor. Offers annual prize and publication of book-length ms with national promotion. Submission must be unpublished as a collection, but individual poems, stories, and essays may have been previously published elsewhere. Considers simultaneous submissions. "Autumn House is a nonprofit corporation with the mission of publishing and promoting poetry and other fine literature. We have published books by Gerald Stern, Ruth L. Schwartz, Ed Ochester, Andrea Hollander Budy, George Bilgere, Jo McDougall, and others." Submit 50-80 pages of poetry or 200-300 pages of prose (include 2 cover sheets requested). Guidelines available for SASE, by e-mail, or online. Competition receives 1,500 entries/year. Winners announced through mailings, website, and ads in *Poets & Writers*, *American Poetry Review*, and *Writer's Chronicle* (extensive publicity for winner). Copies of winning books available from Amazon.com, Barnes & Noble, and other retailers. Deadline: June 30. Prize: The winner (in each of three categories) will receive book publication, $1,000 advance against royalties, and a $1,500 travel/publicity grant to promote his or her book. Judged by Alicia Ostroker (poetry), Sharon Dilworth (fiction), and Dinty W. Moore (nonfiction). **TIPS** "Include only your best work."

AWP AWARD SERIES

Association of Writers & Writing Programs, George Mason University, 4400 University Drive, MSN 1E3, Fairfax VA 22030. **E-mail:** supriya@awpwriter.org. **Website:** www.awpwriter.org. **Contact:** Supriya Bhatnagar, director of publications. AWP sponsors the Award Series, an annual competition for the publication of excellent new book-length works. The competition is open to all authors writing in English regardless of nationality or residence, and is available to published and unpublished authors alike. Guidelines online. Entries must be unpublished. Open to any writer. Entries are not accepted via postal mail. Offered annually to foster new literary talent. Deadline: Postmarked between January 1 and February 28. Prize: AWP Prize for the Novel: $2,500 and publication by New Issues Press; Donald Hall Prize for Poetry: $5,500 and publication by the University of Pittsburgh Press; Grace Paley Prize in Short Fiction: $5,500 and publication by the University of Massachusetts Press; and AWP Prize for Creative Nonfiction: $2,500 and publication by the University of Georgia Press.

THE BASKERVILLE PUBLISHERS POETRY AWARD & THE BETSY COLQUITT POETRY AWARD

descant, Texas Christian University's literary journal, TCU, Box 297270, Fort Worth TX 76129. (817)257-5907. **Fax:** (817)257-6239. **E-mail:** descant@tcu.edu. **Website:** www.descant.tcu.edu. **Contact:** Dan Williams and Alex Lemon. Annual award for an outstanding poem published in an issue of *descant*. Deadline: September-April. Prize: $250 for Baskerville Award; $500 for Betsy Colquitt Award. Publication

retains copyright, but will transfer it to the author upon request.

THE BLACK RIVER CHAPBOOK COMPETITION

Black Lawrence Press, 326 Bingham St., Pittsburgh PA 15211. **E-mail:** editors@blacklawrencepress.com. **Website:** www.blacklawrencepress.com. Contest for unpublished chapbook of poems or short fiction between 18-36 pages in length. Submit via online form. Spring deadline: May 31. Fall deadline: October 31. Prize: $500, publication, and 25 copies.

THE BOARDMAN TASKER AWARD FOR MOUNTAIN LITERATURE

The Boardman Tasker Charitable Trust, 8 Bank View Rd., Darley Abbey Derby DE22 1EJ UK. 01332 342246. **E-mail:** steve@people-matter.co.uk. **Website:** www. boardmantasker.com. **Contact:** Steve Dean. Offered annually to reward a work with a mountain theme, whether fiction, nonfiction, drama, or poetry, written in the English language (initially or in translation). Subject must be concerned with a mountain environment. Previous winners have been books on expeditions, climbing experiences, a biography of a mountaineer, novels. Guidelines available in January by e-mail or online. Entries must be previously published. Open to any writer. Writers may obtain information, but entry is by publishers only (includes self-publishing). Awarded for a work published or distributed for the first time in the United Kingdom during the previous year. Not an anthology. The award is to honor Peter Boardman and Joe Tasker, who disappeared on Everest in 1982. Deadline: August 1. Prize: £3,000 Judged by a panel of 3 judges elected by trustees.

BOROONDARA LITERARY AWARDS

City of Boroondara, 340 Camberwell Rd., Camberwell VIC 3124 Australia. **E-mail:** bla@boroondara.vic. gov.au. **Website:** www.boroondara.vic.gov.au/libraries/boroondara-literary-awards. Contest for unpublished work in 2 categories: Young Writers: 5th-6th grade (Junior), 7th-9th grade (Middle), and 10th-12th grade (Senior), prose and poetry on any theme; and Open Short Story (2,000-3,000 words). Deadline: August 30. Prize: Prizes: Young Writers, Junior: 1st Place: $150; 2nd Place: $100; 3rd Place: $50. Young Writers, Middle and Senior: 1st Place: $600; 2nd Place: $400; 3rd Place: $200. Open Short Story: 1st Place: $1,500; 2ndPlace: $1000; 3rd Place $500.

THE BOSTON AUTHORS CLUB BOOK AWARDS

The Boston Authors Club, Vera Lee, 15 Claremont St., Newtown MA 02458-1925. (617)965-7370. **E-mail:** leev@bc.edu. **Website:** www.bostonauthorsclub.org. **Contact:** Vera Lee. Julia Ward Howe Prize offered annually in the spring for books published the previous year. Two awards are given: one for adult books of fiction, nonfiction, or poetry, and one for children's books, middle grade and young adult novels, nonfiction, or poetry. No picture books or subsidized publishers. There must be two copies of each book submitted. Authors must live within 100 miles of Boston the year their book is published. Deadline: January 15. Prize: $1,000 in each category. Several books will also be cited with no cash awards as Finalists or Highly Recommended.

THE BRIAR CLIFF REVIEW FICTION, POETRY, AND CREATIVE NONFICTION COMPETITION

The Briar Cliff Review, Briar Cliff University, 3303 Rebecca St., Sioux City IA 51104-0100. **E-mail:** tricia.currans-sheehan@briarcliff.edu (editor); jeanne.emmons@briarcliff.edu (poetry). **Website:** www.briarcliff.edu/bcreview. Guidelines available in August for SASE. Inquiries accepted by e-mail. Deadline: Submissions between August 1 and November 1. No mss returned. Entries must be unpublished. Length: 6,000 words maximum. Open to any writer. Results announced in December or January. Winners notified by phone or letter around December 20. "Send us your best. We want stories with a plot." For contest results, send SASE with submission. Submit 3 poems, single-spaced on 8 1/2x11 paper; no more than 1 poem per page. Include separate cover sheet with author's name, address, e-mail, and poem title(s); no name on ms. Include SASE for results only; mss will not be returned. Guidelines online. Deadline: November 1. Judged by the editors of *The Briar Cliff Review*. **Contact:** Tricia Currans-Sheehan, editor. *The Briar Cliff Review* sponsors an annual contest offering $1,000 and publication to each 1st Prize winner in fiction, poetry, and creative nonfiction. Previous year's winner and former students of editors ineligible. Winning pieces accepted for publication on the basis of first-time rights. Considers simultaneous submissions, "but notify us immediately upon acceptance elsewhere. We guarantee a considerate reading." No mss returned. Award to reward good writers and showcase quality writing.

Deadline: Varies per category. Prize: $1,000 and publication to each 1st Prize winner in fiction, poetry, and creative nonfiction.

⬎ THE BRIDPORT PRIZE

P.O. Box 6910, Dorset DT6 9QB United Kingdom. **E-mail:** info@bridportprize.org.uk. **Website:** www.bridportprize.org.uk. **Contact:** Frances Everitt, administrator. Award to promote literary excellence, discover new talent. Categories: Short stories, poetry, flash fiction. 2010 introduced a new category for flash fiction: £1,000 sterling 1st Prize for the best short, short story of under 250 words. Entries must be unpublished. Length: 5,000 maximum for short stories; 42 lines for poetry, and 250 words for flash fiction. Deadline: May 31. Prize: £5,000 sterling; £1,000 sterling; £500 sterling; various runners-up prizes and publication of approximately 13 best stories and 13 best poems in anthology; plus 6 best flash fiction stories. £1,000 sterling 1st Prize for the best short, short story of under 250 words. Judged by 1 judge for short stories (in 2014, Andrew Miller), 1 judge for poetry (in 2014, Liz Lochhead) and 1 judge for flash fiction (in 2014, Tania Hershman).

♻ BURNABY WRITERS' SOCIETY CONTEST

E-mail: info@bws.bc.ca. **Website:** www.bws.bc.ca; www.burnabywritersnews.blogspot.com. **Contact:** Eileen Kernaghan. Offered annually for unpublished work. Open to all residents of British Columbia. Categories vary from year to year. Send SASE for current rules. For complete guidelines see website or burnabywritersnews.blogspot.com. Purpose is to encourage talented writers in all genres. Deadline: May 31. Prize: 1st Place: $200; 2nd Place: $100; 3rd Place: $50; and public reading.

CALIFORNIA BOOK AWARDS

Commonwealth Club of California, 595 Market St., San Francisco CA 94105. (415)597-6700. **Fax:** (415)597-6729. **E-mail:** bookawards@commonwealthclub.org. **Website:** www.commonwealthclub.org/bookawards. Offered annually to recognize California's best writers and illuminate the wealth and diversity of California-based literature. Award is for published submissions appearing in print during the previous calendar year. Can be nominated by publisher or author. Open to California residents (or residents at time of publication). Submit at least 3 copies of each book entered with an official entry form. Open to books, published during the year prior to the contest, whose author must have been a legal resident of California at the time the ms was submitted for publication. Entry form and guidelines available for SASE or online. Deadline: December 31. Prize: Medals and cash prizes to be awarded at publicized event. Judged by 12-15 California professionals with a diverse range of views, backgrounds, and literary experience.

☺ CANADIAN AUTHORS ASSOCIATION AWARDS PROGRAM

6 West St. N, Suite 203, Orillia ON L3V 5B8 Canada. (705)325-3926. **E-mail:** admin@canadianauthors.org. **Website:** www.canadianauthors.org. **Contact:** Anita Purcell. Offered annually for fiction, poetry, and Canadian history. Entrants must be Canadians by birth, naturalized Canadians, or landed immigrants. Entry form required for all awards. Obtain entry form from contact name or download from website. Deadline: January15. Prize: Cash and a silver medal.

CBC LITERARY PRIZES/PRIX LITTÉRAIRES RADIO-CANADA

CBC Radio/Radio Canada, Canada Council for the Arts, *enRoute* magazine, P.O. Box 6000, Montreal QC H3C 3A8 Canada. (877)888-6788. **E-mail:** canadawrites@cbc.ca. **Website:** www.cbc.ca/canadawrites. **Contact:** Christopher DiRaddo, coordinator. The CBC Literary Prizes Competitions are the only literary competitions that celebrate original, unpublished works in Canada's 2 official languages. There are 3 categories: short story, poetry, and creative nonfiction. Submissions to the short story and creative nonfiction must be 1,200-1,500 words; poetry submissions must be 400-600 words. Poetry submissions can take the form of a long narrative poem, a sequence of connected poems, or a group of unconnected poems. Canadian citizens, living in Canada or abroad, and permanent residents of Canada are eligible to enter. Deadline: November. Prize: For each category, in both English and French: 1st Prize: $6,000; 2nd Prize: $4,000. In addition, winning entries are published in Air Canada's *enRoute* magazine and broadcast on CBC radio. Winning authors also get a 2-weeks residency at the Banff Centre. First publication rights are granted by winners to *enRoute* magazine and broadcast rights are given to CBC radio. Submissions are judged blind by a jury of qualified writers and editors from around the country. Each category has 3 jurors.

CHRISTIAN BOOK AWARDS

Evangelical Christian Publishers Association, 9633 S. 48th St., Suite 140, Phoenix AZ 85044. (480)966-3998. **Fax:** (480)966-1944. **E-mail:** info@ecpa.org; mkuyper@ecpa.org. **Website:** www.ecpa.org. **Contact:** Mark W. Kuyper, president and CEO. The Evangelical Christian Publishers Association recognizes quality and encourages excellence by presenting the ECPA Christian Book Awards (formerly known as Gold Medallion) each year. Categories include children, fiction, nonfiction, Bibles, Bible reference, inspiration, and new author. All entries must be evangelical in nature and submitted through an ECPA member publisher. Books must have been published in the calendar year prior to the award. Publishing companies submitting entries must be ECPA members in good standing. See website for details. The Christian Book Awards recognize the highest quality in Christian books and is among the oldest and most prestigious awards program in Christian publishing. Deadline: September 30. Submission period begins September 2.

☺ THE CITY OF VANCOUVER BOOK AWARD

Cultural Services Dept., Woodward's Heritage Building, 111 W. Hastings St., Suite 501, Vancouver BC V6B 1H4 Canada. (604) 829-2007. **Fax:** (604)871-6005. **E-mail:** marnie.rice@vancouver.ca. **Website:** https://vancouver.ca/people-programs/city-of-vancouver-book-award.aspx. The annual City of Vancouver Book Award recognizes authors of excellence of any genre who contribute to the appreciation and understanding of Vancouver's history, unique character, or the achievements of its residents. The book must not be copyrighted prior to the previous year. Submit four copies of book. See website for details and guidelines. Deadline: May 15. Prize: $2,000. Judged by an independent jury.

COLORADO BOOK AWARDS

Colorado Humanities & Center for the Book, 7935 E. Prentice Ave., Suite 450, Greenwood Village CO 80111. (303)894-7951, ext. 21. **Fax:** (303)864-9361. **E-mail:** abu-baker@coloradohumanities.org. **Website:** www.coloradohumanities.org. **Contact:** Reem Abu-Baker. An annual program that celebrates the accomplishments of Colorado's outstanding authors, editors, illustrators, and photographers. Awards are presented in at least ten categories including anthology/collection, biography, children's, creative nonfiction, fiction, history, nonfiction, pictorial, poetry, and young adult. To be eligible for a Colorado Book Award, a primary contributor to the book must be a Colorado writer, editor, illustrator, or photographer. Current Colorado residents are eligible, as are individuals engaged in on-going literary work in the state and authors whose personal history, identity, or literary work reflect a strong Colorado influence. Authors not currently Colorado residents who feel their work is inspired by or connected to Colorado should submit a letter with his/her entry describing the connection. Celebrates books and their creators and promotes them to readers.

tion, biography, children's, creative nonfiction, fiction, history, nonfiction, pictorial, poetry, and young adult. To be eligible for a Colorado Book Award, a primary contributor to the book must be a Colorado writer, editor, illustrator, or photographer. Current Colorado residents are eligible, as are individuals engaged in on-going literary work in the state and authors whose personal history, identity, or literary work reflect a strong Colorado influence. Authors not currently Colorado residents who feel their work is inspired by or connected to Colorado should submit a letter with his/her entry describing the connection. Celebrates books and their creators and promotes them to readers.

CORDON D'OR - GOLD RIBBON ANNUAL INTERNATIONAL CULINARY ACADEMY AWARDS

The 'Accolade of the 21st Century', Cordon d 'Or - Gold Ribbon Inc., P.O. Box 40868, St. Petersburg FL 33743. (727)347-2437. **E-mail:** cordondor@aol.com. **Website:** www.goldribboncookery.com. **Contact:** Noreen Kinney. Contest promotes recognition of food authors, writers, and culinary magazines and websites, food stylists and food photographers and other professionals in the culinary field. See website for full details. Open to any writer. All categories can be found on the website. The only criteria is that all entries must be in the English language. Deadline: December 31. Prize: Cordon d 'Or-Gold Ribbon Crystal Globe Trophies (with stands and engraved marble bases) will be presented to winners. An outstanding winner chosen by the judges from among all entries will also win a cash award of $1,000. Judged by professionals in the fields covered in the awards program.

THE CRUCIBLE POETRY AND FICTION COMPETITION

Crucible, Barton College, College Station, Wilson NC 27893. (800)345-4973 x6450. **E-mail:** crucible@barton.edu. **Website:** www.barton.edu/SchoolofArts&Sciences/English/Crucible.htm. **Contact:** Terrence L. Grimes, editor. Open annually to all writers. Entries must be completely original, never published, and in ms form. Does not accept simultaneous submissions. Fiction is limited to 8,000 words; poetry is limited to 5 poems. Guidelines online or by e-mail or for SASE. All submissions should be electronic. Deadline: May 1. Prize: 1st Place: $150; 2nd Place: $100 (for both poetry and fiction). Winners are also published in *Crucible*. Judged by in-house editorial board.

DANA AWARDS IN THE NOVEL, SHORT FICTION, AND POETRY

www.danaawards.com, 200 Fosseway Dr., Greensboro NC 27445. (336)644-8028. **E-mail:** danaawards@gmail.com. **E-mail:** danaawards@gmail.com. **Website:** www.danaawards.com. **Contact:** Mary Elizabeth Parker, chair. Three awards offered annually for unpublished work written in English. Works previously published online are not eligible. Categories: Novel: For the first 40 pages of a novel completed or in progress; Fiction: Short fiction (no memoirs) up to 10,000 words; Poetry: For best group of 5 poems based on excellence of all 5 (no light verse, no single poem over 100 lines). Purpose is monetary award for work that has not been previously published or received monetary award, but will accept work published simply for friends and family. Deadline: October 31 (postmarked). Prize: Prizes: $1,000 for each of the 3 awards.

EATON LITERARY AGENCY'S ANNUAL AWARDS PROGRAM

Eaton Literary Agency, P.O. Box 49795, Sarasota FL 34230-6795. (941)366-6589. **Fax:** (941)365-4679. **E-mail:** eatonlit@aol.com. **Website:** www.eatonliterary.com. Offered biannually for unpublished mss. Prize: $2,500 (over 10,000 words); $500 (under 10,000 words). Judged by an independent agency in conjunction with some members of Eaton's staff. No entry fee. Guidelines available for SASE, by fax, e-mail, or online. Accepts inquiries by fax, phone and e-mail. Deadline: **March 31** (mss under 10,000 words); **August 31** (mss over 10,000 words). Entries must be unpublished. Open to any writer. Results announced in April and September. Winners notified by mail. For contest results, send SASE, fax, e-mail, or visit website. **Contact:** Richard Lawrence, V.P. Offered biannually for unpublished mss. Entries must be unpublished. Open to any writer. Guidelines available for SASE, by fax, e-mail, or online. Accepts inquiries by fax, phone and e-mail. Results announced in April and September. Winners notified by mail. For contest results, send SASE, fax, e-mail, or visit website. Deadline: March 31 (short story); August 31 (book-length). Prize: $2,500 (book-length); $500 (short story). Judged by an independent agency in conjunction with some members of Eaton's staff.

THE VIRGINIA FAULKNER AWARD FOR EXCELLENCE IN WRITING

Prairie Schooner, 123 Andrews Hall, University of Nebraska-Lincoln, Lincoln NE 68588-0334. (402)472-0911. **Fax:** (402)472-1817. **E-mail:** PrairieSchooner@unl.edu. **Website:** www.prairieschooner.unl.edu. **Contact:** Kwame Dawes. Offered annually for work published in *Prairie Schooner* in the previous year. Categories: short stories, essays, novel excerpts and translations. Guidelines for SASE or online. Accepts inquiries by fax and e-mail. "We only read mss from September 1 through May 1." Winning entry must have been published in *Prairie Schooner* in the year preceeding the award. Results announced in the Spring issue. Winners notified by mail in February or March. Prize: $1,000. Judged by Editorial Board.

FINELINE COMPETITION FOR PROSE POEMS, SHORT SHORTS, AND ANYTHING IN BETWEEN

Mid-American Review, Dept. of English, Bowling Green State University, Bowling Green OH 43403. (419)372-2725. **E-mail:** marsubmissions@bgsu.edu. **Website:** www.bgsu.edu/midamericanreview. **Contact:** Abigail Cloud, editor-in-chief. Offered annually for previously unpublished submissions. Contest open to all writers not associated with current judge or *Mid-American Review*. Deadline: June 1. Prize: $1,000, plus publication in fall issue of *Mid-American Review*; 10 finalists receive notation plus possible publication. 2014 judge: Lindsay Hunter.

✚ FIRST NOVEL CONTEST

Harrington & Harrington Press, 3400 Yosemite, San Diego CA 92109. **E-mail:** press@harringtonandharrington.com. **Website:** www.harringtonandharrington.com. **Contact:** Laurie Champion, contest/award director. Annual contest for any writer who has not previously published a novel. Entries may be self-published. Accepts full-length works in literary fiction, creative nonfiction, memoir, genre fiction, and short story collections. No poetry. Guidelines online. Harrington & Harrington Press aims to support writers, and the First Novel Contest will provide many ways to promote authors through networks and connections with writers, artists, and those involved in the technical production of art. Deadline: August 15. Prize: $500 advance royalty and publication by Harrington & Harrington Press. Judged by the Harrington & Harrington staff for the preliminary round.

A respected author with numerous publications will act as the final judge.

🐟 FISH SHORT MEMOIR PRIZE

Fish Publishing, Durrus, Bantry Co. Cork Ireland. **E-mail:** info@fishpublishing.com. **Website:** www.fishpublishing.com. Annual worldwide contest to recognize the best memoirs submitted to Fish Publishing. Entries must not have been previously published. Enter online or via postal mail. See website for full details. Deadline: January 31. Prize: 1st Prize: €1,000. The 10 best memoirs will be published in the Fish Anthology, launched in July at the West Cork Literary Festival.

FOREWORD MAGAZINE BOOK OF THE YEAR AWARDS

ForeWord Magazine, 425 Boardman Ave., Traverse City MI 49684. (231)933-3699. **Fax:** (231)933-3899. **Website:** www.forewordreviews.com. Awards offered annually. In order to be eligible, books must have a current year copyright. *ForeWord*'s Book of the Year Award was established to bring increased attention from librarians and booksellers to the literary achievements of independent publishers and their authors. Deadline: January 15. Prize: $1,500 cash will be awarded to a Best Fiction and Best Nonfiction choice, as determined by the editors of *ForeWord Magazine*. Judged by a jury of librarians, booksellers, and reviewers who are selected to judge the categories for entry and select winners and finalists in 61 categories based on editorial excellence and professional production as well as the originality of the narrative and the value the book adds to its genre.

TIPS "The best ideas have always come from independent thinkers, and we believe that maxim holds true for written ideas as well."

☺ FREEFALL SHORT PROSE AND POETRY CONTEST

Freefall Literary Society of Calgary, 922 9th Ave. SE, Calgary AB T2G 0S4 Canada. **E-mail:** freefallmagazine@yahoo.ca; editors@freefallmagazine.ca. **Website:** www.freefallmagazine.ca. **Contact:** Lynn C. Fraser, managing editor. Offered annually for unpublished work in the categories of poetry (5 poems/entry) and prose (3,000 words or less). Recognizes writers and offers publication credits in a literary magazine format. Contest rules and entry form online. Acquires first Canadian serial rights; ownership reverts to author after one-time publication. Deadline:

December 31. Prize: 1st Place: $600 (CAD); 2nd Place: $150 (CAD); 3rd Place: $75; Honorable Mention: $25. All prizes include publication in the spring edition of *FreeFall Magazine*. Winners will also be invited to read at the launch of that issue, if such a launch takes place. Honorable mentions in each category will be published and may be asked to read. Travel expenses not included. Judged by current guest editor for issue (who are also published authors in Canada).

GEORGETOWN REVIEW

Georgetown Review, 400 East College St., Box 227, Georgetown KY 40324. (502) 863-8308. **Fax:** (502) 863-8888. **E-mail:** gtownreview@georgetowncollege. edu. **Website:** georgetowncolleged.edu/georgetown-review. **Contact:** Steve Carter, editor. "Our magazine is a collaboration between English faculty at Georgetown College and undergrads who learn the editing business as they go and who always amaze their elders with their dedication and first-rate work." Will consider only original collections of poems written in English. (May include individual poems that have appeared elsewhere.) Students, colleagues, and close friends of the judge, and current students and employees of Georgetown College are not eligible. See website for details on paper and online submission guidelines. Deadline: October 15. Prize: $1,000 and publication; runners-up receive publication.

☉ GOVERNOR GENERAL'S LITERARY AWARDS

Canada Council for the Arts, 150 Elgin St., P.O. Box 1047, Ottawa ON K1P 5V8 Canada. (613)566-4414, ext. 5573. **Website:** www.canadacouncil.ca/prizes/ggla. Established by Parliament, the Canada Council for the Arts provides a wide range of grants and services to professional Canadian artists and art organizations in dance, media arts, music, theater, writing, publishing, and the visual arts. Books must be first edition trade books written, translated, or illustrated by Canadian citizens or permanent residents of Canada and published in Canada or abroad in the previous year. Collections of poetry must be at least 48 pages long, and at least half the book must contain work not published previously in book form. In the case of translation, the original work must also be a Canadian-authored title. Books must be submitted by publishers with a Publisher's Registration Form, which is available by request from the Writing and Publishing Section of the Canada Council for the Arts.

Guidelines and current deadlines are available on our website, by mail, telephone, fax, or e-mail. The Governor General's Literary Awards are given annually for the best English-language and French-language work in each of 7 categories, including fiction, nonfiction, poetry, drama, children's literature (text), children's literature (illustration), and translation. Deadline: Depends on the book's publication date. Prize: Each GG winner receives $25,000. Non-winning finalists receive $1,000. Judged by fellow authors, translators, and illustrators. For each category, a jury makes the final selection.

GRANDMOTHER EARTH NATIONAL AWARD

Grandmother Earth Creations, P.O. Box 2018, Cordova TN 38088. (901)309-3692. **E-mail:** gmoearth@gmail.com. **Website:** www.grandmotherearth.org. **Contact:** Frances Cowden, Award Director. Annual national award open to anyone. Submissions may be published or unpublished. Considers simultaneous submissions. Submit at least 3 poems, any subject, in any form. See website for changes in the rules. Include SASE for winners list. Guidelines available for SASE or online. Winners will be announced in October at the Life Press Writers Conference in August in Cordova, TN. Copies of winning poems or books available from Grandmother Earth Creations. Deadline: July 7. Prize: Offers annual award of $1,250 with varying distributions each year; separate contest for students ages 2-12; $1,250 minimum in awards for poetry and prose; $100 first, etc., plus publication in anthology; non-winning finalists considered for anthology if permission is given.

GREAT LAKES COLLEGES ASSOCIATION NEW WRITERS AWARD

535 W. William, Suite 301, Ann Arbor MI 48103. (734)661-2350. **Fax:** (734)661-2349. **E-mail:** wegner@glca.org. **Website:** www.glca.org. **Contact:** Gregory R. Wegner. Annual award for a first published volume of poetry, fiction, and creative nonfiction. Nominations should be made by the publisher and should emphasize literary excellence. Deadline: July 25. Prize: Honorarium of at least $500. Each award winner has the opportunity to tour the 13 colleges giving readings, meetings students and faculty, and leading discussions or classes. Judged by professors of literature and writers in residence at GLCA colleges.

THE GRUB STREET NATIONAL BOOK PRIZE

Grub Street, 162 Boylston Street, 5th Floor, Boston MA 02116. (617) 695-0075. **Fax:** (617) 695-0075. **E-mail:** info@grubstreet.org. **Website:** grubstreet.org. **Contact:** Christopher Castellani, artistic director. The Grub Street National Book Prize is awarded once annually to an American writer outside New England publishing his or her second, third, fourth (or beyond...) book. First books are not eligible. Writers whose primary residence is Massachusetts, Vermont, Maine, New Hampshire, Connecticut or Rhode Island are also not eligible. Genre of the prize rotates from year to year, between fiction, nonfiction, and poetry. Submissions should include: 2 copies of the author's most recent or upcoming book, in bound galleys or final form; a Curriculum vitae; and a 500-word synopsis of the proposed craft class. See website for details on current prize and genre requirements. Deadline: October 15. Prize: $5,000.

HACKNEY LITERARY AWARDS

1305 2nd Ave. N, #103, Birmingham AL 35203. (205)226-4921. **E-mail:** info@hackneyliteraryawards.org. **Website:** www.hackneyliteraryawards.org. **Contact:** Myra Crawford, PhD, executive director. Offered annually for unpublished novels, short stories (maximum 5,000 words) and poetry (50 line limit). Guidelines online. Deadline: September 30 (novels), November 30 (short stories and poetry). Prize: $5,000 in annual prizes for poetry and short fiction ($2,500 national and $2,500 state level). 1st Place: $600; 2nd Place: $400; 3rd Place: $250); plus $5,000 for an unpublished novel. Competition winners will be announced on the website each March.

⊕ ROSE HAROOTIAN SHORT STORY CONTEST

327 Lowell St., Reading MA 01867. **E-mail:** pattiannah@gmail.com. **Website:** www.pattianna.com/#!rose-harootian-literary-journal/c6b3. **Contact:** Pattianna Harootian. Annual contest to honor short stories. *The Rose Harootian Literary Journal* is made up of the entries submitted to the competition. Entries can be fiction or nonfiction but must be based on at least one character that overcomes adversity to achieve a goal or fulfill a dream, and conclusions must be hopeful, encouraging, and inspiring. Guidelines online. Enter up to 5,000 words. Include a cover page with full name, mailing address, phone number, and e-mail address. Do not include the story title. Deadline: March 31. Prize: 1st Place: $500; 2nd Place: $200; 3rd Place: $50.

THE ERIC HOFFER AWARD (BOOKS)

Best New Writing, P.O. Box 11, Titusville NJ 08560. **Fax:** (609)818-1913. **E-mail:** info@hopepubs.com. **Website:** www.hofferaward.com. **Contact:** Christopher Klim, chair. Annual contest recognizing excellence in publishing. This contest recognizes excellence in independent publishing in many distinct categories. Honors by press type (academic, micro press, small press, and self-published) and category (art, poetry, general fiction, commercial fiction, children, young adult, culture, memoir, business, reference, home, health, self-help, spiritual, legacy fiction, and legacy (fiction and nonfiction) and eBook (fiction and nonfiction). Also awards the Montaigne Medal for most though-provoking book, the Da Vinci Eye for best cover, and the First Horizon Award for best new authors. Results published in the *US Review of Books.* Deadline: January 21. Prize: $2,000. Judged by authors, editors, agents, publishers, book producers, artists, experienced category readers, and health and business professionals.

THE ERIC HOFFER AWARD (PROSE)

Best New Writing, P.O. Box 11, Titusville NJ 08560. **Fax:** (609)964-1718. **E-mail:** info@hofferaward.com. **Website:** www.hofferaward.com. **Contact:** C. Klim, editor. Annual contest for new and unpublished prose. Purchases first publication and one-time anthology rights for winning entries. The Eric Hoffer Award for short prose (i.e., fiction and creative nonfiction - 10,000 words or less) was established at the start of the 21st century as a means of opening a door to writing of significant merit. It honors the memory of the great American philosopher Eric Hoffer by highlighting salient writing. The winning stories and essays are published in *Best New Writing.* Prize: $250; publication contract.

THE JULIA WARD HOWE/BOSTON AUTHORS AWARD

The Boston Authors Club, 15 Claremont St., Newton MA 02458-1925. (617)244-0646. **E-mail:** bostonauthors@aol.com; leev@bc.edu. **Website:** www.bostonauthorsclub.org. **Contact:** Vera Lee. This annual award honors Julia Ward Howe and her literary friends who founded the Boston Authors Club in 1900. It also honors the membership over 110 years, consisting of novelists, biographers, historians, governors, senators, philosophers, poets, playwrights, and other luminaries. There are 2 categories: trade books and books for young readers (beginning with chapter books through young adult books). Works of fiction, nonfiction, memoir, poetry, and biography published in 2010 are eligible. Authors must live or have lived (college counts) within a 100-mile radius of Boston within the last 5 years. Subsidized books, cook books and picture books are not eligible.

INDIANA REVIEW K (SHORT-SHORT/ PROSE-POEM) PRIZE

Indiana Review, Ballantine Hall 465, 1020 E. Kirkwood Ave., Indiana University, Bloomington IN 47405-7103. (812)855-3439. **Fax:** (812)855-9535. **E-mail:** inreview@ indiana.edu. **Website:** indianareview.org. **Contact:** Katie Moulton, editor. Offered annually for unpublished work. Maximum story/poem length is 500 words. Guidelines available in March for SASE, by phone, e-mail, online, or in publication. Open to any writer. Cover letter should include name, address, phone, e-mail, word count and title. No identifying information on ms. "We look for command of language and form." Results announced in August. Winners notified by mail. For contest results, send SASE or visit website. Deadline: May 31. Submission period begins August 1. Prize: $1,000, plus publication, contributor's copies, and a year's subscription to *Indiana Review*.

INSIGHT WRITING CONTEST

Insight Magazine, 55 W. Oak Ridge Dr., Hagerstown MD 21740. **Fax:** (301)393-4055. **E-mail:** insight@rhpa. org. **Website:** www.insightmagazine.org. **Contact:** Omar Miranda, editor. Annual contest for writers in the categories of student short story, general short story, and student poetry. Unpublished submissions only. General category is open to all writers; student categories must be age 22 and younger. Deadline: July 31. Prize: Prizes: Student Short and General Short Story: 1st Prize: $250; 2nd Prize: $200; 3rd Prize: $150. Student Poetry: 1st Prize: $100; 2nd Prize: $75; 3rd Prize: $50.
TIPS "Your entry must be a true, unpublished work by you, with a strong spiritual message. We appreciate the use of Bible texts."

THE IOWA REVIEW AWARD IN POETRY, FICTION, AND NONFICTION

308 EPB, University of Iowa, Iowa City IA 52242. **E-mail:** iowa-review@uiowa.edu. **Website:** www.io-wareview.org. *The Iowa Review* Award in Poetry, Fiction, and Nonfiction presents $1,500 to each winner in each genre, $750 to runners-up. Winners and runners-up published in *The Iowa Review*. Submissions must be unpublished. Considers simultaneous submissions (with notification of acceptance elsewhere). Submit up to 25 pages of prose, (double-spaced) or 10 pages of poetry (1 poem or several, but no more than 1 poem per page). Submit online or by mail. Include cover page with writer's name, address, e-mail and/ or phone number, and title of each work submitted. Personal identification must not appear on ms pages. Label mailing envelope as a contest entry, E.G., "Contest: Fiction." One entry per envelope. Include SASP for confirmation of receipt of entry, SASE for results. Guidelines online. Deadline: Submit January 1-31 (postmark). 2014 Judges: Robyn Schiff, Rachel Kushner, and David Shields.

LEAGUE OF UTAH WRITERS CONTEST

The League of Utah Writers, (435)755-7609. **E-mail:** luwcontest@gmail.com. **Website:** www.luwriters. org. **Contact:** Tim Keller, Contest Chair. Open to any writer, the LUW Contest provides authors an opportunity to get their work read and critiqued. Multiple categories are offered; see webpage for details. Entries must be the original and unpublished work of the author. Winners are announced at the Annual Writers Round-Up in September. Those not present will be notified by e-mail. Submission Period: March 15-June 15. Prize: Cash prizes are awarded. Judged by professional authors and editors from outside the League.

⊕ LES FIGUES PRESS NOS BOOK CONTEST

P.O. Box 7736, Los Angeles CA 90007. **E-mail:** info@ lesfigues.com. **Website:** www.lesfigues.com. **Contact:** Teresa Carmody and Vanessa Place, co-directors. Les Figues Press creates aesthetic conversations between writers/artists and readers, especially those interested in innovative/experimental/avant-garde work. The Press intends in the most premeditated fashion to champion the trinity of Beauty, Belief, and Bawdry. Submit a 64-250 page unpublished ms through electronic submissions manager. Annual NOS (not otherwise specific) book prize given for best ms of poetry, prosem or writing in between. Electronic submissions only. See website for contest guidelines. Deadline: September 30. Prize: $1,000, plus publication by Les Figues Press. Each entry receives LFP book.

LET'S WRITE LITERARY CONTEST

The Gulf Coast Writers Association, P.O. Box 10294, Gulfport MS 39505. **E-mail:** writerpllevin@gmail. com. **Website:** www.gcwriters.org. **Contact:** Philip Levin. The Gulf Coast Writers Association sponsors this nationally recognized contest, which accepts unpublished poems and short stories from authors all around the US. This is an annual event which has been held for over 20 years. Deadline: April 15. Prize: 1st Prize: $100; 2nd Prize: $60; 3rd Prize: $25.

☻ MANITOBA BOOK AWARDS

c/o Manitoba Writers' Guild, 218-100 Arthur St., Winnipeg MB R3B 1H3 Canada. (204)944-8013. **E-mail:** info@mbwriter.mb.ca. **Website:** www.manitobabookawards.com. Offered annually: The McNally Robinson Book of Year Award (adult); The McNally Robinson Book for Young People Awards (8 and under and 9 and older); The John Hirsch Award for Most Promising Manitoba Writer; The Mary Scorer Award for Best Book by a Manitoba Publisher; The Carol Shields Winnipeg Book Award; The Eileen McTavish Sykes Award for Best First Book; The Margaret Laurence Award for Fiction; The Alexander Kennedy Isbister Award for Nonfiction; The Manuela Dias Book Design of the Year Award; The Best Illustrated Book of the Year Award; and the biennial Le Prix Littéraire Rue-Deschambault. Guidelines and submission forms online. Open to Manitoba writers only. Deadline: November 15 and January 6. See website for specific details on book eligibility at deadlines. Prize: Several prizes up to $5,000 (Canadian).

⊘ THE MCGINNIS-RITCHIE MEMORIAL AWARD

Southwest Review, P.O. Box 750374, Dallas TX 75275-0374. (214)768-1037. **Fax:** (214)768-1408. **E-mail:** swr@mail.smu.edu. **Website:** www.smu.edu/southwestreview. **Contact:** Jennifer Cranfill, senior editor, and Willard Spiegelman, editor-in-chief. The McGinnis-Ritchie Memorial Award is given annually to the best works of fiction and nonfiction that appeared in the magazine in the previous year. Mss are submitted for publication, not for the prizes themselves. Guidelines for SASE or online. Prize: $500. Judged by Jennifer Cranfill and Willard Spiegelman.
TIPS "Not an open contest. Annual prize in which winners are chosen from published pieces during the preceding year."

MISSISSIPPI REVIEW PRIZE

Mississippi Review, 118 College Dr., #5144, Hattiesburg MS 39406-0001. (601)266-4321. **Fax:** (601)266-5757. **E-mail:** msreview@usm.edu; rief@mississippireview.com. **Website:** www.mississippireview.com. Annual contest starting April 2. Winners and finalists will make up next winter's print issue of the national literary magazine *Mississippi Review*. Each entrant will receive a copy of the prize issue. Contest is open to all writers in English except current or former students or employees of The University of Southern Mississippi. Fiction entries should be 1,000-5,000 words, poetry entries should be three poems totaling 10 pages or less. There is no limit on the number of entries you may submit. Online submissions must be submitted through Submittable site: mississippireview.submittable.com/submit. No mss will be returned. Previously published work is ineligible. Winners will be announced in late January and publication is scheduled for May next year. Entries should have 'MR Prize,' author name, address, phone, e-mail and title of work on page 1. Deadline: October 1. Prize: $1,000 in fiction and poetry.

NATIONAL OUTDOOR BOOK AWARDS

921 S. 8th Ave., Stop 8128, Pocatello ID 83209. (208)282-3912. **E-mail:** wattron@isu.edu. **Website:** www.noba-web.org. **Contact:** Ron Watters. Nine categories: History/biography, outdoor literature, instructional texts, outdoor adventure guides, nature guides, children's books, design/artistic merit, natural history literature, and nature and the environment. Additionally, a special award, the Outdoor Classic Award, is given annually to books which, over a period of time, have proven to be exceptionally valuable works in the outdoor field. Application forms and eligibilty requirements are online. Applications for the Awards program become available in early June. Deadline: September 1. Prize: Winning books are promoted nationally and are entitled to display the National Outdoor Book Award (NOBA) medallion.

THE NEUTRINO SHORT-SHORT CONTEST

Passages North, Dept. of English, Northern Michigan University, 1401 Presque Isle Ave., Marquette MI 49855. (906)227-1203. **Fax:** (906)227-1096. **E-mail:** passages@nmu.edu. **Website:** www.passagesnorth.com. **Contact:** Jennifer Howard. Offered every 2 years to publish new voices in literary fiction, nonfiction, hybrid-essays and prose poems (maximum

1,000 words). Guidelines available for SASE or online. Deadline: March 15. Submission period begins January 15. Prize:$1,000, and publication for the winner; 2 honorable mentions also published; all entrants receive a copy of *Passages North*.

NEW LETTERS LITERARY AWARDS

New Letters, UMKC, University House, Room 105, 5101 Rockhill Rd., Kansas City MO 64110-2499. (816)235-1168. **Fax:** (816)235-2611. **Website:** www.newletters.org. Award has 3 categories (fiction, poetry, and creative nonfiction) with 1 winner in each. Offered annually for previously unpublished work. For guidelines, send an SASE to *New Letters*, or visit www.newletters.org. Deadline: May 18. Prize: 1st place: $1,500, plus publication; first runners-up: a copy of a recent book of poetry or fiction courtesy of our affiliate BkMk Press. Judged by regional writers of prominence and experience. Final judging by someone of national repute. Previous judges include Maxine Kumin, Albert Goldbarth, Charles Simic, and Janet Burroway.

OHIOANA BOOK AWARDS

Ohioana Library Association, 274 E. First Ave., Suite 300, Columbus OH 43201-3673. (614)466-3831. **Fax:** (614)728-6974. **E-mail:** ohioana@ohioana.org. **Website:** www.ohioana.org. **Contact:** David Weaver, executive director. Writers must have been born in Ohio or lived in Ohio for at least 5 years, but books about Ohio or an Ohioan need not be written by an Ohioan. Results announced in August or September. Winners notified by mail in early summer. Offered annually to bring national attention to Ohio authors and their books, published in the last year. (Books can only be considered once.) Categories: Fiction, nonfiction, juvenile, poetry, and books about Ohio or an Ohioan. Deadline: December 31. Prize: Certificate and glass sculpture. Judged by a jury selected by librarians, book reviewers, writers and other knowledgeable people.

☺ OPEN SEASON AWARDS

The Malahat Review, University of Victoria, P.O. Box 1700, Stn CSC, Victoria BC V8V 2Y2 Canada. **Fax:** (250)472-5051. **E-mail:** malahat@uvic.ca. **Website:** www.malahatreview.ca. **Contact:** John Barton, editor. The Open Season Awards accepts entries of poetry, fiction, and creative nonfiction. Winners published in spring issue of *Malahat Review* announced in winter online, facebook page, and in quarterly e-newsletter, *Malahat lite*. Submissions must be unpublished. No simultaneous submissions. Submit up to 3 poems of 100

lines or less; 1 piece of fiction 2,500 words maximum; or 1 piece of creative nonfiction, 2,500 words maximum. No restrictions on subject matter or aesthetic approach. Include separate page with writer's name, address, e-mail, and title(s); no identifying information on mss pages. E-mail submissions now accepted: season@uvic.ca. Do not include SASE for results; mss will not be returned. Guidelines online. Winners and finalists will be contacted by e-mail. Deadline: November 1. Prize: $1,000 CAD and publication in *The Malahat Review* in each category.

JUDITH SIEGEL PEARSON AWARD

Judith Siegel Pearson Award, c/o Department of English, Wayne State University, Attn: Royanne Smith, 5057 Woodward Ave, Ste. 9408, Detroit MI 48202. (313)577-2450. **Fax:** (313)577-8618. **E-mail:** ad2073@wayne.edu. Offers an annual award for the best creative or scholarly work on a subject concerning women. The type of work accepted rotates each year: drama in 2012; poetry in 2013; nonfiction in 2014; fiction in 2015. Open to all interested writers and scholars. Only submit the appropriate genre in each year. Submissions should be anonymous with the author's name and address on a separate title page. There should be 2 copies of each entry, clearly typed on one side of a 8 1/2x11" paper, double-spaced, and proofread carefully. Submissions must be unpublished. Guidelines available by e-mail. No later or electronic submissions accepted. Deadline: February 21.

PNWA LITERARY CONTEST

Pacifc Northwest Writers Association, PMB 2717, 1420 NW Gilman Blvd., Suite 2, Issaquah WA 98027. (452)673-2665. **E-mail:** pnwa@pnwa.org. **Website:** www.pnwa.org. Annual literary contest with 12 different categories. See website for details and specific guidelines. Each entry receives 2 critiques. Winners announced at the PNWA Summer Conference, held annually in mid-July. Deadline: February 21. Prize: 1st Place: $700; 2nd Place: $300. Judged by an agent or editor attending the conference.

⊕ PRIME NUMBER MAGAZINE AWARDS

Press 53, 411 W. Fourth St., Suite 101A, Winston-Salem NC 27101. **E-mail:** kevin@press53.com. **Website:** www.press53.com. **Contact:** Kevin Morgan Watson, publisher. Awards over $2,000 and publication for winning entries in poetry, flash fiction, short story, flash nonfiction, and creative nonfiction. Details and guidelines online. Deadline: March 30. Submission period begins January

1. Finalists announced June 1. Winner announced on August 1. Prize: 1st Prize in each category: $250 cash; 2nd Prize: $100; Honorable Mention: $50. All winners receive publication in *Prime Number Magazine* online and in the *Prime Number Magazine, Editors' Selections* print annual. Judged by industry professionals to be named when the contest begins.

✪ PRISM INTERNATIONAL ANNUAL SHORT FICTION, POETRY, AND CREATIVE NONFICTION CONTESTS

Prism International, Creative Writing Program, UBC, Buch. E462, 1866 Main Mall, Vancouver BC V6T 1Z1 Canada. **E-mail:** prismwritingcontest@gmail.com. **Website:** www.prismmagazine.ca/contests/. Offered annually for unpublished work to award the best in contemporary fiction, poetry, drama, translation, and nonfiction. Works of translation are eligible. Guidelines are online. Acquires first North American serial rights upon publication, and limited web rights for pieces selected for website. Open to any writer except students and faculty in the Creative Writing Department at UBC, or people who have taken a creative writing course at UBC within 2 years of the contest deadline. Entry includes subscription. Deadline: January 23 (poetry, short fiction); November 28 (nonfiction). Prize: 1st Place: $1,000-2,000; runners-up (3): $200-300 each (depends on contest); winners are published.

RANDOM HOUSE FOUNDATION, INC. CREATIVE WRITING COMPETITION

One Scholarship Way, P.O. Box 297, St. Peter MN 56082. (212)782-0316. **Fax:** (212)940-7590. **E-mail:** creativewriting@randomhouse.com. **Website:** www.randomhouse.com/creativewriting. **Contact:** Melanie Fallon Hauska, director. Offered annually for unpublished work to NYC public high school seniors. 72 awards given in literary and nonliterary categories. Four categories: poetry, fiction/drama, personal essay and graphic novel. Applicants must be seniors (under age 21) at a New York high school. No college essays or class assignments will be accepted. Word length: 2,500 words or less. Applicants must be seniors (under age 21) at a New York high school. Results announced mid-May. Winners notified by mail and phone. For contest results, send SASE, fax, e-mail or visit website. Deadline: February 10 for all categories. Prize: Awards range from $500-10,000. The program usually awards just under $100,000 in scholarships.

✪ THE RBC BRONWEN WALLACE AWARD FOR EMERGING WRITERS

The Writers' Trust of Canada, 460 Richmond St. W., Suite 600, Toronto ON M5C 1P1 Canada. (416)504-8222. **Fax:** (416)504-9090. **E-mail:** info@writerstrust.com. **Website:** www.writerstrust.com. **Contact:** Amanda Hopkins. Presented annually to a Canadian writer under the age of 35 who is not yet published in book form. The award, which alternates each year between poetry and short fiction, was established in memory of poet Bronwen Wallace. Deadline: March 7. Prize: $5,000 and $1,000 to 2 finalists.

ROYAL DRAGONFLY BOOK AWARDS

4696 W. Tyson St., Chandler AZ 85226. (480)940-8182. **Fax:** (480)940-8787. **E-mail:** cristy@fivestarpublications.com. **Website:** www.fivestarpublications.com; www.fivestarbookawards.com; www.royaldragonflybookawards.com. **Contact:** Cristy Bertini. Offered annually for any previously published work to honor authors for writing excellence of all types of literature—fiction and nonfiction—in 52 categories, appealing to a wide range of ages and comprehensive list of genres. Open to any title published in English. Entry forms are downloadable at www.royaldragonflybookawards.com. Prize: Grand Prize winner receives $300, while another entrant will be the lucky winner of a $100 drawing. All first-place winners receive foil award seals and are included in a publicity campaign announcing winners. All first- and second-place winners and honorable mentions receive certificates.

THE MONA SCHREIBER PRIZE FOR HUMOROUS FICTION & NONFICTION

3940 Laurel Canyon Blvd., #566, Studio City CA 91604. **E-mail:** brad.schreiber@att.net. **Website:** www.bradschreiber.com. **Contact:** Brad Schreiber. No SASEs. Non-US entries should enclose US currency or checks written in US dollars. Include e-mail address. No previously published work. The purpose of the contest is to award the most creative humor writing, in any form less than 750 words, in either fiction or nonfiction, including but not limited to stories, articles, essays, speeches, shopping lists, diary entries, and anything else writers dream up. Complete rules and previous winning entries online. Deadline: December 1. Prize: 1st Place: $500; 2nd Place: $250; 3rd Place: $100. Judged by Brad Schreiber, author, journalist, consultant, and instructor.

THE BERNICE SLOTE AWARD

Prairie Schooner, 123 Andrews Hall, PO Box 880334, Lincoln NE 68588-0334. (402)472-0911. **Fax:** (402)472-1817. **E-mail:** PrairieSchooner@unl.edu. **Website:** www.prairieschooner.unl.edu. **Contact:** Kwame Dawes. Categories: short stories, essays and poetry. For guidelines, send SASE or visit website. Only work published in the journal during the previous year will be considered. Work is nominated by the editorial staff. Offered annually for the best work by a beginning writer published in *Prairie Schooner* in the previous year. Celebrates the best and finest writing that they have published for the year. Prize: $500. Judged by editorial staff of *Prairie Schooner*.

JEFFREY E. SMITH EDITORS' PRIZE IN FICTION, ESSAY AND POETRY

The Missouri Review, 357 McReynolds Hall, UMC, Columbia MO 65211. (573)882-4474. **Fax:** (573)884-4671. **E-mail:** contest_question@moreview.com. **Website:** www.missourireview.com. **Contact:** Editor. Offered annually for unpublished work in 3 categories: fiction, essay, and poetry. Guidelines online or for SASE. Deadline: October 1. Prize: $5,000 and publication for each category winner.

KAY SNOW WRITING CONTEST

Willamette Writers, Willamette Writers, 2108 Buck St., West Linn OR 97068. (503)305-6729. **Fax:** (503)344-6174. **E-mail:** wilwrite@willamettewriters.com. **Website:** www.willamettewriters.com. **Contact:** Lizzy Shannon, contest director. Willamette Writers is the largest writers' organization in Oregon and one of the largest writers' organizations in the United States. It is a non-profit, tax-exempt Oregon corporation led by volunteers. Elected officials and directors administer an active program of monthly meetings, special seminars, workshops and annual writing conference. Continuing with established programs and starting new ones is only made possible by strong volunteer support. See website for specific details and rules. There are fivedifferent categories writers can enter: Adult Fiction, Adult Nonfiction, Poetry, Juvenile Short Story, and Student Writer. The purpose of this annual writing contest, named in honor of Willamette Writer's founder, Kay Snow, is to help writers reach professional goals in writing in a broad array of categories and to encourage student writers. Deadline: April 23. Prize: One first prize of $300, one second place prize of $150, and a third place prize of $50 per winning entry in each of the six categories.

SOCIETY OF MIDLAND AUTHORS AWARD

Society of Midland Authors, Society of Midland Authors, P.O. Box 10419, Chicago IL 60610-0419. **E-mail:** loerzel@comcast.net. **Website:** www.midlandauthors.com. **Contact:** Meg Tebo, President. Since 1957, the Society has presented annual awards for the best books written by Midwestern authors. The contest is open to any title published within the year prior to the contest year. Open to authors or poets who reside in, were born in, or have strong ties to a Midland state, which includes Illinois, Indiana, Iowa, Kansas, Michigan, Minnesota, Missouri, Nebraska, North Dakota, South Dakota, Ohio and Wisconsin. The Society of Midland Authors (SMA) Award is presented to one title in each of six categories: adult nonfiction, adult fiction, adult biography and memoir, children's nonfiction, children's fiction, and poetry. Deadline: February 1. Prize: cash prize of $500 and a plaque that is awarded at the SMA banquet in May in Chicago.

SOUL-MAKING KEATS LITERARY COMPETITION

The Webhallow House, 1544 Sweetwood Dr., Broadmoor Vlg CA 94015-2029. **E-mail:** SoulKeats@mail.com. **Website:** www.soulmakingcontest.us. **Contact:** Eileen Malone, Award Director. Annual open contest offers cash prizes in each of 13 literary categories. Competition receives 600 entries/year. Names of winners and judges are posted online. Winners announced in January by SASE and online. Winners are invited to read at the Koret Auditorium, San Francisco. Event is televised. Submissions in some categories may be previously published. No names or other identifying information on mss; include 3x5 card with poet's name, address, phone, fax, e-mail, title(s) of work, and category entered. Include SASE for results only; mss will not be returned. Guidelines online. Deadline: November 30. Prize: Prizes: 1st Prize: $100; 2nd Prize: $50; 3rd Prize: $25.

SOUTHWEST WRITERS ANNUAL CONTEST

3200 Carlisle Blvd. NE, Suite 114, Albuquerque NM 87110. (505)830-6034. **E-mail:** swwcontest@gmail.com. **Website:** www.southwestwriters.com; www.swwcontest.com. Open to adults and students. Annual contest to encourage writers of all genres. Also offers mini-conferences, critique service—for $60/year, offers 2 monthly programs, monthly newsletter, annual writing and bi-monthly writing contests, other workshops, various discount perks, website linking, e-mail addresses, classes and critique service (open to non-members). See website for more information or call or write. Deadline: Entries are open from March 1 to May 1 and may be submitted after May 1 until May 15 with payment of a late fee.

✪ SUBTERRAIN MAGAZINE'S ANNUAL LITERARY AWARDS COMPETITION: THE LUSH TRIUMPHANT

P.O. Box 3008 MPO, Vancouver BC V6B 3X5 Canada. (604)876-8710. **Fax:** (604)879-2667. **E-mail:** subter@portal.ca. **Website:** www.subterrain.ca. Entrants may submit as many entries in as many categories as they like. Fiction: Max of 3,000 words. Poetry: A suite of 5 related poems (max of 15 pages). Creative Nonfiction (based on fact, adorned with fiction): Max of 4,000 words. All entries must be previously unpublished material and not currently under consideration in any other contest or competition. Deadline: May 15. Prize: Winners in each category will receive $750 cash (plus payment for publication) and publication in the Winter issue. First runner-up in each category will received a $250 cash prize and be published in the Spring issue of *subTerrain*.

✪ TORONTO BOOK AWARDS

City of Toronto c/o Toronto Protocol, 100 Queen St. W., City Clerk's Office, 2nd floor, West Tower, Toronto ON M5H 2N2 Canada. **E-mail:** protocol@toronto.ca. **Website:** www.toronto.ca/book_awards. The Toronto Book Awards honour authors of books of literary or artistic merit that are evocative of Toronto. To be eligible, books must be published between January 1 and December 31 of previous year. Deadline: March 28. Prize: Each finalist receives $1,000 and the winning author receives the remaining prize money ($15,000 total in prize money available).

WESTMORELAND POETRY & SHORT STORY CONTEST

Westmoreland Arts & Heritage Festival, 252 Twin Lakes Rd., Latrobe PA 15650-9415. (724)834-7474. **Fax:** (724)850-7474. **E-mail:** info@artsandheritage. com. **Website:** www.artsandheritage.com. **Contact:** Adam Shaffer. Offered annually for unpublished work. Two categories: Poem & Short Story. Short story entries no longer than 4,000 words. Family-oriented festival and contest. Deadline: February 15. Prize: Prizes: Up to $1,000 in total prizes.

WILLA LITERARY AWARD

Women Writing the West, 8547 East Arapaho Rd., #J-541, Greenwood Village CO 80112-1436. **E-mail:** pamtartaglio@yahoo.com. **Website:** www.womenwritingthewest.org. **Contact:** Pam Tartaglio. The WILLA Literary Award honors the best in literature featuring women's or girls' stories set in the West published each year. Women Writing the West (WWW), a nonprofit association of writers and other professionals writing and promoting the Women's West, underwrites and presents the nationally recognized award annually (for work published between January 1 and December 31). The award is named in honor of Pulitzer Prize winner Willa Cather, one of the country's foremost novelists. The award is given in 7 categories: Historical fiction, contemporary fiction, original softcover fiction, creative nonfiction, scholarly nonfiction, poetry, and children's/young adult fiction/nonfiction. Deadline: November 1-February 1. Prize: $100 and a trophy. Finalist receives a plaque. Both receive digital and sticker award emblems for book covers. Winning and finalist titles mailed to more than 4,000 booksellers, libraries, and others. Award announcement is in early August, and awards are presented to the winners and finalists at the annual WWW Fall Conference. Judged by professional librarians not affiliated with WWW.

✪ THE WORD AWARDS

The Word Guild, Box 1243, Trenton, ON K8V 5R9 Canada. **E-mail:** info@thewordguild.com. **Website:** www. thewordguild.com. The Word Guild is an organization of Canadian writers and editors who are Christian, and who are committed to encouraging one another and to fostering standards of excellence in the art, craft, practice andministry of writing. Memberships available for various experience levels. Yearly conference Write Canada (please see website for information) and features plenary speakers, continuing classes and workshops. Editors and agents on site. The Word Awards is for work published in the past year, in almost 30 categories including books, articles, songs, poetry. Please see website for more information.

WORLD'S BEST SHORT-SHORT STORY FICTION CONTEST, NARRATIVE NONFICTION CONTEST & SOUTHEAST REVIEW POETRY CONTEST

English Department, Florida State University, Tallahassee FL 32306. **E-mail:** southeastreview@gmail.com. **Website:** www.southeastreview.org. **Contact:** Brandi

George, editor. Annual award for unpublished short-short stories (500 words or less), poetry, and narrative nonfiction (6,000 words or less). Deadline: March 15. Prize: $500 per category. Winners and finalists will be published in *The Southeast Review*.

WRITER'S DIGEST ANNUAL WRITING COMPETITION

Writer's Digest, a publication of F+W Media, Inc., 10151 Carver Rd., Suite 200, Cincinnati OH 45242. (715)445-4612, ext. 13430. **E-mail:** writing-competition@fw-media.com; nicole.howard@fwmedia.com. **Website:** www.writersdigest.com. **Contact:** Nicki Howard. Writing contest with 10 categories: Inspirational Writing (spiritual/religious, maximum 2,500 words); Memoir/Personal Essay (maximum 2,000 words); Magazine Feature Article (maximum 2,000 words); Short Story (genre, maximum 4,000 words); Short Story (mainstream/literary, maximum 4,000 words); Rhyming Poetry (maximum 32 lines); Nonrhyming Poetry (maximum 32 lines); Stage Play (first 15 pages and 1-page synopsis); TV/Movie Script (first 15 pages and 1-page synopsis). Entries must be original, in English, unpublished*/unproduced (except for Magazine Feature Articles), and not accepted by another publisher/producer at the time of submission. *Writer's Digest* retains one-time publication rights to the winning entries in each category. Deadline: May. Prize: Grand Prize: $3,000 and a trip to the Writer's Digest Conference to meet with editors and agents; 1st Place: $1,000 and $100 of Writer's Digest Books; 2nd Place: $500 and $100 of Writer's Digest Books; 3rd Place: $250 and $100 of Writer's Digest Books; 4th Place: $100 and $50 of *Writer's Digest* Books; 5th Place: $50 and $50 of *Writer's Digest* Books; 6th-10th place $25.

WRITER'S DIGEST SELF-PUBLISHED BOOK AWARDS

Writer's Digest, 10151 Carver Road, Suite #200, Blue Ash OH 45242. (715)445-4612, ext. 13430. **E-mail:** WritersDigestSelfPublishingCompetition@fwmedia. com. **Website:** www.writersdigest.com. **Contact:** Nicole Howard. Contest open to all English-language, self-published books for which the authors have paid the full cost of publication, or the cost of printing has been paid for by a grant or as part of a prize. Categories include: Mainstream/Literary Fiction, Genre Fiction, Nonfiction, Inspirational (spiritual/new age), Life Stories (biographies/autobiographies/family histories/memoirs), Children's Books, Reference Books (directo-ries/encyclopedias/guide books), Poetry, and Middle-Grade/Young Adult Books. Judges reserve the right to re-categorize entries. Judges reserve the right to with-hold prizes in any category. All winners will be no-tifed by October 17. Entrants must send a printed and bound book. Entries will be evaluated on content, writing quality, and overall quality of production and appearance. No handwritten books are accepted. Books must have been published within the past 5 years from the competition deadline. Books which have previously won awards from *Writer's Digest* are not eligible. Early bird deadline: April 1; Deadline: May 1. Prize: Prizes: Grand Prize: $3,000, a trip to the Writer's Digest Conference, promotion in *Writer's Digest* and *Publisher's Weekly*, and 10 copies of the book will be sent to major review houses with a guaranteed review in *Midwest Book Review*; 1st Place (9 winners): $1,000 and promotion in *Writer's Digest*; Honorable Mentions:$50 worth of Writer's Digest Books and promotion on writersdigest.com. All entrants will receive a brief commentary from one of the judges.

WRITERS-EDITORS NETWORK ANNUAL INTERNATIONAL WRITING COMPETITION

CNW Publishing, P.O. Box A, North Stratford NH 03590-0167. **E-mail:** contest@writers-editors.com. **E-mail:** info@writers-editors.com. **Website:** www.writers-editors.com. **Contact:** Dana K. Cassell, executive director. Annual award to recognize publishable talent. Categories: Nonfiction (previously published article/essay/column/nonfiction book chapter; unpublished or self-published article/essay/column/nonfiction book chapter); fiction (unpublished or self-published short story or novel chapter); children's literature (unpublished or self-published short story/nonfiction article/book chapter/poem); poetry (unpublished or self-published free verse/traditional). Guidelines online. Open to any writer. Accepts inquiries by e-mail, phone and mail. Entry form online. Results announced May 31. Winners notified by mail and posted online. Results available for SASE or visit website. Deadline: March 15. Prize: 1st Place: $100; 2nd Place: $75; 3rd Place: $50. All winners and Honorable Mentions will receive certificates as warranted. Judged by editors, librarians, and writers.

WRITERS' LEAGUE OF TEXAS BOOK AWARDS

Writers' League of Texas, 611 S. Congress Ave., Suite 505, Austin TX 78704. (512)499-8914. **Fax:** (512)499-

CONTESTS & AWARDS

0441. **E-mail:** wlt@writersleague.org. **E-mail:** sara@writersleague.org. **Website:** www.writersleague.org. Open to Texas authors of books published the previous two years. Authors are required to show proof of Texas residency, but are not required to be members of the Writers' League of Texas. Deadline: Open to submissions from January 1 to April 30. Prize: $750, a commemorative award, and an appearance at a WLT Third Thursday panel at BookPeople in Austin, TX.

THE YOUTH HONOR AWARD PROGRAM

Skipping Stones Magazine, P.O. Box 3939, Eugene OR 97403. (541)342-4956. **E-mail:** info@skippingstones. org. **E-mail:** editor@skippingstones.org. **Website:** www.skippingstones.org. **Contact:** Arun N. Toke, Editor and Publisher. Original writing and art from youth, ages 7 to 17, should be typed or neatly handwritten. The entries should be appropriate for ages 7 to 17. Prose under 1,000 words; poems under 30 lines. Non-English and bilingual writings are welcome. To promote multicultural, international and nature awareness. Deadline: May 25. Prize: An Honor Award Certificate, a subscription to Skipping Stones and five nature and/or multicultural books. They are also invited to join the Student Review Board. Everyone who enters the contest receives the autumn issue featuring the 10 winners.

PROFESSIONAL ORGANIZATIONS

//

AGENTS' ORGANIZATIONS

ASSOCIATION OF AUTHORS' AGENTS (AAA), 5-8 Lower John Street, Golden Square, London W1F 9HA . E-mail: anthonygoff@davidhigham.co.uk. Website: www.agentsassoc.co.uk.

ASSOCIATION OF AUTHORS' REPRESENTATIVES (AAR). E-mail: info@aar-online.org. Website: www.aar-online.org.

ASSOCIATION OF TALENT AGENTS (ATA), 9255 Sunset Blvd., Suite 930, Los Angeles CA 90069. (310)274-0628. E-mail: shellie@agentassociation.com. Website: www.agentassociation.com.

WRITERS' ORGANIZATIONS

ACADEMY OF AMERICAN POETS 584 Broadway, Suite 604, New York NY 10012-5243. (212)274-0343. Fax: (212)274-9427. E-mail: academy@poets.org. Website: www.poets.org.

AMERICAN CRIME WRITERS LEAGUE (ACWL), 17367 Hilltop Ridge Dr., Eureka MO 63205. Website: www.acwl.org.

AMERICAN INDEPENDENT WRITERS (AIW), 1001 Connecticut Ave. NW, Suite 701, Washington DC 20036. E-mail: info@aiwriters.org. Website: www.americanindependentwriters.org.

AMERICAN MEDICAL WRITERS ASSOCIATION (AMWA), 30 West Gude Drive, Suite 525, Rockville MD 20850-4347. (301)294-5303. Fax: (301)294-9006. E-mail: amwa@amwa.org. Website: www.amwa.org.

AMERICAN SCREENWRITERS ASSOCIATION (ASA), 269 S. Beverly Dr., Suite 2600, Beverly Hills CA 90212-3807. (866)265-9091. E-mail: asa@goasa.com. Website: www.asascreenwriters.com.

AMERICAN TRANSLATORS ASSOCIATION (ATA), 225 Reinekers Lane, Suite 590, Alexandria VA 22314. (703)683-6100. Fax: (703)683-6122. E-mail: ata@atanet.org. Website: www.atanet.org.

EDUCATION WRITERS ASSOCIATION (EWA), 2122 P St., NW Suite 201, Washington DC 20037. (202)452-9830. Fax: (202)452-9837. E-mail: ewa@ewa.org. Website: www.ewa.org.

HORROR WRITERS ASSOCIATION (HWA), 244 5th Ave., Suite 2767, New York NY 10001. E-mail: hwa@horror.org. Website: www.horror.org.

THE INTERNATIONAL WOMEN'S WRITING GUILD (IWWG),P.O. Box 810, Gracie Station, New York NY 10028-0082. (212)737-7536. Fax: (212)737-9469. E-mail: dirhahn@aol.org. Website: www.iwwg.com.

MYSTERY WRITERS OF AMERICA (MWA), 1140 Broadway, Suite 1507, New York NY 10001. (212)888-8171. Fax: (212)888-8107. E-mail: mwa@mysterywriters.org. Website: www.mysterywriters.org.

NATIONAL ASSOCIATION OF SCIENCE WRITERS (NASW), P.O. Box 7905, Berkeley, CA 94707. (510)647-9500. E-mail: LFriedmann@nasw.org. website: www.nasw.org.

NATIONAL ASSOCIATION OF WOMEN WRITERS (NAWW), 24165 IH-10 W., Suite 217-637, San Antonio TX 78257. Phone/Fax: (866)821-5829. Website: www.naww.org.

ORGANIZATION OF BLACK SCREENWRITERS (OBS). Golden State Mutual Life Insurance Bldg., 1999 West Adams Blvd., Rm. Mezzanine Los Angeles, CA 90018. Website: www.obswriter.com.

OUTDOOR WRITERS ASSOCIATION OF AMERICA (OWAA), 121 Hickory St., Suite 1, Missoula MT 59801. (406)728-7434. E-mail: krhoades@owaa.org. Website: www.owaa.org.

POETRY SOCIETY OF AMERICA (PSA), 15 Gramercy Park, New York NY 10003. (212)254-9628. website: www.poetrysociety.org. Poets & Writers, 90 Broad St., Suite 2100, New York NY 10004. (212)226-3586. Fax: (212)226-3963. Website: www.pw.org.

ROMANCE WRITERS OF AMERICA (RWA), 114615 Benfer Road, Houston TX 77069. (832)717-5200. Fax: (832)717-5201. E-mail: info@rwanational.org. Website: www.rwanational.org.

SCIENCE FICTION AND FANTASY WRITERS OF AMERICA (SFWA), P.O. Box 877, Chestertown MD 21620. E-mail: execdir@sfwa.org. Website: www.sfwa.org.

SOCIETY OF AMERICAN BUSINESS EDITORS & WRITERS (SABEW), University of Missouri, School of Journalism, 30 Neff Annex, Columbia MO 65211. (602) 496-7862. E-mail: sabew@sabew.org. Website: www.sabew.org.

SOCIETY OF AMERICAN TRAVEL WRITERS (SATW), 7044 S. 13 St., Oak Creek WI 53154. (414)908-4949. Fax: (414)768-8001. E-mail: satw@satw.org. Website: www.satw.org.

SOCIETY OF CHILDREN'S BOOK WRITERS & ILLUSTRATORS (SCBWI), 8271 Beverly Blvd., Los Angeles CA 90048. (323)782-1010. E-mail: scbwi@scbwi.org. Website: www.scbwi.org.

WESTERN WRITERS OF AMERICA (WWA). E-mail: spiritfire@kc.rr.com. Website: www.westernwriters.org.

INDUSTRY ORGANIZATIONS

AMERICAN BOOKSELLERS ASSOCIATION (ABA), 200 White Plains Rd., Suite 600, Tarrytown NY 10591. (914)591-2665. E-mail: info@bookweb.org. Website: www.bookweb.org.

AMERICAN SOCIETY OF JOURNALISTS & AUTHORS (ASJA), 1501 Broadway, Suite 302, New York NY 10036. (212)997-0947. E-mail: director@asja.org. Website: www.asja.org.

ASSOCIATION FOR WOMEN IN COMMUNICATIONS (AWC), 3337 Duke St., Alexandria VA 22314. (703)370-7436. E-mail: info@womcom.org. Website: www.womcom.org.

ASSOCIATION OF AMERICAN PUBLISHERS (AAP), 71 5th Ave., 2nd Floor, New York NY 10003. Or, 50 F St. NW, Suite 400, Washington DC 20001. Website: www.publishers.org.

THE ASSOCIATION OF WRITERS & WRITING PROGRAMS (AWP), Mail Stop 1E3, George Mason University, Fairfax VA 22030. (703)993-4301. Fax: (703)993-4302. E-mail: services@awpwriter.org. website: www.awpwriter.org.

THE AUTHORS GUILD, INC., 31 E. 32nd St., 7th Floor, New York NY 10016. (212)563-5904. Fax: (212)564-5363. E-mail: staff@authorsguild.org. website: www.authorsguild.org.

CANADIAN AUTHORS ASSOCIATION (CAA), P.O. Box 581, Stn. Main Orilla ON L3V 6K5 Canada. (705)653-0323. E-mail: admin@canauthors.org. Website: www.canauthors.org.

CHRISTIAN BOOKSELLERS ASSOCIATION (CBA), P.O. Box 62000, Colorado Springs CO 80962-2000. (800)252-1950. Fax: (719)272-3510. E-mail: info@cbaonline.org. website: www.cbaonline.org.

THE DRAMATISTS GUILD OF AMERICA, 1501 Broadway, Suite 701, New York NY 10036. (212)398-9366. Fax: (212)944-0420. Website: www.dramatistsguild.com.

NATIONAL LEAGUE OF AMERICAN PEN WOMEN (NLAPW), 1300 17th St. NW, Washington DC 20036-1973. (202)785-1997. E-mail: nlapw1@verizon.net. Website: www.americanpen-women.org.

NATIONAL WRITERS ASSOCIATION (NWA), 10940 S. Parker Rd., #508, Parker CO 80134. (303)841-0246. Fax: (303)841-2607. E-mail: natlwritersassn@hotmail.com. Website: www.nationalwriters.com

NATIONAL WRITERS UNION (NWU), 256 West 38th Street, Suite 703, New York, NY 10018. (212)254-0279. Fax: (212)254-0673. E-mail: nwu@nwu.org. Website: www.nwu.org.

PEN AMERICAN CENTER, 588 Broadway, Suite 303, New York NY 10012-3225. (212)334-1660. Fax: (212)334-2181. E-mail: pen@pen.org. Website: www.pen.org.

THE PLAYWRIGHTS GUILD OF CANADA (PGC), 215 Spadina Ave., Suite #210, Toronto ON M5T 2C7 Canada. (416)703-0201. Fax: (416)703-0059. E-mail: info@playwrightsguild.ca. Website: www.playwrightsguild.com.

VOLUNTEER LAWYERS FOR THE ARTS (VLA), One E. 53rd St., 6th Floor, New York NY 10022. (212)319-2787. Fax: (212)752-6575. Website: www.vlany.org.

WOMEN IN FILM (WIF), 6100 Wilshire Blvd., Suite 710, Los Angeles CA 90048. (323)935-2211. Fax: (323)935-2212. E-mail: info@wif.org. Website: www.wif.org.

WOMEN'S NATIONAL BOOK ASSOCIATION (WNBA), P.O. Box 237, FDR Station, New York NY 10150. (212)208-4629. Fax: (212)208-4629. E-mail: publicity@bookbuzz.com. Website: www.wnba-books.org.

WRITERS GUILD OF ALBERTA (WGA), 11759 Groat Rd., Edmonton AB T5M 3K6 Canada. (780)422-8174. Fax: (780)422-2663. E-mail: mail@writersguild.ab.ca. Website: writersguild.ab.ca.

WRITERS GUILD OF AMERICA-EAST (WGA), 555 W. 57th St., Suite 1230, New York NY 10019. (212)767-7800. Fax: (212)582-1909. e-mail: info@wgaeast.org. Website: www.wgaeast.org.

WRITERS GUILD OF AMERICA-WEST (WGA), 7000 W. Third St., Los Angeles CA 90048. (323)951-4000. Fax: (323)782-4800. Website: www.wga.org.

WRITERS UNION OF CANADA (TWUC), 90 Richmond St. E., Suite 200, Toronto ON M5C 1P1 Canada. (416)703-8982. E-mail: info@writersunion.ca. Website: www.writersunion.ca.

GLOSSARY

#10 ENVELOPE. A standard, business-size envelope.

ADVANCE. A sum of money a publisher pays a writer prior to the publication of a book. It is usually paid in installments, such as one-half on signing contract; one-half on delivery of complete and satisfactory manuscript.

AGENT. A liaison between a writer and editor or publisher. An agent shops a manuscript around, receiving a commission when the manuscript is accepted. Agents usually take a 10-15% fee from the advance and royalties.

ARC. Advance reader copy.

ASSIGNMENT. Editor asks a writer to produce a specific article for an agreed-upon fee.

AUCTION. Publishers sometimes bid for the acquisition of a book manuscript that has excellent sales prospects. The bids are for the amount of the author's advance, adver-tising and promotional expenses, royalty percentage, etc. Auctions are conducted by agents.

AVANT-GARDE. Writing that is innovative in form, style, or subject.

BACKLIST. A publisher's list of its books that were not published during the current season, but that are still in print.

BIMONTHLY. Every two months.

BIO. A sentence or brief paragraph about the writer; can include education and work experience.

BIWEEKLY. Every two weeks.

BLOG. Short for weblog. Used by writers to build platform by posting regular commentary, observations, poems, tips, etc.

BLURB. The copy on paperback book covers or hard cover book dust jackets, either promoting the book and the author or featuring testimonials from book reviewers or well-known people in the book's field. Also called flap copy or jacket copy.

BOILERPLATE. A standardized contract.

BOUND GALLEYS. Prepublication edition of book, usually photocopies of final galley proofs; also known as "bound proofs."

BYLINE. Name of the author appearing with the published piece.

CATEGORY FICTION. A term used to include all types of fiction.

CHAPBOOK. A small booklet usually paperback of poetry, ballads or tales.

CIRCULATION. The number of subscribers to a magazine.

CLIPS. Samples, usually from newspapers or magazines, of a writer's published work.

COFFEE-TABLE BOOK. An heavily illustrated oversize book.

COMMERCIAL NOVELS. Novels designed to appeal to a broad audience. These are often broken down into categories such as western, mystery and romance. See also genre.

CONTRIBUTOR'S COPIES. Copies of the issues of magazines sent to the author in which the author's work appears.

CO-PUBLISHING. Arrangement where author and publisher share publications costs and profits of a book. Also known as cooperative publishing.

COPYEDITING. Editing a manuscript for grammar, punctuation, printing style and factual accuracy.

COPYRIGHT. A means to protect an author's work.

COVER LETTER. A brief letter that accompanies the manuscript being sent to and agent or editor.

CREATIVE NONFICTION. Nonfictional writing that uses an innovative approach to the subject and creative language.

CRITIQUING SERVICE. Am editing service in which writers pay a fee for comments on the salability or other qualities of their manuscript. Fees vary, as do the quality of the critiques.

CV. Curriculum vita. A brief listing of qualifications and career accomplishments.

ELECTRONIC RIGHTS. Secondary or subsidiary rights dealing with electronic/multimedia formats (i.e., the Internet, CD-ROMs, electronic magazines).

ELECTRONIC SUBMISSION. A submission made by modem or on computer disk.

EROTICA. Fiction that is sexually oriented.

EVALUATION FEES. Fees an agent may charge to evaluate material. The extent and quality of this evaluation varies, but comments usually concern salability of the manuscript.

FAIR USE. A provision of the copyright law that says short passages from copyrighted material may be used without infringing on the owner's rights.

FEATURE. An article giving the reader information of human interest rather than news.

FILLER. A short item used by an editor to "fill" out a newspaper column or magazine page. It could be a joke, an anecdote, etc.

FILM RIGHTS. Rights sold or optioned by the agent/author to a person in the film industry, enabling the book to be made into a movie.

FOREIGN RIGHTS. Translation or reprint rights to be sold abroad.

FRONTLIST. A publisher's list of books that are new to the current season.

GALLEYS. First typeset version of manuscript that has not yet been divided into pages.

GENRE. Refers either to a general classification of writing, such as the novel or the poem, or to the categories within those classifications, such as the problem novel or the sonnet.

GHOSTWRITER. Writer who puts into literary form article, speech, story or book based on another person's ideas or knowledge.

GRAPHIC NOVEL. A story in graphic form, long comic strip, or heavily illustrated story; of 40 pages or more.

HI-LO. A type of fiction that offers a high level of interest for readers at a low reading level.

HIGH CONCEPT. A story idea easily expressed in a quick, one-line description.

HONORARIUM. Token payment.

HOOK. Aspect of the work that sets it apart from others and draws in the reader/viewer.

HOW-TO. Books and magazine articles offering a combination of information and advice in describing how something can be accomplished.

IMPRINT. Name applied to a publisher's specific line of books.

JOINT CONTRACT. A legal agreement between a publisher and two or more authors, establishing provisions for the division of royalties the book generates.

KILL FEE. Fee for a complete article that was assigned and then cancelled.

LEAD TIME. The time between the acquisition of a manuscript by an editor and its actual publication.

LITERARY FICTION. The general category of serious, non-formulaic, intelligent fiction.

MAINSTREAM FICTION. Fiction that transcends popular novel categories such as mystery, romance and science fiction.

MARKETING FEE. Fee charged by some agents to cover marketing expenses. It may be used to cover postage, telephone calls, faxes, photocopying or any other expense incurred in marketing a manuscript.

MASS MARKET. Non-specialized books of wide appeal directed toward a large audience.

MEMOIR. A narrative recounting a writer's (or fictional narrator's) personal or family history; specifics may be altered, though essentially considered nonfiction.

MIDDLE GRADE OR MID-GRADE. The general classification of books written for readers approximately ages 9-11. Also called middle readers.

MIDLIST. Those titles on a publisher's list that are not expected to be big sellers, but are expected to have limited/modest sales.

MODEL RELEASE. A paper signed by the subject of a photograph giving the photographer permission to use the photograph.

MULTIPLE CONTRACT. Book contract with an agreement for a future book(s).

MULTIPLE SUBMISSIONS. Sending more than one book or article idea to a publisher at the same time.

NARRATIVE NONFICTION. A narrative presentation of actual events.

NET ROYALTY. A royalty payment based on the amount of money a book publisher receives on the sale of a book after booksellers' discounts, special sales discounts and returns.

NOVELLA. A short novel, or a long short story; approximately 7,000 to 15,000 words.

ON SPEC. An editor expresses an interest in a proposed article idea and agrees to consider the finished piece for publication "on speculation." The editor is under no obligation to buy the finished manuscript.

ONE-TIME RIGHTS. Rights allowing a manuscript to be published one time. The work can be sold again by the writer without violating the contract.

OPTION CLAUSE. A contract clause giving a publisher the right to publish an author's next book.

PAYMENT ON ACCEPTANCE. The editor sends you a check for your article, story or poem as soon as he decides to publish it.

PAYMENT ON PUBLICATION. The editor doesn't send you a check for your material until it is published.

PEN NAME. The use of a name other than your legal name on articles, stories or books. Also called a pseudonym.

PHOTO FEATURE. Feature in which the emphasis is on the photographs rather than on accompanying written material.

PICTURE BOOK. A type of book aimed at preschoolers to 8-year-olds that tells a story using a combination of text and artwork, or artwork only.

PLATFORM. A writer's speaking experience, interview skills, website and other abilities which help form a following of potential buyers for that author's book.

POD. Print on demand.

PROOFREADING. Close reading and correction of a manuscript's typographical errors.

PROPOSAL. A summary of a proposed book submitted to a publisher, particularly used for nonfiction manuscripts. A proposal often contains an individualized cover letter, one-page overview of the book, marketing information, competitive books, author information, chapter-by-chapter outline, and two to three sample chapters.

QUERY. A letter that sells an idea to an editor or agent. Usually a query is brief (no more than one page) and uses attention-getting prose.

REMAINDERS. Copies of a book that are slow to sell and can be purchased from the publisher at a reduced price.

REPORTING TIME. The time it takes for an editor to report to the author on his/her query or manuscript.

REPRINT RIGHTS. The rights to republish a book after its initial printing.

ROYALTIES, STANDARD HARDCOVER BOOK. 10 percent of the retail price on the first 5,000 copies sold; 121/2 percent on the next 5,000; 15 percent thereafter.

ROYALTIES, STANDARD MASS PAPERBACK BOOK. 4-8 percent of the retail price on the first 150,000 copies sold.

ROYALTIES, STANDARD TRADE PAPERBACK BOOK. No less than 6 percent of list price on the first 20,000 copies; 7½ percent thereafter.

SASE. Self-addressed, stamped envelope; should be included with all correspondence.

SELF-PUBLISHING. In this arrangement the author pays for manufacturing, production and marketing of his book and keeps all income derived from the book sales.

SEMIMONTHLY. Twice per month.

SEMIWEEKLY. Twice per week.

SERIAL. Published periodically, such as a newspaper or magazine.

SERIAL FICTION. Fiction published in a magazine in installments, often broken off at a suspenseful spot.

SERIAL RIGHTS. The right for a newspaper or magazine to publish sections of a manuscript.

SHORT-SHORT. A complete short story of 1,500 words.

SIDEBAR. A feature presented as a companion to a straight news report (or main magazine article) giving sidelights on human-interest aspects or sometimes elucidating just one aspect of the story.

SIMULTANEOUS SUBMISSIONS. Sending the same article, story or poem to several publishers at the same time. Some publishers refuse to consider such submissions.

SLANT. The approach or style of a story or article that will appeal to readers of a specific magazine.

SLICE-OF-LIFE VIGNETTE. A short fiction piece intended to realistically depict an interesting moment of everyday living.

SLUSH PILE. The stack of unsolicited or misdirected manuscripts received by an editor or book publisher.

SOCIAL NETWORKS. Websites that connect users: sometimes generally, other times around specific interests. Four popular ones at the moment are MySpace, Facebook, Twitter and LinkedIn.

SUBAGENT. An agent handling certain subsidiary rights, usually working in conjuction with the agent who handled the book rights. The percentage paid the book agent is increased to pay the subagent.

SUBSIDIARY RIGHTS. All right other than book publishing rights included in a book publishing contract, such as paperback rights, book club rights and movie rights. Part of an agent's job is to negotiate those rights and advise you on which to sell and which to keep.

SUBSIDY PUBLISHER. A book publisher who charges the author for the cost to typeset and print his book, the jacket, etc., as opposed to a royalty publisher who pays the author.

SYNOPSIS. A brief summary of a story, novel or play. As part of a book proposal, it is a comprehensive summary condensed in a page or page and a half, single-spaced.

TABLOID. Newspaper format publication on about half the size of the regular newspaper page.

TEARSHEET. Page from a magazine or newspaper containing your printed story, article, poem or ad.

TOC. Table of Contents.

TRADE BOOK. Either a hardcover or softcover book; subject matter frequently concerns a special interest for a general audience; sold mainly in bookstores.

TRADE PAPERBACK. A soft-bound volume published and designed for the general public; available mainly in bookstores.

TRANSLATION RIGHTS. Sold to a foreign agent or foreign publisher.

UNSOLICITED MANUSCRIPT. A story, article, poem or book that an editor did not specifically ask to see.

YA. Young adult books

INDEX

C

865

O

Z